A Political Map

(States drawn in proportion to number of electoral votes)

THE GREAT SOCIETY

3000 miles of unfortified border →

St. Lawrence "seaway"

FRENCH-CANADIAN-

-AMERICANS

VT. 3

ME. 4

N.H. 4

GOOD VOTING RECORD DEMOCRATIC SHIFT HERE

N.Y. 43

HAS MOST ELECTORAL VOTES

MASS. 14

Boston
MELTING POT OF YANKEELAND
J.F.K. BORN HERE

L. Ontario

GOVERNOR HERE IS LIKELY CANDIDATE FOR PRESIDENCY

F.D.R. LIVED HERE

SHAYS REBELLION, 1787

FIRST STATE TO REQUIRE LITERACY TEST

Erie

CONN. 8

R.I. 4

STAYED AWAY FROM CONSTITUTIONAL CONVENTION

New York City
THE MELTING POT —HAS OVER 3 MILLION VOTERS

Dems. Reps.

LONG ISLAND

PA. 29

COAL

N.J. 17

CONSTITUTIONAL CONVENTION — 1787

Philadelphia

1ST PRESIDENTIAL CONVENTION

INTERSTATE COOPERATION IN RUNNING PORT OF N.Y.

THE NEW FRONTIER

W.VA. 7
COAL

VA. 12

Baltimore
MD. 10

DEL. 3

HOME OF CORPORATIONS

...TICS

...UBLICAN COUNTRY

BIRTHPLACE OF 8 PRESIDENTS

Washington, D.C.
GRANTED VOTE FOR PRESIDENT BY 23RD AMENDMENT

Key:

N.C. 13

1 NUMBER OF ELECTORAL VOTES

S.C. 8

TOBACCO POLITICS

THE PIVOTAL STATES

...NEE

STORMY DEMOCRATIC POLITICS

TOTAL NUMBER OF ELECTORAL VOTES 538 FOR 1964 ELECTION

TURN THE RASCALS OUT

A FULL DINNER PAIL

Outline of the above proportional map, super-imposed on an actual map of the United States.

Our government by the people is the product of nearly two centuries of effort by a democratic society to cope with conflict, conduct elections, grapple with issues, and bring the idea of democracy in all its gaudiness and glory to millions of "average" people.

Hence government by the people is a matter not just of laws and constitutions, but clay pipes and medallions, umbrellas and campaign buttons . . . (continued following page 368).

Prentice-Hall, Inc.,   Englewood Cliffs, New Jersey

by   James MacGregor Burns

Williams College

Jack Walter Peltason

University of California, Irvine

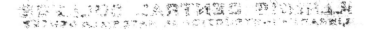

GOVERNMENT BY THE PEOPLE,

THE DYNAMICS OF AMERICAN NATIONAL, STATE, AND LOCAL GOVERNMENT,

6th
Sixth Edition

To Jan, Suzanne, David, Nancy,

Stewart, Timothy, Deborah, Mecki, Jill

GOVERNMENT BY THE PEOPLE   *Sixth Edition*

The Dynamics of American National, State, and Local Government

Burns and Peltason

Design by Walter Behnke

PRENTICE-HALL INTERNATIONAL, INC., *London*

PRENTICE-HALL OF AUSTRALIA, PTY., LTD., *Sydney*

PRENTICE-HALL OF CANADA, LTD., *Toronto*

PRENTICE-HALL OF INDIA PVT. LTD., *New Delhi*

PRENTICE-HALL OF JAPAN, INC., *Tokyo*

36069—C

PREFACE

Teachers of American government carry a double burden these days—both the subject and the discipline are rapidly changing. The mid-1960's have brought more significant developments in our political system than in perhaps any short period since the Civil War. Political science as a discipline is alive with fresh explorations, heightened disputes, new frontiers. As we suggest to the students at the outset of Chapter One, this is an exciting time in which to begin the study of American politics and American government.

This edition hopes to capture that excitment. It tries to do full justice to the new developments both in the discipline and in the subject. We have stressed the enhanced role of the President, the historic actions of the Supreme Court and of the "new Congress," the broadened programs in civil rights and social welfare, the intensified problems of the states and cities. We have also added a new section on political science as a discipline and we have expanded our treatment of political science "frontiers" and political scientists' activities. Since we urge the students to be self-conscious about the discipline, we have tried to be too.

But such additions carry a price—adding even more to an already full treatment of "the most complicated government on earth." Hence in this edition we have developed much more extensively than before the framework of problems that enable the student to make the data more coherent and understandable. We develop these problems systematically in the first chapter, spell them out in more detail in the Part introductions, return to them in the text, and offer some conclusions in Chapter 20.

As in the past, we have asked a number of political scientists to review the current edition in a stringently critical and exacting mood. For their host of specific and general suggestions we thank Professors Bernard C. Cohen of the University of Wisconsin, Philip E. Converse of the University of Michigan, Lewis A. Froman and Martin Shapiro, both of the University of California (Irvine), Duane Lockard of Princeton University, and Michael D. Reagan of the University of California (Riverside). We are also in debt to the hundreds of scholars in the field of political science who by their books, articles, monographs, conference reports, and investigations have made it today a more important discipline than ever. To these hundreds, and the thousands who came before, we give our thanks. Some works we cite, others are not specifically mentioned, but they have become incorporated within our work through their impact on our own intellectual development.

Professor Richard M. Johnson of the University of Buffalo has been of major assistance in criticizing the manuscript, supplying ideas and materials of his own, and in updating the Bibliography. He had the primary responsibility for the revision of Part Six, and made important contributions to all areas.

Professors James A. Burkhart of Stephens College and Raymond L. Lee of Indiana University of Pennsylvania, have produced a most useful workbook, *Guide to Government by the People*, second edition, as a tool for both teaching and learning. The *Guide*, which has been integrated much more closely with this edition of *Government by the People*, is highly recommended to students.

We greatly appreciate the general advice and assistance of Lucius J. Barker of the University of Wisconsin (Milwaukee), who has prepared the new sixth edition of *Teaching Government with Burns' and Peltason's Government by the People*. This teachers manual reflects his own devotion to fine teaching.

We wish to acknowledge especially the imagination, versatility, and resourcefulness of the editorial-production-design team at Prentice-Hall headed by Wilbur E. Mangas and consisting of Walter Behnke, Nancy Hall, and Lois Rankin. James J. Murray III of Prentice-Hall has provided us unfailing assistance out of his fund of experience and judgment. Grace Beiser, Martha Brown, Sue Cooper, Shirley Covington, Helen Dotta, Marie Dunleavy, Thelma MacDonald, and Midge Walker have been of indispensable help in reading proof.

For invaluable advice on this and previous editions we thank Professors Francis M. Carney of the University of California (Riverside); Dwaine Marvick of the University of California (Los Angeles); Richard F. Fenno, Jr., of the University of Rochester; Malcolm E. Jewell of the University of Kentucky; John H. Fenton of the University of Massachusetts; Warren Miller of the University of Michigan; and Ruth Silva of the Pennsylvania State University, who advised on matters in their special fields of competence; Theodore Mitau of Macalester College; Melvin P. Straus of San Jose State University; Clarence A. Berdahl, David J. Danelski, Thomas Page, J. Austin Ranney, Robert E. Scott, and Clyde F. Snider, all of the University of Illinois; Hollis W. Barber, University of Illinois (Navy Pier); Donald C. Blaisdell, City College of New York; Gordon B. Cleveland and James W. Prothro, both of the University of North Carolina; Samuel J. Eldersveld, University of Michigan; George Harvey and Robert F. Karsch, both of the University of Missouri; Mahmut N. Lacin, Sacramento State; Frederic D. Ogden, University of Alabama; Donald R. Larson, Gustav R. Serino, Edward Sofen, and J. Ben Stalvey, all of the University of Miami; and Pauline Yelderman, University of Houston; Professors S. S. Aichele, Temple; Charles Aikin and Victor G. Rosenblum, both of the University of California (Berkeley); Charles R. Cherington, Harvard; Thomas I. Cook, Johns Hopkins; U. G. Dubach, Lewis and Clark; Charles D. Goff, University of Wisconsin (Milwaukee); Fred Greene, Williams; Cecilia Kenyon, Smith; Robert E. Lane, Yale; Clay P. Malick, University of Colorado; Alpheus T. Mason, Princeton; Earl Kohler and E. L. Nowel of St. Petersburg Jr. College; Landon G. Rockwell, Hamilton; Wallace Sayre, Columbia University; Carl O. Smith, Wayne State University; and Joseph R. Starr, University of Maryland. Colleagues at the University of Illinois and at Williams were most generous in their advice and assistance. Professors Charles M. Kneier, University of Illinois; Rolin B. Posey, Northwestern; and Paul N. Ylvisaker, Swarthmore, gave informed advice on the state and local chapters.

The names and dates of court decisions are given in the body of the text, but full citations of all cases mentioned can be found in the Index.

A final note: Both the National and National-State-Local editions have been so organized that they can be adapted for use in several different types of course. For those who want the minimum essentials of American national government, Parts Two through Five (chapters 2–20, pages 31–554) provide a self-contained core coverage for the standard shorter course. For courses covering the basic materials of state and local government also, Part Seven of the larger edition can be in-

cluded. Governmental functions are described in Part Six. Part One and Epilogue
cover materials directly related to the study of American government and permit
more extended coverage, either by themselves or in conjunction with any of the
excellent problem or reading texts now available. Any errors, of course, are the
authors' alone—and we would greatly appreciate being notified of them.

J. W. P.
J. M. B.

Acknowledgments

Color Illustrations

Page i: Campaign assemblage (courtesy Advertising Department of the
National Broadcasting Company and the J. Doyle Dewitt Collection). ii:
Jefferson banner (Smithsonian Institution). iii: J. Q. Adams sewing box,
Clay pipe, Jackson pitcher (all Smithsonian). iv: Harrison banner (New-
York Historical Society), Polk banner (Smithsonian). v: Lincoln poster
(Smithsonian). vi: Grant poster (Warshaw Collection of Business Ameri-
cana). vii: Greeley sheet music and Garfield kerchief (both S. Seidman Col-
lection of Americana), Tilden ribbon (Smithsonian). viii: Cleveland cartoon
(Warshaw Collection). ix: *Judge* cover (New York Public Library Picture
Collection), McKinley Plate (S. Seidman Collection), luncheon placemats
(Warshaw Collection). x: T. Roosevelt poster (New-York Historical Society),
group of buttons (S. Seidman Collection). xi: Taft plate and Wilson sheet
music (both Warshaw Collection). xii: Harding poster (Smithsonian). xiii:
Neckties (Smithsonian), Roosevelt license plate (Franklin D. Roosevelt
Library). xiv: Dewey umbrella and group of buttons (all Smithsonian).
xv: Kennedy-Nixon hats (Smithsonian). xvi: Goldwater bumper stickers and
Johnson button (all Smithsonian).

Cover Illustrations

Clay pipe and Dewey umbrella (Smithsonian Institution), Lincoln medallion
and Taft button (S. Seidman Collection of Americana), Johnson button (J.
Bruce Hall Collection).

CONTENTS

PART 4
The people in politics

PART 5

Policy-makers for the people

PART 6

Big government in action

PART 7
State and local government

PART 1

Democratic government in America

A Problem Guide   The American system of government is probably the most complicated on earth. It is also one of the most interesting, and—since the United States exerts world leadership—one of the most important. Because our system is so complex, however, it is easy to get bogged down in details and to lose perspective. The purpose of these "problem guides" at the opening of each part of this book is to help you gain an overview of the main problems that lie behind the details of government.

The book as a whole will emphasize five sets of problems:

First, *the challenge to democratic government*: How can we answer the claim of communists and other antidemocrats that democratic government is just a cloak for rule by a few selfish interests, that "government by the people" is a luxury to be enjoyed by only a few peo-

ples, that for most of mankind it is ineffective and inappropriate, and that democratic government as we know it in America cannot compete with other types of government throughout the world? Part One poses this problem.

Second, *the problem of constitutional government*: How can we maintain a constitutional government largely shaped in 1787 in the face of the vast and urgent demands of the 1960's? For example, how can we give our leaders enough power to do their jobs well and still prevent them from misusing that power? How can we create genuine teamwork within Washington and between Washington and the state capitals, and at the same time maintain a constitutional system that divides power among a host of officials? Part Two emphasizes this set of problems.

Third, *the problem of individual*

rights: How can democratic government maintain a balance between liberty and order, between diversity and uniformity, between individual rights and collective needs? The philosopher Bertrand Russell has stated this problem well: "How can we combine that degree of individual initiative which is necessary for progress with the degree of social cohesion that is necessary for survival?" This set of problems is treated chiefly in Part Three.

Fourth, *the problem of popular representation:* How fairly do our interest groups, opinion agencies, political parties, and elections reflect the ideas and needs of the American people? For example, how much influence should a popular majority (exerted perhaps through a political party) have as compared with the major interest groups, such as labor and business (exerted perhaps through publicity and lobbying organizations)? How can we meet the demands of organized groups without sacrificing the welfare of the people as a whole? Part Four focuses on this set of problems.

Fifth, *the problem of responsible leadership:* How can we give our leaders enough governmental authority to cope with present and emerging problems and still keep them accountable to the people? For example, should the President have more leeway, at least in foreign affairs? Should we create more unity between President and Congress, or do we want them to check each other? How responsible is Congress to the people—and to what groups of people? Should we make our leaders—executive and legislative and even judicial—more responsible to the majority of the people? If so, how could this be done? Part Five is largely concerned with this set of governmental problems.

But here is an important reminder: Since American government is a "seamless web," it is impossible (and undesirable) to separate one problem sharply from another. Most of these problems are closely interrelated—for example: constitutionalism in Part Two is related to individual liberty in Part Three, representation in Part Four is related to responsible leadership in Part Five. Hence every one of the major problems that we have mentioned is bound to spill over into every part of this book. The guides like that above simply suggest the part of the book in which certain sets of problems are emphasized.

1 GOVERNMENT BY THE PEOPLE?

This is an exciting time to be studying American government. Or so it seems to the authors. A student might feel differently. The word "exciting" he might reserve for the latest sportscar, rock 'n' roll song hit, Italian movie, or Pop or Op art. Or perhaps he feels that no classroom exercise can compete in excitement with the more direct involvement in the political life that makes today's headlines. But consider what has hap-

3

pened in American politics in the short time since a student's political conscious-
ness dawned in his early 'teens.

A 43-year-old Senator named Kennedy boldly defied the tradition that you must
be a middle-aged Protestant even to compete in the presidential sweepstakes and
carried off the grand prize.

Elected on a platform of "get America moving again," that vigorous young
President met some of the built-in checks and balances of the American system
as Congress delayed or killed off many of his main proposals for a New Frontier.

The civil rights struggle, after simmering for years, burst out into the streets and
schoolyards of the nation.

The Americans and the communists confronted each other "eyeball to eyeball"
in Cuba, Vietnam, Berlin, and a dozen other tension points around the world.

One man in Dallas ended the Thousand Days of John F. Kennedy and recast
the shape of American politics.

A new President, labeled a Southerner, a moderate, a compromiser, promptly
took a "northern" stand on civil rights, an advanced position on the responsibilities of government, and an uncompromising position on social welfare measures.

A conservative Senator named Goldwater gained the Republican presidential
nomination over the opposition of moderates who had long controlled it, launched
a counter-attack against the whole trend of the federal government under all the
Presidents since Hoover, and was overwhelmingly defeated everywhere except in
his home state and the deep South.

Lyndon Johnson, whose public experience and political instincts lay mainly in
domestic matters, was drawn increasingly into his roles as foreign-policy maker
and commander in chief.

These were some of the more obviously dramatic events of the 1960's. Less obvious ones might in the long run be more significant. The Supreme Court, traditionally the most passive of the three branches of government, made some of the
most crucial political decisions of the century in civil rights, church-state relations,
birth control, legislative districting. The "solid South" began to vote Republican.
Congress, which had been blocking major presidential proposals for 25 years, after
the election of 1964 often took stronger positions than the President himself on
major items of the Great Society. The concentration of power in the Presidency
seemed to reach a new peak. And behind all this were fundamental social and
economic developments that will be mentioned later in this chapter.

But if these are stirring times for the study of American government, we must
grant that they are also difficult times for such study because of the complexity
and changeableness of the political system. The serious student of modern American government cannot be content with a simple description of President and
Congress and the obvious features of the system. He must do at least four things:

1. He must comprehend *government* as a general phenomenon and see American government as one manifestation of it.

2. He must see American government as one that purports to be a democratic

government and hence must be tested by Western values of free, popular, and constitutional government.

3. He must see this government as part of a broad, changing culture that shapes government and is influenced by it.

4. He must understand the intellectual tool—the *discipline* of *political science*—with which he is conducting his study of American government.

This book deals mainly with the first two of these four items, but we will consider all four briefly in this introductory chapter.

The Subject: Government

One freshman, after reading a book about government, laid it down, threw up his hands, and exclaimed "It's just a big, buzzing confusion to me!" He was right. Government *is* immensely complicated, especially in a large, heterogeneous society. Veteran reporters in Washington sometimes describe the nation's capital as a jungle, crisscrossed by a tangled network of trails. But we can find some kind of order and sense in all this complexity.

The Scope of Government

Let us begin by considering *government* in its broadest scope—as a system of social control, as the ordering of human relations, as both the most formal and the most private and intimate law. So defined, government is much more than what we see in Washington or the state capitals or city hall. It takes many forms. The most common government in the broader sense of the term is the *family*. Other forms of government are an organized religion, a labor union, a corporation. A college club or fraternity is a government—one that makes rules, controls behavior (effectively or not), even inflicts penalties and punishments.

Political scientists, however, are mainly concerned with the more formal government operating amid the informal governments. They are concerned, that is, with *centralized organizations* that maintain *systems of order* over larger communities, with those parts of the social system that are formally designated as the means for the *resolution of conflict* and for the *authoritative allocation of values*.[1] Unlike the family or other informal governments, the "polity" is usually a complex interaction of institutions such as constitutions, legislatures, elections, bureaucracies. Such a formal complex of interacting structures—that for the United States—is the subject of this book. But remember that a formal governmental system such as this cannot be understood as something isolated from the thousands of in-

[1] R. M. MacIver, *The Web of Government* (Macmillan, 1947); David Easton, *The Political System* (Knopf, 1953); William C. Mitchell, *The American Polity* (The Free Press, 1962); David B. Truman, *The Governmental Process* (Knopf, 1951).

formal governments that cluster throughout our society, and with which formal governmental systems continually interact.

Nor can we separate government from people's attitudes toward it. Government is not just a set of leaders, laws, offices, and other tangible things. It is what people expect from it, what they would do with it, how they respect it or fear it or ignore it. There was little protest in 1887 when President Cleveland vetoed a small appropriation to aid farmers stricken by drought to buy new grain seed. People did not expect government to act on such a matter, in those times. Or take the Al Capone days in Chicago. Chicago had a mayor, parties, laws, policemen—it had a government. But the shopkeepers on the south side paid protection money to Capone's henchmen because they respected the government of the mob more than they depended on the government of the city.

Is there any difference between the words "government" and "politics"? As defined above, there is none. Both terms refer to the ordering of social relationships under formal and informal laws and rules.

The Shape of Government

So much for government in the broadest perspective. But just as we cannot climb the Empire State Building and comprehend metropolitan complexity unless we look for rivers, streets, and parks, we cannot understand government unless we see its component parts and how they relate to one another.

Glance through the Table of Contents of this book and you will get a sense of the component parts of the great machine that is the American political system— parts such as the Constitution, federalism, civil liberties, political parties and groups, elections, Congress, President, and so on. These are described one by one because each is a big subject in itself. Yet there is bound to be something artificial about such a description. It is like describing a baseball game by telling first about the catcher, pitcher, first baseman, and so on, then the players on the other team, then the rules, the ball, the gloves, and all the rest, without saying anything about the players in *action*. And yet it is this very interaction, this situational give-and-take among the players, that makes up the essence of the ball game.

So it is with government. All its component parts—constitutions, legislatures, political parties, and so on—affect one another. What we need, then, is some way of cutting across all these component parts to reveal the totality of the political system. One way of doing this is to concentrate on the four "I's" of government: institutions, interests, ideas, and individuals.[2]

1. *Institutions.* A political institution is any organized pattern of behavior that is well established as a continuing part of a political system: secret ballots, gov-

[2] After Pendleton Herring; for an excellent example of how this method of analysis can be used to illuminate the policy-making process, see Stephen K. Bailey, *Congress Makes a Law* (Columbia Univ. Press, 1950).

ernment agencies, courts, press conferences, congressional committees. They have a strong element of permanence; they are often embedded in law or tradition. They are somewhat predictable in a general sense: we know that a presidential election will be held every four years and part of a new Congress elected at the same time, even though we do not know who the President will be or what bills the new Congress will pass.

2. *Interests*. Government operates amid a tangle of interests, with millions of men pushing and hauling in their efforts to reach private and public goals. Workers want more pay; farmers seek higher prices; businessmen demand less government interference; veterans ask higher pensions. Other interests are less economic, as in the case of religious or temperance groups. Groups tend to grow out of interests and to create new interests in turn. Interests affect, and are affected by, the operations of government. The American system would look very different without the business, labor, professional, and hundreds of other groups that exert political pressure.

3. *Ideas*. Men possess thoughts, it is said, but ideas possess men. Ideas come in all shapes and sizes. They may be strong and durable, such as the general American belief in "government by the people," or they may be superficial or short-lived. They may be rational or irrational. An example of the latter was the fervent belief of millions of Germans that the "Aryan" race was superior to any other. Ideas may relate closely to people's economic interests, as in the case of trade-union support of social welfare laws, or they may run directly counter to the material welfare of those holding the belief. Ideas, in short, are forces that in themselves have an impact on politics.

4. *Individuals*. All the above forces operate through, and are transformed by, the people and their leaders. Obviously, America would be a different kind of country had it not been for great Presidents such as Washington and Lincoln, potent senators such as Henry Clay and Robert A. Taft, famous Supreme Court justices such as John Marshall and Oliver Wendell Holmes—and hundreds of industrialists, soldiers, inventors, scholars, financiers, and writers who have left their imprint on American history. America would also be a much different place were it not for the millions of "plain" or "common" men and women—the Smiths, Cohens, Murphys, Muellers, and all the rest—who have elected the Presidents and congressmen, fought the wars, built the railroads and dams, and paid the taxes.

These, then, are four basic forces that interact with one another, like the players in a baseball game, and produce the political system that will be described in the following chapters.

The Focus: American Democratic Government

Democracy—like liberty, equality, and justice—is hard to define precisely. The term has come to mean so many different things and has won such great popularity that even the communists have tried to take it over; communist-controlled eastern Germany, for example, is called the German Democratic Republic. The word itself is made up of two Greek roots—*demos*, the people, and *kratia*, authority—and was used by the Greeks to mean government by the many, as contrasted with government by the few (oligarchy), or by one (autocracy). The word came into English usage in the seventeenth century and was originally used to denote only *direct* democracy, the kind of government that existed in Athens and other Greek city-states, where all enfranchised citizens came together to discuss and pass laws.

The term "democratic government," like the term "democracy," is ambiguous and confusing. Some writers distinguish between *democratic* and *republican* governments, the former meaning governments in which decisions are made *directly* by a majority of the people—as in a New England town meeting—and the latter meaning governments in which the people's wishes are filtered through a series of *representative bodies*, such as Congress. But in this book we shall use the term "democratic government" to mean a representative democracy and shall use "democratic" and "republican" governments interchangeably to mean any government in which those who do the actual governing acquire their power to do so by means of a *fair, free, and vigorous contest for the people's votes*.

So much, then, for what we mean generally by "government by the people." What are the essential values that buttress and perpetuate *democratic* government?

Three Basic Democratic Values

Democracy rests on a belief in the fundamental dignity and importance of the *individual*, in the essential *equality* of human beings, and in the individual's need for *freedom*.

The emphasis on the supreme worth of the individual has run unbroken through democratic thought. It is woven into the writings of Thomas Jefferson, especially in the Declaration of Independence, where he eloquently proclaimed that all men have been endowed by their Creator with certain inalienable rights and that men create governments to secure these rights. Lyndon Johnson and Barry Goldwater agreed in 1964 that all public and private institutions must be designed to protect and promote the integrity and dignity of the individual; they simply disagreed over how best to do this.

This doctrine of *individualism* (not to be confused with the doctrine of laissez faire) rests on the conviction that there is supreme worth in every human being. It demands that we should, in the words of a great philosopher, Immanuel Kant, "so act as to treat humanity, whether in thine own person or in that of any other, in every case as an end withal, never as means only." Individualism makes the individual the central measure of value. The state, the union, and the corporation are valued solely in terms of their usefulness for individuals.

The doctrine of *statism*, on the other hand, makes the state the measure of value, and holds that public policies and governmental forms are good if they promote the well-being of the state. Democratic political theory has refused to glorify the state or to shroud it in metaphysical abstractions. The state is nothing more than the organized political society that operates through government. The welfare of the state has no meaning except in terms of the welfare of the individuals who comprise it.

The second basic premise of democracy is the right of *each* individual to be treated as a unique and inviolable human being. The democrat does not insist, as his critics sometimes imply, that all men are equal in talents, virtues, or capabilities. He does insist that the claims of one individual to his life, liberty, and happiness must be treated as just as important as those of any other individual. He insists that " the poorest he that is in England has a life to live as the richest he," [3] as Colonel Rainboro said back in 1647. The democrat insists that no man be treated as a slave or tool for the use of others.

The third basic premise of democracy is the belief that liberty is desirable, that freedom is good. "Liberty" and "freedom" are slippery words, but as we are using them here they mean that each individual should have the maximum opportunity to select his own purposes in life and to choose the means to accomplish those purposes. The core of liberty is self-determination. "Positive freedom consists," writes Erich Fromm, "in the spontaneous activity of the total, integrated personality." Liberty and freedom mean more than the absence of external restraints; they connote the "power" to act positively toward the goals one has chosen.

Why is freedom desirable? Because the freedom *to make choices* and *to act upon them* is essential to the development of those faculties that make one a human being. Denied this freedom, the individual becomes something less than a man. It is this quality of being able to make rational choices, to select the good from the bad and to decide whether to seek the good, that distinguishes men from other animals. It is only through the use of his freedom that the individual develops a sense of responsibility and self-restraint. It is only by acting as free and responsible individuals that men are able to exploit their full capacity for growth.

From the viewpoint of society, freedom is desirable because both history and logic suggest that liberty is the key to social progress. The greater the area of freedom, the greater the probability of discovering better ways of living. Where men enjoy freedom of inquiry and expression, they are more likely to detect error and uncover truth. Progress is stifled wherever an authoritarian group or even social custom imposes an orthodoxy that none may question. Denial of freedom, moreover, generates personal frustration, which in turn may erupt into aggressive, antisocial behavior.

There is nothing new about these basic principles of democracy. They express ancient ideals of brotherhood, compassion, justice, and the dignity of man— ideals that have deep roots in the civilization of the world.

---

[3] Col. Thomas Rainboro, "Debates on the Putney Project, 1647," from A. T. Mason, *Free Government in the Making* (Oxford Univ. Press, 1949), p. 12.

What We Mean by Democratic Government

Since in all but the most simple societies the day-by-day operation of government must be in the hands of a small group of people, democratic government is essentially a device to determine which of several competing groups shall run the government. In a democracy the electorate chooses the major policy officials in *free* and *relatively frequent elections*. Here we pass over the important question of just what proportion of the adult population must be given a voice in the political affairs of the community in order to conform to democratic ground rules. The proportion must be large enough, however, so that the electorate will represent all the interests and the interests of all.

The elections must be free. There is no meaning to sham elections in which no criticism is permitted and no opposition party allowed to bid for votes. In the Soviet Union it may well be that a large number of Soviet citizens actually support their leaders and consent to their rule. But it is a consent of ignorance, since the ruling elite secures the citizens' support through a monopoly of all the sources of information. The only way the rulers of the Soviet Union may be removed from office is by revolution, assassination, or internal *coup d'état*. In a democratic government the recurring choice of rulers is a matter of routine.

In order for the elections to be free, the citizens must enjoy the right to have *access* to the facts, to *criticize*, to *participate* in political deliberations, and to *organize* for political purposes. This last is of especial importance in modern societies where the units of politics are organized groups. Individuals can become most politically effective by joining with others. Those who hold power can be checked only when the people are free to form pressure groups and political parties, and to use all methods of peaceful persuasion.

A democratic government operates in accord with the *decisions of majorities;* the decisions about who is to run the government and what policies are to become the law of the land are determined by voting. He who gets the most votes wins the election. There is no magic in numerical majorities; but some practical means is needed to determine the outcome of elections and to make decisions. The people do not speak with a united voice; they are divided about candidates and public policies. We do what the majority wants. The majority is not necessarily right, but it is right to do what the majority wishes.

Finally, a democratic government is one in which all citizens have *equal voting power*. This does not mean that all must or will have equal political influence. Some men, by virtue of wealth, talent, or position, will have much greater political power than their fellow citizens. A newspaper publisher undoubtedly has considerably more influence in determining who gets elected to public office and what policies are enacted into law than most who read his paper, but when the votes are counted the publisher has no more nor less voting power than the ordinary citizen. Any other way would negate the very idea of majority rule.

From our analysis of democratic government we can see that the crucial factor determining whether or not we shall consider a government democratic is not how much power the public officials have *but how public officials secure and retain their offices.* The President of the United States wields great power, but this in no way makes our government less democratic—the key point is that the man who is President had to win a free competitive election. The vanquished in a political election are required by the rules of democracy to allow the victorious to govern, but the same rules require the victorious to allow today's minorities to try to become tomorrow's political majorities. You can win a tennis match by jumping over the net and hitting your opponent over the head with the racket, but then you are no longer playing tennis. You can win an election by throwing your opponents in jail, but then you are no longer operating democratically. "To see popular sovereignty, political equality, individual political rights, and majority rule . . . is to see four aspects of the same general principle. . . . More than merely compatible with one another, they are necessary to one another." [4]

So much for the meaning of democratic government. What do we mean by American *constitutional* government?

Constitutionalism—Limited Government

Constitutionalism has to do with the *limits* set on the power of public officials. A constitutional government is one in which there are recognized and generally accepted *limits to the power of those who govern.* In a constitutional government officials have only the authority that the constitution has delegated to them, and any official who exceeds the scope of this authority surrenders his claim to obedience.

Our American government is both democratic *and* constitutional, for there are recognized limits to what government may do, even a government that speaks for a majority. The individual has certain basic rights that he enjoys merely because he is a human being, and not at the pleasure of the government, or even at the pleasure of the majority. Not everyone agrees on the concrete content of these rights, but it is agreed that there are certain things that no government may do and other things that it may do only according to proper and fair procedure. At a minimum, the government may not deprive any person of his life, liberty, or property except by just and fair procedures of law.

Although there have been in the past, under rather unusual circumstances, constitutional governments that were not democratic, it is unlikely that a constitutional government could be maintained in any industrialized modern nation unless it is also democratic. The primary sanctions for insuring that those who hold public power do not exceed the limits of their authority are the rights of unfettered criticism and the necessity of those in office periodically to win elections in order to retain their power. Constitutionalism, with its emphasis on *limited*

---

[4] Thomas Landon Thorson, *The Logic of Democracy* (Holt, Rinehart and Winston, 1962), p. 143.

government, and democracy, with its emphasis on the right of the people to decide who shall wield governmental power, are not exclusive categories but mutually supporting institutions.

What Democratic Government Is Not

Democratic governments come in many varieties, of which the American is only one. Yet some Americans assume that only governments exactly like our own are democratic. They confuse the essentials with the non-essentials. Separation of powers, written constitutions, federalism, and judicial review—to mention just a few of the basic features of American government that will be taken up in this book—are generally supported by Americans as desirable ways of limiting government and making it responsible to the people. But these do not in themselves make our government democratic. The government of England has virtually none of these features; the Canadian, Australian, French, and Swedish governments have them only in part. But in all these countries the majority rule, and minority rights are secure. On the other hand, the Soviet Union has a written constitution and, at least formally, federalism; but the government is in the hands of a self-appointed elite, and those who differ with the rulers usually have the choice of silence or Siberia.

Some Americans assume also that only countries that have our kind of mixed, free-enterprise, competitive economy can have democratic governments. Can free government be maintained, they ask, when the economy is controlled by the government? Democracy has in the past been closely associated with capitalism. It developed along with the rise of the middle class and the growth of the private-enterprise system. Because of this historical connection, many argue that capitalism is necessary to democratic government and that the end of capitalism would mean the end of free government. Others are equally convinced, however, that democratic government does not depend on capitalism. They believe, on the contrary, that effective democracy cannot be achieved until economic power is made subject to governmental control. Political democracy, they say, is impossible without "economic democracy."

In a like manner, some believe that a planned economy is the "road to serfdom," while others consider it to be the road to freedom. Some believe that the welfare state will undermine democratic government, while to others such a program is essential for the preservation of republican government. These positions, and all those in between, are tenable. Plausible arguments can be made and evidence marshalled to support any of them.

But democracy is not capitalism, socialism, the welfare state, planning, the absence of planning, or any other particular economic system, nor does democratic government require any of these. At times our government has followed the favorite policies of business, at times those of labor. In our country the coal industry is privately owned and operated; in England it is owned and operated by the government. But both we and the British have democratic governments because policy is made after free discussion and free elections, and the government does not jeopardize the right of the opposition to oppose. Within limits it is not the *content* of the economic policies that makes a government democratic as much as it is the *procedures* by which they are adopted. A free people has the right to choose socialism, laissez faire, the welfare state, or any mixture they want.

Democratic government, then, is not an economic system but a *way of governing and of being governed*. This does not mean that an economic system is unrelated to the amount of democracy in a country. The point is that democratic government allows the people to discuss different economic arrangements, to test them in terms of democratic ideals, and to change them if they are found wanting. Wise economic policies will help democratic government survive, but democratic government, in turn, enables us to develop wise economic policies.

The Context: Changing American Society

When we study American government we study certain aspects of the behavior of the American people. That is all there is to it—the people, their ideas and customs, and the things they inherit and create. Sometimes we forget this simple but fundamental fact. We become so involved in talking about federalism, or separation of powers, or constitutions, or laws, that we lose sight of the fact that all these things are merely descriptions of *people* and the things *people* produce, that they are shorthand ways to describe how *people* behave, what they believe, what they do.

The way Americans behave politically and the operation of their governmental institutions are obviously related to how they make a living, their fears and anxieties, where they live—in fact, with everything important to them and about them. Since we shall spend most of our time concentrating on the political and governmental aspects of American people, let us first look at the social, psychological, and economic forces that shape politics. What are the salient aspects of American society that condition and influence the nature of American democratic government?

First of all, the United States is a land of infinite diversity. Consider our climate and geography. The continental sweep of our nation embraces burning deserts, thousand-mile-long mountain ranges, humid areas drenched with rain, immense prairies, dust bowls, lake regions, vast forests, and many thousands of miles of coastline. We are a nation of regions vast enough to be called subnations, and each subnation is internally bound by ties of history, politics, economics, and dialect. Each is almost a nation in itself, containing nearly as much diversity as France, Spain, or England.

Ours is a nation of nations in an even more literal sense. America is the fabled "melting pot." We are a nation of Italian-Americans, Irish-Americans, Polish-Americans, Swedish-Americans, German-Americans, Latin-Americans, and many other "hyphenated" groups, along with Negroes, old Yankee groups, Puerto Ricans, Indians, and many others. The millions of immigrants brought the old country with them; they introduced not only differences in languages and customs but also varying religious and political attitudes. They did not discard their old beliefs and languages and customs overnight; on the contrary, they often clung to their separate ways as long as they could. In short, the melting pot did not melt everyone into the same dull gray.

Put these two elements together—sectionalism and a variety of national origins —and the checkered, polyglot nature of America begins to emerge. Add to these the religious diversity—the scores of Protestant sects, the powerful Catholic and Jewish groups; add also the divisive impact of political doctrines that have swept the country, some from Europe, some home-grown; add finally the influence of the competitiveness and individualism that Americans have long praised and practiced—and the heterogeneity of America becomes even more apparent.

Yet there is an underlying homogeneity too. Americans have a common language and venerate national heroes like George Washington and Thomas Jefferson. Wherever we live we listen to the same song hits, read the same comic strips, watch the same movies. Great corporations, labor unions, farm organizations span the nation and affect the lives of people everywhere. To walk down Main Street in our home town, with its bright lights, chain stores, parking meters, traffic jams, is to walk down *any* Main Street in America.

The homogeneity of Americans stems from the fact that regardless of our religion, place of birth, or national origin, we share a common culture, a common language, common heroes, common ideals, a common nationality. On the other hand, no single religion or industry, no single class or profession, is prevalent. We have social checks and balances, a pluralistic outlook, that in many ways is more important than our form of government itself in creating a climate of democracy.

Other social trends, too, have had an effect on government. The movement of our people—first from country to city, and now from city to suburb—has forced politicians to change their campaign appeals. The increased number of older persons has strengthened their political power and directed attention to pensions and programs for the elderly. The incorporation of minorities into the mainstream of American life has led to a keener concern for civil liberties. All these social trends make clear that what happens to Americans happens to American government.

Social Trends

1. *Population changes.* There were about 200 million Americans by the late 1960's. Our population has doubled in the last fifty years. Not long ago the demographers, who study such vital statistics as births, marriages, and deaths, were predicting that our population curve would soon flatten out and that the proportion of young people in the total popu-

lation would decline at a rapid rate. The tremendous increase in population during recent years of prosperity, however, has led to a revision of these estimates. The Bureau of the Census predicts that, barring catastrophic wars or depressions, our population will reach 235 million by 1975.

Our population is also changing in character. For many decades there has been an increase in urban population, as compared with rural, and this trend is continuing. Almost two-thirds of the people live in urban areas as defined by the Census Bureau. Suburban communities are growing at a much faster rate than the central, built-up areas of our cities. The rise of "Suburbia" is having a variety of social and political effects. Population increase is also uneven in different areas of the country. During the 1950's the population of the West, for example, grew much faster than that of the South. Several agricultural states declined in population.

Our population is *aging* as well as growing. The median age in 1900 was 23 years; in 1960 it reached 30. The proportion of people over 65 was 4 per cent in 1900 and is about twice that today. Such changes have important implications for government—for example, in the scope of old-age assistance.

2. *The class system.* In certain ways American society is stratified. Study after study of American communities has revealed a socio-economic class system based largely on wealth. People with similar incomes, occupations, or social positions tend to associate and to form relatively distinct classes. In the typical community at least three basic classes are found—upper, middle, and lower—but usually there are gradations within classes, such as the upper-middle class (wealthy business and professional groups) and the lower-middle class (clerical workers and highly-skilled labor).

The important question is not whether classes exist but whether America is becoming more or less stratified. The day when an individual could rise rapidly from class to class seems to be passing. The "rags to riches" feats of Horatio Alger heroes may have been exaggerated, but they happen even less often today. Increasingly, people seem to follow the occupational and social paths of their parents. On the other hand, there is considerable mobility and flexibility in the largest and most dynamic strata, the middle classes.[5] Here people move "down" or "up" much more freely than in the more stratified upper and lower classes. There are tendencies toward *caste*, too, in American life, especially in the case of minority groups; but the caste system also is in a state of flux, owing to pressures from inside the caste and from outside. Our class system contains within itself the seeds of change.

3. *Mass culture.* The United States, as we have noted, is a medley of diverse groups and subcultures. But the nation and its people have a sense of unity too, and underlying this sense of unity is a mass culture that is common to all the subcultures. Our mass culture is the result of many things—common traditions, folklore, a common language, past and present wars and crises, and the like. It is

[5] J. W. Bennett and M. M. Tumin, *Social Life* (Knopf, 1948), pp. 570–600. See also Don A. Martindale, *American Society* (Van Nostrand, 1960).

produced also by our mass media of communications—films that are shown in every community in the land, magazines that sell millions of copies each issue, and radio and television programs that blanket the nation.

What happens when a mass culture exists along with many subcultures? The mass culture links the subcultures together. But can the mass culture go very deep? According to some sociologists, it lacks roots, consisting as it does of a shifting set of attitudes and values that tend to be simple and fleeting in nature: the fads of teen-agers, the cult of actor worshippers, food fetishes, and self-improvement formulas for everything from hair styles to hypnosis. Such ephemeral common patterns do not provide a core of common fixed meaning and values.

4. *War.* Fourteen million Americans donned military uniforms in World War

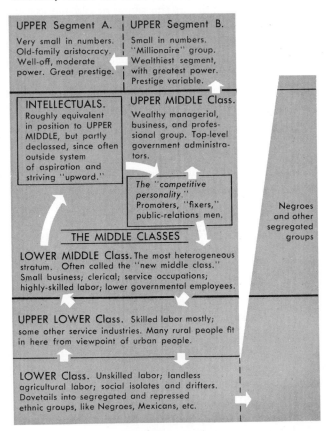

THE AMERICAN CLASS SYSTEM

(Tendency toward Rigidity of this UPPER Stratum through Hereditary Wealth and Social Position.)

UPPER Segment A.
Very small in numbers. Old-family aristocracy. Well-off, moderate power. Great prestige.

UPPER Segment B.
Small in numbers. "Millionaire" group. Wealthiest segment, with greatest power. Prestige variable.

INTELLECTUALS.
Roughly equivalent in position to UPPER MIDDLE, but partly declassed, since often outside system of aspiration and striving "upward."

UPPER MIDDLE Class.
Wealthy managerial, business, and professional group. Top-level government administrators.

The "competitive personality." Promoters, "fixers," public-relations men.

THE MIDDLE CLASSES

LOWER MIDDLE Class. The most heterogeneous stratum. Often called the "new middle class." Small business; clerical; service occupations; highly-skilled labor; lower governmental employees.

UPPER LOWER Class. Skilled labor mostly; some other service industries. Many rural people fit in here from viewpoint of urban people.

LOWER Class. Unskilled labor; landless agricultural labor; social isolates and drifters. Dovetails into segregated and repressed ethnic groups, like Negroes, Mexicans, etc.

Negroes and other segregated groups

From John W. Bennett and Melvin M. Tumin, Social Life, *by permission of Alfred A. Knopf, Inc. Copyright 1948 by Alfred A. Knopf, Inc.*

(Tendency toward Rigidity of this LOWER Class through Constant Economic Underprivilege and Unemployment.)

II, and countless other millions worked in the war program at home. Tens of thousands served in the three-year-long Korean war and more recently in Vietnam. In a sense, we have a whole new subculture—that of millions of men, and some women, working and training in camps and other military installations at home and abroad. It is too early to estimate the impact of continued war crises on Americans, but surely it will leave its mark on our attitudes, customs, behavior, and way of life.

Psychological Trends

All these social trends, though at times contradictory and conflicting, reveal a common trend: the trend toward *bigness*. Ours is a civilization of big cities, big machines, big labor, big business, big bombs, big government. In the shadow of this bigness, the individual stands a tiny and puny figure. To be sure, he created this bigness, but in doing so he may have built a Frankenstein's monster that in turn will destroy him, or at least destroy his power to fashion his life as he wishes.

Little man, big world—this is the nub of the problem. But the problem shows itself in several ways. One is the individual's feeling of *helplessness*. The world is swept by gigantic forces over which he has little sense of control. A second is his feeling of *rootlessness*. Millions of men, living in cities, have little of the feeling of belonging and permanence that their grandfathers experienced in more stable, rural areas. A third aspect, closely related to the other two, is the feeling of *impersonality*. Our social relationships often lack depth and meaning; in the fast pace of urban life our contacts with others may be fleeting and shallow. Individual identity is ignored or crushed.

These feelings of helplessness, rootlessness, and impersonality have influenced our literature and art. Think of Charlie Chaplin in the movie *Modern Times*—the little man controlled by the great machine. Or Franz Kafka's novel *The Trial*, in which the hero, accused of a crime he did not commit and even the nature of which he is uncertain, becomes entangled in a vast nightmarish bureaucracy and is finally destroyed. Social scientists have become increasingly interested in the fate of the little man in the big society. Psychologists have identified three important forces relating to government:

1. *The quest for security.* Man has freed himself from many old bonds, such as slavery and feudalism, and has won for himself certain individual rights and liberties. But in obtaining freedom from the old controls, he has failed to gain the positive freedom of realizing his intellectual and artistic potentialities. Instead, freedom has posed new problems that he feels unable to meet. Living amid modern industrial civilization—with its large-scale organization, its mobility and competitiveness, its impersonality, its sheer bigness—he feels isolated, inadequate, and lonely. Gone is the old framework of custom and authority, of life in small groups and stable communities. The machine age has made man rich in material

things, but he feels insecure, helpless, isolated, anxious, alienated, powerless, lost.

What is the result? Modern man has tried, in the words of the psychoanalyst Erich Fromm, to *escape* from freedom. Faced with impossible situations and decisions, he may turn away from freedom and individuality and try to fuse himself with some outside person or thing to gain a sense of security.[6] He may submit to some self-confident person who has all the "answers" and issues all the orders. One reason Hitler was able to take power in the early 1930's was the feeling of millions of Germans that they were in the grip of giant economic and social forces that they could not understand or control.

2. *The quest for conformity.* Another current tendency, some social scientists feel, is that people are increasingly eager to conform to the standards of men and women around them. In bringing up children, David Riesman noted, parents want their children to be *popular* with *other* children.[7] Mother becomes a chauffeur and a booking agent. The teen-ager's most important possession is a "popularity kit" composed of a knowledge of the latest gadgets, of movie and TV stars, of popular tunes, uniformity in clothes styles, plus an amazing storehouse of small talk on all sorts of subjects. One must conform and adjust. Being an "egghead" or in any way high-hat or "different" is forbidden.

Many adults also seek to conform. Consider, for example, life in some of our bigger organizations, such as government agencies, universities, and especially business corporations. According to one study, success in these organizations forces one to become an "organization man" who conforms to the "system." [8] In a big corporation the trainees, the executives, and even their wives are not supposed to exhibit too much individuality; they are expected to adjust themselves to the needs and life of the corporation, even when they are back home in Suburbia. The pressure to conform is not overtly tyrannical; it is subtle, continuous, and pervasive, and, for that reason, all the more effective. The organization man gains security and "togetherness" but suffers loss of individual responsibility and the freedom to be an *un*common man.

The implications for democratic government are important. Adjusting to others is not the same as individual freedom. The person whose greatest need in life is the approval of his neighbors, whose driving aim is to get along with others at almost any price—such a person may feel lonely in the great crowd. There is a need for autonomy as well as for adjustment, for individuality as well as for conformity. Democratic government cannot last in a homogenized society; civil liberties perish in a society where men will not tolerate political opinions or any other opinion, for that matter, different from their own.

3. *The quest for community.* Closely related to these forces is man's desire for some sense of *direction*, of *belonging*, of *community* with his neighbors. Just as children grow anxious when separated from their parents, says Sebastian de

---

[6] Erich Fromm, *Escape from Freedom* (Farrar & Rinehart, 1941). For political aspects of this problem in one state (Massachusetts), see Murray Levin, *The Compleat Politician* (Bobbs-Merrill, 1962).

[7] David Riesman, *The Lonely Crowd* (Yale Univ. Press, 1950).

[8] W. H. Whyte, Jr., *The Organization Man* (Doubleday, 1957).

Grazia, adults become anxious when separated from their political and religious "fathers"—from their tribal chiefs, priests, gods, kings, and presidents.[9] People *need* such rulers, for the rulers personify the moral codes that help bind citizens together and give them a sense of purpose and direction.

Trouble may result when our moral codes conflict. Our religions, de Grazia says, teach us the need for brotherly love, while Western economic philosophy teaches the need for competitiveness. Modern Western culture, with its stress on individual liberty, tends to leave people confused, insecure, and lacking in purpose. *Men have always felt the need to believe in something or someone.* They have always had leaders who symbolized and helped realize men's highest aspirations and who gave them a sense of community.

What of the impact of these psychological trends on American government? War and fear of war have led to huge government bureaucracies for defense and for veterans' welfare. The quest for security is often cited as one of the factors lying behind the rise of "big government." The psychological insecurity of some Americans, it is said, has led to the success of politicians who play on and exaggerate people's fears in an attempt to win mass followings.

Yet a word of caution: It is difficult to generalize with confidence about psychological trends. Many social scientists disagree that the trends outlined here are so clear or the situation so serious as some of the above views seem to indicate. Other and even contradictory generalizations could be made. It is not certain, for example, that life in the rural communities of a hundred years ago was psychologically secure or that modern urban man feels less rooted than did some of his isolated and culturally poverty-stricken forefathers. Generalizations about psychological trends often depend on which evidence is emphasized. There are many forces working in many directions.

Economic Trends

Perhaps nothing has such a direct impact on American government as the economic needs and satisfactions of Americans. What trends, then, characterize our economy?

1. *Technological progress.* From the Stone Age and the Iron Age, man has passed into an age of glass, plastic fibers, alloys, an age of crop genetics, agrobiology, and mechanized farming, an age of speed and the invasion of outer space. A century ago a commissioner of patents asked Congress to abolish his office because everything had been invented. And yet inventions have come at a faster and faster rate; twice as many patents were granted between 1950 and 1960 as between 1890 and 1900. Less dramatic than these technological strides, but perhaps as important, has been our advance in understanding the human problems of our industrial civilization, such as employer-employee relations.

[9] Sebastian de Grazia, *The Political Community* (Univ. of Chicago Press, 1948), p. ix.

Two recent developments indicate that more industrial revolutions lie ahead. One of these, of course, is atomic energy, a source of vast power that can be harnessed to peacetime as well as wartime uses. The second is automation. Fantastically complicated but reliable machines can do certain kinds of work, including "thinking work," now done by skilled and white-collar people—and do that work much more economically.[10] Such machines, unlike a human operator, do not become bored, unhappy, distracted, bedridden, or rebellious.

2. *Mass production and consumption.* As a result of advanced technology, rich resources, and varied skills, Americans produce and consume more goods than any other people. Physical output has increased at least fivefold in the last fifty years, while the number of employees has only doubled and the length of the work-day has actually dropped by a third. Output per man-hour is still increasing. By the late 1960's our gross national product, stated in terms of constant dollars, had grown from $282 billion in 1947 to well over $500 billion.

Our capacity to consume goods and services is equally gigantic. In the past fifty years the proportion of our income spent on food, liquor, and tobacco has decreased slightly, and the proportion spent on clothing and personal care has stayed about the same. The proportion spent on personal transportation (notably automobiles) and on medical care and insurance, however, has doubled.

3. *Interdependence.* Years ago, the members of a family made most of what they needed with their own hands; today the average urban family hardly produces a tiny fraction of its needs. We depend on the goods and services of thousands of people scattered throughout the country for our daily needs. We have become increasingly *specialized* in our work. Specialization promotes greater efficiency, but it also allows disturbances in one sector of the economy to move quickly to other areas. We sink or swim together.

Related to this interdependence is the concentration of industrial and financial strength in fewer and larger corporations. Despite antitrust laws, the process of consolidation goes on. Today we have scores of "supermonopolies" in basic industries such as banking, railroads, automobiles, insurance, and public utilities, and widespread consolidation in textiles, foods, and the distributive trades. Labor organizations, too, have tended to become more and more centralized and integrated nationally.

4. *A mature or expanding economy?* Dynamic though it is, our economy is showing some signs of old age. We no longer have a western frontier offering limitless opportunities for economic expansion. Immigration today is relatively small compared to what it was fifty or seventy-five years ago. Certain areas of the country are declining economically and some investment outlets have dwindled sharply.

But there are also signs of youthful vigor. Our power to produce continues to increase. Population and national income have soared in the last fifteen years. Some sections of the country—notably the West and Southwest—are expanding

[10] Norbert Wiener, *The Human Use of Human Beings* (Houghton Mifflin, 1950).

at an explosive rate. Even older areas, such as the South and Northeast, have shown amazing powers of economic growth since the end of World War II. Instead of a western frontier, we have a kind of internal frontier that offers virtually limitless possibilities for the investment of money, manpower, and technology.

Indeed, Americans live in grand style. Never before have so many people "had it so good." Ours has been described as an "affluent society" in which our economic problems ironically stem not from scarcities but surpluses.[11] We have a labor force of over 75 million. Our productivity is high, our technological advances are great, and our natural resources are still immense.

5. *Persistence of poverty.* Amid the superlatives, several comments are in order. Although the United States can boast of a wider sharing of wealth than most other nations, certain Americans do not benefit from our high standard of living. Poverty persists. Tenant farmers, migratory workers, low-paid factory workers, chronically unemployed, and especially members of certain minority groups, have little of the material goods of life. Today we "hide" our poor by segregating them from the homes and highways of the rest of the community. But the poor are still with us and in large numbers, as is sporadically brought to the nation's attention when these ghettos of poverty explode in violence and frustration. What is most discouraging is that the rising tide of national wealth flows by these pockets of poverty with little impact on them. In this sub-culture, poverty is more than an economic condition and hence requires more than general economic prosperity for its alleviation.

6. *Public needs.* Despite our national wealth we are still in need of more hospitals, schools, and houses. Our cities lack grace and charm. We spend billions for new and shiny automobiles to drive along dirty, congested streets while breathing polluted air. We cheerfully support gigantic football and baseball stadiums but continue to crowd the mentally ill into dilapidated institutions. How we use our wealth is one of the great political questions facing Americans.

7. *Economic instability.* Our economy continues to be unstable. For over a century our business cycle has climbed and dipped like a roller coaster. We suffered long and severe depressions in the late 1830's, the 1870's, the 1890's, and the 1930's. In between were sharp but minor slumps, in 1884, 1904, 1914, 1920, 1937, 1958, and 1960. We have also had periods of sustained prosperity, however, as during the 1880's and the 1960's.

Is there a trend toward economic stability? Nobody knows. We have acquired a good deal of economic understanding in recent years, and we have established rudimentary machinery for evening out the peaks and canyons in the business cycle. The 1960 recession was one of the shortest and mildest of our history. Some economists, however, are unconvinced that we have yet learned how to achieve long-term stability. And persistent fear of tomorrow's depressions directly affects the way our governments operate.

[11] J. K. Galbraith, *The Affluent Society* (Houghton Mifflin, 1958).

The Discipline: Political Science

Some students are disappointed in college. They are impatient to get on with the business of the world and feel that in the midst of times crying for reform their teachers and texts ask for refined distinctions without a difference. This desire to substitute more exciting ventures for study is a characteristic not unknown to earlier generations of college students. As Justice Oliver Wendell Holmes counseled some law students years ago: "Young gentlemen, you had better learn torts before you twist the Cosmos by the tail."

Other students expect a sharp break with the kind of work they did in secondary schools, but all they seem to be getting is a kind of post-graduate high school. This feeling of lack of intellectual freshness is in part inevitable, for the new material in college must grow out of the old. But there is one important distinction between high school and college. For the mark of the more advanced scholar is his *self-consciousness* about his intellectual *preconceptions, equipment,* and *deficiencies.* And in college, we suggest, you should not merely study a subject, but study yourself studying the subject, not simply find out the "facts," but question the way you are gathering these "facts" and making sense out of them.

To the unsophisticated, a fact is "out there," easy to see, and common sense is sufficient to explain it. His assumptions about how things operate are not very complicated. Everybody has some generalized notions about the dynamics of the political system, a way to make sense out of events, even if not every one is aware of these assumptions. For example, to many people politics is a conflict between the "good guys" and the "bad guys," and the bad guys are always "conspiring" to force through the Congress laws to promote their own selfish interests.

In college we should develop some self-consciousness about our own underlying assumptions, for these assumptions are not neutral—they precondition both what we *look at* and what we *see* when we look. It is because of this phenomenon of "selective perception" that two individuals can live through the same events and each honestly see two different versions of what happened, for each will select out of the environment those things that "fit" with his underlying assumptions.

Political scientists' assumptions—sometimes called frames of reference, standards of relevance, and so on—precondition what we look at and see and teach. Thus we teach students that some senators are Republicans and some are Democrats because our studies indicate that the "fact" of party membership has some relevance to how senators behave. We do not teach our students that some senators are tall and some are short because our notions of politics make this fact irrelevant. But if our assumptions are inadequate, they may divert our attention from data of significance. And one of the primary goals in the study of American government is to become aware of our basic frames of reference and to acquire more adequate ones so that we will have standards of relevance by which we can sort out the trivial from the significant.

The intellectual discipline of political science with which you are working has certain assumptions and tools. The authors of this book are political scientists. Your teacher, whether he is a young man or woman or an older professor, is a political scientist. What you are taught by this textbook and by your teacher is, then, preconditioned by the discipline of political science. What does this discipline consist of?

The World of Political Science

Political science is one of the oldest fields of knowledge—some say the oldest, because it deals with the ordering of affairs among men. Plato and Aristotle were among the earliest political scientists and jointly illustrate one of the classic predicaments (or blessings) of the discipline—its linking factual or empirical description of the political world as it *is* with philosophical speculation and preaching about what the political world *ought* to be.

The history of political science since the Greeks is studded with great names: St. Augustine and St. Thomas Aquinas, the Italian Machiavelli; the Englishmen Hobbes and Locke; the Frenchmen Montesquieu and Rousseau; the Germans Hegel, Marx and Engels, and many others. These men were not merely political scientists; they were philosophers who dealt with fundamental and enduring problems of politics—with the nature of the state, the legitimacy of rulers, the political obligations of the ruled, the right of revolution, the nature of representation. Political science was relatively slow in becoming established in the United States. Often it was hardly distinguishable from the study of law or history or philosophy. Sometimes, political scientists were content merely to collect endless facts, describe the more obvious institutions, pile up minutiae about laws and procedures. There was little attempt to order data in a meaningful way, to speculate boldly, or to hypothesize explicitly. Political science was essentially descriptive. Students might get away with simply memorizing parts of the Constitution and the simpler functions and processes of government.

Political science in the United States has come of age during the last half century. Its development is too full and complex even to be summarized here; much of it is reflected in this book. Today, in midpassage from its rather primitive beginnings

© 1961 by United Features Syndicate.

to the much greater promise of the future, political science in America can be characterized as follows:

1. It continues to deal with the classic questions of politics. "How do we acquire knowledge about politics and about political life? How do we distinguish politics from other aspects of human life? In what ways are political systems similar to one another? In what way do political systems differ from one another? What is the role of authority and power in political systems? How do men behave in politics? What are the special characteristics, if any, of *homo politicus*, political man? What kinds of conditions make for stability, for change, or for revolution in a political system? What is required if social peace is to be maintained and violence to be avoided? What sort of political system is the best? How should we and how do we decide questions about what is 'the best' in politics?" [12]

2. It uses more sophisticated techniques in dealing with immense varieties of data. Without rejecting either classical philosophical speculation or traditional historical analysis, political science exploits techniques developed within its own discipline and sister fields: polls, surveys, oral history, depth interviewing, case studies, participant-observer studies. It is trying to become more scientific in its use of controlled observation and even experimentation, correlations, quantification, mathematical models, probability theory. It is seeking to find patterns and regularities, to generalize more widely, to look more systematically (and less undiscriminatingly) for causal factors.

3. Political science is a profession. This is important, because a profession and professional associations provide continuing centers of communication, discussion, and controversy for their members. Political science has its own heroes and villains, personalities, traditions, jokes, and temper. American political scientists are loosely organized in the American Political Science Association and in several regional and more specialized ones. They meet annually in Chicago or Washington or some other large center, just as morticians and zoologists do. They lecture one another and dispute one another, but they do so within an ongoing universe of discourse that provides some continuity and coherence to their debates.

4. Political science is a house with many chambers. Not only do its disciples concentrate in certain areas, such as American government or world politics or public administration or constitutional law, but they specialize much more intensively within such fields. Some are teachers; others never enter a classroom. Some move freely in and out of their neighboring disciplines of history, anthropology, sociology, psychology, economics; others prefer to "stay within their field." They differ widely in temper, technique, and philosophy. They may be essentially "political theologians," concerned with the enduring questions about political man and the good society; or they may be "political historians," reconstructing in detail the political leaders, politics, and philosophies of the past; or they may be "political engineers," who seek to make government more efficient or honest or representa-

[12] Robert A. Dahl, "What Is Political Science?" in Stephen K. Bailey (ed.), *American Politics and Government* (Basic Books, 1965), p. 4.

tive; or they may be "political anecdotalists," who, as historians of the present, report on specific political activities and problems to the wider public; or they may be "political behaviorists," who try to apply scientific procedures to the analysis of political data and borrow widely from the other social sciences.[13]

5. Political science is marked by internal differences as well as by solidarities. Political scientists have long been divided over matters of method and substance, beginning with Plato and Aristotle. Today the main family quarrel within political science is over the extent to which it can and should be a real science. The "behaviorists," as they have come to be called, do not want to leave political science in the hands of the theologians, engineers, or anecdotalists. They believe that the discipline must develop solid generalizations about the political behavior of human beings, and that the tests of "proof" are those "acceptable according to the canons, conventions, and assumptions of modern empirical science."[14] A political behaviorist typically believes that in dealing with political institutions he should state his findings in "quantitative terms if he can and in qualitative terms if he must."[15] Moreover, he agrees that as a scientist he must distinguish how men *do* act from how he thinks they *ought* to act. In short, the behaviorists try to emphasize the science in the term "political science."

Critics of the behavioral school contend that political science cannot possibly emulate "real" science because of the vast complexity of political life, the fragmentary data of political science, the impossibility of conducting controlled experiments for lack of a laboratory, the crudeness of quantitative measurements (in part because of the difficulty of comparing so many unlike entities in political science), and the problem of attaining objectivity about political phenomena—politicians, laws, institutions—in which a political scientist is also involved as a citizen or as a Republican or Democrat. Above all, the critics fear that the behaviorists would drain political science of its proper moral and ethical concerns. " 'Politics' should refer to power, but the term should also refer to some conception of human welfare or the public good. The achievement of Plato and Aristotle is in part a result of their starting out by asking some of the right questions; above all, what is politics *for?*"[16] Thus, it is said, the emphasis should be on the "political" in political science—meaning by political the key questions of human needs and ethical standards.

[13] From Nelson W. Polsby, Robert A. Dentler, and Paul A. Smith, *Politics and Social Life* (Houghton Mifflin, 1963), pp. 2–5.

[14] Robert A. Dahl, "The Behavioral Approach in Political Science: Epitaph for a Monument to a Successful Protest," *The American Political Science Review* (December 1961), p. 767.

[15] David B. Truman, *Items* (Social Science Research Council, December 1951), pp. 37–39. See also, Heinz Eulau, "Recent Developments in the Behavioral Study of Politics" (Stanford University, Department of Political Science, 1961); James C. Charlesworth (ed.), *The Limits of Behavioralism in Political Science* (American Academy of Political and Social Science, 1962); Austin Ranney (ed.), *Essays on the Behavioral Study of Politics* (Univ. of Illinois Press, 1962); David Easton, *A Framework for Political Analysis* (Prentice-Hall, 1965), pp. 6–9.

[16] Christian Bay, "Politics and Pseudopolitics: A Critical Evaluation of Some Behavioral Literature," *The American Political Science Review* (March 1965), p. 40. See also Vernon Van Dyke, *Political Science: A Philosophical Analysis* (Stanford Univ. Press, 1960), esp. ch. 15.

So much, for the moment, for the main quarrel within the house of political science (we return to this dispute later, especially on pages 274–275). Most political scientists do not grapple with such cosmic questions but attempt through step-by-step, empirical, hard-headed, and controlled research to advance our understanding of some specific process or problem. Here is an example.

Studying Government—Political Scientists at Work

For over thirty years in each of our large metropolitan centers, blue-ribbon commissions have made dozens of studies and all have recommended that governments in the metropolitan region should be reorganized to reduce the number of units and to create a more comprehensive system of metropolitan government. But with few exceptions, the voters have rejected almost every one of these recommendations, and there have been no major alterations in the structure of metropolitan government. How would someone go about finding out why voters persist in ignoring the recommendations of the experts? What questions would he ask? Where would he find the answers? What evidence would he need to support one generalization over another?

One way to answer these questions, perhaps the most commonly used, would be to sit down in one's study and speculate: Human nature is conservative, people don't like to change, politicians are afraid of losing their offices, people are stupid, the recommendations are unwise and the people have the good sense to reject them, and so on. But how are we to know if such speculations are correct?

These speculations could be tested by common sense—that is, by evidence we have gathered during our lifetimes from our own observations, reading, talking with friends. "I have an uncle on the City Council in Chicago and he told me that metropolitan reform committees are front groups for Republican taxpayer associations who are only interested in reducing taxes," and so on. But it is highly probable that our unsystematically gathered evidence—common sense—is biased by the fact that our limited experiences, associations, and observations fail to take into account a large variety of factors. Our real need might be *"un*common sense."

How might a political scientist try to answer such questions? In many ways: interviewing key community leaders; studying reports; surveying public opinion; looking at research findings of other investigators. Two political scientists, Richard A. Watson and John H. Romani, proceeded as follows: Drawing on the accumulated knowledge, they first formulated certain generalizations and plausible explanations, which they then tested by investigating voting records in Cleveland, Ohio. Then on the basis of their findings they reformulated certain generalizations and hypotheses for testing in other communities and under other conditions.[17]

[17] Richard A. Watson and John H. Romani, "Metropolitan Government for Metropolitan Cleveland: An Analysis of the Voting Record," *Midwest Journal of Political Science* (November 1961), pp. 365–390.

Their first generalization was that support for metropolitan reform within the Cleveland area had increased. This point seemed plausible since during the last twenty-eight years there had been ten separate elections pertaining to the issue and considerable public discussion. Furthermore, during this period problems of water supply and transportation (for which metropolitan government might be the solution) had become aggravated, so that more political support for reform measures could reasonably be expected. They found, however, that although the voters gave more support to proposals to appoint commissions, they gave less support to specific reforms recommended by the commissions than they had earlier.

Their second generalization was that the residents of Cleveland proper would give more backing to metropolitan consolidation than would residents of the suburbs. Again this line of thought seemed reasonable. Lower-income groups in the city would be able to tap the financial resources of the suburbs, while people living in the suburbs could no longer avoid paying taxes to support projects within the city. (The assumption here is that voters will perceive "rationally" the economic consequences of consolidation and vote to make the other person pay more and themselves pay less.)

But again looking at the election results, breaking down voters in terms of place of residence, the investigators found just the opposite—suburbanites favored metropolitan consolidation more than did the residents of the central city.

The political scientists then sought to determine what factors within the central city might account for the declining support for metropolitan reform. Searching through the available books and articles, especially the works of Professor E. C. Banfield, they concluded that the influence of recent migrations of Negroes to Cleveland might account for the less favorable attitude toward reform. This conclusion seemed plausible, since Negro leaders in Cleveland had expressed fears that metropolitan reform would shift political power away from Negro voters within the central city to middle-class white voters who control the suburbs.

How to test this generalization? There was no accurate information about the exact location of Negro voters within the Cleveland metropolitan region. The investigators decided to look at the election results in wards represented by Negro councilmen, recognizing that some white voters lived in these wards and that some Negroes lived in wards represented by white councilmen. Nonetheless, because residential segregation prevails in Cleveland, they felt this would be a reasonable way to get at the data.

This time their generalization was supported by the evidence: Increased Negro political strength was accompanied by greater opposition to metropolitan government.

Watson and Romani wished also to determine the impact of income, education, occupation, and location. By the use of statistical techniques they were able to study eight independent variables and found that the division was along class lines: Higher-income, better-educated persons from the managerial group tend to favor reform; those from lower incomes with little formal education and coming from the laboring group tend to oppose. From these findings it is plausible to speculate that business and professional groups look upon metropolitan government as a means to secure more influence in the affairs of the central city, as a device to stimulate business, and contrary to what is sometimes assumed, do not fear an increase in taxes as much as do those of more limited means. Metropolitan reform, then, appears to be an essentially *political* question of who shall govern, and not a matter of taxes and economy alone.

Here is one small step in building up our knowledge. The major contribution of this kind of careful detailed investigation is not what we learn about voting on metropolitan reform in Cleveland, Ohio, during the last quarter century, but the slow accretion of knowledge that will permit development and testing of more generalizations covering a wider range of behavior.

This Book: How to Use It

We suggested at the start that the student of American government must do more than learn the facts of American government. He must see it as an example—though an especially important one—of government in general. He must test it by the democratic standards it purports to satisfy. He must place it in its social and economic context. And he must know something of the discipline of political science within which he works.

This book will help you on some of these tasks more than others. It is, first of all, a description of the background, mechanics, and organization of American government (the Table of Contents affords a quick guide to this). The book will occasionally note aspects of American government that are relevant to other governments, but the relation is sometimes implicit rather than explicit, and for a systematic treatment you should take a course in comparative government. The book does not treat the economic and social context of government extensively—for this one should study economics, history, anthropology, psychology, sociology, or political science courses that borrow heavily from those fields. As for the discipline of political science, this book tries to be self-conscious about its intellectual tools, within space limitations.

Emphasis on Problems

Above all, this book will try to confront you with key problems that require careful analysis and investigation, that raise both questions of basic values and of political analysis. These are:

First—and embracing the other four—the essential problem of democratic government. Is "government by the people" just a pious pretension, or does it in fact exist in the United States? Is democratic government really just a cloak for rule by a small number of leaders and powerful minorities, or is there a connection between what the people want and what the government does? If so, which people?

Second, the problem of *constitutional* government. Does a governmental system largely shaped in the eighteenth century provide an adequate means for the American society to govern itself in the face of the vast and urgent demands of the 1960's? Does our system of dividing authority among a host of officials in order to prevent government from becoming too powerful lead to such a diffuse structure of authority that we lack adequate means to deal with the problems of today?

Third, the problem of *individual rights*. How can a democratic government be used as an instrument to promote liberties rather than to suppress them? Sometimes we use symbolic shorthand to describe this as a problem of maintaining a balance between liberty and order, between diversity and uniformity, between individual rights and collective needs. But care should be taken in reading this shorthand to recognize that the conflicts are not between things called order and liberty, but between *people*, that the conflicts are about *which* rights of *which* people are to be protected and promoted. This whole set of problems is treated chiefly in Part Three.

Fourth, the problem of *representation*. What segments of the American

"When you say that it's all about government, do you mean it doesn't make sense?"

people are represented by our interest groups, opinion agencies, and political parties? Do our electoral arrangements produce results consistent with the desires of the majority? Is the "general interest" best served by a free competition among organized groups or is there a "general interest" beyond and different from simply adding up the claims of organized groups?

Fifth, the problem of *responsible leadership*. If there is some general interest beyond what the people simply seem to want, how can we realize that general interest? How much choice should our elected leaders have? Should the President have more constitutional and political authority, especially in handling foreign affairs? Should we try to make Congress more responsive to popular majorities? Or should we try to *free* President and Congress from popular pressure and control and enable them to respond more to the needs of future generations and not simply to the passing needs of the present? In short, is *responsible* government something more than *representative* government? Part Five is largely concerned with this set of problems.

Some Assumptions about Government by the People

Let us conclude this introductory chapter by following our own advice and looking at our own biases and preconceptions about American democratic government. These will vary from person to person, but the oldest and probably the most potent set of assumptions about "government by the people" might be summarized as the *Popular Rule Model,* as William C. Mitchell has termed it.

1. The great mass of people can effectively run their government provided they are informed, interested, and basically agreed on goals and methods. The people as a whole take the initiative and the government follows their direction.

2. Most people most of the time are rational, so progress is probable if not inevitable. Free and open debate with decisions made by majority vote in elections in which each citizen has one vote—and hence has equal influence—is the best way to get rational solutions to political problems.

3. Elected officials should be made responsive and accountable to the majority and should govern in accord with the wishes of the political majority.

These might be called the classic assumptions about democratic government. To what extent must we revise the Popular Rule Model in the light of 180 years of experience with American democracy? In Chapter 20 we will return to these classic assumptions about democracy, along with the other four problems. In the meantime the student can formulate views of his own as he examines American government and politics in the chapters ahead.

PART 2

The rules and how they grew

A Problem Guide How did Americans create a constitutional system in the 1780's to meet the needs of that day, and how do we maintain constitutional government in the face of the urgent demands of the 1960's? This is the general problem that we will explore in Part Two.

Forty men gathered in Philadelphia in 1787 to write the Constitution under which we are still governed today. They faced the problem of building a national government strong enough to perform its tasks but not so strong as to antagonize the people. They also faced the problem of compromising among many different ideas of government and many different interests and sections. Chapter 2 describes how the framers met these problems.

The Constitution posed further problems, however, that have challenged Americans ever since 1787. Basically, a constitution both grants and controls power. Ideally, it gives the leaders—in our country, the President, congressmen, and so on—enough power to meet the nation's needs, but it also prevents them from abusing this power. It sets up certain "rules of the game" that determine how leaders must win office (for example, through fair elections) and how they must exercise power once they are in office.

Now the Framers—and most other Americans in 1787—feared government, especially a *national government*, even though they knew that some government was necessary. So they designed a national government that could handle the tasks facing the nation but that would not be able to seize or wield too much power. To check national power the Framers depended on these two devices:

(1) *free and fair elections*, so nobody could take elective office unless he was acceptable to a majority of the voters; and (2) an elaborate system of *balancing power*.

This system of balancing power is the heart of our constitutional system. It rests in turn on two other devices: (1) a *distribution of governmental power* among the several branches of the national government (for example, between President and Congress); and (2) a *system of checks and balances* which makes the branches of government responsive to different sources of popular support (for example, election of senators by state electorates and of representatives by numerous small districts based on *population*). This system has stood the test of time and is still very much with us.

But this arrangement creates a set of difficult problems: Is a system of checks and balances that was adequate for the "horse-and-buggy age" good enough for the space age? Does it allow the people direct and strong control over their leaders? By dividing up national power among a great variety of officials, responding to different groups of voters, does it make coordinated public policies too difficult? Does it allow leaders to "pass the buck" so that the voters have trouble finding out who does what, when, and how well? Chapter 3 takes up this set of problems.

A closely related problem is: How flexible and adaptable should our Constitution be? After all, it was drawn up over 175 years ago, and the demands on government are much greater now than they were then. Is the Constitution a timeless charter whose principles and methods are as sound today as ever? Or

should it be possible to amend it easily to keep it attuned to new demands? Chapter 3 discusses this problem too.

Finally, there are the problems created by *federalism*—the division of power between the national and state governments. Our country has undergone vast economic, social, and military changes, and the national government has taken on heavier and heavier burdens. Relatively, the states have lost ground. Is federalism obsolete? Does it deprive the national government of the power it needs to handle its huge tasks? Or is federalism as valid as ever? In either case, who should decide what the states should do, and what the national government should do? What devices have been worked out to foster cooperation among the states, and between the national and state governments, despite the division of power under the Constitution? Chapters 4 and 5 deal with these and related problems.

Taking up these specific problems will help us to think more concretely about the basic problem of Part Two—how can we maintain a constitutional system largely shaped in 1787 in the face of the urgent demands of the 1960's? The answer turns partly on what we mean by "constitutional." Do we mean all the detailed provisions and requirements in the Constitution of 1787? Or do we mean the essential idea of *constitutionalism*—free elections, civil liberties, limited governmental authority, and fair procedures in government? Or do we mean the *main* general feature of *our* Constitution, namely the system of balanced powers? Part Two sets forth these problems, but of course they will reappear throughout the book.

2 THE BIRTH OF A NATION

On a bright and clear Sunday afternoon in May 1787, General George Washington, escorted by three other generals and a troop of light horse, arrived in Philadelphia to the sound of chiming bells and cheering citizens. After depositing his baggage at the fine house where he was to stay, Washington went around the corner to call on an old friend, Benjamin Franklin. It was no coincidence that these two world-famous Americans should have met on this day in Philadelphia. They had many important matters to discuss and much to work out. For Washington, as a delegate from Virginia, and Franklin, as a delegate from Pennsylvania, were in the vanguard of a group of illustrious men who were to spend the hot summer of 1787 writing a new constitution for the thirteen American states.

A constitution that is to endure must reflect the hard experience and high hopes of the people for whom it is written. It cannot emerge merely from the inspiration of a few leaders. Our Constitution is no exception. Those who framed it built with the institutions and ideas that they knew. But they did construct; their creative feat can hardly be exaggerated. They did not, of course, complete the job of constitution-making, for it is a process that never can be completed. It began long before the Constitutional Convention met and it still continues today. Constitutions—even the written ones—are *growing* and *evolving* organisms rather than documents that merely are "struck off, at a given time, by the brain and purpose of man" (as Gladstone once described our Constitution). So we shall leave Washington and Franklin for a moment and look at the materials and concepts out of which our Constitution has grown.

Toward Independence and Self-Government

To trace the Constitution back to its ultimate sources would to be to write an intellectual history of Western civilization. For our purposes it is enough to note that the first immigrants to this continent brought with them English political concepts and institutions. For the next hundred and fifty years these English ideas and institutions were adapted to fit the conditions of the New World. (Sometimes we forget that this nation was part of the British Empire for almost as long as it has been independent.) By July 4, 1776, the colonists had shaped basic governmental arrangements, some of which still serve us today.

Thirteen Schools of Government

It was in the colonies that early Americans first learned something of the difficult art of government. There were three kinds of colonial governments: *royal*, *proprietary*, and *charter*, but in practice the differences were slight. All the colonies had written charters that established the form of government and set forth the rights of colonists. These charters were not subject, many colonists argued, to change by ordinary law. The charters of the eight *royal* colonies had been granted to them by the king and gave the Crown considerable power of supervision. The three *proprietary* colonies—Maryland, Pennsylvania, and Delaware—were each governed in accordance with a charter issued by their respective proprietors, who in turn had received a patent from the king granting the proprietor the right to establish a colony. But by the middle of the eighteenth century the Crown exerted almost the same control over proprietary colonies as it did over royal ones.

The two *charter* colonies—Rhode Island and Connecticut—operated under charters issued by the king confirming the governmental compacts that the colonists themselves had drawn up. These two colonies had the greatest measure of local autonomy. They were required to conform to the laws of England and to recognize the right of the Privy Council in London to review decisions of their courts, but unlike the other colonies their legislatures elected the colonial governor, and they did not have to send their own laws to England for review.

In all the colonies governmental authority was divided among the legislative, executive, and judicial branches. All but one (Pennsylvania) had a *bicameral* (two-house) legislature. The upper house, composed of a dozen or so landed gentlemen and wealthy merchants, advised the governor, heard appeals from colonial courts, and reviewed legislation submitted by the lower chamber. The members of the upper house were *appointed* by the Crown or the proprietor on the recommendation of the governor.

The lower house of the colonial legislature consisted of *elected* representatives; the suffrage varied from colony to colony, but in all it was limited to property-owning adult males; some colonies even had religious requirements. The lower chambers insisted that they alone had authority to raise taxes from the colonists and to appropriate funds. Since they staunchly refused to pass permanent revenue measures, the royal authorities were often forced to make concessions in order to secure the money needed to run the government. The lower houses used this control over the purse to gain further powers; over the years, they gradually assumed power to pass general laws, subject to veto by the upper house, the governor, and imperial authorities in England.

In the royal colonies the governors were appointed by the king and served as his representatives; it was through the governors that instructions from London were transmitted. In proprietary colonies the proprietor selected the governor, but his appointments were subject to confirmation by the Crown, and the governors were pledged to execute the laws of Parliament relating to America. Governors of the charter colonies, Rhode Island and Connecticut, were named by the colonial assemblies.

The royal and proprietary governors were very powerful. They could exercise an absolute veto over legislation, they could dissolve the legislatures, they appointed administrative subordinates, they commanded the colonial militia, and they presided over religious and social activities. Despite their great authority, however, these governors had a difficult job. They had to please both the colonists and the British government, and often ended up pleasing neither.

The judicial system grew more slowly than the other two branches, but eventually both lower and higher courts were established. The judges were appointed by the Crown, although in some colonies they depended on the legislatures for their salaries. In most cases appeals could be taken from colonial courts to the Privy Council in London, an important device of British control to insure that colonial legislation conformed to the laws of England.

Thus it was during the colonial period that the basic pattern of American government was laid down. Relations between the colonies and England familiarized Americans with the division of powers between a central and constituent governments and made federalism a natural development. The role of the Privy Council in enforcing English law as superior to colonial legislation was a fore-runner of the Supreme Court's task of deciding whether state acts violate the Constitution or national law. The familiar separation of powers and the bicameral legislatures also were developing during this time.

Politically-minded Americans became experts at operating, or at times evading, this governmental machinery. By the latter part of the eighteenth century, it was becoming clear that there might soon be a heightened demand for such experts.

The Kindling of Nationalism

Despite all this experience with government within the several colonies, the colonists had little training in *inter*-colonial problems. Under a divide-and-rule policy, London tried to keep the colo-nies separate and dependent on England. The colonists themselves developed little sense of real unity until the events leading to the Revolutionary War stirred latent American patriotism. Until a few years before the Revolution, most colo-nists considered themselves Englishmen, and their national loyalty was to the British Crown. The local loyalty of each was to his own colony, not to America. Beyond this there was some sectional feeling based on familiarity and identity of interests, so that New England, the South, and to a lesser extent the Middle Colonies, became identifiable communities.

Yet even during the colonial period, the demands of war and the need for common defense forced the colonies on occasion to think of problems beyond their own boundaries. The origins of American federalism and the roots of American patriotism reach back into this period. As early as 1643 the New England Confederation was organized to provide unified action against the threats of the Indians, Dutch, and French. The Confederation lasted as an effective organization until 1664. Not for almost a hundred years was there another successful proposal for intercolonial cooperation. Then, in 1754, the British Ministry called the seven northern colonies into conference at Albany to discuss Indian affairs. Benjamin Franklin, aware of an underlying cultural and political identity among the colonies, seized the opportunity to propose a scheme of continental government. Franklin's proposals, known as the Albany Plan, called for the creation of a Grand Council composed of delegates elected by the colonial assemblies and a President General appointed by the king. This central govern-ment was to be given the power to regulate trade with the Indians, make war and peace, and to *levy taxes* and collect customs duties in order to secure military and naval forces.

Meeting under the threat of attack by the French and Indians, the delegates to the Albany Conference avowed that some form of union was necessary to preserve the colonies. They recommended proposals for unity to the colonial assemblies, but not a single assembly approved. Those who controlled colonial affairs saw no need to subordinate their authority to an intercolonial government. Among the people themselves, there were no common American loyalties, no consciously shared experiences, no universally popular ideas. It was to take another thirty years and two wars before a strong central government would be acceptable to the colonists.

But the groundwork was being laid. During the French and Indian War, known in Europe as the Seven Years' War, American war heroes began to emerge. Gradually the colonists became aware of American, as distinct from English or purely regional, interests. And persistent trouble with the mother country served to intensify this sense of American unity.

Prior to the end of the French and Indian War, the imperial authorities had allowed the colonists to handle their own affairs with relatively little interference from London. They had supervised American affairs in a lax and haphazard manner. But one thing the British had done: At considerable expense, they had driven the French from the North American continent and had made new territories available for settlement. The British ministers decided it would only be fair to ask the colonists to pay some of the cost of defending their own frontiers. Steps were taken to raise revenue among the Americans, to enforce trade regulations more rigorously, and generally to tighten English control over colonial affairs. But what seemed logical and just to the English authorities was viewed differently on this side of the Atlantic. Colonial businessmen wanting to develop their own industries, merchants and shippers wishing to trade with nations other than England, planters believing they could get better prices from the Dutch and French than from the English, speculators wishing to buy western land—all these and others chafed under the heavier taxes and harsher restrictions.

What did these restless colonists want? Not very much. They had hardly a thought of independence. They merely wanted Parliament to repeal the onerous laws and to leave the colonists alone as much as possible. Their protests were couched in legal and constitutional phraseology.

To make their protests more effective, these essentially conservative men stirred up the feelings of other elements in the colonies. Many of the small artisans, lesser merchants, and farmers were not directly affected by the tax and trade laws, and many of them did not have the right to vote; nevertheless, the actions of the English government affronted their developing national feeling. Leadership of the protest movement began to pass from the hands of the more restrained group to those who were asking for more radical action, men like Sam and John Adams in Massachusetts and Patrick Henry and Thomas Jefferson in Virginia. These leaders gave more stress to the concepts of the natural rights of men and of government resting on the consent of the governed, and less stress to constitutional and legal arguments. They started to talk about individual liberty and human rights.[1]

These arguments had a double edge. They could be used against the dominant

[1] Cf. J. F. Jameson, *The American Revolution Considered as a Social Movement* (Princeton Univ. Press, 1926).

groups *within* the colonies as well as against the British.[2] Gradually some of the conservatives began to lose their enthusiasm for protest, fearing that revolution might lead not merely to changes in Empire relations but also to domestic reform. Feeling against England, however, did become sharper. The colonists were forced, first for political and then for military purposes, to join together in defense of their common cause. Colonial leaders began to get in closer touch with one another. The Committees of Correspondence, the Stamp Act Congress, and the First Continental Congress stimulated awareness of the common bond and gave the colonists experience in intercolonial cooperation. Finally, in 1775, the Second Continental Congress began to speak for *Americans*.

The Surge toward Independence

Even after minutemen began fighting with redcoats in 1775, many Americans found the idea of independence quite unacceptable and still hoped for reconciliation with England. But the fighting continued through the months, and the English government refused to make concessions to American demands. In August 1775, the king issued a proclamation, declaring the colonies to be in a state of rebellion, and in December 1775, Parliament forbade all trade with the colonies. These actions played into the hands of the radicals and strengthened their cause. Then in January 1776, Thomas Paine issued his pamphlet, *Common Sense*, calling on Americans to proclaim their independence. Seldom in history has a single pamphlet had so much influence. "It rallied the undecided and the wavering, and proved a trumpet call to the radicals." [3]

Those clamoring for independence became stronger. In Pennsylvania the struggle was especially bitter; there the radicals finally gained control, established a new government, drew up a new constitution, and instructed their delegation in Congress to work for independence. On June 7, Richard Henry Lee, following instructions from the Virginia Assembly, moved in Congress "that these United Colonies are, and of right ought to be, Free and Independent States." After bitter debate, Lee's motion was adopted on July 2. The Congress had already appointed a committee, consisting of Thomas Jefferson, John Adams, Benjamin Franklin, Roger Sherman, and Robert Livingston, to prepare a formal declaration of "the causes which impelled us to this mighty resolution." This Declaration of Independence was adopted on July 4, 1776.[4]

The Declaration is more than a justification of rebellion. It is also a statement of the American democratic creed, "designed to justify the past and chart the future." [5] This creed is set forth in succinct and eloquent language:

[2] See Elisha P. Douglass, *Rebels and Democrats* (Univ. of North Carolina Press, 1955).

[3] S. E. Morison and H. S. Commager, *The Growth of the American Republic* (Oxford Univ. Press, 1962), 5th ed., p. 188.

[4] David Hawke, *A Transaction of Free Men: The Birth and Course of the Declaration of Independence* (Scribner's, 1964).

[5] Ralph Barton Perry, *Puritanism and Democracy* (Vanguard, 1944), pp. 124–125.

> We hold these Truths to be self-evident, that all Men are created equal, that they are endowed by their Creator with certain unalienable Rights, that among these are Life, Liberty, and the Pursuit of Happiness.—That to secure these Rights, Governments are instituted among Men, deriving their just powers from the Consent of the Governed, that whenever any Form of Government becomes destructive of these Ends, it is the Right of the People to alter or to abolish it, and to institute new Government, laying its Foundation on such Principles, and organizing its Powers in such Form, as to them shall seem most likely to effect their Safety and Happiness. . . .

Here we find the democratic beliefs in man's *natural rights*, in *popular consent* as the only just basis for political obligations, in *limited government*, and in the right of the people to *revolt* against *tyrannical government*.

Some Intellectual Luggage

To most American patriots in 1776, these doctrines were just plain common sense. Jefferson, who wrote the Declaration, stated in a letter to Henry Lee that he did not feel it his duty to set out "new principles . . . never before thought of," but to "place before mankind the common sense of the subject, in terms so plain and firm as to command their assent, and to justify ourselves in the independent stand we are compelled to take." These ideas had become fully synthesized in America. But in essence they were part of the intellectual luggage that the colonists had brought with them, or later imported, from the Old World.

The man most responsible for popularizing these doctrines was John Locke, whose famous *Second Treatise of Civil Government*, written a century before, had been used to justify the English Revolution of 1688. Locke's arguments were tailor-made for the defense of the American cause. He profoundly influenced the patriot leaders, and his ideas, along with even some of his phraseology, found their way into the Declaration.

Prior to the establishment of organized society and government, Locke had written, man lived in a state of nature. This was not a lawless condition, however, because the natural law was known to all men through the use of reason and was binding on all. (The meaning of natural law has been argued by philosophers for centuries; for our purposes it is enough to think of the laws of nature as inherent, inescapable rules of proper human behavior—laws, in Cicero's words, that are in accordance with nature, apply to all men, and are unchangeable and eternal.) According to the natural law, each individual has a basic, inalienable right to his life, liberty, and that property with which he has mixed his own labor. Whoever deprives another of his natural rights violates the natural law and can justly be punished.

Most men obeyed the natural law, but living in a state of nature was inconvenient. There were always a few lawless souls; and whenever a person's natural rights were violated, he had to enforce the law himself. Furthermore, when people had differences, there was no impartial judge to whom they could turn for a decision. Therefore, being endowed with reason, men decided to end this inconvenience by *contracting* among themselves to form a society and to establish a government for the purpose of protecting each man's natural rights. By the terms of this social contract, each individual promised to abide by the decisions of the majority and to surrender to society his private right to enforce the law.

Government was thus limited by the purpose for which it was established. It had only the authority to enforce the natural law. *When government becomes destructive of man's inalienable rights*, it ceases to have a claim on his allegiance. The people then have the duty to revolt and to create a government better designed to promote their natural rights.

Does this sound like pretty radical doctrine? It must be remembered that while Locke's ideas would give power to the people, they also put checks on that power. In effect, depending on one's interpretation of natural rights, these theories could be used either to strengthen or to weaken the right of the people to control their relations with one another through the agency of government.[6]

Moreover, early Americans were also influenced by other thinkers in the Old World. One of the most prominent of these was Montesquieu, who, in the time of Louis XIV and Louis XV, believed that liberty must be secured *against* government. Montesquieu's importance lies in the fact that he had a very practical scheme to keep government from violating man's natural right to liberty. This was the *separation of powers*. The way to prevent the abuse of power is to check power with power, said Montesquieu, by giving some authority to the legislative branch, some to the executive, and some to the judicial. This kind of built-in mechanism safeguards liberty against government.

These were the ideas that set the intellectual tone during the period when Americans were replacing English authority with their own governments. Broadly speaking, our forefathers leaned more heavily on Locke in setting up government under the Articles of Confederation, more heavily on Montesquieu in framing the Constitution of 1787.

Experiment in Confederation

The American Revolution was primarily a rebellion of colonies against an empire; "in the modern European sense of the word, it was hardly a revolution at all." [7] There were no sharp breaks with the past. The government remained in the hands

---

[6] Willmoore Kendall, *John Locke and the Doctrine of Majority Rule* (Univ. of Illinois Press, 1941), takes the view that Locke, properly understood, advocated majoritarianism. See also Peter Laslett (ed.), *Locke's Two Treatises of Government* (Cambridge Univ. Press, 1960). For a contrary view of Locke as a defender of natural rights to restrain the political majority (the view accepted by most of the framers), see Carl L. Becker, *The Declaration of Independence; A Study in the History of Political Ideas* (Knopf, 1951).

[7] Daniel J. Boorstin, *The Genius of American Politics* (Univ. of Chicago Press, 1953), p. 68.

of a relatively small governing class, the same class that had dominated colonial affairs. There were no great social, economic, or political upheavals.

And yet in significant ways the new governments were different from those existing before the Revolution. The English had tried to regulate the colonists from London; now power was to be held firmly in the hands of state governments. The imperial authorities had trampled on men's liberties; now the new state constitutions incorporated bills of rights, abolished most religious qualifications for voting, and liberalized property and tax-paying requirements.[8]

The most glaring difference between the old colonial charters and the new state constitutions was the *concentration of power* in the *legislatures*. The legislative branches had enhanced their prestige as champions of popular causes. The emphasis on the consent of the governed, borrowed from Locke and others, also stressed the legislature as the repository of that consent. The governorship, on the other hand, smacked of royalty and stirred unpleasant memories. In most of the states the governors were made dependent on the legislature for election, their terms of office were shortened, their veto power reduced, their power to appoint officials curbed. Judges, too, carried overtones of royalty. The new state legislatures saw no reason why they should not override judicial decisions and scold judges whose rulings were unpopular. The legislative branch, complained *Federalist No. 48* later, was "drawing all power into its impetuous vortex."

The Articles of Confederation

What about the central government? The Continental Congress, like the colonial legislatures, had assumed governmental powers at the outbreak of hostilities. Although the Congress appointed General Washington commander in chief of the Continental Army, carried on negotiations with foreign countries, raised and supported troops, and borrowed and printed money, its powers were based only on a revolutionary act. A more permanent constitutional arrangement was needed. Accordingly, in June 1776, the Congress created a committee to draft a constitution. A few days after the Declaration was adopted, this committee submitted a plan for a "league of friendship and perpetual Union," but not until a year later, after months of interrupted debate, did Congress finally submit the Articles of Confederation to the states for their approval. Within two years all the states except Maryland had ratified the Articles; but since unanimous consent was required, the Articles did not go into effect until 1781, when Maryland finally ratified.

The Articles more or less constitutionalized existing arrangements. They frankly established only a league of friendship and cooperation—not a national government. Each state retained its "sovereignty, freedom, and independence, and every

[8] E. P. Douglass, *op. cit.* See also R. R. Palmer, *The Age of the Democratic Revolution* (Princeton Univ. Press, 1959), p. 217–235; Chilton Williamson, *American Suffrage; From Property to Democracy 1760–1860* (Princeton Univ. Press, 1960), p. 92; Robert A. Rutland, *The Birth of the Bill of Rights 1776–1791* (Collier Books, 1962), pp. 84–110.

power, jurisdiction, and right" that was not *expressly* delegated to "the United States, in Congress assembled." The states had jointly declared their independence of the king and had jointly fought against him, but they considered themselves free and independent sovereignties. They were loath to part with any of their newly won powers. After fighting a war against centralized authority, they did not want to create another central government, even though it would be American rather than English. Most of the patriots shared the belief that republican governments could exist only in small states. They feared that a strong central government would fall into the hands of those who would nullify the work of the Revolution.

There was, nevertheless, a universal recognition of the need for "the more convenient management of the general interests of the United States," and for this purpose a Congress was established in which each state was to be represented by not fewer than two nor more than seven delegates. The voting in Congress was by states, each state having one vote regardless of size or contributions to the general treasury. Delegates were chosen by the state legislatures, and their salaries were paid from their respective state treasuries. Since the delegates were state representatives rather than national legislators, they were subject to recall by their state legislatures.

Under the Articles, Congress was given the power to determine peace and war, to make treaties and alliances, to coin money, to regulate trade with the Indians, to borrow money, to issue bills of credit, to build and equip a navy, to establish a postal system, and to appoint senior officers of the United States army (composed of state militias). In short, Congress was given substantially the same powers that the Continental Congress had already been exercising. Approval of nine of the thirteen states was required to make important decisions.

The two most important powers *denied* to Congress were the power to levy taxes and the power to regulate commerce. It was the British government's abuse of these two powers that had precipitated the Revolutionary War. All that Congress could do was to ask the states for funds, and then hope that the state governments would collect taxes and turn the money over to the central treasury. And though the states promised to refrain from discriminating against one another's trade, Congress had no power to prevent such discrimination or to pass positive measures to promote national commerce. Only through treaties could Congress regulate foreign commerce, but here, too, it had no enforcement powers.

Clearly Congress under the Confederation was a feeble body. Furthermore, neither a federal executive nor a federal judiciary existed to enforce what decisions the Congress did make. There was simply the promise of each state to observe the Articles and abide by the decisions of Congress. The Articles—more like a treaty than a constitution—were ratified by the several state legislatures, not by the voters. The Articles could be amended, but again—more like a treaty than a constitution—the approval of all thirteen state legislatures was needed. In some respects the national government was like the United Nations today, although the similarity has often been exaggerated.

Nevertheless, the government created by the Articles of Confederation, however weak, was what most people wanted. They believed that the goals of the Revolution could be achieved only through strong local governments and that centralized authority was dangerous. A truly national government at this time could have been established only by the sword and probably would have been destroyed by the sword. The Articles reflected public sentiment and rested on political reality. As events in this decade in the Congo and elsewhere confirm, a unified national government cannot be created by documents; to survive it must be based on the support of enough interests and individuals within the community or else be held together by force.

Postwar Problems

The war was over and independence won. Could the new nation survive—a nation just becoming conscious of its own nationality? The practical difficulties confronting the infant republic would have tested the strongest and best-entrenched government. Within the limits of its powers, the government of the Confederation did an excellent job: It adopted a program for governing and developing western lands, it established diplomatic relations with other nations, it laid the foundations of a central bureaucracy, and it met the financial problems growing out of the war. By the time the Constitutional Convention assembled, the postwar depression was giving way to a period of business and commercial expansion.

Yet the problems were great and the central government was unable to provide strong leadership. Newly won independence deprived Americans of some of the special trading and commercial privileges they had enjoyed as members of the British Empire. The profitable trade with the English West Indies was prohibited. Congress found it difficult to negotiate favorable trade treaties with other nations because of a general belief in Europe that the states would not comply with the treaties even if they were ratified. The Spanish closed the mouth of the Mississippi at New Orleans to all American goods, and Barbary pirates freely looted American shipping in the Mediterranean. There was no uniform medium of exchange, because each state provided its own money, which fluctuated greatly in value. Paper money issued by Congress to finance the war was circulating at about one-thousandth of its face value. Lacking confidence in the ability of Congress to redeem its pledges, creditors were reluctant to lend money to the central government except at high interest rates. Public securities sold at a fraction of their face value. The states themselves began to default in their payments to the federal treasury. Each state regulated commerce, some discriminating against their neighbors, and the lack of uniformity of trade regulations made it difficult to develop interstate commerce. The end of the war reduced the sense of urgency that had helped to unite the several states, and conflicts among the states were frequent.

Within the states affairs went badly too. Delinquent debtors—primarily farmers, who faced the loss of their property and the prospect of debtor's prison—began to exert pressure on the state legislatures for relief. In several of the states they were successful, and the legislatures extended the period for the payment of mortgages, issued legal-tender paper money for the payment of debts, and scaled down the taxes. Creditors resented these interferences. Throughout the nation the conflicts grew bitter between debtor and creditor, between poor and rich, between manufacturer and shipper.

To add to the difficulties, neither the English nor the states would live up to the terms of the treaty of peace. The English refused to withdraw their troops from the western frontier until American debtors had paid their English creditors and until the states had repaid the Loyalists for confiscated property. Congress lacked the power to force either the English or the states to comply. To the English on the west and the Spanish and French in the south, the new nation, internally divided and lacking a strong central government, made a tempting prize.

Movement for Revision

Was it surprising that, in the face of postwar problems of demobilization, economic changes and expansion, foreign threats, and conflicts among the various sectional and economic interests, some of the democratic ardor of the revolutionary days began to wane? The radicals, who had engineered the Revolution, began to lose power. Most of the conservatives—the property-owners, the creditors, the shippers, the "better people"— had never been satisfied with the Articles of Confederation, considering them too democratic and too feeble. The inability of the Confederation to provide a strong union against foreign dangers, to prevent the states from interfering with business, to pay its creditors, added to the conviction of the conservatives that the central government must be strengthened and that checks must be placed on the state governments. They undoubtedly did, for partisan purposes, "paint dark the picture of the times and blame the supposed woes of the country on the Articles of Confederation," [9] but they were genuinely alarmed. It was, after all, their contracts that the state legislatures were interfering with, their bonds that the central government was unable to pay, their businesses that needed uniform commercial regulations and national protective tariffs, their manufacturing for which they wanted bounties. But beyond this, they were concerned about the dangers of foreign attack, disunion, anarchy, and tyranny.

These fears were sharpened by the growth of a small but powerful group, composed chiefly of men who had never believed in government by the people. These men began to argue publicly that republican government was a failure—that a strong monarchical government was needed to protect persons and property. Washington, who, fortunately for the nation, would have nothing to do with the persistent attempts to make him a king or dictator of the United States, wrote in alarm in August 1786, to John Jay, Director of Foreign Affairs:

[9] Merrill Jensen, *The Articles of Confederation* (Univ. of Wisconsin Press, 1940), p. 245.

What astonishing changes a few years are capable of producing! I am told that even respectable characters speak of a monarchical form of Government without horror. But how irrevocable and tremendous? What a triumph for our enemies to verify their predictions. What a triumph for the advocates of despotism to find that we are incapable of governing ourselves, and that systems founded on the basis of equal liberty are merely ideal and fallacious. Would to God that wise measures be taken in time to avert the consequences we have but too much reason to apprehend.[10]

The politicians, creditors, speculators, merchants, manufacturers, army officers, and others who believed that wise measures should be taken to avert disaster felt that the situation was so critical that it would not be enough merely to amend the Articles of Confederation. They wanted to alter the basic nature of the Union and to create a strong national government with coercive powers. They wanted to place checks on the state legislatures to prevent interference with property rights.

The desire for a strong national government to control internal dissensions was not the only—perhaps not even the most important—reason why the nationalists were anxious to strengthen the central government. As William H. Riker has shown in his careful study of the origins of federalism, the pressures toward unity stemmed from fear of outside military and diplomatic threats.[11] The nationalists were fearful that diplomatic and military intervention by other nations would lead to the disruption of the weak union; they wanted a strong national government to provide diplomatic and military protection. They saw federalism as the only alternative to disunion since a total amalgamation of the states into a single unitary government was politically impossible short of military conquest by the more populous states.

How could closer union be achieved? The nationalists had to move carefully. Although there was growing recognition of the need to amend the Articles in order to give Congress the power to collect taxes and to regulate commerce among the states, many Americans were still suspicious of a central government with coercive powers. Many of the people did not think things were so bad, certainly not bad enough to call for any basic alterations in the governmental structure.

Nevertheless, knotty practical problems—problems of boundaries, navigation, tariffs, and so on—continued to arise, and often these problems were common to most or all of the states. In the fall of 1786 the Virginia legislature, guided by James Madison, invited the states to send delegates to Annapolis to discuss uniform trade regulation. This was the ostensible purpose of the convention, but, as Madison wrote Jefferson, "Many gentlemen both within and without Congress wish to make this meeting subservient to a plenipotentiary Convention for

[10] John C. Fitzpatrick (ed.), *The Writings of George Washington*, XXVIII (Government Printing Office, 1938), p. 503.
[11] William H. Riker, *Federalism: Origin, Operation, Significance* (Little, Brown, 1964), pp. 19–20.

amending the Confederation." [12] Only five states sent delegates. Many who wanted action lost hope. But Alexander Hamilton seized the opportunity to push through the Annapolis Convention a discreetly worded resolution. Congress was requested to ask the states to send commissioners to Philadelphia to "devise such further provisions as shall appear to them necessary to render the Constitution of the Federal Government adequate to the exigencies of the Union." But Congress, apathetic and perhaps suspicious that Hamilton had more in mind than amending the Articles, was loath to act. Some state legislatures appointed delegates, but throughout the states not much more than polite interest was shown. It seemed likely that little would come of the project.

Incident in Massachusetts

In the fall and winter of 1786–1787, however, events in western Massachusetts seemed to justify the dire predictions that the country was on the verge of anarchy. The farmers were in a desperate plight. Many faced imprisonment through inability to meet their mortgages or their taxes. They had unsuccessfully petitioned the Massachusetts legislature for relief. Finally, the angry farmers rallied around Daniel Shays, a Revolutionary War captain, and marched into Northampton, where they blocked the entrance to the courthouse and forcibly restrained the judges from foreclosing mortgages on their farms.

The militia readily put down the uprising, but the revolt sent a shudder down the spines of the more substantial citizens. The outraged General Knox, Secretary of War, wrote to Washington: "This dreadful situation has alarmed every man of principle and property in New England. . . . Our government must be braced, changed or altered to secure our lives and property. . . ." [13] During the winter, as the story of this open rebellion spread through the nation, it took on lurid overtones and, in the minds of many, became a personal threat to life and fortune. Some reacted by abandoning any pretense of support for republican principles. Madison warned that the "turbulent scenes" in Massachusetts had done inexpressible injury to the republican cause and even had caused a "propensity toward Monarchy" in the minds of some leaders. [14]

What could be done? The more respectable leaders were not ready to plunge into either monarchy or disunion. Fortunately, an instrument was at hand that promised a better way to deal with the crisis—the proposed Philadelphia Convention. Shays' Rebellion served as a catalyst, and the movement toward revision of the Articles, which had been brewing for a long time, began to boil. Throughout the states there was a quickening of interest in the recommendation of the Annapolis Convention. Seven states appointed delegates without waiting for Congress to act. Finally Congress jumped on the convention band wagon with a

[12] Quoted by Charles Warren, *The Making of the Constitution* (Little, Brown, 1937), p. 22.
[13] *Ibid.*, p. 31.
[14] Madison to Edmund Pendleton, February 28, 1787. Cited by Warren, *ibid.*, p. 45.

cautiously worded request to the states to appoint delegates for the "sole and express purpose of revising the Articles of Confederation . . . to render the Federal Constitution adequate to the exigencies of Government, and the preservation of the Union." The careful congressmen specified that no recommendation would be effective unless approved by Congress and confirmed by all the state legislatures as provided by the Articles.

Eventually every state except Rhode Island appointed delegates. (The debtors and farmers who controlled the Rhode Island legislature suspected that the very purpose of the convention was to place limits on their power.) Many of the delegations were bound by instructions only to consider amendments to the Articles of Confederation. Delaware went so far as to forbid her representatives to consider any proposal that would deny any state equal representation in Congress. Few people were aware of the portentous changes that were in store.

The Philadelphia Story

The Constitutional Convention was the third step in the birth of the new nation. The first step was the destruction of English governmental authority. The next step was the creation of new state governments to replace the colonial governments. The third step began in Philadelphia in the summer of 1787. The delegates to the convention were presented with a condition, not a theory. They had to establish a national government with enough power to provide for the common defense and to prevent the nation from degenerating into anarchy or despotism.

Although seventy-four delegates were appointed by the various states, only fifty-five put in an appearance in Philadelphia, of whom approximately forty took a real part in the work of the convention. But it was a distinguished gathering. Many of the most important men of the nation were there—successful merchants, planters, bankers, and lawyers, former and present governors and congressional representatives (thirty-nine of the delegates had served in Congress). As theorists, they had read Locke, Montesquieu, and other philosophers. As men of affairs, they were interested in the intensely practical job of constructing a national government.[15] Theory played its part, but experience was to be their main guide.

The Cast

Although most of the Revolutionary leaders eventually supported the Constitution in the ratification debate, only eight of the fifty-six signers of the Declaration of Independence were present at the Constitutional Convention. Among the Revolutionary leaders absent (for various reasons) were Jefferson, Paine, Henry, Richard Henry Lee, Sam and John

[15] Stanley Elkins and Eric McKitrick, "The Founding Fathers: Young Men of the Revolution," *Political Science Quarterly* (June 1961), p. 181.

Adams, and John Hancock. The delegates to the convention were mainly aristocrats. There were no small farmers or working artisans among them. But in the 1780's the common men were not expected to participate in politics, and even today small farmers and workingmen seldom are found in the ranks of Congress. The Constitutional Convention was as representative as most meetings of the time. Of the active participants, the following stand out as the prime movers of the convention:

Alexander Hamilton was, as we have already noted, one of the most impassioned proponents of a strong national government. He had been the engineer of the Annapolis Convention and as early as 1778 he had been urging the necessity for invigorating the national government. Born in the West Indies, he lacked strong local attachments and was dedicated to the vision of a unified and powerful United States. He had come to the United States when only 16, and while still a student at Kings College (now Columbia University) had won national attention by his brilliant pamphlets in defense of the colonial cause. During the war he served as General Washington's aide, and his war experiences confirmed his distaste for a Congress so weak that it could not even supply its troops with enough food or arms. Behind the closed doors of the convention he freely expressed his views, but his advocacy of a central government patterned after that of England was unacceptable. The two other delegates from New York, Robert Lansing and John Yates, were, ideologically, at the opposite pole from Hamilton. Since the voting was by states, Yates and Lansing, when present, controlled the vote of New York. They went home early and Hamilton followed. He returned only at the end of the summer, so New York was unrepresented most of the time.

From Virginia came three of the leading delegates, General George Washington, James Madison, and Edmund Randolph. *Washington* was even at that time "first in war, first in peace and first in the hearts of his countrymen." Although active in the movement to revise the Articles of Confederation, he had been extremely reluctant to attend the convention. He accepted only when persuaded that his prestige was needed for its success. When the Virginia legislature placed his name at the top of their list of delegates, the importance of the convention was made manifest. After Franklin withdrew his own name from consideration, Washington was unanimously selected to preside over the meetings. According to the records, he spoke only twice during the deliberations, but his influence was felt in the informal gatherings as well as during the sessions. His views were well known, and he was counted among those who were convinced of the necessity for a drastic revision of the Articles. The universal assumption that Washington would become the first President under the new Constitution inspired confidence in it.

James Madison, slight of build and small in voice, was only 36 at the time of the convention, but he was one of the most learned members present. Despite his youth, he had helped frame Virginia's first constitution and had served in both the Virginia Assembly and in the Congress. Realizing the importance of the convention, Madison had spent months in preparation by studying the history of

Greek confederacies and Italian republics. During the deliberations, he sat in the front of the room and kept full notes on what was said and done. These notes are our major source of information about the convention. Madison was also a leader of the group who favored the establishment of a real national government.

Of less importance than either Washington or Madison, but still a man of front rank, was *Edmund Randolph*, the 34-year-old governor of Virginia, and, as such, the titular head of the Virginia delegation. His political views were ambiguous and erratic, but he usually voted with Madison. Although he refused to sign the Constitution, he later worked actively for its ratification in Virginia.

The Pennsylvania delegation rivaled that of Virginia. Its membership included Benjamin Franklin and Gouverneur Morris. *Franklin*, at 81, was the convention's oldest member and, as one of his fellow delegates said, "He is well known to be the greatest philosopher of the present age." Second only to Washington in the esteem of his countrymen, he enjoyed a world reputation unrivaled by that of any other American. He was one of the first to hold a vision of a strong and united America. Because of his age and because his opinions were too democratic for most of the delegates, his views were usually given polite attention and then ignored. But at critical moments his sage and humorous remarks served to break the tension and prevent bitterness.

Gouverneur Morris, "a very handsome, bold, and—the ladies say—a very impudent man," was more eloquent than brilliant. He addressed the convention more often than any other person. His views were those of an aristocrat with disdain for both the rabble and the uncouth moneymakers. The elegance of the language of the Constitution is proof of his facility with the pen, for he was responsible for the final draft.

Of course there were many other distinguished delegates present. Luther Martin of Maryland, John Dickinson of Delaware, and William Paterson of New Jersey were not in agreement with a majority of the delegates, but they ably defended the position of those who insisted on equal representation for the smaller states.

The proceedings of the convention were kept secret, and delegates were forbidden to discuss any of the debates with outsiders. This rule was adopted to encourage the delegates to speak freely. It was feared that if a member publicly took a firm stand on an issue, it would be harder for him to change his mind after debate and discussion. Looking ahead to the ratification struggle, the members knew that if word of the inevitable disagreements got out it would provide ammunition for the many enemies of the convention. There were critics of this secrecy rule, but probably it was a wise move. Without it, agreement might have been impossible.

Consensus

The Constitutional Convention is usually discussed in terms of the three famous compromises: the compromise between large and small states over representation in Congress; the compromise between North and South over the counting of slaves for taxation and representation; and the compromise between North and South over the regulation and taxation of foreign commerce. But this emphasis obscures the facts that there were many other important compromises and that on many of the more significant issues most of the delegates were in substantial agreement. While it is impossible to make neat generalizations about the ideas of some forty-odd men, it is clear that certain basic ideas were part of the operating assumptions of the leading delegates. Underlying all the compromises was a general concurrence on certain basic principles.

A few delegates personally favored a limited monarchy, but almost all were convinced supporters of republican government, and this was the only form of government seriously considered at the convention. It was obvious that no other form would be acceptable to the nation. Most important, all the delegates, including those few who favored a monarch, were *constitutionalists* who opposed arbitrary and unrestrained government, whether monarchical, aristocratic, or democratic.

All agreed that society was divided along class lines and that "the most common and durable source of factions" was "the various and unequal distribution of property," as Madison wrote in *Federalist No. 10*. The common philosophy accepted by most of the delegates was that of *balanced government*. They wanted to construct a national government in which no single interest would dominate the others. Since the men in Philadelphia represented groups alarmed by the tendencies of the agrarian interests to interfere with property, they were primarily concerned with balancing the government in the direction of protection for property and business. George Mason of Virginia and Benjamin Franklin warned of the danger of going too far in this direction, but there was an almost universal concurrence in the remarks of Elbridge Gerry (delegate from Massachusetts), "The evils we experience flow from the excess of democracy. The people do not want virtue, but are dupes of pretended patriots."

Likewise there was substantial agreement with Gouverneur Morris' statement that *property* was the "*principal object of government*." John Rutledge of South Carolina not only agreed, but went one step further and stated that "property was the sole end of government." Nor was there dissent from Madison's statement that the meddling by state legislatures with the rights of property had, more than anything else, made the convention necessary.

Benjamin Franklin favored extending the right to vote to nonproperty-owners, but most of the delegates agreed in general with the sentiments expressed by John Dickinson, James Madison, and Gouverneur Morris. Dickinson argued that freeholders (owners of land) were the best guardians of liberty and that only they could be counted on to resist the "dangerous influence of those multitudes without property and without principle." James Madison voiced the fear that those without property would soon become the largest part of the population and, if given the right to vote, would either combine to deprive the property-owners of their rights or would become the "tools of opulence and ambition." Gouverneur

Morris was inclined also to the view that the masses would sell their votes to the rich. The delegates agreed in principle on restricted suffrage, but they differed over the kind and amount of property that one must own in order to vote. Moreover, as the several states were in the process of relaxing freehold qualifications for the vote, the framers recognized that they would jeopardize approval of the Constitution if they should make the federal franchise more restricted than the franchise within the states.[16] As a result, each state was left to determine the qualifications for electing members to the House of Representatives, the only branch of the national government in which the electorate was given a direct voice.

Within five days of its opening, the convention ("with more boldness than legality"), only Connecticut dissenting, voted to approve the Fourth Virginia Resolve that "a national government ought to be established consisting of a supreme legislative, executive, and judiciary." All the delegates were bound by the instructions from Congress merely to suggest amendments to the Articles of Confederation, and some were bound by even more strict instructions from their state legislatures. Yet this decision, approved by a majority of the delegates, to establish a *national government resting on and exercising power over individuals* proposed profoundly to alter the nature of the central government—changing it from a league of states to a national government. Later on, some delegates from the less populous states contended that the convention had no authority to establish a national government that could bypass the states and pass and enforce its own laws through national agencies. But these objections were primarily tactical maneuvers to force the large states to make concessions.

There was little dissent from proposals to give the new Congress all the powers of the old Congress, and all other powers in which the separate states were negligent or in which the harmony of the United States might be disrupted by the exercise of individual legislation. Although the original series of proposals discussed by the delegates, the *Virginia Plan*, called for legislative supremacy, the framers agreed that a strong executive was necessary to provide the energy and direction for the general government that had been lacking under the Articles. And an independent judiciary to provide a practical check on the excesses of democracy was also accepted without much debate. Franklin favored a single-house national legislature, but almost all the states had had two-chamber legislatures since colonial times and the delegates were used to the system. Bicameralism also conformed to their belief in the need for balanced government, the upper house representing the aristocracy and offsetting the more democratic lower house. So the delegates established two chambers in the national government too.

---

[16] John P. Roche, "The Founding Fathers: A Reform Caucus in Action," *The American Political Science Review* (December 1961), pp. 799–816, emphasizes the importance of such political considerations in the framers' deliberations.

Conflict

There were serious differences among the various groups, especially between the representatives of the large states who favored a strong *national* government that they expected to be able to dominate, and the delegates from the small states who were anxious to preserve the *confederate* character of the Union.

The nationalists took the initiative. The Virginia delegation had caucused during the delay before the convention, and, as soon as the convention was organized, was ready with fifteen resolutions. These resolutions, known as the Virginia Plan, called for a strong central government. The legislature was to be composed of two chambers. The members of the lower house were to be elected by the people, those of the upper house to be chosen by the lower chamber from nominees submitted by the state legislatures. Representation in both branches was to be on the basis of either wealth or numbers, thus giving the more populous and wealthy states—Virginia, Massachusetts, and Pennsylvania—a majority in the legislature.

The Congress thus created was to be given all the legislative power of its predecessor under the Articles of Confederation and the right "to legislate in all cases in which the separate States are incompetent." Furthermore, it was to have the authority to disallow state legislation in conflict with the proposed constitution. The Virginia Plan also called for a national executive to be chosen by the legislature and a national judiciary with rather extensive jurisdiction. The national Supreme Court, along with the executive, was to have a qualified veto over acts of Congress.

For the first few weeks the nationalists were in control. But by June 15 additional delegates from the small states had arrived and they began to counterattack. They rallied around William Paterson of New Jersey, who presented a series of resolutions known as the *New Jersey Plan*. This plan struck at the heart of the convention's earlier basic decision to set aside the Articles of Confederation and to establish a national government, for Paterson merely proposed a series of amendments to the existing Articles. He would give Congress the right to tax and regulate commerce and to coerce recalcitrant states, but he would retain a single-house legislature in which all states would have the *same vote, regardless of size*. The New Jersey Plan called for a plural national executive with little power, but it provided for a national Supreme Court with more authority. For the New Jersey Plan contained what eventually came to be a key provision of our Constitution, the supremacy article. The national Supreme Court was to hear appeals from state judges, and the supremacy article would require all the judges—national and state—to treat laws of the national government and the treaties of the United States as superior to the constitutions and laws of the states.

Paterson was maneuvering to force concessions from the large states. He favored a strong central government in principle but not one that would in fact make the big states dominant. And he raised the issue of practical politics: To adopt the Virginia Plan, creating a powerful national government dominated by Massachusetts, Virginia, and Pennsylvania, and eliminating the states as important units of government, would be to court political defeat for the convention's proposals.

But the large states resisted. For a time the convention was deadlocked. The small states argued that states should be represented equally in Congress, at least in the upper house. The large states were adamant, insisting that representation in both houses be based on population or wealth, and that national legislators be elected by the electorate rather than by the state legislatures. Finally, a Committee of Eleven was elected to devise a compromise, and on July 5 it presented its proposals. Because of the prominent role of the Connecticut delegation, this plan has since been known as the *Connecticut Compromise*. It called for: a lower house in which representation would be on the basis of population, the origination in the lower house of all bills raising or appropriating money, and an upper house in which each state would have an equal vote. This was a setback to the large states, who agreed only when the smaller states made it clear that this was their price for union. After equality of representation for the states in the Senate was accepted, most objections to the establishment of a strong national government dissolved.

The problem of representation was complicated by the existence of slavery. Looking back today, we are apt to exaggerate the differences that existed between the North and South over slavery. At that time the question was not one that divided the nation along sectional lines. Slavery was already dying in the North, and there were signs of its demise in the South. Southerners and northerners generally agreed that it was an unfortunate system, that eventually it would have to be removed. There was neither the intense opposition to slavery in the North nor the impassioned defense of it in the South that later developed. States with large numbers of slaves, nevertheless, wanted them to be counted in determining representation in the House of Representatives, but naturally they did not want to count them as property for tax purposes. A compromise was agreed on: that a slave should count as three-fifths of a free person, both in determining representation in the House of Representatives and in apportionment of direct taxes.

Perhaps more important to the southerners was the fear that a northern majority in Congress might discriminate against southern trade. They had some basis for this concern. John Jay, Director of Foreign Affairs for the Confederation, had proposed a treaty with Great Britain that would have given advantages to northern merchants at the expense of southern exporters. To protect themselves, the southern delegates insisted on requiring a two-thirds majority for Senate consent to the ratification of treaties. This sectional check on treaties was supplemented by a provision denying to Congress the power to levy taxes on exports. Another dispute was over the slave trade. To meet the demands of South Carolina and Georgia, Congress was denied until 1808 the right to prohibit the importing of slaves. By that time, it was thought, there would be enough slaves within the United States to supply all demands.

The delegates, of course, found other issues to argue about. Should the national government have lower courts, or would one federal Supreme Court be enough? This issue was resolved by postponing the decision; the Constitution merely states that there *shall* be one Supreme Court and that Congress *may* establish inferior courts. How should the President be selected? For a long time the convention accepted the idea that the President should be elected by the Congress. But it was feared that either the Congress would dominate the President or vice versa. Election by the state legislatures was rejected because of distrust of these bodies. Some of the nationalistic delegates favored election by qualified voters, but others believed that the voters would not be sufficiently informed or dispassionate to make the selection. Finally, after much discussion, the electoral-college system was decided upon. This was perhaps the most original contribution of the delegates, although it was patterned after procedures used by Maryland to select state senators. It is also one of the most criticized provisions in the Constitution (see Chapter 13).

Finally, after three months, the delegates ceased their debating. On September 17, 1787, they assembled for the impressive ceremony of placing their names on the document they were recommending to the nation. All but three of those still present signed; others who opposed the general drift of the convention had already left. Their work over, the delegates adjourned to the City Tavern to relax and celebrate a job well done.

What Manner of Men?

Were the delegates an inspired group of men who cast aside all thoughts of self-interest? Were they motivated by the desire to save the Union or by the desire to save themselves? Was the convention the inevitable result of the weaknesses of the Articles? Was it a carefully maneuvered *coup d'état* on the part of wealthy aristocrats? Was the difference between those who favored and those who opposed the Constitution mainly economic? Or was the difference mainly regional?

All these interpretations—and a few others—have been put forward by students of history and government. During the early part of our history, the members of the convention were the object of uncritical adulation; the Constitution was the object of universal reverence. Early in the twentieth century a more critical attitude was inspired by the scholarship of J. Allen Smith and Charles A. Beard. Smith, in his *The Spirit of American Government* (1911), painted the Constitution as the outgrowth of an antidemocratic reaction, almost a conspiracy, against the rule of majorities. Beard's thesis was that the Constitution represented the platform of the propertied groups who wanted to limit state legislatures and strengthen the national government as a means of protecting property. In his influential book, *An Economic Interpretation of the Constitution* (1913), Beard described the economic holdings of the delegates and argued that their support or opposition to the Constitution could best be explained in terms of their financial interests. Beard explicitly denied that he was charging the Founding Fathers with writing the Constitution for their personal benefit. Rather, he contended that men's political behavior reflects their broad economic interests.

Recently, historians have questioned the soundness of Beard's scholarship and challenged his interpretation of the data. Robert E. Brown points out that there was no great propertyless mass in the United States and that "practically everybody was interested in the protection of property." [17] "We would be doing a grave injustice to the political sagacity of the Founding Fathers," Brown has written, "if we assumed that property or personal gain was their only motive." [18] Forrest McDonald, after looking into Beard's data, has concluded that the "economic interpretation of the Constitution does not work," although he concedes an "economic interpretation renders intelligible many of the forces at work in the making of the Constitution." [19]

Probably no interpretation ascribing an exclusive role to any one facet of human life can be satisfactory. Beard himself recognized that men are motivated by a complex of factors, conscious and unconscious. Self-interest, economic or otherwise, and principle are inextricably mixed in human behavior. The Founding Fathers were neither minor gods for whom self-interest or economic considerations were of no importance, nor men who thought only in terms of their own pocketbooks. They were concerned with the state of the Union and they wanted to protect the nation from aggression abroad and dissension at home. Fortunately, their own interests coincided with the long-run interests of the nation. Stability and strength were needed to protect their own interests—but also to secure the unity and order indispensable for the operation of a democracy.

To Adopt or Not to Adopt

The delegates had gone far. After exceeding their authority by completely setting aside the Articles of Confederation, they had not hesitated to contravene Congress' instructions about ratification, or to ignore Article XIII of the Articles of Confederation. This article declared the Union to be *perpetual* and prohibited any alteration in the Articles unless agreed to by the Congress and by *every one of the state legislatures*—a provision that had made it impossible to amend the Articles. The delegates, aware that there was little chance of securing approval of the new Constitution in all the state legislatures, boldly declared that the Constitution should go into effect for those states that approved as soon as ratified by *conventions* in *nine* states.

But even this method was not going to be easy. Any political pollsters around

[17] Robert E. Brown, *Charles Beard and the Constitution* (Princeton Univ. Press, 1956), p. 198.

[18] *Ibid.*, p. 197.

[19] Forrest McDonald, *We the People: The Economic Origins of the Constitution* (Univ. of Chicago Press, 1958), pp. vii and 415.

in the fall of 1787 would probably have predicted defeat for the Constitution. The nation certainly was not ready to adopt it without a full-dress debate, and soon two camps sprang up. The supporters of the new government, by cleverly appropriating the name of Federalists, took some of the sting out of the charges that they were trying to destroy the states and establish an all-powerful central government. By dubbing their opponents Antifederalists, they pointed up the essentially negative character of the arguments of those who opposed ratification.

The split was in part geographical. The seaboard and city regions tended to be Federalist strongholds. The vast back-country regions from Maine through Georgia, inhabited by farmers and other relatively poor people, were the areas in which the Antifederalists were most strongly entrenched. But, as in all political contests, no single factor, geographical or economic or ideological, completely accounts for the division between Federalist and Antifederalist. For example, in Virginia the leaders of both sides came from the same general social and economic class. In Massachusetts the delegates from the "Dan Shays" territory in the western part of the state voted for ratification. New York City and Philadelphia strongly supported the Constitution, but so did predominantly rural New Jersey.

From our present point of hindsight, many of the criticisms raised by the Antifederalists obviously were unfounded, and many of their fears unjustified. It used to be the fashion among historians and political scientists to picture these opponents of our Constitution as small-minded, selfish men who could not see beyond their own local interests. With the introduction of a more critical attitude toward the Founding Fathers, there was a swing to the other extreme; the Antifederalists were then described as the true defenders of liberty and democracy, fighting the economically motivated aristocratic Federalists. Quite obviously both these generalizations are overdrawn. Each side included able and enlightened men as well as those with less admirable motives, and, judged within the context of the eighteenth century, both Federalists and Antifederalists were confirmed defenders of republican government.

The great debate was conducted with pamphlets, papers, letters to the editors, and speeches. The issue was important, and the interest of those concerned intense, but the argument, in the main, was carried on in a temperate manner. This great debate stands even today as an outstanding example of a free people using the techniques of free and open discussion to determine the nature of their fundamental laws.

The Great Debate

In general, the Antifederalist argument developed along these lines: There is much of merit in the proposed Constitution, but it contains many provisions that show the aristocratic bias of its authors. It lacks many guarantees of the people's fundamental rights. Present conditions are not so bad as the Federalists make out; we are at peace, and there is no danger of internal dissension. What we need is a correction of the Articles of Confederation, but a correction that preserves, as the Constitution does not, the power of the states and the freedom of the people. We should not ratify the proposed Constitution; but after it has been fully discussed and its defects made apparent, another convention should be called to revise the Articles in the light of these discussions.

The Antifederalists were suspicious of the intentions of the delegates to the convention—delegates who had exceeded their instructions, deliberated in secret, and presented a Constitution that established a powerful national government. Said Amos Singletary, delegate from a western town in the Massachusetts ratifying convention, member of the Massachusetts legislature, and a veteran of the Revolutionary army:

> Mr. President, if any body had proposed such a constitution as this in that day [Revolutionary period], it would have been thrown away at once. . . . These lawyers, and men of learning, and moneyed men, that talk so finely, and gloss over matters so smoothly, to make us poor illiterate people swallow down the pill, expect to get into Congress themselves; they expect to be the managers of this Constitution, and get all the power and all the money into their own hands, and then they will swallow up all of us little folks, like the great *Leviathan*, Mr. President; yes, just as the whale swallowed up *Jonah*.

The Federalists, on the other side, argued that there were just two alternatives: adoption of the Constitution or disunion. They insisted that the Confederation was hopelessly defective and, unless it was quickly altered, the Union would be lost. Arguing that union was indispensable to liberty and security, they defended the Constitution as conforming to the true principles of republican government. They admitted that it was not perfect, but held that it was the best that could be obtained, and that the way was open to correct such deficiencies as were uncovered through time and experience.

One of the best attacks produced by the Antifederalists was a series of articles written by Richard Henry Lee, the man who had introduced the resolution in the Second Continental Congress calling for independence. Lee's *Letters of the Federal Farmer*, published in the fall of 1787, were widely circulated throughout the nation. *The Federalist*, on the other hand, is without doubt the best defense of the Constitution produced by the Federalists. Charles and Mary Beard have written, "From that day to this *The Federalist* has been widely regarded as the most profound single treatise on the Constitution ever written and as among the few masterly works on political science produced in all the centuries of history." [20] These essays were written by Alexander Hamilton, James Madison, and John Jay.

---

[20] Charles A. and Mary R. Beard, A *Basic History of the United States* (New Home Library, 1944), p. 136. Gottfried Dietze, *The Federalist: A Classic on Federalism and Free Government* (The Johns Hopkins Press, 1960) is one of the few monographic analyses of these important state papers. There are also two new editions of *The Federalist* available, Benjamin F. Wright (Belknap Press of Harvard Univ., 1961), which contains an excellent introductory essay, and Jacob E. Cooke (Wesleyan Univ. Press, 1961), which provides exhaustive annotations.

Over the name of Publius, they were published serially in the New York papers during the winter of 1787.

Perhaps the most telling criticism of the proposed Constitution made by Lee and others was its failure to include a bill of rights.[21] The Federalists' explanations did not sound highly convincing. They argued that a bill of rights would be superfluous. The general government had only delegated powers, and there was no need to specify that Congress could not, for example, abridge freedom of the press. It had no power to regulate the press. Moreover, the Federalists argued, to guarantee *some* rights might be dangerous because it would then be thought that rights *not* listed could be denied. Contradictorily, they then pointed out that the Constitution protected some of the most important rights—trial by jury in federal criminal cases, for example. Hamilton and others also insisted that paper guarantees were weak reeds on which to depend for protection against governmental tyranny.

The Antifederalists, as well as many who were otherwise generally favorable to ratification, were unconvinced. If some rights were protected, what could be the objection to providing constitutional protection for others? Without a bill of rights, what was to prevent Congress from using one of its delegated powers in such a manner that free speech would be abridged? If bills of rights were needed in state constitutions to limit state governments, why was one not needed in the national constitution to limit the national government—a government farther from the people and with a greater tendency, it was argued, to subvert natural rights? The Federalists, forced to concede, agreed to add a bill of rights if and when the new Constitution was approved.

The Politics of Ratification

Despite the great debate, many people remained apathetic. The only direct voice the electorate had in the writing and adopting of our Constitution was in choosing delegates to the state ratifying conventions. In Connecticut and in New York all adult males were allowed to vote for representatives to the ratifying conventions, and in most of the other states suffrage requirements were liberalized. From 80 to 85 per cent of the adult white males[22] (but only about 20 per cent of the whole adult population) were eligible to vote for delegates; yet only a fraction of those qualified to vote actually did so. "The Constitution was adopted with a great show of indifference."[23]

The political strategy of the Federalists was to secure ratification in as many states as possible before the opposition had time to organize. The Antifederalists were handicapped because their main strength was in the rural areas, under-

[21] Rutland, *op. cit.* See also Alpheus T. Mason, *The States Rights Debates: Antifederalism and the Constitution* (Prentice-Hall, 1964), pp. 4, 66–97.

[22] Chilton Williamson, *op. cit.*

[23] Brown, *op. cit.*, pp. 69, 197. See also A. C. McLaughlin, *A Constitutional History of the United States* (Appleton-Century, 1935), pp. 220–221.

represented in some state legislatures and usually the most difficult to arouse to political action. They needed time to perfect their organization and collect their strength. But the Federalists, composed of a more closely knit group of leaders throughout the colonies, moved in a hurry. "Unless the Federalists had been shrewd in manipulation as they were sound in theory, their arguments could not have prevailed." [24]

Delaware was the first state to ratify; in most of the small states, now propitiated by equal Senate representation, ratification was gained without difficulty. The first large state to take action was Pennsylvania. The Federalists presented the Constitution to the state legislature immediately after the Philadelphia Convention adjourned in September 1787, urging the legislators to issue the call for the ratifying convention to consider adoption of the new Constitution. But the legislature was about to adjourn, and the Antifederalist minority felt that this was moving with unseemly haste (especially since Congress had not even formally transmitted the document to the legislature for its consideration!). They wanted to postpone action until after the coming state elections, when they hoped to win a legislative majority and so forestall calling a ratifying convention. When it became clear that the Federalists were going to move ahead, the Antifederalists left the legis-

lative chamber. With three short of a quorum, business was brought to a standstill. Philadelphia, the seat of the legislature, was a Federalist stronghold. The next morning three Antifederalists were roused from their taverns, forcibly carried into the legislative chamber, sat on, and with a quorum thus obtained, the resolution calling for election of delegates to a ratifying convention was adopted. Under the astute generalship of James Wilson, the Pennsylvania Convention ratified by a vote of 46 to 23 in December 1787, the opposition coming from the western districts.

By early 1788 New Jersey, Connecticut, and Georgia had also ratified. The scene of battle then shifted to Massachusetts, a key state and a doubtful one. John Hancock and Samuel Adams had not declared themselves, and these gentlemen, with their great popular following, held the balance of power. The Federalists cleverly pointed out to Hancock that

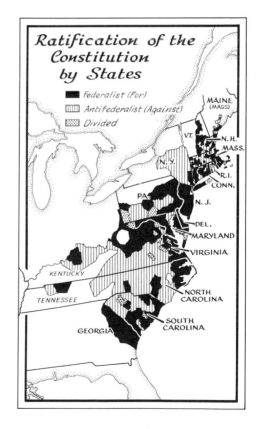

Ratification of the Constitution by States

■ Federalist (For)
▥ Antifederalist (Against)
▨ Divided

[24] Morison and Commager, *op. cit.*, 4th ed., p. 296.

Washington would be the first President, and that therefore the Vice President would undoubtedly be a New Englander. What citizen of New England was more distinguished than John Hancock? Whether or not this hint was the cause, Hancock eventually came out for ratification, and Adams was persuaded to vote for approval after securing a promise that a bill of rights would be forthcoming after adoption. Even so, Massachusetts ratified by the narrow margin of 187 to 168.

By June 1788 Maryland, South Carolina, and New Hampshire had ratified, so the nine states required to bring the Constitution into effect had been obtained. But neither Virginia nor New York had taken action, and without them the new Union would have little chance of success. Virginia was the most populous state and the home of many of the nation's outstanding leaders, and New York was important geographically as well.

The Virginia ratifying convention rivaled the Constitutional Convention in the caliber of its delegates. James Madison was the captain of the Federalist forces, and he had able lieutenants in Governor Randolph and young John Marshall. Patrick Henry, George Mason, and James Monroe within the convention, and Richard Henry Lee outside, led the opposition. Henry attacked the proposed government, point by point, with great eloquence; Madison turned back each attack quietly but cogently—sometimes in a voice so low that the recorder of the debates was unable to hear him. At the critical juncture Washington sent a letter to the convention urging unqualified ratification. This tipped the scale, and Virginia ratified. News was rushed to New York.

The great landowners along the Hudson, unlike their southern planter friends, were opposed to the Constitution. They feared federal taxation of their holdings, and they did not want to abolish the profitable tax that New York had been levying on the trade and commerce of other states. When the convention assembled, the Federalists were greatly outnumbered, but they were aided by the strategy and skill of Hamilton, and by word of Virginia's ratification. New York approved by a margin of three votes.

Although North Carolina and Rhode Island still remained outside the Union (the former ratified in November 1789 and the latter six months later), the new nation was created. In New York, a few members of the old Congress assembled to issue the call for elections under the new Constitution, and then Congress adjourned *sine die*. Throughout the nation citizens paraded and drank toasts to the new ship, *The Constitution*.

3 THE LIVING CONSTITUTION

For a time, some people remained skeptical of the new Constitution. After watching merchants and mechanics march side by side in a parade celebrating ratification, a Bostonian remarked sourly that "it may serve to please children, but freemen will not be so easily gulled out of their liberties." On the other hand, a Philadelphian said that the procession in his city had "made such an impression on the minds of our young people that 'federal' and 'union' have now become part of the household words of every family in the city." This effect on the youth was significant, for it was on the younger generation that hopes for the new government depended.

The new ship of state was launched in favorable seas. The adoption of the Constitution coincided with the return of prosperity; markets for American goods were opening in Europe, and business was pulling out of its postwar slump. Such events seemed to justify Federalist claims that adoption of the Constitution would correct the nation's ills. Within a surprisingly short time the Constitution lost its partisan character. Antifederalists vied with Federalists in honoring it—so much so, said one cynic, that "whenever its eulogium is pronounced, I feel an involuntary apprehension of mischief." Politicians differed less and less over whether the Constitution was good. More and more they began to argue over what it meant.

As the Constitution won the support of Americans, it began to take on the aura of the higher natural law itself. "Here was the document," it has been said, "into which the Founding Fathers had poured their wisdom as into a vessel; the Fathers themselves grew ever larger in stature as they receded from view; the era in which they lived and fought became a Golden Age; in that age there had been a fresh dawn for the world, and its men were giants against the sky; what they had fought for was abstracted from its living context and became a set of 'principles,' eternally true and universally applicable." [1] This adoration of the Constitution—sometimes called the "cult of the Constitution"—was important as a means of bringing unity into the diversity of the new nation. Like the Crown in Britain, the Constitution became a symbol of national loyalty, a unifying symbol that evoked both emotional and rational support from all Americans regardless of their differences. The framers' work became part of the American creed; it stood for liberty, equality before the law, limited government—indeed, for whatever anyone wanted to build into it.

The new Constitution thus became a *symbol*. It is also an *instrument*, a supreme and binding law that both *grants* and *limits* powers. "In framing a government which is to be administered by men over men," wrote Madison in *The Federalist*, "the great difficulty lies in this: you must first enable the government to control the governed; and in the next place oblige it to control itself." As an instrument, the Constitution serves a dual function. It is a *positive* instrument of government, enabling the governors to control the governed. It is also a *restraint* on government, enabling the ruled to check the rulers.

In what ways does the Constitution *limit* the power of the national government? In what ways does it *create* national power? How has it managed to serve both as a great symbol of national unity and at the same time as a somewhat adaptable and changing instrument?

[1] Max Lerner, *Ideas for the Ice Age* (Viking, 1941), pp. 241–242.

Checking Power with Power

It is strange, perhaps, to begin by stressing the ways in which the Constitution *limits* national power. Yet we must keep in mind the dilemma that the framers faced. They wanted a more effective national government, but at the same time they were keenly aware that the people would not accept too strong a national government. Accordingly, they allotted certain powers to the *national* government and reserved the rest for the *states*. In short, they established a system of *federalism* (the nature and problems of which will be taken up in Chapters 4 and 5). But this distribution of powers between the national and state governments, they felt, was not enough. Other ways of limiting the national government were needed.

The most important device to make public officials observe the constitutional limits on their powers is the right of voters to go to the polls and vote out of office those who abuse power. Why were the framers not willing to depend solely on such *political* controls? The answer is simple: They did not fully trust the people's judgment. The people might be misled and vote a demagogue into office. Even more important, the framers feared that a majority faction might use the new central government to deprive minorities of their rights. "A dependence on the people is, no doubt, the primary control on the government," Madison admitted, "but experience has taught mankind the necessity of auxiliary precautions."

What were these "auxiliary precautions"? The framers hoped that two different but related arrangements—*separation of powers* and *checks and balances*—would achieve their supreme goal of preventing public officials from abusing their power and of preventing any one group of people, even a majority, from capturing control of the government and tyrannizing the rest of the people.

Dividing National Power

The first step was the *separation of powers*—that is, dividing constitutional authority among the three branches of the national government. As we have seen, the idea of parceling out power is an old one. Locke had discussed the need for separating powers, and Montesquieu had argued that liberty could last only where powers were distributed among different departments of government. American leaders were familiar with the arguments of both. In *Federalist No. 47* James Madison wrote:

> No political truth is certainly of greater intrinsic value, or is stamped with the authority of more enlightened patrons of liberty, than that . . . the accumulation of all powers, legislative, executive, and judiciary, in the same hands . . . may justly be pronounced the very definition of tyranny.

But the force of Locke's and Montesquieu's logic alone does not account for the incorporation of the doctrine of separation of powers in our basic document.

It was, as we have seen, no novelty, and had been the operating practice in the colonies for over a hundred years. Only during the Revolutionary period was the doctrine compromised and authority concentrated in the hands of the legislature. This experience merely confirmed the belief in the merits of separation of powers. Many of the framers attributed the evils of state government and the want of energy of the central government to the lack of a strong executive who could both check legislative abuses and give energy and direction to administration.

But dividing power in itself was not enough. For there was always the danger— from the framers' point of view—that different officials with different powers might pool their authority and act together. Two modern examples may make this situation clear. In a football team, power is divided—the quarterback has one job, the center another, the guards still another. But all players act in harmony in their efforts to score. In Britain today there are executive, legislative, and judicial officials, but the legislative and executive branches act together in response to directions from the Prime Minister and the Cabinet. Separation of powers by itself would not prevent governmental branches and officials from responding to the same pressures—for example, an overwhelming majority of the voters. If dividing power by itself was not enough, what could be done further?

Checks and Balances—Ambition to Counteract Ambition

The framers' answer was a system of *checks and balances*. This system provides that the President, legislators, and judges, while being mutually dependent on one another in performing their constitutional functions, would be given *political* as well as legal independence. The framers made these officials politically independent of one another by making them responsive to different political forces. The President was to be chosen by a group of *electors*, so that he would have different loyalties and represent different interests from senators chosen by *state legislators*, from representatives directly elected by *local constituencies*, from judges holding office for *life* and appointed by the President with the consent of the Senate.

The framers were also careful to arrange matters so that a majority could win control over only part of the government at one time. A popular majority might take control of the House of Representatives in an off-year election, but the President, representing previous popular sentiment, would still have two years to go. That majority might win the Presidency (difficult, however, because of the electoral-college system, the framers hoped), but other forces might still control the Senate.

Moreover, each branch of the national government is given some responsibilities toward performing the functions of the other, and each is given some authority to control the operations of the other. For the doctrine of separation of powers, combined with checks and balances as in the American system, is one of *interdependence* rather than independence. It is a *blending* and *mingling* of powers. "The great security against a gradual concentration of the several powers in the same department," wrote Madison, "consists in giving to those who administer each department the necessary constitutional means and personal motives to resist encroachment on the others. . . . Ambition must be made to counteract ambition." Thus, the framers provided for interdependence: Congress enacts laws, the President can veto them, and Congress can repass them over his veto. The Supreme Court can invalidate laws passed by Congress and signed by the President, but the Chief Executive appoints the judges with the Senate's concurrence. The President administers the laws, but Congress provides the money for him and his agencies. The Senate and the House of Representatives have an absolute veto on each other. The framers created not a government of separated powers but a "government of separated institutions *sharing* powers." [2]

It was the legislative branch that the framers felt was most likely to take over the whole government. "In republican government," Madison wrote, "the legislative authority necessarily predominates." It was in part to meet this problem that the framers chopped the legislature in two and made the two branches responsible to different constituencies. Thus, said Madison, the two branches were rendered "by different modes of election and different principles of action, as little connected with each other as the nature of their common functions and their common dependence on the society will admit."

Finally, if this did not work, there were the judges. It was not for some years after the Constitution was in operation that the judges obtained the power of *judicial review*—the right to be the official interpreters of the Constitution and to refuse to enforce those laws of Congress that in the judges' opinion were unconstitutional (see Chapter 19). But from the beginning, the judges were expected to check the legislature and the groups that the congressional majority might represent. "Independent judges," wrote Alexander Hamilton in *Federalist No. 78*, would be "an essential safeguard against the effects of occasional ill humors in society. These sometimes extend no farther than to the injury of the private rights of particular classes of citizens, by unjust and partial laws." Independent judges, Hamilton pointed out, were in a monarchy "an excellent barrier to the despotism of the prince," and, in a republic, they were a "no less excellent barrier to the encroachments and oppressions of the representative body."

Could such a system really work? What if a majority of the people should get control of all branches of government and force through radical and impulsive measures? The framers were realists. They knew that if, over a period of years, the great majority of the voters wanted to take a certain step, nothing could stop them. Nothing, that is, except despotic government, and they did not want that. The men of 1787 reasoned that all they could do—and this was quite a lot—was to stave off, temporarily, full control by the popular majority.

It may seem surprising that the people—or at least the large number of them who were suspicious of the new Constitution—did not object to these "auxiliary precautions," which were barriers to action by a popular majority. But most early Americans, like many Americans today, had an innate distrust of government,

---

[2] Richard E. Neustadt, *Presidential Power* (Wiley, 1960), p. 33.

especially a national government. They did not look on government as an instrument they could seize with their votes and use for their own purposes. (Of course, in the eighteenth century, only a small percentage of the population had the right to participate in selecting those who governed them.) They looked on government as something to be handcuffed, hemmed in, and rendered harmless. Thus, separation of powers and checks and balances have come to serve two roles: to *make it difficult for a popular majority to capture control of the government, and to make it difficult for those who govern to exceed their constitutional authority.*

A Study in Contrasts

Most Americans now take this system for granted. To them the separating and checking of power seem to be the very essence of constitutional government. Like Madison, they view the amassing of power in the hands of any one branch of government as the essence of tyranny. Yet it is quite possible for a government to be constitutional without such an apparatus. Consider the British system. The voters elect members of Parliament from districts throughout the nation (much as we elect members of the House of Representatives). The members of the House of Commons have almost complete constitutional power. The Crown appoints the leaders of the majority party to serve as executive ministers, who collectively form the Cabinet. Any time the executive officers lose support of the majority in the Commons, they must resign or call for new elections. The House of Lords once could check the Commons, but now the Lords are almost powerless. There is no High Court with power to void acts of Parliament; the Prime Minister cannot veto them (though he may ask the Crown to dissolve Parliament and call for elections for members of the House of Commons). If, tomorrow, Parliament decided to outlaw mustaches or make everyone wear green clothes, it could do so constitutionally through a majority vote. Its decisions would be carried out by the Cabinet, which constitutionally is simply the organ of Parliament (although *politically* Parliament is largely controlled by the Prime Minister and the Cabinet). And, of course, Englishmen take their system for granted, too.

The British system is based on majority rule—that is, a majority of the voters can elect a majority of the legislators, who can put through virtually without hindrance, the majority's program as long as the parliamentary majority stays together, at least until the next election rolls around. Ours is something else; it usually depends for action on the agreement of many elements of the society, comprising much more than a mere majority. The British system *concentrates* control and responsibility in the legislature; ours *diffuses* control and responsibility among the several organs of government.

But both systems may be described as constitutional government. In both, the rulers are subjected to regular restraints—in Britain to free elections and constant open criticism; in the United States to these *plus* the "auxiliary precautions" Madison mentioned. In both, the constitutional limitations are binding on all those who

AMERICAN SYSTEM OF SEPARATION OF POWERS

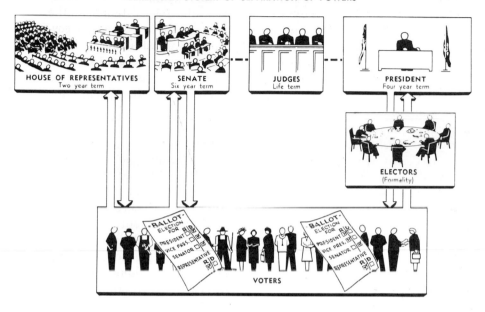

BRITISH SYSTEM OF CONCENTRATION OF RESPONSIBILITY

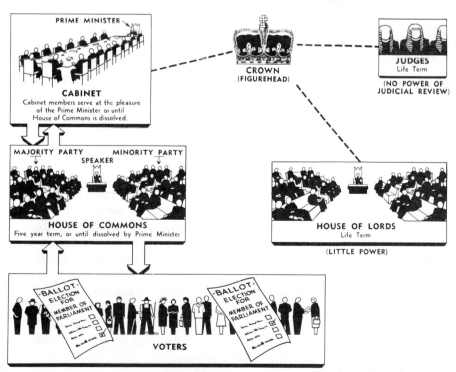

exercise governmental power—on President and Prime Minister, congressmen and members of Parliament, judges, sheriffs, the London bobby and the corner cop. Both systems are constitutional in the basic sense that the rulers are subject to regular restraints. In contrast, an arbitrary government is usually unchecked, sometimes restrained only by the rulers' fear that if the people are pushed too far they might revolt. But revolution today is a small threat when the rulers control modern arms and the means of communication while the people are unarmed.

Which system is better, British or American? Each has its supporters, and some very able Americans have been among the severest critics of our system of checks and balances. Some Englishmen have admired certain aspects of our system—or at least they believed them well suited a nation as safe and prosperous as ours. James Bryce, writing in 1893, pointed out: "Social convulsions from within, warlike assaults from without, seem now as unlikely to try the fabric of the American Constitution, as an earthquake to rend the walls of the Capitol. This is why Americans submit, not merely patiently but hopefully, to the defects of their government. The vessel may not be any better built, or found, or rigged than are those which carry the fortunes of the great nations of Europe. She is certainly not better navigated. But for the present at least—it may not always be so—she sails upon a summer sea." [3] Today, of course, the seas are much more stormy. Today the ship must be navigated with more precision, for the government's responsibilities are much greater.

The attack on our system of checks and balances, and the defense of it, will be described in Chapter 20. It is important to note here, however, that several developments have modified the system.

The Rise of National Political Parties. Political parties have served to some extent as unifying factors, drawing together the President, senators, representatives, and even judges behind a common program. But the parties, in turn, have been splintered and weakened by the workings of the checks-and-balances system.

Changes in Electoral Methods. The framers wanted the President to be chosen by wise, independent-minded men free from popular passions and hero worship. Almost from the beginning, however, the presidential electors have acted as automata, pledged prior to elections to cast their electoral vote for their party's presidential candidate. And senators, who were originally elected by state legislatures, are today directly chosen by the people.

The Establishment of Agencies Exercising All Three Functions: Legislative, Executive, and Judicial. When the government began to regulate the economy, it became clear that agencies had to have some legislative and judicial as well as administrative power. It was difficult, if not impossible, to grant an agency only administrative powers when detailed rules had to be made and judgments rendered on highly complex matters, such as policing air waves or checking the purity of food and drugs.

[3] James Bryce, *The American Commonwealth* (Macmillan, 1910), I, 310. This classic study remains one of the most perceptive interpretations of American government and society.

The Rise of the President as the Dominating, Unifying Element in National Government. Drawing on its constitutional, political, and emergency powers, the office of the Presidency has overcome some of the divisive effects of checks and balances by the growth and exercise of its power.

Despite these developments, the fragmentation of governmental power remains basic in American government, as almost every page of this book will testify.

The Constitution as Instrument of Government

As careful as the Founding Fathers were to limit the powers they conferred on the national government, the main reason they assembled in Philadelphia, after all, was to create a strong national government. They had learned that weak central government, incapable of governing, is a greater danger to liberty than a powerful government. They wished to create a national government within the framework of a federal system and endow that government with enough authority to meet the exigencies of all times. But how much power would be needed and how should it be distributed?

The Founding Fathers were wise and humble men who doubted they had either the right or the wisdom to prescribe the details of how the nation should be governed. They knew that to endure, the government must be capable of meeting the needs of future generations whose problems could not be anticipated. Hence they did not try to put down all the rules in black and white. Instead they made their grants of power general, leaving the way open for succeeding generations to fill in the details and organize the structure of government in accordance with experience.

Consequently, our formal, written Constitution is only the skeleton of our system and is supplemented by a number of fundamental rules that must be considered part of our constitutional system in its larger sense. Without an understanding of the rules of the "informal" Constitution, we would have an incomplete and even misleading picture of our government.

It is primarily through changes in our "informal" Constitution that our constitutional system is kept up to date. These changes are to be found in certain basic statutes of Congress, decisions of the Supreme Court, actions of the President, and customs and usages of the nation.

Keeping the Constitution Up to Date

Congressional elaboration is one of the most important ways of adapting our constitutional system to new problems. Since the framers left authority to Congress to prescribe the details of the structure of the national government, it is unnecessary to amend the formal Constitution every time a change is needed. Examples of congressional elaboration appear in such fundamental legislation as the Judiciary Act of 1789, which laid the foundations of our national judicial system; in the laws establishing the organization and functions of all federal executive officials subordinate to the President; and in the rules of procedure and internal organization and practices of the Congress itself.

Presidential practices have had much to do with the development of our constitutional system. There has been no change in the formal Constitution in this respect, but the constitutional position of the President is different today from what it was in 1789. The Presidency has become the pivotal office of our national government, and the President has become Chief Legislator as well as Chief Executive. This fundamental change in the American constitutional system has come about because of the willingness of several Presidents, especially Jackson, Lincoln, Wilson, and both Roosevelts, to respond to national crises by a vigorous use of presidential power to provide the leadership the people wanted. Other examples of how our Presidents have contributed to the building of our constitutional system are the establishment of the Cabinet, which rests upon traditions going back to President Washington; the precedent established by John Tyler in 1841 that the Vice President acceding to the Presidency after the death of the incumbent becomes President and not merely Acting President; and the precedent established by Wilson that the President may leave the United States and still retain the full powers of his office. The strengthened position of the Vice President and his more important role in national affairs have developed in recent years primarily through the support Presidents Eisenhower, Kennedy, and Johnson have given to their respective Vice Presidents.

Customs and usages of the nation have rounded out our governmental system. Presidential nominating conventions and other party activities, and the residence requirement for congressmen—all to be described in later chapters—are examples of constitutional usages. We can search the written Constitution in vain for any specific mention of these practices, but they are fundamental to an understanding of our constitutional system. In fact, it has been primarily through the *extra*-constitutional development of national political parties and the extension of the suffrage within the states that our Constitution has become democratized. A broader electorate began to exercise control over the national government. The presidential office was made more responsive to the people, and the relationship between Congress and the President was altered. Through the growth of political parties, some of the Constitution's blocks to majority rule were overcome.

Judicial interpretation of the Constitution, especially by the Supreme Court, has played an important part in the continuous process of modernizing the constitutional system. As we shall note in fuller detail in Chapter 19, American judges have the power of *judicial review*, that is, the authority to refuse to enforce those laws that the judges think are in conflict with the Constitution. As a result, the Supreme Court has become the authoritative interpreter of the Constitution.

Judicial review introduces an element of rigidity into our system. Nonetheless, the words of the Constitution are broad and ambiguous enough to allow divergent interpretations. As conditions have changed and new national demands have developed, so too the Supreme Court's interpretation of the Constitution has changed to accommodate these new conditions and to reflect these new demands. In the words of Woodrow Wilson, "The Supreme Court is a constitutional convention in continuous session." The establishment of judicial review itself is a classic example of the importance of judicial interpretation in the development of our constitutional system. The Constitution does not specifically give the judges the power of judicial review. Rather, the Supreme Court in the famous case of *Marbury* v. *Madison* interpreted the Constitution as allowing judges to refuse to enforce those laws that the judges believe to be in conflict with the Constitution.

Because the Constitution is so flexible and because it allows for easy adaptation to changing times, it does not require frequent formal amendment. The advantages of this flexibility may be appreciated when the national Constitution is compared with the rigid and over-specific state constitutions. Many state constitutions, more like legal codes than basic charters, are so long, complex, and detailed that the hands of public officials are often tied. State constitutions leave so little discretion to those who govern that in order to adapt state governments to changing conditions the constitutions must be amended frequently or replaced every generation or so.

A Rigid or Flexible Constitution?

This picture of a constantly changing national constitutional system disturbs many people. They would prefer a fixed Constitution which establishes precise rules alterable only by formal amendment. How, they argue, can you have a constitutional government when the Constitution is constantly being twisted by interpretation and changed by informal methods? This view fails to distinguish between two aspects of the Constitution. As an expression of basic and timeless personal liberties, the Constitution does not and should not change. For example, no government can today, any more than it could yesterday or can tomorrow, destroy the right to free speech and remain a constitutional government. In this sense the Constitution *is* timeless and essentially unchanging.

But in another sense the Constitution can and must change. When we consider it as an *instrument of government* and a *positive grant of power*, we realize that if it does not grow with the nation it serves, it soon will be pushed aside. The purposes of government remain the same: to establish liberty, promote justice, ensure domestic tranquility, and provide for the common defense. But the powers of government adequate to accomplish these purposes in 1787 are simply inadequate in the 1960's. A constitution suitable to promote justice for a small agricultural nation may not be suitable for a large industrial nation. No constitution can long deny to the government the right to do what its people want done.

"We the people"—the people of today and tomorrow, not just the people of 1787—ordain and establish the Constitution. "The Constitution," wrote Jefferson, "belongs to the living and not to the dead." So firmly did he believe this that he advocated a new constitution for every generation. New constitutions have not been necessary, because in a less formal way each generation has taken part in the never-ending process of developing the Constitution.

Because of its remarkable adaptability, the Constitution has survived the rigors of democratic and industrial revolutions, the turmoil of civil war, the tensions of major depressions, and the dislocations of world wars. The problem is, then, to preserve the Constitution in its role as a protector of fundamental liberties, as a preserver of the essentials of justice and democracy upon which our system is based, and at the same time to permit government to operate in accordance with the wishes of the people and to adapt itself to new conditions.

Changing the Letter of the Constitution

The framers of the Constitution knew that future experience would call for changes in the text of the Constitution itself and that some means of formal amendment would be necessary. Accordingly, they set forth two ways to *propose* amendments to the Constitution and two ways to *ratify* them. They carefully saw to it that amendments could not be made by simple majorities.

Proposing and Ratifying

The first method of *proposing* amendments, and the only one that has ever been used, is by a two-thirds vote of both houses of Congress. The second method is by a national convention called by Congress at the request of the legislatures of two-thirds of the states. Shortly before the Civil War there was some discussion about holding a national convention, but nothing came of it. Several scholars have advocated the calling of such a convention to revise the Constitution in the light of modern conditions, and from time to time several states have petitioned Congress in behalf of specific amendments. During the last decade or so, over half the state legislatures asked Congress either to propose or to call a convention to propose an amendment limiting the power of the national government to tax incomes, gifts, and estates. But the state legislatures by themselves, no matter how many of them act, cannot officially propose amendments; all they can do is petition. There is no legal way to force Congress to call a national convention even if the necessary two-thirds of the state legislatures petition for it. In the past, Congress has preferred to propose amendments itself instead of calling a convention to do so. Perhaps Congress remembers the fate of its predecessor at the hands of the convention it called into being in 1787!

After an amendment has been proposed, it must be *ratified*. Again two methods are provided: by approval of the legislatures in three-fourths of the states, or by approval of specially called ratifying conventions in three-fourths of the states. Congress determines which method of ratification shall be used.

A state may ratify an amendment after it has voted against ratification, but once it approves it cannot change its mind and "unratify." States must ratify within a "reasonable time" in order for their action to be effective. Congress determines what is a reasonable time and the modern practice is for Congress, either at the time it submits proposed amendments or as part of the amendment itself, to stipulate that it must be ratified within seven years. If Congress does not place a time limit when it proposes an amendment, Congress determines the effectiveness of state action at the time of ratification. For example, when Congress proposed the child labor amendment in 1924 it did not mention any time limit for ratification. To date, twenty-eight states have ratified; the last was Kansas in 1937. If ten more states should ratify (the three-fourths applies to the number of states presently in the Union, not the number at the time the amendment was proposed), Congress would have to determine if three fourths of the states had ratified within the "reasonable time" that

FOUR METHODS OF AMENDING THE CONSTITUTION

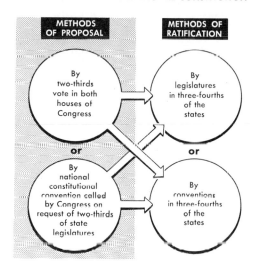

is required in order to make the amendment part of the Constitution.

The submission of amendments to legislatures instead of to ratifying conventions has been criticized because it permits the Constitution to be changed without any clear expression of the electorate's desires. State legislators who do the ratifying may even have been elected before the proposed amendment was submitted to the states. In any event, state legislators are chosen because of their views on schools, taxation, bond issues, and other matters, or because of their personal popularity—they are almost never elected because of their stand on a proposed constitutional amendment.

Despite these objections to ratification by legislatures, the only amendment to be submitted to ratifying conventions was the Twenty-first (to repeal the Eighteenth or Prohibition Amendment). The "wets" rightly believed that repeal had a better chance of success with conventions than with the rural-dominated state legislatures. These strategic considerations rather than any desire to submit the question to the electorate was the important factor, but many commentators mistakenly thought a new precedent had been set, and that in the future Congress would choose the more democratic ratification method.

The major obstacle to the adoption of constitutional amendments has not been ratification but getting Congress to propose amendments in the first place. Although dozens of resolutions proposing amendments are introduced in every session, few make any headway. But what Congress proposes is usually ratified. Of thirty amendments proposed, twenty-four have been ratified. Four of the six unratified amendments were proposed prior to the Civil War; since then, the only amendment that has failed to win the necessary state approval is the child labor amendment. The most recently proposed amendment dealing with presidential succession (see pages 408–409) has just been presented to the state legislatures for ratification.

The President has no formal authority over constitutional amendments. His veto power does not extend to them, although his political influence in getting amendments through Congress is often crucial. Nor may governors veto approval of amendments by their respective legislatures, since the Constitution vests ratification in the legislatures alone.

The entire amending procedure has been criticized because neither a majority of the voters at large nor even a majority of the voters in a majority of the states can formally alter the Constitution. But when a majority of the people are serious in their desire to bring about changes in our constitutional system, their wishes are usually implemented either by formal amendment or by the more subtle methods of interpretation and adaptation.

As we have mentioned, the flexibility of our federal Constitution has reduced the need for formal amendments. If we disregard the Bill of Rights, which for all practical purposes may be considered as part of the original document, the Constitution has been amended only fourteen times, and two of these, the Eighteenth and Twenty-first, involving Prohibition, cancel each other. The fourteen amendments adopted since the Bill of Rights are difficult to classify, but they may be grouped somewhat arbitrarily into the following categories: those (1) whose chief importance is to add to or subtract from the power of the *national* government; (2) whose main effect is to limit the power of the *state* governments; (3) whose chief impact has been to add to or subtract from the role of the *electorate*; and (4) making structural changes in governmental *machinery*.

Changes in National Power

The Eleventh Amendment.
When the Constitution was adopted, it was generally assumed that no private individual could sue a state in federal courts without the consent of the state. But in 1793, when the Supreme Court ruled otherwise in the case of *Chisholm* v. *Georgia*, there was immediate alarm lest citizens flood the federal courts with suits against states defaulting on their debts. The Eleventh Amendment, which became part of the Constitution in 1798, took from federal courts any authority to hear suits *commenced* or *prosecuted* by individuals against the states, except with the consent of the state.

The Thirteenth Amendment. Although this amendment by its own force freed the slaves, its chief significance today is that it gives to Congress power to prevent any attempt to hold a human being in slavery or involuntary servitude (see Chapter 7).

The Sixteenth Amendment. This amendment was also adopted to reverse a Supreme Court decision. In 1895 the Supreme Court, overruling a long line of precedents, for all practical purposes denied to the federal government the power to levy a graduated income tax.[4] The Sixteenth Amendment, which was adopted in 1913, empowers the national government to collect such a tax.

The Eighteenth Amendment. This amendment, adopted in 1919, was the culmination of a long struggle of the prohibitionists against the use of alcoholic beverages. The amendment gave Congress power to enforce the prohibitions of the amendment against the manufacture, sale, or transportation of liquors. Although the amendment was ratified by all but two state legislatures, prohibition did not have the support of large groups of people, especially in urban areas. During the 1920's public indifference made it impossible to enforce prohibition without adopting police-state methods and spending vast sums of money. A thriving bootlegging industry developed, and prohibition, instead of cutting down the consumption of alcohol, served mainly to enrich criminals and to foster a callous attitude toward the law. After thirteen years of disappointment, and the outbreak of the Great Depression (which made new taxes desirable), the *Twenty-first Amendment* was adopted in 1933, repealing the Eighteenth.

Formal amendments, it is clear, have not been very important in adding to or detracting from the power of the federal government. One amendment (the Eleventh) took away power that the national government was not thought to have had; one (the Sixteenth) added power that it was believed to have had; one grant of power (the Eighteenth) was subsequently repealed; and one (the Thirteenth) gave it power that it has never chosen to exercise vigorously and that has been narrowed by judicial interpretation (see Chapter 7).

Limiting State Power

The Fourteenth and Fifteenth Amendments. Along with the Thirteenth Amendment, these two were adopted following, and as a result of, the Civil War. As we have noted, the major purpose of the Thirteenth was to free the slaves; the major purpose of the Fourteenth was to make them citizens and to protect their civil rights; and that of the Fifteenth was to protect their right to vote. Only the objectives of freedom and citizenship were immediately accomplished. But the amendments had other consequences not generally anticipated, the most important being that the Supreme Court for

---

[4] *Pollock v. Farmers' Loan and Trust Co.*

a time used the Fourteenth Amendment to give constitutional sanction to laissez faire (see Chapter 8).

These amendments substantially increased the power of the Supreme Court to review actions of the state governments and might well be placed among those that add to the power of the national government—or at least to the judicial branch of that government.

The Nineteenth Amendment. This amendment, adopted in 1920, deprives the states (and the national government) of the right to deny any citizen the right to vote because of sex. Although women were voting in many states prior to its adoption, the amendment was the final step in providing the constitutional framework for universal suffrage.

The Twenty-fourth Amendment. Ever since 1939 Congress has considered action to eliminate poll taxes either by constitutional amendment or by statute. This amendment, proposed in 1962, allows the four states that still impose a poll tax as a condition of voting to do so for the election of state officers. Since the amendment has relatively little impact on voting requirements, it was ratified without difficulty and became part of the Constitution on January 23, 1964. It forbids any state to require the payment of a poll tax, or any other action in lieu of payment of such tax,[5] as a condition for voting in any election, including a primary, for presidential electors or for members of Congress.

Changing the Power of the Voters

The Seventeenth Amendment. This amendment, adopted in 1913, provides that United States senators be chosen directly by the electorate instead of being selected by the state legislatures. When the Constitution came from the hands of its framers, the House of Representatives was the only branch of the national government that the electorate chose directly. The rise of political parties and the extension of the suffrage within the states brought the presidential office under the control of the voters by the 1830's. From then on it was only a matter of time before the people would demand the right to choose their senators as well.

As the twentieth century opened, the people in many of the states were, in effect, choosing their senators, because the legislatures were simply ratifying the results of popular referendums. But the demand for constitutional change became insistent. It was charged that great sums of money were being used to bribe state legislators into choosing men of wealth and conservative outlook. The Senate came to be dubbed the "Millionaires' Club," and individual senators were tagged as representatives, not of the people, but of the Steel Trust, the Sugar Trust, the Railroad Trust, and so on. Several times the House of Representatives approved an amendment that would require direct election, but the

[5] *Harmon* v. *Forssenius, et al.* (1965).

Senate resisted. Finally, in 1912, the Senate capitulated. The Seventeenth Amendment, passed that year, therefore, rounded out the process by which the political branches of the national government were made more directly responsive to the voters.

The Twenty-second Amendment, adopted in 1951, prevents anyone from being elected to the office of President more than twice. A man succeeding to the Presidency and serving more than two years may be elected President in his own right only once. (Lyndon Johnson came to office after this midterm date and hence is eligible for a second full term.) The chief significance of the amendment, however, is that it limits the electorate. Prior to the third-term election of Franklin D. Roosevelt in 1940, one of the unwritten usages of the American Constitution was that a man should not run and the voters should not elect a man to this high office for more than two terms. In 1940 and again in 1944, a majority of the voters, aided by Roosevelt, "amended" this unwritten rule. But with the adoption of the Twenty-second Amendment, the restriction on the political majority was made formal.

The Twenty-third Amendment. This amendment, ratified in March 1961, grants the citizens of the District of Columbia the right to vote in presidential elections

The United States Senate was called the "Millionaires' Club" before the adoption of the 17th Amendment. (From Puck, *January 23, 1889. Courtesy Roger Butterfield.)*

for the first time since the district was founded in 1802. The amendment provides that the district shall have the number of electoral votes it would be entitled to if it were a state, but in no event more than the least populous state. This means that the District of Columbia will have three votes in the Electoral College, the minimum allowed to the least populous state. The ratification process took only nine months after the amendment finally cleared Congress. Opposition both in Congress and among the states was centered in the South. Presumably because of the implications of the race issue—over half the district's population is Negro—no state of the deep South approved the proposal, and one state, Arkansas, voted against it.

Changing the Constitutional Structure

The Twelfth Amendment. This amendment was adopted in 1804 to correct a deficiency in the original Constitution. The original provisions for the selection of President and Vice President were that electors should be chosen in each state according to the method prescribed by the state legislature. Each elector, without consultation with others, was to vote for the two men he deemed best qualified to serve as President. The person with the most votes, provided the number of votes represented a majority of the electors, was to be President, and the person with the next highest number of votes was to be Vice President. It was generally expected that the electors in the several states would normally cast their votes for the leading members of their own states and that no one would receive a majority. In such cases the House of Representatives, voting by states, was to choose the President from among the five men with the most votes. In the event that two men received the same number of votes, each representing a majority of the number of electors, the House was to choose between them.

"The Suspense Is Terrific" shows everyone waiting for FDR to say yes in 1940. (Courtesy Carl Somdal, Chicago Tribune.)

The rise of national political parties made this system unworkable. By the time the presidential election of 1800 took place, the electors had become party functionaries pledged to vote for the candidates of their own parties. In that year the Republicans, whose candidates were Jefferson for President and Aaron Burr for Vice President, elected a majority of the electors. Each Republican elector, as pledged, cast one of his ballots for Jefferson and one for Burr, so that each man had the same number of electoral votes. As a result, the election was thrown into the House of Representatives, still controlled by the Federalists. For a while, the Federalists toyed with the idea of electing Burr to the presidency; to some Federalist leaders this would have been the lesser of two evils. It was only with the greatest difficulty that Jefferson was finally installed in the White House. Immediately thereafter, the Twelfth Amendment was adopted. Each elector now votes separately for President and for Vice President, and the candidate with the majority of the votes in each case is elected. In the event no candidate receives a majority of the votes for President, the House, voting by states, chooses from among the three men with the most electoral votes. If no man receives a majority of the votes cast for Vice President, the Senate chooses between the two men with the most votes.

The Twentieth Amendment. Popularly known as the "lame-duck amendment," this measure was largely inspired by the late Senator George Norris of Nebraska. Before it was adopted, a President elected in November did not take office until the following March, and congressmen chosen at the same time did not begin to legislate until months after their election. Meanwhile, congressmen who had been defeated in the elections continued to represent—or misrepresent—their constituents in the short and ineffective December-to-March session. The Twentieth Amendment rearranged the schedule of congressional and presidential terms so that congressmen elected in November now begin their duties on January 3, and the President takes office on January 20. This also does away with the short December-to-March session of Congress, which used to specialize in filibusters.

The Changing Constitution—A Case Study

The history of national regulation of child labor offers an interesting example of constitutional change by a combination of all the methods previously discussed. At the beginning of the twentieth century, people were becoming alarmed over the widespread employment of children in heavy and dangerous industries at an age when they still should have been in school. In some working places the conditions were so deplorable, the hours so long, that young children of eight and ten were slowly dying of undernourishment, disease, or overwork. Wages were so low that those who exploited child labor were able to undersell their competitors. To meet the competition, other employers, in turn, were forced to hire children.

Here was an admitted evil; yet, individually, the states were unable to act. If the more progressive states outlawed child labor, they could not prevent the sale within their boundaries of cheap goods produced elsewhere by children, and they could not attract industries seeking cheap labor. Finally, in 1916, after years of agitation, Congress closed the channels of interstate commerce to goods manufactured by, or with the help of, child labor. But the Supreme Court, by a close decision and—according to some—by a tortured construction of the Constitution, in *Hammer* v. *Dagenhart* (1918), struck down the law as an interference with the reserved powers of the states. Congress tried to overcome the constitutional block by placing a tax on goods produced by or with the help of children. In 1922, in *Bailey* v. *Drexel Furniture Company*, the Court ruled this law unconstitutional.

Apparently nothing could be done without a constitutional amendment. In 1924 Congress proposed an amendment that would give to the national government the power to "limit, regulate, and prohibit the labor of persons under 18 years of age." The amendment specifically stated that "the power of the several States is unimpaired by this Article except that the operations of State laws shall be suspended to the extent necessary to give effect to legislation enacted by Congress." But the opponents of the measure, behind the mask of states' rights, were able to prevent ratification by the necessary three-fourths of the states.

By 1937, although the country had experienced a major depression and a marked change in political climate, the Supreme Court was still dominated by judges who represented the views of the 1920's. Congress in 1935 had enacted a law that, if upheld, would indicate that Congress could use its power over interstate commerce to limit child labor. Would the Court approve? After much agitation by the President (see Chapter 19), including a proposal to pack the Supreme Court with justices more responsive to the political majorities of the 1930's, the Supreme Court reversed its ruling on the extent of the power of Congress over interstate commerce.[6] The following year, 1938, Congress once again enacted a law closing the channels of interstate commerce to goods produced by child labor. This time the Supreme Court upheld the law, specifically overruling its decision of 1918.[7] It had taken twenty years, but congressional, judicial, and presidential action had at last succeeded in bringing the Constitution into line with the desires of the people. Since 1937 no state has ratified the child labor amendment, for it is no longer so vitally needed. The Constitution had been "amended" by other means.

The one principal feature of our constitutional system that remains to be examined is *federalism,* one of the most important "auxiliary precautions" against the abuse of power. The United States is not the only or even the oldest federal union, but it was the first to operate successfully a federal system on a continental scale. This has been one of America's major contributions to the science and art of government.

[6] *National Labor Relations Board* v. *Jones & Laughlin Steel Corporation* (1937).
[7] *United States* v. *Darby* (1941).

4 THE DYNAMICS OF AMERICAN FEDERALISM

Federalism 1787-style and federalism of the 1960's are as different as a stagecoach and a space ship. Since 1787 our federal system has been molded by a dynamic society and altered by the thoughts and actions of millions of men. This chapter will explore the nature of American federalism and its constitutional structure. But first we must define our terms.

A *federal system of government* is one in which

a constitution divides governmental powers between the central, or national, government, and the constituent governments (called "states" in the United States), giving substantial functions to each. Neither the central nor the constituent government receives its powers from the other; both derive them from a common source, the Constitution. This constitutional distribution of powers cannot be altered by the ordinary process of legislation—for example, by an act of the national legislature or by act of the several constituent governments. Finally, both levels of government operate through their own agents and exercise power directly over individuals.[1] "In 1964, well over half the land mass of the world was ruled by governments that with some justification, however slight, described themselves as federalisms."[2] Among the modern governments that have a federal system are the United States, Canada, Switzerland, India, Mexico, Australia, and Burma.

A *unitary,* as opposed to a federal, system of government is one in which a constitution vests all governmental power in the *central* government, and in which constituent units exercise only the authority given to them by the central government. What the central government gives it can take away. Britain, France, Israel, and the Philippines are examples of unitary government. The unitary form should not seem strange to Americans for the relation between states and their subdivisional governments, such as counties and cities, is ordinarily of this sort.

Some students distinguish a *confederation* from a federation by defining the former as a government in which the constituent governments by constitutional compact create a central government but do not give it power to regulate the conduct of individuals. The central government makes regulations for the constituent governments but it exists and operates only through their sufferance. The thirteen states operating under the Articles of Confederation fit this definition.

Unless we get the concept of federalism clearly in mind at the outset, we shall fall into confusion when we try to understand how it operates in practice. To add to our difficulties, the founders of our Constitution used the term "federal" to describe what we now would call a confederate form of government.[3] And if this were not confusing enough, today "federal" is frequently used as a synonym for "national"—that is, people often refer to the government in Washington as "the federal government." In an exact sense, of course, the states *and* the national government make up our federal system.

Yet important as it is to get one's terms straight, there is also the danger of being trapped into thinking that there is some ideal type from which we measure deviations. In fact, all governments arrange themselves along a continuum ranging from highly centralized unitary governments through centralized federations to leagues

[1] Based on discussion of A. W. Macmahon (ed.), "The Problems of Federalism," *Federalism, Mature and Emergent* (Doubleday, 1955), pp. 4–5.
[2] William H. Riker, *Federalism: Origin, Operation, Significance* (Little, Brown, 1964), p. 1.
[3] Martin Diamond, "What the Framers Meant by Federalism," in Robert A. Goldwin (ed.), *A Nation of States* (Rand McNally, 1963), pp. 24–41.

of sovereign nations. The precise areal division of powers stems from the existing political forces and the struggles to create multiple levels of access and influence as well as from the needs for administrative efficiency. Every nation is engaged in constantly changing its "mix." The areal distribution of authority is to be assessed not so much by looking at constitutional documents and definitions but at the actual political behavior and practices of the nation under investigation.

Why Federalism?

Why do we have a federal form of government? In part, because in 1787 there was no other practical choice. After confederation had been tried and found wanting, the only choice open to those who wanted a more closely knit union was federation. "No political dreamer was wild enough," said John Marshall in *McCulloch* v. *Maryland*, "to think of breaking down the lines which separate the States and of compounding the American people into one common mass." Perhaps Marshall's statement is too extreme. Hamilton, and George Reed of Delaware, two of the framers, are on record as favoring such a policy, and at least one scholar believes that the framers did intend to establish a unitary government with full power over affairs that affected the whole nation.[4] At any rate, Hamilton knew, as did all the leaders, that the overwhelming majority of the people were too deeply attached to the state governments to permit the states to be subordinated to a central government. Many were even reluctant, as we have seen, to substitute federation for confederation.

Today, a unitary system may be operated democratically even in a large country. But in the United States of 1787 distances were too great, methods of transportation and communication too poor, and techniques of democracy too new to have made possible the operation of a large unitary state by democratic methods. In the absence of widespread cohesion and nationally shared sentiments, such a union could have been held together only by force. Federalism, 1787-style, went as far in the direction of union as public opinion and the technology of the time permitted.

Federalism also has had the great advantage of being the ideal system for "the great enterprise of appropriating the North American Continent to western civilization."[5] It has enabled the Union to expand from thirteen states to fifty without any disruption or revision of the governmental structure. As people moved into a new territory, they drew up state constitutions which were then approved by the Congress and the President. Each new state became a member of the Union with the same powers and responsibilities as the original thirteen; the only changes

[4] W. W. Crosskey, *Politics and the Constitution in the History of the United States* (Univ. of Chicago Press, 1953), 2 vols. Most students of constitutional history remain convinced, despite Crosskey's impressive work, that it was not the intention of the framers to create a consolidated national government.

[5] Edward S. Corwin, "American Federalism—Past, Present, and Future," Princeton University Bicentennial Address, October 7, 1946.

required were the addition of new desks in the Senate and House of Representatives in Washington and new stars on the flag.

The factors that led to the creation of our federal system in 1787 and that sustain it in the 1960's should not be confused with the arguments that are often made about the advantages and disadvantages of federalism. (In large measure we retain federalism because our political party structure is sufficiently decen-

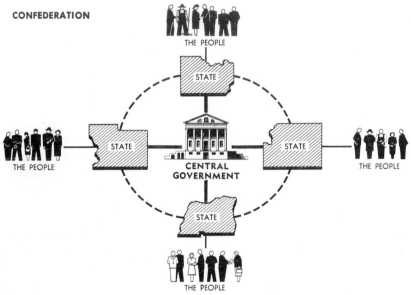

The Confederation was a union of states. The Central Government received power from the states and had no direct authority over the people.

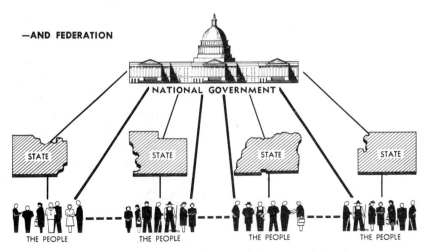

The Federal Union is a union of people. The National Government and State Governments receive power from the people and exercise authority directly over them.

tralized to preserve the independence of the states from the strong pressures that incline us to central controls.) The arguments in behalf of federalism, whatever their merits, provide an ideological tone for political debate that public leaders directly affront at their own peril. The discourse of public debate takes place within the context of all groups insisting that their actions will "strengthen the federal system."

Unity without Uniformity

Even if a unitary state had been politically possible in 1787, it would probably not have been chosen, for federalism was and still is regarded as the appropriate form of government for the people of the United States. It is thought to be ideally suited to the needs of a relatively heterogeneous people who are spread over a large continent, who are suspicious of concentrated power, and who desire unity but not uniformity.

Federalism institutionalizes the American suspicion of concentrated power, for Americans tend to equate freedom and federalism. In the rest of the world federal forms have not been notably successful in preventing the rise of tyrannies and there are many unitary governments that are democratic. Hence it is doubtful if our assumption that federalism is a major factor in preserving democracy can be sustained, but federalism "lessens the risk of a monopoly of political power by providing a number of independent points where the party that is nationally in the minority at the time can maintain itself while it formulates and partly demonstrates its policies and capabilities and develops new leadership." [6] Conversely, if as Madison pointed out in *Federalist No. 10*, "factious leaders . . . kindle a flame within their particular states," national leaders can check the spread of the "conflagration into the other states."

This diffusion of power, of course, has the defects of its virtues—it makes it difficult for a popular majority to carry into effect a national program of action. It permits a local majority in control of state governments to frustrate the natural consensus as expressed by national agencies of government. To control the three branches of the national government sometimes is not enough; power must be won at the state level too. Whether this is an advantage or a disadvantage depends on one's political outlook. To the Founding Fathers it was an advantage. As we know, they did not favor majority rule and they feared that the mass of people "without property or principle" would seize control of the government. Federalism, they hoped, would make such a seizure less probable, since *national* majorities could be checked by *local* majorities. Of course—and this is a point often overlooked—the extent of the nation and the multiplicity of interests within it are the greatest obstacles to the formation of an arbitrary, single-interest majority. But even if such a majority should ever be formed, the fact that it would have to work through a federal system would serve to restrain its powers.

Federalism also provides an arrangement under which all local issues need not

[6] Macmahon, *op. cit.*, p. 11.

be thrust into the national arena, thereby allowing national compromise to be reached on truly national problems. Instead of one big struggle, there are many little struggles for power, and national politicians and parties do not have to iron out every difference on every issue in every state. Hence issues that might prove irreconcilable in Congress are disposed of in the state legislatures. If Congress were the nation's only legislative body, it would be forced to solve all the issues that divide people along religious, racial, and social lines. The continental dimensions of the United States, embracing many diverse cultures, make it difficult to set national norms for ticklish local issues.

Suppose, for example, that Congress had to establish national policy on morals or the content of education. The problem of securing majority agreement might be infinitely complicated. Or take the control of alcoholic beverages. Many persons living in large cities feel that the moderate use of alcohol is one of the amenities of life and that prohibition of its manufacture or sale is an infringement on personal liberty. Many people in rural areas, on the other hand, are convinced that alcohol harms health and morals, causes many social problems, and should be outlawed. Our federal system permits these battles to be fought in the state legislatures. There is no need to try to enforce an inflexible national standard on divergent areas and cultures.

The States as Proving Ground

Federalism is thought to encourage experimentation. Fifty-one governments give us latitude to try out new methods and to compare results. By experimenting with governmental procedures, police administration, budgetary and personnel services, the states provide a wealth of experience from which the best can be adopted. The national government benefited from this experimentation, for example, when it adopted modern budgetary methods in 1921.

The states also serve as training grounds for presidents, congressmen, federal judges, and, to a lesser extent, federal administrators. Generally, more than half of the members of Congress have had prior service in their own state legislatures, and many of our presidents served their apprenticeship as state governors. Few of us can serve the national government as president, congressman, cabinet member, or even as administrator, but many thousands can participate in the operation of their state and local governments.

Federalism is also defended on the grounds that it keeps governed and governors in close and continuing contact and gives the electorate a greater voice in governmental affairs. Analysis makes it clear, however, that the "closeness" of state governments to the people in its several meanings—provision of services directly to the people, participation, control, or identification—is meaningless.[7] Nonetheless, the belief that the states are "closer to the people" than is the na-

---

[7] Mortin Grodzins, "Centralization and Decentralization in the American Federal System," in Robert A. Goldwin (ed.), *A Nation of States* (Rand McNally, 1963), pp. 9–15.

tional government remains part of the conventional wisdom and ideology of American politics.

Whatever the merits or demerits of the case for federalism, this system is a fact of our political life. Federal constitutions, of course, come in many different arrangements. We turn now to examine the constitutional structure of *American* federalism.

Constitutional Structure of American Federalism

The constitutional framework of federalism may be stated simply: The national government, with one important exception, has only those powers *delegated* to it by the Constitution; the states have all the powers that are not delegated to the United States except those *denied* to them by the Constitution; but within the scope of its operation, the national government is supreme. Furthermore, some powers are specifically denied to both national and state governments; others are specifically denied only to the states; still others only to the national government. Here in outline form is the constitutional structure of our federal system.

1. *Powers of the national government.* The Constitution, chiefly in the first three Articles, *delegates* certain specifically *enumerated* legislative, executive, and judicial powers to the national government. In addition to these *express* or enumerated powers, the Constitution delegates to Congress *implied* powers, those powers that may be reasonably inferred from the express powers. Furthermore, in the field of foreign affairs the national government has *inherent* powers that do not depend on specific constitutional grants but grow out of the very existence of the national government.

2. *Powers of the states.* The Constitution *reserves* to the states (see the Tenth Amendment) all the powers not granted to the national government or denied in the Constitution to the states. Powers that have not by express provision of the Constitution or by judicial interpretation been exclusively conferred on the national government may be *concurrently* exercised by the states so long as there is no conflict with national law.

3. *National supremacy.* Although the national government can operate only within limited areas, within these areas it is supreme. Article VI states: "This Constitution, and the Laws of the United States which shall be made in Pursuance thereof; and all Treaties made . . . under the Authority of the United States, shall be the supreme Law of the Land; and the Judges in every state shall be bound thereby; any Thing in the Constitution or Laws of any State to the Contrary notwithstanding." Moreover, all officials, state as well as national, are bound by constitutional oath to support the Constitution. The national government may exercise its full powers over every square inch of the United States, and the states may not interfere with the constitutional activities of national officials.

4. *Constitutional limits*. The Constitution imposes certain restraints on the national or state governments or both, not only to preserve the federal system, but also to protect various individual freedoms. Most of these restraints are set forth in Article I; the Bill of Rights; and the Thirteenth, Fourteenth, and Fifteenth Amendments.

Conflicting Interpretations of American Federalism

This outline oversimplifies and leaves unanswered some important questions. Is ours a union of *states* or a union of *people*? Should the powers of the national government be narrowly or broadly

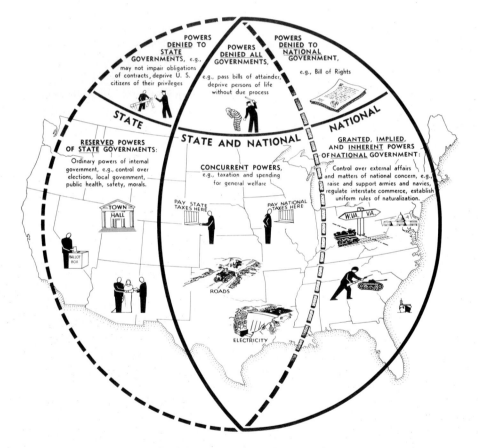

CONSTITUTIONAL DISTRIBUTION OF POWERS

construed? Does the reservation of powers to the state determine the limits of how national power may be used? These questions do not concern just lawyers or scholars. Throughout our history they have been constantly and heatedly debated; in 1861 they even led to war. They grow out of specific, controversial issues. Does the national government have the constitutional power to outlaw slavery in the territories? Do the states have the reserved power to operate racially segregated schools? Can the national government use its power to regulate inter-state commerce in such a way as to determine relations between employers and employees? Can the national government constitutionally insist that states estab-lish congressional districts wholly on the basis of population? Although the de-bates are frequently couched in lofty constitutional language and appeals are made to the great principles of federalism, usually the real struggle is over very practical, immediate, and quite mundane questions of who gets what, where, when, and how, or who does what to whom.

As the issues and times have changed, so have the details of the constitutional arguments. It is a useful oversimplification, however, to classify the approaches to our federal system into two broad schools—states-rights and nationalist.

Among those who have championed the *states-rights* interpretation, albeit with varying emphasis, are Thomas Jefferson, John C. Calhoun, the Supreme Court from the 1920's to 1937, and, today, many white southerners. The states-righters' basic premise is that the Constitution is an intergovernmental compact among the states which thereby created the central government and gave it carefully limited authority. Since the national government is nothing more than the agent of the states, each and every one of its powers should be narrowly construed. In case of doubt whether the states gave a particular function to the general gov-ernment or reserved it for themselves, the doubt should be resolved in favor of the states.

The states-righters hold that the national government should not be permitted to exercise its delegated powers in such a way as to interfere with activities re-served to the states. The Tenth Amendment, it is claimed, makes this emphatic: "The powers not delegated to the United States by the Constitution, nor pro-hibited by it to the States, are reserved to the states respectively, or to the people." This amendment, it is contended, means, for example, that Congress' power to regulate commerce among the states cannot be used to regulate agriculture or to curtail child labor since the Constitution reserves the regulation of agriculture and child labor to the states. Some of the more extreme states-righters have even gone so far as to argue that the states as sovereign entities may exercise their reserved powers to the fullest extent even if they conflict with programs of the national government.

Underlying the states-righters' fundamental position is their insistence that the state governments "are closer to the people" and therefore more accurately reflect their wishes than does the national government, which they view as a distant and essentially external authority. They maintain further that the national govern-ment is inherently heavy-handed and bureaucratic, and in order to preserve our federal system and our liberties the central authority must be carefully circum-scribed.

The *nationalist* position, supported, again with varying emphasis, by Chief Justice John Marshall, Abraham Lincoln, Theodore Roosevelt and Franklin Roose-

velt, and throughout most of our history by the Supreme Court, rejects the whole
concept of the Constitution as an interstate compact. Rather, the Constitution
is a supreme law ordained and established by the people. The national government, it is held, is an agent of the *people*, not of the states, for it was the people
who drew up the Constitution and created the national government. The sovereign people gave the national government sufficient power to accomplish the
great objectives listed in the Preamble. They intended that the central government's powers should be liberally construed and that it not be denied authority
unless there is a clear conflict with express constitutional limits or a clear absence of constitutional sanction.

The nationalists contend that the national government is not a foreign entity
but a government of all the people; each state speaks for only some of the people.
Of course, the Tenth Amendment reserves powers to the states, but as Chief
Justice Stone said, "The Tenth Amendment states but a truism that all is retained
which has not been surrendered." The amendment does not deny the national
government the right to exercise to the fullest extent all the powers given to it
by the Constitution.[8] The supremacy of the national government does restrict
the states, for a government representing part of the people cannot be allowed
to interfere with a government representing all of them.

McCulloch v. Maryland—A Nationalist Victory

In 1819 the Supreme Court had
the first of many chances to choose among these two interpretations of our federal system, in the famous case of *McCulloch* v. *Maryland*. Maryland had levied
a tax against the Baltimore branch of the Bank of the United States, which had
been established in accordance with a law of Congress. McCulloch, the cashier
of the bank, refused to pay on the ground that a state could not tax an instrumentality of the national government. Maryland's attorneys argued in the first
place that the national government did not have the power to incorporate a bank,
but even if it did, the state had the power to tax it.

Maryland was represented before the Court by some of the most distinguished
men of the bar, including Luther Martin, a delegate to the Constitutional Convention who had left early in the deliberations when it became apparent that a strong
national government was in the making. Martin, basing his argument against the
constitutionality of the bank on the states-rights view of federalism, pointed out
that the power to incorporate a bank is not one of the powers expressly delegated
to the national government. He contended that Article I, Section 8, Clause 18,
which gives Congress the right to choose whatever means are necessary and
proper to carry out its delegated powers, should, like all grants of national power,
be narrowly construed. So interpreted, the clause gives Congress only the power

---

[8] Walter Berns, "The Meaning of the Tenth Amendment," in Robert A. Goldwin (ed.), *A Nation of States, op. cit.,* pp. 126–148. For an able statement of the states-rights interpretation see James Jackson Kilpatrick, *The Sovereign States* (Regnery, 1957).

to choose those means and to pass those laws absolutely essential to the execution of its expressly granted powers. Since a bank is not absolutely necessary to the exercise of any of its delegated powers, Congress has no authority to establish it.

What about Maryland's right to tax the bank? Martin's position was simply stated: The power to tax is one of the powers reserved to the states, which they may use as they see fit.

The national government was represented by equally distinguished counsel, chief of whom was Daniel Webster. Webster conceded that the power to create a bank is not one of the express powers of the national government. But the power to pass laws necessary and proper to carry out enumerated powers is expressly delegated to Congress, and this power should be interpreted generously to mean that Congress has authority to enact any legislation convenient and useful in carrying out delegated national powers. Therefore, Congress may incorporate a bank as an appropriate, convenient, and useful means of exercising the granted powers of collecting taxes, borrowing money, and caring for the property of the United States.

As to Maryland's attempt to tax the bank, Webster contended that though the power to tax is reserved to the states, states cannot use their reserved powers to interfere with the operations of the national government. The Constitution leaves no room for doubt: In case of conflict between the national and state governments, the former is supreme.

In 1819 the Supreme Court was presided over by Chief Justice John Marshall, a nationalist and an advocate of a liberal interpretation of the central government's constitutional authority. Speaking for a unanimous Court, Marshall rejected every one of Maryland's contentions. In his usual forceful style, he wrote: "We must never forget that it is a *constitution* we are expounding. . . . [A] constitution intended to endure for ages to come, and consequently, to be adapted to the various crises of human affairs." "The government of the Union," he continued, "is emphatically and truly a government of the people. In form and substance it emanates from them, its powers are granted by them, and are to be exercised directly on them. . . . It can never be to their interest and cannot be presumed to have been their intention, to clog and embarrass its execution, by withholding the most appropriate means." Marshall summarized his views on how the powers of the national government should be broadly construed in these now-famous words:

> Let the end be legitimate, let it be within the scope of the Constitution, and all means which are appropriate, which are plainly adapted to that end, which are not prohibited, but consist with the letter and spirit of the Constitution, are constitutional.

Having thus established the doctrine of implied national powers, Marshall set forth the doctrine of national supremacy. No state, he said, can use its reserved taxing powers to tax a national instrumentality. "The power to tax involves the power to destroy. . . . If the right of the states to tax the means employed by the general government be conceded, the declaration that the Constitution, and the laws made in pursuance thereof, shall be the supreme law of the land, is empty and unmeaning declamation."

The long-range significance of *McCulloch* v. *Maryland* in providing an ideological support for the developing forces of nationalism can hardly be overstated. Although many persons still support the states-rights interpretation, this case went far to establish the doctrines of liberal construction and national supremacy. The arguments of the states-righters, if accepted, would have strapped the national government in a constitutional strait jacket and denied it the powers needed to handle the problems of an expanding nation. In all probability, the Constitution would have been replaced many years ago as succeeding generations were forced, once again, to render the central government adequate to the needs of each new age. Marshall's vision accounts in part for the longevity of our Constitution, today the oldest written constitution in the world—and truly a living constitution.

National Power in Foreign Affairs

Even the states-rights theory of federalism recognizes that in the field of *foreign relations* the national government is not restricted to powers expressly granted or even to those that may be implied. So far as the external relations of the United States are concerned, the national government has *inherent* powers derived only indirectly from the Constitution. It has the same authority in dealing with other nations as it would if it were a unitary government. International politics, not constitutional law, determines the limits of the national government's powers in its relations with the other members in the society of nations. For example, the government of the United States may acquire territory by discovery and occupation even though there is no specific constitutional basis for such acquisition, and may make agreements other than constitutionally defined treaties. Even if the Constitution were silent about foreign affairs—which it is not—the national government would have as "necessary concomitants of its nationality" [9] the right to declare war, make treaties, and appoint and receive ambassadors.

Not only does the national government have inherent power over external relations, but this power "is not shared by the states; it is vested in the national government exclusively." [10] In short, federalism stops at the water's edge. Of course, the fact that ours is a federal system does have an impact on our foreign relations. Relations between the United States and other nations have been embarrassed by the failure of some states to prosecute persons who have injured foreign nationals, by state laws that discriminate against aliens, and by state highway police who stop speeding foreign diplomats. And national officials are often cautious in making agreements with other nations that cover subjects normally handled by states. Still, the Constitution does bestow on the national government *ample* and *exclusive* authority to conduct our foreign affairs.

[9] *United States* v. *Curtiss-Wright Export Corporation* (1936).
[10] *United States* v. *Pink* (1942).

Treaties and the Federal System

The national government's power to make treaties, vested in the President with the advice and consent of two-thirds of the Senate, is *not unlimited*. The Supreme Court has "regularly and uniformly recognized the supremacy of the Constitution over a treaty." [11] The national government cannot, by treaty, abridge rights guaranteed by the Constitution. It could not, for example, deprive a person of his First Amendment rights by treaty or by a law to implement a treaty any more than it could do so by any other law. Treaties and the laws passed to implement treaties, like all other laws, must conform to the Constitution. Furthermore, Congress may, at any time, as far as its application within the United States is concerned, abrogate a treaty.

The reserved powers of the states, however, do not set bounds to the national government's treaty power. Treaties made under the authority of the United States, and laws passed by Congress to carry treaties into effect, are *superior* to state constitutions and state laws. A *self-executing treaty*, one that operates of itself and goes into effect without the need of any further action by Congress, is regarded by the courts on the same (but not higher) level as any other national law. The framers felt that the national interest was superior to the interest of any state and that if a conflict arose between a national treaty and state policy, the state policy should give way.

In short, so long as treaties do not abridge a specific provision of the Constitution, the President and the Senate may make agreements with foreign nations regulating subjects, or giving Congress the power to regulate them even though the regulations are not within the lawmaking power directly granted by the Constitution to the national government. This doctrine had been familiar for many years, but in 1920 the Supreme Court's decisions in *Missouri* v. *Holland* made its implications clear. The story of this important case is as follows:

In 1914 Congress had passed a law dealing with the hunting of birds migrating between the United States and Canada. Two federal district courts held this law unconstitutional on the ground that Congress had no authority, express or implied, to regulate wildlife. The Supreme Court did not review these decisions, but a few years later Congress enacted an even more stringent law governing the hunting of such birds. This measure, however, was passed in order to comply with a treaty between the United States and Great Britain (acting for Canada). This time the Supreme Court did review the law and upheld its constitutionality. Justice Holmes, speaking for the Court, said that, assuming Congress could not in the absence of the treaty have enacted this legislation, it did not follow that the same law to implement a treaty would also be unconstitutional. The treaty did not contravene any prohibitory words in the Constitution. It could not be declared unconstitutional because of some "invisible radiation from the general

[11] *Reid* v. *Covert* (1956).

terms of the Tenth Amendment." Since the treaty was constitutional, Congress had power to pass whatever laws were necessary and proper to implement it.

After World War II, with the United States' increasing activity in foreign affairs, some people expressed alarm that the doctrine of *Missouri* v. *Holland* would permit the national government to use the treaty power to authorize the regulation of matters normally handled by state governments. They have urged, so far unsuccessfully, that the Constitution be amended to limit the national government's power to make agreements with foreign nations and international agencies. Opponents of such an amendment, generally referred to as "the Bricker Amendment" since it was actively sponsored by former Senator John Bricker of Ohio, have argued that it would severely restrict America's role as the leader of the free world and that fears of the alteration of our constitutional structure by the treaty power are without historical or political justification.

The Constitutional Position of the States

The powers of the states are also derived from the Constitution, which reserves to them all powers not granted to the national government subject only to the limitations of the Constitution. Of course, states may not use their reserved powers to frustrate national policies. (It should be recognized that local units of government are merely agents of the states exercising powers given to them by the states. What states cannot constitutionally do, local units cannot do. In our discussion of national-state relations and the constitutional structure of federalism, the local units are subsumed in all references to states.)

The Constitution, as we have noted, contains certain explicit limitations upon state power in behalf of individual liberties. In addition, the Constitution forbids the states to make treaties, impair the obligation of contracts, coin money, and pass bills of attainder or *ex post facto* laws (see Chapter 8). States may not, except with the consent of Congress, collect duties on exports or imports or make compacts with another state.

What if the Constitution does not vest a particular power exclusively in the national government or specifically limit state power? Does the mere vesting of a particular power in the national government by itself withdraw that power from the states? There is no general answer to this question. The Supreme Court has ruled that the very nature of some powers granted to the national government is such that they are exclusive powers—to determine the rules of naturalization, for example. On the other hand, granting to the national government the power to tax does not preclude state taxation even of the same item. Both national and state governments have *concurrent* powers to tax, and as long as a state tax measure does not conflict with a national law or treaty or unduly burden a function of the federal government, it may be considered constitutional.

The commerce clause granting to Congress the power to regulate interstate and foreign commerce illustrates the complexities of the situation. Some of the most difficult questions of constitutional law arise over the extent to which this clause limits the reserved powers of the state. Obviously, congressional regulation of this commerce takes precedence over any state enactments. But what if Congress has said nothing? May the states regulate interstate commerce? The answer would be simpler if the Supreme Court had adopted the position that the commerce clause totally excludes any state regulation. But the Court has ruled that the states may—when Congress has not acted—regulate those local aspects of interstate commerce that do not require uniform national treatment; they may apply their laws, designed to protect the public, to interstate commerce, if those laws do not unduly burden, obstruct, or discriminate against such commerce.

Who is to say whether a particular measure discriminates against interstate commerce or that the subject in question requires uniform national treatment? When Congress has not acted, the Supreme Court is the "arbiter of the competing demands of state and national interest." In each case, the Court must make the decision, after weighing state and national considerations. State laws imposing speed limits on trains within city limits and requiring the elimination of grade crossings have been upheld, but laws requiring trains to stop at every crossing have been invalidated.[12] The Court has upheld the right of a state to refuse a permit to an interstate motor carrier because the resulting congestion on the highways would create a hazard.[13] On the other hand, it has held that a state unconstitutionally interfered with interstate commerce when it refused to grant a permit to an interstate motor carrier because of fear of excessive competition.[14]

Does all this sound complicated? It is. But complications are inevitable under federalism. For federalism means that someone—mainly legislators and judges—must apportion duties to different governments in an increasingly unified country.

Obligations of the National Government to the States

The Constitution obliges the national government to guarantee to each state a *republican form of government*. It does not define what is meant by a republican form—the framers undoubtedly used the term to distinguish it from a monarchy on the one hand and a purely direct democracy on the other—and the Supreme Court has consistently held that the enforcement of this constitutional clause is a congressional obligation.[15] Congress determines whether a state has a republican form of government when it decides whether or not to permit the congressional representatives of that state to take their seats in Congress.

In addition to guaranteeing to each state a republican form of government, the national government is obliged by the Constitution to protect the states against

[12] *Erb* v. *Morasch* (1900); *Erie R. Co.* v. *Board of Public Utility Commissioners* (1921); *Seaboard Air Line Ry. Co.* v. *Blackwell* (1917).

[13] *Bradley* v. *Public Utilities Commission of Ohio* (1933).

[14] *Buck* v. *Kuykendall* (1925); see also *Southern Pacific* v. *Arizona* (1945) and cases mentioned therein.

[15] *Pacific States Telephone and Telegraph Co.* v. *Oregon* (1912).

domestic insurrection. Congress has delegated authority to the President to send troops to quell insurrections on the request of the proper state authorities. This gives the President the power to determine which of contending factions is the proper authority in a state. President Tyler's decision was binding on the courts when in effect he threatened to send federal troops to protect the Rhode Island government against the "domestic insurrection" of a rival government contending for the right to speak for the state.[16]

Horizontal Federalism—Interstate Constitutional Relations

What obligations does the Constitution impose on the states in their *dealings with one another?* Three clauses of the Constitution, taken from the Articles of Confederation, require the states to give full faith and credit to one another's public acts, records, and judicial proceedings; to extend to one another's citizens the privileges and immunities of their own citizens; and to return persons who are fleeing from justice in sister states.

Full Faith and Credit. The full-faith-and-credit clause is one of the most technical provisions of the Constitution. Speaking in general terms, it requires each state to enforce civil judgments of other states and to accept their public records and acts as valid documents. (It does not require states to enforce the criminal laws of sister states; in fact, in most cases for one state to enforce the criminal laws of another would be unconstitutional.) The clause applies especially to noncriminal judicial proceedings. Suppose Smith obtains a $5000 judgment against Jones from the Pennsylvania courts, but then Jones moves to California and refuses to pay up. Although California will not automatically enforce the judgment of the Pennsylvania courts, thanks to the full-faith and credit, Smith does not have again to convince a California judge or jury that he is entitled to damages from Jones. In appropriate proceedings the California courts will give full-faith and credit to the Pennsylvania judgment without inquiring into the merits of the legal dispute.[17]

Some idea of the complexity of the problems growing out of the full-faith-and-credit clause is suggested by the question, "How much faith and credit must a state give to a divorce decree, a civil judgment, granted by another state?" Clearly, a divorce granted by a state to two bona-fide residents must be given full faith and credit by all the other states, even though they might not themselves have granted the divorce for the grounds alleged. On the other hand, what if Mrs. A, a citizen of North Carolina, goes to Reno, Nevada, in order to avoid the divorce laws of her own state, stays just the six weeks necessary to establish residence in Nevada, obtains a divorce in a proceeding in which Mr. A is not represented, and returns to North Carolina? Must North Carolina give full faith and

---

[16] *Luther v. Borden* (1849).
[17] Harold W. Chase, "The Lawyers Need Help with 'the Lawyer's Clause'," in Gottfried Dietze (ed.), *Essays on the American Constitution* (Prentice-Hall, 1964), pp. 104–110.

credit to the divorce? Not necessarily, for the Supreme Court has held that under certain circumstances it is permissible for the courts of other states to rule that the divorce-granting state lacked jurisdiction over the parties; hence, there would be no validly obtained divorce decree to which full faith and credit must be given. In our example, North Carolina would not be required by the Constitution to recognize Mrs. A's divorce, though in Nevada it would be unquestioned.

Interstate Privileges and Immunities. States may not deny to citizens of other states the full protection of the law, the right to engage in peaceful occupations, or access to the courts. States may not tax citizens of other states at a discriminatory rate or otherwise arbitrarily interfere with the use of their property within the state. In short, states must extend to citizens of other states the privileges and immunities of their own citizens. However, this does not extend to political rights such as voting, serving on juries, or admission to publicly supported institutions such as schools or hospitals.

Extradition. The Constitution asserts that a state shall, when requested by the governor of the state from which a criminal has fled, deliver him to the proper officials. Congress has supplemented this provision by making the governor of the state to which the fugitive has fled responsible for returning him. Despite the use of the word "shall," the federal courts will not order governors to extradite (return) persons wanted in other states. A few years ago the Governor of New Jersey, horrified at the conditions under which men lived in a chain gang, refused to hand over a fugitive to Georgia officials. There was nothing that Georgia could do about it. Normally, however, extradition is handled in a routine fashion. Furthermore, Congress has closed this "gap" in part by making it a federal crime to flee from one state to another for the purpose of avoiding prosecution for a felony.

In addition to these three obligations, the Constitution also requires the states to settle their disputes with one another without the use of force. States may carry their legal arguments to the Supreme Court or may negotiate *interstate compacts.* Compacts may also be used to establish interstate agencies and to solve joint problems (see Chapter 5). Before interstate compacts become effective, the approval of Congress is required, an approval that is sometimes given in advance. After a compact has been signed and approved by Congress, it becomes binding on all signatory states, and its terms are enforceable by the Supreme Court. Not all agreements among states, however, require congressional approval—only those, the Supreme Court held in 1893, "tending to increase the political power of the States, which may encroach upon or interfere with the just supremacy of the United States." [18]

[18] *Virginia* v. *Tennessee* (1893).

The Supreme Court as Umpire of the Federal System

The Supreme Court has often been called the umpire of the federal system. This role is not merely an exercise in constitutional doctrine. For as the late Robert H. Jackson wrote before he became a Supreme Court justice, "This political role of the Court has been obscure to laymen—even to most lawyers. It speaks only through the technical forms of the lawsuit, which are not identified with politics in its popularly accepted sense. Yet these lawsuits are the chief instrument of power in our system. Struggles over power that in Europe call out regiments of troops, in America call out battalions of lawyers. When the Court decides where power will be recognized, it often thereby settles whether that power can ever effectively be exercised. A given power held to reside in the states becomes at once power subdivided into forty-eight sections, each circumscribed by state boundaries—a power which can easily be defeated, evaded, or cancelled by playing one state against another. The same power held to reside in the nation is quite another matter in its effectiveness." [19]

The Court is not the only arena of conflict between those who want the national government to act and those who prefer keeping the authority in the states. Congress has much to say about the distribution of functions and the extent to which state regulations will be permitted.[20] The President has been the major national officer to speak for national majorities. And Supreme Court decisions have little significance unless they are consonant with the stand of either Congress or the President. John Marshall's great decisions in behalf of expanded national authority, for example, had little impact during his own lifetime on the actual role of the national government.[21] But the judges are not mere passive reflectors of the political currents; by their decisions they participate in the political life of the nation and in the resolution of the many battles that are fought using the language of national-state conflict.

The Supreme Court, itself a branch of the national government, has often been accused of bias. "The States," it has been charged, "have had to play against the umpire as well as against the national government itself." [22] Though the states have had their innings, over the long pull the Court's decisions have favored national powers. Especially in recent years, Congress has shown more of a tendency than the Supreme Court to respond to local pressures and to favor local regulations. And the local majorities that control the state governments have been severe in their criticism of the Court for its decisions curtailing their authority.

Despite the frequent criticism of the Supreme Court by some outraged groups who control the machinery of state government, not many would deny the Su-

[19] Robert H. Jackson, *The Struggle for Judicial Supremacy* (Knopf, 1941), p. xi.
[20] See Paul A. Freund, "Umpiring the Federal System," in Macmahon, *op. cit.*, p. 160.
[21] Riker, *op. cit.*, p. 103.
[22] O. P. Field, "States versus Nation, and the Supreme Court," *The American Political Science Review*, April 1934, p. 233.

preme Court the power to review state actions. Support for Supreme Court review of actions of state and local governments rests upon a different basis than does the argument for Supreme Court review of acts of Congress or the President. As Justice Holmes once remarked, "I do not think the United States would come to an end if we lost our power to declare an Act of Congress void. I do think the Union would be imperiled if we could not make that declaration as to the laws of the several states." [23] Or, as Justice Story wrote many years earlier, such a review is necessary to maintain "uniformity of decisions throughout the whole United States, upon all subjects within the purview of the constitution. . . . Judges of equal learning and integrity, in different states, might differently interpret a statute, or a treaty of the United States, or even the constitution itself." There must be a "revising authority to control these jarring and discordant judgments, and harmonize them into uniformity." [24]

This review of the formal constitutional structure of American federalism contains little that would have startled the generation of 1787, for the *formal structure* of our federal system is little changed. The way we actually operate this system, however, is drastically different.

Growth of the National Government

The words of the Constitution, wrote Justice Holmes in *Missouri* v. *Holland*, called into life a being whose development "could not have been foreseen completely by the most gifted of its begetters. It was enough for them to realize or to hope that they had created an organism; it has taken a century and has cost their successors much sweat and blood to prove that they created a nation." [25] The Constitution established a framework in which a national government could develop, but it was some time before a viable national community to support this national government actually existed.

As we saw in the case of *McCulloch* v. *Maryland*, John Marshall argued that ours is a union of *people*, that the central government is both in theory and in fact a national government resting directly on the people. But there were many, foremost of whom was John C. Calhoun, who dissented. These dissenters argued that the central government was only a *federal*, not a national, government, created by the states and receiving all its powers from the states acting in their organized sovereign capacities. When the Constitution of the Southern Confederacy was written, its Preamble pointedly declared, "We, the People of the Confederate States, each State acting in its sovereign and independent character do ordain and establish this Constitution. . . ."

The question was ultimately decided at Appomattox Court House, but from the beginning the logic of events vindicated the nationalists. It has made no dif-

[23] O. W. Holmes, *Collected Legal Papers* (Harcourt, Brace, 1920), pp. 295–296.
[24] *Martin* v. *Hunter's Lessee* (1816).
[25] *Missouri* v. *Holland* (1920).

ference whether the party in power has been Federalist, Jeffersonian, Whig, Republican, or Democratic—the national government's sphere has constantly expanded. The platforms of both major parties today reflect the wishes of the major interest groups and continue to call for programs that require greater activity by the central government. The political pressures calling for an expansion of national functions are so powerful that even President Eisenhower, who was pledged to return functions to the states, was unable to do so. A special Joint Federal-State Action Committee was able to designate only two rather trivial federal functions that might be returned to the states.[26] Even these recommendations—for cessation of federal aid for vocational education and for building municipal waste-treatment plants—ran into such heavy opposition that nothing came of them. It seems a safe bet that the domain of the federal government will continue to grow, no matter which party is in power.

Basis of the Growth

How has the expansion occurred? Not by amendment. The formal constitutional powers of the national government are essentially the same today as they were in 1789. But the Supreme Court (building on Marshall's work in *McCulloch* v. *Maryland*), the Congress, the President, and—ultimately—the people, have taken advantage of the Constitution's flexibility to permit the national government to exercise the powers needed to fight wars and depressions and to serve the needs of a modern industrial nation. The full scope of the central government's constitutional powers has been used to support this expansion of functions, but there are three major constitutional pillars on which the expansion has developed.

The War Power. The national government traditionally has been responsible for protecting the nation from external aggression, and, when necessary, for waging war. In a world community that knows total war, the power needed to provide for the common defense is of a scope never dreamed of in 1787. With the possibility of attack always present, the national government cannot wait until war is declared. It must keep the nation strong enough to prevent wars if possible and to win them if they break out. Military strength no longer depends primarily on troops in the field, but on the ability to mobilize the nation's industrial might and to apply its scientific knowledge to the tasks of defense. Everything from the physics courses taught in the schools to the conservation of natural resources and the maintenance of a prosperous economy affects the nation's war-making potential (see Chapter 23).

In wartime, the national government has to organize, coordinate, and channel all human and natural resources to the end of destroying the war-making power of the enemy. It then becomes not only proper, but absolutely necessary, to con-

---

[26] *Report of the Joint Federal-State Action Committee* (Government Printing Office, 1957).

script men, requisition property, control prices, encourage scientific studies, allocate resources, maintain the supporting economy, and bolster public morale. And when the fighting ceases, the government must cope with the problems of demobilization and reconversion. After disrupting national life by converting manpower, materials, and machines to war, it is responsible for achieving the return to peacetime living as smoothly as possible. It must give aid to veterans and correct the many war-caused or war-aggravated maladjustments in the economy—such as housing shortages.

In brief, the national government has the power to wage war and to do what is necessary and proper to wage it successfully. In total war this means almost total power.

The Power to Regulate Interstate and Foreign Commerce. This is the second constitutional pillar supporting the expansion of the national government's functions. Congressional authority extends to all commerce *that affects more states than one* and to all those activities, wherever they exist or whatever their nature, whose control is necessary and proper to regulate interstate and foreign commerce. The term "commerce" includes all commercial intercourse, the production, buying, selling, and transporting of goods. The power to regulate is the power to prescribe the rules by which this commerce is governed—that is, the right to foster, prohibit, promote, protect, defend all commerce that affects more states than one.

The commerce clause packs a tremendous constitutional punch. It has not been construed to cover *only* commercial or business transactions. Rather, the national government has been able to find in these few words constitutional justification for regulating a wide range of human activity and property. Two examples: It is a federal crime to use the channels of interstate commerce to sell adulterated goods, to steal automobiles, to rob a bank, to kidnap, and to transport women for immoral purposes. It is a federal offense for hotel-keepers who serve interstate travelers to refuse service to any person because of race, color, religion, or national origin.

Today there are few aspects of our economy that do not affect commerce in more states than one. When Farmer Filburn plants wheat in his own back yard to feed his own children and chickens, his actions affect the price of wheat in the interstate market, and therefore his activities are within the scope of congressional authority. When a large steel company fires men because they belong to a labor union, it enhances the danger of industrial strife and threatens the flow of goods in interstate commerce. Thus, national laws regulating employer-employee relations in industries that affect interstate commerce have been upheld as necessary and proper means to protect the free flow of this commerce.

Some people have accused the Supreme Court of making strained and unrealistic interpretations of the commerce clause in order to find constitutional justification for national regulation. But the Court has simply recognized the obvious facts of our economic life and has refused to make its decisions in an "intellectual vacuum." Wheat planted in people's back yards does, as a matter of economic fact, affect the interstate commerce in wheat. A strike in Pittsburgh or Detroit does affect commerce in California and New York.

The Power to Tax and Spend for the General Welfare. Congress lacks constitutional authority to pass laws solely on the ground that the laws will promote the general welfare, but it may raise taxes and spend money to promote the general welfare. This distinction between legislating and appropriating frequently makes little practical difference; the distinction is primarily of legal significance. For example, Congress lacks constitutional power to regulate education or agriculture directly, but Congress has the power to appropriate money to support education or to pay farmers subsidies, and by attaching conditions to its grants of money Congress may regulate what it could not constitutionally control by legal fiat.

Congress has power to appropriate the money directly to the states by what are known as *grants-in-aid.* These grants are generally conditional—that is, the states must match with their own money some of the federal funds, create an agency to supervise the spending, and submit to federal inspection. Or Congress may bypass the states and give the money to individuals, local governments, or private organizations. For example: Congress has appropriated money to be used by colleges for student loans and graduate fellowships and to individual scholars for research.

Since Congress puts up the money, it has a strong voice in determining how it shall be spent. By withholding or threatening to withhold funds, the national government can influence state operations or regulate individual conduct. Unless farmers agree to certain restrictions, they are not eligible for federal loans or other subsidy programs. Unless states agree to build highways that meet federal standards, they are not eligible for federal grants. The 1964 Civil Rights Act provides that, "No person in the United States shall, on the ground of race, color, or national origin, be excluded from participation in, be denied the benefits of, or be subjected to discrimination under any program or activity receiving Federal financial assistance." Federal authorities are directed by the act to develop regulations that will insure that federal funds, whether loans or grants, are not being used to support programs from which persons are excluded because of race or national origin. School districts that continue to segregate pupils because of race will lose substantial federal aid, hospitals that deny admission or segregate patients because of race will not be eligible for federal funds, universities that segregate or discriminate against students or faculty because of race will not be able to participate in the many federal programs that provide scholarships, fellowships, research funds, and building support.

In addition to using its power to appropriate for regulatory purposes, Congress may use its power to tax. For example: Congress has laid heavy taxes on white-phosphorus matches, on the sale of sawed-off shotguns, on the sale of narcotics, not to raise money but to regulate specific activities. Similarly, Congress requires professional gamblers to secure an annual federal license and to pay a federal tax on their gross receipts. Since gambling is illegal in forty-nine states, gamblers have a choice of paying the federal tax and thereby alerting state and local officers to their illegal activities or not paying the federal taxes and thereby running the risk of federal prosecution for tax evasion.

Congress has also used its taxing powers "to induce" states to adopt certain kinds of programs. For example, Congress has levied a tax on employers but allows them to deduct from the amount they owe the national government the state taxes they pay to support state unemployment compensation. Since the employer has to pay this money anyhow, all the states have been induced to establish unemployment compensation programs.

These three constitutional powers—the war power, the power over interstate commerce, and the power to tax and spend for the general welfare—have made possible a tremendous expansion of federal functions. If all the laws Congress has passed in pursuance of these powers were wiped off the statute books, the size of the federal government and the scope of its functions would shrink drastically.

Reason for the Growth

Why has this expansion of federal functions occurred? Certainly not because of the superior logic of the affirmative side in the age-old debate: "Resolved: that the powers of the federal government should be increased." Nor has it come about because of the desire of "that man" or "those men" to consolidate power in Washington. Such glib explanations, so prevalent in political campaigns, overlook many fundamental factors. Rather, "big government" has come about because of deep-seated changes in our society and as the result of the pushing and hauling of interest groups.

Since 1789 we have grown from a poor, sparsely populated, agricultural society to a rich, densely populated, industrial nation. Our meager, slow transportation and communication network has been replaced by one that is vast, rapid, and increasingly expanding. The farmer who used to eat what he raised now produces for people who live thousands of miles away. The small, local businessman who owned, organized, and operated his business has been joined and has even been supplanted by large-scale business owned by thousands of persons throughout the nation and operated by a nationally organized corporation. Our labor force has grown from unorganized artisans to nationally organized, mass-production workers. The United States has grown from a weak, isolated debtor nation to a powerful creditor who plays a central role in the world community.

Clearly, such profound alterations in any society would have a powerful impact on the government of that society. People's attitudes toward the national government have changed, too. While the government of the Confederation was viewed in the 1780's as a distant, even foreign government, today most people identify their fortunes much more closely with Washington than they do with their own state governments.[27] The railroad, telegraph, telephone, radio, airplane, and tele-

[27] See George Belknap and Ralph Smuckler, "Political Power Relations in a Mid-West City," *The Public Opinion Quarterly*, Spring 1956, p. 80. See also, V. O. Key, Jr., *Public Opinion and American Democracy* (Knopf, 1961), pp. 99–120.

vision have made the activities of federal officials familiar to all. Most people do not even know when their state legislature is in session, but what goes on in Washington is known throughout the land in a matter of minutes. The President, his family, their troubles and habits are objects of dinner-table conversations. Likewise, citizens of other states are no longer considered strange. The highway, automobile, and house on wheels have made us a nation on the move. Almost two hundred years of common experiences, especially the fighting of two major wars, have cemented the Union and made Washington the focus of attention.

An urban-industrial society, moreover, requires much closer regulation than does an agricultural-rural one. A thousand people in the country might need only one policeman, since informal pressures can be counted on to keep them in line. The same number of people living in the city, with its impersonal and diversified make-up, might require five policemen to enforce social sanctions. The states have also had to expand their functions, but because many of our problems have become national in scope, even greater responsibilities have devolved on the national government. In recent decades the national government has gradually taken over a greater role in business regulation, law enforcement, conservation, education, housing, and civil rights, among others. Much of what was local in 1789, or even in 1860, is now national. It is axiomatic that the unit of government dealing with a problem should be coextensive with the problem. States could supervise the relations between a small merchant, who bought and sold his products within the local market, and his few employees. But only the national government can supervise the relations between a nationally organized industry that buys and sells its materials all over the world and its thousands of employees organized into national unions.

With the industrialization of the United States there also came about a concentration of economic power, first in the form of business units and later in the form of labor unions. These units, along with professional organizations, are private governments exercising *political* as well as *economic* power. The concentration of economic power required a corresponding coalescing of political power; if the unit of public government is not as powerful as the unit of private government it is meant to supervise, the regulated often regulates the regulator. The activities of a Walter Reuther or an American Telephone and Telegraph Company are too far-flung and their power too formidable to enable the states to provide the needed social control. In 1966 General Motors had twice the total "revenue" and four times as many employees as the state of California. Big business, big agriculture, big labor, all must add up to big government.

As industrialization progressed, various powerful interests began to make demands on the national government. First the business groups, who were largely responsible for building industrial America, called on the government for aid in the form of tariffs, a national banking system, a uniform and stable currency, and subsidies to railroads, airlines, and the merchant marine. Once the business groups obtained what they wanted, however, and felt strong enough to take care of themselves generally, they began to oppose governmental aid to other groups.

But then the farmers learned that the national government could give them much more aid in solving their economic problems than could their states, and they too began to demand help. The farm groups used their powers to secure such laws as regulation of the railroads, antitrust legislation, paper currency, parcel post, and finally, government support for farm prices. By the beginning of the present century, the urban groups in general, and organized labor in particular, began to press their demands. Workers found that they could not organize unions with a hostile government issuing injunctions and calling out troops. They began to work for restrictions on injunctions and for friendly administrations. Finally, with increased industrialization and urbanization, the working groups and city dwellers found that, for political reasons, they normally received more help from the national government than from the states.

How has the new world role of the United States contributed to the growth of the national government? Until recently, the United States played a small part in maintaining order in the world community. Because of our isolated geographic position, a favorable balance of power in Europe, and a relatively stable world in Asia, we easily maintained our security without the need for a positive foreign policy. All this, of course, has changed. Today the United States has to work at the job of maintaining order and stability in the world; we no longer get a free ride. The defense of the free democratic world requires a great deal of effort and money on the part of the national government. The funds spent for direct national security, aid to allies, aid to veterans, and for interest on a debt largely acquired fighting past wars, account for approximately 80 per cent of the central government's annual budget, and the activities of well over half of its employees.

Failures of the States

Finally, in order to account for the growth of the national government, we must turn to what have to be called the failures of the states. Many of our fifty states were arbitrarily blocked out on the map, with little reference to underlying geographic, social, or historical realities. With the passage of time, growing discrepancies have developed between these artificial state boundaries and new conditions. Many natural regions, such as river valleys, are cut in half by the surveyor's line. Many large cities have grown up along state boundaries, which means that a cohesive metropolitan area is fragmented between two or three states—New York City, Kansas City, and Washington, D.C., for example. When the people of a river valley or a metropolitan region want to act through their governments to conserve human and natural resources, they often find that no one state has jurisdiction to deal with the problems of the entire area. A few states are too large; most are too small. They vary in size from Alaska to Rhode Island and in population from California to Alaska. Regardless of size or population, however, they all support the same elaborate governmental organization.

Some states lack the resources to satisfy even minimum public needs. Worse, many of the problems affecting citizens most directly are of such extent that only the national government can handle them. Faced with the Great Depression of the 1930's, the states had neither the financial resources for relief nor the power over a wide enough area to stimulate recovery. The national government, with its much greater tax resources and almost unlimited borrowing power, was literally forced to act.

The increased confidence of Americans in the national government has been paralleled by a diminishing sense of identity with the respective states. This is due in part, as we have noted, to the greater mobility of our population. Also, most states had no independent existence prior to becoming members of the Union.

But even within the limits of their jurisdiction and their resources, many of our state governments, through their failure to provide the programs desired by the public, have failed to retain the loyalty of large numbers of their citizens. Some time ago, J. Melville Broughton, a former governor of North Carolina, wrote: "Those of us who believe in the fundamental principles of states' rights and local self-government may as well concede frankly that much of the almost terrifying expansion of federal encroachment upon the original domain of the States has come about because state governments failed to meet the challenge of the new day. Inadequate educational opportunities, archaic labor laws and regulations, unrelieved hardships and inequities suffered by the working people, low-pitched politics and unjust class and race discriminations have, all too frequently, caused the people to . . . call for relief from the Federal Government. . . ." [28]

Although we hear much about the waste and extravagance of the national government, Washington is almost a model of perfection when compared to some state capitals which are graft-ridden, inefficient, and unable to provide the services that the people expect. Generally speaking, "the most critically defective part of our present system is the state government." [29] Some states, of course, are doing an excellent job of providing a high level of public service. But there are others that serve as instruments, not of the majority, but of powerful local interests.

Even if we had ideal state governments throughout the country, the national government's functions would continue to expand in response to national needs. And it is not even clear that adequate performance by the states will reduce substantially the assumption of activities by the national government. For in some instances, the successful introduction by some of the states of new programs has led to the demand for national action to bring the full benefit of these programs to the people in all the states.[30]

The primary reasons, then, for the expansion of federal functions are the industrialization and urbanization of the United States, the consequent concentration of economic power, the resulting national problems that require action by a national government with sufficient resources and extensive jurisdiction, external threats to our national existence, and the deficiencies of the states.

[28] "The Future of the States," *State Government*, March 1943, pp. 55–56.
[29] G. C. S. Benson, *The New Centralization* (Farrar & Rinehart, 1941), p. 157.
[30] See Grodzins, *op. cit.*, p. 19.

5 PROBLEMS OF AMERICAN FEDERALISM

In discussing federalism, we must beware of the "billiard-ball" concept of the state and national governments as hard, solid objects that collide with sharp impact. Actually these governments *mesh* with one another, for they are made up of people who govern, and are governed by, other people. To talk of states rights is but a shorthand way of referring to the rights of people who live in states and to the authority of officials elected by them. Texans, not Texas, have rights.

107

To put it another way, national and state governments are merely arenas in which differing groups engage in political combat over public policies. Congressmen and state legislators often respond to the same groups and express the same ideas, and we have "national-state cooperation." At other times, congressmen and state legislators represent sharply different combinations of interest, and we have "national-state conflict." This conflict between the two levels of government is just one facet of the continuing struggle among groups that makes up our politics. "Federalism does not involve a struggle between the nation and the states, but rather a struggle among interests who have favorable access to one of the two levels of government." [1]

The Politics of Federalism

From the day the colonists first set foot on the soil of the New World, Americans have been arguing about the "proper" division of powers between central and local governments. But from then to the present it has been impossible to disentangle substantive issues of politics from these discussions. From time to time various governmental commissions and private study groups have attempted to make impartial and objective determinations of the "proper" distribution of functions between the national and state governments. But the experts are discovering, just as the Founding Fathers did in 1787, that there are no objective, scientific standards distinguishing between national and state functions. The questions are *political* in nature. Hence, national action is favored by those who anticipate that national officials will be responsive to what they conceive to be in the general interest. But those who believe that state officials will be most likely to support their goals are the champions of states rights. The attachments of groups to one or the other level of government change in time; and they change less through conversion on abstract constitutional issues than through changed estimates of ability to influence one or the other level of decision.

At one time or another northerners, southerners, businessmen, farmers, workers, Federalists, Democrats, Whigs, and Republicans have thought it "improper" to vest a particular function in the national government. They opposed "control by Washington" in the name of maintaining the federal system. But underlying the debates were such issues as slavery, labor-management relations, government regulation of business, civil rights.

When the Federalists were in control of the central government and, in behalf of merchants and creditors, established a national bank, assumed state debts in full, proclaimed the neutrality of the United States in the French-English struggles, and passed the Alien and Sedition laws, the Jeffersonian agrarians and debtors protested each move as a violation of "states rights." But when these same Jeffersonians captured the national government and placed embargoes on

[1] Harmon Zeigler, *Interest Groups in American Society* (Prentice-Hall, 1964), p. 48.

shipping, purchased Louisiana, and fought the War of 1812, it was the New England Federalists who picked up the cry of "states rights." When the Republican party threatened the slave economy in 1861, the South arose to defend "states rights." When the industrial interests used their influence with the national government to raise the tariff, secure land grants for railroads, and tax state bank notes out of existence, the exporters and agrarians championed "states rights."

With the advent of the New Deal and the growth of organized labor's influence at the national level, most business groups became devotees of the rights of states. The national government came to be controlled by persons in whom many businessmen had little confidence and over whom they had less influence. They discovered that state legislatures and state courts are more likely than their national counterparts to make decisions favored by businessmen. As Professor Swisher has written, "It behooves us . . . to take thought before drenching our handkerchiefs when the National Association of Manufacturers and the American Bar Association bewail the prostrate position of the states before the federal colossus. These mourners are not shedding tears over the lamentable conditions of New Hampshire and North Carolina and Montana and Texas but over the enterprise caught in the grip of the federal regulatory hand. . . ." [2] On the other hand, labor leaders have found national agencies more responsive to their claims. It is not surprising that while business groups are quick to defend the states against what they call the "federal octopus," labor leaders emphasize the need for national action and charge the states with being dominated by "special interests."

In recent years those who favor segregation have rightly recognized that those who control southern state and local governments are also likely to favor segregation. They fear that national officials, responding to different political majorities, will favor integration. Naturally, segregationists sing of the virtues of local governments close "to the people," they are quick to emphasize the dangers of "overcentralization," and they argue at length that the regulation of civil rights is not a "proper" function of the national government. On the other side, those who want segregation abolished emphasize the "propriety" of national power being used because they recognize that state governments controlled by segregationists will never on their own initiative move against segregation.

So it is that political issues are involved in discussions of national-state relations. Nevertheless, almost all observers, however sharply they differ on particular issues, agree that a country the size of the United States needs strong and active state governments and that maintaining a balance between national and state governments is a major problem of federalism.

[2] Carl B. Swisher, *The Growth of Constitutional Power in the United States* (Univ. of Chicago Press, 1946), p. 33.

The Problem of Maintaining the Balance

The awful spectacle that disturbed Hamilton—"a nation without a national government"—need frighten us no longer. The national government's activities have greatly expanded, and they probably will continue to do so. What can be done to make state governments even stronger instruments of public service?

Modernized State and Local Governments

We hear so much about the growth of national governmental functions that we sometimes overlook the growth of state activities. State and national power is not a seesaw on which one side must be up while the other be down. An increase in the authority of one does not necessarily detract from the authority of the other. On the contrary, the entrance of the national government into new fields has in many cases strengthened the states and helped them to improve their services. Despite the lamented "weakening of states" and the constant cries about national interference, states are today, measuring by the amount of money spent and the number of functions performed, stronger units of government than they were in 1787. Indeed, since the end of World War II, activities of states and their subdivisions have been increasing at a faster rate than the nondefense activities of the national government.[3] As Governor Rockefeller of New York has pointed out, ". . . The striking fact in our domestic political experience since World War II has not been the growth of federal government—but the far more rapid expansion of state and local government to meet growing social needs. . . . The role of the state within American federalism is far from 'obsolete.' It is as dynamic and promising as is the federal idea itself." But as Governor Rockefeller warned, "The essential political truth is that—today more than ever—the preservation of states' rights depends upon the exercise of states' responsibilities."[4]

Clearly, then, one of the most promising approaches to maintaining a federal system is to improve, simplify, and modernize the state governments. Many reforms designed to vitalize state governments have long been advocated—such as reorganizing administrative machinery, streamlining legislative procedures, keeping up to date the basis of representation in state legislatures to reflect the growing urban population, shortening the ballot, and making officials responsive to wider segments of the electorate. Although recommendations for reform are often filed and forgotten, several states—New Jersey, New York, and Virginia, for example—have made considerable progress. But much remains to be done.

[3] U.S. Commission on Intergovernmental Relations, *A Report to the President* (Government Printing Office, 1955), p. 36.

[4] Nelson A. Rockefeller, *The Future of Federalism* (Harvard Univ. Press, 1962), pp. 11, 14, 54.

Regional Administration of Federal Functions

Centralization of policy-making need not lead to centralization of administration. Policies and programs can be adopted at the national level, but their administration can be decentralized. Today only 11 per cent of all federal employees work in the Washington metropolitan area. This decentralization permits greater local participation in national programs and encourages adjustment of policies to local conditions.

Hitherto, each agency in Washington tended to set up its own field headquarters in accordance with the demands of its own activities and with little thought to the established field units already created by other federal agencies. While the United States is now blanketed by a great number of federal administrative regions, some of them overlapping, there is a growing tendency for one agency to use the regional divisions created by another. Perhaps in time we shall have regional national capitals throughout the United States.

Another kind of federal decentralization is represented by the Tennessee Valley Authority, which Congress established in 1933 to develop the resources of the Tennessee Valley, and which is described more fully on pages 682–684. Originally, many people within the Tennessee Valley, along with government officials in the area, opposed the creation of the authority for fear that it would dwarf and dominate state governments. But from the outset, the TVA has championed "grassroots" administration and has cooperated closely with state and local officials. Wherever possible it has even delegated responsibility to state and local agencies. State departments of health, conservation, education, highways, and other agencies have joined with the TVA to raise the level of government throughout the valley.

Thus the pattern of federalism is constantly being altered. We have a variety of regional organizations across the nation, some the result of federal action, others of federal-state cooperation, and, as we shall presently note, still others the result of action by individual states. These regional organizations supplement the constitutional division between the central government and the states. At present, they are mainly concerned with the administration of single programs; but conceivably in the future, as they assume more functions of national, state, and local governments, they could be given representative institutions—legislatures, executives, and courts—and a new dimension would be added to our federal union.

"Federalism without Washington"—Interstate Cooperation

The states are not forced to wait for the national government to take the initiative in dealing with problems that require regional action. Several states together can deal with problems too large for any one to handle alone. If the states were more effective in solving their own regional problems, there would be less need for the national government to step in (aside, perhaps, from giving financial aid). One instrument they can use is the *interstate compact.*

Until the twentieth century, interstate compacts were used only to settle boundary disputes between states, but since 1900 over twenty interstate agencies have been established by compact.[5] One of the more successful of these is the Port of New York Authority, established by New Jersey and New York. This agency supervises and operates the harbor as a unit, and recently it has been given the job of coordinating the operation of airports in the area. Other promising interstate compact agencies are those created to deal with education, abatement of water pollution, conservation of oil and gas, parole and probation, and conservation of fish.

In addition to these more formal interstate compact agencies, state officials often get together to handle a particular problem: for example, to establish joint operations of police radio broadcasting nets or to coordinate plans for highway safety. These efforts have on occasion given rise to regular organizations, such as the Interstate Commission on the Delaware River Basin, composed of representatives from New York, New Jersey, Pennsylvania, and Delaware, or the Conference of Southern Governors. In addition to these regional conferences, state officials have joined together in various nationwide organizations— the American Legislators' Association, the National Association of Attorneys General, of State Budget Officers, of State Purchasing Officials, and others. Each state now has a Commission on Interstate Cooperation. Most of the interstate agencies are coordinated through the Council of State Governments, which serves as a secretariat, collects data, sponsors research, and publicizes results. This kind of cooperation is bringing about greater uniformity among the states and higher standards in the administration of laws within the states.

Genuine interstate cooperation could lead ultimately to greater uniformity of laws throughout the country. Although diversity is a virtue of federalism, it can also be a fault. For example, the wide diversity in traffic rules, even in neighboring states, makes it virtually impossible to drive across the nation without unknowingly violating some law along the way. The story of Harry Harper, an Iowa farmer, is not unusual. Harper "started out for St. Louis, Missouri, to sell a load of melons he had grown. During his journey he was stopped by the Iowa Highway Patrol at night and required to put three green lights on his truck. After driving across the state line into Missouri, the Missouri police stopped him and told him it was illegal in Missouri to have three green lights on his truck, so he had to take them off." [6]

Diversity of state laws on insurance, contracts, negotiable instruments, judicial procedures—in fact, on the whole scope of business transactions—increases

[5] Richard H. Leach and Redding S. Sugg, Jr., *The Administration of Interstate Compacts* (Louisiana State Univ. Press, 1959), p. 6.
[6] Related by Frank Bane and reported in W. Brooke Graves, *American State Government,* 3rd ed. (Heath, 1946), p. 914. Used by permission of D. C. Heath and Company.

operating costs and makes it difficult to do business on a national basis. Labeling laws designed to protect consumers against fraud, for example, are so diverse that manufacturers often have to use special labels in order to sell their products in different states.

The application and interpretation of all these laws by the fifty-one court systems in the United States create another level of confusion. What law applies to a contract signed in California, delivered in New York, between citizens of Wisconsin and Minnesota, about property located in New Jersey? This is not a fanciful question, but an example of the actual problems confronting judges in their everyday decisions.

How can we create some measure of uniformity among state laws? Members of the American Bar Association in 1892 organized the Conference of Commissioners on Uniform State Laws. Under the guidance of this conference, composed of commissioners appointed by the state governors, committees have been established to recommend uniform laws to the state legislatures. All the states have adopted the Negotiable Instrument Law and the Warehouse Receipt Act, and some states have adopted other uniform laws including those dealing with stock transfers, narcotics, and criminal extradition. These attempts to bring about uniformity of the laws also have the desirable effect of raising standards because the best practices tend to spread throughout the states. But despite occasional successes, over sixty years' work has not significantly decreased the diversity of state laws. Furthermore, even after all the states adopt a particular code, there is no guarantee that uniformity will in fact result. Fifty separate state court systems may be likely to interpret their codes in their fifty separate ways.

How successful, then, have the states been in their efforts to cooperate? On balance, "Federalism without Washington" has not brought about the results that its sponsors had hoped for. One of the difficulties has been too much emphasis on simply forestalling centralization. Horizontal cooperation—that is, cooperation at the state level—has perhaps made its greatest contribution "in providing central staff research and educational facilities to strengthen the competence with which the governments at a particular level do their job, so that governmental bankruptcy alone cannot justify the transference of authority to higher levels of government." [7] Horizontal federalism has brought only marginal results. What, then, about cooperation between national and state governments?

Cooperative Federalism

Recent scholarship has made it abundantly clear that "There has in fact never been a time when federal, state, and local functions were separate and distinct. . . . All nostalgic references to the day of state and local independence are based upon mythical views of the past. . . . Government does more things [today] than it did

[7] James W. Fesler, *Area and Administration* (Univ. of Alabama Press, 1949), p. 40.

in 1790 or 1861; but in terms of what government did, there was as much sharing of functions then as today." [8]

Cooperation among national and state governments takes many forms. When a secret service agent is helped by state and local police to nab a counterfeiter, we are benefiting from cooperative federalism. A public health official tracking down carriers of disease uses both federal and state services. Many federal agencies, such as the United States Public Health Service, the United States Office of Education, and the Bureau of the Census, conduct surveys and gather statistics for state officials. Other agencies train local employees and help enforce state laws. This kind of cooperation avoids duplication and provides better services at less cost.

In some cases, the administration of federal programs is delegated to state governments. The TVA encouraged state and local officials to help run parts of the TVA program. The administration of the selective service system is primarily a responsibility of state and local officials. Some people favor a broad extension of state administration of national programs, arguing that the national government should lay down general policies but delegate administration to state and local governments. President Johnson's "War on Poverty" programs—discussed in Chapter 26—are in many respects joint federal-state ventures of this nature. It is doubtful, however, if this can be done except on a limited scale. "State administrations that are not in sympathy with the National Government will cause considerable difficulty; and it is doubtful whether United States Senators will favor administrative methods that give their potential or actual rivals, the state Governors, the power of patronage over national programs in their States." [9]

In addition, when national programs are turned over to state governments, there is the risk that they will not be administered in accordance with national policies. Philip Selznick, in his discerning study, *TVA and the Grass Roots* (1949), presented evidence that TVA's policy of working with local governments often amounted to handing over the TVA to powerful local groups. And Paul H. Appleby, an experienced administrator, says: "If a program is Federal and if the responsibility is Federal, the authority should be Federal and the administering bureaucracy should almost always be Federal." [10]

Conversely, there is some opposition to state administration of national policies on the grounds that it turns the states into administrative districts of the federal government. Nevertheless, where responsibility for programs is only partly national, delegation of administration to the states would seem feasible, especially if the states were to modernize their practices so that they could efficiently handle the jobs given to them.

[8] Grodzins, *op. cit.*, pp. 6–7. See also Daniel J. Elazar, *The American Partnership: Intergovernmental Cooperation in the Nineteenth Century United States* (Univ. of Chicago Press, 1962).
[9] William Anderson, "Federalism—Then and Now," *State Government*, May 1943, pp. 107–112.
[10] Paul H. Appleby, *Big Democracy* (Knopf, 1945), p. 87.

Grants-in-Aid

More promising than turning over complete administration of federal policies to the states is the joint operation of programs through the device of the *grant-in-aid*. There are some programs for which the states have chief constitutional responsibility, but in which the entire nation has an interest. By an accident of geography, for example, some children may be deprived of an adequate education, and many people can be denied good health services, for states in which they live may either lack adequate resources to provide minimum essential services, or else the dominant groups within the state lack the desire to do so. These problems can no longer be considered of only local concern. Young people who have been deprived of educational opportunities, or whose health has been impaired, are national liabilities.

Much of our national wealth is concentrated in the industrialized areas—northeastern, midwestern, and far-western states. As a result, other areas, especially the rural South, find it difficult to raise funds for public services. This may be only one reason why public services in some states are below the national level, but it is an important reason.[11]

What can be done? The national government could in many cases take over the entire responsibility for the programs. But as an alternative to complete national control, Congress, through the grant-in-aid, has tried to secure a national minimum level and to encourage the states into taking action on their own. With its broader tax base, it taxes the wealth where it is located and turns the money over to the states for programs that Congress feels should be more adequately supported. This system of federal grants-in-aid goes back at least as far as 1802, but it got its real start in 1916 when Congress gave money to the states for the construction of "rural post roads." During the depression of the 1930's the number of federal grants greatly increased. Today the national government gives money to the states for agricultural extension work, land-grant colleges, elementary and secondary education, old-age assistance, aid to dependent children, aid to the blind, and aid to crippled children, to mention only some of the more important federal grants-in-aid programs. The Appalachia Project (see pages 670–672) directs such grants to the nation's largest depressed area. On the average, the states now receive from the national government about one-fifth of the money they spend.

Most of these grants are *conditional*, however—that is, the states must reciprocate and match the federal funds with state funds, establish agencies to expend the funds, submit plans for advance approval, permit inspection by national officials of the completed work, and place the employees who administer the grant under a merit system.

Since most grants require the states to match the federal dollars, the poor states,

[11] Richard E. Dawson and James A. Robinson, "The Politics of Welfare," in Herbert Jacob and Kenneth N. Vines (eds.), *Politics in the American States* (Little, Brown, 1965), p. 403.

even with federal assistance, are often unable to provide the same services as their richer sisters. For example, a totally disabled worker in recent years might receive as much as $137.34 a month in Massachusetts or as little as $43.41 in Mississippi. To help correct these inequalities, formulas for the distribution of federal funds have been proposed that take the relative needs of the several states into account. Quite naturally, the wealthy states that contribute most of the money to the federal treasury are not happy when a larger proportion goes to the less fortunate areas.

One of the dangers of federal grants is that states may be tempted to match federal money for prescribed purposes even when they could better spend their limited resources for something else. States can now receive federal dollars for the funds they spend on highway construction, but in many states, perhaps, the money could be better spent for schools or mental hospitals. The lure of federal funds tends to destroy the flexibility of state programs and makes the states take a back seat in planning their own expenditures. Is there a way out of this dilemma?

More Flexible Grants?

The national government has been urged not to make state grants for specific programs but to give *unconditional* subsidies to be used as each state wishes. This approach has been followed in other federal systems—Canada and Australia, for example. It has also been suggested that Congress make its grants to the states in terms of *broad categories*—highways, education, public assistance, and public health—instead of retaining the present system of detailed grants; with this innovation states would have more flexibility and initiative to work out their own programs.[12]

Others have opposed either broader grants or unconditional subsidies.[13] They contend that such subsidies might not be used to provide necessary services and that states would continue asking for additional grants for specific programs. "A policy of unconditional subsidies with no matching requirements would be likely to undermine the sense of financial responsibility," argued a presidential Commission on Intergovernmental Relations. The tendency would be for states and localities "to look more and more to the national government to perform the disagreeable task of extracting money from the taxpayer."[14]

Underlying the question of how federal grants-in-aid should be made is the basic difference between those who feel that the state legislatures might spend money more wisely if they had more discretion, and those who believe that Congress is more likely to determine the "proper" use of the funds. Since the political demands behind most federal grants are for expanding particular ac-

---

[12] U.S. Commission on Organization of the Executive Branch of the Government, *Overseas Administration, Federal-State Relations, Federal Research* (Government Printing Office, 1949), p. 36.

[13] U.S. Commission on Intergovernmental Relations, *op. cit.*, pp. 132–133.

[14] *Ibid.*

tivities—highways, public education, public health, and so on—rather than with a more abstract concern for improving the operations of state governments, it seems unlikely that there will be any fundamental changes in the nature of the federal grant-in-aid system.

Grants-in-Aid: A Trial Balance

After a careful study of the federal grant system, V. O. Key, Jr., came to the conclusion that it

> . . . strengthens the states and thereby strengthens but profoundly modifies the federal system. . . . The achievements of direct federal administration are not so striking as to make federal assumption an inviting alternative to the grant system. The governance of a nation of continental proportions is a matter for which no simple blueprint and specifications are available. The grant system builds on and utilizes existing institutions to cope with national problems. Under it the states are welded into a national machinery of sorts and the establishment of costly, parallel, direct federal services is made unnecessary. A virtue of no mean importance is that the administrators in actual charge of operations remain amenable to local control. In that way the supposed formality, the regularity, and the cold-blooded efficiency of a national hierarchy are avoided.[15]

The Commission on Intergovernmental Relations confirmed Key's judgment. So has the Advisory Commission on Intergovernmental Relations.[16] The grant system is here to stay. Its constitutionality is beyond question, in more than one sense. The Supreme Court has ruled that neither a state nor a taxpayer has the right to contest the constitutionality of a grant.[17] Today, discussion centers around more specific questions: Just what functions should be supported by federal money? What conditions should be tied to the grant? How should grants be administered?

The federal grant is not the solution to all problems, of course. And certainly the system is subject to abuse. Federal money is not "free"; all services must be paid for by the taxpayers. Nevertheless, an intelligently administered program of grants-in-aid can bring greater strength to the states and better services to the people.

Bypassing the States—National-Local Cooperation

A more controversial example of cooperative federalism involves relations between national and local governments that bypass the states. According to the traditional theory of American federalism,

[15] V. O. Key, Jr., *The Administration of Federal Grants to States* (Public Administration Service 1937), pp. 375, 383.

[16] Advisory Commission on Intergovernmental Relations, *The Role of Equalization in Federal Courts*, 1964, p. 81.

[17] *Massachusetts* v. *Mellon* (1923).

the national government should deal with local governments only through the states. It is true that in a constitutional sense local governments are creatures of the states. But to "refer to Chicago as but an arm of Illinois or to New York City as but an arm of New York is as unrevealing as to call the General Motors Corporation an instrument of Delaware or the Southern Pacific Company an instrument of Kentucky, under whose laws it is organized." [18]

Although sooner or later everything the national government does affects the operations of local governments, it was not until the Great Depression that the national government began to deal directly with city officials. Today cities receive federal aid for building and operating mass transportation facilities, for building streets and airports, for civil defense, for slum clearance and housing, urban renewal, and other projects.

State officials have sharply criticized this circumventing of the states; on the other hand, of course, city officials favor direct federal help. Many large cities —actually "city-states" in many respects—fail to receive sympathetic treatment from state legislatures dominated by rural representatives who not only have little sympathy or understanding for city problems but are often downright hostile to city politicians. As a result, as President Eisenhower told the Conference of State Governors, "Today, for help in urban problems, committees of Mayors are far more likely to journey to Washington than to their own state capitals." [19] Mayor Richard Daley of Chicago told a congressional committee, "I think a city the size of Chicago should be able to go directly to its Federal Government with its programs, because we find in many instances the greater responsiveness and greater understanding." Another mayor, Charles P. Taft of Cincinnati, agreed, stating simply, "I would rather do business with Washington." [20]

This difference in attitude between big-city officials and state officials reflects a more general conflict. The big-city constituencies are more likely to have influence at the national level—especially with the President and the Executive branch —than they have with their own state governments. It is not surprising that state officials sometimes get caught in the squeeze between national and city officials. In part the conflict between city and state government grew out of the under-representation of large city populations in the state legislatures. With the balance of legislative power shifting to the urban areas as a result of Supreme Court decisions beginning with *Baker* v. *Carr*, state governments may come to serve as more effective intermediaries between national and local governments. However, as Robert S. Friedman has pointed out, reapportionment will mainly increase the voice of suburbia rather than the central city and "will not solve the problems of the central city in all respects. In fact in such matters as distribution of state funds

---

[18] C. B. Swisher, *American National Government* (Houghton Mifflin, 1951), p. 908.

[19] Text of Address by the President at the State Dinner of the 1957 Governors' Conference, June 24, 1957, in *Report of the Joint Federal-State Action Committee* (Government Printing Office, 1957), p. 20.

[20] Hearings on "Federal-State-Local Relations" before a Subcommittee of the Committee on Government Operations, House of Representatives, 85th Cong., 1st Sess., October 16–22, 1957, pp. 391, 641.

to localities it might even hurt." Friedman believes that for states to work out more productive relations with their own cities requires greater *home rule* for cities as well as reapportionment.[21]

Cooperative federalism means all things to all men. To some it is a midway station on the road to greater power for the national government; to others it is a way of strengthening the states; but above all it is an example of what Tocqueville noticed over a hundred years ago: "I have never been more struck by the good sense and the practical judgment of the Americans than in the manner in which they elude the numberless difficulties resulting from their Federal Constitution."[22]

Trouble Spots of Federalism

The truck driver who is stopped at the state boundary because his vehicle is six inches too long, the governor who would like to sign a new tax measure but is warned that industry may move out of the state if he does so, the woman who discovers that she is legally divorced in one state but not in another—these people, like the rest of us, face the problems of federalism. What are some of these problems and what steps have been taken to solve them?

Law Enforcement

Not many years ago the local constabulary had little difficulty in dealing with crime. Everybody knew everybody else and detection of the guilty was a relatively simple process. Whenever help was needed in capturing a fugitive, the sheriff could rally law-respecting citizens by raising the "hue and cry." Today, in our mobile society where anonymity makes capture difficult, criminals move swiftly across the nation by automobile or airplane, cutting across one jurisdictional boundary after another. Our multitude of police agencies, with overlapping responsibilities, give criminals an advantage that they are quick to exploit. On the national level, postal inspectors, "T" men, "G" men, and twenty-three other specialized federal police have limited authority to enforce specified federal laws. State police operate within the boundaries of their own states and, within the state, city police, county sheriffs, and township constables often spend as much time competing for glory as they do in crime detection. What happens outside their own jurisdiction is sometimes of little interest to police officers. Frequently, troublemakers are simply chased out of town.

In 1951 a Senate committee investigating crime uncovered many instances of the failure of police agencies to cooperate even in the most obvious ways. The

[21] Robert S. Friedman, "The Reapportionment Myth," reprinted from *National Civic Review*, April 1960, in Edward C. Banfield (ed.), *Urban Government* (The Free Press, 1961), pp. 64–65.

[22] Alexis de Tocqueville, *Democracy in America*, Phillips Bradley (ed.) (Knopf, 1946), I, p. 167.

committee pointed to a case of a gambling house that straddled the Missouri-Kansas border. Whenever the Missouri police staged a raid, the gamblers merely moved to the back of the house, which was located in Kansas. Whenever the Kansas police knocked on the back door, the gamblers returned to the front of the house, which was located in Missouri. The fact that the Missouri police never arranged a simultaneous raid with Kansas police officers suggests stupidity, negligence, or corruption.

Failures of state and local police to cope with criminals have led to demands for national action. Congress has made it a federal offense to use the channels of interstate commerce to steal, to kidnap, to transport women for immoral purposes; for shipment of firearms to or by convicted felons; for shipment of information or equipment used in illegal gambling; for shipment of explosives for purposes of destroying churches or public buildings. In each instance the demands for this extension of the police duties of the national government came about as a result of failure of states to deal adequately with the problem. In recent years the failure of some state and local police authorities to protect the rights of Negroes has added fuel to the growing demand for more vigorous federal police protection.

The constant expansion of federal police jurisdiction, if carried far enough, could be dangerous. The concentration of control over the police in a central agency is a primary characteristic of totalitarian police states. However, there is much that can be done short of giving complete authority over law enforcement to the national government. Something could be done, for example, about the hundreds of inadequate, overlapping police agencies. Here again, cooperative federalism is needed. Already progress is being made. The FBI fingerprint file, with over 21 million prints, is available to all law-enforcement officers, who in turn record their own collection of prints with the FBI. Federal officers enforcing national law turn over to state officials any evidence of the violation of state laws. Some states have coordinated their police radio networks, and neighboring states often grant reciprocal arrest privileges to out-of-state officers who are in "hot pursuit" of offenders.

Law Avoidance

Federalism also helps people who can hardly be called criminals to evade state laws. State sales taxes on cigarettes, liquor, and gasoline, for example, can often be avoided simply by crossing the state line. "Last-chance" gasoline stations that dot the highways just before one enters a state with higher taxes are evidence of this everyday tax evasion. When metropolitan cities are located near state boundaries, persons who earn their living in one state and benefit from its public services can in certain cases avoid paying city and state taxes by commuting to work from the adjoining low-tax state.

A more spectacular form of law avoidance is carried on by those who have the money and time to go to Reno for six weeks to avoid their own state divorce laws.

Nevada does a thriving divorce business and, in a sense, sets the divorce standards for the wealthy members of the entire nation. Moreover, despite the efforts of the Supreme Court to protect each state's right to control the matrimonial affairs of its own citizens and at the same time to accommodate the national interest in seeing that states respect the full-faith-and-credit clause, there is greater confusion than ever about the validity of divorces. Some observers favor uniform divorce standards throughout the nation. But since all fifty state legislatures could probably never agree on the same standards, federal action would be required. Congress has no power to pass laws regulating marriage and divorce, but the Supreme Court may have left the way open under the full-faith-and-credit clause for Congress to determine the grounds for divorce that would be recognized by all states.

Evasion of business laws is another problem. New Jersey, in earlier years, and Delaware today, have been the Renos of the world of corporation charters. Many corporations that do most of their business and sell most of their securities in other states have responded to advertisements such as this:

> Charters—Delaware Best, Quickest, Cheapest, Most Liberal. Nothing needs to be paid in. Do business and hold meetings anywhere. Free forms. Colonial Charter Company, Wilmington, Delaware.[23]

Corporations gaining such charters in Wilmington maintain nominal one-room-one-desk headquarters there simply to evade the stricter charter laws (designed to protect stockholders, consumers, and the public) of the states in which they do business. Periodically, it is proposed that all corporations carrying on an interstate business be required to incorporate under national law, but so far nothing has come of these proposals. Congress also could require all corporations using interstate commerce or the mails to incorporate in the state in which they maintain their real headquarters or do the bulk of their business. But until such action is taken, the situation will remain as it has been.

Interstate Competition

In their zeal to attract business, some states and cities offer free factory sites, tax exemptions, free water, and laws that make it difficult for labor to organize unions. Often these concessions to business are made at the public expense. Many states hesitate to levy taxes to pay for better schools or to increase aid to the needy for fear that the higher taxes may drive industries away to states with lower rates, even though there is no conclusive evidence that the tax rate is a cause of business migrations. Similarly, states are often reluctant to enact minimum-wage laws or to extend welfare programs because the additional cost may place their industries at a competitive disadvantage to those in states without such provisions.

[23] W. Z. Ripley, *Main Street and Wall Street* (Little, Brown, 1927), p. 29, cited by G. C. S. Benson, *The New Centralization* (Farrar & Rinehart, 1941), p. 28.

Competition among the states has also retarded the development of state conservation programs. Each state hesitates to require industries to follow conservation procedures—for example, preventing water pollution—for fear that the resulting expenses will cause local business firms to lose out to those operating in states with a "get-rich-quick-and-never-mind-the-future" philosophy. Although interstate agreements, especially in the oil and gas industry, have led to some conservation programs, such agreements have been made only when conservation coincides with more immediate economic interests—for example, controlling the supply of a commodity to prevent the depressing of prices.

Maintaining the National Market

One of the major goals of the Constitution was to create a free-trade area within the United States. To a large extent this goal has been achieved. Certainly one of the major reasons for the remarkable economic development of this nation has been the absence of state barriers to trade and commerce. Throughout the years, however, some state regulations have imposed restraints on the free flow of commerce. Some of these regulations are designed to protect consumers from fraud, some are in the form of health and quarantine regulations, and others are attempts to collect a fair share of taxes from those who use the roads or other tax-supported facilities. However, many laws passed ostensibly to protect persons from disease or fraud, or to protect animals and crops from infection, are actually designed to give home industries the advantage of the home market.

The interstate-commerce clause of the Constitution deprives states of any power to tax interstate commerce as such, but they may levy fees for the use of their highways and require out-of-state trucks to secure licenses, permits, and registration tickets. So long as the fee bears some reasonable relation to the use of highways, it is not unconstitutional. Although no state has yet tried to collect registration fees or permits from nonresident passenger vehicles, they all have some form of charge for out-of-state trucks. The most common forms are: registration fees, mileage taxes, consumption-of-gasoline taxes, and levies on the receipts received for hauling goods. One survey reports that a trucker traveling from Alabama to South Carolina in a five-to-six-ton truck would have to pay fees totaling several hundred dollars.

These burdens are to some extent lightened by reciprocity agreements, but only nine states grant complete freedom from fees by such agreements. States are entitled to receive some payment for the use of their highways by those who do not pay the normal state taxes. But many state highways are in part financed by federal grants drawn from federal tax funds, and the burdens placed on the free movement of goods are ultimately paid through increased costs by all the people of the nation.

True to the traditions of John Marshall, the Supreme Court has struck down some laws whose purpose is to discriminate against the commerce of other states. Many discriminatory practices, however, are never brought to the Court. Moreover, the Supreme Court has a difficult task. While it must protect interstate commerce from discriminatory treatment and must prevent the "Balkanization" of our national economy, it cannot permit business firms to hide behind the commerce clause in order to avoid paying their share of taxes or to escape compliance with regulations necessary to protect the public health, welfare, safety, and morals.

The Future of Federalism

There are many who consider federalism as only a midway station between a confederation and a unitary state. These critics argue that modern techniques of transportation and communication have destroyed the barriers of time and distance that originally gave rise to federalism. In short, they insist that federalism has become obsolete.

Harold J. Laski, the late British political scientist, socialist writer, and critic of American federalism, argued that federalism

> . . . is insufficiently positive in character; it does not provide for sufficient rapidity of action; it inhibits the emergence of necessary standards of uniformity; it relies upon compacts and compromises which take insufficient account of the urgent category of time; it leaves the backward areas a restraint, at once parasitic and poisonous, on those which seek to move forward. . . .

Here is the crux of his argument:

> Giant capitalism has . . . concentrated the control of economic power in a small proportion of the American people. . . . For forty-eight separate units to seek to compete with the integrated power of giant capitalism is to invite defeat in every element of social life where approximate uniformity of conditions is the test of the good life.[24]

Laski charged that our national government lacks the constitutional authority to control vested business interests and that the state governments are reluctant to regulate them lest these business interests withdraw their patronage and go elsewhere. He predicted that public pressures would force positive national action, eventually leading to the abandonment of federalism. But Laski was not so much predicting the end of our federal system as he was arguing for its abolition. Favoring more vigorous national regulation of business and more positive government management of the economy, he believed that the federal system stood in the way of achieving these goals.

William H. Riker, after a systematic study of federalism, agrees with Laski that federalism has created benefits to economic interests, but he concludes these bene-

[24] H. J. Laski, "The Obsolescence of Federalism," *The New Republic*, May 3, 1939, pp. 367–369.

fits "pale beside the significance of the benefits to Southern segregationist whites
. . . who have been given the freedom to oppress Negroes, first as slaves and later
as a depressed caste. . . . The judgment to be passed on federalism in the United
States is therefore a judgment on the values of segregation and racial oppression." [25]

Perhaps we attribute to federalism difficulties for which it is only partly responsible. We are a nation of continental proportions with a rich variety of sections
and groups. Even if the federal form of government were abolished tomorrow, there
would still be a South and a New England. Giant capitalists and trade unionists
would remain strong, and white supremacists would still oppose the passage and
enforcement of civil rights laws. Even without federalism there would be local
units of government, and local majorities would use these units to resist national
majorities. True, the ideology of states rights and the general support for federalism
permit segregationists and others who dominate state governments to work for
their goals in the name of local self-government, but such appeals are not unknown
in governments that operate under the unitary forms. And as far as the constitutional structure of federalism is concerned, today *the national government has all
the constitutional power it needs to deal with virtually every problem of national
extent.*

[25] William H. Riker, *Federalism: Origin, Operation, Significance* (Little, Brown, 1964), pp.
152–153.

PART 3

Civil liberties and citizenship

A Problem Guide How can we maintain the proper balance between liberty and order, between diversity and uniformity, between individual rights and collective needs? This is the main problem taken up in Part Three. To many Americans the safeguarding and broadening of individual freedom—of civil liberties and civil rights—is the most important task of a democratic society. These are the lofty and historic rights of the Western tradition—freedom of religion, freedom of speech, freedom of assembly, freedom of the press, equality under the law.

When we think of protecting these freedoms of the individual, we usually think of protecting them against *government*. This is only natural, for government historically has often been the great "engine of tyranny." We are all familiar with the struggles of oppressed peoples and individuals against government— Americans in 1776, Hungarians (in a far worse context) against communist repression only a few years ago. But in a democracy the protection of the rights of the individual against the government is only part of the problem (though probably the major part). The other part of the problem concerns the rightful power of government *over the individual*. A person's freedom from governmental oppression is of little use, after all, except in a peaceful, orderly society. And government must have some power over individuals if it is to maintain peace and order.

Motorists meet this problem whenever they go out for a drive. Every minute they face the heavy hand of government —GO SLOW, 25-MILE ZONE, STOP, NO U-TURN. But few drivers complain, because they know that without these restrictions driving would be so suicidal that they would lose a greater freedom—the freedom to drive safely. In effect, the motorist is willing to relinquish some freedoms for other, more important freedoms.

The problem, then, is how to balance individual rights against collective needs, remembering always that individual freedom and social order are necessary to each other. Chapter 6 describes how Americans have tried to achieve this balance in several important areas—freedom of religion and of speech and of the press, for example. Which goals—individual liberties or collective needs—should receive priority if they come into conflict with each other? When and under what conditions should one or the other receive priority? Who should decide—judges, legislators, or someone else? Achieving this balance is especially difficult today, for our chief collective need is national survival, which means, among other things, emphasis on military strength and internal security. How much individual liberty may we allow in face of our need for military security? To what extent, in a *democracy*, may we allow military security to threaten individual freedom? This problem is the focus of the second half of Chapter 6.

We have been talking about individual liberties, such as freedom of speech; there is also the matter of *civil rights*, such as the right to equal opportunity in education and to vote. Chapter 7 takes up the constitutional guarantees and political battles behind the idea that no man should suffer pains and penalties because of his race, religion, national origin, or other qualities irrelevant to his individual merit. Chapter 8 describes a different but equally important type of right—the right not to be deprived arbitrarily of life, liberty, and property—for example, free-

dom from unjustified arrest. Both sets of rights—*civil* rights and (mainly) *procedural* rights—pose the problem of the balance of individual rights against collective needs.

There is a final basic problem in this Part—*which government*, state or federal, should determine the balance among and between individual rights and collective needs? What if one government—say, the state government—should fail to protect a man's civil rights? Should the national government step in and protect those rights? Hence the problem of *federalism* is crucial to the problem of freedom in America. This problem—the relation of *governments* to one another in protecting individual freedom—is emphasized in both Chapter 7 and Chapter 8.

Implicit in this discussion is one very important point: Individual freedom may be threatened directly by *other individuals* as well as by government. For example, a man trying to speak from a soapbox may be knocked down by a mob, just as he may be arrested by a policeman. It is also possible that the policeman might protect him *against* the mob —a case of *government* guarding the liberty of one individual against other individuals. Hence it is always advisable, when considering a problem of individual freedom, to ask the question: *Whose* civil liberties are to be protected, against *what*, by *whom* (for example, what agency of government), and *how*?

Chapter 8 deals also with the status and rights of immigrants, aliens, and citizens. The Constitution does not guarantee the right of admission to the United States; aliens do not enjoy all the privileges of American citizens. But quite a few important problems of individual liberty are involved in our treatment of noncitizens.

6 THE FIRST AMENDMENT AND THE FIRST FREEDOMS

"Congress shall make no law," declares the First Amendment, "respecting an establishment of religion, or prohibiting the free exercise thereof; or abridging the freedom of speech, or of the press; or the right of the people peaceably to assemble, and to petition the Government for a redress of grievances." Here in bold and imposing terms are the fundamental supports of a free society—freedom of conscience and freedom of expression.

127

Although the framers drafted the Constitution, in a sense it was the *people* who drafted our basic charter of liberties. The Constitution drawn up at Philadelphia included no specific guarantee of freedom of speech and religion and other basic freedoms—an omission that aroused suspicion and distrust among the people at large. In order to win ratification, the Federalists promised to correct this oversight, and in the very first session of the new Congress they lived up to their promise. Congress proposed amendments that were ratified by the end of 1791 and became part of the Constitution. These ten amendments are known as the Bill of Rights.

Note that the Bill of Rights is addressed to the *national* government. As John Marshall held long ago, in *Barron* v. *Baltimore* (1833), the Bill of Rights limits the national but not the state governments. Why not the states? In the 1790's the people were confident they could control their own state officials. Furthermore, most of the state constitutions already had a bill of rights. It was the new and distant central government that the people feared.

But as it turned out, those popular apprehensions of 1790 were largely misplaced. The national government, responsive to tens of millions of voters from a variety of races, creeds, religions, and economic groups, has shown less tendency to curtail civil liberties than have state and local governments. It was not long after the Bill of Rights had been adopted that people began to recognize the mistake of exempting state governments from the prohibitions of the national Bill of Rights and thereby allowing state regulation of our liberties. True, each state constitution also includes a bill of rights, but for the most part state judges have not been inclined to apply these bills of rights to protect civil liberties.

How to plug the gap created by the exemption of the states from the Bill of Rights? With the adoption of the due-process clause of the Fourteenth Amendment in 1868, which *does* apply to the states, litigants tried to persuade the Supreme Court to construe this clause to mean that the *states* are limited in the same way that the Bill of Rights limits the *national* government. At a minimum, they contended, freedom of speech should be brought within the confines of the Fourteenth Amendment.

For decades the Supreme Court refused to interpret the Fourteenth Amendment in this way. Then in 1925, in a historic decision, *Gitlow* v. *New York*, the Supreme Court announced:

> For present purposes we may and do assume that freedom of speech and of press—which are protected from abridgment by Congress—are among the fundamental personal rights and liberties protected by the due process clause of the Fourteenth Amendment from impairment by the states.

Gitlow v. *New York* was a decision of major, almost revolutionary, significance. Since that date the Fourteenth Amendment has placed the same restraints in behalf of free speech on states (in a constitutional sense, all subdivisional units of a state, such as cities, counties, and school districts, are part of the state) that the First Amendment places on the national government. By 1947 the Supreme Court had brought all the other liberties of the First Amendment under the protection of the Fourteenth. Since then many, but not all, of the other provisions of the Bill of Rights have thus been made applicable to the states. (See pages 213–214).

Although Congress is governed by the absolute language of the First Amendment to pass no law abridging free speech, press, and religion whereas states are limited by the relative language of the Fourteenth not to deprive a person of speech, press, or religious freedom without due process of law, this difference in constitutional language has had no significance. For all practical purposes the Fourteenth imposes on the states the same restrictions that the First Amendment imposes on the national government.

Today virtually all Americans agree that governmental power should not be used to interfere with the freedoms of speech and conscience. Yet the country seems to be almost constantly involved in quarrels about specific application of these restraints. It is all very well to venerate our liberties in general. The trouble arises when we move from generalities to specifics. And in few areas are the problems more difficult to resolve than those concerning religious freedom.

"Each May Worship in His Own Way"

The right to hold any or no religious belief is an absolute right: One's religious beliefs are inviolable, and no government in the United States has any authority whatsoever to compel the acceptance of, or to censor, any creed. Thus a unanimous Supreme Court struck down a provision of the Constitution of Maryland requiring a declaration of belief in the existence of God as a test to hold public office.[1]

The right to advocate one's religion by speech or writing—like the right to use speech or writing for any other purpose—may be curbed only when there is danger of substantial injury to the rights of others. In fact, the Supreme Court has shown greater concern for religious than for political advocacy, perhaps because Congress is specifically enjoined by the First Amendment (and the states through interpretation by the Fourteenth) to make no law "prohibiting the free exercise" of religion.

The *practice* of one's religion has less protection than its *advocacy*. As the Supreme Court has said, "It was never intended that the First Amendment . . . could be invoked as a protection against legislation for the punishment of acts inimical to the peace, good order and morals of society." [2] Religious convictions do not exempt one from complying with otherwise valid laws designed to protect the public peace, health, safety, and morals. The Supreme Court has sustained laws forbidding the practice of polygamy, as applied to Mormons; laws requiring

[1] *Torcaso v. Watkins* (1961).
[2] *Reynolds v. United States* (1879).

vaccination of school children, as applied to Christian Scientists; laws forbidding business activities on Sunday in order to promote health and rest, as applied to Orthodox Jews.[3]

On the other hand the Court has struck down laws denying unemployment benefits to those who refused to accept jobs requiring them to work on Saturday, their Sabbath.[4] The Court reasoned that refusal to work on Saturday harms no one, and the state had shown no compelling public interest justifying this infringement on the free exercise of religion. The dissenting justices argued that to require a state to exempt persons for religious reasons from otherwise valid regulations is to require the state to favor religion and thus to violate the Establishment Clause. For the Constitution not only forbids Congress and the states to prohibit the free exercise of religion, it also stipulates that "Congress (and the states) shall make no law respecting an establishment of religion."

"No-Preference" v. "Wall-of-Separation"

What does this prohibition against the establishment of religion mean? To oversimplify, there are two general constructions of this clause: the *no-preference* doctrine and the *wall-of-separation* doctrine. Those who accept the former hold that our Constitution forbids national and state governments to aid any particular religion, but *if no preference is shown among different creeds*, they may aid and encourage religious activities. The second construction, and the one adopted by the Supreme Court, is that the Constitution creates a wall of separation between church and state and forbids governments to aid, encourage, or support *any* or *all* churches, *any* or *all* religious activities. As Justice Black said in *Everson* v. *Board of Education* (1947):

> Neither a state nor the Federal Government can set up a church. Neither can pass laws that aid one religion, aid all religions, or prefer one religion over another. Neither can force nor influence a person to go to or to remain away from church . . . or force him to profess a belief or a disbelief in any religion. . . . No tax in any amount, large or small, can be levied to support any religious activities or institutions, whatever they may be called, or whatever form they may adopt to teach or practice religion. Neither a state nor the Federal Government can, openly or secretly, participate in the affairs of any religious organizations or groups and vice versa. In the words of Jefferson, the clause against establishment of religion by law was intended to erect "a wall of separation between Church and State."

The Supreme Court reaffirmed the Everson doctrine (McCollum case, 1948) when it declared unconstitutional the Champaign, Illinois, Board of Education's program of allowing privately chosen instructors to teach religion to students

---

[3] See *McGowan* v. *Maryland* (1961) and related cases and cases cited therein.
[4] *Sherbert* v. *Verner* (1963).

whose parents approved during school hours and in public school rooms. The Supreme Court ruled: "Here not only are the State's tax-supported public school buildings used for the dissemination of religious doctrines. The State also affords sectarian groups an invaluable aid in that it helps to provide pupils for their religious classes through the use of the State's compulsory school machinery. This is not separation of Church and State." [5]

Many applauded the Supreme Court's stand in favor of the "wall of separation" doctrine, but others criticized. In the face of this criticism the Supreme Court (*Zorach v. Clauson*, 1952) sustained New York City's released-time program, despite the fact that the only difference between it and the Champaign program was that it provided for the released-time classes to be held outside the public school building in rooms made available by the various churches. Although insisting that they were not overruling Everson and McCollum, Justice Douglas' opinion for a six-man majority appeared to be at odds with the "wall-of-separation" doctrine. He wrote:

> The First Amendment . . . does not say that in every and all respects there shall be a separation of Church and State. . . . We are a religious people whose institutions presuppose a Supreme Being. . . . When the state encourages religious instruction or cooperates with religious authorities by adjusting the schedule of public events to sectarian needs, it follows the best of our traditions.

Since Zorach, however, the Supreme Court has specifically disavowed any intention of supporting the "no-preference" doctrine.[6] In 1962 (*Engel v. Vitale*), and in 1963 (*Abington School District v. Schempp*), the Court ruled that nondenominational prayers, reciting the Lord's Prayer, or reading the Bible, all violate the Establishment Clause if made part of the program of public schools. Distinguishing ceremonial and patriotic exercises or the objective study of religion and the Bible from frankly religious ceremonies, Justice Black in the first decision declared for the Court: "In this country it is no part of the business of government to compose official prayers for any group of the American people to recite as part of a religious program carried on by government. . . . Neither the fact that the prayer may be denominationally neutral, nor the fact that its observance on the part of the students is voluntary can serve to free it from the limitations of the Establishment Clause as it might from the Free Exercise Clause." Justice Clark, speaking for the Court, in the second decision, repeated: ". . . violation of the Free Exercise Clause is predicated on coercion while the Establishment Clause violation need not be so attended. . . . To withstand the strictures of the Establishment Clause there must be a secular legislative purpose and a primary effect that neither advances nor inhibits religion."

In view of its insistence upon separation of chuch and state, why has the Su-

[5] *Illinois ex rel. McCollum* v. *Board of Education* (1948).
[6] *Torcaso* v. *Watkins* (1961).

preme Court permitted states and cities to enforce Sunday closing laws? The Court majority conceded that these laws originally had a religious purpose and effect of encouraging people to attend church, but the majority was persuaded that today they have a secular purpose and effect, to provide a day of rest, recreation, and family togetherness.[7]

Only a few subjects arouse as much concern as does the question of the proper relation between governments and churches. The Supreme Court's rulings in this area have engendered many debates and comments. Some public school authorities have even gone so far as to announce that they would continue to include prayers and Bible readings as part of the school program, despite the Supreme Court. In Congress there has been pressure for a constitutional amendment to permit religious programs in the public schools. However, those who favor the Supreme Court's construction of the Constitution have been able to block the proposed amendment. For the moment at least, the Supreme Court's construction of the Establishment Clause remains official and authoritative.[8]

To conclude that any kind of governmental aid to religion is unconstitutional does not, however, answer all the questions. The question remains: What is aid to religion? May a state provide free textbooks, hot lunches, and use tax money to pay the bus fare for children attending church-operated as well as public schools? In all these instances the Supreme Court has ruled that these practices are not aids to religion, which would be unconstitutional, but aids to *education* and to the *welfare* of children, which the Constitution does not forbid.

For many years conflict over the wisdom and constitutionality of using federal funds to build schools, pay teachers, and purchase equipment in church-operated as well as public schools was one of the major reasons why Congress failed to provide comprehensive federal aid for elementary and secondary schools. Some congressmen would not support such a program unless federal funds were also made available to church schools; other congressmen would not support such a program if federal funds *were* made available to church schools.

Then in 1965 Congress skirted the issue and enacted the Elementary and Secondary Education Act of 1965 (see pages 675–676), which provides federal funds for almost everything except raising teachers' salaries or building classrooms. Students and teachers in private schools, including those operated by religious organizations, are eligible to participate in the federally supported public school programs and may use the books and other materials that the public schools own and purchase with federal funds. Whether this form of indirect aid to parochial schools will survive constitutional challenge remains to be seen. Whatever ruling the Supreme Court makes will be sharply criticized. Yet it is worth noting, despite the intense emotions and the difficult problems, in a world where many nations are sharply divided into religious factions, "the amicable accommodation of re-

[7] *McGowan v. Maryland* (1961).
[8] William M. Beaney and Edward N. Beiser, "Prayer and Politics: The Impact of Engel and Schempp on the Political Process," *Journal of Public Law*, Vol. 13 (1964), pp. 475–503.

ligious difference in America has been a significant achievement of our political experience." [9]

Free Speech and Free Men

Most democrats assume that government by the people is based on the individual's right to speak freely, to organize in groups, to question the decisions of the government, and to campaign openly against it. Only through free and uncensored expression of opinion can the government be kept responsive to the electorate and can governmental power be transferred peacefully. Elections, separation of powers, and constitutional guarantees are meaningless unless each person has the right to speak frankly and to hear and judge for himself the worth of what others have to say.

Despite the fundamental importance of free speech in a democracy, some seem to believe that speech should be free only for those who agree with them. A national poll indicated that one American in three did not seem truly to believe in free speech, feeling, for example, that the newspapers should not be permitted to criticize the government, even in peacetime.

Why, one might well ask, should evil or ignorant men be permitted to spread falsehoods and confuse the minds of others? Why should they be allowed to utter dangerous ideas that subvert the very foundations of our democratic society?

The Best Test of Truth

Believers in democracy insist on free debate and the unlimited exchange of ideas because they feel that no group has a monopoly on truth, that no group has the right to establish in the field of politics absolute standards of what is true and what is false. A man may be convinced that he is right, that truth is on his side, but in the midst of debate he appeals to no philosopher-king, commissar, or oracle of wisdom, but to the power of his reason. As Justice Holmes wrote: "The best test of truth is the power of the thought to get itself accepted in the competition of the market." The insistence upon free speech for others stems from the recognition that men are not infallible, that perhaps the other person is right, or at least, that "I might be wrong."

Free speech is not simply the personal right of an individual to have his say, *it is also the right of the rest of us to hear him.* When John Smith out in California is denied the right to speak, the Bill Browns all over the United States are denied the right to hear what he had to say and to judge its worth for themselves. John Stuart Mill, whose *Essay on Liberty* is an illuminating defense of free

[9] Alan P. Grimes, *Equality in America: Religion, Race, and the Urban Majority* (Oxford Univ. Press, 1964), p. 4.

speech, put it this way: "The peculiar evil of silencing the expression of opinion, is that it is robbing the human race. . . . If the opinion is right, they are deprived of the opportunity for exchanging error for truth; if wrong, they lose, what is almost as great a benefit, the clearer perception and livelier impression of truth, produced by the collision with error." [10]

Freedom of speech is not merely freedom to express ideas that differ slightly from ours; it is, as the late Justice Jackson said, "freedom to differ on things that go to the heart of the matter." Some people profess to believe in free speech, but they draw the line at ideas they consider abhorrent or dangerous. But what is a dangerous idea? Who decides? Socrates was forced to drink a cup of hemlock for expressing dangerous ideas. And Christians were persecuted for holding dangerous ideas. The heresies of yesterday are often the orthodoxies of today. In the realm of political ideas who can find an objective, eternally valid standard of right? The search for truth is an endless one. It involves the possibility—even the inevitability—of error. The search cannot go on unless it proceeds unfettered in the minds and speech of men. This means, in the words of Justice Holmes, not only free thought for those who agree with us "but freedom for the thought we hate."

In short, to forbid the expression of ideas on the ground that they are dangerous is to set oneself up as an infallible judge of what speech should be permitted. Such presumptuousness stifles the fearless exchange of opinions and short-circuits the procedures of democratic government that are protected by the First Amendment. All this, at least, is the assumption of democrats.

Constitutional Guarantees

Despite the fact that the First Amendment emphatically denies the national government the power to pass *any* law abridging freedom of speech, the amendment has never been interpreted in such sweeping terms. Liberty of expression is important—but it is not absolute. Like almost all rights, the right to freedom of speech and press is limited by the fact that its free exercise "implies the existence of an organized society maintaining public order without which liberty itself would be lost in the excess of unrestrained abuses." [11] How is the line to be drawn between permissible and unconstitutional restraint on freedom of expression?

In discussing the constitutional power of government to regulate speech, it is useful to distinguish among belief, speech, and action. At one extreme is the right to *believe* as one wishes, a right about as absolute as any can be for men living in organized societies. Despite occasional deviations in practice, the traditional American view is that *thoughts* are inviolable, and no government has

[10] John Stuart Mill, *Essay on Liberty, The English Philosophers from Bacon to Mill*, Edwin A. Burtt (ed.) (Modern Library, 1939), p. 961.
[11] *Cox v. New Hampshire* (1941).

the right to punish a man for his beliefs or to interfere in any way with his freedom of conscience.

At the other extreme from belief is *action,* which is constantly constrained. We may *believe* it perfectly all right to go sixty miles an hour through an intersection, but if we do so we will be punished. We may *believe* that it is proper to build glue factories in residential districts, but government will probably stop us from doing so. Since one man's action directly affects the liberty and property of others, "his right to swing his arm ends where the other fellow's nose begins."

Speech stands somewhere between belief and action; it is not an absolute, or almost absolute, right like belief, but it is not so exposed to governmental restraint as is action. There are certain narrowly limited classes of speech that "by their very utterance inflict injury or tend to incite an immediate breach of peace" which government may justifiably prevent or punish; these are the obscene, the libelous, the fighting words. What about speech outside these narrow categories?

The Holmes-Brandeis Clear-and-Present-Danger Test

The first test adopted by the Supreme Court to distinguish between protected speech and that which could be regulated was announced by Justice Holmes in *Schenck* v. *United States* (1919): "The question in every case is whether the words are used in circumstances and are of such a nature as to create a clear and present danger that they will bring about substantive evils that Congress has a right to prevent." Furthermore, "no danger flowing from speech can be deemed clear and present," wrote Justice Brandeis (concurring in *Whitney* v. *California,* 1927), "unless the incidence of the evil is so imminent that it may befall before there is opportunity for full discussion."

Holmes and Brandeis, although conceding that speech is not an absolute right, felt it to be so fundamental that under our Constitution no government has authority to suppress speech or punish a man for what he has said unless the connection between the speech and illegal action is so close that the speech itself takes on the character of the action. The Holmes-Brandeis clear-and-present-danger formula is primarily a rule to determine the sufficiency of the evidence. It requires that before being allowed to punish a man for what he has said or written, a government must prove clearly that his speech presents an imminent danger of a major substantive evil. Note, it is not *any* clear and present danger that justifies conviction, but only danger of a substantive evil the government has a right to prevent—for example, rioting and destruction of property, or forceful overthrow of the government.

Let us see how the clear-and-present-danger test might be applied. Suppose, for example, a legislature has made it illegal to utter scurrilous and abusive remarks about members of another race. Under the clear-and-present-danger doctrine, a man could be punished for making such remarks only if at his trial the government has convincing evidence that his particular scurrilous remarks *clearly* and *presently* might have led to a riot or some other serious substantive evil that the government rightfully may prevent.

The Dangerous-Tendency Doctrine

Although the clear-and-present-danger doctrine was the first to receive formal Supreme Court support, the *dangerous-* or *bad-tendency doctrine* stemming from the common law is the older, and it too at various times has been the official doctrine of the Court, most notably in *Gitlow* v. *New York* (1925). According to adherents of the dangerous-tendency doctrine, the Constitution does not require government to stay its hand until there is a clear and present danger flowing from a particular speech, but it may outlaw speech that has a *tendency* to lead to a substantive evil. Furthermore, those who espouse this view contend that it is primarily a legislative and not a judicial responsibility to determine what kinds of speech have a dangerous tendency. Once the legislature has made it a crime to say or write certain things that have a dangerous tendency, persons may be punished who have used the forbidden words, even if there is no immediate danger flowing from their particular speech. For the legislature has already decided that such words are dangerous.

Now let us take the same example as above and apply to it the dangerous-tendency doctrine. The legislature has already determined that scurrilous and abusive remarks about members of another race are dangerous, and since it is not unreasonable to conclude that such comments have a *tendency* to stir up riots, all that is necessary in this case to convict a person is to show that he in fact made such comments.

The Preferred-Position Doctrine

Another test, the *preferred-position* doctrine, was the official view of the Supreme Court during the 1940's, and is today supported by several of the justices. This doctrine is an extension of the clear-and-present-danger formula—indeed, some of its supporters come close to the position that freedom of expression is an absolute right. Those who espouse the preferred-position interpretation believe that First Amendment freedoms occupy a preferred position in our constitutional hierarchy and that courts have a special responsibility to scrutinize with extra care laws trespassing on these freedoms. Whereas legislative majorities are free to experiment and adopt various schemes regulating our *economic* lives, *when they tamper with freedom of speech they close the channels of the political process by which error can be corrected.* The majority is free via the legislature to adopt any policies it wishes, provided it leaves untouched the procedures by which new majorities may be formed. Hence, any law that on its face limits the First Amendment freedoms is presumed to be unconstitutional. Only if the government can show that limitations on speech are absolutely necessary to avoid extremely imminent and extremely serious substantive evils are such limitations to be tolerated.

If the preferred-position doctrine were applied to our example above of a law against abusive racial remarks, the law would be declared unconstitutional. Restraints on such abusive speech are not absolutely necessary to prevent riots, according to this doctrine, and whatever danger may flow from such abusive remarks does not justify a restriction on free comment. Moreover, supporters of the preferred-position doctrine contend that it is not merely the application of this law to a particular speaker that is unconstitutional, but that the law itself violates the Constitution.

These three doctrines are subject to a variety of interpretations and applications. And they are not the only formulas that the Supreme Court uses to measure the constitutionality of laws regulating speech. Among the other "tests," or "doctrines," or "rules of thumb," perhaps the most important are, in summary:

Prior Restraint. Of all the forms of governmental interference with speech, judges are most suspicious of those that impose prior restraint—that is, that require approval or a license before a speech can be made, a newspaper published, a motion picture shown. As Justice Brennan pointed out, "Because the censor's business is to censor, there inheres the danger that he may well be less responsive than a court . . . to the constitutionally protected interests in free expression." [12] Since it is often onerous to secure judicial reversal of a censor's decision, that decision may in practice be final and his views of what the public should be allowed to see or read conclusive. The Supreme Court has not gone so far as to declare all forms of prior censorship unconstitutional, but "any system of prior restraints of expression comes to this Court bearing a heavy presumption against its constitutional validity." [13] The judges insist on unusual justifications and elaborate safeguards before giving constitutional approval.

Vagueness. Any law is unconstitutional if it is so vague that it fails to alert men to what is forbidden or if it fails to set standards to guide those who must administer it. Laws touching First Amendment freedoms are required to meet an even more rigid standard. The Court opined in one decision: "The overly broad statute . . . creates a 'danger zone' within which protected expression may be inhibited. So long as the statute remains available to the State the threat of prosecutions of protected expression is a real and substantial one. Even the prospect of ultimate failure of such prosecutions by no means dispels its chilling effect on protected expression." In another: "Because First Amendment freedoms need breathing space to survive, government may regulate in the area only with narrow specificity." [14]

[12] *Freedman* v. *Maryland* (1965).
[13] *Bantam Books, Inc.* v. *Sullivan* (1963).
[14] Respectively, *Dombrowski* v. *Pfister* (1965); and *NAACP* v. *Button* (1963).

Least Means. Outside the area of First Amendment freedoms, judges ordinarily will not invalidate a law just because the legislature might have chosen some other means to deal with a particular problem. But if the law impinges on the First Amendment, "even though the governmental purpose be legitimate and substantial, that purpose cannot be achieved by means that broadly stifle fundamental personal liberties when the end can be more narrowly achieved. The breadth of legislative abridgement must be viewed in the light of less drastic means for achieving the same basic purpose." [15] To illustrate: It is perfectly proper for a city council to protect the people from fraudulent door-to-door salesmen, but it may not do so by an ordinance forbidding all persons to ring a doorbell unless they are invited to the house by the occupant. There are other means to protect persons against fraud that would not impinge on the right of free communication.

The Balancing Doctrine. All judges, whatever language they use to express their opinions, weigh a variety of factors in making their decisions. But in recent years the "balancing doctrine" has come to take on a more restricted meaning and to refer to a particular doctrine, especially as espoused by the late Justice Frankfurter and presently by Justice Harlan. Dozens of opinions and hundreds of articles have been written attempting to support or condemn the balancing doctrine and to explain what it means; it is impossible to give an accurate impression of the doctrine in what must be a capsule form.[16] But essentially the balancing doctrine is a protest by those who think the First Amendment should not be read in absolute terms, who reject the notion that First Amendment freedoms are any more sacred than any other constitutional freedoms, who believe that judges should not apply different standards to measure the constitutionality of laws impinging on First Amendment freedoms than are used to measure any laws, and who think that judges have no mandate to protect these freedoms any different from their responsibilities in any other area. Rather, these judges argue, laws regulating First Amendment freedoms, like all laws, must be judged by balancing the interests to be secured by the regulation against the amount of freedom that is lost or impaired. Thus Justice Harlan, claiming to use the balancing test, ruled that Congress' concern to preserve the national against communist subversion overbalances a witness' right before a congressional investigating committee to refuse to answer questions about his possible involvement with the Communist party.[17]

But doctrines do not decide cases—judges do. Doctrines are judges' starting points, not their conclusions. Judges are always searching and seeking and explaining; hence the Supreme Court may undergo doctrinal changes whenever it deals with issues that lack a national consensus. Whatever the current doctrines,

---

[15] *Shelton* v. *Tucker* (1960).
[16] See for example, Dean Alfrange, Jr., "The Balancing of Interests in Free Speech Cases: In Defense of an Abused Doctrine," *Law In Transition Quarterly*, Vol. II (Winter, 1965), pp. 1–29, and the many articles cited therein by Laurent Frantz and Wallace Mendelson, the most vigorous protagonists of the balancing test.
[17] *Barenblatt* v. *United States* (1959).

whether it be clear and present danger, preferred position, or balancing of interests, each case requires judges to weigh a variety of factors. *What* was said? Obscene speech, libelous statements, fighting words are not in the same category as political disputations. *Where* was it said? On the street corner, in a living room, over the radio? *How* was it said? In a flammable manner? What was the *intent* of the person who said it? To encourage people to violate the laws, to stir them to violence, or merely to cause them to think? What were the *circumstances* in which it was said? During time of war, in front of a hostile audience? *Which* government is attempting to regulate the speech? The city council that speaks for a few people, or the Congress that speaks for a wide variety of people? (Only one *congressional* enactment has ever been struck down because of conflict with the First Amendment.) *How* is the government attempting to regulate the speech? By prior censorship, by punishment after the speech, by administrative procedures? *Why* is the government attempting to regulate the speech? To protect the national security, to keep the streets clean, to protect the rights of unpopular religious minorities, to prevent criticism of those in power? These and scores of other considerations are involved. The social interests must be weighed in each case. And there is the further question of how much deference judges should show to the legislature's attempt to adjust these social interests. In short, no test has been devised that will automatically weigh all the factors.

Freedom of the Press

"Upon what meat doth this our democracy feed?" asks Herbert Brucker, a noted newspaper editor. "It feeds upon facts brought into the minds of its citizens by the press, the radio, and the supplementary media of information." [18] So important is this system of disseminating information, says Brucker, that it constitutes the indispensable "fourth branch" of the national government. Today, information is seldom spread through street-corner meetings or public assemblies, the historic centers of debate. Rather, it is broadcast wholesale by the press, television, radio, movies, and other communication media. On the whole, the Supreme Court has been zealous in guarding freedom of the press from governmental restriction. But how broad is this freedom?

The case of *Near* v. *Minnesota* (1931) provided a partial answer to this question. A Minneapolis newspaper charged, among other things, that a known gangster controlled racketeering in the city and that the chief of police was receiving graft. Under a Minnesota law authorizing injunctions against "malicious, scandalous, and defamatory" action, the newspaper was permanently enjoined from being published. The editor appealed ultimately to the Supreme Court. "The question," said Chief Justice Hughes, speaking for a closely divided court, "is whether a statute authorizing such proceedings in restraint of publication is consistent with the conception of the liberty of the press as historically conceived and guaranteed. . . . The fact that the liberty of the press may be abused by mis-

[18] Herbert Brucker, *Freedom of Information* (Macmillan, 1949), p. 10.

creant purveyors of scandal does not make any the less necessary the immunity
of the press from previous restraint in dealing with official misconduct." The
Court held the Minnesota law to be an infringement of the liberty of the press.
This case made clear that government may not set up advance censorship except
in extraordinary circumstances.

Sometimes freedom of the press comes into conflict with another basic right,
trial by an impartial judge and jury in a calm and judicial atmosphere. When
newspapers and other mass media report in vivid detail the facts of a lurid crime
and secure press releases from the prosecutor, it may be impossible to hold a
trial in an atmosphere free from hysteria or to secure a jury that can decide in
an impartial manner. In England the weight is on the side of fair trial. British
courts do not hesitate to hold in contempt newspapers that comment on pending
criminal proceedings. In the United States the weight is on the side of free comment. The Court has sustained the right of the press to criticize judges, even to
the point of allowing editors to threaten judges with political reprisals unless they
deal with defendants in a certain fashion. As Justice Douglas put it, "Judges are
supposed to be men of fortitude, able to thrive in a hardy climate" (*Craig* v.
Harney, 1947).

Juries, on the other hand, are more susceptible to prejudicial comments and
events. In 1952 a defendant was given a new trial because, after his indictment,
a congressional investigating committee held open hearings that the judges believed so inflamed public opinion that a fair trial was impossible. Similarly, the
Supreme Court has reversed convictions where prejudicial newspaper publicity
and prosecutors' statements to the press, or the televising of the accused reading
a confession, have so aroused a community that a jury selected from the community could not be impartial.[19]

What about televising criminal trials? Is a defendant deprived of due process
if over his objection the judge allows television cameras into the courtroom? Four
justices of the Supreme Court are of the view that the mere fact that the trial is
being televised is so likely to influence the behavior of judge, jury, witnesses, and
defendants and is so inherently contrary to the idea of quiet and calm deliberation,
that televising of trials is a violation of due process. The other justices would ban
television from a courtroom only if there is evidence that its impact upon the
particular judge, jury, or witness in the peculiar circumstances of the trial in question interferes with a fair trial.[20]

Is there a freedom of the press to *obtain* news as well as to print it? Recently
threats to freedom of the press arising out of so-called "censorship at the source"
have aroused public concern. Governments have always withheld information,
especially during time of war. But as the "cold war" has reached into more and
more sectors of life—education, for example—public officials have classified all

[19] *Delaney* v. *United States*, US S.C.A. (1952); *Irvin* v. *Dowd* (1961); *Rideau* v. *Louisiana*
(1963), and cases cited therein. See also Justice William O. Douglas, "The Public Trial and the
Free Press," *American Bar Association Journal*, Vol. 46, (1960), p. 840.
[20] *Estes* v. *Texas* (1965).

sorts of information as "restricted" or "secret," so that it becomes a crime to divulge it. Also, federal agencies have used a 1789 statute authorizing executive officials to conceal government documents from newsmen, sometimes even from congressmen. This "housekeeping statute" has been used even where information is not classified as military or secret. For example, the Department of Defense at one time ordered officials not to release information unless it would "constitute a constructive contribution to the primary mission of the Department of Defense."

In 1958 Congress amended the 1789 statute by stipulating that it is not to be construed as authorizing the withholding of information from the public or limiting the availability of records. The President signed the 1958 act, but only after saying that he did not interpret it to alter the President's inherent constitutional power to withhold information whose release he considered not in the public interest. Despite the 1958 law, the President still has this "prerogative." [21]

Libel and Obscenity

If one person publishes false and malicious comments about another, he may be forced to pay damages, but through a progressive tightening of the constitutional standards, the danger of civil damages or criminal prosecution for libel no longer constitutes a serious threat to free communication. The Supreme Court has made it a constitutional rule that no person may be made to pay damages or be punished for any comments he makes about a public person or public affairs unless it can be proved that the comments were made with actual malice—that is, with knowledge of their falsity or with reckless disregard of whether they were true or false. The mere fact that a statement is wrong or even defamatory of official reputation is not sufficient to sustain a charge of libel against a public official.[22]

What about group libel statutes making it a criminal offense to publish materials defaming races, religions, or groups? A closely divided Supreme Court sustained such an Illinois law (*Beauharnais* v. *Illinois*, 1952), the majority arguing that it was a reasonable measure to avoid race riots and that libelous comments are not within the protection of the Constitution. The dissenting justices contended that since there was no evidence of any danger of disorder arising from the publication in question, the state had exceeded its constitutional authority. Group libel laws, the minority charged, restrain public discussion because they make people afraid of expressing adverse judgments about members of other races or religions. In view of more recent decisions, the minority may carry the day if the issue is again presented to the Court.

Obscene publications are not entitled to constitutional protection. But what is the test of obscenity and who is to apply it? Obscenity has often been broadly interpreted; books by such distinguished writers as Edmund Wilson, Lillian Smith,

---

[21] Francis E. Rourke, *Secrecy and Publicity: Dilemmas of Democracy* (Johns Hopkins Press, 1961), p. 60.

[22] *New York Times Co.* v. *Sullivan* (1964); and *Garrison* v. *Louisiana* (1964).

D. H. Lawrence, James Joyce, and even Aristophanes, have been held obscene.

The Supreme Court (*Roth* v. *United States*, 1957) has insisted upon a narrow definition of obscenity. The justices have warned that sex and obscenity are not synonymous and that only materials patently offensive or indecent and "which deal with sex in a manner appealing to prurient interest" may be judged obscene. Moreover, books and other materials must be judged as a whole rather than on the basis of a few scattered passages, their impact must be assessed in terms of normal adults, and their decency must be determined on the basis of contemporary community standards.[23] The Supreme Court has also held that a state cannot make it a crime merely for a bookseller to offer an obscene book for sale; the state must show that he knowingly did so.[24] Otherwise the public would be deprived of an opportunity to purchase perfectly proper books, since booksellers would tend to place on their shelves only those books they had personally inspected and would avoid offering any book which someone might consider objectionable.

States are primarily responsible for regulating obscene literature and those who publish or knowingly sell such materials run the risk of state prosecution. The national government, through its control over customs and postal matters, also attempts to prevent the circulation of obscene materials. In 1958 Congress amended the criminal code to make it easier to convict persons for sending obscene publications through the mails by allowing trial in any judicial district through which the offending publication was sent from point of origin to point of delivery. Until the law was so amended, the government could prosecute only in the district from which the mail originated, chiefly urban centers where juries are likely to be more tolerant of reading matter than in some rural communities. Under the new amendment, the government can choose the district where convictions are most likely.

In addition to federal criminal prosecutions, the Postmaster General has claimed authority to exclude obscene publications from the mails, revoke second-class mailing privileges of publications alleged to be obscene, and cut off all incoming mail to a person sending obscene matters through the mails. The basic assumption underlying these claims is that the use of the mails is a privilege that the government may terminate at its discretion. But this assumption has been questioned by the courts in the last several years, and judges have been clamping down on the Postmaster General's discretion.[25] In 1959 an attempt by the Postmaster General to bar from the mails the unexpurgated version of D. H. Lawrence's famous novel, *Lady Chatterley's Lover*, was checked by the courts; and earlier the Post Office Department in the face of threatened judicial action backed down from its proposed ban on the mailing of Aristophanes' *Lysistrata*. Then in 1965

[23] *Manual Enterprises* v. *Day* (1962).
[24] *Smith* v. *California* (1959).
[25] See, for example, *Hannegan* v. *Esquire, Inc.* (1946) and *Summerfield* v. *Sunshine Book Company* (1954); and James C. N. Paul and Murray L. Schwartz, *Federal Censorship: Obscenity in the Mail* (The Free Press, 1961).

the Supreme Court—on a different issue—rejected the doctrine that the use of the mails is a privilege that the government may confer or take away at its discretion. As Justice Holmes had written, ". . . the use of the mails is almost as much a part of free speech as the right to use our tongue." Congress, said the Supreme Court, cannot condition the right of an addressee to receive foreign communist political propaganda on his returning an official notice saying that he wants to receive it. "The regime of this Act," said the Court, "is at war with the 'uninhibited, robust, and wide-open debate' and discussion that are contemplated by the First Amendment." [26] This is the first, and so far only, time that the Supreme Court has ruled that Congress has violated the First Amendment.

Motion Pictures. Until 1952 motion pictures were considered a form of entertainment and not a method of communication, and therefore were not protected by the free speech and press guarantees of the Constitution. Seven states and numerous cities required all exhibitors to submit all films to censors who determined without any legal restraints what could and could not be shown. Then in 1952 (*Joseph Burstyn, Inc.* v. *Wilson*) the Supreme Court brought the movies under the protection of the Constitution when it held that New York authorities lacked constitutional power to prevent the showing of a film because the authorities thought it to be "sacrilegious." Not only does "sacrilegious" lack precise meaning, the Court held, but government has no right to censor movies solely because they may offend some people's religious sensibilities. Since the Burstyn decision the Supreme Court, in case after case, has upset attempts to ban motion pictures that various censors have alleged "tended to corrupt morals," or were "harmful," or presented "acts of sexual immorality as desirable." [27] About the only grounds on which a government may prevent the showing of a film is proof that it is obscene.

The Supreme Court has allowed films to be treated differently from books or newspapers and has refused to hold that prior censorship of films is necessarily unconstitutional under all circumstances.[28] However, laws calling for prior submission of all films to a review board are constitutional only if the review board is required promptly to grant a license or promptly to go to court for a prompt judicial hearing and determination that the film in question is obscene, and the burden is on the board to prove to the court that the film is in fact obscene.[29] Justices Black and Douglas would not even have allowed this kind of prior restraint. They argued that the public is adequately protected by the authority of the government to prosecute in a court of law those who show obscene films, and

[26] *Lamont* v. *Postmaster-General* (1965).
[27] See Paul C. Bartholomew, "Movie Censorship and the Supreme Court," *Michigan State Bar Journal* (August 1961), pp. 10–16. See also Alan F. Westin, "The Miracle Case: The Supreme Court and the Movies," in Edwin A. Bock and Alan K. Campbell (eds.), *Case Studies in American Government* (Prentice-Hall, 1962), pp. 83–131.
[28] *Times Film Company* v. *City of Chicago* (1961).
[29] *Freedman* v. *Maryland* (1965).

that any form of censorship, no matter how speedy, is just as unconstitutional for films as it would be for newspapers.

Censorship of films and books may be imposed by a variety of means other than formal action. In some cities local police have been known to threaten an exhibitor or a bookseller with criminal prosecution if he persists in showing pictures or selling books of which the local police disapprove. Such a threat is often enough to compel exhibitors to stop showing the picture or selling the book. Of course any group is free to stay away from pictures or books that they dislike, even to try to persuade others to stay away. What the Constitution forbids is the use of the coercive powers of *government*.

Other Means of Communication

Radio and Television. The number of frequencies that can be used for broadcasting and telecasting is limited. Chaos would result if the national government could not use its power over interstate commerce to allocate the airways and to issue licenses for broadcasting and television. The regulating agency, the Federal Communications Commission, has not tried to exercise direct power of censorship over political views or ideas presented over the airways, and doubtless it would be stopped by the courts if it did. But the First Amendment does not include "the right to use the facilities of a radio without a license" (*National Broadcasting Co.* v. *United States,* 1943). Nor does the First Amendment prevent the Federal Communications Commission from refusing or canceling a license if, in its opinion, the broadcasting station is not serving the public interest, convenience, or necessity. Federal regulation of radio and television does, however, protect these media from *state* regulation. When Philadelphia officials tried to censor motion pictures shown on television, a United States Court of Appeals ruled that the federal regulation was exclusive (*Dumont Laboratories* v. *Carroll,* 1950).

Handbills. The distribution of religious and political pamphlets, leaflets, and handbills to the public—a historic weapon in the defense of liberty—is constitutionally protected. The Supreme Court has been quick to strike down ordinances interfering with this right. Of course, cities may prosecute those who engage in fraud, or libel, or who deliberately litter the streets, but keeping the streets clean does not justify interference with the right to pass out political or religious literature. When Los Angeles tried to outlaw the distribution of anonymous handbills, the Supreme Court ruled that the city's interest in identifying those who might be responsible for fraud, false advertising, or libel was not substantial enough to justify a ban on all anonymous handbills.[30] When it comes to commercial handbills or advertising matter, however, there is no such sweeping constitutional protection, and such activities are exposed to much greater government regulation.

[30] *Talley* v. *California* (1960).

Picketing. This is a means of speech traditionally used by workers to convey their messages to the public. At the same time, it is an economic weapon in the struggle between labor and capital. In 1940 the Supreme Court ruled in *Thornhill v. Alabama* that picketing was a form of communication protected by the First and Fourteenth Amendments; therefore, a state law forbidding all peaceful picketing carried on for any purpose was an unconstitutional invasion of freedom of speech. However, the Court has held, provided state action is not precluded by federal law, that even peaceful picketing can be restricted if it is conducted for a purpose that is against public policy as declared either by the state legislature or by state judges.[31] Since federal law is so comprehensive and since the Supreme Court has construed it to preempt many areas from state regulation, the power of states to interfere with labor union picketing is much narrower than it appears if one looks only at decisions relating to freedom of speech.[32]

Sound Trucks. Which is more important—the right to an undisturbed Sunday afternoon nap or the right to use a sound truck to publicize a message? In 1948, by a five-to-four decision, the Supreme Court held in *Saia v. New York* that the Fourteenth Amendment was violated by a city ordinance requiring an official permit from the chief of police before one could use a sound truck. Justice Douglas, speaking for the majority, said that sound trucks are "indispensable instruments of effective public speech, and . . . such abuses as they create can be controlled only by statutes narrowly drawn." The very next year, however, the authority of this ruling was thrown in doubt by another five-to-four ruling in *Kovacs v. Cooper* upholding a municipal ordinance forbidding any sound truck that emitted "loud and raucous noises." The Court majority believed that this ordinance provided a definite enough standard to guide administrators, and that it was a justifiable exercise of the police power "to protect the well-being and tranquility of a community." These two cases are an excellent example of the narrow and delicate balance between civil liberties and the needs of an ordered community.

Freedom of Assembly

The right to assemble peaceably applies not only to meetings in private homes and meeting halls, but also to meetings held in public streets and parks, which, the Supreme Court has said, ". . . time out of mind have been used for purposes of assembly . . . and discussing public questions." (*Hague v. C.I.O.*, 1939.) But people are not free to incite riots, to block traffic, to hold parades or to make speeches in public places during rush hours; and the government may make reasonable regulations to preserve order.

[31] *International Brotherhood of Teamsters* v. *Vogt* (1957) and cases cited therein.
[32] Martin Shapiro, *Law and Politics in the Supreme Court* (The Free Press, 1964), pp. 75–142.

The courts will look carefully at regulations and police action that obstruct the right of public assembly, especially in circumstances that raise a suspicion that a law is not being applied even handedly. The Supreme Court is unwilling to approve regulations authorizing public authorities to determine at their own discretion which groups will be allowed to hold public meetings, or laws that are so vague that they give police broad discretion to determine whom to arrest and courts latitude to determine whom to convict. Governments may control the use of the streets, but they must do so by precisely drawn and fairly administered regulations. The Supreme Court, for example, sustained a Louisiana statute that made it an offense to picket or parade in or near a courthouse with the intent to influence a judge, juror, witness, or court order or to impede the administration of justice. On the other hand, the Court struck down another Louisiana statute that defined disturbing of the peace so broadly that it would permit arrest merely for holding a meeting upon a public street or public highway.[33]

What of unpopular groups whose peaceful public meetings and non-violent demonstrations in the public streets and parks arouse others to violence? May police arrest them and judges convict the demonstrators? If the answer were yes, then the right of unpopular minorities to hold meetings would be seriously curtailed. It is almost always easier for the police to maintain order by curbing the peaceful meetings of the unpopular minority than to move against those threatening the violence. On the other hand, if police never have the right to order a group to disperse, public order is at the mercy of those who may resort to street demonstrations just to create public tensions and provoke street battles.

The Supreme Court has refused to give a categorical answer; it depends on the circumstances. Several years ago the Court upheld the conviction of a sidewalk speaker who continued to talk after being ordered to stop by the only two policemen present. There was no evidence that the police interfered because of objection to what was being said. But in view of the hostile response of the audience, the police were fearful that a fight might ensue that they could not contain or prevent.[34] Judges have also approved of the police breaking up demonstrations in front of public school buildings by segregationists who by taunts and threats have tried to intimidate school authorities, parents, and children attempting to carry out a court-ordered desegregation program. On the other hand, the Supreme Court has refused to approve police interference in circumstances where there is a strong suspicion that the local authorities failed to make a good-faith attempt to protect *peaceful* demonstrations that were not interfering with substantial rights of others. For example, 187 Negro high school and college students were arrested for holding a mass meeting in front of the South Carolina State House to protest denial of their civil rights. A crowd of about 300 onlookers watched the demonstration. The police protected the demonstrators for about forty-five minutes and then gave the students fifteen minutes in which to disperse. When they refused to do so, they were arrested and convicted for breach of the peace. The Supreme Court stressed

---

[33] *Cox v. Louisiana* (1965).
[34] *Feiner v. New York* (1951).

that this was not a prosecution for violation of a precise and narrowly drawn statute limiting or prescribing specific conduct, such as interfering with traffic. All that had happened was that the opinions being expressed had been sufficiently opposed by a majority of the community as to attract a crowd and necessitate police protection. "The Fourteenth Amendment," said the Court, "does not permit a State to make criminal the peaceful expression of unpopular views." [35] Justice Clark, the lone dissenter, argued that the right to express views does not include the right to do so under circumstances where law-enforcement officers conclude in good faith that a dangerous disturbance is imminent.

An explanation of the Supreme Court's attempt to draw a line between legitimate use of public authority to preserve order and the unconstitutional use of public authority to suppress the right to assemble only begins to state the problem. The Court cannot police the nation. In thousands of local communities what really determines the extent to which people are free to exercise their constitutional right to assemble peacefully and to express unpopular views is the conduct of the local law enforcement authorities and they, in turn, reflect the views and values of the communities they serve. Despite Supreme Court opinions, local demonstrators still are arrested and demonstrations stopped. Thousands of dollars and months later, convictions may be reversed if the case is carried all the way to the Supreme Court. In the meantime the protestors are silenced. Again, we have an example of the fact that the Supreme Court can *lead*, but it cannot *secure* constitutional rights unless its decisions are backed by the dominant political views and values and forces of the nation.

Freedom of Association

The right to organize for the peaceful promotion of political causes is not precisely mentioned in the Constitution, but in 1958 the Supreme Court made specific what has long been implied: "It is beyond debate that freedom to engage in association for the advancement of beliefs and ideas is an inseparable aspect of the 'liberty' protected by the Constitution." [36]

Of course this right, like other rights, under certain conditions may be regulated. The Supreme Court has sustained a congressional requirement that certain kinds of communist organizations register the names of their members with the Attorney General. The Court conceded that the publicity resulting from this disclosure would impair the ability of communists to recruit members and would subject individual communists to social ostracism and economic reprisal. The Court majority was impressed, however, by the evidence before Congress that communist organizations are not ordinary political groups seeking to promote goals by peaceful means, but organizations dominated by the Soviet Union working to overthrow the United States government by unlawful means.[37]

[35] *Edwards* v. *South Carolina* (1963).
[36] *NAACP* v. *Alabama* (1958).
[37] *Communist Party* v. *Subversive Activities Control Board* (1961).

The Supreme Court has quite differently treated the attempts by some southern states to prevent persons from joining the National Association for the Advancement of Colored People. This organization, which proceeds in large measure by pressing lawsuits, has aroused considerable hostility among white citizens in areas where segregationist traditions are strong. And southern states and cities have tried by a variety of means to discourage persons from joining the NAACP, even to the extent of trying to outlaw the organization.

One of the most frequently attempted anti-NAACP tactics is to force the NAACP to reveal the names of its members. In many regions, if it becomes known that a person belongs to the NAACP, he risks loss of employment, economic reprisal, even physical coercion. Under such circumstances disclosure of membership lists would interfere with the right to join a lawful organization. Unless the state can show some compelling public purpose, the Supreme Court has ruled, it may not force the NAACP to hand over membership lists.[38] Along these same lines, the Supreme Court ruled that Arkansas could not demand a list of all organizations to which its teachers belong, the list ostensibly required to determine their fitness to teach. The Supreme Court concluded that the state could get the information it was entitled to without having to impose a requirement which would discourage membership in lawful but unpopular organizations.[39]

What about the freedom *not* to associate? To oversimplify a complex problem, a majority of the justices apparently feel that under certain circumstances a legislature may constitutionally authorize compulsory membership in a union or a bar association provided no individual is compelled to have his dues spent for political causes.[40]

Subversive Conduct and Seditious Speech

"If there is any fixed star in our constitutional constellation," Justice Jackson said, "it is that no official, high or petty, can prescribe what shall be orthodox in politics, nationalism, religion, or other matters of opinion. . . ." Any group that abides by the basic rules of democracy can champion whatever position it wishes, whether vegetarianism, socialism, or even communism. But what about the American Communist party? Its leaders are unwilling to abide by democratic methods. Their organization is an instrument of a foreign power whose aggressive policies threaten the free world.[41] Yet they claim the right under the Constitution to carry on their propaganda and other activities.

Here is a perplexing problem for American democratic government. How can the United States protect itself against communists and other anti-democrats and

[38] *Bates v. Little Rock* (1960); *NAACP v. Alabama* (1958); *NAACP v. Button* (1963).
[39] *Shelton v. Tucker* (1960).
[40] *International Association of Machinists v. Street* (1961) and *Lathrop v. Donohue* (1961).
[41] See decision of Subversive Activities Control Board, which after fourteen months of hearings concluded that the Communist party is dominated by the Soviet Union and ordered it to register as a "communist-action organization." F.R. Vol. 18, No. 83, p. 2513, April 30, 1953.

at the same time preserve traditional American freedoms? The weapons in the battle against disloyalty are hazardous—there is a constant risk that they will backfire. If used clumsily, they may do more to undermine individual freedom and the security of the United States than can the communists themselves. Let us look first at the least dangerous weapons—those aimed at disloyal *actions*.

Traitors, Spies, Saboteurs, Revolutionaries

Laws punishing disloyal *actions* raise no constitutional questions nor do they infringe on civil liberties, except when they are loosely drawn or indiscriminately administered. The framers of the Constitution—themselves considered traitors by the English government—knew the dangers of loose definitions of treason. Accordingly, they carefully inserted a constitutional definition of the crime of treason by stating that it consists only of the overt acts of giving aid and comfort to the enemies of the United States or levying war against the United States. Furthermore, in order to convict a person of treason, the Constitution requires the testimony of two witnesses to the overt treasonable acts or else confession in open court.

Against what other forms of disloyal action does the national government have constitutional power to protect itself? It has the power to make it a crime to engage in espionage or sabotage, to overthrow the government by force, or to conspire to do any of these things.

This power to proceed against disloyal action, however, is not unlimited. Some constitutional lawyers suggest that perhaps Congress went too far in the Internal Security Act of 1950, which outlaws any conspiratorial action, peaceful or violent (except proposals for constitutional amendments), designed to contribute substantially to the establishment of a foreign-controlled dictatorship in the United States. So far the Department of Justice has made no attempt to prosecute any person under this provision, which, unlike other anti-subversive laws, is not aimed at specific acts or merely at the use of violence or other unlawful means, but attempts to outlaw political goals.

"Fire!"

From The Herblock Book (Beacon Press, 1952).

Seditious Speech

It is one thing to punish men for what they *do*; it is quite another to punish them for what they *say*. The story of the development of free government is in large measure the story of making clear this distinction between speech and other kinds of activity, and of restricting the power of government to define and punish seditious speech. Until recent centuries, seditious speech was so broadly defined that all criticism of those in power was considered criminal. As late as the eighteenth century in England, seditious speech was defined to cover any publication intended to incite disaffection against the king or the government or to raise discontent among the people or to promote feelings of ill will between different classes.[42] And it did not make any difference if what was said was true. On the contrary, "the greater the truth the greater the libel." For if one charged the king's ministers with being corrupt and in fact they were corrupt, such a charge would more likely cause discontent among the people than if it were false.

The adoption of the Constitution and the Bill of Rights did not result in a quick, easy victory for those who wished to establish free speech in the United States. In 1798, only seven years after the First Amendment had been ratified, Congress passed the first national sedition law. These were perilous times for the young Republic, for war with France seemed imminent. The Federalists, in control of both Congress and the Presidency, were so stung by the criticisms of the Jeffersonian Republicans that they persuaded themselves that national safety required a little suppression of speech. The Sedition Act made it a crime to utter false, scandalous, or malicious statements intended to bring the government or any of its officers into disrepute or "to incite against them the hatred of the good people of the United States." [43]

The Sedition Act of 1798 marked a definite advance over the English common law, for it made truth a defense and allowed the jury to determine the seditious character of the utterances. (At about this same time in England these same procedural reforms were also being adopted.) But Federalists, like most officials wielding the power to suppress, regarded all criticism of their actions as scandalous, malicious, and false, and they used the law to punish their political opponents for criticizing the policies of the Federalist administration.

The popular reaction to the Sedition Act helped defeat the Federalists in the elections of 1800. They had failed to grasp the core of the democratic idea that a man may criticize the *government of the day*, he may work for its downfall, he may oppose its policies, and still be loyal to the *nation*. If the Sedition Act had been left on the statute books and applied in its full measure, neither a "loyal opposition" nor a free government would have been possible.

[42] Zechariah Chafee, Jr., "The Great Liberty: Freedom of Speech and Press," in Alfred H. Kelly (ed.), *Foundations of Freedom in the American Constitution* (Harper, 1958), p. 79.

[43] See James Morton Smith, *Freedom's Fetters; The Alien and Sedition Laws and American Civil Liberties* (Cornell Univ. Press, 1956).

The Sedition Act of 1918

Not until World War I did such a severe measure again become the law of the land. In 1918 Congress made it a crime to print, write, or publish any "disloyal, profane, scurrilous, or abusive language about the form of government of the United States or the Constitution . . . or any language intended to bring the form of government of the United States, or the Constitution of the United States, or the military forces . . . or the flag . . . or the uniform of the Army and Navy . . . into contempt, scorn, contumely, or disrepute."

This drastic measure was not aimed at talk that might lead to specific kinds of illegal activity. Rather, it made *the speech itself illegal*. Like the Sedition Act of 1798, this law made it a crime not only to advocate illegal activities, but even to criticize the government. Loosely drawn and poorly administered, it was applied at a time when many people, emotionally aroused by the war, were willing to restrict the liberties of their fellow citizens. As a result of the combined effort of state laws against anarchy and sedition and federal laws against interfering with drafting men for the army, it became a crime "to advocate heavier taxation instead of bond issues, to state that conscription was unconstitutional . . . to say that the sinking of merchant vessels was legal, to urge that a referendum should have preceded our declaration of war, to say that war was contrary to the teachings of Christ." [44] A 21-year-old girl was sentenced to 15 years in jail for taking part in the scattering of pamphlets attacking President Wilson and opposing American intervention in Russia. [45] During the "red scare" that followed the war, judges and juries punished hundreds of people who expressed ideas to which their neighbors objected.

The Smith Act of 1940

The next sedition law, the first to apply in peacetime since the Sedition Act of 1798, was the Smith Act of 1940. Unlike earlier sedition laws, it does not make mere criticism of the government a crime, nor does it contain such loose language as "bring into contempt" or "cause discontent." The core of the offense to which this law applies is to advocate the overthrow of the government by force with the intent to bring about this overthrow. It forbids persons to advocate forceful overthrow; to distribute, with disloyal intent, matter teaching or advising the overthrow of government by violence; and to organize knowingly or to help organize any group having such purposes. According to some authorities, the act introduces for the first time into federal criminal law the concept of *guilt by association*, by making it a crime for an

[44] Zechariah Chafee, Jr., *Free Speech in the United States* (Harvard Univ. Press, 1941), p. 51; John P. Roche, *The Quest for the Dream* (Macmillan, 1963), pp. 26–76.
[45] *Abrams* v. *United States* (1919).

individual to be a member of any organization that advocates forceful overthrow of the government when the individual *knows* that this is its purpose and joins with the intent to help the organization bring about the violent overthrow of government (even though he himself might not so advocate).

The Supreme Court construed the Smith Act and considered the constitutionality of its several provisions in a series of important cases during the 1950's. In *Dennis* v. *United States* (1951), a majority of the justices rejected the contention that the Smith Act could not be constitutionally applied to the leaders of the Communist party who had been charged with conspiring to advocate the violent overthrow of the government. Chief Justice Vinson, speaking for the majority, adopted the position of Circuit Judge Learned Hand that the probability of success of the speech in question should not serve as the sole criterion, but the question is "whether the gravity of the evil, discounted by its improbability," justified such invasion of speech as is necessary to avoid the danger. The Court gave great weight to the fact that the Communist party leaders were not isolated zealots scattering a few insignificant pamphlets but members of a rigidly disciplined organization and part of a world-wide conspiracy whose purpose was to destroy democracy. Justices Douglas and Black dissented. They pointed out that there had been no evidence introduced to indicate that the Communist party leaders were teaching "methods of terror and seditious conduct," but only that they had organized people to teach them Marxist-Leninist doctrines. Moreover, the evidence did not show that this teaching presented any clear and present danger to the government. "The communists in America," Justice Douglas wrote, "are miserable merchants of unwanted ideas; their wares remain unsold. The fact that their ideas are abhorrent does not make them powerful. . . . The invisible army of petitioners is the best known, the most beset, and the least thriving of any fifth column in history. . . . Unless and until extreme and necessitous circumstances are shown our aim should be to keep speech unfettered and to allow the process of law to be invoked only when the provocateurs among us move from speech to action."

The Yates and Scales Cases

Following the Dennis Case, the Department of Justice and in many states local prosecutors proceeded to go after the second-string communist leaders, more than 100 of whom were jailed. Then the Supreme Court called a halt to the easy conviction of communist leaders. In *Pennsylvania* v. *Nelson* (1956), the Court ruled that the Smith Act precluded state prosecutions for seditious advocacy against the *national* government. In *Yates* v. *United States* (1957), the Court, speaking through Justice Harlan, held that the Dennis decision had been misunderstood. The Smith Act did not outlaw the advocacy of the abstract doctrine of violent overthrow. "That sort of advocacy," Justice Harlan explained, "even though uttered with the hope that it may ultimately lead to violent revolution, is too remote from concrete action to be regarded as the kind of indoctrination preparatory to action which was condemned in Dennis. The essential distinction is that those to whom the advocacy is addressed must be urged *to do* something, now or in the future, rather than merely *to believe* in something." The Supreme Court denied that it was reversing the Dennis case, but certainly it severely restricted the scope of that decision.

After the Yates decision, many students of constitutional law felt that the Supreme Court would not sustain the provision in the Smith Act that makes it a crime to belong knowingly to an organization that advocates the violent overthrow of the government. But in *Scales* v. *United States* (1961) the Supreme Court, by a five-to-four vote, ruled that the membership clause is constitutional. It did so, however, after narrowly construing it to apply only if there is clear evidence that the accused "specifically intended to accomplish the aims of the organization by resort to violence. A person who joins the Communist party, however active he may be, may not be prosecuted under the membership provision unless there is proof that he joined with intent to bring about the overthrow of government as speedily as circumstances would permit."

So construed, the membership provision of the Smith Act is even more limited in coverage than the advocacy provision and in essence can be applied only against those who are attempting to overthrow the government by force, activity that was made criminal long before the passage of the Smith Act.

From this brief survey of laws aimed at seditious advocacy it seems clear that *seditious speech if narrowly defined to cover only the advocacy of concrete acts of violence is not constitutionally protected.* Such narrowly construed antisedition acts leave communists and other totalitarians free to work for their political objectives so long as they abandon force or its advocacy.

The Internal Security Act of 1950

With steadily increasing tension between the United States and the Soviet world, many have pressed for even more stringent restrictions on communist political activity than the Smith Act imposes. When the "cold war" turned into a hot one in Korea, Congress responded with the Internal Security Act of 1950, popularly known as the McCarran Act. In addition to the as yet ineffective provision previously mentioned, which outlaws conspiratorial action designed to establish a totalitarian dictatorship in the United States, the Internal Security Act also strengthens laws against espionage and sedition, adds to alien registration requirements, makes it more difficult for communist aliens to enter or remain in the United States, and establishes procedures for detaining, in the event of a national emergency, any person who can "reasonably" be expected to engage in acts of sabotage or espionage. But the most significant parts of the act were the attempt to strip the veil of secrecy from communist political activity and to impose certain disabilities on communists.

The act created the Subversive Activities Control Board which determines on the request of the Attorney General whether a particular organization is a communist action, communist front, or communist infiltrated organization as defined by the act. A communist *action* organization, for example, is defined as one that is substantially directed by the USSR or operates primarily to advance the objectives of world communism. After the Subversive Activities Control Board issues a final order declaring an organization to be a communist organization and this order has been sustained by the courts, various disabilities are imposed on the organization and its members. For example, action and front communist organizations must register annually with the Attorney General, listing names of officers and accounting for all money spent and received, including its sources; submit information about printing equipment; and so on. In addition, certain sanctions are imposed on members of registered organizations.

The Court met this issue squarely in 1965. In an 8–0 decision it held that individual members of the party could not be forced to register under the McCarran Act.[46] Individuals ordered to register could cite the self-incrimination provision of the Fifth Amendment since, the Court stated, "an admission of membership may be used to prosecute the registrant under the membership clause of the Smith Act." The Court left open the question of whether the *party* could be compelled to register, but this question was bound to reach the High Court in due course. The official spokesman of the Communist party hailed the court's decision as "vindication," but the decision caused little stir among most Americans. With its dwindling membership and old-fashioned Marxist war cries, the party seemed too weak to benefit much from the decision.

The Supreme Court has declared unconstitutional the only other provision of the Internal Security Act that has as yet come before it. This provision made it a criminal offense for any member of a registered communist organization to apply for or use a passport, regardless of the extent of his involvement in the affairs of the organization or his reason for going abroad. Such a sweeping provision, said the Supreme Court, "too broadly and indiscriminately transgresses" the liberty to travel which is part of the liberty protected by the Fifth Amendment against unreasonable governmental interference.[47]

A generation after the adoption of the Internal Security Act the constitutionality and effectiveness of many of its provisions remain highly questionable.[48]

The Communist Control Act of 1954

The purpose of the Internal Security Act of 1950 was to bring communists out into the open. But even before this act could be applied, Congress decided to take more drastic action. Although for some time there had been agitation to outlaw the Communist party and its successors, no action was taken until 1954, partly because of doubts about the constitutionality of such a measure, partly because of doubts about its effectiveness.

In that year Congress declared that even the overt political activities of the Communist party serve as a front behind which the party can seduce individuals into the service of world communism and work toward the violent overthrow

[46] *Albertson* v. *Subversive Activities Control Board* (1965).
[47] *Aptheker* v. *Secretary of State* (1964).
[48] Ralph S. Brown, Jr., *Loyalty and Security* (Yale Univ. Press, 1958), p. 472.

of the government of the United States. (Such a conspiracy, of course, is illegal; and evidence to support this finding, if properly presented in court proceedings, would be sufficient under existing law to throw the conspirators into jail.) The party's very existence, declared Congress, renders it a "clear, present, and continuing danger to the security of the United States." Therefore, in the Communist Control Act of 1954, Congress deprived the Communist party and its successors of "any of the rights, privileges, and immunities attendant upon legal bodies created under the laws of the United States" or any of the states.

The act does not make it a crime to be a communist (although members of the party may be subjected to the penalties that the Internal Security Act imposes on members of communist action organizations). The major effect of the law has been to deprive the Communist *party* of the right to seek places on election ballots for its candidates. For the first time in our history, a political party has been outlawed by the national government, and a group has been denied the opportunity to use the traditional instruments of democracy.

Disloyalty

Spies, saboteurs, and those who advocate the forceful overthrow of the government may be tried and punished under existing laws. But what about persons who commit no crimes and yet are sympathetic to the cause of communism, or who have joined organizations that the Attorney General believes to be subversive? Should they be permitted to work for the government, serve in the armed forces, work in defense plants, secure passports? Apparently most Americans believe that they should not, and a whole host of disabilities has been imposed upon such persons.

J. Edgar Hoover has estimated that there are less than 10,000 communists in this country and perhaps ten times that many who are sympathetic to their cause. In order to forestall this group from securing public employment, receiving government-financed fellowships, joining the merchant marine, or working in defense plants, about twenty million Americans have been subjected to some kind of federal loyalty check. In addition, Congress and at least six state legislatures have established committees to investigate un-American activities. These committees have checked into the loyalty of public employees, newspapermen, teachers, scientists, and others, and have "exposed" those whom the committee members believe to be un-American.

Federal Loyalty-Security Programs

Since 1939, communists, Nazis, and fascists have been disqualified from federal employment. During World War II, all applicants for government jobs were carefully investigated, and access to classified and secret information was denied to all except those who had been cleared. Then in 1947 President Truman, responding to public concern over disclosures of communist espionage, by executive order created the first comprehensive and systematic federal loyalty-security program.

This program, as modified by acts of Congress, presidential executive orders, and Supreme Court decisions, now requires an investigation of each applicant for a position in the federal executive branch, the extent of the investigation varying with the nature of the job he is being considered for. The applicant will be denied employment if evidence is uncovered that he would not be a good security risk because of untrustworthiness, liability to blackmail, drunkenness, and so on.

Federal employees holding sensitive positions—those directly involving national security—may under a 1950 act of Congress be summarily dismissed if at any time evidence is uncovered that brings their security status into question. The employee is entitled to a hearing, but the government is under no legal obligation to disclose the name of his accusers or the precise nature and source of the information being used against him. President Eisenhower extended these procedures to cover all federal executive employees, but the Supreme Court ruled that Congress had intended to apply such drastic dismissal regulations only to persons holding "sensitive positions." [49] The government may dismiss other of its employees, however, under civil service regulations, but these regulations provide more safeguards for the rights of the "accused."

Congress has also been concerned with the loyalty of citizens who are not federal employees. It has created a security program for employees of defense contractors. At one time, students seeking federally supported scholarships or educational loans had to sign an affidavit that they were not disloyal. Because of the opposition of leading educators and the refusal of many universities to participate in this program, Congress in 1962 repealed this requirement. It has since substituted a law that makes it a federal crime for any student who belongs to a communist organization to apply for or to hold a scholarship or loan supported by federal funds. Every enrollee in the Job Corps must take an oath swearing allegiance to the United States and any recipient of funds under the Economic Opportunity Act of 1964 must sign an affidavit that he does not believe in, teach, or belong to any organization that advocates the overthrow of the government by illegal or unconstitutional methods.

The states also have incorporated loyalty programs. Although few positions occupied by state and local officials directly affect our national security, almost all our states require loyalty oaths from public employees, and some even require oaths from attorneys, students in the state university, public accountants, occupants of public housing projects, and persons applying for unemployment compensation. One state includes wrestlers and fighters, on the grounds, according to the executive secretary of the state athletic commission, that "we didn't want to license a professional boxer and wrestler who might become a hero in the eyes of youthful fans and then discover he was a communist." [50]

---

[49] *Cole* v. *Young* (1956).

[50] See testimony before Subcommittee on Constitutional Rights of the Senate Committee on the Judiciary, Hearings, *Security and Constitutional Rights*, 84th Cong., 2nd Sess., November 17, 1955, p. 350.

Few object to oaths requiring one to swear or to affirm loyalty to the United States. But state loyalty oaths reverse the normal presumption of loyalty and proceed on the assumption that one is disloyal unless he swears to the contrary.[51] Of the several kinds of loyalty oaths required by the states, the more carefully drawn are limited to statements that the person does not advocate the overthrow of government by unlawful means or knowingly belong to any organization that does. But some of the oaths are much more sweeping.

While avoiding a direct ruling on constitutionality, the Supreme Court has narrowly construed federal security laws and executive orders. It has sustained loyalty oaths for public employees provided the oaths are narrowly drawn so as to disqualify from employment only persons who *knowingly* advocate violent over-throw of government or who *knowingly* join organizations that do so.[52] The Court has shown even less sympathy for the attempts by government to inquire into the political reliability of private citizens; for example, the Court held that California could not constitutionally require churches and veterans to sign loyalty affidavits in order to receive tax exemptions normally given by the state to churches and veterans.[53] In light of this decision and other recent rulings, it is likely that if properly challenged, the Supreme Court would invalidate or narrowly construe congressional enactments that condition participation by private citizens in federal programs on the filing of loyalty affidavits or that make it a crime for members of communist organizations to apply for federal scholarships or loans.[54]

The Operation and Impact of Loyalty Programs

Many of the objections to loyalty-security programs have to do with the procedures used. The government is allowed to judge loyalty on the basis of hearsay evidence. Frequently neither the "accused" nor the board sifting the evidence knows where the charges came from or who the informants are. Sometimes the hearings go far afield. Not untypically, in one security hearing, a witness was asked, "Do you consider Dr. V— as a religious man?" and "Was he an extremist on equality?" At another hearing, one of the charges against the person under investigation was that years ago he had attended a dinner of an organization that had since been cited as a communist front, a dinner also attended by many Washington notables.[55]

One of the most frequently criticized aspects of loyalty-security hearings has been the government's use of unidentified informants. Although many critics concede that the government may be justified in refusing to disclose the names of regularly established informants because disclosure would destroy their usefulness in counter-espionage work, they see no reason why the government should

[51] See Milton Greenberg, "Loyalty Oaths: An Appraisal of the Legal Issues," *The Journal of Politics*, Vol. 20, 1958, pp. 487–514.
[52] *Wieman* v. *Updegraff* (1952).
[53] *Speiser* v. *Randall* (1958).
[54] See especially *United States* v. *Archie Brown* (1965).
[55] See *Vitarelli* v. *Seaton* (1959) and *Greene* v. *McElroy* (1959).

be allowed to use derogatory information supplied by casual informants—next-door neighbors, fellow employees, former classmates, and so on—unless they are willing to disclose their identities and be subject to cross-examination. Such was the recommendation of the Commission on Government Security, created by Congress in 1955 and composed of men appointed by the President, the President of the Senate, and the Speaker of the House of Representatives.[56]

But no matter how fairly they are administered, programs calling for a check on the political activities of millions of Americans may create an atmosphere of suspicion that does more harm, it is feared, than could be done by communists in positions not involving national security. Unquestionably the morale of civil servants suffered in the early 1950's. A task force of the Second Hoover Commission reported: "There is fear that honest and loyal employees can be destroyed by unsupported or trivial derogatory charges; there is fear that security authorities can be stampeded; and there is fear that security charges are at times a means of making 'political' removals." [57]

Are the various security-loyalty programs necessary? Most citizens seem to believe that the tactics of communists and the necessities of the cold war require unusual precautions to keep communists and "politically unstable" persons out of sensitive areas such as the Central Intelligence Agency, Atomic Energy Commission, State Department, Defense Department, and other vital agencies. But there is far less agreement on the need for intensive investigations into the beliefs and political actions of thousands of persons in nonsensitive positions in or out of government.

Where We Stand in the Battle against Disloyalty

As a result of the Smith Act, the Internal Security Act, the Communist Control Act, federal employee security-loyalty programs, and state oath requirements, communists and those suspected of communistic sympathies are now subject to many restrictions. They may be prosecuted for advocating the overthrow of government by force. They may be required to register their group memberships and be subject to certain disabilities. They are denied the right to run for elective office or to operate as a political party. A communist alien may not enter the United States, but if already inside he may be deported from the United States, and he is not allowed to become an American citizen. Communists cannot work for the federal government, for most state and local governments, or for defense industries. They cannot teach in most school systems, cannot serve as labor union officials, cannot practice law. In addition to these governmentally-imposed restrictions, they must cope with disabilities that stem from public abhorrence of their ideas and activities.

[56] *Report of the U.S. Commission on Government Security* (Government Printing Office, 1957), pp. 669–671.
[57] U.S. Commission on Organization of the Executive Branch of the Government, *Task Force Report on Personnel and Civil Service* (Government Printing Office, 1955), p. 121.

Some feel that certain of these restrictions are unjustified. Although they would use every resource to ferret out and punish anyone guilty of espionage or conspiracy to overthrow the government by force, they would not penalize persons who have combined for political action nor deny anti-democrats the right to use the regular methods of democratic government. They would place no restrictions on communists except those absolutely necessary to protect national safety. These critics of governmental restrictions are moved, not by love for communists, but by the conviction that democracy itself is endangered when any group is punished because its ideas are abhorrent to the majority. As Justice Jackson stated it, ". . . the right of every American to equal treatment before the law is wrapped up in the same constitutional bundle with those of the communists."

Those who support governmental limitations on communist activity argue that the communists are not entitled to any rights, since they are at war with our whole democratic system. They insist that the communists, unless they are carefully controlled, will take advantage of their status as a legitimate political party to camouflage their underground activities. Only by denying communists their veil of secrecy can innocent persons be protected. Democratic government, it is contended, must curtail the freedom of those who would destroy freedom.

All recognize that we must act to protect ourselves against those who are conspiring to destroy our democratic system. On the other hand, all recognize that we must be careful not to jeopardize the rights that we have developed in order to prevent the growth of tyranny. An undemocratic but relatively insignificant minority does not justify panic. In fact, it is in times of national peril that our traditional liberties must be most steadfastly strengthened and protected.

7 EQUALITY UNDER THE LAW

Certain liberties are essential to the operation of democratic government. But these liberties are not merely means of attaining self-government; they are ends in themselves. They exist not for the government; rather, the government exists to protect them. Our forefathers called them natural rights—today we speak of human rights—but the belief is still the same, the belief in the moral primacy of men over government and in the dignity and worth of *each* individual.

160

The Declaration of Independence proclaims in ringing terms, "We hold these truths to be self-evident, that all men are created equal, that they are endowed by their Creator with certain unalienable rights, that among these are life, liberty, and the pursuit of happiness. That to secure these rights, governments are instituted among men. . . ." The Declaration does not talk about the equality of white, Christian, or Anglo-Saxon men, but of *all* men. This creed of individual dignity and equality is older than the Declaration of Independence; its roots go back at least as far as the teachings of Judaism and Christianity. To act by this creed, to bring practice into conformity with principles, has long been a central preoccupation of Americans.

"Our inability to achieve [an] . . . accommodation of racial differences has been our most conspicuous political failure." [1] Today no problem is more compelling than that of insuring to every American his basic *civil rights*—his right to enjoy his life and liberty and to pursue his happiness—without discrimination because of his race, religion, national origin, or any other irrelevant characteristic. American democracy, despite its many triumphs, has not extended civil rights to all people, especially not to Negroes. From the time he is born until he dies, a Negro suffers handicaps that no other American has to face—handicaps imposed on him by other Americans. This lack of racial equality is an injury that every American must live with day by day.

What should we do to protect civil rights? This question has been of significance in our presidential elections; it gives rise each year to battles in Congress and to debates in state legislatures and city councils. What we do, or fail to do, has significance beyond our national borders. Our attacks on communist totalitarianism throughout the world lose some of their force in the light of the obvious chinks in our democratic armor. Colored peoples in Asia and Africa, our potential allies, follow the treatment of American Negroes with more than casual interest. And it is not only the colored people who are concerned, for all who hear us talk of democracy may lose faith in a government that denies in fact the very rights that it promises in theory. For as Father Hesburgh, President of the University of Notre Dame and a member of the Civil Rights Commission, has said, "Americans might well wonder how we can legitimately combat communism when we practice so widely its central folly: utter disregard for the God-given spiritual rights, freedom and dignity of every human person." [2]

Our denial of equal rights not only negates the equality that the Declaration of Independence champions—it is also contrary to the commands of the Constitution. For under the Constitution each person has the right to live and work and participate in public affairs, free of discriminatory laws. The Constitution provides two ways of protecting these civil rights: first, by seeing to it that *government* itself imposes no discriminatory barriers; second, by granting the

[1] Alan P. Grimes, *Equality in America: Religion, Race, and the Urban Majority* (Oxford Univ. Press, 1964), p. 41. See also John P. Roche, *The Quest for the Dream* (Macmillan, 1963).

[2] United States Commission on Civil Rights, *Civil Rights, Excerpts from the 1961 Report* (Government Printing Office, 1962), p. 100.

national and state governments authority to act positively to protect civil rights against interference by *private individuals*. In this chapter we shall be concerned with both these aspects, government as a *threat* to civil rights and government as the *protector* of civil rights.

The Life—and Death—of Jim Crow

Laws requiring the segregation of Negroes and whites date only from the end of the nineteenth century.[3] Prior to that time it was social custom and economic status, rather than law, that kept the two races apart. Then toward the end of the nineteenth century, segregationists insisted that laws were needed to maintain racial segregation. Before long, southern states and cities had made it a crime for whites and Negroes to ride in the same car on a train, attend the same theater, or go to the same school. "Jim Crow" laws, as they came to be called, soon blanketed southern life. How could these segregation laws be adopted and enforced in the face of the Fourteenth Amendment, which declares: "No state [including any subdivision thereof] shall . . . deny to any person within its jurisdiction the equal protection of the laws?"

Before turning to the question of the constitutionality of segregation laws, let us look briefly at this more general problem of the power of government to classify. Most laws classify, but what the Constitution forbids is *unreasonable* classification. (Although there is no equal-protection clause limiting the national government, unreasonable classification on its part is made unconstitutional by the due-process clause of the Fifth Amendment.) A classification is unreasonable when there is no relation between the classes it thereby creates and permissible governmental goals. For example, a law prohibiting redheads from voting would be unreasonable, because there is no relation between red hair and the ability to vote. On the other hand, laws denying to persons under 21 the right to vote, to marry without the permission of their parents, or to drive a car are reasonable because (to most adults, at least) there seems to be a relationship between maturity and voting, marrying, and driving. Similarly, the Supreme Court has held the following classifications to be reasonable: classification of persons on the basis of income for tax purposes, classification of property according to its use for zoning purposes, classification of persons by sex for purposes of regulating hours and conditions of employment.

Classifications based on religion, national origin, or race, especially the last, however, have caused great controversy. The courts have always been particularly suspicious of these classifications, allowing them only in the most unusual cases—for example, when the government can demonstrate some exceptional justification and show some relation between race or religion or national origin and the permissible goal. Since the end of World War II the Supreme Court has

[3] C. Vann Woodward, *The Strange Career of Jim Crow* (Oxford Univ. Press, 1955).

come pretty close to the view that *all* racial classifications are inherently arbitrary and unconstitutional. But that gets ahead of our story.

Is Segregation Discrimination?: *Plessy v. Ferguson*

With the ratification of the Fourteenth Amendment and the abolition of slavery, it became unconstitutional for governments to discriminate against Negroes or any other racial or religious groups. But in 1896 the Supreme Court in *Plessy v. Ferguson* endorsed the view that racial *segregation* did not constitute discrimination, and that states by law could require the separation of races in public places so long as *equal accommodations* for all were provided. Even equal accommodations were not required except in the case of services provided out of public funds or in a limited category of public utilities, such as trains and buses. Under this celebrated *separate-but-equal* formula, several states, most of them in the South, enforced segregation in transportation, places of public accommodation such as inns, restaurants, and theaters, and in schools and colleges.

Even if the Supreme Court had declared segregation unconstitutional in 1896, a decision so contrary to the popular feeling of the time would have had little immediate impact. The Negro was considered by many whites, North and South, to be a childlike person. Southern political leaders openly and unapologetically espoused white supremacy. In 1896 one Negro was lynched, on the average, every fifty to sixty hours; few citizens, black or white, raised a voice in protest.

Perhaps, indeed, the Plessy decision was forward-looking within the context of its time, for it did require equality as the price a state should pay if it wished to adopt a program of compulsory segregation. But for many years the "equal" part of the formula was meaningless. States segregated Negroes into unequal facilities and Negroes lacked a political voice to protest. The Supreme Court required only a slight nod on the part of the states in the direction of equality. In 1899, for example, the Court found no denial of equal protection in the fact that a county provided a high school for white citizens but none for the sixty colored children in the district.[4] The passage of time did not lessen the inquality. In 1950, in all the segregated states, there were fourteen medical schools for whites, none for Negroes; sixteen law schools for whites, five for Negroes; fifteen engineering schools for whites, none for Negroes; five dentistry schools for whites, none for Negroes.

By the 1950's, however, the discriminatory impact of governmentally imposed segregation was no longer unchallenged. Through urbanization and industrialization the South had become more integrated with the rest of the nation. Large numbers of Negroes had migrated to northern cities, and their votes had become important in national elections. World Wars I and II and the New Deal had opened more jobs for Negroes and improved their economic conditions. Above

[4] *Cumming* v. *County Board of Education* (1899). See also J. W. Peltason, *Fifty-eight Lonely Men: Southern Federal Judges and School Desegregation* (Harcourt, Brace, 1961), p. 248.

all, these changes created a Negro middle class to whom segregation as a symbol of servitude and a cause of inequality had become a primary target. Negroes were no longer passive recipients of white men's favors, but active and politically powerful citizens. There was a growing, persistent, and insistent demand for the abolition of color barriers.

Beginning in the late 1930's Negroes had started to file lawsuits challenging the separate-but-equal doctrine as a sham. They cited facts to show that in practice separate-but-equal always resulted in discrimination against Negroes. However, the Supreme Court justices were not yet willing to upset the doctrine directly. Rather, they began to undermine it. No longer satisfied with mere token equality, the Court began first to scrutinize each situation and in case after case to order facilities to be equalized.

In 1950, the Supreme Court, though specifically refusing either to affirm or reject the doctrine of *Plessy* v. *Ferguson*, ruled (*Sweatt* v. *Painter*) that Negroes otherwise qualified could not be denied admission to state law schools. A segregated legal education, said the Court, was not in fact equal to a nonsegregated one and could never be made equal. To segregate Negroes into schools from which the state excluded members of the white race, which numbered 85 per cent of the population—including most of the lawyers, witnesses, jurors, judges, and other officials with whom Negroes would be dealing when they became members of the bar—in itself discriminated against Negroes.

On the same day it handed down the decision in the Sweatt case, the Supreme Court held that once a state admitted a Negro to a graduate school, it could not segregate him within the school (*McLaurin* v. *Oklahoma*). Clearly, the legal underpinnings of segregation were getting shaky. If a state could not segregate within a school, could it do so between schools? If segregated legal education is always discriminatory, why would this not be the case for *all* kinds of education? Although for a while the Court continued to avoid a specific overruling of the separate-but-equal doctrine, no one could doubt the direction of its decisions. But how far would it go?

The End of Separate-but-Equal:
Brown v. Board of Education

Finally, in 1952, the Supreme Court agreed to consider five cases involving elementary and secondary schools that unhesitatingly challenged the separate-but-equal doctrine. For two years the Court carefully considered the issues. By Monday, May 17, 1954, the last decision day before the end of the Court's term, no decision had been forthcoming. No one except the Supreme Court justices themselves knew for sure if this would be the day the decision would be announced. But by 9 A.M., when the doors opened to the great main hall, a capacity crowd had already formed.

At 11:00 the doors to the courtroom itself were opened. At 11:45 the lawyers came in and took the front benches. The high-ceilinged, marble-columned courtroom awed the audience into silence. Promptly at noon the red velvet curtains parted behind the nine chairs on the dais, the audience rose, and the Chief Justice and his eight black-robed associates took their seats. The more knowledgeable of the spectators pointed out to their neighbors that Associate Justice Robert Jackson, who was recovering from a heart attack, had left his hospital room in order to be present. This must be the day.

For fifty-two minutes three justices took turns reading decisions, but they were not the ones that had drawn the crowd to the courtroom. Then at 12:52 P.M. the Chief Justice picked up a printed document and began to read in a clear voice: "Does segregation of children in public schools solely on the basis of race, even though the physical facilities and other tangible factors may be equal, deprive the children of the minority group of equal educational opportunity? *We believe it does.*" Citing psychological findings as well as legal sources, the Chief Justice continued:

> In these days it is doubtful that any child may reasonably be expected to succeed in life if he is denied the opportunity of an education. . . . To separate [children] from others of similar age and qualifications solely because of their race generates a feeling of inferiority as to their status in the community that may affect their hearts and minds in a way unlikely ever to be undone.

The Supreme Court justices, knowing their decision conflicted with long-established southern customs and recognizing the formidable problems involved, postponed for a year any final decree. Then in May 1955, after hearing suggestions from state attorneys-general, the High Court issued its implementation decree. The Supreme Court directed local school authorities to proceed "with all deliberate speed" to make a prompt and reasonable start toward admitting Negroes to public schools on a racially nondiscriminatory basis. The Court stated, however, that local officials could take time to make necessary administrative adjustments and need not immediately desegregate schools under their jurisdiction. The Supreme Court did not itself formulate precise instructions, but rather returned the cases to the federal district judges (who could best take into account the great variety of local conditions) to supervise the implementation of desegregation by local school authorities.[5]

Following its rulings in the Brown case,[6] the Supreme Court struck down law after law requiring racial segregation. The upshot: Any kind of governmental action at any level and in any area that denies any person access to any facility because of his race is unconstitutional. And except for elementary and secondary schools, governmental laws and regulations imposing racial classifications may not be constitutionally enforced even briefly during a transitional period.

[5] *Brown v. Board of Education* (1955).
[6] Also known as the School Segregation Case.

Desegregation and Defiance

Outside of the South, church leaders, labor leaders, newspaper editors, teachers, and many others applauded the Supreme Court's decision. Inside the South a few white southerners regarded the decision as a milestone in the long struggle to achieve equal treatment and to bring into reality the promise of the American Revolution. A much larger number, especially those who lived in cities, although not approving of the decisions, felt that the law must be obeyed and school authorities should proceed to comply with the Supreme Court's ruling. In many cities school boards announced that they would begin to desegregate.

Then the more ardent segregationists organized a political attack on the Supreme Court and its decision. The Supreme Court, they argued, had ignored strongly held racial attitudes. Negroes were not ready for integration, they claimed, and the Supreme Court's decision was bad law and bad policy. "No decision of the Supreme Court," said former Governor (now Senator) Herman Talmadge of Georgia, "is entitled to any greater moral weight than its content merits." [7] In Congress, representatives of the deep South attacked the Supreme Court and supported moves to "curb the Court." Southern state legislatures, dominated by legislators from the small towns and rural areas where segregationist sentiments are most deep-seated, reached back to pre-Civil War precedents and asserted the right to "interpose" and resist the Supreme Court mandates; some even claimed the right to declare the Court's decisions null and void. A host of organizations sprang up to fight for continued school segregation, including the White Citizens Councils that claimed a membership of half a million persons. These organizations not only insisted that school boards had no duty to obey the Supreme Court, but that boards should resist desegregation by every possible means. Although decrying force, Council leaders urged parents to barricade and boycott schools in order to prevent Negro children from attending schools previously reserved for whites. White moderates, especially those living in rural areas, began to find it dangerous to express opinions or develop programs of action. Public officials who took a moderate stand were often defeated at the polls. Many school boards refused to initiate desegregation programs.

Most Negroes' only resort was to the courts. They had the important assistance of the National Association for the Advancement of Colored People, but Negroes who became parties to legal proceedings ran the risk of losing their jobs, even of physical harm. And in almost every southern state, legislation was enacted to suppress or to obstruct the NAACP so that it could not help Negro parents and children take the necessary legal action to force desegregation.

During much of this period President Eisenhower (and the Democratic Congress) "remained above the battle." Only if a governor or a school board directly

[7] Herman E. Talmadge, "School Systems, Segregation and the Supreme Court," *Mercer Law Review*, Vol. VI, 1955, pp. 189–200.

challenged a specific court injunction or only if open violence flared in the face of a federal court injunction did federal authorities intervene. Civil rights advocates urged the President and Department of Justice to lend a helping hand. Unless the federal government became more active, they argued, it would be an unequal contest between a few Negro parents and the NAACP on one side against the entire resources of the state on the other. School districts would continue to operate segregated schools for decades. But the Department of Justice felt it lacked authority to intervene, and in 1957 southern senators were able to prevent Congress from adopting a law that would authorize it to do so.

Nevertheless, Negroes continued to file school desegregation suits and the authorities continued to resist. School officials tried to circumvent desegregation orders by such tactics as assigning pupils to segregated schools, but ostensibly for reasons other than race, by closing schools to which Negroes had been assigned, by using the pretext of violence as justification for delaying action.

The Supreme Court stood firm. Eventually federal judges struck down all the evasive schemes. In the Little Rock Case (*Cooper* v. *Aaron*, 1958), in an opinion signed by all members of the Court individually—an unprecedented move to indicate their unanimity and strength of conviction—the Court stated: "The constitutional rights of children not to be discriminated against in school admission on grounds of race or color . . . can neither be nullified openly and directly by state legislators or state executives or judicial officers, nor nullified indirectly by them through evasive schemes for segregation whether attempted ingeniously or ingenuously." Community opposition, even violent protests, said the Court, could not justify any delay: "Law and order are not . . . to be preserved by depriving the Negro children of their constitutional rights." And in 1963, the Supreme Court pointedly stated, "Given the extended time that has elapsed, it is far from clear that the mandates of the several Brown decisions . . . would today be fully satisfied by types or plans or programs for desegregation of public educational facilities which eight years ago might have been deemed sufficient." [8] As school district after school district, despite resistance and violence, was forced to desegregate, it became evident that resistance did not lead to the retention of segregation, but only to social unrest and economic injury to the community.

1963—A Turning Point

A decade after the Supreme Court declared public school segregation to be unconstitutional, most Negro children in the deep South still attended segregated schools. For it is one thing to declare something unconstitutional; it is another to alter human behavior. What was needed was a political-legal movement to counter the resistance of those who supported segregation and were defying the courts. Such a mass-based civil-rights movement was slowly developing.

By 1963, the struggles in the courtrooms were being supplemented by a massive

[8] *Watson* v. *Memphis* (1963).

social, economic, and political movement. What had been before then largely a conflict involving the emotions and commitments mainly of the more highly educated and economically secure Negroes, all of a sudden gripped the feelings of thousands of men and women from domestic servant to Nobel prize winner.

The Negro Revolt of 1963 did not come unannounced and its immediate background did not stem directly from the struggle to desegregate the public schools. In a real sense it began when the first Negro slave was educated three hundred years ago. But its more immediate origin was in 1955 in Montgomery, Alabama, when the Negro community engaged in a persistent boycott of the city buses to protest segregation on the buses. The boycott worked. And from the Montgomery incident the civil rights movement produced its first charismatic leader: the Reverend Martin Luther King, who through his Southern Christian Leadership Conference and his doctrine of non-violent resistance, provided a new dimension to the struggle for civil rights. By the early 1960's, the Committee on Racial Equality (CORE) and the Student Non-violent Coordinating Committee (SN-CC) added new organizational forces to support and sponsor sit-ins, freedom rides, live-ins, and mass demonstrations.

In the summer of 1963 the forces of social discontent created a national crisis. It started with a demonstration in Birmingham, Alabama, that was countered by the use of fire hoses, police dogs, and mass arrests. It culminated in a march in Washington, D.C., where over 100,000 people heard King speak of his dream of the day when children "will live in a nation where they will not be judged by the color of their skin, but by the content of their character." By the time the summer was over there was hardly a city that had not had a demonstration, protest, sit-in; in many, there were riots. This direct action had some effect. In many cities civil rights ordinances were enacted and existing legislation broadened. More schools were desegregated that fall than in any year since 1956. At the national level President Kennedy made a dramatic address to the nation and urged Congress to enact a comprehensive civil rights bill. But Congress did not act. Late in 1963, the nation's grief over the death of John Kennedy, who had become identified with civil rights goals, added political fuel to the drive for federal action. President Johnson made the adoption of civil rights legislation the highest priority of his program.

On July 2, 1964, after months of debate and the use of cloture to end a southern filibuster in the Senate (see page 441), President Johnson signed the Civil Rights Act of 1964 into law. The enactment of the most comprehensive and forceful civil rights law in the nation's history marked the culmination of a long drive and the beginning of a new era in the civil rights struggle.

The Civil Rights Act of 1964 and School Desegregation

Among its many provisions, the Civil Rights Act of 1964 authorizes the Attorney General to take an active role in school desegregation suits. On signed complaints and where he is satisfied that the aggrieved individuals are unable to initiate lawsuits because of lack of funds or because they may be subject to economic injury or physical harm, the Attorney General may initiate legal proceedings in behalf of the United States. No longer do Negro parents have the full burden of securing compliance with the Constitution.

Of even greater significance is the use of the congressional power of the purse. The 1964 Act authorizes the Office of Education to give technical and financial assistance to local school systems that request such help in order to desegregate their schools. The act also stipulates that federal funds—of major importance since the adoption of the Elementary and Secondary Education Act of 1965— will be withdrawn from any school district or public institution of higher education that refuses to desegregate. School desegregation is far from being an accomplished fact. But today school segregation is not only unconstitutional, it is fiscally costly and increasingly a political liability. It has become more trouble for many school boards to try to maintain segregation than to desegregate.

Color Bar at the Polls

Equality at the polls is one of the most important civil rights still denied to many Negroes, for their social, economic, and legal rights depend largely on their success in gaining—and exercising—the right to vote.

The Constitution leaves to the states the power to determine suffrage qualifications, but states are subject to a variety of constitutional restraints in exercising this power. The Fourteenth Amendment forbids states to deprive any person of the equal protection of the laws and thus limits their power to establish discriminatory suffrage qualifications. For example, the Supreme Court (*Carrington* v. *Rash*, 1965) held that Texas violated this clause when it prohibited "any member of the Armed Forces of the United States who moved to Texas from voting in any election." "The uniform of our country . . . must not be the badge of disfranchisement for the man or woman who wears it," the Court declared, and "a state may not fence out from the franchise a sector of the population for fear of how it will vote." Similarily, a state law that gave whites the right to vote but denied it to Negroes otherwise qualified would also violate the equal protection clause since racial classifications for voting are unreasonable.

The Fourteenth Amendment also declares that if any state, for any reason other than participation in rebellion or other crime, deprives male citizens 21 years and over of the right to vote, the state is to suffer a proportionate loss of representation in the House of Representatives. Congress, however, has never made any attempt to enforce this section of the Fourteenth Amendment.

The Fourteenth Amendment, in addition to restricting a state's right to discriminate against Negro voters, also authorizes Congress to enact any legislation necessary and proper to enforce the prohibitions of the amendment. Federal authority can be used to prevent any kind of governmental action designed to keep Negroes from voting because of their race.

What the Fourteenth Amendment does implicitly, the Fifteenth does explicitly: "The right of citizens of the United States to vote shall not be denied or abridged by the United States or by any State on account of race, color, or previous condition of servitude." The Fifteenth Amendment also empowers Congress to enact any law necessary and proper to enforce the prohibitions of the amendment.

For over a decade after the Civil War, the provisions of the Fourteenth and Fifteenth Amendments were backed up by federal troops. Negroes, in alliance with northern Radical Republicans ("carpetbaggers") and certain white southerners ("scalawags"), assumed full control of some state governments. The new regimes passed good laws as well as bad, but they were loathed by "patriotic" white southerners.

Then came the counter-revolution. Even before federal troops were withdrawn from the South in 1877, white Democrats had begun to regain power. Organizing secret societies like the Knights of the White Camelia and the Ku Klux Klan, the aroused southerners set out to restore southern government to white rule. Often they resorted to threats, force, and fraud, to midnight shootings, burnings, and whippings. Many Negroes concluded that it would be healthier to stay away from the polls than to insist on their vote, and the carpetbaggers began to retreat north.

Circumventing the Fourteenth and Fifteenth Amendments "Legally"

Once they had regained control of southern state governments, southern Democrats resolved to continue to keep the Negro from voting. At first they continued to rely only on social pressures and threats of violence. But toward the end of the nineteenth century, for the first time since the Civil War, in many parts of the South there were two strong parties, the Democrats and the Populists. White supremacists were fearful that the competing political parties might bid for the Negro's vote and the Negro might come to have a balance-of-power role. They searched for "legal" ways to disfranchise the Negro. To continue to rely on extra-legal and illegal means had other disadvantages: It undermined the moral fabric of the society, and for many years southerners feared that a too flagrant use of force and fraud might cause the President and Congress to intervene.[9]

Southern leaders reasoned that if laws could be passed which, while ostensibly not denying Negroes the right to vote because of their race, deprived them of it on other grounds, the Negroes would find it difficult to challenge the laws in the courts. Some whites protested, saying that such laws could be used against whites as well as Negroes. But the likelihood that the laws would keep poor whites from voting did not disturb the conservative leaders of the Democratic

[9] Frederic D. Ogden, *The Poll Tax in the South* (Univ. of Alabama Press, 1958), pp. 30–31.

party in control of some southern states, for they were often just as anxious to undermine white support for the Populist party as they were to disfranchise Negroes. Leaders in the Black Belt, where Negroes constituted a large minority and sometimes even a majority, skillfully played on memories of Negro rule and northern intervention. "The disfranchisement movement of the 'nineties,' " says V. O. Key, "gave the southern states the most impressive system of obstacles between the voter and the ballot box known to the democratic world." [10] And, "The southern states have a kind of defense in depth against the would-be Negro voter," says Dayton McKean; "If one barrier falls before courts or legislature there is another behind it." [11]

The White Primary. The Fourteenth and Fifteenth Amendments forbid *states* to deprive Negroes of the right to vote. But in the South, for most state and local offices the decisive political contests are the *primary* elections within the Democratic party (see Chapter 13); in most sections, Republicans are so scarce that the Democratic nominee is usually an easy winner in the fall elections. Obviously, exclusion of the Negro from the Democratic primary would deprive him of much influence in politics. And for many years the white primary was the most important disfranchising technique. The constitutional argument was that the primary was set up by a political party, not by the state, and a political party, as a voluntary association, has as much right to exclude people from its activities as does the Elks, or the Daughters of the American Revolution, or any other social group.

Then in 1944 the Supreme Court in *Smith* v. *Allwright* took a realistic look at the white primary and concluded that where primaries are essential steps in the selection of public officials they comprise a basic part of governmental machinery, and that discrimination by the party is as unconstitutional as discrimination by the state.

Some states tried to circumvent the Smith decision. South Carolina, for example, made party primaries completely private and repealed all its laws—147 of them—controlling party nominations. But the maneuver failed. A federal district judge held that if the state turned over the control of elections to a political party, the party is no longer a private club. "It is time," he said, "for South Carolina to rejoin the Union." [12] Other devices such as primaries before the primaries were also struck down by the courts as subterfuges.

Racial Gerrymandering. In 1957 the Alabama legislature redefined the city limits of Tuskegee in such a way as to remove from the city all but four or five of the 400 Negro voters. The legislature hoped to take advantage of the fact that heretofore federal courts had been unwilling to set aside election district boundaries. But the Supreme Court (*Gomillion* v. *Lightfoot*) ruled that this racial

[10] V. O. Key, Jr., *Southern Politics* (Knopf, 1949), p. 555.
[11] Dayton D. McKean, *Party and Pressure Politics* (Houghton Mifflin, 1949), p. 66.
[12] *Brown* v. *Baskin* (1948) and *Terry* v. *Adams* (1953).

gerrymandering so clearly violated the Fifteenth Amendment that the lower courts were instructed to set it aside.[13]

Negroes, along with white urban voters, have also been under-represented in southern state legislatures. In southern cities many Negroes do vote but their votes, along with those of white city voters, have less of an impact on the southern legislatures than the over-represented white rural southerners, the groups who are most insistent on segregation and most opposed to extending to Negroes the right to vote. Until recently there was no legal remedy to overcome this discrimination against urban voters in the drawing of election districts.

Then in 1962, in *Baker* v. *Carr*, the Supreme Court ruled that federal judges do have jurisdiction to hear complaints of city voters who have arbitrarily been denied fair representation in the state legislatures. Two years later, in *Reynolds* v. *Sims*, the Supreme Court held that both chambers of the legislature must be apportioned on the basis of population and that the only constitutionally valid standard for determining legislative representation is population. These decisions, although not directly aimed at discrimination against Negro voters, by providing more equitable representation of urban voters will increase the voice of white moderates and Negro voters in the state legislatures.

The Poll Tax. The best-known, though perhaps the least important, disfranchising device is a tax that need not be paid unless one wants to vote. (This type of poll tax is to be distinguished from head taxes levied by some states whether one votes or not and payment of which is not a prerequisite to vote.)

The poll tax puts a price tag on the ballot. The price is not high but its payment places an additional obstacle in the path of the voter. In Mississippi, for example, the tax must be paid two years in a row, and comes due in January, a long time before there is any campaign to focus attention on the ballot. The poll tax probably keeps the ballot from more whites than Negroes and today is of major significance in reducing the suffrage only in Alabama and Mississippi.

The poll tax is on the way out. Since 1920, North Carolina, Louisiana, Florida, Georgia, South Carolina, Tennessee, and Arkansas have abolished it; it exists only in Alabama, Mississippi, Texas, and Virginia. The Twenty-fourth Amendment forbids any state to deny a person the right to vote in "any primary or other election" for President, Vice President, United States Senator or Representative because of failure to pay any tax, but left states free to require such taxes as a condition for voting for state and local offices. As part of the Voting Rights Act of 1965, Congress came close to an outright ban on the poll tax for *any* election for *any* office on the grounds that the tax is not intended to establish a qualification for voting but to impose a burden upon the right to vote as a means of circumventing the Fifteenth Amendment.

Opponents of an outright ban did not defend the poll tax but argued that Congress lacked the constitutional authority, especially in the face of the language of the Twenty-fourth Amendment, to impose an outright ban on all poll taxes.

---

[13] See Bernard Taper, *Gomillion* v. *Lightfoot; The Tuskegee Gerrymander Case* (McGraw-Hill, 1962), for a detailed account.

Rather, they contended, it is the discriminatory use of the tax to keep Negroes from voting that is unconstitutional, and such practices should be challenged in the courts. The matter was compromised by a congressional declaration that in view of the fact that the payment of a poll tax in some states and localities is a device to abridge the right to vote, the Attorney General should institute "forthwith" court action against the enforcement of poll taxes or any substitute for such taxes enacted after November 1, 1964, that had the purpose or effect of abridging a person's right to vote. Twenty-five hours after President Johnson signed the Voting Rights Act of 1965, the Justice Department filed suit in the federal court in Jackson, Mississippi, charging that the Mississippi poll tax constituted a "substantial restriction on the right of otherwise qualified persons to vote. . . ." Similar suits quickly followed in other southern states.

Discriminatory Applications of Registration Requirements such as Literacy, Understanding, and Good Character Tests. As the white primary, poll taxes, racial gerrymandering, and other laws that on their face clearly denied Negroes the right to vote have been declared unconstitutional, those wishing to deny Negroes the right to vote have placed primary reliance on registration requirements. On their face, these requirements appear to be perfectly proper. It is the manner in which they are administered that keeps Negroes from the polls, for they are often applied by white election officers, while white policemen stand guard, with white judges hearing appeals—if any—from decisions of registration officials.

Registration officials often seize on the smallest error in an application blank as an excuse to disqualify a hopeful voter. In one Louisiana parish, after four white voters filed affidavits in which they challenged the legality of the registration of Negro voters on the grounds that these voters in their applications had made an "error in spilling" (*sic*), registration officials struck 1,300 out of approximately 1,500 Negro voters from the voting rolls.[14] In other instances, Negroes have been denied the right to register because in listing their ages, they did not stipulate the precise number of days.

Literacy tests have also been used to deny Negroes the right to vote. Most southern states, as well as states elsewhere, require citizens wishing to register to demonstrate that they can read or write. Literacy tests, as such, are perfectly proper and constitutional, but it is in their application that they are abused, for the registrars have such wide discretion in determining who is "literate" and who is not.

Some southern states, either as an additional requirement or as a substitute for literacy tests, require an applicant to demonstrate to the satisfaction of election officials that he understands the national and state constitutions and that he is a person of good character. Even more than literacy tests these understanding tests encourage discrimination against Negro voters. Whites may be asked simple questions about the Constitution; Negroes may be asked questions that would baffle a Supreme Court Justice. In Louisiana, where illiterates were allowed to

[14] *Report of the United States Commission on Civil Rights, 1959* (Government Printing Office, 1959), pp. 103–104.

qualify to vote if they could pass an understanding test, 49,603 illiterate white voters were able to persuade election officials they could understand the Constitution, but only two Negroes were able to do so.

Intimidation. The white primary, the poll tax, racial gerrymandering, and in recent years, through intervention of the Department of Justice, the grosser forms of discrimination in registration are no longer so readily available to those attempting to keep Negroes from voting. But in some rural areas and small towns, intimidation and even threats of physical violence are still used to "persuade" Negroes that they should not attempt to register and vote. Even these devices, however, are ceasing to be effective. With educated leadership and more cohesive organization, Negroes can no longer be easily intimidated, and those who try to break up Negro registration drives now know that their activities are likely to be exposed to the world via television, newsreels, and the press. Moreover, there is always the danger of federal intervention.

In summary, and in the words of President Johnson: "Every device of which human ingenuity is capable has been used to deny this right. The Negro citizen may go to register only to be told that the day is wrong, or the hour is late, or the official in charge is absent. And if he persists and if he manages to present himself to the registrar, he may be disqualified because he did not spell out his middle name or because he abbreviated a word on the application. And if he manages to fill out an application, he is given a test. The registrar is the sole judge of whether he passes this test. He may be asked to recite the entire constitution, or explain the most complex provisions of state laws. And even a college degree cannot be used to prove that he can read and write. For the fact is that the only way to pass these barriers is to show a white skin."

The National Government Acts

Although for over twenty years federal courts, under the leadership of the Supreme Court, have scrutinized carefully laws and procedures in cases brought by Negroes who had been denied the right to vote, this case-by-case procedure did not open the voting booth for millions of Negroes, especially those living in rural areas of the deep South. As the United States Civil Rights Commission reported, "Suits must proceed in a single court at a time, and they are time consuming, expensive, and difficult. After one law or procedure is enjoined, the state or county would adopt another." [15] Faced with growing and insistent economic, social, and political pressures from Negroes and with a growing national consensus that the right to vote should be guaranteed by the national government, Congress since 1957 has enacted civil rights laws that have progressively expanded the national government's role in securing for Negroes the right to vote.

[15] United States Commission on Civil Rights, *Report* (Government Printing Office, 1959), and 1961 *Civil Rights, Excerpts*, p. 18.

The Civil Rights Acts of 1957 and 1960 still left the major responsibility to the courts. The Department of Justice was empowered to seek federal injunctions. Federal judges were authorized to hold prompt hearings and appeals were allowed directly from these courts to the Supreme Court. Federal judges were permitted to appoint registrars actually to register Negro voters if on application of the Attorney General the judges found a pattern or persistent practice of discrimination to exist; thus each Negro did not have to file a lawsuit in order to get a chance to vote.

In the Civil Rights Act of 1964, Congress took another step. Without going outside the courtroom framework, Congress strengthened the basic federal civil rights statute that applies to voting. The 1964 Act (further strengthened by the Voting Rights Act of 1965) stipulates that no person shall be denied the right to vote because of inability to read or write in English if he demonstrates that he has successfully completed the equivalent of the sixth grade in an accredited school under the American flag. In elections in which federal officials are nominated or elected, oral literacy tests are prohibited, as is the denial of the right to vote because of irrelevant and minor errors or omissions on application forms. The American flag was stipulated by the 1965 Voting Rights amendment in order to protect the right to vote of Puerto Ricans who have moved to the mainland, but many of whom are not able to pass literacy tests given in English.

In 1965 the Supreme Court declared unconstitutional the use of understanding tests where voting registrars are given discretion to determine who has passed and who had failed. The Court also ruled that a written citizenship test could not be substituted for an understanding test unless all voters, including those previously registered, are subject to the same test.[16]

The 1964 Civil Rights Act hardly had been enacted when events in Selma, Alabama, dramatically showed the inadequacy of dependence on the courts as the major federal instrument to prevent racial barriers in polling places. The voter registration drive in that city by Martin Luther King and his associates produced police arrests, further demonstrations, marches on the state capitol, and the murdering of two civil rights workers, but there was no major dent in the color bans at the polls.

The Selma protests culminated in President Johnson's making a dramatic address to the nation and to the Congress in which he called for final federal action to insure to each person that he would not be deprived of his right to vote in any election for any office because of the color of his skin. Congress responded with an even stronger measure.

The Voting Rights Act of 1965

The Voting Rights Act of 1965 is a major departure from the approach of the prior civil rights acts which depended first on legal action, and then, after the lawsuit was over, on state and local officials to carry the court order into effect. The Voting Rights Act of 1965

[16] *Louisiana* v. *United States* (1965).

authorizes *direct action* by *federal executives* to register voters and to see to it that these voters are allowed to cast their ballot and that the ballot is honestly counted.

Today the suppression of Negro voters is concentrated in about 100 rural counties in Alabama, Florida, Georgia, Louisiana, Mississippi, North Carolina, South Carolina, and Tennessee.[17] The Voting Rights Act of 1965 concentrates on these areas. In states or political subdivisions in which less than 25 per cent of voting-age Negroes are registered to vote, or in areas in which less than 50 per cent of the voting-age population of Negroes was registered to vote on November 1, 1964, or actually voted in the 1964 presidential elections, and which required on that date a literacy, understanding, or good character test, the Attorney General may, *without intervening court action*, call upon the Civil Service Commission to appoint federal examiners. Outside of the areas covered by these "triggering formulas," the Attorney General must secure approval for the appointment of federal examiners by carrying his complaint of voter discrimination to a federal court.

Federal examiners are to ignore literacy and other tests that have been used by local registration officials to discriminate against Negroes and to make their own examination to see which voters are otherwise qualified under the laws of the state or political subdivision to which they are assigned. And to keep states from constantly changing voter requirements in order to prevent Negroes from registering, in the areas to which federal examiners are appointed new voting laws are not to be effective unless approved by the Attorney General or by a three-judge district court for the District of Columbia. Each month, up to forty-five days before any election, federal examiners transmit to the appropriate election officials a list of voters they have determined are qualified to vote.

If election officials turn away from the polls any voter that the federal examiners have determined is entitled to vote, the examiners may go into a federal district court and secure an order impounding all the ballots until persons entitled to vote are allowed to do so. In addition, the Attorney General may appoint poll-watchers to enter voting places, and ballots are counted in order to insure that the votes of all qualified persons are properly counted. Existing criminal provisions of civil rights laws were also strengthened by specifically making it a federal offense, punishable by five years in prison and a $5,000 fine, for anybody, private citizen or public official, to intimidate or otherwise interfere with any person attempting to exercise his right to vote.

States or political subdivisions subject to the Voting Rights Act of 1965 may seek exemption from it only by proving to a three-judge district court for the District of Columbia that during the last five years they have not in fact kept Negroes from voting because of their race. It is significant that Congress placed this matter outside the jurisdiction of the federal district judges sitting in the states and subdivisions subject to the Act. Some of the latter judges had shown an unwilling-

[17] United States Commission on Civil Rights, *Civil Rights, op. cit.*, p. 15. See also H. D. Price, *The Negro and Southern Politics* (New York Univ. Press, 1957), and Margaret Price, *The Negro and the Ballot in the South* (Southern Regional Council, 1959).

ness in past legal proceedings to scrutinize carefully state and local regulations discriminating against Negro voters or to apply with vigor civil rights statutes.

What the Voting Rights Act of 1965 means is that federal authority displaces state authority over voting in the affected counties, and the federal government enrolls and protects the right to vote of all those who are qualified to do so. States still determine the qualifications for voting, but in areas where there is a long history of the use of state and local authority to violate the Fifteenth and Fourteenth Amendments, Congress has determined that the only necessary and proper way to enforce these amendments is for the national government to step in and directly handle voter registration.

The Results

Are Negroes winning their long fight for the ballot? They are, slowly, though the pace is quickening. Outside the South neither social pressures nor legal barriers discriminate against Negro voters. And in most southern cities there are no obstacles. Today the problem is most acute in a few areas and in these areas the Voting Rights Act of 1965 will have its most dramatic impact.

The rate of increase of Negro voting in the South, after increasing sharply in the 1940's as a result of Supreme Court decisions setting aside the most obvious discriminatory practices, was checked temporarily because of intensified hostility to the Supreme Court's school desegregation decisions. But with the renewed pressures by Negro voters and the growing intervention of federal power, the weight of Negro voting is increasing. Reapportionment of state legislatures, also a result of Supreme Court action, has also enhanced the political voice of Negroes, since rural domination and urban under-representation in southern legislatures meant that Negroes who were allowed to vote in the cities along with their white brethren did not secure as much representation in the legislatures as their voting power entitled them to.

The Negro vote is already an important factor in southern cities. In at least a dozen such cities Negroes are serving on city councils or boards of education. In the upper South and even in some deep South states such as Georgia, Negroes are being elected to the state legislatures. In a growing number of areas and election contests, public officials no longer find that it is always politically profitable to be identified with the more extreme white supremacists.

Many southern whites want the Negro to have the ballot, but not immediately. Hodding Carter, editor of a Mississippi newspaper, has said that Negroes must have more education before they vote, so that they will learn to vote, not "by color and for color," but in terms of enlightened self-interest. He wants more schools for Negroes, decent housing, better health facilities. "We want all this too," say Negro leaders, "but how can we get it unless we can vote for it at the polls?" Increased voting by Negroes and better education for Negroes must go hand in hand, one fortifying the other. But full Negro voting will not come automatically even after all external barriers have been destroyed. Negro voters—like voters everywhere—also stay away from the polls because of ignorance and inertia. For even in the North and in southern cities where Negroes are free to vote if they wish, many do not. Negro political apathy is much like that of white voters, but it is perhaps more pronounced because of a sense of inferiority and of the importance of "staying out of trouble," products of decades of deference and subordination. In the last analysis, the solution is both to insure the Negro the right to vote, and also to help him, like any other citizen, to see that he has a duty to participate in democratic politics.

The Struggle for Color-Blind Justice

Of all the sectors of the civil rights front, perhaps the most difficult to deal with by legislation, and the one in which the role of the national government is most limited, is the administration of justice. The Constitution reserves to the states the primary responsibility for the administration of justice, with the national government's function being chiefly restricted to supervision of action by the states to secure compliance with constitutional standards. Beginning in the 1930's the Supreme Court started to apply the Fourteenth Amendment to reverse all convictions by state and local governments where there is evidence that Negroes fail to receive fair treatment.

If state or local police and prosecutors brutalize or intimidate Negroes, about the only federal statute that authorizes federal prosecution of these officials is the Civil Rights Act of 1866. This act makes it a federal offense, punishable by a fine of not more than $1,000 and imprisonment for not more than one year, for any person acting under color of law willfully to deprive any person of a right secured or protected by the Constitution of the United States.

In 1939 the Department of Justice created a Civil Rights Section to enforce the Civil Rights Act of 1866. Since that date it has tried to bring to justice public officials who willfully deprive persons of their constitutional rights. But the act is difficult to enforce, as is illustrated by the following revolting episode.

Late one night in 1944, a car stopped in front of the home of Robert Hall, a citizen of the United States and of Georgia. Three men got out of the car: Screws, the county sheriff, Jones, a policeman, and Kelly, a special deputy. The men had been drinking. A few days before, Screws had threatened Hall that he was going to get him, and Hall was terrified. Screws flashed a warrant charging Hall with the theft of a tire. Hall resisted, but the three men pushed him into the waiting car. The car pulled up in the courthouse square, Hall got out, and immediately the three men "began beating him with their fists and with a solid-bar blackjack about eight inches long and weighing two pounds." [18] Hall was handcuffed and defenseless, and the three men continued to beat him for fifteen

[18] *Screws v. United States* (1945).

to thirty minutes. Then the unconscious Hall was dragged feet first through the courthouse into the jail and thrown on the floor. He died within an hour.

Here was a clear case of murder, but as the days went by no action by state authorities was taken against the three men. Hall was a Negro. The matter was brought to the attention of the Civil Rights Section, but it waited for the state to punish the guilty men. Still no action. Finally, the Department of Justice started to move. Under the Civil Rights Act of 1866, the penalty for willfully subjecting any inhabitant, under color of any law, to the deprivation of any rights, privileges, or immunities secured or protected by the Constitution and laws of the United States is a fine of not more than $1,000 and prison sentence for not more than one year. Admittedly this was puny punishment for such a heinous crime, puny even when combined with the possible two-year imprisonment for conspiring to violate a federal law. But at least it would serve notice that the federal government was not powerless to protect rights guaranteed by the Constitution against abuse by state officials.

The federal officials, careful lest they arouse local resistance to outside interference, assigned only southern attorneys to the case. An indictment was secured against Screws and his companions for willfully causing Hall to be deprived of rights secured to him or protected by the Fourteenth Amendment, specifically the right not to be deprived of life without due process of law; the right to be tried by due process upon the charge on which he was arrested; and, if found guilty, the right to be punished in accordance with the laws.

The case proceeded. In his charge to the jury, the judge said that if the jurors believed that the facts were established, then the "defendants would be depriving Hall of certain constitutional rights guaranteed to him by the Constitution of the United States and consented to by the State of Georgia."

The jury's verdict, "Guilty." But the case was not over. Screws turned to the court of appeals, which affirmed the decision of the trial court. The case then went to the Supreme Court. A majority of the justices felt (there were five separate opinions) that the trial judge had erred in failing to instruct the jury that Screws and his companions could be held guilty of the crime only if they had "willfully" intended to deprive Hall of his constitutional rights, that it was not sufficient that Screws had a generally bad intent.

The case was returned to the district courts for a retrial. Screws and his friends were duly retried. This time they were acquitted. And as the United States Commission on Civil Rights stated, "The episode did not seriously tarnish the reputation of Claude M. Screws. In 1958 he ran for the State Senate and was elected." [19]

The Department of Justice has been more successful in other cases. In 1947, for example, Crews, a Florida town marshal, arrested a Negro and, after beating him with a heavy whip, forced him to jump from a high bridge into a river. The Negro drowned. Crews was successfully convicted of violating the civil rights statute, and this time the conviction was sustained.[20] In another case, a private

[19] United States Commission on Civil Rights, *Justice, op. cit.*, p. 9.
[20] *Crews v. United States* (1947).

detective (but authorized by law to act as a special police officer) was convicted of extracting a confession from a prisoner by physical brutality.[21]

Civil Remedies against Public Officials

In addition to *criminal* statutes, the Civil Rights Act of 1871, as amended in 1964, authorizes persons whose constitutional rights are being abridged by state or local officials to sue these officials for damages in federal courts or to seek federal court injunctions. Persons brutalized by police officers may resort to federal courts to seek protection, even if redress is theoretically available in state courts. Since this is a civil and not a criminal statute, damages can be won and injunctions obtained without having to prove, as is true of criminal prosecutions, that the officers had a specific intent to deprive a person of his federally protected constitutional rights.

Negroes, working mainly through the NAACP, have had some notable successes using the civil remedies of the Act of 1871. But private litigants often have difficulty in gathering evidence to challenge the local authorities, and it can even be dangerous for them and for the lawyers who represent them. One white lawyer, for example, told the United States Commission on Civil Rights:

> I was born in North Carolina and raised in the hills of Eastern Tennessee, and I am in favor of the Civil Rights Statutes but must live with this as silent as the grave. I see my clients beat, abused and run over all of the time and there is nothing much I can do, because when I try in Federal Court I wind up with the hell beat out of me.[22]

The Department of Justice, which has the resources to obtain the evidence and the ability to withstand the pressures, has generally been given more and more authority by Congress to assist Negroes in protecting their civil rights. The 1964 Civil Rights Act permits the Attorney General to intervene in any civil rights suit whenever he thinks the case is of public importance. The more active role by the Department of Justice in civil rights cases has alerted state and local officers to the fact that they violate at their own peril the rights and privileges protected by the Constitution, but as the Civil Rights Commission has reported, "Little can be done directly to prevent police brutality itself until the police are more carefully selected, trained and controlled."[23]

Racially Motivated Crimes

The Fourteenth Amendment applies only to discriminatory conduct supported, sponsored, or encouraged by the use of the power of *government*. What if a private citizen murders or intimidates a Negro because he has tried to exercise his constitutional rights? This has be-

[21] *Williams* v. *United States* (1951). See also Burke Marshall, *Federalism and Civil Rights* (Columbia Univ. Press, 1964), pp. 45–48.
[22] United States Commission on Civil Rights, *Justice*, Report 5, 1961 (Government Printing Office, 1962), p. 69.
[23] United States Commission on Civil Rights, *Justice*, p. 9.

come a major national issue, for during the last decade more than a dozen civil rights leaders, mostly Negroes but some whites, have been murdered and scores have had their homes bombed, but few persons have ever been punished for these acts. State officials sometimes refuse to prosecute; even when they do so juries fail to convict.

The national government has limited constitutional authority to prosecute in its own courts private individuals accused of racially motivated crimes. The Thirteenth Amendment, unlike the Fourteenth, does apply to all persons and not just those acting under the color of law. This amendment by its own force freed the slaves in 1865, and prevents all forms of involuntary servitude. (This amendment, along with Section II of the Twenty-first, is unique in that by its own terms it directly and immediately applies to private individuals as well as to public officials.) The amendment authorizes Congress to pass whatever laws are necessary and proper to prevent slavery no matter who tries to impose it. Some have argued that since racial discrimination is a badge of servitude, under the Thirteenth Amendment Congress may enact a comprehensive federal code against any kind of racial discrimination whatever its source. But the Supreme Court has given the Thirteenth Amendment a more limited meaning; the amendment merely authorizes Congress to legislate against slavery narrowly defined and peonage. (Peonage is a condition of compulsory servitude based on indebtedness of the worker to the employer.)

Congress has other constitutional power, however, to protect American citizens in the exercise of their constitutional rights, especially rights stemming from federal laws or having to do with the relations between American citizens and the national government itself: such things as the right to petition Congress or to travel freely throughout the United States.

Whatever its constitutional power, Congress has so far not chosen to permit extensive federal protection from, or prosecution for, racially motivated crimes. About the only general federal law that applies is the antiquated Civil Rights Act of 1870 (the Ku Klux Klan Law) that makes it a federal crime, punishable by ten years of imprisonment and $5,000 fine, for two or more persons to *conspire* to deprive a citizen in the enjoyment of any right or privilege secured to him by the Constitution or federal laws. Heretofore the courts have so narrowly construed this statute that it has seldom been used. It is not too difficult to predict, however, that there will be growing pressures for a more active federal role if state and local governments fail to apply justice even-handedly or allow persons to go unpunished for intimidating or murdering Negroes and whites trying to help Negroes secure their civil rights.

The Color Bar to Homes, Jobs, and Public Accommodations

Until recently, those who wanted to keep Negroes from buying homes, or eating lunches in the same stores or working in the same plants with white persons, could use the power of government to enforce these discriminatory practices. Laws and regulations that interfere with equal access to homes, jobs, or public accommodations are now unconstitutional. Yet Negroes still have difficulty buying homes, getting jobs, or securing service in public places. Such discriminatory action by private individuals does not of itself violate the Constitution. For the Fourteenth Amendment only forbids discrimination by *states*, including, of course, all units of the states, and the Fifteenth Amendment only forbids discrimination by *national* authorities. Unless discrimination is openly sanctioned or supported by the state, the Fourteenth Amendment offers the victim no protection or redress at all.

In recent decades, however, the Supreme Court has significantly expanded the concept of "state action" in support of discrimination. For example, it has ruled that though there is nothing unconstitutional about making or signing racially restrictive covenants (provisions attached to deeds restricting the sale or use of property to certain groups), court *enforcement* of such covenants is *state* action and therefore unconstitutional.[24] In another line of cases the Supreme Court has held that trade unions whose right to engage in collective bargaining is protected by the government may not discriminate.[25] The Court has held that those who lease space in public buildings to operate restaurants are subject to the Fourteenth Amendment prohibitions against state discrimination.[26] And, as we have seen, the Supreme Court has come very close to the position that the holding and conduct of elections in which public officials are nominated or elected is a *governmental* function and hence whoever discharges these functions is restrained by the Constitution.

A more difficult constitutional issue grew out of the arrest for trespassing of Negroes who, to protest denial of service, refused to leave lunch counters and other facilities privately owned but opened to the public. They contended that arrest by the police and conviction by the state courts would be an unconstitutional use of state power to support discrimination. Others argued that if owners of privately owned businesses wished to refuse service to Negroes, the state could protect their right to do so. The Supreme Court had no difficulty in deciding that if state laws or actions in effect forced the operator of the place of public accommodation to refuse nonsegregated service to Negroes, a state could not prosecute persons for peacefully attempting to secure their rights. What would happen in a community where there is no governmental pressure on the place of public accommodation to discriminate is a question that may not be presented. With the passage of the Civil Rights Act of 1964 few businesses any longer have a legal right to discriminate against their customers because of race.

State Civil Rights Programs

Although private acts of discrimination are not unconstitutional, these acts may be *illegal*. Just as the states have the authority to protect a person's property rights against infringement by others,

[24] *Shelley* v. *Kraemer* (1948) and *Barrows* v. *Jackson* (1953).
[25] *Conley* v. *Gibson* (1957).
[26] *Burton* v. *Wilmington Parking Authority* (1961).

so they have the authority to protect civil rights. And so does the national government (as noted below).

Should governments use their powers to make it illegal for landlords, employers, trade unions, private schools, and others to discriminate against persons because of their race or religion? "No," say some people. Prejudice cannot be eradicated by laws. Others respond that if laws cannot eradicate prejudice itself, they *can* eliminate the *product*—actual overt discriminatory action that deprives people of their right to be treated as human beings and American citizens.

In the South, as we have noted, state laws require segregation, and they are still being enforced despite their unconstitutionality. But other states *outlaw* segregation and other kinds of racial or religious discrimination. Discrimination by owners and operators of places of public recreation and accommodation has long been a tort (civil wrong) under the common law, and thirty-two states have special statutes making it a criminal or civil offense for places of public accommodation to refuse to serve patrons because of their race, religion, or place of national origin. Twenty-two states apply these civil rights statutes to private employers, and the same number prohibit unions from controlling membership on the basis of race or religion. Some states have made it illegal for university authorities to discriminate racially or religiously against students seeking to enter colleges or universities, except, of course, in the case of application of religious standards by church-operated schools. Some cities forbid landlords to discriminate. Almost all northern states forbid discrimination in public employment.

The weakness of some of these civil rights statutes is that they make no special provision for enforcement other than by regular court action instituted by public prosecutors or through the initiation of law suits by the person being discriminated against. Frequently, the persons who are denied a job or service have neither the knowledge to bring the matter to the attention of prosecutors nor the money to undertake a civil suit. Moreover, many prosecutors have been somewhat less than eager to take action.

The ineffectiveness of criminal laws against discrimination and of dependence on damage suits brought by the aggrieved persons has led to a new development in the enforcement of civil rights.[27] New York in 1945 created a commission charged with investigating and hearing complaints in instances of alleged discrimination, and since then eighteen additional states and numerous cities containing over half of the total population of the United States have established such special civil rights commissions with the exclusive duty of acting against discrimination.

The New York procedures are typical. The Commission for Human Rights is responsible for enforcing the state laws forbidding racial, religious, and national-origin discrimination by employers, labor unions, places of public accommodation, and governmentally aided housing projects. (Laws covering discrimination in educational institutions are enforced by the Commissioner of Education and Board

[27] "Anti-Discrimination Commissions," *Race Relations Law Reporter*, October, 1958, pp. 1085–1108 (Vanderbilt Univ. School of Law); *Summary of 1960 and 1961 State Discrimination Laws* (Commission on Law and Social Justice of American Jewish Congress, 1962).

of Regents.) Any person suffering such discrimination may file a complaint with the commission. If, after investigation, the commission finds the complaint is justified, it first tries to remove the cause through "conference, conciliation, and persuasion." If these efforts fail, a formal hearing takes place before at least three members of the commission. If the commission discovers evidence of violation of the law, it orders the offender to cease and desist from such practices. Violation of a commission order is punishable by imprisonment for not more than one year or by a fine of not more than $500 or both. The courts may review decisions of the commission on questions of law. The commission has seldom had to resort to its coercive powers, and through a program of education and publicity it has done much to improve human relations in this most difficult of all fields.

Other states and cities have similar procedures.In some places the commissions have advisory rather than regulatory powers and cannot punish offenders. Although commissions operate in most of the border states with many southern traditions, as yet none have been established in southern areas.

National Protection against Private Discrimination

What of the national government? It was the hope of some of the congressmen who proposed the Fourteenth Amendment that its ratification would authorize federal action against nongovernmental discrimination, but this hope was quickly dashed by the Supreme Court. In 1875 Congress made it a federal offense for any owner or operator of a public conveyance, hotel, or theater to deny accommodations to any person because of his race or color. In the Civil Rights Cases (1883), the Supreme Court invalidated this law on the ground that the Fourteenth Amendment applies only to *state* action and does not give Congress authority to forbid discrimination by *private* individuals. The Civil Rights Cases brought to a temporary halt federal protection against nongovernmentally imposed discrimination. By 1888 Congress had ceased to have any interest in such laws, and the matter was left to the states.

The trouble was that the states where most of the discrimination took place did nothing. The Presidency was the first agency of the national government to become sensitive to the aspirations of Negroes. Since the 1940's Presidents have used their executive authority to extend civil rights. President Roosevelt ordered all contractors and sub-contractors of the federal government to agree not to discriminate against any employee or applicant for employment because of race, religion, color, or national origin. Today the Secretary of Labor supervises a vigorous program to insure compliance by several million government contractors. President Truman ordered discrimination to cease in federal employment and the abolition of segregation in the armed forces. President Kennedy signed an order to prevent federal funds from being used to support housing programs that are not available to Negroes. The Interstate Commerce Commission and the Civil Aeronautics Board ordered interstate carriers to cease segregating their passengers. But all these actions have been swallowed in significance by the adoption of the Civil Rights Act of 1964.

Civil Rights Act of 1964—
Places of Public Accommodation, Title II

For the first time since Reconstruction Congress, through the Civil Rights Act of 1964, authorized the massive use of federal authority to combat privately imposed racial discrimination. Title II forbids discrimination in *places of accommodation*. Since the Supreme Court's decision in the Civil Rights Cases of 1883 cast some doubt about the power of Congress under the Fourteenth Amendment to legislate against discrimination by operators of places of public accommodation, Congress based Title II on the commerce clause.

Title II makes it a federal offense to discriminate against any customer or patron because of his race, color, religion, or national origin. It applies to any inn, hotel, motel, or lodging establishment (except establishments with less than five rooms and occupied by the proprietor, in other words, small boarding houses); to any restaurant or gasoline station that offers to serve interstate travelers, or which serves food or products, a substantial portion of which have moved in interstate commerce; and to any motion picture house, theater, concert hall, sports arena, or other place of entertainment that customarily presents films, performances, athletic teams, or other sources of entertainment that are moved in interstate commerce. Title II also applies to any establishment that attempts to discriminate or segregate in response to state law or order of any public official.

The Attorney General may initiate proceedings as well as intervene in cases initiated by aggrieved individuals. States with laws against discrimination in places of public accommodation are given thirty days to see if they can bring about compliance. Federal judges may refer complaints to the Community Relations Service (see page 187) in order to seek voluntary compliance. But if these procedures fail, judges are to provide prompt hearings with direct appeals to the Supreme Court whenever the Attorney General believes the case is of general public importance.

Within a few months of its enactment into law, the Supreme Court unanimously sustained the constitutionality of Title II. "That Congress was legislating against moral wrongs . . . does not detract from the overwhelming evidence of the disruptive effect that racial discrimination has had on commercial intercourse." Nor does it matter that if considered in isolation a particular inn's or motel's business may be considered primarily a local business. "If it is interstate commerce that feels the pinch, it does not matter how local the operation that applies the squeeze." The Court had before it evidence that Negroes were unable to engage freely in interstate travel because of denial to them of facilities to eat, sleep, and purchase supplies.[28]

Faced with the adoption of Title II, the determination of the Department of Justice to enforce it, and an organized program of testing by Negroes to publicize

[28] *Heart of Atlanta Motel* v. *U.S.*, 1964.

lack of compliances, most larger establishments in most cities, including those in the South, have opened their doors to all customers. Smaller establishments and especially those in the rural South still have not done so and are not likely to do so until legal, economic, and social pressures are brought to bear directly on them.

Civil Rights Act of 1964— Employment, Title VII

Title VII of the Civil Rights Act of 1964 makes it an unfair employment practice for any employer or trade union in any industry affecting interstate commerce to discriminate in any fashion or to segregate any person because of race, color, religion, sex, or national origin. (Religious institutions such as schools may use religious standards, and exceptions may be made to the ban against discrimination because of religion, sex, or national origin where there are bona fide occupational qualifications reasonably necessary to the normal operation of a particular business or enterprise. For example, it is not an unlawful employment practice for an employer to refuse to hire a woman to perform a job that requires unusual physical strength.) The law, which went into effect on July 2, 1965, applies the first year to firms and unions with 100 or more employees or members and each year drops down by 25 to include additional firms until July 1968 when it will cover employers or unions with 25 or more employees or members.

Employers and trade unions subject to the act are required to keep records and make them available to federal authorities and to take whatever steps are necessary to bring about non-discriminatory hirings. The Equal Employment Opportunity Commission, consisting of five members appointed by the President with the consent of the Senate, has overall responsibility for bringing about compliance. The commission is instructed to work with state authorities and to use conciliation and persuasion wherever possible. The commission may not itself order an employer or trade union to comply, but if it fails to persuade, those who have been discriminated against and the Attorney General may bring civil suits in the federal courts. If the Attorney General feels that a firm or trade union is engaged in a willful and persistent pattern of resistance, he may request a prompt hearing before a three-judge federal court from which direct appeals to the Supreme Court are possible.

The Federal Presence and Civil Rights

The recently expanded involvement of the national government in the field of civil rights has produced many different federal agencies with responsibilities in this field. In addition to those previously mentioned, the more prominent of these federal civil rights agencies are:

United States Commission on Civil Rights. Created by the Civil Rights Act of 1957. Consisting of six national leaders, the commission serves as a national clearing house. Its public hearings and reports to the Congress have focused national and congressional attention on the more flagrant violations of civil rights, and its recommendations have had a major impact on congressional legislation and executive actions.

Community Relations Service. Created by the Civil Rights Act of 1964 as a unit within the Department of Commerce, in 1966 it was due to be shifted to the Department of Justice in accordance with President Johnson's recommendation. It serves as a conciliation service working with community leaders where conflict among the races often has shown the lack of any kind of local machinery to bring leaders from both races together. Federal courts also refer to the service complaints presented by lawsuits to desegregate public accommodations to see if voluntary compliance can be obtained.

There are dozens of other civil rights agencies. In addition, Title VI of the Civil Rights Act of 1964 directs "each federal department and agency which is empowered to extend federal financial assistance to any program or activity, by way of grant, loan, or contract to take the necessary action to insure that no person in the United States shall, on the ground of race, color, or national origin, be excluded from participation in, be denied the benefits of, or be subject to discrimination under any program or activity receiving Federal financial assistance."

Though sometimes overlooked in discussions of federal civil rights activities, the Economic Opportunity Act of 1964 and other anti-poverty programs that provide federal funds and technical assistance to states, local communities, and private agencies to support a variety of programs to motivate individuals and provide them with job skills, may prove to be the most important federal civil rights program. For Negroes more than any other group have felt the impact of technological change that has made obsolete large numbers of unskilled jobs. Discriminated against, forced into urban ghettos, and suffering from the social ills of all groups that have been subjected to these conditions, many Negroes are unable to take advantage of the opportunities for employment that are progressively being made available to them. Through the programs provided under the Economic Opportunity Act, many will be given training and counseling to develop the attitudes, skills, and ambitions that will permit them to break out from the vicious cycle of discrimination and poverty.

It is easy to get lost in the maze of federal and state civil rights laws, to become confused by the refined distinctions made in courts of law, and to perceive the struggle to secure civil rights as one involving only constitutional and legal questions. But we are what we are, and the laws and constitutional provisions are what they are, because of a complicated interaction among social, economic, legal, and political developments.[29]

[29] Grimes, *op. cit.*, pp. 41–85.

The federal presence in civil rights was a long time in coming. As we have seen, after the Civil War the federal government did briefly try to secure for the recently freed slaves some measure of protection. But Negroes were largely uneducated, illiterate, and completely dependent on the white community for their bread. Unlettered and undemanding, they were an insignificant political force. In 1877 the federal government withdrew from the field and left Negroes to their own resources. For decades, Negroes did not count politically or economically or socially and as a result they were segregated and discriminated against.

With the growth of an educated Negro middle class, the struggle for civil rights was renewed. By the 1930's, as a result of the migration of Negroes to the North, the industrialization and urbanization in the South, the Great Depression, and the New Deal, Negroes began to emerge as a significant political group in presidential elections. In the South they still lacked a political voice and had to depend almost exclusively on the lawsuit as their only weapon to protect their rights. But with growing economic independence, leadership, and the vote, and because of the special nature of the electoral college (see pages 366–369), by the 1930's no man in the White House or any who aspired to live there could afford any longer to ignore the aspirations of Negroes.

On many occasions Presidents used their executive authority to secure greater protection for Negroes, and they urged Congress to act. The commitment of our Presidents to the cause of civil rights became translated into the appointment of federal judges who began to give a more generous construction to the constitutional claims of Negroes, and to reverse earlier decisions that had narrowly construed civil rights laws. The Supreme Court began to apply the Fourteenth Amendment to protect rights of Negroes, as had been the intent of those who proposed it.

At the end of World War II—a war against racism—the nation began a national debate over civil rights. Negro leaders and many others urged Congress to adopt federal laws to protect civil rights. White southerners and many others contended that federal civil rights laws would upset the federal system and lead to a dangerous centralization of power. They insisted that national legislation would be ineffective and create more problems than it solved. A national program could not be enforced if it overrode local public opinion, they contended. Let the states do the job, they argued, for they can protect civil rights by laws adapted to the attitudes of the local citizenry. Anyway, they added, "you can't legislate morality."

Champions of national action argued that states had failed to protect civil rights, and, in fact, in many areas the state governments themselves were the major instruments of discrimination. Furthermore, the denial of civil rights is not merely a local matter, for it has national and international implications. The national Constitution promises to every person who lives in the United States that he will receive equal treatment before the law without respect to his race, religion, or national origin, and it is up to the national government to see that this promise is kept. Whatever the speculative merits of local rather than national action, as a matter of practical political fact, observance of civil rights will be extended only by the *national majority* using the power of the *national government*. For as one southerner has noted, "no one concrete step toward full rights for the southern Negro—whether in voting or education—has been achieved without the intervention of the national government." [30]

By the end of the 1950's, the debate over whether the national government had a responsiblity to protect civil rights was over. The question became, What should it do? For the gradual development of a national consensus, and most important, the mobilization of the Negroes themselves, meant that Congress could not delay for long. Until 1957 the House of Representatives had frequently adopted civil rights bills, but the intense opposition of southern Democrats and the indifference of many conservative Republicans, combined with Senate rules that gave an advantage to a determined minority, made it impossible to get any positive Senate action. When Congress assembled in 1957, however, the political situation had changed. In the 1956 elections there was a substantial movement of Negro voters into the Republican column, especially in the cities. For the first time in our history neither party could consider the "Negro vote" safe, and neither party wanted to be tagged as being opposed to civil rights. The southern Democrats, although still powerful enough to force concessions, were no longer able to block all civil rights legislation. They had lost allies in the Border States, and with the addition of Hawaii and Alaska, there were four more votes for civil rights legislation in the Senate.

In 1957 Congress adopted the first civil rights law since Reconstruction. Again in 1960, 1964, and 1965, came additional legislation. Today the full weight of the national government in all its branches, reflecting a widespread and politically powerful national consensus, is working to bring to fruition the ideals proclaimed in 1776. Each year more and more Negroes will vote. As more of them become educated, they will comprehend more clearly the connection between voting and better schools, houses, and jobs. And with better jobs, better houses, and better education, more and more Negroes will come to insist upon the abolition of segregation. The impact of the political voice of the Negro will be felt long before every Alabama field hand and Atlanta hotel maid becomes politically self-conscious.

What is happening in the United States is one facet of the world-wide "revolution of rising expectations." Colonialism is dead. White supremacy is dying. There is no stopping place between the granting of a few rights and full citizenship. Once the first Negro was educated, once slavery was abolished, America made her choice. Negroes will demand and secure the same rights as other citizens. No other Americans have asked for more than this, or settled long for less.

[30] James W. Prothro, "A Southerner's View of a Southerner's Book," *The Reporter*, September 20, 1956, p. 46.

8 RIGHTS TO CITIZENSHIP, LIFE, LIBERTY, AND PROPERTY

Public officials have great power. Under certain conditions they can seize our property, throw us into jail and, in extreme circumstances, even take our lives. Under some conditions they can take away our citizenship. It is necessary to vest great power in those who govern; it is also dangerous. It is so dangerous that to keep officials from becoming tyrants we are unwilling to depend on the ballot box alone. For we know that political controls have little impact when a hysterical majority uses governmental power to deprive unpopular minorities of their rights.

Because such public power can be dangerous, we parcel it out in small chunks and surround it with elaborate restraints. No single official can by himself decide to take our life, liberty, or property. And officials must proceed according to established forms. If they act outside the scope of their authority or contrary to the law, be they the President or policeman, they have no claim to obedience.

The Constitution also protects our rights to become and to remain citizens, a right basic to the concept of self-government. True, all nations, free and non-free, have rules that determine nationality, the condition of membership in, owing allegiance to, and being the subject of a nation-state; but in democratic theory citizenship is something more than mere nationality, something more than merely being a subject. Citizenship in a democracy is an "office," and like other offices carries with it certain powers and responsibilities.

The Constitution Protects Citizenship

It was not until 1868, with the adoption of the Fourteenth Amendment, that this basic right of membership in the body politic was given constitutional protection. This amendment makes "all persons *born or naturalized* in the United States and subject to the jurisdiction thereof . . . citizens of the United States and of the State wherein they reside." Thus, with the minor exception, for example, of children born to foreign ambassadors and ministers (but not consuls), all persons born in the United States are citizens of this country regardless of the citizenship of their parents. (Congress has defined "the United States" to include Puerto Rico, Guam, and the Virgin Islands.) Members of Indian tribes were not made citizens of the United States by the Fourteenth Amendment, but Congress has by law conferred citizenship on persons born in the United States to members of Indian tribes.

The Fourteenth Amendment confers citizenship according to the principle of *jus soli*—that is, by place of birth. In addition, Congress has granted under certain conditions citizenship at birth according to the principle of *jus sanguinis*—that is, by blood. Thus a child born of an American parent living abroad becomes an American citizen at birth provided at least one of his citizen parents had been physically present in the United States or one of its possessions prior to the child's birth. In order to *retain* citizenship derived through only one citizen parent, a person must come to the United States before he is twenty-three and must live here for at least five years between his fourteenth and twenty-eighth birthday.

Citizenship may also be acquired by naturalization, collective or individual. The granting of citizenship to Puerto Ricans in 1917 by an act of Congress is an example of collective naturalization. Individual naturalization requirements are determined by Congress.

Today any non-enemy alien over 18 years of age (children under 16 who are lawful residents become citizens when their parents become citizens) who has been lawfully admitted for permanent residence (except a military deserter, draft dodger, or alien who has refused to serve in the armed forces because of allegiance to another country), who has resided in the United States for at least five years and in the state for at least six months (relatives of citizens and aliens in the armed services have lower residence requirements), is eligible for naturalization. He files a petition of naturalization, verified by two witnesses, with the clerk of a court of record, federal or state. An official of the Immigration and Naturalization Service examines the petitioner to insure that he has met the residence requirements, can read, write, and speak English, is of good moral character, understands and is attached to the fundamentals of the history, the principles, and the form of government of the United States and is well disposed toward the good order and happiness of this country, and that he does not now nor within the last ten years, believe in, advocate, or belong to an organization that supports opposition to organized government, overthrow of government by violence, or the doctrines of world communism or any other form of totalitarianism.

The examiner makes his report to the judge. The final step is a hearing in open court. If the judge is satisfied that the petitioner is qualified, the applicant renounces all allegiance to his former country and swears to support and defend the Constitution and laws of the United States against all enemies, and to bear arms in behalf of the United States when required by law. (Those with religious beliefs against the bearing of arms are allowed to take an oath to serve in the armed forces as a noncombatant or to perform work of national importance under civilian direction.) Then the court grants a certificate of naturalization.

Loss of Citizenship

Naturalized citizenship may be revoked by court order if the government can prove that it was procured by concealment of a material fact or by willful misrepresentation. In addition, citizenship, however acquired, may be lost by expatriation. A citizen may expatriate himself—that is, give up his American citizenship—and he may do so by conduct that Congress has determined to be incompatible with undivided allegiance to the United States. In addition, Congress seems to believe that it has the power to strip a person of his citizenship as a penalty for the commission of certain kinds of crimes. However, the Supreme Court has questioned this notion. The justices have had difficulty in articulating their arguments and in developing a coherent and consistent majority position, but in essence the Court has ruled that what the Constitution gives—and it gives citizenship both to a natural-born and a naturalized citizen—Congress may not take away as punishment for crimes.

Of the eleven types of conduct that Congress has stipulated to be construed as expatriating acts, four have been recently challenged in the courts. The only one sustained by the Supreme Court is a provision that automatically takes citizenship away for voting in a foreign political election. A bare majority of the Supreme

Court ruled that Congress could constitutionally adopt such a law as a necessary and proper means of regulating our foreign relations. But the Court ruled Congress could not make conviction by a court-martial of desertion during time of war grounds for expatriation. Desertion does not necessarily indicate allegiance to another country and the Eighth Amendment forbids the imposition of loss of citizenship as punishment.[1]

The Supreme Court also ruled that Congress could not make departing from or remaining outside the United States in time of war or national emergency in order to avoid military service an automatic act of expatriation. To impose such a punishment without any judicial or administrative proceeding is to deprive a person of the safeguards provided by the Fifth and Sixth Amendments. (Even if Congress should provide a jury trial, it is still doubtful if it could strip a person of citizenship for draft evasion.) Again the Supreme Court has ruled that Congress could not deprive naturalized citizens of their citizenship merely because they reside abroad in the country of their national origin for more than three years. Natural-born citizens may live outside the United States for as long as they wish without jeopardizing their citizenship.

Among other kinds of expatriating conduct still operative—at least not declared unconstitutional as yet—are such acts as being naturalized in a foreign state, taking an oath of allegiance to another country, accepting a job in a foreign state that is open only to citizens of that state, and serving in the armed forces of another state without the approval of the Secretary of State and Secretary of Defense. In addition, Congress has declared that conviction of treason, attempting to overthrow the government by force, or conspiring to advocate forceful overthrow should also lead to loss of citizenship.

What of the person who wishes to renounce formally his citizenship? If outside the United States, he may do so before an American diplomatic or consular official. A person living in the United States may formally renounce his citizenship only during time of war and only with the approval of the Attorney General.

Rights of American Citizenship

American citizenship confers some very special rights. First of all, an American citizen obtains state citizenship merely by residing in a state. (Residence, as used in the Fourteenth Amendment, means "domicile," the place one calls "home." The legal status of domicile should not be confused with the fact of physical presence. A person may be living in Washington, D.C., but be a citizen of California—that is, he may consider California "home." Domicile or residence, as used in the Fourteenth Amendment, is a question primarily of intent.)

[1] *Perez* v. *Brownell* (1958); *Trop* v. *Dulles* (1958); *Kennedy* v. *Mendoza-Martinez* (1963); *Schneider* v. *Rusk* (1964); John P. Roche, "The Expatriation Decisions: A Study in Constitutional Improvisation and the Uses of History," *American Political Science Review* (March, 1964), pp. 72–80.

It is from state citizenship that many of our most important rights flow. For example, states determine—subject to constitutional limitations—who shall vote, not merely for state and local officials, but also for national officials. Although states could confer the right to vote on aliens, no state today does so and citizenship is an essential (but not sufficient) requirement to vote and to hold office.

Do American citizens have some rights other than the right to become a citizen of the state in which they reside? The Supreme Court in the *Slaughter House Cases* (1873), carefully distinguished between privileges of *United States* citizens and of *state* citizens, holding that the only privileges attaching to national citizenship are those that "owe their existence to the Federal Government, its National Character, its Constitution, or its laws." These privileges of United States citizenship have never been completely enumerated, but they include the right to use the navigable waters of the United States; to assemble peacefully and to petition the national government for redress of grievances; to be protected by the national government on the high seas; if qualified to do so under laws, to vote in national elections and to have one's vote counted properly; and to travel throughout the United States.

The right to travel, the basic freedom of persons to move from place to place, has in recent years become the subject of considerable litigation. Except for persons under legal restraint—committed to jail, subject to the draft, out on bail, and so forth—all American citizens may travel throughout the nation and no state may impose any barriers to this freedom of movement. During World War II, however, the national government forced American citizens whose only offense was to be of Japanese ancestry to move from their homes to relocation centers. The Supreme Court reluctantly approved this denial of their liberty, accepting as reasonable the decision of military commanders that such measures were necessary to prevent sabotage and espionage. But the Supreme Court insisted that after the loyalty of these people was established, restrictions that were not legally imposed upon all other persons could not be placed on their freedom to travel.[2]

Do American citizens have a right to travel abroad, or is that a privilege that the government may limit at its discretion? Until World War I no passports were required, though one could be obtained as a convenience if wanted. Other nations then began to demand passports before they would grant visas to our citizens. Under present law and presidential directives, when the United States is at war or during the existence of a national emergency proclaimed by the President, it is unlawful, except as otherwise provided by the President, for any citizen to depart from or enter the United States unless he bears a valid passport. Since 1941 presidential proclamations have brought these provisions into effect and, except for departure to a few nations—Mexico and Canada, for example—no citizen can lawfully leave the United States without a passport.

For many years the Secretary of State refused to give passports to citizens if he believed they were going abroad "to further the Communist cause." Before a passport application would even be considered, a non-communist affidavit was required and, in determining whether or not a citizen was eligible, the Depart-

---

[2] *Korematsu v. United States* (1944) and *Ex parte Endo* (1944).

ment of State reserved the right to use information, the source and nature of which were not revealed to the citizen whose right to passport was being considered. Then in 1958 (*Kent* v. *Dulles* and *Dayton* v. *Dulles*) the Supreme Court, avoiding the underlying constitutional issues, ruled that Congress had not given the Secretary authority to withhold a passport because of a citizen's political beliefs or associations. The Supreme Court (*Aptheker* v. *Secretary of State*, 1964) also declared unconstitutional a provision of the Internal Security Act of 1950 which made it a crime for any member of a registered communist organization to apply for a passport on the grounds that automatically to deny a citizen the right to travel—whatever the reasons for his travel and whatever his own relationship to the organization might be—just because he is a member of a communist organization "sweeps too widely and too indiscriminately across the liberty guaranteed in the Fifth Amendment."

The Department of State still contends that it may deny passports to persons whose travel abroad in the judgment of the Secretary of State may "be prejudicial to the orderly conduct of foreign relations of the United States or otherwise be prejudicial to the interests of the United States." But the Department no longer uses confidential information in passport hearings, so a person may now know what evidence is being used to deny him a passport and he is given a chance to be heard.

To the surprise of some observers, the Supreme Court, speaking through Chief Justice Warren (*Zemel* v. *Rusk*, 1965), upheld the right of the Department of State to restrict where American passport-holders may travel by refusing to validate passports for Cuba, China, and other "iron curtain countries." The Court majority felt that Congress had the authority, and had delegated it to the Secretary of State, to impose area restrictions whenever and wherever the Secretary felt that travel by American citizens is not in the best interest of the United States.

Although Congress may restrict the right of American citizens to travel abroad, the right to come to the United States and to live here is not subject to such restraint, and in these days of war and tyranny perhaps the most precious right of an American citizen is this right to live in the United States. Aliens have no such right.

Right to Live in the United States

Congress has complete constitutional power to decide which aliens shall be admitted to the United States and under what conditions they shall remain. Despite the fact, as President Franklin D. Roosevelt reminded the Daughters of the American Revolution, that "all of us are descended from immigrants and revolutionists," Congress has made it difficult for aliens to enter the United States, though compared to other nations admission to the United States takes on a more generous connotation.

Beginning in 1875 Congress imposed the first of the so-called "qualitative" limitations to exclude certain types of "undesirables." But the major restriction did not come until World War I and the 1924 Immigration Act that set a top limit on the number of immigrants and created the national-origins quota system. Congress recodified our immigration laws in the Immigration and Nationality Act of 1952 but retained the essential features of the national-origin quota system.

The law set an over-all annual limitation of around 156,000, which was divided among each nationality in proportion to the number of people of that nationality who were living in the United States in 1920. As a result, the countries of southern and southeastern Europe and of Asia had very small quotas. Since the largest annual allotments went to countries from which few people wanted to emigrate, and the smallest to those where there were a large number waiting, considerably less than the permissible 156,000 quota immigrants came to the United States each year. National-origin limitations did not apply to natives of independent countries of the Western Hemisphere, to spouses and minor children of American citizens, and a few others. In addition Congress enacted temporary emergency measures to admit outside the quotas persons who had been displaced and uprooted from their homes by war and political upheavals, and each year hundreds of private bills were enacted to admit individual aliens whose special plight had aroused the attention of a congressman.

Then in 1965, after years of political pressures, Congress adopted a new immigration act that marks a major departure in our immigration policies. The quota system is to be phased out over a three-year period ending in 1968. In its place, a ceiling of 170,000 "regular" immigrants a year is to be established for all countries outside of the Western Hemisphere, with a limitation of 20,000 from any one country in a single year. For the first time a quota is to be imposed on immigrants from nations in the Western Hemisphere—not more than 120,000 a year for the entire hemisphere. Within these over-all quotas, preferences are created for members of the arts and professions, for refugees driven from their homes by political or racial

"The Last Yankee"—A cartoon attacking unrestricted immigration, 1888. *(Courtesy Library of Congress.)*

persecution, and for relatives of American citizens. Minor unmarried children, spouses, or parents of American citizens may enter without regard to quota limitations.

Once here, aliens remain in this country at the sufferance of the national government. Aliens who enter illegally may be expelled without much ado. Since the Supreme Court has ruled that deportation, despite its drastic consequences, is a civil rather than a criminal proceeding, the constitutional safeguards that protect persons accused of crimes do not come into play. Thus aliens may be deported for acts that were not grounds for banishment when they were performed, and may be deported for a variety of reasons, such as two convictions for crimes involving moral turpitude, joining an organization that advocates revolutionary doctrines, or for engaging in activities that the Attorney General believes are "subversive to the national security." Although the Supreme Court in recent years has narrowly construed congressional statutes dealing with deportation of aliens, the basic constitutional authority of Congress to deport has not been questioned.

In summary, aliens enter and remain in the United States subject to congressional regulation. Citizens of the United States have a constitutional right to live in the United States and to move freely about within this nation and under most circumstances to travel abroad.

The Constitution, however, does not limit most of its protective provisions to citizens. More often it speaks of the rights of *persons* and constitutional guarantees apply regardless of the citizenship of those whose rights are involved. For example, Congress and the states have no more right to interfere with the freedom of religion of aliens living in the United States than they do with the freedom of religion of citizens. And the Constitution protects from arbitrary governmental interference the rights to property, life, and liberty of all persons.

Constitutional Protection of Property

By "property rights" we mean the rights of the individual to own, use, rent, invest, or contract for property. Property has no rights; it is the individual's right in property to which we refer. From Aristotle, through the English philosopher Harrington, to the Founding Fathers, there has run a persistent emphasis on the close connection between liberty and private ownership of property, between property and power. This emphasis has been reflected in American political thinking and American political institutions. A major purpose of the framers of our Constitution was to establish a government strong enough to protect each person's right to use and enjoy his property, and, at the same time, a government so limited that it could not encroach upon that right. For example, the framers were disturbed by the efforts of some state legislatures in behalf of debtors at the expense of creditors (see Chapter 2). So in the Constitution they forbade states to make anything except gold or silver legal tender for the payment of debts or to pass any law "impairing the obligation of contracts."

The Contract Clause

The obligation-of-contracts clause of Article I, Section 10, was aimed at state laws extending the period during which debtors could meet their payments or otherwise relieving them of their contractual obligations. The framers had in mind an ordinary contract between private persons. But in characteristic fashion Chief Justice Marshall later expanded the meaning of this clause to include transactions to which the state government itself was a party. So, when the Georgia legislature annulled a grant of a large tract of land fraudulently made by an earlier legislature, the Supreme Court declared that the annulling act was an unconstitutional impairment of the obligation of contract.[3] Then in 1819 the Supreme Court ruled that charters creating corporations are contracts. Thus, whatever privileges a charter conferred on a corporation appeared to be irrevocable and untouchable by any subsequent law.[4]

In effect, the contract clause was being used to protect vested property at the expense of the power of the states to guard the public welfare. State regulations of business enterprises ran a serious risk of being declared unconstitutional. Gradually, however, the Court began to restrict the coverage of the contract clause. Finally, in 1880, in the case of *Stone* v. *Mississippi*, the Supreme Court ruled that all contracts are subject to the states' *police power* and could be regulated when necessary to protect the public health, safety, welfare, or morals. In 1934 the Supreme Court declared that even contracts between individuals—the very ones the contract clause was intended to protect—could be reasonably modified by state law in order to avert social and economic catastrophe resulting from the depression.[5]

But in the 1880's, just as the contract clause ceased to be an important block to state regulation of property, the due process clause took over.

Due Process of Law

Perhaps the hardest parts of the Constitution to understand are those clauses in the Fifth and Fourteenth Amendments that forbid the national and state governments, respectively, to deny any person his life, liberty, or property without due process of law. These due process clauses have resulted in more Supreme Court decisions than has any other clause in the Constitution. Even so, it is impossible to give due process any exact and completely satisfactory explanation. Indeed, the Supreme Court itself has refused to give it precise definition.

There are two types of due process: *procedural* and *substantive*. The *procedural* kind is the older, for it grew out of Magna Carta and embodies the ancient notion that no man should be deprived of his life, liberty, or property

---

[3] *Fletcher* v. *Peck* (1810).
[4] *Dartmouth College* v. *Woodward* (1819).
[5] *Home Building and Loan Association* v. *Blaisdell*.

unless he has violated the law and has had a fair trial. It requires, to paraphrase Daniel Webster's famous definition, that government render judgment against a man only after he has had a hearing in which the essentials of justice have been preserved. For the most part, procedural due process has its application in the administration of *criminal justice*, as we shall see below.

Substantive due process has to do not with the procedures but the *content* of law, which it requires to be reasonable and fair. Whereas procedural due process primarily restrains the executive and judicial branches, substantive due process mainly limits the lawmaking branch. Substantive due process means that even if a law has been legally passed and is being properly applied, nonetheless if the law itself is unreasonable it is unconstitutional. Or to put it still another way, procedural due process places limits on the *manner* in which governmental power may be exercised, but substantive due process withdraws certain *subjects* from the reach of public regulation regardless of the procedures used.

For an extreme example of denial of substantive due process, suppose that a state legislature should adopt a law requiring employers to pay all their employees precisely the same salary that is paid to the president of the firm. An employer being prosecuted for violating this law might well object that the law is unreasonable, that even though he is being given a fair trial, to make him comply with the law would be to deprive him of his property without due process. He would be raising the substantive interpretation of due process.

Substantive due process dates from the 1880's. The Supreme Court from about 1880 to 1937 was composed for the most part of conservative gentlemen who considered almost all social welfare legislation unreasonable and hence contrary to substantive due process. They used the due process clause to strike down laws regulating hours of labor, establishing minimum wages, regulating prices, forbidding employers to discharge workers for union membership, and many other laws the legislatures thought were needed. The Supreme Court, elevating the doctrine of laissez faire into a constitutional principle, vetoed laws adversely affecting property rights unless the judges could be persuaded that such laws were absolutely necessary to protect public health or safety.

But what is "reasonable"? What is "necessary"? The trouble with the substantive interpretation of due process is that the view of the reasonableness of a law depends on a man's economic, social, and political views. In democracies, *elected* officials are supposed to be responsible for accommodating the clashing notions of "reasonableness" and for deciding what regulations of liberty and property are needed to promote the public welfare. When the Supreme Court substituted its own idea of "reasonableness" for the legislature's, it was acting like a superlegislature. But how competent were *judges* to say what the nation's economic policies should be?

Under the impact of this criticism the Supreme Court since 1937 has largely abandoned substantive due process as a check on legislative regulation of the economy (but not as a check on legislative regulations of civil liberties). The Court now consists of justices who believe that determining the reasonableness of laws regulating the uses of property is a legislative and not a judicial duty.

As long as it sees some connection between such a law and the promotion of the public welfare, the Supreme Court will not interfere, even if the justices personally believe the law to be unwise.

Eminent Domain

Many government regulations affect the value of the property we own, sometimes making it worth more, sometimes less. For example, a zoning law restricting a particular area to residential uses may decrease the immediate value of a particular individual's property. Maybe he was about to use his land for a gas station, but now he cannot do so. The government does not have to remunerate the owner for such losses, so he loses money —but the rest of the community may gain.

What if the government goes beyond reasonable regulation and *takes* property? Both the national and state governments have a constitutional right to do so, to exercise what is known as the power of eminent domain. But the Constitution requires that property be seized only for public purposes—for example, to build a highway or school or military installation—and that the owner must be paid a fair price. If there is any dispute about what price is fair, the final decision is made by the courts.

To sum up, where do we stand today in terms of constitutional protection of property? The obligation-of-contracts clause no longer is a major barrier to state regulation of property, and substantive due process has been abandoned as a judicially enforced limit on legislative regulation of our economy. The constitutional limits to the power of eminent domain remain as important as ever. But our right to use our property is not above regulation in the public interest. What regulations are needed is determined by the legislatures; the national courts will intervene only if the laws are outrageously arbitrary and outrageously unreasonable or are being applied without procedural due process.

Freedom from Arbitrary Arrest, Questioning, and Imprisonment

James Otis' address in 1761 protesting arbitrary searches and seizures by English customs officials was the opening salvo of the American Revolution; as John Adams later said, "American independence was then and there born." It is not surprising to find that the Fourth Amendment states:

> The right of the people to be secure in their persons, houses, papers, and effects, against unreasonable searches and seizures, shall not be violated, and no Warrants shall issue, but upon probable cause, supported by Oath or affirmation, and particularly describing the place to be searched, and the persons or things to be seized.

What Is an Unreasonable Search and Seizure?

Despite what one might think from looking at television police dramas, lawmen have no right to invade homes and break down doors, and they may not search homes or people without warrants except under certain narrowly defined conditions. If police have probable cause to believe that an automobile contains contraband or incriminating evidence, they may search the automobile even if they lack a search warrant, for the obvious reason that the automobile might not be there when the police return. And if they have a lawful right to arrest a person either because they have an arrest warrant or because they have probable cause to believe that he is committing or has just committed a crime, during the course of the arrest they may search him and the immediate area under his control. In all other circumstances, the police need a search warrant. Furthermore, not any warrant will do. The police must furnish information and persuade a magistrate that there is probable cause for an arrest and search. The warrant he issues must describe what is to be searched and to be looked for. A mere blanket authorization to search indiscriminately violates the Fourth (and Fourteenth) Amendments.[6]

Combining the Fourth Amendment prohibition against unreasonable searches and seizures with the Fifth Amendment injunction that no person shall be compelled to be a witness against himself, and as the only effective way to secure the right of privacy protected by the Fourth Amendment, the Supreme Court has come up with the rule that evidence unconstitutionally obtained cannot be used against persons from whom it was seized. To allow the use of this evidence would be in effect to force persons to testify against themselves. With such evidence excluded, police officers have every incentive to comply with the requirements of the Fourth Amendment when they make arrests and searches.

What of *state* courts? Until 1961 the Supreme Court held that state officers (and of course local officers, since in a constitutional sense officers of local units of government are covered by the term "state officers") who made unreasonable searches and seizures deprived the affected person of his property without due process of law contrary to the Fourteenth Amendment, but that it was not a denial of his liberty without due process of law for a state court to convict him on the basis of evidence unconstitutionally taken from him.[7] Then in *Mapp* v. *Ohio* the Supreme Court reversed itself and ruled that the Constitution requires the *states* as well as the national courts to exclude from trials evidence obtained in an unconstitutional manner. Today any conviction based on such evidence in any court violates the Constitution.

Apparently, however, the distinction still remains between the use in state courts of evidence obtained merely by violating the *laws* and the use of evidence secured unconstitutionally. This distinction has special significance in connection

[6] *Aguilar* v. *Texas* (1964).
[7] *Wolf* v. *Colorado* (1949).

with wire tapping. In *Olmstead* v. *United States* (1928) the Supreme Court, over the dissent of four justices, narrowly construed the Fourth Amendment to cover only physical, tangible objects and ruled that federal officers who secure evidence by tapping telephone lines do *not* violate the Fourth Amendment. Subsequent to this decision, however, the Congress made it a federal crime to do so. Thus it is not a violation of the Fourth Amendment of the *Constitution* for federal police to secure evidence in this manner, but it is still *illegal* for them to do so. And the Supreme Court will not permit the use in federal courts of evidence secured by lawless methods, no matter who secured it.[8] Although state officers commit a federal crime when they tap telephone wires, so far, at least, the Supreme Court has not been willing to hold that the Constitution forbids states to use evidence obtained by wire tapping or other illegal methods unless there has been an unconstitutional search and seizure.[9] (A note to conclude this picture of a tangled web of affairs: State officers who engage in wire tapping need have little fear of being prosecuted by the Department of Justice, for the Department itself has been trying to persuade Congress to authorize *federal* police to tap telephone wires under certain circumstances so that they may introduce in federal courts the evidence thus uncovered.)[10]

The primary protection of the Fourth (and Fourteenth) Amendment is against interference by police officers. In 1959 the Supreme Court held in a five-to-four decision that a person could be fined for refusing to allow a health inspector to make a daytime house search even though the inspector had no warrant.[11] The Court majority distinguished between permitting health inspectors to make forcible entry without warrants—forbidden by the Constitution—and fining a householder unless he would let inspectors enter—not forbidden by the Constitution. To the dissenting justices the decision was of little significance and to them the entire procedure was unconstitutional.

The Third Degree

The questioning of suspects by the police is a key procedure for solving crimes—and also one that can easily be abused. Police sometimes forget or ignore the constitutional rights of suspects, especially of those who are frightened and ignorant. Torture, detention incommunicado, and sustained interrogation to wring confessions from suspects are commonly used by police states. Unfortunately, such tactics are not unknown in the United States.

Judges, especially those on the Supreme Court, have used their power to try to stamp out police brutality. The Supreme Court has ruled that even though there may be sufficient evidence to support a conviction apart from a coerced

---

[8] *Elkins* v. *United States* (1960).
[9] *Schwartz* v. *Texas* (1952) and *Pugach* v. *Dollinger* (1961).
[10] *Benanti* v. *United States* (1957).
[11] *Frank* v. *Maryland* (1959).

confession, the admission in evidence of a coerced confession violates the due process clause and vitiates the entire proceeding. Hence, any conviction by either *national* or *state* courts on the basis of a trial in which a confession secured by physical torture or psychological coercion has been introduced is unconstitutional.[12]

The federal rules of criminal procedure and the laws of all our states require officers promptly to take those whom they have arrested before a magistrate. Police have no lawful right to hold a person for questioning prior to this hearing before a magistrate. The magistrate informs the person in custody of his constitutional rights and allows him to get in touch with friends and to seek legal advice. However, police are often tempted to question first. Sometimes they lack evidence to make an arrest stick but feel that if they can interrogate the suspect before he knows of his constitutional rights they can frighten him into confessing.

The Supreme Court has adopted a rule against the use in federal courts of any confession, whether voluntary or involuntary, made while a person was being illegally detained by federal officers. In 1957 the Supreme Court reaffirmed this doctrine in the *Mallory* case, a case that made front-page headlines because it involved an especially heinous crime, and because the application of the exclusion rule resulted in the release of a confessed criminal. But the Court has stood fast despite criticism by some police chiefs and congressmen, and has even ruled (*Massiah* v. *United States,* 1964) that incriminating statements deliberately elicited by federal agents from a suspect while out on bail waiting trial deprived the suspect of his right to counsel under the Sixth Amendment, and that statements so elicited could not constitutionally be used as evidence against him in his trial. Moreover, in its *Escobedo* decision (1964), the Supreme Court held that if local police question a suspect who has asked to consult with counsel, and who has not been warned of his constitutional right to keep silent, the suspect is denied the assistance of counsel he is entitled to under the Fourteenth Amendment. As a result, no statement extracted by the police during such an interrogation can be used against the defendant at his trial. The Supreme Court is edging close to forbidding all police interrogation of persons suspected of crime in the absence of counsel, especially when police fail to warn a suspect that he has a constitutional right to remain silent.

The Right to Remain Silent

During the seventeenth century in England, Star Chamber and High Commission courts were used to force confessions of heresy and sedition from religious dissenters. The judges of these courts assumed that unless suspects brought before them would take expurgatory oaths they were guilty. It was in response to these practices that the British privilege against self-incrimination developed, and it was because the framers of the Bill of

[12] *Payne* v. *Arkansas* (1958).

Rights were familiar with the history of these odious oaths that they included within the Fifth Amendment the provision that no person shall be compelled to testify against himself in criminal prosecutions. The protection against self-incrimination is designed to strengthen a fundamental principle of Anglo-American justice —that no man has an obligation to prove his innocence. Rather, the burden is on the government to prove him guilty.

Literally read, the privilege against self-incrimination applies only in criminal prosecutions, but it has always been interpreted to protect any person subject to questioning by any agency of government. Hence, a witness before a congressional committee or before the Interstate Commerce Commission or before the Immigration and Naturalization Service, for example, may refuse to answer incriminating questions. But to invoke the privilege, it is not enough that the witness' answers might be embarrassing or lead to public disapproval or to loss of job or might incriminate others; there must be a reasonable fear that the answers might support a criminal prosecution or "furnish a link in the chain of evidence needed to prosecute" him for a crime.[13] A witness may refuse to answer even if his responses would not indicate guilt, for the right extends to answers that might lead to *prosecution* even if the witness thinks the prosecution would not lead to conviction.

If defendants refuse to take the stand in their own defense, the judge must warn the jury not to draw any adverse inferences from the defendant's silence. However, if a defendant elects to take the stand, he cannot claim the privilege against self-incrimination to prevent cross-examination by the prosecution.

In 1965 (*Malloy* v. *Hogan*) the Supreme Court ruled, "The Fourteenth Amendment secures against state invasion the same privilege that the Fifth Amendment guarantees against federal infringement—the right of a person to remain silent unless he chooses to speak in the unfettered exercise of his own will, and to suffer no penalty . . . for such silence." In a subsequent decision the Court went on to rule (*Murphy* v. *Waterfront Commission*) that fear of prosecution by either national or state officials is sufficient justification to invoke the privilege against self-incrimination and refuse to answer questions put by any governmental agency, national or state.

Until the Supreme Court brought the privilege against self-incrimination within the scope of the Fourteenth Amendment, and until it permitted the privilege to be invoked to prevent incrimination by either national or state governments, a person could find himself "whip-sawed" between national and state authorities: He could not refuse to answer questions put to him by national authorities for fear of state prosecution, or refuse to answer questions put to him by state authorities for fear of federal prosecution. Federal and state authorities working together could use the machinery of one government to compel evidence to be used in the courts of the other government. The 1965 rulings of the Supreme Court put a stop to these practices.

Sometimes authorities would rather have answers from a witness than prosecute him. Congress has often granted immunity from subsequent prosecution in

[13] *Blau* v. *United States* (1950).

order to secure evidence. The most sweeping such law is the Immunity Act of 1954, covering national security matters, and subsequently amended to include testimony about narcotics. Under this act a majority of either House of Congress, two-thirds of a congressional committee, or a United States district attorney may petition a federal district judge to grant a witness immunity against federal or state prosecution for crimes uncovered by his compelled testimony. Once given this immunity, since answers can no longer lead to incrimination, a witness must answer questions or risk punishment.

Under the supremacy clause, Congress may confer absolute immunity on witnesses from federal or state prosecution, but a state may not immunize a witness completely from prosecution by federal authorities. However, in 1965, the Supreme Court ruled that when a state grants a witness immunity, federal officials may not use the evidence uncovered by the state proceedings. Under these circumstances the Court ruled that a state could punish witnesses who refused to answer after being granted immunity from state prosecution.

The Writ of Habeas Corpus

Even though the framers did not think a Bill of Rights necessary, they considered certain rights important enough to be included in the original Constitution. Foremost is the guarantee that the *writ of habeas corpus will be available unless suspended in time of rebellion or invasion.* Since permission to suspend the writ of habeas corpus is found in the article setting forth the powers and organization of Congress, presumably only Congress has the right to suspend it. When President Lincoln assumed this privilege on his own during the Civil War, Congress subsequently and retroactively authorized him to do so.

There are several kinds of writ of habeas corpus and, as developed in the United States, the device has several uses. Simply stated, it is a court order to any official having a person in his custody, directing him to produce the prisoner in court and explain to the court the reasons for confining him. A person held in custody applies under oath (usually through his attorney) stating why he believes that he is being held unlawfully. The judge then orders the jailer to show cause why the writ should not be issued. Testimony can be taken if there is a dispute over the facts. If the judge finds that the prisoner is being unlawfully detained, he orders the prisoner's release.

The case of Messrs. Duncan and White is a good example of one use of the writ. Duncan and White were civilians who had been convicted by military tribunals and were being held by military authorities in Hawaii during World War II. They filed petitions for writs of habeas corpus in the District Court of Hawaii, citing both statutory and constitutional reasons to prove that the military had no right to keep them in prison. The court then asked the military officers to show cause why the petition should not be granted. The military replied that Hawaii had become part of an active theater of war, that the writ of habeas corpus had been suspended, that martial law had been established, and that consequently the District Court had no jurisdiction to issue the writs. Moreover, the military answered, even if the writ of habeas corpus had not been suspended, it should not be issued in this case because the military trials of Duncan and White were valid. After hearing both sides, the District Court, in an action eventually approved by the Supreme Court, agreed with Duncan and White, and issued writs ordering their release.[14]

State courts do not have the power to issue writs to federal officials. But a federal judge may issue writs to *state* officers whenever it appears that a person is being held in violation of a federal law, treaty, or the Constitution. The applicant must first show that he has exhausted his remedies at state law, and persons are released only in the most unusual circumstances. Even so, a good many habeas corpus cases come before federal judges. Recently, protest has been growing against the habeas corpus jurisdiction of federal district judges. Some state officials have asked that the federal district courts be denied the power to set aside state court judgments in criminal cases. On the other hand, many oppose any action to restrict the full use of this important procedure, which gives to all persons within the United States easy access to the courts and protection against arbitrary arrest and imprisonment.

Ex Post Facto Laws and Bills of Attainder

The Constitution in express terms forbids both the national and state governments to pass ex post facto laws or enact bills of attainder (Article I, Sections 9 and 10).

An *ex post facto law is a retroactive criminal law that works to the detriment of an individual*—for example, a law making a particular act a crime that was not a crime when committed, or a law increasing the punishment for a crime after it was committed. The prohibition of ex post facto laws does not prevent the passage of retroactive civil laws—for example, increasing income tax rates as applied to income already earned—nor does it prevent the passage of retroactive penal laws that work to the *benefit* of an accused—for example, a law decreasing a punishment or changing the rules of evidence to make conviction more difficult.

A *bill of attainder is a legislative act inflicting punishment on specified individuals without judicial trial*. Bills of attainder have been rare in American history, but Congress has enacted two in the last two decades.

In 1943 Representative Martin Dies, then chairman of the House Committee on Un-American Activities, denounced from the floor of Congress thirty-nine officials as "crackpot, radical bureaucrats." He singled out three of these men for special abuse. Shortly afterward, Congress attached a rider to an appropriation bill naming these three employees and ordering that they should receive no salary from the federal government until the President had reappointed them and the Senate had confirmed their nominations. President Roosevelt, convinced

[14] *Duncan v. Kahanamoku* (1946).

that Congress had acted unconstitutionally, refused to resubmit their names. The three men kept on working and sued for their salaries in the Court of Claims, which upheld their claim. The Supreme Court, affirming that decision, ruled (in *United States* v. *Lovett*, 1946) that by accusing the men of disloyalty and denying them their pay Congress had punished them without a trial and thus had violated the constitutional prohibition against bills of attainder.

In 1959 Congress first repealed a provision of the Taft-Hartley Act that conditioned a union's access to the National Labor Relations Board on the filing of affidavits by its officers that they were not members of or affiliated with the Communist party, and then Congress enacted a law making it a crime for a member of the Communist party to serve as an officer or an employee of a labor union. Chief Justice Warren, speaking for a five-man majority, pointed out that Congress possesses power under the commerce clause to enact legislation designed to protect that commerce from political strikes. However, the 1959 enactment did not set forth a general rule, but designated by name members of a particular political group and imposed a punishment upon them. This was a bill of attainder. The Chief Justice wrote, "Congress possesses full legislative authority, but the task of adjudication must be left to other tribunals." [15]

Rights of Persons Accused of Crime

That the innocent will go free and that the guilty will be punished, that rich and poor, educated and ignorant will secure justice under law—these are among the most ancient and honorable goals of free nations.[16] Some feel that the rights of persons accused of crime are less important than other civil liberties, but, as Justice Frankfurter observed, "The history of liberty has largely been the history of observance of procedural safeguards." These safeguards, moreover, have frequently "been forged in controversies involving not very nice people." Their purpose is not "to convenience the guilty but to protect the innocent."

John T. Crook and the Federal Courts

The rights of persons accused of crime by the national government can be found in the Fourth, Fifth, Sixth, and Eighth Amendments. In order to get some idea of the application of these constitutional safeguards, let's follow the fortunes and misfortunes of John T. Crook (a purely fictitious name).

Crook sent circulars through the mails soliciting purchases of stock in a nonexistent gold mine. This action is contrary to at least three federal laws. When postal officers uncovered these activities, they went to the district court and

[15] *United States* v. *Archie Brown* (1965).
[16] For a comprehensive treatment of the rights of persons accused of crime, see David Fellman, *The Defendant's Rights* (Rinehart, 1958).

secured warrants to arrest Crook and to search his house for copies of the circulars. They found Crook at home, arrested him for using the mails to defraud, and seized some of the circulars. Crook was promptly brought before a federal district judge, who set bail at $1,500 and ordered him held over until the convening of the next federal grand jury in the district. After posting bond, Crook was permitted his freedom so long as he remained within the limits of the judicial district.

When the next grand jury was convened, the United States district attorney brought before the twenty-three jurors evidence to indicate that Crook had committed a federal crime. Grand jurors are concerned not with a man's guilt or innocence, but merely with whether there seems to be enough evidence to warrant bringing him to trial. No person has a right to appear before a grand jury, but he may be *invited* or *ordered* to do so. If a majority of the grand jurors agree that a trial is justified, they return what is known as a "true bill" or "indictment." Except in cases arising in the military forces, the national government cannot force any person to stand trial for any serious crime except on grand jury indictment. In our particular case, the grand jury was in full agreement with the United States district attorney and returned a true bill against Crook.

A copy of the indictment was served on Crook and he was again ordered before a federal district judge. A poor and ignorant man, Crook did not know that he had a constitutional right to the *assistance of counsel*, and that even if he could not afford to pay for an attorney the national government could not bring him to trial without legal assistance. The judge saw to it that he was informed of his right and after being told that Crook had no money, the judge appointed a lawyer to undertake his defense. The Constitution also guarantees to the accused the right to be *informed of the nature and cause of the accusation* so that he can prepare his defense; consequently, the federal prosecuting officers had seen to it that the indictment clearly stated the nature of the offense, and they had given copies to Crook and his lawyer. After consulting with his lawyer, Crook entered the plea of "not guilty."

After indictment, Crook's bail was raised to $3,000. Now the federal government was obliged to give him a *speedy and public trial*; the word "speedy" should not be taken too literally, however, especially since Crook had to be given time to prepare his defense. His lawyer pointed out that he had the right to a *trial by an impartial jury* selected from the state and district where the alleged crime was committed, but that his right could be waived and the trial could be held before a judge alone. After some thought, however, the attorney advised him to take his chances with a jury.

Crook told his lawyer that he had had dinner with George X. Witness on the night on which he was charged with sending the damaging circulars. But when Witness was approached, he said that he was unwilling to testify at the trial. The attorney took advantage of Crook's constitutional right to *obtain witnesses in his favor,* and had the judge subpoena Witness to appear at the trial and testify.

Witness could have refused to testify on the grounds that his testimony would tend to incriminate him, but he agreed to testify. Crook himself, however, chose to use his constitutional right not to be a witness against himself and refused to take the witness stand. He knew that if he did so, the prosecution would have a right to cross-examination, and he was fearful of what might be uncovered. The federal judge conducting the trial cautioned the jury against drawing any conclusions from Crook's reluctance to testify—although nothing could prevent the jurors from being affected. All prosecution witnesses appeared in court and were available to defense cross-examination, since the Constitution insists that the accused has the right to *be confronted with the witnesses against him*.

At the conclusion of the trial, the jury rendered a verdict of "guilty." The judge then raised Crook's bail to $5,000 and announced that he would hand down a sentence on the following Monday. The Eighth Amendment forbids *excessive*

CIVIL LIBERTIES: AN AMERICAN HERITAGE

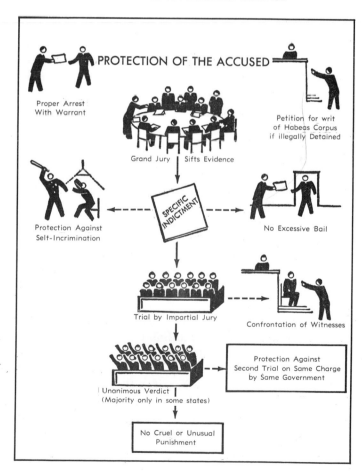

From Our Constitutional Freedoms by Robert E. Cushman, published by the Public Affairs Committee, Inc., and the National Foundation for Education in American Citizenship.

bail, the levying *of excessive fines*, and the *inflicting of cruel and unusual punishments*. But in view of Crook's past record and the nature of the offense, the bail could not be considered excessive; nor when the judge, in accordance with the law, gave Crook the maximum punishment of $5,000 fine and five years in jail, could it be considered cruel and unusual punishment.

Since the Constitution forbids the federal government to place anyone *twice in jeopardy for the same offense*, Crook could not be tried again by federal courts for this crime. But double jeopardy does not apply to actions initiated by the defendant. Crook's lawyer appealed to the court of appeals on the ground that the judge had improperly instructed the jury. If the court of appeals had sustained the appeal, which it did not, and ordered a new trial, no double jeopardy would have been involved. Finally, the Supreme Court refused to review the case and Crook went to jail.

In addition to the protection of the specific provisions of the Constitution, Crook was entitled to certain safeguards insured by the more general terms of the *due process clause*. Due process, which requires that persons receive fair treatment, goes beyond mere forms of procedure. Even if all the specific provisions of the Constitution are scrupulously followed, a trial might be unfair if, for example, the judge were, in his words and manner, obviously antagonistic and biased against the accused. Or suppose the jury returned a verdict of guilty on the basis of perjured testimony. Although there would be no specific procedural error in these cases, the trial would not have been fair, justice would not have been done, and the due process clause would have been violated.

The State Courts and the National Constitution

After three years in the federal penitentiary, Crook was paroled. But his freedom was short-lived. The next day he was arrested by state officers, brought before a state judge, and charged with violating the state statutes against fraud. He protested that he had already been tried and punished by the federal government for using the mails for fraudulent purposes, and he pointed to the Fifth Amendment provision that no person shall "be subject for the same offense to be twice put in jeopardy of life or limb."

The judge answered that the double jeopardy provision is contained in the Fifth Amendment and the Fifth Amendment does not apply to the states. Any way, the judge told Crook, "the Supreme Court of the United States has said that double jeopardy prevents only two trials by the *same* government for the same offense." [17] Crook, who had learned something about constitutional rights while serving in the federal penitentiary, then argued that the Fourteenth Amendment, which *does* apply to the states, forbids them to prosecute persons for offenses for which the persons have already been tried by the federal government. But the judge pointed to a 1959 Supreme Court decision (although perhaps some-

[17] *United States* v. *Lanza* (1922).

what undermined by more recent decisions, it still has not been reversed) in which the Court had even sustained a state conviction of a man for robbing a bank after he had previously been *acquitted* by a federal court of the same offense.[18]

What constitutional rights can Crook claim in the state courts? In the first place, every state constitution contains a bill of rights listing practically the same guarantees against state abridgement that the Bill of Rights in the national Constitution contains against national abridgement. By and large, however, state judges have been less inclined than federal judges to construe constitutional guarantees of their own state constitutions liberally in favor of those accused of crime.

To what extent does the national Constitution protect courtroom freedoms from state abridgement? The Bill of Rights does not apply to the states, but the Fourteenth Amendment does, and it contains two clauses of great importance in courtroom procedures—the *due process* and the *equal protection* clauses.

The equal-protection-of-the-laws clause protects persons accused of crime against discriminatory state action. Hence, in those cases where the state provides trial by jury, it must be a fair and impartial jury. A jury, either grand or petit (trial), from which Negroes have been barred because of their race would not be able constitutionally to try a Negro, for this would deny him equal protection of the laws. (Such action would also violate the civil rights of Negroes denied the opportunity to serve on juries.) Nor could a state provide different punishments for persons of different races or religions.

The "Nationalization of the Due Process"

Although a persistent minority of Supreme Court justices has long argued that the due process clause of the Fourteenth Amendment should be construed to apply to states exactly the same restrictions that the Bill of Rights applies to the national government, a majority of the Supreme Court has refused to accept this doctrine. Rather, the official doctrine of the Court is that only those rights that are "implicit in the concept of ordered liberty," that are so important that neither "liberty nor justice would exist if they were sacrificed" are, so to speak, automatically included within the Fourteenth Amendment. Outside the scope of these rights, the test in each case is whether the procedures adopted by a state are fundamentally fair, and not whether the procedures are those prescribed for the national government by the Bill of Rights.

This formula is known as the *Palko Test* or the doctrine of "selective incorporation," since it was formulated by Justice Cardozo for the Court in *Palko v. Connecticut*. Using the Palko Test, the Supreme Court distinguished between rights such as those of First Amendment freedoms—speech, press, religion—that are so fundamental that there can be no liberty or justice if they are lost, from requirements such as indictment by grand jury and trials before a jury of twelve. Replacement of these latter rights by other procedures would not necessarily be a denial of

[18] *Bartkus* v. *Illinois* (1959).

justice or inevitably hostile to the fabric of ordered liberty. In England, for example, many persons are tried by judges without juries, yet we cannot say that this is necessarily a denial of justice. Hence, as far as the Fourteenth Amendment is concerned, states may try persons without juries if they wish (none so wishes for serious crimes), provided some other fair procedures are used.

The Palko Test still remains the official Supreme Court doctrine. However, since 1964 the Supreme Court, without squarely adopting the doctrine of total incorporation, has incorporated provision after provision of the Bill of Rights into the due process clause of the Fourteenth Amendment. Today the Fourteenth Amendment includes every provision of the Bill of Rights except the Second and Third Amendments; the requirements of grand jury indictments; the double jeopardy feature of the Fifth Amendment; the requirement of trial by jury in the district where the crime is committed; the use of compulsory processes for obtaining witnesses in favor of the accused of the Sixth Amendment; the Seventh Amendment; and the requirement against excessive bail of the Eighth Amendment.[19] Some of the provisions not now incorporated are likely to be brought within the protection of the Fourteenth Amendment as soon as an appropriate case comes before the Supreme Court. It seems difficult to believe that the Supreme Court will continue to permit states to place persons twice in jeopardy for the same offense now that other provisions of the Bill of Rights have been incorporated into the meaning of due process. The Supreme Court, however, may refrain from a complete acceptance of the doctrine of total incorporation in order to allow the states to use such procedures as indictment by information, for there are many who believe that this procedure is better than grand jury indictments.

Dissenting justices, such as John Marshall Harlan and other critics, argue that the "onward march of the . . . discredited incorporation doctrine" undermines our federal system. The Constitution, they contend, leaves each state free to adopt whatever procedures its own legislature and courts desire, provided these procedures result in fundamental fairness, and Supreme Court justices should refrain from subjecting "state legal processes to enveloping federal judicial authority." [20]

The Court majority and their defenders respond that the vague, subjective test of fundamental fairness requires the Supreme Court "to intervene in the state judicial process with considerable lack of predictability and with a consequent likelihood of considerable friction." The failure of state courts either to apply the provisions of their respective state constitutions or properly to construe Supreme Court rulings with respect to due process led to such shocking examples of injustice that the Supreme Court had to set forth clear and imperative constitutional standards. With the elaboration for state courts of the same rules that have long been followed by national courts, the state judges will know in advance how to proceed, and there should be much less need for the Supreme Court to set aside state decisions on review or for federal district judges to have to use their habeas

---

[19] *Mapp* v. *Ohio* (1961); *Malloy* v. *Hogan* (1964); *Robinson* v. *California* (1962); *Gideon* v. *Wainright* (1963); *Pointer* v. *Texas* (1965).
[20] *Pointer* v. *Texas* (1965).

corpus jurisdiction to free from state custody persons who have been denied constitutional rights by the state. "And, to deny to the states the power to impair a fundamental constitutional right is not to increase federal power, but, rather, to limit the power of both federal and state governments in favor of safeguarding the fundamental rights and liberties of the individual." [21]

Relation between Bill of Rights and the Fourteenth Amendment Due Process Clause

Provisions of National Bill of Rights which apply to states because included within the Fourteenth Amendment

FIRST AMENDMENT

No law establishing a religion.	*Applies to states.*
Freedom of religion.	*Applies to states.*
Freedom of speech and press.	*Applies to states.*
Freedom of assembly and petition.	*Applies to states.*

SECOND AMENDMENT

Right to keep and bear arms not to be denied.	*Does not apply to states.*

THIRD AMENDMENT

No soldiers to be quartered in private homes during time of peace, and in time of war only as the law allows.	*Does not apply to states except where the taking of private property is involved (see Fifth Amendment below).*

FOURTH AMENDMENT

No unreasonable searches and seizures.	*Applies to states.*

FIFTH AMENDMENT

No indictments for serious offenses except by a grand jury. (Does not apply to members of armed forces.)	*Does not apply to states.*
No person shall be twice placed in jeopardy for the same offense.	*Does not apply to states. No specific Supreme Court ruling, but probably the Court would declare unconstitutional several trials of person for same offense if no errors of law were committed in the first trial.*
No person shall be compelled to be a witness against himself in criminal prosecution.	*Applies to states.*
No witness may be compelled to answer questions which will incriminate him (by interpretation from provisions mentioned just above).	*Applies to states.*
No person shall be denied life, liberty, or property without due process of law.	*Same provision specifically applied to states by Fourteenth Amendment.*
Private property may not be taken except for public use and with just compensation.	*Applies to states.*

[21] Justice Goldberg concurring in *Pointer v. Texas.*

SIXTH AMENDMENT

Accused persons to have speedy and public trial.	*Applies to states.*
Trial by impartial jury.	*Jury trial not required; but if there is one, the jury must be impartial and states may not exclude members of defendant's race or national origin because of their race or national origin.*
Trial in district where crime committed.	*Does not apply to states.*
Accused must be informed of nature and cause of accusation.	*Applies to states; essential for a fair trial; criminal statutes must not be vague or ambiguous.*
Accused must be confronted with witnesses against him.	*Applies to states.*
Accused must have compulsory process for obtaining witnesses in his favor.	*Does not apply to states.*
Accused must have right to the assistance of counsel in criminal prosecutions.	*Applies to states.*

SEVENTH AMENDMENT

Jury trials in suits of common law.	*Does not apply to states.*

EIGHTH AMENDMENT

Excessive bail shall not be required.	*Does not apply to states; however, denial of bail or imposition of excessive bail under some circumstances could result in denial of due process.*
Excessive fines shall not be imposed, nor cruel and unusual punishments exacted.	*Applies to states.*

NINTH AMENDMENT

Listing of some rights not to disparage existence of others.	*Not applicable to states.*

TENTH AMENDMENT

Powers not given to national government and not denied to states are reserved to states or to the people.	*Not applicable to states.*

NOTE:

The fact that the Fourteenth Amendment may not deny a state the right to do certain things does not automatically mean the state is free to do those things. The bill of rights in a *state* constitution frequently denies a state the power to do what the *national* Constitution would permit.

How Just Is Our System of Justice?

What are the major criticisms of the American system of justice? How have they been answered?

Too Many Loopholes. In our zeal to protect the innocent and to place the burden of proof upon the government, it is argued, we have established so many elaborate procedures that justice is delayed, disrespect for the law is encouraged, and guilty men are allowed to go unpunished. Justice should be swift and sure without being arbitrary. But under our procedures a criminal may go unpunished because (1) the police decide not to arrest him, (2) the judge decides not to hold him, (3) the prosecutor decides not to prosecute him, (4) the grand jury decides not to indict him, (5) the jury decides not to convict him, (6) the judge decides not to sentence him, (7) an appeals court decides to reverse the conviction, or (8) the executive decides to pardon, reprieve, or parole him.

As a result, some complain, the public never knows whom to hold responsible when laws are not enforced. The police can blame the prosecutor, the prosecutor can blame the police, and they can all blame the grand jury.

And yet there is more to justice than simply securing convictions. We must remember that all steps in the administration of criminal laws developed out of centuries of trial and error and that each of them has been constructed to provide protection against particular abuses. History warns against entrusting the awful instruments of the criminal law to a single functionary. For this reason responsibility is vested in many officials. And as long as all these safeguards are maintained, no one need fear for his life or liberty because of the overzealous or despotic action of another.

The most debated step in the administration of justice is the grand jury. Many students feel that the grand jury is unnecessary. W. F. Willoughby has summarized these criticisms of the grand jury as follows: that it

> . . . is in the nature of a fifth wheel; that real responsibility for the bringing of criminal charges is in fact exercised by the prosecuting attorney, the grand jury doing little or nothing more than follow his suggestions; that it entails delay . . . ; that it renders prosecution more difficult through important witnesses getting beyond the jurisdiction . . . or through memory of facts becoming weakened by lapse of time; that it entails unnecessary expense to the government; and that it imposes a great burden on the citizen called upon to render jury service.[22]

As a result of such criticisms, the grand jury has been largely replaced in England. And in this country twenty-eight of our states allow the prosecuting attorney to dispense with grand jury indictments for all but the most serious crimes. The prosecutor simply files an *information* affidavit that he has evidence in his possession to justify a trial.

But the grand jury has its defenders, who see it as necessary to protect innocent persons against arbitrary prosecutors. Although in a formal sense a man is still presumed to be innocent even after he has been charged with committing a crime, in actual practice indictment injures a person's reputation and subjects him to the expense and strain of defending himself. And "the charge that the grand jury is dominated by the prosecutor is not substantiated by the available evidence."[23] Furthermore, grand juries have the power—and there are many in-

[22] W. F. Willoughby, *Principles of Judicial Administration* (Brookings Institution, 1929), p. 186.
[23] Robert Scigliano, "The Grand Jury, the Information, and the Judicial Inquiry," *Oregon Law Review*, June 1959, p. 303.

stances where they have used it—to carry out their own independent investigations and to act when a lax prosecutor is permitting crimes to go unpunished. The grand jury is one of the few agencies with the power to limit the almost unfettered discretion of the prosecuting officers.

Too Unreliable. Critics who complain that our system of justice is unreliable point to trial by jury as the chief source of trouble. Trial by jury, they argue, leads to a theatrical combat between lawyers who base their appeals on the prejudice and sentiments of the jurors. "Mr. Prejudice and Miss Sympathy are the names of witnesses whose testimony is never recorded but must nevertheless be reckoned with in trials by jury." [24] Too often verdicts are influenced by the jurors' dislike for an attorney's personality or for a defendant's appearance. In addition, because of mass circulation of newspapers, untrained jurors are easily swayed by the prejudices and sentiments of the community and lack the training to distinguish between fact and fiction. No other country relies as much as does the United States on trial by jury. In short, according to this argument, the jury system is an unreliable method of sorting the guilty from the innocent.

Defenders of the system reply that trial by jury provides an invaluable check by nonprofessionals over the actions of judges and prosecutors. Justice is too important to be left to the professionals. True, juries are sometimes swayed by their feelings, but the record of judges is not substantially better. The jury system, moreover, helps to educate citizens and enables them to participate in the application of their own laws. The jury trial, said Justice Murphy, has the beneficial effect of "leavening justice with the spirit of the times." Abuses in the system call for improvement, not abolishment.

Too Inflexible. The elaborate and detailed procedures of our system of justice, some critics complain, stem from the day when people wanted to limit the behavior of royal officials over whom they had no other control. But now there are better methods of preventing abuse. Modern newspapers and other media of information also reduce the danger that officials will act despotically. Then, too, hemming in the administrators of criminal laws with detailed procedures denies them the discretion that modern criminology calls for. Each criminal should be dealt with as an individual, and the findings of sociology, psychology, and criminology should be applied to protect the community and to rehabilitate the criminal. More attention should be paid to selecting better prosecutors and judges, and to insuring them the discretion they need to administer justice.

Again, defenders of the system reply that the day of arbitrary officials has not passed. They cite cases in which prosecutors, judges, and juries have deprived individuals of justice or have failed to prosecute the guilty. So long as we have to deal with men as they are, rather than as they should be, we must limit the

[24] Jerome Frank, *Courts on Trial* (Princeton Univ. Press, 1949), p. 122.

discretion of those who apply criminal law and trust to the Constitution itself to provide the system with the necessary flexibility.

Discriminates against Minorities and the Poor. There are two parts to this indictment. First, it is argued that the high cost of justice gives an advantage to the man who can afford the best legal advice and who can pay for the appeals and other expenses connected with preparing his defense. The second part of the indictment is that minority groups, especially Negroes, do not receive equal treatment before the law.

Perhaps on no problem has the Supreme Court worked harder during the last several decades than to give reality to the ideal of equal justice under the law. The Court has laid down a whole series of rules to give a poor man the same treatment before the courts as a rich man. In *Gideon v. Wainright* (1963), the Supreme Court ruled that just as the Sixth Amendment requires federal judges to assign counsel to all impoverished persons accused of serious federal crimes, so does the Fourteenth Amendment require state judges to be sure that all persons accused of state crimes are adequately represented by trained legal counsel. (Until *Gideon*, the national Constitution required states to provide counsel only in cases involving capital punishment or in which peculiar circumstances—youth or ignorance of the defendant, for example—made the assignment of counsel especially necessary for a fair trial.) The Supreme Court has also insisted that no appeal procedure be allowed to make it more difficult for a poor defendant to secure an appeal than a rich one. For example, if a state requires transcripts for appeals, it must see that such transcripts are made available to those who cannot afford to purchase them.[25] Congress, too, has acted. In 1964 Congress finally made federal funds available to pay fees and cover some of the costs of attorneys assigned by a federal court to assist indigent defendants, thereby making it more likely that the assigned counsel will be able to provide a more adequate defense.

Discrimination against minorities, especially Negroes, in the administration of justice remains a major defect of our system. Police brutality is a serious problem in the United States, with Negroes feeling the brunt of it. As the United States Commission on Civil Rights reports, this brutality is largely confined to state and local police and prison forces, but no section of the nation has a monopoly. Practice of racial exclusion for juries persists "even though it has long stood indicted as a serious violation of the Fourteenth Amendment." [26] Negroes are subject to more severe punishment than whites for the same crimes, and in some regions whites who commit crimes against Negroes are not indicted by grand juries or convicted by white jurors who share the defendants' attitudes. Courts and police are inevitably composed of men who reflect the prejudices and values of the so-

[25] Anthony Lewis, *Gideon's Trumpet* (Random House, 1964).
[26] United States Commission on Civil Rights, *Justice*, Report No. 5 (Government Printing Office, 1962), pp. 26 ff.

ciety of which they are a part. Even when surrounded by elaborate legal and procedural safeguards, personal attitudes and sentiments are not shed by judges and
juries on entering the courtroom. When poverty and prejudice exist in the community, they will affect all institutions of the community. And yet there are few
agencies that do as much as the courts to isolate prejudice and to compensate for
poverty. As the Commission on Civil Rights stated, "There is much to be proud
of in the American system of criminal justice. For it is administered largely without regard to the race, creed, or color of the persons involved. . . ."

In summary, some observers believe that our system of justice could be improved
without sacrificing the essential safeguards. But others believe along with the
late Justice Rutledge that "the old time-tried 'principles and institutions of the
common law' perpetuated for us in the Bill of Rights" are a "basic charter of
personal liberty, and there should be no experimentation with them under the
guise of improving the administration of justice." [27]

The Supreme Court and Civil Liberties

In our discussion of civil liberties and civil rights, it has become clear that the
judges, especially those on the Supreme Court, play a significant role in enforcing constitutional guarantees. In fact, this combination of judicial enforcement
and written guarantees of enumerated liberties is one of the basic features of the
American system of government. The full significance of this combination has
only recently been recognized (though at times exaggerated). Some of the framers,
for example, thought of the Bill of Rights merely as a statement of general principles to guide government officials. But the Bill of Rights is now regarded as a
judicially enforceable limitation on legislative and executive powers.

This emphasis on constitutional limitations and judicial enforcement is an example of the "auxiliary precautions" that James Madison felt were necessary to
prevent arbitrary governmental action. Other free nations tend to rely more on
free elections and political checks to protect their rights. But in the United States
we look to judges to hear appeals from people who feel that their freedoms are
being jeopardized. All judges, not only those on the Supreme Court, have taken
an oath to measure the actions of public officials against the appropriate *constitutional*, as well as legislative, provisions.

English judges have authority to restrain executive officials from depriving people of their legal rights, but they do not have the power to declare legislative acts
unconstitutional. Moreover, Englishmen place primary reliance on an alert and
aroused public opinion, operating through elected officials, to safeguard their
liberty. The late Justice Jackson once commented: "I have been repeatedly impressed with the speed and certainty with which the slightest invasion of British

[27] Concurring opinion, *In re Oliver* (1948).

individual freedom or minority rights by officials of the government is picked up in Parliament, not merely by the opposition but by the party in power, and made the subject of persistent questioning, criticism, and sometimes rebuke. There is no waiting on the theory that the judges will take care of it. . . . In Great Britain, to observe civil liberties is good politics and to transgress the rights of the individual or minority is bad politics. In the United States, I cannot say this is so." [28]

In the United States, our emphasis on the *judicial* protection of civil liberties focuses attention on the Supreme Court. The High Court gets the headlines, but it is the judges of lower courts, both national and state, policemen, prosecutors, newspaper reporters, and other citizens who are on the firing lines. Only a small number of controversies get to the Supreme Court. It is the inferior court judge and the policeman on the beat who have to translate the doctrines of the Supreme Court and apply them to hundreds of cases. It is the police officer who, acting for his local community, has to decide on the spot whether a particular speaker is inciting people to riot or merely exercising his freedom of speech.

To focus attention on the constitutionality of laws is to risk ignoring consideration of their merits. Much that is constitutional may still be unwise, and it is often more important to ask *should* it be done rather than ask may it *constitutionally* be done. Moreover, to consider civil liberties only in the context of constitutionality may cause us to ignore other factors of critical significance in determining the extent of our liberties. We cannot protect freedom merely through lawsuits and legal decisions. A society plagued by depression, hysteria, and fifth columnists offers a poor prospect for keeping freedom, no matter what is set down in the Constitution or what the judges may decide. Efforts to prevent poverty and insecurity, to preserve order and stability, may have more to do with maintaining our constitutional freedoms than the actions of our judges.

We must not, of course, underestimate the contribution of the nine justices of the Supreme Court in defending civil liberties. Even aside from their decision-making power, their opinions are influential in clarifying the law and determining people's attitudes. And perhaps of greatest significance, the Supreme Court of the United States as an instrument of the national majority has been able to prevent local majorities in control of a state legislature or state judicial system from using their authority to deprive local minorities of constitutional rights. For in recent decades the Supreme Court has been the cutting edge of a growing national consensus in favor of equal rights. The Court acted first to end state-imposed racial segregation, to break control of rural minorities over state legislatures, and to curb local police brutality in interrogations and administration of justice.

But the Supreme Court is of little consequence unless its decisions do reflect a national consensus. The judges by themselves cannot guarantee anything. Neither can the First Amendment. As the late Justice Jackson once asked: "Must

[28] Robert H. Jackson, *The Supreme Court in the American System of Government* (Harvard Univ. Press, 1955), pp. 81–82.

we first maintain a system of free political government to assure a free judiciary, or can we rely on an aggressive, activist judiciary to guarantee free government? . . . [It] is my belief that the attitude of a society and of its organized political forces, rather than its legal machinery, is the controlling force in the character of free institutions. . . . [Any] court which undertakes by its legal processes to enforce civil liberties needs the support of an enlightened and vigorous public opinion. . . ." [29] In short, only so long as we desire liberty for ourselves and are willing to restrict our own actions in order to preserve the liberty of others can freedom be maintained.

[29] *Ibid.*

PART 4

The people in politics

A Problem Guide   A central problem in realizing "government by the people" in a mass society is *popular representation*. Part Four raises the crucial question—who really governs in democratic society? Do *all* people take part? Do some people have more political influence than others? Through what instruments do people express themselves politically—interest groups, mass media, political parties? How are the people organized to take part in "government by the people?" And how do these different types of political organizations and forms of representation square with the ideals of democratic government?

The basic inquiry in Chapter 9 concerns the formation and expression of political attitudes. What is the nature and role of public opinion in the free society? Who are the shapers of opinion—TV news commentators, newspaper columnists, politicians? How much influence do such persons have over our political behavior? Do they really represent popular political opinion?

The next two chapters, 10 and 11, develop the problem of popular representation in its principal forms—voting and interest group activity. One key issue here is the extent of representation. Millions of Americans do not vote because they are barred from the polls; other millions do not vote because going to the polls does not seem worth the effort. Some Americans' views are actively reflected by influential organizations. Others seem to find few, if any, organized groups promoting their interests. How serious are these problems in a democracy? How much equality of political influence do we have in America?

Chapter 12, on political parties, deals with this same problem of *fair represen-*

tation but in connection with another part of our political system. Under a two-party system, in theory at least, the party that wins a majority of the votes then proceeds to represent the interests of that popular majority in government. How effectively does the winning party speak for the majority of voters that elected it? That raises another question: *Can* the parties be strengthened so that they may represent their supporters more effectively? (Whether or not the parties *should* be strengthened is taken up in Chapter 20.) And what about the minority party—can it do the job of *opposing* the majority as well as it should?

A final problem of Part Four is the fairness and efficiency of the electoral system. We might think that electoral machinery would be neutral, but it is not. Some election arrangements make it difficult for people to vote. Others—for example, the electoral college—give some voters more weight than others in the election of office-seekers. How fair is our system of nominating political candidates —especially the President? Chapter 13 raises such problems, which all relate to the basic question in Part Four, the question of equality of political influence for the sake of fair representation in government.

Sometimes this problem of fair representation is described in terms of "special interests versus the general interest." The "special interests" are often pictured as small, selfish groups that "gang up" on the rest of the people, who represent the "general interest." Actually, the problem is more complex. As used here, the term "special interest" means merely the interest (the goal or attitude) of considerably less than the whole. It is special in the sense that it immediately and directly favors and is sought by a part rather than the totality. The "general interest" simply means the goal or attitude of all, or most, of the people.

9 PUBLIC OPINION: THE VOICES OF THE PEOPLE

Government by the people is supposed to be government in accordance with the will of the people. So it is, but what *is* the will of the people? What does government do when people disagree? What does it do when opinions change? What does it do when most of the people are indifferent about some issues, while a minority is active and noisy? Should government itself try to influence opinion? If so, how far should it go?

Let us look at these questions from the vantage point of, say, a senator in Washington. He wants to be the servant of the people. But he is not sure what the people want. He cannot really tell from his mail, because he is not sure that the letter-writers actually reflect opinion back home. He is suspicious of public opinion polls. He is not sure just what issues he was elected on, since he argued for and against so many propositions in his last campaign. Besides, it is five years since he was elected, and many important events have taken place in that time. He listens for the voice of the people, but the people do not speak with a single voice. No wonder he straddles the fence. From his point of view, the *people* are straddling the fence.

But governments must act. Decisions must be made. Somehow, out of the confusion of raucous voices and dead silences, politicians must shape fairly precise and positive policies. To see the relation between political opinions and governmental actions, we must look first at the variety of people involved.

Millions of Publics

Imagine that the following incident takes place: A group of college students at a state university decides—all in a spirit of frivolity—to announce to the press that they are forming a local chapter of the League of the Militant Godless. The story appears in a newspaper. Immediately a variety of responses occurs. The other students merely smile. They sense a joke. The president and dean of the college do not smile. They feel that this may be meant as a joke, but they are afraid of the effect it may have on the "public." Local church groups are indignant. Religion is not a matter for pranks, says one minister in a sermon. Local townspeople are divided; some see the incident as a joke, but others feel that the students have gone too far. Several legislators at the state capital denounce the affair as another sign of communist influence in the colleges. Some people read about the incident in the newspapers, shake their heads, and forget about it. Others hear about it indirectly, and perhaps complain that there are too many reds at the state college. A few parents of undergraduates write letters of protest to the college president. But most people, even in the state, never hear about the incident at all. At any rate, after a few weeks have gone by the incident is all but forgotten.

No Mass Mind

Now it would be wrong to say that one general public opinion, or a single mass mind, was involved here. Actually there were a number of *different public opinions* simply because there were a number of *different publics*. These publics reacted in several ways, largely in accordance with their physical nearness to the incident, the extent of their understanding of the incident, their own occupational position or social group, their preoccupation or interest in the incident, and, above all, their basic attitudes. The other students, for example, were close to the incident and understood its frivolous nature. The college administration, the ministers, and the legislators had an actual or assumed stake in the incident. The townspeople reacted largely as a close-knit group with set attitudes toward student activities. Most people remote from the incident remained uninformed and uninterested.

Translate all this into a real live national issue, and one sees the tremendous complexity of public opinion and the many publics involved. The President makes a speech about labor legislation, and his words fall differently on the ears of union members, businessmen, union leaders, farmers, Democrats, Republicans, and so on. The Secretary of Agriculture announces a new farm program, and he gets mixed reactions not only from the large non-farming public, but also from the farm public itself—that is, from cotton farmers as against wheat farmers, from large farmers as against small farmers. A senator calls for the end of government subsidies; many businessmen applaud because they want lower taxes, but businessmen who are receiving subsidies, as in the case of ship operators, do not applaud. These are examples merely of different *interests*—but the whole process is immensely complicated by the different attitudes that people have by reason of their economic and social status, their group loyalties, their occupation, their degree of understanding or information.

What, then, are some of the important aspects of public opinions—and of the various publics that hold them?

Some Kinds of Political Attitudes Are Fairly Stable. People's attitudes toward certain matters may change slowly, if at all, even though the world may be changing around them. This is especially true of loyalty toward one's own group and hostility toward competitive or hostile groups. For example, political party preferences, like religious preferences, vary little over the years, as the table below suggests. In general, people remain more loyal to their groups, including their political parties, than toward issues or policies that they cannot relate to those groups.

Party preferences help to stabilize other political attitudes: The political party

Party Self-Identification: 1952–1964

Party preference	1952	1954	1956	1958	1960	1962	1964
Strong Democrat	22%	22%	21%	23%	21%	23%	26%
Weak Democrat	25	25	23	24	25	23	25
Independent Democrat	10	9	6	7	8	8	9
Independent	5	7	9	8	8	8	8
Independent Republican	7	6	8	4	7	6	6
Weak Republican	14	14	14	16	13	16	13
Strong Republican	13	13	15	13	14	12	11
Apolitical	4	4	4	5	4	4	2
	100%	100%	100%	100%	100%	100%	100%

Source: Survey Research Center, University of Michigan.

serves as a reference point. A strong Democrat is apt to conclude that the Democratic candidates are men of integrity and to view more favorably their policy proposals than would a man without any party identification or with a preference for the Republicans. In the midst of the 1956 campaign, when the Suez crisis exploded, persons who had planned to vote for Stevenson viewed the crisis as proof that Eisenhower was not doing a good job and that Stevenson was needed. But voters who had planned to support Eisenhower saw the crisis as the kind of emergency that demanded the skill and experience of a man like Eisenhower. "Most voters merely fitted the new information," points out Warren Miller, "into an old partisan frame, used the new situation further to justify their previous decision, and voted the way they had intended to vote all along." [1]

Partisanship does not only color our response to what political leaders do; strong partisans also are likely to impute to their party leader support for ideas and issues that the voters favor even though the candidate himself does not. And even when a voter leaves his party to vote for the candidate from the opposition, he often assumes that the man he favors really supports the position that the voter imputes to his own party.

Public Opinion on Some Issues Is Fluid. Certain kinds of political attitudes can change dramatically, almost overnight. Isolationist feeling in 1941, for example, dwindled significantly following the attack on Pearl Harbor. Changes occur less in response to the exhortations or even the acts of political leaders than to "nonpolitical" events: a depression, frustrations in Vietnam, the movement of people from country to city. The intensity and durability of an opinion turns largely on its *saliency*—whether it is "relatively important, at the focus of attention, crowding out other items, a pivot for organizing one's thoughts and acts." [2] What was controversial yesterday may not arouse much interest today. A few decades ago the nation was divided over the issue of the federal government's responsibility to maintain full employment. Following the Korean War "McCarthyism" was the center of national attention and political leaders carefully calculated whether to support or oppose it. By 1957 charges and counter-charges about subversion ceased to attract much attention. Sometimes people get bored with issues, but more often the objective situation may change.

People Vary Greatly in the Intensity of Their Beliefs. Some are mildly in favor, for example, of federal aid to education, others are mildly opposed; still others are fanatically for or against. Such variations in intensity have important political results. The attitudes of the passive can probably be easily changed. Those with strong feelings may try to organize in groups, to win votes, to campaign. (It is plausible to suppose that the more intense one feels about an issue the more likely

---

[1] Warren Miller, "The Political Behavior of the Electorate," *The American Government Annual,* 1960–1961 (Holt, Rinehart and Winston, 1960), p. 53.
[2] Robert E. Lane and David O. Sears, *Public Opinion* (Prentice-Hall, 1964), p. 15.

he is to "do something" about it; however, we have some evidence that many people "satisfy their needs" by talk, and do nothing else.) And some people may have no interest in the matter at all.

The Public Is Made up of Numberless Sub-Publics. This is simply another way of stating what we found in the reaction to our college prank—that different publics were uncovered or created. These sub-publics vary in their interest in a given issue, their level of understanding, their basic attitudes, their religion, their section or locality, their economic or social position, their national origin, their cultural inheritance, their education, and in a host of other ways. Moreover, these thousands of sub-publics cut across one another in a thousand different ways, in turn creating literally millions of "sub-sub-publics."

The public is often indifferent to political issues. We must distinguish between the public and the "Attentive Public." Frontpage headlines tell of a crisis in Laos, the story is featured in television specials, it makes a lead article in *Time*, and it becomes the center of a conversation at the student union. Lights burn late in the White House and students organize to send telegrams. To look at all this activity, one might conclude that the "issue" has excited public attention. But careful research often reveals that "the public" could not care less. In a vague way the mass of the public may have a hazy notion of what is involved, but little interest. During the Suez crisis in 1956 editorial writers speculated about its impact on the electorate, but the Survey Research Center found that less than 10 per cent of the voters responded in any way at all to the crisis.

Some who discover that the general public is more concerned about sports than politics, that the New York *Daily News* has more customers than the *New York Times*, and that "The Man from U.N.C.L.E." draws far more viewers than a political debate become cynical and contemptuous of the "masses," or they charge that behind the facade of our democratic system a "power elite" manipulates the public. Such pessimists fail to recognize that there are important links between the "Attentive Publics" and the public, and that the attentive publics are not unified monolithic entities but reflect the range of interests of the public itself.

Public Opinion May Be Latent. Even though public attitudes on a particular issue have not crystallized, they are important. For they can be evoked and converted into action if certain things are done. Latent public opinion may have little direct impact on political decisions, but it has long-run political consequences for it sets rough boundaries within which the attentive publics and political leaders must operate. When leaders conclude that a public policy would give their opponents an opportunity to activate latent opinion, the issue is seldom debated—for example, United States recognition of Communist China. Rightly or wrongly, leaders assume that this issue would provoke such hostile reactions from the public to make it too hot to handle. But latent opinion is an opportunity for political leaders as well as a danger. Especially in time of crisis, as Key says, presidents or other leaders "may capture the attention of the ordinarily inattentive public, provide cues of direction and clarification, and amass support" for their policies.[3] Or as Lasswell has summed it up, "Crisis concentrates attention; noncrisis disperses it."

Political Attitudes among the Most Informed Tend to Cluster. Those who oppose federal aid to education are more likely than those who favor it to oppose a federal social security program to provide medical care; those who feel strongly that the federal government should protect civil rights of Negroes are more apt than those who do not to be in opposition to motion-picture censorship. Again, this generalization has to be qualified. Politicians and editorial writers sometimes assume that the public can be placed into broad categories ranging from the most conservative on the one side to the most liberal on the other, and after once identifying a citizen as a "conservative," that one can predict from this "latent" political attitude how he will respond toward various issues. But Campbell and his associates in their careful studies of national samples have found that only two per cent of the sample could be classified as persons who look at political men and events in terms of a liberal-conservative scale. "Most people," V. O. Key, Jr., writes, "have no latent ideological outlook along a liberal-conservative scale to be activated by the manipulation of the appropriate symbol." [4] But political *leaders* are more likely to think and act in symbolic terms and hence their political attitudes are more likely to cluster.

The American-Idea System

What is basic in our political idea system? One eminent sociologist, Gunnar Myrdal, has found that the American people despite their diversity have a common set of beliefs. This American creed he calls "the cement in the structure of this great and disparate nation." [5] It has its roots in the era of "Enlightenment" when early Americans were absorbing the new philosophy of liberty, equality, and fraternity. It also has roots in Christianity—in the biblical teachings about man's need for freedom and equality, for justice and dignity. Americans, in short, believe in democracy.

Americans actually order their lives, however, according to a more specific set of beliefs which somehow they square with their basic creed. These particular beliefs are extremely numerous and complex, but we can list a few of them. After making an exhaustive study of a typical American city (Muncie, Indiana) in the 1930's, two investigators found that most of the citizens of "Middletown," as the authors called it, shared such beliefs as the following: [6]

[3] V. O. Key, Jr., *Public Opinion and American Democracy* (Knopf, 1961), p. 285, which is also the source of the Lasswell quotation.

[4] *Ibid.,* p. 281.

[5] Gunnar Myrdal, *An American Dilemma,* rev. ed. (Harper, 1962), p. 3. For a more recent, astute view of America from abroad, see the volume by the French Dominican priest, Father R. L. Bruckberger, *Image of America* (Viking, 1959).

[6] R. S. Lynd and H. M. Lynd, *Middletown in Transition* (Harcourt, Brace, 1939), pp. 402–486.

That, when in doubt, people should act like other people.

That America is a land of progress, and that increasing size is a sign of progress.

That progress should not be speeded up artificially.

That the middle way is the best way.

That good will and sincerity will solve most problems.

That a man should try to get ahead of his fellows, but not in an unfair way.

That if a man does not get on, it is his own fault.

That people should place *their* family, *their* community, *their* state, *their* nation first.

That American ways are better than foreign ways, and Americans superior to foreigners.

That the small businessman is the backbone of the American economic system.

That capital and labor have basically the same interests.

That such problems as corruption in government can be solved mainly by electing better men to office.

Notice that some of these ideas may contradict one another. The reason is partly that ideas arising in one era are carried over uncritically into new situations. "Men's ideas, beliefs, and loyalties—their nonmaterial culture—are frequently slower to be changed than are their material tools," it has been said. "It is precisely in this matter of trying to live by contrasting rules of the game that one of the most characteristic aspects of our American culture is to be seen." [7]

Here are some of our contrasting rules:

Everyone should try to be successful. *But:* The kind of person you are is more important than how successful you are.

The family is our basic institution and the sacred core of our national life. *But:* Business is our most important institution, and, since national welfare depends upon it, other institutions must conform to its needs.

Religion and the finer things of life are ultimate values and the things all of us are really working for. *But:* A man owes it to himself and his family to make as much money as he can.

Life would not be tolerable if we did not believe in progress and know that things are getting better. We should, therefore, welcome new things. *But:* The old, tried fundamentals are best; and it is a mistake for busybodies to try to change things too fast or to upset the fundamentals.

Honesty is the best policy. *But:* Business is business, and a businessman would be a fool if he didn't cover his hand.

Education is a fine thing. *But:* It is the practical man who gets things done.

The American judicial system insures justice to every man, rich or poor. *But:* A man is a fool not to hire the best lawyer he can afford.

No man deserves to have what he hasn't worked for. It demoralizes him to do so. *But:* You can't let people starve.

[7] R. S. Lynd, *Knowledge for What?* (Princeton Univ. Press, 1939), p. 59.

Of course there are differences between the profession of the American basic ideological creed and its practice, and even those who profess belief in democracy differ markedly about what democracy is. Public opinion surveys and investigations by psychologists suggest that persons with little education and low levels of political sophistication tend to take a simplified view of politics, fail to show tolerance toward those with whom they disagree, and find it difficult to grasp democratic norms (see Chapter 10).

Where Do Our Opinions Come From?

Living in a democracy can be a pretty confusing business. Everyone seems to be trying to get our ear or catch our eye so that he can press on us his point of view. Under a dictatorship life is much simpler. There is officially one public opinion—the word that comes down from the head man. Some of the lesser citizenry growl and mutter under their breath, but they are in no position to take a public stand. In a democracy we sometimes complain about the babel of voices that shriek at us in the newspaper and over the air waves, but we sense, too, that this babel is a sign of a free society, and one of its foundation posts.

If we look sharply, however, we can see a pattern even in the complex workings of public opinion in a democracy. Along with the basic ideas described above, there are certain forces that have a massive part in the shaping of men's ideas. There are certain methods of persuasion and propaganda common to all opinion-molders.

Opinion-Shapers

First of all, our opinions are molded by the *culture* we live in—by the over-all beliefs and behavior that characterize American society. Chapter 1 described the shifting economic and social foundations of our society, the impact of these changes on individual and group attitudes and behavior, and certain psychological factors. It will be useful to keep these factors in mind in considering the nature of public opinion. Our society is vast and highly diverse. What influences produce a pattern of opinion within our complex culture?

Probably the most important opinion-molder of all is the *family*. We begin to form our picture of the world at our mother's knee, or listening to father talk at breakfast, or hearing the tales that our older brothers and sisters bring back from school. What we learn in the family are not simply political opinions, but the basic attitudes that will shape our future opinions—attitudes toward our neighbors, toward other classes or types of people, toward local rules or customs, toward society in general. "The family is bound up with all the great crises and transitions of life," says MacIver. "It is the primary agent in the molding of the life-habits and the life-attitudes of human beings." [8] Some of us may rebel against the ways of the close

[8] R. M. MacIver, *The Web of Government* (Macmillan, 1947), p. 23. See also David Easton and Robert D. Hess, "The Child's Political World," *Midwest Journal of Political Science* (August 1962), pp. 229–246.

little group in which we live, but most of us conform. Thus the family is a sort of link between the past and the present. It translates the world to us, but it does so on its own terms. And it is not only the family of our parents, but after our formative years, the influence of one's spouse, "which now supplements but does not displace childhood familial influence. . . . When there is disagreement between one's spouse and one's parents, there is a greater chance that the contemporary influence will win out over the historical one, rather than vice versa." [9] Husbands, incidentally, appear to influence their wives more than the reverse.

School is another great influence on our attitudes. Studies have shown that in general the more education youngsters have, the more they depart from parental beliefs. In part this tendency may result from teachers' attitudes that may be different from parents'. In one school that emphasized the "democratic creed"— equality, tolerance, civic participation—there was a decided increase of support for that creed among students.[10] But we probably learn as much outside the classroom as in it, for we are reacting not merely to teachers and books but also to the behavior—the manners, dress, talk, attitudes—of other children. The same is true of our church, another opinion-making institution. We are influenced by sermons and symbols, and by other members of the congregation. *Direct personal contact is always a key agency of influence.*

College has an even more decisive influence than high school on the political attitudes of many students. In a pioneering study in the late 1930's a social psychologist found that Bennington College students, most of whom came from Republican, high-income families, tended over their four years in college to move closer to the prevailing liberal, New Deal norms of the college community.[11] Was this just a temporary change, under the influence of the Bennington faculty—or even just a way of currying favor with liberal faculty members and student leaders? A follow-up study twenty years later showed that the students had generally adhered to their changed political attitudes. Of course students will not necessarily shift in a liberal direction; at a later time and in a different institution the movement might be in the opposite direction. Or, as in the 1950's apparently, the students might move more toward apathy, conventionality, and ambiguity.

During and after school other influences are coming to bear. We begin to look at the newspaper—perhaps only at the comics, sports, headlines, and pictures at first, but later we read news stories and possibly the editorial page. Indeed, we can hardly avoid some contact with the newspaper, for it has been estimated that only one out of every twenty families in urban areas reads no daily newspaper. The total circulation of American newspapers is well over 50 million copies a day. There are countless foreign-language newspapers, and thousands of weeklies, ranging from mass-circulation magazines we are all familiar with, such as *Newsweek,*

9 James C. Davies, *Human Nature in Politics* (Wiley, 1963), p. 177.
10 Edgar Litt, "Civic Education, Community Norms, and Political Indoctrination," *American Sociological Review* (February 1963), pp. 69–75.
11 Theodore M. Newcomb, *Personality and Social Change* (Dryden Press, 1943). See also Alex S. Edelstein, "Since Bennington: Evidence of Change in Student Political Behavior," *Public Opinion Quarterly* (Winter 1962), pp. 564–577.

Life, and *The Saturday Evening Post,* to more specialized journals, along with the multitude of slicks and pulps that are sold every day. Walter Lippmann has called the newspaper the "bible of democracy, the book out of which a people determines its conduct."

Studies have consistently shown that motion pictures are often the most effective means of communication and persuasion. For years, pictures shown in theaters were extremely influential in the shaping of American opinion. While 30 or 40 million people watch movies on a typical evening, most of these do their viewing in front of a television set. By bringing picture and sound into the home, television has become the most effective of the mass media. The attraction of television for children and young people is well known, and of those who attend commercial movie theaters, it is estimated that two-thirds are under thirty years of age. Thus, we tend to be exposed to both powerful instruments of opinion at an age when our attitudes are most malleable. The motion picture industry has long been criticized, for example, for stressing the sensational rather than the significant. The late Edward R. Murrow told broadcasters that if historians a hundred years hence were to view a typical week of television they would find "recorded in black and white, or color, evidence of decadence, escapism, and insulation from the realities of the world in which we live." [12]

To name these major opinion-forming agencies is not to exhaust the list of influences that focus on us as we grow into citizenhood. Books, for example, play an important though often intangible role. Nor is it to do justice to the many groups or persons, such as political parties, interest groups, governments, politicians, businessmen, bureaucrats, and corporations, that seek to use the media of communication and persuasion for their own ends.

How much influence do all these forces have in molding opinion? Are they as formidable as they seem?

How Influential Are the Editors?

Consider the press. It can be argued that the newspapers really do not influence opinion very much, because the editors often think one way and the people vote the opposite way. The four elections of Franklin D. Roosevelt to the Presidency are often cited to support this view. It has been estimated that Roosevelt was backed by 40 per cent of the press (in terms of total circulation) in 1932, by 36 per cent in 1936, by 20 per cent in 1940, and by 17 per cent in 1944. Yet he won all these elections decisively, and he swept some urban areas where he had little or no newspaper support. John F. Kennedy's victory in 1960 is another case in point. Only one-third of American daily newspapers, representing less than one-sixth of the total daily circulation, backed Kennedy, the most any Democratic candidate had received since 1944, yet he won, if only barely. And city bosses have flourished for years in the face of con-

---

[12] Edward R. Murrow, "A Broadcaster Talks to his Colleagues," *The Reporter* (November 13, 1958), p. 32.

tinued denunciation by local newspapers. It is also pointed out that the vast majority of newspaper readers do not bother to look at the editorial page.[13]

These arguments, however, do not wholly meet the issue. The real question is not whether the press directly influences our choices at the polls, but whether it gives us a conception of the world about us that indirectly influences our political behavior. Our views are shaped, in Lippmann's words, by the "pictures inside our heads." The newspaper, in its frontpage make-up, its headlines, its use of pictures, its playing up of some news and playing down of others, its distortion or suppression of important information, helps form those "pictures inside our heads." Thus, while it is significant that Roosevelt won out against the majority of the newspapers, the really central question is the extent to which he had to modify his program and actions in the face of public opinion even before he began campaigning. The press has a long-run, continuous influence on opinions that may not be obvious in a particular election. "The steady flow of the propaganda of the media between elections probably strikes people at a time when their defenses are less effectively mobilized than they are during presidential campaigns." [14]

Other media, such as radio, television, and movies, can also be effective in molding political attitudes. It is sometimes thought that radio and television, being ostensibly neutral in politics, and the movies, having no political views as such, cannot be viewed in the same light as the press, which often bears an obvious party label (the New York *Herald Tribune*, for example, identifies itself as an independent Republican newspaper). On the contrary, radio, television, and movies, as part of our eyes and ears, help mold our underlying attitudes and thus our decisions at the polls, just as the daily newspaper does. Indeed, the fact that they have no obvious party ties or open intention of influencing voters may actually increase their effect. A David Brinkley or a Johnny Carson, speaking over the radio and television to millions, may tell a story about Washington doings that will influence the votes of many more people than the speech of a leading party politician over another major network. A movie depicting Soviet brutality in dramatic and grisly terms may affect attitudes toward American foreign policy more decisively than a statement by the Secretary of State.

Mass Media and Local Leaders

It seems clear, then, that the combined weight of mass media—the press, movies, radio, and television—in opinion-making is very large. Some social scientists believe that these agencies are coming to have more influence than the family itself in shaping attitudes. It is difficult to prove this contention, however, because the particular influence of the home or the press cannot easily be isolated for study. For example, if reading a

---

[13] See articles in *Journalism Quarterly*: Charles E. Swanson, "What They Read in 130 Daily Newspapers," (Fall 1955), pp. 411–421; and Percy H. Tannenbaum, "The Effects of Headlines on the Interpretations of News Stories" (September 1953), pp. 189–197.
[14] Key, *op. cit.*, p. 403.

Democratic newspaper for many years influences a father, and he influences his son, which is the dominant factor, home or newspaper?

We do have a little evidence, however, on the relative roles of television and newspapers in national campaigns. A study of the 1952 elections concentrating on members of the United Automobile Workers found that more of them distrusted newspapers than television as a source of information. In an earlier study of Erie County, Ohio, voters indicated that the radio was a more important source in helping them make up their minds than the newspapers. On the other hand, Eisenhower supporters in the 1952 election and Dewey voters in 1944 said newspapers were more important to them. Perhaps these studies show not that television and radio are more important sources but that the newspapers which in 1944 favored Dewey and in 1952 favored Eisenhower were selected by those who favored the candidates, whereas the Democrats selected out of the vast information available the more neutral views presented on radio and television.

For this much does seem clear: Out of all the thousands of speeches, hundreds of articles, millions of news stories, billions of political pamphlets, many voters ignore much or all of them. Those who listen to the speeches on television are the ones who are also likely to read the news stories. However, we all tend to select those speeches and those stories that support our predispositions.

The television debates of 1960 between Kennedy and Nixon were highly dramatic; they also may have had further effects. For the first time in modern campaigning, strong Republicans and strong Democrats were exposed to the speeches of their political *opponents*. Republicans who without the debates might have tuned in only to hear Nixon, and Democrats who otherwise might never have been exposed to the Republican candidate, were compelled by the debates to confront the candidate and arguments of the other party. Few strong partisans changed their minds, but some with less intense feelings probably did so.[15]

But whatever the role of press and television and other media may be, we must not lose sight of the fact that it is above all *direct, face-to-face contacts* that influence people, whether in family, neighborhood, or group. Studies have shown that the more *personal* the means of communication, the more effective it is in changing opinions. For example, it seems clear that (other things being equal) face-to-face conversation has more effect than a radio speech, and a radio speech is more effective than a newspaper account of it. Radio singer Kate Smith once sold almost $40 million of bonds in one day, undoubtedly because her regular listeners felt she was talking directly to each of them.

Does this mean that personal methods of communication have more effect on opinions than institutional methods, such as newspapers? Possibly, but the problem is not that simple. For the local opinion leaders, who influence their friends through face-to-face conversations, may have got their ideas from a newspaper or magazine

---

[15] See Sidney Kraus (ed.), *The Great Debates: Background-Perspective-Effects* (Indiana Univ. Press, 1962); and two articles in *Public Opinion Quarterly* (Fall 1962); Richard S. Salant, "The Television Debates: A Revolution That Deserves a Future," pp. 335–350; and Stanley Kelley, Jr., "Campaign Debates: Some Facts and Issues," pp. 351–366.

and may pass those ideas on to other people virtually unchanged. If a friend drops in and sells me on the need for a sales tax, and if he in turn got the idea from a popular magazine, what is the source of the influence on me? The shaping of opinions is not a one-way or even a two-way affair. Opinions are the product of many interrelated forces, each acting on others. It seems safe to say, however, that the mass media of communication, while they may influence local opinion leaders, will never be a substitute for them.

"How to Win Friends and . . ."

We live in what has been called the Propaganda Age. Propaganda is, of course, nothing new, but in the twentieth century it has truly come into its own. The reasons are not hard to find. The mass media described above have become enormous enterprises: newspapers with circulations in the millions, air waves spanning the continent, movies showing in almost every city and town in the nation. The techniques of communication have been vastly improved in a few decades, and the art of propaganda itself has been refined in our century. Harold Lasswell has said, "A new skill group has come into existence in modern civilization . . . skill in propaganda has become one of the most effective roads to power in modern states." We need think only of Adolf Hitler to see the truth of this statement.

What Is Propaganda?

Is propaganda bad? Not necessarily. Indeed, it is difficult to say just where propaganda leaves off and education starts. Effective education may include some propaganda (in favor, let's say, of basic democratic values, the virtues of which must in part be taken on faith). And if propaganda is defined as a "method used for influencing the conduct of others on behalf of predetermined ends," then almost every person who writes or talks with a purpose becomes a propagandist. Lasswell has described propaganda as a technique of social control—"the manipulation of collective attitudes by the use of significant symbols (words, pictures, and tunes) rather than violence, bribery, or boycott." Obviously propaganda in these terms may be used for good causes as well as evil ones.

Americans are almost constantly exposed to propaganda techniques, and advertisers exploit these techniques to the full. (It has been said that Adolf Hitler borrowed some of his propaganda methods from American publicity experts.) Advertisements are cunningly designed by "practical psychologists" to appeal to our basic attitudes, especially to our desire for *recognition* by others (above all, by members of our own group), for *prestige*, and for *security*. Constant repetition is the hallmark of effective propaganda. Malcom M. Willey writes: "In straight advertising, for example, the morning newspaper will carry the [advertising] copy; it will appear again in the street car (or even in the flip device in the taxicab); at the office a letter or a telegram may supplement what already has been said; the menu and the matches of the restaurant will serve as another medium of transmission; the afternoon paper repeats what the morning issue has already said; billboards are employed to catch a wandering eye; the radio program has its sponsor; the motion picture has not been free of advertising influence; and more recently the neon sign takes the 'message' far into the night." [16] This bombardment of potential buyers from all directions seems to get results.

As with the advertiser, so with the politician. The latter, seeking votes instead of sales, makes use of every agency of communication—ranging from skywriting to automobile stickers—that will influence men's attitudes and actions. Despite the variety of channels employed, however, certain methods are characteristic of propaganda, especially political propaganda.

Some Propaganda Techniques

Name-calling—giving an idea a bad label—is used to make us reject and condemn the idea without examining the evidence.

Glittering generality—associating an idea with a "virtue word"—is used to make us accept and approve the idea without examining the evidence.

Transfer carries the authority, sanction, and prestige of something respected and revered over to something else in order to make the latter acceptable.

Testimonial consists of having some respected or hated person say that a given idea or program or product or person is good or bad.

Plain folks is the method by which a speaker tries to convince his audience that he and his ideas are good because they are "of the people," the "plain folks."

Card-stacking involves selecting truths or falsehoods, logic or illogic, to give the best or the worst possible case for an idea, program, person, or product.

Band wagon—with this, the propagandist tries to convince us that all members of a group to which we belong accept his program and that we must *therefore* follow our crowd and "jump on the band wagon." [17]

A political talk has been analyzed in the above terms, with the names of the various devices italicized in parentheses:

> Ours (*Plain folks*) must be a moral (*Glittering generality*) platform from which there is preached (*Transfer*) a positive (*Glittering generality*) policy based upon the principles of religion (*Glittering generality, Transfer*) and of patriotism (*Glittering generality*). For God (*Transfer*) and country (*Transfer, Glittering generality*). For Christ (*Transfer*) and the flag (*Transfer, Glittering generality*)—that is our motto as we prepare for action, for Christian American (*Transfer, Glittering generality*) action. . . .

[16] M. M. Willey, "Communication Agencies and the Volume of Propaganda," *Annals of* the American Academy of Political and Social Sciences, Vol. 179, 1935, p. 197.

[17] Slightly paraphrased from A. M. Lee and E. B. Lee (eds.), *The Fine Art of Propaganda* (Harcourt, Brace, 1939), pp. 23–24. The speech analysis was also taken from this source.

Propaganda Is Politics

Propaganda is often denounced as dishonest and dangerous, but it is also part of the currency of a democratic politics. As Edelman has written: "If politics is concerned with who gets what, or with the authoritative allocation of values, one may be pardoned for wondering why it need involve so much talk. An individual or group can most directly get what it wants by taking it or by force and can get nothing directly by talk." But force leads to counter-force, and the employment of language "is exactly what makes politics different from other methods of allocating values. . . . Force signals weakness in politics, as rape does in sex. Talk, on the other hand, involves a competitive exchange of symbols . . . through which values are shared and assigned and coexistence attained. It is fair enough to complain that the politician is not deft in his talk, but to complain that he talks is to miss the point." [18]

In any event, propaganda is not an invincible weapon. Moreover, after a time the people—in a democracy, at least—somehow seem to get a picture of things as they are, if only through ordinary, day-to-day experience. Against the propaganda of the *word* is the propaganda of the *deed*. Facts to some extent speak for themselves. And if they are backed up by propaganda, they become doubly potent in shaping men's attitudes and behavior. In the long run, then, well-publicized *truth* is the most telling propaganda.

But how can we get at the truth?

A Free Market Place for Ideas?

In Justice Holmes' classic sentence, "The best test of truth is the power of the thought to get itself accepted in the competition of the market." This is a doctrine that most Americans would heartily endorse. But do we have a free market place for ideas in the United States? Or do monopolistic practices exist in the market of opinion just as they do to some extent in the economic market place? Certainly we have a free market in the sense that the government does not control the main agencies of opinion. But the absence of governmental control does not in itself guarantee an open and competitive market.

Trends in the Opinion Industries

Even in the case of our own justly famed free press there are at least three disturbing tendencies.

Concentration. We live in an era of "dying dailies." Newspaper circulation keeps rising, but the number of newspapers keeps decreasing. While our population

[18] Murray Edelman, *The Symbolic Uses of Politics* (Univ. of Illinois Press, 1964), p. 114.

doubled between 1910 and 1960, the number of dailies in the country dropped by a third. What has been the result? Many states have not a single city with competing daily papers. Many others are without Sunday newspaper competition. A dozen companies owning big newspapers control over a quarter of our total daily circulation. Daily newspaper competition survives in only sixty of the country's 6,000 cities—and in two-thirds of these the competition is only between morning and afternoon papers.

This concentration of ownership and control has led to a *standardizing* of news and editorial opinion. Newspapers get the bulk of their out-of-town news from great newsgathering organizations like the Associated Press and the United Press International. The AP, for example, sells news to papers controlling over 95 per cent of the total circulation in the United States. The country newspaper—once considered the citadel of rugged, independent journalism—has often become merely the local distributor of opinion "canned" in New York or Chicago. Over 100 newspaper chains control almost half the total daily circulation in the country.

Some argue that absence of competition is not necessarily detrimental. If a single newspaper has a monopoly, they contend, it does not have to pander to the lowest taste of the public in order to compete for readers. The editor need not fear that if he antagonizes local advertisers or groups within the city he will lose business to his rival. Moreover, in some cities with competing newspapers the level of journalism is not as high as in some single newspaper cities, as for example, the case of Louisville with the *Louisville Courier*. But the "evidence does not support the contention of single-ownership advocates that these papers *as a class* have been taking advantage of their more favorable economic position to improve their news, editorial, and feature content." [19]

Commercialism. A newspaper is a business. To survive it must sell copies, for its income depends on sales and advertising. Many publishers feel, perhaps quite rightly, that they must give the public what it wants. If the readers like screaming headlines, comics, scandal, sex, crime, features, and fiction at the expense of full and balanced news stories and editorial discussion, a newspaper can hardly hold out against its customers. Such a policy, however, means that an editor may cater to the political prejudices of his readers. By giving them what they want, he may deny them the chance to break out of their political bias and apathy. And he may block off the expression of controversial views for fear of alienating influential sections of his public.

Conservatism. Newspaper publishers are businessmen. They are worried by the things that worry every businessman, such as labor demands, costs, sales, taxes, dividends, profits. As businessmen, they tend to take a conservative point of view. It is not surprising that their business attitudes are reflected in their editorial columns, and sometimes in the slanting of news. Nor is it surprising that liberal candidates

---

[19] Raymond B. Nixon and Robert L. Jones, "The Content of Non-Competitive versus Competitive Newspapers," *Journalism Quarterly* (1956), pp. 299–314, quoted by Key.

and proposals so often meet stout resistance from the press. Such a situation leaves a plethora of orthodoxy on editorial pages. Yet democracy demands the airing of *competing* views.

Occasionally, too, advertisers bring pressure to bear on publishers. The story of a strike in a local plant may be suppressed, or the news of the indictment of a large corporation for unfair practices may be buried in the back pages. The real problem, however, is not outright pressure or conspiracy but the *community of interest* that exists between the big businessman who is a publisher and the other big businessmen who advertise. An English poet put this point satirically:

> You cannot hope to bribe or twist,
> Thank God, the British journalist;
> But seeing what the man will do
> Unbribed, there's no occasion to.

"If modern journalism tends to speak the language of corporate business instead of that of the little fellow," says Herbert Brucker, well-known editor, "it does so not because it is corrupt and venal but because it is itself a big business, a powerful institution with its interests vested in conservative economics." [20] On the other hand, many conservative publishers print the views of liberal columnists.

Certain newspapers have special political importance. *The New York Times* and the *Washington Post*, along with the *Christian Science Monitor* and the *Wall Street Journal*, although relatively small in circulation compared to tabloids, are read by political, business, and educational leaders. They are the major instruments for supplying political leaders with open forums for political debate. They are noted for their fair and full coverage of controversial events, and for their ability to confine editorial opinions to the editorial page. As V. O. Key, Jr. points out, these newspapers, especially the *Times*, serve "a special function in communication among the major political actors and the lessor activists." [21]

Proposals for Reform

Nevertheless, the problem of monopolistic tendencies—or at least of imperfect competition—in the market place of ideas remains a significant one. Certain solutions have been put forward. One would be to call on editors and publishers to clean their own houses, to police their own industry. It is urged that the press draw up *codes* of fair conduct binding on all, that working newspapermen be given a greater voice in the management and editorial policy of the newspaper. The difficulty is that such codes would not be enforceable, and the worst offenders would be those least likely to conform to them.

Another proposal calls for the establishment of *competing newspapers* wherever possible. Unfortunately, starting a new journal becomes increasingly difficult as

---

[20] Herbert Brucker, *Freedom of Information* (Macmillan, 1949), p. 68.
[21] Key, *op. cit.*, p. 405.

the years go by. Some time ago it was possible for William Allen White to establish a famous newspaper—the *Emporia* (Kansas) *Gazette*—with a few hundred dollars and a lot of determination. To set up a newspaper today in a middle-sized or large city takes hundreds of thousands, perhaps millions, of dollars.

Finally, *government intervention* has been urged as a means of promoting full competition. In 1947 a Commission on Freedom of the Press, headed by then Chancellor Robert M. Hutchins of the University of Chicago, recommended that the federal government, if private agencies failed to do the job, should set up its own communications agencies—a government-owned newspaper, perhaps to tell the people of its plans and policies. To encourage criticism of the press from within and without, the commission proposed the creation of a "new and independent agency" to "appraise and report annually upon the performance of the press." Further, it urged that the antitrust laws be used to maintain competition among the larger newspapers. The commission concluded:

> The urgent and perplexing issues which confront our country, the new dangers which encompass our free society, the new fatefulness attaching to every step in foreign policy and to what the press publishes about it, mean that the preservation of democracy and perhaps of civilization may now depend upon a free and responsible press.[22]

These recommendations raise a vital question: Can government take steps to make the press more competitive and more responsible without imperiling our basic freedoms? There is no easy answer. Yet our experience with another great agency of opinion—broadcasting—may throw some light on the problem.

Problems of Radio and Television

Since their infancy, radio and television have been under some kind of government regulation. When radio broadcasting first began in the early 1920's, a free-for-all occurred because broadcasters sometimes used the same wave lengths at the same time, deafening the listener with a chaos of sound. By 1927, sharp protests had brought government action. Today, by law, a broadcaster or a telecaster cannot operate without a license from the Federal Communications Commission, a federal regulatory agency (see Chapter 25). Those granted such licenses are obliged to use the public-owned airwaves and to conduct their operations in the public interest. The FCC has the power to refuse to grant or renew a license if it decides the station is not providing programs which serve the public interest.

The FCC has the ticklish task of *policing* the broadcasters without *censoring* them. On the one hand the Communications Act of 1934 specifies that nothing therein shall be understood to give the commission the power to interfere with the

---

[22] Robert D. Leigh (ed.), *A Free and Responsible Press* (Univ. of Chicago Press, 1947), pp. 105–106.

right of free speech by radio and television. And the commission has no power to make regulations governing the content of particular programs. On the other hand, in considering applications for the renewal of licenses, the commission may and does take into account the content and character of the broadcaster's past programs in order to determine if he has used his license in the public interest. If only prize fights and cowboy shows are telecast, its license renewal might be questioned.

In practice the FCC has not vigorously regulated the programs of television and radio broadcasters, and the industry operates largely under its own rules. The FCC discourages excessive concentrated control over newspaper, television, and radio facilities in a community and enforces the statutory requirement that if a station's facilities are made available to one candidate for a public office they must be opened to all candidates for that office on the same terms. (Congress suspended this rule in 1960 to the extent of permitting television stations to give time to the presidential candidates of the two major parties without having to give equal time to candidates of all the splinter parties.) Under present regulations station owners may speak their own minds politically, but within reasonable limits they must make time available to persons or parties on the opposite side.[23]

The radio and television facilities in America represent a halfway house between private control and state operation. Great Britain and Canada have tried a different approach to the problems of radio and television. The British Broadcasting Corporation and the Canadian Broadcasting Corporation are government enterprises, but other channels are privately owned and commercially-operated. The BBC, financed by an annual tax on radio and television sets, is rarely accused of partisanship; more often listeners complain that its efforts to avoid taking sides have led to overcautiousness and timidity.

Television, the young giant of the opinion industry, has already made it clear that government cannot pursue a simple hands-off attitude toward it. For example, television potentially is a superb vehicle for education. Its roving cameras can spotlight meetings of the United Nations, forums, debates, round tables, good plays, music, and painting. In the classroom, television can effectively supplement (but usually not substitute for) the teacher, the blackboard, and the textbook. But television channels are limited, and they are greatly in demand for military, police, air, and sea communications, as well as for regular commercial purposes. Should certain channels be reserved for education? If so, who will sponsor educational programs? The government? This raises the problem of governmental interference. Advertisers? It is doubtful that they should be allowed to influence the content of education. Universities and foundations? They may lack the large sums needed. The federal government must solve this problem, for it is the Federal Communications Commission that allots the channels. Whatever it does, it cannot duck the issue.

Disclosures of the rigging of television quiz shows and other questionable practices combined with growing discontent by some segments of the public over television's tendency to provide only programs which will sell the most soap or beer

[23] See Newton N. Minow, *Equal Time: The Private Broadcasters and The Public Interest* (Atheneum, 1964), pp. 25–34.

have aroused demands for a more vigorous insistence by the FCC that licensees
better serve the public interest. Moreover, President Kennedy appointed as chairman
of the FCC Newton N. Minow who warned the telecasters that they had an obligation to the public and accused them of turning television into a "wasteland."
Industry spokesmen, denying this charge, raised the specter of government
censorship, but nonetheless they have stepped up the number and quality of
"public service" news and informational programs. The advent of the Early Bird
satellite and the possibilities of world-wide television add another dimension to
the problem.

However, in the main, the fault of our government has been excessive caution
in the market place of ideas, rather than undue interference. But this fault is a
reflection of great virtues. Dictators have shown that the free market becomes an
absurdity when the government clamps down a rigid censorship and establishes its
own monopoly over ideas. It is a ticklish task for democratic government to keep
the channels of communication clear of obstruction without itself becoming the
most perilous obstruction of all.

Taking the Pulse of the People

"What I want," Abraham Lincoln once said, "is to get done what the people
desire to have done, and the question for me is how to find that out exactly." This
perplexing question faces every politician, in office or out. Another President,
Woodrow Wilson, once complained to newspapermen that they had no business
to say, as they often did, that all the people out their way thought so and so: "You
do not know, and the worst of it is, since the responsibility is mine, I do not know,
what the people are thinking? The usual way, of course, is to look at the election
yet I have got to act as if I knew. . . ."

What Do the People Want?

How can the politician find out
what the people are thinking? The usual way, of course, is to look at the election
results. If John Brown wins over James Smith, presumably the people want what
John Brown stands for. Thus if Brown is an out-and-out prohibitionist, and Smith
is a 100-per-cent wet, evidently the majority of the people support some kind of
prohibition.

But we know that in practice things do not work out this way. Elections are
rarely fought out on single issues like prohibition, and candidates rarely take clear-
cut stands. Elections usually turn on many diverse issues, and candidates are often
deliberately vague. It is impossible, moreover, to separate issues from candidates.
Take the presidential election of 1960, for example. Was President Kennedy elected
because he captured the popular imagination with "The New Frontier"? Or because of his farm policies? Or because of strong labor support? Or because he pro-

jected himself well on television and people liked his family? Or because of his opponent's errors? The answer, of course, is that he won for some of these reasons, and for many others. Which brings us right back to the basic question—what do the people want?

This is where straw votes and public opinion polls come in. It is only natural that people should try to measure the popular mind with tools more exact than election results. In this country public opinion polls are over a century old, but their main development has taken place in the last two or three decades. Some of the techniques were worked out by market research analysts hired by businessmen to estimate potential sales for their products. The techniques were then adapted to measuring opinions on general issues. Today there are over 1,000 polling organizations, the most famous of which are the American Institute of Public Opinion, which puts out the Gallup poll, the Elmo Roper agency, and the Survey Research Center at the University of Michigan. Many newspapers conduct local straw votes, and parties, private associations, and governments have been polling people for many years.

Problems of Sampling

Everybody conducts polls, or more precisely, most of our judgments are based on samples of evidence. The choice is not between polling (sampling) or not polling, but between biased or representative sampling. Most of us in a majority of cases draw conclusions from *biased* samples. For example: the Congressman who reports that he is opposed to H.R. 506 and who is sure that the voters are too because his mail has been running six to one against the bill; the reporter who writes that students are becoming more conservative, based on interviews with a dozen students on the Yale campus; the coed who predicted that Nixon would win, based on her discussions with several of her classmates. We can have little confidence in such guesses.

Suppose a politician or a social scientist wants to measure opinion more precisely. The first thing is to determine the *universe*, that is, the whole group whose opinion he is interested in—every adult, all students on this campus, all students in the United States, voters in City X. If the universe consists of only thirty units—all students in a particular class—the most precise way to find out what they think on a particular issue would be to poll every one of them. But for most politically significant problems this is impossible, so pollsters *sample* the universe they are interested in. The accuracy of the results turns largely on securing a sample *representative* of the total universe. If drawn properly so that each unit in a universe has an equal chance to be included, a relatively small sample can provide accurate results. Beyond a certain point, an increase in the size of the sample reduces only slightly the "sampling error"—that is, reduces the range between the divisions found in the sample and those of the universe.

Even a large sample can be highly inaccurate if it is unrepresentative. For example, in 1936 the *Literary Digest* sent tens of thousands of "ballots" through the mail to persons whose names were taken from telephone directories and lists of automobile owners. The results were inaccurate because the sample, large as it was, did not include persons who did not own telephones or cars or who had not bothered to return the ballot. (In the 1936 election, telephone owners voted significantly different from nontelephone owners.)

One way to develop a representative sample would be to shuffle all the units of a universe and draw the sample at random. But this type of *random sampling* is impossible for most political surveys. Instead we use *census tracts*—where these are available—which give the number of residences and their locations. By shuffling census tracts and drawing out at random the required number, and then sending interviewers to every fifth or tenth or twentieth house, one would have a random sample. A less complicated, but less reliable, sample is "quota sampling." Here an attempt is made to secure a sample which reflects those variables among the population which it is thought might affect opinion. One polling organization, in testing opinion that is thought to be affected by income status (for example, views on the income tax), makes up a sample based on two wealthy persons, fourteen members of the upper-income class, fifty-two from the middle-income groups, and thirty-two from the poor. Interviewers are merely instructed to interview so many in each group until they have reached the quota for that group.

An even better way to develop a sample, especially if your purpose is not so much to determine merely what a universe of population thinks but to study more deeply the dynamics of political behavior is to *weight* the sample. Thus a group may be of great importance politically but may be too thinly represented in a cross-section sample for effective analysis. By weighting the sample, the analyst can include enough respondents to allow further analysis. The Survey Research Center, studying the 1964 election, wanted more than its normal 150 Negroes. So the Center surveyed Negroes at triple weight, thereby getting 450 who could be further divided into sub-groups for deeper analysis. There is no risk to representativeness in such a procedure provided the analyst reduces the fractional weight of each observation when he generalizes about the population as a whole.

Another difficulty in securing accurate results from a survey is in phrasing the questions to be asked. As everyone knows, if you ask the question in just the right way, you can get the answer you want. Ask a man if he favors labor unions and he may say "no." Ask him if he favors organized efforts by workers to improve their well-being, and chances are he will answer "yes." Or trouble may arise in the alternatives that a question presents. Clearly, asking a person, "Do you favor the United States entering a world government, or do you prefer our traditional independence in determining our own affairs?" is loading the dice. Polling organizations go to great efforts to make their questions fair; some of them conduct trial runs with differently worded questions.

One way to avoid this difficulty is to ask the multiple-choice—or "cafeteria"—type of question. Here the respondent has his choice of several answers. For example, a Gallup poll asked, "How far do you, yourself, think the federal government should go in requiring employers to hire people without regard to race, reli-

"Do you, or do you not, favor U.S. participation in some form of world government, under which each nation would forfeit a certain amount of its sovereignty?" (Courtesy Collier's and David Huffine.)

gion, color, or nationality?" The respondent could answer: *All the way; None of the way; Depends on type of work; Should be left to state governments;* or *Don't know.* A variation of this type—the "open-end question"—allows the respondent to supply his own answer. He may be asked simply, "How do you think we should deal with the problem of disloyalty in government?" The answers to this type of question are, of course, hard to tabulate accurately.

Interviewing itself is a delicate task. Tests show that the interviewer's appearance, clothes, language, and way of asking questions may influence the replies. Inaccurate findings may result from the bias of the interviewer, or from his failure to do his job fully and carefully. And the persons interviewed may be the source of error. Respondents suspicious of the interviewer's motives may give false or confused answers. Their memories may be poor—for example, how they voted in a past election. To cover up ignorance they may give neutral answers, or appear undecided. Or they may give the answers that they think the interviewer would like them to give.

Polls may give a false impression of the firmness and intensity of opinion. As we have seen, opinions may be volatile and fleeting. Moreover, polls do not differentiate among people; they give equal weight to a follower and to an opinion leader who may in the end influence other voters. Studies at the Survey Research Center at Michigan suggest that public opinion is not like an iceberg, where the movement of the top indicates the movement of the great mass under water. The visible opinion at the top may be moving in a different direction—indeed it may even be differently located—from that of the great mass of opinion that is far less visible. In short, it is far easier to measure the surface waves and eddies of public opinion than its depth and intensity.

Polling is subject to other limitations. Since any attempt to gather data through sampling must take account of a "sampling error," polls should never be considered exact. Then too, a sample survey of population dispersed over a wide geographical area is unlikely to represent satisfactorily any highly local characteristic of the population. "It is impossible to analyze adequately the complex fabric of social

245

organization through the survey method alone, because the process of sampling tends to lift the individual respondent out of his social context." [24] Obviously the larger the sample and the more careful the polling, the better the results—but also the more costly the investment in money, manpower, and time.

Despite all these difficulties, polling is so useful a device for sounding out opinion that it is employed by a variety of organizations. During elections, parties conduct polls to discover their strong points and weak points. Interest groups run polls to back up their claims that the people—or at least their own members—favor or oppose a certain bill.

Interpreting the Results

To the average American pre-election forecasting is the most intriguing use of surveys. Everyone likes to know in advance how an election will turn out, whether it's Uncle Charlie who is placing an election bet, or a national party chairman, or a stockbroker watching the market. During the campaign pollsters submit regular "returns" on the position of the candidates. On the whole, the record of the leading forecasters has been good, as the table on this page shows. The most sensational slip came in 1948. During the presidential battle between President Truman and Governor Dewey, the polls repeatedly indicated that Mr. Truman was running far behind. The President denounced these "sleeping polls," but the pollsters stood pat on their statistics. Early in September one of them actually announced that the race was over. Gallup gave the President 44.5 per cent of the popular vote in his final forecast and Roper's prediction was 37.1 per cent. Actually, Mr. Truman won 49 per cent of the popular vote, and the pollsters were subjected to general ridicule. Since then the pollsters have been more cautious in making predictions from their polling data.

Some Recent Presidential Polls

Year	Actual Dem. Vote	Roper Poll	Gallup Poll
1936	60.2	61.7	53.8
1940	54.7	55.2	55.0
1944	53.8	53.6	53.3
1948	49.4	37.1	44.5
1952	45.+	43.0	46.0
1956	42.0	40.0	40.5
1960	49.4	47.0	49.0
1964	61.4		61.0

Election forecasters face some specially difficult problems. Actually, all they are polling is "intentions." Some of the respondents may change their plans at the last minute. Some may vote contrary to how they say they will vote, or they may simply fail to go to the polls. The forecasts must estimate which and how many of the people will vote, as well as how they will vote. In 1948 voting turned out to be lighter than expected, and an unusually large number of people cast ballots for state and local candidates but not for

[24] A. A. Campbell and George Katona, "The Sample Survey: A Technique for Social Science Research," in Leon Festinger and Daniel Katz (eds.), *Research Methods in the Behavioral Sciences* (Dryden, 1953), pp. 15–55.

national ones. Happily for the forecasters, however, a pattern is observable in these false expectations. Almost invariably more people expect that they will vote than actually show up at the polls on election day. Hence the forecasters have elaborate correction procedures to eliminate a certain proportion of the respondents who say that they will vote but have characteristics that in the past have cut down their attendance at the polls. Another "patterned irregularity" is that more people say that they will defect to the other party at the beginning of the campaign than actually do so on election day. This "coming-back-home" phenomenon is closely predictable—but the speed of the change is not.

Political polls have taken on increasingly more significant functions in our political system. Candidates use polls to determine where to campaign, how to campaign, and even if they should campaign. In the years and months preceding a national convention, politicians watch the polls to determine which among the hopefuls has "political appeal." Kennedy used polls systematically in both his pre-convention and election campaigns, as Johnson did in his contest with Goldwater. Questions have been raised about this use of polls.[25] Should candidates run for office only when it seems safe to do so? If a candidate believes in a cause, should he not defend it publicly in order to present a meaningful choice to the voters?

Surely the polls at best are no substitute for elections. Faced with his ballot, the voter must translate his opinions into concrete decisions between personalities and parties. He must decide what is important, and what is unimportant. Then, out of the welter of views of all the voters, a decision emerges for some candidate who will act in terms of some program, however vague. For democracy is more than the expression of views, more than a simple mirror of public opinion. It is also the *choosing* among issues—and the governmental action that must follow. Democracy is the thoughtful participation of people in the political process; as Lasswell says, it means *using* heads as well as *counting* them. Elections, with all their failings, at least establish the link between the many voices of the people and the decisions of their leaders.

Politics and Public Opinion

We can sum up our discussion of public opinion with a few thumbnail conclusions:

1. Public opinion has many characteristics. In some respects it tends to be compact and stable; in others fluid and varied. One must speak not merely of public opinion, but of many public opinions.

2. The public itself is many-sided in its make-up. Some people are fickle in their views; others are steady and unmoving. Actually there are many millions of publics, divided in a thousand different ways.

3. Despite its diversity, public opinion is given a certain orderliness by the

[25] See discussion with Elmo Roper and George Gallup, in *Opinion Polls* (Center for the Study of Democratic Institutions, 1962).

fact that most Americans are subjected to common influences—family, schools, press, radio, television, and so on.

4. Much public opinion is formed by deliberate manipulation of attitudes by people with all sorts of purposes, good and bad. The development of highly efficient means of communication and persuasion has enlarged the role of the propagandist, but his influence is by no means unlimited.

5. In the offering of ideas we do not have a wholly free market. In the press and other media we find tendencies toward concentration, commercialization, and conservatism. Most Americans probably want a free market, but there is no easy way to get it. The relation of government to the market is the most difficult problem of all.

6. We have fairly reliable methods for roughly measuring people's attitudes at a given time. But these methods cannot take the place of elections.

Sampling as a Research Tool

Social scientists use surveys not just to find out what people think but also to test hypotheses and to investigate the dynamics of political behavior. To use these sophisticated tools requires advanced training. But all citizens must interpret and process data; and although they use less refined techniques, like social scientists the citizen must be careful in interpreting "the facts." Two problems deserve brief mention: .

The problem of *significance*. Suppose a political scientist after tabulating results from a well-constructed survey discovers that sixty per cent of the Democrats favored an income tax, but only forty per cent of the Republicans. How does he know if this is a significant difference? How does he know that if he asked another 100 Democrats and another 100 Republicans this difference in their attitude toward the income tax would persist? He must use statistical tests to determine if his results have any significance. As a rough rule of thumb, many statisticians consider that if the results secured could happen by chance at least once in twenty times, the results are not statistically significant.

The problem of *multi-variables*. Suppose a political scientist is trying to determine what factors are related to a high interest in politics. He discovers that 70 per cent of the men in his sample have a high interest in politics but only 30 per cent of the women. Although this difference is statistically significant, before he concludes that political interest depends on sex he decides to test another variable. It seems unlikely, he speculates, that the biological difference between men and women could account for this difference in political interest. More likely, he thinks, is that in our society more women stay at home than do men and perhaps this is the factor which accounts for increased political interest. So he cross-tabulates his data. This time he groups his respondents by whether they have jobs which keep them at home or whether they have jobs which take them to an office or a factory. He finds that both men and women who have jobs that keep them at home have a lower political interest than do either men or women who do not stay at home, and the difference is statistically significant. His hypothesis is verified.[26]

By this type of multi-variant analysis, social scientists are beginning to explore not only how people behave in politics but to understand why they so behave.

What is the relation of government to all this? Obviously, government is not an innocent bystander in the constant play and interplay of political attitudes. It is closely related to the whole process. It has a stake in the way attitudes are formed, in the methods used to form them, such as television, and in the uses of propaganda. A democratic government is especially interested in the degree of competition in the market place of ideas, and in the ways that polling organizations try to measure public opinion.

Above all, government is concerned with the make-up of public opinion itself. To stay in office, politicians must respond—or at least seem to respond—to changing opinions. They must have some sense of the scope of popular attitudes, their intensity, their stability or instability. Measuring public opinion in its many forms—perhaps by a sort of sixth sense—is the essence of the politician's job. To be successful he must have the knack of peering behind propaganda fronts and gauging the real public opinion, of spotting the areas of ignorance, the areas of apathy, the areas of understanding, the areas of action.

But all politicians do not respond to public opinion in the same way. Government is made up of thousands of different men, with varying attitudes, ambitions, and loyalties. Obviously, a President responsible to the whole nation and a senator elected by a state will often react differently to public opinion. The senator will react differently from a member of the House of Representatives. And perhaps an administrative official will take still another view. Many factors lie behind the diverse attitudes of officials—their position in the government, the people by whom they are elected or appointed, the amount of security they enjoy, the date of the next election or appointment, the balance of forces in their home district or in the office of their superior, their own basic attitudes and expectations.

Nor does government merely *respond* to public opinion; it also *creates* it. Government is not merely the broker for outside pressures or putty in the hands of mighty groups. Our "strong" Presidents and even less dynamic ones like Coolidge and Eisenhower have known the uses of public opinion.[27] Congressional investigation committees have learned how to make headlines with their revelations. The job of the political leader is to guide political attitudes and mediate among them as well as to follow them. This dual role enables the politician to provide the great need of modern democracies—responsible leadership. Knowing how to respond to public opinion and how to help shape it is much of the art of democratic leadership.

[26] This discussion is drawn primarily from Jane Werner Watson, *The Sciences of Mankind: Social Scientists at Work* (Golden Press, 1960), pp. 111–115.
[27] Elmer E. Cornwell, Jr., *Presidential Leadership of Public Opinion* (Indiana Univ. Press., 1965).

10 POLITICAL BEHAVIOR: THE AMERICAN VOTER

Politics is sometimes called "the great American game." Thousands of politicians take part in it; millions of people follow the election fights and decide who will win and who will lose. Yet the real nature of the game remains a mystery. Why does one candidate win and another lose? Why are so many Americans merely spectators? What causes some people to go to the polls and vote when others do not? How do we decide to vote the way we do? Man is a political animal, yet man knows all too little about his own political behavior—or misbehavior.

Of course, there are a lot of pet theories—theories that are resurrected in every election by the newspapers and by the politicians themselves. Experience often deals harshly with these theories, but they live on. Take the old saying, "As Maine goes, so goes the nation." This has been disproved in election after election. (In 1936, Jim Farley said, "As goes Maine, so goes Vermont.") But it was years before the old adage died. Again, it has long been political gospel that mid-term congressional elections foreshadow the results of the next presidential election, but the 1948 and 1956 results upset this theory—at least for a while. Other frequently encountered observations seem more durable. That most labor union members tend to vote for Democratic candidates while most doctors are politically aligned with the Republican party is a verifiable generalization. There are, however, subtle but important variations even within these categories.

We are still groping for some understanding of our own political behavior. In recent years there has been a systematic effort to answer some of these basic questions of political life. Political scientists, social psychologists, cultural anthropologists, and others are making new studies that in time may throw a flood of light on the political process. Their tools questionnaires, voting statistics, polls, interviews, intensive studies of particular campaigns, and so on—are slowly being improved. We are gaining new insights into the way relations among members of groups, between leaders and followers, and among members of families affect political activity.

Here again the keynote is change. Sometimes political change comes very quickly, as when voting returns seem to shift crazily from year to year. Far more important are underlying changes that may produce a series of voting shifts over the years. Thus we are still affected by basic forces that were unloosed in the "realigning election" of 1896.[1] In this decade we are in a period of flux in national politics. The 1964 election campaign was a very different type of struggle from most presidential election campaigns of this century. In this chapter we will deal more with the earlier elections because 1964 seemed such an exceptional one. But will it be exceptional for the future? If conservative Republicans retain control of Republican presidential conventions, ideological battles between the parties may be the rule rather than the exception—and one more enduring change will have registered itself in American politics.

Who Votes?

The history of the suffrage in the United States has been a continuing struggle to extend the right to vote from a small group of property-owning males—perhaps

[1] Walter Dean Burnham, "The Changing Shape of the American Political Universe," *The American Political Science Review* (March 1965), pp. 7–28.

one person out of every twenty or thirty—to the great bulk of the adults. In this chapter we will consider who actually votes, and how and why, rather than with who has the *right* to vote. But let us pause to note, without indulging in patriotic self-congratulations, that we could not even be discussing voting behavior if a lot of men and women had not fought to extend the right to vote over the last century and a half.

Three great struggles have been fought over this issue. The first was against *property* tests for voting. Conservatives like Chancellor Kent of New York argued that universal male suffrage would jeopardize the rights of property, that if poor people gained the right to vote they would sell their votes to the rich. The democratic, egalitarian mood of America, eastern immigration and the western frontier, and the eagerness of politicians to lower voting barriers so they could pick up votes—all these led to a series of struggles in the states and to the end of property (and taxpaying) restrictions by the mid-nineteenth century. The second great struggle was for *womens' suffrage.* Husbands argued that women had no place at the polling booth, that husbands could vote for the interests of the whole family —but these arguments had a hollow ring. The aroused women conducted noisy parades, drew up petitions, organized a Washington lobby, picketed the White House, got arrested, went on hunger strikes in jail. They won the vote in some states and finally achieved a breakthrough in 1920 with the passage of the Nineteenth Amendment. The third struggle—for Negro suffrage—is still going on (see Chapter 7). We will doubtless see more tumult and violence particularly in the states of the deep South and in Negro ghettos in large northern cities, before this right too becomes guaranteed.

Still, the overwhelming number of Americans, including Negroes, have the right to vote. What do they do with it?

THE PRESIDENTIAL VOTE SINCE 1912

Adapted from The New York Times.

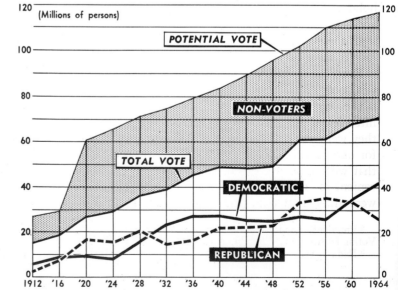

Millions of Nonvoters

On the average, the proportion of
Americans who vote is smaller than that of the British, French, Italians, West
Germans, Scandinavians, or Canadians (although the figures are not strictly comparable). Talk as we will about the right to vote, the hard fact remains that millions of Americans do not want to vote or somehow fail to get to the polls on
election day. Our elections have not always been characterized by low voter
participation. Eighty-six per cent of the adult enfranchised males voted in 1876.
Beginning in the early 1900's voter participation declined steadily, increasing
slightly in the era of Franklin D. Roosevelt.[2] In those democracies where people
have the right not to vote if they wish, there will always be some nonvoters. But
the startling feature of nonvoting in America is its extent. In the 1964 presidential
election almost two fifths of the potential voters did not go to the polls. About half
of them will stay at home in the congressional elections of 1966 and 1970. Participation in state and local elections is usually even lower.

Why do people fail to vote? Even aside from outright denials of the right to
vote, "Many election laws and administrative practices are unreasonable, unfair,
and outmoded. They obstruct the path to the ballot box, disfranchising millions
who want to vote."[3] About eight million could not vote in 1960 because they had so
recently moved from one state or county to another that they were unable to meet
residence requirements. To reduce this involuntary nonvoting, a President's
Commission recommended that: voter registration be made easy for citizens, for
example by authorizing registrars to canvass house by house; that state residence
requirements be reduced to six months and local residence requirements to 30
days; that voting lists should be kept current; that states provide absentee registration; that literacy tests be abolished; that election day be proclaimed a national
holiday; that absentee voting by mail be allowed; that poll taxes be eliminated;
and—not least—that states consider lowering the voting age to 18 years. But even
if all these recommendations (and others) were adopted, many persons would still
fail to show up at the polls.

Every study confirms the findings of Merriam and Gosnell, two pioneer investigators, who on the basis of interviews discovered that simple lack of interest
is the primary reason for nonvoting. Although about one in every eight of those
interviewed said that they were ill at the time and about the same number said
they were away from the voting district, 10 per cent simply disbelieved in voting
for one reason or another—they were "disgusted with politics," or they thought
that women should not vote, or something of the sort. Some found it too inconvenient to vote; a few—mostly women—did not want to disclose their ages. Some
were afraid that they would lose business or wages while they went to the polls.

[2] President's Commission on Registration and Voting Participation, *Report* on Registration and
Voting Participation (Government Printing Office, 1963), p. 6.
[3] *Ibid.*, p. 11.

A salesman said he was more concerned with his business than with politics. A housewife said she did her washing that day. A mother explained simply, "Got a lot of children." A young musician confessed that he had had one of his temperamental spells on election day. Some nonvoters said they had intended to vote but had forgotten all about it.[4]

Most nonvoting probably results from a combination of inconvenience and low interest. That is, a young man really would take the trouble to vote on election day—but he forgot to register to vote two months earlier. Or an elderly woman would vote if the polls were around the corner—but the polls are actually two miles away and she lacks easy transportation. One reason that Europeans turn out in larger numbers than Americans is that they have avoided a lot of the red tape (especially registration procedures) that afflicts our system.

Who Fails to Vote?

The extent of voting varies among different types of persons, areas, and elections. Voting studies generally agree on the following patterns, which are listed here roughly in order of declining importance:

1. *The higher a person's income, the more likely he is to vote.* Our common sense might expect the opposite—that low-income people would have a strong incentive to vote because of the benefits they can gain from government. Why do low-income people vote in fewer numbers than the wealthy? For a medley of interrelated reasons. They have less economic security; they feel less of a sense of control over their political environment; they feel at a disadvantage in social contacts and their social norms tend to de-emphasize politics. They are subject to cross-pressures; on the one hand, their experiences and their class position push them toward political action, but they are also exposed to strong upper-class and conservative influences through the press, radio, churches, and the like. Low-income class nonvoting thus is part of a larger political and psychological environment that discourages political activity, including voting.[5]

2. *The college educated vote more than the noncollege educated.* "Practically speaking," writes Warren Miller, "almost everybody who has been to college votes." [6] Even college-educated persons who profess little interest in or knowledge about political issues turn out to vote. People with college backgrounds exist in a climate of opinion in which voting is considered a civic duty; they tend to be more

[4] C. E. Merriam and H. F. Gosnell, *Non-Voting* (Univ. of Chicago Press, 1924). Paul F. Lazarsfeld *et al.*, *The People's Choice* (Duell, Sloan, and Pearce, 1944), pp. 45–46. See also S. M. Lipset, *Political Man* (Doubleday, 1959); Robert E. Lane, *Political Life* (The Free Press, 1959); Bernard R. Berelson, Paul F. Lazarsfeld, and William N. McPhee, *Voting* (Univ. of Chicago Press, 1954), pp. 331–347.

[5] See Lane, *op. cit.*, pp. 50, 233–234; Angus Campbell, Philip E. Converse, Warren E. Miller, and Donald E. Stokes, *The American Voter* (Wiley, 1960); and Lipset, *op. cit.*, pp. 203–205.

[6] Warren Miller, "The Political Behavior of the Electorate," *American Government Annual, 1960–1961* (Holt, Rinehart and Winston, 1960), p. 50.

exposed to ideas, active people, newspapers, political leaders. The college education itself may have an independent effect in itself in exposing the graduate to political ideas and personalities. Persons with only a grade-school education vote less than high-school alumni.

3. *Middle-aged people tend to vote more than the younger and older.* Many young people are busy getting established, moving about, having babies, raising young children. The new husband is occupied with getting ahead; the young wife is immersed in home affairs. They find little time for politics. The more established, between thirty-five and fifty-five, are more active; then voting falls off sharply in the sixties and seventies owing partly to infirmities of old age. The higher incomes enjoyed by middle-aged citizens (on the average) may also spur them to greater participation.

4. *Men tend to vote more than women.* This variation—not very great in most elections—exists in many foreign countries as well. In recent presidential elections about 61 in every 100 women have voted, about 75 in every 100 men. Women feel less social pressure to vote than men, are subject to more cross-pressures concerning which way they should vote, and so tend to withdraw. Morality issues like prohibition generally bring out a high women's vote, and college-educated women tend to be more active in political party work than college-educated men. There are indications that the traditional differences in the rate of voting between men and women is decreasing.

5. *Republicans tend to vote more than Democrats.* In the 1952 election, for example, only eight per cent of those who regarded themselves as "strong Republicans" failed to vote, while 24 per cent of those who regarded themselves as "strong Democrats" stayed at home.[7] This gap too may be narrowing.

6. *Partisans tend to vote more than independents.* "By far the most important psychological factor affecting an individual's decision to vote in his identification with a political party."[8] When the election outcome is doubtful, strong partisanship is even more likely to induce a person to vote. A partisan is likely to have a personal interest, and to be concerned about the outcome.

Summing up, if you are a young woman, with a low income, and little sense of partisanship, the chances that you will turn out even for an exciting presidential election are far less than if you are a wealthy man, in your fifties, a strong Republican partisan. Thus nonvoting influences are cumulative, or additive. But there also appear to be certain psychological or attitudinal differences between nonvoters and voters. Even when sex, age, education and income are controlled, the chronic nonvoter more characteristically than the voter is a person with a sense of inadequacy, more inclined to accept authority, more concerned with personal and short-range issues, less sympathetic toward democratic norms, and less tolerant of those who differ from himself.[9]

---

[7] Angus Campbell, Gerald Gurin and Warren E. Miller, *The Voter Decides* (Harper, 1954), pp. 70–73.
[8] The President's Commission, pp. 9–10.
[9] Lane, *op. cit.*, p. 342.

Effect of Different Types of Elections

Political institutions have their impact on nonvoting. So does the total political context. Among these are:

1. *National elections tend to bring out more voters than state or local campaigns.* Presidential elections attract the greatest number of voters. Off-year congressional elections almost invariably draw fewer persons to the polls. City and other local elections tend to attract an even smaller number. And participation is lowest in party primaries. Even when voters are marking a ballot that offers a variety of national and local contests, some voters will check their presidential choice but not bother with others. This is one reason why our governmental officials chosen by somewhat different electorates often represent different points of view. In a local election, for example, where there is little public interest, a local political organization finds it easier to control the outcome of city elections than it would the vote for national officials.

2. *Meaningful contests tend to bring out more voters.* Voting is higher when the electorate clearly perceives that the choices between candidates and parties may make a difference. In recent decades in Italy, voters often have had a choice among the Communist, the quasi-fascist, or the democratic parties. These party differences, reflecting intense conflicts within the Italian society, are significant and dramatic; they affect the daily lives of millions. It is not surprising that most Italians turn out to vote. When Americans have faced—or thought they faced— great choices about the political shape of the future, as in the elections of 1916, 1936, and 1940, they too have turned out in fairly heavy numbers.

3. *Voting tends to be lowest in areas in which there is little two-party competition.* Thus, the lowest voting figures are apt to be found in states such as Mississippi, Georgia, and South Carolina, although undoubtedly the restraints on Negro voting are more important than lack of party competition. Recently there has been a marked upswing of voting in the South. The growth of two-party politics in the South, the appeal of Goldwater Republicanism, and greater participation by Negroes are all having their effect.[10]

How serious is the low rate of voting? Does it indicate that our democratic system is in danger and should we encourage—perhaps even force—everyone to vote? No, answer many authorities. F. G. Wilson suggests that it is not a low rate of voting that signals a danger for a democratic system, but a high rate.[11] A pioneering Swedish student of voting behavior concluded after a survey of voting studies around the world that a high turnout warns of such intense

---

[10] Converse, Campbell, Miller, and Stokes, "Stability and Change in 1960: A Reinstating Election," *The American Political Science Review* (June 1961), pp. 269–280.

[11] F. G. Wilson, "The Inactive Electorate and Social Revolution," *Southwestern Social Science Quarterly*, Vol. XVI, 1936, pp. 73–74.

differences among groups that the democratic system may be destroyed.[12] A measure of nonvoting, it is argued, is a sign of widespread satisfaction, indicating that many people generally accept the status quo and have more interesting things to do than to get involved in politics.

Clearly there would be little to be gained from pushing into the polls people who have little knowledge about or interest in the election. And *sudden* upsurges in voting precipitated by a social crisis or by the pull of an authoritarian leader are a danger sign, especially since large numbers of nonvoters are mobilized with little sympathy for democratic values. For all surveys and investigations suggest that persons with low levels of political sophistication tend to take a simplified view of politics, fail to show tolerance toward those with whom they disagree, and find it difficult to grasp democratic norms. And it is also clear that the level of voting merely as a raw statistic has little significance—compare the 99.9 per cent turnout rates in the Soviet Union with those in the United States or England, for example.

What counts is the *kind* of participation. As long as all groups in our society are represented by the electorate, some nonvoting may not be cause for concern. But a large number of uninterested, apathetic, uninformed nonvoters provides a potential source of votes to be exploited by authoritarians and a potential factor contributing to instability in time of national crisis.

How to increase participation gradually? Moralistic preaching about the duties of citizenship fails to reach its chief target. It would be better to concentrate on political and institutional changes: Raise the level of education and economic well-being. Shorten the ballot by cutting down the number of unimportant elective positions. Simplify registration and residence requirements. Above all, make the parties more competitive in state and local as well as national elections.

So much for the nonvoter. What about the people who *do* vote?

How We Vote

Sometimes Americans are called fickle voters who switch from party to party as blithely and as often as women change fashions. Actually, however, the great majority of Americans stick to one party year after year, and their sons and grandsons vote for the same party long after that. Politically, these voters are "set in their ways." As a result, both parties can count on the support of an almost irreducible minimum of voters who will go Republican or Democratic almost by habit.

Of course, there are still millions of so-called independent voters who tack back and forth from party to party. They help make our elections the unpredictable and breathless affairs that they so often are. Still, even in the variations from year to year one finds certain persistent elements. Looking closely at the complex mosaic of American politics, we can see *patterns* of voting habits that help us understand *how* we vote, and a little about *why* we vote as we do.

[12] Herbert Tingsten, *Political Behavior: Studies in Election Statistics* (London: P. S. King & Son, 1937), pp. 225–226.

Patterns of Voting

1. A pattern of *state* voting. Since the Civil War, Vermont has given its electoral votes to the Democrats only in 1964, and Maine has done so only twice since 1912. Mississippians and South Carolinians, on the other hand, have given a fifth of their presidential popular votes to Republicans only twice, and usually much less. Between these extremes some states have tended to be Republican in national elections, as in the case of Oregon, Kansas, Pennsylvania, and New Hampshire, or to be Democratic, as with several Rocky Mountain states, some border states, and of course the Solid South. Most states, however, are doubtful; they cannot be considered safe by either party. Indeed, some doubtful states are consistent only in their inconsistency.

2. A pattern of *sectional* voting. The South is the most famous example. The Democratic solidarity of the states that formed the Confederacy has been breached in six presidential races: in 1928, when Al Smith, a Catholic, headed the Democratic national ticket; in 1948, when President Truman was campaigning on a civil rights platform; in 1952, when Stevenson lost some southern states; in 1956, when Eisenhower carried all but seven states in the nation; in 1960, when 14 Democratic electors from Mississippi and Alabama refused to vote for Kennedy; and in 1964 when the only states Goldwater carried (except for his own Arizona) were Alabama, Georgia, Louisiana, and Mississippi. North of the Solid South lies a band of border states that lean toward the Democrats. Republican sectionalism is not so clear cut. Much of New England and the upper Midwest tends to be firmly Republican in presidential years. Recently, however, there have been Democratic inroads in the off-year elections, such as Democratic successes in Maine and Vermont. The 1962 "off-year" elections showed a continuing swing toward a party balance *within* sections; for example, a Democrat won the governorship of Vermont for the first time since the Civil War, and the Republicans captured the governorship of Oklahoma for the first time in the state's history.

3. A pattern of *national* voting. In most states party popularity rises and falls with the national popularity of the party. National trends, in other words, are reflected in trends in most of the states. States and sections are subject to a variety of local influences, but they cannot resist the great tides that sweep the nation. This is especially true of changes in economic conditions. Our national economy is so integrated that people in every state tend to feel the effects of highs and lows in the business cycle. As a result, the percentage of the vote for a party in many states is a gauge of national voting behavior. "As the nation goes," says Louis H. Bean, "so goes Massachusetts . . . New York . . . Pennsylvania . . . Illinois . . . Ohio . . . Michigan . . . Wisconsin . . . Minnesota . . . California . . . and so goes almost any state outside the South." [13] In other words, the relation between the Democratic vote in these states and the national Democratic vote tends to remain constant. In the case of Illinois, for example,

[13] Louis H. Bean, *How to Predict Elections* (Knopf, 1948), pp. 105–106.

one usually need add a few percentage points to its Democratic percentage to get a rough gauge of the national Democratic percentage. Iowa usually stays about seven percentage points below the national Democratic level. Except for some southern states, this kind of pattern was evident again in 1964.

4. A pattern of voting for candidates for *different offices* in the same election. Well over half the voters usually vote a straight ticket—that is, they throw their support to every one of their party's candidates. If one candidate is an especially able vote-getter—as Johnson was in 1964, for example—the party's whole slate may gain. Thus it is said that weaker candidates ride into office on the coattails of stronger ones. The pulling power of a presidential candidate's coattails seems to help elect members of his own party to office during presidential election years; Democrats, for example, won many more seats in Congress in 1936, 1944, and 1948 than in the off-year elections in between, as did Republicans clinging to Eisenhower's coattails in 1952. It is not easy to tell, however, which candidate rides on whose coattails, or just how important the relation is.[14]

5. Finally, a pattern of voting over *time*. There seem to be great political tides that flow back and forth as decade follows decade. The general mood of the nation for the past century has seemed to alternate broadly between liberalism and conservatism; it has been suggested by one historian, for example, that the periods 1841–1861, 1869–1901, and 1918–1931 were marked by a general emphasis on property rights, and the other periods by a stress on human rights. Another historian predicted that the 1960's would be a liberal period following the relative conservatism of the 1950's.[15] Moreover, the Republican and Democratic parties have alternated in power (especially in their control of the House of Representatives) with a fair degree of regularity.

Behind the Tides

What causes the political tides to rise and fall? The business cycle, for one thing. A drop in business activity has often preceded a loss of congressional seats by the party in power; the latest case was in 1958. But we cannot be sure that business cycles *cause* political cycles. Sometimes the two cycles diverge in erratic fashion. Psychological, political, traditional, sectional, international, and other forces may muddle the effect of economic forces.

If, then, there are patterns in American politics, these patterns are rough, and they are often blurred by capricious and unexplainable variations. Indeed, the patterns may exist for many years and then disappear. For example, before the

[14] D. B. Truman, "Political Behavior and Voting," *The Pre-Election Polls of 1948* (Social Science Research Council, 1949), pp. 239–244. See also John W. Meyer, "A Reformulation of the 'Coattails' Problem," in William N. McPhee and William A. Glaser, *Public Opinion and Congressional Elections* (The Free Press, 1962).

[15] A. M. Schlesinger, "Tides of American Politics," *Yale Review*, Vol. 29 (1939), pp. 217–230; A. M. Schlesinger, Jr., "The Shape of National Politics to Come" (privately circulated memorandum, 1959).

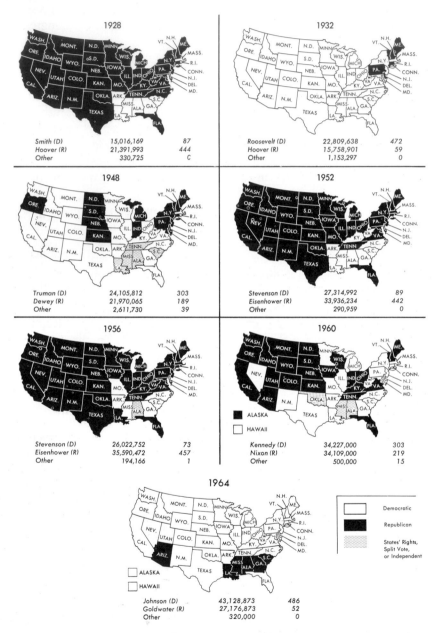

SEVEN PRESIDENTIAL ELECTIONS 1928–1964

1928

Smith (D)	15,016,169	87
Hoover (R)	21,391,993	444
Other	330,725	C

1932

Roosevelt (D)	22,809,638	472
Hoover (R)	15,758,901	59
Other	1,153,297	0

1948

Truman (D)	24,105,812	303
Dewey (R)	21,970,065	189
Other	2,611,730	39

1952

Stevenson (D)	27,314,992	89
Eisenhower (R)	33,936,234	442
Other	290,959	0

1956

Stevenson (D)	26,022,752	73
Eisenhower (R)	35,590,472	457
Other	194,166	1

1960

ALASKA
HAWAII

Kennedy (D)	34,227,000	303
Nixon (R)	34,109,000	219
Other	500,000	15

1964

ALASKA
HAWAII

Democratic

Republican

States' Rights,
Split Vote,
or Independent

Johnson (D)	43,128,873	486
Goldwater (R)	27,176,873	52
Other	320,000	0

*Patterns of voting. (Adapted from Dayton D. McKean,
Party and Pressure Politics. Boston: Houghton Mifflin,
1949.)*

1948 election a change in party control of Congress in an off-year election had regularly preceded a change in party fortunes in the following presidential election. But the Democrats, who lost control of Congress in 1946, won both houses of Congress and the Presidency in 1948; and despite 1954 Democratic congressional victories, the Republicans captured the White House, though not Congress, in 1956. So perhaps we will hear less of this "pattern" in the future.

Perhaps this murkiness in American politics is a good thing. Perhaps it shows that we are not caught in inevitable and relentless forces beyond our control. As yet unfathomable factors of chance and human nature still have their place. Even the opinion polls, with all their careful scientific techniques, must reckon with these factors. As someone said following Truman's startling victory in 1948, no one can expect to deliver the American people, neatly packaged, tied, and ticketed. Men of determination in either party, campaigning skillfully and energetically, can overcome "inevitable" political trends.

Why We Vote as We Do

Suppose we were able to find ten voters who represented a tiny but fairly accurate cross section of the American electorate. Suppose—shortly after an exciting and close presidential election—we asked them to tell us in a few words why they voted as they did. And suppose they gave us the *real* reason they voted as they did. What kind of answer would we get? Studies of voting indicate that their answers might go something like this:

MR. ANDERSON (*fruitgrower*): "I voted Republican. I always do. I'm a businessman, you see, and the Republicans have a sound, businesslike point of view. All the fruitgrowers around here voted that way."

MRS. SMITH (*housewife*): "I supported the Democratic candidate. My husband said he was going to vote that way. He doesn't tell me how to vote, but I leave the politics to him. He always seems to vote Democratic anyway."

MARY BROWN (*stenographer*): "Well, I didn't know what to do. I wasn't much interested, frankly, but all the girls at the office seemed to think the Democrats are doing a good job, so that's the way I decided to go."

HARRY VENUTI (*young barber*): "Me? Democratic. The Venutis always vote Democratic. We go along with Tom Murphy—he's a big wheel in the party here, and he's a nice fellow too. He's done us some good turns."

DR. WHITE (*local surgeon*): "I voted Republican. I don't like these medical programs the Democrats keep talking about. They'll hurt all us doctors if they go through."

JOHNNY BLACK (*factory worker*): "I voted for the Republican candidate for President even though I'm a Democrat. All the boys in the plant were talking Democratic and one of the boys on the union committee gave us a pep talk about supporting the Democrats. But I voted Republican for President—he seemed more sincere. I just didn't warm up to the candidate of the Democrats."

MRS. MURPHY (*housewife*): "I was on the fence a long time. I read the speeches in the paper, watched on television, and finally I went Democratic. Except for Senator ————. He's been in a long time and people say he's very conscientious."

MR. SCOTT (*industrialist*): "Republican, of course. We can't take these high taxes much longer. Besides the Republican candidates are obviously higher type men. They are statesmen, not politicians. I voted a straight Republican ticket."

BILL JOHNSON (*unemployed*): "I didn't know what to do. My family's Republican, but the Democrats seem to want to do something to get men back to work. So I split my vote—Democratic for President, Republican for Congressman."

SALLY RICE (*salesgirl*): "Well, I didn't even plan to vote. I'm not much interested in politics. But I was so mad after some people booed the Republican candidate at the movies the night before that I went out and voted for him. I just voted for a couple of candidates—I didn't know all those other names."

Voting Behavior

In what ways are these ten persons representative of Americans as a whole in the manner in which they made up their minds?

First and foremost, over half of the ten supported their *party* almost automatically, and this voting by habit is true of most American voters. No matter what the candidates or issues, no matter whether wars or depressions are taking place, millions of voters in both parties can be relied on to put their X's in the same party column election after election. Since party identification is amazingly stable over the years,[16] each major party is sure to poll a big national vote. This traditional vote is not necessarily blind or irrational. In many cases, voting for the same party over the years may represent a person's rational view of his self-interest, as in the case of Mr. Anderson above or Harry Venuti. In any case, habitual voting, or what more precisely may be called "party identification," is by far the most important cause of how people vote. If you want to predict someone's vote in the next election and you can ask him only one question, the best one to ask is "What party do you belong to?"

But party identification is by no means the only factor. Some people, like Mr. Black, departed from their traditional party affiliation to vote for the candidate of the opposition. Most of the time even when we claim to vote for "the man and not the party," our warmness or coldness toward the candidate is related to whether or not he belongs to the party we do. But not always. An Eisenhower whose personality was so appealing to millions was able to win the vote of many Democrats.

Secondly, most of our ten voted the same way as their *families* or *friends* or *workmates* were going to vote. On election day Americans mark their ballots in

---

[16] Campbell, *et al.*, *op. cit.*, ch. 6.

private, yet voting is essentially a *group* experience. We tend to vote as apple-growers, union members, Legionnaires, prohibitionists, Catholics, Constitution reverers, isolationists, or as members of other existing or potential groups. The most homogeneous of all groups in molding the opinions of its members is probably the parental family.[17] In Erie County it was discovered that among husbands and wives, both of whom planned to vote, twenty-one couples out of every twenty-two agreed on their choice. Parents and children tended to vote the same way too; only one pair in twelve divided. As might be expected, in-laws were less in agreement, but even here four out of five agreed in their party choice.[18] The reasons for this uniformity are twofold. Members of the family shape one another's attitudes (often unintentionally); and members of the same family are naturally exposed to similar economic, religious, class, and geographical influences. The husband seems to be head of the house politically as well as otherwise. Most wives talk the election over with their husbands. Men, on the other hand, "do not feel that they are discussing politics with their wives; they feel they are telling them." [19]

A third factor related to voting is *income*. Most studies of voting behavior confirm what everyday observation has already indicated: The highest proportion of persons who prefer the Republican party are in the upper-income brackets, especially those with incomes over $10,000 a year. But we cannot make too much of this factor, indeed of *any* single factor. In 1952 and 1956 Eisenhower's great personal popularity seemed to blur differences in income, and the correlation between income and voting preference which developed out of the 1932 Depression tended to disappear. Do the voting returns of the 1950's indicate a decline in class voting—that is, in the tendency of the lower socio-economic groups to vote Democratic, and of the higher to vote Republican? A recent study concludes that there is no evidence of a long-term realignment of the rough class base of the political parties.[20]

Several other factors may be noted briefly. *Where one lives* apparently has a relation to how one votes; Republican strength outside of the South is most concentrated in the small cities. *Race* and *religion* are also related to voting, with Negroes voting more heavily for the Democrats, as do Catholic voters. Some of these factors can be seen in the table on page 264.

[17] Herbert McClosky and Harold E. Dahlgren, "Primary Group Influence on Party Loyalty," *The American Political Science Review* (September 1959), p. 775.

[18] Lazarsfeld, *The People's Choice*, p. 141. See also T. M. Newcomb, *Social Psychology* (Dryden, 1950), pp. 531–534. For some interesting exceptions to this tendency, see E. E. Maccoby, R. E. Matthews, and A. S. Morton, "Youth and Political Change," *Public Opinion Quarterly*, Vol. 18 (1954), pp. 23–29; and Campbell, *et al.*, *The Voter Decides*, pp. 109–206.

[19] Lazarsfeld, *op. cit.*, p. 141. For some recent studies in this area, see articles by H. W. Riecken, C. W. Wahl, and R. D. Luce in the provocative collection of essays, Eugene Burdick and A. J. Brodbeck (eds.), *American Voting Behavior* (The Free Press, 1959); McClosky and Dahlgren, *op. cit.*, pp. 757–776; and Lane, *op. cit.* And see generally James C. Davies, *Human Nature in Politics* (Wiley, 1963).

[20] Robert R. Alford, "The Role of Social Class in American Voting Behavior," *The Western Political Quarterly* (March 1963), pp. 180–194.

The Demography of the Vote in
Recent Presidential Elections (by
Percentage)

Demographic Characteristic	1948 Dem.	1948 Rep.	1956 Dem.	1956 Rep.	1960 Dem.	1960 Rep.	1964 Dem.	1964 Rep.
Religion								
Protestant	47*	53*	37	63	38	62	55	45
Catholic	66*	34*	51	49	78	22	76	24
Jewish			75	25	81	19	90	10
Race								
White	53*	47*	41	59	49	51	59	41
Negro	81*	19*	61	39	68	32	94	6
Union Labor Families	74†	26	57	43	65	35		
Young Voters (Age 21–29 yrs.)	62†	38	43	57	54	46	64	36
Sex								
Women	53*	47*	39	61	49	51	62	38
Men	56*	44*	45	55	52	48	60	40

Table from *American Government Annual* (Holt, Rinehart and Winston), 1961 Volume, p. 74; 1965 Volume, p. 24.
* Figures accompanied by an asterisk are taken from Angus Campbell *et al.*, *The Voter Decides* (Row, Peterson, 1954), pp. 70–71. Data given there were converted from a percentage of the total sample to a percentage of those voting, ignoring the "Other" column. All other data are taken from releases of the American Institute of Public Opinion (The Gallup Poll).
† Includes Democratic, Progressive, and States' Rights votes.

But we cannot make too much of these categories. The shift from Democratic to Republican presidential voters between 1948 and 1956 was not peculiar to one or two groups, but was in fact common to all economic classes, religions, and racial groups. In 1956, for example, the Negro vote was still primarily pro-Democratic, but Eisenhower picked up more than twice as many votes among Negroes as Dewey had won in 1948. Although Catholics still vote more Democratic than do Protestants, a majority cast their votes for Eisenhower in 1956. Some elections, of course, tend to divide the electorate more evenly along economic lines (as in 1936) than do others (1952). Sometimes noneconomic forces are crucial. In the 1960 election, for example, religion became a highly publicized issue. Although President Kennedy won a larger ratio of the votes among Catholics than is normal for Protestant Democratic presidential candidates, he lost a much higher number of southern white-Protestant votes than is normal for the Democratic presidential candidate. Still, even in 1960, the basic party vote was the key factor; Kennedy won mainly because he was a Democrat and the Democrats regained the majority they lost to Eisenhower during the 1950's.[21]

To identify the political preferences of sociological groups may give a mis-

[21] Philip E. Converse, *et al.*, "Stability and Change in 1960: A Reinstating Election," *op. cit.* See also Andrew R. Baggaley, "Religious Influence on Wisconsin Voting, 1928–1960," *The American Political Science Review* (March 1962), p. 66 ff.

leading picture of voting behavior, for over time these distinctions alter, and they fail to take into account the impact of national and international developments and the personality factors of the individual voter and the way he responds to candidates. ". . . Events, communications, and attitudes—may all be more or less independent of group memberships and social classifications," points out Warren Miller. They all make important contributions to the individual's political behavior. But their importance is inevitably minimized or neglected in group-oriented descriptions of electoral behavior. Even to describe people as Democrats or Republicans does not tell us for sure how a voter will behave. "A sense of being a Democrat or being a Republican is not necessarily at all the same as voting for the candidate which a party has sponsored." President Eisenhower, for example, could not have been elected or re-elected if it had not been for millions of Democrats who voted for him.

Thus, we may speak in general terms and say that if Mr. Jones is a wealthy businessman, Protestant, living in a small Ohio town, married to a Protestant, and the son of a Republican, the chances are very good that Jones will vote Republican. Unless radical alterations occur in our party structures or in our society generally, we can predict that such a person as Jones will vote Republican in a future election before we know either the candidates or the issues. But this does not mean that people's voting behavior can be predicted with certainty or that voting is a simple mechanical addition to set factors. Some men like Jones vote Democratic.

It is a healthy sign that our political parties do not reflect too accurately basic social, economic, geographical, and religious differences. The fact that some Jews are Republicans, that some wealthy men are Democrats, that neither party can claim a monopoly of any group, keeps the parties from reinforcing and exaggerating differences. Lipset observes, "Where parties are cut off from gaining support among a major stratum, they lose a major reason for compromise." [22]

All Kinds of Independents

Regularly a quarter to a third of the voters could be classed as independents. Unable to identify themselves consistently with one party or candidate, some independents cross and re-cross party lines from election to election. Some "split" their ticket and vote for some candidates from one party and other candidates from another party. Some people call themselves independents because they think it is socially more respectable, but actually they vote with the same degree of regularity for one party as do others who are not so hesitant to admit party loyalty.[23] So there are all kinds of independ-

[22] Lipset, *Political Man, op. cit.*, p. 31.
[23] Samuel J. Eldersveld, "The Independent Vote: Measurement, Characteristics, and Implications for Party Strategy," *The American Political Science Review* (September 1952), p. 737. In one study reported by Eldersveld one-half of those who claimed to be independents were *not*, by objective criteria.

ent voters. A study indicates that younger voters who live in middle-size cities, with above average income, and with a college education, tend to be more independent than other groups, but that the independent vote is rather evenly distributed throughout the population.[24] On the average, about one out of every five voters calls himself independent, and twelve million independent-minded voters are a fact for any politician to reckon with.

Is the independent voter the more informed voter? There has been heated debate over this question, but much of it fruitless because everything depends on what kind of independent we are talking about. If independents are defined as those who fail to express a preference between parties, the "independent voter" tends to be less well-informed than the partisan voter, for such independents include chronic nonvoters, apathetic people, and the like. But if we mean by independents those who switch parties between elections, we find some

"Me, I vote the man, not the party. Harding, Coolidge, Hoover, Landon, Dewey. . ." (Copyright 1956, Crowell Collier Publishing Company, by Bill Mauldin.)

who are highly informed and who carefully pick and choose at the polls. In short, some independents are like our Mrs. Murphy, who tried to hear all sides of the argument before voting. Others resemble Sally Rice, who voted almost by whim.

Variations in party strength may be due less to independent voters' shifting from one party to another than to the acquisition of new voters from the ranks of nonvoters or of younger people voting for the first time. In 1952, however, voters shifting their allegiance from one party to another were of crucial importance. According to a careful study, former Democrats who voted for Dwight D. Eisenhower held the balance of power in the 1952 election. "While sizable numbers of 1948 nonvoters were coming into the ranks of 1952 voters, dividing their favors rather equally between the two presidential aspirants, smaller numbers of people who had voted in 1948 were withdrawing from the political arena to become nonvoters in 1952. The net result of these additions and subtractions left the Republicans with an added 6 per cent of the population supporting their cause. In the same way, the Democrats picked up slightly more than 2 per cent of the population. As these sizable, but to some extent compensating, shifts were occurring, some 11 per cent of the citizens were deciding to change their votes

[24] *Ibid.*, pp. 743, 751.

from 1948 Democratic to 1952 Republican. . . ." [25] All told, the study concludes, some 25 per cent of the final Republican vote came from 1948 Democrats—a striking indication of the potential power of this kind of independent.

Does Campaigning Change Votes?

From our discussion of voting behavior, we might conclude that all the speeches of vote-seekers, all the hullabaloo of their campaigns, had little effect compared with the other forces at work. In part this conclusion would be true. A campaign usually *converts* only a small fraction of the electorate. But it has other important effects. It *reinforces* the convictions of those already tending one way or another. And it *activates* people—that is, it arouses their interest, exposes them to particular candidates and ideas, shapes their attitudes, and stimulates them to vote on election day.

Even television may not influence voting as much as some have thought. In 1952 two students of politics took advantage of a "happy accident"—a government freeze on the construction of new television stations—to study voting in comparable Iowa counties, some of which received television clearly and others poorly. They found no significant differences between the two sets of counties either in voting turnout or in the division of the vote between the parties.[26]

Still, events between elections, and underlying attitudes, traditions, and pressures, are far more important than the campaign. Does this situation discourage the vote-seeking politician? Not at all. He knows that he is dealing in margins, often in close margins. He knows that a hundred unknown intangibles will shape the final outcome. Great political forces are delicately balanced—perhaps a good push by his party and himself will tip them in the right direction.

Leaders and Followers

Not long ago an interviewer from the Survey Research Center of the University of Michigan asked some questions of the wife of a machinist in Kentucky.[27] The dialogue went like this:

> "What do you like about the Democrats?"
> "That's Stevenson, ain't it?"
> "Yes, that's his party."
> "No, I don't know anything about Stevenson but I do like the party."

[25] Angus Campbell, Gerald Gurin, and Warren E. Miller, "Political Issues and the Vote: November, 1952," *The American Political Science Review* (June 1953), p. 369. This study was based on data gathered through nationwide sample surveys (conducted in October and November 1952) of over 2000 persons. See also *The American Voter*, pp. 142–145.

[26] H. A. Simon and Frederick Stern, "The Effect of Television Upon Voting Behavior in Iowa in the 1952 Presidential Election," *The American Political Science Review* (June 1955), pp. 470–477.

[27] Campbell, *et al.*, *The American Voter* (Wiley, 1960), pp. 239–240.

"What is it that you like about the Democratic party?"

"There's always been more Democrats running for President than there has been for the other party, and they've got in more."

"Is there anything else you like about the Democratic party?"

"No."

"What do you dislike about the Democrats?"

"I don't know anything about the Democratic party. . . . Well, for one thing, they were hard on the farmers. . . . No, I always liked the Democratic party until Truman was in. He said that he was going to do things for the farmers and he backed out."

"What do you like about the Republicans?"

"That's Stevenson, ain't it? I get them mixed up."

"No, that's Eisenhower's party."

"Well, one thing, I heard he lowered taxes."

"Is there anything else you like about the Republican party?"

"And he's a good man—I hope he gets in this time."

"Anything else you dislike about the Republicans?"

"No, I can't think of anything."

"Anything you like about Stevenson?"

"No, I just don't like Stevenson."

"Anything you like about Eisenhower?"

"I don't know of any."

Obviously this woman knows little about national affairs. Yet we cannot dismiss her as an ignoramus. She had some idea about the relation of politics and economic problems—note her reference to farmers and to taxes. She may be inarticulate about why she liked Eisenhower, but the feeling was there and was perhaps important to her. She probably votes, at least occasionally.

In any event, this housewife is typical of millions of Americans, who, lacking solid information and clear views, usually vote under the influence of other people—their parents, the newspaper editor, the local party boss, or someone else. In their voting they tend to be *followers*—if they vote at all.

Multivoters

At the other extreme are the leaders who influence the followers. These we might call "multivoters"—persons whose influence over other voters is so great that they in effect control more than one voter. This influence may or may not be intended. The head of a family may be a multivoter simply because he holds the respect and confidence of his wife and children. The party worker, on the other hand, deliberately sets out to win votes from friends and neighbors in his ward. In either case the personal, face-to-face contact is highly effective.

Is there any way to measure the varying extent to which people take part in politics? Some years ago pollsters asked a series of questions of a cross section of adult Americans.[28] Do you discuss public issues, like taxes or foreign policy, with your friends? Do you belong to an organization that sometimes takes positions on such issues? Have you ever told your representative about your views? How often have you voted? Have you taken part in political campaigns? The answers were graded; the highest score possible was twelve, the lowest zero. How well did these typical people do?

The results of these and other studies indicate that almost 70 per cent of American adults are politically inactive. Another 20 per cent take some part in political, civic and social life. About 10 per cent are among the "influentials." Who are the dormants? They are much like the nonvoters described above—more women than men, less educated, with lower income, more Democrats than Republicans, younger in years. The top tenth of very active people includes a far more than average number of executives, professional people, and persons with college educations. And the evidence suggests that the inactive people are less likely to feel themselves members of, or affected by, the community they live in. They have less sense of identity with politics, believe that "it makes no difference anyway," and have little understanding of how the system operates.

Still, political leaders are not simply a small group of like-minded persons at the top. They are found at all levels within the community. And the leader in the local community may be a follower in the county or state. The head of a local labor or business organization is perhaps a follower of a state or national labor or business leader. Thus there are *overlapping hierarchies* of leaders and followers.

Local Leaders

Through their face-to-face contacts, local opinion leaders have an influence that national leaders, with their less personal relationship, cannot always match. Many voters, moreover, pay more attention to local opinion leaders than to the radio or newspaper. "In comparison with the formal media of communication," says Lazarsfeld, "personal relationships are potentially more influential for two reasons: their coverage is greater and they have certain psychological advantages over the formal media," such as the newspaper.[29] Opinion leaders can get through to persons who rarely expose themselves to the radio or printed page. And their technique—consciously or not—is far more effective. Listening to a candidate or reading a campaign poster, the follower may suspect that someone is trying to sell him a bill of goods. But the seemingly casual remarks of the opinion leader may catch him off guard. The leader can talk in terms that the follower understands, can find the right time to deliver his opinions, can tailor his argument to suit the follower's personality or beliefs. In politics, just as in business, face-to-face contact lowers sales resistance.

[28] J. L. Woodward and Elmo Roper, "Political Activity of American Citizens," *The American Political Science Review* (December 1950), pp. 872–885.

[29] Lazarsfeld, *The People's Choice*, p. 150.

Successful political leaders understand all this. Half a century ago Boss Plunkitt, a Tammany district leader, was quoted as saying:

> There's only one way to hold a district; you must study human nature and
> act accordin'. You can't study human nature in books. Books is a hindrance
> more than anything else. If you have been to college, so much the worse for
> you. You'll have to unlearn all you learned before you can get right down to
> human nature, and unlearnin' takes a lot of time. Some men can never forget
> what they learned at college. Such men may get to be district leaders by a
> fluke, but they never last.
>
> To learn real human nature you have to go among the people, see them
> and be seen. I know every man, woman, and child in the Fifteenth District,
> except them that's been born this summer—and I know some of them, too. I
> know what they like and what they don't like, what they are strong at and
> what they are weak in, and I reach them by approachin' at the right side.
>
> For instance, here's how I gather in the young men. I hear of a young feller
> that's proud of his voice, thinks that he can sing fine. I ask him to come
> around to Washington Hall and join our Glee Club. He comes and sings, and
> he's a follower of Plunkitt for life. Another young feller gains a reputation as
> a baseball player in a vacant lot. I bring him into our baseball club. That fixes
> him. . . . I don't trouble them with political arguments. I just study human
> nature and act accordin' . . . .
>
> As to the older voters, I reach them, too. No, I don't send campaign litera-
> ture. That's rot. People can get all the political stuff they want to read—and
> a good deal more, too—in the papers. Who reads speeches, nowadays, anyhow?
> It's bad enough to listen to them. You ain't goin' to gain any votes by stuffin'
> the letter boxes with campaign documents. . . .[30]

Do "multivoters" and Boss Plunkitts raise doubts about the possibility of "government by the people"? We will return to this question in Chapter 20.

Voting Studies: A Research Frontier

Since at least the time of Aristotle political scientists have been trying to understand both the "what" and the "why" of politics. The "what" has been relatively
easy; scholars have made detailed compilations and descriptions of election returns,
political credos, the history of legislative enactments, administrative decision-
making; indeed, no major area of political life has been left unexplored. The
"why" has been much more difficult. Why does one man, from a particular social
background, forge ahead relentlessly to political fame and fortune, while another
man, from the same background, remains apolitical all his life? Why do some
people vote for the same party year after year, while others shift back and forth?
Why do millions of persons desert their old political beliefs to embrace strange new
doctrines like Marxism or Nazism? Why does one Supreme Court justice, ap-

[30] W. L. Riordon, *Plunkitt of Tammany Hall* (McClure, Phillips, 1905), pp. 33–34.

pointed by a liberal president and expected to take liberal positions, turn conservative; and another justice does quite the opposite? Why do some nations have stable democracies and others a constant series of "men-on-horseback"? Why do some people rebel against those in power while others tolerate tyrants? Why do legislatures dominate some political systems and executives dominate others?

The question of *why* of course challenges historians, economists, psychologists, sociologists, anthropologists—indeed, all scholars in some way—as well as political scientists. And even the simplest event raises a host of possible answers as to why it happened. E. H. Carr, the distinguished English historian, provides an example: [31]

> Jones, returning from a party at which he has consumed more than his usual ration of alcohol, in a car whose brakes turn out to have been defective, at a blind corner where visibility is notoriously poor, knocks down and kills Robinson, who was crossing the road to buy cigarettes at the shop on the corner. After the mess is cleaned up, we meet—say, at local police headquarters—to enquire into the causes of the occurrence.

Why did the accident happen? Because Smith was semi-intoxicated? Or because of the car's brakes? Or because of the blind corner? Or because Robinson smoked cigarettes? Or because Jones, or Robinson, or both, were careless? Perhaps any or all of these. Then we might ask: Which are the direct, and which the indirect, causes? Which are purely chance and which are likely to recur? And ultimately the political scientist might ask: Which causes could be removed (the blind corner, the defective brakes), and which could not (Jones' alcoholism, Robinson's desire for cigarettes)?

The purpose of this section is to show social scientists, including political scientists, at work in one of the corners of one of the great areas marked "why?" —namely, why do Americans vote the way they do? We cannot do justice to the enormous range and variety of these voting behavior studies; but to get some idea of what a professional social scientist does, of his tools, his skills, his fund of knowledge, his problems, let us look at some of the work that has been done in voting and opinion studies.

The Cutting Edge: Some Earlier Voting Studies

Concern with why men vote the way they do is nothing new. Scholars and journalists have speculated, have based generalizations on their own observations, have argued that it is "logical" to assume that men vote this way instead of that for a whole host of what appear to be plausible reasons. But only recently has it been possible to find answers to these questions by looking at "hard data" and using more precise tools.

[31] Edward Hallett Carr, *What Is History?* (Knopf, 1962), p. 137. Carr develops further problems of historical causation from this example.

In the 1920's a young graduate student at Columbia, Stuart A. Rice, came under the intellectual influence of a sociologist who stressed quantitative research, such as the use of election statistics. Rice decided to apply quantitative methods to a study of the American farm-labor movement, in which he had been active as a young man. The resulting study of this movement led a publisher to suggest to Rice that he apply these methods to other political problems. Within three weeks Rice wove together some previously published findings with research that he had ready to be published. His work appeared in 1928 as *Quantitative Methods in Politics*.

Rice raised many questions. What differences in political attitudes existed between urban and rural voters? How do political attitudes spread across areas? How do they change over time? To what extent are peoples' attitudes affected by their stereotypes—that is, by set opinions of what labor leaders, senators, communists, and so on, are like? In an experiment, when William Jennings Bryan was visiting Dartmouth to denounce the theory of evolution, Rice compared his students' attitudes before and after Bryan's visit.

Rice modestly admitted that his book was only a start. Public opinion polls were still in their infancy, experimental work in social psychology was still primitive, and his data were limited. More important, however, he helped stimulate further research in voting. The 1930's saw the appearance of studies of urban-rural tensions in the election of 1896, of the extent to which labor supported Andrew Jackson in certain wards of Boston, of voting trends in particular cities or counties. The results were interesting and suggestive, but far from conclusive. There was little systematic testing of hypotheses over a long series of elections. Findings for one state might have little relation to another. The studies did not explain the reasons for individual voting choices. The "why" of voting behavior was still not clear.[32]

Appropriately, a psychologist now came to the fore in scholarly efforts to understand individual voting behavior. During the 1930's Paul F. Lazarsfeld had headed the Office of Radio Research, which had done pioneer work on how people make up their minds about what goods they buy. Earlier, in Vienna, Lazarsfeld had studied the psychology of choice, especially the occupational choices of young people. What he now proposed to do was to survey repeatedly a *sample* of households to see how their choices of brands of goods could be related to their exposure to advertising. Unable to find commercial support for such a group study, he obtained funds from the Rockefeller Foundation for a panel study of the 1940 presidential campaign, as a way to test his technique of interviewing a panel over and over again. The result was a notable volume, *The People's Choice*, by Lazarsfeld and two associates.[33]

---

[32] On these earlier voting studies see Samuel J. Eldersveld, "Theory and Method in Voting Behavior Research," *The Journal of Politics* (February 1951), pp. 70–87, and Peter H. Rossi, "Four Landmarks in Voting Research," in Eugene Burdick and Arthur J. Brodbeck (eds.), *American Voting Behavior* (The Free Press, 1959), pp. 5–54.

[33] Lazarsfeld, *The People's Choice, op. cit.*

The place chosen for the study was Erie County, Ohio; the occasion was the stirring election of 1940 between Roosevelt and Willkie. A carefully selected panel of six hundred respondents were interviewed seven times—a Herculean task—and four matched control groups were each interviewed twice. Lazarsfeld and his colleagues emerged with many significant conclusions. Choosing candidates, it seemed, was quite different from choosing goods; voters had long-standing attachments to certain parties and had in effect decided how to vote long before the presidential campaign had begun. Many of them were apathetic; they did not even want to enter the "electoral market place." Other notable findings were that voting was heavily affected by family, work-place, and neighborhood influences and hence was more a *group* than an individual act; that many voters under "cross-pressures" became indecisive and failed to vote at all; that the candidates' campaigns tended to reach their own supporters rather than people in the opposite camp and those who were undecided; and that there was a "two-step flow of influence" in the mass media—from the media, to local opinion leaders, to the rank and file.

On their main question—why people voted as they did—the authors concluded that religion, socio-economic status, and place of residence (rural or urban) were the most important factors. They constructed an "Index of Political Predisposition" to show these forces in their combined impact:

Socio-economic Status	Protestants		Catholics	
	Rural	Urban	Rural	Urban
A, B (well-to-do)	1	2	3	4
C+ (middle)	2	3	4	5
C− (lower middle)	3	4	5	6
D (lower)	4	5	6	7

The greater the rank number of a given cell, the greater the frequency of Democratic voting preference among the members of that cell.

The People's Choice was greeted as a major advance in understanding the "why" of voting, but both the authors and the critics agreed that there were certain failings and omissions. In 1948 Lazarsfeld, Berelson, and McPhee conducted an even more elaborate study of Elmira, a small industrial city in upstate New York, in the presidential campaign of that year. They used a larger panel, 1,000 instead of 600, but they interviewed it only four times. Field researchers also analyzed Elmira's newspapers, political party organization, and interest groups. The result, after six years of labor, was a community and election study, entitled simply *Voting*, with far more breadth and depth than the earlier one.[34] Attention centered on the group context of voting behavior, the role of issues in the battle

[34] Bernard R. Berelson, Paul F. Lazarsfeld, and William N. McPhee, *Voting* (Univ. of Chicago Press, 1954).

between Truman and Dewey, and the impact on behavior of the community and its institutions. The treatment of the two major parties and of the unions not only illuminated Elmira's politics, but shed light on the role of parties and unions in the nation as a whole. Once again the authors stressed major factors like religion and income, but they paid more attention to the *structure* of the community. Many scholars considered *Voting* the most useful and sophisticated community opinion and voting study that had been done.

As voting studies proliferated during the 1950's, they came under increasing criticism from "anti-behavioralists" and others who were skeptical of the achievements and pretensions of the voting studies. In large part this criticism reflected the basic division within the discipline noted in Chapter 1, the division, that is, over the extent to which political science could become a "real" science. But critics had some further specific questions. Voting studies, they said, were sharply limited in their applicability; if field researchers investigated Erie County in 1940, all they learned about was Erie County in 1940. Critics charged also that the studies came up with *correlations* rather than *causation*. If Catholics with low incomes tend to vote Democratic, this does not prove they vote Democratic *because* they are Catholics with low incomes. Finally, said some critics, the voting studies put too much emphasis on man's social milieu, whereas his behavior is not wholly, or even mainly, determined by his environment. What if a man is a Protestant, or lives in the country? This does not mean that he must behave like a Protestant or like a rural dweller. Man is simply too complex and mysterious to respond predictably to external stimulus, like Pavlov's dog salivating automatically to the sound of a bell. Above all, according to this view, man is a *reasoning* animal—he can think rationally about his problems without being totally controlled by his environment.

Inside the Mind of the Voter

Of all these criticisms, those who study voting behavior have been most sensitive to the view that voters respond less directly to their social milieu—to their family, social groups, religion, occupational circle—than to *attitudes* that both influence and are influenced by their group memberships. The early studies, with their emphasis on the role of groups, had been heavily influenced by political sociologists; the new emphasis would call more for psychologists (and for political scientists with some understanding of social psychology) who could discern and perhaps measure the psychological forces that operated between the individual voter and the social situation.

Happily, this very emphasis marked the next major advance in voting studies. During World War II the Program Surveys Division of the United States Department of Agriculture had conducted studies of grass-roots opinion and attitudes in connection with farm programs. After the war some of the Division's researchers moved to the University of Michigan and set up the Survey Research Center, which rapidly took leadership in public opinion research. Its work was largely socio-psychological in orientation—that is, it was "guided by the philosophy that the immediate determinants of an individual's behavior lie more clearly in *attitudes* and his *perceptual organization* of his environment than in either his social position or other 'objective' situational factors." [35] A man might be poor and live in a city slum, for example, without seeing himself as a low-income urbanite; how he saw himself, and why he behaved politically as he did, would depend on *his* picture of reality, not on reality as someone else saw it.

Beginning in 1948 the Center conducted surveys of opinions and voting in every presidential campaign, based on a national probability sample of 2,000 respondents.[36] Since the survey was nationwide, and since it was repeated again and again (using some of the same respondents), the studies met two of the main criticisms of the earlier efforts. Most important, they measured a number of psychological attitudes as "intervening variables linking behavior with a host of antecedent factors." [37] The major intervening variables were support for one of the political parties ("party identification"), concern with national governmental policy issues ("issue orientation"), and liking for the presidential candidates ("candidate orientation"). By measuring attitudes on these matters the studies could predict with fair accuracy not only how people voted but—equally important—who would be likely to vote.

To what extent did these "psychological" voting studies answer the basic question of "why"? Some readers were skeptical. To be sure, they said, the studies showed that those who were Republican and who "liked Ike" would come out and vote for Eisenhower to a high degree—but did this prove very much? It was like saying that students who liked bodily contact and throwing a pigskin around would "try out" for the football squad in large numbers. But the "political psychologists" felt that they had done more than explain immediate antecedent factors; they felt that they had found basic influences that lay behind the immediate causes for a person voting as he did. For example, surveys may show that a woman in Virginia is still voting in reaction to the events of the Civil War, or that a laborer in Massachusetts is a confirmed Democrat because of his experiences in the Depression. A psychological approach, in short, can isolate both the original motivating factor and the voter's reaction to it, in a single theory of causation. This theory is shown in diagrammatic form.

A nationwide survey would obviously reveal the background of a voter only in a short and hazy manner. Is it possible to study a smaller number of persons, but far more intensively? Three Harvard-educated psychologists tried this tack in the mid-1950's. They selected ten "normal" men in the greater Boston area, subjected them to a battery of psychological tests, and interviewed them inten-

[35] Rossi, in Burdick and Brodbeck, *op. cit.*, p. 37 (emphasis supplied). See also Davies, *op. cit.*, Ch. 4.

[36] The most important of these studies are Angus Campbell, Gerald Gurin, and Warren E. Miller, *The Voter Decides* (Row, Peterson, 1954), and Angus Campbell, Philip E. Converse, Warren E. Miller, and Donald E. Stokes, *The American Voter* (Wiley, 1960).

[37] *The American Voter*, p. 120. The authors advance an interesting metaphor of the "funnel of causality" (pp. 31–32).

sively for a total of about 30 hours each over a span of three or four months. The purpose was to collect *all* the available information about the subjects. The authors concluded, among many other things, that there was no rigid or easily discernible relation between a person's personality and his opinions (or voting), that opinions that develop in a person are "multiple in their determinants," that the same opinions can serve several functions for their holder (for example, helping him to adjust to groups in which he participates, and also helping him

CIRCUITS OF CAUSALITY

Typical paths along which external events, communications media, group members, and partisan attitudes interact and influence political behavior.

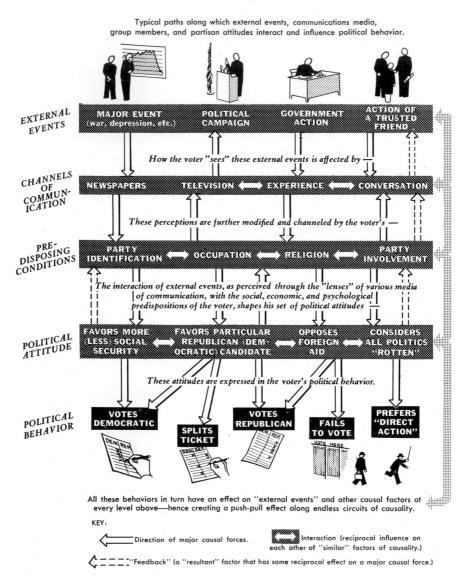

All these behaviors in turn have an effect on "external events" and other causal factors at every level above—hence creating a push-pull effect along endless circuits of causality.

KEY:

⟵ Direction of major causal forces.

◀▬▶ Interaction (reciprocal influence on each other of "similar" factors of causality.)

⟵ --- "Feedback" (a "resultant" factor that has some reciprocal effect on a major causal force.)

to cope with his own unresolved inner problems), that the whole process of opinion formation was tremendously complex.[38] In effect, they indicated that opinion and voting studies have a long way to go before answering the real question of "why" in voting.

Evidently, then, we are only at best in midpassage in the study of voting behavior. Some would say that there is no end to the passage, or that we will end up somewhere we do not expect—certainly not in the realm of a real science. At this point we can talk, like the weatherman, only in terms of tendencies and probabilities. Two things, though, are certain. One is that political scientists can advance in this field only in cooperation with other types of social scientists, such as those mentioned above. The other is that if the problems are complex, the challenge and opportunity to the young political scientist are enormous.

[38] M. Brewster Smith, Jerome S. Bruner, and Robert W. White, *Opinions and Personality* (Wiley, 1956).

11 THE DYNAMIC ROLE OF INTEREST GROUPS

The United States has been called a nation of joiners. Europeans sometimes make fun of us for setting up all sorts of organizations, from antiprofanity leagues to zoological clubs. We ourselves are often amused by the behavior of our groups—the noisy conventions of veterans' associations, the solemn rites of great fraternal organizations, the oratory of patriotic societies, the gossip of local sewing circles, the pomposity of

278

reform leagues. Yet most of these groups are deadly serious in their aims, and they play an enormous role in politics. Moreover, joining is not an exclusively American trait. It is a common trait of human beings—and a biological factor as well.

How many groups are there in America? There is no way of knowing accurately. Families are groups—the most basic and important groups of all—and there are at least forty million families in the United States. We have a quarter of a million local religious congregations, countless athletic teams, tens of thousands of trade unions, over two thousand trade associations. And all these are groups in the broadest sense of the term—that is, the members of each group share some common *outlook* or *attitude*, and *interact* with one another in some way.[1]

Nor can we measure the variety of groups in America, although we know that it is tremendous. One observer has made a list of odd organizations to give a hint of this variety: [2]

> The Nonsmokers Protective League of America
> Simplified Spelling Board
> American Sunbathing Association
> Blizzard Men of 1888 (to commemorate a famous storm)
> American Hackney Horse Association
> Toastmasters International

One person may belong to a great variety of groups and organizations. A typical college student is a member of the college community as a whole. But he may also belong to the sophomore class, the Tau Delta Tau fraternity, the basketball squad, the second floor of his dormitory, the Geology Club, the discipline committee, and classes in English, physics, French, and government. He belongs to other groups at home—his family, neighborhood, religious congregation, and so on. This student is a member of all these groups but he is not *equally* a member of them. His loyalty to his family, his class, or his fraternity may greatly outweigh his loyalty to all the other groups.

His father may be a member of an even greater array of groups—not only his family, congregation, and neighborhood, but perhaps, also, the Rotary Club, a philatelic society, the Masons, a downtown law firm, the American Automobile Association, a taxpayers' association, the Republican party, a bowling league, the American Bar Association, the state bar association. Do the individual's allegiances to a wide variety of groups of this sort ever come into conflict with one another? Indeed yes. The AAA may demand better roads, while the taxpayers' association wants less governmental spending. The neighborhood this person lives in may be largely made up of Democrats whereas he is a Republican. Even without such conflicts, belonging to a variety of groups puts a great strain on his time and his pocketbook.

[1] D. B. Truman, *The Governmental Process* (Knopf, 1951), ch. 2. The basic approach of this chapter is drawn largely from this volume and from the pioneer work, A. F. Bentley, *The Process of Government* (Univ. of Chicago Press, 1908).

[2] From E. E. Schattschneider, *Party Government* (Farrar & Rinehart, Inc., 1942), p. 26.

The fact that groups are so numerous and varied raises a number of questions that go to the very heart of democratic politics in America: Why are some groups strong and organized, others weak and diffused? What happens when competing groups overlap in membership, as in the cases just mentioned? How are groups organized, led, and governed? How do they gain influence? What is their relation to the party system, to elections, to government as a whole?

Politics is concerned with the workings of all groups, but we can simplify our effort to answer these questions by limiting ourselves to a particular type, the *interest group. This is any group whose members, as a result of sharing certain attitudes, make claims on other groups in order to realize aims arising from these attitudes.* Interest groups are of many types. Some are formal *associations* or *organizations.* Others have no formal organization at all—a young people's interest group, for example. Various interest groups may even exist *within* a given interest group. Thus inside the American Bar Association there may be several interest groups in conflict over a particular issue. An interest group may be either broader or narrower than a particular organization. The American Federation of Labor and Congress of Industrial Organizations, for example, is opposed to a labor reform measure. But not all members of the AFL-CIO oppose the labor reform bill, and some people who are *not* members oppose it. The interest group working to amend or abolish this measure, then, is composed of most members of the AFL-CIO, but not all, along with some people outside the formal labor organization.

Politics is largely a conflict among competing groups with conflicting ideas of what is in the "general interest." In political arguments we inevitably talk about special interests versus the general welfare. But in political analysis it is better to talk about *this* group's idea of the general welfare as compared with *that* group's idea. As political partisans we are all committed to particular ideas and values, but as social scientists we cannot pretend to set up a clearly defined national interest. For this is really the question at issue—"What *is* the general interest?"

Unions for All—Occupational Groups for All

It is only natural that men working together should combine in some sort of association. They tend to have common attitudes and interests, and directly or indirectly they deal with one another during their working day and after. This is true not only of factory workers, but also of businessmen, farmers, doctors, lawyers, and many others. In a sense we all belong to unions, whether we are presidents of insurance companies, apple-growers, baseball umpires, professors, plumbers, or what not. Such unions come in all shapes and sizes, with all sorts of programs, memberships, and interests.

Men interact and unite on a nationwide and statewide basis as well as in local groups. They can do so easily and effectively because of modern methods of communication and transportation. Milk producers in Vermont and Wisconsin, druggists in Boston and Seattle, and garment workers in New York and Chicago can talk with one another in a matter of minutes, or meet in a matter of hours. In fact, members of each group *must* work together if they are to promote their common interests. They can find strength only in unity, and they can meet common, nationwide problems only by organizing on a nationwide basis. The typical large association comprises a mosaic of local and state bodies, heading up in the national organization. Usually it is the product of slow and painful growth through decades. The labor movement illustrates the rise of many separate groups struggling to national status and influence after a period of trial-and-error organization.

Workers

The earliest trade union locals in the United States were founded during Washington's first administration. For several decades "mechanics" and other workers organized local groups in the larger cities, but often these failed in the face of hard times, the hostility of employers, or the indifference of the workers themselves. Yet the urge for closer union remained powerful. As the economy became nationally integrated, the local unions in different states began to join hands with one another. Slowly taking root, the unions began to participate actively in politics. The Working Men's party, the first labor party, was born shortly before Andrew Jackson took office. An ambitious attempt to establish one big union of all types of workers came shortly after the Civil War with the founding of the Knights of Labor, which included in its membership factory workers, farmers, and others—in fact, everyone except gamblers, stockbrokers, lawyers, and bankers! The Knights adopted a progressive platform, lobbied in state capitals, and joined forces in turn with Greenbackers, Populists, and Bryan Democrats. At one point, they claimed 700,000 members. But the experiment failed. Lacking unity, the Knights lost out both in political and economic battles, and had virtually disappeared by the end of the century.

The *American Federation of Labor* was formed in 1886 by skilled workers—carpenters, machinists, and the like—who felt that their particular needs were overshadowed by the vastness of the Knights of Labor. Organized in tight craft unions, these workers surrendered only limited power to the national AFL, which continued as a true confederation of strong and independent-minded national unions. Headed by the astute Samuel Gompers, an ex-cigarmaker, the AFL stressed the economic weapon of the strike rather than all-out political battles. When compelled to enter politics as a result of hostile governmental action, the AFL tried to reward labor's friends and punish its enemies. Thus, it followed a balance-of-power policy, steering shy of any firm party connection. As a result, the Federation was often assailed by socialists and others who felt that labor should take a more aggressive political stand.

Following World War I the AFL lost strength as a result of anti-union drives, unemployment, and its own failure to organize the millions of unskilled workers in the huge mass-production industries of the nation. Under the impact of the New Deal, its membership soared, but disunity increased too. Failing to induce the AFL craft leaders to organize the mass-production industries, a group of AFL leaders, led by John L. Lewis of the miners, set up the Committee for Industrial Organization. The AFL soon ejected them as "dual unionists," and the CIO then continued as the *Congress of Industrial Organizations*, composed largely of workers in the steel, auto, rubber, textile, electrical, and maritime industries. Faced with vigorous competition for members, the AFL made stronger organizing attempts, and for a short period won back the miners' union after Lewis deserted the CIO.

In 1955, after long negotiations, the AFL and CIO merged at the top levels. Since that time, their member unions have combined at the national, state, and local levels. The merged national organization has today about 15 million members. It dominates the world of labor, but there are important groups outside the fold. The miners, teamsters, and one or two other large unions are—at the moment at least—independent. There are thousands of local unions that are not affiliated with any national union. And there are millions of workers who have no regular union at all, but do have some kind of employees' organization. The objectives of all the different organizations, however, are much the same—to improve wages and working conditions, to extend social security, and to ward off hostile governmental action.

Farmers

Farmers, too, have their "unions." Despite their individualism and their physical separation from one another, they have long seen the need for combining to protect their interests. An early farm group—the South Carolina Agricultural Society—was founded even before our Constitution was written; since then, thousands of local and state associations have sprung up. The oldest nationwide farm group today is the *National Grange* (Patrons of Husbandry). Founded in 1867 by a group of federal employees, the Grange started out as a secret society to promote social and intellectual activities, but it soon became embroiled in the political movements that swept rural areas in the 1870's. Rebelling against low farm prices, railroad monopolies, grasping middlemen, and high taxes, the Grangers turned to political action, such as lobbying. After helping to gain certain reforms, such as railroad regulation and various direct aids to farmers, the Grange declined in influence and membership. Once a fighting organization with over a million members, the Grange today is reduced in membership and is the most conservative farm group in the nation. Strongest in the northeastern states, it works for price-support policies and other governmental protection for its farm members.

The largest farm group today is the *American Farm Bureau Federation*, which claims over a million members, most of them in the corn belt. It is set up on the usual local, state, and national bases, but from its start early in this century it has been organized around the government agents who helped the farmers in rural counties. As experts teaching improved farm methods, the county agents were in close touch with farmers, and they served as the virtual organizers of the local Farm Bureaus.[3] The Federation today is almost a semigovernmental agency, but it retains full freedom to fight for such goals as price support, conservation measures, and expansion on farm credit facilities. It maintains the strongest farm lobby in Washington.

"Nah, that's not a candidate—that's a farmer." (Herblock in The Washington Post.)

Another important but smaller organization is the *Farmers Union,* founded in 1902, which claims to speak for the family-sized farm. The Farmers Union works for legislation that will protect the small farmer, such as government aid to family-sized farms, the gradual breakup of large farms, and minimum wage laws for farm labor—as well as the usual aims of price supports, rural electrification, easier loan policies, and the like. Largely based on cooperatives of various types, the Farmers Union is centered in the Missouri River Valley. It has taken a special interest in the problems of dust-bowl farmers.

A great number of other farm organizations are based on the interests of farmers who produce specific commodities: the National Beet Growers Association, the American Soybean Association, the American Wool Growers Association, and many others. These groups are relatively small, but they wield significant power when they want. After journeying through the states that maintain the sugar bloc in Congress, John Gunther wrote: "Only 3 per cent of American farmers grow sugar beet and cane; the entire processing industry employs no more than twenty-five thousand people. But sugar is spread through many states—beets grow in seventeen, cane in two—which gives it thirty-eight senators out of ninety-six, and they can certainly make a noise." [4]

Most farm organizations profess to be nonpolitical; actually, all of them are

[3] Wesley McCune, *The Farm Bloc* (Doubleday, Doran, 1943), p. 165. See also C. M. Hardin, *The Politics of Agriculture* (The Free Press, 1952).

[4] John Gunther, *Inside U.S.A.* (Harper, 1947), p. 221.

in politics. Farmers have exerted influence on government not only through their associations; they have entered politics directly by organizing their own parties. The Greenback party in the 1870's and 1880's fought for currency inflation to ease the distress of farm debtors; at its peak it polled nearly one million votes and sent 15 congressmen to Washington. The Populist party did even better in the nineties, but the Democratic party under Bryan stole most of its thunder and its support. Farm votes made up much of the strength of Senator Robert La Follette's Progressive movement in 1924. Farm parties have controlled a number of state governments for long intervals.

Businessmen

Businessmen's "unions" are the most varied and numerous of all. Over 2,000 trade associations and other business groups operate on a national or interstate basis, and there are at least 3,000 local business groups. The nature of the hundreds of trade associations is almost as varied as the different products and services that are sold. Automobile manufacturers and pin manufacturers both have their national associations; so do canners, cotton manufacturers, retail kosher butchers, road builders, tobacco merchants. Manufacturers of amusement tickets, clothing tickets, and transit tickets have three separate organizations. The list is almost endless. Businessmen group themselves by size and general function as well as by trade. The National Federation of Independent Business, for example, is spokesman for the little businessman. The National Retail Dry Goods Association speaks for a variety of retailers.

Two general, nationwide organizations of businessmen are especially important. One is the *Chamber of Commerce of the United States*, which was organized in 1912. The Chamber is a federation of federations—it is composed of about 5,000 local chambers of commerce and trade associations representing over 25,000 business firms. Its members have so many different interests and attitudes that the Chamber must stay aloof from many of the squabbles that divide business internally. It tries to represent business as a whole by opposing antibusiness governmental measures or the demands of other groups, such as labor. A typical set of Chamber of Commerce resolutions might call for lower taxes, a curb on labor excesses, governmental economy, and less centralization of government. The Chamber publicizes its views widely.

Loosely allied with the Chamber on almost all issues is the *National Association of Manufacturers*, a unified organization of about 21,000 manufacturing firms and corporations. Organized in the wake of the depression of 1893, the NAM today speaks for the more conservative elements of American business. Reflecting the attitudes of employers of large numbers of workers, it is more outspoken than the Chamber of Commerce in supporting restrictive labor legislation and opposing certain social legislation. The NAM sponsors an annual convention of industrialists—the Congress of Business—and is run by a large part-time board of directors and by a full-time secretariat. The association uses a variety of outlets for its "public information," including motion pictures, cartoons, editorials, advertising, and radio speeches.

Traditionally, businessmen have shied away from open political activity. But in recent years, partly because of labor's energetic political activity, several big corporations have been experimenting with ways to speak out more effectively on political issues affecting their interests and encouraging their executives and clerical people to become more active in politics. The American Can Company, for example, has been mapping a program to educate its employees in practical politics and to urge them to be active in the party of their choice; the Ford Motor Company is intensifying its efforts to educate its managers on political issues, especially major issues before Congress; and General Electric has set up a Government Relations Service to help the company acquire a working knowledge of public affairs.

Professional Men

Alongside the giant groups of farmers, workers, and businessmen, organizations of professional people look small, but still they are important. And they are equally varied in type. About 400 professional organizations with national membership exist in the country today, ranging from accountants to veterinarians, and including architects, beauticians, midwives, optometrists, and undertakers. Large professions are divided into many subgroups; thus teachers are organized in the National Education Association, the American Association of University Professors, and particular subject groups, like the Modern Language Association. Many professions are closely tied in with government, especially on the state level. Lawyers, for example, are licensed by the states, which have set up certain standards of admission to the state bar, often as a result of pressure from lawyers themselves.

Some professions enjoy special influence because of the prestige of their members. Doctors—the "men in white"—are a case in point. Their chief organization, the American Medical Association, has played a notable role in opposing governmental intervention in the field of medicine. It has lobbied before Congress, put out literature, urged its members to talk to their patients, and assessed each of its 176,000 members $25 to build up a war chest for its fight against compulsory health insurance. In 1962 the A.M.A. established a political arm, the American Medical Political Action Committee, to oppose proposals to finance medical care for the aged through the Social Security system. The doctors are engaged in the political battle—yet somehow they seem to be above politics, perhaps because of their prestige in their communities—and this probably increases their influence. The professional societies do not claim the mass membership of an AFL-CIO or a Farm Bureau Federation, but their prestige and expertness help make up for their lack of numbers.

The Crisscross of Interests

We have been talking about the interaction of individuals within some kind of common occupation. It would be good if we could stop here in our exploration of groups, for these occupational interests are complex enough in themselves. But we have seen only part of the picture. Man does not live by bread alone; he has other interests and attitudes beyond the essentially economic ones, and they can inspire powerful organizations. One of the strongest political forces in American history—the Anti-Saloon League—was aroused not by direct economic motives but simply by a spirit of reform and morality.

Once we look on men as holding nonoccupational as well as occupational interests, the group picture becomes even more complicated and untidy. We have been discussing groups that are somewhat clear-cut and separate from one another; it is a rare person who is at once a farmer, a trade-union member, and a businessman. But most people are members both of occupational and nonoccupational groupings—the businessman who is also a Methodist, for example. Moreover, a person may easily belong to several different nonoccupational groupings, as does a Catholic who is also a Legionnaire, a trade unionist, and a member of the League to Abolish Capital Punishment. Thus we end up with a most elaborate crisscross of interests—a great scrambled collection of attitudes and loyalties working with or across one another in a thousand different ways.

Veterans

Which is the most important of the nonoccupational interest groups? The answer to this question varies according to the time and the situation. In certain medieval societies the church groups were most important. In a South American country today the military organizations might be dominant. In the jumble of interest groups in the United States no single one is supreme. Since we live, however, in the wake of two world wars in which our country was heavily involved, the veterans are numerous and they are well organized. "In the next generation," said President Truman in the closing days of World War II, "the veterans of this war are going to run this country." [5]

The largest veterans' organization today is the American Legion, claiming over 2.5 million members. Founded in Paris at the end of World War I, the Legion gradually became entrenched in thousands of local communities. Thus it was able after World War II to attract many of the recent veterans, despite the efforts of several new outfits, including the American Veterans of World War II (Amvets) and the American Veterans' Committee. The AVC attracted a good deal of attention when it based its program on the principle, "Citizens First, Veterans Second," and adopted a platform intended to benefit lower-income groups generally and not

[5] Harry S. Truman, speech in Portland, Oregon, June 25, 1945.

veterans alone. Its failure to attract a large membership suggested that most veterans wanted their own organizations to act essentially for their own interests. The second largest organization today is the Veterans of Foreign Wars, claiming over a million members. Like most interests the veterans are subdivided into specialized groups—for example, the Disabled American Veterans and organizations of veterans by religion or nationality.

Veterans have many reasons to organize. They share memories of common experiences in wartime, and the local post is a handy place for the "boys to get together." Having donned uniforms for their country, many veterans feel a right and duty to speak out on governmental matters, especially on matters of patriotism and "Americanism." Above all, they have an economic interest in joining together. Veterans have demanded—and obtained—bonuses, pensions, free education, cheap loans and insurance, and a variety of other favors, even including free hunting licenses, exemptions on certain taxes, and honor guards for veterans' funerals. These favors are not new. "They saved the country, and now they want it," said an exasperated public official about the Grand Army of the Republic, the big post-Civil War veterans' organization. Veterans' lobbies are among the most influential in Washington today.

National, Racial, and Religious Groups

Nationality groups are another important factor in American politics. Today, the American "melting pot" includes almost 10 million foreign-born persons and almost 25 million native whites of mixed or foreign parentage. Over 150 nationwide organizations of Americans of German, Irish, Italian, Polish, Scandinavian, and many other national origins represent several million members. These groups have put their stamp on American politics. The Irish dominate the politics of many cities, such as Boston; Germans and Scandinavians are especially influential in the north-central states; French Canadians are a cohesive group in many New England areas; New Mexico's state legislators debate in Spanish as well as English. Parties carefully balance their tickets to appeal to all national elements. Party tickets in New York, with their representatives of different nationalities, look like a list of United Nations delegates. Nationality groups take positions on general political issues, but they are concerned especially with such matters as easier naturalization laws and increased immigration quotas.

These nationality groups may gradually lose political leverage as their members become increasingly absorbed into the mainstreams of American life. Our many *racial* groups may have the same experience—but the largest racial group of all may be the last to lose its separate identity. This group consists of the nineteen million American Negroes. Decades of discrimination and segregation—political, economic, and social—forced Negroes to set up an almost separate life of their own on the less agreeable side of the color line. Their most important group is the National Association for the Advancement of Colored People, established in 1910 to fight lynching and peonage and to press for the right to vote.

Today, with over 500 branches, the NAACP works for a variety of economic and social objectives. Its special concern now is to implement the Supreme Court's 1954 decision on public school segregation and the 1964 and 1965 legislation on civil rights, especially voting rights. It cooperates with the Urban League, a federation of local groups, which is mainly interested in broadening economic opportunities. Other organizations, such as CORE (Committee on Racial Equality), have been created to coordinate demonstrations against chronic segregation. In the last twenty years, Negroes have become increasingly active in politics. For decades they tended to back the Republican party, but the depression of the 1930's and the support of New Dealers and Fair Dealers for civil rights brought large numbers of Negroes over to the Democratic party. The anti-civil-rights stand of southern Democrats, however, will help maintain the traditional nonpartisanship of Negro organizations. In any event Negroes, like whites, are not agreed on aims or methods. Indeed, their color is perhaps less of a unifying force than a common religious creed is to Irish-Americans.

Religion plays a part in American politics. Over half the people in the United States belong to some religious organization; there are more than 66 million Protestants, 44 million Roman Catholics, 5 million Jews.[6] Of these three groups, Protestants are the least united, for they are subdivided into large denominations, such as the Methodists and Baptists, and these denominations are in turn broken up into numerous bodies. The National Council of Churches speaks for some of these groups in its pronouncements on a wide variety of issues. As a result of its unity and discipline, the Roman Catholic Church is probably at least as influential in politics as the Protestants. Some of its political activities are conducted by such Catholic groups as the Knights of Columbus (a fraternal order a million strong), the Association of Catholic Trade Unionists, and the Catholic War Veterans. The Jews, too, are active politically, as shown by the influence they mustered in their fight for a national home in Palestine.

Religious bodies are interested in almost every type of legislative matter—especially in education, foreign affairs (for example, our relations with certain other nations, like Spain), social welfare legislation, and various social problems like gambling, child labor, divorce, birth control, euthanasia, vice. The special responsibility of the church in matters of morals gives it considerable influence in a broad range of state and local legislation.

We have now seen something of the shape and size and variety of the larger interest groups in the United States. It would of course be possible to list many other types of association. There are the women's groups, like the League of Women Voters. There are the countless reform groups, such as the Woman's Christian Temperance Union, the Townsend movement, and the National Municipal League. There are groups concerned with particular problems, such as the Foreign Policy Association. A complete list would shade off into thousands of struggling groups that live for a few years, sometimes realize their objectives, and

---

[6] For a balanced treatment of the churches as interest groups see Murray S. Stedman, Jr., *Religion and Politics in America* (Harcourt, Brace & World, 1964), esp. ch. 5.

then die. It would include not only existing groups but *potential* groups that would spring into being if certain events occurred, such as a new depression.

But our list is long enough. It is time to look more closely at the inner workings of organized groups, to see what makes them behave as they do.

Interest Groups in Ferment

Our picture of interest groups shows a cluster of organizations large and small, old and new, rising and falling, visible and invisible, of endless number and variety. The most important thing about this picture is that it is a mobile one. There is nothing static about group organization in America. Sometimes the changes within groups and between groups are almost imperceptible; sometimes they are sensational enough to become front-page news. Thus John L. Lewis made headlines when he set up the CIO, when he deserted it, when he joined the AFL, when he left it. On the other hand, the slow gradual effect of religious beliefs on church relationships may be less conspicuous but equally significant over a period of time.

Groups are plastic. In their internal and external relationships they are responsive to the deep economic and social currents that flow through America and the world about it. Successive changes in industrial organization, for example, first allowed the AFL to become dominant in labor organization, and then forced it to yield ground to a rival union. Improved agricultural techniques have created new patterns of life on the farm, new relationships among farm groups. The rise of big government has affected the functions of group leaders. The migration of thousands of Negroes from the South to northern cities has brought changes in their economic and social opportunities and in their role in politics.

The relation of groups to other forces is two-way. Thus big government affects interest groups; but the reverse is true, too—interest groups help create and shape big government. Indeed, the process is more than a two-way one; it is multidirectional and many-sided. What we have is a gigantic web of interactions, stretched among interests, associations, governments, beliefs, techniques, and many other elements. A movement anywhere in this web will set the whole elastic network in motion. It is equally certain, however, that in this interrelationship some groups have much more power than others, just as different politicians have varying influence in government.

The Basis of Group Power

What determines the political effectiveness of an interest group? The main internal elements are two: *size* and *unity*. Obviously numbers are important. An organization with three million members will overshadow one with three thousand. But numbers do not amount to much if the group is so divided internally that the members fail to work together. Just as a small but disciplined army can rout a far larger but disorderly one, so can a compact group make its way against rival organizations, and even against the electorate as a whole.

The question then becomes: What makes a group cohesive? What causes its members to vote the same way? At least three elements are involved here.

By far the most important is the *attitude and make-up of the membership*. If the members of an organization are undivided in their loyalty to it, that group will have an enormous advantage in the political arena. When the leaders can absolutely depend on the full backing of their followers, an organization is able to put its full force into pursuing its aims. Communist groups are said to be made up of people who devote all their time and energy single-mindedly to their cause; if this is true, it explains why the communists seem to exercise influence out of proportion to their numbers. But most Americans are not made that way. They cannot possibly give their lives over to one group—not even to their families. Most Americans are members of many groups; their loyalties are divided. They cannot be depended on to go all-out for any cause.

It is this fact of overlapping membership that largely determines the cohesiveness of a group. Organization leaders run up against the problem time after time. A union official, for example, asks a dozen of his members to come to a meeting the next night. Several say they will show up. But one says that he has to be with his bowling club that night. Two others have to stay home with their families. Another has a church supper. Even those who finally do show up at the union meeting are not "100 per cent supporters." They are asked, perhaps, to vote for a particular candidate in a coming election. Some of them will. But one of them may decide to vote for the other candidate because they are next-door neighbors, or because they are both Italo-Americans, or both Republicans, or both Legionnaires. Or perhaps he will not know what to do, and will not vote at all.

Usually a mass-membership group comprises three types of members: First, a relatively small number of formal leaders, who may hold full-time, paid positions, or at least devote much of their extra time, effort and money to the group's activities.[7] Second, a "hard core" of members who are highly involved in the group organizationally and psychologically; they identify themselves with the group's aims, show up at meetings, cheerfully pay their dues, do a lot of the "leg-work." Third, people who are members of the group essentially in name only; they do not participate actively; they do not look on themselves as Teamsters or Rotarians or Legionnaires;[8] they cannot be depended on to vote in elections or otherwise act politically as the leadership wants. For every top leader, there might be, in a typical organization, a few hundred hard-core activists and 10,000 inactive members.

A second factor in the cohesion of a group is its *organizational structure*. Some groups have no formal organization. Others consist of local organizations that have joined together in some sort of loose state or national federation. In such cases the local organizations retain a measure of separate power and independence, just as the states did when they entered the Union. Thus, there is a form of federalism

[7] V. O. Key, Jr., *Public Opinion and American Democracy* (Knopf, 1961), pp. 504–507.
[8] Angus Campbell, *et al.*, *The American Voter* (Wiley, 1960), pp. 308–309.

in some organizations (like the AFL-CIO and AMA) that may hinder unity.

A sort of separation of powers may be found as well. The national assembly of an organization establishes—or at least ratifies—policy. An executive committee meets more frequently. A president or director is elected to head up and speak for the group. And permanent paid officials form the organization's bureaucracy. Power may be further divided between the organization's main headquarters and its Washington office. An organization of this sort tends to be far less cohesive than a centralized, disciplined group such as the Army or some trade unions.

Closely related to this factor is a third one—the nature of the *leadership* of the group. In a group that embraces many attitudes and interests, the leaders may either weld the various elements together, or else sharpen their disunity. The leader of a national business association, for example, must tread cautiously between big business and little business, between exporters and importers, between chain stores and corner grocery stores, between the makers and sellers of competing products. Yet he must not be a cipher—a mere punching bag for different interests—for above all he must *lead*. He must show how to achieve whatever goals can be agreed on. Thus the group leader is in the same position as a President or a congressman, though his constituency is different. He must act diplomatically in his efforts to patch up differences among the subgroups. He must know when to lead his followers, when to follow them. He is at the head of the parade—but if he gets *too far* ahead the paraders may follow someone else down a side street.

Finally, the power of a group is affected by the nature of the *political* and *governmental* system in which it operates. Because of our federal system, a group consisting of three million supporters but concentrated in a few states will have less influence than another group consisting of the same number of supporters but spread out into a large number of states. (If the supporters are spread too widely, however, they might have the least impact of all.) A group whose goals are contrary to widely accepted values will have tougher going than another group which can clothe its demands in acceptable ideology. And as we shall see in later chapters, governmental structures are significant because they allow some groups direct access to governmental decision-makers and other groups much less. The seniority system in Congress, for example, gives special influence to groups based in one-party areas, while the electoral-college system gives groups located in evenly-divided populous states more influence. And the party system too has its impact upon the political influence of groups. A system based on centralized and disciplined parties, like Britain's (see Chapters 3 and 12), may be better able than the American system to withstand pressures of highly organized minorities than our government with its decentralized parties.

Does this picture of group power suggest that the "mass" organizations are beset by many weaknesses and cannot act like a disciplined army? Quite so. The bark of these groups may be much bigger than their bite. As Key says, "When the president of an organization announces to a congressional committee that he speaks for several million people, the odds are that a substantial proportion of his members can be shown to have no opinion or even to express views contrary to those voiced

by their spokesmen." [9] Much of the group leader's efforts must be devoted not to
influencing nonmembers of the group but persuading his own "peripheral" members
to support the group's line. But we should not push this point too far. There is
evidence that the longer a person has belonged to a union, the more likely he is to
identify strongly with it.[10] The group organizationally has some influence in solidi-
fying its members, strengthening their attitudes toward group goals, and inducing
them to take part more actively in politics, as the following table suggests:

**Union Membership in Relation to Level
of Political Participation**

| Participation | Skilled | | Unskilled | |
Level	Union	Nonunion	Union	Nonunion
High 4	28%	23%	19%	8%
3	49	48	52	44
2	5	7	3	5
Low 1	18	22	26	43
	100%	100%	100%	100%
Number	267	195	69	105

Data Source: Survey Research Center, Univ. of Michigan, 1952.

To be sure, the differences between the participation levels of union and nonunion
members may seem marginal, but the vote-seeking politician knows that he wins
or loses by margins hovering around the magic figure of "50 per cent plus one"
of the vote.

The Group Leader

Leaders of organizations use a va-
riety of methods to hold their followers together. Directing the affairs of every
group are a few insiders or old-timers who control the administrative machinery,
such as admission to membership, financial affairs, correspondence, and committees.
This active minority actually runs the organization. It holds the strings that make
the members work in some unity. In exercising discipline and control, the leaders
can withhold certain services (such as lobbying assistance) from rebellious members. Sometimes they can expel members who do not follow the party line; this
sanction is important if members lose their jobs when they lose their membership,
as with the closed union shop. The leaders may also control the organization's
propaganda. The active minority usually puts out the newspaper or magazine that
goes to the members. It arranges the meetings and works up the agenda.

[9] Key, *op. cit.*, p. 525.
[10] *Ibid.*, p. 506.

The leaders of a group tend to stay in control year after year. Bossism or oligarchy exists in most groups, including political parties.[11] An organization that is secure in its leadership can confront its enemies and pursue its program with unity and single-mindedness. On the other hand, unchanging leadership may contribute to decay, demoralization, disunity. In order to stay in power it may resort to illegal means, or it may be enthusiastically re-elected or reappointed each year by a rank and file grateful for successes achieved.

Labor unions are a revealing—though by no means the only—examples of the balance of democracy and oligarchy in interest groups. On the one hand, most unions follow democratic procedures, such as regular elections, a good deal of free speech, grievance machinery, and open and much publicized conventions. On the other hand, many unions have been undemocratic in fact. Opposition has been suppressed on the convention floor, occasionally by violence. Opposition views have been barred from the union newspaper. Union presidents have been able to turn the union professional staffs into their personal political machine. Occasionally, ballots have been "lost" or miscounted.[12] Yet unions may be at least as democratic as most private associations—their failings may simply be more conspicuous because of their more open procedures and the old ideal of "union democracy" by which they are tested. And recently two of the largest industrial unions—the Steel Workers and the Electrical Workers—voted out of office leaders who had held power for many years.

We must keep in mind too the hard question of how much *should* labor or other group leaders represent simply the narrow interests of their groups. A union or business or veterans leader might follow impeccably democratic procedures and speak unerringly for his group—and end up as simply a narrow-minded spokesman for some parochial interest. In fact, some leaders *misrepresent* their membership not because they are dictatorial but because they have some feeling for the broader interests outside their group. Surprising gaps have been discovered between the political positions adopted by some leaders and the attitudes of their members. Here we encounter one of the problems of *representation* that make up the theme of this part of this book.

This balance of power is also upheld by external forces that operate in the whole community. One of these is democracy itself. Americans generally want to have a share in running their government—so naturally they want to have a say in the way their organizations are managed. Actually, most groups are little democracies (although they may have their share of undemocratic practices). There are periodic elections; meetings are run in a parliamentary fashion; a member has the right to stand up in a meeting and say what he wishes. If an organization violates demo-

---

[11] See Robert Michels, *Political Parties: A Sociological Study of the Oligarchical Tendencies of Modern Democracy* (Jarrold, 1915). For a discerning treatment of oligarchic rule within groups, see Grant McConnell, "The Spirit of Private Government," *The American Political Science Review* (September 1958), pp. 754–770.

[12] For a list of nine recent studies of union government and democracy, and a discriminating comment on them, see Oliver Garceau, Book Note, *The American Political Science Review* (December 1963), pp. 982–985.

cratic procedures year after year, it comes into bad repute. Some of its own members may turn against it. Other organizations become hostile and may refuse to play ball with it.

Probably the most powerful factor preventing one group from upsetting the balance of power is the existence of other groups. Organization invites counter-organization. The increased influence of one group forces competing groups to strengthen themselves. Decades ago, for example, nationwide corporations helped create nationwide labor unions, which in turn stimulated the organization of national business federations. If tomorrow people over 60 were to form a powerful organization to put over a super bonus plan, people under 60 would organize against it through their existing organizations or through new ones. A sort of organizational arms race takes place, and every member feels that the devil may take the hind-most.

Groups in the Political Struggle

Seen in these terms the power of organized groups does not turn only on internal factors, such as the size and unity and leadership of groups. It also turns on external factors—the nature of the environment, the attitudes of people everywhere, the strength of other groups. Adding up all these factors, what are the main advantages and disadvantages of the major groups in the American political struggle?

Numerically, businessmen are in a minority in the United States, yet they wield great power. This power has several foundations. First, the business community is fairly cohesive. "It is almost as if the business leadership were in a continuous political caucus," says one astute political observer. "Conventions, committee sessions, board meetings, and corporate staff conferences, with their interlocking and overlapping memberships, build a system of face-to-face relations knitting the business community together. The airplane and the corporation expense account bring literally thousands of businessmen into conference every day, and they in turn have their relations back home with the less mobile elements of the business community." [13]

Second, business beliefs are shared by many Americans who are not businessmen. Business values have been stamped on American culture. [14] Many people identify themselves with business. Even after the depression and the New Deal, business leaders enjoyed higher public prestige than labor leaders, according to polls. Given this situation, it becomes easier for people to accept such ideas as "What is good for business is good for you."

Third, businessmen have money, and money means influence. It can be used to pay for propaganda, to support political parties, to finance lobbies, to influence

[13] V. O. Key, Jr., *Politics, Parties, and Pressure Groups*, 5th ed. (Crowell, 1964), p. 90.
[14] The nature and extent of the domination of American thought and practice by business values was vividly described by Thorstein Veblen in a series of pioneering studies, especially in his *The Theory of the Leisure Class* (Macmillan, 1899).

public officials directly or indirectly. Fourth, business has important allies who share its community of interest—namely, lawyers, editors, and other professional and white-collar people. Finally, businessmen have important skills, such as the ability to explain their case, experience in competition, and the like.

Business suffers certain disadvantages, too. Businessmen are in a numerical minority, and in the long run votes count most in a democracy. The very concentration of business that promotes unity tends to make business a target. Americans tend to be suspicious of bigness and monopoly. Business is also a convenient scapegoat. When business falls off and jobs are scarce, it is easy to blame "Wall Street."

Other groups have their own strengths and weaknesses. Industrial workers are large in numbers, and they have become more organizationally and politically conscious. But they are divided into organized and unorganized, white and black, skilled and unskilled. Moreover, many American workers refuse to identify themselves or their interests with an "inferior" class. In 1956, only 2 per cent of American white males considered themselves members of the lower classes; 59 per cent, however, identified themselves as members of the working class, and 36 per cent with the middle class.[15] Furthermore, it is hard for labor to make alliances with farm or business groups, because the latters' views of trade unionism may be somewhat unfavorable.

The farmers' strategic situation is almost the reverse of labor's. They are declining in numbers relative to the whole population. But their advantages are significant. The geography of American federalism gives them extra political strength, for farmers are spread through all fifty states. Furthermore, farmers enjoy high esteem; in the popular mind they are frugal, hard-working, independent—the backbone of the nation. Like labor, however, the farmers are divided.

These strategic factors are not static. The external factors especially tend to change over time. Business at one time may enjoy enormous prestige, as during the prosperous 1920's, when Calvin Coolidge could say that "the business of America is business." A few years later, it may be relegated to the national doghouse. Labor is usually stronger during a time of ferment and reform than during a period of prosperity.

The Weapons of Group Influence

Groups use a wide range of political techniques to reach their goals. Their capacity to use these techniques is heavily affected by the factors we have just discussed—the size of the group, its cohesion or lack of it, its organizational structure, the skills of its leaders, the external situation. Like a good football team, every group must exploit the particular advantages that its material makes possible. Just as a team of lightweights may have to stress deception rather than power drives, so a small but well-organized group will probably rely on skillful lobbying rather than mass elec-

[15] P. E. Converse, "The Shifting Role of Class in Political Attitudes and Behavior," in Eleanor Maccoby, *et al.*, *Readings in Social Psychology* (Holt, 1958), p. 288.

tion appeals. In plotting their political tactics, most groups use one or more of the following techniques.

Propaganda

All interest groups are propagandistic. They exploit the media described in Chapter 9—radio, press, film, leaflets, signs, and—above all—word of mouth. Business enjoys a special advantage in this arena, and businessmen have the money to hire propaganda machinery. Being advertisers on a large scale, they know the technique of delivering their message effectively. Most important, they generally have easy access to the means of propaganda, such as the press. The NAM spends over $2 million a year in national advertising. It puts out four periodicals—one goes to 36,500 educators, another to 40,000 leaders of women's clubs, another to 30,000 farm leaders, another to clergymen. According to the NAM, during one nine-month period it "turned out 816,110 copies of 45 pamphlets, booklets, leaflets, etc." A speakers' training program, motion pictures (shown to 4,620 audiences), and meetings with leaders of other main groups, such as farmers and veterans, are other features of this program of opinion-molding. In any four years, says McKean, the NAM "will spend more for this all-around publicity than any political party. And the material is technically excellent—very shrewdly and carefully prepared—whereas much party propaganda is crude and poorly adapted to its recipients." [16] Supplementing the NAM's efforts are those of the Chamber of Commerce, trade associations, and individual corporations.

Other groups have become increasingly aware of the uses of propaganda. Organized labor is a notable example. When a business organization places full-page messages in newspapers across the nation, unions often find the funds to hire similar space for an answer. Recently the AFL-CIO bought time on national radio networks to present its views, and it put out highly effective pamphlets, especially on political and legislative matters. Although labor has not yet matched the propaganda skills of business, it is devoting more money and attention to this political technique. Other interest groups, such as doctors and teachers, are making use of publicity methods. The American Medical Association spent over $163,000 in 1961 in a campaign against extension of Social Security to support hospital care for persons over 65.

How effective is group propaganda? It is impossible to measure precisely the impact of propaganda campaigns, for too many other factors are involved. But we know enough to be skeptical of some of the extravagant claims made for group propaganda. For example, organized labor strongly denounced the Taft-Hartley act and similar "anti-labor" legislation for years after its passage, but surveys in 1952 showed that the great majority of the public *and of union members* either wanted to keep the new law or had no opinion about it, or what to do about it. Also, the more a group publicizes its position, the more it runs

---

[16] Dayton D. McKean, *Party and Pressure Politics* (Houghton Mifflin, 1949), p. 493.

the danger of arousing the opposition and stimulating *its* propaganda potential. Sometimes a highly specialized interest group—for example, the drug manufacturing industry—may improve its "public image" by a skillful advertising campaign. But the impact of a general propaganda campaign to affect mass attitudes on general issues may be small. The best policy for a group may not be to "go it alone," but to form alliances with other groups or with a political party.[17]

Electioneering

Almost all large organizations avow that they are "nonpolitical." The American Legion's constitution flatly bars political activity. Actually, almost all organized groups are involved in politics in one way or another. What group leaders really mean when they say that they are nonpolitical is that they are *nonpartisan*. A distinguishing feature of organized interest groups is that they try to keep their feet in both camps by working through both parties. Usually this means working for individual candidates in elections. The policy that labor has followed for years—helping friends and defeating enemies— is the policy of almost all organized interest groups.

This policy is put into action in different ways. Occasionally an organization openly endorses a candidate and actively works for his election. Thus, in 1924 many labor unions endorsed "Fighting Bob" La Follette for President; the CIO officially backed President Roosevelt in 1944 and Lyndon Johnson in 1964. More often the organization formally stays neutral, but prominent officials take a public stand. In 1944, eleven members of the AFL's executive council worked actively for Roosevelt. Because of such factors as overlapping membership, an organization may set up a front organization to carry on its political activities, as in the case of the Committee on Political Education formed by the AFL-CIO.

Individual labor unions, with somewhat homogeneous memberships, sometimes can afford to take a rather firm position on candidates. Other organizations are more handicapped by the diversity of their members. A local retailers' group for example, might be composed equally of Republicans and Democrats, and many of its members might refuse to take an open position on a candidate for fear of losing business. In such cases more subtle means may be equally effective. At meetings word is passed around that Candidate X is sound from the organization's point of view. Perhaps the hat is passed around, too, and a contribution made to the cause. Members of the organization may serve as local opinion leaders in drumming up support for him.

How effective is electioneering by interest groups? No generalization is possible, because everything depends on the kinds of factors we have been discussing: the group's size, unity, objectives, political resources, leadership, and above all the political context in which it is operating. It can be said in general, though, that the power of the big mass-membership organizations such as labor, business, and

[17] Samuel Halperin, *The Political World of American Zionism* (Wayne Univ. Press, 1961), ch. 13.

veterans to mobilize their full strength in elections has been exaggerated in the press. Too many cross-pressures are operating in the pluralistic politics of America for any one group to assume a really commanding role. Some groups reach their maximum influence only by allying closely with one of the two major parties— but this means losing some of their independence and singleness of purpose.[18]

Another method of trying to win elections is to form a separate party. Again and again groups have decided that keeping a foot in the camps of both regular parties often leads to a choice—from their point of view—between Tweedledum and Tweedledee on election day. Third parties in the United States, however, have tended to be self-defeating (see Chapter 12). The strength of interest groups has been siphoned off into minority party politics, while the two old parties have retained control of the government.

Some groups have tried a third method—trying to infiltrate the organization and machinery of the *major parties*. They have placed their members on local, state, and national party committees and have helped send them to party conventions as delegates. For years, one vice president of the AFL was prominent in Republican activities and another was equally active for the Democrats.

Obviously, burrowing from within is not a new tactic; but it is being used more and more often, and with increasing success. The AFL-CIO's Committee on Political Education is a good example. Technically, COPE is nonpartisan, assisting pro-labor candidates in both parties. Actually, COPE has come to concentrate most of its effort in the Democratic party. Not only does it endorse party candidates, like any organized interest, but in many states it has gone on to exercise electioneering functions that the parties ordinarily monopolize. COPE pays close attention to registration (see Chapter 13) in order to insure a large vote. It takes part in primary campaigns as well as in the later election contests. It puts out posters and leaflets, holds schools on political action techniques, provides automobiles to carry voters to the polls. COPE reported spending almost $800,000 in the 1960 elections; most of this went to Democratic candidates.

Lobbying

Lobbying is a long-used weapon of interest groups. Generations of Americans have been stirred by exposés of the "social lobby" and "invisible government," of bribery and corruption and midnight revels, of invisible agents holding the strings that make politicians dance. Some of this feeling is based on folklore, but much of it on fact. From the time of the Yazoo land frauds 150 years ago, when a whole legislature was bribed and the Postmaster General was put on a private payroll as a lobbyist, to the latest logrolling activity in Congress, Americans have enjoyed denouncing the "unscrupulous" lobbyists.

Over 1,000 lobbyists are active in Washington today, but few of them are glamorous, unscrupulous, or very powerful. Most of the organizations maintaining lobbyists are highly specialized outfits such as the National Fertilizer Asso-

[18] See Harmon Zeigler, *Interest Groups in American Society* (Prentice-Hall, 1964), esp. ch. 8.

ciation, Retired Officers Association, Institute of Shortening and Edible Oils, Associated Tobacco Manufacturers, Texas Water Conservation Association, and a host of others. Lobbyists for these associations are usually hard-working attorneys, with long experience in Washington ways; their job is to watch a handful of bills and to keep in touch with a few administrative officials. Since lawmaking today is a highly technical matter, these lobbyists—or legislative counsel, as they like to be called—play a useful part in modern government. The harried congressman or administrator, threading his way through mountains of paper and seeking to appease conflicting interests, gladly turns to them for their views and information.[19]

Lobbyists for the big groups, such as farmers, labor, and business, operate on a loftier scale. Their specialty is knowing just how to throw their political weight around. These lobbyists are better known throughout the country than some senators, better paid, better staffed, and more secure in their positions. The groups they represent have such broad interests that they must watch a wide variety of bills touching every phase of government. They are expert in raising such a clamor that they seem to be speaking for vast numbers of people. They exert pressure in Congress wherever they can find vulnerable points—regular committees, appropriations committees, individual legislators, even on the floor of the House and Senate (see Chapter 16). They know how to mobilize their organizations back home so that a storm of letters, telegrams, and petitions descends on Washington. They know how to draw up laws, to testify before committees, to help speed a bill through its long legislative journey, or to slow it down. They are experts in the art of influence.

Sometimes lobbyists stay in the background and make use of the legislator's own constituents. The following "Hints on Lobbying" sent by one organization to its members reveal this technique.

1. Interview the legislator at home if you are a constituent. If seeing him at the Capitol, impress on him that you live and vote in his district.

2. Be sure to have read the bill and to know the question with which it deals.

3. Find out main facts about legislator before interviewing him—his party, committee membership, business or profession, etc.

4. Be nonpartisan with legislator of opposite party from your own. In any case make clear our organization's nonpartisanship.

5. Don't pin legislator down to position for or against. Establish friendly relations. We will have to continue working with him in the future.

6. Use good salesmanship techniques. Our organization will be judged by the kind of interview you have.

7. Don't be "superior" even if you know far more about the question than he does. You are not there to score a point but to help get the measure passed!

8. Be patient and keep your temper.

[19] On lobbying as a communication process, see Lester W. Milbrath, *The Washington Lobbyists* (Rand McNally, 1963). Also see Zeigler, *op. cit.*

9. Attend House and Senate galleries when bill comes up on the floor.

10. If possible, establish friendly relations with chairman and key members of at least one committee.

How many voters does a particular lobbyist represent? Nobody really knows. For one thing, his strength varies with the issue; on one matter his whole organization will be united, on another it will not be. Moreover, polls and voting studies indicate that the strength an interest group can muster on election day is often exaggerated. But the real question is what the congressman *thinks* the group can do at the polls. Here he is at a disadvantage, for he is always feeling in the dark. As later chapters suggest, he is highly vulnerable to anything that hints of organized power, of purposeful and united action. The administrator, too, is always uncertain about how much congressional strength lobbyists can muster to deprive his agency of funds or even abolish it forever. The great weapon of the lobbyist is that he *seems* to be representing unseen millions of voters. He must remember the old maxim, "Never admit that it is only you who are talking."

Litigation

When groups find the usual political channels closed to them, they may seek other ways to influence public policy. The courts have become increasingly the center of such efforts. The NAACP, for example, has made court litigation a basic part of its political strategy. Through its Legal Defense and Educational Fund the NAACP has instituted and won numerous cases in its efforts to improve the legal protection of Negroes. The long-time special counsel for the Fund, Thurgood Marshall (later United States Solicitor General), was so successful in winning cases before the Supreme Court in the 1940's and 1950's that he earned the title "Mr. Civil Rights." [20] Other groups have been similarly effective in this regard. The Jehovah's Witnesses and other religious minorities have achieved outstanding success in pressing their claims in court and have thereby had a powerful effect on the doctrine of religious freedom. Urban interests, finding themselves under-represented in the state legislatures and in Congress, turned to the courts after finding rurally dominated state legislatures closed to them.

Direct involvement in lawsuits is just one technique of group activity in litigation. Another is the device of *amici curiae*, friends of the court. Here the organizations present briefs supporting one side or the other in cases before the courts, hence gaining a forum for stating their organizational interests. The American Civil Liberties Union, the American Jewish Congress, AFL-CIO, and the National Lawyers Guild have been most active in the use of the *amicus curiae* procedure. A much more specialized device employed by interests to get their story before the courts is use of legal periodicals. Since judges and justices read these journals to

[20] For a recent summary of the growing literature on this weapon in the group struggle, see Zeigler, *op. cit.*, ch. 11.

keep abreast of legal scholarship and frequently cite articles as authority for their rulings, groups sometimes seek to have articles presenting their views published in these scholarly journals.[21]

In addition to the use of litigation there are other political weapons:

Direct Action. This tactic includes a variety of activities ranging from coercion to general pressure—strikes, boycotts, passive resistance, mass demonstrations. The strike has been employed in the United States mainly by trade unions to win concessions from employers, but strikes and other kinds of economic coercion can be used for political purposes. In some communities Negroes active in the civil rights movement have been denied credit or dismissed from their jobs. In recent years Negroes and white civil rights activists have used the same weapon to counterattack their adversaries by organizing boycotts of buses and stores. Negro and white college students organized freedom rides to bring about compliance with Interstate Commerce Commission regulations on inter-city buses. Sit-ins have been staged to protest the refusal of business establishments to serve Negroes at lunch counters. And in dozens of communities mass demonstrations and marches have dramatized suppression of the right to vote, police brutalities, denial of job opportunities, and other grievances.

Force and the Threat of Force. Normally we think of these as weapons of nation-states rather than of groups within the nation. But if one compares relations between the United States and Canada, for example, with the *internal* politics of some Latin American or African nations, the distinction between international and intranational politics is not so sharp.[22] Of course, within a highly developed nation such as the United States the use or threat of force to secure political goals is illegal. Nevertheless, force is always a weapon of last resort in politics. In the Whiskey Rebellion of 1794 Pennsylvanians refusing to pay excise taxes took up arms against troops directed by President Washington himself. And the nation's most notable failure was our inability to resolve the conflict over slavery except by force. Yet the most remarkable thing about our history has been our ability to resolve our conflicts without the organized use of force.

Today the threat of force has been used by scattered persons and crowds to keep Negroes from voting in some areas and to keep Negro and white children from attending desegregated schools. In some cities persons attending desegregated schools did so under threat of bodily harm and at times federal marshals or troops have had to be used to prevent organized resistance to federal court orders. Over a dozen Negro and white civil rights leaders have been murdered. Undoubtedly the

[21] Jack W. Peltason, *Federal Courts in the Political Process* (Doubleday, 1955), p. 52. For an account of the NAACP's attack on the restrictive covenants see Clement E. Vose, *Caucasians Only* (Univ. of California Press, 1959). See also Chester A. Newland, "Legal Periodicals and the United States Supreme Court," *Midwest Journal of Political Science* (Feb. 1959), pp. 58–74.

[22] Chadwick F. Alger, "Comparison of Intranational and International Politics," *American Political Science Review* (June 1963), p. 406.

fear of bodily harm has deterred some Negro parents from permitting their children to be one of those to take the lonely first step toward a "white" school, but by and large these tactics have reacted to bring additional resolve and support for civil rights advocates.

Interest Groups and Democratic Government

Almost everyone likes to denounce pressure groups—especially somebody else's pressure group. Editorial columns are filled with protests that big business, or big labor, or the farm bloc, is taking over the country. This viewing with alarm has put organized interest groups under a cloud. Some people even look on them as a perversion of democracy—as a blot on the otherwise fair system of popular representation. Various proposals have been advanced to do away with these allegedly evil interests, or at least to clip their wings.

It is easy enough to answer these gloomy critics. Obviously, organized groups are here to stay. So long as there is a modicum of freedom left in America, men will associate on some basis or other. Life without group activity would be unthinkable. Actually we owe a great deal to the richness and fullness of group life in America. Our progress in technological, cultural, and political areas would have been impossible without it. Yet there are two criticisms of organized interest groups in America that we must consider.

Interest Groups: Attack and Defense

Certain organizations, it is said, are becoming *too strong*. Once upon a time, big business was the chief target of this criticism, but more recently farmers and unions have been pictured as the new Goliaths. Are these fears justified? Our discussion above suggests that they are grossly exaggerated. The larger an association becomes, we noticed, the more it includes members of other groups with other allegiances. The stronger a group becomes, the more stimulus there will be for other groups to counter-organize. The real defense against group tyranny in America lies in the groups themselves.[23] So long as we have a great number and a rich diversity of groups, and so long as we preserve our liberties, no single interest or combination of interests can take over America. The competition would simply be too great.

A second criticism is that interest groups are *unrepresentative*. There is a good deal of truth in this charge. In the first place, group leaders often fail to speak for their own members. In the second place, group leaders sometimes ignore the many people with related interests outside their own group, as in the case of agricultural associations acting for a narrow segment of the farm population. In the third place—and most important of all—many elements of the population are not represented in formal organizations at all, or at best are badly under-repre-

[23] Truman, *The Governmental Process*, ch. 16.

sented. Not all groups receive the consideration they deserve in the clash of organized interests. Notable examples of unorganized or under-organized interests are consumers, nonunion laborers, farm workers, and certain professional and white-collar groups. Inevitably, government will tend to over-represent the strongly organized.

But we must be careful not to push this criticism too far. Our government is still organized on a *territorial* or *geographical* basis; we have made no attempt to build occupational representation into the structure of government. Furthermore, Americans who are under-organized can always resort to the polls, or ultimately they can organize their own associations. Admittedly this is a slow process, but it is a process that has occurred again and again in American history as less organized elements have striven to make up for their weakness by political counter-organization. In the economic sphere, for example, when business became too strong, unions and consumer groups rose to hold it in check. Or if manufacturers try to raise prices unduly, powerful chain stores threaten to turn to other sources of supply or even to build or buy factories of their own. This doctrine of "countervailing power," [24] operates also in the political sphere; no one group can become too strong, for under a system of private checks and balances among group interests other groups will become politically active and united in opposition. The result is a system of rough justice in the representation of groups.

Control of Lobbying—A Case Study

However exaggerated, the criticisms of the activities of organized interest groups cannot be ignored. And they have not been. For years Americans have been trying to curb the excesses of the "pressure groups." The attempt to control lobbying—which, as we have seen, is the primary weapon of interest groups—is a revealing example of the difficulties involved in trying to regulate dynamic groups in a democracy.

Attempts to control lobbying began at least a century ago. In 1877 Georgia wrote into its constitution the simple provision that "lobbying is a crime." Early in this century a number of states passed acts to regulate lobbyists, requiring that legislative counsel or agents officially register as such, and that they file statements of expenses paid or promised in connection with promoting legislation. Under the Federal Regulation of Lobbying Act of 1946, every person hired to influence or defeat bills in Congress must register and disclose the name and address of his employer, how much he is paid, and who pays him. Every three months he must file a further statement listing the names of publications that have carried his publicity, and the bills he supports or opposes. Organizations whose main purpose is to influence legislation also must furnish information, which is printed regularly in the *Congressional Record*. It seems clear however, that the 1946 act has not diminished the extent of lobbying; its registration provisions, moreover, have been construed by the courts to apply only to direct pressure on legislators.

[24] J. K. Galbraith, *American Capitalism* (Houghton Mifflin, 1952).

Actually, the aim of such legislation is to turn the spotlight of publicity on the expenditures and activities of lobbyists. How successful has the attempt been? The national lobby law has furnished a vast amount of detailed information about lobbyists—who they are, who sponsors and finances them, what bills they seek to pass or block. This information has given the public some idea of the amount of money involved; in the first four years the act was in effect, lobbyists collected about $60 million and spent approximately $30 million. About 500 persons and organizations had filed, but many hundreds of others had not, on one pretext or another.

Some hold that publicity is not enough, that what we need is *actual regulation* of lobbying. Most lobbyists, these critics argue, have no fear of publicity, but on the contrary actually welcome it. There is much doubt, however, that Congress will try to restrict lobbyists. For one thing, such an attempt might drive the lobbyists underground, where their influence might be more insidious and just as effective. Regulation might run into serious constitutional objections based on the rights guaranteed by the First Amendment. But more important, most students of the problem feel that lobbyists serve an important and desirable function, and that nothing more than publicity is needed.

These observers point out that lobbyists are a sort of "third house" of Congress. While Senate and House are set up on a *geographical* basis, lobbyists represent people directly in terms of their *economic* or other interests. The representative speaks for voters as members of, say, the third district of Ohio; the lobbyist speaks for people as manufacturers or steelworkers or veterans or fruit-growers. Small but important groups, such as bankers, can get representation in this "third house" that they might not be able to get in the other two. In a nation of large and important interests, this kind of *functional* representation, if not abused, is highly useful as a supplement to geographical representation. The lobbyists pour vitally needed information and ideas into the legislative mill. Some European nations have gone so far as to set up legislative branches to provide functional representation; our informal "third house" is a welcome compromise between such extreme measures and no functional representation at all.

The Real Problem: Representation

The real problem raised by the activities of interest groups in America is their frequent failure to represent broader segments of the community, organized or not. This problem in turn involves the broader question of representation. Even the strongest organized interests are still minorities—they are not big enough to embrace all the people, or even most of them. Yet they dominate national legislation. A few years ago an influential congressman was quoted as saying, after the late President William Green of the American Federation of Labor had asked him to vote for a food subsidy bill, "I have always followed Mr. Green on labor bills. But this is not a labor bill. This is a farm bill. On this bill I follow the farm leaders." Undoubtedly such a course is good pressure-group politics. But is it good *majority-welfare* politics?

Groups tend to be competitive, and in the noisy clash of special interests the welfare of the great mass of Americans is sometimes drowned out. The dynamic elements of group life that contribute so much to a healthy America give rise at the same time to dangerous stresses and strains. Groups can cement individual *fragments* of the American people, but what will pull together the *people as a whole*, including both the organized and unorganized? Many agencies fulfill this need—our common traditions and ideas, the role of national leaders like the President, and the overlapping character of the groups themselves. On the organizational level, the political party might fill this great function, but it too is often divided and weakened by internal disunities (see Chapter 12). The problem of maintaining internal unity is especially acute in a day when government needs broad and firm support from the people in handling critical problems at home and abroad. We will return to this problem in Chapter 20—but first we must examine the party forces that play upon our government, and the governmental machinery that both reflects and in turn affects these forces.

12 THE CHANGING PARTIES

American politics is something like a deep river. The undercurrents of party attachment and voting behavior move along slowly in old and familiar channels. The sub-surface currents—shifting attitudes toward candidates and issues—are somewhat more volatile and unpredictable. On the surface of the river, storms may cause the water to overrun the old banks and cut new channels, but underneath the great flow of water may con-

306

tinue unchanged. The 1960's are a time of storm and commotion on the surface of American politics. How long we feel the effect of such an election as that of 1964 will depend on quiet mutations in the pace and direction of the deep currents underneath the rush of waters.

Our two great national parties seem to be among the more permanent and unchanging features of the great tide of American politics. Both these parties are well past their centennials. Only once in the past century has there been a major threat to the two-party system, and that exception—Theodore Roosevelt's desertion of the Republicans in 1912—was short-lived. But if we look below the surface we will note other party systems besides the two-party one.[1] Although most state and local parties also call themselves Democratic or Republican, they may be separated from, or even hostile to, the national organizations. Many such parties are actually the personal organizations of a powerful governor or mayor. And behind the two-party system nationally, as we will note later in this chapter, we can discern the structure of a *four*-party system that closely affects policy-making in Washington.

Yet when all the qualifications are made, at the national level ours is a two-party system in which the Republicans and Democrats, and only these two, have any real chance to gain power; one of these parties normally can muster the majority to enable it to control Congress or to elect the President without any help from a third party, and over a period of time the two parties alternate in power.

Why do we have a two-party system? Nobody knows for sure. Jefferson thought that men naturally divided into Whigs and Tories. Lord Bryce said they inevitably split into nationalists and states-righters. Some have said that "advanced Anglo-Saxon peoples" sensibly adopted tidy political systems; perhaps the sentry in *Iolanthe* was mocking them when he sang:

> Then let's rejoice
> That Nature always does contrive
> That every boy and every gal
> That's born into the world alive
> Is either a little Liberal
> Or else a little Conservative.

Probably the explanation lies largely in the nature of our electoral system. Most of our elections are set up on the basis of our single-member districts in which the candidate with the most votes wins. Since only one candidate can win, the largest and second-largest parties monopolize the victories, and the third party, being deprived of the rewards of office, eventually gives up the fight. The system of electing the President, the grand prize of American politics, operates in this fashion on a national scale. In order to win the Presidency, it is necessary for a party to win a

[1] Austin Ranney and Willmoore Kendall, "The American Party Systems," *The American Political Science Review* (June 1954), pp. 477–485. Also Joseph A. Schlesinger, "The Structure of Competition for Office in the American States," *Behavioral Science* (July 1960), pp. 197–210.

majority of the electoral votes; that requires a national organization and party support in more than one region. The two major parties alternate in their possession of the Presidency; deprived of patronage and power, third parties tend to wither away. The ability of some third parties to last for two or three decades has been due largely to their hold on congressional and state offices in certain sections of the country, as in the case of the Wisconsin Progressives in the 1920's and 1930's.

Two important results stem from our two-party system. First, both parties must be broad alliances of many different interests. Parties are the means whereby groups pool their efforts to reach at least some of their goals. Successful party leaders must be group diplomats—they must know how to mediate among more or less hostile groups so that agreement can be reached on general principles. The implications of this tendency are obvious: National unity is not simply a mystical thing—it is the capacity to rise above differences (at least for a while) and pull together. Parties want to *win elections*. In order to win, each of

"I have the same trouble!" From The Herblock Book (*Beacon Press, 1952*).

them emphasizes the *common beliefs* that *unite* men and plays down the issues that divide them. Parties help reconcile unity and diversity.

A second result of the two-party system is that both parties tend to be moderate in their platforms.[2] Under a multiparty system the parties range all the way from extreme conservatism to extreme radicalism. With two big parties, these extremes are normally avoided. Each party must embrace a variety of groups, and above all each must try to attract the crucial middle-of-the-road vote that easily switches from one side to the other. Not only do the parties seek wide support, but the different interest groups try not to alienate either party. This moderating tendency helps unite the country.

Let us glance briefly at the growth of the American party system to see how these two tendencies—toward unity and toward moderation—have worked out in practice over a century and a half of party development.

[2] E. E. Schattschneider, *Party Government* (Farrar & Rinehart, 1942), pp. 85 ff.

The Grand Coalitions

The story of American parties is closely bound up with the economic, political, and social history of the whole nation. The full telling of that story would take a four-foot shelf in itself. Here we must oversimplify. Looking at American parties as alliances of interests, we see three great phases. The first, lasting until the Civil War, is the Age of the Democrats. The second, stretching through the first decade of this century, is the Age of the Republicans. The third, beginning in 1930, might be called a New Age of the Democrats.

The peculiar American brand of rough-and-tumble politics did not begin in Revolutionary days. Well before '76 there were divisions of interest between economic and sectional groups; there were political clubs and committees; there were meetings, parades, songs, oratory, and even fisticuffs, just as today. But the effect of the Revolution and the post-Revolutionary struggles was to crystallize political interests and allegiances into more coherent and lasting form. The great service of George Washington was to give the fledgling government a sense of unity by his ability to rise above faction and party. He had hardly taken the oath of office, however, before there were signs of an emerging party split. On one side was Alexander Hamilton, who was not only Washington's Secretary of the Treasury but the leader of the Federalists. As a supporter of the Constitution, strong central government, and "sound" financial policies, Hamilton was spokesman for the bankers, traders, and manufacturers of the day.

Rise of the Democrats

On the other side was Thomas Jefferson and a motley collection of small farmers, frontiersmen, laborers, debtors, small proprietors, slaveowners—in general, an agrarian group. Jefferson, the first national party leader, resigned as Secretary of State in Washington's second administration to devote full time to the job of welding together a great party following. He accomplished this task by negotiating with local party leaders in New England, New York, Virginia, and other sections, and by expounding a philosophy of equality, agrarianism, and limited government that appealed alike to northern farmer, southern planter, and western frontiersman. By the turn of the century this combination had overcome the Federalists. As President, Jefferson continued to serve as party chief, using the party to put his program through Congress. The Federalists had feared that Jefferson would be a radical, demagogic leader, but—as required of a multi-interest leader under a two-party system—in office he was conciliatory and moderate.[3]

Here was the first of the grand coalitions. It started out as the Democratic-

[3] William N. Chambers, *Political Parties in a New Nation* (Oxford Univ. Press, 1963), p. 177.

Republican party, but soon dropped the "Democratic," later split into Republican and Democratic elements, and ended up as the Democratic party. During this sixty-year period, ending with Lincoln's election, the party changed in many ways. Millions of new voters were casting ballots. Americans were moving westward, and the party had to move with them. Republican leaders in office, like John Quincy Adams, seemed to drift away from the leveling sentiments of Jefferson. The rising democratic elements, led by Andrew Jackson, gave the party a southern and westward cast. Nevertheless, the party retained two of its main features. First, it won elections. The Whigs—who came to be the main opposition party—were able to elect only two Presidents, and only then by nominating war heroes. Second, it continued to play coalition politics. Its following embraced sizable numbers of cotton planters, slaveowners, small farmers in the West, workmen in eastern mills.

How does a major party lose power? In the case of the Democrats, two things happened. The party itself was split by the irrepressible conflict over slavery, and the opposition hammered out a superior combination of voting groups. The 1850's were a time of party upheaval. The Democrats, sharply split between northerners and southerners, broke into fragments. The Whigs' coalition, composed of large sections of the propertied class, big slaveowners and planters, nativists, and antislavery people, had never been stable enough or large enough to turn the tide against the Democrats. But now the conservative elements of the Whig party, especially in the South, went over to the Democrats. Other Whigs looked around for a new party.

Era of the Republicans

The new winning alliance—the Republican party—was founded in 1854 (not by Abraham Lincoln, who was still a Whig). Initially the party was radical in many respects, appealing to farmers, workers, and small businessmen. To the revolutionary air of the "Marseillaise" the Republicans sang:

> Arise, arise, ye brave,
> And let your war-cry be
> Free speech, free press, free soil, free men,
> Frémont and victory.

In 1856, the Republicans lost with Frémont to a Democratic coalition still strong enough to win, but four years later Lincoln led the Republicans to victory on a platform that opposed further extension of slavery and favored internal improvements, including a "satisfactory homestead measure" for farmers and "liberal wages for workingmen and mechanics." Lincoln received 40 per cent of the popular vote in 1860, but his common appeal to North and West won him the electoral votes of all the states outside the South.

After the war, the Republican party consolidated and broadened its coalition of interests. Its liberal homestead policies helped solidify the support of farmers, especially in the Midwest, and of immigrants eager for land. Its humanitarian appeal and its high-tariff stand continued to attract many eastern workers. Its aids to business, such as sound money policies and railroad grants, won the support of financiers, industrialists, and merchants. As the party of Lincoln, it gained a hold on the newly freed Negroes that was long to remain secure. Veterans of the northern armies were part of this coalition; for decades units of the Grand Army of the Republic worked closely with the party machine and reaped their reward in the form of pensions. Above all, the Republicans were the "party of the Union," with a national appeal that seemed to transcend the lines of class, group, or section.

For five decades after 1860 this coalition was to give every presidential race to the Republicans, except for Cleveland's victories in 1884 and 1892. Not that all was smooth sailing for the Grand Old Party. It suffered from the exposure of corruption that marred Grant's administrations. It was shaken by internal divisions between East and West, between conservative businessmen and not-so-conservative farmers and workers, between reform-minded Liberal Republicans and stand-patters, between party regulars (Stalwarts) and party independents (Halfbreeds), and between many different combinations of these interests. Yet the GOP remained a grand coalition. The secret of its success lay in finding, by design or by chance, leaders who could assuage conflicting elements. For example, when important labor and rural elements were on the verge of deserting the party toward the end of the century, it was a group diplomat, William McKinley, who reasserted the party's broad appeal. When the upsurge of reformism and muckraking in the following years presaged a change in political moods, it was a progressive Republican, Theodore Roosevelt, who reoriented the party's appeal.

The Loyal Opposition

Meanwhile, what had happened to the Democrats? Discredited—in the minds of many—by the Civil War, this party survived with its hard core in the South. Acting as the loyal opposition after the Civil War, the Democrats capitalized on the mistakes and excesses of the party in power. Along with winning the Presidency twice, and nearly winning it several times, the party occasionally took control of Congress and frequently captured state governments. Its platforms championed the principles of low tariffs, states rights, civil service, currency reform. But the Democrats were not able to consolidate national power. Part of the trouble was their failure to win over dissident groups, like the Greenbackers, that spent their energies in third-party movements in behalf of such "radical" changes as bimetallism and business regulation. But the main difficulty was that the Republicans, riding the wave of a long-term economic boom, were in accord with the main temper of the times. Even in 1896, when the Democrats under William Jennings Bryan finally formed an

A SHORT CARTOON HISTORY OF THE REPUBLICAN PARTY

1874—*The Republican Elephant appears; the party symbol is introduced by Thomas Nast in Harper's Weekly. (Courtesy Harper's Weekly and Thomas Nast.)*

1900—*Bryan was bowled over like Don Quixote by McKinley's promise to keep the workman's dinner pail full. (Gillam in* Judge.)

1956—*Eisenhower scores another great personal triumph but cannot pull his party to victory. (Herblock in* The Washington Post.)

1964—*Moderates are left out in the cold when Goldwater receives the Republican nomination. (Scott Long in* The Minneapolis Tribune.)

alliance with the Populists, the GOP re-established control of the White House after one of the most turbulent election fights in American history.

For all their noisy battles during the century, both parties had remained true to the rule that under a two-party system neither side can afford to be extremist. Both parties embraced liberal and conservative elements, both reached out for the support of members of the major interest groups, especially of the dominant business groups. Democrats Tilden and Cleveland shared the major political and economic assumptions of Republicans Hayes and Harrison. Indeed, one of the main complaints of the third parties of the day was that both major parties were in a conspiracy of agreement over policy, disagreeing only over how to split up the spoils of office.[4] Both parties, however, were sensitive to shifting public sentiment. Thus during 1896–1912, a period of unrest and protest, the progressive wings of both parties were dominant much of the time.

In 1912 the Republican coalition split as cleanly as the Democratic coalition had in 1860. The conservative wing under President Taft kept a tight grip on the party machinery; the disgruntled progressives deserted the GOP and nominated Theodore Roosevelt on the ticket of a new Progressive party. The Democratic party, led by Woodrow Wilson, won fewer popular votes than the Republicans and Progressives combined, but it swept the electoral college. As President, Wilson used Jeffersonian precedents in putting through Congress a series of notable measures including a new income tax law, a revised banking system, fair-trade and antimonopoly legislation, and lower tariffs. As party chief, Wilson aimed his "New Freedom" program at the "common man"—labor, farmers, small businessmen—and at the solid South.

Wilson's coalition was not broad or firm enough, however, to stay in power for long. The Democrats barely won the Presidency in 1916 over a reunited Republican party, with Roosevelt back in the GOP fold. And the 1920's, in the wake of World War I, were years of supremacy for the Republicans as the "party of prosperity." To be sure, the Republicans had during this period no specialist in group diplomacy like McKinley or Roosevelt. Yet Harding, Coolidge, and Hoover triumphed easily over their Democratic opponents, perhaps because the business philosophy of the Republicans was in direct accord with the business mood of the era. The Democrats were an uneasy alliance of urban, Catholic, and "wet" groups as opposed to rural, Protestant, and "dry" elements. No matter whether they presented a liberal or a conservative candidate, they could not break the GOP's hold on masses of farmers, businessmen, and even workers.

The Great Depression changed all this. The bleak years of job-hunting and breadlines created a new political temper and new political alignments. People in all classes and groups turned away from the GOP. The Democrats, under Franklin D. Roosevelt, offered some kind of New Deal to the "forgotten man" and plenty of voters felt themselves forgotten. Roosevelt not only strengthened the farmer-labor-southern alliance that Wilson had led; he put together a grand coalition of these groups plus Negroes, unemployed, middle-class people, national

[4] See Matthew Josephson, *The Politicos* (Harcourt, Brace, 1938).

and racial minorities—a coalition that in 1936 gave the Democrats the electoral votes of every state except two. Roosevelt was chief legislator as well as chief executive. Under his generalship Congress enacted a series of laws to provide a new deal for American labor, farmers, small businessmen, old people, and other groups. This grand coalition was strong enough to re-elect Roosevelt three times. That it was not simply F.D.R.'s personal following was indicated when Harry Truman, who lacked some of Roosevelt's superb political skills, led the Democrats to an unexpected triumph in 1948.

A New Age of the Democrats?

The election of 1952 was a sweeping victory for the Republican candidate, Dwight D. Eisenhower, and the Republicans won control of the national House and Senate. Was this the start of a new era of Republican supremacy? Some observers were doubtful. It was an *Eisenhower* victory, they said, resulting from his wartime record and his great popularity.

The 1956 election was both a test of President Eisenhower's personal popularity and a test of the strength of the Republican party. On the first test the results were crystal clear. Running against Adlai E. Stevenson—the same man he had defeated in 1952—Eisenhower boosted his electoral-vote margin to 383 and his popular-vote margin to over nine million, compared with margins of 353 electoral votes and less than seven million popular votes over Stevenson four years before. Despite Eisenhower's victories, the Republicans did not fare so well as a *party*. They lost control of both houses of Congress in the 1954 midterm elections and failed to regain congressional majorities in 1956 even though Eisenhower won. In 1958 the Republicans suffered a debacle reminiscent of New Deal days. The Democrats won thirteen more Senate seats, forty-seven more House seats, and five more governorships. The Grand Old Party was heartened, however, by winning the governorship of New York behind the energetic campaigning of a new figure on the political scene, Nelson Rockefeller.

Thanks to the Twenty-second Amendment, Democrats never had to fear that President Eisenhower, still very popular in the latter part of his Administration, might run for a third term. Vice President Richard M. Nixon, had gained such a head start among the party faithful that he won the Republican party nomination at the convention in Chicago without difficulty. On the Democratic side, a young senator from Massachusetts, John F. Kennedy, had been campaigning for the nomination ever since the Democratic presidential defeat in 1956. Darting around the country in airplanes, he and his aides patiently lined up delegates, kept his name and face constantly in the mass media, and carried a string of presidential primaries in the early months of 1960. After winning on the first ballot at the Democratic convention in Los Angeles, Kennedy awarded the vice-presidential nomination to his chief convention opponent, Senate Majority Leader Lyndon Johnson of Texas.

The contest that followed between Kennedy and Nixon was one of the most dramatic in American history. Kennedy's main strategy was to call for the nation to "move forward" after the "stagnation" of the Eisenhower years, to emphasize his standing as a Democrat and his belief in New Deal-Fair Deal principles, and to carry the attack to his opponent, especially in a series of television debates. Nixon's main strategy was to defend the Eisenhower record, to play up his own experience and to play down Kennedy's, and (knowing of the Republicans' minority position) to appeal directly to Democrats and independents as well as to Republicans. The television debates, the religious issue, and a climactic television marathon by the Vice President enlivened the campaign. And the vote-counting, too, was dramatic, for the outcome was the closest in modern American history: Kennedy 303 electoral votes (from 23 states), and 34,221,463 popular votes; Nixon 219 electoral votes (from 26 states), and 34,108,582 popular votes. Fifteen "independent" electors from the South voted for Senator Harry F. Byrd of Virginia. Kennedy's popular majority was only one-tenth of one per cent greater than Nixon's.

Kennedy's election, along with the election of a strongly Democratic Congress, posed an urgent question for the Republicans. Were they doomed to be a minority indefinitely? How could they, without a popular hero like Eisenhower, break the Democrats' grip on the national government? A fundamental difference over political strategy now divided the Republican camp. Conservative members of the party, headed by Senator Barry Goldwater of Arizona, contended that the only way for the GOP to win was to stop being a "me-too" party, to stop offering the voters a "watered down version of the Fair Deal and New Frontier," to stop truckling to the "Eastern Establishment," to make a stronger appeal to the conservative West and South, and to take a more independent line on foreign policy than was possible under the bipartisan foreign policy approach. Liberal Republicans disagreed. They warned that the party would lose votes if it moved to the right; that a conservative appeal would antagonize Negroes, immigrant, and working groups in the big cities; that the South and West simply did not have enough votes to carry the electoral college; that the Republicans should adhere to their great progressive tradition of Lincoln and Theodore Roosevelt; and that foreign affairs in the 1960's were too critical to permit playing party politics beyond the water's edge.

By 1964 a battle royal was under way between Goldwater on one side and moderates headed by Rockefeller, Governor William Scranton of Pennsylvania, Governor George Romney of Michigan, and former Senator Henry Cabot Lodge of Massachusetts on the other. In past years governors of large populous states such as these had dominated the GOP, especially at national conventions, and had usually overcome the "congressional Republicans" in Washingon. But now these governors were too few; they were too late with too little. Moving early against a divided and irresolute field, Goldwater piled up delegate strength in state party conventions and committees where his zealous supporters were able to out-work and out-organize the opposition. Goldwater did not fare so well in the presidential primaries except for the very last one, and largest one, California, where he won

86 delegates in a close victory over Rockefeller. The Arizona Senator was nominated on the first ballot at the Republican convention in San Francisco. When the Democrats unanimously nominated President Johnson—who in his eight months in office had moved squarely into the Roosevelt-Truman-Kennedy tradition —the stage was set for a clear test of the conservative strategy.

The Republican nominee did not duck the requirements of his strategy. He voted against the Civil Rights Act of 1964. He pressed his campaign efforts in the South, West and Midwest rather than in the East. He argued for economic and social policies that were clearly more conservative than the Democrats'. Johnson's strategy was different. Exploiting his position as President to the hilt, he tried to unite liberals and moderates, Democrats and independent Republicans, northerners as well as southerners, behind his "Great Society."

The election outcome seemed to be a decisive repudiation of the Goldwater strategy. Not only did Johnson receive the greatest total vote, the greatest margin over an opponent (43.1 million versus 27.2 for Goldwater), and the highest percentage of the total vote (61), in history, but he helped pull into office the most Democratic and the most liberal Congress since 1936. The Democrats added two senators and 37 representatives to their already topheavy majorities in both chambers. Goldwater achieved a sensational breakthrough in the deep South, carrying Alabama, Georgia, Louisiana, South Carolina, and Mississippi—the last with a remarkable 87 per cent of the vote. But he lost all other states except his own state of Arizona, many of them by one-to-two minorities.

What had gone wrong with the Goldwater strategy? Explanations were varied: that he was trying to play partisan, divisive politics when the nation was basically united behind a liberal, bipartisan consensus; that he overdid his appeal to the South; that he spoiled his strategy by reckless foreign policy pronouncements that enabled Johnson to shift the grounds of the debate; that he wrote off too quickly the great urban states that loom so large in the electoral college. The election was a fascinating test of whether or not highly organized and zealous conservatives could arouse the great "lost vote" that the Goldwaterites contended had not shown up in the "meaningless" battles between moderate Democrats and Republicans. Goldwater had in effect challenged one of the oldest rules of American politics—the rule that a successful presidential candidate must be a group diplomat heading a moderate, widely based party embracing many group interests—and he had failed. The rightists simply could not mobilize very much support in the middle of the political spectrum.[5]

What lies ahead for the Republicans and for the two-party system? In the late sixties the Republicans were still suffering from the scars of 1964. They could not mobilize enough strength on Capitol Hill to block Johnson's major bills. They were still divided over political strategy and policy programs. They were still failing, as

[5] On the difference in the campaign between "mass opinion" and the opinion of letter writers (who tended to be more ideological) in relation to the Goldwater strategy, see Philip E. Converse, Aage R. Clausen, and Warren E. Miller, "Electoral Myth and Reality: The 1964 Election," *The American Political Science Review* (June 1965), pp. 321–336. See also ch. 11.

Theodore H. White wrote, "to capture the imagination of the American people." [6]
But they had some assets—their new found strength in the South, the continued
loyalty of millions of voters, and a number of governors who might make attractive
candidates in 1968. Chastened by defeat, the Republicans were also in a mood to
experiment with new techniques and organization. The election of John V. Lindsay
as mayor of New York City suggested that a Republican could win in urban areas
with heavy Democratic registration if the GOP leadership modernized its party
issues and attracted moderate and liberal voters. History indicated that some
day the party balance would right itself but history did not indicate how long the
process might take. Meantime the era of the Democrats continued.

Functions of Political Parties

The party in power has the for-
mal responsibility of *governing*. The party out of power has the job of *opposing*
the "ins"; it is supposed to play a bright spotlight on any errors the incumbents
commit. While no party is foolish enough to denounce the party in power for
every action it takes, in general the "outs" are supposed to keep before the people
an alternative line of action.

Whether, in fact, parties do what the formal theory of party government indicates they are supposed to do is a different question. Our parties usually perform
faithfully the basic "watchdog" duty; they are not so effective in presenting an
agreed on alternative program. The party that wins an election does not necessarily
govern as a *party* and the public seldom blames a party as a total institution for
the failures of those in office.

What are the consequences, intended and otherwise, that flow from our party
system? The foregoing history of the party system, brief though it is, shows that
our parties have managed to pull America's warring groups into a consensus that
has helped us to live together with a minimum of open conflict. In other words,
our party system is an important mechanism for the *peaceful resolution of conflict*.
This unifying role of the parties was well shown in the years before the Civil War.
Most of the other bonds between North and South—for example, between northern
and southern members of the same religious denominations, business organizations,
reform groups—snapped even before the parties broke apart. Party leaders, in their
desire to win national office, were forced to search for formulas that would keep
their parties united. The moderating role of the party system has been demonstrated recently by the fact that, except for the 1964 presidential elections, the
ideology of both parties has moved in the same general direction, as both parties
put forward platforms and candidates reflecting the "mainstream" of American
political views.

In trying to gain votes, parties *simplify the alternatives*. Usually they present the
public with a choice between two relatively understandable solutions to the question, although most controversial matters admit of a variety of approaches. The

[6] Theodore H. White, *The Making of the President 1964* (Atheneum, 1965), p. 385.

two major parties limit the choice of candidates as well as issues. Hence voters can choose between a few alternatives instead of a bewildering variety of men and platforms.

In trying to gain votes, parties help *to stimulate interest in public affairs*. An election contest is exciting. Parties use all the media—radio, television, press, posters, leaflets, meetings, and the like—in order to saturate the voters with their arguments. After a polite interval following the election, the opposition party maintains a drumfire of faultfinding against the party in power. Public discussion promoted by partisans may not fit the ideal model of a debating society, but in the real world it is the best means for the *resolution of conflict*. And thousands, perhaps millions, have been mobilized to participate in public affairs through the machinery of parties.

Partisan activity has also been an important *source of public welfare*, especially in the past. Local party organizations, in their desire to win votes, gave the needy jobs, loans, free coal, picnics, recreational facilities, and helped those in trouble with such matters as pensions, unemployment benefits, taxes, and licenses. William S. Vare, leader of the Republican machine in Philadelphia, used to brag that his organization was "one of the greatest welfare organizations in the United States." In every election precinct, he said, his committeemen were at the beck and call of the people day and night and service was rendered "without red tape, without class, religion, or color distinction." The creation of the Welfare State has robbed parties of most of their charitable activities, but the chance to be a bridge between an impersonal government official and the ordinary voter provides big-city organizations with an opportunity to retain their support from underprivileged citizens.

Our parties have also served as important *channels of upward mobility for integrating* those on the "outside" into the American consensus. Decades ago it was the Irish-Americans who found in partisan activity a way to achieve status. Parties today, especially in the larger cities, are providing a channel of upward mobility for Negroes, although types of political action other than party activity—militant civil rights action, for example—have increasingly been attracting their attention, especially the attention of young Negroes.

The most important and vital function of our party system is to provide an essential link in the governmental and electoral processes so that the decisions made by public officials do in some measure reflect the desires of the electorate. The simplified model of our party system—the majority of the voters elect to office one party which then carries out the mandate of the majority of the voters—can be misleading. Nonetheless, the need of the partisan to win more votes than anybody else if he is to secure and retain power is the *link between the mass public and the governing elites*. Politics has been defined as the authoritative allocation of values, or as the determination of who gets what, where, when, and how. The party system is the most important agency in *democratizing*—to use a non-elegant word—*our allocation of values*.

Our parties do not, as organized units, supply this link between the electorate and the policy-makers so much as they provide the arenas in which individual office-seekers compete for votes. And since the first step is to secure the support of one's own partisans, the process of candidate selection is extremely significant.

Choosing Candidates

From the very beginning, parties have been the mechanism by which candidates for public office are selected. The earliest method was the *caucus*, a closed meeting of party leaders. The caucus was used in Massachusetts only a few years after the *Mayflower* landed and played an important part in pre-Revolutionary politics. John Adams, in 1763, described with some distaste a caucus in Tom Dawes' garret:

> There they smoke tobacco till you cannot see from one end of the garret to the other. There they drink flip, I suppose, and there they choose a moderator, who puts the questions to the vote regularly; and selectmen, assessors, collectors, wardens, firewards, and representatives are regularly chosen before they are chosen by the town. . . .

After the Union was established, party groups in the national or state legislatures served for several decades as the caucus. The legislators in each party simply met separately to nominate candidates. Our first presidential candidates were chosen by senators and representatives meeting as party delegates.

"King Caucus," however, soon fell into ill repute. Its meetings smacked of secret deals and logrolling; moreover, the caucus could not be fairly representative of the people where the party was in a minority, since only officeholders were members. Andrew Jackson's supporters boycotted the Republican caucus of 1824 because, they argued, the outcome was rigged by the congressional insiders. Although there were efforts to make the caucus more representative, gradually a system of *party conventions* took its place. The convention was made up of delegates usually chosen directly by party members in towns and cities. The conventions served several purposes. They chose the party standard-bearers. They debated and adopted a platform. And they provided a chance to whip up party spirit and perhaps to paint the town red.

But the convention method in turn came in for grave criticism. It was charged— and often quite rightly—that the convention was subject to control by the party bosses and their machines. At times, delegates were freely bought and sold, instructions from party members were ignored, meetings got completely out of control.

To "democratize" party selections, the *direct primary* was adopted by state after state in the early years of this century. This system simply gives every member of the party the right to vote on party candidates in a primary election. The state usually supplies the ballots and supervises the primary election, which takes place some time before the general election in November. The direct primary was hailed by many Americans as a major cure for party corruption but, as we shall see, it did not cure all the existing evils, and it led to new ones.

Today the primary is the main method of picking party candidates, but the nominating convention is available in one form or another in about one-fourth of the states. The convention has also been retained by three states as a principal nominating device and nationally, of course, for picking presidential candidates. In either case, the party carries the main burden of activity, although many of its electoral activities are closely regulated by law. In the general election, too, the party has a central role. It campaigns for its candidates, mobilizes its machinery in their behalf, helps finance them, and on election day it produces cars, advice for the voters, and workers at the polls to watch the counting of the ballots.

The Role of Third Parties

Minor parties have many of the same electoral and propaganda functions as the big parties, except that they cannot perform the crucial feat of mobilizing a majority of voters at the polls. In one respect, however, minor parties play a special role: They draw public attention to controversial issues that the major parties either ignore or straddle. Such notable minor parties as the Locofocos, the Greenbackers, the Socialists, the Prohibitionists, and the Progressives of 1912 and 1924, in performing this function, have acted as "vehicles for the expression of political discontent." [7]

Disgusted with the conservative policies of both Republicans and Democrats, farmers in the last century organized parties of their own. These parties were short-lived, but they compelled the major parties to modify their programs. In this century some labor groups have repeatedly turned to the third-party technique. In 1912 and 1920 the Socialist party polled over 900,000 votes, but these were its high-water marks. The Liberal party in New York City occasionally has enjoyed some balance-of-power influence. Over the years third parties have been organized by special-interest groups, such as anti-slavery people, Prohibitionists, Christian Nationalists, Vegetarians (who nominated a candidate for President but never got on the ballot), and many others.

Although six minority-party candidates won about 125,000 votes in the 1964 presidential election, not since 1948 have third parties had a significant role in a presidential campaign. In many cases, however, the minor parties have won wide support for their ideas, only to see a major party filch their best planks to adorn its own platform. The Grangers campaigned for a regulation of unfair railroad rates. The Greenbackers demanded a graduated income tax. The Populists proposed a constitutional amendment providing for the direct election of United States senators. The Socialists called for an end to child labor, for public works systems, old age and unemployment insurance, the adoption of the initiative and referendum. All these proposals, once they had gained significant popular support, were taken over by the major parties and enacted into law. Minor parties, however, deserve much of the credit for popularizing the ideas.

[7] M. S. Stedman and S. W. Stedman, *Discontent at the Polls* (Columbia Univ. Press, 1950), p. 168.

The failure of third parties has not been due simply to the ability of major parties to steal their thunder. That failure is due in part to the extremism of third parties, their tendency to break up over issues of party dogma, their concentration on propaganda rather than political action at the grass roots. Moreover, the major parties have erected legal barriers against third party action. For example, in some states the number of signatures on petitions needed to place a third party on the ballot is very high. All these factors, plus the primary role of the single-member district system noted above, explain the fact that no minor party has succeeded in dislodging a major party in national politics at least since the Civil War.

Party Machinery and How It Runs

On paper our parties look like armies. They have the form of a pyramid, with millions of party members and thousands of local party officials at the base, and a few national party heads at the top. Like the army, they have a hierarchy of leaders and followers, running from the national committee at the top down to town and precinct committees at the bottom. Actually, this analogy is false, for the essence of an army is discipline from the top down. And this sort of central discipline is precisely what our parties lack. They have been well described as "loose associations of state and local organizations, with very little national machinery and very little national cohesion." [8]

Why are our parties decentralized and undisciplined? There are many reasons. Perhaps the most important is the *federal* basis of our government. Earlier in the book we suggested that the Constitution has shaped our political system, just as politics in turn has affected the structure of government. Here is an excellent example of this circular relationship. Parties tend to organize around *elections* and *officeholders*. Since our federal system sets up elections and offices on a national-state-local basis, our parties are organized on a similar basis. Just as state and local governments are largely independent of the national government, so the state and local parties are somewhat independent of the national party organizations. Thus, the Constitution has given us federalism in our *parties* as well as in our *government*. The nature of our party organization in turn has had a vital impact on the workings of our government, as we shall see in Part Five.

National Party Organization

The supreme authority in both major political parties is the national convention. The convention meets every four years and has four major duties: to nominate the party's candidates for President and Vice President; to write the party's national platform; to adopt the

[8] "Toward a More Responsible Two-Party System," A Report of the Committee on Political Parties of the American Political Science Association, *Supplement, The American Political Science Review* (September 1950), p. v.

rules of the party; and to go through the formality of electing the national committee. (In Chapter 13 we shall look more closely at the convention.) But the convention is in session only briefly; most of the time party business is handled by party executives.

The Democratic National Committee is composed of something over 100 members—one man and one woman from every state and a few members representing areas like Puerto Rico. The Republican National Committee is also composed of one man and one woman from each state, along with territorial representatives. In addition, the Republicans make each Republican state chairman a member of their National Committee if his state cast its electoral vote for the Republican presidential candidate in the preceding election, or if a majority of his state's congressional delegation (House and Senate counted together) are Republican, or if his state has a Republican governor. In form, the committeemen of both parties are elected every four years by their respective national party conventions. Actually, they are chosen by state party conventions or by party committees or by party primaries.

The national committeemen often are influential in their states, but the committee itself is not very important. In fact, it rarely meets. (One of its main jobs is to choose the city where the national convention will meet, a choice usually dictated by the nature of the convention hall and facilities and by the amount of cash offered by cities for the privilege of acting as host to the convention.) The party organization is usually run by the chairman of the committee and by appointed, full-time officials.

The main job of the *chairman* is to manage the presidential campaign. Although in form he is elected by the national committee, actually he is chosen by the party's presidential candidate at the close of the quadrennial convention. It is through him that the presidential candidate—and perhaps later the President—runs the party nationally. By the same token, a defeated presidential candidate may have little control over the national chairman, or the national committeemen may elect a new head who responds to the balance of forces within the committee. Usually the national chairman is the chief dispenser of patronage for the President, using his control of the relatively few but politically important federal jobs that are not covered by civil service to promote zeal and discipline in the party. If a President and a chairman cannot get along with each other, it is the chairman who must go, as with President Franklin D. Roosevelt and Democratic chairman James A. Farley in 1940. Thus the chairman becomes, in V. O. Key's words, "a technician, a specialist in campaign management and machine tending, who exercises his power only so long as he enjoys the confidence of the presidential nominee." [9]

It is the national chairman, backed by the President, who gives the party a measure of unity and direction when the party is in power. When the party loses a presidential race, it often has no real central leadership. The defeated nominee is called the titular leader, but he usually has little real power over the organization, partly because he has no jobs to hand out. As a result, the party out of power nationally may come under the control of congressional leaders.

[9] V. O. Key, Jr., *Politics, Parties, and Pressure Groups*, 3rd ed. (Crowell, 1952), p. 342.

The *Congressional and Senatorial Campaign Committees* aid congressmen in their campaigns for re-election. Today the Republican Senatorial Campaign Committee is composed of senators chosen for two-year terms by their fellow Republican senators. The Democrats through their party leader in the Senate normally choose their men for a two-year term. The men selected are usually from states in which there will be no senatorial election. The Congressional Campaign committees, composed of members chosen by each party group in the House of Representatives, are organized in somewhat similar fashion.

After candidates have been nominated, the committees send them money, provide speakers, supply campaign material, and the like. Normally they concentrate their efforts in doubtful districts and states where an expenditure of money and time can do the most good. During presidential election years, the activities of the national committee tend to overshadow the work of the Congressional and Senatorial Campaign committees. But during off-year elections, these committees often provide the only campaign that is nationally directed.

Both a cause and a result of party disorganization is the manner in which candidates are nominated. Ordinarily, politicians seeking the party nomination run on their own, while the party remains, outwardly at least, neutral toward the aspirants. Lacking organized party support, each candidate builds a personal organization; and since scores of candidates are usually running for a dozen or more offices, from

FORMAL AND ACTUAL PARTY ORGANIZATION

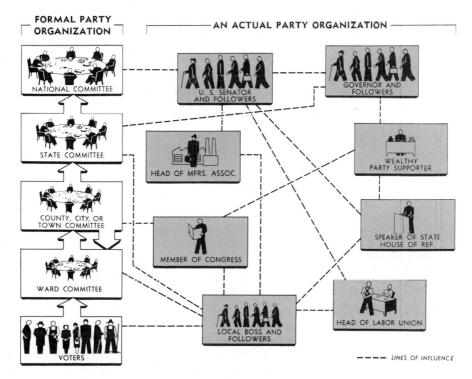

governor to small local jobs, the party becomes a confused arena filled with countless guerrilla bands sniping at one another. Candidates campaign on their own, raising their own money and putting out their own publicity. In the hurly-burly of the primary campaigns there often develop sharp rivalries between Democrats or between Republicans—rivalries that may carry over into the general election, even though the party should be unified in order to put up a strong fight. Such individualistic politics is not always the case; indeed, contests within the primaries are not always the rule.[10] In cities dominated by one party—Chicago, for example—the minority party finds it difficult sometimes to persuade a politician even to run against the slates of candidates put up by the "organization."

State Party Organization

At the next lower level in the party hierarchy are the *state committees*, which in general resemble the national committees. They are manned by committeemen chosen locally in counties or other areas. Most state committees are not powerful; they are often dominated by the governor, a United States senator, or a coalition of strong local leaders, just as the President dominates his party's national committee. The state chairman is sometimes the creature of the governor or senator; occasionally, however, he is really the party's boss on the state level and is able to pick—and control—governors, senators, and other key officials. Many state parties are as undisciplined and decentralized as the national party.

Below the fifty state committees, each party hierarchy broadens out into countless district and county committees. These, too, vary tremendously in their functions and power. The New York county chairmen are often powerful bosses like the late Ed Flynn of the Bronx, and many county chairmen elsewhere make up the party slates for a host of offices such as county commissioner, sheriff, treasurer, and the like. Some county chairmen, however, are mere figureheads.

At the Grass Roots

It is at the base of the party pyramid—at the city, town, ward, and precinct level—that we find the grass roots of the party in all its richness and profusion and variety. In some localities party politics is a round-the-clock, round-the-year occupation. This is where party politics, to quote Mr. Dooley, "ain't bean bag," but a "professional spoort, like playin' baseball f'r a livin' or wheelin' a truck." The party's sergeants and corporals—the local ward and precinct leaders—do countless favors for their constituents, from

---

[10] Austin Ranney, "Candidate Selection and Party Cohesion in Britain and the United States," paper prepared for delivery at the 1965 Annual Meeting of the American Political Science Association, September 8–11, p. 5. See also Frank J. Sorauf, *Political Parties in the American System* (Little, Brown, 1964), pp. 98–104; and *Party and Representation* (Atherton Press, 1963), chs. 3–5.

fixing parking tickets to organizing clambakes. But such strong local party organization is exceptional. Most local party committees are small, poorly financed, and inactive except during the few hectic weeks before election day. Party activities are not professional but amateurish.[11] The party committeemen are less interested in policy and program than in gaining recognition and favors from candidates and officeholders.

Our party systems are highly complex. For example, the Kansas party organization embraces a state committee, congressional district committees, county committees, state senatorial district committees, state judicial district committees, and precinct committees. The organization of other state parties is hardly less elaborate. Why such complexity? As we have seen in earlier chapters, party politics tends to be highly individualistic and personalized. It would be more nearly correct to say that we have *candidate* politics or *officeholder* politics rather than party politics. That is to say, political activity tends to focus on men seeking or holding political power, and on the groups around them, rather than on a unified, hierarchical party system. Since our constitutional arrangements provide for a multiplicity of officeholders at a number of levels of government, our parties are bound to be complicated. The diversity of our country and the absence of strong direction and control by the national party headquarters mean that party systems also vary a good deal from state to state. In Great Britain, although there are often sharp clashes within the parties and although local constituency organizations vary in ideological stance, the structure of party organization is about the same in Yorkshire, London, Glasgow, and Wales. In our country, the differences between the Democratic party in New York and in Alabama, both in terms of program and procedure, and between the Republican organizations in New York and Illinois, are quite sharp.

This situation inevitably opens a gulf between national party headquarters and state and local parties. Deepening this gulf is the fact that most election laws are enacted and enforced by the states, not by the national government. "Political parties, as legal entities," says one authority, "are by and large state parties. . . . The national superstructure over the state party organizations, in a sense, derives its power from their consent." [12] Moreover, some states hold their state and local elections in different years from national elections. New York, for example, elects its governors for four-year terms in even-numbered years between presidential elections, and New York City elects its mayors in odd-numbered years.

The gulfs between national and state parties vary from state to state and from year to year. One factor tending to link national and local parties is mutual self-interest; each has a stake in the other's victory. Perhaps more important, most states—especially the more urban ones—are affected by political trends affecting the nation as a whole, as we saw in Chapter 10.

---

[11] The actual effectiveness of local party work has not been systematically tested. See Phillips Cutright, "Measuring the Impact of Local Party Activity on the General Election Vote," *Public Opinion Quarterly* (Fall 1963), pp. 372–386; and Raymond E. Wolfinger, "The Influence of Precinct Work on Voting Behavior," *Ibid.* (Fall 1963), pp. 387–398, for suggestive studies.

[12] Key, *Politics, Parties, and Pressure Groups*, p. 306.

A Decline in One-Party States?

In the past, most of our states have been dominated by one party. Democratic party control of southern states and Republican party control of northern New England were but extreme examples of the prevailing system. Parties were mainly sectional—Democrats strong in certain states versus Republicans strong in other states—so that real party competition did not exist within the states. In the past fifty years, however, competitive two-party systems have developed within most states. Oregon and Vermont, for example, are no longer guaranteed for the Republicans, nor are all southern states assured for the Democrats, as the 1962 and 1964 elections re-emphasized.

Party trends in the South are especially interesting. As a result of industrialization, urbanization, migration of northern whites into the South and of Negroes out of it, increased Negro voting, and other economic, social, and political developments, a more competitive two-party system is slowly rising in the South.[13] One southern student distinguishes between the "Inner South" comprising the "black belt" from Georgia to Mississippi, and the "Outer South" composed of the encircling states.[14] The latter, with fewer Negroes and more large cities, is fast moving toward a two-party alignment like that in the rest of the nation. The former went strongly for Goldwater in 1964, but its flirtation with the Republican party may be a brief one, depending on the party's position on civil rights. Thus the southern shift toward Republicanism in 1964 could be a surface eddy or a basic undercurrent, depending on changes in the broader flow of American politics.

American Parties and American Democracy

American political parties are vital to American democracy. They do the jobs that have to be done in any healthy system of representative government. They build a bridge between people and their government. They shore up national unity by bringing conflicting interests into harmony. They soften the impact of the extremists on both sides. They stimulate and channel public discussion. They find candidates for the voters and they find voters for the candidates. They help run elections. Parties shoulder much of the hard, day-to-day, work of democracy.

Yet today our party system is under attack. And one of the most common complaints is that the two parties do not stand for anything.

---

[13] Alexander Heard, A *Two Party South?* (Univ. of North Carolina Press, 1952).

[14] William Buchanan, "Cracks in Southern Solidarity," *The Antioch Review* (Fall 1956), pp. 351–364. See also Alan P. Sindler, "The Unsolid South: A Challenge to the Democratic Party," in Alan Westin (ed.), *The Uses of Power* (Harcourt, Brace & World, 1962).

The Two Parties—Tweedledum and Tweedledee?

The charge goes something like this: We all know that party platforms are evasive and obscure. Every four years spokesmen of interest groups appear before a bored committee on resolutions, and then a national platform is hastily pieced together. The typical platform seems to be designed to pick every stray vote rather than to speak out in a forthright manner on the vital questions of the day. The voter has almost no alternatives. Platforms are so vague, candidates' statements so ambiguous, that voters have no basis on which to choose. According to an old saying, party platforms are like train platforms—something to get in on, not to stand on.

As a result, the two major American parties have no significance, it is said. During the business-oriented period of the twenties, the welfare-oriented period of the thirties, and the national security-oriented period of the forties and fifties, both parties adhered to the same basic values and sought the same basic goals in a virtually "bipartisan fashion." This would not be a weakness, it is argued, if the similarity between the two parties represented a basic agreement among all Americans. But since no alternatives are presented to the voters, the parties become agents of transition from one period to another only after a crisis has occurred.[15]

In short, it is charged that compared to British and German and French parties, which take definite, definable positions on matters of policy and ideology, American parties are fuzzy, formless things. How accurate is this characterization?

In an *organizational* sense party membership does not mean a great deal. In contrast to most parties abroad, the Republican and Democratic parties are not composed of regular, dues-paying members. In most states one does not join the party in any formal sense, as he must when he becomes a member of a union or a college debating group. He simply enrolls as a Democrat or Republican, or requests a ballot of either party (which automatically enrolls him) at the party primaries. And if he finds the party not to his liking, he can easily drop out and become an independent, or "join" the other party. Some people over the years change their party registration back and forth like a woman changing hats.

But *psychologically* the story is quite different.

For one thing, many people see their own party or the opposition party as standing for something. "People tend to have a broad image of parties," Key reports. "They see a party as generally dedicated to the interests of a particular set of groups within society, or as committed to a broad range of policy objectives." [16] To be sure, their ideas of party philosophy and orientation may be rather crude, but they seem to make sense. For example, most business and professional people see the Republican party as the party that best serves their interests, while skilled and unskilled workers look on the Democrats as the party best serving them. When polled,

---

[15] Harvey Wheeler, " 'Duocracy' or the Imperfect Competition in our Party System," in J. R. Fiszmon (ed.), *The American Political Arena* (Little, Brown, 1962), pp. 302–306.
[16] V. O. Key, Jr., *Public Opinion and American Democracy* (Knopf, 1961), p. 433.

workers offer such comments as: "The Democratic party is for the working people. . . . Poor people have a better chance with the Democrats. . . . The Democrats give more help to the laboring class. . . . Yes, they don't be no depressions, when them Democrats is in. They just lets that money roll on and that's what I likes. . . ." As for the Republicans, workers are quoted as saying: "The Republicans always stand for big business. . . . They are all for the big man; people with money. . . . It is a big business party. . . . They are all right for the big shots in Wall Street. . . ."

In the second place, many people *believe* that there are important differences between the two parties. As we say on page 225, party identification remains stable over the years. Most people do not shift from one party to another from election to election. Furthermore, the Survey Research Center has consistently found about forty per cent of their national sample responding affirmatively to the question: . . . "Do you think there are any important differences between what the Democratic and Republican parties stand for?" Another ten per cent indicates that there are differences, but none of great moment. (The sharp divisions between Johnson and Goldwater in 1964 probably strengthened these perceptions of party difference, but they may dwindle again if the Republicans repudiate the Goldwater strategy in 1968 or 1972 and return to a more moderate opposition role.) How can people see stronger party positions and stronger party differences than really exist? People who are strong Democrats or Republicans are likely to look at events "through the eyes of their party." This phenomenon is called "perceptual distortion," and the more partisan a person is, the more he may select and distort his party's positions.[17]

The Role of Party Leadership

We have been discussing the party membership as a whole, but we must remember that the party is made up not of just a mass of followers but of a variety of people ranging from "round-the-clock activists" to the almost completely passive. The leadership of a party, like that of any group, almost always comprises the full-time officials and leaders, a core of activists, and a larger number of fairly active members. The most important party leaders are usually the president, senators, governors, the elected chairman, and other party officials.

Just as the Republican rank-and-file differs from Democratic members in socioeconomic background, so do the party leaders. A study of the occupational backgrounds of candidates for nomination for county office in three Indiana counties, for example, showed that a quarter of the Republican candidates had professional backgrounds and half had managerial, while only twelve per cent had been manual workers; of the Democrats, on the other hand, over forty per cent had been manual

[17] Angus Campbell, *et al.*, *The American Voter* (Wiley, 1960), p. 133. See also Key, *Public Opinion and American Democracy*, p. 453.

workers, and only one-fourth managerial.[18] Such contrasts, while suggestive, are not striking; it may be much more significant that most leaders in both parties come from middle-class, white-collar backgrounds.

What is the relation of party leaders and party followers? In the social scientist's language, "mutually interactive or dependent." The very passivity of many followers who cherish the party label gives the party leader a wide area within which to determine party policy. For example, a newly nominated presidential candidate not only may pick a new national chairman if he wishes; he can interpret the party platform almost as he wishes. But the party leader, like all group leaders, cannot go too far. He cannot antagonize big sections of his own following. And he may manage to get his opinions superficially accepted without really changing deep-seated attitudes of the rank-and-file. For "American parties," as Key says, "are poorly equipped to inform and shape the opinions of their followers. Formation of party policy is itself haphazard. . . . In the periods between campaigns machinery for the formation of the minority party position is either nonexistent, or many party spokesmen enunciate various policies both conflicting and consistent but invariably confusing." [19]

What about leadership in the minority or opposition party? This party has a very special duty: to probe, to criticize, to present alternative approaches, and to act on those alternatives if elected. But our opposition parties are not well organized to perform this function. At the national level the "out" party has no authorized leader to attack the "ins"—except after it has named a presidential nominee. Its leadership is usually dispersed among congressional leaders, governors, former presidents, future hopefuls. When the Democrats control one branch of the government and the Republicans another, the job of opposing is almost impossible, for each party can blame the other if things go badly. During Eisenhower's administration the Democrats established an Advisory Council composed of eminent Democrats such as Truman and Stevenson, and this council did a good job of proposing alternative policies to those of the Republican administration. But Democratic congressional leaders ignored the Council, and it was dropped when President Kennedy took office. An All-Republican Conference was established in 1962, but Republican congressional leaders view it with suspicion, and its usefulness appears to be limited.

A Four-Party System?

It can be argued that, despite outward appearances, the American national party system is essentially a four-party system rather than a two-party one. According to this view, it is absurd to suppose

[18] Frank Munger, "Two-Party Politics in the State of Indiana" (unpublished MS thesis, Harvard University, 1955), p. 275, cited in S. M. Lipset, *Political Man* (Doubleday, 1959), p. 289.

[19] Key, *op. cit.*, p. 452.

that conservative Southern Democrats and liberal Northern Democrats make up one party, their common party label notwithstanding. Nor are conservative mid-western and border-state Republicans members of the same party as eastern internationalists and urbanites like Nelson Rockefeller. Actually, it is contended, there are four parties, each with its distinctive institutional, doctrinal, sectional, and electoral make-up. They are:

Congressional Republicans. This party is led by the committee and elected Republican leaders in the House and Senate. It is strongest in northern rural areas, especially in the Midwest. It opposes big economic-aid programs, lower tariffs, wider presidential power in foreign affairs (as in its support for the Bricker amendment). Its most noted recent leaders have been men like Robert A. Taft, Charles Halleck, Gerald Ford, and the ranking Republican members of the major fiscal committees in the Congress, such as the Senate Finance Committee and the House Ways and Means Committee. Led by Goldwater, this party overcame the presidential Republicans in the 1964 convention and captured the presidential nomination.

Presidential Republicans. This party is the party of Theodore Roosevelt at the start of the century, and more recently of Wendell Willkie, Thomas Dewey, Eisen-hower, and Rockefeller. It usually controls Republican national conventions, where congressional leaders (for example Taft) have little chance of winning. Its great center of strength is the White House, just as the congressional party dominates the House and Senate. Its policies, as in Eisenhower's case, are moderately liberal and internationalist. The presidential party electorally comes into its fullest strength in presidential elections, just as the congressional parties have more weight in the more restricted voting of the "off-year" elections.

Congressional Democrats. This party is as conservative as the congressional Republicans on economic matters, much more conservative on civil rights and segregation, but perhaps somewhat more internationalist on foreign economic policy. It has the same institutional strength in Congress as the congressional Republicans. Its leaders in recent years have been men like Senator Byrd of Virginia, chairman of the Senate Finance Committee, and Representative Howard W. Smith, also of Virginia, chairman of the Rules Committee in the House. Its power in Congress rests on the mainly rural, one-party districts in the South, which enable members of Congress to accumulate seniority and hence rise to top com-mittee positions.

Presidential Democrats. This is the party of Woodrow Wilson, Franklin D. Roosevelt, Truman, Stevenson, Kennedy, and Johnson. Like the presidential Re-publicans, it dominates the national party convention and the executive branch of the national government. In doctrine it is the most liberal and internationalist of the four parties.

To see the American parties as a four-party system is to see our national government not as "party government," as in Britain, but as a continuously shifting coalition of four parties. The two congressional parties, for example, often coalesce in opposition to liberal social and economic policy, and are denounced as an "Unholy alliance of Republocrats." Perhaps the most striking example of bipartisanship is that between the two presidential parties on foreign policy; thus Eisenhower and Kennedy broadly agreed on foreign policy, and it was easy for Franklin Roosevelt to find two prominent internationalist Republicans, Stimson and Knox, to join his cabinet during a time of international crisis in 1940. President Johnson and such Republicans as Henry Cabot Lodge have collaborated closely on Vietnamese policy. This too is an alliance of "Republocrats"—but of a different type.

The four-party system has been less conspicuous under Johnson than under his predecessors, for after the congressional Republican defeat in 1964 the President was able to unite the bulk of the two presidential parties and elements of the Congressional Democrats behind his "consensus." Yet the basic four-party tendencies remained evident in congressional voting and in the jockeying for advantage in the 1968 elections. Whether the four-party system would slowly give way to a two-party system—or even to a dominant one-party system under Johnson, as some feared—would depend on changes in fundamental factors, especially in the institutions on Capitol Hill that fortified the two congressional parties.

Two Basic Party Weaknesses

Many of the complaints against the American party system are either inaccurate or overdrawn. An example is the charge that democracy is flouted within the parties. Inside the party machinery a small group of leaders may control day-by-day events. But seen in perspective, it is apparent that these leaders must satisfy most of the voters most of the time if they wish to retain their "power." Competition *among* parties rather than democracy *within* them is the safeguard.

When all is said and done, however, two major criticisms of our party system remain. One is that *party machinery* in virtually all the states is *unwieldy* and *out-of-date*. It is true that the *informal* party structure—for example, the party leadership of the President—in part makes up for the ramshackle nature of the formal organization. But powerful forces are constantly at work dividing and weakening party unity and effectiveness. The national committee, which should do the job of month-to-month governing of the party, is almost powerless. Financially, the national party usually exists from hand to mouth. It is often heavily in debt, especially in the years directly following a presidential campaign, and recovers mainly by raising funds from party "fat cats."

A situation underlying this party weakness is indeed curious: *The party has no real rank-and-file membership*. To be sure, individuals may "join" a party by voting in a primary or registering as a party member. But they assume no obligations; they pay no dues; they rarely take part in party discussions of candidates or platforms. A person is usually far more active in his favorite lodge or hobby club than he is in the organization that assumes responsibility for governing the nation—the Democratic or Republican party. Our national parties, in short, have plenty of generals, lieutenants, and sergeants, but practically no privates enlisted in the party cause.

The other major criticism is that of *party irresponsibility*—in the sense that persons elected to office on party platforms are completely free to ignore these platforms without any accounting to party leaders. Indeed, this criticism takes on all the more importance today because of the vital role that parties *could* play in the challenging era in which we live. Today, more than ever before, governmental policies must be coordinated and coherent. One part of the government cannot pursue an inflationary policy, for example, while another is following an anti-inflationary program. Today policies must be *programmatic*—that is, they must fit into a comprehensive and consistent plan. The party—simply because it nominates and elects our chief policy-making officials—is the ideal agency to force these officials in every branch of government to pull together.

But the party does not do this job. It does not even perform the much more elementary task of making politicians live up to whatever hazy and inconsistent promises they make. This basic party weakness affects our whole government. We shall look again at the implications of this weakness (in Chapter 20) after considering how our politicians get into office and how they try to stay in office once they have won power in Washington.

13 APPEAL
TO THE VOTERS

The preceding four chapters have dealt with the main ingredients of American politics. We have looked at *voting behavior*—which people vote and fail to vote, how they vote, and why. We have noticed how *opinions* are born and shaped, the various sub-publics that hold these opinions, the way opinions can be measured. We have seen something of the role of *interest groups*—their number and complexity, the way they cut across one another and form sub-groups, their internal and external relations, their methods of gaining and wielding influence. We have considered *parties* as grand coalitions of interest groups, doing a variety of important jobs though not always doing them well, sometimes powerful in local activities but poorly coordinated as national agencies.

We have had to consider these factors one at a time, but we must not deceive ourselves into regarding them as separate entities. They are not. Parties, groups, voting behavior, public opinion—all affect one another closely. The forming of political opinions, for example, and the way people vote are largely matters of *group* allegiance and activity, as we have seen. Parties are inseparable from groups, and their role and effectiveness are deeply affected by voting behavior. The close relation between public opinion and voting is obvious. We must see these political processes as a vast network of interrelationships, each process affecting others and in turn being affected by them, all part of a shifting balance of action and counteraction.

The workings of politics seem all the more complex because they so often go on *invisibly*. We cannot actually see Mr. Smith's mind at work as he decides whether or not to vote, or how to vote; we cannot possibly discern the thousands of interrelationships among a number of groups, several political parties, and a maze of political attitudes. But there is one occasion, at least, when some of the labyrinthine attitudes and actions are brought to the surface and exposed to the public view. This occasion is an election.

In the election campaign we get some feel for the dominant attitudes of the community, the activities of groups, the role of the party. In the election results we get some idea of the extent of certain attitudes, the power of parties and groups, the tendencies of voters, and the number of nonvoters. At least a dim light is thrown on the vast subterranean elements of the political process. In the election itself, the people—who often find it hard to keep their eyes on the many players and the many balls in the great game of politics—finally get the score.

Elections are not merely the showdown for the restless political forces described in the past four chapters. They are also vitally affected by the constitutional and legal factors described earlier in this book. For example, a striking aspect of American elections is that they occur on several levels—local, state, and national. The "federalism" of our elections has an important effect on their outcome and meaning, as we shall see. Again, presidential elections would be different without the electoral college. Constitutional provisions allowing the *states* to administer voting, and the way *states* arrange the balloting, also influence elections. Thus we see again the indivisibility not only of politics in the narrow sense, but of our whole political, legal, and institutional system.

What Every Voter Should Know

It would be pleasant if elections were simple affairs. But they are not. The manner in which they are conducted differs widely from state to state. Their sheer number is amazing—well over a hundred thousand elections a year in all states for all offices, according to the Census Bureau. Voting is a chore as well as a privilege. The Constitution authorizes the state legislatures to regulate the time, place, and manner of congressional elections, but Congress may alter these regulations and may also stipulate the day on which presidential electors shall be chosen and the day on which they should cast their votes. In other words, the Constitution has left the regulation of elections for President and Congress almost entirely up to the states. And, of course, each state has direct control over the election of its own and local officials.

Knowing election angles has long been a specialty of political insiders and bosses, but by a little research the interested citizen can also equip himself with the weapon of knowledge. For in elections, too, knowledge is power. Following are merely the ABC's of voting.

Registration

Almost every state requires that a person must be *registered* if he wants to vote. A registered voter is one who has appeared before election officials during a set period and has established his right to vote. In most states an otherwise qualified voter may register to vote if he is over 21, an American citizen, and has lived in the state for one year; in some states this residence requirement is shorter and in some states (mostly in the South) longer. The would-be voter also must have lived in the election district for a set period, often for six months. Once registered, a person's name appears on registration lists and is checked off when he votes. Residence requirements are designed to give the voter a chance to inform himself about state and local conditions before he votes. Some such requirements, however, have been used to deny the ballot to migratory workers or to minority groups, such as Negroes.

Registration is of two types, *permanent* and *periodic*. Under the former system, now used by most states, once the voter is on the list he stays on it as long as he remains in the election district and meets any other requirements established. In a few states a person is dropped from the list if he fails to vote in two successive elections; he must re-register in order to vote again. Permanent registration is easy on the voter, but hard to administer, for election officials must see to it that those who have left the district, have died, or have been committed to public institutions, are removed from the list.

The system of periodic registration requires voters to re-register from time to time.

This system keeps the registration lists up to date, but it is inconvenient for the voters, expensive, and a deterrent to large voter turn-out. Some states allow absentee registration by persons who must be absent from the state for certain reasons.

Primaries

Taking part in the selection of party candidates is often as important as voting in the election itself. As we have seen, in almost all the states candidates are chosen in *direct primary elections* rather than in conventions. In almost all states, primaries are financed out of the public treasury, run by the regular election officials, and held in the same polling places

Al Capp on the importance of registering.

as the regular election; moreover, the voters are protected by the same legal safeguards. To get on the primary ballot a candidate usually must file a petition signed by a required number of voters. In practice this means that almost anyone can get on the ballot if he does enough leg work, and the voter may find a large number of names listed on the primary ballot.

Who can vote in a party primary? In most states voters must publicly acknowledge membership in a party in order to help pick that party's nominees. Party membership in the United States is a rather ambiguous matter, and the tests are not very severe. In some states a voter may declare his party allegiance when he registers to vote; in others the voter enrolls as a party member simply by showing up at the party primary to vote. In some states, mainly in the South, voters appearing at the primary must pledge, before receiving the ballot, that they supported the party's nominee at the last election, or will at the next, or both. In any case, a voter may change his party affiliation between elections by following prescribed procedures.

All this refers to the *closed* primary, in which the party seeks to close the door of the polling place to all but those who are, in one way or another, party adherents. But a number of states—eight by latest count—have an *open* primary system, under which any qualified voter may participate in the primary of any party he prefers without having to reveal publicly his party affiliation. Except in the state of Washington, however, a voter may participate in only one party's primary. In some open systems the voter receives the ballots of all the parties and then fills out the party ballot he prefers; in others he receives one ballot that lists the candidates of all parties for all offices.

Several states use a combination convention-primary system. Party conventions—usually called *pre-primary conventions*—or committees propose a candidate for each office. The candidate gaining the convention's endorsement then runs in the ensuing primary along with any other aspirants who may wish to compete without that endorsement. This procedure informs the voter of the official party choice of candidates but still leaves him free, if he wishes, to support any other candidate who may enter the race.

All primary systems allow supporters of one party to enter—or "raid"—the primary of another. The aim may be to nominate the weakest candidate in a rival party's camp, although it is difficult to point to many examples of where this has happened. The *open* primary, exposed to the depredations of one-day Republicans and next-day Democrats, makes raiding particularly easy. For this reason the open primary is deplored by party officials and advocates of more strongly disciplined parties, although recent research finds no relation between the openness or "closedness" of primaries and subsequent support for the party in office, at least with respect to legislators.[1] The open primary is preferred, however, by those who like to have a free choice on primary day as to the party contests in which they vote, or who for some reason prefer not to reveal their party affiliation.

The *runoff primary* is used in about ten southern or border states. In most of these states the Democratic nomination automatically leads to election, because of the weakness of the Republican opposition. Sometimes so many candidates file in the Democratic primary that the leader may capture only 20 or 30 per cent of the total vote. Under the runoff, if no candidate wins a majority in the first election, the two highest candidates run against each other in a second primary.

In the so-called *nonpartisan primary*, no party designations are permitted; candidates who can qualify simply file and the two candidates who receive the most votes run against each other in the general election. *Cross-filing* also has a nonpartisan or at least a bipartisan tinge. Formerly used most notably in California, it allows a candidate to enter the primaries of more than one party. A candidate may win *both* major primaries and thus in effect win the election, as former Governor Earl Warren did in California in 1946. California has since abolished cross-filing, however.

[1] Ira Ralph Telford, "Types of Primary and Party Responsibility," *American Political Science Review* (March 1965), pp. 117–118.

Balloting

Nowhere are fairness and accuracy more important than in the handling of elections. In balloting, the *Australian ballot system* has long been accepted as a model. Under this system—used in Queensland as early as 1857—the government (rather than the parties or candidates, as had been the earlier practice) prints uniform ballots on good-quality paper, listing the names of all the candidates. Ballots are given to voters only on election day, only at the official polling place, and only by public officials. The ballots are marked secretly, folded, and deposited unopened in a ballot box. We tend to take these arrangements for granted nowadays, but each one was adopted only after hard experience. For example, the use of good-quality paper balks the old trick of issuing tissue-paper ballots that enabled sharp-eyed party workers to see where a voter put his mark after the ballot was folded. Certain aspects of ballots and voting are worth noting:

The office-group, or *Massachusetts type, ballot* lists together the names and party designations of all candidates for the same office. Candidates for the highest office, such as President and governor, usually come first and then state and local candidates. Since this type of ballot makes it impossible to vote a straight ticket with a single mark, it encourages independent and split-party voting.[2] It also, however, leads to voter fatigue and to failure to vote for the offices at the bottom of the ballot.

The party-column, or *Indiana type, ballot* groups candidates by *party* in columns. A voter can vote for all the candidates of a party, from President to sheriff, simply by making his mark in a large circle or box next to the party's name and emblem. Or he may "scratch his ticket"—that is, go from column to column marking his choice for each office. The party-column ballot encourages straight party voting.

Stickers and write-ins are devices for making last-minute changes in the ballot—for example, when a candidate withdraws or dies after the ballots have been printed. The voter may either paste in a gummed sticker or write in the name of the candidate of his choice. These devices are allowed in some states as a means of voting for some candidate other than the offerings of the parties on the ballot, but write-in or sticker campaigns are rarely successful.

Absentee voting. Almost all the states allow certain persons, such as servicemen, to vote away from home. In order to prevent fraud, however, absentee voting has been made so difficult and cumbersome that often only the most zealous citizen will go to the trouble of sending in an absentee ballot.

Stuffing the ballot box. This is a type of ballot fraud, but the term often is used to denote all methods of fraud. There have been—and still are—so many of these as to defy description; they involve frauds in marking ballots, in collecting them, and in counting them. The "endless chain" or "Tasmanian Dodge" indicates the ingenuity of the corruptionists. A person buying votes will manage somehow (there

[2] Angus Campbell and Warren E. Miller, "The Motivational Basis of Straight and Split Ticket Voting," *The American Political Science Review* (June 1957), pp. 293–312.

are various ways) to secure an unmarked ballot. He fills this out, gives it to the bought voter, who enters the polling place, receives a ballot, deposits the previously marked one, and brings out the unmarked one for the vote buyer to fill out and hand to his next man. By this method the corrup tionist knows that the ballots are being cast just as he wishes.

Voting machines. Originally patented in the United States by Thomas A. Edison, the voting machine is designed to stop ballot frauds and to make vote-counting accurate and speedy. The machines are expensive, and some voters seem to find them difficult to manipulate, but their advantages have led to their use or authorization in over half the states.

Herblock in The Washington Post.

The Long Ballot and the Short

The "long ballot" represents reality, the "short ballot" mainly a hope. In filling out the long ballot, which is used by most of the states, the baffled voter must decide among a fantastic array of candidates for legislative and administrative offices. In one case a ballot was twelve feet long and contained almost five hundred names. Tree warden, coroner, secretary of state, county treasurer, highway inspector—candidates for these and many more offices are crowded onto the ballot, along with lengthy questions or propositions to be accepted or rejected by the voters. The more insignificant the office, the fewer the voters who know the qualifications of the candidates, and the greater the likelihood that party organizations or interested groups can elect their favorites, good or bad.

There has long been a movement to shorten the ballot by restricting officials popularly elected to those concerned with broad policy determination. But progress has been slow, and the "tablecloth" or "bedsheet" ballot is still common. Many states have, however, adopted the *presidential short ballot*, which, instead of listing the names of all the electors of each party, carries only the names of the presidential and vice-presidential candidates to whom the electors are pledged. By casting one vote for President and Vice President, the voter in effect chooses the entire party slate of electors.

To conclude: This description of voting arrangements has been essentially a catalogue of things that the conscientious voter ought to know. But as *political scientists* we should understand that most of them have some effect, planned or not, on voting behavior and hence on the allocation of political power. Unfortunately, research on these effects has been so limited and scattered that we still lack solid evidence and conclusions. There is some indication that registration requirements and procedures are a major factor in the extent of nonvoting in the United States; [3] that party primaries tend to divide parties and their leaderships to a greater extent than do party conventions; that different types of ballots, as noted, encourage or discourage straight-party voting; that even the use of voting machines instead of paper ballots has a discernible effect on voting outcomes. Further analysis of these problems, exploiting the vast amount of data available through polls and election returns, represents a major research frontier in political science.

Money and Elections

Money in politics is an important but shadowy subject. Suppose we could listen to a group of congressmen in Washington discussing in confidence what their campaigns had cost. Their conversation might go like this:

> *Midwestern congressman:* I believe it was $4,872 I spent in the last election. I paid my own traveling expenses in the district; I didn't count that in the total. . . .
>
> *Urban congressman* with competitive district: Campaigns are a lot more costly in a metropolitan area where you have television and the mass media methods. We don't have much of a party organization in my area. My organization has to carry the whole ticket and so, in effect, I have to raise the money. To be candid, in my district it costs a lot more to run a campaign than you can legitimately spend.
>
> *Mid. cong.:* Is that honest?
>
> *Urban cong.:* That is a proper question and one that disturbs me because I don't believe you can be elected in some of these districts, mine included, within the spirit of the law. You can do it within the technicalities. What we had to do was technically legal—we created a whole slew of committees, each one of which would take over a portion of the campaign. I honestly didn't have control of that, and if anyone asked me to take an oath and testify to that effect I could do so. But it would not be true to say that is within the spirit of the limitations on expenditures. The laws are impossible to adhere to in a metropolitan area.
>
> *Mid. cong.:* How much does it really cost?
>
> *Urban cong.:* I had to run the campaign for the party in my area. My cam-

---

[3] For example, Donald R. Matthews and James W. Prothro in two articles in *American Political Science Review*, "Social and Economic Factors and Negro Registration in the South" (March 1963), pp. 24–44, and "Political Factors and Negro Voter Registration in the South" (June 1963), pp. 355–367, find that political and legal factors have a probable effect on Negro registration, but socio-economic factors have an even greater probable effect.

paign last time ran over $60,000. It is a big district, of course, but that is a lot of money. . . .

Eastern congressman from "safe" district: The differences in campaign costs always puzzle me. I assume by the stunned silence when our colleague mentioned he spent less than $5,000, that it was thought to be small. I only spent about $2,000 in my campaign. . . .

Urban congressman in the West: My district is large and similar to that of ————. If you include the costs of the primary, I too spent about $60,000 last time. I know that one of the senators in my state spent at least $1 million in his campaign. Legally speaking, he would be limited to somewhere around $30,000. Now it is obvious that you cannot cover a large state like ours in the various media for $30,000. Something should be done to make election costs more realistic. You couldn't put on an advertising campaign for selling dog food in one city for that amount.[4]

Obviously elections cost money—often a great deal of it. Reported expenditures by national party organizations in 1964 presidential and congressional campaigns totaled over 27 million dollars. Candidates for the Senate and House of Representatives reported spending over 4.8 million in 1960. Many millions more were spent locally on state, county, and city contests. These are the expenditures reported under the law; much—perhaps most—of the spending is never reported. In 1960 between 165 to 175 million dollars were spent by candidates, their friends, and other interested people for nominating and electing all public officials in the United States.[5] A campaign for governor or senator in a large state can easily cost over half a million dollars.

Where does the money go? A half-hour program on a coast-to-coast television network costs (depending on the coverage) from $50,000 to $100,000. A one-minute television spot in a medium-sized city may cost $50. A full-page ad in a big-city newspaper costs $2,500. Campaign buttons cost three cents each, and candidates distribute tens of thousands of them. One mailing to every voter in a medium-sized state might cost $20,000.[6] Gasoline, telephone, printing, posters, rental of headquarters, hiring paid help—all these and many other items send expenses soaring.

One reason elections cost so much in the United States compared with other countries is the sheer length of the campaigns. There are really *two* campaigns—one for nomination and then one for election—and each of them lasts months. A presidential aspirant may campaign for eight or ten months before the conventions, as Kennedy did in 1960 and Rockefeller and Goldwater did in 1964. Candidates for governor and senator may spend far more money on their primary campaigns than on their final election campaigns—and the primary campaign ex-

[4] These are actual statements taken from a discussion, sponsored by the Brookings Institution, among members of Congress on various aspects of congressional life and the legislative process; see Charles L. Clapp, *The Congressman: His Work as He Sees It* (Brookings, 1963), pp. 335–337.

[5] Report of the President's Commission on Campaign Costs, *Financing Presidential Campaigns* (Government Printing Office, 1962), p. 9. See also Alexander Heard, *The Costs of Democracy* (Univ. of North Carolina Press, 1960).

[6] From Ivan Hinderaker, *Party Politics* (Holt, 1956), pp. 579–581.

penses come out of their own pockets and from their friends, not from the party. In Great Britain, by contrast, candidates for Parliament campaign for about three weeks and depend almost wholly on their parties for money.

Where the Money Comes From

Donations to the party treasury come from many sources. In presidential campaigns the national headquarters of the parties take in millions of dollars. Those who have given most to the Republicans in recent presidential elections have been manufacturers; bankers; and utilities, insurance, mining, and oil interests; to the Democrats, brewers, distillers, contractors, builders, the professions, merchants, and amusement and related interests. Wealthy family groups often make big donations. In 1960, the duPonts gave over $51,000 to the Republicans, the Pews $59,000, the Rockefellers, $91,000. Enjoying less support from such big givers, the Democrats ran a series of Jackson Day dinners throughout the country, charging from $5 to $100 per plate. Labor usually gives far more to the Democrats than to the Republicans. A little money comes to both parties from small donors, but most of the campaign chest is filled by large contributors. In 1960, for example, both parties together reported they received over $28 million, and well over half of this came in donations of over $1,000. Only about 5 or 10 per cent of the voters give any money at all to their parties or candidates.

State and local parties also receive direct gifts, but much of their money comes from candidates and especially from officeholders. Sometimes candidates give money to local parties in exchange for help from the parties. Assessing appointed officeholders often is a lucrative source of income to the parties. Although usually kept under cover, the shakedown may be very important. It was revealed in Philadelphia, for example, that three to five per cent of city workers' salaries was collected by the Republican city committee, and one to

"It's terrible how the big money guys run politics." (Herblock in The Washington Post.)

two per cent by the ward committees where the employees lived. Some years ago the Democrats in Indiana ran a notorious "2 Per Cent Club" on the same model.

Why do people give? Mainly because they want something, usually for themselves. City jobholders want to stay in office. Candidates want the party's good will and support. Big donors often want the party's men in office to follow certain policies. Businessmen are concerned about taxes, tariffs, and subsidies. Labor may want the repeal of anti-union legislation. Distillers may hope to get dry laws repealed. Builders want government contracts; suppliers want to sell to government agencies; insurance companies want to write policies covering government property. Some big donors hope to gain prized positions, such as ambassadorships. Often what contributors want is nothing tangible but simply an "entree" or access to those in power in case the need arises[7]

The motive for giving is not always direct self-interest, however. Thousands of contributors simply believe the party of their choice will govern best for the whole people. Still, the number of small contributions by the "average citizen" is lamentably low. Most party and campaign contributions come from big donors with an axe to grind. The Goldwater cause in 1964 attracted a large number of small contributions (over $5 million in direct mail appeals, it was reported), but this was exceptional.

Regulation of Party Finance

The national and state governments have made frequent, but not very successful, attempts to publicize party finances and to limit contributions and expenditures through *corrupt practices legislation* and other laws. Organizations receiving or spending money to influence the election of national officials in two or more states under certain conditions must file statements with the clerk of the House of Representatives giving the names of all persons contributing over $100, of all persons to whom payments of more than $10 have been made, and a total of all receipts and all expenditures. The national government and most of the states have long prohibited contributions from certain types of corporations, and in 1947 the Taft-Hartley Act barred *any* corporation or labor organization from giving or spending money in connection with elections to national offices or in conventions of primaries choosing candidates for such offices.

Campaign spending is supposed to be sharply limited. Under federal law, a candidate for representative may not spend more than $2,500, a candidate for senator not more than $10,000 or, as an alternative, three cents per vote cast for all candidates for the office at the last general election, but no more than $25,000 for a senator and $5,000 for a representative. The Hatch Act of 1939 and later

---

[7] A. Heard, *op. cit.* For excellent material on this general problem, including recommendations from political scientists and others, see "Federal Voting Assistance Act of 1955," *Hearings Before the Subcommittee on Privileges and Elections, Committee on Rules and Administration, United States Senate, 84 Congress, 1st Sess.,* on S. 636 (Government Printing Office, 1955).

amendments limit spending by any single political committee to $3 million a year and contributions by individuals to each candidate or nationally affiliated party committee to $5,000 annually, and it forbids forced contributions from government office-holders to candidates or parties. This act also makes it "unlawful for any person employed in the executive branch of the federal government, or any agency or department thereof, to use his official authority or influence for the purpose of interfering with an election or affecting the result thereof." Such federal employees can vote but they cannot take an active part in party affairs or political campaigns.

How effective are these regulations on campaign finance? The consensus is: not very. Much of the legislation is filled with loopholes and is poorly enforced. Full publicity is often evaded by filing reports after the election is over or by submitting inadequate or even false reports. Corporations make campaign contributions through personal offerings of executives and their families, labor unions through more or less voluntary offerings by their mem-

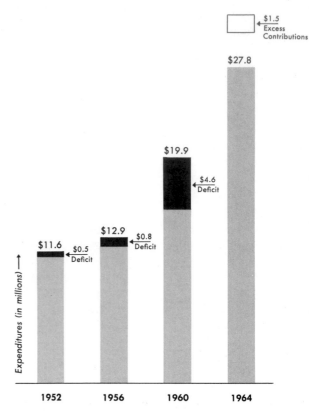

Combined Democratic-Republican expenditures at the national level. This was money (in millions of dollars) actually spent by committees operating in more than one state, not including money transferred to other organizations. (Adapted from figures provided by the President's Commission on Campaign Costs, 1962; and from the United States Congress, 1964.)

bers. The lawmakers, politicians themselves, have made no attempt to pass really rigorous or airtight laws in this field, and it is not certain that such an attempt would be successful, given traditional American attitudes toward such laws.

In 1962 the President's Commission on Campaign Costs under the leadership of political scientist Alexander Heard recommended among other things these steps to help finance national presidential campaigns:

1. In order to encourage lower- and middle-income persons to contribute to political parties, for an experimental period covering two presidential campaigns

those who contribute to the national committee of a major political party or to a state committee of such a party be allowed to credit against their federal income tax half of what they contribute up to $10 a year. Or alternatively, a contributor could claim up to $1,000 a year as a regular deduction.

2. That the present meaningless ceiling on individual contributions and expenditures by political committees be abolished. Instead, a Registry of Election Finance should be established to provide an effective system of public disclosure. Political parties or other groups and large contributors (individuals or families contributing $5,000 a year or more) would be required to file periodic reports of where they got their money and how they spent it.

3. That corporations and labor unions be encouraged to make bipartisan contributions but that the existing prohibitions on corporations and trade unions against making direct, partisan, campaign contributions and expenditures be strictly enforced.

A major problem, the Committee concluded, was the general attitude toward money in politics: "A chronic difficulty . . . has long been the lurking suspicion that contributing to political parties is somehow a shoddy business. This is unfortunate. Improvement of public understanding of campaign finance is essential." [8] The existing system poses serious problems, including the fact that it makes candidates dependent on a relatively small number of individuals or on organizations for the money they need to finance their campaigns.

Mr. Douglas Runs for Senator

When we think about elections we usually picture exciting national campaigns, fighting speeches watched by millions of televiewers, political caravans crossing the nation in a blaze of publicity. But not all campaigns for national office are like this. A candidate for Congress often finds that a campaign means a lot of dull legwork and exhausting rounds of speeches to small audiences. "When you get away from the national arena," Pearson and Allen have written, "political campaigning gets right back to the old horse-and-buggy days. . . . What really counts is the all-important ingredient of personal contact." How a member of Congress wins office is important; watching him as a campaigner helps us understand him as a member of the Senate or House. It is impossible to generalize about senatorial and congressional campaigns because of the variety of states and districts involved.[9] The following true-life tale of his first race for the Senate in 1948 by

[8] Report of the President's Commission on Campaign Costs, *Financing Presidential Campaigns*, p. 2.
[9] For excellent case studies, presented in detail, of the actual campaigns of two candidates for Representative, see S. K. Bailey and H. D. Samuel, *Congress at Work* (Holt, 1952), pp. 112–135. See also the illuminating studies of primary and election campaigns, "Eagleton Institute Cases in Practical Politics," sponsored by the Eagleton Foundation Advisory Board at Rutgers University and published by McGraw-Hill.

The candidate runs for office. (Roy Doty; © 1965 by The New York Times Company. Reprinted by permission.)

Once the candidate has entered the race he must please everyone . . .

A sore throat and temperature of 102° cannot keep him from campaigning . . .

He must be against the Taft-Hartley Law and a champion of labor . . .

A few ill-chosen words on the golf course can antagonize the church vote.

And at the same time finance his campaign with management's contributions.

And a moment of absent-mindedness will cost him the support of the vets . . .

Senator Paul H. Douglas, then a University of Chicago economist, suggests some of the problems of campaigning and the candidate's reaction to them: [10]

Running for Office Means Just That

The contrast between American and British campaign practices is summed up in the verbs used to describe the activities of candidates. In Great Britain one "stands" for office. In the United States we "run" for it.

As a candidate for the United States Senate from Illinois, I have a vivid sense of that word "run"—and for this reason:

Illinois holds some 8,300,000 people, divided evenly between Chicago and its suburbs on the one hand, and "down-state" on the other. And in both areas the people come from all the world's racial and religious stocks, settled in massive blocks of tens of thousands. The ways in which they make their living are as varied as the people themselves.

In industry—and moving from north to south—there are giant railroad yards, meat packing plants, steel mills and machine shops, oil fields and coal mines. Farming, on the other hand, and moving from south to north, includes cotton planting in "Little Egypt," where the soil shows signs of exhaustion; the superb corn fields of mid-Illinois, and pedigreed dairy cattle in the northern regions.

Add together the natural variety of interests which comes from such a setting and the task facing a candidate in Illinois can be seen. I have been "running" for office in every corner of the state almost incessantly ever since I was recommended by the state committee for nomination in January. And I have been "sprinting" since I was formally nominated by the Democratic party in April.

Following the state committee's action in January of this year I got hold of a jeep station wagon, had it equipped for sound and took to the road. In the primary campaign during the three months that followed I made 250 speeches and visited eighty out of our 102 counties. Since the primaries last May, I have made approximately 700 speeches in over 300 towns and cities in every county in the state. And the formal campaign doesn't open until Labor Day. A word hasn't been invented yet to describe the form of running that takes place between then and November.

My style of campaigning follows this pattern: I pull up my sound-equipped jeep wagon at a

He can lose the election by being seen in a non-union barber shop.

Is it all worth it? Only the returns on election day can tell.

[10] *The New York Times Magazine*, September 5, 1948, p. 5 ff.; reprinted by permission of *The New York Times Magazine* and of Senator Douglas.

factory gate during a change in shifts, or on a village street, or somewhere else near the main flow of people. I introduce myself to whatever crowd gathers, and then summarize the main themes of the campaign. Afterward I move among the clusters of people to shake hands and to distribute campaign litera- ture which they can read at leisure. In this way I've spoken to about 225,000 people and have shaken hands with over 100,000 of them. . . .

There is a reason for this direct work. The average voter wants to see the candidates for office and form a visual as well as auditory judgment of them. But the voter is either too busy to go to formal political meetings, or he dis- counts them as being long winded, hot and blatantly partisan. It becomes necessary, therefore, for the candidate to go direct to the voters

On Being the Object of Abuse

Physical exertion is, however, the least of the burdens a candidate must bear. He must expect in advance to be abused and misrepresented. Indeed, the way the courts have interpreted the libel laws of the nation, political leaders are set up as fair game for any attack short of murder. The whole spirit of those laws says to the candidate for elective office: "Brother, whatever happens to you—you asked for it!" It is only human, of course, for a candidate to be nettled now and then by the bare-faced lies that are spread about him. And in my own case, on being subjected to them, I at first shared the thoughts of young Count Rostov in "War and Peace." As he saw the French lancer come at him in his first engagement, young Rostov asked: "Is it really true that this man wants my life—I whom my mother loves?"

It was a source of dismay—and also the beginning of wisdom—to discover that not everyone loved me!

Since I aim to be a liberal progressive, I find myself being attacked by both the extreme left and the extreme right. The communists whisper that I am anti-Semitic, anti-Negro, an advocate of a preventive war against Russia and the tool of bankers and industrialists. The extreme right, on the other hand, calls me a Socialist and a crafty fellow-traveler. It might seem that such mutually contradictory attacks would largely cancel themselves out, but in practice each group aims its propaganda at the circles which are closest to it, with the result that various sections of the population can at the same time believe in conflicting and slanderous reports.

It is this personal abuse which deters most competent men from running for public office. It is as though certain types of politicians tried to make the going so rough that they would shut off competition from all except their own kind, who are protected by the proverbial rhinoceros hide. . . .

Pressures on the Candidate

In my campaigns I've also been brought face to face with the forces which make politicians "crooked." Though I have no wealth, I have been able to earn enough in private pursuits to support my family. Yet not every politician is so situated. If he has no private means and is not skilled in a trade or profession, then the expenses of campaigning and the demands that are made upon him when he is elected exert a tremendous pressure on him to cut a few corners. . . .

With respect to the "crooked" politician, many voters who are the first to denounce him are also the first to stake out a claim to the fruits of his corruption. The way they do this is an unwitting one. Hundreds of individuals and organizations in a city or state—devoted to the very best of causes—expect the elected politician to contribute to those causes, to buy tickets to their functions or political advertisements in their fund-raising programs. The politician who balks at these demands is met with a veiled or open threat that the voting strength of the organization will be turned against him at election time.

It could be said that the politician should gladly suffer defeat and remain honest. But being human, most politicians want to stay in office, and so some make "deals" with unlawful sources of income in order to meet the demands of lawful organizations performing fine community activities—including the waging of campaigns against "crooked" politicians.

And yet, as between the politicians on the one hand with their genuine "liking for people," and the class of reformers on the other hand who think of good government as being merely a good bookkeeping process, my personal preference, like Lincoln Steffens', runs to the former type—with all their lamentable faults.

On Taking an Honest Stand

The greatest danger to the functioning of the democratic process comes in the area of ideas and social policies. There is a subtle temptation, which operates on every candidate, to say things he doesn't believe in order to get votes, or for the same reason, to urge contradictory policies before different groups. It is this aspect of political activity which I would call most "crooked." . . .

By the most pragmatic of tests, I have found that a straightforward and consistent approach to any problem brings higher personal rewards than a policy of double-talk. For instance, I have been a lifelong advocate of unionism and collective bargaining. Yet in this campaign I've reminded union audiences many times about the ways in which their movements could be improved. In every case I found the response of labor to be an approving and hearty one.

Closely related to this danger of being all things to all men is the added danger of treating people as votes and not as persons—as means to the end of winning an election rather than as ends in themselves. As a college student I was thrilled by Immanuel Kant's rule that one "should treat humanity, whether in one's self or in another, always as an end, never as a means." This imperative means that one should really care for people, whether they are partisans for or against you, or in the "no opinion" group. It means a constant view of politics as having one aim—the promotion of justice—justice for all men—and not the mere acquisition of power for one man.

I have dwelt at length on the trials of a campaign without mentioning its rewards. There are many of these rewards—which are independent of how things turn out at the polls. In talking face to face with people you get a renewed personal assurance of the essential decency and fairness of the human race. Most men in fact try to do good and avoid evil. Abundant proofs can be offered, of course, of the many times when community passions have twisted matters so that men in the mass act contrary to their own ultimate interests. Yet the search for truth is not killed off. It reasserts itself as the stronger force in our life and in time bears its fruits.

A second gain from these campaigns is a better appreciation of how vital our democratic process actually is. It is an unending source of joy to see thousands upon thousands of men and women of all ages and in all stations of life lend their efforts to the advancement of political causes. These people are not paid workers. They do not stand to benefit directly from a political victory for their candidate. But they do appreciate the indirect benefits of victory—the creation of an America which better fits their own dreams. . . .

For all its demands, a vigorous "politics" in which everyone takes sides is, paradoxically, the best way to bring about a fuller sense of the community of interest. But underneath all this is needed a sense of the basic unity which should bind men together and should provide a feeling of good-will to all.

Fundamentally men are brothers and the heat and passion of political struggle should not make us forget that fact.

How to Be Nominated for President

To attain the Presidency a man has to run two races and win them both. First he must be nominated at his party's national convention, and this is sometimes the harder of the two jobs. Then he must get a majority of the nation's electoral votes.

The first "national" convention was probably held in 1808, when a few Federalist leaders met secretly in New York to nominate candidates for President and Vice President. In 1831, under Jackson's leadership, the first real national convention was held by a major party. Today the national convention is a famous and unique political institution. Every four years each party convention enjoys— usually for about a week—world attention; covered by batteries of cameras and microphones and by hundreds of newsmen, every incident in the great convention hall is carried to millions in this country and abroad.

Make-up. Each party has the double task of giving convention representation to the states roughly in proportion to the size of their electorates, and of giving a "bonus" to states that have a heavier concentration of party strength. The two parties keep changing their rules for apportionment of votes among the states in an attempt to do both these things.

The latest Democratic allotment method, adopted in the 1964 convention, gives every state three convention votes for every electoral vote, and awards extra convention votes to each state roughly in proportion to the extent that that state voted for the preceding Democratic presidential candidate (*i.e.,* Johnson in 1964).

Tying the bonus to *presidential* voting alone, this allotment in effect cuts down the convention strength of southern states who have typically rolled up huge majorities for Democratic candidates for governor and senator but much smaller votes for Democratic presidential candidates. Under this arrangement 2,944 delegates plus 108 national committee members cast 2,316 convention votes in the 1964 Democratic convention (some delegates have only half a vote so that more Democrats will be able to take part in the convention).

The Republicans have a different means of awarding bonus votes. They allow each state a number of delegates proportionate to its size, and then allow it extra delegates in proportion to its *Republicanism*. States receive extra representation

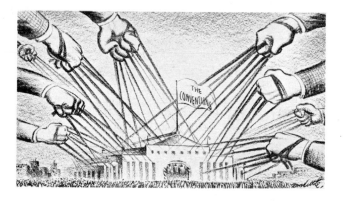

Convention delegates respond to the pulls of many interests. (Tom Little; ©️ 1965 by The New York Times Company. Reprinted by permission.)

roughly in proportion to how strongly they voted for the last Republican presidential candidate *or* Republican candidates for United States senator or representative. Under this arrangement 1,308 delegates each had a single vote in the 1964 Republican convention. The key difference between this arrangement and the Democrats' is that the Republicans reward voting for both President and Congress, while the Democrats do so for President alone.

Each party also seats delegates from Puerto Rico and the Virgin Islands, and the Democrats also include the Canal Zone, even though these areas cast no electoral votes for President. And even before adoption of the Twenty-third Amendment, each party had a delegation from the District of Columbia.

Choosing Delegates. The method of selecting delegates is set by *state* law and varies considerably from state to state. In about two-thirds of the states, delegates are chosen by party *conventions* or committees. In about one-third, which includes most of the populous states, delegates are picked in state *presidential primaries.* A few states use a combination of the two methods. The *convention* system tends to put selection of the delegation into the hands of a party "inner circle." This may be no problem where the party is vigorous and the leadership representative, but that is often not the case. Most Republican party organizations in the South, for example, have tended to be little "closed corporations" controlled by a few

Republican officeholders in Washington with the help of patronage. In such situations the question of who has the right to speak for the rank and file of the party becomes very obscure. This was a main cause of the fierce fight between the Taft and Eisenhower forces in the 1952 Republican convention, culminating in the unseating of the Taft delegations from Georgia, Louisiana, and Texas, and the seating of the Eisenhower forces.

Presidential Primaries, the other chief method of choosing delegates, come in many forms. The basic system is for delegates to be elected directly by persons voting in state presidential primaries, which take place variously from March through June of election year. But the primaries vary widely in the extent to which they enable the voter to indicate his preference for the party's presidential nominee by his vote for a candidate for delegate. At one extreme, a voter may choose between rival delegate aspirants definitely pledged to specific candidates, and he may also indicate his *personal preference* for President by checking or listing the name of his favorite. At the other extreme, a voter may have only the choice of approving a slate of faithful party delegates whose preferences for the presidential nomination are completely unknown to him. Most systems fall between these extremes.

Here are some examples of the main types of presidential primary: [11]

"*Let's see—four oranges plus three apples, minus one monkey wrench, times two bushels—*" (*Herblock in* The Washington Post.)

1. *Presidential preference vote with election of national convention delegates made by state convention.* The primary ballot provides for expression of preference between prospective nominees, but the state convention chooses the delegates. (Maryland, Indiana.)

2. *Combined expression of preference and vote for pledged national convention candidates.* The primary voter expresses his choice for an aspirant and a slate of delegates pledged to him. In some states delegates are chosen by congressional district, thus the state delegation can be divided

[11] V. O. Key, Jr., *Politics, Parties, and Pressure Groups* (Crowell, 1964), p. 409–410.

among all of the competing candidates. (Minnesota, Wisconsin, South Dakota.)

3. *Separation of preference vote and delegate selection.* Some states require the voter to mark his ballot twice, once to express his candidate preference and once to indicate his choice of delegate slate. (New Hampshire.)

4. *Direct election of unpledged delegates with no presidential preference vote.* (Pennsylvania, Nebraska.)

This variety of methods of choosing delegates, combined with the variety of power patterns in state parties, makes it impossible to generalize about the nature of the final delegations. Some may be under the thumb of a powerful state party leader. Others may be "split wide open." Some may be willing to "go down the line" for some presidential candidate. Others may veer from candidate to candidate. Most state delegations mirror the factions in the state party, but sometimes a strong and well-organized group will gain control of the whole delegation.[12]

One thing is clear. The mere adoption of a presidential primary system does not guarantee a delegation that will reflect rank-and-file wishes. Turnout in presidential primaries, as in most primaries, tends to be low. Often presidential candidates simply ignore state primaries, as Adlai E. Stevenson did in 1952, and still win the nomination. Herbert Hoover fared badly in state primaries in 1928 but won both the nomination and the election. Sometimes, on the other hand, success in presidential primaries is decisive, as in the case of Adlai Stevenson's string of state victories in the spring of 1956, and Kennedy's strength in the 1960 primaries.

The system is undermined by the tendency of many state delegations, no matter how chosen, to support a "favorite son"—a prominent state leader but often not of "presidential timber"—who is a convenient person for whom to ballot while the delegation leaders bargain with the main candidates. It can be said for presidential primaries, though, that they have stimulated interest in the early stages of presidential nominations, have opened up the machinery to rank-and-file participation where the voters have been interested enough to use it, and have enabled the country to get some idea—though not a very accurate one—of the popularity of rival candidates in some of the states.

Organizing the Convention. The chairman of the national committee presides over the national convention until temporary officers are chosen; these in turn officiate until the convention elects permanent officers. A committee on *credentials* has the power to make recommendations to the convention in the case of disputed seats; a committee on *permanent organization* recommends permanent officers for the convention; a committee on *rules* reports out the rules governing the convention proceedings; a committee on *resolutions* draws up the party platform and recommends that it be adopted by the convention. The actions of each

[12] For a carefully prepared proposal for state presidential primary improvement, see Manning J. Dauer, William A. F. Stephenson, Harry Macy, and David Temple, "Toward a Model State Presidential Primary Law," *The American Political Science Review* (March 1956), pp. 138–153.

of these committees may be—or at least seem to be—of crucial importance to some one of the contestants. For example, the credentials committee may recommend unseating delegates friendly to a particular candidate and seating his rival's, as in the Republican convention in 1952.

Voting. In the national conventions voting is by simple majority. During most of its existence, the Democratic party had the "two-thirds rule" requiring that fraction of the total vote for the nomination of presidential and vice-presidential candidates. This rule, supported mainly by southern Democrats who feared being outvoted by the northern majority in the party, led to endless deadlocks—in one case a candidate was nominated only after 103 ballots. Finally, in 1936, the Democrats under President Roosevelt's leadership succeeded in abolishing the rule. Under certain circumstances Democratic conventions authorize the *unit rule*, under which the entire vote of a state delegation is cast as the majority of the delegation wishes. Since few state parties now instruct their delegations to act as a unit, the unit rule has become of limited importance. The Republican national convention does not permit the unit rule.

Pre-convention Campaigns

The pre-convention campaign usually starts at least a year or two before the convention itself. The candidate—who may be a well known governor, cabinet member, senator, or perhaps an eminent general—is likely to assume the appearance of indecision for a time, while his scouts are busy sounding out party sentiment from Maine to California. The candidate has his choice of several pre-convention strategies, depending on his political position. He can announce his candidacy months before the convention and try openly to capture state delegations. He can keep silent if he prefers not to show his hand early, especially if it is not a strong one. He can concentrate on gaining a following among the party rank and file and the voters at large through public appearances, television speeches, and the like. He can try to build his strength mainly by lining up delegates through various arrangements or deals. Goldwater successfully employed the first, third, and fourth of these strategies in 1964, while Governor Scranton used the second for a long time—too long a time, many felt.

John Kennedy's pre-convention campaign of 1957–1960 may become a classic example of the activist strategy—and an example that many future presidential hopefuls will emulate.[13] Kennedy began his campaign soon after Stevenson lost to Eisenhower for the second time in 1956. After three years of intensive speaking and politicking throughout the country, and amid mounting attention from the press, Kennedy announced his candidacy in January 1960. The odds seemed heavily

[13] This case study is drawn chiefly from Theodore C. Sorensen, *Kennedy* (Harper & Row, 1965), ch. 5; and Theodore H. White, *The Making of the President 1960* (Atheneum, 1961), ch. 5.

against him. He was in his early forties and a Catholic. The old Democratic party "establishment"—former President Truman and the veteran Fair Deal leadership —were against him. Most Senate Democrats favored Lyndon Johnson; most House Democrats, Senator Stuart Symington. Liberal Democrats and intellectuals leaned heavily toward Stevenson. Many city "bosses" and most Democratic Governors opposed Kennedy.

Kennedy's response was to seek every delegate vote that was possibly available, with special emphasis on the presidential primaries. He would build his party strength "from the bottom up." In the early weeks of 1960 he stepped up his campaign tours and sent advance men into the key primary states. He paid special attention to Democratic Governors, both because of their influence over state delegations and because some of them were candidates themselves, or at least favorite sons. A confidential report to Kennedy on the early attitudes of some governors went as follows (without revealing names here): [14]

GOVERNOR A: . . . strong for Kennedy, partly because he considers himself a Vice-Presidential possibility. . .

GOVERNOR B: . . . for Stevenson first and Humphrey second . . . probably cannot be enthusiastic about Kennedy but may face tough fight for re-election and need help in areas where Kennedy is strong. . .

GOVERNOR C: . . . irritated by tremendous Kennedy strength in his state . . . might be interested in Cabinet post if does not run for Senate . . . enjoys being wooed and is looking for support to be keynoter [at the convention] or nominator [of Kennedy]. . .

GOVERNOR D: . . . reportedly has been reached by the Johnson people though still far from committed. . .

GOVERNOR E: . . . probably favors Johnson . . . also presumed to have Vice-Presidential ambitions. . .

GOVERNOR F: . . . presumably will have no voice in delegation. . .

GOVERNOR G: . . . reportedly made a deal with Symington . . . can be wooed. . .

GOVERNOR H: . . . favors either Kennedy or Johnson. . .

GOVERNOR I: . . . a Catholic with Vice-Presidential ambitions, he knows they will never be realized with Kennedy. . .

GOVERNOR J: . . . committed to Humphrey . . . would be interested in Vice Presidency if Humphrey did not want it. . .

What primaries should Kennedy enter? This was the candidate's main tactical problem. Other candidates' home states had to be written off—for example, Humphrey's Minnesota. Some primaries, clearly, Kennedy would have to invade to show his vote-getting capacity. Other states presented more awkward problems. California's Governor Edmund "Pat" Brown had himself some hope of the presidential nomination—or at least the vice-presidential—and he wanted to keep control of his delegation for that reason, or for bargaining purposes. Kennedy indicated to Brown and other "neutralist" governors that he would invade their

[14] Sorensen, *op. cit.*, p. 126.

primaries unless guaranteed at least a good chunk of the delegation. Such bargaining and threatening was simple in theory, but applying these tactics to the infinitely complex politics of several large states was a hard test of Kennedy as a politician. In the end, except for Ohio and California, he entered every binding presidential primary where no legitimate favorite son was running and he entered most of the nonbinding primaries as well.

The story of Kennedy's "grand slam" of the contested primaries—Wisconsin, West Virginia, Maryland, Oregon—is well known. Less known but equally important was his capture of delegations chosen in state party conventions or committees. Some sharp bargaining was necessary. In Michigan, for example, Kennedy had to make clear that its Democratic party leaders would be recognized in future party decisions, and he had to make clear his own views on forty-odd national issues. Other states presented other claims. But one thing the state politicians could not ignore—Kennedy's popularity in the primaries (and in the polls). The more primaries he won, the more state politicians realized that they had better get on the bandwagon. So in the end Kennedy's state primary campaigns and his state convention bargaining converged in a victory on the first roll call at the Democratic national convention.

Convention Battles

In each national convention the grand object is simple: to win a straight majority of the votes cast on the first or any other ballot. This job is most difficult, however, for the delegates arrive in the convention city in all stages of commitment, non-commitment, or semi-commitment to one candidate or another. Some delegates are pledged to a candidate only on the first ballot; others pledge themselves to one man until "the crack of doom." Some state delegations observe the unit rule; others split their vote according to the position of individual delegates.

As the convention opens, the air is filled with talk of favorite sons; of stalking-horses, who are used as fronts for strong candidates wishing to keep some strength in reserve; and of dark horses, who "stand restively and fully accoutered in their paddocks waiting, watching, and hoping that the favorites will kill each other off, and that the convention in desperation will lead them to the starting post." [15] The big test of a candidate is his *availability*, which turns on whether he has demonstrated vote-getting power, whether he seems to have presidential stature, whether or not he is closely tied to a narrow faction in the party, whether he comes from a politically strategic state or section, and—above all—whether or not he has alienated some vital religious, ethnic, or economic group. Governors have usually met the availability test better than senators, partly because the former can more easily dodge specific stands on national issues than the latter. But this aspect

---

[15] P. H. Odegard and E. A. Helms, *American Politics*, 2nd ed. (Harper, 1947), p. 532. See also Paul T. David, Ralph M. Goldman, and Richard C. Bain, *The Politics of National Party Conventions* (Brookings, 1960).

of availability may be changing, for in 1960 the voters seemed more interested in senatorial candidates who had dealt with international problems.

The doctrine of availability was well illustrated in the choosing of a Democratic nominee for Vice President in 1944. It was generally known that the convention's choice might well succeed President Roosevelt in the White House. According to Bronx leader Edward J. Flynn, he and a number of other Democratic bosses canvassed the field. Vice President Wallace was too liberal, and old-line Democrats did not like him. Speaker Rayburn of Texas would antagonize the crucial Negro vote. "Byrnes, who was the strongest candidate," says Flynn, "wouldn't do because he had been raised a Catholic and had left the church when he married, and the Catholics wouldn't stand for that." Truman, on the other hand, was known to the public and had made few enemies; "he came from a border state, and he had never made any 'racial' remarks. He just dropped into the slot." [16] Kennedy followed somewhat the same reasoning in choosing Johnson in 1960, although he had to cope with some grumbling from organized labor.

Both party conventions follow the same ritual. First there is a keynote speech, which lauds the party and bombards the enemy in equally flamboyant terms. Then come the election of convention officials, the reports of committees, the adoption of a platform. Some of these activities, such as the election of the permanent chairman and the seating of contested delegations, are occasions for tests of strength among leading candidates. After hearing statements from representatives of interested groups, the resolutions committee presents a proposed platform to the convention. Usually the planks are debated by the delegates, although sometimes they are accepted perfunctorily. Though drawn in generalities, negative in tone, and sometimes meaningless in detail, the platform indicates the way the wind is blowing. And on some issues, such as prohibition in the Democrats' 1928 and 1932 conventions and civil rights in their 1948 and 1956 conventions and in the 1964 Republican convention, stormy debate may ensue and planks may be accepted or defeated by close votes.

By the third or fourth day the convention is ready for the main business. Candidates are placed in nomination in fulsome speeches making them out as angels blessed with every virtue—above all, the ability to win elections. In placing Dewey's name before the Republican convention in 1944, a delegate orated:

> We are here to restore the Presidency of the United States to the American people. (Applause.) We are here to bring Washington, D.C., back into the United States. (Applause.) We are here to make the American people masters in their own household. (Applause.) For that job we have the means and we have the man. (Applause.) I give to you the nominee of the Republican party, the spokesman of the future, Thomas E. Dewey!

In the same year Senator Alben W. Barkley nominated Roosevelt in the Democratic convention with these words:

[16] Edward J. Flynn, *You're the Boss* (Viking, 1947), pp. 180–181.

> I present to this Convention for the office of President of these United States the name of one who is endowed with the intellectual boldness of Thomas Jefferson, the indomitable courage of Andrew Jackson, the faith and patience of Abraham Lincoln, the rugged integrity of Grover Cleveland, and the scholarly vision of Woodrow Wilson—Franklin D. Roosevelt.

Pandemonium breaks forth when the name of each candidate is mentioned. Delegates march about singing and cheering in demonstrations that may last half an hour or so. Short seconding speeches come next. Then the balloting begins.

Meantime the candidates have been maneuvering for position. From their headquarters in nearby hotel rooms has emerged a stream of claims of delegate strength, counter-claims, denials, rumors, charges, and counter-charges. If one candidate comes to the convention with a big lead in delegate strength, the other candidates will attempt to head him off by combining their forces. For if the convention can be deadlocked, a stampede may start toward even a weak candidate. Anyone controlling delegate votes must make the crucial decision of when to throw his strength to a candidate. If he throws his votes too soon, he may give them to a candidate who loses out in the end. If he waits too long, some candidate may acquire enough strength elsewhere. The trick is to deliver at the right time to the winning man; the reward may be the Vice Presidency or some other prize.

The task of the leading contenders is even more delicate. They must mobilize enough strength in early balloting to prove their power. They must also increase their votes with every new balloting to show that they are gaining. If their total drops on any one ballot, their cause may be lost. Franklin Roosevelt's capture of the Democratic nomination in 1932 shows the intricacies of the process. With Jim Farley's invaluable help, F.D.R. received 666¼ votes in the first balloting (more than a majority, but in 1932 the Democrats still observed the "two-thirds rule"). He gained 11½ votes in the next balloting, but only 5 more in the third. Some observers thought he had reached his peak. But in the next few hours while the weary convention was in adjournment, Farley managed to bring over the Texas and California delegations controlled by John Garner—an objective he had been working toward for months by holding out the Vice Presidency to Garner as bait. This switch brought a break in the opponents' ranks, and a stampede to Roosevelt on the next ballot. Farley said later that if Illinois had come over to Roosevelt after the first or second ballot, the Vice Presidency would have gone to that state.

Once a candidate wins a majority, some delegate who has voted against him normally moves that the nomination be made unanimous. This is done, and then another long ovation breaks out. The victorious candidate, who usually has been directing his forces from a nearby hotel suite, may appear before the convention a short while later. Smiling wife by his side, spotlighted by movie and television cameras, the happy candidate thanks the delegates for their vote of confidence and promises a winning fight.

Nominating a vice-presidential candidate usually comes as an anti-climax. The delegates are tired, broke, and anxious to get home. While the vice-presidential nominee is formally chosen in a rollcall vote, in almost all cases the newly picked presidential nominee and his backers actually make the selection, and the convention is glad to endorse it. An effort is ordinarily made to "balance the ticket" by selecting for vice president a man who represents a different wing of the party, geographical area, or party faction from the presidential nominee. Sometimes the selection is partly the result of a trade by which a party faction gives its ballots to the man who wins the presidential nomination in exchange for the "consolation prize." In 1956 Stevenson tried to set a precedent by "throwing open" the Democratic convention and allowing the delegates to choose his running-mate without any interference on his part. But in 1960 both Kennedy and Nixon reverted to the traditional practice of the new presidential nominee choosing his own man—and they also followed tradition in selecting men who would "balance" them geographically and doctrinally. Johnson and Goldwater chose geographical— but not doctrinal—balance in 1964.

Should the National Convention Be Reformed?

One of the most-criticized party institutions is the national convention. It is charged that every party candidate is picked by party bosses in a series of unprincipled deals in "smoke-filled rooms," and that they usually come up with a compromise candidate who represents the dead level of party mediocrity. The manner of choosing the delegates is also under attack. Both conventions and primaries are rigged and run by state bosses, it is said, and presidential primaries are so complicated that they baffle the voter and discourage him from taking part.

The main defense of the convention system is simple: It works. During the last hundred years, it is argued, the convention system has brought before the country men of the caliber of Lincoln, Cleveland, McKinley, Wilson, Smith, Willkie, both Roosevelts, Stevenson, Eisenhower, Kennedy, and others. The genius of the convention system is that it usually produces a candidate who represents party consensus instead of merely some wing of the party. This is important, it is said, for only such a man can enjoy the united support of the party in the campaign and in the White House. Moreover, it is said, the convention increasingly manages to select the man who is the overwhelming choice of the party rank and file and who is, indeed, a national favorite rather than a "dark horse." [17] When a party convention nominates a candidate lacking consensus and moderate support at the grass roots, as the Republicans did in choosing Goldwater in 1964—this argument continues—the party pays a heavy price in the November election.

Some favor the convention but would like to see it improved in operation. Former President Eisenhower, for example, has said that the American people have been "horrified" by convention bedlam and disorder. He called for cutting down the number of delegates to about a thousand; restricting demonstrations to five minutes; maintaining absolute order in the hall; and keeping all reporters and cameramen off the floor. Experienced politicians opposed such changes on the

[17] W. G. Carleton, "The Revolution in the Presidential Nominating Convention," *Political Science Quarterly* (June 1957), pp. 224–240.

grounds that Americans liked the conventions the way they are, even with all the tumult, and that both the delegates and the public wanted reporters and cameramen on the floor—the delegates because they liked the publicity, and the public because it wanted an intimate close-up of what was supposed to be going on in state delegations and smoke-filled rooms. Still others favor keeping the present quadrennial "sideshow" but establishing annual or biennial policy conferences or conventions that could concentrate on the discussion of issues and the framing of platforms, without the distraction of having to choose nominees.

Some critics of the convention would abolish it completely and substitute a nationwide direct *presidential primary system*. President Woodrow Wilson in 1913 advocated legislation providing for primary elections to take place simultaneously throughout the country, in which the voters in each party would vote directly for their favorite without the intervention of nominating conventions. This system would do away with much of the confusion and inefficiencies of the present system. The proposal, which might require a constitutional amendment, has been criticized, however, by those who feel that one nationwide direct primary would disrupt party solidarity and effectiveness. We need consensus *within* the party, they say, so that all major elements—geographical, economic, ideological—can take part in its affairs. We need division *between* the major parties so that the people will have a more meaningful choice at the polls. A nationwide primary system, critics assert, would give us the reverse.

Both the critics and the supporters of national conventions agree on at least one thing: that methods of *selecting convention delegates* should be improved. The whole system needs to be simplified and clarified. Reform does not necessarily mean that party *conventions* must be dropped. Both the primary system and the state convention system can be democratic methods of choosing delegates. Both may become "boss-controlled," however. Whether they become one or the other depends on whether or how the voters use them. Even the most democratic methods will not do the job if they lack the propulsive power of wide participation by the people.

How to Be Elected President

Immediately after nominating the vice-presidential candidate, the convention adjourns. The presidential candidate may choose a new party chairman, who usually serves as his campaign manager. The rest of the summer is spent planning electioneering tactics and arrangements. Campaign headquarters are geared for action. By early fall the presidential race is on.

Campaign Strategy

Grand strategy differs from one election to another, but most campaigns combine certain standard ingredients:

The Build-up. The personality of the candidate may be as important as the platform he runs on. If a candidate has serious personality defects, they must either be played down or transformed into virtues. The dour Calvin Coolidge had to be humanized before the presidential campaign of 1924. Franklin D. Roosevelt in 1936 had been pictured by the opposition as an arrogant dictator; his campaign tour was designed in part to show him as a warm and pleasing personality close to the people. Many in 1960 considered Kennedy too young to run for President; he had to show his maturity and judgment by his handling of bills before the Senate committees on which he served.

The candidate's desirable features are played up. In 1944 Dewey was presented as an aggressive young executive, in contrast with the tired old group in power; in 1952 Eisenhower was presented as a man who could unite the American people behind a middle-of-the-road program. In the end, the man offered to the people has become almost a myth. As Boss Penrose once said, "Always after a man is nominated they bring out the royal robe and put it on him, and that covers up all the cracks and nail-holes."

Taking the Stump. By the end of September both candidates are dashing about the country by train, plane, and automobile. There was a time when candidates conducted front-porch campaigns, receiving friendly delegations at their homes. But that day seems gone forever. Today the campaign must be carried straight to the voters. Presidents Hoover, Franklin Roosevelt, and Eisenhower stayed in the White House until late in their campaigns for re-election to show their devotion to duty, but they took the stump before the end. The candidates' campaign trains and caravans have been seen by too many Americans to need description here. Often overlooked,

"The big guy in front is Joseph T. Cochrane. Call him Joe. You met him in Marysville three weeks ago. Talk about hunting. He goes after deer every fall. Man on left is Leo Brown. Sixteenth District in his pocket. Don't ask him about his wife. She's ditched him. Fellow with mustache is Jim Cronin. Watch your step with him. He's Cochrane's brother-in-law, and . . ." (Drawing by Peter Arno; © 1946 The New Yorker Magazine, Inc.)

however, is the planning that goes into the choice of itinerary. Candidates sometimes try to steer clear of areas where they might be embarrassed by a local issue or an intraparty fight.

Where to Stump. The electoral-college system has a strong influence on campaign strategy. Under this system, as we shall see, the presidential contest is not decided by the pooled votes of all those casting ballots throughout the nation, but solely by the ballots of presidential electors. *All* the electoral votes of a state go to the candidate who gains the most popular votes in that state. As a consequence, candidates concentrate their attention on big, closely divided states. This means that the Democratic candidate may write off Maine and Kansas and his Republican foe probably does the same with part of the South. Consequently, the candidates make most of their appearances in states like New York, California, Pennsylvania, Massachusetts, Illinois, and Ohio, for the election outcome may easily be decided by a large bloc of electoral votes from such states as these. But Richard Nixon campaigned in every state, including Alaska and Hawaii, in 1960.

Building Group Support. The essential strategy of the campaign is to build up a winning alliance of interests—mainly sectional, economic, ideological, national-origin, racial, religious. Some of these interest groups are antagonistic to one another—for example, a Democratic candidate must seek to win the support of northern Negroes without alienating too many southern whites. Since most large organizations, such as the American Legion or the National Grange, will not commit themselves as organizations, the trick is to induce their leaders to take part in special election groups, such as Veterans for Goldwater or United Farmers for Johnson. Each party headquarters maintains active bureaus designed to mobilize support from organized groups. Campaign literature is slanted to appeal to housewives, businessmen, farmers, veterans, workers, and so on. The candidate himself must pitch his appeals so that they attract the support of divergent and overlapping groups.

Choosing Issues. This is one of the basic arts of campaigning. Issues may not be more important than personalities—but actually the two are inseparable. The candidate has a wide choice of alternatives, for he is not bound by his party's platform; indeed he can openly repudiate or modify planks of the platform if he wishes, as Landon did in 1936. One basic question arises: Should the candidate take a stand on specific issues, or should he speak in generalities? Either way, he is bound both to win and to lose some votes. Traditionally, evasion of issues has been considered an effective tactic, but the success of Truman and Kennedy in taking fairly definite stands in recent elections may presage a change. Usually the candidate tries to develop a basic theme, which is repeatedly played on, with variations to suit the place and hour. But there is a good deal of improvisation as candidates and campaign managers sense last-minute changes in public feeling from their audiences and from opinion polls.

"How does he stand on reciprocal trade agreements? That's what I want to know." (Drawing by Robert Day; © 1958 The New Yorker Magazine, Inc.)

Offensive and Defensive Tactics. Is it better to concentrate on attacking the enemy and ignoring his charges? Or should the opposition be answered charge for charge? Is it possible to put the opposition on the defensive? How? Do Americans really vote *for* candidates or *against* them? These questions plague any campaign strategist. Of course, a candidate for re-election is often on the defensive, for his public record is on display before the voters. But it is always possible to ignore the opposition's attacks and concentrate on one's own achievements. An effective tactic is to ignore the opposition's most damaging charges and to answer his weakest and wildest ones. In 1940, for example, Roosevelt said nothing about the third-term issue, but he answered at length the reckless statement of a minor Republican official that the President's only supporters were "paupers, those who earn less than $1,200 a year and aren't worth that, and the Roosevelt family."

Splitting the Opposition. According to an old political maxim, a candidate should always try to separate his opponent from the party rank and file. Willkie in 1940 tried to make a distinction between New Dealers and Democrats. Johnson in 1964 tried to sharpen the differences between Goldwater and moderate Republicans. Campaigners also try to divide the groups that seem to be united behind their opponent; thus Dewey made a point of his support from organized labor, and Roosevelt made use of businessmen's organizations set up to back him. Another splitting device is to focus the attack on a minor figure in the opposition camp, or on the sinister forces that are said to be in command. Republicans play up city bosses, leftists, "eggheads," arrogant bureaucrats; Democrats concentrate on big business, special interests, utilities, Hooverites, and the like. The great weakness of this device is that too much fire directed toward minor figures may leave the candidate himself unscathed.

Auxiliary Organizations. While the candidate is parading himself before the voters, he must rely on his national, state, and local party organizations to carry the heavy burden of routine work. His own campaign headquarters must raise money, issue propaganda, coordinate party efforts throughout the nation, and operate special divisions to seek the vote of large groups, such as Negroes, labor, and farmers. An important organizational question is whether to use auxiliary organizations independent of the party. In 1940, for example, Republicans and Independents set up thousands of Willkie Clubs, many of which had somewhat distant relations with the Republican organization. The advantage of auxiliaries is that they can appeal more effectively to independent voters. The disadvantage is that they are likely to duplicate the efforts of the party regulars, and even generate serious friction. In general, a presidential candidate must rely heavily on the party machinery throughout the nation; for he does not have time to build up a nationwide personal organization. The Citizens for Eisenhower in 1952 and 1956, however, were probably more effective than most such organizations.

Surveys. Old-line politicians have been skeptical of the dependability of polls, partly as a result of the pollsters' debacle in 1948. But in recent years candidates have been making increasing use of carefully conducted surveys of voters' attitudes and intentions. Kennedy employed surveys effectively both in his pre-convention and election campaigns. Through the use of polls Johnson discovered in the spring of 1964 that the voters approved most of his record on economic and social, or "bread-and-butter," issues; that they were most concerned about cold-war frustrations; that the widely feared "backlash" over the civil rights struggle was a potential threat but not yet an existing threat; and that no matter whom Johnson chose for his running mate, the President would win by about the same margin. When one of Johnson's close personal aides was arrested for misconduct at the height of the campaign, the President requested an immediate poll, which revealed that the incident had not had a significant impact on voters' intentions. The Goldwater headquarters polled the voters systematically during the fall.

Timing. This is one of the most important and mysterious techniques of all. Candidates try to pace their campaigns to reach a climax just before the election. Eisenhower's promise late in October 1952 to make a personal trip to Korea if elected was perfectly timed for maximum appeal. Although it is doubtful that election climaxes can be planned with complete success, both candidates usually converge on the populous areas of the East shortly before election day. The final campaign speech usually takes place on the Saturday before the Tuesday election; on election eve, however, the candidates make a sober and restrained appeal to the people to do their duty at the polls next day.

An American politician can face no ordeal more exhausting or exacting than a presidential campaign. The late Adlai E. Stevenson, the unsuccessful Democratic candidate in 1952 and 1956, told how it felt to campaign.

> You must emerge, bright and bubbling with wisdom and well-being, every morning at 8 o'clock, just in time for a charming and profound breakfast talk, shake hands with hundreds, often literally thousands, of people, make several inspiring, "newsworthy" speeches during the day, confer with political leaders along the way and with your staff all the time, write at every chance, think if possible, read mail and newspapers, talk on the telephone, talk to everybody, dictate, receive delegations, eat, with decorum—and discretion!—and ride through city after city on the back of an open car, smiling until your mouth is dehydrated by the wind, waving until the blood runs out of your arms, and then bounce gaily, confidently, masterfully into great howling halls, shaved and all made up for television with the right color shirt and tie—I always forgot—and a manuscript so defaced with chicken tracks and last-minute jottings that you couldn't follow it, even if the spotlights weren't blinding and even if the still photographers didn't shoot you in the eye every time you looked at them. (I've often wondered what happened to all those pictures.) Then all you have to do is make a great, imperishable speech, get out through the pressing crowds with a few score autographs, your clothes intact, your hands bruised, and back to the hotel—in time to see a few important people.
>
> But the real work has just commenced—two or three, sometimes four hours of frenzied writing and editing of the next day's immortal mouthings so you can get something to the stenographers, so they can get something to the mimeograph machines, so they can get something to the reporters, so they can get something to their papers by deadline time. (And I quickly concluded that all deadlines were yesterday!) Finally sleep, sweet sleep, steals you away, unless you worry—which I do.
>
> The next day is the same.
>
> But I gained weight on it. Somehow the people sustain you, the people and a constant, sobering reminder that you are asking them to entrust to you the most awesome responsibility on earth. It was a glorious, heart-filling, head-filling odyssey for which I shall be forever grateful to my party, to my staff and to my fellow Americans. Their faces are a friendly, smiling sea of memory stretching from coast to coast.[18]

The Electoral-College System—Mechanics

To win the Presidency, a candidate must put together a combination of electoral votes that will give him a majority in the electoral college. This unique institution has no professors or football team, never meets, and serves only a limited electoral function. Yet it has an

---

[18] Adlai E. Stevenson, *Major Campaign Speeches, 1952* (Random House, 1953), pp. xxi–xxiii. Reprinted by permission of Random House, Inc. Copyright 1953 by Random House, Inc.

importance of its own. Although the framers of the Constitution devised the electoral-college system because they wanted the President chosen by *electors* exercising independent judgment, subsequent political changes have transformed the electors into straight party representatives who simply register the electorate's decision.

The system today works as follows: In making his presidential choice on election day, the voter technically does not vote directly for a candidate but chooses between slates of *presidential electors*. Each slate is made up of men selected by the state party (in most states in party conventions) to serve this essentially honorary role. The slate that wins the most *popular* votes throughout the *state* gets to cast *all* the *electoral* votes for the state (a state has one electoral vote for every senator and representative).

The electors on the winning slate travel to their state capital a few weeks after the election, go through the ceremony of casting their ballots for their party's candidates, perhaps hear some speeches, and go home. The ballots are sent from the state capitals to Washington, where early in January they are formally "counted" by the House and Senate and—to the amazement of nobody—the name of the next President is announced.

Counting of the electoral votes has not always been just a formality. In 1876 there was a serious and potentially explosive dispute over which slate of electoral votes from several southern states should be counted. The election was so close that the outcome was at stake. The Senate was Republican; the House, Democratic. Finally a Commission of Fifteen was elected, composed of eight Republicans and seven Democrats. By a vote of eight to seven, the Commission ruled that the Republican electors in the disputed states had been properly elected; so Hayes became President over Tilden.

The House and Senate also must act when no candidate secures a *majority* of the electoral votes. This is not likely as long as there are only two serious contending parties, but it has happened twice in the case of President and once in the case of Vice President. The House chooses the President from among the top three candidates; each *state delegation* has one vote, and a majority is necessary for election. If no man receives a majority of the electoral vote in the vice-presidential contest, the Senate picks from among the top two candidates; each senator has one vote, and again a majority is required.

The Electoral-College System—Politics

The operation of the electoral college, with its statewide electoral slates, sharply influences the Presidency and presidential politics. In order to win a presidential election, a candidate must appeal successfully to urban and suburban groups in populous states such as New York, California, Pennsylvania, Illinois, and perhaps a dozen others. A Republican candidate usually enters the fray sure of the backing of rural states such as Vermont, Kansas, Oregon, and the Dakotas. Under ordinary circumstances the Democratic candidate knows that he can depend on the support of the "solid South" and some of the border states. Under the electoral-college system, as we have seen, a candidate either wins *all* a state's electoral votes or *none*; hence the presidential candidate ordinarily will not waste his time campaigning in states unless he has at least a fighting chance of carrying them; nor will he waste time in states that are assuredly on his side. Consequently, the fight usually narrows down to the big states where the balance between the parties tends to be fairly even.

Obviously the presidential candidate must win over—or at least not antagonize —the masses of voters in industrial centers. He must show sensitivity to their problems—working conditions, housing, wages, social security, and relations with foreign nations, especially nations whose sons and daughters have come by the million to our shores. Moreover, the candidate's appeals must at the same time transcend local and petty matters and dramatize the great national issues. He will, of course, address himself to groups such as farmers, workers, veterans, and the like, but he will try to seize on the issues that unify these groups on a nation-wide basis. The candidate, in short, strikes out for a *national majority* rooted in the largest states and sacrifices many narrow issues in order to exploit the broader ones. Candidates for Congress, on the other hand, often win votes by pressing local and sectional claims against those of the rest of the nation.

The presidential election of 1964 did not fit the traditional pattern, as we have noted. Goldwater made a strong appeal to the solid conservative vote in both parties rather than trying to appear as a "consensus" candidate. He virtually wrote off the large industrial states of the Northeast. He fought essentially a divisive rather than a unifying campaign. Johnson, on the other hand, campaigned as a consensus candidate, took a breezily optimistic and positive stand on most issues, tried to pitch his appeal to all sections and major groups, and sought to unify the people behind his administration. Goldwater's stunning defeat in the fall is likely to fortify and perpetuate some of the old rules of the presidential game—perhaps to a greater extent than they really deserve.

The Politics of Electoral-College Reform

In 1960 an elector in Oklahoma chosen on the Republican ticket refused to cast his electoral vote for Nixon and gave it to Senator Byrd of Virginia. Although such departures from constitutional custom are rare and have never affected the outcome of an election, almost everyone agrees that it is dangerous to have a system that allows individual electors to vote for whomever they wish despite the results of the popular vote in their state. In a close election a small group of persons could frustrate the wishes of the majority of the electorate.

It would probably not be too difficult to secure agreement on the desirability of abolishing individual electors, but there is real difference of opinion whether we should alter the present winner-take-all method of counting electoral votes. True, the unit-vote system could lead to the election, as it has twice in our history, of a President who received fewer popular votes than his opponent. However, the more usual impact is to exaggerate the margin of electoral votes of the winning candidate. Thus, even when the popular vote is close, the electoral vote margin of the winner is substantial. Take the 1960 election: Kennedy's popular vote margin out of almost 69 million votes was only 112,000 but he received 303 electoral votes to Nixon's 209. In the absence of the electoral-college unit-vote system there might have been a much greater disposition on the part of the Republicans to challenge the returns.

In order to make the electoral vote correspond more closely to the popular vote, some have advocated a constitutional amendment that would give each candidate the same proportion of the electoral votes of a state as he won of its popular vote. For example, if a candidate secured one-third of the popular vote in a state having twelve electoral votes, he would win four of the electoral votes.

What would be the consequences of such an amendment (generally known as the Lodge-Gossett amendment)? Many northern Democrats are opposed because they believe it would strengthen the position of rural-small-town conservatives. They argue that the present system compels presidential candidates to fight especially hard to win the support of the big pivotal states such as New York, Illinois, and California, since candidates face the prospect of winning or losing a big batch of electoral votes in such states. As a result, presidential candidates pitch their appeals in these states to the great balance-of-power groups that tend to be composed largely of urban voters—organized labor, Catholics, nationality groups, and Negroes, who usually give majorities to Democratic candidates. The electoral college thus forces presidential candidates—and ultimately the President —to be especially responsive to the problems and interests of these groups. Since Congress over-represents the conservative, rural areas, they ask, why should not the President over-represent urban, liberal areas? President Kennedy, when a senator, opposed electoral reform partly for this reason.

For precisely the opposite reasons some southern Democrats and conservative Republicans favor the Lodge-Gossett amendment (or some other system that would break up the unit-vote procedures—for example, having one elector chosen in each congressional district). They argue that the present system gives too much influence to the balance-of-power groups in the northern and western states. In 1960, for example, a shift of 1 per cent of the popular vote would have altered the electoral vote in eleven states.

But not even all southern Democrats or Republicans favor changing the present system. Some Republicans are worried that a Lodge-Gossett type amendment might give Democratic candidates too great an advantage, since it would probably result in a fairly even division of electoral votes in the larger northern and western states with the Democratic candidate receiving a winning margin from the "solid South."

Although the proposed alteration in the electoral college would seem to benefit southern Democrats, even some of them are skeptical. For the present system helps them to maintain a one-party system. Republicans ordinarily have little incentive to campaign in rural Georgia or Mississippi or Alabama, for under most

. . . Straw hats, beer, the bloody shirt, campaign songs have played their part in American history, along with more elevated issues reflecting deeper economic and social forces.

These pages capture some of the pageantry and pugnacity, blarney and energy that have characterized American democracy during 175 years of partisan elections.

During the nation's early years politicians did not actively campaign for the Presidency. This banner, appearing after Jefferson's victory in 1800, hailed the fall of Federalist John Adams and the victory of Jefferson's Republicans.

Gradually politics became more "popular" and more earthy, the electorate broader and more diversified. In the 1820's John Quincy Adams was extolled on a sewing box,

Henry Clay on a pipe—

but neither could withstand the triumphant Democratic forces which swept into office behind General Andrew Jackson.

The Federalists had long since died away and—after a period of one-party politics—a new party, the Whigs, challenged Jacksonian Democracy. The national party balance became more even in the 1840's, and the Whigs grasped the new style of democratic politics in choosing a war hero of their own, General Harrison. Four years later the Democrats won with James K. Polk, the first convention "dark horse."

A decade later Whigs and anti-slavery groups formed a new Republican party; the nation was rent in two when the Republicans won with Abraham Lincoln in 1860.

The Republicans, with plenty of war heroes of their own, and with a "bloody shirt" to wave, held the Presidency during the post-Civil War years. The Democrats could not find a winning strategy in either reformers like Horace Greeley or conservatives like Samuel J. Tilden. Though the latter won a popular plurality in 1876, he suffered defeat when a Republican-controlled special commission decided a tie in the electoral college.

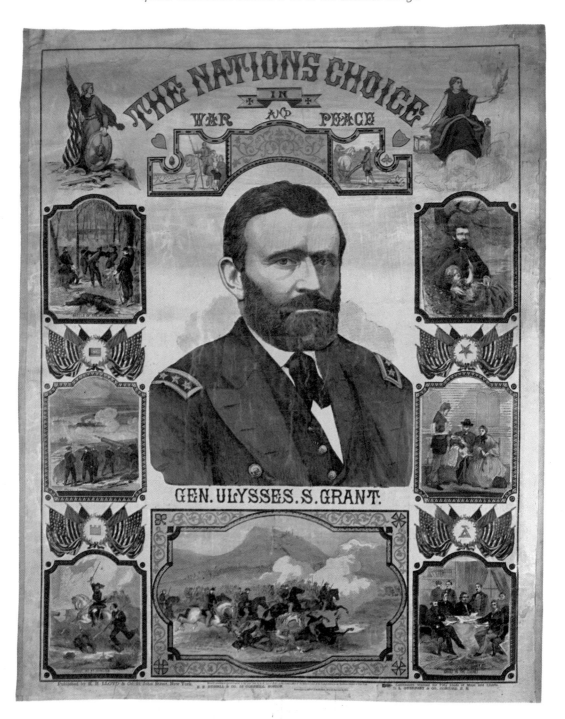

OUR NEXT PRESIDENT

Horace Greeley's March

as played by

GRAFULLAS SEVENTH REG? BAND.

NEW YORK HORACE WATERS 481 BROADWAY,
Publisher of Sheet Music, Music Books &c.
MANUFACTURER & DEALER IN PIANOS, MELODEONS & ORGANS.

TILDEN
AND
HENDRICKS
HAVE BEEN
ELECTED
AND SHALL BE
INAUGURATED.

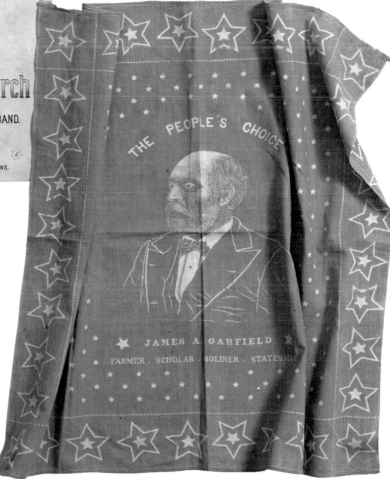

THE PEOPLE'S CHOICE

JAMES A. GARFIELD

FARMER . SCHOLAR . SOLDIER . STATESMAN

Republicans consolidated their hold on business-men, factory workers, farmers, veterans, Negroes—and also on the issue of prosperity. But the party balance was righting again, and the Democratic nominee, Grover Cleveland, won in 1884 and 1892. Putting the depression issue into politics, like this, would return to haunt the Republicans during the Great Depression of the 1930's.

Bryan confronted McKinley in the great "realigning contest" of '96, as the East (and the eastern press) lined up solidly behind the Republicans. Women still could not vote in national elections, but candidates' wives (pictured here on luncheon placemats) shared the political spotlight.

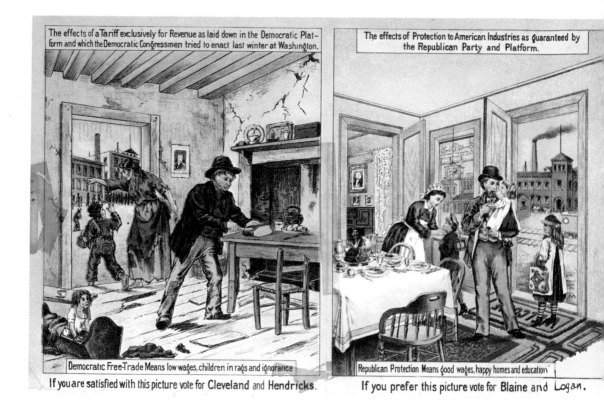

The effects of a Tariff exclusively for Revenue as laid down in the Democratic Platform and which the Democratic Congressmen tried to enact last winter at Washington.

The effects of Protection to American Industries as guaranteed by the Republican Party and Platform.

Democratic Free-Trade Means low wages, children in rags and ignorance

Republican Protection Means good wages, happy homes and education

If you are satisfied with this picture vote for Cleveland and Hendricks.

If you prefer this picture vote for Blaine and Logan.

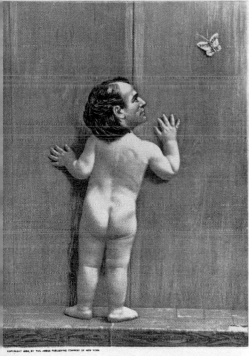

VOL. 31 NO. 783   OCTOBER 17 1896   PRICE 10 CENTS

Judge

ENTERED AT THE POST OFFICE AT NEW YORK AS SECOND CLASS MATTER COPYRIGHT 1896   BY THE JUDGE PUBLISHING CO.   TITLE REGISTERED AS A TRADE MARK

COPYRIGHT 1896, BY THE JUDGE PUBLISHING COMPANY OF NEW YORK

LITTLE BILLY BRYAN CHASING BUTTERFLIES.
(After popular photograph by Schloss.)

Wᵐ McKINLEY

After McKinley's assassination at the turn of the century (the third presidential assassination in 35 years), Theodore Roosevelt tried to move the Grand Old Party in new directions.

During the 1890's it became the vogue to picture the candidates on celluloid buttons.

The GOP split between Roosevelt and Taft in 1912 enabled an ex-college professor, Woodrow Wilson, to carry the Democrats back to the White House for the first time in 20 years. After World War broke out in Europe, a song-writer rallied to Wilson, but his lyrics carefully straddled the issue of intervention.

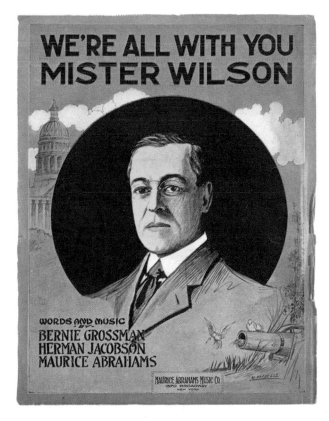

The "return to normalcy" in the 1920's meant also a return to Republican rule. Harding, Coolidge, and Hoover presided over a prosperous nation—until 1929.

Millions of Americans hoped Roosevelt would bring back prosperity—

but some were more concerned about bringing back beer.

After 13 stirring years of reform and recovery under Roosevelt, the nation suddenly found
itself with a new President in
the closing months of World
War II. Harry Truman led the
nation into a "cold war" period
—and won a surprise victory
over a strong Republican ticket
in 1948.

Like the Whigs in 1840, the
Republicans in 1952 made a
breakthrough with a popular
army general, Dwight Eisenhower, who swept into office over
Governor Adlai Stevenson of
Illinois.

The Democrats were still the dominant party. In 1960 John Kennedy, a Catholic, defied political tradition and won a razor-edge victory over Richard Nixon, in the "year of the great debates."

In 1964's historic test between an avowedly conservative and avowedly liberal candidate, Barry Goldwater won the battle of the bumper stickers—

but Lyndon B. Johnson won "all the way" except in the South, and carried his party to overwhelming victories in House and Senate.

circumstances even if they should double the Republican vote, the Democratic advantage is so great that these Republican popular votes ordinarily cannot be translated into electoral votes. (The 1964 presidential election is the great exception.) But under the Lodge-Gossett proposals, a Republican vote in the South would count as much as a Republican vote in New York and hence both parties would be encouraged to campaign throughout the nation and not concentrate just on the pivotal states. Since a two-party system in the South would make it much more difficult for rural whites to maintain control over southern governments, they too are not enthusiastic about electoral-college reform.

Thus, although everyone criticizes the present electoral college, no one is precisely clear what consequences would flow from changing it. Even those who believe they know what the consequences would be are not agreed on their desirability. Under the circumstances, major reform of the electoral college system is unlikely.

Who Won the Election?

The election is over. The victors and the losers exchange gracious messages. Placards and posters blow away in the autumn storms. Soon the successful candidates are taking office in White House, Congress, statehouse, and city hall. These are the winners. But aside from the victorious candidates, can we say who really won the election?

No Total Victors

Did a *party* win it? Only to a limited extent, at best. No party (fortunately) ever sweeps all the national, state, and local elections, nor does any party ever elect all the members of one chamber, like the House of Representatives. And sometimes one party captures one or both chambers of Congress while the opposition party wins or retains the Presidency, leading to divided party rule. Never in the United States does one party seize control of the legislative and executive branches of the national government to the extent that the winning party in Britain takes command in Parliament and Cabinet. Indeed, we cannot speak of party control in any real sense. At most, we can speak of control or influence by various factors or individuals in the party. The point is that the elected candidates are not elected by or responsible to a single monolithic party, but rather to groups inside and outside the party. The party as such did not win the election.

Can we say, then, that any particular *group* won the election? Of course, certain groups will say that they were the ones that elected the winning candidates. But these claims are exaggerated. Few organized groups are big enough by themselves to muster enough votes for a majority. And big groups, whether economic, religious, or any other, do not vote as a bloc. The most we can say is that the election was won by a combination of *segments* of groups, or of *subgroups*.

Was the election a victory for a particular *principle* or set of ideas? Here again the answer must be "no." Certainly many persons will make this claim. We will hear over the radio or read in the paper that the election results were a victory for civil rights or for anti-union laws or a repudiation of the bureaucrats or of Wall Street. But an election is rarely, if ever, a mandate for particular policies. The party platforms are vague catchalls, and the candidates' promises are often obscure and inconsistent. An electoral majority is made up of many different elements with a variety of views. At best, the election reflects general attitudes of important segments of the voters.

Who, then, did win the election? What do the election results mean? Of course, the winners of the election may have been—at least in the long run—the whole nation, all the people. In a narrower and more immediate sense, the winners were the elected candidates and the voters supporting those candidates—*to the extent that the candidates can follow through on their followers' expectations*. The election results mean simply that the voters have made choices among candidates—choices that give only a rough idea of what the voters are thinking. Election results are not blueprints for future action, but crude guidelines to the general drift of popular feeling, and indications of popular backing for a *general direction* of government. "A vote," says Lippmann, "is a promise of support. It is a way of saying: I am lined up with these men, on this side." [19]

What Elections Are

To understand election results, then, we must remember what elections are and what they are not. Elections are not simply a grand rally of the people, who on their own initiative debate issues, produce candidates, and decide among them. Elections are struggles among party and group leaders who go to the voters for support. The voters are of all types, organized and unorganized, active and passive, concerned with world-wide issues and with petty ones. Elections are not the spontaneous acts of a mass of people but the periodic mobilization of voters by leaders at many levels.

[19] Walter Lippmann, *The Phantom Public* (Harcourt, Brace, 1925), pp. 56–57.

"Don't expect me to get this real accurate, Bub." From The Herblock Book *(Beacon Press, 1952).*

"Maybe I ought to listen. This is the year I start voting."
(Drawing by Tobey © 1960 The New Yorker, Inc.)

Elections are only one of the ways in which the voters can have a say in their government. The people intervene in other ways between elections—by writing to their congressman and to the editor, by signing petitions, by arguing and griping, by organizing in groups. This does not mean that elections are unimportant or uninspiring. Quite the contrary. "A presidential election," William B. Munro once said, "is merely our modern and highly refined substitute for the ancient revolution; a mobilization of opposing forces, a battle of the ins against the outs; with leaders and strategy and campaign chests and all the other paraphernalia of civil war, but without bodily violence to the warriors. This refinement of the struggle for political control, this transition from bullets to ballots, is perhaps the greatest contribution of modern times to the progress of civilization." [20]

[20] William B. Munro, *The Invisible Government* (Macmillan, 1928), p. 17. For an interesting development of the view that politics is simply the manipulation of rather passive voting groups by elites vying for power, see J. A. Schumpeter, *Capitalism, Socialism, and Democracy* (Harper, 1942), chs. 21–23.

Elections set the course of government only in part. Elected officeholders share power with appointed ones, such as judges and administrative officials. All these officials, elected and appointed alike, do not exercise power freely but only within channels set by the forces discussed earlier in this book—the forces of tradition and practice, of laws and institutions, of popular wants and expectations. In the following chapters we turn to our national policy-makers and see how they share and exercise power in the never-ending ferment of ideas, interests, individuals, and institutions.

PART 5

Policy-makers for the people

A Problem Guide   The main problem posed by Part Five is *responsible leadership*. By "leadership" we mean the readiness and ability of officials to act effectively in meeting the problems facing the country. By "responsible" we mean the ability of voters sooner or later to hold these officials accountable for their actions.

The Presidency, discussed in Chapters 14 and 15, poses sharply these twin problems of responsibility and leadership. The powers of his office and his assured rule for at least four years give the Chief Executive the tools of leadership, and strong Presidents have used these tools boldly. Has the Presidency gained *too much power* for a "government by the people"? These questions in turn raise the problem: To whom is the President responsible? Presumably to the majority of the voters, but the Electoral College, as we saw in Chapter 13, tends to make the President especially responsive to the big urban states with their balance-of-power voting blocs.

This problem of responsible leadership arises in the treatment of Congress in Chapters 16 and 17. How quickly and effectively can Congress take the lead in meeting problems? Except in times of crisis, it may be handicapped by the procedures described in Chapter 16, such as the committee system and the power to filibuster. To whom is Congress responsible? Mainly to the voters, of course. But to *what* voters? The problem here is that individual members of Congress may respond to special and local groups in their states and districts. Should Congress respond more strongly to a broader interest, such as a majority of the *national* electorate?

What about civil servants and federal

judges? These officials are not directly chosen by the voters and they are not expected to "lead" in the usual sense. In fact, however, bureaucrats and judges, too, must on occasion lead—for example, the official who takes some clearly desirable action when not specifically authorized by law, or the Supreme Court in the famous school desegregation case of 1954. To whom are these officials responsible? To the President? To Congress? To the electorate? To their own professional standards? To all these, of course. —but what if officials must choose between different kinds of responsibility? These questions arise in Chapters 18 and 19.

There is one key problem running through all the chapters in this part: the problem of majority rule—that is, whether or not President and Congress should be responsible directly and primarily to the majority of voters that elected them to office. Since our political leaders win power through political parties seeking majority support, this problem in turn raises the further question of how strongly, if at all, the winning party should control the leaders in of-

fice. Should we make our leaders, executive and legislative and even judicial, more responsible to the majority of the people? In short, do we want some kind of "party government"? Or do we want a looser, more decentralized political system that gives more power to shifting coalitions of minority groups working through or around our parties? This problem—and its implications for responsible leadership—is explored in Chapter 20. Chapter 20 also deals with the other four basic problems outlined in Chapter 1, including the assumptions of democratic government.

Clearly *representation*—the focal problem of Part Four—and *responsibility*—the main problem of this part—are closely intertwined. In studying representation we were looking at the problem of how the voters are organized (or *dis*organized or *un*organized) to influence political leaders. In studying responsibility we are trying to discover what voters—in groups, in localities, in parties—the leaders are responsible to, and just how they are responsible. In short, responsibility and representation are opposite sides of the same coin.

14 THE PRESIDENCY: POWERS AND PARADOX

Not long ago President Lyndon B. Johnson celebrated the 175th anniversary of George Washington's taking the oath of office. In his proclamation President Johnson stated that the Presidency had long since come to transcend its occupants, that it "has made every man who occupied it, no matter how small, bigger than he was; and no matter how big, not big enough for its demands." This was an arresting statement. For here was the President of the United States saying that the presidential office was much more than the man who happened to occupy it, that the *Presidency* had become a power—and perhaps something of a problem—in itself.

This view would have come as something of a shock to George Washington and the other framers of the Constitution. They had carefully created a presidential office with limited powers. They wanted mainly a national executive who would stay clear of parties and factions, enforce the laws passed by Congress, deal' with foreign governments, and help the states put down disorders such as Shays' Rebellion. And yet they did not want the President to be too weak either. They spent many days debating the twin questions: How strong should the executive power be? And what relation should the executive have to the new Congress?

Day after day the delegates argued. Some, like Alexander Hamilton and James Wilson, wanted a strong executive, independent of the legislature—an executive who would lend "energy, dispatch, and responsibility" to the new government. Others, like Roger Sherman, wished to have the "executive magistracy" appointed by Congress and wholly subject to the legislative will. So fearful were the delegates of a strong President that they decided several times for appointment of the chief executive by Congress—a move that would have made the President the tool of Congress and probably would have given us a European type of parliamentary government. Others wanted to weaken the executive by setting up a plural Presidency composed of two or three men of equal power, or by allowing the President only one four-year term. But still others warned urgently against a weak President who could not hold his own with Congress.

In the end the delegates compromised. On the one hand the President would be single rather than plural, eligible for re-election, and independent of the legislature. On the other, he was hemmed in by the system of checks and balances: His major appointments had to be approved by the Senate; Congress could override his veto by a two-thirds vote; he could make treaties only with the consent of two-thirds of the Senators; and his power to appeal directly to the voters was muzzled by the electoral-college system. Even this Presidency with its mixed set of powers worried many Americans in 1787. "It squints toward monarchy," Patrick Henry complained. But those concerned about presidential power were reassured by the fact that the wise and magisterial George Washington was slated to be the first President.

Such was the origin of the office that has become the mainspring of American government. As the executive has taken on vast powers, the old questions that preoccupied the framers have been central in the continuing debate over the shape of American government. How strong should the executive be? What should be its relation to Congress? We will return to these questions after considering how the Presidency has grown and how the President carries out his crucial roles today.

The Growth of the Presidency

The growth of the Presidency has not been steady. During its first century much depended on the personality of the President and the nature of the times. Washington served essentially the role that the framers hoped, yet his administration, under the urgings of Alexander Hamilton and other activists, took strong leadership in foreign affairs and in fiscal policy. Thomas Jefferson, who had been a strict constructionist of the Constitution and had criticized it in 1787 for granting the President too much power, proved to be one of the stronger Presidents. He led the new Republican party to power, exercised pervasive leadership over Congress, and took the bold step of purchasing Louisiana without seeking the advance approval of Congress. Andrew Jackson dramatized the political potency of the Presidency in

his battle with "Nicholas Biddle's Bank" and with his foes on Capitol Hill. Abraham Lincoln, who as a Whig in earlier days had been hostile toward presidential power, acted virtually as an executive dictator during the Civil War. He spent money, drafted soldiers, increased the size of the Army and Navy, and suspended the writ of habeas corpus—all without authorization from Congress.

Tom Little; © *1965 by The New York Times Company. Reprinted by permission.*

But presidential power ebbed and flowed during the nineteenth century. Strong Presidents were followed by weak ones. James Madison and James Monroe inherited Jefferson's Republican party but they were unable to use the party as a source of presidential control. Martin Van Buren and later Democrats wanted to carry on in the Jacksonian tradition, but they could not equal Old Hickory's vigor, courage, and popular appeal. After Lincoln's vast expansion of presidential powers, the office dwindled in importance. President Andrew Johnson was impeached and nearly convicted. Powerful men on Capitol Hill even gained control of major executive powers—especially of the President's control of hiring and firing administration officials and of taxing and spending. The President had a tiny staff, and of course the whole executive establishment remained rather small. A Vanderbilt spent more money on his private program of scientific farming and forestry than was spent by the whole United States Department of Agriculture!

The expansion of presidential power has been more rapid and sustained in this century. To be sure, the ebb and flow in the power relations of President and Congress has continued—thus the vigorous, dominating Theodore Roosevelt was followed by William Howard Taft, the eloquent, idealistic Woodrow Wilson by Warren G. Harding. But even Dwight Eisenhower, pledged to the notion that the President should share his powers with Congress, found that conditions demanded strong presidential leadership. Today the Presidency seems to have assumed a lasting role as the focus of leadership in American government. Today the Presidency is at the peak of its prestige. It is the center of action, the presiding office of the Free World, "probably the single most important governmental institution in the world." [1] What are some of the basic forces behind the rise of the powerful modern Presidency?

Challenge and Crisis. The President can respond to crises more quickly and forcefully than can a Congress of two houses and several hundred legislators. Almost every major domestic or foreign emergency has been seized upon by activist Presidents to make decisions; these decisions in turn set precedents that can be used by later Presidents. Critics have denounced Presidents for ignoring or overriding Congress, but few have been able to challenge Lincoln's defense of his near-dictatorship: "Was it possible," he asked, "to lose the nation and yet preserve the Constitution? By general law, life and limb must be protected, yet often a limb must be amputated to save a life, but a life is never wisely given to save a limb."

Foreign Affairs. The Constitution gave the President great authority in foreign affairs so that he could act swiftly and the nation could speak with a single voice. But even the perspicacious framers could hardly have expected that the world would grow so small and the President so predominant. He can act with secrecy, speed, and force. The shrinking of the globe has produced a vast amount of multilateral diplomacy which in turn has required central coordination by the President. The sheer management of the tremendous burden of foreign affairs would be beyond the capacity of Congress today, or even of the Senate alone.

Popular Need for Leadership. People will turn, especially in times of distress, to the single leader rather than to obscure members and factions of a legislature. Partly this is a psychological need for an authority figure, for some one who can produce miracles or at least tell people what to do. Partly it is a popular wish to give authority to a clearly identifiable person so that he can be held accountable. People fear presidential power in the abstract but often demand that specific Presidents—a Lincoln or a Roosevelt—take action even though constitutional checks and balances are disrupted. On the eve of the twentieth century a historian noted that "the greatness of the presidency is the work of the people, breaking through the constitutional form." [2] The President's ability to command radio

---

[1] David E. Haight and Larry D. Johnston, *The President: Roles and Powers* (Rand McNally, 1965), p. 1.

[2] Henry Jones Ford, *The Rise and Growth of American Politics* (Macmillan, 1898), p. 292.

and television, and the attention lavished on his personality and family by news-papers and magazines, have doubtless made the people feel more dependent than ever on the solitary figure in the White House.

Economic and Social Trends. The United States has become a highly urbanized and interdependent society, as we noted in Chapter 1. Such a society puts enor-mous pressure on government to cope with economic and social crises, to head off problems that loom on the horizon, to act quickly and decisively. Such pres-sures tend to focus on the President, who can act with national authority and deftly time his moves. Theodore Roosevelt directly intervened to settle a major anthracite strike in 1902, and recently the White House has often been the center of dramatic, last-minute negotiations on the eve of a strike that could paralyze a vital national industry. Franklin Roosevelt acted boldly to ward off financial col-lapse in 1933, and today no President would dare to sit by idly in the face of an economic recession or even a sharp slump in the stock market. Eisenhower sent troops into Little Rock, as Kennedy did into Mississippi. Recurring crises in the cities—civil rights tension, poverty, crime, urban decay—are certain to gen-erate continuing pressures for presidential action.

Is the expansion of presidential power irreversible? From the very beginning Americans have condemned this growth as a violation of the constitutional checks and balances. Henry Clay's attacks on Jackson are part of our great political litera-ture. During the administrations of recent, strong Presidents, the criticism has become sharper and more persistent. In 1964 Barry Goldwater charged that be-lievers in a strong Presidency held a "totalitarian philosophy that the end justifies the means." "What, then," asked the Republican presidential candidate, "is the best distribution of power for our society? Our answer to this question has tra-ditionally been a *balance* of power among the various parts of the society. . . . I submit that this balance is being upset today by the trend toward increasing con-centration of power in the Presidency. . . . *The more complete and concentrated executive power becomes, the greater will be the temptation to employ it to wipe out all opposing power.*" [3] Senator Goldwater pressed this argument so forcefully that the 1964 election became in part a test of whether the voters supported—or at least acquiesced in—the modern use of presidential power.

We will return to this controversy later. But first, to get a better idea of the size and complexity and scope of the President's job, we must consider the chief executive in each of his six great roles—as chief politician, chief administrator, chief legislator, chief foreign policy-maker, commander in chief, and chief of state. Truly "the President is many men." But although we shall explore each of these roles in turn, they must not be viewed as separate or compartmentalized. On the contrary, only in the *interweaving* of these different roles can we see the full tapestry of presidential power, as we will note at the end of this chapter.

[3] Barry Goldwater, "Powers of the Presidency," *Yale Political Review* (Fall 1964), p. 18.

Chief Politician

First and foremost, the President is the leading politician—the most visible and potentially the most effective mobilizer of influence in the American system of power. "Politician" is a nasty word to many Americans, and some Presidents have tried to be "above politics." President Eisenhower once remarked that there were many things about his work that he found intriguing, but as for politics in the usual sense, "I have no great liking for that." But a President cannot escape politics. As a candidate he has made promises to the people. As party leader he carries the hopes of a great political organization. To get things done he must work with many people who have somewhat differing loyalties and responsibilities. Inevitably the President is embroiled in legislative politics, judicial politics, bureaucratic politics, and of course foreign politics.

Despite his tremendous powers a President very rarely can command. He spends most of his time persuading people to do what he thinks ought to be done. Of course he has great persuasive power—it is not easy for the average politician or official to resist a President—but in the long run people think mainly of their own interests and obligations. In a government of separated institutions sharing powers,[4] some congressional leaders and even some bureaucratic leaders are beyond the political reach of the President because they have their own "constituencies"—a House committee, for example, or a powerful interest group. Presidents cannot simply bark out orders like a first sergeant. Before Eisenhower became President Harry Truman said of him: "He'll sit here, and he'll say, 'Do this! Do that!' *And nothing will happen.* Poor Ike—it won't be a bit like the Army. He'll find it very frustrating." [5] *All* Presidents have found it frustrating.

The President must simply be more skillful at manipulating influence than his rivals. He must know how to marshal all the powers of his office, his own prestige, his reputation for political skill, and even his capacity to inflict political injury on his opponents, in order to carry out his policies. Above all he must know how to bargain—to offer something to men who have their own political ambitions just as he does. Here again the President has the trump hand because he has so much to offer—high positions, presidential recognition, assistance to another politician on some pet project, and little courtesies and favors that can mean a great deal—an invitation to a state dinner, a special birthday note, a ride in the presidential limousine or jet. But the President's political resources are not limitless, and in a government that has so many leaders the drain on his resources is very high.

Besides the authority and trappings of his office, the President has two other special sources of political influence—his influence over public opinion and his role as party chief.

[4] Richard E. Neustadt, *Presidential Power* (Wiley, 1960), p. 33.
[5] Quoted in *ibid.*, p. 9.

The President and Public Opinion

No other politician—and few television or film stars—can achieve a closer contact with the people than does the President. Typically he has been an active public man for years and has built up a host of followers. He has won a nomination and an election and hence has been under the public gaze for months on end. But the White House is the finest platform of all—a "bully pulpit," as Theodore Roosevelt called it. The President has his television studio, which he can use, as Lyndon Johnson has done, to appeal directly to the people for understanding and support in the face of foreign crisis. He can summon the press when he wishes; accept an invitation to speak (he has a wide choice!); arrange a "nonpolitical" speaking tour; and he can time all these moves for maximum advantage.

The press conference is an example of how systematically the President can employ the machinery of communication. Years ago the conferences were rather casual affairs. Franklin Roosevelt ran his conferences informally and was a master at withholding information as well as giving it. Under Truman, the conference had become "an increasingly routinized, institutionalized part of the presidential communications apparatus. Preparation became elaborately formalized, as did the conduct of the meetings themselves in their new setting [a State Department auditorium]. Finally, the nature of the meetings as private encounters between the Chief Executive and the newspaper representatives was rapidly changing into a semi-public performance (soon to be completely public) whose transactions were increasingly part of the public record." [6] Kennedy authorized the first live telecast of a press conference and used it frequently for direct communication with the people. Johnson has preferred non-televised meetings with reporters—sometimes while walking at a fast clip around the White House—but the big televised press conference has become a key element of presidential politics.

The President also has advantages in *gauging* public opinion. He sees the newspaper polls, often before they are published. He receives reports on political attitudes from local party leaders. He can get some idea of public opinion from the letters that pour into the White House, the crowds that greet him on his travels, conversations with visitors. Every President, says a former White House aide, must be a "keen judge of public opinion. He must be able to distinguish its petty whims, to estimate its endurance, to respond to its impatience, and to respect its potential power. He must know how best and how often he can appeal to the public—and when it is better left undisturbed." [7] The President must interpret public opinion not only to follow it but to *lead* it.

Despite these advantages, the President finds difficulties in both gauging and

---

[6] Elmer E. Cornwell, Jr., *Presidential Leadership of Public Opinion* (Indiana Univ. Press, 1965), p. 175.

[7] Theodore C. Sorensen, *Decision-Making in the White House* (Columbia Univ. Press, 1963), p. 49.

shaping public opinion. As we have mentioned (Chapter 9), public opinion is unstable and murky and hence always somewhat baffling and unpredictable. And when the people do speak with a loud, clear voice, the President may have to ignore it. Some programs may be basically unpopular and the President may have to move ahead in the absence of dependable support. He must know not only what to do but *when* to do it. Thus it is said that Kennedy's appeal for fall-out shelters in the 1961 Berlin crisis overcame the existing apathy over civil defense, "but it also unleashed an emotional response which grew to near-hysterical proportions (before it receded once again to near-apathy)." [8] And the President can often mobilize opinion behind *his own* actions without affecting the support for other men's actions. Thus a presidential appeal for support of a civil rights measure in Congress might influence many voters—but perhaps not the constituents of key southern Senators who might control the actual fate of the bill. In short, Presidents may not have much *selective* influence over public opinion.

Party Chief

A second main source of influence for the President is his political party. All Presidents since Washington have been party leaders, and generally the stronger the President, the more use he has made of party support. Men like the two Roosevelts, Wilson, Kennedy, and Johnson have fortified their executive and legislative influence by mobilizing support within their party. Yet no President has fully dominated his party, and the story of all Presidents, including the most famous, includes party failures as well as party triumphs. How does the President direct his party? Where does his influence stop—and why?

The President is wholly master of the party organization at the *national* level. He has no formal position in the party structure, but his vast influence as President over vital national policies and over thousands of appointments commands respect from national party leaders. President and party need each other. He needs the party's backing throughout the government in order to enact his program. The party needs his direction, his prestige, and the "political gravy" that flows from the White House.

The strings of the national organization all lie in the President's hands. Formally, the national party committee picks the national party chairman; actually the President lets the committeemen know whom he wants—and they choose him. Today the President can hire or fire national party chairmen much as he shifts department heads or even his own staff. Usually his pronouncements on national party policy are more authoritative than any party committee's, even more significant than the party platform itself. The great test of the President's influence in the party is his power to gain renomination if he wishes it, and all recent Presidents have met this test. Taft won renomination in 1912 despite the opposition of Theodore Roosevelt and the Progressives, as did Hoover in 1932

[8] *Ibid.*, pp. 46–47.

despite the depression, and Truman in 1948 despite sharp divisions in his party.

Yet the President's power over his party has limits. If he controls the national organization, he has only varied influence over the state and local parties. And his power often comes to an end precisely where he needs it most. He has little influence over the selection of party candidates for Congress and for state and local office. The reason is in part his *limited control* of *state* and *local organizations*; even more, it is that *party organizations* themselves do *not control their candidates in office*. They do not control them because most candidates, as we have seen, win office less through the efforts of the organized party than through their own individual campaigning in both the primary and general election. The situation of course varies from place to place. In cities with strong Democratic party leaders, like Chicago or Albany, a Democratic President may have great influence over the choice of candidates for Congress because (1) he has power over the machine, and (2) the machine picks faithful party men, elects them to office, and expects them to support the President. But most party organizations are not of this type. Because they are largely dominated by state and local leaders, because they may receive patronage from state and local governments, they can operate independently of the national leadership in Washington.

Franklin Roosevelt's "purge" of 1939 is a dramatic example of the limits of the President's power. Despite his own sweeping victory in the 1936 election and the lopsided Democratic majorities in Congress, Roosevelt ran into heavy opposition from many Democratic senators and representatives in 1937 and 1938. Angered by this opposition within the party, Roosevelt decided to use his influence to bar the nomination of anti-New Deal candidates in the 1938 congressional primaries. He announced that not as President but as "head of the Democratic party, charged with the responsibility of carrying out the definitely liberal" 1936 Democratic party platform, he would intervene where party principles were clearly at stake.

Roosevelt won a significant victory in New York City when he repudiated the anti-New Deal chairman of the House Rules Committee and helped a pro-Administration Democrat win nomination. But elsewhere—mainly in the South—Roosevelt was defeated. In Georgia he intervened against the venerable Walter George, a long-time Senate leader and a conservative. Speaking directly to Georgia voters, in the presence of Senator George, Roosevelt declared that effective government depended on cooperation between other party leaders and himself—"cooperation, in other words, within the majority party, between one branch of Government, the Legislative branch, and the head of the other branch, the Executive. That is one of the essentials of a party form of government." Senator George replied to the President that he "accepted the challenge." He easily won renomination against the man that Roosevelt had put into the primary race.

The moral is plain. The President's control over his party has limits, no matter how strong and skillful he is. He cannot, under most circumstances, reach into local party organizations and control their nominations or the policies of their leaders. The President of course is not helpless. He can give a candidate a good deal of recognition and publicity in Washington. He can grant—or deny—campaign assistance and even (indirectly) financial assistance. If he does campaign for his candidate, he will probably encounter less criticism for "invading" the district than Roosevelt did 30 years ago. But his practical influence is sharply limited.

The upshot is that the President often must bargain and negotiate with party leaders as he does with other independent power centers. In most cases he cannot employ the kind of party discipline available to a British prime minister. Lacking full support from the whole party, the President usually falls back on his own personal organization that originally enabled him to gain the presidential nomination. The most effective political organization in the United States in 1960 was not the Democratic party but the "Kennedy organization" led mainly by the Kennedy brothers and their staffs. Despite their own emphasis on their roles as party leaders, Presidents appeal to independents and even opposition party members to gain and hold power.

Thus President and party need each other—but they also conflict with each other. The President protects his own organization within the party, makes deals with the opposition party, plays down his own party when events compel him to "rise above partisan politics." The national party has its own long-term interests and traditions that may differ somewhat from White House concerns, and the party is not strong enough to elect a President by itself, nor is it able to mobilize support for the President's program from all its members on Capitol Hill. The bargaining, the cooperation, and the tension between President and party reflect some of the basic forces toward unity and toward diffusion in the pluralistic politics of America.

Chief Administrator

Over a century and a half ago, when Jefferson was President, the federal government employed 2,120 persons—Indian commissioners, postmasters, collectors of customs, clerks, tax collectors, marshals, lighthouse-keepers, and the like.[9] Today, by latest count, the President heads a colossal establishment of over 2.5 million federal civilian employees. These employees work in more than 1,800 units of federal administration—departments, services, bureaus, commissions, boards, governmental corporations, and other agencies. They work not only in Washington but throughout the world. Their salaries and wages alone amount to well over ten billion dollars a year.

All this is big government—the result of decades of sporadic expansion of government activities resulting in turn from the attempts of Americans to cope with big problems, such as armed threats at home and abroad, gigantic increases in population, technological changes, depressions, social unrest, and the interdependence and complexity of our national life.

The Constitution charges the President to "take care that the laws be faithfully executed." But the President can be only a part-time administrator, for his

[9] L. D. White, *The Federalists* (Macmillan, 1948), pp. 255–256.

other tasks demand most of his attention. Even if he could devote all his time to running the administrative establishment, it would still have to be organized for leadership and control. It is, of course, so organized. These more than 1,800 agencies are set up in great pyramids, each with its own hierarchical structure. Orders —theoretically at least—flow from President to department head to bureau chief down to the offices, services, and smaller units where they are carried out (see Chapter 18). This is the "line," so-called. The President, like all the top brass, is also assisted by a staff, whose job it is to advise and assist him in managing the administration. This *line* and *staff* organization—inherent in any large administrative unit, whether the Army, the General Motors Corporation, or the Veterans Administration—is worth a closer look.

The President and His Cabinet

Directly in line under the President are the executive departments: State; Treasury; Defense; Interior; Agriculture; Justice; Post Office; Commerce; Labor; Health, Education, and Welfare; and Housing and Urban Development. The State and Treasury departments were established in 1789, the government's first year of existence. The War Department was also set up that year, but, along with the Navy Department, it was reorganized into the Defense Department in 1947. Health, Education, and Welfare was created in 1953 out of a number of existing agencies, as was Housing and Urban Development in 1965.

The heads of these eleven departments form the President's Cabinet. Actually the Cabinet has always been a loosely designated body and it is not always clear who belongs to it. The U.S. Ambassador to the United Nations, for example, in addition to his other duties, also holds Cabinet rank. Heretofore it has made little practical difference to determine precisely who belongs to the Cabinet, but with the adoption of the proposed Twenty-fifth Amendment (see page 409) the Cabinet, defined in the amendment as "the principal officers of the executive departments," for the first time will be given a constitutional responsibility as a collective body.

It would be hard to find a more unusual or nondescript institution than the Cabinet. It has existed since early in Washington's administration; yet it is not even mentioned by name in the Constitution or, until the Twenty-fifth Amendment is accepted, is it referred to as a collective group. In recent years the Vice President has sat with the Cabinet, but even the chiefs of the great agencies such as the Veterans Administration are not members. However, Presidents often invite high officials—for example, the Budget Director or the chairman of the Civil Service Commission—to attend Cabinet meetings. Cabinet membership carries high prestige and most Presidents have met regularly with their Cabinets; yet the discussions are often casual, perfunctory, and even listless. Presidents have turned to their Cabinets for advice on a variety of matters; yet votes are rarely taken and the President can ignore Cabinet sentiments if he wishes. (Lincoln, finding the whole Cabinet opposed to him, could say with impunity, "Seven nays, one aye—the ayes have it.") Eisenhower tried to make the Cabinet a more important agency but with little success. Kennedy rarely used his Cabinet for major decisions. President Johnson has returned slightly to the Eisenhower pattern, but he uses his Cabinet meetings less to secure advice than to make sure that all Cabinet officials "understand" administration policies and hence can present a unified public front in behalf of the President's programs.

It is also difficult to generalize about how the President chooses his Cabinet members. The President handpicks his Cabinet members with little senatorial interference, yet they are not often the President's closest supporters. Occasionally a President will select a member of the opposition political party, as did Kennedy and Johnson when they named prominent Republicans as Secretary of the Treasury. Political considerations are paramount, and the President usually tries to give representation to various factions of his party—to its liberal and conservative wings, and to different sections of the country. Business, farm, and labor groups must be appeased in the appointment of the Secretaries of Commerce, Agriculture, and Labor respectively. Most Presidents face a dilemma in Cabinet-making. To choose a weak group may throw the whole administration into disrepute. To choose strong men with powerful political backing may lead to quarrels within the President's official family.

Nevertheless, the Cabinet has a character and importance of its own. Membership in it continues to be the ambition of many politicians. On occasion the meetings are devoted to matters of top policy. And the discussions gain from the fact that Cabinet members usually bring lengthy political and policy-making experience to bear on the problems at hand. Most administrative problems—at the White House level—are really legislative and political problems.

The Cabinet may in time become a team that both sustains the President and renders him more responsible to the people. But at present the American Cabinet bears little resemblance to the Cabinet described by Harold J. Laski as a "place where the large outlines of policy can be hammered out in common, where the essential strategy is decided upon, where the President knows that he will hear, both in affirmation and in doubt, even in negation, most of what can be said about the direction he proposes to follow."

What Cabinet unity there is tends to break down as soon as the members leave the Cabinet room. "In matters of prestige, partisan politics, and legislative relations alike," concludes a recent study, "the Cabinet as a collectivity has only a symbolic value, a value which readily disappears when the need for action supersedes the need for a show window. In the day-to-day work of the Cabinet member, each man fends for himself without much consideration for Cabinet unity. His survival, his support, and his success do not depend on his fellow members. His performance is judged separately from theirs. This condition is but another result of the combination of the centrifugal tendencies of our political system with the low degree of institutionalization which characterizes the Cabinet." [10]

[10] R. F. Fenno, Jr., *The President's Cabinet* (Harvard Univ. Pres, 1959), p. 247.

If the Cabinet's role is so limited, how does the President direct his far-flung administrative machine? He meets frequently with individual department and agency chiefs. Crucial decisions are sometimes reached in small, informal conferences between the President, the heads of two or three major departments and agencies, and staff members. Another factor in the President's control of administration is his ultimate power—subject to some limitations noted below—to hire and fire his main lieutenants as he deems fit. The Senate must ratify major appointments, but by tradition the President is allowed considerable freedom to pick his immediate subordinates—and to get rid of them.

Of a total federal civil personnel of about 2.5 million, the President, with the concurrence of the Senate, hires about 16,000. (He can appoint a limited number without Senate assent.) He chooses the department and agency heads who in turn employ other thousands of civil servants. Aside from his power to hire and fire, the President directly or indirectly controls promotions, demotions, and transfers, especially at the top levels. The Supreme Court, has upheld (in *Myers* v. *United States*, 1926) the power of the President to remove executive officers at will but has ruled that he has no constitutional power to discharge certain officials with part judicial and part legislative functions.

The single most important means of Presidential control, however, is the White House staff.

The Men around the President

Americans hear various stories about secret, invisible men who are said to control the President. Stories of a palace guard or a White House gang make good feature material for any newspaper columnist or TV commentator. The simple fact is that the President needs help. He must have advisers to help him handle the momentous questions that crowd into the White House. Much of his effectiveness turns on their loyal, disinterested, expert services.[11] So the Washington commentators are right in emphasizing the importance of the men who advise the President. But they are wrong when they imply that there is anything sinister or un-American about this practice. All Presidents from Washington to Johnson have relied heavily on their own staffs.

The President's immediate staff, the *White House Office*, does not have fixed form; indeed, part of its value lies in its flexibility and adaptability. Most Presidents, however, have an appointments secretary, who lets the right people see the President and keeps the others away; a press secretary, who handles publicity and deals with the scores of newsmen and photographers assigned to the White House; a correspondence secretary, who watches the President's mail and often drafts important letters for his chief; a legal counsel, who advises the President on a variety of matters of broad policy (not merely on legal matters); a diplo-

[11] See discussion in Louis Koenig, *The Invisible Presidency* (Holt, Rinehart and Winston, 1960); and Francis H. Heller, *The Presidency: A Modern Perspective* (Random House, 1960), ch. 2.

matic aide, who acts as the President's eyes and ears on the many-sided diplomatic front in Washington; military aides, who sometimes have policy as well as ceremonial functions; and several other key legislative, administrative, and political assistants. The President's top assistants may have far more influence than the equivalent Cabinet member; for example, the President may lean more heavily on his foreign policy assistants for an opinion on an urgent international matter than on the Secretary of State.

Just outside this inner circle of the White House Office are a complex of agencies and their heads who report directly to the President and are roughly grouped together in what is called *The Executive Office of the President*. Today in addition to the White House Office, the Bureau of the Budget, Council of Economic Advisers, National Security Council, National Aeronautics and Space Council, Office of Emergency Planning, Office of Economic Opportunity, Office of the Special Representative for Trade Negotiations, and Office of Science and Technology are located in the Executive Office of the President (see pages 403–406). Each of these agencies and their heads report directly to the President since their responsibility is to help the President carry out his duties.

Not all the assistants in the White House Office or in the Executive Office of the President are, of course, of equal influence, and sometimes men without any formal governmental post have direct access to the President. All our Presidents have drawn around them small groups of men in whom they have confidence: Andrew Jackson had his kitchen cabinet; Abraham Lincoln his personal advisers; Woodrow Wilson his Colonel House; Franklin Roosevelt his Harry Hopkins; Dwight Eisenhower his Sherman Adams; John F. Kennedy his brother Robert, who was also Attorney General; and Johnson his young aide Bill D. Moyers.

Why does the President lean so heavily on his personal staff and political advisers? Why does he not use the Cabinet or heads of vital departments for the day-by-day advice? The answer is simple. The staff can give the President the help he wants. It can do so because the President can, for the most part, juggle his staff membership and organization in a way that will be most helpful to him. He chooses the men he wants; he chooses them for their experience, their ability to work as part of a team, and above all for their loyalty to himself. Nowhere else—not in Congress, not in his Cabinet, not in his party—can he find the loyalty, the single-mindedness, and the team spirit that he can build, if he is a leader, among his close aides. Such a staff is important to him and to the country—so important that it has come to be widely accepted that the President should have the utmost freedom in organizing his staff as he wishes.[12]

Chief Legislator

Since the national government is divided into the executive, legislative, and judicial branches, many people assume that the President has only administrative functions, the Senate and House only legislative, and the judiciary only judicial.

[12] See Koenig, *op. cit.*, esp. ch. 6.

Actually, as we have seen, the essence of the system is an *intermingling* of powers. The President is a prime example. The Constitution grants him certain policy-making power—that is, legislative power. And a century and a half of national growth and recurrent crises have vastly increased that power. Today he and his aides ordinarily have more influence over national policy than any single congressman or group of congressmen; truly the President is chief legislator.[13]

The Constitution ordains that the President "shall from time to time give to the Congress Information of the State of the Union, and recommend to their Consideration such Measures as he shall judge necessary and expedient." From the start, strong Presidents have exploited this power. Washington and Adams came in person to Congress to deliver information and recommendations. Jefferson and many Presidents after him sent written messages, but Wilson restored the practice of delivering a personal, and often dramatic, message. Franklin Roosevelt in particular made personal appearances as a means of drawing the attention of the whole nation to his program—with the invaluable help of radio and camera. The President can also dramatize his policies by calling either or both houses of Congress into special session, although the legislators need not act if they do not wish to.

Less obvious but perhaps equally important are the frequent written messages dispatched from the White House to Capitol Hill on a vast range of public problems. Often mumbled indistinctly by a clerk, these messages may not create much stir at the moment, but they are important in defining the administration's position and giving a lead to friendly legislators. Moreover, these messages are often accompanied by detailed drafts of legislation that may be put into the hopper with hardly a change. These administration bills, the products of bill-drafting experts on the President's own staff or in the departments and agencies, may be mauled and mutilated by Congress—but many of the original provisions may survive unscathed.

The Power to Say "No"

The President can *veto* a bill by returning it with his objections to the house in which it originated. Congress, by a two-thirds vote in each chamber, may then pass it over his veto. If the President does not sign or veto the bill within ten weekdays after he receives it, the bill becomes law without his signature. If Congress adjourns within the ten weekdays, however, the President, by taking no action, can kill the bill. This is known as the *pocket veto*.

The veto is sometimes a strong, sometimes a feeble, weapon. Its essential strength lies in the ordinary failure of Congress to muster a two-thirds majority of both houses in favor of a policy that the President has told the people he dis-

[13] For description of the institutionalization of the President's legislative role see Richard E. Neustadt, "Presidency and Legislation: Planning the President's Program," *The American Political Science Review* (December 1955), pp. 980–1021.

likes. Yet a Congress that can repeatedly mobilize such a majority against a President can virtually take command of the government. Such was the fate of President Andrew Johnson. Faced after 1866 with a House of Representatives almost three to one against his reconstruction policies, he was virtually helpless as bill after bill was passed stripping him of his powers; in fact, he barely escaped being ousted from office. Eisenhower, on the other hand, though faced with a Democratic-controlled Congress for six of his eight years as President, had only two of his 181 vetoes overturned (most of them were pocket vetoes, however).

In ordinary times, Congress can manipulate legislation to reduce the likelihood of a presidential veto. For example, it can attach irrelevant but controversial provisions, called *riders*, to vitally needed legislation; the President must either accept or reject the whole bill, for he does not have the power to strike out individual items in the bill—that is, he does not have the *item veto*. Appropriations are a special case in point. In one appropriations bill the lawmakers may combine badly needed funds for the armed forces and a host of costly pork-barrel items, but the President must take or reject the whole bill. Governors of most states do have the power of item veto, and it has long been urged that the President should too. President Eisenhower and previous chief executives requested Congress to pass legislation providing for the item veto.

For his part, the President can use the veto power in a positive as well as a negative way. He can announce openly, or let it be known quietly, that a bill under consideration by Congress will be turned back at the White House door unless certain changes have been made. He can use the *threat* of a veto against some bill Congress badly wants in exchange for another bill that he wants. It is said that Franklin Roosevelt sometimes asked his assistants for "something I can veto" as a reminder to congressmen of the ever-present threat of this power.[14] But the veto is essentially a negative weapon, of limited use to a President who has a positive program. For it is the President who usually is pressing for action. It is Congress that has the real power to say "no."

Filling in the Details

Most federal legislation today deals with highly complex situations. A labor law, for example, may affect a great variety of industries, a number of different unions, all kinds of labor-management relationships, and diverse attitudes and traditions in different parts of the country. Agricultural legislation may deal with certain farm problems in general, but in practice the law affects big farmers and small ones, prosperous ones and marginal ones, cotton farmers, wheat farmers, applegrowers, and so on. No matter how wise Congress might be, it could not write a law that would automatically adapt itself to such different situations. Indeed, to try to do so would be to put the administrator into a strait jacket and to make the law unworkable. Hence Congress often must content itself with prescribing general standards and delegating to the Presi-

[14] Richard E. Neustadt, *Presidential Power* (Wiley, 1960), p. 84.

dent and administrators the job of *filling in the details of the laws*. Such sub-ordinate legislation is usually issued in the President's executive orders and in circulars, orders, rules, regulations, directives, and so on, issued by departments, regulatory boards, and other agencies.

Much of this delegation of legislative power involves making decisions within rather narrow limits. For example, a law may permit the President to alter tariff or minimum-wage standards to some extent, but only in terms of a standard laid down by Congress. Yet such standards vary greatly in precision. The Trade Agreement Act of 1934, its extensions, and especially the Trade Expansion Act of 1962, empower the President to make trade agreements with foreign nations lowering existing tariff rates by as much as 50 per cent and under certain conditions to abolish completely tariffs on some items. Other acts authorize him to suspend the eight-hour day for federal employees, to issue civil service rules, to prevent the export of certain raw materials.

An even wider delegation of legislative power is contained in the several Reorganization Acts. Since 1939 Congress by a series of measures has given the President authority to reduce and rearrange certain federal agencies through plans that come into effect 60 days after being sent to Congress unless disapproved by a majority of either the House or the Senate. Here is a delegation of power that amounts almost to a reversal of the usual formal relation between Congress and the Chief Executive. (Perhaps this is simply formal recognition of what in practice has come to be the relation between Congress and the President, the President initiating legislation, the Congress approving or vetoing it.)

Thus Congress, while setting objectives and standards, in practice allows the President not only to fill in the details but even to decide when action shall be taken. It is one thing to delegate the carrying out of specific provisions; it is something else to delegate the power to say when and whether a law will be invoked or applied. Why has Congress seen fit to delegate such sweeping powers? The reason is partly the willingness of the legislators to face the facts of modern life and to allow the President to do quickly and effectively what they could do, at best, haltingly and ineffectively. The reason is also that Congress is often so dominated by warring factions that it cannot find common ground on which to act. It defers to the President because he can act. The Constitution, it is true, prevents Congress from giving away its "essential" legislative powers. This is one of the reasons why the Supreme Court invalidated the National Industrial Recovery Act (*Schechter v. United States*, 1935). But so long as Congress lays down some kind of standard, the Supreme Court has been willing to approve extensive delegation of power.

Thousands of Legislators

Just as Congress must delegate legislative power to the President, so he must *re*delegate policy-making power to hosts of administrators down the line. Obviously the Secretary of State has a decided influence on policy, as do other department heads, along with bureau, division, and section chiefs. In a sense, there is no level in the administrative hierarchy at which discretion really ends. Even a secretary may make policy decisions on what matters or visitors her superior should turn to first—or at all. A sort of settling-down process sets in. Routine, noncontroversial decisions are made at the lower levels, vital and difficult ones at the top echelons. But at any time the most routine matter may be called to the public's attention, perhaps by a newspaper columnist or a congressman. Then the matter will be pulled out of the lower echelon and given consideration by a bureau or department chief—perhaps it will even go to the White House.[15]

In short, there are thousands of legislators throughout the government—and millions more outside, such as editors, lobbyists, and ordinary citizens, who exert pressure on a democratic government. Control of legislation cannot be diagramed neatly, with Congress on top, the President in the middle, and a pyramid of department, bureau, and division heads below. Rather, it is a *circular* system, with President and congressmen cooperating on some matters, fighting over others, and both influencing—and being influenced by—the administrators throughout the administration and by political forces outside.

Moreover, history and politics have bestowed on certain agencies a degree of independence from the White House. The Federal Bureau of Investigation in the Department of Justice, the Bureau of Reclamation in the Interior Department, and the Corps of Engineers in the Department of the Army are agencies somewhat insulated from the White House because of the prestige of their chiefs or the closeness of the agencies to blocs in Congress and to interest groups outside. The independent regulatory commissions (see Chapter 18) are a special case. Congress has delegated legislative (and judicial) powers to agencies like the Interstate Commerce Commission, the Federal Trade Commission, and the National Labor Relations Board in an attempt to keep partisan Presidents from interfering with their decisions. The President appoints the commissioners, with the consent of the Senate, but his power to discharge them is limited to that which Congress is willing to authorize. Hence they are often at liberty to make policies at variance with those of the administration. Here is one more set of little legislators in the Washington scene.

Thus, the President shares his legislative power not only with Congress but also with administrators in the executive branch that he himself heads. The extent to which he wields legislative power turns not only on his formal constitutional position and powers, but also on his political position and powers. His political powers turn on many factors. How effective is he in appealing to the public? To what extent can he dramatize official business? How magnetic is he on radio or television? How good is his timing? How active and articulate are his lieutenants—his Cabinet members and key agency heads? How close are his relations with congressional leaders? Can he mobilize public opinion on crucial issues? Does his influence reach into states and districts throughout the country so that he can "build fires" under recalcitrant legislators?

[15] Paul H. Appleby, *Policy and Administration* (Univ. of Alabama Press, 1949), p. 82.

Obviously a President's power turns to a great extent on his public prestige and standing. But in the daily task of getting things done in Washington, his effectiveness turns also on his *professional* reputation in a city peopled by thousands of expert politicians. These professional politicians are in Congress, the foreign embassies, the executive departments, the interest group association headquarters, the White House itself. Because the President's power, and his employment of it, is by far the most important single influence in Washington, these professionals must watch him narrowly. Does he carry through on what he promises people? Does he reward those who help him and punish—or at least withhold favors from—those who do not? How well does he bargain with other power centers? To what extent, in short, is he on top of the struggle for power, or submerged in it, or remote from it? The President's political skill and his political power are interrelated; Washington politicians must anticipate as best they can his ability and will to make the most of the bargaining advantages he has. Out of what others think of him and his power emerge his opportunities for influence with them.[16]

Chief Foreign Policy-Maker

The framers of the Constitution foresaw a special need for speed and single-mindedness in our dealings with other nations. The Constitution makes the President the exclusive spokesman for the United States. It gives him control over relations with foreign powers. It vests in him command of the two major instruments of foreign policy, the diplomatic corps and the armed services. It gives him responsibility for negotiating with foreign powers. It permits him to make commitments in behalf of the United States. The Constitution specifically assigns to the President the authority to appoint with the consent of the Senate all United States representatives to foreign nations, and to "receive ambassadors and other public ministers."

The power to appoint ambassadors and to receive them involves the vital power of *recognition*. The President has *complete discretion* to recognize or not to recognize new governments or states. In 1902 Theodore Roosevelt recognized the new state of Panama a few hours after a revolt had been staged with the help of United States forces. President Wilson withheld recognition from Mexican governments of which he disapproved, and President Hoover tried to restrain Japan by refusing to recognize its puppet Manchukuo. In 1933 President Roosevelt recognized the government of the Soviet Union, whose existence the United States had officially ignored for sixteen years. Presidents Truman, Eisenhower, Kennedy, and Johnson have withheld recognition from Red China.

Executive Agreements

The Chief Executive shares his treaty-making power with the Senate. Presidents have found an easy way, however,

---

[16] Neustadt, *op. cit.*, p. 60.

to bypass the Senate under certain conditions. This is the *executive agreement*. Well over half the international agreements signed by the United States have been achieved by this procedure, which involves simply an act by the President without any participation whatsoever by Senate or House. Some executive agreements have signalized famous events, such as the Boxer Protocol of 1901, the Atlantic Charter, and the "destroyer-bases" agreement. In addition to executive agreements based on the President's own constitutional powers, Congress often confers authority on the Chief Executive to make agreements with other nations. The reciprocal trade program is an important example. Of course, executive agreements, like treaties, may be set aside by the legislature. But unless they are, they seem to have much the same legal validity as treaties in the eyes of the courts. To be sure, treaties possess a "constitutional and moral control over the conscience and conduct of the American people," [17] but agreements made by Presidents with the prestige of a Franklin Roosevelt or a Dwight Eisenhower or a John Kennedy have an authority all their own. In the last twenty years Presidents have concluded about 2,000 executive agreements, compared to fewer than 300 treaties.

The famous destroyer deal with Britain was a striking example of the uses of executive agreements. In 1940 Britain urgently needed destroyers to protect her shores and convoys. President Roosevelt and his advisers, convinced that prompt action was vital, feared that the Senate might not act fast enough in ratifying a treaty, or might not act at all. By executive agreement the President traded fifty over-age American destroyers to the British in return for long-term leases on military and naval bases in the Western Hemisphere. The move won a good deal of popular support; presented with a *fait accompli*, Congress made no attempt to repudiate the agreement.

How much power does the chief executive have over foreign relations? The Supreme Court has repeatedly upheld strong presidential authority in this area. In the *Curtiss-Wright* case in 1936 the Court referred to the "exclusive power of the President as the sole organ of the Federal Government in the field of international relations—a power which does not require as a basis for its exercise an act of Congress, but which of course, like every other governmental power, must be exercised in subordination to the applicable provisions of the Constitution." These are sweeping words. Yet Congress itself does have significant power in foreign relations. It controls the funds to back up our policies abroad. It is a forum of debate and criticism. And it can "take back" powers that it has delegated the President in the realm of foreign affairs.[18]

The President has not only the authority but the capacity to act. For example, he has at his command unmatched sources of information. To his desk come facts channeled from the entire world. Diplomatic missions, military observers, under-cover agents, personal agents, and technical experts gather tons of material which

---

[17] George B. Galloway, *Congress at the Crossroads* (Crowell, 1946), p. 269.
[18] For a penetrating analysis of presidential-congressional relations in foreign relations, see D. S. Cheever and H. F. Haviland, Jr., *American Foreign Policy and the Separation of Powers* (Harvard Univ. Press, 1952).

Powers of the President as chief foreign policy maker. (Adapted from Blair Bolles, "Who Makes Our Foreign Policy?" By permission of the Foreign Policy Association, Headline Series No. 62.)

GRAPHIC ASSOCIATES

are analyzed by experts in the State Department and elsewhere. Since the President draws on the informed thinking of hundreds of specialists, his pronouncements have a tone of authority. The President and his experts are sometimes wrong, and many gaps appear in their information, but his sources of information give him a clear advantage over Congress.

Diplomacy, moreover, frequently requires quick action. The President can act swiftly; Congress cannot. Diplomacy often has to be secret; as Harold Laski has said, diplomatic negotiations, like a proposal of marriage, must be made in private even if the engagement is later discussed in public. The President can act secretly; Congress cannot. For these and other reasons, Congress has granted the President wide discretion on questions affecting foreign policy and military security. Today the President has leeway in such matters as controlling foreign trade and exchange, restricting imports and exports, barring the transfer of ships to foreign registry, buying military supplies without bids, restricting immigration—even aside from his vast constitutional powers as commander in chief in time of crisis (see next section). Congress thus has given up tremendous amounts of its power over foreign policy. It has done so not only because of the advantages the President enjoys in this sphere—the *unity* of his office, its capacity for *secrecy* and *speed*, and its superior sources of *information*. It has done so also because it has recognized that the United States must present a united front in dealing with other powers. It is hardly surprising, then, that the President looms large in world politics. A foreign observer has said that, in the capitals of other nations, "What is the United States going to do?" usually means "What is the President going to do?"

But the limits to presidential power should not be overlooked. Checks and balances operate in foreign policy-making and cannot be ignored. For example, Congress must *finance* the President's policies—a power of special importance when so much of our foreign policy consists of economic and military aid to other countries.

Commander in Chief

"The President shall be Commander in Chief of the Army and Navy of the United States," reads Section 2 of Article II of the Constitution. Even though this is the first of the President's powers listed in the Constitution, the framers intended that his military role be a limited one. As Hamilton pointed out in *The Federalist*, the President as commander in chief would be far less powerful than a king. The President's authority, Hamilton said, "would amount to nothing more than the supreme command and direction of the military and naval forces"; he would be a sort of first general and first admiral of the new nation. As things have turned out, however, the President has become far more powerful, as both the custodian and wielder of the nation's armed forces, than Hamilton foresaw.[19]

Today the President has wide powers as commander in chief during peacetime; in wartime his authority increases sharply.

In Peacetime

The President is supreme military commander. He appoints, with the consent of the Senate, all officers of the armed forces, from ensigns and second lieutenants to five-star generals. This is a vitally important function; it means that largely on the President's shoulders rests the job of determining whether the Grants, Pershings, and Marshalls will boss our military forces and plan the over-all strategy, or whether mediocre men will rise to the top. He can also dismiss the "top brass," as when President Truman relieved General MacArthur of his Far Eastern command in 1952. The President also has charge of such matters as defense plans and the disposition of forces, but these military decisions he generally leaves to the chiefs of staff and other commanders.

The President's peacetime powers are limited by the same factors that restrict

[19] E. S. Corwin, *The President: Office and Powers* (New York Univ. Press, 1957), p. 283.

him as chief administrator and chief legislator—the checks and balances within government and the strength of the opposition. Congress has the power to raise armies, to enact military regulations, and to appropriate money. In practice, Congress delegates a good deal of military rule-making to the commander in chief, but the legislators can revoke such grants if they wish. Congressmen also make full use of their right to investigate, to question, and to criticize, especially when the military chiefs come around requesting additional funds. Occasionally, members of Congress try to take a hand in strategic and diplomatic activities, often with unhappy results.

The Constitution delegates to Congress the authority to *declare* war (with the consent of the President), but the commander in chief in practice *precipitates* war. This supreme power of war*making* has been used by the chief executive time and time again. President Polk in 1846 ordered American forces to advance into disputed territory; when Mexico resisted, Polk informed Congress that war existed by act of Mexico, and a formal declaration of war was soon forthcoming. President McKinley's dispatch of a battleship to Havana, where it was blown up, helped precipitate war with Spain. In 1918, when no state of war existed between the United States and Russia, President Wilson sent American forces to Siberia to join Allied troops fighting the Bolsheviks. The United States was not formally at war with Germany until late 1941, but prior to Pearl Harbor President Roosevelt ordered the Navy to guard convoys to Great Britain and to open fire on submarines threatening the convoys. President Truman had no specific authorization from Congress in 1950 when he ordered American forces to resist aggression in Korea. Neither did President Eisenhower when he dispatched forces to Lebanon in 1958; nor did President Kennedy when he ordered a troop build-up during the Berlin crisis of 1961, or when he sent forces into Southeast Asia in the spring of 1962, or when he ordered a naval quarantine of Cuba in the fall of 1962; nor did President Johnson when he bolstered American forces in Vietnam in 1965 and sent troops into Santo Domingo.

Thus, in the context of modern times, Congress' formal authority to declare war has become obsolete. In Korean and South Vietnamese types of hostilities, formal declarations of war are no longer made. If a total war should come, the aggressor is unlikely to make a formal declaration of war before the bombs have fallen. After they have fallen a formal declaration of war is likely to be impossible, and if possible meaningless.

The President's War Powers

When war comes—short of a nuclear holocaust that would destroy organized society—the central need in a democracy is for unity, teamwork, discipline—in addition to the preservation of our basic liberties. The people want leadership and instinctively they turn to the President. He can tap a vast reservoir of power in planning broad strategy, raising military and industrial manpower, mobilizing the nation's economy.

In wartime the White House becomes GHQ for *governmental* as well as for military and industrial mobilization. Political power, which is ordinarily dispersed throughout the national government, is largely centered in the President. He becomes a sort of constitutional dictator. For example, he makes secret diplomatic agreements with foreign powers, far surpassing in importance many treaties that in peacetime would require senatorial consent. He authorizes the allotment of billions of dollars of funds appropriated by Congress. He takes final responsibility for crucial military decisions—as in the case of Roosevelt's decision in World War II to concentrate our armed might against Hitler before finishing off Japan. Constitutional forms are not abandoned, of course. They still exist—at least on paper. But in wartime the people become unified behind one goal—victory—and the solidarity of the people compels a unity in the government behind the President. Opposition congressmen may continue to snipe at the commander in chief's nonmilitary plans or policies, such as domestic economic policy or postwar peace goals, but they will not ordinarily obstruct his war program, even though they may lack confidence in it.

These vast powers of the President in wartime are not a recent development. It was Lincoln himself, struggling to overcome the crisis of civil war, who set the vital precedents for presidential quasi-dictatorship. Congress was not in session when Lincoln was inaugurated in March 1861; despite the emergency (or perhaps because of it) the new President did not even call Congress into session for four months. Congress during wartime has handed the President great chunks of authority. In World War I, President Wilson was given power to control the production, purchase, and sale of various fuels and foods, and to requisition them if he wished. In World War II, Congress again delegated vast authority to the President, who redelegated it to price, production, manpower, and transportation czars, who in turn were coordinated by super-czars. Mr. Roosevelt used Lincolnian as well as Wilsonian precedents. In 1942, when Congress refused to repeal a provision in the price control act that protected the farmers, the President demanded that Congress act within a month—or he would. This action of Roosevelt's has been called "a claim of power on the part of the President to suspend the Constitution in a situation deemed by him to make such a step necessary." [20] In any event, Mr. Roosevelt's maneuver worked; Congress meekly repealed the provision.

Under the Constitution, a wartime President can direct military operations (taking the field himself if he wishes), establish military government in conquered lands, and end hostilities by means of an armistice. Under authority likely to be granted by Congress, he can raise armies, lend or give money or goods to other countries, take over strikebound plants, requisition property needed for defense, ration goods and set prices, shift military functions from one agency to another, censor mail, control vital imports and exports, and so on. The list is long—and a compliant Congress will delegate even more emergency powers if the President requests them.

Certain forms of the Constitution may seem to be suspended. But two basic constitutional rights remain—or at least have remained in all our wars so far. One is

[20] E. S. Corwin, *Total War and the Constitution* (Knopf, 1947), p. 64; see also Nathan Grundstein, *Presidential Delegation of Authority in Wartime* (University of Pittsburgh, 1961).

the ultimate control of the President by the people. In no war so far—not in the Civil War when Lincoln had to campaign for re-election, nor in World War II, when Roosevelt had to do the same—have elections been suspended. And so far, despite certain restrictions, our basic liberties of free speech and free press have survived the hard test of war.

Chief of State

As commander in chief the President represents the whole nation. He is not directing the war for the benefit of Republicans or Democrats, of businessmen, farmers, or workers, of easterners, northerners, or southerners. He is acting for all the people. His military role, his ceremonial function, and his national responsibilities combine to make him a powerful chief of state representing *the whole nation and rising above the claims of majority or minority groups.*

Such was the role the framers of the Constitution hoped the President would fulfill. Looking on him as a sort of chief magistrate, they gave him judicial duties as well. These duties stem from the "power to grant reprieves and pardons for offenses against the United States, except in cases of impeachment." This *pardoning power* leaves the President a good deal of discretion. He can withhold a pardon altogether, or simply grant a reprieve (a delay in executing sentence), or lighten the sentence, such as by substituting life imprisonment for the death penalty, or grant a pardon subject to certain qualifications, or give a full pardon, which makes the offender, in the eyes of the law, as innocent as if he had never committed the offense. Neither Congress nor the courts can overrule a pardon. Since a President receives about 1,600 applications for pardons a year, he must lean heavily on advice from the Department of Justice. The pardoning power also includes *amnesty*, a device for pardoning a specific group of persons at one stroke. In the 1860's Presidents Lincoln and Johnson granted amnesties to southerners who had taken part in secession.

Even the Founding Fathers could hardly have foreseen the extent to which the President would become the *ceremonial* head of the nation. No doubt they expected him to receive ambassadors in the manner of a king, and to issue proclamations on matters of national, nonpartisan concern. But today his ritualistic role surpasses all this. He pitches out the first baseball of the season, buys Christmas seals, gets his Red Cross membership card, presses buttons that start big power projects, attends the Army-Navy football game, hurries to the scene of national catastrophes, speaks on the Fourth of July and other patriotic occasions, reviews parades, and receives delegations of Boy Scouts, veterans, 4-H members, students, and the like.

Often these actions may be part of a deliberate effort to humanize the man and the job, a reaching for popular support. But there is also the tendency of people to turn to him. Even in a democracy—perhaps *especially* in a democracy—the people need a leader. They need someone who will personalize government and authority, who will simplify politics, who will symbolize the protective role of the state, who will seem to be concerned with them. How else explain the gifts they shower on him, the tens of thousands of letters that pour into the White House, especially in time of crisis, the sense of private grief felt by masses of people when a President dies? The President is head of the political family; as a sort of father image he sustains a deep-seated desire for a leader and protector.

The role of the *national* leader, then, is vital in the United States. American acceptance of leadership does not rest essentially on blind worship, as in the case of fascists or communists, but on an awareness that in a competitive society the exceptional leader should be allowed to emerge from the mass, take a commanding position, and receive a vote of confidence (at least at the outset). Gunnar Myrdal, a brilliant Swedish social scientist who studied American society, has remarked on the "patterns of strong and competitive personal leadership and weak followership" in the United States. He sees our type of "individual leadership as a great strength of this nation, but the passivity of the masses as a weakness." [21]

All these factors, constitutional, political, and psychological, serve to accentuate the President's role as chief of state, as leader of the nation. Yet under ordinary conditions, the President as leader of *all* the people keeps running headlong into the President trying to act for *part* of the people.

The Double Role

The point is that the President's functions are fundamentally inconsistent with one another. On the one hand he is a party leader, the spokesman and representative of a popular majority more or less organized in the party that he heads. As party chief he not only directs the national party organization; he also uses his powers as chief legislator to effect the party's program. On the other hand, as commander in chief and chief of state he must act for *all* the people, regardless of group or faction. As chief administrator he must faithfully administer the laws, whether these laws were passed by Democratic or Republican majorities in Congress; yet in choosing his subordinates and in applying the law, he tends to think first of the interests of his popular majority.

How do the two Presidents live with each other? Sometimes the relationship is uneasy. For example, the President may wish to address the nation on an important problem. As *President* he is entitled to free time on the radio and TV networks. But if an election is in the offing, the opposition often charges that the President is really acting in his capacity as *party chief* and that his party should pay for the radio or TV time. The same question comes up in connection with the President's inspection trips, especially when he uses them as occasions for political talks and general politicking. The President is often accused, too, of executing laws in a partisan manner, of putting party regulars into administrative offices, of issuing executive orders favorable to the interests of the majority he leads.

During normal times, however, the President usually manages to combine his roles of chief of state and party leader without too much difficulty. The people

[21] Gunnar Myrdal, *An American Dilemma* (Harper, 1962), pp. 709–719. See also Eric Hoffer, *The True Believer* (Harper, 1951).

expect him to hold both roles, and he moves from one to the other as conditions demand. We are accustomed to seeing the President operate as national leader in conferring with a foreign envoy, only to don partisan clothing an hour later in conferring with party leaders. Late in the 1964 campaign, President Johnson was embarrassed by the arrest of a key aide on a charge of misconduct. During the same week, however, Communist China exploded a nuclear device and there was a shake-up in Soviet leadership. When the President went on television, it was to deal with these international events.

During times of emergency the problem tends to solve itself. A crisis at home or abroad demands leadership. People in both parties instinctively turn to the White House for decision and action. The President doffs his party robes and emerges as national leader or chief of state, as Kennedy did in 1962 when he suddenly broke off campaigning in the congressional elections and returned to Washington to take charge of the threat of Russian missile bases in Cuba. Two basic changes take place. First, as we have seen, the President assumes extraordinary powers. A serious crisis invariably results in an "increase in the prestige and competence of the President." [22] The President's hold on the people is so strong, his responsibility for action is so great, that Congress almost always follows where he wishes to lead. To meet the crisis he is given wide freedom of action. The normal checks and balances in government are largely suspended.

Even more significant, the normal opposition to the President vanishes—or at least breaks into fragments. To be sure, critics remain. But most of the criticism involves relatively petty matters—problems of mechanics, of methods, of procedures. There remains little organized opposition to the broad goals and programs that the chief of state champions. If any party or group opposes him, it may be suspected of seeking to sap the solidarity of the great majority. Such an opposition element may even be accused of lacking in Americanism. Under such conditions the opposition is likely to vanish.

All this may be inevitable. But is it healthy in a democracy? As chief of state, the President is responsible to the nation as a whole. Consequently, he has wide latitude in making his decisions and shaping his program. In a sense, his freedom is so great that it embarrasses him. He lacks the guidelines that help chart the course of the "party President." Some decisions he must make virtually alone. Being responsible to his majority is one thing. Being responsible to the whole people as chief of state is something else. This plight leads us straight into the general problems and prospects of the Presidency.

The Roles Combined: Presidential Government

Like mechanics going over an automobile, we have been looking first at one function of the Presidency and then another. But we must see the Presidency as a combined operation. A President cannot conduct foreign policy or direct his political party without consideration for his roles as chief administrator or chief

[22] C. L. Rossiter, *Constitutional Dictatorship* (Princeton Univ. Press, 1948), p. 217.

of state. The roles may fortify each other or threaten each other. Thus the President gains influence over Congress from his role as party chief, but his obligations to his party may handicap his efforts to "rise above politics" and appeal to the whole electorate as chief of state.

The whole Presidency, in short, is far more than the sum of its parts. We have created a system of *presidential government* that may go down in history as the most striking American contribution in this century to the art of governing large democracies. Presidential government is also more than the various Presidents who come and go. It is the perpetuation and enlargement of a set of great powers; it is also the institutionalization of a vast executive establishment. Each of these developments is worth a closer look.

Presidential Powers

The President of the United States assumes the following responsibilities:

1. Shares with Congress power over the 2.5-million man executive establishment but has been strengthening and centralizing his own authority in recent years;

2. Has a crucial initiative in policy-making and legislation and exercises a limited constitutional veto and a broader *political* veto over measures passed by Congress;

3. Is the chief economic decision-maker through his control over the budget, the federal financial institutions, and federal spending;

4. As chief politician runs his own party at the national level, establishes the ground on which the opposition party must debate and maneuver, challenges, curbs, cooperates, and bargains with major political interest groups, appeals directly to the mass public through the most powerful instruments of propaganda and persuasion;

5. Can on his own decision plunge the nation into little wars, big wars, or cold wars with or without any formal participation by Congress;

6. Almost wholly monopolizes power over foreign policy subject only to advice, occasional resistance over appropriations, and sporadic harassment from Capitol Hill;

7. As the chief personage, symbolic leader, and spokesman of the whole nation gains continuous publicity from the press and becomes a hero to millions of his supporters throughout the nation;

8. And combines all these powers in a single institution and a single person for maximum effectiveness in the mobilizing of influence at home and abroad.

The Presidential Establishment

Tourists passing by 1600 Pennsylvania Avenue often remark on the charm and simplicity of the White House. The mansion itself is small compared to those of many foreign potentates, and the administrative offices are neatly tucked away in the low west wing. Actually this west wing houses the President's main office (he also has a study on the second floor of the mansion) and the offices of about a dozen presidential aides who collectively, along with their chief, are the center of initiative, action, and decision in American government. And to the west of the west wing, across a small closed-off street, sits the main bureaucracy of the presidential office in a great old stone building, which used to house the entire State Department and military officialdom and now accommodates the bulk of the Executive Office of the President. The rise of this office is one of the great "success stories" of our governmental bureaus.

Hardly a century ago, President Grant had one private secretary, one stenographer, two executive clerks, one steward, and one messenger. He had to borrow generals from the War Department to help handle his duties. Presidents received little more office assistance until the emergency days of the New Deal, when Roosevelt, on the advice of administrative experts, expanded his personal staff. Under the Reorganization Act of 1939, the President established the Budget Bureau in the *Executive Office* of the President, which has come to embrace the central staff and administrative offices around the White House. Under Eisenhower, the executive office reached a peak in organization, numbers, and power. His "immediate" staff included the assistant to the President, three deputy assistants, two secretaries, three special counsels, three administrative assistants, nine special assistants to the President, and numerous outside advisers, expert consultants, and the like. Kennedy and Johnson kept this structure essentially intact. Today it numbers about 2,000 people.

We can understand this super-organization of the Presidency if we think of the Executive Office as a cluster of staff agencies that enable the President to take initiatives and make decisions in crucial sectors that cut across the separate bureaus and departments. Presidential aides insist that they are simply the eyes and ears of the President, that they make few important decisions, and that they never insert themselves between the Chief Executive and the heads of departments, who are usually Cabinet members. Presidential aides and staff assistants are supposed to keep out of the limelight and, in the old phrase, to have a "passion for anonymity." In fact, as long as they have the confidence and support of the President, the men in the White House are part of the mainspring of government. Hence we can see them as occupying central command posts from which they instruct, prod, and bargain with administrators and legislators.

Administrative Command Post. The key agency here is certainly the Budget Bureau. The Director of the Budget is not simply a glorified bookkeeper; he advises the President in detail on the real needs of the hundreds of government agencies, how much money they should be allotted in the budget, and what kind of job they are doing. He and his assistants pare down the appropriations requested by the agencies to fit the President's fiscal program. They also try to improve the planning, management, and statistical work of the agencies. The Bureau makes a special effort to see that each agency conforms to presidential policies in its dealings with Congress by requiring clearance for policy recommendations to the legislature.

A budget is many things, for it deals with the purposes of men in a highly political environment. "Serving diverse purposes, a budget can be . . . a political act, a plan of work, a prediction, a source of enlightenment, a means of obfuscation, a mechanism of control, an escape from restrictions, a means to action, a brake on progress, even a prayer that the powers that be will deal gently with the best aspirations of fallible men." [23] But to the President the budget is mainly a means of control over administrators who can "gang up" with one another or with congressional or state politicians to thwart the presidential program and the President's control. Through the long budget-preparing process (see pages 692–694) he uses the Budget Bureau as a way to conserve and centralize his own influence. But the Bureau is more than the instrument of any single President; it is a continuing institution that has systematized its own roles, procedures, and routines, and hence it works at the heart of presidential government.

If control of money is vital to the President, control of men would seem to be more important. But the President has not enjoyed full control over "hiring and firing" in the executive branch. The Senate, of course, has had the power to confirm or reject major appointments, and during the period of "congressional government" after the Civil War Presidents had to struggle to keep their power to appoint and dismiss. Major control of appointments in the middle and lower ranks was vested in an independent Civil Service Commission in an effort to thwart political or patronage appointments. In recent years Presidents have gained more control of personnel, in part as the result of the warnings of organizational experts that the Chief Executive cannot really be Chief Executive unless he can hire the top men he wants and establish personnel policies down the line. Under Lyndon Johnson the chairman of the Civil Service Commission has become the President's chief "talent scout" and in effect a member of the presidential staff.

Economic Command Post.   Ever since New Deal days the President has been responsible for planning against depressions and taking emergency action in the face of a sharp decline. This is not a constitutional but a *political* responsibility; a President knows that if he fails to act he will suffer the fate of Herbert Hoover, who was denounced for years by the Democrats for his alleged inaction during the Great Depression. The President's main staff unit in this area is the Council of Economic Advisers. The council was established under the Employment Act of 1946, which placed responsibility on the federal government for stabilizing the economy and maintaining high levels of employment. Composed of three members appointed by the President with the consent of the Senate, the council with the help of a small staff advises the President as to the health of the economy, analyzes existing programs, recommends new economic policies, and each year prepares for the President an economic report that enables him to review for Congress the nation's economic condition and set broad guidelines for the future. (The Budget Bureau recently has come to share some of the council's function

[23] Aaron Wildavsky, *The Politics of the Budgetary Process* (Little, Brown, 1964), p. v.

of formulating tax and credit policy and of working up programs for education, welfare, agriculture, and resource development.)

The council's role has changed since its early years. Originally it was expected to be a somewhat disinterested group of experts who would give the President independent advise and might even differ with him in public. The first chairman disputed with his colleagues and with the President and later resigned. Today the council is considered a staff arm of the President. While the members are supposed to adhere to professional standards, they are expected to support the President in testifying before Congress and to resign if they disagree with him (none has). Thus the council is one more example of the centralization of power under the President and of the institutionalization of the Presidency.

The council is an advisory, not an operating agency. In making economic decisions, the President also works with and through the Treasury Department, the Commerce Department, the State Department, the Federal Reserve Board, and many other agencies. He may also deal with interests and with the public directly, as in the cases of frequent presidential warnings against excessive wage and price increases, and of Kennedy's dramatic public attack on Big Steel for raising steel prices. In the face of a threatened strike that would cripple the economy, the President often invites labor and business leaders to the White House, where he can directly apply pressure for a settlement. But in dealing with economic czars, bureaucratic specialists, and academic economists the President is immensely strengthened by having a body of economic advisers who are loyal to *him*.

Political Command Post.   Since every act of the President has political implications, the whole executive office is a kind of political command post. But many presidential actions are political in the narrower sense: making major appointments, planning campaigns, dealing with his party's national chairman and headquarters, mobilizing and directing presidential influence on Capitol Hill. A number of White House aides specialize in these operations. Their role ranges from helping plan the President's legislative priorities and program to deciding what state and local politicians will be allowed appointments with the President (and thus allowed to gain headlines and prestige back home). Partly because the President often does not want to *seem* involved in politics even when he *is* involved, his political staff is the least formalized and institutionalized part of the White House.[24]

Security Command Post.   This is probably the most complex part of the President's decision-making apparatus. The President presides over the National Security Council, which is composed also of the Vice President, the Secretary of Defense, the Secretary of State, and others, and which is described on pages 565–566. The council has proved a useful place for discussing broad strategic matters and coordinating action, but it suffers from the fact that most members and participants in it represent departmental views and special agency interests. The President badly

[24] See Richard E. Neustadt, "Approaches to Staffing the Presidency: Notes on FDR and JFK," *The American Political Science Review* (December 1963), pp. 855–863.

needs a single adviser who can take the same kind of "presidential perspective" as the budget director or the economic advisers, and who can coordinate actions among agencies and expedite action.

This is the job of the Special Presidential Assistant for National Security Affairs, who directs a small, highly secret command post in the basement of the White House. This office is a tiny, combined Defense and State Department all in one. Like other staff men, this special assistant is supposed to coordinate action rather than make decisions on his own. But as the arm of the President, he does in fact take part in decisions that in turn are carried out in the departments. Much depends on the man who fills this job. Under Kennedy and Johnson that man was Mc-George Bundy, former dean of the Faculty of Arts and Sciences at Harvard. Bundy served the Presidents as a catalyst of ideas, coordinator of information, evaluator of proposals, and spur to sluggish agencies. His role was mainly advisory, but he often shared major decision-making with the Secretaries of State and Defense. It was expected that Bundy's departure from the White House might bring a decline in the importance of the "little Defense-State Department," but that in the long run it would continue to be of cardinal importance to Presidents.

This special assistant is especially useful to the President because he can coordinate actions not only in the big departments but also in a host of smaller ones that touch on national security matters. He can also work closely with other parts of the Executive Office, especially the Central Intelligence Agency, which reports formally to the National Security Council. However long Bundy may last in his job—and presidential aides are notoriously expendable—his function in the White House will continue, for it has become indispensable in enabling the President to keep control of national security policy.

The Paradox of the Presidency

The size and complexity of the presidential office, the President's mutually supporting and sometimes conflicting roles, the great powers and traditions of the office, the popular expectations of the office—all these lend force to President Johnson's remark that the Presidency is much bigger than any President. They also point up a paradox of the Presidency. On the one hand, the Presidency has become so institutionalized that we have in effect a system of *presidential government*—a heavily organized office with an enduring structure of power and an exacting set of constitutional duties and political obligations. Presidential government will continue no matter who may occupy the famous "oval office." On the other hand, the Presidency is vitally affected by the personality, background, temperament, loyalties, ideology, and working habits of the Chief Executive and the men around him. Hence we must look in the next chapter at presidential personality, tenure, and disability before we can assess the place of the President in democratic government.

15 THE PRESIDENT: PERSONALITY AND PROBLEMS

The assassination of John Kennedy demonstrated anew the decisive role of personality in the White House and the President's closeness to the people. It is estimated that the Sunday ceremonies in the Capitol Rotunda were witnessed in 85 per cent of the television homes of America, and that next day over 90 per cent of all American television sets—the highest total in television history— brought over 100 million people to the funeral and burial services. Television and films relayed the ceremonies to many millions abroad. Kennedy's death reached people who usually ignore politics and even top political personalities. "Mourning and sadness encapsulated children" as well as adults; there was about the same proportion among grownups and children of headaches, loss of appetite, trouble going to sleep, and the like.[1]

The sheer pressure on the President is a cruel test of his temperament, resilience, and sheer physical stamina. A student of the Presidency has listed the personal qualifications demanded by the job: [2]

> *Bounce.* The President must have that "extra elasticity" that enables him to thrive on a harsh diet of work and responsibility.
>
> *Affability.* "The President's heart must be not only stout but warm. . . . The Presidency is a people's office. . . ."
>
> *Political skill.* The President must be able to win popular support for his programs, to deal with powerful rivals in Congress, with party and interest-group leaders.
>
> *Cunning.* The President must know the arts of politics—how to dodge and maneuver, when to be silent and when to speak out, when to lead the people and when to follow them.
>
> *The newspaper habit.* If the President does not want to be isolated from the outside world, he must have direct lines to information and ideas beyond his immediate staff. A secretary's briefing is no substitute for reading several newspapers with different outlooks, and even glancing at the feature columns and cartoons.
>
> *A sense of history.* The President must feel responsible to the generations who bequeathed us a great nation and to the generations still to come.
>
> *A sense of humor.* At least two recent Presidents have said that they "could not have survived in office if they had been unable to laugh at the world and themselves."

If the Presidency is the "toughest job on earth," it is also the most powerful position in the Free World. Hence there are dangers inherent in an office on which so much depends: the President's hectic pace, physical exhaustion, exposure to potential enemies with inherently inadequate protection. His death or breakdown would make imperative a quick and effective transfer of power.

When a President Dies

What happens when the President dies or is unable to do his job? The Constitution provides that when the President is removed from office, dies, retires, or is unable to discharge the duties of his office, the Vice President takes office. The

[1] Roberta S. Sigel, "Death of a President and School Children's Reaction To It—An Exploration Into Political Socialization," Wayne State University, 1965.

[2] C. L. Rossiter, *The American Presidency* (Harcourt, Brace, 1956), pp. 135–137. The quoted material is taken directly from this illuminating volume, the other comment is condensed or adapted from it.

framers were wise to provide for a Vice President, for four Presidents have been assassinated and four have died in office. Congress has power to decide what official shall succeed to the Presidency if there is no Vice President. For a long time the law provided that the Vice President should be succeeded by the Secretary of State—and he by the next ranking Cabinet members in a prescribed order. In 1947, however, Congress provided that the Vice President would be succeeded first by the Speaker of the House, then by the president pro tempore of the Senate, and only then by the Cabinet members. This change was criticized for giving Congress too great a role in presidential succession.

If the President dies, the Vice President becomes not merely acting President but President in the full sense. What happens when the President is too ill to discharge his duties? Should the Vice President take over? This could be a critical question, for Garfield was disabled for almost three months before he died, Wilson for long periods during the last sixteen months of his second term, and Eisenhower on three separate occasions. But in no case did the Vice President take over, partly because he lacked the full confidence of the stricken President.

Congress has now faced up to these problems. Under the proposed Twenty-fifth Amendment, when the Vice Presidency becomes vacant, the President nominates a Vice President of his own choice, who takes office on confirmation by a majority vote of both houses of Congress. Thus the new Vice President is likely to be a man in whom the President has full confidence. When the President finds that he—the President—is unable to discharge his duties, the Vice President takes over as *acting* President. When the President feels that he can do his job but the Vice President and a majority of the Cabinet believe that he cannot, the Vice President becomes acting President. When a President has been disabled and believes that he is fit again, and when the acting President and a majority of the Cabinet disagree, the latter may notify Congress of their dissent and Congress must resolve the question. A two-thirds vote of both houses would be necessary to keep the Vice President as acting president; otherwise the President would resume full powers.[3]

The Vice President's Job

Under the Constitution, the Vice President serves as President of the Senate, voting only in the case of a tie vote. Since he temporarily delegates the job of presiding to some senator, however, his legislative duties are not very arduous. Usually his power in the Senate is limited. Lyndon Johnson as Majority Leader of the Senate was one of the most influential men ever to hold that post; as President of the Senate, despite behind-the-scenes activity, he ceased to be a major force in the Senate.

At first sight the Vice President might seem to be an ideal officer both to take some of the burdens off the President's shoulders and and to serve as a liaison with

[3] For a critical view of the new procedure on the ground that it would unduly decrease the role of Congress in presidential succession, see George D. Haimbaugh, Jr., "Vice-Presidential Succession: A Criticism of the Bayh-Celler Plan," *South Carolina Law Review* (No. 3, Vol. 17, 1965), pp. 1–19.

Congress, or at least with the Senate. In practice, however, at least until recently, the office of Vice President has never been utilized by the President. One of them once described the Vice President as "a man in a cataleptic fit. He is conscious of all that goes on but has no part in it." [4]

The basic trouble is that the President can brook no rivals and often prefers to work through men of his own choosing who are directly accountable to him and are subject to his dismissal. Although the President in effect chooses his Vice President, the latter is often picked to balance the ticket—that is, to represent a wing of the party other than that of the presidential candidate. If the presidential candidate is a liberal, the vice-presidential candidate often comes from the more conservative wing of the party; if the head of the ticket has a special appeal to the urban north, the number-two man will often be chosen to bring support from the rural south or west. In the face of the political fact that the Vice President represents a wing of the party that is usually not in accord with the President, attempts to make the Vice President something more than a figurehead have usually come to naught.

Recently, however, the Vice Presidency has taken on important duties. President Eisenhower's illnesses and President Kennedy's assassination dramatized the importance of the office. President Eisenhower deliberately attempted to give Vice President Nixon a more prominent role in his administration. Nixon chaired Cabinet committees and took highly publicized goodwill trips abroad. But despite the fact that the Vice President conscientiously deferred to the leadership of President Eisenhower, frictions developed and Vice President Nixon in effect did not have as much influence in the Eisenhower administration as did Eisenhower's own staff. President Kennedy also attempted to involve Vice President Johnson in the affairs of his administration. Still, the man who was but one heart beat away from the most powerful office in the free world had—while that heart still beat—less influence over public policy than a veteran United States senator, a chairman of a House Committee, or even a confidential assistant to the President.

Having suffered some of the frustrations of the Vice Presidency, Lyndon Johnson resolved to make his own Vice President a key political and legislative associate. He knew that he must pick a 1964 running mate who would be completely loyal to him and hence could claim his complete confidence. Johnson rejected Robert F. Kennedy, despite the young Attorney General's appeal as inheritor of the Kennedy name and tradition, and chose his old associate in the Senate, Hubert H. Humphrey. The President went farther. According to one report, he made Humphrey understand before offering him the job that the Vice President must have no public disputes with the President; that he must clear his speeches with the White House; that he must not lobby for special interests; that he could disagree with the President before a decision was made but afterwards must support him; and that he must share secrets with the President that the President could not even tell his wife.[5] Humphrey accepted these conditions, and later received major assignments

[4] E. S. Corwin, *The President: Office and Powers* (New York Univ. Press, 1957), p. 73.
[5] Theodore H. White, *The Making of the President, 1964* (Atheneum, 1965), pp. 285–286.

from his chief. Whether President and Vice President can become full partners amid the tempestuous, divisive, and constantly changing political pressures is today a fascinating study in American government as well as in political personality.

Kennedy, Johnson, and the Presidency

Perhaps more than any of his predecessors, John F. Kennedy brought definite views of the nature and exercise of power to the Presidency, "I am no Whig," he said the year before his election; he believed, unlike the Whigs, that the Presidency must be the energizing and unifying force to make the divided governmental system work. And more than any other President, Kennedy campaigned for the office on the basis of how the President should exercise his power as well as what policies he would pursue.

The President, he told a crowd in Queens during the campaign, is "the center of action under the American constitutional system." He pictured the "five different responsibilities of a President of the United States: commander in chief, the party leader, the legislative leader, the leader in foreign policy, the leader in domestic policy. . . ." [6] He was critical of President Eisenhower for failing to exploit the full sweep of presidential power, for delegating too much authority to subordinates, for slighting other political resources of the office. He said during the campaign:

> I want to be a President who has the confidence of the people—and who takes the people into his confidence—who lets them know what he is doing and where we are going, who is for his program and who is against. I hope to set before the people our unfinished agenda—to indicate their obligations—and not simply follow their every whim and pleasure.
>
> I want to be a President who acts as well as reacts—who originates programs as well as study groups—who masters complex problems as well as one-page memorandums. I want to be a President who is the Chief Executive in every sense of the word—who responds to a problem, not by hoping his subordinates will act, but by directing them to act—a President who is willing to take the responsibility for getting things done, and take the blame if they are not done right. . . .
>
> I am not promising action in the first 100 days alone—I am promising you 1,000 days of exacting presidential leadership. [7]

Kennedy as Chief Administrator

On taking office President Kennedy was aware of the two basic patterns of presidential management of the executive branch. One was best typified by Franklin D. Roosevelt. Long experienced

[6] "Speeches, Remarks, Press Conferences, and Statements of Senator John F. Kennedy, Aug. 1 through Nov. 7, 1960," *Final Report* of the Committee on Commerce, U.S. Senate, 87th Cong., 1st Sess., 1961, p. 904. This volume, and its counterpart on Nixon's speeches, is an invaluable source.

[7] *Ibid.*, p. 910.

in government and politics, Roosevelt had not been content to operate as a chairman of the board. He had administered the office in a highly personal way; he often acted through his staff assistants rather than department heads; he pounced on administrative details far down the line; he acquired information from a "myriad of private, informal, and unorthodox channels and espionage networks" rather than standard official sources; and instead of delegating power clearly and neatly, he liked to "keep grants of authority incomplete, jurisdictions uncertain, charters overlapping." [8]

The other pattern was well exemplified by President Eisenhower's methods. As perhaps befitted a military man, the General liked to follow orderly procedures, to avoid tangled lines of communication and delegation, to "go through channels." He believed in a strong staff system that would take much of the load off his own shoulders. He appointed Sherman Adams, a former governor of New Hampshire, as "the" Assistant to the President—in effect a powerful chief of staff overseeing the executive department.

Kennedy greatly preferred the Roosevelt technique, not because he liked disorder or confusion, but because he wanted, whenever possible, to keep power and policy in his own hands. He had read with favor a study of presidential power by a young Columbia political scientist, Richard Neustadt, who contended that the President must not let power slip from his own hands, that he must not become too dependent on his staff, that he must check official reports against private reports, that he must not become a prisoner of his office.[9] By building competition and diversity and even disorder into his administration, the President would be in a better position to be the real instead of the titular head of the administration.

The new President moved quickly to establish his authority as Chief Executive. "The capacity to act decisively at the exact time action is needed," he said ten days after his Inauguration, "has too often been muffled in the morass of committees, timidities, and fictitious theories which have created a growing gap between decision and execution, between planning and reality. . . ." He spurned suggestions that he should have a "First Assistant" or a "Chief of Staff" like Adams; rather he took care that his staff aides should have essentially equal power and access to his office. He abolished a host of coordinating committees and interdepartmental boards, begun in previous administrations, that he felt stifled action. Instead of meeting frequently with the Cabinet, he dealt with department heads as an *ad hoc* group of administrators meeting irregularly on matters of mutual concern.

Observers differed over the effectiveness of Kennedy's technique of administration. Some contended that he was taking too much on his own shoulders, that his personal intervention in administrative matters left his officials perplexed and sometimes at a loss as to what to do, that it was difficult to know sometimes whether the department or the White House was responsible for decisions. The failure of the effort to back up the invasion of Cuba in 1961 was blamed by some

[8] Arthur M. Schlesinger, Jr., *The Coming of the New Deal* (Houghton-Mifflin, 1959), pp. 522–523.
[9] Richard E. Neustadt, *Presidential Power* (Wiley, 1960).

on tangled lines of communication and decision making between the State and Defense Departments and the White House. Others felt that the Kennedy system had proved itself. The White House was able to move speedily and simultaneously on many fronts. While there was little of the genial disorder and creative disarray that characterized the Roosevelt administration, an effective team of White House aides working together closely accomplished miracles of output. No invisible staff men or anonymous department officials were running the government behind the scenes; the President had the power and he assumed the credit or blame, as in the aftermath of the 1961 Cuban crisis. There was never any real question of who was in charge. It was the President—quite rightly, perhaps, for of all the thousands of administrators he was the only one elected by, and directly accountable to, the people.

Kennedy as Chief Legislator

General Eisenhower had come to the White House in 1953 with a genuine regard for Congress and a respect for the tradition of governmental checks and balances. But soon disillusionment set in. Congress, though Republican-controlled, began opposing the administration in many time-honored ways—investigating it, holding up presidential appointments (in the Senate), cutting down requested appropriations, voting down White House measures. Later in his administration, with the Democrats controlling Congress, the President took somewhat stronger personal leadership, calling publicly for his legislative program and wielding his veto power freely against some measures passed by the Democrats. But he rarely threw himself into the thick of the battle on Capitol Hill, preferring to leave the in-fighting to friendly congressmen and agency chiefs.

Kennedy too had somewhat mixed views about the President's role as legislator. "I believe that our system of checks and balances, our whole constitutional system, can only operate under a strong President," he said in 1959. "The Constitution is a very wise document. It permits the President to assume just about as much power as he is capable of handling. If he fails, it is his fault, not the system's. I believe that the President should use whatever power is necessary to do the job unless it is expressly forbidden by the Constitution. . . ." [10]

As Kennedy faced his legislative tasks after his election, the political arithmetic of Congress seemed to him to call for presidential caution. In the 1960 congressional elections the Democrats had lost 22 seats in the House—most of them held by liberals and moderates. The lineup of 263 Democrats and 174 Republicans would give him a clear Democratic party majority, of course, but almost 100 of the Democrats were southerners largely hostile to his program. The President decided on a policy of moderation and restraint. To be sure, he threw his weight into the battle to enlarge the Rules Committee (see pages 434–435), but he made it clear

[10] James M. Burns, *John Kennedy: A Political Profile* (Harcourt, Brace & World, 1959), p. 275.

to the southerners that he would not demand extensive civil rights legislation, at least for a time. And he withheld strong backing from Senate liberals in both parties who were trying to modify that great barrier to civil rights measures, the filibuster.

The President's legislative tactics in general followed this pattern: First of all, he made clear, through frequent messages to Congress, addresses to the people, comments in press conferences, and specific drafts submitted to Congress, just what he hoped that Congress would do. The President's legislative aides then helped mobilize congressional support, mainly through persuasion rather than pressure. While there were few outright "deals"—that is, exchanges of White House favors for specific votes—the White House aides were able to hold out the expectation of recognition on matters close to a congressman's heart: funds for projects back home, patronage, defense contracts, administration help on bills especially important to the congressman, and the like. Meantime, the President tried to create a climate of friendly relations with Congress. The President's basic tactic in dealing with Congress, then, was to use both the carrot and the stick—but much more the former than the latter. He bargained and compromised with the members of Congress rather than trying to high-pressure them.

The over-all result of President Kennedy's first congressional session was mixed. On policies that aroused a bipartisan consensus over accepted types of social and economic reform—wages and hours, public housing, social security, development of depressed areas—the Administration won passage of major bills. But on "New Frontier" efforts to "get the country moving forward" in new directions, the President made little progress. General aid to education, the financing of medical care for the aged through social security, extensive tax reform, stand-by powers for the President in coping with the threat of recession, orderly urban and transportation development, long-term financing of foreign aid, and other measures were locked in congressional committees, or stalled in the labyrinthine legislative channels, or defeated on the floor.

Kennedy's experience with the congressional sessions of 1962 and 1963 was even more disappointing to the administration. He suffered defeats on administration measures to create a Department of Urban Affairs and Housing with Cabinet status; once again on health insurance for the aged financed through social security ("Medicare"); major tax reform (a limited tax revision program passed); supply-management controls for wheat, corn, and other feed grains, combined with a long-range program of cropland retirement; and general federal aid to education. The President won two striking victories, however, in the passage of the Trade Expansion Act and of a large program of grants for higher education; the education bill was signed into law by President Johnson after Kennedy's assassination.

What verdict could be rendered on President Kennedy as Chief Legislator? Some felt that the President's tactics of caution and compromise had been wrong, that he should have aroused the country to put pressure on Capitol Hill. Others believed that the administration had done a good job considering the circumstances, but that "blarney, bludgeon, and boodle," as it was called, was not enough.

The one-party districts in the rural North and South, the seniority system, fili-buster, the Rules Committee, and all the other impediments in Congress were simply too strong for a President dealing with a power system beyond his power to overcome: a coalition of the "Congressional Republican" and the "Congressional Democratic" parties on the Hill. Such a formidable power system, some felt, demanded not more manipulation and bargaining, but a frontal assault by the President to clear away the institutional barriers to his program.

Whether the President would try to cope with his legislative problems by traditional tactics of personal influence, or by new political strategies, depend in part on his own role as leader of the "presidential" Democratic party.

Kennedy as Party Leader

Of all the presidential roles, Kennedy had probably conceived that of party leader with the least clarity and certainty. To be sure, he was fully prepared to take leadership of the national Democratic party as soon as he won the nomination. This he did by seeing that John M. Bailey of Connecticut, an early supporter, was appointed national chairman. And he stated in the campaign, "I do not intend, if successful, to ignore party leadership or party responsibility—and I do not intend to forget that I am a Democrat." But in almost the same breath he said, "I have no wish to be known as a narrowly partisan President, or as a private interest President—I want to be President of all the people." [11] Once he took office, moreover, he faced practical difficulties in playing his part as party leader.

For one thing, Congress' Democratic majority was not a *Kennedy* majority. Hence it was often necessary to appeal to liberal (or "presidential") Republicans to supply the necessary margin of votes. But the more Kennedy played up his role as Democratic leader, the more he might antagonize such support. In the second place, the President knew that he would face many foreign crises, for the handling of which he would need bipartisan support in Congress and among the electorate.

This ambivalence over party leadership was evident throughout Kennedy's three years in office. He worked closely with Democratic party leaders in Congress, attended many party rallies througout the country, campaigned in support of Democratic candidates in the 1962 elections, and gave firm support to major pledges that the Democratic party had made in its 1960 platform. On the other hand, he did little to strengthen the party at the grass roots, he gave a good deal of recognition to friendly Republican congressmen, and in general he greatly stressed his role as national leader over that of party leader.

What kind of verdict will history render on Kennedy as chief politician? Two years after his death only tentative judgments are possible. His own campaign for the Presidency may well be rated as one of the best planned, most expertly conducted, and best organized political operations in American political history.

[11] "Speeches of Senator John F. Kennedy," *op. cit.*, p. 910.

His legislative tactics on Capitol Hill will probably be considered less successful. Some will conclude that he was too cautious and deferential toward Congress and the congressional structure of power, though as John P. Roche noted, his elaborate solicitude toward Congress "was that of a kindergarten teacher who suspects that one of the children has secreted a hand grenade on the premises." On the other hand, Kennedy's critics will have to demonstrate how he could have pursued any other tactic with a Congress that was hostile to most of his bolder proposals. Doubtless it will be his capacity to inform the people, to marshal public opinion, to time his major actions, to move quickly and yet prudently in emergencies, and to conduct his office with style, humor, and zest that will secure Kennedy's reputation among the great Presidents.

Johnson: A New Political Style?

Lyndon B. Johnson's sudden elevation to the Presidency in November 1963 brought to 1600 Pennsylvania Avenue a man of considerably different political background from John F. Kennedy's. While Kennedy had used the Senate mainly as a springboard to the Presidency, Johnson had carved out his political reputation in the upper chamber. He had been, above all, a "Senate man." As Democratic Majority Leader, he had shown a remarkable capacity to exert personal influence over Democratic senators of highly diverse points of view, and over some Republicans. He had been willing, during Eisenhower's Presidency, to cross party lines on occasion in order to get measures enacted, despite the protests of some liberal Democrats who accused him of deserting the Democratic national platform. He prided himself on being a moderate Democrat who was able to unite the liberal and conservative factions of his party.

In some respects Johnson infused the Presidency with his own personality and methods. As legislative and party leader, he relied heavily on numerous face-to-face conferences with a great variety of politicians, and on telephone calls to key people, conducted throughout the day and into the night, from his office, his limousine, and even his helicopter. He tried to use his old "Senate persuasiveness" on committee chairmen and other leaders of Congress. He also resisted any attempt to tie him to any definite political label or philosophy. As a senator he had said in 1958: "I am a free man, an American, a United States Senator, and a Democrat, in that order. I am also a liberal, a conservative, a Texan, a taxpayer, a rancher, a businessman, a consumer, a parent, a voter, and not as young as I used to be nor as old as I expect to be—and I am all these things in no fixed order." The new President adhered to this position, at least at the start of his administration.

Still, the continuities of the Presidency as an institution seemed even more significant than the change of personality in the White House. For one thing, as a Democrat, Johnson inherited Kennedy's problems and policies. He quickly made it clear that he would support the Kennedy program in Congress. He called for early passage of the tax reduction and civil rights bills, and endorsed many other Kennedy proposals: expanded social welfare programs; Medicare; general federal aid to education; less discriminatory immigration barriers; youth employment legislation "to put jobless, aimless, hopeless youngsters to work on useful projects"; stepped up housing and urban renewal programs. President Johnson spoke out for fiscal policies that would stimulate the economy and reduce unemployment. To be sure, he called vigorously for government economy, especially in the defense establishment, and for a smaller budgetary deficit, but these were policies that Presidents had preached (if not always practiced) for many years.

The new President also inherited leadership of the "presidential Democratic party." Although he hoped to unify the two major Democratic wings or parties, it was clear that he would follow the strategy of Franklin Roosevelt, Harry Truman, and John Kennedy in appealing to labor, consumer, and ethnic blocs in the big urban states. It was not difficult for Johnson to make this appeal, for he had started political life as a protegé of Franklin Roosevelt, and he had long reflected some of the Populist, "anti-Wall Street" feeling that was strong in Texas earlier in the century.

Johnson as Chief Politician

Like Kennedy, Johnson had spent almost all his adult life in politics and knew the mazes and pitfalls of the political jungle. The political style of the two men was quite different. Kennedy was urbane, sophisticated, and sometimes even a bit detached as he went about his political chores, while Johnson seemed so forceful, earthy, and transparently political that some criticized him for being little more than a wheeler-and-dealer and arm-twister, even in the White House. But whatever the differences in style, the political aims of the two Presidents were similar—to gain support from Congress and the voters for a huge program of legislation and executive action, and to win another popular mandate in the next election.

Johnson inherited a host of Kennedy measures that had become stalled in Congress. The new President made the customary public obeisance to Congress. "As one who has long served in both houses of the Congress," he told a joint session five days after first taking the oath of office, "I firmly believe in the independence and the integrity of the Legislative branch. And I promise you that I shall always respect this. It is deep in the marrow of my bones." But behind the scenes Johnson and his legislative aides marshaled influence on Capitol Hill as vigorously as his strongest predecessors. In the 1964 and 1965 sessions of Congress the new President scored a series of stunning legislative victories: two major civil rights measures, school aid, Medicare, a revised immigration policy, aid to Appalachia, highway beautification, federal aid to arts and humanities, establishment of a new Department of Housing and Urban Development.

How much of Johnson's success on Capitol Hill was due to his special political skills and experience, how much to the basic political situation? Washington correspondents made much of the President's "feel" for Capitol Hill, his old friendships with congressional leaders, and his uncanny knack of knowing just what combination of charm, argument, pressure and various forms of "political persuasion" would win over an influential congressman or senator. Others contended that Johnson was lucky in the time that he came to power, for civil rights and other social legislation was about to achieve a breakthrough under Kennedy, and that Kennedy's martyrdom accentuated public support for his major measures. It was agreed on all sides that the most decisive factor was the outcome of the 1964 congressional elections, for Goldwater had pulled down to defeat a number of Republican congressmen who were replaced by liberal Democrats. Hence for the first time since the election of 1936 a Democratic President won an effective majority for his program. The question remained whether Johnson could continue to make good use of his majority on Capitol Hill, or whether he would meet the fate of his political hero, Franklin Roosevelt, who failed to mobilize his big Democratic majority of 1936 behind his New Deal programs.

Johnson as Chief of State

Like all Presidents, Johnson somehow managed to appear to "rise above politics," to be "President of all the people," even when he was most partisan and political. Yet no President dedicated himself more ardently and persistently to a concept—the Great Society—that would represent a consensus of all interests. Johnson's view was that if only people would respond to his plea "Come, let us reason together," agreement would be reached and forward action taken. His skillful conduct of the presidential transition during the sad days of November and December 1963; his effort to cut federal spending and taxes at the same time that he expanded social welfare programs; his attack on poverty and discrimination; his ability to win extensive support from business; and above all his colossal luck in running against a doctrinaire conservative in 1964—all these fortified Johnson's politics of consensus.

Johnson used consensus politics skillfully to win support for his program. In the 1964 election he pre-empted the middle of the road and gained the great bulk of the independent vote as well as a large fraction of the normally Republican. He won sizeable Republican backing on Capitol Hill for his legislative program. He showed a genius for discerning the formulas that united people, as in his White House settlement of issues that had divided railway executives and labor for decades. Himself a product of the South and West, he made perhaps the strongest presidential appeal in history to the Negroes, ethnic groups, and industrial workers of the North. Abroad he maintained the bipartisan foreign policy that had long enjoyed support from both presidential parties. Two years after Johnson's proclaiming of the Great Society, some were predicting a new "Era of Good Feeling" for Americans.

Others were less sure. Consensus politics, it was argued, was essentially a kind of brokerage politics that consisted of buying off major groups with small concessions, rather than moving boldly toward a well-defined great society. An attempt to find agreement on major policies would mean a loss of excitement and imagination and experimentation in national government. Experience suggested that in the long run consensus was impracticable as well as undesirable—in the long run people will divide over major issues and Presidents must take a stand. "The experience of past Presidents," one observer summed it up, "suggests that eventually Johnson will have to make unpleasant choices that may cost him some of his broad-based support. He is a master of the political balancing act, but, for an activist President, there are limits to the politics of harmony—and Johnson, on the basis of his record, not to mention his restless temperament, is clearly an activist President. Moreover, no President elected on a party ticket and dependent on the support of interest groups can wholly escape a partisan identity.

"But the public will to have a nonpartisan President is very strong. . . . By temperament, by experience, by the circumstances of his first coming to the presidential office, and by the nature of the election that confirmed him there, President Johnson seems to be unusually alert both to the need and to the possibility of reconciling the two contradictory roles incorporated in his office." [12] In short, it was conceivable that the aims and personality of the President himself might be the weakest ingredient in the presidential politics of consensus.

Is the Presidency Becoming Too Powerful?

Lyndon Johnson's vigorous exercise of presidential power sharpens the old question: How much power *should* the President have? This question is hard to answer because we cannot be certain just what powers the President *does* have. The Constitution, as we have seen, is somewhat vague on the matter. It seems to grant the President a broad executive power without defining that power. Some scholars point out that the Constitution vests "the executive power of the United States" in the President but gives Congress only the legislative power "herein granted." They argue that the President has wide powers to protect the public interest in emergencies without specific legal authority or even at the cost of over-riding existing laws. Despite considerable controversy over the matter, and the Supreme Court's rebuff of President Truman's attempt to exert "inherent powers," there seems to be a kind of "inherent power" in the Presidency, vast but undefined, that an aggressive President could exploit in time of crisis. The President also has a good deal of undefined power as the chief maker of foreign policy—a situation that has advantages in a crisis, but that makes it difficult to define presidential power.

[12] C. Peter Magrath, "Lyndon Johnson and the Paradox of the Presidency," *The Yale Review* (June 1965), p. 493.

Theories of Presidential Power

Presidents have had different ideas about their job. Two of them have given their views with great frankness. Theodore Roosevelt wrote in his *Autobiography* that he had insisted on:

> . . . the theory that the executive power was limited only by specific restrictions and prohibitions appearing in the Constitution or imposed by the Congress under its Constitutional powers. My view was that every executive officer, and above all every executive officer in high position, was a steward of the people. . . . I declined to adopt the view that what was imperatively necessary for the Nation could not be done by the President unless he could find some specific authorization to do it. . . . Under this interpretation of executive power I did and caused to be done many things not previously done by the President and the heads of the Departments. I did not usurp power, but I did greatly broaden the use of executive power.[13]

This has been called the *stewardship* theory of presidential power. William Howard Taft, on the other hand, took a rather narrowly *constitutional* view of presidential power. He wrote in 1916:

> The true view of the Executive functions is, as I conceive it, that the President can exercise no power which cannot be fairly and reasonably traced to some specific grant of power or justly implied and included within such express grant as proper and necessary to its exercise. Such specific grant must be either in the Federal Constitution or in an act of Congress passed in pursuance thereof. There is no undefined residuum of power which he can exercise because it seems to him to be in the public interest. . . .[14]

Franklin D. Roosevelt's conception of his powers—sometimes called the *prerogative theory*—was that the President in the face of emergencies had the same power that John Locke once argued that kings had—the power, in Locke's words, "to act according to discretion for the public good, without the prescription of the law and sometimes even against it." [15] The destroyer deal, for example, conflicted with several laws.

Is the Presidency Powerful Enough?

Now for the other side of the ledger. The President's power is so great that it is easy to forget all the limits on his freedom. We have seen that as chief administrator and as chief legislator:

[13] T. R. Roosevelt, *An Autobiography* (Macmillan, 1913), pp. 388–389.
[14] W. H. Taft, *Our Chief Magistrate and His Powers* (Columbia Univ. Press, 1916), p. 139.
[15] E. S. Corwin, *The Constitution and What It Means Today*, 10th ed. (Princeton Univ. Press, 1948), pp. 84–85.

The President must share *policy-making* power with congressmen, administrators, and others.

He must share his *treaty-making* power with the Senate.

He must share his *appointing* power with congressmen, especially senators.

His power to *dismiss* agency heads is limited.

He is powerful in his *party*, but by no means all-powerful, particularly at the lower echelons.

Above all, the President is held in leash by the political situation in which he operates. No matter how strong a leader he may be, he is not a free agent. Not only must he deal with key congressmen, Cabinet members, important bureaucrats, the Vice President, party chiefs, and perhaps even leaders of the opposition party but he must also cope with the great political forces operating around the White House—public opinion in all its complexity, pressures from organized interests, demands from his own party. He must negotiate endlessly among individuals and among interests. Always he must act—but without stepping on too many toes. Always the fierce light of public opinion, magnified by press, radio, and television, beats on the White House. Truly, the President has one of the toughest jobs on earth.

In recent years a significant curb has been put on the President's power: He has been made ineligible for a third term. Although the framers provided for indefinite re-eligibility, Washington quit after two terms and set a precedent that Presidents followed for a century and a half. In 1940, however, Franklin Roosevelt challenged this unwritten law and sought a third term. His victory in effect "repealed" the tradition, but the repeal was not to last long. In 1951 the thirty-sixth state ratified the Twenty-second Amendment, which now bars the President from being elected for more than two terms. It will be interesting to see if this change will survive should an immensely popular President want a third term some day. The amendment will probably weaken Presidents during their second term, because powerful political leaders in Congress and in the administration will feel less obliged to support a man they know will be out of power on a certain date.

Problem and Prospects

Have we come to the point where we are willing to accept the President as master of our fate and fortunes in time of crisis? Certainly we have rejected the concept of rigid checks on the Chief Executive, especially during times of crisis. For example, in June 1950, a few days after North Korean troops invaded South Korea, President Truman, acting on his own, ordered American forces to resist aggression. Equally significant, the few senators who criticized him for not first going to Congress found no support except in the extreme isolationist press. President Kennedy consulted congressional leaders, but not Congress as a whole, when he ordered a naval quarantine of Cuba in 1962, and this time there was practically no criticism. Nor was there congressional opposition in 1965 when President Johnson suddenly ordered armed forces to intervene in Santo Domingo. Today more than ever before, the President, as Woodrow Wilson once said, "is at liberty, both in law and conscience, to be as big a man as he can."

The growth of presidential power is not the result of White House conspiracies. It stems from social changes, economic crises, wars, the rise of political parties, the frequent failure of Congress to act effectively in the face of national problems, the deep popular demand for leadership and action. Nor is it unique to the United States. Executive power has grown sharply in this century in Western nations, such as France, and in most developing nations. Today in the United States, more than ever before, continually recurring and deepening wars and economic dislocations demand drastic and far-reaching action by the man in the White House.

How dangerous is the tendency toward "one-man rule" in time of crisis? So far the danger has not been great. Perhaps we have been lucky. The great wartime leaders of the United States—Lincoln, Wilson, F.D.R.—were democrats in the best sense. They did not want power for power's sake, but simply as a means of overcoming national peril. Aside from one or two lapses, they maintained the basic democratic institutions of civil liberties and free elections. We may not always be so lucky. Some day we may elect a President who in time of crisis would find some pretext to postpone elections or stifle free speech. Indeed, we may elect a man who would deliberately create an emergency for the very purpose of suppressing the opposition.

The problem will grow more sinister if the twentieth century continues to be a time of endless emergencies. But one thing seems sure. We cannot eliminate the threat by trying to cut the President down to size. To do this would be to blunt the very weapon—presidential power—that has served us so well in past emergencies. Nor should we try to raise Congress into full rivalry with the President, for that would give us divided government, which may be intolerable in time of crisis. A thoughtful student of the problem, generally satisfied with the workings of the office, has advised us, "Leave Your Presidency Alone!" [16]

The problem has two edges: On the one hand we must see to it that the President is our servant, not our master, that he leads us only in the direction we wish to go. On the other hand, we need to help the President. He must have enough authority to do his job.[17] He must be free of some of the obstacles that now confront him. Above all, he needs the wise counsel of men who take a broad, national point of view, who can both guide him and sustain him. He cannot always find such associates in the Cabinet, for the members, though men of his choosing, seldom have national prestige of their own. He cannot often find them in Congress, because even congressmen of the same party have their own political loyalties and responsibilities. He cannot easily find them in his own party, because our parties tend to create sectional rather than national leaders.

[16] Rossiter, *The American Presidency*, p. 161.
[17] Louis Brownlow, *The President and the Presidency* (Public Administration Service, 1949), pp. 114–115.

The need, in essence, is for *leadership*. The Presidency can be a vast reservoir of leadership, as Franklin D. Roosevelt realized. "The Presidency is not merely an administrative office," he said. "That is the least of it. It is more than an engineering job, efficient or inefficient. It is pre-eminently a place of moral leadership. All our great Presidents were leaders of thought at times when certain historic ideas in the life of the nation had to be clarified. . . . That is what the office is—a superb opportunity for reapplying, applying in new conditions, the simple rules of human conduct to which we always go back. Without leadership alert and sensitive to change, we are all bogged up or lose our way."

But what is the proper scope for such leadership? We will come to grips with this question after we have looked in the next four chapters at our other national policy-makers.

16 THE HOUSES OF CONGRESS

Clearly, the President has come to hold the commanding position in American government. This development is just the opposite of what the framers of the Constitution planned. They lived in a time when parliamentary assemblies were dislodging kings and royal minions, when the new legislatures embodied some of the revolutionary aspirations of the common man. The framers expected that Congress would be the main channel of popular impulses, while the President would act as a moderating and stabilizing force. They were not quite sure how to set up the executive branch, as we have seen, but they had no major doubts about Congress. It was to be the "first among equals" in the new government. It was to be the branch that spoke for the people, and the framers took special pride in their judicious separation of power between an upper chamber representing people by areas and a lower chamber representing people by number.

What has happened to the dream of Congress as the great "people's branch" of the government? Is its eclipse by the President simply part of a world-wide trend toward stronger executives? Certainly the past century and a half has not dealt kindly with parliaments. The German Reichstag became a mere cheering section under Hitler; the Supreme Soviet in Russia rigidly follows the party line; De Gaulle has held the French Parliament carefully in check; and the House of Commons in Britain is essentially a chamber for debating policy and rolling up an almost guaranteed majority for the Prime Minister. Congress has survived as an independent body, but not without almost ceaseless criticism from the start. A century and a quarter ago Alexis de Tocqueville was struck by the "vulgar demeanor" of the House of Representatives. Woodrow Wilson as a graduate student in political science won his scholarly reputation with a book, *Congressional Government*, that was one long critique of the national legislature. We used to hear "Senator Claghorn," a noisy, doltish fellow, on the radio, and we see "Senator Phogbound" in the comic strips. Hardly a year goes by without the appearance of a highly critical study of Congress, often by congressmen themselves. And Congress puts its worst foot forward. Students visiting the House are often disappointed by the absence of real debate, and over in the Senate only a handful of members may be on the floor.

Still, Congress is very much a going body. On January 3 each year, 535 men and women meet in the chambers of the Capitol in Washington to inaugurate a new session of Congress. These 435 representatives and 100 senators are members of a legislature that, whatever the changes in its role, has met to debate and enact laws every year for 175 years. What are the powers of Congress today? What are the relations and make-up of the two houses? How are laws made? And what criticism and defense can be made of Congress in its recent and present roles?

Congress: The Structure of Power

Let us start with Congress as it operates today. If Congress has lost its major role as chief legislator, it has strengthened its role in overseeing the executive branch and in helping constituents with their problems. Congress still retains some major powers.[1] It can defeat presidential proposals and indeed even whole programs ad-

---

[1] See Samuel P. Huntington, "Congressional Responses to the Twentieth Century," in David B. Truman (ed.), *The Congress and America's Future* (Prentice-Hall, 1965), pp. 5–31.

vanced by a President. Under the first article of the Constitution, Congress has authority to levy taxes, borrow money, regulate commerce among the states, declare war; and even though the initiative has largely passed to the President, the Chief Executive must gain the support of Congress in taking action in these fields. Under the Constitution, as we have seen, Congress can propose amendments to the Constitution, and through its separate houses can impeach and try the President and other federal officials and may launch investigations into almost any subject it wishes. Finally, Congress has power over its own establishment—for example, to determine whether or not newly elected members may take their seat, to discipline erring members, and to make procedural rules.

Over the decades Congress fashioned an elaborate organization to cope with its legislative duties and other burdens. This organization was designed in part to distribute work efficiently. It was also designed to distribute political power in different ways to different people. The student of Congress must understand both how Congress works and how its structure of power affects "who gets what, when, and how" both within and outside the congressional establishment.

Committees—The Little Legislatures

The main work of Congress is done in committees and subcommittees. Deluged by several thousand bills in a year, Congress could not do its job unless it delegated work to these "little legislatures." There are four types of congressional committees. *Special* or *select* committees ordinarily make specific investigations rather than introduce legislation; after submitting their report they are dissolved. When problems arise that need joint consideration, the House and Senate occasionally create *joint* committees composed of members of both chambers. *Conference* committees, a special kind of joint committee, are appointed by the presiding officers of the House and Senate when the two chambers disagree over legislation; their functions are discussed on page 460. By far the most important are the *standing* committees, which do the main work of framing legislation.

The House of Representatives has twenty standing committees with an average membership of about thirty. Among the most important of these committees are the great spending and taxing committees, namely Appropriations and Ways and Means, and—for a special reason described below—the Rules Committee. Standing committees are divided into subcommittees with jurisdiction over particular subjects. Standing committees have great powers. To them are referred all bills introduced in the House. They can kill bills, pigeonhole them for weeks, amend them beyond recognition, or speed them on their way. They are, as Speaker Reed once said, "the eye, the ear, the hand, and very often the brain of the House."

The House especially depends on the work of its committees. They are important also because of their power to kill a bill merely through inaction. If a committee fails to report a bill, the only way it can be brought to the floor of the House is through a *discharge petition* signed by a majority of the House membership. Many petitions are filed; few gain the necessary number of signatures.

Indirectly, however, the threat of a petition sometimes helps move bills out of committee.

The Senate has sixteen standing committees composed of seven to twenty-seven members; each senator normally serves on only two committees. Among the most important Senate committees are Foreign Relations, Finance, Appropriations, and Government Operations; the last supervises and investigates the executive agencies. Senate committees have the same great powers over the framing of legislation as do those of the House.

Committees frequently hold open hearings, where spokesmen from executive departments, representatives of interest-group organizations, experts of various sorts, and mere private citizens testify formally on pending legislation. These hearings may be far more interesting to the visitor than sessions of House or Senate, and the committee proceedings published verbatim by the government afford rich material on the operations of government. The most important work of the committees, however, is done in *executive session*, from which visitors are barred. These sessions are centers of vital decision-making. Their nonpublic character "promotes the free interplay of ideas among committee members. Compromises and alternatives can be shaped in a fluid environment."[2] Committee decisions are made by majority vote.

Standing committees are bipartisan. The chairman and a majority of the members are elected from the majority party, and the minority party is represented roughly in relation to the proportion of its members in the entire chamber. Getting on a politically advantageous committee is important to members of Congress. A representative from Nebraska, for example, would much rather serve on the Agriculture or Public Works Committee than on the Merchant Marine and Fisheries Committee. Members usually stay on the same committee from one Congress to the next, but freshmen who are given minor appointments may, when they gain seniority, move to more important committees.

How are committee members chosen? In the House of Representatives a Committee on Committees of the Republican membership allots memberships to Republican freshmen. This committee is composed of one member from each state having Republican representation in the House; this member is chosen by his own state delegation but is almost always the senior member of the delegation, and he has as many votes on the committee as there are Republicans in his delegation. Hence, this committee is dominated by the senior members from the large-state delegations. On the Democratic side assignment to committees is also dominated by veterans, since the Democratic members of the House Committee on Ways and Means handle this job for the Democrats, in negotiation with senior Democrats from the respective state delegations. In both parties the procedures "are so constituted as to be virtually immune to immediate pressures brought about by electoral changes."[3]

[2] Bertram M. Gross, *The Legislative Struggle* (McGraw-Hill, 1953), pp. 309–310. See also Ralph K. Huitt, "The Congressional Committee: A Case Study," *The American Political Science Review* (June 1954), pp. 340–365.

[3] Nicholas A. Masters, "Committee Assignments in the House of Representatives," *The American Political Science Review* (June 1961), p. 350.

In the Senate, veterans also dominate the committee assignment process, with each party having a small steering committee for this purpose. In both chambers it is necessary for the chamber to ratify the recommendations of party leaders, which is done routinely.

In making committee assignments, the party leaders are guided by a variety of considerations, but a major factor is to give each new congressman an assignment that will help him get re-elected. Thus, "Although it might . . . seem desirable . . . to place an urban congressman on the Agriculture Committee to protect consumer interests," in fact, urban congressmen seldom request such an assignment and even if they do, preference will be given to congressmen from farm areas.[4] Assignment to key committees such as Appropriations or Ways and Means are normally handed out only to men who have some seniority in Congress and who have persuaded party leaders that they are "responsible"—that is, they can be counted on to abide by the rules of the legislative way of life.

Clearly, committees are not only a means of dividing up the workload. They are also separate little centers of power. Consider Appropriations, one of the most powerful single committees in the House. Analyzing this committee, Fenno discovered that it is characterized by a remarkable agreement among its members over key issues. Leadership in the committee is stable; members tend to remain on the committee a long time; they have worked out a way of life emphasizing conformity, give-and-take, and hard work. Subcommittee chairmen become specialists on the budgets and programs of the agencies within the scope of their subcommittee's jurisdiction and often exercise more influence over administrative policy than any other single congressman. For example, the chairman of the Appropriations Subcommittee on Foreign Aid has more influence over that program than has the chairman of the House Committee on Foreign Affairs. The several appropriations subcommittees defer to one another's recommendations and back up the decisions of the parent committee in an atmosphere of "you support my recommendations and I'll support yours."[5]

Crucial in protecting this separate little system of power is the committee chairman, who has authority to set up subcommittees and to appoint subcommittee chairmen. What other powers do chairmen have and how are they appointed?

Committee Leaders—The Rule of Seniority

Although every member of a committee has one vote, the committee chairman is almost always the most influential member, for he holds certain formal as well as informal powers. "It is difficult to exaggerate the power of a committee chairman," Berman says. "Even

[4] *Ibid.*, p. 354.

[5] Richard F. Fenno, Jr., "The House Appropriations Committee as a Political System: The Problem of Integration," *The American Political Science Review* (June 1962), pp. 310–324. See also George Goodwin, Jr., "Subcommittees: The Miniature Legislatures of Congress," *ibid.* (September 1962), pp. 596–604; and Charles O. Jones, "The Role of the Congressional Subcommittee," *Midwest Journal of Political Science* (November 1962), pp. 327–344.

on committees with comparatively democratic procedures, chairmen are generally able to exercise firm control, and what the committee does is seldom different from what the chairman wants it to do. Events have not served to outdate the description by Woodrow Wilson of those who command the committees: petty barons who 'may at will exercise an almost despotic sway within their own shires, and may sometimes threaten to convulse even the realm itself.' . . . The most awesome power of a chairman is his ability to prevent his committee from acting and thus prevent Congress from acting." [6] Chairmen may refuse to call a meeting, or schedule a meeting at an inopportune time for their opponents; they control the agenda of committee meetings, dominate committee procedure, and have power to recognize—or not recognize—those who wish to speak. Like the chairman, the other ranking committee members of both parties are particularly influential because they draw upon experience in committee work, legislative and parliamentary know-how, and wide contacts in Congress and outside.

Chairmanships are awarded by the rule of *seniority*. The member of the *majority* party who has had the longest continuous service on the committee becomes chairman. (The member of the minority party with the longest continuous service on the committee is the *ranking minority member*.) The chairman may be at swords' points with his fellow partisans in Congress, he may oppose his party's national program, he may even be incompetent—still, he has the right to the chairmanship under the workings of seniority.

The Politics of the Seniority Rule

The rule of seniority means that chairmen are not chosen by their own committees, by their party, or by the House or Senate as a whole. They are really picked by the voters in their districts and states, who give them seniority by sending them back to Congress in election after election. Thus, the key makers of national policy in Congress are locally chosen and locally responsible. The seniority rule puts a premium on careful cultivation of the district. It bestows the most influence in Congress on those constituencies that are politically stable or even stagnant—where party competition is low, where a particular interest group or city or rural machine predominates. It stacks the cards against areas where the two parties are more evenly matched, where interest in politics is high, the number of votes large, and competition between groups keen. These are the very areas most likely to reflect quickly and typically the political tides that sweep the nation.

What groups does the seniority system benefit? When Democrats control a chamber—especially the House—committee and subcommittee chairmen tend to be disproportionately southerners from rural and small-town areas, along with a few products of city machines. When Republicans are in control, the midwestern rural areas tend to gain a disproportionate number of chairmanships. Whatever party controls, the chairmanships go mostly to the rural areas: In a recent Congress

[6] Daniel M. Berman, *In Congress Assembled* (Macmillan, 1964), pp. 121–122.

the 217 most urban districts produced only 26 per cent of the House chairmen while the 218 least urban districts accounted for 74 per cent. The imbalance is even greater if one takes into account the relative importance of the committees.

Since in both chambers the seniority system works against the urban and more liberal districts, the rule of seniority tends to make the voice of Congress a conservative one, especially in the lower chamber. It also creates conflicts between Congress and the White House. For the committee chairmanships are most likely to be in the hands of men who are least likely to support the policies sponsored by the President, whatever his party. President Eisenhower, for example, during his first two years in office, had to deal with Republican committee chairmen who had been accumulating seniority during the years of Democratic supremacy and who generally represented different groups in the Republican party than did the President. And President Johnson has had to work with committee chairmen predominantly from the southern or western wing of his party, many of whom oppose key items of the President's legislative program: for example, Senator James Eastland of Mississippi is chairman of the Senate Judiciary Committee to which all civil rights bills are referred. Senator Eastland is a vigorous opponent of the civil rights plank of the Democratic National Party Platform, of civil rights measures favored by the President, and of civil rights measures favored by a majority of his own party in the Senate.

The seniority system also undermines national party cohesion. Chairmen of the committees are not accountable to their own national party for the exercise of their authority. In the words of one student, the system "divides the authority of the party leaders [those elected by the party in Congress, such as the Speaker or majority leaders; see below] and prevents them from carrying out a general program of party legislation. It may even defeat the projects to which the majority of a party has been publicly pledged. . . . It makes the party system a less effective instrument than it might and should be in organizing majorities within the House for serving the manifest needs of the people of the country." [7]

Seniority is defended on the grounds that it prevents disputes among congressmen and elevates the most experienced members to committee leadership. It is attacked on the grounds that it puts power into the hands of veteran members who may be out of touch with the new needs and problems of the nation. Basically, the argument concerns political rather than technical matters. Rural interests naturally tend to favor the system. It is opposed by groups such as organized labor, supporters of civil rights legislation, and other urban-based interests, who feel that it gives the farmers and their conservative representatives too much power in Congress. However, the share of noncompetitive districts held by the North has increased in recent years [8] and in view of other changes it may well be

[7] A. N. Holcombe, *Our More Perfect Union* (Harvard Univ. Press, 1950), p. 185. For a scholarly treatment of the subject that warns against exaggerating the impact of the system, see George Goodwin, Jr., "The Seniority System in Congress," *The American Political Science Review* (June 1959), pp. 412–436. For a participant's defense of the system see Emanuel Celler, "The Seniority Rule in Congress," *Western Political Quarterly* (March 1961), pp. 160–167.

[8] Raymond E. Wolfinger and Joan Heifetz, "Safe Seats, Seniority, and Power in Congress," *The American Political Science Review* (June 1965), pp. 337–349.

that shortly the rule of seniority will enhance the influence of urban-based northern interests. If so, it will be interesting to see if those defending and those opposing the rule of seniority switch sides.

The House of Representatives

The framers of the Constitution intended the Senate to represent areas rather than numbers, but this was to be offset by making the House of Representatives roughly reflect population. But even the lower chamber does not represent population accurately. How can this be? The explanation is found in the way congressional districts are set up.

By act of Congress, the membership of the House is set at 435. In keeping with the Constitution, the membership is distributed by Congress among the states according to population with each state receiving at least one. (After each ten-year census the Bureau of the Census submits a report that becomes official unless Congress acts to the contrary.) Congress has left almost complete control over the drawing of congressional districts to the *state legislatures*.

In theory, congressional district boundaries should be as nearly equal in population as practicable, fairly compact, and boundaries should not cut across unified areas such as cities. But such a theory assumes that the goal is to make the state's congressional delegation as representative as possible of the state's population and to give each voter an equal voice in the House of Representatives. In practice, the creation of congressional districts is immensely complicated by political considerations and is the product of a variety of personal, group, and party forces jockeying for advantage.

The Politics of Districting

One result of this jockeying has long been *gerrymandering*. The term was coined a century and a half ago when Elbridge Gerry of Massachusetts carved out a district that had the shape of a salamander and was quickly dubbed a "Gerrymander." The term now applies to any attempt by a party or faction controlling a state legislature to draw the boundaries of districts in such a way that that party or group enjoys a *close but safe margin of support in many districts*, while the opposition's votes are *concentrated* in a *few districts* and thus wasted. Since both parties freely indulge in this practice, some districts have fantastic shapes. "If you let your imagination go while thumbing through the maps of Congressional districts," it has been said, "you may readily fancy that you have seen a dumbbell, a tomahawk, a skull, a worm, the M.G.M. lion, and characters from the comic strips."

Another result of the politics of districting is sometimes called the "silent gerrymander." A state losing one or more representatives ordinarily must establish new district boundaries. It must also redistrict if it gains representatives, although it may do nothing and elect its new representative "at large"—that is, the whole state becomes his district—and the existing districts remain intact. If there is no change in the size of the congressional delegation, a legislature may make no effort to adjust its districts to population shifts *within* the state. An urban district may double in population and still have only one representative, while rural districts that have declined in relative population may keep their past representations. Until recently, Michigan's biggest district, for example, had 802,994 persons, the smallest only 177,431. To be sure, we have nothing as unrepresentative as the famous "rotten boroughs" of Britain, where one town, half submerged under water and numbering only fourteen voters, had two members in Parliament, while great cities such as Birmingham had none. But Britain long ago cleared up these inequities, while some people fear that our own are becoming worse.

A third type of political districting is very different from the old-fashioned gerrymander. This is the effort to build safe seats and hence to cut down political *competition*. A state legislature could make every congressional district approximately equal in population, but still carve up the state with such expertness that some districts remain hopelessly noncompetitive. Actually, the hottest fights over districting take place mainly within the dominant party, between the state party leaders whose concern is to strengthen the state party as a whole and incumbent congressmen and their allies who are trying to fortify their own positions. State party leaders want as many congressional districts as possible to be fairly secure for their own party but not overwhelmingly safe since they seek to spread their party's strength widely in order to win as many congressional elections as possible. The individual congressman, on the other hand, wants to build up his majorities as high as possible. He remembers the occasional horrible example of an "entrenched" congressman being unseated, and no matter how "safe" his seat he prefers it to be even safer. Given the diffusion of power in the state party, the congressman can often get his way, checked only by the ambitions of other incumbent congressmen. The resulting noncompetitive seats are in many ways more significant than traditional gerrymandering.

The main results of the politics of districting has been to reduce the number of competitive seats in the House and to over-represent the rural areas. The reason for the latter is twofold: First, since population shifts have been mainly from rural to suburban and city areas, simple failure to redistrict strengthens rural representation, primarily at the expense of the suburban areas; and second, most state legislatures, themselves products of gerrymandered state legislative districts which over-represent rural areas, tend in drawing congressional district boundaries to favor their own rural supporters. City and suburban people were of course unhappy about this arrangement. But they could do little more than protest. The state legislatures, themselves the product of rural over-representation, were not likely to reform themselves. Nor was Congress, for the same reason. The Supreme Court in *Baker* v. *Carr* had provided relief for voters discriminated against in the creation of *state* legislative districts, as we have seen, but this did not directly affect *congressional* districting.

Then in 1964 came a dramatic challenge to gerrymandering of congressional districts. The Supreme Court, reversing an earlier decision, ruled that the Constitution required that "as nearly as is practicable one man's vote in a Congressional election is to be worth as much as another's." [9] This was a mighty blow for the idea that one man equals one vote. Soon state legislatures were grudgingly redrawing congressional districts to conform more closely to the court's ruling that districts must be relatively equal in population. Congress followed up the court's action in 1965 by taking on a bill establishing 15 per cent as the maximum percentage by which the population of any congressional district could deviate (either greater or lesser) from the average size of the state's districts. The bill provided also—a direct slap at the gerrymander—that districts must be contiguous and as compact as possible.

How much difference would these actions make? Two years after *Wesberry* it seemed clear that the days of the classic gerrymander were numbered. The "silent" gerrymander would still have some effect, if only because redistricting would always lag somewhat behind the flow of population, but its effect would be small. The third type of political districting—creating noncompetitive districts—might last much longer. The reason for this is that districts can be fairly equal in size and fairly compact but still be noncompetitive. Take the curious case of Massachusetts. This state had fairly equal congressional districts even before *Wesberry*. And in state elections the two parties compete on fairly equal terms. But in the 1964 congressional elections seven Massachusetts congressmen won re-election by margins ranging from 60 to 80 per cent of the two-party vote, and the other five congressmen had no opposition at all! Not one district in Massachusetts, in short, was closely competitive. A remarkable number of congressional districts in other states are noncompetitive.[10] But even this kind of political gerrymandering may decline over the long run, as state legislatures come to represent different interests.

Congressional districting raises major questions about Congress as a representative and responsible agency of "government by the people." We encounter similar questions as we turn to the *internal* operations of the House of Representatives.

The Rules Committee—Traffic Cop or Roadblock?

To get a bill through the House you cannot simply drop it into the hopper and expect it to wend its way through some committee and onto the floor. The House handles several thousand bills a year—so many that there must be traffic police to help direct the heavy stream. Important bills, especially those favored by committees or perhaps by the President, must be given priority handling. Granting such priority is the special business of the Rules Committee of the House. This committee is one of the regular

[9] *Wesberry* v. *Sanders* (1964).

[10] For aspects of reapportionment see Andrew Hacker, *Congressional Districting: The Issue of Equal Representation* (Brookings, 1963); Lewis A. Froman, Jr., *Congressmen and Their Constituencies* (Rand McNally, 1963); and Charles O. Jones, "Inter-party Competition for Congressional Seats," *Western Political Quarterly* (September 1964), pp. 461–476.

standing committees of the lower chamber, but it has exceptional power. It can grant or withhold a special rule—and a bill without a special rule may easily get lost in the thick traffic on Capitol Hill. The Rules Committee may grant a rule that makes it difficult or easy for a bill to be "amended to death" on the floor. Thus its special rule for handling the bill may permit or forbid amendments, set the length of debate, and otherwise expedite or slow up the bill. And this power in turn gives the Rules Committee tremendous bargaining power with the elected House leaders, with other committees, and with the administration.[11]

What kind of traffic cop is this? If the committee were fairly representative of the rank and file of the House, its power would seldom be questioned. But it is not. The committee is dominated by veteran congressmen who have been re-elected time and time again from "safe" (noncompetitive) districts regardless of the ebb and flow of national politics. And in recent years a coalition of conservative Republicans and conservative Democrats have dominated the Rules Committee and made it difficult for Presidents, be they Truman, Eisenhower, or Kennedy, to deliver on their campaign promises. Liberals in both parties denounced the committee for being unrepresentative, unfair, dictatorial, and negative. Its defenders contended that the committee did just what the framers of the Constitution wanted our system to do—prevent the House from responding too readily to new popular majorities. Its famous and long-time chairman, Howard W. Smith, a conservative Democrat from Virginia, contends that the committee serves another function—it kills or delays bills that congressional sponsors secretly do not want but feel they must openly support because of pressures from lobbyists or from their constituents.

For years House liberals attacked the committee and tried to reform it, but without much success. In 1949, hard on the heels of Harry Truman's surprise election victory in November 1948, the House established the 21-day rule, which allowed a committee chairman to call up a bill if the Rules Committee delayed it more than 21 days; but two years later the conservatives regained the upper hand and abolished the reform. In 1961, following John Kennedy's presidential campaign promises to "get America moving again," the reformers tried to "purge" from the committee a southern Democrat who had deserted his party's national ticket and supported Richard Nixon in the campaign. This effort failed. The liberals, with the assistance of Speaker Sam Rayburn, were able to gain an enlargement of the committee to provide a bit more representation for liberals, but in practice this new "Kennedy majority" on the committee was rather precarious.

The critics of the Rules Committee achieved something of a breakthrough when the 89th Congress convened in January 1965. Their numbers swelled by the sweeping Democratic victories against Goldwater Republicans the preceding fall, liberal Democrats won passage of two reforms. One was the 21-day rule, which permitted the *Speaker* to recognize a committee chairman to introduce a measure for House consideration if it had been before the Rules Committee for 21 days without having been granted a rule. A second rules change made it more difficult for the

---

[11] For a study that emphasizes the bargaining role of the committee see James A. Robinson, *The House Rules Committee* (Bobbs-Merrill, 1963).

Rules Committee to delay sending a bill to conference committee (see page 460). The changes became part of the basic House rules and would not need to be re-adopted at the beginning of each Congress. But they could be eliminated by specific House action if at a later time the members so wished. One thing was certain: Representatives would continue to argue over House rules because these rules are part of the political process in the Congress.[12]

House Procedure on the Floor

Bills are often drafted by representatives of interest groups or by experts in the executive departments and sometimes even by congressmen; but no matter who drafts them they must be introduced by a member of the House. The Speaker then refers them to a standing committee for study and action. Once a bill has passed through the committee stage, how is it handled on the floor of the House of Representatives? In contrast to the smaller, more informal Senate, the large membership of the House makes imperative quick and orderly methods. Some of the important procedures are as follows.

Calendars. Bills reported out of committee to the floor of the House are assigned to one of three main calendars, or schedules. Finance measures—tax or appropriations, for example—are put on the *Union* calendar. All bills that are nonfiscal but still of a public character are placed on the *House* calendar. Private bills—bills dealing with individuals' problems, such as a veteran's pension—go on a *Private* calendar. These and other calendars serve as a traffic-directing system designed to give each bill its fair turn. But there are also various means for taking up bills out of their calendar order. For example, House rules may be suspended by a two-thirds vote on certain days; or important bills may be brought up at any time by the Rules Committee; or immediate action on a measure may be won by unanimous consent.

Committee of the Whole. This committee, made up of all members of the House, is another means of expediting business. By sitting as the Committee of the Whole, members are able to operate more informally and quickly than under the regular House rules. For example, a quorum in the Committee of the Whole is 100, compared with a majority of all the members under the House rules. More important, there are no roll calls. Congressmen sometimes vote differently when a record is kept of their vote than they would otherwise. Very rarely does the whole House reject the recommendations of this committee, though it has the power to do so.

[12] See Hugh Douglas Price, "Race, Religion, and the Rules Committee," in Alan F. Westin (ed.), *The Uses of Power* (Harcourt, Brace & World, 1962), p. 20; James A. Robinson, "The Role of the Rules Committee in Regulating Debate in the U.S. House of Representatives," *Midwest Journal of Political Science* (February 1961), pp. 59–69; and "The Role of the Rules Committee in Arranging the Program of the U.S. House of Representatives," *Western Political Quarterly* (September 1959), pp. 653–669.

House Cloture. In contrast to the smaller upper chamber, the House is too large to let everyone have his full say. Debate may be cut off simply by majority vote. This ready method of cloture (or closure) makes filibusters impossible. Most speakers are allowed only a few minutes, usually by prior agreement between party leaders on both sides.

Voting. Ordinarily, voting is conducted quickly in the House either by a viva-voce (voice) vote, or by a standing vote. Occasionally, though, some faction may want to make members go on record as to their stand on a controversial measure; in this case voting is conducted by the slower method of a vote by tellers (the members are checked off as they file past the Speaker's desk), or, upon demand of one-fifth of members present, by the still slower method of a roll call (the clerk calls each member by name).

The Speaker

The Speaker's formal authority is not what it was fifty or seventy-five years ago when such men as Thomas B. (Czar) Reed or (Uncle) Joe Cannon controlled committee assignments and wielded almost complete control over House deliberations. Revolts of the rank and file in

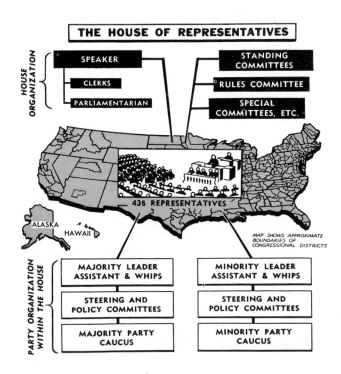

Organization of power in the House of Representatives.

1910 stripped the Speaker of most of his old-time authority. Still, he remains the single most important leader of the House.

The Speaker's formal authority grows out of the fact that he can grant or withhold recognition to those who wish to speak, he settles parliamentary disputes (with the help of a specialist in procedure), he appoints members of select and conference (but not standing) committees, and in general directs the business on the floor.

Much more significant is the Speaker's political and behind-the-scenes influence. Although formally chosen by the House of Representatives, he is in fact picked by the majority party. Once in office, unlike the nonpartisan presiding officer of the British House of Commons, the Speaker is openly a party leader and is expected, subject to the rules of the game, to use his office to support the program of his party.

The late Speaker Sam Rayburn had unusual power. Because of his tremendous personal influence over his fellow Democrats, his support frequently proved decisive in key legislative battles. His decisions, like those of any Speaker, were of course subject to being overruled by the House, but as long as he kept the support of his own party, he was a man of enormous influence. When "Mr. Sam" did not want the House to do something, it seldom did it. His successor, John McCormack of Massachusetts, former Majority Leader of the House Democrats, does not enjoy the same kind of personal influence. But as Speaker he is a man of consequence.

Party Officers and Meetings

Next to the Speaker the most important party officer in the House is the *Majority Floor Leader* who, like the Speaker, is chosen by the majority party caucus, but unlike the Speaker is an officer only of his party and not of the House proper. The Majority Floor Leader helps plan party strategy, confers with other party leaders, and tries to keep members of his party in line. The minority party elects a *Minority Floor Leader*, who usually steps into the speakership when his party gains a majority in the House. Assisting each floor leader are the *party whips* (the term derives from the "whipper-in" who in English fox hunts kept the hounds from leaving the pack). The whips serve as liaison between the House leadership of each party and the rank and file; they inform members when important bills will come up for a vote, exert mild pressure on them to support the leadership, and try to insure maximum attendance on the floor when critical votes are imminent.

At the beginning of the session and occasionally thereafter, each party holds a *caucus* (or conference, as the Republicans call it). The caucus, composed of all the party's members in the House, meets privately to elect party officers, approve committee assignments, discuss important legislation, and perhaps try to agree on party policy. Decisions are usually made by simple majority. In theory, the caucus is the directing party agency; in fact, this party group plays a small part in lawmaking. A decision of the Democratic caucus is binding only when approved by two-thirds of the members. When it involves a matter of constitutional interpretation (as do most measures), or when conflicting promises have been made back home (and all sorts of promises have been made), the decision is not binding at all. Republicans are not bound by any conference decision. Hardly more important than the caucus are the *steering committees*, made up of the party leadership, which do little steering but have some influence on party policy and tactics.

The House also produces a variety of groupings that come and go, some with and some without formal organization. State delegations often meet to consider business that affects the entire state. Sometimes representatives organize around common ideological concerns. For example, after the 1958 elections a group of liberal Democrats, frustrated by institutional roadblocks and by the domination of the House by the Republican-Southern Democratic coalition, formed the Democratic Study Group. The Kennedy victories and the Democratic sweep of 1964 added to the strength of the group, which now is formally organized and has become a major instrument in securing significant alterations in rules and procedures of the House. It has bargained for better representation for liberal Democrats on major House committees and has worked in behalf of legislation reflecting its liberal views.

The most striking characteristic of the House (and as we will see, of the Senate) is the dispersion of power. Committee leaders, the Rules Committee, the elected party officials, factional chieftains—each set of leaders shares in making the key decisions in the House. There are no "czars" today; to get things done the leaders must negotiate and bargain with one another. The strongest leadership is exercised by the White House through party leaders, but even the President cannot dictate. The advantage of bargaining is that a large number of representatives must be consulted and minority groups given recognition. The disadvantage is that measures may be watered down or defeated or delayed, and accountability for action or inaction confused and thus responsibility eroded. Recently there have been signs of greater party solidarity in the House,[13] but strong centralized leadership is unlikely so long as both parties have so little organizational strength in congressional districts across the nation.

The Senate

In many respects the Senate resembles the House. There is the same basic committee structure (but no powerful Rules Committee in the Senate); the seniority system; the elected party leadership and rather weak party committees—in short, the same dispersion of power. But the Senate is a smaller body of 100 members, who hold staggered six-year terms. Only one-third of the senatorial terms expire in each Congress. Hence the Senate, unlike the House, is always organized. It is an ever-continuing body.

[13] See, for example, Randall B. Ripley, "The Party Whip Organizations in the United States House of Representatives," *The American Political Science Review* (September 1964), pp. 561–576.

The most striking difference, of course, is that each state has two senators no matter what its size. Alaska, with 250,000 inhabitants, has the same senatorial representation as California, with about 75 times that population. A majority of votes in the Senate can be cast by senators representing less than 20 per cent of the voters. Sections such as northern New England, the Rockies, and parts of the South are over-represented, while the Middle Atlantic states and other populous areas are politically short-changed in the upper chamber.

The President of the Senate is the Vice President of the United States. Despite his exalted position, he has much less control over the Senate than the Speaker has over the House. He is not a member of the Senate—not quite a member of the exclusive "senatorial club"—and can vote only in case of a tie. He must recognize members in the order in which they rise. The Senate also elects from among its own membership a *president pro tempore* who presides in the absence of the Vice President. He is of course really chosen by the majority party. As a member of the Senate, he can vote on all issues.

Party machinery in the Senate is somewhat similar to that of the House. There are party conferences (in the Senate, both parties have given up the term "caucus"), majority and minority floor leaders, and party whips. In the Senate each party has a *policy committee*, composed of the leaders of the party, which is theoretically responsible for the party's over-all legislative program. (In the Senate the party steering committees only handle committee assignments.) The Democratic policy committeemen are appointed by the Democratic floor leader with the approval

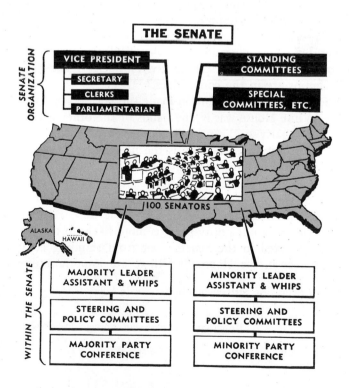

Organization of power in the Senate.

of the Democratic Senate Conference and serve indefinitely, while their Republican counterparts are elected by the party conference for two-year terms. Unlike the House steering committees, the Senate's policy committees are formally provided for by law and each of them has a regular staff and a significant budget. While the Senate policy committees have some influence on legislation, they have neither asserted strong legislative leadership nor managed to coordinate party policy.[14]

The Majority Leader, however, is usually a man of influence within the Senate and sometimes in the nation. He has the right to be the first Senator to be heard on the floor and, in consultation with the minority floor leader, determines the Senate's agenda. He has much to say about committee assignments for members of his own party. But the position confers less authority than the speakership in the House, and the leader's influence depends on his political skill and the national political situation. Some majority leaders had little influence in the Senate and were relatively unknown in the nation. Others made it an important post. It was as majority floor leader that Senator Taft became "Mr. Republican." President Johnson, when Majority Leader, dominated the Senate and was even called "The Second Most Powerful American."

Senator Lyndon Johnson's dramatic development of the leadership position in the Senate, partly because of his parliamentary skill, gave the Senate more centralized leadership than it had ever known in its history. Many hoped that Johnson's action would transform the position so that the Senate would have a means of organizing itself, identifying issues, and overcoming the divisive impact of the seniority leaders. But his successor, Senator Mike Mansfield of Montana, has farmed out more of his responsibilities and has displayed much less of a desire to bring Johnson's style of leadership to his position. He is quoted as saying, "I'm not the leader, really. They don't do what I tell them. I do what they tell me. . . . We've had a dispersal of responsibility. How can I know everything that's going on? The brains are in the committees." [15]

Both Senators Taft and Johnson made the position of Majority Leader powerful when the White House was in the hands of the other party. When the President is of the same party as the majority floor leader of the Senate, the Senate leader has less opportunity to stand out as the national spokesman for his party. When the President and Senate leader are of the same party, moreover, the latter must of necessity be not just a leader of the Senate, but a member of the administration team. He serves as a liaison between Senate and White House. On the other hand, his role within the Senate may be easier since he is reinforced by the President, and hence the Senate majority party is more likely to operate as a unit.[16]

Bills are reported to the Senate floor from standing committees in much the same fashion as in the House, but there are important differences in procedure

---

[14] Hugh A. Bone, "An Introduction to the Senate Policy Committees," *The American Political Science Review* (June 1956), pp. 339–359. See also Ralph K. Huitt, "Democratic Party Leadership in the Senate," *The American Political Science Review* (June 1961), pp. 333–344.

[15] Quoted by James A. Robinson, *Congress and Foreign Policy-Making* (Dorsey, 1962), pp. 215–216.

[16] David B. Truman, *The Congressional Party* (Wiley, 1959), pp. 279–329.

on the two floors. The Senate's Rules Committee has none of the delaying or blocking power of its counterpart in the House. The Senate has only two calendars, and these are usually followed rather closely. It uses its Committee of the Whole only for considering treaties. It has more time for debate and can carry on its business in a more informal manner. Measures in the Senate are normally debated in the order in which they are reported by committees, or else are taken up for discussion by unanimous consent.

Rule 22—The Filibuster

Another major difference between the two chambers is that debate is sharply limited in the House, and is almost unlimited in the Senate. Once a senator gains the floor, he has the right to go on talking until he relinquishes it voluntarily or through exhaustion. This right to unlimited debate may be used by a small group of senators to *filibuster*— that is, to *delay the proceedings of the Senate in order to prevent a vote*. Except in very limited circumstances, debate in the Senate does not have to be germane. A senator may, if he wishes, read the *Congressional Record* at great length or, as the late Senator Long once did, entertain his colleagues with recipes for "Louisiana potlikker," turnip greens, and cornbread.

How may a filibuster be defeated? The majority can keep the Senate in continuous session in the hope that the filibustering senator will have to give up the floor. But if three or four senators cooperate, they can keep going almost indefinitely. They merely ask one another long questions that will permit their partners to take lengthy rests. So long as they keep on their feet, debate can be terminated under Senate Rule 22 only by *cloture*. Under the rule of cloture, if 16 members sign a petition, two days later the question of curtailing debate is put to a vote. If *two-thirds* of the senators on the floor vote for cloture, no senator may speak for more than one hour; then the motion before the Senate must be brought to a vote.

The Senate has acted favorably on cloture petitions only seven times since such a procedure was adopted in 1917, despite many filibusters. The most spectacular filibusters of recent years have been by southern senators determined to block civil rights legislation. The all-time record for one senator holding the floor was achieved in 1957 by Strom Thurmond of South Carolina who, with little help from "questioners," talked for 24 hours and 18 minutes. During the debate on the Civil Rights Act of 1960 a group of southern senators filibustered from February 15 to March 10. At one point in their efforts to block the legislation, the participants talked through nine days of continuous sessions. In the spring of 1962 southern senators again organized a filibuster which lasted 13 days and ended with a defeat of a bill designed to eliminate discriminatory administration of literacy tests. Of course, southern anti-civil rights senators are not the only ones who have resorted to filibustering. Senator Morse, an avowed proponent of changing the rules to forbid filibusters, has not hesitated to take advantage of the privilege whenever it serves his purpose. In 1962 Senator Morse and nine other liberal senators filibustered to try to block the Communications Satellite Bill of 1962, which they felt gave too much authority to the American Telephone and Telegraph Company over a communications system developed in large part from federal tax funds. However, for the first time since 1927, by three more than the required votes of two-thirds of the senators voting, the Senate invoked cloture and terminated the filibuster.

The number of actual filibusters is not a proper measure of their significance. For the *threat* of a filibuster by an organized minority may hang over the Senate's business. Often the knowledge that a bill might lead to a filibuster is enough to force a compromise satisfactory to its opponents. Sometimes the Senate leadership, knowing that a filibuster would tie up the Senate and keep it from enacting needed legislation, does not even bother to bring a bill to the Senate floor.

Should the Senate amend Rule 22 to make it easier to end filibusters? The merits and demerits of the question are often discussed in more general theoretical terms, such as, majority rule versus minority rights, but there is a *policy* issue behind these debates—civil rights. Advocates of federal civil rights legislation know that unless they can force through a revision of Rule 22 it is more difficult to secure the kind of legislation they wish.

But how to amend Rule 22? A motion to amend the rule is itself subject to a filibuster. In order to get around this roadblock, a bipartisan coalition of liberal senators have tried unsuccessfully to develop a new tactic, the so-called "opening-day" procedure. Traditionally the Senate, unlike the House, does not adopt new rules each time a new Congress is organized; it proceeds on the theory that the Senate is a continuous body, since only one-third of its members are elected for each Congress, and thus the rules of the preceding Senate are still in effect. However, several times in recent years at the beginning of a new session of Congress liberal senators have introduced a new Rule 22—for example, permitting cloture by a constitutional majority. They have argued that debate on the motion for a new rule can be terminated by majority vote, and that Rule 22 of the preceding Senate cannot constitutionally bind a majority of the senators in the new Congress. So far a majority of the senators have not supported this position. Undoubtedly attempts will continue to be made to use these "opening-day" anti-filibuster tactics, especially when the presiding officer of the Senate, usually the Vice President, promises to give his support.

Significant as the filibuster is, its impact should not be exaggerated. Even in the area of civil rights it is gradually becoming less of a barrier. Today there are 100 senators, and those from the border states can no longer be counted on to vote against civil rights legislation. True, southern senators can use the filibuster and the threat of it to stop civil rights bills or to force modifications, but they know that if they are too obstreperous they may force the Senate to alter Rule 22. And a really determined majority can overcome a filibuster, either by wearing the speakers down, or by mobilizing the necessary votes for cloture. Both in 1964 and 1965 senators voted cloture to enact the vital civil rights measures of those years.

Political Role of the Senators

The two houses of Congress resemble each other in their concern with local and special-interest legislation, their intricate legislative and parliamentary procedure, their tendency toward voting by blocs and interest groups in defiance of party ties. Yet the upper chamber has a character all its own.

Senators are a somewhat different breed of political animal from the average representative. Most of the members of the upper house represent larger and more populous areas than do representatives. They have much more political elbow room if only because of their six-year term. A representative, elected by a smaller constituency both geographically and numerically (in most cases), may feel somewhat cramped by the necessity of devoting himself to the needs of a few interest groups and a handful of local party bosses. A senator, on the other hand, who represents a broader and more varied constituency, has more freedom to maneuver and is less vulnerable to minute shifts in opinion among smaller groups.

Senators tend also to wield greater power in their state political parties. Sometimes they virtually dominate those parties, as in the case of Huey Long of Louisiana, Joseph Guffey of Pennsylvania, Nelson Aldrich of Rhode Island, or, more recently, Robert A. Taft of Ohio and Harry Byrd of Virginia. Their party position often rests partially on their control of federal patronage dispensed to the state, and their patronage power largely rests in turn on the constitutional provision requiring Senate confirmation of major presidential appointments.

This power of the Senate to confirm nominations is important *constitutionally* as a part of our checks-and-balances system. It is even more important *politically*, for under the system of *senatorial courtesy* the individual senator has virtually a veto power over major appointments in his state (provided the President belongs to his party). The arrangement is a simple one. When presidential nominations are received in the Senate, they are referred quietly to the senator or senators from the state involved. The senator may, if he wishes, declare that the nominee is "personally obnoxious" to him, and the Senate almost always respects this declaration and rejects the appointment. Being personally obnoxious does not necessarily mean that the nominee is dishonest, or has insulted the senator on some occasion. It usually means that the nominee has not played ball with the senator *politically*, has been a member of a hostile personal organization in the state—perhaps that of the President. In any event, the upshot is that the President usually makes sure before submitting a nomination to the Senate (especially nominations for appointments located in the state, such as federal judgeships) that the nominee will be acceptable to his party's senator or senators from the state involved. The system of senatorial courtesy has important practical results. It strengthens the senators' role both in national administration and in state politics, and it weakens national party leadership and discipline.

The Senate's Power over Treaties

Another source of the senators' unique position is the fact that *two-thirds of the senators present* must give their consent before the President may ratify a treaty.

The framers of the Constitution probably wanted the President and senators to sit down together and jointly work out treaties. At any rate, George Washington tried this experiment. The story goes that he once visited the Senate to discuss a treaty with the southern Indians; when an obstreperous senator moved to refer the President's proposals to committee, Washington "started up in a violent fret," complaining that "this defeats every purpose of my coming here." No President since has conferred directly with the Senate; nonetheless, the senators help frame treaties as well as ratify them. The voices of influential senators are heard in foreign capitals as well as at home. Above all, the threat of Senate repudiation of a treaty makes it desirable for the President to solicit their views in advance. As a result, the Secretary of State usually works closely with the Foreign Relations Committee of the Senate and occasionally with the Foreign Affairs Committee of the House. Influential senators often undertake personal missions abroad and serve on delegations to the United Nations and other international bodies.

How important is the Senate's power over treaties? Secretary of State John Hay once complained that "a treaty entering the Senate is like a bull going into the arena; no one can say just how or when the final blow will fall—but one thing is certain—it will never leave the arena alive." The statistics suggest that Mr. Hay's remark was too severe. Even though a two-thirds majority is needed for treaty ratification, the Senate has unconditionally approved over 80 per cent of the approximately 1,100 or more submitted to it and many of the others were finally passed with amendments or reservations. And yet it is true that some of the rejected treaties were of supreme importance; for example, Senate disapproval of the Taft-Knox arbitration treaties of 1911–1912, of the Treaty of Versailles (involving United States membership in the League of Nations), and of the protocol for participating in the World Court, had a decided effect on the world role of the United States. Moreover, on many occasions Presidents have failed to negotiate treaties, have modified treaty provisions in advance of Senate consideration, or have even recalled treaties already submitted, in the face of opposition from various senators.

The Senate—and to a lesser degree the House—also influences foreign policy through investigations. A widely publicized investigation of munitions-makers by the Nye Committee in 1934 undoubtedly intensified isolationist and pacifist feeling and helped pave the way for neutrality legislation in the 1930's. In 1951 a Senate investigation of the dismissal of General Douglas MacArthur by President Truman raised the whole question of American foreign policy in the Far East and forced the administration to clarify its position. Occasionally, congressional committees or subcommittees make junkets overseas to look into the operations of American agencies.

Until recently, at least, the Senate has been the congressional spokesman on foreign policy, and the House has been decidedly a junior partner. The Senate's superiority stemmed from its treaty-ratifying authority and its veto power over presidential appointments of ambassadors, ministers, and other important officials. Partly because of the difficulty and unpredictability of the two-thirds treaty rule, however, partly because of pressure from the House, and partly because the House must approve appropriations necessary to implement most foreign policy programs, there has been a marked trend toward joint action by Senate and House.[17] The European Recovery Program, Point Four, the Indian grain program, the Formosa Resolution—to mention but a few—were undertaken by legislation rather than by treaty. Some senators resent this "encroachment," as well as the President's frequent use of *executive agreements* (see Chapter 14), and periodically demands are heard in the Senate that no obligations be made except by formal treaty procedure.

The Senate as a Court

The Senate also has a *judicial* function. It sits as a court in judgment on officials who have been impeached. The initiative in impeachment proceedings is taken by the House of Representatives, which passes a resolution charging a civil officer (any federal official, including judges but not military officers or members of Congress) with "treason, bribery, or other high crimes and misdemeanors." A committee of House members then prosecutes the impeached official before the Senate. On such an occasion the Senate takes on a judicial character—it issues writs, subpoenas witnesses, and administers oaths. (When a President is on trial, the Chief Justice of the United States presides.) A two-thirds vote is required for conviction; the penalty is removal from office and possible ineligibility for any other federal office. The Senate has sat as a court of impeachment on twelve occasions and has given a verdict of "Guilty" four times. The most dramatic trial—and the only one involving the Chief Executive—was that of President Andrew Johnson, who in 1868 escaped conviction by only one vote after the Senate had sat for three months.

Senate Solidarity

In view of the Senate's political and constitutional powers, it is no wonder that the individual member is a person to be reckoned with. Even Presidents at times have had to defer to the wishes of some veteran senator who is entrenched in a state political organization and at the same time heads a powerful legislative committee. Such a man looms large on the Washington scene. His speeches receive nationwide attention, his name comes to stand for a particular public policy, such as economy, military preparedness, social legislation, or a big air force.

In a sense, the Senate is a mutual-protection society. Each member tends to

[17] See Robinson, *op. cit.*

guard the rights and perquisites of his fellow senators—so that his own rights and perquisites will be protected in turn. Any legislative body is a close-knit social and occupational group, and the members must learn to live with one another. This group feeling is especially strong in the Senate, with its small size and hallowed traditions. Senatorial solidarity often cuts across lines of party and issue. Two senators may attack each other rather sharply on the floor, only to be seen a short time later strolling together in the corridors outside. This sense of solidarity enables the Senate to show a united front against any outside force, such as the President, that seems to be challenging its privileges and powers.

The Senate, in short, is something of a club. Indeed, within recent years reporters and political scientists have discerned a club *within* the Senate—an "inner club," without name or officers, made up of "Senate types" who dominate the politics and procedures of the upper chamber. Republicans Everett M. Dirksen of Illinois and Bourke B. Hickenlooper of Iowa are Senate types as are Democrats Harry F. Byrd of Virginia and Richard B. Russell of Georgia. These "inner club" members of both parties bolster the solidarity of the Senate, despite partisan differences. Senator Joseph S. Clark of Pennsylvania charged on the floor of the Senate in 1963 that there was a "Senate establishment" that was almost the antithesis of democracy. "It appears to be quite unresponsive to the caucuses of the two parties, be they Republican or Democratic. It is what might be called a self-perpetuating oligarchy with mild, but only mild, overtones of plutocracy." [18] On the other hand, the Senate is a tolerant institution, and short of going too far, as did Senators Huey Long and Joe McCarthy, the Senate even supports those of its members who refuse to abide by the rules of the "inner club," who champion lost causes, and who play a more lonely role, as have such "outer club" members of the past as Robert La Follette and George Norris, and of today as Wayne Morse and Paul Douglas.[19]

Two other factors lie behind a senator's sense of authority and independence. One is his six-year term of office. Members who win election four times—and many of them accomplish this feat—see six presidential terms come and go. No wonder veteran senators exhibit a sense of permanence and position even when dealing with the President. Perhaps more important is the right of almost unlimited debate. The *filibuster* not only symbolizes the power of the individual senator—it also provides a basis of that power. One senator, moreover, can easily disrupt the bills and business of his fellow members by spiking efforts to expedite action, by the simple means of shouting "I object" every time the presiding officer calls for unanimous consent to a particular motion. "Live and let live" might be the Senate's motto— and might help explain why it has become one of the most powerful and yet individualistic assemblies in the world.

[18] Joseph S. Clark, *The Senate Establishment* (Hill and Wang, 1963). See also Donald R. Matthews, *U. S. Senators and Their World* (Univ. of North Carolina Press, 1960); and W. S. White, *Citadel* (Harper, 1957).

[19] White, *op. cit.* (1957); Matthews, *op. cit.* See also Ralph K. Huitt, "The Outsider in the Senate: An Alternative Role," *The American Political Science Review* (September 1961), pp. 566–575.

The House v. The Senate

When the framers created a two-chamber national legislature, they anticipated each would represent sharply different interests. The Senate was to be a small chamber of men elected indirectly by the people and holding long, overlapping terms. The House of Representatives, elected *in toto* every two years, was to be the direct implement of the people. The Senate did provide a conservative check on the House, especially in the late nineteenth and early twentieth centuries when it was "a bastion of conservatism, something of a 'rich man's club,' and highly resistant to liberal or progressive sentiment." [20] But many factors, chiefly political, have altered the character of the House and the Senate. In recent years, especially since World War II, except for the civil rights legislation, the House has become a conservative check on the more liberal Senate.

How has this come about? One reason is the large number of relatively safe seats in the House that we noted above. By a recent estimate, out of a total of 435 congressional seats, only about 125 are really contested each year. This means that aside from great election sweeps such as those of 1936 and 1964, these representatives are quite safe in their little enclaves. Safe seats tend to be from districts that consist of a relatively smaller number of different kinds of constituency interests than competitive seats.

At the same time that the number of safe noncompetitive House districts has been increasing, the number of safe noncompetitive Senate seats has been *decreasing* as the number of statewide electorates with a two-party character is growing. Some senators, especially southerners, enjoy safe seats, but not to the same extent as in the House. Moreover, the urbanization of the nation has left most states with large and growing metropolitan areas. Hence a senator's constituency is usually more populous than a representative's and consists of a wider variety of interests.[21] Compare, for example, the conservative Republican representatives from upstate New York, who have little fear of offending those who live in New York City, with Republican Senator Jacob Javits, who must be concerned above all with the mass of voters in the New York City area.

Summarizing this chapter, we note that (1) Congress has surrendered its great creative law-making role to the President but has retained important functions of discussion, investigation, and assistance to constituents; (2) the most important work of Congress is done in committees, whose chairmen are appointed on the basis of seniority and tend to be conservative or middle-of-the-road in their stands on legislation; (3) each chamber has special devices for protecting minorities, most

---

[20] H. D. Price, "The Congressman and the Electoral Arena," in David B. Truman (ed.), *The Congress and America's Future* (Prentice-Hall, 1965).

[21] Froman, *op. cit.*, ch. 6, "Why the Senate is More Liberal Than the House." Froman finds that the tendency of legislative leaders to be more conservative than the rank-and-file, and the stronger hierarchical organization of the House are other reasons for the difference between the two chambers.

notably the Rules Committee in the House and the right to filibuster in the Senate; and (4) important differences between the two chambers are their size, basis of representation, length of members' terms, and the recent and rather surprising tendency, in the light of the framers' intentions, for the Senate to be the more liberal chamber of the two.

Thus the structure of power of President and Congress is a complex and changing one. At times in the past the House has been the great positive agency of the national government; today the Senate and White House often propose, the House vetoes. This relationship could shift in the future as blocking devices in each chamber may be changed. Whatever the changes, however, the fundamental structure of power envisaged by the framers of the Constitution will continue. For that structure of power is based on the checks and balances system—on the representation of different sets of voters by President, Senate, and House. Whatever the organizational changes *within* Congress or the Presidency, there is little prospect of basic change in the separate election of President, senators, and representatives. We will return to the implications of this situation for *representation* and *responsibility* in Chapter 20.

17 CONGRESSMEN AT WORK

Congress is composed of politicians who have succeeded in winning office. As politicians, the senators and representatives live amid the pulls and pressures of their constituents, powerful interest groups, party leaders in and out of Congress, and the President. To understand Congress, we must see its institutions and procedures as part of what has been called the "legislative struggle." Let us look at this struggle in terms of the pressures,

powers, and problems that affect a typical congressman—Representative Smith—
in his work on Capitol Hill.

Mr. Smith Goes to Washington

When Mr. Smith leaves his home for Washington, he carries with him political
debts and political hopes. In a way, his biggest debt is to the majority of voters
in his district who elected him to office. His chief hope is to keep the support of a
majority of the voters and thus to stay in office. How can he do this? It is not just
a matter of living up to the platform for which his supporters presumably voted.
He does not really know just who his supporters are, or just what policies they
favored. He does not really know how to keep their backing. Conditions will change.
Some of his supporters will turn against him; others will return to the ranks of
the nonvoters.

Represent Whom?

The chances are that Mr. Smith
will work most actively for those who most directly helped him win the election.
If his campaign was typical, his victory in that election did not seem to hinge
chiefly on his attitude toward broad national issues, for the voters were not
occupied with such issues, or their views were vague and diffused. If they had been
interested in national problems, Mr. Smith's job of staying in office might be easier,
for he could simply vote "right" on each bill as it came up. As it is, Mr. Smith, like
most of his fellow legislators, decides that one way to stay in office is to maintain
close and friendly contacts with the leaders of the personal organization that he set
up during his campaign.

Some of his most effective support came from *leaders of organized groups* in his
district—particularly occupational interest groups. He owes a debt to these persons,
and he finds in Washington that he is expected to pay that debt. The associations
that he dealt with locally—the labor organizations, or the Farm Bureau Federation,
or the American Legion—are well represented in Washington, and their legislative
agents are quick to arrange a meeting with Mr. Smith and acquaint him with their
programs. Although an organization may have taken positions on broad national
issues, such as foreign policy or taxation, it is mainly concerned with specific bills
conferring benefits on its members. On these bills—which are little known to his
constituents as a whole—Mr. Smith is expected to vote favorably. His support is a
means of paying his political debt, and he knows that his actions will be reported
to the organization's members back home.

Mr. Smith also enjoyed the support of *local party leaders*. He probably has no
great sense of obligation to the party in his district, for an effective local party
hardly exists. But he does owe a debt to the individual party leaders back home,
who worked for him and used their party contacts in his behalf. These local party

leaders are not, for the most part, concerned with national legislation, but they are greatly interested in patronage and favors. They look to Mr. Smith for both. As a freshman representative, he does not control much patronage in Washington, but he is permitted to fill certain jobs in the congressional establishment—an elevator operator, perhaps, or messenger—and he probably can find other jobs in the administrative departments. More important are the federal appointments in his district over which he may have some influence: postmasters, tax collectors, United States marshals, federal attorneys, and other positions not fully covered by nonpartisan civil service laws. Of course, Mr. Smith has little or no patronage if the President belongs to the opposition party. And even if his own party is in power, he may have to share the patronage with one or two senators. Actually, this never-ending scramble for jobs is one of the most trying aspects of his work. Every time he gives out a position, he suspects glumly that he is making nine enemies and one ingrate.

Mr. Smith's loyalty to local party officials does not necessarily extend to the national party organization. To be sure, he keeps in touch with party leaders *in* Congress, and he must clear his patronage through his national party chairman. Beyond these contacts, however, he sees very little of the party organization in Washington, for the national committee rarely meets or tries to set policy. Occasionally, Mr. Smith hears from the national chairman on a legislative matter that the party considers important. But he feels small sense of obligation. The national party gave him little if any help in the campaign, and he knows that voting as his district seems to want him to vote will probably win him more friends than following the national party line.

As a congressman, Mr. Smith keeps all these considerations in mind. This does not mean, however, that he is merely a calculating machine, with various forces punching the keys. For Mr. Smith brings to Congress certain political convictions of his own. He may feel that labor has too much power, that big business should be curbed, that the cost of government should be reduced. No matter what pressures converge on him in Washington, Mr. Smith neither can nor wishes to shake off the ideas that have been part of his environment since birth. In short, Mr. Smith's official acts are not simply a result of the pressures acting *on* him. They are also a result of the pressures acting *within* him.[1]

The Congressman Looks at His Job

Undoubtedly, Mr. Smith finds a great many satisfactions in his job. He is an important person back home and one of his party's leaders. In Washington he is paid $32,000 a year and an allowance for travel and other expenses. And he enjoys some rather special privileges: He has absolute immunity for whatever he says on the floor of Congress or before a congressional committee; he is privileged from arrest during attendance at Congress or in going to or from Congress, except in cases of treason, felony, or breach of the peace; and under his postal frank he may use the mails without charge to

[1] See Stephen K. Bailey, *Congress Makes a Law* (Columbia Univ. Press, 1950), pp. 192–193.

write to his constituents and even to send out election
literature—a privilege denied to his election opponent,
of course. He enjoys a good deal of legislative assistance,
including the help of the Legislative Reference Service,
consisting of recognized experts in a variety of national
problems.[2] Beyond all this there is the excitement and
challenge of the job, the feeling of taking part in great
events, and the attraction of being able to help others.

But there are drawbacks, especially for the eager young
freshman who wants to do big things, and in a hurry.
He must work with the system if he wants to get anywhere, and the congressional system is hard to learn and
even harder to work. He has to spend an enormous amount
of time catering to the needs of individual constituents.
In addition to the many chores he performs in behalf of
his constituents, there is always the mail, which is a
heavy burden. To get a bill onto the floor, to gain membership on a good committee, to retain independence
while working within the system, to do a good job but
still have enough time with one's family—each of these
efforts means a struggle. Above all, the congressman
grieves over the difficulty of his legislative role. "I am
appalled," says one, "at how much congressmen are expected to do for the nation. We have to know too much.
We have to make too many decisions. . . . No matter
how hardworking and conscientious a congressman is,
no matter how much homework he does, he just can't
master these problems. We just don't have the time to
keep informed properly."

But few congressmen retire voluntarily. If nothing else,
they receive a superb education in politics. "What makes
this thing so fascinating," according to one Representative, "is that it is a human panorama. Tremendous psychological forces are working all the time and human
relations are in play constantly. It is so complex you
couldn't actually draw the lines of interrelationship. There
is the element of friendship, there is every degree of respect and relationship. What makes one man follow another man's lead? That is what makes it so fascinating."[3]

9:00—Congressman arrives at office.

9:01—Telephone rings. Talks, signs mail.

9:58—Rushes off to committee meeting.

10 to 12—Hearing. At noon goes to floor.

1:00—Starts lunch. Call-bell rings.

[2] Kenneth Kofmehl, *Professional Staffs of Congress* (Purdue Univ.
Press, 1962), pp. 154–155, also contains an analysis of the entire
range of staff assistance.
[3] This and the previous quotation are from Charles L. Clapp, *The
Congressman: His Work as He Sees It* (Brookings, 1963), pp. 104–
105, 435, an illuminating picture of Congress as seen by members.

3:00—Page bring note. Lady outside.

4:00—At office, sees home-state students.

4:15—Call to floor again.

7 to 12—Does homework.

6:30—Dinner with wife.   "   12:00—And so to bed.

A day in the life of a congressman.
(Roy Doty; © 1965 by The New York
Times Co. Reprinted by permission.)

535 Ombudsmen

Mr. Smith knows that one way to win the support of his constituents is by doing countless individual favors. His office is well set up for this task. He has the service of several secretaries and stenographers, as well as a full-time legislative aide. Most important, government agencies are eager to respond to Mr. Smith's requests. Still, one representative has complained that a congressman is just a glorified messenger boy, employment agency, trouble shooter, gladhand extender, convention goer, veterans' affairs adjuster, financial wet nurse, good samaritan, and recoverer of lost baggage!

Frustrating and time-consuming as these chores are, they are not only important for a congressman's own re-election, but they provide a vital governmental role. In this era of big government, which often seems cold and impersonal, congressmen serve as friendly mediators between the citizen and the bureaucrats. In some Scandinavian countries a special official, the *Ombudsman*, receives and investigates complaints in behalf of the individual citizen who feels that he has a grievance against governmental officials. The United States has 535 legislators who serve industriously as *ombudsmen* for their local constituents.[4] But it is not easy for Mr. Smith to be so

4 H. D. Price, "Congressmen and the Electoral Arena," in David B. Truman (ed.), *The Congress and America's Future* (Prentice-Hall, 1965).

philosophical about this client-caretaking. He has come to Washington to legislate—and sometimes he feels that lawmaking is the least of his duties.

The Smith Bill Runs the Gantlet

The diagram on pp. 458–459 indicates the formal stages a bill must go through to
become law. But the *political* as well as the procedural aspects of lawmaking must
be kept in view. Let's suppose that Representative Smith decided to sponsor a bill.

It was not until his third term of office that Mr. Smith was able to sponsor
legislation on which he had set his heart from the beginning. This was a bill to
raise and broaden minimum-wage standards. Usually even a third-termer would
not have the chance to sponsor an important piece of legislation requested by the
President and party leaders. Mr. Smith, a member of the Education and Labor
Committee, got the chance only because the chairman of the committee was
opposed to the bill, the next-ranking member was ill, and two other senior members
did not want to commit themselves to specific changes in minimum-wage standards
until a later time.[5]

The first step was a meeting with the President. Mr. Smith and several other
members of the committee had a fifteen-minute interview with him in the White
House. The President, who did most of the talking, offered no suggestions on the
details of the proposed legislation; he simply asked that the coverage of the bill be
as broad as possible. He also requested that the committee work closely with the
Secretary of Labor to maintain smooth relations between Congress and the executive on this matter. After the exchange of a few pleasantries, the congressmen left.

Drumming up Support

Mr. Smith was glad to sponsor
the bill because minimum wages had been one of his campaign issues. But now
that he was ready to champion it, he found little interest in the matter back home.
Local labor leaders and liberal groups endorsed the proposed legislation, of course,
but without creating much of a stir. Mr. Smith wanted publicity. He saw that he
himself would have to create it. At his suggestion, a committee of liberals, union
leaders, and small businessmen began a campaign for the bill in his district. Letters
appeared in newspapers. Resolutions were adopted calling on Mr. Smith for action.
Hundreds of people signed petitions demanding a raise in minimum standards. At
the height of the campaign, Mr. Smith appeared at a mass meeting and promised to
fight for the bill. He returned to Washington with cheers still ringing in his ears.

The next step was the difficult one of writing the bill. Mr. Smith took a rough

---

[5] This description is drawn chiefly from Bailey, *op. cit.*, and J. M. Burns, *Congress on Trial*
(Harpers, 1949), ch. 5, "The Story of Three Bills." Descriptions of the handling of actual bills
will be found in Chapters 17, 25, 26 and below. See also Daniel M. Berman, *A Bill Becomes A
Law* (Macmillan, 1962).

draft over to the Department of Labor—and found that officials there had already drawn up their own bill, complete with preamble and a dozen clauses. Mr. Smith was disturbed to find that the administration bill, as the Labor Department people called it, went much further than his. For example, Mr. Smith wanted to exempt from inclusion in the bill small retail businesses employing only members of the owner's family; the administration bill covered such workers. An inconclusive argument ensued. It was agreed to hold another meeting in a week.

During the next few days Mr. Smith got some telegrams from the union leaders in his district in support of the administration bill. Surprised and disturbed, Mr. Smith telephoned them to ask why they had changed from their previous positions. They answered that they had talked the matter over with their national headquarters. At the next meeting the Labor Department officials brought with them two national union leaders and a representative from the White House. Mr. Smith was assured by his visitors that the administration draft was supported by the President and by the national AFL-CIO. He soon gave in on some of the major points. He insisted, however, that the new compromise draft retain one of his provisions exempting fruit-canners (who were fairly strong in his district) from any change in hours standards. He warned that unless this provision was kept in, he would not sponsor the bill. He got his way on this matter. After getting legislative counsel to help him polish up the bill, Mr. Smith introduced the measure into the lower chamber by placing it in the hopper on the clerk's desk which is near the Speaker's rostrum.

The clerk, acting for the Speaker, promptly gave the bill a number—H.R. 2102 —and referred it to the Committee on Education and Labor. Then ensued an irritating delay of six weeks. The trouble was—and Mr. Smith knew it—that the committee chairman did not want to act on the bill. First the bill got lost somewhere in the chairman's office. When finally found, the bill had to wait while the chairman held hearings on some other measures. It was only after Mr. Smith appealed to the Speaker and Majority Leader, and after the Labor Department asked help from the President, that the chairman finally announced that hearings on the bill would commence.

Running Interference

Meanwhile Mr. Smith was busy making plans for presenting the case for his bill. (He knew that the committee chairman would see to it that the bill's opponents had a chance to speak.) To lead his parade of witnesses he enlisted the Secretary of Labor, the head of the AFL-CIO, and the senator who had introduced a companion bill to H.R. 2102 in the Senate. A good strategist, Mr. Smith knew that the hearings should not give the impression that labor was for the bill and business and agriculture opposed. So he tried to split the opposition. Fearing that the big organizations of farmers employing hired hands might oppose the bill, he got a promise from the National Farmers Union that it would send an official to endorse H.R. 2102. Knowing that some small manufacturers in his district feared low-wage competition in the South, he asked them to urge their national association of small businessmen to take sides. But the national association had a number of influential members from the South in its ranks, so Mr. Smith was unable to get its support. Instead, some representatives of northern industry agreed to testify.

At first the hearings went splendidly for Mr. Smith and his bill. The "big names" spoke briefly for H.R. 2102, and committee members did not wish to cross-examine them too vigorously. Then trouble developed. After the Farmers Union spokesman endorsed the bill, the chairman called on representatives of the other major farm organizations, who stated that the great majority of farmers did not want an increase in minimum wages because it would raise their labor costs. By asking leading questions, the chairman brought out the fact that his witnesses spoke for many more farmers than did Mr. Smith's. That was bad enough—but then another committee member attacked one of Mr. Smith's liberal businessmen as a former member of two communist-dominated organizations. Mr. Smith was glad that he was able immediately afterward to present the president of a World War II veterans' organization, who spoke in favor of the bill. His hope of gaining business support was further dashed, however, when the National Association of Manufacturers advanced some amendments that—in Mr. Smith's mind at least— would cripple the bill.

The hearings lasted six days. Despite frequent clashes between committeemen and witnesses—and sometimes among committeemen themselves—the hearings played a valuable role. Many useful suggestions were made. A great deal of important economic and statistical material was put into the record. And virtually every interest group involved was able to offer views orally or in writing. True, over half the committee members were absent most of the time, but they could consult the voluminous printed record later on.

Following the open hearings, the committee met in secret *executive session*. Mr. Smith had already begun to count noses. He knew that of the twenty committeemen of his own (majority) party, twelve favored the bill, five opposed it, and three were doubtful. Of the ten members of the minority party, six seemed hostile to the bill, two friendly, and two on the fence. Mr. Smith knew that he needed a majority of at least sixteen—and seventeen or eighteen would be safer— in reporting out the bill, for Congress rarely approves a bill without a favorable committee report. The first executive session, in which the bill was discussed section by section, gave him a chance to see just where his fellow committeemen stood. Soon afterward he conferred with the Majority Leader of the House, who then induced the President to invite to lunch three of the doubtful members of the majority party and two of the straddlers—but not the chairman, who was considered beyond hope. At the luncheon table, the President did not try to pressure his guests, but he made his own position clear, described the need for party unity, and incidentally agreed to straighten out some patronage matters that were troubling one or two of the representatives.

Mr. Smith also saw to it—with the help of labor and liberal organizations—that the erring members were deluged with letters and telegrams in behalf of the bill. Most of these communications came from within the members' districts. The combined approach worked. At the next executive session, three of the President's four guests were generally in favor of the measure. The real danger now was the adoption of crippling amendments. While announcing their support of the general principles of the bill, member after member demanded amendments that would exempt certain areas, occupations, or classes of workers. Helplessly Mr. Smith watched while his colleagues kept the log rolling, each supporting another's amendment so that his own amendment would go through in turn. After three such meetings the bill was a tattered remnant of what it had been. Indeed, it had been so weakened that in the final committee vote the bill received the support of half the opposition party members and of all Mr. Smith's party members, including even the chairman.

Into the House

For a time Mr. Smith considered dropping the whole matter. He was reminded, however, that the bill might be strengthened on the floor of the House, and perhaps in the Senate too. He already had a favorable committee report before the House. He decided that the next step was to try to get favorable action from the Rules Committee.

Here Mr. Smith's bill came up against one of its biggest hurdles. The Rules Committee was composed of veteran representatives, a majority of whom were members of the majority party but often sided with the minority. Not only did Mr. Smith need a go-ahead sign from Rules, but he also wanted a rule that would prevent his bill from getting loaded down with amendments during House debate. For three weeks Rules refused to act at all, but when Mr. Smith and other representatives began to talk about prying a rule out by a *discharge petition* (requiring signatures of a majority of the members), the Rules Committee granted a rule. Under the terms of the rule, debate was to take four hours, divided between proponents and opponents of H.R. 2102. The rule also provided, however, that anyone on the floor could offer amendments.

Mr. Smith was floor manager of the bill; with the Majority Leader he worked out a schedule that allotted thirty minutes to himself and brief five-minute speeches to other supporters of H.R. 2102. The rest of the time was parceled out by minority party leaders to opponents of the bill. The Speaker was to use these two lists in recognizing representatives who wanted to speak on the bill. Meanwhile Mr. Smith was busy lining up support. He arranged with a White House official for a formal message from the President endorsing the objectives of the bill and asking for stronger provisions. Labor organizations set up a nationwide Committee on Social Rights, which issued propaganda for the bill. Lobbyists visited representatives in their offices and buttonholed them in the corridors. Delegations of businessmen and workers arrived in Washington from the lawmakers' districts. A torrent of mail descended on Capitol Hill. The opposition was equally active.

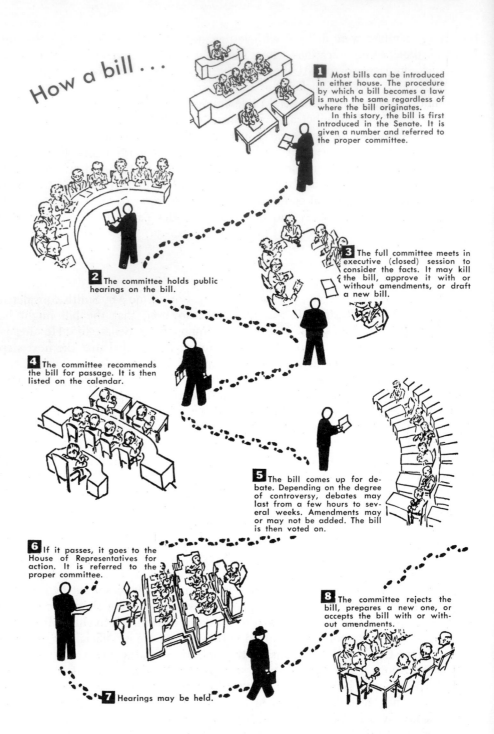

How a bill . . .

1 Most bills can be introduced in either house. The procedure by which a bill becomes a law is much the same regardless of where the bill originates.
In this story, the bill is first introduced in the Senate. It is given a number and referred to the proper committee.

2 The committee holds public hearings on the bill.

3 The full committee meets in executive (closed) session to consider the facts. It may kill the bill, approve it with or without amendments, or draft a new bill.

4 The committee recommends the bill for passage. It is then listed on the calendar.

5 The bill comes up for debate. Depending on the degree of controversy, debates may last from a few hours to several weeks. Amendments may or may not be added. The bill is then voted on.

6 If it passes, it goes to the House of Representatives for action. It is referred to the proper committee.

7 Hearings may be held.

8 The committee rejects the bill, prepares a new one, or accepts the bill with or without amendments.

Adapted from Journal of the National Education Association.

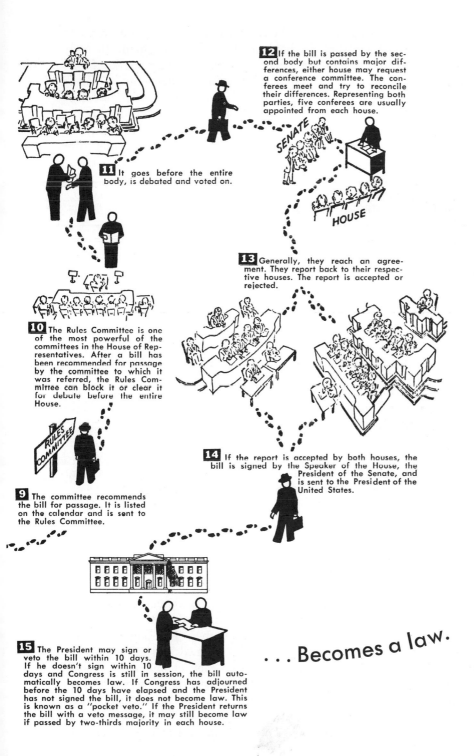

12 If the bill is passed by the second body but contains major differences, either house may request a conference committee. The conferees meet and try to reconcile their differences. Representing both parties, five conferees are usually appointed from each house.

SENATE

HOUSE

11 It goes before the entire body, is debated and voted on.

13 Generally, they reach an agreement. They report back to their respective houses. The report is accepted or rejected.

10 The Rules Committee is one of the most powerful of the committees in the House of Representatives. After a bill has been recommended for passage by the committee to which it was referred, the Rules Committee can block it or clear it for debate before the entire House.

RULES COMMITTEE

9 The committee recommends the bill for passage. It is listed on the calendar and is sent to the Rules Committee.

14 If the report is accepted by both houses, the bill is signed by the Speaker of the House, the President of the Senate, and is sent to the President of the United States.

15 The President may sign or veto the bill within 10 days. If he doesn't sign within 10 days and Congress is still in session, the bill automatically becomes law. If Congress has adjourned before the 10 days have elapsed and the President has not signed the bill, it does not become law. This is known as a "pocket veto." If the President returns the bill with a veto message, it may still become law if passed by two-thirds majority in each house.

. . . Becomes a law.

By the time the debate opened, almost all the representatives had made up their minds; the real question was whether the bill would be amended to death and abandoned. The worst threat was an amendment that would have excluded from H.R. 2102 all employees involved in the raising, processing, or delivering of farm or related products. This catch-all, which Mr. Smith knew would cut out the heart of the bill, had the backing of a formidable group of representatives from farm states, the opposition party, and low-wage areas. Only by inducing the Speaker to leave the rostrum and make a personal appeal on the floor, and by warning the farm representatives that labor would vote down agricultural legislation unless they supported H.R. 2102, was Mr. Smith able to save the bill. The final threat came on a motion to *recommit* the bill to committee—in effect a motion to kill it. When this attempt narrowly failed, the members voted overwhelmingly in favor of the measure.

When Senate and House Disagree

Mr. Smith's long battle was over—or half over, for H.R. 2102 would still have to clear the Senate. There the bill normally would go through the same steps as in the House—introduction (by a senator who agrees to sponsor the bill jointly with Mr. Smith), long committtee hearings, executive committee meetings, debate on the floor, and all amid political conflict throughout the nation. There is no Rules Committee in the Senate to hold up the bill, but a filibuster might stall it on the floor. The senators, moreover, might be somewhat less responsive to direct pressure from home because of their longer terms.

Let us suppose, however, that Mr. Smith's bill passed the Senate but in substantially different form from the version passed by the House. This is likely, for, as we have seen, the Senate and House often differ. Such differences, moreover, can create an acute problem, since each chamber has veto power over the other. Only if both houses pass an absolutely identical measure can it become law. How do the legislators resolve their disagreements?

The answer is the *conference committee*. If neither house will accept the other's bill, a special committee of members from each chamber settles the differences. Appointed to the conference committee by their presiding officers, the members are usually the first lawmakers who handled the bill in their respective chambers. The most senior senator usually serves as chairman of the conference committee, which has anywhere from three to nine members from each house. Both parties are represented, with the majority party having a larger number. The proceedings of this committee—not open to the public—are usually a shrewd and elaborate bargaining process. Concessions must be made not only to each chamber but to the more powerful groups within the chambers. Brought back to the respective chambers, the conference report can be accepted or it can be rejected (often with further negotiations ordered), but it cannot be *amended*. Each set of conferees must convince its colleagues that any concessions made to the other house were on trivialities, and that nothing basic in their own version of the bill was surrendered.

How much leeway does a conference committee have? Ordinarily the conferees are expected to stay somewhere between the alternatives set by the different versions; for example, if the House version of Mr. Smith's bill should set a minimum wage of $1.75 and the Senate bill $2.00, the conference committee would hardly come up with $2.25. But on many matters, where there is no clear middle ground, conferees are sometimes accused of "exceeding their instructions" and producing a new measure. Indeed, the conference committee has even been called a "third house of Congress" that arbitrarily revises Senate and House policy in secret session. Despite such criticism, however, some kind of conference committee is indispensable to the workings of a bicameral legislature such as Congress.

Congressmen as Investigators

Both senators and representatives are on a constant quest for facts, ideas, and advice. They need information and opinion in making laws, in publicizing governmental activities, in attacking the other party or other political officials, in overseeing the administrative agencies. They obtain their information from committee hearings, the President, administrative agencies, other congressmen, interest groups, letters from constituents, the Library of Congress and its Legislative Reference Service, and from many other sources.

Why Congress Investigates

Hearings by standing committees or by their subcommittees are probably the most important source of information and opinion. Such inquiries provide an arena where experts can submit their views and data, statements and statistics can be entered into the record, and congressmen can quiz a wide variety of witnesses. When an important and controversial bill is under consideration, hearings will last for weeks, and a host of administrative officials, lobbyists, technical experts, interested citizens, and members of Congress will testify. Sometimes the hearings receive front-page billing in newspapers throughout the land; more often they are little publicized unless a well-known person is testifying. Congressmen cannot go to all the hearings, of course, but by means of verbatim records of the hearings they can follow the proceedings as they wish.

Committees investigate not only to collect facts and opinions. Many inquiries are largely *political* in nature—they are designed to help or hinder some bill or party or official. Members of Congress may have information already at hand, but they know that the effective publicizing of those facts before reporters and fellow congressmen may dramatize existing evils and the need for reform. For example, many of the corrupt practices of some labor racketeers "revealed" by Congress in 1959 were well documented in studies and reports; but the "exposés" in Washington helped create the right political climate to allow Congress to act. Hearings, in short, are often directed toward the people in an effort to mobilize public opinion.

Some investigations by regular committees have another purpose—the *over-seeing* of administration. A committee can summon any administrative official, from Cabinet officer to stenographer, to testify in public or private hearings. Some officials greatly fear these inquiries; they dread the loaded questions of hostile congressmen, and the likelihood that some administrative error in their agency may be uncovered and publicized.

Both the congressman and the administrator suffer certain handicaps in such hearings. The congressman is usually not expert in the field (although some members become highly expert after years of service on a particular committee), and he has a thousand other problems on his mind. The official knows his field, but he may not see the broader problems, and he feels ill at ease among unsympathetic legislators.[6] Despite occasional misunderstandings and abuses, however, the routine investigations of administration are an important means of checking administrative action. In this sense, investigations are an important part of the system of checks and balances.

The Constitution gives Congress major investigative powers. Private witnesses can be subpoenaed and required to testify. If the investigation is reasonably connected with matters over which Congress has power, and if the questions asked are pertinent to the purposes of the investigation, witnesses who fail to answer may be punished for contempt of Congress. Still, proceedings are more informal than in a court of law. Since the purpose of an investigation is to gain information, not to prosecute, persons before such committees are not, legally speaking, in jeopardy of life or limb. The elaborate safeguards of the judicial process are not always needed, and if required they might deny essential information to Congress and country.

"Grand Inquisitions"?

We have been talking about the day-to-day inquiries conducted by regular standing committees or their subcommittees. Special investigations made by standing, special, or select committees to probe particular questions present many of the same problems as the more routine inquiries, but in exaggerated form. Special investigations have long been undertaken by Congress. The first one took place in 1793, after General St. Clair's military expedition against the Indians had ended in disaster. Some representatives wanted to let President Washington look into the causes of the failure. But the House, taking matters into its own hands, set up a special investigating committee to act for Congress.

Since then, there have been many famous investigations. Corruption in public office has been repeatedly exposed; infringements of civil liberties uncovered;

[6] Roland Young, *This Is Congress* (Knopf, 1943), pp. 228–229.

harmful banking, stock exchange, and utility practices publicized; bureaucratic practices checked; "un-American" practices denounced. A particularly famous investigating committee was the Truman Committee, which, during World War II, probed into waste and inefficiency, made many constructive suggestions, and helped put its chairman into the White House. The number of investigations has also grown—in 1964, for example, Congress authorized almost 200 separate probes

—and the cost has multiplied several-fold in the past decade. Special investigating committees have all the powers of standing committees except that they normally may not introduce legislation. At the same time, they usually enjoy far greater publicity —and investigations thrive on publicity. These committees operate in the spotlight, and their proceedings are often covered by newsreel and television cameras and reported by a host of newsmen.

Tom Little; © *1965 by The New York Times Company. (Reprinted by permission.)*

Yet right here is where the danger lies. So eager are some investigators for sensational results that they often permit abuses that bring the congressional power of investigation into disrepute. This is nothing new. Early in the last century a committee was criticized for excessive zeal—probing the executive, it "pointed out little items, sniffed about dark corners, peeped behind curtains and under beds, and exploited every cupboard of the Executive household with a mousing alacrity, not so eager to correct abuses as to collect campaign material for damaging some candidate." [7] Recently some investigators have been so zealous in seeking publicity that they have indulged in defamation of character, bullying and mistreatment of witnesses, and outright partisanship. Sometimes even the better-intentioned have conducted mere fishing expeditions in the hope that something might turn up.

Are there any constitutional limits to Congress' power to compel private citizens to answer questions? The Supreme Court in 1957 (*Watkins* v. *United States*) cautioned Congress that the First Amendment limits its power to investigate, that no committee has the power "to expose for the sake of exposure," that Congress and its committees are not courts to try and punish individuals, and that "no inquiry is an end in itself; it must be related to, and in furtherance of, a legitimate task of Congress." Nonetheless, only a minority of the Supreme Court has shown any disposition to provide a judicial check on legislative investigations

[7] Quoted in Irving M. Ives, "In Place of Congressional 'Circuses,'" *The New York Times Magazine*, August 27, 1950, p. 20.

in behalf of First Amendment rights.[8] The judicial checks used so far are twofold: the Fifth Amendment protection against self-incrimination has been construed broadly to protect witnesses who are willing to risk public censure by invoking the amendment to refuse to answer questions; and the Supreme Court has narrowly construed the crime of contempt of Congress in order to avoid punishment of witnesses for refusing to answer questions unless these questions were *clearly pertinent* to the functions of an authorized committee.

The Power of the Purse

The gradual assumption by the legislature of the power to levy taxes and appropriate money is the story of the gradual establishment of democratic government. Although legislative investigations grab the headlines, by far the greatest weapon of Congress in maintaining control over the executive branch is its power to appropriate money. And under the Constitution only Congress can levy federal taxes and appropriate money. All tax bills constitutionally must first originate in the House and by custom so must appropriation measures also; but since the Senate can amend everything except the title of these bills, this distinction between the two chambers is of little consequence.

The President too initiates appropriations requests. Under the Budget and Accounting Act of 1921, the President with the aid of the Bureau of the Budget, presents a budget each year to the Congress early in January. (The fiscal year runs a year ahead of the calendar year, from July 1 through the subsequent June 30. Thus fiscal year 1967 began July 1, 1966.)

The appropriations requests from the President are first presented to the Appropriations Committee of the House of Representatives. This committee operates through twelve subcommittees each with its own staff. The head of the subcommittee is a veteran congressman who has almost the final word with the agencies within the jurisdiction of his subcommittee. Congress may have authorized the program, but each year the subcommittee members go over the budget, often instructing the agency head in detail how they want the money spent, and reminding him that he will be called to account next year.[9]

The subcommittee makes its report to the full Appropriations Committee which in turn recommends appropriations bills to the House. Each measure is debated on the floor of the House, sometimes for two or three days. When the bill is sent to the Senate, it is referred to the Senate Appropriations Committee. Smaller than its counterpart in the House, the Senate committee usually concentrates on controversial items and functions as an appeals body, allowing agency spokesmen to argue for restoration of funds slashed by the House.

---

[8] *Barenblatt* v. *United States* (1959); *Wilkinson* v. *United States* (1961); *Braden* v. *United States* (1961). See also Carl Beck, *Contempt of Congress* (Hauser, 1959).

[9] Richard F. Fenno, Jr., "The House Appropriations Committee," *The American Political Science Review* (June 1962), pp. 310–324; Aaron Wildavsky, *The Politics Of The Budgetary Process* (Little, Brown, 1964), pp. 47–62.

The President must either veto or accept the whole appropriations bill as it comes from the Congress; unlike most state governors he cannot veto individual items. Practically speaking, this gives him no choice but to sign the measure. The President, however, may instruct an agency not to spend funds even if Congress has appropriated them and continues to press for their expenditure.

Appropriations measures are subject to the same type of political pulling and hauling as other items in the legislative process. The President, whose chief concern is with the national and international responsibilities of the nation and with the fiscal and monetary impact of the federal budget, has one set of objectives. Congress as a whole may share the President's objectives, but it acts on appropriations chiefly by delegating the responsibilities to individual congressmen whose goals are often at cross purposes with that of the President. The congressman may be eager to push through a project for the benefit of his district, or to oppose a program for an agency which he finds objectionable. And of course the officials in the executive departments and the interests supporting them want maximum appropriations for their programs.

Despite the fact that individual congressmen often complain that the President's budget is too large, the result of congressional handling of the budget is often the enactment of appropriations larger than the President has asked, as each congressman adds to the budget funds for his particular district and for his favored programs. Moreover, the sheer size and detail of the budget tends to force congressmen's attention to details. Billions of dollars for one program will be passed with little debate, while congressmen argue for hours about the expense allowances of American diplomats abroad. (If a congressman were to spend an hour studying each million dollars of expenditures, it would take him over twenty years to go over the annual budget.)

On the basis of recommendations of various study commissions, Congress in recent years has been moving from a less detailed budget to one more broadly based on *performance* or *program* classifications, especially in the area of defense appropriations. Since budgetary procedures are at the heart of the political process, alterations in these procedures are alterations in how the process operates and hence have political consequences; they are *political*, not just administrative, changes. And as long as the budget of the national government amounts to tens of billions of dollars and congressional power is dispersed among a couple of dozens of leaders each of whom has an independent political base, congressional control over appropriations is likely to remain fragmented, sporadic, and incremental.

What's the Matter with Congress?

Congress is the nation's whipping boy. Newspaper editors, radio commentators, politicians, and plain citizens seem never to tire of berating individual legislators, blocs, or Congress as a whole. Cartoonists delight in portraying congressmen as timid, ignorant, selfish, and narrow-minded.

Much of this abuse is unjustified. Critics of Congress often seem to forget that our national legislature is particularly exposed to unfair attacks. In the first place, Congress does its work directly under the public eye. Unfortunate incidents—quarrels, name-calling, evasive actions, inaccurate statements—that might be hushed up in the executive branch are almost always observed by the alert journalists covering Congress for the whole nation. In the second place, Congress by its very nature is controversial and argumentative. Its members take stands on both sides—sometimes on half a dozen sides—of every important question, and the average citizen holding one opinion is likely to be intolerant of lawmakers holding other views.

Some of the abuse, moreover, stems from confusion *about* Congress as well as from confusion *in* Congress. There is lack of agreement on what the primary functions of Congress should be. Should it concentrate on making policies, debating them, investigating problems, or curbing the President and bureaucrats—or on something else? "Congress is in a legislative dilemma," it has been said, "because opinion conceives of it as a legislature. . . . An assembly need not legislate to exist and to be important. . . . The primary work of legislation must be done, and increasingly is being done, by the three 'houses' of the Executive branch: the bureaucracy, the administration, and the President. . . . Far more important than the preservation of Congress as a legislative institution is the preservation of Congress as an autonomous institution." [10] Huntington suggests that Congress should concentrate on constituent service and administrative oversight or—if it truly prefers a more traditional legislative role—it must undertake massive reform to reverse "trends toward insulation, dispersion, and oversight." [11] Others reject the notion of Congress abandoning its more traditional legislative role. But whatever Congress does it gets criticized. When it blocks Presidential proposals, those who favor the proposals accuse Congress of being a "roadblock." When Congress approves presidential proposals, those who oppose the proposals accuse Congress of being "a rubber stamp."

Confusion *in* Congress arises from the different jobs it does, the complexity of the procedure, the sheer number of legislators, the variety of viewpoints, the maze of party and group conflicts. At a baseball game almost anyone can understand the duel between pitcher and batter. In Congress a dozen pitchers throw a dozen balls to a dozen batters. Such complexity is not basically a result of procedural inefficiencies in Congress but of our constitutional and political system that divides up authority, checks power with power, and disperses political leadership. We will return to this problem in Chapter 20, after looking at two other parts of our system of checks and balances: the federal bureaucracy and the federal judges.

[10] Samuel P. Huntington, "Congressional Responses to the Twentieth Century," in David B. Truman (ed.), *The Congress and America's Future* (Prentice-Hall, 1965), p. 29.
[11] *Ibid.*, p. 31.

18 THE BUREAUCRATS

Government officials are people. We hear so
much these days about arrogant bureaucrats and
red-tape artists that it is well to keep this fact
in mind. The bureaucrat is the postman who just
stuck your mail in the door, Miss Green who
teaches sixth grade at P.S. 19, the cop directing
traffic on Elm Street, the judge who lives down
the way. He is the man fighting a forest fire in
Wyoming, the diplomat negotiating a treaty in

467

Argentina, the tax collector checking figures in New Orleans, the bureau chief
hurrying to the White House, the scientist studying a rare disease at a great medical center. These are people with hopes and worries, ambitions and frustrations,
abilities and failings—just like all the rest of us.

Flaying the bureaucrat is an old American custom, and to an extent is a wholesome one. And yet we need to remind ourselves that all large organizations, governmental or not, are run by bureaucrats. Bureaucracy is a characteristic form of
modern organization. We hear much of the "dead hand of bureaucracy," but
bureaucracy as a type is neutral. It can be efficient or inefficient, democratic or
autocratic, alert or stagnant. *Some* governmental bureaucracies—like *some* private
ones—are on balance inefficient (although inefficiency is very hard to measure).
Why, then, is the criticism of bureaucrats in government so loud and persistent?
Partly because Americans have a deep-seated fear of big government, partly because public officials work in a goldfish bowl under the sharp eyes of congressmen, columnists, radio and television commentators, and lobbyists.

In this chapter we are mainly interested in the 2.5 million people who make
up the executive branch of the federal government. Certain facts about these
people need to be emphasized at the outset:

1. Only a small part of the 2.5 million work in Washington. The great majority are employed in regional, field, and local offices scattered throughout the
country. California alone has well over a quarter of a million federal employees.
The stereotyped picture of a huge bureaucratic horde concentrated in Washington
is a false one.

2. More than half of these 2.5 million civilian employees work for the Army,
Navy, Air Force, or some other defense agency. The continuing world crisis has
put its stamp on our bureaucracy.

3. Only a small part of the bureaucrats—perhaps 10 per cent—work for so-
called welfare agencies, such as the Social Security Administration or the Rural
Electrification Administration. The welfare state may be a major point of controversy in our party battles, but it has a minor place in today's big government. A
still smaller proportion of government employees work in regulatory agencies,
such as the Interstate Commerce Commission.

4. Federal employees do not run to any one type. They are not all Democrats,
or all Republicans. They are not all college-educated. They are not all conservatives, or all liberals. They come from all parts of the country, have a variety of
religious faiths and political views, represent a great range of national origins.

5. Their work in government is equally varied. Not all these officials pound
typewriters or stamp forms or issue regulations, as the newspaper cartoons would
have us think. Over 15,000 different personnel skills—about two-thirds as many
as are found in all private business—are represented in the federal.government.
Like Americans generally, most government workers are specialists in some occupation or profession. Unlike Americans as a whole, however, most federal em-

ployees are white-collar workers—stenographers, clerks, lawyers, office heads, inspectors, and the like.

How important are the bureaucrats? In a sense, of course, they are all-important. They are the core of big government. Without officials and employees, government would be a collection of politicians and lawmakers—generals without armies. Government without a bureaucracy is unthinkable. So influential are the officials that sometimes the political heads seem insignificant. Alexander Pope said over 200 years ago:

> For forms of government let fools contest,
> Whate'er is best administer'd is best.

But this sentiment goes too far. *Forms of government* help shape the political world in which the administrator lives; they influence the kind of decisions made, and the way they are carried out. Administration in the United States is different from administration in Russia, Spain, or Nepal.

Actually we cannot separate administration from politics. The two are inextricably linked. Our job is not to put each in a separate sphere, but to see the interrelationship between the two. Our job is to ask questions: How is administration carried on? What kinds of problem do administrators face? What are their powers? How are they made accountable to the electorate? In short, *how can the bureaucrats do their jobs and yet remain our servants and not our masters?*

The Shape of Administration

Big government is complex government. The executive branch is a cluster of eleven departments, twenty-one government corporations, and forty-six independent agencies, together embracing over 1,800 bureaus, divisions, branches, offices, services, and other sub-units. In size, five big agencies, the Departments of Army, Navy, and Air Force, the Post Office, and the Veterans Administration, tower over all the others. Most of the agencies are responsible to the President, but some are partly independent of him. Virtually all the agencies exist by act of Congress; the legislators could abolish them either by passing a new law or by withholding funds. The power of Congress to set up departments and agencies is implicit in the Constitution. The framers simply assumed—without actually specifying— that Congress might establish such functions and organizations as it saw fit.

In its first session in 1789, Congress created the Departments of Foreign Affairs (later changed to State), War, and Treasury. During the next one hundred years the government grew slowly but fairly steadily. World War I brought a mushrooming of federal agencies, and many of these survived into the postwar years. World War II brought an even greater expansion, as the government mobilized armed forces of 15 million men, fought a war on many fronts, and controlled large areas of the nation's economy. The executive branch shrank after World War II, but not back to its prewar size, and increased sharply again during the Korean War.

Formal Organization

A soldier writes to his family that he is a member of the first squad of the second platoon of Company B of the 1st Battalion of the 426th Regiment of the 95th Division of the III Corps of the Ninth Army. A friend of his works in the personnel office of the parts section of the Flint Division of the Buick Department of General Motors. A "government girl" in Washington tells her father that she is in the stenographic section of the administrative service of the Budget and Finance Division of the Bureau of Supplies and Accounts of the Department of the Navy in the Department of Defense.

Bigness Means Organization. The larger the number of people and the more complex the job, the more highly organized the agency will be. In establishing a new agency, Congress may lay down a general structural plan in legislation, the President may give further shape to it in executive orders and in private instructions, and the head of the agency and his assistants will extend the organizational skeleton of the new agency down to small units. But the executive branch as a whole, it has been said, grew up "without plan or design like the barns, shacks, silos, tool sheds, and garages of an old farm." Although different functions produce different types of organization, in general the main agencies of government are composed of departments, corporations, independent agencies, and their subunits—bureaus, divisions, offices, and so on down the line—together with a network of regional and local offices.

The *departments* are headed by Secretaries (except Post Office, which is headed by the Postmaster General; and Justice, which is headed by the Attorney General). These Secretaries also are Cabinet members (except for the Secretaries of the Army, Navy, and Air Force, who report to the President through their chief, the Secretary of Defense) and thus are directly responsible to the President. While the departments vary greatly in size, they have certain features in common. Often an undersecretary takes part of the administrative load off the Secretary's shoulders. One or more assistant secretaries direct major programs. Like the President, the Secretaries have personal assistants who help them in planning, budget, personnel, legal, public relations, and other staff functions. The departments are, of course, subdivided into bureaus and smaller units, but the basis of division may differ. The most common basis is *function*; for example, the Commerce Department is divided into the Bureau of the Census, the Patent Office, the Weather Bureau, and so on. Or the basis may be *clientele* (for example, the Bureau of Indian Affairs of the Interior Department), or *work processes* (for example, the Economic Research Service of the Agriculture Department), or *area* (for example, the Alaskan Air Command of the Department of the Air Force). The basis of organization of most departmental units—and indeed of the departments themselves —is mixed.

The score or more of *government corporations*, such as the Tennessee Valley Authority and the Federal Deposit Insurance Corporation, are "mongrel" organizations. A sort of cross between a business corporation and a regular government agency, the government corporation was designed to make possible a freedom of action and flexibility not always found in the regular federal agencies. For example, corporations have been free from certain regulations of the Budget Bureau and the Comptroller General. They also have had more leeway in using their own earnings as they pleased. And yet the fact that the government *owns* the corporations means that it retains basic control over their activities. Recently, Congress has deprived the corporations of much of their freedom, and they have taken on some of the character of regular departments—they are no longer free from the need to get annual congressional appropriations, for example. They remain, however, useful means of keeping certain government activities (especially financial) somewhat apart from the routine, congested, and centralized federal agencies and from excessive congressional and presidential control, particularly in time of emergency.

The *independent agencies* comprise many types of organization and many degrees of independence. Broadly speaking, all agencies that are not corporations and that do not fall under an executive department (such as Treasury or Interior) are called independent agencies. Many of these agencies, however, are no more independent of the President and Congress than are the executive departments themselves. The huge Veterans Administration is not represented in the Cabinet, for example, but its chief is directly responsible to the President.

Another type of independent agency, however, really deserves the adjective. This is the *independent regulatory board* or *commission*—agencies like the Securities and Exchange Commission, the National Labor Relations Board, the Interstate Commerce Commission. Congress deliberately set up these boards to keep them somewhat free from White House influence in exercising their quasi-*legislative* and quasi-*judicial* functions. Congress did not want the President, for example, to interfere in the ICC's setting of railroad rates or deciding whether its rules had been violated by railroad companies. Congress has protected their independence in several ways. The boards are headed by three or more commissioners with overlapping terms, they often have to be bipartisan in membership, and the President's power of removal is curbed. But this independence is limited. No agency can be completely separate from its governmental and political surroundings (nor should it be). And many of the boards have found that the more independence they have of the President, the more dependent they are on Congress or on the interests they regulate.[1]

Within the departments, corporations, and independent agencies are a host of subordinate units. The standard name for the largest sub-unit is the *bureau*,

[1] R. F. Cushman, *The Independent Regulatory Commissions* (Oxford Univ. Press, 1941), especially ch. 10, is a classic treatment of this problem.

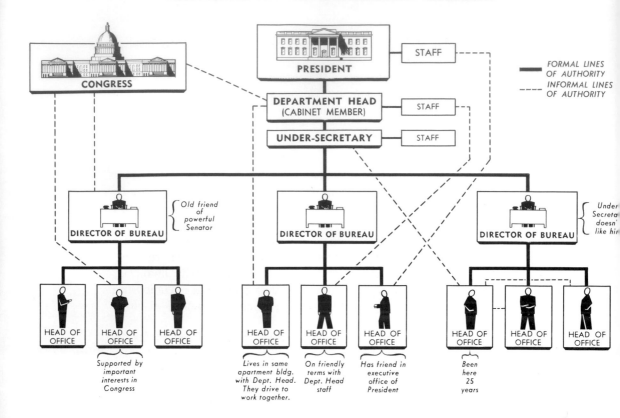

although sometimes it is called an office, administration, service, or what not. Bureaus are the working agencies of the federal government. In contrast to the big departments, which are often mere "holding companies" for a variety of agencies, the bureaus usually have fairly definite and clear-cut duties, as do the Bureau of Customs and Bureau of Narcotics of the Treasury Department, the Bureau of Indian Affairs of the Interior Department, the Bureau of Motor Carriers of the ICC. Most bureaus are overshadowed by their mother agencies, but some of them, like the Federal Bureau of Investigation and the Bureau of Reclamation, enjoy a popular prestige and political position of their own. Below the bureaus are hundreds of branches, services, sections, and other units that perform even more specialized operations.

The *field service* of the federal government embraces a vast number of regional, state, county, and local units. The local post office is part of the field service, as is the local recruiting center or veterans office. As the action end of government, the field service runs into many vitally important problems. Ticklish questions of coordination constantly arise. How can cooperation in the region be promoted between several federal offices with overlapping duties but responsible to different departments in Washington? How far is it possible and desirable to depart from national regulations in meeting local situations? Which decisions should be made on the spot, and which should be referred to Washington? How much collaboration should be tried with state and local governments? Washington administrators face problems, too: how far to decentralize, what decisions should be delegated to the field, what type of field organization is best suited to their needs (there are many types), how to combine local flexibility with national direction and responsibility.

Informal Organization

All this elaborate organization of the executive branch gives order and system to administration. It assigns certain functions to certain units, places one official (or sometimes more) at the head of each unit and makes him responsible for its performance, allows both specialization and coordination, permits ready communication, and in general makes our far-flung administration somewhat controllable and manageable. But this formal organization can be highly misleading if taken too seriously. The detailed organization chart on the office wall of some administrator may represent hope and intention rather than reality.

Why? Because men and women are not standardized units. They differ in attitude, motive, ability, experience. And their very diversity leads to all sorts of complications. Relationships among officials in an agency may be based on *influence* rather than on formal authority. Leadership may be lodged not at the top but in a variety of places. A certain group of officials may have considerable influence, while another group, with the same *formal* status, may have much less. The loyalties of some officials may cut across the formal aims of the agency.

Let us consider an imaginary but typical bureau. The bureau chief is an old-line administrator who has served through four presidential administrations. He is cautious and unimaginative. He has a rival in the person of an assistant to the secretary who heads the whole department. Some officials in the bureau look to this assistant for leadership; they share his enthusiasm and support his plans, and they hope that he may take over the department some day and give them the power and position they feel they deserve. But the bureau chief has his own set of motives and attitudes; moreover, he enjoys the backing of a powerful bloc in Congress that will defend him if he is attacked. He has built a personal organization, made up of two or three division chiefs, an attorney, the personnel officer, and his own staff, and this personal following is intensely loyal to him.

This, perhaps, is an extreme case; but it shows how *informal* organization can have a major effect on administration. A subordinate official in an agency, for example, might be especially close to his chief simply because they went to the same college or play poker together, or because the subordinate knows how to ingratiate himself with his chief. A staff official may have tremendous influence, not because of his formal authority, but because his experience, fairness, common sense, and general personality lead men to turn to him for advice. In an agency headed by a chief who is weak, unimaginative, phlegmatic, and incompetent, a vacuum may develop that encourages others to try to take over. The private secretary of an official, through her charm, tact, and understanding of her boss' job and the politics of the agency, may gain great influence in an organization. The elevator man has no formal power at all, but he is a vital link in the informal communications network in the agency, and his rumor-mongering distinctly affects the morale of the employees. Such informal organization and communication cutting across regular channels is inevitable to some degree in any organization, public or private. Even the Army, with all its hierarchy and regimentation, abounds with these elements.

Building the Team

The government administrator is not nearly so free in building his team as is the private businessman. Government has long followed prescribed methods of recruiting, examining, classifying, promoting, and dismissing personnel. For many years America had a notorious appointment system that was summed up in the slogan, "To the victor belong the spoils." When a new party came to power, its leaders and followers felt they had a right to take over desirable government jobs. The excuse was a double one. Parties should have patronage, it was said, to encourage members to work for the party, and to answer the people's demand for a new broom to sweep Washington clean. Men like Andrew Jackson argued, moreover, that a frequent turnover of officials would keep government democratic. Besides, they said, the duties of public officials were so plain and simple that any intelligent person could perform them.

Later in the century a sharp reaction set in against the spoils system. The job of government was becoming increasingly complex, and interested citizens, some of them organized in the National Civil Service Reform League, were agitating for reform. Presidents, too, were chafing under the pressures of hordes of jobseekers. Public opinion crystallized when President James A. Garfield was assassinated in 1881 by a disappointed office-seeker. Two years later Congress passed the Pendleton Act, which set up the beginnings of a merit system under a three-man bipartisan board, the Civil Service Commission. The act placed certain types of employees under a new classified service, which could be entered only by passing a competitive examination. Congress put relatively few employees under the new merit system, but it gave the President power to expand the classified service. As a result of a series of executive orders over the years, about three-quarters of the federal employees today hold jobs that are covered by a merit system and protected from patronage.

Today the administrator must work closely with the Civil Service Commission in staffing his agency. With about 4,000 employees of its own, the commission acts as a central agency in recruiting, examining, and appointing government workers. It advertises for new employees, prepares and administers oral and written examinations throughout the country, and makes up a register of names of those who pass the tests. When an agency wishes to employ a person, the commission certifies to it three names taken from the top of the appropriate register. The administrator has some voice in the type of examination given, and he has some freedom of choice under the rule of three, but obviously his discretion is greatly limited.

The centralization of personnel direction in the Civil Service Commission disturbs administrators eager for freedom and flexibility in their agency operations. They charge that the commission is entangled in red tape, uses old-fashioned personnel methods, and lacks initiative and imagination. Whatever its defects, over the years the Civil Service Commission has helped to keep most federal jobs out of the spoils system. Still designed to be nonpartisan, the commission is composed of three members (no more than two of the same party) with six-year terms.

This is not to say, however, that appointment to the classified service is based on merit considerations alone. There is still a strong feeling in the United States that government jobs are a form of reward.[2] The best example of this feeling is *veterans' preference*. Today five points are automatically added to the examination grades of all veterans, and they receive other special considerations. Disabled veterans, their wives, and their widows, are given a ten-point bonus. These provisions, supported by veterans' groups in and out of Congress, have aroused much controversy. Some have charged that veterans' preference is a racket; others say that the government owes a debt to the ex-servicemen and that it can easily find able recruits among them. At any rate, veterans' preference is probably here to stay. It is not surprising that about half the federal employees today are veterans.

Hiring is only the first step in building the administrative team. The administrator must see that appointees get into the right positions, that they are trained effectively, that their jobs are classified properly in terms of the nature and responsibility of the work. Here, too, the administrator shares his power with the Civil Service Commission. Around each of these fields, such as job classification, an elaborate procedure—indeed, virtually an administrative science—has grown up.

Managing the Team

In directing his agency, the good administrator is always conscious that he is directing people. As a practical psychologist, he must remember that people's actions are influenced not merely by instructions from the top. He must also remember that:

1. *People respond to many incentives.* Chester I. Barnard, an outstanding businessman and author of a classic volume on administration, has listed some of these as material rewards (money), the chance for prestige or power, agreeable working conditions, pride of workmanship, happy relations with workmates,

---

[2] H. A. Simon, D. W. Smithburg, V. A. Thompson, *Public Administration* (Knopf, 1950), pp. 323–324.

conformity to habitual practices, sense of taking part in something big, and patriotic or religious feeling.[3]

2. *People in administrative units tend to have a powerful feeling of group identity and defensiveness*. Most government workers are members of cohesive groups marked by excellent communication (that is, employees see one another throughout the working day), a sense of oneness, and a feeling of mutual protection. This in-group feeling has important practical effects. For example, the group may react in a hostile way to interference from outside the organization, particularly to attempts to reorganize it. At the same time, the desire of each person to have the respect and affection of his fellow workers is a big factor in promoting harmony, morale, and efficiency.

3. *People respond to influences from outside the agency as well as from within*. Government employees do not identify themselves wholly with the administrative unit to which they belong. They come to work as members of many groups—as southerners, veterans, Negroes, taxpayers, Catholics, and so on. The administrator faces the same problem of overlapping membership as the leader of a party or interest group.

4. *People—in the United States especially—have a mixed attitude toward authority*. Generally, government employees, like employees everywhere, will accept the orders of their superiors. But there are limits. Americans are individualists—they have their own opinions and they do not like to be pushed around. Much depends on the manner in which authority is exercised, and on the relations between administrator and employees.[4]

To put the whole matter another way, the administrator finds that the morale and efficiency of his unit are affected by *informal* as well as *formal* organization. He must be *people*-minded, not simply *stereotype*-minded.[5] In directing his agency, he must operate through informal channels of communication and organization as well as through formal channels. He ignores people's personalities— including their quirks and "bugs"—only at his peril.

On the other hand, the administrator has the benefit of certain powers or tools in running his unit. Much of his authority stems simply from his position as boss of the agency; his instructions are usually followed without question, and the agency is set up so that a stream of directions runs from the top to subordinate units. The administrator also has some power over promotions within the agency. Through this power he can reward able service and raise the ablest men and women to more responsible positions. Here, too, set procedures must be followed. Agencies are under pressure from the Civil Service Commission to give promotions only after examinations, some of which the commission itself conducts. Promotions are based also on an elaborate system of efficiency ratings which are given employees by their supervisors and which can be appealed to boards of

---

[3] C. I. Barnard, *The Functions of the Executive* (Harvard Univ. Press, 1938), pp. 142–148.
[4] Simon, Smithburg, and Thompson, *op. cit.*, pp. 70–71, 180–217.
[5] A. H. Leighton, *The Governing of Men* (Princeton Univ. Press, 1945), ch. 3.

review if employees question the fairness of their ratings. Administrators may gain some flexibility through transfers of personnel to and from their agencies, although transfers must be handled carefully because of their relation to morale.

Finally, the administrator can discharge unsatisfactory employees. Despite a popular notion to the contrary, government workers *can* be fired. The process, however, is hedged in by many rules to prevent arbitrary dismissals. During their first six months of employment, new appointees are on probation, and they can easily be dropped at the end of the period (though very few are). After the probationary period, however, an employee can be removed only "for such cause as will promote the efficiency of the service." He must be furnished with a written statement of the charges against him and be given time to reply. Some inefficient employees have used cumbersome appeal procedures to protect their jobs. In one case a stenographer appealed to four separate boards, while hanging on to her job for seventeen months before she finally quit. But such cases are exceptional.

Administrators as Decision-Makers

A policeman stops a student who fails to bring his car to a full halt before crossing a highway. The student admits that he did not come to a full halt, but he argues that he did look both ways before entering the highway, and he did slow down enough so that he had to shift into second gear. The officer lets him off with a lecture and a warning. Why? The law requires that the student be arrested and pay a fine. But the officer knows that a full halt is not necessary at this particular corner, so long as the driver is reasonably careful.

Here is a simple example of administrative discretion and decision-making. The officer is not an automaton. He is an experienced man of good sense. In this case he exercised two functions basic in the administrative process: He established his own rule and he made a judicial decision. In his own way he was participating in *administrative legislation* and *administrative adjudication.*

The Constitution gives legislative powers to the President and Congress, and judicial powers to the courts. Under today's big government some of these powers must be delegated to officials throughout the executive branch. Some officials have tremendous discretion, some have very little. Democratic government permits delegation of broad powers, but seeks to safeguard the manner in which those powers are exercised.

Big Decisions

Every day in hundreds of ways federal bureaucrats make decisions that affect our jobs, our pocketbooks, our lives. We may or may not know about these decisions. The Board of Governors of the Federal Reserve Board issues a ruling that affects the size of the down payment we must make on a new car. The Rural Electrification Administration decides to supply electricity to farmers in one valley but not in another. The director of the Bureau of Labor Statistics formulates a new method of computing price indexes—one that may affect the government's anti-inflation policies. The Attorney General decides to prosecute a large corporation under the antitrust law. Officials in charge of civil service examinations change their methods of testing. Safety officials in the Civil Aeronautics Board issue a new and more stringent set of air safety regulations.

Wars and near-wars have vastly broadened the decision-making powers of administrative officials, especially in agencies involved in making war and peace. Obviously, the Secretary of State in dealing with foreign powers makes decisions that gravely affect the chances of peace or war. The Atomic Energy Commission and the Defense Department jointly or separately decide on crucial policies that bear on our capacity to win a war. If war comes, the fate of the nation hangs on decisions of commanders in the field. Many military decisions are secret, but some are public and even become subjects of wide discussion.

To say that bureaucrats make important decisions, however, is not to say that they have a wide number of alternatives from which to choose. An administrator may have been given broad discretion by both Congress and the President, and yet feel constricted by other forces. For an administrator, like a congressman or a President, works amid a complex set of political pressures. In making a key decision he must try to anticipate the attitudes of his own agency, of experts inside and outside the agency, of other agencies involved in the decision, of interest groups affected by the decision, of the press, of the attentive public as a whole,[6] of the party in power and the opposition party, of Congress and the President, perhaps even of foreign governments. He must take into account all kinds of complex organizational and psychological relationships.[7] Furthermore, he often must act in a hurry and on the basis of incomplete knowledge.

Administrative Lawmakers

Given these many influences and pressures, there is always the chance that bureaucrats may act for personal profit, or, more likely, may ignore the interests of the many for the benefit of the few. Congress has long realized that as governmental problems become more numerous and complex, administrators must make more and more important decisions. The lawmakers also know—or at least most of them do—that there is no easy way to reverse this trend. But Congress has sought to surround the decision-making process with safeguards, both because it is jealous of its own control over lawmaking and because it wants to prevent the abuse of delegated power. There is not much Congress can do in a formal and systematic way to regulate the decisions made by key officials who must face new and unprecedented problems—especially when those officials are acting under broad powers granted to the President. But

[6] G. A. Almond, *The American People and Foreign Policy* (Harcourt, Brace, 1950), ch. 7; James N. Rosenau, *Public Opinion and Foreign Policy* (Random House, 1961).

[7] See H. A. Simon, *Administrative Behavior* (Macmillan, 1947); Victor A. Thompson, *Modern Organization* (Knopf, 1961).

in the cases of agencies that regulate and control private interests on a regular and long-term basis, an effort has been made to set up certain safeguards.

Well over 100 agencies have the power to issue rules and regulations affecting the public. Most of these agencies are *regulatory agencies*, like the Interstate Commerce Commission, which has powers over the nation's railroads, or the Federal Communications Commission, which polices the nation's radio and television waves. The most important regulatory functions have been placed in independent boards and commissions, but on occasion Congress has assigned them to line agencies such as the Department of Agriculture. Congress has a special interest in the regulatory agencies, for they must interpret the laws passed by Congress and fill them out to meet specific problems. For example, Congress has recognized the right of employees to "organize and bargain collectively through representatives of their own choosing." Such a general provision leads to a hundred new questions and definitions, such as the nature of unions, the rights of employers, the definition of unfair labor practices, the rights of nonunion employees, the scope of collective bargaining, and so on. And these all-important interpretations must be made by a *regulatory agency*—in this case the National Labor Relations Board.

Safeguards against abuse of power are of several types:

1. The agencies interpret and enforce *laws of Congress*, and if they misinterpret a statute Congress can always amend it to make its intent clearer. The basic legislative power of Congress compels the agencies to identify the will of Congress and to interpret and apply laws as the congressmen would wish. Congress can also exercise this control through investigation and appropriation.

2. Congress has closely regulated the *procedure* to be followed by regulatory agencies. Under the Administrative Procedures Act of 1946, agencies must publicize their machinery and organization, must give advance information of proposed rules to interested persons, must allow such persons to present information and arguments, must allow parties appearing before the agency to be accompanied by counsel and to cross-examine witnesses.

3. Under certain conditions, final actions of regulatory agencies may be appealed to the courts.

4. Administrators in regulatory agencies, as in all agencies, are surrounded by informal political checks as well as formal ones. They must keep in mind the demands of professional ethics, the advice of experts, the attitudes of congressmen, President, interest groups, political parties, private persons, and so on. In the long run, these safeguards are the most important of all.

Administrators as Judges

Among the hardest problems facing administrators are those that call for judgment and judiciousness in settling disputes or mediating among conflicting claims. The Secretary of Defense, for example, might have to reconcile the demands of two rival services, such as the

Navy and Air Force. The Secretary of Agriculture might need to intervene in a conflict between two interest groups, such as growers and wholesalers of grain. A bureau chief might have to referee a jurisdictional squabble between two division heads. To umpire such disputes may call for the wisdom of Solomon, at the very least for fairness and understanding.

The regulatory agencies bear the main burden of making judicial decisions when disputes arise between two or more private interests, such as business groups, or between private interests and the government. Congress has delegated power to make such decisions to the regulatory agencies, a power that transforms the agencies into courts, the administrators into judges. They receive complaints, hold hearings, listen to witnesses and lawyers, study briefs, and make decisions, much like any other court.

Much of this judicial business is handled informally, through the voluntary settlement of cases at lower levels in an agency. The Interstate Commerce Commission, for example, arranged voluntary settlements of all but five out of 3,500 complaint cases in one year. The National Labor Relations Board, even though it administers a very controversial law, made formal decisions in only 4 per cent of more than 12,000 cases involving unfair labor practices during the first four years of its existence.[8] Informal settlements of this sort make life a lot easier in the bureaucratic jumble of Washington. They dispose of disputes relatively quickly and inexpensively, and they take an immense burden off the courts. Moreover, they are handled by men who are experts in such technical areas as transportation, labor relations, and radio communication. And yet many persons—especially lawyers pleading cases before the regulatory agencies—have expressed concern over the extent of the judicial power vested in the agencies. They complain that the administrators violate due process of law by holding private and informal sessions, by failing to give interested parties an adequate hearing, by basing their decisions on insufficient evidence.

Partly in response to these complaints the Administrative Procedures Act of 1946 provided for broader judicial review of administrative decisions. The courts have always had the power to overturn administrative judgments on points of *law*, as in cases where an agency had exceeded its authority, or misinterpreted the law, or had simply been unfair. Under the 1946 act, the courts seem to have acquired more authority to examine questions of *fact*—that is, to go over the mass of technical evidence examined by the agency. While this tendency has not gone very far, it points up the problem of maintaining the balance between judicial control and administrative efficiency and expertness. The 1946 law also provides for procedural safeguards, such as more formalized hearings and proper notice of action.

Finally, the act tackled another long-debated problem—the high concentration of both legislative and judicial power in regulatory agencies. This administrative

[8] Attorney General's Committee on Administrative Procedure, *Final Report, Senate Document 8*, 77th Cong., 1st Sess. (Washington, 1941), p. 35. For an admirable treatment of administrative action, see Emmette S. Redford, *Administration of National Economic Control* (Macmillan, 1952).

absolutism, as some have called it, seems to run counter to the great doctrine of the separation of powers. The act provides that there should be a greater separation *within* regulatory agencies so that the same officials will not act as both judges and prosecutors. Thus, officials who investigate cases and present them for action are not to have any part in deciding them. The act did not, however, provide that the agencies be divested of legislative or judicial duties. It could not. In an era of big government and big problems, Congress and the courts must delegate much of this job to the administrators—or else the job will not be done at all. Administrators will continue to act as lawmakers and judges as long as the functions of government are technical, complex, many-sided, and voluminous. And this means for a long time.

Those who worry about the concentration of judicial power in the agencies usually express the fear that administrators will do too much *prosecuting* and not enough impartial *judging*. Yet the opposite tendency may prevail. In some cases regulatory agencies become so occupied with umpiring disputes that they pay insufficient attention to prosecuting offenders. They tend to sit back and wait for complaints to be filed instead of taking the initiative in ferreting out violations of the law. They become "judicialized." Such a course may seem to be the safe thing to do; to some extent the regular courts have forced regulatory agencies to organize themselves mainly as judicial bodies. The result of this tendency may be inadequate protection of the very groups these agencies were set up to safeguard.

Administrators in Action—Two Cases

We have seen something of the complex of pressures and loyalties amid which a bureaucrat must work. We have seen that the good administrator must have some of the qualities of the politician, the lawmaker, the judge, the expert, the team quarterback. Day after day he must make decisions involving issues of policy, problems of organization, matters of law—and above all *people*. The following two cases, based on actual administrative experience, illustrate some of the painful choices that a bureaucrat may have to make, whether he is in Washington or in the field.

Mr. Brown's Dilemma

George Brown is chief of the Bureau of Erosion of the Department of Conservation.[9] He is still in his early forties; his appointment to the post was a result both of his ability and of luck. When the old bureau chief retired, the President wanted to bring in a new chief from outside the agency, but influential members of Congress pressed for the selection

[9] The person and agencies (except for the Budget Bureau) in this case are fictitious, but the facts of the case are drawn from actual happenings in Washington.

of an ex-senator who had represented a farm state. As a compromise, Brown, then a division head, was promoted to bureau chief. A graduate of a midwestern agricultural college, Brown is a career official in the federal service.

Early in March of Brown's second year in the new post, his boss, the Secretary of Conservation, summoned him and the other bureau heads to an important conference. The Secretary informed the group that he had just attended a Cabinet meeting, that the President had called for drastic economies wherever possible, and had specifically asked each department to effect at least a 10 per cent cut in spending in the coming fiscal year. The President, the Secretary reported, was convinced that there was a great popular demand for retrenchment.

Brown quickly calculated what this cutback would mean for his agency. For several years, the Bureau of Erosion had been spending about $45 million a year to help farmers protect their farmland. Could it get along on about $40 million, and where could savings be made? Returning to his office, Brown called a meeting of his personnel, budget, and management officials, together with his four division chiefs. After several hours of discussion it was agreed that savings could be effected only by decreasing the scope of the program—which would involve ending the jobs of about 1,200 of the Bureau's employees.

A few weeks later Mr. Brown presented a $40 million budget to Secretary Jones, who approved it and passed it on to the White House. The President went over the figures in a conference with the Director of the Bureau of the Budget, and a few weeks later the budget for the whole executive department, incorporating the Erosion Bureau's $40 million, was transmitted to Congress.

Meanwhile Brown was running into trouble. News of the proposed budget cut had leaked immediately to the personnel in the field. Nobody knew who would be dropped if the cut went through, and some of the abler officials were already looking around for other positions. Morale fell. Hearing of the cut, farmers' representatives in Washington notified local farm organizations throughout the country. Soon Brown began to receive letters asking that certain services be maintained. Members of the farm bloc in Congress were also becoming restless.

Shortly after the President's budget went to Congress, Representative Smith of Colorado asked Brown to see him. Smith was Chairman of the Agriculture subcommittee of the House Appropriations Committee, and thus was a potent factor in congressional treatment of the budget. Brown immediately went up to the Hill. Smith began talking in an urgent tone. He said that he had consulted his fellow subcommittee members, both Democratic and Republican, and they all agreed that the Erosion Bureau's cut must not go through. The farmers needed the usual $45 million and even more. They would practically rise up in arms if the program were reduced. Members of Congress from agricultural areas, Smith went on, were under tremendous pressure. Leaders of farm groups in Washington were mobilizing the farmers everywhere. Besides, Smith said, the President was unfair in cracking down on the farm program; he didn't understand agricultural problems, and he was not cutting other expenses.

Then Smith came to the point. Brown, he said, must vigorously oppose the budget cut. Hearings on appropriations would commence in a few days and Brown as bureau chief would of course testify. At that time he must state that the cut would hurt the bureau and undermine its whole program. Brown would not have to volunteer this statement, Smith said, but just respond to leading questions put by the congressmen. Brown's testimony, he felt sure, would help clinch the argument against the cut because congressmen would respect the judgment of the administrator closest to the problem.

Mr. Brown's Decision

Brown returned to his office in a state of indecision. He was in an embarrassing position. He had submitted his estimates to the Secretary of Conservation and to the President, and it was his duty to back them up. An unwritten rule demanded, moreover, that agency heads would defend budget estimates submitted to Congress, whatever their personal feelings might be. The President had appointed him to his position, he reflected, and had a right to expect loyalty. On the other hand, he was on the spot with his own agency. The employees all expected their chief to look out for them. Brown had developed happy relations with "the field," and he squirmed at the thought of having to let over 1,000 employees go. What would they think when they heard him defend the cut? Even more important, he wanted to maintain friendly relations with the farmers, the farm organizations, and the farm bloc in Congress.

Brown turned for advice to an old friend in the Bureau of the Budget. This friend urged him to defend the President's budget. He appealed to Brown's professional pride as an administrator and career servant, reminding him that every student of administration agreed that the chief executive must have central control of the budget and that agency heads must subordinate their own interests to the executive program. As for the employees to be dropped—well, that was part of the game. A lot of them could get jobs in defense agencies; civil service would protect their status. Anyway, they would understand Brown's position. In a parting shot he mentioned that the President had Brown in mind for bigger things.

The next day Brown had lunch with a senator, wise and experienced in Washington ways, who had helped him get his start in the government. The senator was sympathetic. He understood Brown's perplexity, for many similar cases had arisen in the past. But there was no doubt about what Brown should do, the senator said. He should follow Representative Smith's plan, of course being as diplomatic as possible about it. This way he would protect his position with those who would be most important in the long run.

"After all," the senator said, "Presidents come and go, parties rise and fall, but Smith and those other congressmen will be here a long time, and so will these farm organizations. They can do a lot for you in future years. And remember one other thing—these people are elected representatives of the people. Constitutionally, Congress has the power to spend money as it sees fit. Why should you object if they want to spend an extra few million?"

Leaving the Senate Office Building, Brown realized that his dilemma was deeper than ever. The arguments on both sides were persuasive. He felt hopelessly divided in his loyalties and responsibilities. The President expected one thing of him. Congress (he was sure Smith reflected widespread feeling on Capitol Hill) expected another. As a career man and professional administrator, he sided with the President; as head of an agency, however, he wanted to protect his team. His future? Whatever decision he made, he was bound to alienate important people and interests. There was no way to compromise, because he would have to face a group of astute congressmen.

It was Brown's realization that the arguments in a sense canceled one another out, that in the end helped him to make his decision. For he decided finally that the issue involved more than loyalties, ambitions, and programs. Ultimately it boiled down to two questions. First, to whom was he, Brown, legally and administratively responsible? Obviously to the Chief Executive who appointed him and who was accountable to the people for the actions of the administration. And secondly, which course of action did he, Brown, feel was better for the welfare of all the people? Looking at the question this way, he felt the President was right in asking for economy. As a taxpayer himself, Brown knew of the strong sentiment for retrenchment. To be sure, Congress must make the final decision. But to make the decision, Brown reflected, Congress had to know the attitude of the administration, and the administration must speak with one voice for the majority of the people or it could hardly speak at all. Despite continued pressures and mixed feelings, Brown stuck to this decision.

Assignment in Indonesia

In August 1945, shortly after the Japanese surrender, the Republic of Indonesia declared its independence from the Netherlands.[10] A difficult political situation immediately arose. The Dutch wanted to keep their rich islands; the Indonesians wanted their freedom—just as strongly as did Americans in 1776. For several months the Dutch and Indonesian forces skirmished, especially in Batavia, the capital. The United States, deeply interested in the area for economic and strategic reasons, followed a policy of neutrality.

Representing the United States in Batavia was a consul general who had served in the Indies for twelve years before the war. Sixty years old, he had enjoyed pleasant relations with Dutch officials before the war and tended to feel sympathetic toward their position. As an old hand he was experienced in Indonesian affairs but he tended to be somewhat prejudiced and set in his ways. In February 1946, the consul general was joined by a vice-consul, William Jones, who was sent

---

[10] This case is drawn from an actual autobiographical account by the vice-consul involved, prepared for, and published by, the Committee on Public Administration Cases (Washington, 1950), under the title *Indonesian Assignment*.

out by the State Department to undertake economic analysis and reporting. At this time Washington had a particular need for full and accurate information on the economic situation in Indonesia to help in developing important foreign policies.

Jones was of a different stamp from his chief. A young economist, trained in American universities and in the State Department, he had studied the prewar pattern of colonialism and had developed strong sympathies for the nationalist cause. He had no established ties with the Foreign Service; indeed, his actual appointment was in the Foreign Service Reserve (see Chapter 22). While at the State Department, moreover, Jones had learned that there was some official concern over the consul general's pro-Dutch views.

Within a few months after his arrival, the new vice-consul was busy preparing economic reports on the Indonesian islands. His relations with his chief were most cordial. But soon a difficult situation began to develop. To get complete information Jones needed to approach Indonesian as well as Dutch officials. But the consul general wanted him to see only the Dutch. He stressed the ticklish political situation that existed and warned Jones to move slowly. Eager to maintain friendly relations with his superior, Jones followed instructions, but he had an uneasy feeling that he was not doing a full job of reporting to Washington.

Some time later a confidential airgram arrived from the State Department requesting an extensive economic report on Indonesia, adding that "if possible, and with the utmost discretion, Dutch, Indonesian, and British sources should be consulted as far as feasible." Jones was elated to have the assignment, but puzzled about how he should proceed. Should he consult the Indonesian authorities?

Jones had several alternatives. He could consult the consul general, who would surely say "no"; this course would protect Jones' position in the Department and his friendly relations with his chief, but it would lessen the value of the report. Or he could go ahead with the report, inform the Department that he had not consulted the Indonesians, and let Washington specifically request such consultation if it was still desired. This was the safest course all around, but it would mean a delayed report and perhaps a less satisfactory one. Finally, Jones could use the airgram to justify consultations with the Indonesians, at whatever risk to his relations with his chief and to Dutch-American relations.

Jones decided on the third course. Before doing so he spoke to a high Indonesian official, who assured him that he would receive useful material from the Republic and in confidence. Jones' decision proved a happy one. His talks with the Indonesians (as well as with the Dutch and British) were fruitful, and he was later commended by the State Department for the report he submitted. Yet he had to pay the price. His relations with the consul general cooled markedly—not a trivial matter in a small office thousands of miles from home. Nevertheless, Jones was satisfied with his decision. He felt that he had been loyal to his profession and to the interests of his country, though at the expense of loyalty to his superior. It is clear, however, that had Jones been a veteran career man, with family responsibilities, and with no particular sympathy for the Indonesians, his decision might have been very different.

Can We Control the Bureaucrats?

The foregoing case histories lead to three important generalizations:

1. Bureaucrats are people, not robots, and as people they are subject to many influences.
2. Bureaucrats do not respond merely to orders from the top but to a variety of motives stemming from their own personalities, formal and informal organization and communication, their political attitudes, their educational and professional background, and others.
3. Bureaucrats are important in government. Some of them have tremendous discretion and make decisions of great significance—and the cumulative effect of all their policies and actions on our daily lives is enormous.

Put these factors together and a crucial question arises. How can we keep this powerful bureaucracy responsive to the "people"? How do we insure that bureaucrats remain public servants and do not become the public's master? And underlying all these questions, to which people should the bureaucrats be held accountable—the majority who elected the President, the majority reflected by the Congress, the organized interests?

Chains of Command

The predominant, but by no means the only, school of thought is that the President should be placed clearly and unequivocably in charge. The President is the chief administrator. Of all the 2.5 million bureaucrats, the American people directly hire and fire only one—the President. The presidential office, it is argued, must see that popular needs and expectations are converted into administrative action. If the nation votes for a conservative President who favors restricted intervention in the economy by federal agencies, that policy can be effected only if the bureaucracy responds to presidential direction. Or if the electorate chooses a President who favors a more vigorous regulation of business, the majority's wishes can be translated into action only if the bureaucrats support the presidential policies.

Yet as we have seen over and over again, under the American system of *constitutional* checks and *political* balances a single political majority winning a presidential election does not acquire control of the national government, not even the executive branch itself. For under our Constitution the President is not the undisputed master of the executive structure. Congress too has its say and wishes to keep it. Congress sets up the agencies, broadly determines their organization, provides the money, and establishes the ground rules. Congress constantly reviews the activities of the bureaucrats by appropriations hearings, special investigations, or informal inquiry. And as we have seen, the Senate helps choose the men who run the agencies.

Moreover, it is not Congress as a whole that shares the direction of the executive structure with the President. More accurately, it is the individual congressmen to whom Congress has delegated its authority. These congressmen, primarily chairmen of committees, often specialize in the appropriations and policies of a particular group of agencies—often the agencies serving constituents in the congressman's own district. But some legislators stake out a claim over more general policies; Congressman Carl Vinson, for example, made the Navy Department his "specialty." These congressmen, who see Presidents come and go and secretaries of this or that pass through Washington, come to feel that they know more about the agency than does the President (and often they do). While Congress as an institution may prefer to have the President in charge of the executive branch so that they may hold him responsible for its operation, the congressional seniority leaders often prefer to "protect" the agencies from presidential direction in order better to maintain their own influence over public policy. Sometimes this is institutionalized: The Army Chief of Engineers, for example, is by law given authority to plan public works and report to Congress without referring to the President.

As we have seen, Congress has deliberately decided that the independent regulatory agencies should not be directly responsive to the President's control. Since these agencies make rules and decide disputes, Congress wants them to be arms of the Congress. So in addition to making these commissions multiple in membership, Congress has given their commissioners long and staggered terms. Although the President fills vacancies with the consent of the Senate, Congress has restricted his right to remove the members of these quasi-legislative, quasi-judicial agencies. The Supreme Court (*Humphrey's Executor* v. *United States*, 1935) upheld the right of Congress to do so, and recently went further to rule (*Wiener* v. *United States*, 1958) that the President lacks any power to remove these officers unless Congress has specifically authorized him to do so.

Political Checks on the President

Important as these institutional breaks in the President's chain of command are, they are only part of the picture. In addition, political checks block the President. Some of the agencies have so much support among interest groups and Congress that a President would hesitate to move against them. The Federal Bureau of Investigation under the popular J. Edgar Hoover, for example, is politically so powerful that any President would take serious political risks if he should attempt to curtail its operations or to impose policies against the wishes of Mr. Hoover. In addition, the agencies that perform services for certain groups—the so-called *clientele agencies* such as the Rural Electrification Administration or the Veterans Administration—have powerful support. Close relations develop between the agency and the clients it services. If a President, trying to enforce his idea of the general interest, seeks to restrict the agency, he may come into conflict with an influential group that is not without allies in the Congress.

What of the bureaucrat? Is he merely an innocent bystander in the mêlées? There are those who think he should be. They want to "neutralize" the civil service. That bureaucrats—at least those in the lower ranks—should be neutral as between partisan politics has long been accepted policy. Not only has civil service largely overcome the patronage system, but the Hatch Acts of 1939 and 1940 extended the idea of neutrality by forbidding federal civil servants "to take any active part in political management or in political campaigns." The aim has been both to prevent the building of a gigantic machine of federal office holders and to protect the bureaucrats against having to donate money to parties or candidates in order to retain their jobs. The laws allow them to discuss politics in private and to vote, but no other partisan activities. Despite some criticism that it is unwise to isolate 2.5 million people from politics and unfair to deny them the same political freedoms as anyone else, neutralization of the civil service from political party battle seems to be a fixed feature.

Yet partisan disputes between Democrats and Republicans are not the only items of political conflict. And the Hatch Act does not mean that bureaucrats have become political nonentities. Bureaucrats have their own ideas of what is desirable public policy. The bureaucracy is not a static force; it has political influence of its own. It seeks to maintain its own organizational system, and group loyalties to agencies and programs are forces to be reckoned with. The influence of the bureaucracy is built on the political skills of the administrator and his staff, the relations with legislative and executive officials, the amount of support the bureau can command from interest groups and the attentive public. As we have seen, a large bureau finds public acceptance, interest-group backing, and a place in the web of government that give it a measure of political power of its own.[11]

In summary, the role of the bureaucrats in the American system of government is not to be solved merely by structural alterations. For the system of command will always end not just in the White House but in a variety of places on Capitol Hill. There are conflicting claims, including those of the bureaucrats themselves, each insisting that the administrator act "in the public interest," each with a different definition of that interest. Defining that interest is the crucial problem.

Organization Theory—A Research Frontier

The study of organizations or administration (or as it is now coming to be called, management sciences, organization sciences, organizational behavior, or organization theory) is a relatively young discipline and is in many respects still unorganized. "Organization theory means different things to different people," report

---

[11] For a discerning study of this problem and related questions, see Simon, Smithburg, and Thompson, *op. cit.*, especially chs. 18 and 19.

two of its most distinguished investigators.[12] The sociological orientation—but influenced also by the work of political scientists—stems from the pioneering work of Max Weber who developed analytic distinctions among various types of authority relationships: the *traditional*, the *charismatic*, and the *legal-rational*. This last Weberian type identifies bureaucratic structure in which authority flows from the *office* rather than from the characteristics of the *person* who occupies the office. Today many scholars are investigating the consequences that flow from hierarchical organization and the impact of such structures both on persons who work within them and on the larger society of which they are a part. Much attention is directed to "informal organization" outside of the organization chart (see p. 473) with a growing awareness that authority is a relationship that depends as much on the behavior of those to whom an order is directed as it does on the behavior of the one who issues it, that behavior is influenced not merely by instructions from the top but by many other incentives, such as prestige or power or attitudes of fellow workers.[13]

A New Discipline with Old Roots

At the beginning of this century Frederick Taylor launched the scientific-management movement when he developed tools for the measurement of the efficiency of task performances. Stemming from the epic Hawthorne Experiments, the "human-relations" literature stresses the subjective and "non-rational" factors, the face-to-face interpersonal relations that take place in small groups within formal structures. Today scholars, primarily social psychologists, are involved in experimental studies of such complex factors as morale and productivity.

The organization theorists whose work is of most immediate relevance to the political process are those working on administrative behavior within complex organizations. Under the banner of the Science of Public Administration, Luther Gulick and other pioneering scholars early in this century—basing their work on analytic distinctions first made by Goodnow and Wilson between policy and administration—developed a formal model of administration from which they deducted certain principles: *unity of command*—every officer should have a superior to whom he reports and from whom he takes orders; *chain of command*—there should be a firm line of authority running from the top down, and of formal responsibility, running from the bottom up; *line and staff*—the staff advises the executive, but gives no commands, whereas the line has operating duties; *span of control*—a hierarchical structure should be established so that no one person supervises more agencies directly than he can effectively handle; *decentralization*—administrators should delegate decisions and responsibilities to lower levels.

[12] Richard M. Cyert and James G. March, *A Behavioral Theory of the Firm* (Prentice-Hall, 1964), p. 16. See also William J. Gore, *Administrative Decision-Making: A Heuristic Model* (Wiley, 1964), pp. 30–35; and Herbert Kaufman, "Organization Theory and Political Theory," *The American Political Science Review* (March 1964), pp. 5–14.

[13] James G. March and Herbert Simon, *Organizations* (Wiley, 1958).

These classical principles of public administration were thought to promote efficiency and economy, to secure firm control by superiors over subordinates, and by establishing links between politically accountable policy-makers and administrative agencies to make administration responsive to the demands of the elected officials.

How Good Is the Classic Model?

The classic model remains the most influential "ideal" for those involved in administration. However, scholars have become increasingly skeptical of the validity of these principles either as guides for practitioners or as models for investigators. One difficulty is that the principles cannot be tested. As Herbert A. Simon wrote in his highly influential *Administrative Behavior:* "Administrative description suffers . . . from superficiality, oversimplification, lack of realism. . . . It has refused to undertake the tiresome task of studying the actual allocations of decision-making functions. It has been satisfied to speak of 'authority,' 'centralization,' 'span of control,' 'function,' without seeking operational definitions of these terms. . . . A fatal defect of the current principles of administration is that, like proverbs, they occur in pairs. For almost every principle one can find an equally plausible and acceptable contradictory principle." [14]

Another and related challenge to the classic "rational" approach to decision-making is *incrementalism.* The "incrementalists" question the idea that men rationally approach problems with definite objectives in mind and with a clear sense of alternative ways of reaching those objectives. Men—even public administrators—simply do not know enough about the alternatives, their own goals and values are not clear enough, the situations they face are too complex, for such a broad and "rational" approach, according to this argument. Rather they are likely to go one step at a time, to feel their way, to cling to one familiar method rather than to consider carefully all the other methods, to "morselize" problems and attack them piece-meal, to adjust and compromise with institutions rather than overturn them and reconstruct them wholesale. Not only is this the way men *do* act, according to the incrementalists, it is the way they *should* act if they wish to go about their affairs in a sensible and effective manner.[15]

Today scholars are making intensive case studies of how decisions are made. They are developing generalizations for study and for prescription. We still lack sure knowledge to guide administrators or to speak with high confidence about the precise consequences that flow from organizational arrangements, but we have learned that the classic principles *that we used* to proclaim with such assurance conceal as much as they reveal.

[14] *Op. cit.,* p. xiv.
[15] David Braybrooke and Charles E. Lindblom, A *Strategy of Decision* (Free Press, 1963). See also a review of this volume, Lewis A. Froman, Jr., *The American Political Science Review* (March 1964), pp. 116–117.

19 THE JUDGES

Foreigners are often amazed at the great power Americans give their judges, especially federal judges. In 1848, the French aristocrat Alexis de Tocqueville wrote after his visit to America, "If I were asked where I place the American aristocracy, I should reply without hesitation . . . that it occupies the judicial bench and bar. . . . Scarcely any political question arises in the United States that it is not resolved, sooner or later, into a judicial question." [1] A century later the English laborite Harold Laski observed, "The respect in which the federal courts and, above all, the Supreme Court are held is hardly surpassed by the influence they exert on the life of the United States." [2]

Why do American federal judges have great influence and prestige? One reason is their power of judicial review—that is, to make the authoritative interpretation of the Constitution. Only a constitutional amendment—and the judges would interpret the amendment—or the Supreme Court itself can modify the Court's doctrine. Mr. Justice Frankfurter once put it tersely, "The Supreme Court is the Constitution."

When the judges interpret the Constitution, they are making policy decisions. Though the arguments will be clothed in constitutional terminology, the judges are resolving important social, economic, and political issues. Should the government regulate the economic market place? Should the activities of totalitarian political parties be restricted? Defeated at the polls or in the legislative halls, individuals may carry this kind of issue to the judicial chambers through the device of the lawsuit. "We are very quiet there," said Justice Holmes of the Supreme Court, "but it is the quiet of a storm centre."

Even without the power to interpret the Constitution our judges would be influential decision-makers. Constitutional questions, indeed, are not involved in many of the more important cases that come before the judges, cases that nonetheless result in the construction of statutes and the development of rules that affect the conduct of countless numbers of people.[3] Litigation is important as a technique for resolving policy, judicial participation is crucial in the policy-making process— but both of these are incidental results that flow from the primary function of courts: to serve as impartial tribunals for the settlement of legal disputes. Many of these disputes raise no major policy issues and are of little interest to any except the immediate parties to the case. But in settling peacefully the innumerable controversies that arise among individuals and between individuals and the government, judges play as notable a role as in deciding the more momentous cases that help shape the grand outlines of American politics.

The Shape of Federal Justice

The authority of federal judges, like that of congressmen and Presidents, is derived ultimately from the Constitution. But unlike congressmen and Presidents, federal judges receive very little power directly from that document. All the authority of federal judges except the original jurisdiction of the Supreme Court (see page 494) is given to them by Congress. The Constitution in Article III merely sets the out-

---

[1] Alexis de Tocqueville, *Democracy in America*, 2 vols. Phillips Bradley (ed.) (Knopf, 1946), I, pp. 278, 280.
[2] Harold J. Laski, *The American Democracy* (Viking, 1948), p. 110.
[3] Martin Shapiro, *Law and Politics in the Supreme Court* (The Free Press, 1964), pp. 1–49.

side limits. Congress determines which, if any, federal court is to exercise some or all of the judicial authority of the United States.

The purpose of the framers of the Constitution in delegating judicial power to the central government was to enable it to maintain its supremacy, to meet its national responsibilities, and to provide tribunals for cases where state judges might not be appropriate. Therefore, they gave to the national courts the power to hear and decide cases in law and equity if:

1. They arise under the Constitution, a federal law, or a treaty.
2. They arise under admiralty and maritime laws.
3. They arise because of a dispute involving land claimed under titles granted by two or more states.
4. The United States is a party to the case.
5. A state is a party to the case (but not including suits commenced or prosecuted against a state by an individual or a foreign nation).
6. They are between citizens of different states.
7. They affect the accredited representatives of a foreign nation.

The Organization of Federal Courts

The Constitution provides for only one Supreme Court, leaving it up to Congress to ordain and establish inferior federal courts. (The Constitution also allows Congress to determine the size of the Supreme Court as well as of lower courts.) A Supreme Court is a necessity if the national government is to have the power to frame laws superior to those of the states. The lack of such a tribunal to maintain national supremacy, to insure uniform interpretation of national legislation, and to resolve conflicts among the states was one of the glaring deficiencies of the central government under the Articles of Confederation.

The framers did not feel that a complete system of *lower* courts was indispensable to an effective federal system. Hence they avoided that controversial issue, and the structure as well as the authority of the national judiciary is largely controlled by Congress. The First Congress divided the nation into districts and created lower national courts for each district. That decision, though often supplemented, has never been seriously questioned. Today the hierarchy of the national courts, of general jurisdiction, consists of *district courts, courts of appeals,* and one *Supreme Court.*

The Supreme Court is the most glamorous and venerated court in the country— the national symbol of justice. Its members are known to the public, its decisions headlined in the press. It has the last word in interpreting the meaning of the Constitution and of federal laws; it is potentially the court of ultimate appeal for cases falling within the competence of national courts; it supervises the administration of justice by the federal courts. But the workhorses of the federal judiciary are the eighty-seven district courts within the states, the district court in the District of Columbia, and the territorial district court in Puerto Rico. Each state has at least one district court; the larger states have as many as the demands of judicial business and the pressure of politics require (though no state has more than four). Each district court is composed of at least one judge, but there may be as many as twenty-four. District judges normally sit separately and hold court by themselves. There are three hundred and three district judgeships, all filled by the President with the consent of the Senate; all district judges, except those of the territorial courts, hold office during good behavior.

District courts are trial courts of *original jurisdiction*. They are the only federal courts that regularly employ grand (indicting) and petit (trial) juries. Many of the cases tried before district judges involve citizens of different states, and the judges apply the appropriate state laws. Otherwise, district judges are concerned with federal laws. For example, they hear and decide cases involving crimes against the United States, suits under the national revenue, postal, patent, copyright, trademark, bankruptcy, and civil rights laws.

District judges are assisted by clerks, bailiffs, stenographers, law clerks, court reporters, probation officers, and United States commissioners. All these persons are appointed by the judges. The commissioners, who serve for four-year terms and are paid from fees, handle some of the preliminaries. They issue warrants for arrests, and often hear the evidence to determine whether an arrested person should be held for action by the grand jury. If so, the commissioner may set the bail. A United States marshal, appointed by the President, is assigned to each district court. Although the U.S. marshal no longer exercises general police jurisdiction (except in television horse operas), the modern-day Matt Dillons and Wyatt Earps maintain order in the courtroom, guard prisoners, make arrests, and carry out court orders, such as summonses for witnesses or even at times, as in the fall of 1962 in Oxford, Mississippi, carrying out orders of a federal court in the face of violence.[4] A United States district attorney is appointed by the President for each district court, but he operates under the Attorney General's supervision and not the district judges'.

Although a few important decisions of the district court may be appealed directly to the Supreme Court, most decisions may be carried only to a United States court of appeals. The United States is divided into eleven judicial circuits, including the District of Columbia as a circuit, each of which has a court of appeals consisting of three to nine circuit judges, seventy-eight in all. Like all judges of courts exercising the judicial power of the United States, circuit judges are appointed by the President with the consent of the Senate. The United States courts of appeals have only appellate jurisdiction; they review decisions of the district courts within their circuit and also some of the actions of certain of the independent regulatory agencies, such as the Federal Trade Commission. Each court of appeals normally hears cases in panels of three judges. One Supreme Court justice is assigned to each circuit, but today his duties as circuit justice are only nominal.

District courts, courts of appeal, and the Supreme Court—these are the three

[4] Rita W. Cooley, "The Office of U.S. Marshal," *Western Political Quarterly* (March 1959), pp. 123–140.

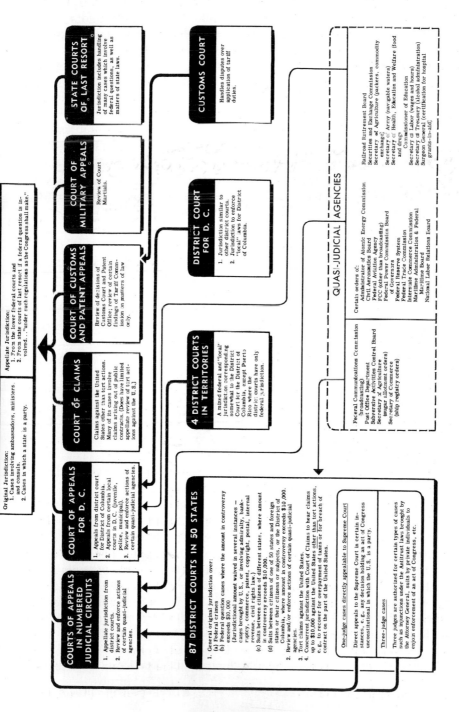

U. S. SUPREME COURT

Original Jurisdiction:
1. Cases involving ambassadors, ministers, and consuls.
2. Cases in which a state is a party.

Appellate Jurisdiction:
1. From the lower federal courts and
2. From state courts of last resort if a federal question is involved . . . "under such regulations as the Congress shall make."

STATE COURTS OF LAST RESORT

Jurisdiction includes handling of many cases which involve federal questions, as well as matters of state laws.

CUSTOMS COURT

Handles disputes over application of tariff duties.

COURT OF MILITARY APPEALS

Review of Court Martials.

COURT OF CUSTOMS AND PATENT APPEALS

Review of decisions of Customs Court and Patent Office; review of certain findings of Tariff Commission on matters of law only.

DISTRICT COURT FOR D. C.

1. Jurisdiction similar to other district courts.
2. Jurisdiction to enforce "local" laws for District of Columbia.

COURT OF CLAIMS

Claims against the United States other than tort actions. Many of its cases involve claims arising out of public contracts. (Does have limited appellate review of tort actions against the U.S.)

4 DISTRICT COURTS IN TERRITORIES

A mixed federal and "local" jurisdiction corresponding somewhat to the District Court for the District of Columbia, except Puerto Rico where the district courts have only federal jurisdiction.

COURT OF APPEALS FOR D. C.

1. Appeals from district court for District of Columbia.
2. Appeals from certain local courts in D. C. (juvenile, police, municipal).
3. Review and enforce actions of certain quasi-judicial agencies.

COURTS OF APPEALS IN NUMBERED JUDICIAL CIRCUITS

1. Appellate jurisdiction from district courts.
2. Review and enforce actions of certain quasi-judicial agencies.

87 DISTRICT COURTS IN 50 STATES

1. General original jurisdiction over:
   (a) Federal crimes
   (b) Federal question cases where the amount in controversy exceeds $10,000.
   (Jurisdictional amount waived in several instances — cases brought by U.S., or involving admiralty, bankruptcy, commerce, patent, copyright, postal, internal revenue, civil rights law.)
   (c) Suits between citizens of different states, where amount in controversy exceeds $10,000.
   (d) Suits between citizens of one of 50 states and foreign states or their citizens or subjects, or the District of Columbia, where amount in controversy exceeds $10,000.
2. Tort claims against the United States.
3. Review and/or enforce actions of certain quasi-judicial agencies.
4. Concurrent jurisdiction with Court of Claims to hear claims up to $10,000 against the United States other than tort actions, e.g., to recover for overpayment of taxes or for breach of contract on the part of the United States.

One-judge cases

Direct appeals to the Supreme Court in certain instances, e.g., any decision holding an act of Congress unconstitutional in which the U.S. is a party.

Three-judge cases

Three judges are authorized for certain types of cases such as injunctions under the Antitrust laws brought by the Attorney General, suits by private individuals to enjoin enforcement of an act of Congress, etc.

Direct appeals to the Supreme Court

QUASI-JUDICIAL AGENCIES

Federal Communications Commission (broadcasting)
Post Office Department
Subversive Activities Control Board
Secretary of Agriculture (sugar allotment orders)
Secretary of Commerce (ship registry orders)

Certain orders of:
Administrator of Atomic Energy Commission
Civil Aeronautics Board
Federal Aviation Agency
FCC (other than broadcasting)
Federal Power Commission Board of Governors
Federal Reserve System
Federal Trade Commission
Interstate Commerce Commission
Maritime Administration & Federal Maritime Board
National Labor Relations Board

Railroad Retirement Board
Securities and Exchange Commission
Secretary of Agriculture (packers, commodity exchange)
Secretary of Army (navigable waters)
Secretary of Health, Education and Welfare (food and drug)
Commissioner of Education
Secretary of Labor (wages and hours)
Secretary of Treasury (alcohol administration)
Surgeon General (certification for hospital grants-in-aid)

495

major kinds of federal courts. The lower court judges are required to follow the precedents established by the Supreme Court. But the federal judicial system is not a monolithic unit in which orders flow from the top down with all federal judges speaking with a single voice. The judges of the district court living and working in one federal district—who are local citizens, appointed by the President with consent of the Senate but in fact selected by the local dominant groups—often take a different point of view toward legal disputes from that of the members of the Supreme Court, who are more likely to reflect the values of the presidential constituency. And since of the thousands of disputes only a small number reach the Supreme Court, the judges of the lower federal courts are important policy-makers. Moreover, just as the Constitution is subject to interpretation, so are Supreme Court decisions. District judges and circuit judges have considerable discretion in determining the precise contours of a "binding" Supreme Court decision.[5] The President may be, as we have seen, chief administrator, but his control over the federal bureaucracy is less than total. So the Supreme Court stands at the top of the federal judiciary, but the judiciary, like other agencies of American government, reflects and is subject to an ever-shifting competition among different concepts of the public interest.

Special Courts, Legislative Courts, and Administrative Tribunals

In addition to the federal constitutional courts of general jurisdiction, Congress has also created constitutional courts of special jurisdiction: the Court of Claims, the Customs Court, and the Court of Customs and Patent Appeals. The Court of Claims consists of a chief and four associate judges, with jurisdiction over all property and contract damage suits against the United States. The court sits in Washington, but commissioners of the court travel throughout the United States taking evidence. The United States Customs Court, consisting of nine judges, has jurisdiction to review rulings of collectors of the customs. Its decisions in turn may be appealed to the Court of Customs and Patent Appeals, a five-member court, which, in addition, reviews decisions of the Patent Office, and on a more restricted scale, certain rulings of the United States Tariff Commission.

The United States Court of Military Appeals is the "GI Supreme Court." This is a *legislative* rather than a *constitutional* court (significant mainly in that its judges need not be appointed for life). It is composed of three civilian judges appointed for fifteen years by the President with the consent of the Senate. This court applies *military law*, which is separate from the body of law that governs the rest of the federal courts. Congress develops the rules and judicial organization to protect the rights of persons in the military forces. The Constitution specifically denies to such persons the constitutional right to grand-jury indictment; and the

[5] Walter F. Murphy, "Lower Court Checks on Supreme Court Power," *The American Political Science Review* (December 1959), pp. 1017–1031.

weight of opinion, though there is considerable dissent, appears to be that the other rights of persons accused of crime listed in the Fifth and Sixth amendments do not apply to persons in the armed forces.

During World War II, there was sharp and persistent criticism of military justice. The old court-martial system, concerned primarily with promoting military efficiency, vested autocratic powers in the hands of the commanding officers. Then Congress, realizing that a good many Americans would be subject to military justice for some period of their lives, passed in 1951 a comprehensive revision of the military judicial system and established a Uniform Code of Military Justice. The Uniform Code was an attempt to balance the needs of the military and the demands of justice. It strengthened the rights of persons brought before courts-martial and specified that major court-martial decisions be reviewed by a board composed of three lawyers.

The Court of Military Appeals, which sits at the top of the military court hierarchy, must review all decisions involving a flag officer, a general, imposition of the death penalty, and questions certified to it by one of the judge-advocate generals. When petitioned by the accused, it has discretionary power to review decisions involving bad-conduct discharges or more than one year's imprisonment. The Supreme Court has not yet made clear the exact extent of civil courts' authority to review decisions of military courts, but it has indicated that their authority is exceedingly limited—probably no more than to determine whether the military courts had jurisdiction and have given fair consideration to the claims of justice.[6]

Many administrators and administrative agencies also hear and decide cases and exercise what amounts to quasi-judicial power, even though these agencies rank as neither constitutional nor legislative courts. For example, a person or company injured by the allegedly unfair competitive practices of a business engaged in interstate commerce may bring a charge to the Federal Trade Commission. Attorneys appear, present briefs, introduce evidence, and carry out regular court routine; eventually the commissioners hand down a decision—just as though they were actual judges. Appeals on questions of law and procedure in these hearings may be taken to the court of appeals and eventually to the Supreme Court.

State and Federal Courts

What is the relation between the federal and state courts? The common impression that *all* federal courts are superior to *any* state court is wrong. The two court systems are related, but they do not exist in a superior-inferior relationship. Over some kinds of cases only the *state* courts have jurisdiction, over other kinds *both* court systems have jurisdiction, and over others only the *federal* courts have jurisdiction. Moreover, except for the limited habeas corpus jurisdiction of the district courts, the Supreme Court is the only federal court that may review state court decisions, and it may do so only under special conditions.

[6] *Burns v. Wilson* (1953).

State courts have *sole* jurisdiction to try all cases not within the judicial power granted by the Constitution to the national government. As to the judicial power that is granted to the national government, Congress determines whether it shall be *exclusively* exercised by national courts, *concurrently* exercised by both national and state courts, or denied to either or both national and state courts. For example, Congress has stipulated that prosecutions for violations of federal criminal laws, suits for penalties authorized by federal laws, and cases involving foreign ambassadors are within the exclusive jurisdiction of national courts. On the other hand, legal disputes between citizens of different states involving more than $10,000 may be tried in either national or state courts. If the amount is less, the case can be tried only in state courts. (Of course, federal courts may have jurisdiction over suits between citizens of different states for some other reason, for instance if the dispute arises under national law.)

Administration of the Federal System

Until recently, little attempt was made to integrate the administration of the federal judicial system. Today, the *Judicial Conference of the United States*, consisting of the chief judge of each court of appeals and the Chief Justice of the United States, is the administrative head of the federal system. It meets at least once a year and establishes policies for the Administrative Office of the United States Courts, which carries out the daily administrative chores and submits to Congress the budgets of all courts except the Supreme Court.

Within each of the circuits, the judges of the court of appeals and the circuit justices (the Supreme Court justice assigned to the circuit) constitute a judicial council, which meets at least twice a year to discuss common problems. The chief judge of each court of appeals also summons an annual judicial conference of all circuit and district judges within the circuit. Sometimes members of the bar are invited in to talk over problems.

One of the central purposes of this integration of the federal judicial system is to promote efficient use of "judgepower." Each federal judge is appointed to a specific judgeship. But one court may be swamped with cases while another may have little or nothing to do. Integrated administration makes it possible to assign a judge temporarily to some court other than his own, thereby evening out the work load. For example, the chief judge of each court of appeals may request a district judge to serve on the court of appeals or may send him to another district, or he may request a circuit judge to hold district court.

Federal Prosecutions

Judges decide cases; they do not prosecute persons. That job, on the federal level, falls to the Department of Justice and, more specifically, to the Attorney General, to the Solicitor General, and to the hundreds of United States attorneys and assistant attorneys throughout the country. A United States attorney is appointed to each district court by the President with the consent of the Senate; he is appointed for a four-year term, but he may be dismissed by the President at any time. These appointments are of great interest to senators who, through senatorial courtesy (see page 443), exercise significant influence over them. Assistant attorneys are appointed by the Attorney General. Assisted by the Federal Bureau of Investigation, the district attorneys start criminal proceedings against persons who break federal laws, and they may help initiate civil actions for the government. In a criminal case, the district attorney presents to a grand jury evidence that a national law has been violated. If the jury brings an indictment, the attorney conducts the government's case against the accused.

Within the Department of Justice, special divisions—such as the Criminal Division, Civil Division, Antitrust Divison, Civil Rights Division, for example—coordinate the work of the attorneys in the field, develop cases, and send out specialists to assist the attorneys. Of special importance is the Solicitor General, who appears for and represents the government before the Supreme Court. Moreover, no appeal may be taken by the United States to any appellate court without his approval.

Contrary to the practice in most states, prosecutions by the national government are centralized under the supervision of the Chief Executive. It is noteworthy, however, that the attorneys are lodged in the executive branch and the judges, of course, in the judicial, thus preserving the principle of separation of powers. In many European countries, both judges and prosecutors are part of the same organization, the ministry of justice.

What Cases Reach the Supreme Court?

When an irate citizen insists that he will take his case to the highest court of the land even if it costs him his last penny, he probably overestimates the cost of justice and underestimates the difficulty of securing Supreme Court review. The Supreme Court has both original and appellate jurisdiction. Its original jurisdiction stems directly from the Constitution, and is limited to cases in which a state is a party or to cases that affect forcign ambassadors, consuls, and other public ministers. Its appellate jurisdiction, like that of all federal courts, is given to it by Congress. Congress has authorized the High Court to review some decisions of both state and lower federal courts.

Cases may be carried from the state courts to the Supreme Court only if a *federal question* (the interpretation of the Constitution, or a federal law or treaty) is involved, and only if an answer to that question is necessary in order to dispose of the case. Before the Supreme Court will accept jurisdiction, the litigant must have taken the case to the highest *state* court in which a decision under *state* law can be made in that particular case. If the state court declares a federal law or treaty *un*constitutional or upholds a state law *against* a substantial challenge that it conflicts with a federal law, treaty, or the Constitution, the Supreme Court *must* review the case when asked to do so by the disappointed litigant. Cases of this kind are said to go to the Supreme Court *on appeal*. In all other state cases involving federal questions, however, the litigant disappointed by the state decision has only the right to petition the Supreme Court to issue *a writ of certiorari* (pronounced sûr'shi-o-ra'ri), ordering the state court to hand up the records of the case. But the Court does not have to grant the writ unless at least four justices feel that the case is important enough to require their attention.

The Supreme Court has the same discretion in determining which cases coming up from the federal courts of appeals it shall review. Only if a court of appeals strikes down a state law because it is contrary to a federal law, treaty, or the Constitution, does a person disappointed by a decision of the court of appeals have the *right* to a Supreme Court review. Of course, any disappointed litigant may petition the High Court for a writ of certiorari, but in most cases his petition will be rejected. The Supreme Court turns down about 80 per cent of the petitions it receives, selecting for review only those cases that involve issues of significant public interest. Furthermore, not too much should be made of the distinction between cases that go to the Supreme Court on appeal and those that go on writ of certiorari. Although in form a disappointed litigant has a right to appeal those cases that fall within the appeal category, the Supreme Court has to determine if the appeal involves a substantial federal question, and many appeals are dismissed for that reason. Thus it is not enough in any case that Jones thinks he should have won the case against Smith. The *Supreme Court* determines which cases it shall consider.

The Supreme Court usually selects for review cases in which there seems to be a conflict between the rulings of the courts of appeals, or cases in which the lower courts seem to have departed from sound methods of judicial proceeding or which involve questions of considerable public importance. If the High Court had to review all cases from the courts of appeals and all cases involving federal questions from the highest state courts, it would still be deciding cases today that originated in the 1920's. The discretion enjoyed by the Supreme Court justices also enables them to select those issues that they feel are most significant and timely, and to duck those issues they do not wish to meet.

How the Supreme Court Operates

At 10 A.M. on the days when the Supreme Court is in session, the eight associate justices and the Chief Justice, dressed in their judicial robes, file into the Court. As they take their seats—arranged according to seniority, with the Chief Justice in the center—the clerk of the Court introduces them as "the Honorable Chief Justice and Associate Justices of the Supreme Court of the United States." Though he concludes "May God save the United States," this is traditional—not editorial. Those present in the chambers then sit down, the counsel taking their places along tables in front of the bench, the attorneys for the Department of Justice, dressed in morning clothes, at the right. Counsel for each side is limited to a one-hour argument—in some cases even less—and the Court scrupulously enforces the time limits. Lawyers before the Court use a lectern to which two lights are attached. A white light flashes five minutes before time is up; when the red light goes on the lawyer must stop instantly even in the middle of a word.[7] The justices freely interrupt the lawyers to ask questions, to inquire for more information. Sometimes, to the annoyance of the attorneys, the justices talk among themselves. The entire procedure is formally informal and is designed to bring out the facts and issues in the case as quickly as possible. Although forensic flourishes are not unknown, oratory is discouraged and arguments before the High Court are usually matter-of-fact and direct. Eloquence is less important than soundness.

The cases that come before this most famous court in the world fall into three main categories: (1) Cases involving citizens or companies of different states. Here the Supreme Court is concerned to see that the federal courts have applied the state laws fairly. These decisions rarely reach the headlines. (2) Cases involving interpretation of a federal law. (3) Cases involving a question of constitutional power. These last two types are the cases that make the Court famous—or infamous.

The justices are in session from the first Monday in October through June. In their gleaming Corinthian building, they listen to oral arguments for two weeks and then adjourn for two weeks to consider the cases and write their opinions. Six justices must participate in each decision, and cases are decided by a majority. In the event of a tie vote, the decision of the lower court is sustained, although the case may be re-argued.

Each Friday the justices meet in conference. During the week they have heard the oral arguments, read and studied the briefs, and examined the petitions. Before the conference, each justice receives a list of the cases that will be discussed. Each brings to the meeting a red leather book (carefully locked) in which the cases and the votes of the justices are recorded. The Friday conferences are highly secret affairs; what goes on in these meetings has to be gleaned from the infrequent comments of members of the Court. The Chief Justice presides; it is in these closed sessions that he has an opportunity to influence his colleagues. Chief Justice Hughes ran these conferences like a stern taskmaster, keeping the Justices talking to the point, moving the discussion along, and doing his best to work out compromises. Frowning on dissents, he tried to achieve a unanimous vote in order to give greater weight to Court decisions. Chief Justice Stone, on the other hand, perhaps influenced by his New England town-meeting background, encouraged each justice to state his own point of view, and let the discussion wander as it would.[8]

Although the procedure varies, these conferences are marked by informality and

[7] Henry J. Abraham, *Courts and Judges* (Oxford Univ. Press, 1959), p. 25; and by the same author, *The Judicial Process* (Oxford Univ. Press, 1962).

[8] John P. Frank, *Marble Palace: The Supreme Court in American Life* (Knopf, 1958), p. 81. See David J. Danelski, "The Influence of the Chief Justice in the Decisional Process," in Walter F. Murphy and C. Herman Pritchett (eds.), *Courts, Judges and Politics* (Random House, 1961), pp. 499–508, for a carefully researched analysis.

vigorous give-and-take. The Chief Justice usually opens the discussion by briefly stating the facts, summarizing the questions of law, and making suggestions for disposing of the case. He then asks each member of the Court, in order of seniority, to give his views and conclusions. After full discussion a vote is taken, with the least senior justice voting first.

The decision itself is of vital interest to the parties concerned, but the grounds on which it is made are often more important to the general public. Except for routine cases that can be disposed of by well-settled principles of law, the High Court always announces the reasons for each decision. If the Chief Justice is not among the majority, the senior justice must write the *Opinion for the Court* himself or assign the task to one of his colleagues. This opinion is then circulated for comments and suggestions. Often a justice may agree with the majority on the decision but differ on the reasoning. He may then write his own opinion, which is known as a *concurring opinion*. Justices who are among the minority normally select one of their number to write a *dissenting opinion*, although each dissenter is free to write his own opinion. Dissenting opinions have no force in disposing of the case or as precedents, but they are not futile gestures. "A dissent in a court of last resort," wrote Chief Justice Hughes, "is an appeal to the brooding spirit of the law, to the intelligence of a future day when a later decision may possibly correct the error into which the dissenting judge believes the court to have been betrayed. . . . Nor is this appeal always in vain. In a number of cases dissenting opinions have in time become the law." [9]

Supreme Court opinions usually state the facts, present the issues, give the reasoning, and announce the decision. The Court's opinion on the ruling of law is binding on all lower federal courts and, when pertinent, on all state courts. Sometimes the justices wander off in their opinions and talk about issues not involved in the case before them. Chief Justice John Marshall, for example, in the case of *McCulloch* v. *Maryland* (see Chapter 4), stated that he thought the national government could tax the states. Since the question actually before the Court was whether the states could tax the federal government, Marshall's remark was *obiter dictum*—that is, reasoning and ruling on an issue not before the Court. *Obiter dicta* often provide valuable clues to the views of the justices; they are not, however, binding on other courts.

The Judges—Guardians of the Constitution

Judicial review is an American contribution to the art of government, though an independent judiciary is a means of enforcing constitutional limitations in all free governments. If an Englishman or an American is thrown into prison without cause, either can appeal to the courts of his respective country for protection. When Parliament passes a law, however, no English judge has the authority to declare it

[9] Charles Evans Hughes, "The Supreme Court of the United States: Its Foundation, Methods, and Achievements," *American Bar Association Journal* (April 1930).

null and void because *he believes* it to violate the English constitution. Not the courts but Parliament is the guardian of the English constitution. But in the United States the courts, ultimately the Supreme Court, are the keepers of the constitutional conscience—not Congress and not the President. How did the judges get this tremendous responsibility?

Origins of Judicial Review

The Constitution itself says nothing about who should be the final arbiter of disputes that might arise over its meaning. It does not specifically grant such power to the Supreme Court. Whether the members of the Convention of 1787 intended to bestow on the courts the power of judicial review is a question that has long been debated. There is little doubt that the framers intended the Supreme Court to have the power to declare *state* legislation unconstitutional, but whether they intended to give it the same power over *national* legislation is not clear. The late Professor Edward S. Corwin, an outstanding authority on the American Constitution, concluded that unquestionably "the framers anticipated some sort of judicial review. . . . But it is equally without question that the ideas generally current in 1787 were far from presaging the present vast role of the Court." [10] Why, then, did the framers not specifically provide for judicial review? Probably because they believed the power rested upon certain general provisions that made specific statement unnecessary.

Certainly Alexander Hamilton intended the Supreme Court to have the power to set aside congressional legislation. He favored, as he said in *Federalist No. 78*, a strong and independent judiciary as a check upon the majority, as an "excellent barrier to the encroachments and oppressions of the representative body." He wanted judges appointed for life to protect the private rights against "the occasional ill-humors in society" that might lead the Congress to pass laws interfering with the propertied minority.

Not all Americans in the eighteenth century looked so kindly upon the courts. During the conflict with England the patriots invoked the doctrine that the courts should refuse to enforce the laws of Parliament that were against "natural equity" and the English constitution. But after the Revolution, when some state judges dared to void acts of the state legislatures on the grounds of conflict with a "higher law," there was widespread protest. Only a few persons thought of the courts as instruments to enforce constitutional limitations in behalf of the liberties of the people. Most of those who favored judicial review hoped to check the power of popular majorities.

The First Congress adopted—without much debate—the Judiciary Act of 1789, in which it was assumed that the Supreme Court had the power to refuse to enforce congressional legislation that the justices believed to be unconstitutional. Early in its history the Supreme Court did in several cases review acts of Congress, and in

[10] Edward S. Corwin, "The Constitution as Instrument and as Symbol," *The American Political Science Review* (1936), p. 1078.

1794 it apparently even declared an act of Congress invalid, but little attention was paid to this incident.

The Federalists—the men who wrote the Constitution and controlled the national government until 1801—generally supported the courts and favored judicial review, but their opponents, the Jeffersonian Republicans, were less enthusiastic. In 1798 and 1799 Jefferson and Madison (the latter by this time had left the Federalist party) came very close in the Virginia and Kentucky Resolutions to arguing that the state legislatures and not the Supreme Court had the ultimate power to interpret the Constitution. This would seem to imply that the Supreme Court did not even have the final authority to review *state* legislation, something about which there had been little doubt.

When the Jeffersonians defeated the Federalists in the elections of 1800, it was still undecided whether the Supreme Court would actually exercise the power of judicial review. "The idea was in the air, the ingredients to support a doctrine of judicial review were at hand, and a few precedents could even be cited"; nevertheless, judicial review was not an established power. Then in 1803 came the case of *Marbury* v. *Madison*, a case intimately related to the political struggles between the Federalists and the Jeffersonians.

The Case of *Marbury* v. *Madison*

The elections of 1800 marked the rise to power of the Jeffersonian Republicans. President John Adams and his fellow Federalists did not take their defeat easily; indeed, they were greatly alarmed at what they considered to be the "enthronement of the rabble." But there was nothing much they could do about it before leaving office—or was there? The Constitution gives the President, with the consent of the Senate, the power to appoint federal judges to hold office during "good behavior"—virtually for life. If the judiciary should be manned by good Federalists, reasoned Adams and his party followers, they could stave off the worst consequences of Jefferson's victory. These Federalists were not motivated solely by partisan purposes; for some time they had contemplated reform of the judicial structure. But between their defeat in November 1800 and the expiration of their terms on March 4, 1801, they worked with renewed zeal.

By the end of February 1801 the Federalist lame-duck Congress had created dozens of new federal judicial posts. By March 3, Adams had appointed, and the Senate had confirmed, deserving Federalists to all these new positions. Adams signed the commissions and turned them over to John Marshall, the Secretary of State, to be sealed and delivered. Marshall had just received his own commission as Chief Justice of the United States, but he was continuing to serve as Secretary of State until Adams' term expired. Working right up to nine o'clock on the evening of March 3, Marshall sealed but was unable to deliver all the commissions. The important ones were taken care of, however, and only those for the justices of the peace for the District of Columbia were left undelivered. It was late and the Chief Justice had a big day ahead: He was going to administer the presidential oath of office to his distant cousin and political enemy Thomas Jefferson. He retired to his lodgings and left the commissions to be delivered by his successor.

Jefferson was highly aroused by this Federalist packing of the judiciary. When he discovered that some of the commissions had not been delivered, he told the new Secretary of State, James Madison, to hold up seventeen of those still in his possession. Jefferson could see no reason why the District needed so many justices of the peace, especially Federalist justices.

Among the commissions that were not delivered was one for William Marbury. After waiting in vain, Marbury decided to seek action from the courts. Searching through the statute books, he came across Section 13 of the Judiciary Act of 1789, which authorized the Supreme Court "to issue writs of mandamus, in cases warranted by the principles and usages of law, to . . . persons holding office, under the authority of the United States." A *writ of mandamus* is a court order directing an official to perform a nondiscretionary or ministerial act. Delivering a commission is a ministerial act; the Secretary of State is a person holding office under the authority of the United States; so why not, thought Marbury, ask the Supreme Court to issue a writ of mandamus to force Madison to deliver the commission? He and his companions went directly to the Supreme Court and citing Section 13, they so asked.

What could Marshall do? If the Court issued the mandamus, Madison and Jefferson would probably ignore it. The Court would be powerless, and its prestige, already low, might suffer a fatal blow. On the other hand, by refusing to issue the mandamus, the judges would appear to vindicate the Republican party's claim that the Court had no authority to interfere with the executive. Would Marshall issue the mandamus? Most people thought so; angry Republicans talked of impeachment.

On February 24, 1803, five dignified gentlemen in judicial robes took their seats in a small, dingy room in the basement of the Capitol.

John Marshall's Decision

The first part of the opinion was as expected. Marbury was entitled to his commission, said Marshall, and Madison should have delivered it to him; a writ of mandamus could be issued by the proper court against even such an august officer as the Secretary of State.

Then came the surprise. Although Section 13 of the Judiciary Act purports to give the Supreme Court original jurisdiction in just such cases, this section, said Marshall, *is contrary to Article III of the Constitution.* This article gives the Supreme Court original jurisdiction in *only* those cases in which an ambassador or other foreign minister is affected or in which a state is a party. This is a case of original jurisdiction, but Marbury is neither a state nor a foreign minister. If we follow Section 13, wrote Marshall, we have jurisdiction; if we follow the Constitution we have no jurisdiction.

Then, in characteristic fashion, Marshall stated the question in such a way that the answer was obvious—namely, should the Supreme Court enforce an unconstitutional law? Of course not, he concluded; the Constitution is the supreme and binding law, and the courts cannot enforce any action of Congress that conflicts with it.

The real question remained unanswered. Congress, in passing the law, and the President, in signing it, had also read the Constitution, and according to *their* interpretation (which was also reasonable) Section 13 was compatible with Article III. Where did the *Supreme Court* get the right to say they were wrong? Why should the *Supreme Court's* interpretation of the Constitution be preferred to that of Congress and the President?

Marshall, paralleling Hamilton's argument in *Federalist No. 78*, reasoned that the Constitution is law, that judges—not legislators or executives—interpret law; therefore, the judges should interpret the Constitution. "If two laws conflict with each other, the courts must decide on the operation of each," he said. Obviously the Constitution is to be preferred to any ordinary act of Congress.

Case dismissed.

Jefferson fumed. For one thing, Marshall had said that a court with the proper jurisdiction could issue a writ of mandamus even against the Secretary of State, the President's right-hand man. But there was little Jefferson could do about it, for there was not even a specific court order that he could refuse to obey. Thus, in a single stroke Marshall had given the Republicans a lecture for failing to perform their duties, and had gone a long way toward acquiring for the Supreme Court the power of judicial review of acts of Congress—all in a manner that made it difficult for the Republicans to retaliate.

Marbury v. *Madison* is a masterpiece of judicial strategy. Marshall, contrary to modern canons of judicial interpretation, went out of his way to declare Section 13 unconstitutional. He could have interpreted the section to mean that the Supreme Court could issue writs of mandamus in those cases in which it did have jurisdiction. He could have interpreted Article III to mean that Congress could add to, though not subtract from, the original jurisdiction that the Constitution gives to the Supreme Court. He could have dismissed the case for want of jurisdiction without discussing Marbury's right to his commission. But none of these would have suited his purpose. Jefferson and his fellow Republicans had been threatening to use the impeachment powers to remove Federalist partisans from the federal bench. Marshall was fearful for the Supreme Court's future, and he felt unless the Court spoke out it would become subordinate to the President and Congress.

Marshall's decision, important as it was, did not by itself necessarily establish for the Supreme Court the power to review and declare unconstitutional acts of the Congress. *Marbury* v. *Madison* could have meant simply that the Supreme Court had the right to interpret the scope of *its own* powers under Article III, but that Congress and the President had the authority to interpret their own powers under Articles I and II, respectively. However, Marshall's decision has not been interpreted by court or country in this way (though it was not until the *Dred Scott* case in 1857 that another act of Congress was declared unconstitutional). Had Marshall not spoken when he did, the Court might not have been able to assume the power of judicial review. The vital precedent had been created. Here we have a classic example of constitutional developments through judicial interpretation. There is no specific authorization in the Constitution for the Supreme Court's power to declare congressional enactments null and void; yet today it is a vital part of our constitutional system.

The Supreme Court in American History

The importance of the Supreme Court in shaping the contours and policies of the American Republic has hardly been less than that of Congress and the President. A story of over 170 years cannot be told briefly without distortion. Yet we can see the rhythm of the law by highlighting the general attitudes of the most prominent of the more than ninety men who have served on the High Bench.[11]

The Formative Period: John Marshall and Roger B. Taney

Until John Marshall became Chief Justice in 1801, the Supreme Court had been a minor branch of the federal government. During the first ten years of its history, three Chief Justices came and departed without finding the position of sufficient importance to challenge their talents. Then came Marshall, a leading Federalist lawyer. During his thirty-four years as Chief Justice, he elevated the judiciary to a position of importance coordinate with that of Congress and the President.

After 1811 a majority of his fellow justices were nominally Jeffersonians, but Marshall's strong personality and intellect, combined with the fundamentally conservative character of the men appointed to serve with him, enabled the Chief Justice to dominate the Supreme Court to an extent never since equaled. Under his leadership the Court "struck blow after blow in support of the doctrine that the United States was a sovereign nation and not a mere confederacy of sovereign states." [12] Marshall, representing a political party whose views grew less popular with the passage of each year, continued to uphold the authority of the national government and to protect the rights of property. His classic opinions for the Court in _Marbury_ v. _Madison_, _McCulloch_ v. _Maryland_, _Gibbons_ v. _Ogden_, and _Cohens_ v. _Virginia_ remain among the most influential opinions ever handed down by any court.

Roger B. Taney (pronounced "Tawney"), Marshall's successor, also started his political life as a Federalist, but he became an ardent supporter of Andrew Jackson, whom he served as Attorney General and as Secretary of the Treasury. When Jackson appointed Taney to the High Bench in 1835, only two men remained from the

[11] J. R. Schmidhauser, "The Justices of the Supreme Court: A Collective Portrait," _Midwest Journal of Political Science_ (February 1959), pp. 1–57.

[12] Alfred H. Kelly and Winfred A. Harbison, _The American Constitution_, revised edition (Norton, 1955), p. 272.

great days of the Marshall Court, and under Taney the ideas of Jacksonian democracy began to work their way into the Court's opinions. The break between the Marshall and Taney Courts is often exaggerated. Taney and his colleagues were just as devoted to the protection of property as was the Marshall Court. The Taney Court was concerned especially with property rights in land and slavery. And Taney did not differ with Marshall on the supremacy of the national government. Nevertheless, there were important differences between the dominant spirit of the Taney Court and that of its predecessor. In a limited retreat from Marshall's nationalism, the Supreme Court now began to stress the power of the states. The Taney Court was more inclined than its predecessor to recognize the rights of legislative majorities to regulate the uses of private property (especially property that was given special privilege by the states).

It is unfortunate that Taney's *Dred Scott* decision toward the end of his twenty-nine years as Chief Justice has obscured his many earlier constructive opinions. The *Dred Scott* case is now generally recognized as a misguided attempt by the Supreme Court to interfere in a political controversy in order to resolve the issue of slavery. The majority opinion—that the national government did not have the power to exclude slavery from the territories—merely aggravated the conflict and did the Court itself a grave disservice.

Civil War and Reconstruction

During the decade in which Salmon P. Chase presided over the Supreme Court, 1864–1874, the Court tried to avoid the cross fire between President Johnson and the Radical Republicans in Congress. The Radical Republicans were in control, and they rode roughshod over those who got in their way. Nevertheless, the Chase Court declared ten acts of Congress unconstitutional, as contrasted with the two acts that had been held void in the preceding eighty-four years.

The High Court could not, however, insulate itself from the rough and tumble of postwar party politics, as the *Legal Tender Cases* made clear. To pay for the Civil War, Congress authorized the Treasury to issue greenbacks (paper currency), and it taxed state bank notes out of existence. The right of Congress to authorize paper currency not redeemable in gold or silver was vigorously challenged, and in 1870 (*Hepburn* v. *Griswold*) a bare majority of Supreme Court justices declared the Legal Tender Act unconstitutional. President Grant, however, had an opportunity to appoint two new justices, and soon (in 1871) the Supreme Court reversed its decision of the preceding year and upheld the Legal Tender Act.[13] President Grant's appointees "voted the right way."

The primary concern of the Supreme Court during the Chief Justiceship of Morrison R. Waite, 1874–1888, was to re-establish the equilibrium between the states and the national government that had been upset by the Civil War and Reconstruction. In the name of the federal system, the Court nullified the Fourteenth Amend-

[13] *Legal Tender Cases* (1871).

ment as a constitutional prop for a positive national program of protection for civil rights. At the same time the Court, despite the bitter dissent of a minority, refused to expand its own powers by using the due process clause to judge the reasonableness of state regulation of business enterprise. The Supreme Court should not become, said the Court, "a perpetual censor upon all legislation of the States." [14]

The Supreme Court Becomes a Super Legislature

Between the Civil War and the New Deal, Republicans were in the White House for all but sixteen years. Regardless of party affiliation, most of the Presidents and influential senators believed in the existence of unalterable economic laws beyond the sphere of governmental control. They looked with suspicion on any proposal that interfered with the rights of men to invest their capital or to hire workers, deeming such suggestions dangerous, socialistic, populistic, and anarchistic. These were the men who selected most of the members of the Supreme Court.

The appointment of Melville Fuller as Chief Justice in 1888 marked the beginning of a new period in the Court's history. Between 1888 and 1937 the Supreme Court became "an aristocracy of the robe and twisted the due process clause into a moat around all forms of private property." The Supreme Court became a censor of legislation which, in the justices' opinions, unreasonably interfered with the use of private property. The Court also gave such a restrictive interpretation of congressional power over interstate commerce that effective federal regulation of the economy was forestalled. The Court, by judicial interpretation, took the teeth out of the Sherman Antitrust and Interstate Commerce Commission laws, and vetoed all attempts by Congress to outlaw child labor in this country.

In 1895 the Supreme Court demonstrated, perhaps too clearly, its concept of itself as the protector of property against the "revolutionaries." By a five-to-four decision, the Court, reversing an old and theretofore unquestioned precedent, made it impossible for the federal government to levy an income tax. Justice Field, in a concurring opinion, brought to the surface the majority's feelings about such dangerous experiments. The income tax was an assault on capital, he wrote, "it will be but the stepping stone to others, larger and more sweeping, till our political contests will become a war of the poor against the rich; a war constantly growing in intensity and bitterness." [15] In 1913 the Sixteenth Amendment was ratified reversing this decision.

The Supreme Court's assumption of power as a super legislature was contested by a minority of the Supreme Court justices. Justice Oliver Wendell Holmes spent many of his thirty years on the Court (1902–1932) protesting against his colleagues' habit of writing their own economic predilections into the Constitution. Although he was not Chief Justice and was often in dissent, Holmes became the most famous member of the Court. Though he himself was a conservative with little faith in social reform by legislation, with Olympian detachment he refused to let his own

---

[14] *Slaughter-House Cases* (1873).
[15] *Pollock* v. *Farmers' Loan and Trust Co.* (1895).

social views become the measure of a law's constitutionality. In 1916 Louis D. Brandeis, appointed by President Wilson, joined with Holmes in protesting the major direction of the Supreme Court's opinions and in exposing the reasons behind the decisions of the Court majority. Brandeis' constitutional and social philosophy was radically different from that of Holmes, but it often produced the same results. When Harlan Fiske Stone became a member of the Court in 1925, he joined with the two dissenters, and "Holmes, Brandeis, and Stone dissenting" became a familiar phrase in the law reports.

The New Deal and After

Charles Evans Hughes was a majestic-looking man, the very model of a model Chief Justice. He was a liberal-conservative who used his great talents to guide the Supreme Court during the stormy period (1930–1941) when it collided with Roosevelt's New Deal. The Hughes Court was split into fairly consistent conservative and liberal blocs. Four of the justices—Sutherland, Van Devanter, Butler, and McReynolds—held views that reflected the conservative political attitudes dominant in the times when they were appointed. Showing no reluctance to veto legislation that ran counter to their own economic and social attitudes, they looked upon the New Deal as an unconstitutional and dangerous interference with the rights of property and the constitutional system. On the other hand, Justices Brandeis, Stone, and Cardozo (the distinguished jurist who replaced Holmes in 1932), though they found constitutional objections to some New Deal legislation, could find nothing in the Constitution that prevented the national government from doing what was necessary and proper to fight the depression. Chief Justice Hughes and Justice Owen Roberts, both Hoover appointees, held the balance of power. They wavered, then joined the conservatives in ruling that much of the New Deal was unconstitutional.

President Roosevelt counterattacked vigorously. After the smoke of battle had cleared, it was found that Justice Roberts and the Chief Justice had altered their positions. Moreover the conservatives—who had held on all during Roosevelt's first term—now began to leave the Court. By 1939 a liberal majority controlled the Supreme Court, and by 1941 all the old guard had been replaced by Roosevelt appointees. The "New Court," as it was called after 1937, soon knocked down the barriers that its predecessors had erected against social and economic reform. The Holmes, Brandeis, and Stone dissents became the ruling doctrine of the Court. The "New Court" returned to Marshall's broad construction of Congress' power over interstate commerce, and to the doctrine that the Fourteenth Amendment was not intended to give the Supreme Court justices "carte blanche to embody [their] economic or moral beliefs in its prohibitions."

Though tolerant of governmental regulation of business enterprise, the "New Court" became increasingly intolerant of any attempt to restrict civil liberties, especially attempts by the state governments. Between 1937 and 1946 the Supreme

Court handed down many important decisions protecting the civil liberties of individuals.

Harlan Fiske Stone's elevation to the chief justiceship by President Roosevelt in 1941 did not mark any basic change in the Court's doctrines. By that date eight of the nine members of the Court were Roosevelt appointees. Many critics of the New Deal accused the President of creating a rubber-stamp court. To be sure, all his appointees shared the general political position symbolized by the New Deal, and none of them agreed with the constitutional doctrines of conservatives like Sutherland or McReynolds. But they were far from united. In fact, more dissenting opinions were penned after 1940 than at any previous time in the Court's history. In many cases as many as five justices felt impelled to write separate opinions, often sharply attacking one another's views. The justices, most of whom had previously been active in politics, discussed the philosophical and political premises of their decisions to a much greater extent than had any of their predecessors.

Under the leadership of Chief Justice Fred M. Vinson (1946–1953), the Supreme Court continued to sanction governmental regulation of business, labor, and agriculture. The Court pushed forward in behalf of civil rights for minority groups, but in the face of the tensions of the Cold War the Court retreated from the strong civil liberties stand it had espoused under Chief Justice Stone. The High Court construed the Smith Act to ease the way for the Department of Justice to prosecute communists; it refused to consider cases challenging the right of congressional committees to interrogate private citizens about their political views; and it dodged constitutional questions raised by loyalty-security programs. In short, the Supreme Court deferred to the judgment of Congress and the state legislatures that national security required some sacrifice of civil liberties.

The Warren Court—Civil Liberties to the Fore

When Chief Justice Vinson died, President Eisenhower appointed Earl Warren, former governor of California and former Republican vice-presidential nominee, to the vacant position. Under Chief Justice Warren's leadership the Supreme Court has continued to deal with a wide variety of constitutional and statutory issues,[16] but its chief concern has been with questions involving civil liberties and civil rights.

If the Warren Court had done nothing else, its place in history would be secure—it would be enough to say that this was the Court that made the Constitution color-blind. But the Court has been active on many fronts: It has incorporated most of the provisions of the Bill of Rights into the Fourteenth Amendment and thereby provided a national standard for the administration of justice; it broke the log-jam that for decades kept legislative bodies unrepresentative of the electorate; it struck down many state statutes and a few congressional enactments,

[16] Glendon Schubert, "The 1960 Term: A Psychological Analysis," *The American Political Science Review* (March 1962), p. 100.

and narrowly construed others, in order to prevent what the justices consider infringements of civil liberties. The Warren Court's active and almost eager decision-making has brought the Court into frequent conflict with those who dislike its decisions or who object to its dealing with issues that the critics think should be left to the legislatures.[17] Congress has considered legislation to "curb" the Court by restricting its jurisdiction, and amendments to override some of the decisions. So far the only retaliatory congressional action has been the reduction of a proposed salary increase for Supreme Court justices.

The Warren Court has often been divided, but in one area the justices have stood together. All the justices, whether appointed by Roosevelt, Truman, Eisenhower, or Kennedy, have firmly insisted that under the Constitution of the United States the power of government can never be used to deny equal rights under the law to any person because of his race. Whether the question be the right to vote, to attend public schools, to equal justice in courts, with rare exceptions the Supreme Court's decisions have been unanimous and the general direction of its rulings consistent.

On other issues the Supreme Court is more closely divided, teetering back and forth from case to case. The divisions among the justices are not rigid and vary from issue to issue. A condensed description is necessarily oversimplified and omits the many subtle issues and differences. But there are, speaking in general terms, two groups: Chief Justice Warren; Justice William J. Brennan, Jr., another Eisenhower selection; two Roosevelt appointees, Hugo L. Black and William O. Douglas; and Arthur Goldberg (until his resignation in 1965 to become Ambassador to the United Nations), appointed by Kennedy, make up a fairly consistent civil-liberties bloc that holds that the Supreme Court has a special mandate to protect civil liberties. This bloc has had the votes necessary to control most decisions.

Until his retirement, the late Justice Felix Frankfurter headed the other bloc, one that is much less inclined to find governmental action to be an infringement of civil liberties. Since his retirement, Justice John Marshall Harlan, nominated by Eisenhower, has taken over the leadership of this group. These justices argue that politically responsive elected officials have the major responsibility for balancing conflicting values and that judges should exercise caution and restraint. A legislative decision that the public well-being requires some restraints on civil liberties is not lightly to be questioned. Justice Harlan can often count on the support of Justice Potter Stewart, an Eisenhower selection, Justice Tom C. Clark, a Truman appointee, especially if national security or law enforcement matters are involved, and Justice Byron White, a Kennedy selection, especially on matters that do not involve freedom of speech. However, on some issues and on some occasions, one

---

[17] For the most part, those who object to such decisions are also those who think that the Court is overstepping its boundaries. However, Charles Hyneman, in *The Supreme Court on Trial* (Atherton, 1963), raises issues relating to the proper role of the Court within the context of democratic theory unrelated to concurrence or difference with the particular substantive decisions.

or more of the Harlan bloc, including Harlan, vote with the civil libertarians, especially if it can be done without having to interpose a constitutional veto.[18]

The never-ending task of determining what the Constitution means today and tomorrow is a process in which the voters participate. By selecting John F. Kennedy over Richard Nixon and Lyndon B. Johnson over Barry Goldwater (the latter made his opposition to key Supreme Court decisions one of his campaign issues) the voters decided, among other things, that the justices President Kennedy appointed and those whom President Johnson will appoint are more apt to be liberal-to-moderate Democrats than moderate-to-conservative Republicans.

Judges as Technicians

The Constitution does not require judges to be lawyers. Yet all Supreme Court justices, as well as other federal judges, have been members of the bar. No businessman, farmer, or union leader has ever served on any federal court. The reason is not hard to uncover. Although ignorance of the law is no excuse for the wrongdoer, knowledge of the law is a professional discipline, a technical subject that can be mastered only after long study.

What kind of law do federal judges apply? Where do they find it? [19]

The Law

Sometimes judges apply *constitutional law*. Since the Constitution contains only 7,000 words and can be read in a half-hour or so, it might be assumed that any person could learn constitutional law after a little study. But even the Constitution has become a possession of the specialists, and to read the document itself sheds little light on constitutional law. Indeed, Professor T. R. Powell, one of Harvard's most distinguished teachers, is reported to have warned his students not to read the Constitution because it would "confuse their minds." Constitutional law is full of phrases like "the clear and present danger rule" and "selective absorption" that are not to be found in the written words of the Constitution. They come from the decisions of the Supreme Court. Constitutional law, in other words, consists of statements about the interpretation of the Constitution that have been given Supreme Court sanction.

[18] Schubert, *op. cit.*; Robert G. McCloskey, "Deeds Without Doctrine: Civil Rights in the 1960 Term of the Supreme Court," *The American Political Science Review* (March 1962), pp. 71–89; Benjamin F. Wright, "The Rights of Majorities and of Minorities in the 1961 Term of the Supreme Court," *The American Political Science Review* (March 1963), pp. 98–115; Walter F. Murphy, "Deeds Under A Doctrine in the 1963 Term," *The American Political Science Review* (March 1965), pp. 64–79. See also Paul C. Bartholomew, review of the work of the Court in the March 1961, March 1962, December 1962, December 1963, and December 1964 issues of the *Western Political Quarterly*, and the annual review of the work of the Supreme Court in the *Harvard Law Review*.

[19] See Epilogue to find out where the lay citizen can look up the law.

In many instances it is *statutory law* that controls the judges' decisions. This is law formulated by the legislature, although it also includes treaties and executive orders; it is law that comes from authoritative and specific lawmaking sources. The legislature has no choice but to state the rules in general terms, for it cannot anticipate all the questions that will arise over their meaning. Even the most specific law must be applied to an infinite variety of concrete situations. The initial interpretation is often made by an administrator, but the final interpretation, short of an actual change in the law, is made by the judges.

Again, intelligence alone is not enough to interpret even the simplest of laws. The law must be interpreted according to the application of legal principles. In general, judges try to discover *legislative intent*—what the legislators intended to do. When possible, this is done by studying the words of the statute in question. Sometimes, however, judges must look to legislative journals, legislative debates, and committee hearings for clues to the intention of the legislators. A layman might try to consult the men who drafted, introduced, or considered the bill in committee, for they might seem to be the most informative and reliable source of legislative intent. But according to the judges' rules, which in large part they make themselves, this is not permissible.

What happens if there is no statutory law governing a case that comes before a court? What if the legislature has not formalized any rule to apply to the dispute? Then the judges must apply the *common law*. Common law is judge-made law. It has an ancient lineage reaching back through centuries of judicial decisions. It originated in England in the twelfth century when royal judges began traveling around the country settling disputes in each locality according to prevailing custom. Gradually these principles became the same for the entire nation. The common law continues to develop according to the rule of *stare decisis*, which means, "let the decision stand." *Stare decisis* requires that once a rule has been established by a court, it shall be followed in all similar cases. It makes the decisions of judges of superior courts binding not only on all subordinate courts in the same judicial system, but also on their own successors.

The American common law began to branch off from the English system in the seventeenth century. Today we have 49 separate common-law systems, or 50, counting the federal interpretation of state law. (In Louisiana the legal system is based on the other great western legal tradition, the *civil law*. The civil law gives more emphasis to codes of lawgivers and less to past judicial decisions. In Louisiana the civil law has been greatly influenced by and intermingled with the common law.) There is no federal common law. Whenever federal judges have to decide disputes between citizens of two states and there is no applicable state statute, they apply the common law as interpreted by the state courts. But when there is no state interpretation, federal judges strike out for themselves. The common law governs many disputes, and even where it has been superseded by statute, the statutory law is usually a modification and codification of the old common-law rules and is normally interpreted according to the common-law tradition.

Federal judges also apply *equity*. Like common law, equity is a system of judge-made law that had its origins in England. Early in the development of the common law, it was discovered that in certain circumstances the common law did not insure justice. Under the common law, for example, a person whose property rights are about to be injured has no choice but to wait until the injury has taken place and then to seek money damages. But the injury may do irreparable harm for which money damages cannot provide adequate compensation. Accordingly another set of rules was worked out to be used where the law was inadequate. Under equity, a person may go to a judge, show why the common-law remedy is inadequate, and ask for equitable relief—an injunction, for example, to prevent an act that threatens irreparable harm. If the wrongdoer persists, he may be punished for contempt of court.

Other Types of Law

Admiralty and maritime law is also applied by federal judges. This is a highly complex and technical body of rules applicable to cases arising in connection with shipping and water-borne commerce on the high seas and, by decision of the Supreme Court,[20] on the navigable waters of the United States.

A relatively new kind of law that has become increasingly prominent in the decisions of federal judges is *administrative law*. Congress has, within the last several decades, delegated to administrators and administrative agencies so much rule-making authority that today there is, in volume, more administrative than statutory law. Administrative law consists of the rules and regulations issued by administrative agencies that deal with the operations of the government or that determine private rights. An example is the Federal Trade Commission regulation that forbids interstate advertisers to use the word "free" in such a way as to mislead the reader. The rules and decisions of administrators may be reviewed by federal judges, and judges are often called upon to determine whether the administrators have acted properly and within their authority.

Law may also be classified as *criminal* or *civil*. Criminal law, which is almost entirely statutory, defines crimes against the public order and provides for punishment. Government has the primary responsibility for enforcing this type of law. The great body of criminal law is enacted by states and is enforced by state officials in the state courts, but the criminal business of federal judges is by no means negligible, and it is growing. The Constitution insists upon certain minimum procedures in the trial of criminal cases (see Chapter 8), and these procedures have been supplemented by law. The Supreme Court, as supervisor of the administration of justice in the federal courts, has adopted other rules that federal judges must follow.

Civil law governs the relations between individuals and defines their legal rights. For example: Jones, who has a trademark for "Atomic Pills," discovers that Smith is advertising "Atomic Tablets" in national magazines. If Jones wishes to protect

[20] *The Genessee Chief* (1852).

his trademark, he may proceed against Smith before a federal judge. But the government can also be a party to a civil action. Under the Sherman Antitrust Act, the federal government may initiate civil as well as criminal action to prevent violations of the law.

The Scope of Judicial Power

Some people seem to think that judges roam around the country ferreting out injustice. Perhaps they visualize a judge reading through the morning paper, looking for evidence of law violations or for legislation passed by Congress that he should declare unconstitutional. This is not the way judges operate. They have only *judicial power*—the power "to decide and pronounce a judgment and carry it into effect between persons . . . who bring a case before [them] for decision." [21] The Supreme Court has steadfastly refused to permit the constitutional courts to exercise any nonjudicial functions. These courts cannot make any decisions "not binding on the parties or subject to later . . . alteration by administrative action." Hence, the Supreme Court will not give any advisory opinions to Congress or the President; it will act, and permit other constitutional courts to act, only when it is presented with a controversy over which it has jurisdiction.

Not all disputes are within the scope of judicial power. Judges decide only *justiciable* disputes, those that grow out of actual cases and that are capable of settlement by legal methods. A rabid Dodger fan might engage in a violent dispute with a booster of the Cardinals, but no judge will use his judicial authority to determine which is the better team. Not even all governmental questions or constitutional problems are justiciable. For example, judges will not determine which government of a foreign state should be recognized by the United States. The Constitution gives this authority to the President, and judges will not question his decision. Similarly, the Supreme Court has ruled that some claims of unconstitutionality raise political and not justiciable questions. What does the Court mean by "political"? It means an issue that requires knowledge of a nonlegal character, that requires the use of techniques not suitable for a court, or that the Constitution addresses to the political branch of government. Examples of political questions are: Which of two competing state governments is the proper one? What is a republican form of state government? [22]

Judges will not use their power unless the controversy is a real one. Two people cannot trump up a suit merely to contest the actions of the legislature. For example, in 1889 a man named Wellman tried to purchase a railway ticket the day after the Michigan legislature had fixed the rates. The ticket agent refused to sell a ticket at the new rate and Wellman brought suit. During the trial Wellman did not contest the railway company's testimony. It became clear that Well-

---

[21] Justice Miller, *Constitution* 314, quoted by Justice Day for Supreme Court in *Muskrat* v. *United States* (1911).
[22] *Luther* v. *Borden* (1849); *Coleman* v. *Miller* (1939).

man wanted the railway company to win; he made no attempt to present fully the facts in the case. The Supreme Court said, however, "It was never thought that, by means of a friendly suit, a party beaten in the legislature could transfer to the courts an inquiry as to the constitutionality of a legislative act." [23] (This, of course, is exactly what is done in a nonfriendly suit. In such cases, however, the two parties have an interest in getting the full facts before the Court.)

Can anybody challenge a law? Not unless he has "sustained or is immediately in danger of sustaining a direct injury. It is not sufficient that he has merely a general interest common to all members of the public." [24] Furthermore, the injury must be substantial. In 1921 Congress passed a law providing for federal grants to the states to help reduce maternal and infant mortality. When a Miss Frothingham heard about the law she was indignant. It was, she thought, clearly unconstitutional, for this activity was reserved to the states and beyond the power of the national government. She instructed her attorneys to seek an injunction to prevent Secretary of the Treasury Mellon from disbursing money in accordance with the law. Did she have the right to maintain the suit? Yes, her lawyers argued, because if the unconstitutional appropriations were made, it would increase the burden of future taxes and thereby take her property without due process of the law. The Supreme Court decided, however, that Miss Frothingham's interest in the money in the Federal Treasury was too minute, and the effects of appropriation on future taxation too remote and uncertain, to give her any standing to contest the act.[25]

Judges are careful to decide only what is necessary to dispose of the case before them, especially when the constitutionality of an act of Congress is in question. The Supreme Court has frequently shown extreme reluctance to rule on constitutional questions. As Mr. Justice Brandeis wrote: "It is not the habit of the court to decide questions of a constitutional nature unless absolutely necessary to a decision of the case. . . . The Court will not 'formulate a rule of constitutional law broader than is required by the precise facts to which it is applied. . . .' The Court will not pass upon a constitutional question although properly presented by the record, if there is also present some other ground upon which the case may be disposed of. . . . [It] is a cardinal principle that this Court will first ascertain whether a construction of the statute is fairly possible by which the question [of constitutionality] may be avoided." [26]

Judges do not always remain strictly within the limits set by these restrictions. At times the Supreme Court justices, despite their professed reluctance to do so, have had little hesitancy about striking down laws of Congress. Disputes have been trumped up entirely for the purpose of getting a Court decision; the *Dred Scott* case, for example, appears to have been a dispute of this kind. Other cases have been presented in which it is questionable whether the parties actually

---

[23] *Chicago & Grand Trunk Railway Co.* v. *Wellman* (1892).
[24] *Ex parte Levitt* (1937).
[25] *Frothingham* v. *Mellon* (1923).
[26] Concurring opinion in *Ashwander* v. *T.V.A.* (1936).

stood in an adverse relationship. Despite these breaches, the judges generally are careful to stay within their proper field of operations.

Laymen are often impatient with what they consider to be legal technicalities. But judges are not free agents with the power to right any and all wrongs according to their own sense of justice. "We do not sit," wrote Justice Frankfurter in the *Terminiello* case, "like a kadi under a tree dispensing justice according to considerations of individual expediency. . . ." In the long run, a court's violation of the settled rules of judicial procedure would probably lead to more uncertainty, to more abuse of judicial power, and to more delay than does the slow but inexorable movement of justice. "Some of these rules," Justice Frankfurter has admitted, ". . . may well appear overrefined or evasive to the laity. But they have the support not only of the profoundest wisdom. They have been vindicated, in conspicuous instances of disregard, by the painful lessons of our constitutional history." The rules restricting judges are designed to prevent them from interfering in matters beyond their competence and to confine them to the functions for which they were established.

"Judges as Politicians"

"Do judges make law? 'Course they do. Made some myself," remarked Jeremiah Smith, former judge of the New Hampshire Supreme Court.[27] Today such statements raise few judicial eyebrows. But just a few generations ago, such frankness would have shocked many of the leading gentlemen of the bench and bar. Despite glaring evidence to the contrary and the realistic statements of outstanding judges and lawyers, the orthodox position was that judges *discovered* but never made laws. According to this orthodoxy, the judges' own views of pupil policy were irrelevant since their only function was to apply the rule or principle applicable to the case before them. Judging, it was insisted, was solely a matter of knowledge of the law, and the personal values of the judges did not enter into the picture. According to the "discovery" theory of the law, a judge is bound by the rule of *stare decisis*. A judge merely *discovers* the right precedents; and when there are no precedents, he extends the old principles.

How Judges Make Law

In deciding most cases, however, it is easy enough to find precedents to support a decision for either party. There are competing principles, each of which might appropriately support a decision. In choosing between them, the judge acts very much like a legislator. The judge also has a range of choice when he interprets statutory law, for most statutes give no clear guide to legislative intent. Although judges profess to search for legislative

[27] Quoted in Paul A. Freund, *On Understanding the Supreme Court* (Little, Brown, 1949), p. 3.

intent, how is one to discover the intention of all the congressmen and the President who make the law? Legislative intention is, as Professor Max Radin has written, "a transparent and absurd fiction." [28] Even where legislative history affords clear guides to the intent of the legislators, James M. Landis has pointed out, "strong judges prefer to override the intent of the legislature in order to make law according to their own views." [29] According to Judge Learned Hand, who was one of America's great jurists, the words of a statute that a judge must construe are "empty vessels into which he can pour nearly anything he will."

How judges make law is well illustrated by an example that is extreme but not unique. In 1890 Congress passed the Sherman Antitrust Law, declaring, "Every contract in restraint of trade and commerce among the several States is illegal." But the legislators left it to the judges to determine the concrete meaning of this law. In order to discover, for example, whether the law outlaws contracts pertaining to *manufacturing* that ultimately will restrain interstate commerce, one must look not to the words of the law or even to legislative history, but to the decisions of the Supreme Court. This was the question in *United States v. E. C. Knight Co.* (1895), the first case under the Sherman Act to come before the High Tribunal. The government had asked the Court to set aside a contract among a group of companies that gave them control over the refining of 98 per cent of the sugar in the United States. But a majority of the Supreme Court justices declared that the act did not outlaw such a contract. The sugar companies, they said, had restrained manufacturing—not interstate commerce—and the restraint of interstate commerce that might result was indirect. By this interpretation the Supreme Court took the heart out of the Sherman Antitrust Law, though the rationale of the Knight case was undercut by the Supreme Court a few years later. In 1911 the Court further "amended" the Sherman Act by ruling that, despite the words of the statute, Congress had intended to make illegal only "unreasonable contracts." [30]

The Supreme Court acts even more clearly as a lawmaker in interpreting the Constitution than in interpreting statutes. Yet the old "discovery theory" insisted that the power of judicial review was merely the power to follow the obvious intent of the Constitution. In 1936 Mr. Justice Roberts, speaking for the Court, fell back on this orthodox doctrine, frequently referred to as the theory of mechanical jurisprudence, to answer those who were criticizing the justices for writing their own value preferences into the Constitution. He wrote:

> It is sometimes said that the court assumes a power to overrule or control the action of the people's representatives. This is a misconception. . . . When an act of Congress is appropriately challenged in the courts . . . the judicial branch . . . has only one duty,—to lay the article of the Constitution which is involved beside the statute which is challenged and to decide whether the

[28] Max Radin, "Statutory Interpretation," *Harvard Law Review* (April 1930), pp. 863–885.
[29] James M. Landis, "Statutory Interpretation," *Harvard Law Review* (April 1930), pp. 886–893.
[30] *United States v. American Tobacco Co.* (1911).

latter squares with the former. All the Court does, or can do, is to announce
its considered judgment upon the question. . . . The court neither approves
nor condemns any legislative policy.[31]

This explanation of the judicial process has been called "the slot machine
theory." Although it has been discredited, echoes of the doctrine are still frequently
heard. As late as 1958 Chief Justice Warren, who on other occasions has acknowl-
edged the judges' creative role in balancing conflicting values, fell back on mechanical jurisprudence when he wrote:

> When it appears that an Act of Congress conflicts with one of the pro-
> visions [of the Constitution], we have no choice but to enforce the paramount
> commands of the Constitution. . . . We cannot push back the limits of the
> Constitution merely to accommodate challenged legislation. . . . We do well
> to approach this task cautiously. . . . But the ordeal of judgment cannot be
> shirked.[32]

Mechanical jurisprudence ignores the fact that the judges must choose which
of the several meanings of the Constitution shall be adopted. It rests on the false
assumption that the Constitution has a single, clear, precise meaning and that
laws come already tagged with labels of "unconstitutionality." Of course no one
argues that unconstitutional laws should be enforced. But in the very cases in
which Roberts and Warren described their function as merely enforcing the clear
commands of the Constitution, other Supreme Court justices were equally convinced that the particular laws in question did not conflict with the Constitution.
True, the meaning of many parts of the Constitution is obvious. If Congress
passed a law extending the term of United States senators beyond six years, its
unconstitutionality would be apparent to everyone. If constitutional interpretation
amounted only to this, judges would have no special claim as guardians of the
Constitution. But it is not the specifically worded clauses of the Constitution that
present questions of interpretation. Rather it is those open-ended clauses, those
few words whose meaning cannot be interpreted solely with a dictionary. Judges
have few external guides, for example, in trying to determine the meaning of due
process or the First Amendment.

In giving specific meaning to ambiguous provisions of the Constitution, Supreme Court justices are not seriously restricted by the doctrine of *stare decisis*.
The doctrine is even less controlling in the field of constitutional than in the
field of statutory interpretation. The legislature can correct judicial errors of
statutory interpretation, but only the Supreme Court or a constitutional amendment can alter the Court's "erroneous" or "misguided" construction of the
Constitution. Justices are, therefore, less hesitant to overrule decisions on constitutional matters. Even when they do not wish to repudiate openly an earlier

[31] *United States* v. *Butler* (1936).
[32] *Trop* v. *Dulles* (1958).

doctrine, it is easy to "distinguish" each new case from the old ones and thus permit a new ruling. The first Mr. Justice Harlan told a group of students, "I want to say to you young gentlemen that if we [the Supreme Court] don't like an act of Congress, we don't have much trouble to find grounds for declaring it unconstitutional." [33]

Recently, some scholars, most notably Professor Herbert Wechsler, have called on Supreme Court justices to apply "neutral principles" in the sense that the justices should not be concerned with which particular person or group asserts a claim—all would agree with this—but more importantly, that the justices should be neutral as between principles. As many have pointed out, this is essentially a revival of mechanical jurisprudence in a more sophisticated garb. Constitutional cases of consequence require confrontation of principles and judges must *choose* between them.[34]

To recognize the facts of judicial life—that judges must choose between competing values, that, in the words of Max Lerner, "Judicial decisions are not babies brought by constitutional storks"—is not to criticize the judges. Nor is it to say that the judges have unlimited discretion in deciding cases, or that they can give free rein to their own views. They are restricted, as we have seen, by precedent and procedures, by the severe discipline of the law itself, and above all by the total political system of which they are but a part. Those who insist that judicial decisions are only reflections of the personal biases of the judges ignore as many factors as do those who insist that these biases have no impact on judicial decision-making.

Activists v. Self-Restrainers

Not all judges are convinced of the possibility or of the desirability of achieving objectivity or of withdrawing from the field of policy-making. These judges, roughly characterized as "judicial activists," insist that political choice is inevitable and inherent in judging, and that judges should make no false pretense of objectivity. Rather, they should recognize that they are making policy, and they should consciously exercise their judicial power to achieve social justice.

The judicial "self-restrainers" take another view. They recognize the judge's difficulty in rising above his own biases, but they insist that objectivity is the goal that he should aim for. As the people's *political* representatives, the legislators and executives, they argue, have the chief responsibility for working out the accommodation of interests that is the essence of legislation. The self-restrainers insist that judges must be very careful to avoid injecting their own wishes into the judicial process, since it is not their responsibility to determine public policy.

[33] Quoted by E. S. Corwin, *Constitutional Revolution, Ltd.* (Claremont and Associated Colleges, 1941), p. 38. See also John P. Roche, "Judicial Self-Restraint," *The American Political Science Review* (September 1955), pp. 762–772, and Frank, *Marble Palace*, pp. 20–41.

[34] Herbert Wechsler, "Toward Neutral Principles of Constitutional Law," *Harvard Law Review* (November 1959), p. 1.

Judges should be especially hesitant to check the full play of the democratic process. As Justice Stone wrote in his dissenting opinion in the Butler case, "Courts are not the only agency of government that must be assumed to have the capacity to govern," and "The only check upon our own exercise of power is our own sense of self-restraint. For removal of unwise laws from the statute books, appeal lies not to the courts but to the ballot and to the process of democratic government."

Some people take a position midway between the activists and the self-restrainers. They believe that judges should not invalidate economic and social laws affecting *property rights*, but should have full authority to void laws restricting *civil liberties*, such as free speech. Their argument for this compromise position goes like this: The political majority should not be stopped from experimenting with social and economic arrangements. If mistakes are made, new majorities will arise to correct them. But majorities should not be permitted to tamper with basic liberties. For if they go too far, the very instruments for publicizing and correcting the mistakes—such as free speech and free press—will not be able to operate effectively. The Constitution does not embody any particular economic theory, and legislative majorities are free to adopt any they wish. But the Constitution *is* committed to the political theory of free debate, and it is the judges' special responsibility to prevent legislative tampering with the democratic processes.

These divergent views about the proper role of the judiciary have been formulated more explicitly in the recent opinions of the Supreme Court than they were when the "discovery theory" was prevalent. Yet judges cannot be fitted into neat categories; accusations that the judges are being influenced by their own political biases often stem from a dislike of the Court's opinions rather than from disagreement over the proper scope of the judiciary. Prior to 1937, when the Supreme Court majority was announcing constitutional doctrines that protected the business community, supporters of these doctrines insisted that the justices were merely applying the clear dictates of the Constitution. On the other hand, those who disliked the conservative tenor of the doctrines accused the justices of usurping the legislative function, of making their own partisan views the measure of constitutionality. From 1937 to the present, the shoe has been on the other foot. Those who dislike the decisions sustaining government regulation of the economy and striking down laws supporting racial segregation have accused the justices of being "New Dealers," "partisan politicians," and "incompetent judges." Those who like the decisions and approve of the new doctrines insist that the justices have merely returned to the true meaning of the Constitution.[35]

Judges must make choices among conflicting values. By the very nature of their duties, judges—especially those on the Supreme Court—are forced into the storm center of politics and policy-making. What problems does this fact raise for democratic government?

[35] For a vivid account of how one Chief Justice was almost continuously involved directly in judicial, legislative, and even party politics, see Alpheus Thomas Mason, *William Howard Taft: Chief Justice* (Simon & Schuster, 1965).

Judges and Democratic Government

Judges are at one and the same time legal technicians, and, in the broad sense, politicians. As legal technicians, it is their legal competence that controls their decisions; as policy-makers, it is their political attitude that counts. As impartial dispensers of equal justice under the law, judges should not be dependent on the pleasure of the executive, the legislature, or the parties to a case. As determiners of basic public policy, judges should be politically responsible and publicly accountable. As legal experts applying legal principles to the solution of justiciable controversies, judges should be above politics. As policy-makers, judges should be—and inevitably are—in politics.

The Constitution takes into account the confusion occasioned by the blending of these dual and inextricably related functions in the person of a judge. In some of its provisions it looks to the independence of the judiciary: Judges are appointed by the President with the consent of the Senate to serve for life terms; Congress is forbidden to decrease their salaries during their term of service. On the other hand, judges are made dependent on Congress for the money they need to operate, and for their authority to hear and decide cases. Congress creates the inferior courts, determines the size of all courts, and may remove judges by impeachment and conviction.

How Independent Should the Judges Be?

This relation between courts, Congress, and the President is the familiar pattern of separation of powers and checks and balances. The principle of separation of powers, however, is more vital for the independence of the judiciary than it is for the other branches. Many who urge the consolidation of legislative and executive powers in the same agency still insist on an independent judiciary. In the first place, it is an ancient and seldom-questioned maxim of justice that no man be trusted as both prosecutor and judge. The active enforcement of the law, the investigation of crimes, and the prosecution·of wrongdoers are executive functions. If judges depended on the pleasure of the executive, then two incompatible functions would be consolidated in the same agency. Secondly, "a government of laws and not of men" is one in which public officials as well as private individuals operate under and in accordance with the law. To check the illegal actions of these officials would require an appeal to an independent judiciary.

Judges must also be free to apply the law impartially, even against the most popular person in a community or in favor of the most hated. Sometimes justice requires a judge to favor a person who has aroused the active hostility of his neighbors or to rule against one who has a strong popular following. He must have the independence to apply the law fearlessly—especially when the community has been swept by emotions that make it intolerant of restrained action.

Independence is always a matter of degree, and even if the judges' sole duty were to serve as legal experts, complete isolation from the community and lack of all popular control would not be desirable. Yet few would question the value of an independent judiciary when judges are thought of as *legal technicians*.

But if few people have ever seriously questioned the arrangements that give national judges great independence, many, including Presidents Jefferson, Jackson, Lincoln, and both Roosevelts, have tilted with the defenders of *judicial review*. (Here the reference is to judicial review of acts of the President and the Congress, coordinate branches of the national government. No President has questioned the necessity of the Supreme Court review of acts of *state* and *local* officials to insure compliance with the United States Constitution.) Although most people admit the necessity of having independent judges, some have questioned the need to give these independent judges the power to veto the desires of the majority as expressed through their elected representatives. All agree that an unconstitutional law should not be enforced. The question remains, *is the Supreme Court's interpretation of constitutionality to be preferred to that of Congress or the President?*

The most important parts of the Constitution, as we have noted, are vague and leave room for difference of opinion. Of the three branches of government, it is argued, the Supreme Court is the least responsive to the public will. If the Constitution is supreme because it is an expression of the people's ideas, then those agents who most directly represent those ideas have the best right to interpret the Constitution. Why should five men (i.e., a majority of the Court) holding office for life have the power to tell Congress and the President, elected by the people, what they may or may not do?

Other opponents of judicial review have pointed out that John Marshall's logic in *Marbury* v. *Madison* could be turned against him. Confronted with a Supreme Court decision that he considered unconstitutional, a President might reason that his duty would be to follow the Constitution and to refuse to enforce the Court's decision.

But despite the persistent attacks on judicial review, most Americans continue to view it as a desirable feature of our governmental system. Generally speaking, Americans have never been willing to put full trust in the majority. An independent judiciary with the power of judicial review has been the major institutional sign of this fear of unchecked legislative and popular majorities. The belief in judicial review reflects and rests on the belief that the Constitution, like natural law, contains certain fundamental principles with which no majority should tamper. It is argued that the independence of judges from temporary majorities is their strength in protecting these rights, not their weakness. Justice Jackson phrased it, in a somewhat different context, this way, "One's right to life, liberty, and property, to free speech, a free press, freedom of worship and assembly, and other fundamental rights may not be submitted to vote; they depend on the outcome of no election." [36]

[36] *West Virginia State Board of Education* v. *Barnette* (1943).

But just how independent in fact are the judges? Are they so independent that given their power of interpreting the Constitution and the laws, they are the masters of the majority? For the moment—yes; in the long, and not so very long, run—no.

"The Constitution Is What Most of Us Say It Is"

The most important way in which political majorities bring their weight to bear on the judiciary is through the election of the President and senators who, in turn, appoint the judges. National majorities have the loudest voice in the selection of Supreme Court justices, since the President has the greatest leeway in selecting its members. The choice of judges for the federal district courts is more widely shared, for the rule of senatorial courtesy is applied to these appointments. Senators of the state in which the judge is to sit, provided they are of the same party as the President, have an informal veto over the appointment. Until recently the senators often sent a list of names to the President from which he (through his Attorney General) nominated a man for Senate consideration. "But more recent data . . . indicate that there has been at least a slight move of the pendulum toward the President." [37] The Attorney General now takes a more active role in selecting nominees for consideration by the Senate, but still he must find men acceptable to the senators from the state in which the judge is to sit. It is not surprising that lower federal judges often reflect a different consensus of values than do those appointed to the Supreme Court.

In the case of lower federal courts, party considerations are of crucial significance. Presidents have seldom selected a person from the opposition party. Nor have party considerations been ignored, though they are of much less importance, in the naming of Supreme Court justices. Here the determining factors are the basic social, economic, and judicial attitudes of the individual. Every President since Washington has felt that his responsibilities demanded that he nominate to the Supreme Court men who could be depended on to make the "right" decisions, meaning decisions compatible with the views of the popularly elected President. President Theodore Roosevelt voiced this attitude in a letter to Senator Lodge about Judge Holmes of the Massachusetts Supreme Judicial Court, whom he was considering for the United States Supreme Court. Roosevelt wrote:

> In the ordinary and low sense which we attach to the words "partisan" and "politician," a judge of the Supreme Court should be neither. But in the higher sense, in the proper sense, he is not in my judgment fitted for the position unless he is a party man, a constructive statesman, constantly keeping in mind his adherence to the principles and policies under which this nation has been built up. . . . Now I should like to know that Judge Holmes was in entire

[37] Joel B. Grossman, *Lawyers and Judges: The ABA and the Politics of Judicial Selection* (Wiley, 1965), p. 27. See also Harold Chase, "Federal Judges: The Appointing Power," paper delivered at the 1964 meeting of the American Political Science Association.

sympathy with our views, that is with your views and mine. . . . I should hold myself guilty of an irreparable wrong to the nation if I should [appoint] any man who was not absolutely sane and sound on the great national policies for which we stand in public life.[38]

Presidents have occasionally been disappointed in the men they have appointed to the Supreme Court. Once on the bench, some justices have departed from the "sound policies" that the Presidents expected them to support. But by and large, through their selection of the personnel of the federal judiciary, Presidents and Senates have *eventually* been able to bring the Court's decisions into line with the general attitudes of contemporary political majorities.[39]

The difficulty, however, is that the judge's life tenure often keeps him in office long after the political climate has changed, and he continues to represent views of the era in which he was appointed. Some justices have even stayed on the Court to prevent incumbent Presidents from appointing successors. Chief Justice Taft, for example, feared to resign lest the "radical" Hoover be allowed to appoint someone in his place. In 1929 he wrote, "I am older and slower and less acute and more confused. However, as long as things continue as they are, and I am able to answer in my place, I must stay on the court in order to prevent the Bolsheviki from getting control. . . ." [40]

In most cases the Court's tardiness in adjusting to changing political climates is the normal result of the long tenure of the justices. Jefferson, for instance, became President only to discover that the judiciary was entirely manned by Federalists who represented the doctrines Jefferson had just defeated in the election. Many of these Federalist judges had no scruples against using their power to attack Jefferson's political doctrines.

Faced with this opposition, Jefferson and his followers tried to use the impeachment power to modernize the judiciary. Although judges hold office during good behavior, they may be impeached for "treason, bribery, or other high crimes and misdemeanors." Despite his belief in the doctrine of strict construction, Jefferson wished to interpret liberally the impeachment clause and to develop it as a device for keeping the judiciary in line with current views. The Federalist judges had not committed treason, high crimes, or misdemeanors, though some of them were guilty of conduct unbecoming a judge and of using their positions for frankly partisan purposes. Yet Jefferson felt that judges who held political views not in harmony with those of the political majority should not be permitted to thwart the wishes of the people and should be subject to some kind of political control. As a result, his supporters in the House of Representatives impeached Justice Chase, and Chief Justice Marshall was apparently to be next on the list. Although Chase had been an intemperate Federalist partisan, he had com-

[38] Henry Cabot Lodge, *Selections from the Correspondence of Theodore Roosevelt and Henry Cabot Lodge,* I (Scribner's, 1925), pp. 518–519.
[39] David J. Danelski, *A Supreme Court Justice Is Appointed* (Random House, 1964).
[40] Letter to Horace Taft, November 14, 1929, quoted by H. F. Pringle, *The Life and Times of William Howard Taft,* II (Farrar & Rinehart, 1939), p. 967.

mitted no crimes, and the Senate refused to sustain the impeachment charge. Since that date, impeachment has never been used to remove judges except, in a very few cases, for criminal or patently unethical practices.

Congressional control over the structure and jurisdiction of the federal courts has been used more successfully to influence the course of judicial decisions. Although thwarted in their attempts to impeach the judges, the Jeffersonians abolished the circuit courts that the Federalist Congress had created just prior to leaving office. In 1869 the Radical Republicans in Congress used their constitutional power to alter the Supreme Court's appellate jurisdiction in order to snatch from the Court a case it was about to review involving legislation of dubious constitutionality (*Ex parte McCardle*). They also reduced the size of the Court to prevent President Johnson from filling two vacancies. After Johnson left the White House, Congress increased the size of the Court to permit Grant to select two justices. As we have seen, Grant selected men who made it possible to reverse the Supreme Court invalidation of the Legal Tender Act. Historians are still debating whether Grant packed the Court. Certainly he was not unaware that his two appointees shared his sentiments about the desirability of reversing the earlier decision.

F.D.R. v. the "Nine Old Men"

President Franklin D. Roosevelt's battle with the Supreme Court is a more dramatic attempt by a political leader to influence the course of judicial decisions. President Roosevelt took office on March 4, 1933, in the midst of the Great Depression. Under his leadership, Congress passed in quick succession a series of important laws designed to give Americans a "New Deal." By 1935 these measures began to come before the Supreme Court. In the next sixteen months the Supreme Court invalidated eight out of the ten measures that came before it. In 1936, despite the Supreme Court's judgment that the New Deal was unconstitutional, Franklin D. Roosevelt won an overwhelming victory at the polls. An irresistible force seemed to be moving toward an immovable object. One or the other would have to give way.

Early in 1937, as the conflict between the President and the Supreme Court was approaching its climax, a variety of proposals were put forward to limit the judges' power. One suggested amendment would require a two-thirds vote of the justices before the Supreme Court could declare acts of Congress unconstitutional; another would permit Congress to override Supreme Court decisions by a two-thirds vote. But President Roosevelt decided that it would be impossible to secure ratification of such a constitutional amendment or, at any rate, that it would take too long. On February 5, 1937, he presented to Congress his own program to reorganize the federal judiciary. The most significant recommendation was that the President be given the right to appoint an additional justice for each member of the Court over the age of seventy who chose not to retire after ten years' service. The maximum size of the Supreme Court was to be set at fifteen. The ostensible purpose of the recommendation was to make the Supreme Court more efficient so that it could keep up with its work. The real purpose was obvious. The President wished to modernize the Supreme Court by "packing" it.

Clearly the Supreme Court, dominated by very conservative justices, was blocking the program endorsed by a majority of the voters. But the electorate that had given that program an overwhelming vote of confidence was less enthusiastic about the President's attack on the Supreme Court. Opponents of the New Deal were able to mobilize opinion against the President by capitalizing on the symbol of the Supreme Court as the inviolable guardian of the Constitution standing above the noisome sea of politics. The President was accused of wanting to be a dictator and, like Hitler and Mussolini, to subjugate the judiciary to his own will. Many persons who agreed with the President that something should be done to restrict the power of the Supreme Court could not accept the method he suggested. Others believed that while the President's proposal could conceivably be an expedient solution to the immediate problem, its ultimate and fundamental result would be to weaken an important instrument for protecting individual liberties.

Yet the President was not without resources. Although many could not agree on what should be done, they could not deny that Supreme Court justices were blocking legislation endorsed by the electorate. The President had the support of powerful groups, but the Supreme Court itself dealt the final blow to the President's program to "pack" the Court. It simply reversed its direction. Between March and June 1937, in the midst of the debate over the President's proposal, the High Court upheld a state minimum wage law, the Farm Mortgage Act, the amended Railway Labor Act, the Wagner Act, the Social Security Act. Justice Roberts and Chief Justice Hughes, who theretofore had voted with the conservatives, switched their support to the liberals.[41] Here was the famous "switch in time that saved nine." No longer did the Supreme Court stand in the way of social and economic legislation. The President's reform proposal was rendered superfluous, as far as the immediate crisis was concerned, and it was defeated in Congress.

Did the Supreme Court follow the election returns? There is no way of knowing why Justice Roberts and the Chief Justice changed their position. But they could hardly have been blind to the 1936 election returns. They might well have interpreted these returns to mean that if the Supreme Court persisted in denying to the national and state governments the power that a majority of the people wanted them to exercise, it might be the Supreme Court and not the New Deal that would have been overturned.

[41] Merlo J. Pusey in his biography, *Charles Evans Hughes*, 2 vols. (Macmillan, 1951), chs. 69–71, holds that Hughes did not change his position. But see E. S. Corwin's review of this book for contrary position, *The American Political Science Review* (December 1952), pp. 1167–1173.

The Supreme Court under Fire

The most recent attempt to alter the course of judicially made policies stems from the Supreme Court's pro-civil liberties decisions. After the 1954 School Segregation Decisions, southern Democrats opened a furious attack on the Court, but most northern conservatives, though disturbed by the Supreme Court's failure to interpose any objections to legislative regulation of business enterprises, refrained from joining these denunciations. Southern Democrats, despite the sound and fury of their comments, were making no headway. So long as the Court was merely taking on defenders of racial segregation, it was in little danger of retaliatory action.

But in 1956, when the Court took a more positive civil-liberties stand in behalf of so-called political defendants, many security-minded congressmen shifted over to its list of vocal critics. In August 1958 the chief justices of thirty-six state supreme courts rebuked the Supreme Court for paying too little attention to the rights of states. Early in 1959 the American Bar Association's House of Delegates threw its considerable prestige into the fray by adopting a critical report charging the Supreme Court with deciding cases "in such a manner to encourage or increase communist activity." In Congress dozens of proposals were introduced "to do something about the Supreme Court." [42] These varied from impeachment resolutions to suggestions that the Constitution be amended to make justices elective, to bills depriving the Court of jurisdiction to hear cases involving threats to national security.

Southern Democrats let their Republican allies carry the attack by playing down the issue of segregation. None of the anti-Court bills given serious congressional consideration would directly have affected the Supreme Court's decisions dealing with racial segregation. But the attack served the southern Democrats' purposes by giving credence to their charges of "judicial tyranny."

Although, as we have seen, attacks on the Supreme Court are not novel, this most recent controversy is unprecedented because for the first time *conservative* congressmen were mounting the offensive. In 1937 it was a New Deal President versus the Supreme Court—in 1957 it was conservative congressmen versus the Supreme Court. Many of those who in 1936 were roundly denouncing President Roosevelt for trying to influence the work of the Supreme Court were among the most active proponents of anti-Court legislation. On the other hand, many liberals who felt that President Roosevelt was justified in attacking the Court in 1937 accused the conservative critics of trying to undermine our constitutional system.

Defenders of the Court were able to avert anti-Court legislation, and the elec-

[42] See R. J. Steamer, "Statesmanship or Craftsmanship: Current Conflict Over the Supreme Court," *Western Political Quarterly* (June 1958), pp. 265–277; Sheldon D. Elliott, "Court-Curbing Proposals in Congress," *Notre Dame Lawyer* (August 1958), p. 597. For a detailed analysis of this most recent controversy, see Walter F. Murphy, *Congress and the Court* (Univ. of Chicago Press, 1962).

tions of 1958 resulted in the defeat of some of the Court's most outspoken critics. Proposed amendments to restore the constitutionality of religious exercises in the public schools and to permit a state to base representation in one house of their legislature on factors other than population have also been checked, though proponents of these amendments have not given up their struggle for them. As noted, so far the only "punishment" that the opponents of the Supreme Court have been able to inflict is a reduction in the justices' proposed pay raise. (The Constitution forbids a reduction in established salaries.)

The full impact, however, of the controversies over the Supreme Court are not to be measured only by the fate of "anti-Court" or "corrective" legislation. In 1937 President Roosevelt's plan to pack the Court was defeated, but the Court altered its interpretation of the Constitution. There is always the possibility that the attacks may cause the Supreme Court justices, consciously or otherwise, to moderate their decisions.

Other "controls" over the Supreme Court stem from the obvious fact that compliance with the announced rulings of the Court does not automatically follow their enunciation. A ruling by the Supreme Court can be "interpreted" into insignificance by lower-court judges, it can be ignored by state and local officials, it can be "misunderstood" by police officers, and under some circumstances it even may be openly defied. Unless the President, the Congress, and the great body of the American public insist upon compliance with the policies proclaimed by the Supreme Court, those who intensely oppose these policies often find ways to continue to do what the Supreme Court has proclaimed to be illegal or even unconstitutional.[43]

True, the Constitution is what the judges say it is. But ultimately the Constitution is what the people want it to be.[44] The Supreme Court is able to make its decisions effective only to the extent that these decisions are supported by a considerable portion of the electorate. The main thrust of judicial policies cannot remain too far outside the main channels of American public life. The American democratic system has reached a pragmatic compromise between the desire for the independence of the judges and the desire to provide political checks on their policy-making activities. Judges have no armies or police to execute their rulings. They have no authority to levy taxes to pay their salaries. In the long run, they must adapt themselves to the nature and demands of government by the people. Ultimately, the power they enjoy rests upon their retention of public support. No better criterion for determining the power of a government official has ever been invented.

[43] Gordon M. Patric, "The Impact of a Court Decision; Aftermath of the McCollum Case," *Journal of Public Law* (Fall 1957), pp. 455–464; Frank J. Sorauf, "*Zorach v. Clauson:* The Impact of a Supreme Court Decision," *The American Political Science Review* (September 1959), pp. 777–791.

[44] Robert A. Dahl, "Decision-Making in a Democracy: The Supreme Court as a National Policy-Maker," *Journal of Public Law* (Fall 1957), p. 285.

20 GOVERNMENT BY THE PEOPLE: PROBLEMS AND PROSPECTS

The 1960's are a time of change and challenge in the American system of government. The President has become more than ever the fulcrum of decision and action; but in the same period Congress has displayed unusual vigor in passing a sheaf of laws that immensely broadens the responsibilities of the federal government. Not content with its epochal *Brown* decision of 1954, the Supreme Court has gone on in this decade to act on the

531

thorniest questions of legislative representation, church-state relations, and individual liberty. Our system of federalism has been almost revolutionized as the national government has become the senior partner—some would say the threatening "big brother"—of almost every state and city in the land. A broad national consensus has arisen over the federal government's responsibilities for maintaining economic prosperity and social welfare at home and for strengthening friendly nations abroad—a consensus that was sharply challenged but not broken by the election of 1964. And the urbanization and suburbanization of the nation, long reflected in the politics of the Presidency, have become more manifest in the House of Representatives as congressional districts have been "de-gerrymandered."

But if the shape of government changes, the basic questions and problems remain much the same. The authors posed five sets of problems in Part One (pages 1–2) and proposed to return to them following our survey of the ideas, interests, institutions and individuals that make up our national political system. The first of these questions—whether we have "government by the *people*," whether indeed such government is possible under modern conditions—we will take up in the last section of this chapter. Let us consider first the second of the five questions: How can we maintain a late-eighteenth century system of checks and balances in the face of late-twentieth century needs for efficient and effective government?

Can Constitutional Government Be Efficient Government?

For centuries "strong men" of various types have seized power from republican governments on the grounds that they were so bumbling and creaking and overloaded with constitutional checks and balances that they could not act. In the United States, especially in crisis times, voices have proclaimed that the country needed a dictator to clean up the "mess in Washington"—there is always a mess in Washington in someone's view—and to get things done. More thoughtful people have criticized the vast, often slow-moving federal bureaucracy, the power of the judiciary to stall and block action, and the complex and time-consuming machinery linking the federal, state, and local governments. But the great bulk of criticism has centered on Congress, the heart of our constitutional republic.

Congress under Attack

Critics can cite many facts to demonstrate the Congress is woefully inefficient. Procedure in both chambers—especially the Senate—is slow and cumbersome. A small group can hold up action in the House; one man can delay the majority in the Senate. The many committees, with their scores of subcommittees, operate ponderously. Congressmen spend much of their time on time-wasting activities, such as running errands for constituents or making speeches to an almost empty chamber. Simply calling the role in the House can take three-quarters of an hour of valuable time. One result of the inefficiency is that congressmen are constantly overworked. Above all—goes the charge—Congress does not pull in harness with the President and hence teamwork in government is lessened.

Defenders of Congress answer these charges by pointing to the sheer volume of congressional work; Congress will consider several thousand bills in one session and enact hundreds of them. They point also to the congressional debates and to the committee hearings—much of it of a high order of excellence. But in general, students of Congress grant that its procedures are overly time-consuming and even archaic. It is significant that some of the most outspoken critics of Congress are congressmen themselves.[1]

Every generation or so Congress makes an effort to modernize its procedures. In 1946 it streamlined the committee system by reducing the number by about half in each chamber and thus enabling members to concentrate on a smaller number of policy areas. Congress also strengthened the committees' professional assistance and staffs; required committees to hold regular meetings and keep better records of proceedings; and to prevent delay and obstruction required committee chairmen to report promptly any measures approved by their committees. But the reorganization effort of 1946 did not have the effect that some hoped. It streamlined committees, critics pointed out, but the committees simply spawned a host of subcommittees. Congress continued to go about its business in much the same way as in ages past.

A New Effort to Modernize

Pressure for congressional improvement mounted in the early 1960's, as Congress held up or killed off many of President Kennedy's legislative proposals. A new Joint Committee on the Organization of Congress was established in 1965 under the co-chairmanship of Senator Mike Monroney and Representative Ray J. Madden. The joint committee consists of six members from each chamber. While predominantly representative of the "congressional establishment," a few congressmen on the committee belong to the Democratic Study Group, which favors major changes in congressional procedure. The joint committee, however, operates under rules that bar it from proposing any changes in the Senate or House rules and is thus precluded from considering reforms that could drastically affect the internal power structure of either chamber. Hence the committee is likely to restrict its proposals to less controversial problems, such as improvements in services and staff.

Perhaps more likely to have a significant impact on Congress is a study of the

---

[1] See, for example (Representative) Richard Bolling, *House Out of Order* (Dutton, 1965); (Senator) Joseph S. Clark, *Congress: The Sapless Branch* (Harper & Row, 1964); and (Senator) Kenneth B. Keating, *Government of the People: The Challenge of Change* (World Publishing Co., 1964).

national legislature now under way and sponsored by the American Political Science Association. The study group, composed of sixteen leading political scientists, was established with the cooperation of some congressional leaders. It will concentrate on clarifying "various assumptions regarding the role of Congress in our system, identifying and analyzing major problems of Congressional operation and explaining the character and probable consequences of realistic alternatives for structural or procedural change." [2]

It is significant that the political scientists began their study by clarifying the assumptions about the role of Congress in our system. For the question is: What part do we *want* Congress to play in our system? Congress may delegate such time-consuming functions as running the affairs of the District of Columbia and it could adopt electric voting, but the significant questions are not mechanical. They are political and philosophical.

Is Efficient Government Free Government?

In Chapter 1 the authors urged that students of politics—indeed, all college students—pause regularly to challenge their own assumptions. Here is a case in point. In the last section the authors have been blandly proceeding on the assumption that efficiency in government is a good thing. But how much value should we attach to efficiency as compared with other goals? Obviously we all want congressmen to save their time and our money—that is, we want efficiency in the narrow sense. But what about efficiency in the broader sense—what about *effectiveness*? Do we want a "stronger" Congress? Do we want more teamwork between executive and legislature? Do we want more partnership between national and state government?

In short, do we want a more powerful government even if it might jeopardize our highly prized civil liberties—liberties *against* government?

Liberty against Government

The answer of most of the framers of the Constitution was, of course, No. As we have seen, they feared an overly effective government, just as they did a weak government, and certainly they did not want the rulers in the nation's capital and in the states to "gang up" against the people and their liberties. Freedom was mainly to be protected *against* government, not through it. The framers were proud of their handiwork—an elaborate constitutional system that nicely balanced the powers of government agencies against one another—which in effect meant balancing certain groups and interests against one another. The effect during most of our history has been what the framers wanted—slow, deliberate, at times even ponderous government.

[2] Evron M. Kirkpatrick, Executive Director of the American Political Science Association, in *The American Political Science Review* (June 1965), p. 544.

Perspectives change. The framers tended to think of government as kings and ministers who were not politically accountable to the electorate and who were likely to suppress legislatures, arrest citizens for criticizing the authorities, search homes without warrants. Today many of us think of government as our own elected officials responsible and responsive to *us*. We see restraints on our liberties flowing not from what public officials do, but from social and economic conditions of poverty and illiteracy and from the actions of other individuals: employers who might fire workers for trying to unionize, landlords who may refuse to rent homes to Negroes because of their race, vigilantes who may threaten students for working for civil rights. We have learned that, as Hobhouse said, liberty is a matter not just of the increase or decrease but of the *reorganization* of restraints. Indeed, we have used our political power to demand that those we elected to office employ the authority of government to extend *our* liberties and rights.

Yet the authors, apparently in common with most Americans, would not overweigh the value of effective government at the expense of safe government. Elected officials, like all men, tend to view the nation's welfare from their own special and limited perspective. Some of them—revenue officials and government prosecutors, for example—have great powers when dealing with individual citizens. In our judgment, the defense of liberty against government requires not only that such officials follow due process of law and observe procedural safeguards for the individual, but that independent political bases be created for those who oppose the officials, their policies, and their methods. Perhaps the strongest inhibition on rulers is the fear that they will be driven out of power, or that their actions will be closely scrutinized, or that arbitrary methods will be checked by judges. Hence the major safeguards against oppressive governmental actions are an opposition party that strongly and continuously opposes congressional investigations of arbitrary executive actions or practices, congressional leaders who do not depend on the President's favor for remaining in office, judges who can require enforcement officials to justify their actions, and other arrangements that were developed over the centuries to limit rulers.

Civil Liberties—the Supreme Value?

The implication of the above, and of Part Three in general, is that individual liberty should be the supreme value in "government by the people." Certainly this was the implication of the original American demand for independence from Britain. In writing the Declaration of Independence, Jefferson held that certain truths were *self-evident*—including that men were endowed by their Creator with certain unalienable rights, and that among these were life, liberty, and the pursuit of happiness. But here again we should reassess our own preconceptions.

The authors are civil libertarians in the broad sense, but even so, they would not take an absolutist position about such prized values as freedom of speech and of the press. Although the First Amendment commands Congress to make no law abridging these and certain other freedoms, there are always the competing claims of prudence, reasonableness, and common sense. Clearly, we should not allow the right of free speech to be abused by those who would use it to overthrow the government by force during wartime, even though we would allow subversives every procedural right in defending their actions. Clearly, we would not allow a freedom of the press that would permit men knowingly to sell obscene magazines to children, or permit newspapers to publish secret military information. For the Constitution itself, after all, does not single out liberty as the only value; the objectives were also to establish justice, insure domestic tranquility, provide for the common defense, as well as to "secure the blessings of liberty." And such values often come into conflict.

Hence we must balance all individual liberties against the collective security and needs of society; we must also balance certain individual liberties against other individual liberties. The question is always which rights of which people are to be protected by what means and at what price? Opposed to the idea of absolute prohibition of governmental interference of free speech and press, says Hyneman, "is the so-called balancing doctrine—the contention that the nation's interest in freedom of speech and press is in competition with its interests in some other valued things that sometimes are endangered by unrestrained expression, that the competing interests ought to be evaluated and balanced out, and therefore that a test of reasonableness ought to be applied in litigation where abridgement of speech or press is charged." [3]

We must also balance traditional rights against other rights that have become increasingly important in a crowded urban society. The right of privacy as such is not mentioned in the Bill of Rights, but many city dwellers today might consider it as important as freedom of expression. Here values and interests come into conflict. "Consider the simple case of courtship and the hospital. Value 1—Romance. Value 2—Quiet for hospital patients. Means to romance—the serenade from the sidewalks and the call to trysting place when the nurse sticks her head out the window. Means to quiet for patients—a city ordinance which, admittedly abridging the freedom of communication, makes it a penal offense to play a banjo, sing joyfully or plaintively, or call out in a loud voice on sidewalk or street adjacent to hosiptal grounds. Two central points, then, in the evaluation of means to valued ends." [4]

Liberty has limits. Even though the authors would place freedom of expression at the top of their hierarchy of values, there still are other competing values. And within these values there are questions concerning how conflicting specific claims can best be settled. "The practical question," as John Stuart Mill said, is "where to place the limit—how to make the fitting adjustment between individual independence and social control." Government must represent our quest for liberty; it must also represent other goals and values of a free people.

[3] Charles S. Hyneman, "Free Speech: At What Price?" *The American Political Science Review* (December 1962), p. 847.
[4] *Ibid.*, pp. 851–852.

Representation: How Much and for Whom?

On the face of it, representative government would seem to be a simple as well as a desirable thing. Government officials, chosen in fair and competitive elections, do what the people want done; if they do not, the people will oust them at the next election. Unhappily, representation is not such a simple and clear-cut process.

In the first place, representation is impossible in the literal sense. If you want lower taxes and better highways—as most voters do—are you being better represented if government cuts taxes or builds more highways? If every man actually has a host of conflicting desires, fears, and vague yearnings—as most of us do— how can government possibly "re-present" those complex sets of attitudes in making policy? And even if it could for one person, how could it for countless millions, with their further millions of combinations and permutations of desires and attitudes? Clearly "government by the people" cannot be a perfect reflection of literally billions of specific personal wants. These must be aggregated to serve as a basis of action—but how can and should they be aggregated?

Secondly, leaders in government do not directly represent the people *en masse*. All kinds of agencies intervene between the people and their "representatives": interest groups, political parties, agencies of public opinion, election systems. We looked at the agencies in Part Three, and a compelling conclusion was that they are not necessarily representative of the majority of the people. Parties are often controlled by officeholders and party leaders rather than by the rank and file membership. Public opinion is subject to manipulation; even the most careful polls cannot reproduce public opinion in all its complexity. Elections reflect different sets of popular attitudes depending on the nature of the election system.

Finally, even if people could be directly represented *en masse*, questions would arise about *how* they were to be represented. This is partly a matter of sheer mechanics. One can set up an election or decision-making system that lets every person act *directly for himself*: the New England town meeting, for example. Or a system that mainly represents people in their different *localities*. Or a system that represents people in their various *economic* or *vocational groups*: guild representation, or syndicates and corporations, as under Mussolini. Or a system that especially represents *minorities*: giving veto power to each sizeable minority so that majorities cannot act without the consent of the minority. Or a system that represents the *majority*: once 50 per cent plus 1 of the voters (or legislators) have agreed on a candidate or a policy, the minority must acquiesce or face sanctions.

In short, different kinds of institutions imply different kinds of representation. Congress is a case in point.

Is Congress Representative?

How representative Congress is depends again on how we use the word. Certainly Congress is not a microcosm of the community. Even as an institution—aside from the problems listed above—it is not an accurate sample of 200 million Americans. Occupationally, it notoriously over-represents the "talking" classes of lawyers, businessmen, and teachers (four-fifths of the members of a recent typical Congress had one of these three occupational backgrounds) at the expense of such groups as factory workers and domestic servants.

On the other hand, Congress is a crude but effective representative of minorities. Virtually every important minority group or opinion finds expression there. Congress is composed of—and speaks for—Catholics, Jews, and Protestants; rich men and poor men; easterners, westerners, and southerners; veterans, trade unionists, and so on. The fact that certain occupational groups are under-represented is perhaps not vital; many a congressman who has never worked in a factory speaks eloquently for the millions of Americans who have. At the very least, Congress provides a forum where scores of groups and ideas can find expression.

More serious is the question of whether Congress systematically over-represents the interests and values of rural, small-town America as against the metropolitan-suburban communities. "The country at large has become urban, suburban, and metropolitan," it has been said. "Its economic, social, educational, technological activities are increasingly performed by huge national bureaucratic organizations. But on Capitol Hill the nineteenth-century ethos of the small town, the independent farmer, and the small businessman is still entrenched behind the institutional defenses which have developed in this century to insulate Congress from the new America. . . . The Executive branch has thus grown in power [because] it has become more representative." [5]

Defenders of Congress admit this distorted representation. But, they ask, what branch of government does not mal-represent the people? The workings of the Electoral College clearly make the President over-represent urban-metropolitan views and interests, as we have noted (see pages 366–369). The Supreme Court, composed of men appointed by Presidents for life, is institutionally a generation behind the time in its attitudes and decisions. Federal administrative agencies represent a host of special interests, such as farmers and the aged, but what about representing the general welfare?

The Case for Non-representation

Such questions are hard to answer, partly because of a hidden assumption that we should now expose. This assumption is that the test of a democratic governmental system is how closely

---

[5] Samuel P. Huntington, "Congressional Responses to the Twentieth Century," in David B. Truman (ed.), *The Congress and America's Future* (Prentice-Hall, 1965), p. 16.

it can approximate an accurate reflection of the wishes of the people. We have already noted that such accuracy is impossible. But even if it were possible, would it be desirable? Does "government by the people" have to be a government that tries to respond to the peoples' complex, obscure, and shifting attitudes and interests?

Perhaps the oldest formulation of this issue is whether a legislator should function merely as an *instructed delegate* from the voters in his district or as an *independent agent* using his own best judgment and voting on the basis of the best information and expertise available to him. Over a century and a half ago the great English legislator, Edmund Burke, speaking to his constituents in Bristol, stated that while a representative should keep in close touch with his district,

> His unbiased opinion, his mature judgment, his enlightened conscience, he ought not to sacrifice to you, to any man. . . . Your representative owes you, not his industry alone, but his judgment; and he betrays, instead of serving you, if he sacrifices it to your opinion.

A dramatic example of non-representation in a wider field was the late Winston Churchill's stand on foreign policy during the late 1930's. As a member of Parliament Churchill warned that Hitler was a clear and present threat to Britain and that Britain must rearm and rebuild collective defenses against Nazi Germany. He had little support from his own Conservative party, from the press, or from the people in general. Neville Chamberlain's conciliatory policies toward Hitler won wide support. Churchill was as un-representative of immediate public and party opinion as he was brilliantly representative of his nation's long-term interests.

Clearly in a democracy, however, the politician usually takes a stand somewhere between representing the district's immediate, day-to-day, local interests, and trying to act for a broader constituency over a longer period. On some issues he has no choice; the district may have such a strong, single interest, such as tobacco-growing or steel-making, or it may have such unified attitudes, for example against civil rights, that for the representative to ignore his district would be to commit political suicide—which would also mean ending his ability to be a "statesman" on other matters of less importance to his constituents. The question we turn to now is: How does the form of government, the type of institutional machinery, influence the way in which he represents his district and his nation?

Concurrent Majority Rule

The main practical choice in setting up representative institutions in a democracy is between (1) a system that gives special representation to minority groups, that acts only by consent of the large organized interests, that proceeds slowly through a process of conciliating and accommodating the major interests; and (2) a system that strongly represents a popular majority, that can act rapidly once it has gained such majority support, and that guarantees the minority only the right to agitate and put up candidates and try to win elections. The first type of system was exemplified in the Articles of Confederation; the second type, as noted in Chapter 1, is exemplified in the British system. The first system—the doctrine of *concurrent majority rule*—has long been part of American political theory. Over a century ago John C. Calhoun stated the theory in extreme form. Calhoun wanted to safeguard the diversity of the American nation. He wanted to protect minority rights against the unchecked rule of numerical majorities. Of course, he had good reason to support such a theory, for he was desperately anxious to prevent the North from oppressing the planter interests in the South. But the fact that he represented a minority interest made his theory no less impressive.

Our system of concurrent majority rule today is not so extreme as Calhoun would have wanted. Very few single interests, if any, hold a complete and final veto over the rest of the community. But the main features of the system are with us, and the system shows itself in every one of our major governmental and political institutions. Minority blocs in Congress strengthen their power through their control of committees, the filibuster in the Senate, and other devices for obstructing the majority. Business is done by trading votes (logrolling) among the main interest groups involved. Powerful minorities show their hand also in the Supreme Court, in the bureaucracy, and in the Cabinet. Even a candidate for President is unlikely to be successful if he has antagonized some minority groups, such as Negroes, Catholics, or farmers.

Above all, our system of concurrent majority rule reveals itself in our *party system*. Neither major party stands for a definite ideology or program. Both major parties follow shifting courses and straddle important issues as they seek to pick up votes from this group and that. Both parties appeal to every major interest. Both parties attract all types of people—labor, businessmen, farmers, old people, young people, reformers, standpatters, rich, poor, upper class, middle class, working class, Negro, Irish, and so on. Whatever issue becomes popular, whatever group becomes powerful, both parties adapt their principles and move to catch what votes they can. Unlike the ideological parties of Europe, American parties are mainly concerned not with expounding programs but with getting enough votes to win office.

Government by concurrent majority rule, in short, is a sort of "broker rule." Brokers act essentially as go-betweens; likewise, broker rule is a system of government in which leaders mediate between interest groups, veering now right, now left, as political pressures rise and fall. Instead of acting for a firm, united party majority with a fairly set program, either liberal or conservative, the government tries to satisfy virtually all minority groups by giving them a voice in decisions and a veto over actions. In the pushing and hauling of political groups, the government does a sort of delicate balancing act. Its condition is always one of dynamic equilibrium.

The System Defended

Broker rule has its supporters. Many thoughtful Americans believe that government by concurrent majorities is the price we pay—and not a very large price—for the maintenance of unity in a great, sprawling, diverse nation such as ours. Their arguments go something like this:

1. The system protects minorities. Broker rule does not hurt interest groups of any size because by definition it acts only with their support—or at least their acquiescence. At the same time, the system defends individual rights, which often find expression in minority action.[6]

2. Broker rule safeguards our diversity. Our varied nationality, religious, economic, and ideological groups are both the pride and strength of America. Our system of government should reflect the rich diversity of our group life. "The very multiplicity of interests," Merle Fainsod has said, "their freedom to maneuver and combine, and the open character of the society in which newly felt demands may always find organizational expression insure against the possibility of a frozen society and the rise of centers of intransigence within it." In short, our society is *pluralistic*; should our government not be pluralistic too?

"*Gad, when I think of the power the people have . . . it just isn't fair. . . .*" (© 1965, Los Angeles Times. Reprinted by permission.)

3. Broker rule tames down the extremists on both sides by giving them a stake in government—and by giving them favors from government. By thus absorbing groups on the right and left, the system minimizes conflict and hardship.[7]

4. Broker rule permits a dynamic, flexible political system just as laissez faire encourages a competitive, dynamic economy. Power is not concentrated at the top, but is distributed throughout society. Everyone—not just a few key people—gets a chance to take part in the job of running the government.

5. Clearly, broker rule is the price of unity. It prevents our political parties from becoming hopelessly divided on ideological grounds, because each party embraces a diversity of interests stretching across the political spectrum. The parties serve as unifying agents. When they fail to do so, the nation is likely to

[6] Pendleton Herring, *The Politics of Democracy* (Norton, 1940), pp. 92–94.
[7] Herbert Agar, *Pursuit of Happiness* (Houghton Mifflin, 1938), p. 198.

become involved in civil war, as it did in 1861. "A federal nation," says one historian, "is safe so long as the parties are undogmatic and contain members with many contradictory views. But when the people begin to divide according to reason, with all the voters in one party who believe one way, the federal structure is strained." [8]

Broker Rule Criticized

Many Americans dislike certain features of broker or concurrent majority rule. They complain:

1. Broker rule is unrepresentative. True, it tends to give every big minority interest a voice in decisions. But leaders of organized interests are often not truly representative of the members of those groups. And what about the millions of Americans not organized in vocal, self-seeking groups? Does not broker rule ignore them?

2. Broker rule results in parties that do not stand for much of anything. The choice between them is often one between Tweedledum and Tweedledee. If people think that their parties will not take strong stands on important issues, they may begin to suspect that democratic government evades problems instead of solving them. If this suspicion hardens into conviction, they may turn to extremist leaders and parties, especially in time of social conflict and economic depression.

3. Broker rule may be all very well for a laissez-faire economy and a loose social organization, such as we had in the nineteenth century. But the world today is putting heavy demands on government, and these demands cannot be met by a polity of pressure groups. According to some observers, "the expanding responsibilities of modern government have brought about so extensive an interlacing of governmental action with the country's economic and social life that the need for coordinated and coherent programs, legislative as well as administrative, has become paramount." [9] The shifting, unstable alliances of minority interests cannot do the job of translating nationwide policies into firm decisions and actions.

4. Broker rule does *not* protect diversity. Heterogeneity, minority interests, and individual rights thrive best in a society that is productive, stable, and secure. A depression-ridden, frightened society cannot afford—or at least does not tolerate —diversity. Only positive action can keep the nation productive and strong. If democratic government cannot act, people may turn in frustration to more drastic solutions. In short, strong—not weak—government is necessary to safeguard democracy, which in turn protects diversity. [10]

5. Nor does broker rule lead to unity in the long run. On the contrary, by

[8] Herbert Agar, *The Price of Union* (Houghton Mifflin, 1950), pp. 689–690.
[9] "Toward a More Responsible Two-Party System," A Report of the Committee on Political Parties of the American Political Science Association, *The American Political Science Review*, Vol. XLIV (1950), Pt. 2, p. 31. For a trenchant critique of this and other theories of how to define the public interest, see Glendon A. Schubert, *The Public Interest* (The Free Press, 1960).
[10] See Max Lerner, *It Is Later Than You Think* (Viking, 1938).

responding to pressures it sets group against group, section against section. Broker rule does not achieve genuine unity, but only temporary agreements and fleeting coalitions. By responding to minority pressures so readily, it fails to achieve a basic consensus of a majority of the people, and such a consensus is the only basis of real unity.

Whatever position one takes between these two views, the implications of the problem are significant. The issue is no longer simply that of direct and faithful representation of the people. The broader question is: How much discretion should leaders have *not* to respond to what the people seem to want at a given time, provided that some day, in some election, they will have to account for their record in office?

Responsibility and Leadership

The issue, then, is not so much representation as *responsibility*. By responsibility we mean two things. First, and more narrowly, we mean the final accountability of leaders to the led, presumably in some election, even though in the meantime the leaders have a great deal of freedom to act. Second, we mean a leader's concern for the general welfare of the *whole nation*, not just the interests of his constituents, and with the nation's long-term interests, not just its fleeting desires—that is, whether he acts responsibly from the long hindsight of history. How can we provide our leaders with enough power to exercise responsibility in both senses and yet keep them accountable to the people?

Among the many answers to these questions, two are especially important for students of American government: *majority rule* through *party government*, and *executive* (or *presidential*) *leadership*.

Majority Rule and Party Government

Proponents of majority rule believe that leaders should be largely if not wholly accountable to the popular majority that won the last election. They value *strict majority rule*—the idea that when a majority of the voters elect a set of leaders to power, the new government essentially represents that majority and is responsible for enacting its wishes into law. In short, the victorious leaders have no obligation to respect the wishes of the unsuccessful popular minority—except to protect civil liberties and free elections so that the minority can try to become a majority some day. Broker rule, on the other hand, shuns strict majority action. In its allegiance to concurrent majority rule, it stresses representation of all the major groups in the society. The government acts not for a relatively solid and identifiable group of voters ranged on one side of the fence ideologically, but for all sorts of groups and for both parties.

Many Americans fear strict majority rule. They believe that the majority holds in it the seeds of tyranny. Broker rule, they suggest, minimizes conflict by absorbing forces on the right and left. Majority rule would result in violent wrenches as first one set of leaders and then a very different set of leaders came to power. The majoritarians deny this. They maintain that majority rule must be safe because the majority, by definition, embraces a tremendous variety of attitudes and interests, even though it may not include every group across the political spectrum. Since the majority is a broad one, the leaders must act in the interests of a tremendous diversity of voters. Thus a popular majority carries built-in checks and balances.[11] Minorities—not majorities—tend to be extremist. Above all, contend the majoritarians, a government that need only win and keep the support of a majority can *act*. It does not need to gain the assent of every minority group before dealing with some rising problem or developing crisis. Occasionally leaders of majorities may be wrong or may act rashly, but they do not commit the fatal error of not acting at all.

Majoritarians recognize that the people cannot act on their own. They can act only through political organization and leadership. The obvious political organization for a majority is the *political party*. Historically, great popular movements have turned to parties—the Jeffersonian Republicans, the Jacksonian Democrats, the rising anti-slavery Republicans, the New Deal Democrats—as the key political link between popular majorities and control of the government. Parties have a special advantage in that they provide a common organization for leaders in different parts of the government—especially for the Presidency and Congress—and hence can serve as a unifying force.

So in theory, at least. In fact, believers in majority rule and strong parties have had to recognize that, as we saw in Chapter 12, parties in the United States are loose associations of state and local groups, lacking strong national machinery or real national cohesion. National and state party organizations are virtually independent of each other. Leadership is diffused. And yet the *potential* of our political parties is tremendous. They can be whatever the people want them to be; no constitutional amendments need be passed, no basic governmental institutions changed. And this is the time that the party potential must be realized. For today, the government must draw up and enact a broad range of social, economic, and foreign policies. Strong parties are needed to help formulate, coordinate, and develop popular support for these vital programs.

To party reformers the issue is *responsibility*. They maintain that parties should be more representative of the general public and of their own members. Parties should be less responsive to pressures from organized minority groups and local politicos, and more concerned with developing positive policies reflecting a broad national consensus of party membership. The party in power must be responsible for enacting the policies on which it won election. It must be willing to discipline its members in office—especially those in Congress—if they desert the party platform. All this goes for the opposition party, too. It must act as the critic of the

[11] H. S. Commager, *Majority Rule and Minority Rights* (Oxford Univ. Press, 1943), pp. 57 ff.

party in power, constantly developing and presenting alternative policies. It must serve as a strong and united loyal opposition.[12]

Several specific proposals have been made for enhancing party responsibility.

1. *Build up and improve the national party organization.* The national convention should continue as the party's main organ, but it should become more representative and more active. It should meet every year or two instead of every four years, as at present. A new party council of about fifty members should serve as the full-time governing organ of the party. The council would plan party strategy, interpret the platform, and run the organization. Above all—in the case of the party in power—it would take responsibility for pushing through the party platform—a task that involves coordinating the whole party, national, regional, state, and local.

2. *Make the party platform mean something.* No one today takes party platforms very seriously. They are collections of pious hopes and vague promises. A newly nominated presidential candidate may interpret his party's platform as freely as he wishes during the campaign and later. Party platforms, it is proposed, should be drawn up at least every other year to keep them abreast of the times. State and local platforms should be consistent with the national platform. A broad range of groups within the party, including congressmen, should take part in platform-making, and the adopted platform should be binding on all members.

3. *Strengthen the party in Congress.* Advocates of more responsible parties see Congress as the graveyard of party hopes and party pledges. Congressional party organization, they suggest, should be tightened up. The separate leadership groups in both the Senate and the House should be merged into one responsible leadership committee for each party in each chamber. These four committees would submit proposed policies to the party members and would direct the legislative program. The caucus should meet more often, and its decisions should carry greater weight. Party rebels should be prevented from serving as chairmen of important committees, even if it means violating the seniority rule. At any rate, individual chairmen, the House Rules Committee, and senatorial filibusters should be curbed.

4. *Develop party activity at the grass roots.* Supporters of stronger national parties believe that the problem is largely one of political participation. They know, for example, that the only way to make congressmen more responsible to the party is to make the party mean more to the congressmen. The local party, with the full support of national party leaders, should build a strong democratic organization to carry the burden of congressional campaigns. Local party groups should meet more frequently to discuss and initiate policy. Party membership should be made more meaningful by imposing certain obligations on all members, such as paying dues and taking part in party activities.

[12] The arguments for party government described here are taken largely from "Toward a More Responsible Two-Party System," cited above.

The Price of Party Responsibility

So much for the specific proposals for enhancing party responsibility. We still must face the question: Would party responsibility lead to a more democratic system of government? Would it foster responsible leadership?

The party reformers answer "yes." They believe that an invigorated party system would forge a stronger link between the people and the government. The men in power would be the leaders of the majority party. They would be bound by the wishes of the party rank and file, as embodied in the platform. If they ignored basic party policy, they would risk losing the support of sections of the party, and perhaps the next election as well. Thus the millions of party members would not only *sustain* the government, they would also *constrain* it, by forcing it to abide by its mandate at the previous election. The opposition party would therefore serve as another check on the rulers. By holding out and presenting alternative policies and by continuously criticizing the government, the opposition would strive to win over a majority of the voters at the next election. The opposition party, like the party in power, would then act as a responsible organization.

Not all political scientists agree with this diagnosis or with the proposed cure. Some say these proposals underestimate the present extent of party responsibility. They cite cases where the parties have presented clear alternatives to the voters. They fear, too, that more discipline in the parties would cut down party compe-

One failing of our party system is that the party out of power nationally does not have the kind of leadership that the President can provide for the party in power. (Tom Little; © 1965 by The New York Times Company. Reprinted by permission.)

tition in certain areas, for the national leaders of a strong party might enforce doctrines that were unpopular in certain localities (for example, racial equality in the South).[13] Not party discipline but *party competition* is the great need, according to this view. "Our parties are big and clumsy and loosely hung together," says Professor Ruth C. Silva, "because our country is big and clumsy and loosely hung together."

What about an alternative means of achieving responsible leadership?

Presidential Leadership and Responsibility

Party government would bring a radical change in the American system because the parties would try to unite what the framers wanted to divide. The Constitution, as we noted in Chapter 2, made different leaders—President, senators, representatives—responsive to different and conflicting constituencies. "Ambition" was made to "counteract ambition." Party reformers hope that parties could become strong enough to elect and provide continuing political support for all the leaders of government in the same party, whether in the White House or on Capitol Hill. Critics of party reform contend that strong parties and party government will never come about precisely because of the anti party aims of the framers. The different and conflicting constituencies still stand, just as the framers planned. Indeed, instead of unifying leaders, parties themselves become disrupted as party leaders and candidates respond to different constituencies. No party could be strong enough, it is argued, to unify presidential and congressional Republicans or northern and southern Democrats.

In any event, ask the critics, why try the long, hard method of party reform when a much better instrument is at hand to act for the popular majority, to expedite governmental action, and even to unify clashing interests? This is the Presidency. We have discussed presidential leadership in Chapters 14 and 15; let us consider it now in terms of the value of *responsibility*.

Defenders of presidential power contend that, first of all, the Presidency fully meets the test of accountability. The Chief Executive must win an electoral majority to gain power. In office he is clearly responsible for his administration; he cannot pass off the blame to anyone else. For four years he operates in the bright spotlight of television, questioned by the press, attacked by the opposition, searchingly examined by the columnists and pundits. And after four years he must face the people again. The people then can apply more general tests of accountability. Did the President observe the basic rules of the game, such as maintaining civil liberties and keeping the public informed? Did he abide by the Constitution? And is he willing to take responsibility for his stewardship?

But responsibility means more than accountability to a particular electorate in a particular election. It means accountability for the welfare of the nation in

[13] Julius Turner, "Responsible Parties: A Dissent from the Floor," *The American Political Science Review* (March 1951), pp. 143–152.

the long perspective of history. As we have suggested above, it may mean at times *not* being immediately accountable to, or representative of, the people because the leader sees something the people may not see. He is responsible to history, or to fundamental national values, or perhaps just to his own conscience. Lyndon Johnson described this kind of responsibility a few months after he entered the White House when he observed that the President "is not simply responsible to an immediate electorate." The President continued: [14]

> He knows over the long stretch of time how great can be the repercussions of all that he does or that he fails to do, and over that span of time the President always has to think of America as a continuing community.
>
> He has to try to see how his decisions will affect not only today's citizens, but their children and their children's children unto the third and fourth generation. He has to try to peer into the future, and he has to prepare for that future. . . .
>
> The President of this country, more than any other single man in the world, must grapple with the course of events and the directions of history. What he must try to do, try to do always, is to build for tomorrow in the immediacy of today. . . .

This view of presidential leadership has its critics. If the President acts according to such vague tests—the verdict of history, the welfare of our children's children —what is to stop him from acting as freely as he wishes? Why could he not become a virtual dictator on the grounds that some day he would be vindicated? Such criticism invites two comments. Whatever his broader responsibility, the President will and must be accountable to an electoral majority at the end of his term. Even if he does not run again, he will want his party to win. Second, the President in a democracy needs a strong and durable opposition. This is perhaps the weakest link in the American democratic structure, as we have noted. Perhaps the most compelling task for the party reformers is not to establish "party government," which can never replace our present system of presidential government, but to foster a well-organized, well-financed *loyal opposition* that can consistently, responsibly, and vigorously attack the President's program and offer alternatives.

The People, Yes?

"Is 'government by the people' just a pious pretension," we asked at the end of Chapter 1, "or does it in fact exist in the United States? Is democratic government really just a cloak for rule by a small number of leaders and powerful minorities, or is there a connection between what the people want and what the government does? If so, which people?"

It would be easy, from the evidence in this book alone, to attack the theory and

[14] Remarks to American Society of Newspaper Editors, The White House, April 17, 1964.

practice of government by the people. We have noted that our constitutional system prevents popular majorities from controlling government, that public opinion is often ignorant or emotional, that the individual voter is often apathetic and ill-informed, that political parties often evade issues rather than confront them, that the supposedly popular institution of Congress is mal-apportioned and inefficient, that the President has tremendous powers and can ignore the people's wishes as well as respond to them.

Some political scientists, sociologists, and others have been so impressed—or depressed—by the unreality of the "Popular Rule Model" (see page 30) that they prefer another set of assumptions about American democratic government, which can be summarized as the "Power Elite Model." Its best known and "purest" advocate was a brilliant sociologist, the late C. Wright Mills.[15] According to this model:

1. Mass man and mass society lack the basis of power.

2. Those who control the basis of power—control of key economic decisions, military authority, influence over the mass media—form a "power elite." This elite can, within very broad limits and at a relatively low "political price," make pretty much the decisions it wants to, behind the facade of "government by the people."

3. President and Congress and the other formal leaders have little function except to ratify decisions made elsewhere in the "power structure."

The Pluralist Model

Most political scientists take a position somewhere between the "popular rule" and the "power elite" models. As they look at the evidence—community studies, voting behavior, public opinion polls, case studies of how decisions are actually made—they see the people as far too complex to be simply categorized as informed or uninformed, sensible or silly. There is neither a simple power elite ruling an impotent mass, nor the classic ideal of popular self-government based on interest, knowledge, and participation.

After their intensive study of Elmira, for example, Berelson and his colleagues concluded that *individual voters* were indeed uninvolved in politics, not well-informed, parochial, unable to think clearly and "rationally," but that the *system of democracy* did seem to meet certain requirements for a going political society. "The individual members may not meet all the standards but the whole nevertheless survives and grows. This suggests that where the classic theory is defective is in its concentration on the *individual citizen*. What are undervalued are certain collective properties that reside in the electorate as a whole and in the political and social system in which it functions." [16] These are the balances between in-

<hr />

[15] See his *The Power Elite* (Oxford Univ. Press, 1956). See also William C. Mitchell, *The American Polity* (Macmillan, 1962), pp. 74–94, on which much of this discussion is based.

[16] Bernard R. Berelson, Paul F. Lazarsfeld, William N. McPhee, *Voting* (Univ. of Chicago Press, 1954), p. 312.

"That's the trouble with a monarchy—they can't vote you out of office." (Courtesy The Saturday Review and Mirachi.)

volvement and indifference, stability and flexibility, progress and conservation, consensus and cleavage, individualism and collectivism.

A comparable conclusion was reached by Almond and Verba after an intensive study of five western nations, including the United States. Here again the investigators found a contrast between the classic ideals of civic participation and rational thinking, and the reality of political passivity, narrowness, and irrationality. They agree with Schattschneider that "the problem is not how 180 million Aristotles can run a democracy, but how we can organize a community of 180 million ordinary people so that it remains sensitive to their needs. This is a problem of *leadership, organization, alternatives and systems of responsibility and confidence.*" [17] They conclude that tendencies toward political apathy and intensity, toward support of the status quo and support of change, toward consensus and cleavage, and toward other conflicting qualities are distributed widely throughout society and even within individuals, and hence tend to balance one another. After all, a democracy cannot govern a citizenry every one of whom is passionately aroused politically any more than it can a people that is completely inert and ignorant.[18]

Thus, according to such studies, it is in the balancing of opposite tendencies in a large public that we find the safeguards of democracy. These are the social and psychological checks and balances that parallel—and strengthen—the constitutional ones. Extremist tendencies are balanced and hence cancelled.

Both of these studies, and many others, prove the vital necessity of responsible leadership in a democracy. The people by themselves cannot take the initiative or carry the momentum of government. Leaders arise through the democratic process and once in power must have considerable leeway in exercising authority.

[17] E. E. Schattschneider, *The Semi-Sovereign People* (Holt, Rinehart and Winston, 1960), p. 138.
[18] Gabriel A. Almond and Sidney Verba, *The Civic Culture* (Princeton Univ. Press, 1963), ch. 15.

The crucial institution is the electoral system. "An electoral system, designed to turn power over to a particular elite for a limited period of time, can achieve a balance between power and responsiveness: the elites obtain power, yet this power is limited by the periodic elections themselves, by the concern for future elections during the interelection period, and by a variety of other formal and informal checks." [19] In this sense the ideal of government *by* the people must recognize a place for government *of* the people.

On the basis of such considerations, many political scientists conceive of American politics in terms of a third model, the "Pluralist Model," which also reflects concepts of some of the framers of the Constitution, most notably James Madison.

1. Man is a rational and an emotional and subjective individual moved by symbols, prejudices, and limited perspectives as well as by knowledge and reason.

2. Politics is best "conceptualized" not as a debate among autonomous individuals engaged in the rational pursuit of the public interest, but of individuals combining and recombining into groups, each with a differing concept of the public interest.

3. The most important issues of politics are value conflicts with differing groups and individuals having differing concepts of the public interest. It is precisely because there is no objective way to solve such conflicts, because there is no scientific certainty about what is and what is not in the public interest, that the democratic way of governing is best. The well-educated person's concept of the public interest is just as likely to be limited as is the less well-educated person's concept.

4. Democratic politics is not a way to solve problems, but to work out accommodations. "What characterizes a political problem is that no answer will fit the terms of the problem as stated. A political problem therefore is not solved, it may be settled, which is a different thing altogether." [20] Political problems are settled by the application of an accepted principle, lacking this by authority, or most often in a democracy by bargaining and compromise.

5. Democracy is preserved not so much by the convictions of the mass but by the agreement among the "influentials" on the basic rules of the game. It is the common commitment of these "influentials" to seek political victories in accord with the democratic norms and the competition among these "influentials" that makes democracy possible.

6. Decisions are made, even in a democracy, by a relatively small group of decision-makers, with most of the public on most issues being unconcerned and uninvolved. Yet there is a rough correspondence between what public officials do and the interests of most of the people because of competition among the governing elites, who periodically must please most of the people most of the time in order to secure the right to make decisions. Elections may not determine public

[19] *Ibid.*, p. 477.
[20] Bertrand De Jouvenel, *The Pure Theory of Politics* (Yale Univ. Press, 1963), p. 207.

policies, but they "legitimatize" the right of one segment of the elite to make these policies.

7. The Popular Rule Model of democracy may have a useful function, but it does not correspond with reality and there is the danger that if it is accepted too uncritically, it will lead to cynicism.

Conditions of Democratic Government

If these are the kinds of qualities needed for an effective and durable democratic government, what are the basic economic and social conditions that foster such qualities? Social scientists differ over the necessary "mix" of qualities—indeed, this is one of the most interesting frontiers of political science and allied disciplines—but there is considerable agreement that democratic government in part depends for success upon the following conditions:

Educational Conditions. Before democratic government can operate effectively for any length of time in a large nation, most of the people must at least be able to read and write. A recent study shows that in the more democratic European and English-speaking nations most of the people are literate, in contrast with the high rate of illiteracy in dictatorial Latin-American nations. Moreover, Latin-American democracies have a significantly higher percentage of literacy than the Latin-American dictatorships.[21] Other studies show a high correlation between education and such democratic ideas as belief in tolerance for the opposition. But a word of caution: A high level of education does not "cause" or "guarantee" democratic government, as the examples of Nazi Germany and Soviet Russia readily illustrate, and some relatively less-educated peoples such as the Indians have democratic governments. Nonetheless, a high level of education contributes to the stability of democracy.

Economic Conditions. A relatively prosperous nation, with security and an equitable distribution of wealth, provides the best milieu for democracy. Starving men are more interested in food than in the franchise. Where economic power is concentrated, political power is likely to be concentrated, too. The study noted above confirms the long-held theory of political scientists that the more well-to-do nations have a greater chance of sustaining democratic governments than do those with widespread poverty.[22] In modern times wealthy nations have been the urban and industrial ones. And though the evidence is by no means conclusive, modern social scientists tend to question Jefferson's belief that democratic stability is best

[21] Seymour M. Lipset, "Some Social Requisites of Democracy: Economic Development and Political Legitimacy," *The American Political Science Review* (March 1959), pp. 76–77, 96.
[22] *Ibid.*, p. 76.

preserved by preventing the growth of cities. Not only do urbanization and industrialization lead to economic well-being, but they also bring a breakdown of isolation and homogeneity, and promote a cosmopolitan outlook.[23]

Social Conditions. In a society fragmented into large, solid, warring groups that differ on fundamental questions, government by discussion and compromise becomes difficult. When the issues at stake between ideologically separated groups are considered by them to be vital, they may prefer to fight rather than accept the verdict of the ballot box. But when society consists of many overlapping associations and groupings, individuals are not as likely to identify themselves completely with a single group and to give their total allegiance to it. Joe Brown, for example, is a Methodist, Legionnaire, Rotarian, southerner, Democrat, electrician, and a member of the $6,000-a-year economic bracket. On some issues Joe thinks as a Methodist, on others as a southerner, and on still others, as an electrician. Bill Jones is a Methodist, Legionnaire, and Rotarian—but he is also a Republican, an auto dealer, and a member of the $12,000-a-year bracket. Sometimes he acts more like a Republican, sometimes more like a Legionnaire. Jones and Brown differ on some issues but agree on many others. Certainly the differences between them are not likely to be greater than their common interest in maintaining democracy.

Democracy is also more likely to survive where other social institutions reinforce democratic habits. The family, the church, the lodge, the union, the school, for example, are institutions regulating important areas of life affected by and affecting government. If these institutions support and reinforce the idea of government by democratic procedures, then the habits of discussion, compromise, respect for differences are developed and strengthened by constant use. In the family, for example, there appears to be a close reciprocal connection (not necessarily causal) between the authoritarian family and authoritarian political attitudes.

Ideological Conditions. Out of these educational, economic, and social conditions there must also develop widespread acceptance of the ideals of democracy, the willingness of an overwhelming proportion of the people to agree to proceed democratically. This quality is *democratic consensus.* A perceptive discussion of democratic theory states: "Prior to politics, beneath it, enveloping it, restricting it, conditioning it, is the underlying consensus on policy that usually exists in the society among a predominant portion of the politically active members. Without such a consensus no democratic system would long survive the endless irritations and frustrations of elections and party competition." [24]

To sum up: A society that offers the best chances for democratic success is one with an educated and fairly prosperous electorate without concentrated wealth, with relative freedom from bitter class, religious, or sectional antagonisms, with

[23] *Ibid.,* p. 96.
[24] Robert A. Dahl, *A Preface to Democratic Theory* (Univ. of Chicago Press, 1956), p. 132.

many private loyalties and associations, with other social institutions that buttress the principles and practices of democracy, all tending to produce a democracy consensus. But no one of these conditions—nor even all of them—guarantees democracy. There is no foolproof double-your-money-back guarantee for freedom.

PART 6

Big government in action

A Problem Guide **A Problem Guide**   In Part Six we come to the *action* aspect of our political system—what government actually *does*. In these six chapters we shall explore the tremendous number and variety of federal functions, ranging from crucial foreign policy decisions to the more routine domestic tasks, such as regulating interstate commerce. As we study these functions, we shall see that they raise anew all the five major sets of problems that we have explored in this book. These problems, originally listed before in Chapter 1, are worth reviewing here to see how they relate to the functions of the national government.

First, *the challenge to democratic government*. Do federal functions—the tasks that are finally carried out by Washington officials and others—prove the communist argument that democratic government is just a cloak for rule by a few capitalistic interests rather than the people as a whole? Do the actual operations of government suggest that a democratic system cannot effectively perform the big tasks of strengthening and stabilizing the economy, aiding the underprivileged, promoting peace between business and labor, coping with farm problems, and the like? Chapters 24, 25, and 26 provide the factual background necessary for considering such questions.

Second, *the problem of constitutional government*. Because of the anarchical balance-of-power relation among nations, our leaders must be able to move quickly to head off crisis or to meet it head on. They must have power to mobilize and manage our armed forces without getting the consent of the voters or even the consent of the legislators, and sometimes without announcing their plans ahead of time. Under such conditions, what happens to our traditional constitutional processes of open debate and slow, deliberative action? Foreign and military programs require unity of purpose and action. Can we afford, then, the traditional splintering of power between the executive and legislative branches, the traditional supremacy of civilian over military leaders? Such problems are sharply raised in Chapters 21, 22, and 23.

Third, *the problem of individual rights.* This set of problems is not put so squarely in Part Six as in earlier chapters. But the increasing role of the federal government does raise the basic question of whether big government narrows or broadens individual liberty and initiative. Do the security requirements of a continuing cold war gradually impair our freedom? Are we witnessing "creeping socialism" that may deprive Americans of their traditional rights against government? Or can federal functions, such as aid to education, help *expand* liberty? Such questions are implicit in Chapters 24, 25, and 26.

Fourth, *the problem of popular representation.* For whom does the federal government perform its immense variety of tasks? Does it serve major needs of the people as a whole, or does it actually operate on behalf of hundreds of special interests? Does federal regulation of interest groups such as business or labor—regulation ostensibly undertaken for the general welfare—actually turn out to be protection of that group at the expense of the public interest? The material in Chapters 24 and 25 raises such questions. The problem of whether our fiscal machinery—raising, lending, spending money, and so forth—is capable of serving the interests of the whole nation is taken up in Chapter 26.

Fifth, *the problem of responsible leadership.* The officials administering federal functions have great discretion and power. Do the people as a whole, acting through elected civilian officials, have adequate control over bureaucrats, technicians, military men? In matters of foreign and military policy, should federal officials be accountable to the people as a whole through *bipartisan* procedures, or to the party in power favoring foreign policies endorsed by a majority of the people, or to various organized minorities or interest groups? Or—the other side of the same coin—does our governmental system allow our leaders enough power to act quickly and comprehensively when such action is needed, at the same time holding those leaders ultimately accountable to the people for their performance in office?

21 FOREIGN POLICY: POLITICS AND PROBLEMS

One momentous fact dominates foreign-policy making in this country: The United States exists in a world of sovereign and independent nations. There is no world government that can guarantee to each of these nations its security, liberty, or property. There is little formal machinery for settling disputes. In contrast to the relatively ordered relations of people *within* the United States, the relations with other nations tremble in a state of semi-anarchy. World order rests on a precarious balance-of-power system and on some convergent patterns of self-interest from which flow a handful of international rules and customs.

Some day the present system of sovereign states may come to an end. A single nation may conquer the world and impose, as Hitler tried to do, a "new order" directed from one super capital. Or the peoples of the world may some day join hands and establish a world government capable of making and enforcing law for everyone everywhere. But these are future possibilities, not present-day realities. For good or for ill, the present system of independent states is the international framework in which the United States must strive to achieve its objectives.

What are these objectives? Have they·changed significantly over the nineteen decades of our national existence? Who determines the objectives and the means of reaching them? What fundamental role is played by organized interests, political parties, public opinion? What is the role of the United Nations in our foreign policy making? How democratic is our procedure of making foreign policy?

The United States in a Changing World

The chief objective of American foreign policy has been to safeguard the security of the United States. Given the nature of the world we live in, our objective could be none other than this. To be sure, American politicians have often preferred to speak in high moral terms about "safeguarding world peace" and "helping our little brown brothers" rather than to talk the blunt language of power politics. But beneath the high-flown rhetoric, the central purpose of protecting national interest has been fairly consistent.

But promoting the "national interests" of the United States provides no better guidelines to foreign policy makers than the standard of "the public interest" furnishes to those who make domestic policies. Total security is never obtainable even if it were definable. The United States lacks the resources, even if it had the will, to make the rest of the world respond to our wishes. Our policy-makers try to influence, direct, and shape events; but the rest of the world shapes and influences us. And in recent decades the world about us has been in a process of constant and rapid changes.

Security in the Nineteenth Century

In his famous *Farewell Address*, George Washington said: "Europe has a set of primary interests, which to us have none, or a very remote relation. Hence she must be engaged in frequent controversies, the causes of which are essentially foreign to our concerns. Hence, therefore, it must be unwise in us to implicate ourselves, by artificial ties, in the ordinary vicissitudes of her politics, or the ordinary combinations or collisions of her friendships or enmities." Quoted over the years by thousands of politicians, these words keynoted American foreign policy making for decades.

During a good part of the nineteenth century this formula of "minding our own business" worked fairly well—not because American officials had some special knack of "keeping out of foreign entanglements," but because Americans benefited from a world balance of power. Our ". . . Isolationism was but the shadow on the wall of a global equipoise."[1] The factors in that balance were threefold: Britannia ruled the waves, Europe was stable, and our oceans shielded us from attack.

The British navy controlled strategic sea lanes from Gibraltar to Hong Kong. And Britain stood between our virtually undefended shores and the other major powers. Any threat by a continental nation to the United States was a threat to Britain. At the same time, the European countries could neither permit Britain to regain control over her former colonies, nor allow any nation to threaten South America, because such action would upset the balance of power. That balance rested on a diffusion of military strength and on an elaborate network of treaties and understandings. Shaky though the structure was, it endured for a century.

The United States was not insulated completely from international power politics, of course. Americans fought a war with Britain at the beginning of the nineteenth century and a war with Spain at the end of it. We had frequent brushes with other great powers. We fought a war with Mexico. President Lincoln and Secretary of State Seward had their hands full trying to prevent foreign intervention during the Civil War. There were disputes with England over fisheries and boundaries, with France over her adventures in Mexico, with Germany and England over Venezuela. And yet the essential security of the United States was not seriously threatened in the hundred years after 1815.

Then, in the chaotic years after 1914, the relatively stable world of the nineteenth century came tumbling down around us.

Security in the Sixties

It is impossible to review here the past eventful fifty years. It is important, however, to survey the strange new world with which American foreign policy makers must somehow cope.

Europe is no longer the pivot of world politics. Britain, France, Italy, and Germany are still important powers, but they are highly vulnerable to both economic and military stress. Dominating world politics are two super powers, the United States of America and the Union of Soviet Socialist Republics. This polarization of power has tended to pull the other nations into the orbits of the giants. The rise of Communist China and the widening gulf between Peking and Moscow is adding still another dimension to this world power struggle.

This sharp division between immense power blocs is perilous enough in itself.

[1] F. L. Schuman, *International Politics*, 6th ed. (McGraw-Hill, 1958), p. 590.

But along with it—and greatly intensifying it—is an ideological split. The new religion of communism stands as a challenge to believers in the values of democracy and freedom. Soviet propaganda asserts that democracy in the West is actually rule by imperialistic, warmongering militarists and profiteers who would drown the world in blood for their own selfish ends. The Voice of America proclaims that communism in practice means rule by a self-elected elite, tyranny over the many, slave-labor camps, and secret trials. The conflict between the communist and the noncommunist nations is more than a traditional power struggle between nations; it is also a battle for the minds of men.

Another fact of international politics that may be far more significant in the long run is the "awakening" of the peoples of Asia, the Middle East, and Africa. Nearly two billion people live in these lands. For centuries they have for the most part accepted squalor, hunger, and sickness as inevitable conditions of life. In the nineteenth century many of them were introduced to western ideas of liberty, equality, and progress, and western technical and scientific methods. Today that introduction is bearing fruit in national movements, reforms, and revolutions. Membership in the United Nations has more than doubled since its founding in 1945, largely as a result of the emergence of newly independent nations. This process of emergence is by no means complete. Countries in Latin America, Asia, the Middle East, and Africa are convulsed by social ferment and rebellion.

The super powers have not ignored the explosive potentialities of this "revolution of rising expectations." The Soviet Union and Red China have been quick to take advantage of mass unrest and social revolution, and communist propaganda sometimes has a powerful appeal for people who are promised "pie in the sky" and believe they have nothing to lose but their chains. The democracies have been slower in sensing the profound consequences of the end of colonialism. But for defensive reasons, if not others, the United States and its allies have been forced to give economic and military aid to the governments in these areas and to step up their propaganda against Soviet communism. All this is a far cry from the day when American activities took place in sleepy consulates and embassies handling trivial duties that brought Americans into contact with a tiny fraction of the native population.

Finally, the world has seen immense technological changes in the past half-century. While ideologies have been tearing the world apart, technology has tended to make it one. The techniques of communications, transportation, and war have brought the continents of the world closer together than were the thirteen states of the Union in 1790. Scientific successes by both Russia and the U.S. in the exploration of outer space have emphasized a common interest in the unknown. Techniques of war have been revolutionized. Russian rockets located on the northern shore of Europe can lay waste the industrial areas of the United States. Polaris submarines prowl the seas, and our bases are on constant alert, with Minutemen missiles ready to go at a moment's notice. Our geographical isolation, which, along with our powerful friends, once gave us a "cushion of time and distance," is no longer. Even the Arctic has become a strategic frontier.

New Times, New Problems

Such is the world that our foreign policy makers look out on, a world sharply split ideologically but closely knit technologically, a world in which tens of millions of people are demanding a larger role, a world in which the decisive events of our times are those that affect our relations with other nations.

Has our thinking kept pace with these vast changes? In the nineteenth century a policy of isolationism worked, and twentieth-century America inherited a deep belief in "no foreign entanglements" as the best means of safeguarding our national security. Then, with shocking suddenness, national security seemed to demand that the United States play a positive and active part on the world stage. Slowly, grudgingly, almost belatedly, Americans, led by such men as Woodrow Wilson, Henry Stimson, Franklin D. Roosevelt, Cordell Hull, Wendell Willkie, Arthur Vandenberg, Harry S. Truman, Dwight D. Eisenhower, stirred themselves into action. The world situation will continue to change, and new conditions will doubtless demand new thinking and new techniques.

Recently, our foreign policies have become increasingly linked with our domestic policies. The issue of federal protection of civil rights, for example, is sometimes discussed simply as a question of domestic politics or states' rights. But in the perspective of world politics, the problem takes on a new dimension. The United States spends billions of dollars trying to win the friendship of the colored peoples in Africa and Asia. At the same time, every denial of civil rights to Negroes is seized upon by our enemies to create ill-feeling against the United States in these areas. Or take "domestic" economic matters. A high level of production not only supplies Americans with goods, it helps sustain our economic and military power abroad. A depression in this country dislocates the economies of other nations, vindicates communist predictions of "capitalist doom," causes political turmoil abroad as well as at home.

The makers of foreign policy in the United States must face all these facts of international politics. As if these were not difficult enough, they must also face the uncertainties and complexities of American politics at home. Thus in planning some new policy toward a foreign nation, American officials must consider not only the political situation in that nation, the attitude of our allies, the reaction of Soviet Russia and her satellites, and the effect on western military strength; they must also consider the attitude of the opposition party in this country and of the interest groups concerned (including the national-origin groups) and the state of public opinion. No wonder foreign policy making is the most challenging and critical job facing Americans and their rulers today.

Who Makes Foreign Policy?

It is the awesome responsibility of those who formulate our foreign policy to determine the basic objectives vital to our national interests and to formulate programs to achieve these objectives. The chief instruments of these foreign policy makers are military force, economic power, propaganda, and negotiation. They must determine what particular combination of these instruments should be brought into play.

Who is it that makes our foreign policy? The answer, of course, is the elected representatives of the people—namely, Congress and the President. In earlier chapters of this book, we discussed the roles of these representatives in foreign policy making, and we shall return to them in later pages. But first we must look at the other officials who help the President make foreign policy.

The President's Right-Hand Man

The Constitution scatters responsibility for foreign policy making among President, Senate, and the House of Representatives. But the initiative rests with the President. The President's role depends not only on his great constitutional powers, but also on his political influence, the attitudes of congressmen, and the very nature of foreign policy making. But the job is too big for the President to perform without help.

The President's chief adviser is the *Secretary of State*, the most important member of the President's Cabinet and chief of the Department of State. The Secretary of State is politically important too. Many people who cannot identify any other member of the Cabinet know his name. The influence of the Secretary of State is suggested by the names of many famous American foreign policies or actions—the Hay Open Door Policy, the Kellogg Pact, the Stimson Doctrine, the Hull Reciprocal Trade Program, the Marshall Plan.

Officially the Secretary of State helps the President to make decisions. In actual practice the Secretary formulates a great deal of foreign policy himself and then secures the President's backing. According to Secretary of State Cordell Hull, "with the present immense network and mass of details involved in conducting our foreign relations, the President finds it impossible to keep familiar with more than the principal acts of the State Department. The Secretary of State must do the rest." But just how much influence the Secretary exercises depends largely on the President's personal desires. Presidents Harding, Coolidge, Hoover, and Eisenhower turned over to their Secretaries almost full responsibility for making important policy decisions. Other Presidents have taken a more active part; indeed, at times they have been their own Secretaries of State. Wilson, both Roosevelts, and Johnson are examples. Even so, important decisions on foreign policy are so numerous that both President and Secretary of State must usually play important roles.

The Secretary has a large department to administer. He receives many visits in Washington from foreign diplomats. He attends important international conferences and usually heads our delegation in the General Assembly of the United Nations. He makes key statements on foreign policy, sometimes speaking directly to the people. He visits other nations to confer with chiefs of state and foreign ministers. He deals directly with our ambassadors and ministers in other countries. As a leading member of the Cabinet, he may have a hand in shaping general administration policy.

In all these activities the Secretary of State serves as the President's "right-hand man." But he must also command support in Congress. Unless he enjoys con gressional confidence, the foreign policies proposed by the President may have rough going on Capitol Hill.[2] For this reason one of the Secretary's top assistants is assigned to keep congressmen in touch with the Secretary's policies and to serve as a channel of communication between the legislators and the Secretary. Broadly speaking, however, the Secretary is at the mercy of power relationships in Washington—the relations between President and Congress, the political strength of the President, the attitudes of key congressmen, all reflecting the temper of the country. In recent years, Don K. Price writes, "The Secretary of State has seemed to be the official scapegoat for a nation which resents the sacrifices of two world wars and the frustration of idealistic hopes which carried it to victory but failed to establish a firm basis for peace."[3]

The President's Left-Hand Men

Decades ago, the President needed to call only on the Secretary of State for advice in determining foreign policy aims and formulating programs and policies. But today foreign policy is intimately related to every phase of governmental activity—finance, transportation, agriculture, commerce, and, of course, military activity. Suppose, for example, the President needed to make a decision on a matter of international trade. The specialized knowledge and expert help he would need are scattered throughout the executive structure, in the departments of the Treasury, Commerce, Labor, and Agriculture, in the Federal Trade Commission, and in the United States Tariff Commission. The first Hoover Commission Task Force on Foreign Affairs pointed

[2] For an illustration of the importance of congressional confidence in the Secretary of State for the President's program, see Richard F. Fenno, Jr., *The President's Cabinet* (Vintage, 1959), pp. 203 ff.

[3] Don K. Price (ed.), *The Secretary of State* (Prentice-Hall, 1960), p. 1. See also Arthur M. Schlesinger, Jr., *A Thousand Days: John F. Kennedy in the White House* (Houghton Mifflin, 1965), for a critical view of the capacity of the Secretary of State and his department to respond to presidential needs and perspectives during the Kennedy years.

out that if the President wished to review United States policies toward Brazil, he would find the financial data in the Treasury, trade and commerce data in the State and Commerce departments and in the Tariff Commission, agricultural information in the Department of Agriculture, and military data in the Department of Defense.

About fifty agencies are concerned in one way or another with foreign policy, and virtually all of them are called upon to furnish advice and make decisions. Sometimes these decisions are of great importance. The Secretary of Defense, for example, probably has had as much effect on our relations with Cuba, South Vietnam, and the Dominican Republic as has the Secretary of State. In the Eisenhower administration the Secretary of the Treasury had more to say about the budget for military forces than did either the Secretary of State or the Secretary of Defense. In 1965 the Secretary of the Treasury, not the Secretary of State, conducted the discussions with other nations over steps to solve problems flowing from the international balance of payments. In one sense the entire executive structure serves as the President's left hand in making foreign policy.

Next to the State Department, the Defense Department is the chief source of advice on foreign policy. Since the main goal of American foreign policy is maximum security for the United States, military factors are involved in almost every major foreign policy decision. It is not surprising that military men and military agencies have a strong voice in shaping that policy. Moreover, the line between military and foreign policy is often hard to draw, for foreign policy makes little sense unless it is coordinated with military policy. The military were in direct control of occupied areas such as Japan and guided the development of the North Atlantic Treaty Organization. Generals are assigned to important diplomatic positions, are given command of international military forces, and are called upon to testify before Congress and to speak to the people on controversial foreign policies. The influence of a MacArthur, a Marshall, or a Maxwell Taylor on foreign policy is incalculable.

Linking the Right and Left

During the Kennedy and Johnson administrations, a good deal of the coordination of these diverse facets of foreign policy making has been performed within the White House Office. The *Special Assistant to the President for National Security Affairs* now heads a sizable staff of experts that keeps the President apprised of happenings within the government and abroad which affect American foreign policy (see pages 565–566). But recent special assistants have had their counterparts in earlier administrations: Wilson's Colonel House; Roosevelt's Harry Hopkins; Truman's Averell Harriman. The arrangement was much more institutionalized in recent presidencies. Under Eisenhower this linkage of left and right hands was most effectively accomplished—and made less dependent upon personalities—by the utilization of the *National Security Council*.

On the average of once a week, about fifteen men file into the Cabinet Room in the West Wing of the White House.[4] They carry papers marked "top secret." The President usually presides at council meetings, since it is he who must make the decisions. The council merely recommends. The other statutory members are the Vice President, Secretary of State, Secretary of Defense, and Director of the Office of Emergency Planning. The Chairman of the Joint Chiefs of Staff and the Director of Central Intelligence are always there as advisers, and Eisenhower asked the Secretary of the Treasury and Director of the Bureau of the Budget to serve. In addition, the President frequently requests other officials, such as the Attorney General and the Director of the United States Information Agency, to sit in on the meetings. The Special Assistant to the President for National Security Affairs is there, as is the Executive Secretary of the council staff.

The council has the responsibility of helping the President integrate foreign, military, economic, fiscal, internal security, and psychological policies that affect national security. Members of the council are expected to act not merely as representatives of their departments "but as a collegiate body seeking over-all policies rather than compromises of agencies' positions." Only as the director of the Central Intelligence Agency, however, does the council have any formal legal duty as a unit. Its main job is to assist the President in balancing our foreign risks and commitments against our domestic and military strength.

The Planning Board does most of the work for the National Security Council. Presided over by a Special Assistant to the President, the Board is supposed to identify clearly the elements of disagreement, spell out alternative policy courses, and insure that the busy men—most of whom are Cabinet officers—who make up the National Security Council are fully informed. For as Senator Henry M. Jackson put it: "You know the typical week in the life of a Cabinet officer—7 formal speeches, 7 informal speeches, 7 hearings on the Hill, 7 official cocktail parties, 7 command dinner engagements. It is a schedule which leaves no time. . . . What they can do, should do, must do—and all they should be asked to do (on the National Security Council)—is to pass judgment on sharply defined policy issues." [5]

National Security Machinery—
Criticisms and Proposals for Reform

Since the end of World War II and especially in recent years, knowledgeable Americans have engaged in a governmental "great debate" over the adequacy of present arrangements for formulating

[4] The National Security Council's operations under the Eisenhower administration have been described by two who have served as Special Assistant to the President for National Security Affairs. See Dillon Anderson, "The President and National Security," *Atlantic* (January 1956), pp. 42–46; and Robert Cutler, "The Development of the National Security Council," *Foreign Affairs* (April 1956), pp. 441–458. See also Paul Y. Hammond, "The National Security Council as a Device for Interdepartmental Coordination: An Interpretation and Appraisal," *The American Political Science Review* (December 1960), pp. 890–910; and Schlesinger, *op. cit., passim.*

[5] "How Shall We Forge a Strategy for Survival?" Address before the National War College, April 16, 1959, included in U. S. Senate Committee on Government Operations, Subcommittee on National Security Policy Machinery, *Organizing for National Security*, Vol. 2 (Government Printing Office, 1961), p. 271.

national security policies. There have been two Hoover Commission reports, two Brookings Institution studies, dozens of congressional hearings, investigations, and reports, not to count the numerous articles and books by research organizations and independent scholars.

Under President Eisenhower the National Security Council, at least in form, was the central pivot for making defense and foreign policy. A series of sub-units and subcommittees of the NSC were established to insure implementation of NSC proposals approved by the President. But many critics, such as Senator Henry Jackson, chairman of a Senate subcommittee that has carried on intensive investigations of the national security machinery, charged that the NSC system was a dangerously misleading facade: "The American people and even the Congress get the impression that when the Council meets, fresh and unambiguous strategies are decided upon. This is not the case. . . . The NSC spends most of its time readying papers that mean all things to all men." [6]

President Kennedy, in response to these criticisms and to his own desire to maintain firm control over national security policies, came to rely much less on the NSC than did President Eisenhower. Rather, Kennedy coordinated security policies through his own Special Assistant for National Security Affairs and a small personal staff, but tried to avoid having his staff interpose itself between the President and the Secretary of State. His administration "deliberately rubbed out the distinction between planning and operation" since it was felt that the President's purposes could be "better served if the staff officer who keeps in daily touch with operations in a given area is also the officer who acts for the White House Staff in related planning activities." [7]

Despite his desire to avoid needless committees and specialized machinery, President Kennedy's administration found it necessary to create a variety of special task forces—high-level, specific action-oriented groups. During the Cuban missile crisis of 1962 President Kennedy improvised an Executive Committee for the National Security Council consisting of his Special Assistant for National Security Affairs, the Secretaries of State and Defense, and the President, which not only coordinated policies, but kept day-by-day direction of policies in its own hands. President Johnson has continued in the Kennedy tradition and even retained the same men in the top posts. The National Security Council remains as a channel through which broad issues of national security policy come forward for presidential decision. But ultimately the President has the final constitutional authority to coordinate national security policies, and whatever the formal arrangements, each President has the duty and discretion to determine for himself how he shall meet this crucial responsibility.

[6] *Ibid.*, p. 272.
[7] Letter from McGeorge Bundy to Senator Jackson, quoted in full in Subcommittee, *op. cit.*, Vol. I, pp. 1335–1338.

Intelligence and Foreign Policy

What is the significance of yesterday's election in Brazil? How many trained infantrymen are there in Hungary? What is the morale of the North Vietnam peasants? What should we do about communist pressures on Berlin—send a diplomatic note, seek a resolution in the United Nations, use military power, propaganda, or something else? Before policy-makers can answer such questions, they must know a great deal about other countries—their probable reactions to a particular policy, their strengths and weaknesses, and—if possible—their strategic plans and intentions. Moreover, the makers of foreign policy must be familiar with the geographical and physical structure of the nations of the world; with the people—their numbers, skills, age distributions; the status of their arts, technology, engineering, and sciences; and their political and social systems.

Clearly, policy-makers must be able to counter the moves of other nations, and have some idea of the direction in which they are going to move. They need, in other words, "high-level foreign-policy intelligence." Those who gather and analyze this material are among the most important assistants to the policy leaders. The term "intelligence work" conjures up visions of spies and undercover agents, but at least 95 per cent of the information comes from open sources. Yet secret intelligence often supplies the crucial and coordinating data.

Intelligence work involves three operations: surveillance, research, and transmission. Surveillance is the close and systematic observation of developments the world over. Research is the "attempt to establish meaningful patterns out of what was observed in the past and attempts to get meaning out of what appears to be going on now." [8] Transmission is getting the right information to the right people at the right time.

Many agencies of the government are engaged in intelligence work.[9] But each of these agencies is primarily interested in gathering information within its own particular field of activity. When all the bits of information gathered by the many agencies are pieced together, they often reveal what is not evident when they are viewed separately.

The *Central Intelligence Agency*, better known as the CIA, serves directly under the National Security Council. CIA correlates and evaluates information gathered by other agencies, provides for its distribution, and itself gathers intelligence from all over the world. Located at Langley, Virginia, 20 minutes from the White House, in the next to the largest federal building (the Pentagon is the largest), the CIA has over 10,000 employees (the precise number is a secret) and spends anywhere from 500 million to a billion dollars a year

[8] Sherman Kent, *Strategic Intelligence for American World Policy* (Princeton Univ. Press, 1949), esp. p. 4.

[9] For a detailed discussion, see Harry H. Ransom, *Central Intelligence and National Security* (Harvard Univ. Press, 1958).

(compared with $250 million for the Department of State). The work of this agency is so secret that its appropriations are concealed even from Congress by being distributed through the federal budget; its director may write a check for millions of dollars without explaining what he wants it for except in a general way to the President, and he may hire and fire without regard to civil service regulations.

According to some observers, a most difficult problem is to keep the CIA from becoming another Department of State. The CIA function is to gather and analyze intelligence, but throughout the world its hundreds of agents, some secret and some not, have been known to claim to speak for the United States; and they have actively participated in the making of foreign policy, sometimes on their own without the knowledge even of the Secretary of State. CIA engineered the overthrow of governments in Iran, Laos, and Guatemala; took charge of the ill-fated attempt to invade Castro's Cuba; [10] and helped secure the downfall of the Diem regime in South Vietnam.

After the Cuban fiasco in 1961, President Kennedy took steps to restore the CIA to its intelligence function. He reactivated the President's Foreign Intelligence Advisory Board, a small committee composed of the heads of agencies involved in intelligence work, and ordered the board to conduct a continuing review of CIA's work. In Congress, however, an attempt to create a congressional watchdog over the CIA failed. With the security of the nation at stake, Congress felt that it would be inadvisable to give even a few congressional leaders access to CIA's secrets.[11]

The various interdepartmental committees, the National Security Council, the Central Intelligence Agency, are all attempts to improve the intelligence machinery. The executive structure is probably better organized to meet its responsibilities now than it has ever been in the past, but a close student of intelligence operations has pointed out that organization alone cannot correct all deficiencies: "In both the Pearl Harbor and Cuban crises there was plenty of information. But in both cases, regardless of what the Monday morning quarterbacks have to say, the data were ambiguous and incomplete. There was never a single, definitive signal that said, 'Get ready, get set, go!' but rather a number of signals that, when put together, tended to crystallize suspicion. The true signals were always embedded in the noise or irrelevance of false ones." [12] Whatever the organizational pattern, intelligence requires men to interpret the signals, and even with the best organization and the best men, our decision-makers will often have to act on the basis of incomplete information.

---

[10] Haynes B. Johnson, *The Bay of Pigs* (Norton, 1964). See also Theodore Sorensen, *Kennedy* (Harper and Row, 1965); and Schlesinger, *op. cit.*

[11] Most of the above is based on Andrew Tully, *CIA, the Inside Story* (Morrow, 1962).

[12] Roberta Wohlstetter, *Cuba and Pearl Harbor: Hindsight and Foresight* (The Rand Corporation, 1965), p. 36; see also, Roberta Wohlstetter, *Pearl Harbor: Warning and Decision* (Stanford Univ. Press, 1962).

The Politics of Foreign Policy Making

Under government by the people, foreign policy making cannot be divorced from public opinions, from the pressures of interest groups, from the operations of political parties. Those who attack the idea of democratic government in general find particular reason to decry popular control of foreign relations. The people, they say, are especially ignorant, selfish, fickle, narrow-minded, and impetuous in their attitudes toward foreign nations. These critics can find evidence to support their position. But government by the people assumes that the people can make the ultimate decisions, that ultimately they can choose the "right" course of action, that at the very least they can tell "when the shoe pinches."

Public Opinion and Foreign Policy

While there is wide variation in the manner and extent to which the American public participates in the foreign policy process, three "publics" seem to exist in foreign policy making. The largest, estimated to be as high as 90 per cent of the adult population [13] and identified as the *mass public*, knows virtually nothing of foreign affairs, despite its grave importance. The hard core of chronic know-nothings that we noted in Chapter 9 is even larger in respect to foreign affairs. In 1948, during the Berlin blockade, the Survey Research Center found that 37 per cent of the people did not even know of any trouble in Berlin. During the Berlin crisis in 1959 a *New York Times* survey showed that many people did not even know that Berlin was located inside East Germany.[14] In February 1953 only 41 per cent of a national cross section of adults was able to give any approximately correct answer to the question: "Can you tell me what is the main job of the State Department in Washington?" [15] In 1964 the Survey Research Center found that 28 per cent of the people interviewed did not know that there is a communist regime in China.

The second level of the foreign policy public is the *attentive public*. Comprising perhaps 10 per cent of the population, this group maintains an active interest in foreign policy through membership in world affairs organizations and through reading publications devoted to such problems. The third and smallest level is the *opinion makers*—those who transmit information and judgments on foreign affairs and mobilize support in the two other publics.

To illustrate the relationship between these three "publics," one analyst has developed this instructive analogy of a huge theater with a tense drama being played out on the stage.

---

[13] Alfred O. Hero, *Americans in World Affairs* (World Peace Foundation, 1959), p. 10.
[14] *The New York Times* (March 22, 1959), Part IV, p. 8.
[15] William A. Scott and Stephen B. Withey, *The United States and the United Nations* (Manhattan, 1958), pp. 32, 176.

The mass public, occupying the many seats in the balcony, is so far removed from the scene of action that its members can hardly grasp the plot, much less hear all the lines or distinguish between the actors. Thus they may sit in stony silence or applaud impetuously, if not so vigorously as to shake the foundations of the theater. Usually, however, they get thoroughly bored and leave. . . . The attentive public, on the other hand, is located in the few choice orchestra seats. Its members can not only hear every line clearly, but can also see the facial expressions of the actors. Thus they become absorbed in the drama, applauding its high spots and disparaging its flaws. Indeed, their involvement is such that during the intermission they make their views known to any occupants of the balcony who may have wandered into the lobby. As for the members of the opinion-making public, they are the actors on the stage, performing their parts with gusto and intensity, not infrequently in an effort to upstage each other. Many are directing their performance at some specific portion of the orchestra audience. Others, those with especially strong vocal cords, try to make themselves heard as far as the balcony. All are keenly aware that the quality of their performance will greatly affect their bargaining power when they seek higher salaries or better parts in future productions.[16]

Over the years the plot may change, but the drama continues as the majority in the balcony remain uninvolved.

Why are so many people indifferent or uninformed? A hundred years of effortless security have left their mark on American attitudes. The feeling still persists that what happens outside the boundaries of the United States is of less importance than what happens inside. We still tend to exaggerate the importance of our geographic isolation. Most Americans learn their geography from American-centered Mercator-projection maps whose distortions confirm their feeling that the United States lives in a world of its own. Some people still feel that diplomacy and foreign affairs have only to do with the squabbles of far-off Europeans and Asians.

In addition to these specific historical-cultural factors are some general causes of indifference and ignorance: Foreign affairs are more remote than domestic problems. People have more first-hand information about inflation than about Chinese communism. The worker in the factory and the boss in the front office know what labor-management relations are about, and they have strong opinions on the subject. They are less concerned about the consequences of civil war in Algeria. Not only are the issues of foreign policy more remote, they are also highly complex.

Many people, uninformed and uninterested, react to foreign-policy issues on the basis of moods that have no intellectual structure or factual content.[17] These

---

[16] James N. Rosenau, *Public Opinion and Foreign Policy* (Random House, 1961), pp. 34–35.

[17] This material is drawn from Gabriel A. Almond, *The American People and Foreign Policy* (Harcourt, Brace, 1950); Rosenau, *op. cit.*; and Hero, *op. cit.* In a more recent edition of his book (Praeger, 1960), Almond has noted a "greater stabilization in foreign policy awareness and attention" in recent years.

mood reactions are unstable; optimism gives way to pessimism, idealism to cynicism. So long as there is no glaring threat to American interests, the public mood is one of withdrawal from international affairs; but the moment danger appears, the mood shifts to a demand for full-scale intervention. Then, as the danger *appears* to subside, the mood shifts back to withdrawal.

The common denominator of the mass public oversimplifies the problems of foreign politics. It tends to reduce all issues to the one issue that is most urgent at the moment. It thinks of the participants in terms of heroes and villains. It favors quick and easy remedies—fire the Secretary of State, lower trade barriers, get rid of Khrushchev, and all will be well. Even the more informed members of the attentive public are also subject to mood responses and oversimplification, but as the level of interest and information rises, the degree of sophistication increases.

Popular indifference toward international politics means that the official policy-makers often have to dramatize the issues in order to arouse public support for their programs. On the other hand, in periods of public excitement, fear of rash public opinion causes policy-makers to be overcautious. To secure American participation in the United Nations, for example, the State Department carried on an intensive publicity campaign, and in so doing gave many people the impression that the United Nations would insure peace and order in the world. To arouse public support for the Truman Doctrine, people were told of the looming "crisis." But then officials had to spend their energies cooling down public opinion to ease demands for hasty action. This overselling of policies may lead to a "giddy-ap and whoa" approach to foreign relations.

The instability of public moods makes it difficult for official policy-makers to plan ahead, to take the long view after full consideration of the military, political, diplomatic, psychological, and other subtle factors involved in every major decision. The unorganized mass public does not, of course, make foreign policy. Yet public opinion determines the broad limits within which others make the decisions. Public attitudes—the political climate in general—determine the political possibilities open to the policy-makers. The President and the congressional leaders know that they must secure active public support for programs that call for large expenditures of money or for commitments that involve risk of grave danger. Even when the public plays a negative role in the making of foreign policy, that role may still be important. The people have effective ways of making their attitudes felt both at election time and between elections.

Congressmen are sensitive to what they perceive to be popular feeling. The relations between the public and congressmen are direct, well-known, and influential. What of the Department of State? "The Department . . . and the American public are neither old nor intimate friends," writes John Dickey.[18] Until recently, those responsible for foreign policy regarded themselves as answerable only to the Presi-

[18] John S. Dickey, "The Secretary and the American Public," in Don K. Price (ed.), *The Secretary of State* (Prentice-Hall, 1960), p. 139.

dent. Not so today. Now the Department of State makes a systematic effort to keep the public informed, and just as importantly, to keep itself informed about the state of public opinion.

On major issues of foreign policy the President, through television addresses, messages to Congress, and public speeches, tries to "educate" the public. The Secretary of State holds regular press conferences. The Assistant Secretary for Public Affairs heads the Bureau of Public Affairs, whose Office of Public Services operates an extensive informational program. The office sends speakers, over 1,000 a year, to explain American policy to private organizations, and receives and answers over 100,000 letters a year. The Office of Media Services publishes leaflets and pamphlets on many topics of general interest, including the weekly *Department of State Bulletin* and the biweekly *Foreign Policy Briefs*.[19]

The department is just as interested in finding out what the public thinks as it is in explaining its policies to the public. The Policy Plans and Guidance Staff analyzes polls, reads resolutions and publications of organized groups, and digests daily more than ninety newspapers and sixty magazines. At one time the Staff contracted for scientific surveys so that it would be able to find out public views. But in 1957, angry congressmen cut off funds for these surveys after one poll showed general public support for foreign aid at a time when congressional mail was critical. Although this incident merely demonstrated the well-known fact that congressional mail may be unrepresentative of general opinion, congressmen felt that the survey information was being used by the Department of State to discredit congressional attitudes and as propaganda in behalf of the foreign aid programs.[20]

Public opinion does condition the making of foreign policy (even if diplomats are misinformed about the state of public opinion), and conversely, officials mold public opinion. These interrelations are dramatically illustrated by the events of the late 1930's. By 1937 President Roosevelt and his advisers had become convinced that Germany, Italy, and Japan threatened American security. They believed that the power of the United States had to be thrown behind England and France if the aggressors were to be prevented from controlling the Eurasian Continent. They hoped that a strong stand by the United States would swing the balance of power in favor of the democracies and deter the aggressors. In October 1937, President Roosevelt made his famous "quarantine the aggressor" speech in which he cautiously stated his position. But the public response, both inside and outside congressional chambers, was hostile. Most Americans still seemed to cling to the doctrines of nonintervention, neutrality, and freedom from entangling alliances. The people insisted upon neutrality laws that tied the executive's hands in the hope that if war came in Europe, we could stay out. So the President proceeded to move cautiously. Aided by the unfolding of events in Europe, he began to

[19] Robert E. Elder, *The Policy Machine: The Department of State and American Foreign Policy* (Syracuse Univ. Press, 1959), pp. 129–133.

[20] See full account in MacAlister Brown, "The Demise of State Department Public Opinion Polls: A Study in Legislative Oversight," *Midwest Journal of Political Science* (February 1961), pp. 1–17.

"educate" the public to support a more vigorous program. As public opinion became more favorable, the President gradually used the powers of his office to give as much aid and comfort to the democracies as public opinion would tolerate. But even as late as 1941, just prior to Pearl Harbor, public opinion was sharply divided. A large and vocal part of the population opposed the President's program. He had to move without the vigor and dispatch that many observers thought the crisis called for. The division of public opinion also obscured the intentions of the United States. Japanese and German leaders misjudged the significance of this division. They thought it meant that we would not have the unity needed to fight a war.

In Chapter 9 we noted that the American public is composed of hundreds of smaller publics, and that what we call "public opinion" is the complex interrelation and interaction of hundreds of interests, organized and unorganized. If the unorganized American public is indifferent to foreign politics, the same cannot be said of the organized publics and their spokesmen.

Organized Interests and Foreign Policy

The group and opinion leaders sprinkled through society—the priests and preachers, newspaper, radio, and TV commentators, teachers and public speakers—form an elite, an attentive public whose support is actively sought by the official policy-makers. State Department officials and the officials of the major interest groups often work together. The Department of State maintains relations with over four hundred national citizens' organizations, consulting with them and sending them materials and background information.[21]

What groups are most interested in foreign affairs? First of all there is a small, but very influential, group of citizens' organizations devoted to increasing the public's knowledge and understanding of international politics. These organizations do not agitate for the adoption of particular policies, but they do provide information and stimulate the discussion of issues. Many of them issue their own publications, and in their meetings they bring together influential citizens and public officials. The Council on Foreign Relations and the Foreign Policy Association are examples of organizations that have assumed such leadership responsibility. Other citizen organizations operate in much the same manner, although they are not exclusively concerned with foreign affairs. The League of Women Voters, for example, takes stands on particular issues and carries on campaigns to raise the level of citizen understanding.

Foreign policies so affect the domestic scene that inevitably the major interest groups of agriculture, labor, and business are closely involved. The big interest

---

[21] See analysis of group influence on Foreign Policy in Bernard C. Cohen, *The Influence of Non-Governmental Groups on Foreign Policy-Making* (World Peace Foundation, 1959); and Alfred O. Hero, *Voluntary Organizations in World Affairs Communication* (World Peace Foundation, 1960).

groups may represent such a wide cross-section of the general public, however, that they speak for broad national interests. Pacifist, patriotic, and veterans' organizations are also closely concerned with foreign policy. The patriotic and veterans' groups, for example, support large military appropriations whereas the pacifists oppose them. Farm, labor, and business interests have heavy economic stakes in foreign policy. Developments abroad affect businessmen's profits, farmers' markets, workers' jobs and wages.

Religious and national-origin publics are particularly interested in certain phases of foreign policy. These groups have intense feelings about some issues, and they are often strategically located to affect the outcome of elections. Although some scholars are skeptical about the importance of these groups, politicians are sensitive to the wishes of these articulate interests.[22] Some Americans of Irish origin, reflecting feelings aroused by English-Irish relations, are hostile toward Anglo-American cooperation. Many Americans of German origin voted against Roosevelt in 1940 because of his strong stand against Germany.[23] The attitude of Roman Catholics has been a significant factor in shaping American policy toward Spain both during the Spanish Civil War and after World War II. American policy toward Israel has been intimately affected by the pressures of American Zionists.

It is difficult to generalize about the impact of special interest groups on American foreign policies. Their influence appears to vary by type of issue and from time to time. At moments of international crisis the President is able to mobilize so much public support for his policies that specialized groups find it difficult to exert much influence.[24] Outside of the crisis areas, careful investigations into some areas of policy, such as reciprocal trade, fail to find that special groups have had a decisive role in the formulation of foreign policy.[25] And what is most difficult of all to determine is the impact on policy stemming from the policy-makers' *anticipations* of special interest group reactions.

Parties and Foreign Policy

Parties, as such, do not play a major role in shaping foreign policy, for two reasons: First, many Americans would prefer to keep foreign policy out of politics; party politics, they say, should "stop at the water's edge." Second, parties take even less clear and candid stands on foreign policy than they do on domestic policy. All the party weaknesses discussed earlier in this book operate in full measure in foreign policy making. Party platforms often obscure the issues instead of highlighting them; many congress-

[22] Louis L. Gerson, *The Hyphenate in Recent American Politics and Diplomacy* (Univ. of Kansas Press, 1964), p. 243.

[23] See also Lawrence H. Fuchs, "Minority Groups and Foreign Policy," *Political Science Quarterly* (June 1959), pp. 161–175.

[24] Nelson W. Polsby, *Congress and the Presidency* (Prentice-Hall, 1964), pp. 25–26.

[25] Raymond A. Bauer, Ithiel de Sola Pool, Lewis Anthony Dexter, *American Business and Public Policy: The Politics of Foreign Trade* (Atherton, 1963), p. 396. See also Cohen, *op. cit.*, p. 2.

men fail to follow even a very general party "line"; and the parties fail to discipline even the most outspoken rebels.

On the other hand, congressional voting in the 1950's did indicate that on some foreign-policy issues significant differences did exist between the major parties. Speaking very generally, congressional Democrats, especially northern Democrats, were more likely to support commitment of American troops and resources to back up our European allies, American participation in international organizations, proposals for foreign aid, and large military appropriations; and they gave first priority to European rather than to Asiatic defense against communism. Republicans, however, tended to look with suspicion on foreign aid programs, opposed tariff reductions, regarded more skeptically American participation in international organizations, viewed our European allies more critically, were more reluctant to support large military appropriations except during "all-out" war, and favored the use of American power in Asia rather than in Europe.[26] Additional investigations are needed before we can state with assurance whether these or some other partisan differences persist in the 1960's.

Should parties be concerned with foreign policy? At the end of World War II sentiment grew stronger for a "bipartisan approach" to foreign policy. An ambiguous term, bipartisanship seems to mean (1) collaboration between the executive and the congressional foreign policy leaders of both parties; (2) support of presidential foreign policies by both parties in Congress; (3) withdrawal of foreign policy issues from debate in political campaigns. In general, bipartisanship is an attempt to remove the issues of foreign policy from partisan politics. In its defense, it is argued that despite the internal differences that divide Americans, they all share a common interest with respect to other nations. During times of national danger we readily unite behind policies necessary to preserve the national well-being, and such unity is needed to support our foreign policies. American foreign policy, it is asserted, was ineffective following World War I because it became entangled in the partisan struggle between Democrats and Republicans.

Between 1942 and 1950, the leaders of the two parties, both in and out of Congress, worked closely together on foreign policy. Once policies were agreed upon, they received broad support from both parties in Congress and were not seriously debated in the political campaigns. Democrats supported the policies largely out of loyalty to the Democratic administration, and the Republicans at least partly because of their respect for Senator Vandenberg, the Republican foreign policy spokesman.[27] For the most part, the bipartisan policy was limited to programs calling for American participation in the United Nations and to policies of economic and military support for our European friends. Policy with respect to the Far East, however, won little bipartisan support.

[26] See Robert A. Dahl, *Congress and Foreign Policy* (Harcourt, Brace, 1950), pp. 229, 284–287. See also Ralph H. Smuckler, "The Region of Isolationism," *The American Political Science Review* (June 1953), pp. 386–401.

[27] For interesting perspectives on the role of Vandenberg in this period see Arthur H. Vandenberg, Jr., and Dean Acheson, "From Doubt to Leadership," in James D. Barber (ed.), *Political Leadership in American Government* (Little, Brown, 1964).

After 1950 bipartisanship began to break down. The problems of Asia took over the foreign affairs stage. During the 1952 elections Republicans bitterly attacked the Korean policies of the Truman administration and made foreign policy a central issue. However, with the election of President Eisenhower, the bipartisan approach reappeared. Except for the first two years of his first term, the Congress was controlled by Democrats, whose support President Eisenhower needed for legislation and appropriations. In the 1960 presidential elections Nixon and Kennedy jabbed at one another over the details of American policy on Quemoy and Matsu, but there were no major differences between them over our foreign policies. President Johnson and Secretary Rusk have included Republican congressional leaders in foreign policy discussions, and although some Republicans have criticized several of the President's foreign policy programs, by and large the Republicans have given it their full support. Goldwater's defeat in 1964 after his attacks on bipartisanship seemed to strengthen Johnson's "consensus foreign policy," at least for a time.

Is a Democratic Foreign Policy Possible?

Over a century ago, de Tocqueville wrote that democracies were decidedly inferior to other types of governments in the conduct of their foreign relations. "Foreign politics," he observed, "demand scarcely any of these qualities which are peculiar to a democracy; they require, on the contrary, the perfect use of almost all those in which it is deficient. . . . [A] democracy can only with great difficulty regulate the details of an important undertaking, persevere in a fixed design, and work out its execution in spite of serious obstacles. It cannot combine its measures with secrecy or await their consequences with patience." [28] More recent observers have expressed somewhat similar misgivings over the handling of foreign relations in the American democracy. Hans Morgenthau, for example, has observed that policy-makers "either . . . must sacrifice what they consider good policy upon the altar of public opinion, or they must by devious means gain support for policies whose true nature is concealed from the public." [29] How serious is this criticism? What role does the general electorate play in the making of foreign policy?

How Much Popular Control?

Democratic foreign policy making does not require that a general election be held before every decision is made. Everyone cannot be an expert; the people as a whole cannot actively take part in drawing up policy. "In the case of foreign affairs," it has been said, "where the

[28] Alexis de Tocqueville, *Democracy in America,* the Henry Reeve text (Knopf, 1945), Vol. 1, pp. 234–235.
[29] Hans Morgenthau, "The Conduct of American Foreign Policy," *Parliamentary Affairs* (Winter, 1949), p. 147.

given elements in a situation consist largely of the attitudes and intentions of foreign communities, to expect a very high level of information on the part of the electorate is utopian." [30] But it is equally unrealistic to conclude that the policy-makers can or should ignore the electorate. Foreign policies that commit American manpower and resources will have little success if Americans, through ignorance, apathy, or downright opposition, refuse to back them up. The electorate cannot fashion policy, but the voters can set limits on the extent of the policies they are willing to support. The people, too, have a positive responsibility to keep themselves informed on foreign issues. No matter how able the top officials, foreign policy cannot be formulated over the long run without the support of an informed electorate. Undoubtedly we need better ways of spreading information, of enlarging the opportunities for consideration and discussion.

Granting all this, however, the basic trouble in the United States is perhaps not so much democracy or democrats, but our particular set of institutional arrangements. Weak parties, strongly organized interests, halting legislative procedures—these difficulties disrupt democratic control of foreign policies in the same way that they threaten effective popular control of domestic policies. Indeed, some thoughtful observers believe that our governmental and political weaknesses in the foreign policy area are far more serious than in the domestic. We do not enjoy the margin for error, they argue, that we enjoy in internal affairs.

Presidential Power

In the face of these difficulties Americans have evolved two methods of achieving effective national action in foreign affairs. One is to vest wide powers in the President. The framers of the Constitution gave the Chief Executive a decisive role in foreign relations, as we have seen, and with the passage of time he has taken on new powers, such as frequent resort to executive agreements. This method has advantages. The President can act swiftly and decisively. He can see the more general interest above the clamor of the crowd and the tugging of special interests. He must face the people in elections, but not so often that he need follow public opinion instead of leading it. But there are disadvantages too. The President may bear responsibilities that are a tremendous load for one man. In a time of crisis—a time when he may see factors that most of the people do not see—the President may have to withhold information, or at least his own true opinions, from the people. Many of those who approved President Roosevelt's course in the year or two before Pearl Harbor would agree that the President, "when confronted by an apathetic public and a critical foreign menace, felt compelled to deceive the people into an awareness of their peril."

To what extent should the President be a leader in shaping our foreign policy? To what extent a follower? These questions go to the heart of democratic gov-

[30] Max Beloff, *Foreign Policy and the Democratic Process* (The Johns Hopkins Press, 1955), p. 58.

ernment. One answer, as we noted in Chapter 20, is that the President should act as leader of the majority party and should be responsible to that party. But again, institutional arrangements for party rule are lacking in this country. This brings us to the second method of evading the weakness of the American system of government.

Bipartisanship and Responsibility

The second method of evading the weaknesses of our government in foreign policy making is *bipartisanship*. Although bipartisanship means different things to different people, it is essentially an arrangement by which administration leaders consult with minority party leaders before making important decisions, *and by which both parties share responsibility for those decisions and their consequences.*

Bipartisanship has enormous appeal. In this era of chronic crisis, it seems to symbolize a people standing shoulder to shoulder as they face their enemies abroad. It provides more continuity of policy, and it insures that a wider variety of leaders and interests are consulted in foreign policy making. Psychologically, it helps to satisfy the instinct of people to turn to one another for reassurance. Its motto—"Partisan politics stops at the water's edge"—is comforting to the many Americans worried about disunity.

But the idea of bipartisanship has come under sharp attack. Critics charge that bipartisanship denies a basic tenet of democracy—the right of a people to choose between alternative lines of action. According to this argument, in a free society men should be allowed and even encouraged to differ. The need in a democracy is not to stifle differences, or to ignore them, or to elude them. The need is to express the differences in a meaningful way, to find the will of the majority, to permit the government to act and the opposition to oppose. This is where parties come in. They present alternatives. Because they want to win as many votes as possible, parties find common denominators in the views of millions of people. Because we have a two-party system, each party distills the essence of agreement from a medley of conflicting opinions. The party that wins a majority takes office. The losing party has the equally important job of furnishing opposition.

Thus parties—and partisanship—are vital to democracy. "Why should we abandon them at the water's edge?" ask the opponents of bipartisanship. Certainly not because Americans are agreed on foreign policy. The nation abounds with differences, as recent crises have made clear. Surely not because we hope to show a united front to our enemies. We cannot deceive them with a pretense of agreement. With their trained observers stationed in Washington and throughout the country, they know our differences as well as we do. Besides, our party divisions should be something to flaunt with pride—not something to be slammed into the closet whenever foreigners seem to be looking at us.

Even more serious, the critics conclude, bipartisanship erodes responsibility.

A great virtue of partisan government is that the men in office can be held to account simply because they hold authority. But when the leaders of both parties have their hands on the tiller, responsibility fades. After things go badly politicians begin the grand game of passing the buck. The leaders of each party maintain that it was the other gang that really steered the ship onto the rocks. Instead of a sober consideration of alternative courses of action, there is a frantic hunt for scapegoats.

Despite these criticisms, Americans will probably continue to resort to bipartisan arrangements in foreign policy making. The reason is clear. Our constitutional system encourages bipartisanship. The two-thirds requirement for ratification of treaties forces the President to rely on the support of the minority party. Moreover, in a time of international tension and crisis, democracies must *act*. Any device that will permit action without violating constitutional forms is indispensable. Bipartisanship permits action. So does broad presidential power. These methods may flout democratic ideals of responsibility and popular control, but they seem to be part of the price we must pay for living in a disorderly world of sovereign nations.

22 CONDUCTING FOREIGN RELATIONS

High-level foreign policy leaders deal mainly with the key issues of state. They work at the top of an iceberg-shaped governmental structure; the organization below them is wide and deep. The day-by-day administration, the handling of routine problems, and the decisions that do not immediately involve great discretion are in the hands of others. These thousands of men and women greatly influence high-level policies by gathering and evaluating data and by making the scores of little decisions out of which the big ones are often compounded. The President, Congress, the Secretary of State, and the people depend on these officials for information and advice, and for the execution of policy once it has been determined. What finally emerges as a policy decision is the product of many minds.

The Role of the State Department

The State Department is the key agency in the day-by-day routine of foreign relations. This department has five traditional duties. (1) It provides the President with the *information* he needs to conduct international relations. The department, through its missions abroad, collects data on political and economic events. The daily volume of telegraphic traffic alone between State and the embassies is estimated at 400,000 words! The department sorts and analyzes these reports, sends some to other interested departments, and some to the CIA. (2) The department assists the President in forming and implementing *policy*. It evaluates the information, makes recommendations to the President, the National Security Council, and others, or it makes decisions in the name of the President. (3) The department has the primary responsibility for *representing* the United States in our dealings with other nations and international organizations. Messages to and from other nations are routed through the department. (4) The department has the primary but not exclusive responsibility for carrying on *negotiations* with other nations and international organizations. Only 25 per cent of the United States representatives in 390 recent international meetings were from the Department of State, but in most cases the heads of the delegations were State Department men. (5) The department *coordinates* the activities of the many groups, agencies, and interdepartmental committees participating in the formulation and execution of foreign policy.

Organization

The organization of the Department of State reflects its two major activities: to advise on the formulation of policy and to handle the daily relations of the United States with other nations and international organizations. For many years the department handled its duties with a small staff. But with the steady growth of new activities and the emergence of the United States as a major world power, the organizational structure gradually became unwieldy. To improve its operations, the department has been reorganized eight times since January 1944. Though many critics still insist that the more it changes the more it stays the same, the department has probably become somewhat better organized to handle the problems of the modern world—although it remains a "vast, sprawling aggregation of specialists, career men, political appointees, and bureaucrats from other agencies—so much so that it is no longer feasible to present any meaningful chart of its structure smaller than a bed sheet." [1]

The policy-making and advisory activities of the department are centered in a team of high-ranking officers. At the top, of course, is the Secretary. Second in command is the Under Secretary, who, in addition to responsibility for the development and supervision of foreign economic policy, serves as Acting Secretary during the Secretary's absence. An Under Secretary for Economic Affairs works with the Secretary as a general policy adviser. Two Deputy Under Secretaries assist in the management and organization of the department. Specialized assistance to the Secretary of State comes from the Counselor, who is the senior policy adviser and consultant in the department, the Legal Advisors, and fourteen Assistant Secretaries. The Counselor is also chairman of the Policy Planning Council, a group of high-level officials who are freed from operating responsibilities so that they may evaluate current policy and formulate long-range policies. An Assistant Secretary for Congressional Relations supervises a small staff and points up the department's concern with maintaining proper liaison with the legislators.

The actual operations of the Department of State are organized along both functional and geographic lines. Seven bureaus, each under the direction of an assistant secretary, are responsible for major activities that cut across geographical boundaries: International Organization Affairs, Security and Consular Affairs, Economic Affairs, International Scientific and Technological Affairs, Intelligence and Research, Public Affairs, Congressional Relations, and Educational and Cultural Affairs.

Five regional bureaus, each under an assistant secretary, have become the pivot of the department's operations. Each bureau embraces a geographic area (Inter-American Affairs, European Affairs, Far Eastern Affairs, Near Eastern and South Asian Affairs, and African Affairs). Each bureau is broken into offices and these in turn are subdivided into what are known as country desks. The desk man is expected to have a thorough understanding of "his" country. "Almost every scrap of information which government agencies collect on an area and many policy papers from other agencies proposing action . . . cross the country desk, at a rate of 250 to 350 documents per day. . . . The Department's 114 country desk officers remain the eyes and ears, the brain and the voice, of America. . . . They keep daily watch over events in 179 political entities from Aden through Zanzibar." [2]

Inside the Department of State, but in a real sense not a part of it, are two so-called "semi-autonomous" agencies—the Agency for International Development and the Peace Corps.

The *Agency* for *International Development* (which took the place of the International Cooperation Administration, which took the place of the Foreign Operations Administration, which took the place of the Mutual Security Agency, which took the place of the Economic Cooperation Administration) operates

[1] Frederick L. Schuman, *International Politics*, 6th ed. (McGraw-Hill, 1958), p. 183.
[2] Robert E. Elder, *The Policy Machine* (Syracuse Univ. Press, 1959), p. 22.

under a director who reports to the Secretary of State. With its own staff of over 15,000 persons, AID handles this country's economic and technical assistance and coordinates most of the military aid programs. AID places greater emphasis on loans than on grants and insists that each country seeking American aid first put its own house in order to insure that the aid will lead to improved economic well-being for all the people, not just a privileged few. AID operates on the assumption that using our economic power to strengthen independent nations will improve the security of this country.

The *Peace Corps*, first established by President Kennedy by executive order in 1961 and then confirmed by Congress, is designed to place American volunteers in the newly developing nations to help fill the critical need for skilled manpower. The Peace Corps recruits, trains, and places volunteers willing to serve for periods of from one to three years. The volunteers teach, work in agricultural extension, community development, construction, medical services, and a wide range of other activities (see Epilogue).

The *United States Arms Control* and *Disarmament Agency* is not within the Department of State but its Director reports to the Secretary and the President on arms control and disarmament negotiations. The ACDA was established in 1961 to deal with the whole range of disarmament problems. It conducts research and sends representatives to, and prepares information for, disarmament negotiations. The 1963 test-ban treaty was based on an ACDA draft. In 1963 ACDA also took the lead in developing an agreement with the Soviet Union for the "hot-line" communications system to reduce the danger of an "accidental war" by insuring that Moscow and Washington would always be in contact.

The *United States Information Agency*, known as USIA, operates under the general policy guidance of the Secretary of State and the National Security Council; it controls all facets of our foreign informational programs. It maintains field offices in over one hundred foreign countries. The Voice of America broadcasts are well-known, but they are only a part of an elaborate program of explaining American foreign policies to people abroad. It was during World War II that the United States for the first time seriously began to use propaganda as an instrument of policy. Under the Office of War Information, an independent agency, propaganda was used in order to soften enemy morale and gain the support of neutral countries. All kinds of propaganda, "white" (objective and balanced), "black" (slanted), and "gray" (mixed), were used. Today the emphasis is on the use of *white* propaganda. In addition to radio broadcasts, the United States maintains libraries in foreign countries—recently the targets of anti-American violence in Indonesia and elsewhere— containing books and magazines about this country and its culture; we also conduct an elaborate program to help foreign students come to the United States for their education. Democracies in general and the United States in particular have been reluctant to establish propaganda bureaus, but the success of the Soviet Union in painting the United States as a country dominated by capitalist warmongers has forced us to engage in "campaigns of truth." The propaganda instrument is especially important in gaining the support of peoples in colonial areas where programs must be designed in terms of local idea-systems.[3]

The creation of "semi-autonomous" units reflects a compromise in the never-ending debate between those who believe the State Department should make policy but, except for the traditional instrument of diplomacy, leave its execution to others, and those who insist that we must coordinate all facets of foreign policy in a single agency.[4] Some believe that just as we unified the armed services into a single Defense Department, so we should unify the foreign policy agencies into a single Department of Foreign Affairs under a Secretary of Foreign Affairs. Into this new superdepartment they would place, each with its own secretary, the Department of State, a Department of Information and Cultural Affairs (consisting of the USIA and the educational and cultural bureaus now in the Department of State), and a Department of Foreign Economic Operations (consisting of the Agency for International Development).[5] Although Congress and President Johnson have given no indication of supporting a new Department of Foreign Affairs, Johnson has increased the control of the Department of State and the Secretary of State over the "semi-autonomous" agencies. But whatever the scheme of organization, foreign affairs touches so many interests and activities that inevitably some of them will be handled outside the Department of State.

Americans Overseas

American diplomacy is older than the United States. Even before the Revolution, Benjamin Franklin was sent as our representative to France by the Continental Congress. Today the United States maintains two hundred seventy-four posts abroad.

During our early years as a nation, the caliber of our overseas representation was high. Men like John Adams, Thomas Jefferson, and James Monroe served American interests in foreign capitals. But following the War of 1812, diplomatic posts were in the main used to reward persons for political activities. High diplomatic assignments were given to wealthy men who had contributed to the campaigns of victorious presidents. Since the salaries of diplomats were small and their expenses large, only men of independent means could afford to take

[3] Charles A. Thomson and Walter H. C. Laves, *Cultural Relations and U.S. Foreign Policy* (Indiana Univ. Press, 1963); and Wilson P. Dizard, *The Strategy of Truth: The Story Of The U.S. Information Service* (Public Affairs Press, 1961).

[4] For examples, see U.S. Commission on Organization of the Executive Branch of the Government, *Task Force Report on Foreign Affairs* (Government Printing Office, 1949), p. 15; The Brookings Institution, *The Administration of Foreign Affairs and Overseas Operations* (1951), p. xix; Arthur W. Macmahon, *Administration in Foreign Affairs* (Univ. of Alabama Press, 1953), p. 34 ff; U.S. Commission on Organization of the Executive Branch of the Government, *Overseas Economic Operations, A Report to the Congress* (Government Printing Office, 1955), p. 42.

[5] H. Field Haviland, Jr., *et al.*, *The Formulation and Administration of United States Foreign Policy* (The Brookings Institution, 1960), pp. 3–4. A Report for the Committee on Foreign Relations of the United States Senate.

posts in the more important nations. The *consular* offices were in particular demand because of "the fees that went into the consul's pocket; at big ports such as Hamburg and London, the yearly plunder often exceeded the salary of the President of the United States." [6] Various minor reforms were made, but it was not until 1924 that a modern career service was established. In that year the Rogers Act consolidated the diplomatic and consular service and provided for a Foreign Service of the United States established on a career basis. The service was further modernized and reorganized after World War II.

The elaborate protocol surrounding diplomacy gives an unwarranted impression of daintiness and mystery to the profession. Historical and popular novelists make out that diplomacy is the work of adroit and gallant heroes, voluptuous heroines, and scheming diplomats. Of course some diplomats are handsome and adept at making pretty compliments to beautiful ladies, but diplomacy is, as an experienced diplomat has written, a "grim business . . . a laborious business, singularly free from glamour and mystery."

The American Foreign Service

The American Foreign Service is the eyes and ears of the United States. Although a part of the State Department, the service represents the entire government and performs jobs for many other agencies. Almost 90 per cent of its reports go to departments other than State. Its main duties are to carry out foreign policy as expressed in the directives of the Secretary of State, gather data for American policy-makers, protect Americans and American interests in foreign countries, and cultivate friendly relations with foreign peoples. Although theoretically the service is only an instrument to assist policy leaders, the importance of the foreign service officer and his reports for policy-making are reflected in the quip, "foreign policy is made on the cables."

The Foreign Service is composed of ambassadors, ministers, officers, reserve officers, and staff.[7] At the core of the service are the Foreign Service officers, comparable to the officers of the regular army in the military services. It is a select, specially trained body of men and women who are expected to take an assignment at any place in the world on short notice. There are approximately 3,600 such officers; in most years over 200 junior officers are appointed. They have their own training school, the Foreign Service Institute, where new officers and their wives are briefed and where experienced officers get advanced instruction. Officers have either diplomatic or consular duties and provide the general direction of our missions abroad. As a small elite group, the Foreign Service has a high *esprit de corps*.

The Foreign Service is one of the most respected and most criticized branches

---

[6] J. Rives Childs, *American Foreign Service* (Holt, 1948), p. 6.

[7] See Epilogue for discussion of method of appointment and preparation for entering the Foreign Service, and detailed background in William Barnes and John Heath Morgan, *The Foreign Service of the United States* (Department of State, 1961).

of the national government. Recently the criticism seemed to outweigh the respect, and the service's morale suffered accordingly. In loyalty-security hearings, officers were asked to justify remarks sometimes taken out of context from confidential reports made years ago to their superiors. Critics accused the service of being infiltrated by communist sympathizers; others charged that it was dominated by a high-society elite who were still under the impression that diplomacy was 'the business of "gentlemen." It is more important, said the critics, that our diplomats understand the social and economic problems of the Chinese peasant, for example, than to know how to behave at a fashionable cocktail party. The charges about communist infiltration were undoubtedly overdrawn, as were claims that the service was preoccupied with refined manners. The latter charges probably stemmed in part from the conventional stereotype of a diplomat. Still, most of the personnel of the service did come from the same general social background—a fact that cut down on the effectiveness of their total reporting, for every reporter, no matter how objective he tries to be, selects and evaluates what he sees on the basis of his own attitudes and "picture of the world."

Prior to 1954 most stateside positions within the Department of State were held by civil service employees whose salary and retirement systems were less favorable than those of the Foreign Service but who had no obligation to serve outside the United States. Since the Foreign Service was small, there was little opportunity to bring officers back for a tour of duty in Washington. Consequently, it was charged that they had lost contact with American domestic conditions. At the same time, the civil service employees with little or no service abroad often failed to understand other nations, appreciate foreign conditions, or sympathize with the job of the men working abroad. Friction occurred be-

"The U.S. Embassy? Just follow us, we're on our way there right now." (Drawing by O'Brian, Copr. © 1958 The New Yorker Magazine, Inc.)

tween the two groups: The Foreign Service officers felt that their system of selection and obligation to serve abroad made them an elite corps; the civil service
employees felt that the Foreign Service officers were limited in viewpoint and
got excessively high salaries, sometimes for doing the same kind of job assigned
to civil service people.[8]

Between 1949 and 1954 five commissions or special committees studied the For-
eign Service. All recommended that there should be a single service to staff both
overseas and Washington positions, all persons being obliged to serve where needed.
The most recent group to endorse this proposal was the Secretary of State's Public
Committee on Personnel, popularly known after the name of its chairman as the
Wriston Committee, which was appointed after the attacks on the loyalty of the
Foreign Service had led to a decline in morale and to a loss of public confidence.
The committee emphasized that the integration of the civil service and the Foreign
Service would bring into the Foreign Service highly trained specialists to balance
the Foreign Service tradition of selecting and training "generalists." The com-
mittee also recommended that the service avoid choosing so many of its men
from the Harvard-Yale-Princeton axis and improve its training program.[9]

Finally, in 1954, Congress authorized an expansion of the service to bring
within the Foreign Service most of the State Department's policy positions.
Holders of these positions, wherever qualified, were given a chance to accept a
Foreign Service commission, carrying with it both a higher salary and the obligation to serve abroad. It was hoped that this expansion of the Foreign Service
would give Foreign Service officers a stateside assignment at least after every
six-year tour abroad.

Except for clerical, custodial, and administrative jobs, key positions in the
State Department are now held by members of the Foreign Service. The Foreign
Service Reserve, really misnamed, permits the Secretary to appoint specialists to
serve for a temporary period. Foreign Service Staff now consists of technical,
clerical, and custodial personnel. Steps are also being taken, in compliance with
the other recommendations of the Wriston Committee, to recruit more men and
women from colleges, to make the examinations less costly, and to place less emphasis on "personality" and "foreign service characteristics." [10]

Operations Overseas

The United States has missions
in the capital cities of almost all nations with whom we carry on diplomatic relations. In addition, we maintain permanent missions at the North Atlantic Treaty

[8] U.S. Commission on Organization of the Executive Branch of the Government, *Foreign Affairs* (Government Printing Office, 1949), p. 62.
[9] Report of the Secretary of State's Public Committee on Personnel, *Toward A Stronger Foreign Service*, Department of State Publication 5458 (Government Printing Office, 1954).
[10] For a fuller treatment of personnel in the service see Barnes & Morgan, *op. cit.*, Parts IV and V; Elder, *op. cit.*, pp. 181–214; and Zara S. Steiner, *The State Department and the Foreign Service* (Princeton University Center of International Studies, 1958).

Organization, European regional organizations, and the United Nations. The heads of these missions, designated by the President with the consent of the Senate, hold the ranks of ambassador, minister, or *chargé d'affaires*. Historically, ambassadors were sent to the larger and more important countries, but now we maintain embassies (each headed by an ambassador) in almost all countries. Until recently, diplomatic posts were filled primarily by political appointees, some of whom had little knowledge of foreign affairs. As late as 1958 we were represented in France, Italy, Germany, and ten other important capitals by ambassadors, none of whom could speak the native tongue. Today, despite the tremendous expansion in the number of nations to which we now send representatives, more than 70 per cent of the chiefs of missions are Foreign Service officers, many of whom are competent in the language of the nation to which they are assigned. The average tour of duty of chiefs of missions in recent years has been under three years, too short a time, however, for them to develop high language competence in all posts or to secure a deep understanding of the complex problems of the nations to which they are assigned.

Diplomatic missions located in capital cities are chiefly concerned with political and economic relations between governments. *Consular offices*, though part of the Foreign Service, are largely concerned with the activities of individuals. Consuls are not official representatives to other governments, but serve as public agents to promote the commercial interests and protect the citizens of their own state. Their powers and privileges are determined by arrangement with the countries concerned. Consular officers are ranked in descending order: consul general, consul, vice-consul, and consular agents. The latter are not members of the Foreign Service and operate in less important places.

In order to get a better idea of the many duties of the Foreign Service, let us look at the activities of a typical American mission.

Americans in New Delhi

On Shantipath—"Path of Peace" —in New Delhi stands a handsome modern building designed by an American architect in an eastern style. This is the American Embassy, in its diplomatic enclave in India's capital city. The entire United States mission operates out of eight office buildings in this enclave and outside, spends almost $3 million a year directly on its own activities, helps administer over $650 million in loans and grants to India, and employs about 1,800 Americans and over 3,000 Indians. A dozen local units of major Washington departments and agencies—Commerce, Agriculture, the Peace Corps, for example—are attached to the Embassy. The Ambassador —and New Delhi has received such distinguished American envoys as J. Kenneth Galbraith and Chester Bowles—is the ranking American representative in India and is responsible for coordinating all activities of the mission.

The Embassy is divided into three major sections: The *Division of Political-Economic Affairs*, created in 1965, is unique among American embassies; it consolidates the former Political, Economic, and Political-Military Affairs Division. This division is divided into the External Section, which informs the State Department of developments in India's political, military, and economic relations with other nations, and the Internal Section, which analyzes and reports on India's internal economic policies and political affairs—for example, parliamentary debates, election results, economic development, language and communal problems, Kashmir. The *Consular Division* coordinates the activities of the various consular offices throughout India, which provide Americans in India the same services as secretaries of chambers of commerce, justices of the peace, notaries public, commissioners of immigration and naturalization, and Veterans Administration officials furnish at home. It examines applicants for admission to the United States, issues permits to exporters of goods to the United States, administers customs laws, and the like. The *Administrative Division* runs the financial, personnel, and other administrative services of the mission.

Two key agencies are organized separately from the Embassy but operate under the Ambassador's general direction. The USAID (U.S. Agency for International Development) Mission in India is the largest in the world, as is the economic aid program in India. USAID gives both development grants and loans for industry, agriculture, health, education, and other activities. It has made grants for malaria and smallpox eradication, craftsman training, dairy development, crop production. The U.S. Information Service in India is also the largest USIS post in the world. USIS sponsors exchanges of persons and cultural programs in India; visits by American specialists; science, art, and book exhibits; and film shows. The Information Section is a huge publishing operation in itself. It puts out the *American Reporter*, a newsy fortnightly filled with features and pictures about American and Indian affairs; *Span*, an attractive monthly magazine that stresses current issues in both countries and cooperation between them; a cultural and intellectual quarterly; and vast numbers of press releases, texts of important speeches, feature stories, and photographs for use by Indian newspapers and magazines.

And then there is the Peace Corps. Once again, India has more "PCV's" (Peace Corps Volunteers) than any other country—around 1,000. As in other countries, the PCV's work far from the glittering embassy—in the grass roots on such matters as auto mechanics, health, rural community action, and farming.

Other Americans Overseas

The Foreign Service has competitors. Of the tens of thousands of Americans employed abroad, exclusive of the armed services, only about 17,000 are Foreign Service personnel. Prior to 1939 the Departments of Commerce, Agriculture, Treasury, and others had their own overseas staff. In that year, however, the principle was established that there should be but one foreign service, and that all American employees in a foreign country should be responsible to the chief of mission. Services of the Commerce and Agriculture Departments were merged with those of the Foreign Service. During the war, however, many agencies set up their own offices. The diplomatic missions in many cases were overshadowed, and friction and lack of coordination resulted. The American ambassador in England was not even kept informed of various matters affecting Anglo-American relations, and was all but superseded by the American lend-lease expediter.

After World War II many of these agencies were abolished and some of their duties and personnel were assigned to diplomatic and consular missions. But as postwar programs developed, the principle that the United States should have but one overseas arm was again violated and separate overseas missions were frequently established. In the decade since the Second Hoover Commission recommended the creation of a single integrated foreign service system (except for the military) with overseas personnel of all agencies incorporated into the embassy and subject to the authority of the ambassador, the number of separate agencies representing the United States overseas has increased rather than diminished. The United States Information Agency, the Agency for International Development, and the CIA have their own overseas career services. In many countries a Military Assistance Advisory Group reports directly to the Pentagon, and in some countries there are operating military commands. In some countries, because of our representation at international agencies, there is more than one American ambassador: For an extreme example, there are four American ambassadors in Paris—the ambassador to France, to NATO, to the Organization for Economic Cooperation and Development, and to the Development Assistance Committee.

As a matter of official protocol, the ambassador is the President's representative and outranks all other Americans, including even the Vice President and Secretary of State when they visit the country of his mission. Recent Presidents have issued directives to clarify the ambassador's primacy and his responsibility for coordinating all American activities in the country of his mission. In many nations, the ambassador chairs a regular committee known as "The Country Team," consisting of the heads of all agencies operating within the country. But in fact the primacy of the ambassador remains a polite fiction. Overseas personnel continue to deal directly with their organizational superiors in Washington, especially on important matters of budget and program. The Jackson Subcommittee recommended that Washington officials consult with our ambassador before assigning key personnel to the country of his mission and give him a voice in budgetary decisions that affect programs in the nation to which he is assigned. It is unlikely, however, that coordination of our agencies overseas can proceed any faster than the efforts to coordinate programs in Washington.

The United States and International Organizations

The United States is an international joiner. Today it belongs to all the most important world organizations, and its representatives attend all major international conferences. The story of how the United States failed to join the League of

Nations but took the leading role in the formation of the United Nations is well-known. But not so many people realize that the international organization, and the international conference are major weapons of American diplomacy. In addition to the United Nations and its related agencies, the United States is a member of well over two hundred international organizations of various types. Slowly but steadily certain functions are being transferred from the national to the international level.

In its own hemisphere the United States is a member of the *Organization of American States*, a regional agency consisting of 20 American republics. (Canada has never been a member and Castro's Cuba was expelled in 1962.) A *Council* of the Organization forms a continuing group. It consists of one representative from each member state with the rank of ambassador. Decisions of the Council are not subject to a veto, but decisions of security matters are made by a second organ of the OAS, *Meetings of the Ministers of Foreign Affairs*. Any threat of aggression is dealt with by the ministers, two-thirds of whom are necessary for decisions to be binding on all members, except that no state can be required to use its armed forces without its own consent. *Inter-American Conferences* meet about once every five years and special conferences are called occasionally. The famous Pan-American Union serves as the General Secretariat for OAS. There are also several specialized organizations that operate within the framework of OAS, including the Inter-American Economic and Social Council, the Inter-American Cultural Council, and the Inter-American Defense Board.

The United Nations

The United States maintains a permanent diplomatic mission at the headquarters of the United Nations. This mission is headed by a chief holding the rank of ambassador who has Cabinet status, and includes three other leading diplomats, all appointed by the President with the advice and consent of the Senate. In addition, the President, with the consent of the Senate, appoints five representatives to the General Assembly, who serve for the duration of a particular session. The chief of the mission is responsible for coordinating the actions of our many delegates to other divisions of the U.N. Within the Department of State, a separate Bureau of International Organization Affairs coordinates American policies and activities with other federal agencies, helps to prepare instructions to our representatives, serves as technical adviser to them, spreads information to the public and the department regarding the United Nations, and assumes general responsibility for American participation.

The United Nations is an organization designed to bring nations together to maintain international peace and security, to develop friendly relations, to achieve international cooperation in solving world problems, to promote and encourage respect for human rights, and to harmonize the actions of nations in attaining these common goals. Although basically an association of nations, the United Nations is an international legal personality with the power to make treaties and competence to claim reparations for injury to its agents. It maintains its own legal staff, operates its own headquarters, and has its own flag. The major United Nations organs are the Security Council, the General Assembly, the Social and Economic Council, the Trusteeship Council, the Secretariat, and the International Court of Justice.

The United Nations' failure to solve each and every dispute among the nations of the world, and its inability to resolve the conflict between the East and West, have caused some Americans to become disillusioned with it. Part of their disillusionment stems from their failure to understand the nature of the organization. The United Nations is essentially the collective name of over 110 nations who have organized themselves in order to facilitate cooperation. It is a diplomatic technique that simplifies the problem of multilateral consultation. The United Nations, unlike the United States of America, is not an entity separate and above its member states. Its power is the power of the nations of the world. What the United Nations can do is what the member nations want to do.

The United Nations is a useful organization for diplomatic consultation. It provides techniques and machinery for discussion, for working out joint plans of action, and for establishing international machinery to handle world-wide problems. As such it has been a useful device by which the United States has been able to carry on its relations with the other nations of the world. But the United Nations, like every other agency of international politics, is affected by the fact that the world is divided into separate national sovereignties.

Conducting Foreign Relations—Three Case Studies

Foreign policy is not made according to any set formula. A great deal depends on the nature of the issue, the speed with which the problem arises, the personality of the President, the political situation, and the accidents of history. Seldom does Congress initiate policy; more often it is the President, the Secretary of State, the Joint Chiefs of Staff, or an ambassador. Each problem calls for new decisions; each decision creates new problems. The initiative is sometimes in the hands of our government, but unfortunately it is more often in the hands of other governments. To search for the origins of any particular policy, to isolate the critical areas, to focus on the alternatives, is not our purpose here. In the following cases we shall merely suggest the way in which the machinery works.

The Marshall Plan

In 1947 all Europe was in dire need of economic assistance. Much was already being done by the United States through the various branches of the government. But it seemed likely that unless a greater and broader program was adopted, European economies would be subject to such stresses and strains that the situation would become highly unstable.

On March 8, 1947, Under Secretaries Acheson and Clayton discussed the emergency with the President. On May 8, Acheson in a speech at Cleveland, Mississippi, outlined the situation. This was the administration's trial balloon to sound out public and congressional opinion. The department, meanwhile, consulted Senator Vandenberg, who warned that a carefully prepared long-range program had to be worked out. The State Department's Policy Planning Staff advised that European nations should take the initiative and work out the plan. Secretary of State Marshall approved, but insisted that all Europe, including Russia, be included in the program. Meanwhile, the State Department experts published a study on *The Development of the Foreign Reconstruction Policy of the United States*.

On June 5, the Secretary made a commencement address at Harvard University. Instead of an "as I look at your bright and shining faces" speech, Secretary Marshall took advantage of the opportunity to make a major policy statement. He described the serious situation in Europe and the need for American help. But the initiative, he said, must come from Europe. The United States should aid in the drafting of a European recovery program and later support such a program.

The U.S.S.R. and her satellites refused to participate, but the other European nations "seized the proposal with both hands." Soon, sixteen nations met in Paris and formed the Committee of European Economic Cooperation. Within the United States, groups of specialists, calling on consultants and experts outside the government, made reports covering every phase of European recovery. The State Department studied these reports and advised the President. Congress was not in session, but on November 10 Secretary Marshall appeared before a joint session of the Senate Foreign Relations Committee and the House Committee on Foreign Affairs. He outlined a program calling for an appropriation of over $6 billion for the first fifteen months of the program, which was to run for four years.

President Truman then called a special session of Congress. The legislators were presented with a proposed bill by the State Department, and administration officials made numerous appearances before committees and addresses to the public. Three special committees, composed of over 350 State Department employees, were set up in the department to work out the details of the program.

Congressmen had their own ideas. Many of them were unconvinced that such vast expenditures were needed to protect American national interests. Then, occurring between February 23–25, 1948, the communist coup in Czechoslovakia startled the world. Congress quickly approved the legislation, but not without amendments. The House included Franco Spain in the program, contrary to the wishes of the President and the Department of State, but aid to Spain was defeated in conference committee.

The Foreign Assistance Act of 1948 was passed on April 3. The next step was to secure the appropriations. The chairman of the House Committee on Appropriations was interested in saving money, and despite the fact that the House had previously approved the program, he recommended and the House approved a billion-dollar reduction in the program. Senator Vandenberg used his great prestige to have the amount restored, and except for the fact that the money was authorized for only a year instead of fifteen months, the final program was substantially as requested. The administration of the program was vested, however, not in the Department of State, but in a separate Economic Cooperation Administration.

The Marshall Plan was initiated by the President and the State Department, but approved by Congress, both houses of which were controlled by the opposite party to that of the Chief Executive. The leaders of the State Department and of Congress worked closely together, consulting on the details and collaborating in securing approval. Not all decisions, however, require congressional approval or permit public discussion, as the following cases indicate.

A Decision Not to Go to War

On March 20, 1954, General Paul Ely, then French Chief of Staff, arrived in Washington to tell the President, Secretary of State Dulles, and Chairman of the Joint Chiefs of Staff Admiral Arthur W. Radford that unless the United States intervened Indo-China would be lost to the communists.[11]

Some time immediately thereafter—the exact date is unknown—the National Security Council was called into special session. There Admiral Radford, Vice President Nixon, and Secretary Dulles agreed that Indo-China must not be allowed to fall into communist hands lest it set off a "falling row of dominoes" across all Southeast Asia. The council decided that if necessary the United States should intervene, provided it could obtain the support of its allies and the French would grant Indo-China its independence. A policy paper was prepared, initialed "D.D.E." by the President to make it official.

The President had the constitutional power to put this policy into effect, but, as we have noted, President Eisenhower usually refused to make any major foreign-policy commitment without prior congressional approval. So on April 3, 1954, eight congressmen, the foreign-policy leaders of both parties, were called to a secret conference with Secretary Dulles. When they entered the State Department's fifth-floor conference room, they found that Admiral Radford and several high Defense Department officials were also present. The Secretary told the congressmen that the President wanted a joint resolution from Congress permitting the President to use air and naval power in Indo-China. (Constitutionally, the President as commander in chief already had this power.) Admiral Radford warned the congressmen that French forces under siege in Dienbienphu could not hold out much longer and that the fall of Indo-China would endanger all of Southeast Asia. If Congress passed the resolution, the Admiral said, the Navy and Air Force would be used for a single strike to attempt to break the siege.

---

11 The materials on the Indo-China decision are drawn from Chalmers M. Roberts, "The Day We Didn't Go to War," *The Reporter* (September 14, 1954), pp. 31–35.

The congressmen, both Republicans and Democrats, asked, "Would this mean war?" Would Communist China intervene on the other side? Radford, who long believed that a showdown with the Chinese communists was inevitable and who felt that the sooner it came the better, minced no words: "Yes." Would land forces have to be used? No one could say for sure. As the talk continued, only Senator Knowland, Republican Senate leader, supported Dulles and Radford, and it became clear to the congressmen that the other Chiefs of Staff did not agree with Radford. Dulles, moreover, had not consulted our allies; he explained that it would take too long and that emergency action was needed if Dienbienphu was to be saved. Finally, the congressmen told Dulles that before they would try to get a joint resolution from Congress, which would in effect commit the nation to war, the Secretary should first line up the allies. Even Knowland now was cool to intervention.

Within a week Dulles had talked with the diplomatic representatives in Washington of Britain, France, Australia, New Zealand, the Philippines, Thailand, and the three Associated States of Indo-China. Dulles urged these nations to be ready at the time of U.S. military action with a statement defending our intervention and warning the Chinese communists against entering the war. Messages flashed back and forth. Our allies were opposed.

Dulles flew to London to talk personally with Prime Minister Churchill and Foreign Secretary Anthony Eden, but he could find little enthusiasm for American plans. Nor were the British any more ready to favor American military intervention after Dulles proposed the creation of a Southeast Asia Treaty Organization to serve as the vehicle for "united action." When Dulles returned to Washington and called for a drafting meeting on April 20 to set up SEATO, London instructed the British Ambassador not to attend.

A few days later Dulles flew back to Paris. The situation was more alarming than ever; when Radford arrived in Paris he told Dulles that only a massive air attack could save Dienbienphu. On April 24 Dulles and Radford informed Eden that if the allies would agree, the President was prepared to go to Congress the next day, ask for a joint resolution, and then set the military strike for April 28. Under Secretary of State Walter Bedell Smith, who also supported intervention, gave the same proposal to the French Ambassador in Washington.

Eden balked. He said that coming on the eve of the Geneva Conference—which had been called in part to discuss means to end the seven-year Indo-China war—American military action would be disastrous. He was convinced it would lead to the use of ground troops and the spread of fighting to Communist China. Eden agreed, however, to carry the matter before the English Cabinet. But on Saturday, April 24, word came from the British Cabinet: "No support." On the following Tuesday, Churchill told the House of Commons that the British government was not prepared to undertake any military action in Indo-China. Reluctantly, Dulles concluded that the United States would not intervene. Dienbienphu fell, and eventually an agreement was reached to end the Indo-China war. But that agreement brought only a temporary cessation of hostilities in what became the divided nation of Vietnam.

Intervention in Santo Domingo

Late in April, 1965, President Johnson summoned congressional leaders to the White House for an emergency meeting. He bluntly told them that he had ordered the landing of a detachment of marines in the Dominican Republic to protect American interests endangered by a civil war that had been raging there for over four days. He pointedly did not ask for authority to take this action but wanted Congress to know about it before the public did. Shortly thereafter the President went before the American people on TV and radio: ". . . I have ordered the Secretary of Defense to put the necessary American troops ashore in order to give protection to hundreds of Americans who are still in the Dominican Republic and to escort them safely back to this country." This first direct military intervention in Latin America by the United States since marines landed in Nicaragua in 1927 incited charges at home and abroad of "Yankee imperialism" and "gunboat diplomacy."

What lay behind this intervention? Administration officials in the 1960's had hoped that the Dominican Republic would become a "showcase of democracy," as millions of Alliance for Progress dollars were channeled into the country. Political instability frustrated these dreams. The Dominicans had known only one period of calm—from 1930 until 1961 under the iron hand of Dictator Trujillo. An assassin's bullet ended his regime, but a broadly based popular rule did not develop.

From 1961 to 1965 the nation saw four coups and five changes of government. In December, 1962, a valid election was won by Juan Bosch, an idealistic, well-known Latin American literary figure. A powerful military junta headed by General Wessin y Wessin sent Bosch to a Puerto Rican exile the following September; the military had feared that Bosch's left-leaning regime was opening the door too widely for communist participation in the nation's affairs. The military leaders installed a new civilian regime, which ruled until April 1965, when a group of junior military officers and Bosch supporters led by Colonel Francisco Caamaño Deñó seized the radio station, announced that the nation was in a state of siege, and asked the citizenry to rise up and help return the country to constitutional rule. Arms were freely distributed to the people. A military junta, led again by Wessin, regained control from the civilian government and attempted to crush the uprising. Within a week a reported 2,000 Dominicans were dead.

It was in this atmosphere that Ambassador William Tapley Bennett, Jr., requested help from Washington. The 2,400 Americans and many foreign nationals needed protection and evacuation, the ambassador pleaded by telephone, as he himself sought refuge from shattering glass under his embassy desk. The CIA also reported to President Johnson that over fifty communists were known to be among the rebel ranks, although the extent of their involvement was not immediately known. The President acted. Some 500 marines from the aircraft carrier *Boxer* were sent ashore. Within two weeks a force of 32,000 American fighting men were on the scene, along with a flotilla of ships and 275 aircraft. This intervention brought most of the fighting to a halt. Rebel leader Caamaño and an estimated

12,000 rebels were confined to a two-square-mile sector of Santo Domingo. An American-imposed corridor prevented the junta troops from moving in on the rebels. A truce and an uneasy calm lasted for some months. The pressing need involved maintaining vital governmental services and negotiating a settlement between the warring factions. American dollars were used to meet the payrolls of civil servants and the military of both the junta and rebel factions. American troops distributed food and medicine to the citizenry.

Finding a government suitable to both factions turned out to be nearly an insoluble problem. President Johnson dispatched a personal envoy, John Bartlow Martin, who had been U.S. ambassador to Santo Domingo during the Bosch regime and who was a personal friend of the deposed leader. As a result of his mission, the three-man junta headed by Wessin was replaced by a more broadly based five-man junta composed of both civilians and military. Heading this group, which became known as the Government of National Reconstruction, was Brigadier General Antonio Imbert Barreras. Imbert was in some measure a national figure, since he had participated in the assassination of Trujillo, and it was hoped that he might be acceptable to the rebels. His close association with Wessin's military faction, however, precluded support from the rebels.

Thus the United States was not only interposing itself between rival military and political factions, it was also going so far as to help form a compromise government. Was this not a violation of the OAS Charter? After all, Article 15 states that no member country ". . . has the right to intervene, directly or indirectly, for any reason whatever, in the internal or external affairs of any other state." The United States' position was a difficult one to defend, especially since it was currently predicating its Vietnam policy on the principle of self-determination. To gain a measure of legitimacy for the action, President Johnson instructed Ellsworth Bunker, U.S. representative to the OAS, to propose the creation of a precedent-setting, inter-American peace force which would take America's place as a Dominican policeman. Under this plan, member states would send troops to serve under a unified command. As these troops became available, the U.S. would withdraw its forces. Many nations of Latin America had disapproved of the U.S. action and acceptance of this plan was not a foregone conclusion. A great deal of U.S. pressure, however, resulted in approval by a 14 to 5 vote, barely the two-thirds margin necessary for acceptance. Voting against this plan were Mexico, Peru, Chile, Ecuador, and Uraguay, with Venezuela abstaining. After the vote, Johnson sent veteran trouble-shooter Averell Harriman to the various capitals to stimulate participation in the peace force. By the end of the second month of the crisis, Brazilian General Alvim had relieved the American commander, and the 18,000 man peace force had started taking on a genuine inter-American complexion.

OAS action, while relieving somewhat the onus of U.S. occupation, did not solve the problem of bringing political stability to the embattled nation. The U.S. continued its unilateral action in this regard. In May, President Johnson dispatched a top-level team of advisers to Santo Domingo: his Special Assistant for National Security Affairs McGeorge Bundy along with high officials from the Departments of State and Defense. This was more than a fact-finding mission. It was a sales effort in behalf of the new U.S. candidate for provisional president, Antonio Guzmán, who had been Bosch's Minister of Agriculture. A few days before, Guzmán had been flown to Washington, approved by officials, and returned to Santo Domingo. On the way south, the Bundy mission stopped off in Puerto Rico and secured Bosch's approval of Guzmán. In Santo Domingo, rebel chief Caamaño agreed to Guzmán's presidency, but Imbert disagreed on the grounds that he was a mere Bosch puppet and completely unacceptable to the junta. Besides, Imbert viewed *his* government as a broadly based one worthy of support, and he felt it should be allowed to wipe out the rebels. Thus the Bundy mission ended in failure.

In June a three-man OAS peace team arrived in Santo Domingo to help OAS Secretary General Jose A. Mora negotiate a settlement. This was the seventh peace-seeking mission in six weeks. This team recommended that a provisional government of non-political businessmen and professors rule under a special institutional act prepared by local jurists. It also felt that the OAS should remain on the scene to keep peace and to supervise elections in six to nine months. By July both sides had agreed upon a provisional president, Héctor García Godoy, foreign minister under Bosch. Negotiations snagged, however, on other important-matters, such as who would control the military. Imbert, of course, insisted that his associates would exercise military leadership in the new government. As in the past, the military in the Dominican Republic occupied a pivotal position.

The Johnson Administration found that military intervention was infinitely simpler than finding a workable political arrangement. It is clear that U.S. action was in the last analysis a continuation of the policy of containment; Washington would not tolerate any more Castros or Cubas in Latin America. In his public statements, President Johnson felt the action had served its purposes:

> I think the Dominican Republic was a successful achievement. One hour after the order, troops had been landed. We brought out 5,614 people from 46 countries without a skinned ankle. . . . But we don't have a Cuba. I told them, I told the other countries, we're not going to sit here on our tails and have these people take over. We're going to have some kind of an agreement and we're going to have an election, which no Communist government would ever have allowed them to have.[12]

The imminence of a communist take-over was not universally recognized. Juan Bosch, in whose behalf the revolt was originated, characterized this as ". . . a democratic revolution smashed by the leading democracy of the world." Should the President have consulted more closely with Congress—even asked for formal authorization? Did quick unilateral action by the United States prevent a communist take-over in the Dominican Republic? Or did the U.S. actually prevent a popularly based government from returning to power? Did U.S. action save or permanently disable the OAS as an instrument of inter-American endeavor? The crisis had raised these old questions in a new context.

[12] Quoted in *Newsweek*, August 2, 1965, p. 21.

23 TO PROVIDE FOR THE COMMON DEFENSE

At 8:15 on the morning of August 6, 1945, an A-bomb hurtled down toward the city of Hiroshima. At that moment there were 340,000 people living there. One minute later only 280,000 were left alive; of these, 20,000 more were to die from injuries. A total of 80,000 men, women, and children were killed by this single bomb; tens of thousands more were injured and maimed. This was a small bomb. Two day later another bomb, an "improved model"—was dropped on Nagasaki.

599

Seven years later in the Central Pacific, a deserted island was destroyed by a fusion-type bomb—the hydrogen bomb, a device whose power far surpassed the earlier A-bomb. Spectacular improvements in nuclear weapons technology since then has all but exhausted the supply of superlatives. Capable of delivery by intercontinental missile, the modern thermonuclear device, with its devastating blast and deadly fall-out, has added a dimension of destruction to modern warfare that strains the imagination.

The extent of the destruction which man may wreak upon himself is virtually limitless. We live in a world in which literally hundreds of millions could be killed in a single night. While there is much dispute over precise numbers and extent of destruction, an entirely conceivable attack on the United States in the late 1960's could kill about 140 million people in the first 60 days. The number would continue to mount over a longer period as fall-out, lack of food, shelter, and medicine all took their toll.[1] Winston Churchill warned that it might no longer be possible "for nations to fight each other and survive as nations, or even for armies to fight a battle and have at the end of it enough men on either side to fight another." [2] The age of absolute weapons has arrived.

To some, the fact that men are able to destroy their fellow men by the millions brings the hope that they will forego such a foolish venture. To others, it means that modern civilization is doomed. But most agree that the United States must pay a high price to maintain security in a world of absolute weapons. Not only is the United States open to attack every minute of the day and night, but in any major war we would undoubtedly be the prime target. No longer will we have a year or two to mobilize our military might while our traditional allies hold the enemy from our shores. If an all-out thermonuclear war comes, it will be too late to start to build up our military strength. What, then, are the elements of a defense program?

First and foremost, we have to be powerful enough not only to win the next war, but to avoid it. We need military power of such proportions that any potential aggressor would be reluctant to attack the United States or its allies. This military power must be ready at a moment's notice to strike a stupendous retaliatory blow.

Second, in addition to massive retaliatory forces, we need mobile units for limited wars, to resist aggressions of a local nature, and to achieve objectives in situations where it would be suicidal to use major nuclear weapons.

Third, not only must we have powerful offensive forces, but also strong defenses at home to complement our deterrent military power. If we make an inviting target, the enemy may be persuaded to believe that he could knock us out in a single blow and destroy our ability to retaliate.[3]

---

[1] Arthur T. Hadley, *The Nation's Safety and Arms Control* (Viking, 1961), pp. 34–35. See also Secretary Robert S. McNamara's testimony before the House Armed Services Committee, Feb. 18, 1964, *The New York Times*, Feb. 19, 1964, p. 10.

[2] Paraphrase of Churchill by Roger Hilsman, *Military Policy and National Security*, William W. Kaufmann (ed.) (Princeton Univ. Press, 1956), p. 44.

[3] See J. David Singer, "Stable Deterrence and its Limits," *Western Political Quarterly* (September 1962), pp. 449–464, for a discussion of the elements of deterrence.

Friends and Neighbors

Our power includes that of other nations whose security is inextricably interwoven with our own. And the most important of our allies are the more than 300 million people of Western Europe. Here is concentrated an industrial and economic unit second in its productivity only to the United States and the Soviet Union, and whose rate of growth in recent decades has been faster than our own or the Soviet Union's. Here are bases, plants, airports, navies, armies, with a great military and industrial potential. True, with development of intercontinental missiles the Soviet Union could direct an attack on this nation without occupying Western nations, and we are no longer so dependent on European bases for our own striking force, but unless Western Europe is firmly defended, this great potential could fall into the hands of the communist world and in the long pull of the Cold War competition, its loss would vitally threaten our own security.

One of the most important links in the American defense effort is the North Atlantic Treaty among the United States, Canada, United Kingdom, France, Italy, Belgium, Denmark, Iceland, Luxembourg, the Netherlands, Norway, Portugal, Greece, Turkey, and West Germany. These nations have agreed "by means of continuous and effective self-help and mutual aid" to develop their own capacities to resist armed attack. Each nation has pledged itself to regard an attack on any member of the treaty community as an attack on all.[4]

NATO has at its disposal several military commands, of which the best known is the Supreme Headquarters, Allied Powers, Europe (SHAPE) under the direction of an American commander. Although the United States is not required by the terms of the treaty to provide military assistance, it has taken the lead in supplying troops and munitions, including nuclear weapons, for NATO forces. In addition, the United States furnishes machines, tools, and technical assistance to its allies in order to increase their ability to contribute to mutual defense. While United States policy-makers envision a stronger NATO through a truly integrated multilateral force, national differences have so far precluded such thorough combination.[5] France in particular has been a restless and even wayward partner. The organization has functioned in the Cold War period; how well it would respond to wartime emergency is a matter of conjecture and differing opinion.

The Southeast Asia Treaty Organization, popularly known as SEATO, forms another link in the American defense system. The United States, France, the United Kingdom, Australia, New Zealand, the Philippines, Pakistan, and Thailand are pledged to consider communist aggression against any member nation or against Cambodia, Laos, or South Vietnam as a threat to their own security and to meet

---

[4] Alvin J. Cottrell and James E. Dougherty, *The Atlantic Alliance* (Praeger, 1964).

[5] Hanson W. Baldwin, "NATO's Uneven Steps Toward Integration," *The Reporter* (March 11, 1965), p. 32 ff. See also Wilfrid L. Kohl, "Nuclear Sharing in NATO and the Multilateral Force," *Political Science Quarterly* (March 1965), p. 88 ff.

the common danger in accord with their own constitutional processes. In case of nonmilitary aggression or attacks by noncommunist nations, these nations have agreed to consult on common action. Each nation maintains a permanent representative in Bangkok, Thailand, the permanent headquarters of SEATO. The council, composed of foreign ministers, is the governing body and meets at irregular intervals. The inability of SEATO to deal effectively with communist aggression in Southeast Asia, however, has raised doubts about the efficacy of this link in our defensive chain.

Our security arrangements in Latin America have been previously mentioned. To the north, the United States has a defense alliance with Canada that predates World War II and recognizes that the two countries are a strategic entity. We have bilateral agreements of cooperation with countries in the Central Treaty Organization of the Middle East (CENTO)—Pakistan, Iran, Turkey, and the United Kingdom—and have bilateral agreements of mutual defense and assistance with Nationalist China, Korea, Japan, and the Philippines.

Politicians, Bureaucrats, and Armed Forces

Both the President and Congress are responsible for the common defense, and both have the powers needed to discharge that responsibility. Constitutionally, Congress controls the purse; the President directs the sword. Congress declares war; the President runs it. Congress appropriates the money and determines the size, structure, and organization of the fighting forces; the President is the commander in chief of these forces and determines where and when military power will be used.

Although Congress, the President, the State Department, and the National Security Council make over-all policy and integrate our national security programs, the day-by-day work of developing and executing our military policy is the job of the Department of Defense.

Pentagonia

The world's largest office building, the famed Pentagon, is the headquarters of the United States Defense Department, a department so big that in comparison it makes even the American Telephone and Telegraph Company look like a small-town business. The Department spends about $50 billion a year, 8 per cent of the entire nation's gross national product. At work in the Pentagon are nearly 25,000 persons, including the Secretary of Defense and about 350 generals and admirals. Over 170 security officers guard the restricted areas in which the nation's military plans are made. This vast building is a communications center in constant touch with our armed forces throughout the world.

Prior to 1947 there were two separate military departments, War and Navy. But the lack of coordination between them during World War II led to demands for unification. In 1947 the Air Force, already an autonomous unit within the War Department, was made an independent unit, and the three military departments—Army, Navy, Air Force—were placed under the "general supervision" of the Secretary of Defense.[6] The Unification Act of 1947, a hesitant first step, was a bundle of compromises between the Army, which favored a tightly integrated department, and the Navy, which wanted a loosely federated structure. It also reflected compromises between congressmen who felt that disunity and interservice rivalries were undermining our defense efforts, and, on the other hand, congressmen who feared that a unified defense establishment would defy civilian control and smother dissenting views.

The 1947 act had not been long in operation before it became apparent that the Department of Defense, which was supposed to be the nation's sword, looked more like a pitchfork. All that the 1947 act had really accomplished was to bring the military services under a common organization chart. Instead of having moved from two military departments to one, we had ended up with three. Despite further centralizing moves, congressional amendments in 1949, and presidential directives in 1953, each service retained considerable autonomy and the Defense Department was unable to develop an integrated military program.

In 1958, when headlines featured factional struggles among military services while the Russians were sending up sputniks, President Eisenhower came forward with Defense Department reorganization proposals. He urged Congress to appropriate all funds to the Secretary of Defense rather than to the separate military departments, and to give the Secretary full control over the armed services, including the authority to transfer or abolish combatant functions and to establish direct lines of command between his office and operational forces in the field. The President recommended that a Director of Defense Research and Engineering be appointed to operate directly under the Secretary of Defense with power to coordinate development of weapons systems. The President also asked that the Joint Chiefs of Staff be strengthened by giving its Chairman a vote, that the staff be enlarged, and that each service chief be allowed to delegate his command duties so that he could devote most of his time to the work of the Joint Chiefs.

The President's plan to unify further the Defense Department by increasing the authority of the Secretary of Defense and by centralizing the Joint Chiefs was subjected to heavy congressional fire. Many congressmen, fearful of creating a "Prussian-type" military establishment, argued that instead of concentrating greater authority in the Defense Secretary, what was needed was a cleaning out of the large number of assistant secretaries of defense and assistants to the assistant secretaries, positions which had been spawned in the Defense Secretary's office. They contended that with layer upon layer of civilian staffs, with so many initials to obtain on every action, and with so much red tape, nothing was getting done.

President Eisenhower felt so strongly about his proposals for Defense Department reorganization that he used the prestige and influence of his office to promote

[6] For a comprehensive analysis see Paul Y. Hammond, *Organizing for Defense: The American Military Establishment in the Twentieth Century* (Princeton Univ. Press, 1961).

their accomplishment. In the end, the Defense Department Reorganization Act of 1958 gave the President most of what he wanted. Congress, however, refused to approve the appropriation of funds to the Secretary of Defense. Furthermore, at the prompting of the Naval Air Force, Marine Corps, and National Guard (who it was pointed out, live in constant fear that somebody will abolish them),[7] Congress insisted that the Secretary of Defense notify the House and Senate armed services committees if he contemplates any major change in combatant functions. If within thirty days either committee disapproves, each chamber has another forty days to stop the order from taking effect.

Congress also refused to repeal a provision, which President Eisenhower called "legalized insubordination," authorizing a secretary of a military department or a member of the Joint Chiefs to make any recommendations he wishes to Congress about Defense Department matters even if contrary to Defense Department policy. Eisenhower's view, as that of other Presidents, is that he is the commander in chief, that the Secretary of Defense is his deputy, and that it is the duty of all military men to support before Congress and the country the agreed-on policies of the Defense Department regardless of their own judgment.

McNamara and "Creeping Unification"

Under Presidents Kennedy and Johnson there have been no major structural changes in the Department of Defense, but the appointment of Robert McNamara as Secretary of Defense by President Kennedy and his continued service under President Johnson has led to greater changes in the operation of the Defense Department than were effected by any act of Congress.

Secretary McNamara brought to the Department a small group of men, chiefly trained as economists and analysts. "Perhaps never before had so much civilian talent, sophisticated in military strategy, been assembled under a Defense Secretary, himself known for exceptional intellect combined with the ability to make difficult decisions with dispatch." [8] Secretary McNamara and his "Whiz Kids," as they came to be called, with strong support from the White House, proceeded to unify the supply and intellegence activities of the services, create unified military commands, and bring a more effective degree of unification to the Department than Congress had been willing to sanction by legislation. "Systems analysis" has been introduced as a means of evaluating weapons and allocating funds among various commands and services. Secretary McNamara and his staff have had their own ideas about strategic policies; unlike many past civilian leaders of the Defense Department they have raised questions about military strategy and overruled military men when they felt that the "top brass" lacked sound reasons. The Secretary, supported by Presidents Kennedy and Johnson, even redistributed military funds in order to

[7] Ivan Hinderaker, "The Eisenhower Administration: The Last Years," in *American Government Annual, 1959–1960* (Holt, 1959), p. 82.

[8] Harry Howe Ransom, *Can American Democracy Survive Cold War?* (Doubleday, 1963).

redress what he believed had been an unbalanced reliance by the Eisenhower administration on nuclear power.[9] With the build-up of flexible, conventional military power, the United States has more options available to it in order to support its foreign policies.

Some congressmen and some military chieftains have been critical of Secretary McNamara's iron-handed control of the Defense Department, of his centralization of authority in his own office and away from the civilian secretaries of each department and the military heads. Whether the "McNamara Revolution" will have a lasting impact on the Defense Department is yet to be established. But it has demonstrated that the power of the Secretary of Defense is more a function of his political position—chiefly of his support by the President—than it is of his legal authority or hierarchical position.[10]

Key Military Agencies

The *Armed Forces Policy Council* is the Defense Department's "little cabinet." It is composed of the department Secretary, deputy secretary, the three civilian secretaries of the military departments, the Director of Defense Research and Engineering, the Chairman of the Joint Chiefs of Staff, and the chief of staff of each of the services. It advises the Secretary on matters of broad policy.

The *Joint Chiefs of Staff* serve as the principal military advisers to the President, the National Security Council, and the Secretary of Defense. They comprise the military heads of the three armed services, the commandant of the Marine Corps—whenever a matter comes up directly concerning the Marine Corps—and a chairman, all appointed by the President with the consent of the Senate for a two-year term, and eligible in peacetime for only one reappointment. Behind double steel doors in the Pentagon the Joint Chiefs shape strategic plans, work out joint supply programs, review major supply and personnel requirements, formulate programs for joint training, make recommendations to the Secretary of Defense on the establishment of unified commands in strategic areas, and provide American representation on the military commissions of the United Nations, NATO, and SEATO.

The Chairman of the Joint Chiefs takes precedence over all other military officers. He presides over the meetings of the Joint Chiefs, prepares the agenda, directs the staff, and informs the Secretary of Defense and the President of issues on which the Joint Chiefs have been unable to reach agreement.

In the past, the Joint Chiefs at times were unable to develop united strategies or to agree on the allocation of resources. There is more to disputes among military services, however, than mere professional jealousies. The technological revolution in warfare has rendered obsolete existing concepts about military missions. In the past, it made sense to divide command over land, sea, and air forces, but today

---

[9] William K. Kaufmann, *The McNamara Strategy* (Harper, 1964).

[10] John C. Ries, *The Management of Defense: Organization and Control of the U.S. Armed Service* (Johns Hopkins Press, 1964), p. 198.

"technology makes a mockery of such distinctions." [11] Under the impact of ever-changing military technology and the outmoding of traditional divisions of roles and missions, each service supports a concept allowing it to claim a decisive role, each "seeks to control weapons which will enable it to carry out that role; virtually independently of operations of other services." [12]

The Army, for example, argues that missiles are a form of artillery and should be developed by the Army. The Air Force insists they are merely an extension of the airplane and should be developed by the Air Force. The Navy argues that it needs to develop missiles for its submarines. The artificial division of military missions among the services also leads to many other disputes. For example, the Air Force opposes the diversion of airplanes to serve as an airlift for the Army on the grounds that planes are most needed for strategic and tactical purposes. But the Army wants planes so that it may rapidly move its forces to theaters of combat.

Sometimes interservice rivalries break out in the Congress and the press. Quasi-official organizations such as the Association of the United States Army, the Navy League, and the Air Force Association lobby openly in behalf of their particular service. Behind the scenes the military men themselves are active. The President, as we have mentioned, has tried to keep interservice disputes inside the administration.

[11] Henry A. Kissinger, *Nuclear Weapons and Foreign Policy* (Doubleday, 1958), p. 228.

[12] William R. Kintner, *et al.*, *Forging a New Sword: A Study of the Department of Defense* (Harper, 1958), p. 172.

"I'll never forget his ringing words: 'Damn the Appropriations Committee—full speed ahead!' . . ." (Drawing by Ed Fisher; © The Saturday Review.)

But the military commander who deeply feels that administration policy threatens the national security is in something of a quandary. He is taught to respect civilian supremacy and to obey his civilian superiors. But which civilian superiors? The President as commander in chief? Or should he—as he has a legal right to do—report to Congress, which is also a civilian superior? A few officers, such as General James M. Gavin, former chief of the Army missile program, resolve the dilemma of conflicting loyalties to President, Congress, and conscience by resigning so that they will be free to carry their views to the nation. More commonly, military men who wish to express dissents from official policy get their views to Congress by resorting to the normal Washington practice of "leaking" information to the press. Furthermore, in facing congressional committees it is not difficult for officers to support policies of the Defense Department only in a formal sense and to allow their real views to come across.

The continuation of interservice differences has led some to advocate the replacement of the Joint Chiefs by a single chief of staff, the complete integration of all military into a single branch, and the reassignment of forces in terms of strategic missions rather than means of locomotion. Although such a system has had the support of many high-ranking Army and some Air Force officers, it is opposed by most Navy officers and most congressmen. Under Secretary McNamara there has been considerable integration of military forces under single commands for each strategic mission, but without any alterations in outward forms. Strategic policy, much like that of any other area, is the result not of a collective process of rational inquiry, but of a mutual process of give and take.[13] Whether strategic policies are worked out within the Defense Department, the White House, or Congress, the decisions result from a political process in which some measure of consensus is essential and conflicts among the participants are not necessarily evil. As one admiral put it: "How curious it is that the Congress *debates*, the Supreme Court *deliberates*, but for some reason or other the Joint Chiefs of Staff just *bicker!*" [14]

Nuclear Policy in the Space Age

During the first years of the atomic age, no basic changes in military strategies seemed to be called for. Our atomic monopoly reinforced our traditional policy of not maintaining large standing armies. Even after the Soviet Union exploded its first atomic bomb, the situation was not seriously altered. We believed that our technological superiority would keep us ahead of the Soviets for many years to come, and that from our overseas bases we could rain down hundreds of bombs in the event of attack. At the same time, our defense system would reduce the

[13] Samuel P. Huntington, *The Common Defense: Strategic Programs in National Politics* (Columbia Univ. Press, 1961), preface and *passim*.

[14] Quoted by Huntington, p. 170, from Vice Admiral H. E. Orem, "Shall We Junk the Joint Chiefs of Staff?" 84 U.S. Naval Institute Proceedings (Feb., 1958), p. 57. See also David W. Tarr, "Military Technology and The Policy Process," *Western Political Quarterly* (March 1965), pp. 135 ff.

enemy's ability to deliver these expensive weapons to American targets. Although wars would be terribly costly, it was still possible to talk about "winning" such wars.

Then, on October 4, 1957, the Moscow radio announced that the Soviet Union had placed in orbit the first earth satellite. The space age was born and the military implications were terrifyingly clear. The Soviet Union had beaten us to the punch and was perfecting the intercontinental missile. Not only that, but the Soviet Union had an ample supply of nuclear weapons. A balance of terror suddenly loomed. The enemy had sufficient power to destroy us, and the fact that we could do the same to him provided little comfort to Americans. It has become clear that atomic weapons cannot be used except under extreme provocation and—we hope—the most remote circumstances.

"No fair—I can't afford a gun." From Straight Herblock (Simon & Schuster, 1964).

A Military Strategy for the 1960's

The emergence of the Soviet Union as a major nuclear power and the explosion by France and Red China of their own nuclear weapons presaged the proliferation of nations capable of destroying the world. These ominous developments forced the United States to rethink its military strategy. Most agreed that even after massing sufficient retaliatory power to destroy the enemy, it would be dangerous to relax, for he might achieve a technological breakthrough giving him a temporary advantage, such as a system to stop missiles or reduce the dangers of radiation.

Army spokesmen, however, as well as many students of foreign policy, were critical of the tendency to place so much emphasis on massive weapons at the expense of mobile tactical forces capable of being used in "limited wars." They contended that the desire to balance the national government's budget by reducing the Army and relying on relatively less expensive air-atomic power had left us dangerously exposed to local aggressions. Neither the United States nor the Soviet Union, they argued, is likely to start a thermonuclear war of mass destruction, since such a war would lead to their own extermination. Such a war is "morally, politically, and practically unjustifiable." Furthermore, these critics argued, to rely only on massive retaliation and weapons of mass destruction actually increases the likelihood of all-out war. For if the Soviet Union is led to believe that these are our only weapons and that we plan to use them, the Russians might be tempted to shoot first, especially if they have a temporary missile superiority. But even more likely, leaders of the Soviet Union know that the United States will not let loose a catastrophic conflict merely to prevent localized aggressions such as those in Laos in 1959, or Berlin in 1961, or Cuba in 1962, or South Vietnam in 1965. The risk of unleashing an all-out war would be too great, and it would bring the condemnation of the entire world down on the United States. Nor, according to this view, is atomic power suitable to stop Soviet conquest of Western Europe, because its use would also destroy our allies. Hence, the Army and others argued, we must spend more on forces that can be used restrictively in order to prevent the enemy from nibbling at the edge of the free world.[15]

Air Force spokesmen and most Navy men, on the other hand, contended that to slow down the build-up of our atomic weapons would be dangerous. They argued that we had not achieved decisive superiority; and until we did, the Soviet Union would be tempted, despite the risks involved, to take advantage of any superiority it might gain. The Soviets have intercontinental missiles and a formidable air defense, so that an all-out effort was needed to overcome their missile superiority. Until we caught up, we must depend on our strategic air power and atomic submarines and not divert any resources to limited-war forces. Some spokesmen for airpower—but not necessarily for the Air Force—argued that mass armies are obsolete, that airpower can be used for limited conflicts, and that by concentrating on airpower and missiles we will be able to get more defense for less money. They believed it was foolish to commit our forces to peripheral small-scale wars—"brushfires"—and that we needed only have the ability to retaliate massively if the enemy started trouble.

The election of President Kennedy and the appointment of Secretary McNamara resolved for the moment these differences over military policies, for one of President Kennedy's highest priorities was "to get the nuclear genie back in the bottle," by providing other forces as means of exerting American influence. President Johnson has supported this program and during recent years there has been a dramatic shift in emphasis toward building up conventional, flexible, and mobile military forces.

These conflicts over appropriate military strategies clearly illustrate the interrelations among military and foreign policies. A military program that places major reliance on massive retaliation, for example, makes allies less important than does a policy of maintaining forces able to resist invasions without resorting to mass destruction. A foreign policy pledging help to nations threatened by communist-backed guerrillas is meaningless unless we have the kind of military power to back the pledge.

[15] Kissinger's book cited above has been influential in presenting the point of view of those who believe we should strengthen our limited-warfare forces. See also Matthew B. Ridgway, *Soldier* (Harper, 1956), pp. 295–361.

Second Line of Defense

In the past, our nation's practice was to rely on a small standing force that would be joined in an emergency by all able-bodied men. The sturdy farmer could be called to snatch his musket from the mantelpiece and rush to the battlefield. Today, however, our armed forces are a complex organization of trained specialists. It takes many months, even years, to train a man to serve with the modern fighting machine. A stout heart and a straight-shooting gun are not enough. The time lag between the decision to create a large military organization and its actual existence as a fighting unit can be fatal.

Today, standing behind the combat forces is a second line of defense, the Ready Reserves, consisting of the National Guard, the Army, Navy, Air Force, and Coast Guard Reserves. In a thermonuclear war these reserves would probably be of restricted use, but in a limited war such as that in Korea, and Vietnam, we have seen that these reserves can be quickly called to duty by the President. These reserve personnel take part in weekly drills and attend summer camps so that they will be ready to serve with a minimum of additional training.

An important component of the Ready Reserves is the National Guard, composed of the organized militias of the states.[16] Except when called into federal service, the Guard is under the command of the governors of the respective states. The governors commission the officers, and through their adjutant generals supervise the training of the militias. The national government, however, provides most of the money for their training and equipment, and has established minimum standards.

A state-controlled militia is an established tradition. In fact, in 1787 the states insisted on the adoption of the Second Amendment to prohibit the national government from depriving them of the right to maintain their own militias. During the War of 1812 some states would not even let their militias be used outside their own boundaries. Today, however, the national government exercises far-reaching supervision over the National Guard. Congress has the authority to call state militias into federal service, and it has given the President power to call the National Guard into immediate federal service. Once this is done, the Guard becomes an integral part of the national fighting forces subject only to such limitations as Congress may impose.

The chief purpose of the Guard today is to provide a trained reserve for the national military forces. Its service to the states is less important, for the state police have taken over many of its former duties. For this reason, and because the states have not always done a good job of training, it has been suggested that the National Guard be "federalized" and combined with the organized reserves to

---

[16] See W. H. Riker, *Soldiers of the States: The Role of the National Guard in American Democracy* (Public Affairs Press, 1957). See also Martha Derthwick, *The National Guard in Politics* (Harvard Univ. Press, 1965).

provide one reserve unit as an integral part of the federal defense establishment. Every such proposal, however, has drawn little support and much opposition in Congress.

A reconsideration of our Ready Reserve program soon followed the "foul-ups" that occurred when the Ready Reserves, including two National Guard divisions, were called into active service to make clear our determination during the Berlin crisis in 1961. It became apparent that the Reserve program was inadequate, that many units could not be relied on because of lack of sufficient training, and that mobilization of Reserves generated political pressures and discontent. The Kennedy administration proposed that in order to have a reserve force ready for "cold" war as well as "hot" war uses, it would be necessary to have a more highly trained but smaller reserve component. To effect this program, President Kennedy, through Secretary McNamara, proposed that some National Guard units be abolished. The political outcry from some state governors and mayors of cities in which the units were located was so great that the administration backed down. Under President Johnson, Secretary McNamara tried to accomplish the same objective by merging the highest priority Army Reserve units with the Army National Guard and abolishing all other ready reserve units. Again opposition in Congress was strong. Finally, the Defense Department accomplished its objectives by using existing statutory authority to disband "lower priority" Reserve units and to accelerate the training and equipment of selected National Guard units. For it is increasingly clear that a large and costly reserve suitable for the "slow, deliberate World War II type of mobilization plan" does not meet our present need for "quick reaction forces."

Science and Security

When the atomic bomb was dropped on Hiroshima, few could any longer doubt that science had become a decisive element in a defense program. Wars are fought and won in large measure in a nation's scientific laboratories.

The nature of war has been altered by the invention of the proximity fuse, the snorkel submarine, radar, sonar, the guided missile, and nuclear weapons. The scientist's contribution to the war effort during World War II is well-known. But what is not so well-known is that the scientists drew "heavily on the accumulated stockpile of fundamental scientific knowledge that was all but exhausted when fighting stopped." [17] Further advance has depended upon the extension of fundamental scientific knowledge, on what is sometimes called "pure science." Such science is not preoccupied with finding more powerful explosives or better devices to guide missiles, but with unlocking the mysteries of the world in which we live.

It is essential, therefore, to create the conditions under which scientific inquiry can best operate. Hitler's misunderstanding of the importance of scientific research led him to expel from Germany those who did not conform to the "New

[17] Vannevar Bush, *Modern Arms and Free Men* (Simon & Schuster, 1949), p. 27.

Order." Our own preoccupation with *applied* science, and particularly with applications that have military significance, could tend to exhaust our fund of scientific knowledge without replenishing it. For this reason the government has established a National Science Foundation, which through scholarships and other forms of assistance helps to train scientists without regard to the immediate military value of their possible contributions.

The military departments themselves have tapped the knowledge and skill of scientists in commercial laboratories and universities.[18] In addition to this, the scientist has played an increasingly greater role as an adviser to the policy-maker.[19] This problem of integrating scientific and military knowledge is an essential but difficult task. Military men, like other professionals, tend to be cautious in adopting new techniques. In the past, almost every new weapon of war—gunpowder, submarine, tank, airplane, proximity fuse—had to be pushed on the military by civilians.

Should scientific knowledge be kept secret, or disseminated as widely as possible? Some scientific knowledge must be kept secret. Yet to stamp every new research finding "top secret" in the interests of national security would be disastrous, for scientific progress depends on the wide sharing of information. Many scientists, wishing to exchange data with their colleagues, question whether we are not losing more than we gain by our excessive concern over secrecy. Moreover, the withholding of information sometimes deprives the policy-planners themselves of essential knowledge.

Protecting the Home Front—Civil Defense

The United States will probably not be as fortunate in any future war as it has been in the past. An attack on the American mainland is now technically possible; and in case of a full-scale war, our factories, transportation centers, atomic plants, and other vital installations would be prime targets. The defense circle, authorities believe, cannot be closed without an adequate program for defending the home base. Until 1953, when the Soviet Union exploded its H-bomb, the military tended to neglect defensive power. Today, however, the Continental Air Command operates on a twenty-four alert, instantly ready to send planes into the air. Warning systems have been improved. Missile centers are in place, and work continues on developing anti-missile missiles.

With the development of intercontinental missiles even the best warning systems cannot guarantee more than fifteen minutes notice. Even the finest defense will not be able to prevent some of the enemy missiles from getting through. The most optimistic estimate is that 30 per cent of the missiles approaching the United States could be stopped. A more realistic figure is perhaps half that.

[18] Gene M. Lyons, "The Growth of National Security Research," *Journal of Politics* (August 1963), pp. 489 ff.
[19] R. Gilpin and C. Wright (eds.), *Scientists in National Policy-Making* (Columbia Univ. Press, 1964). See also Avery Leiserson, "Scientists and The Policy Process," *The American Political Science Review* (June 1965), pp. 480 ff.

The industrial power of the United States is concentrated in the area north of the Ohio and east of the Mississippi, and along the West Coast. And many of our basic industries are in coastal cities particularly vulnerable to attack. We could decentralize industry and create duplicate facilities dispersed through the United States, but large-scale decentralization is not feasible because of strong political pressures and the enormous sums that would be needed.

Americans have been reluctant to face up to the questions of civil defense. Not until the Korean conflict was the issue even discussed, and little has since been done. As late as 1966 nothing had happened to alter a 1956 *New York Times* survey of our major cities (probable prime targets of the enemy) which showed that Chicago is "helpless," Bostonians have "almost no chance of survival," Cleveland is a "sitting duck," Seattle is "not ready," and Fort Worth is "woefully unprepared." [20]

Confronted by the obvious inadequacies of our civil defense program, President Kennedy assigned the operating responsibilities for the program to the Department of Defense, leaving the planning and coordinating role to a small staff in the Office of Emergency Planning in the Executive Office of the President. Moreover, the President urged Americans through private initiative and state and local governmental action to provide family fall-out shelters. Momentarily there was a flurry of action, but it quickly became apparent that an adequate shelter program could not be developed by individual action, and that the state and local governments would not spend the billions of dollars necessary for civil defense. Until the national government acts, little civil defense is likely; and it seems that national action can be expected only during an emergency period. With a decline of international tension following the Berlin crisis of 1961, public concern for civil defense seemed to evaporate. This apathy was reflected in congressional refusal to appropriate requested sums for the President's nationwide shelter program. Concern flared up after the Cuban crisis of 1962, only to die down once again. The civil defense program has remained in limbo since that time.

Many Americans are opposed to civil defense preparations. They argue that not only would a fall-out shelter program be useless, but the costs would divert resources from more positive programs to maintain peace, and that active preparation such as a fall-out shelter program might so frighten a potential aggressor as to induce him to strike first. Others respond that although "there is no certainty that any nation can survive an all-out nuclear attack," we must face up to the fact that a war is possible. True, if there is such a war millions will die whatever we do. Nor would life be pleasant for those who might survive. But with advance preparations, millions of others might be saved. Secretary McNamara, for example, has testified that an all-out attack on military and urban targets in the United States would result in the death of an estimated 149 million Americans. With a $5 billion expenditure for a full fall-out shelter program another 30 million lives might be saved. An additional $17 billion for anti-missile defenses and $3 billion for manned bombers would cut the casualities to an estimated 78 million lives.[21] Many also feel that civil defense

---

[20] *The New York Times* (January 4, 1956), Part 4, p. 1.
[21] Secretary McNamara's Testimony, *op. cit.*

preparations are essential to avoid war. For if the aggressor recognizes that this nation is defenseless, he may be encouraged to believe that by a single strike he can gain victory.

Arms Control and National Security

For many, the promise of avoiding a thermonuclear war lies not with the development of a deterrent capacity based on military weapons and elaborate civil defense, but rather through arms control and disarmament. A world in which conflicts are resolved without resort to force has been an objective of man for many centuries. Realization of such a hope in the near future indeed seems dim as both sides in the East-West conflict continue to build massive military systems. Nevertheless, disarmament and arms control are much-debated goals and a part of policy planning.

The policy of deterrence holds that a conflict of values is the root cause of the East-West confrontation and that military force is but a reflection of that basic conflict. Proponents of arms control and disarmament share to some degree this view, but argue that armaments themselves are also a fundamental cause of international tension. They warn of the immense risks of the deterrence system—human error, a failure in the warning network, a "misguided" missile, the inevitable expansion of the number of nations with nuclear weapons. But they paint an even grimmer picture of a future without arms control—one with heightened tension brought by more devastating nuclear warheads and longer-ranged, more accurate delivery vehicles; the threat of biological, chemical, and even radiological weapons; the constant surveillance of "spy" satellites; ever-increasing defense budgets and ever-increasing commitments of human resources to weapons technology.

Some advocates of disarmament feel this possibility can be forestalled only by general and complete renunciation of force with the elimination of virtually all military power. The Soviets purport to favor comprehensive disarmament but as yet have given no sign of willingness to move meaningfully toward that goal. A vocal minority in the West proposes that in order to save the world from nuclear destruction, the West must, unilaterally, take a significant first step in disarmament. A skeptical majority suspects that the communists would not reciprocate but rather take advantage of our vulnerability.

A more feasible alternative to the arms race is limited disarmament, generally known as arms control. Beginning with nuclear weapons, gradual arms reduction by both sides has two immediate objectives: first, to reduce the likelihood of war, and if unsuccessful in this, second, to diminish the violence of armed conflict. Within this policy, mutual arms reduction would be accomplished through negotiations.[22]

The United States, Britain, and the Soviet Union began talks in 1958 to seek a

---

[22] For a balanced overview of arms control and disarmament see: Hadley, *op. cit.*; Donald G. Brennan (ed.), *Arms Control, Disarmament and National Security* (Braziller, 1961); and Louis Henkin (ed.), *Arms Control, Issues for the Public* (Prentice-Hall, 1961).

treaty banning nuclear tests. Simultaneously, the three powers began a voluntary moratorium on testing. Although France, not involved in the test ban negotiations, detonated a nuclear device in 1960, the moratorium was honored by the major powers for almost three years, until the Soviet Union resumed tests. Following the Russian tests, the United States and Britain initiated their own series. Despite testing on both sides, negotiations continued in Geneva.

On August 5, 1963, the United Kingdom, the Soviet Union, and the United States agreed on a treaty to ban all nuclear explosions in the atmosphere or in any other place if there was any danger of radioactive debris. The treaty permits nations to engage in underground testing and has an escape clause permitting nations on the basis of three months notice to withdraw from the obligations of the treaty, but its ratification by the United States and the Soviet Union and its subsequent adherence by more than 100 nations is the first concrete step toward nuclear disarmament. However, there are two notable exceptions to the list of nations adhering to the test ban, France and China, both of whom have tested bombs and contaminated the atmosphere since the treaty was signed by all the other nations. It is likely that a broadening of the test ban to cover other testing situations will be a channel through which easing of East-West tensions will be sought.

National security is not the product of a single approach—military, economic, or political. Thus, while the concept of deterrence clearly dominates defense policy today, it is not pursued independently of economic assistance or even arms control. Deterrence and disarmament are both strategies of national security.

Security and Liberty—Not by Power Alone

So long as the United States exists in a world of sovereign, independent nations, it must look to its defenses. As we have seen, this means large standing military forces, adequately trained reserves, the application of scientific and other knowledge to military problems, a strong and stable economy, an alert and trained citizen body, and powerful allies.

To fail to do what is necessary to provide for the common defense would be disastrous. But it would be equally disastrous to depend solely on military power to provide security. Not even the United States has sufficient resources, even if the people had the stomach for it, to control the destinies of the international community. Politics is conflict, but it is also cooperation, and power should be used to help build the kind of world community in which armies and tanks will one day be archaic.

What should be the role of the military in a democratic society? A fear of the military is deeply rooted in American traditions. The framers of the Constitution, recognizing that military domination was incompatible with free government, wove into the Constitution several precautions. The President, an elected officer, is commander in chief of the armed forces. With the Senate's consent, he commissions all officers; Congress makes the rules for the governance of the military services; and appropriations for the Army are limited to a two-year period. Congress has supplemented these precautions by requiring that the Secretary of Defense and the heads of the military departments be civilians, and by devising elaborate procedures to prevent the military from controlling the selection of men for West Point, Annapolis, and the Air Force Academy.

In the past, professional military men were largely ignored. During time of peace, their recommendations were shrugged off, or the generals were accused of wanting war. A career in the armed services was not attractive. The military mind was stereotyped as conservative, stodgy, and concerned mainly with protocol. Failure to heed the words of our professional soldiers, sailors and airmen has cost us much. In the future what they have to say will probably be given serious consideration. At the other extreme there is the danger of elevating them into positions where what they have to say is accepted uncritically. This would be disastrous both for the preservation of liberty and for the promotion of security.

War and defense today, more than ever before, are too important and too complex to leave to the generals. As we have seen, security programs require the talents of the bureaucrat, social scientist, natural scientist, labor leader, engineer, industrialist, and all other professionals. What the military expert knows must be meshed with what others know. But he may not know enough to be trusted with the running of our defense program.

Militarism v. Democracy

Maintaining civilian supremacy over the military today is harder than ever. There is no longer a clear separation between military and civilian spheres of activity. As national security problems are brought to the fore, the generals, often reluctantly, are called upon to pass judgment on issues that in the past have not been thought to be within the scope of their competence. At the same time, their civilian superiors find it more difficult to secure the information they need to exercise control. In many cases it is the military who decide what information must remain top secret. Congressmen and the general public are at a disadvantage in exercising supremacy over the military.

The dangers to liberty arising from the garrison state—a nation that is constantly prepared for total war and that is organized to exert its military might—were recognized by Alexander Hamilton when he wrote: "Safety from external danger is the most powerful director of national conduct. Even the ardent love of liberty will after a time give way to its dictates. The violent destruction of life and property incident to war, the continual effort and alarm attendant on a state of continual danger, will compel nations the most attached to liberty to resort for repose and security to institutions which have a tendency to destroy their civil and political rights. To be more safe, they at length become willing to run the risk of being less free." [23]

[23] *Federalist* No. 8, The Modern Library edition (Random House, 1937), p. 42. For a recent treatment of the problem, see Samuel P. Huntington, "Civilian Control and the Constitution," *The American Political Science Review* (September 1956), pp. 676–699.

Professor Harold D. Lasswell has summarized the impact of militarization upon individual freedom as follows: "To militarize is to governmentalize. It is also to centralize. To centralize is to enhance the effective control of the executive over decisions, and thereby to reduce the control exercised by courts and legislatures. To centralize is to enhance the role of the military in the allocation of national resources. Continuing fear of external attack sustains an atmosphere of distrust that finds expression in spy hunts directed against fellow officials and fellow citizens. Outspoken criticism of official measures launched for the national defense is more and more resented as unpatriotic and subversive of the common good. The community at large, therefore, acquiesces in denials of freedom that go beyond the technical requirements of military security." [24]

The threat of militarization comes not only from the military, however. As John McCloy wrote in dissent to one of the recommendations of the Hoover Commission's task force on security organization, "I doubt whether we need fear the men in uniform in this regard [seeking unfettered power] any more than the man or men in civil clothes to whom we have given far greater authority. Indeed, as many examples as there are of authority usurped by generals or admirals, I believe history records as many instances of usurpation on the part of civilians with at least as many disastrous results." [25]

The United States has been fortunate. It has never developed a military caste. Its generals and admirals have demonstrated statesmanlike qualities, including respect for civilian authority. American soldiers have been imbued with democratic principles of civilian supremacy. Now that the skills required of military men are so varied, it becomes all the more necessary to educate them not only to be good soldiers but also to be good democrats. For it is by "civilizing" the military that much can be done to prevent militarizing the civilians.[26]

In his last message to the nation as President, Dwight Eisenhower pointed out that this country is now committed to a vast armament industry and maintains "a defense establishment employing 3.5 million persons and spending huge sums." He warned:

> This conjunction of an immense military establishment and a large arms industry is new in American experience. The total influence—economic, political, even spiritual—is felt in every city, every State house, every office of the Federal government. We recognize the imperative need for this development. Yet we must not fail to comprehend its grave implications. Our toil, resources, and livelihood are involved; so is the very structure of our society.[27]

[24] Harold D. Lasswell, "Does the Garrison State Threaten Civil Rights?" *Civil Rights in America*, The *Annals* of the American Academy of Political and Social Science (May 1951), p. 111.

[25] *Task Force Report on National Security Organization*, p. 59.

[26] For a different interpretation see Samuel P. Huntington, *The Soldier and the State* (Harvard Univ. Press, 1957), especially ch. 17. Also Harry L. Coles (ed.), *Total War and the Cold War: Problems in the Civilian Control of the Military* (Ohio State Univ. Press, 1962).

[27] *The New York Times* (January 18, 1961), p. 22.

24 GOVERNMENT AS REGULATOR

It is impossible to draw a sharp line between the activities of the national government in waging war and peace on the one hand and its so-called domestic functions on the other. The two are inextricably intertwined. The foreign policies administered by the State Department have a direct impact on American businessmen and farmers. Fighting a war mobilizes both the nation's economy and the whole peacetime bureaucracy. Our foreign economic policies directly affect employment, wages, prices, and taxes at home. Here we discuss domestic activities separately from foreign affairs only for purposes of convenience.

Americans have always been quick to criticize their country's foreign policy, but no one has ever seriously questioned that foreign policy must be made by the *national government*. Even the most waspish critic of bureaucratic inefficiency has never urged that foreign affairs be turned over to businessmen, for example, or that the job of defending the country against attack be turned over to the state governments. Everyone agrees that the national government must manage the relations of Americans with other peoples.

But when it comes to the dealings of Americans with *one another*—that is a different matter. On domestic questions people differ not only over *what* policies should be adopted, but also over *whether* government should act at all, and if so, *which* government. And even if they agree that government should act, the dispute shifts to new grounds of controversy: How far should government go? What kinds of control or procedure should it use? And so the debate rages on and on—in editorial pages, over the air, in legislative chambers, and on the platform.

This chapter and the next two will describe some of the functions of our national government. These chapters will provide illustrations of the major techniques of governmental action, but no attempt will be made to analyze in detail the operations of all federal agencies or all federal programs. Such a catalogue would be dull, uninformative, and quickly outdated. Our concern is not so much with what particular governmental bureaus do or the precise description of a particular agency's organization, but to convey some idea of the general forms of the national government's many activities and to indicate some persistent problems.

In this chapter we shall explore the national government's regulatory role—regulatory in the narrow sense of trying to limit the activities of some of its citizens, to prevent "bad" practices, to restrict one interest from interfering with the rights of others (as defined, of course, by the men in power). This is government in a somewhat negative or restrictive sense. In the next chapter we shall turn to some of the promotional functions of government. But although we use the term "promotion" to mean something different from regulation, it is impossible to make a sharp distinction between the two activities. Regulation means setting restraints on individuals and groups, directly compelling them to take, or not to take, certain actions. Promotion means encouraging, strengthening, safe-guarding, or advancing the interests of particular persons, groups, industries, or sectors of the economy. But to regulate one interest may be to promote another. Similarly, promotion can be used to regulate interests. Promotion savors a little more of the carrot, regulation of the stick, but often either one, or a combination, can be used to carry out a public policy.

A traditional type of governmental regulation is of course the regulation of human behavior to *prevent crime*. In the United States such regulation has been largely the job of state and local governments. The national government has been concerned with crime prevention mainly in connection with such activities as delivering mail or collecting taxes. Increasingly in recent years, however, fighting crime has been extended to more activities and has become an important national function; for instance, the recent civil rights laws discussed in Chapter 7 have added greatly to the national government's responsibilities in this regard. The Department of Justice which employs the services of the Federal Bureau of Investigation and other agencies, has the main responsibility for investigating federal crime and prosecuting criminals. The Secret Service in the Treasury Department has special crime-fighting responsibilities, such as investigating counterfeiting. Other members of the "federal police" are postal inspectors, narcotics agents, treasury inspectors, and border patrols. Under the kind of cooperative federalism described in Chapter 5, these federal officials work closely with state and local police. Paradoxically, though law enforcement of this sort is one of the most ancient functions of government, it is a relatively new responsibility of the national government. Since crime seems to be a big interstate business, however, the national government will probably become more and more involved in policing the country.

The main regulatory task of the national government is not crime-prevention, but the policing of powerful interests, such as business and labor. But two words of caution before we take up these regulatory functions: First, government is not the only regulating agency. Regulatory control is also exercised by families, friends, church, and the over-all social environment, as we saw in earlier chapters. Second, the type of activity described in this chapter is only one type of regulation. Government also acts as a regulating agency in some of its newer functions, as we shall see later.

Regulating Business

Businessmen today operate in a complex web of national, state, and local laws. It was not always thus. Business has never been altogther free of restrictive legislation, of course, but during much of the latter part of the nineteenth century our national policy was to leave business alone. Most of the nation's leaders, and the country at large, believed broadly in laissez faire—or hands off. Given their head, businessmen set about developing a nation that was enormously rich in natural resources. The heroes of the 1870's and 1880's were not politicians but business magnates— the Rockefellers, Morgans, Carnegies, and Fricks. "From rags to riches" became the nation's motto.

Then, toward the end of the century, a reaction set in. Sharp depressions rocked the nation's economy and threw men out of work. Millions of people, including workers and farmers, labored long hours in factory and field for little money. "Muckrakers" revealed that some of the most famous business leaders had indulged in shoddy practices and corrupt deals, taking a "public-be-damned" attitude. A demand for government regulation of business sprang up, and a series of national and state laws were passed to correct specific abuses. These laws followed no methodical plan or philosophy; rather, they were adopted on the pragmatic assumption that each problem could be handled as it arose.

Antitrust Policy: Background

We Americans have mixed feelings about big business. On the one hand we are easily impressed by bigness—the tallest skyscraper, the largest football stadium, the biggest corporation—and the efficiency and power that seem to go with bigness. On the other hand, we often assert that our economic system functions best under conditions of fair competition among small businessmen. This dichotomy has been reflected in our attempts to prevent monopoly and restraint of trade.

The popular clamor for government control late in the nineteenth century culminated in attacks on monopoly. The trust-busters argued that little business was being squeezed out by huge trusts in oil, sugar, whisky, steel, and other commodities. In 1890 Congress responded to this sentiment by passing the famous Sherman Antitrust Act. Designed to foster competition and stop the growth of private monopolies, the act made clear its intention "to protect trade and commerce against unlawful restraints and monopolies." Henceforth, persons making contracts, combinations, or conspiracies in restraint of trade in interstate and foreign commerce could be sued for damages, required to stop their illegal practices, and subjected to criminal penalties.

Presidents Cleveland and McKinley showed little interest in enforcing the Sherman Act. Indeed, a Supreme Court decision in the Sugar Trust Case (1895) considerably limited the scope of the act by ruling that a sugar-refining company which produced 98 per cent of the sugar used in the United States was primarily engaged in *manufacturing* rather than *interstate commerce*, and hence could not be regulated by the national government.[1] But in 1901 Theodore Roosevelt became President. Wielding a "big stick," he responded to the growing sentiment against the "giant octopus" of monopoly. Yet even Roosevelt talked more than he acted. Like most Americans he had conflicting attitudes toward bigness. Mr. Dooley, the Chicago bartender-philosopher, poked fun at Roosevelt's vacillation by pretending to quote him as saying: "Th' trusts are heejous monsthers built up be th'enlightened intherprise iv th'men that have done so much to advance progress in our beloved country. On wan hand I wud stamp thim undher fut; on th'other hand not so fast." During the Taft and Wilson Administrations the trusts were prosecuted more vigorously, and court rulings gave the rather vague provisions of the act more definite meaning. Certain consolidations were permitted unless a clear intent to monopolize was proved. Voting trusts, pools, and some collusive practices were sharply curbed.

The Clayton Act in 1914 further clarified antitrust policy. It outlawed specific abuses affecting interstate commerce, such as charging different prices to different buyers, the granting of rebates, and the making of false statements about competitors in order to take business away from them. Corporations were prohibited from acquiring stock (amended in 1950 to include assets) in competing concerns if such acquisitions substantially lessened interstate competition, and interlocking

[1] *United States* v. *E. C. Knight Co.* (1895).

directorates in large corporations were banned. Labor had been enraged by a Supreme Court ruling that applied the Sherman Act to a union boycott against the products of a nonunion manufacturer; the Clayton Act exempted labor from the 1890 act and was greeted by unions as their Magna Charta. Later legislation exempted various business activities from the Sherman Act.

Antitrust activity languished in the 1920's. Times were prosperous; the Republican administrations were actively pro-business; and the Department of Justice, charged with enforcing the Sherman Act, paid little attention to it. During the Depression popular resentment mounted against big business as abuses were revealed. At first the Roosevelt administration tried a new method of industrial self-government under the National Industrial Recovery Act of 1933, which tried to promote cooperation among businessmen by allowing them to work out codes of fair competition. This was seen as a virtual suspension of government antitrust policy. The NIRA, however, was invalidated by the Supreme Court in 1935.[2]

Subsequent years saw a revival of trust-busting. In the late 1930's a well-publicized committee of congressmen and New Deal experts, the Temporary National Economic Committee, made an elaborate investigation of economic concentration and monopoly. It unanimously urged that enforcement be strengthened "to cope with the gigantic aggregations of capital which have become so dominant in our economic life." Under the leadership of Thurman Arnold, a former Yale professor, the antitrust division of the Justice Department was given a larger staff to commence trust-busting in earnest. In one year, 1940, the government instituted 345 suits; of the 280 suits that were terminated, the government won 265.

Bigness—Curse or Blessing?

Although antitrust activity flagged during World War II, it was revived by postwar administrations, and it is evident that "vigorous antitrust enforcement has become a bipartisan policy."[3] The Eisenhower administration brought against major electrical firms indictments that led to the imprisonment of seven executives for price-fixing activity. The antitrust division during the Kennedy and Johnson administrations has brought similar indictments against eight major steel producers for fixing extra charges on carbon sheet steel.

Much of the division's attention in recent years has been focused upon corporate

[2] *Schechter Poultry Corp.* v. *United States* (1935).
[3] Merle Fainsod, Lincoln Gordon, and J. C. Palamountain, Jr., *Government and the American Economy* (Norton, 1959), p. 616.

A typical cartoon of a half-century ago against the "trusts."

mergers. While mere size of a corporation is not viewed as an offense against the antitrust laws, the division has carefully scrutinized the effect that a merger may have upon the market. As the former Kennedy and Johnson antitrust chief described this policy, ". . . the relative market size of the enterprise involved clearly is important. An acquisition or merger by a company already very large in relation to its market is far more likely to lessen competition substantially or tend to create a monopoly in violation of the antitrust laws than a similar transaction by a small company. But size alone is not controlling. Competition, rather than size, is the ultimate criterion." [4]

The main burden of measuring business practices by the antitrust yardstick falls to the federal courts. In hammering out the extent of permissible corporate power consistent with antitrust laws, the judges over the years have found these factors to be relevant: "The number of firms in the market; their effective size from the standpoint of technological development, and from the standpoint of competition with substitute materials and foreign trade; national security interests in the maintenance of strong productive facilities, and maximum scientific research and development; together with the public interest in lowered costs and uninterrupted production." [5]

In striking down mergers and sustaining antitrust prosecutions, the Supreme Court in recent years has indicated its agreement with the executive interpretation of the antitrust laws. In the DuPont Case the Supreme Court held that the big chemical comany's stock ownership in General Motors gave DuPont an advantage in the market for automobile fabrics and finishes that threatened competition in that market, and DuPont was ordered to divest itself of its GM stock over a ten-year period.[6] In the Brown Shoe Case the Court noted that what must be considered was a merger's ". . . probable effects upon the economic way of life sought to be preserved by Congress. . . . Congress desired to promote competition through the protection of viable, small, locally owned business. Congress appreciated that occasional higher costs and prices might result. . . . It resolved these competing considerations in favor of decentralization." [7] Thus the executive and the judiciary have been of one mind in the 1960's in preventing corporate size from impairing competition.

Should bigness as such be outlawed? Yes, say some Americans; others, like David E. Lilienthal, former Chairman of the Atomic Energy Commission, say no. Lilienthal believes that "in Big Business we have more than an efficient way to produce and distribute basic commodities, and to strengthen the Nation's security; we have a social institution that promotes human freedom and individualism." [8] Rather than outlaw bigness, Lilienthal would encourage it, since he believes that big business makes several positive contributions: It stimulates competition in ideas, products, and services; through research it develops more and better products; it strengthens constructive labor-management relations; it produces greater stability of employ-

[4] Lee Loevinger, "Antitrust Is Pro-Business," *Fortune* (August 1962), p. 136.
[5] *U.S.* v. *Aluminum Co. of America* (1944).
[6] *U.S.* v. *E. I. du Pont de Nemours & Co.* (1957).
[7] *Brown Shoe Co., Inc.* v. *U.S.* (1962).
[8] D. E. Lilienthal, *Big Business, a New Era* (Harper, 1953), p. ix.

ment; it increases industrial output; it promotes conservation of natural resources; and it creates new opportunities for independent and small businessmen. Any danger that big business will abuse its power has been reduced to manageable proportions, argues Lilienthal, by the expanded role of government in economic affairs in recent years.

Who controls the large corporations? In a classic study, Berle and Means showed that corporation ownership has been divorced from corporation control.[9] The ownership of stock in large corporations is widely dispersed, leaving control in the hands of a small group of managers. To whom are these managers responsible? If they are not truly responsible to the owners, should they be made more responsible to all the people through the national government? Although this problem does not directly relate to the monopoly problem, it touches on the whole role of the national government in regulating business.

Traffic Cop for Competition

Most Americans believe in vigorous but fair and open competition. In a simple economy, competition virtually enforces itself; buyers and sellers know one another and follow the old principle of *caveat emptor*—let the buyer beware. By the turn of the century, however, the American business economy was becoming so large and impersonal that a demand arose for the government to police competition. Big business was especially suspect for its trade practices; the same Congress that passed the Clayton Act in 1914 also enacted the Federal Trade Commission Act. When Wilson was campaigning for election, he had said that one vice of the trusts was their tendency to stop men of genuine ability but limited capital from making their way under the competitive system. The new act was a sort of "Magna Charta" for businessmen opposed to unfair and injurious methods of competition.

Because our industrial life is so diverse, Congress put enforcement of the law in the hands of a five-member Federal Trade Commission, an independent regulatory board whose job is to apply the act to specific practices. As its membership slowly changed (the term of office is seven years), the FTC's conception of its job changed too. In the 1920's the commission exercised its powers rather mildly, but more recently it has taken a stricter view toward business practices and has been given new responsibilities by Congress. Today the FTC exercises a wide range of powers. It may outlaw many diverse activities.

1. *Unfair or deceptive practices.* A businessman who sells in interstate commerce must not misrepresent his products. For example, in a recent well-publicized case the FTC enjoined a television commercial that allegedly showed sandpaper being

[9] A. A. Berle, Jr. and Gardiner C. Means, *The Modern Corporation and Private Property* (Macmillan, 1932). For an interesting picture of the "checks and balances" in the American economy that, in the author's opinion, tend to prevent excessive concentration of power, see J. K. Galbraith, *American Capitalism: The Concept of Countervailing Power* (Houghton Mifflin, 1952); see also A. A. Berle, Jr., *Power Without Property* (Harcourt, Brace & World, 1959).

shaved to demonstrate the "super-moisturizing power" of a shaving cream. The demonstration utilized not sandpaper but a prop consisting of sand applied to plexiglass, which of course made the job easier. The Commission's ruling that this was a deceptive trade practice was subsequently upheld by the Supreme Court.[10]

2. *Tying contracts.* The Radio Corporation of America was forbidden to require radio manufacturers to buy from RCA all vacuum tubes needed for first use in radio sets. On the other hand, when the General Motors Corporation required its Buick and Chevrolet agents to use only GM replacement parts in repair work, an FTC ban on this practice was overturned by the Supreme Court.

3. *Price discrimination.* It is unfair to sell below cost in an effort to destroy weaker competitors and thus secure a monopoly position. This practice had been a favorite one with the "robber barons" of old.

4. *Monopolistic practices.* There are a host of these—buying up supplies in order to stifle competition, conspiring to set uniform selling prices and conditions, harassing competitors (such as by bribing their employees or bringing vexatious law suits), and selling below cost in order to hinder competition. The FTC works closely with the Justice Department in trying to curb practices that improperly restrain trade among the states.

5. *Dangerous practices.* The FTC, for example, can regulate the interstate marketing of apparel to bar the use of highly flammable materials. Very recently the FTC first announced, then delayed, an order that would have required a health warning statement on cigarette packages and advertisements. Congress took over this explosive issue and approved a rather innocuous health warning on cigarette packages, but specifically forbade the FTC to require any such statements in advertisements for at least three years.

Some of the FTC's decisions have had a profound effect on our whole system of trade. Take the case of "Pittsburgh plus." For years steel producers had a friendly arrangement—called the basing point system—whereby the same prices were charged to all steel fabricators throughout the country no matter where they were located and where their steel came from. For example, if you were a Chicago fabricator buying steel from a Chicago mill, you would have to pay a Pittsburgh base price plus transportation charges from Pittsburgh even though no transportation was involved. The FTC watched this collusive arrangement in steel and other industries, such as cement, and then held hearings that lasted for three years. On the basis of almost 100,000 pages of oral testimony and exhibits, the FTC in 1943 issued a cease and desist order against the basing point system in the cement industry. The case went to the Supreme Court, which in 1948—eleven years after the FTC investigation first got under way—upheld the commission's action. Even this decision did not end the story. Supporters of the basing point system carried the battle to Congress, where bills were introduced to legalize the system, and they have exerted pressure on the Federal Trade Commission to modify its stand.

[10] *Federal Trade Commission* v. *Colgate-Palmolive Co.* (1965).

Policing the Money Market

The American economy rests on a vast system of investment and credit. Our resources could not have been developed had people not been willing to invest money in factories and machinery. The credit system—the "economic promises men live by"—has helped make possible enormous investments and the development of the economy. Before World War I there were hardly half a million investors in this country, but during the war and the 1920's millions of little people began to buy securities. Investment trusts and brokerage houses mushroomed.

For many years individual states had tried to cope with some of the abuses of the money markets, such as outright swindling. But it took the stockmarket crash of 1929 and the collapse of the rosy hopes of millions of investors to bring vigorous national action. Investigation during the Depression revealed that abuses had been many and varied. Worthless or questionable securities had been unloaded on the public through various kinds of fraud. Insiders had used confidential information to arrange deals for themselves at the expense of thousands of fleeced lambs. Investment bankers had sponsored stock issues that created unsound corporate structures. An enormous amount of speculating on margin (buying stocks on credit) had helped precipitate the 1929 crash. Pools, rigging the market, and preferred lists were other means of manipulating the money markets. More specifically, there was the wash sale, whereby one speculator agrees to sell a stock, and another agrees to buy it, at a point higher than it normally would command, in order to give the impression of a stronger market for the stock. There was the matched order, whereby two innocent brokers are hired, one to sell a stock and another to buy, to give the appearance of an active market for the stock.

The Federal Securities Act of 1933 and the Securities Exchange Act of 1934 were passed in response to wide bitterness and disillusionment over "Wall Street" practices. The 1933 act required the registration of all issues of stocks, bonds, or other securities offered in interstate commerce or by mail, along with a registration statement providing full information for potential investors. The 1934 act regulated the buying and selling of securities on exchanges throughout the country. To administer both acts, Congress established the Securities and Exchange Commission, an independent regulatory board of five men with five-year terms. All firms having listed securities must file regular reports with the SEC and with the exchanges. The main objective of these acts is to give full publicity to stock-market transactions, but they also outlaw manipulation and other unsavory practices of the past. The SEC can investigate suspicious activities in the market and even has the power to impose new trading rules on exchanges.

The commission has special powers over *public utility holding companies*— corporations that control networks of operating companies. Formerly, holding companies could escape regulation by incorporating in one state to take control of operating companies in another. Many abuses developed, such as siphoning funds from operating utilities into holding companies. There was also a problem of concentration. An investigation revealed that thirteen large holding-company groups controlled three-fourths of the entire privately owned electric utility industry, and over 40 per cent was concentrated in the hands of the three largest groups. To meet this problem, Congress in 1935 passed the Public Utility Holding Company Act. Not only must holding companies register full information with the SEC, but many of their transactions, such as issuing and buying securities, may be made only with the commission's consent. Congress also required the holding companies to get rid of their extraneous operating companies and to confine themselves each to a single integrated system.

Transportation

In August 1787, the framers of the Constitution were debating how much power they should give the new national government to regulate commerce. One day, as a relief from their labors, they junketed to the banks of the Delaware River to watch John Fitch demonstrate his sensational steamboat. "As we look back, it seems that Fitch and the Founding Fathers were working at different parts of one unfolding problem." While Fitch's experiment would bring the states into closer economic relations, the framers were granting Congress power to "regulate commerce with foreign nations, and among the several States. . . ." [11] Today Congress has virtually complete power to regulate interstate commerce, including transportation.

National power over interstate commerce is a far more powerful weapon today than the framers could have expected. For today that power extends to hundreds of thousands of miles of railways, to water-borne commerce, to networks of pipelines, to motor and air transportation. Congress controls not only the movement of persons, things, and words from state to state; it also has broad powers over the conduct of industries that *affect* interstate commerce.

Regulating (and Protecting) the Railroads

It is hard for us today to realize how deeply railroads were involved in the politics of the late nineteenth century. At first the national government's policy was to help railroads and during the years 1862–1866 alone Congress granted over 100 million acres of land to the railroad builders. But as evidence of corrupt use of these lands and of high rates charged by the railroads came to the public's attention, demands for national regulation became insistent. To many Americans of that time, the railroads were nothing but ogres intent on ruining the little man. Farmers had especially bitter grievances. They charged that railroads extorted outrageously high rates, conspired with one another to prevent competition, discriminated against certain localities and persons, corrupted officials, evaded taxes, watered their capital, and stole money that farmers

[11] Charles Fairman, *American Constitutional Decisions* (Holt, 1948), p. 173.

had invested in the railroads. Angry and desperate, the farmers turned to political action. The powerful Grange movement that swept the West in the 1870's and 1880's was a response to the tactics of railroads as well as to monopoly, middlemen, and the "ominous power of eastern financiers."

The Grange movement helped to secure a number of state laws regulating railroads. The railroads fought the new laws through appeals to the courts, and the Supreme Court in 1886 held that the commerce clause of the national Constitution deprived states of any authority to regulate transportation even within their own boundaries if it was part of commerce among the states.[12]

Shippers and small businessmen joined the farmers to demand that Congress fill the void and provide national regulation. The result was the Interstate Commerce Act of 1887 which set up the Interstate Commerce Commission, the first independent regulatory commission to be created by Congress and the beginning of a new era of more positive federal regulation of business.

The 1887 act was only a modest beginning. It gave the Interstate Commerce Commission authority to prevent railroads from charging special rates, rebating, and practicing other methods of discrimination, such as charging more for a short haul over a line where there might be less competition than for a long haul. At first a hostile Supreme Court narrowly restricted the Interstate Commerce Commission's authority over rates, but as a result of subsequent grants of jurisdiction, it became a powerful agency.

The ICC is composed of eleven commissioners who hold seven-year overlapping terms and with a large staff of over 2,400 regulate railroad rates and services, mergers, safety practices, corporation structures, and in fact, the entire railroad business. In addition, the ICC has jurisdiction over motor carriers operating in interstate commerce, water carriers in domestic service (such as ships operating on canals or rivers), and certain pipelines.

Today, however, the ICC's major concern is no longer to prevent railroads from taking advantage of those who use their services, as much as it is to help the railroads avoid financial bankruptcy in the face of increased operating costs and competition from buslines, trucklines, airlines, pipelines, shiplines, and the private automobile. By the Transportation Act of 1958, Congress authorized the ICC for a limited time to guarantee loans for railroads to maintain and improve their services and gave the commission additional authority to permit railroads to abandon local services on which they were losing money even if a state regulatory agency opposed.

Regulating the Airlines

The power to regulate air transportation is shared by the Civil Aeronautics Board and the Federal Aviation Agency. The five-member board is an independent agency that grants licenses to airlines, and regulates fares, rates, mergers, and other competitive practices. The board investigates accidents involving civil aircraft and determines their causes.

[12] *Wabash Ry. Co. v. Illinois* (1886).

It also regulates rates for carrying air mail and in so doing considers the need of each air carrier for enough revenues from mail and other sources to enable it to maintain air transportation needed for commerce, the postal service, and national defense.

The Federal Aviation Agency enforces the safety regulations established by the Civil Aeronautics Board and has other specialized regulatory duties, but is chiefly promotional. It aids the air transportation industry by developing and evaluating systems to improve its facilities; it also administers the Federal Airport grants-in-aid for the development of public airports.

Who Shall Haul What?

The ICC has jurisdiction over railroads, interstate buses, trucks, and inland water carriers. The CAB and FAA regulate airlines. And still other agencies regulate and subsidize transoceanic carriers (the Federal Maritime Commission and the Maritime Administration). The transportation industry is not subject to regulation by a single agency and there is no over-all transportation plan. Congress has never declared a broad and definite transportation policy. It has preferred to deal with problems piecemeal, pragmatically, as they arose. Partly as a result of the lack of a basic policy, the administrative machinery for direction of transportation is broken up, as agencies—largely independent of a central directing force, such as the President, and subject to varying political pressures—go their own way. There is some virtue in this freedom from unified executive power, but it means that there is no one agency responsible for proposing and enforcing a united transportation program for the nation.

The situation and prospects of the four principal modes of domestic transportation are not identical, but most authorities agree that uncoordinated, step-by-step attention to specific industry problems has not been adequate. Recommendations in the direction of a more comprehensive approach have included more realistic tax policies for all carriers, a re-examination of rate structures and rate-making, and the creation of a clear policy for users of such federally provided facilities as inland waterways. A former member of the CAB graphically demonstrated the urgency of such measures to offset the present fragmentary approach by predicting that ". . . if we keep on trying to plan our national transportation system this way, we will wake up in a national emergency one day and find that it won't do the job."

The Politics of Petroleum

Oil and natural gas are vital resources widely used and produced in a large number of states. Although the production, distribution, and sale of petroleum products are not public utilities in the traditional sense, the federal government is very much concerned with the industry. Some have charged that because of the powerful voice of the oil producers, especially in the United States Senate, the federal government has failed to protect the consumer and has become an instrument to promote the fortunes of the producers. They charge that the federal income tax laws, by granting producers a higher "depletion" allowance than other industries, gives special benefits to them. Spokesmen for the industry insist that the depletion allowances are essential incentives.

Regulation of the actual production of oil in the United States is primarily in the hands of the states, but the federal government provides needed support. Originally there was little government regulation. An oil pool would be discovered and producers would put down as many wells as possible to draw out the oil as fast as they could in order to prevent others from drawing from the pool. Such exploitation is wasteful. The drilling of many wells reduced natural pressure and left underground millions of barrels of oil that could be recovered only by more costly processes. Moreover, much of the oil was wasted by burning or running off into the ground. And at the same time, the discovery of a big oil field with unlimited production would cause so much oil to be placed on the market that the price would drop.

The problem became so acute during the Depression with the discovery of the huge East Texas Oil field that state governors took emergency action, even to the extent of calling out the National Guard. This led to a more formal type of regulation. Today, twenty states are members of the Interstate Compact to Conserve Oil and Gas. Although states are not legally compelled to do so, it is to their economic advantage to establish quotas for each well in the state on the basis of monthly forecasts of consumer demands made by the Bureau of the Mines in the Interior Department. The federal government lends its support to the Interstate Compact by making it a federal offense to ship in interstate commerce "hot oil"— that is, oil produced in excess of the state quota. The federal government also helps to maintain the price of American oil by imposing quotas on importers as to the amount and kinds of foreign oil they may bring into the United States.[13]

Presumably, competition among the oil companies protects the consumer. When it comes to natural gas, however, there is no such competition at the consumer level. Here the federal government's regulatory role is more positive. The Federal Power Commission, a five-man independent regulatory agency, in addition to regulating rates and services of electric utilities engaged in selling or sending electricity across state boundaries, polices the rates and services of companies that transmit natural gas across state boundaries or offer its sale for interstate resale. The actual sale of natural gas by a local utility to consumers is regulated by state agencies.

Until 1954 the Federal Power Commission made no attempt to regulate the rates charged by independent producers of natural gas to the interstate pipeline companies.[14] There are several thousand such producers located primarily in the

[13] Robert H. Salisbury, "Agriculture and Natural Resources," in J. W. Peltason and James M. Burns (eds.), *Functions and Policies of American Government* (Prentice-Hall, 1962), pp. 203–204. An overview of the political behavior of the petroleum industry is Robert Engler, *The Politics of Oil: A Study of Private Power and Democratic Directions* (Macmillan, 1961).

[14] For a careful and detailed analysis of all phases of this controversy, see Edith T. Carper,

Southwest, but a relatively small number of them produce most of the natural gas. Although the Federal Power Commission did regulate rates charged by the interstate pipeline companies, and state utility commissions regulated what the local utilities charged the consumer, the price paid by the consumer "floated" on top of the producer's unregulated prices.

Producers of natural gas insisted (and still insist) that no regulation was necessary. Competition, they maintained, protects the consumer; moreover, the natural gas industry does not require utility-type price regulation. The Federal Power Commission was divided on the matter. Then in 1950 the natural gas industry was able to persuade the Senate to refuse to reconfirm the appointment of Leland Olds to the commission. The defeat of Olds, a vigorous spokesman for regulation, gave the nonregulation forces control over the FPC, even though President Truman vetoed a bill that would have specifically exempted from FPC jurisdiction authority to regulate rates charged by producers.

The FPC persisted in refusing to regulate producers. Then in 1954 the Supreme Court ruled that not only did the commission have authority under the law to set "just and reasonable rates" for gas entering the interstate pipelines, but that it had a duty to do so. The natural gas producers returned to Congress where they have always had more support than in the courts or executive departments. Congress adopted a bill exempting them from FPC regulation. President Eisenhower was on record as favoring the natural gas industry proposal, so it looked like smooth sailing for the industry. However, when a senator revealed that some proponents of the bill had used unethical lobbying tactics, President Eisenhower vetoed the bill.

The FPC is struggling to develop formulas appropriate for the industry, for the problem of rate regulation is substantially different from those of electric utilities. Some FPC commissioners are not anxious to regulate the rates, but in time, as more commissioners are appointed to reflect the view of the consumer, as has been the case during the Kennedy and Johnson administrations, a more positive federal regulation of the natural gas industry is likely. But as this brief case study illustrates, in the American system, with its multiple centers of decision-making, an interest as powerful as the natural gas industry is not without its resources in protecting itself from federal regulation.

Labor-Management Relations

As we have seen, governmental regulation of business has been essentially *restrictive*. Most of the laws and rules have served to curb certain business practices and channel the dynamic force of private enterprise into socially useful channels. But regulation cuts two ways. In the case of American workers, most laws in re-

---

"Lobbying and the Natural Gas Bill" in Edwin A. Bock and Alan K. Campbell (eds.), *Case Studies in American Government: The Inter-University Case Program* (Prentice-Hall, 1962), pp. 175–222.

cent decades have tended not to *restrict* labor but to *confer rights* and *opportunities* on it. Actually, many labor laws do not touch labor directly; instead, they regulate its relations with employers, including contract provisions.

Most business leaders would probably like to see government return to its old hands-off policy (though with certain exceptions, noted in the next chapter). But not labor leaders. For if governmental regulation were to be wiped out, they fear that business would impose far stricter regulations of its own—longer working hours, for example.

Labor and the Government

Labor has not always looked on government with a friendly eye. Traditionally, workers have viewed federal and state judges with particular suspicion. Early in the American experience, judges, steeped in the common law, tended to follow the *conspiracy doctrine*—the idea that men must not combine to injure others. Since organized labor's traditional weapon has been the strike, this doctrine could be used by anti-union judges to prevent workers from acting effectively. Some judges freely issued injunctions against strikes, boycotts, and other kinds of union activities. Moreover, the courts often *interpreted* laws in a way that hurt labor. As we saw earlier in this chapter, the Supreme Court turned the Sherman Antitrust Act against labor, even though the workers thought it had been passed to curb business combinations rather than their own unions. Finally, the courts held unconstitutional a number of acts designed to improve the worker's lot. Perhaps the most famous example was the Supreme Court's invalidation of a New York law limiting employment in bakeries to sixty hours a week and ten hours a day on the grounds that the law interfered with freedom of contract and therefore violated the due process clause of the Fourteenth Amendment.[15]

But during the first half of this century, governmental protection and promotion were gradually extended over the whole range of labor activity and organization. This change was the result of two basic political developments—labor's growing political power, and the awareness of millions of Americans in all walks of life that a healthy and secure nation depends in large measure on a healthy and secure labor force. Both these developments were reflected in the election of pro-labor Presidents, such as Wilson and the two Roosevelts, and of friendly legislators in Senate and House and the state capitols.

Labor's basic struggle was for the *right to organize*. For many decades trade unions had been held lawful by acts of state legislatures, but here again the courts had chipped away at this right by legalizing certain anti-union devices. The most notorious was the yellow-dog contract, by which anti-union employers, before they would hire a new worker, made him promise not to join a labor organization. If labor organizers later tried to unionize the worker, the employer, on the basis of

[15] *Lochner* v. *New York* (1905).

yellow-dog contracts, could apply for injunctions from the courts to stop the organizers. This was a great stumbling block in the path of American unions. Chafing under this restriction, labor in 1932 secured the passage of the Norris-La Guardia Act, which made yellow-dog contracts unenforceable in federal courts. Granting labor the right to organize, the act also drastically limited the issuance of labor injunctions in other respects.

By 1932 labor had won other kinds of protection from the federal government, especially over conditions of labor. Almost a century before, in 1840, the government had established the ten-hour day in its navy yards, and later Congress shortened the working day of governmental employees to eight hours and required the eight-hour day for railroad employees and for seamen. Nevertheless, progress was slow, partly because of the courts. In 1918 the Supreme Court invalidated a national law prohibiting the interstate transportation of goods produced by child labor, and a constitutional amendment to give Congress this power had not got very far. By 1932 the United States still lagged far behind several European countries in the protection afforded to labor.

A New Deal for Labor

In 1932, on the eve of the Roosevelt administration, the AFL was down to barely two million members—partly a result of unemployment during the Great Depression. Its political influence was small. But the new administration was sympathetic toward labor. During the 1930's organized labor rose to a position of tremendous economic and political power. Under the New Deal, labor achieved both an array of protective legislation and governmental help in its campaign to organize the unorganized. The CIO split off from the AFL and unionized a number of vital industries, such as steel, automobiles, and rubber, but the AFL itself reformed its ranks and became larger and stronger than ever.

The National Industrial Recovery Act of 1933 laid the stage for the New Deal's labor policies. This act was essentially a means of giving business a shot in the arm by allowing industries to work out codes of fair competition. Such codes, however, involved labor standards, such as wages, hours, and child labor, and the unions were given a part in the code-making process. Moreover, Section 7a of the act contained the famous provision that "employees shall have the right to organize and bargain collectively through representatives of their own choosing, and shall be free from the interference, restraint, or coercion of employers of labor, or their agents, in the designation of such representatives or in self-organization or in other concerted activities for the purpose of collective bargaining or other mutual aid or protection." Under the stimulus of the NRA and the subsequent upturn in business, the unions blossomed. New members flocked into unions and violent organizational strikes occurred in many parts of the country.

The NRA was short-lived, for the Supreme Court declared the act unconstitutional in 1935. But the New Deal Congress, determined to maintain national protection and encouragement of labor, passed a series of acts in the next few years that amounted to a sort of NRA for labor. These acts were widely diversified.

Public Contracts. The Walsh-Healey Act of 1936 requires that all national government supply contracts in excess of $10,000 must provide that no worker employed under such contracts shall be paid less than the prevailing minimum wage as determined by the Secretary of Labor and overtime for all work in excess of eight hours per day or forty hours per week; that convict labor will not be used; and that child labor (boys under sixteen and girls under eighteen) will not be employed.

Wages and Hours. The Fair Labor Standards Act of 1938 went much further. It set a maximum work-week of 44 hours, to be successively reduced to 42 and then to 40 hours, for all employees engaged in interstate commerce, or in the production of goods for interstate commerce (with certain major exemptions). Employees could work beyond these limits only if paid at 1½ times the regular rate. Minimum wages were set at 25 cents an hour, but were to rise by jumps to 40 cents. In 1949 the minimum was raised to 75 cents an hour; in 1956 to $1.00 an hour; and in 1961, to $1.25. Congress is considering extending coverage to farm workers

USE OF LEISURE TIME, 1900–1975

1900

WORK TIME	60 hours weekly
LEISURE TIME	24 hours weekly
RECREATION SPENDING PER PERSON	Less than $10 a year

TODAY

WORK TIME	40 hours weekly
LEISURE TIME	44 hours weekly
RECREATION SPENDING PER PERSON	$200 a year

1975

WORK TIME	37 hours weekly (est.)
LEISURE TIME	47 hours weekly (est.)
RECREATION SPENDING PER PERSON	$350 a year (est.)

(Adapted from Pictograph, Inc. © 1964 & 1965 by The New York Times Company. Reprinted by permission.)

and other major groups. The Equal Pay Act of 1963 amended the Fair Labor Standards Act to compel employers to pay equal wages within an establishment to men and women doing equal work on jobs requiring equal skill, effort, and responsibility and performed under similar working conditions. Not only did the Supreme Court uphold the constitutionality of the Fair Labor Standards Act, but in later decisions it broadened the scope of the act.

The Fair Labor Standards and Walsh-Healey acts are administered by the Wage and Hour and Public Contracts Divisions of the Department of Labor; these two divisions are jointly administered by a head appointed by the President (with the consent of the Senate). They maintain a crew of inspectors who check business firms to insure compliance with the law, but their administrator has frequently asked Congress for more funds to permit more intensive inspection.

Child Labor. The Fair Labor Standards Act prohibited child labor (under 16 years of age or under 18 in hazardous occupations) in industries that engage in, or that produce goods for, interstate commerce. These provisions are enforced by the Wage and Hour and Public Contracts Divisions and the Bureau of Labor Standards (in the Labor Department).

Labor Relations. Section 7a of the NRA was resurrected in the National Labor Relations Act, which was passed in 1935 only two months after the Supreme Court struck down the former act. In the preamble, the Wagner Act (so called after its chief sponsor, Senator Robert Wagner of New York) declared that workers in industries affecting interstate commerce (with certain exceptions) should have the right to organize and bargain collectively, and that inequality in bargaining power between employers and workers led to industrial strife and economic instability. The act made five types of action unfair for employers to practice: (1) interfering with workers in their attempt to organize unions or bargain collectively; (2) supporting company unions (unions set up and dominated by the employer); (3) discriminating against membership in unions; (4) firing or otherwise victimizing an employee for having taken action under the act; (5) refusing to bargain with union representatives. The act was intended to prevent open-shop employers from using violence, espionage, propaganda, and community pressure to resist unionization of their plants.

The Wagner Act also set up machinery to decide contests over what union should represent a given group of employees. Such conflicts—which became numerous and bitter when the CIO broke away from the AFL in the mid-1930's—were to be settled by secret ballot and majority rule. To administer the act, a board of three members, now five members, holding overlapping terms of five years each, was set up. Under the act, the National Labor Relations Board (NLRB), an independent regulatory commission, has the ticklish job of determining the appropriate bargaining unit—that is, whether the employees may organize by plant, by craft, or on some other basis. The board operates largely through regional officers who investigate charges of unfair labor practices and may issue formal complaints, and through trial examiners who hold hearings and submit reports to the board in Washington.

Striking a Balance

From the start the Wagner Act was a center of controversy. It strengthened the unions and helped them seize greater economic and political power. In 1936 a committee of eminent attorneys declared that the measure was unconstitutional. Taking heart from this "opinion," many corporations simply ignored NLRB decisions. Unions, unwilling to wait for the slow-moving procedures of the law, organized a series of violent strikes, including the much-criticized sit-down strikes. In April 1937, during President Roosevelt's campaign to pack the Supreme Court, the Court by a five-to-four vote upheld the constitutionality of the Wagner Act.[16] The fight then shifted to Congress, where senators and representatives attacked the NLRB through denunciations, investigations, and slashes in its appropriations.

What had caused all this uproar? Three things: First, from the outset the board applied vigorously the pro-labor provisions of the act. For example, the act prohibited the employer from interfering with employee unionization; the board interpreted this to mean that employers could not even make public statements advising workers not to join unions. Such rulings raised a storm of protest from employers. Second, the board got caught in the struggle between the AFL and CIO. Whichever way it decided certain representation cases, it was bound to antagonize one labor faction or the other. Some of these cases, moreover, were highly consequential; in one decision the board designated the CIO Longshoremen's Union as the bargaining agent for all West Coast ports, although the AFL claimed majority support of employees in particular companies. Third, the purpose of the act was widely misunderstood. Employers and editorial writers solemnly charged the measure and the board with being biased in favor of labor, when the very aim of the act had been to improve the workers' bargaining power.

The controversy was sharpened by criticism of several union practices. These practices were not new, but now that labor was achieving greater power they came in for more public attention. One was featherbedding. Faced with labor-saving devices that cut down on the number of workers needed to do a given job, some unions demanded that the original number of workers be paid, even if they had nothing to do and merely stood around. For example, James C. Petrillo, former head of the AFL Musicians' Union, barred his members from making records, taking part in television broadcasts, or making transcriptions that could be played over the radio. Then there was the charge that unions were in the hands of dictators. Some union leaders stayed in office for years, even decades, and then passed control to other members of their family. To be sure, many union leaders had no more control over their unions than did many business executives over their enterprises, but, as we saw in Chapter 11, people's attitudes toward labor leaders are often hostile. And unions are supposed to be run in a democratic manner. Moreover, protected

[16] *National Labor Relation Board* v. *Jones & Laughlin Steel Corp.* (1937).

by the *closed shop* (a contract under which only union members can be hired),
some union heads seemed to have as much power to discipline members as had
the more ruthless employers of old. And a few unions were out-and-out rackets.
Investigations revealed intimate connections between certain union leaders and the
underworld.

Most unions continued to be run honestly and democratically. Nevertheless,
public opinion, fed by anti-union propaganda, seemed to swing against labor after
World War II. Not only labor excesses but a wave of great industry-wide strikes
intensified demands in Congress for a law that would equalize the obligations of
labor and management. In 1946 the Republicans won majorities in House and
Senate, paving the way for modification of the Wagner Act.

The Taft-Hartley Act

The upshot was the Labor-Man-
agement Relations Act of 1947, commonly called the Taft-Hartley Act after its
sponsors. This act, which applies with certain exceptions to industries affecting
interstate commerce:

> 1. Outlawed the closed shop, and permitted the *union shop* (under which
> newly employed workers must join the union within a stated time period) only
> under certain conditions.
> 2. Required unions to file affidavits that their officers are not communists,
> if such unions want to secure federal action on complaints against employers
> (since repealed).
> 3. Outlawed jurisdictional strikes (strikes arising from disputes between
> unions over which has the right to do a job), secondary boycotts, political
> expenditures by unions in connection with federal elections, excessive union
> dues or fees, and strikes by federal employees.
> 4. Made it an unfair labor practice for unions to refuse to bargain with
> employers.
> 5. Permitted employers and unions to sue each other for violation of con-
> tracts in federal courts.
> 6. Allowed the use of the labor injunction on a limited scale, reversing the
> policy set by the Norris-La Guardia Act.
> 7. Revamped the National Labor Relations Board, increasing its member-
> ship to five and strengthening the semi-independent position of the board's
> general counsel.

Organized labor greeted the new measure as a "slave-labor" act and vowed that
it would use its political power to wipe the act from the statute books. Senator Taft
saw the bill as "an extraordinary reversal along the right lines toward equalizing
the power of labor unions and employers." Most observers recognized the measure
as neither a slave-labor act nor as a cure-all. While acknowledging the seriousness
of some labor practices, they expressed fears that the Taft-Hartley Act, despite its
conservative sponsorship, may have pushed the government too far into the
hitherto voluntary area of collective bargaining.

The Labor Reform Act of 1959

During the late 1950's public attention focused less on relations between union and management and more on the internal affairs of unions. A Senate "rackets" committee investigating labor activities found in some unions glaring cases of corruption, dictatorial control by a few bosses, loose financial practices, and other deplorable practices. Heavily publicized, the committee's disclosures aroused popular demand for reform. At the same time, businessmen and others, with the backing of the Eisenhower Administration, wanted new restrictions on labor's use of the boycott and picketing. Union leaders hotly opposed reform on the grounds that it would harass good unions and have no effect on the bad ones. After two years of deadlock over the issue, Congress in 1959 passed the Labor Reform Act of 1959, which:

1. Requires labor organizations to file comprehensive reports with the Secretary of Labor on all financial transactions and on the workings of its constitution and bylaws.

2. Under a "bill of rights" section, grants union members the unqualified right to vote in union elections by secret ballot, to speak up freely in union meetings, to get open hearings in discipline cases, and to sue in federal courts if they feel that they are not getting fair play under union rules.

3. Requires secret elections at least every three years for local union officers and at least every five years for national union officers, and bars from union office ex-convicts, embezzlers of union funds, communists, and any union leader with conflicting business interests.

4. Plugs loopholes in the Taft-Hartley Act's provisions against the secondary boycott. For example, the new act outlaws the "hot cargo" weapon used by unions like the Teamsters to refuse to handle cargoes to or from firms involved in labor disputes.

5. Outlaws organizational picketing if the employer has validly recognized another union, or if there had been an NLRB election within the preceding year.

Most labor leaders "went along with" the Labor Reform Act of 1959, because they could not deny that a number of unions and their officials had been irresponsible. But organized labor continued to be strongly opposed to the Taft-Hartley Act. Their opposition focused on Section 14(b) of the act, which permitted states to outlaw union shops. Union leaders contended that this section was a deliberate effort to undermine their organizing efforts, especially in the South, where most of the states had taken advantage of the provision and had outlawed the union shop. Labor did not have the votes in Congress to repeal 14(b) until 1965, when the top-heavy Democratic majorities, under President Johnson's leadership, supported a repeal bill. Under its provisions "right-to-work" laws in nineteen states would be voided, with the result that in any firm where the union induced the management to agree to a union shop, for example, a worker who did not join the union within thirty days could be discharged.

Keeping Labor-Management Peace

The Federal Mediation and Conciliation Service, with mediators located in seven regional offices, stands ready to help settle labor-management disputes in any industry affecting interstate commerce (except railroads and airlines, which are covered by the Railway Labor Act), either on request of one of the parties to the dispute or whenever the dispute threatens to cause a substantial interruption of interstate commerce. Through tact and persuasion, the trouble shooters of the Federal Mediation and Conciliation Service induce unions to call off strikes and persuade employers to make concessions. The service has no power to dictate terms; the parties to the dispute are free to ignore the conciliators and their suggestions. If mediation fails, the parties may ask the service to assist in the selection of an arbitrator; under this arrangement the parties agree in advance to accept the arbitrator's decision.

The Taft-Hartley Act also set up new machinery for handling disputes affecting an entire industry, or a major part of it, where a stoppage would threaten national health or safety. When such a strike breaks out, the following steps are authorized:

1. The President appoints a special board to investigate and report the facts.
2. The President may then instruct the Attorney General to seek in a federal court an 80-day injunction against the strike.
3. The court grants this injunction if it agrees that the national health or safety is endangered.
4. If the parties have not settled the strike within the 80 days, the board informs the President of the employer's last offer of settlement.
5. The NLRB takes a secret vote among the employees to see if they will accept the employer's last offer.
6. If no settlement is reached, the injunction expires, and the President reports to Congress with such recommendations as he may wish to make.

How successful has the Taft-Hartley Act been in helping maintain labor peace? It has been invoked several times against strikes in vital sectors of the economy, such as atomic energy, coal, shipping, steel, and telephone service, sometimes successfully, sometimes not. President Kennedy's Advisory Committee on Labor-Management Policy, a group representing labor, management, and the general public, recommended that the President be given more authority and flexibility to deal with major strikes. Specifically, the committee recommended that the President be allowed to declare a national emergency, order an end to the strike for up to 80 days, and appoint an emergency dispute board that would have authority to make recommendations for the settlement of the dispute. There would be no judicial intervention unless one of the parties appealed to the courts from the President's declaration of a national emergency.

These recommendations, which stop considerably short of compulsory government arbitration of disputes, nonetheless would authorize the President to take a more active role in settling major strikes. Informally, President Johnson and his

Secretary of Labor have taken an active role in attempting to mediate a number of strikes, as did the Kennedy administration before them. Yet the basic issue remains unsolved: Strikes are part of the price we pay for a system of free collective bargaining, but under what conditions does the price become so high that the federal government should be authorized to intervene, stop the strike, and determine the terms of settlements? Congress—and the nation—will be dealing with this issue for a long time.

The policies of collective bargaining are but part of a broader set of issues. Labor is deeply concerned not only with the traditional conditions of work such as hours, wages, and pensions, but also with job security itself, now threatened by technical change and automation. Business is faced not only with rising costs but intense foreign competition, primarily from Western Europe and Japan. These problems clearly are not private. The public is directly affected by altered patterns of competition, quality of goods, prices, and unemployment. The impact of monopoly power of either a business or a union is felt throughout society. A healthy labor-management climate seems to require a willingness on the part of the immediate participants, the people, and their government to take a broad view of specific problems.

The Politics of Regulation

Karl Marx, the theorist of "capitalist decay," maintained that the long-run interests of all capitalists were the same. He argued that the proletariat had a similar unity of interest, and that eventually the exploiting class would give way to a government of the workers. Relations among the new proletarian rulers would be so harmonious that eventually the state would just wither away.

A look at the American economy today is enough to dispel the idea of a united group of businessmen facing a united group of workers. Admittedly, there is conflict between businessmen and workers. But such conflict is obscured by a vast complex of antagonistic interests operating *within* economic groups. The American political scene reflects not only the struggle of employer against worker, but also the struggles of consumer against producer, of businessmen against businessmen, of labor against labor, of section against section. And all these interests are intertwined and interlocked in such a way as to make the whole picture very complex indeed.

The Clash of Interests

In Chapter 11 we noted some of the characteristics and weapons of the larger economic interests. Here it might be well to look more closely at the competition among interest groups in the light of the problem of governmental regulation.

Some of the sharpest contests take place within the world of business. Consider, for example, the railroad interests. Early attempts to regulate the railroads reflected chiefly a struggle between the railroads and consumers. But other interests more and more were drawn into the struggle—for example, financial control groups, railroad investors, railroad equipment and supply industries. Later, the railroads began to meet intense competition from other forms of transportation, and railroad politics became even more intricate than before.

Today a political battle constantly simmers between railroad carriers and the trucking business, and occasionally this battle erupts in full-page advertisements in leading newspapers. The railroads argue that the trucking business offers unfair competition. The fact that government builds and maintains the nation's highways, they protest, means that motor transportation is subsidized, while the railroad must provide their own facilities. The truckers reply that they contribute heavily to highway maintenance through gasoline and other taxes—and so the battle rages. The railroads also complain of the subsidies granted airlines and water shippers.[17]

The internal rivalries of labor also affect the politics of regulation. Labor, as we noted, is by no means a unified, monolithic body; it is a cluster of unions of all kinds, sizes, and interests, along with many unorganized workers. The cleavages that develop within the ranks of organized labor were dramatically revealed in the 1930's when the CIO broke away from the AFL. But less conspicuous rivalries are also important. One of these is between workers employed in rival industries. For example, the Railroad Brotherhoods and the Teamsters' Union often clash on national transportation policy simply because industrially these two groups compete with each other. Sometimes, of course, unions ignore such competitive situations. Ford, General Motors, and Chrysler may compete in selling cars, but this rivalry has little effect on the solidarity of the United Auto Workers Union, which embraces workers from all three corporations.

The struggle of the interests also influences regulatory *procedures.* Recently, for example, the Civil Aeronautics Board decided to formulate a plan for federally subsidized local air service for seven midwestern states that were facing a transportation crisis because of contraction of railroad services. So many airlines, mayors, presidents of chambers of commerce, and others were affected by the plan that there were almost 100 parties to the case and almost 200 witnesses testified before one of the board's examiners. This expert, after reading through pleadings, transcripts, exhibits, and briefs that, piled up, were five and a half feet high, announced his plan for air service for the area—in two volumes totaling 658 pages. More exceptions and briefs were filed by the interests affected. Then the case went before the Civil Aeronautics Board and took on more of a political atmosphere, for 16 senators, 22 representatives and 3 governors testified along with spokesmen for the airlines concerned. The board finally announced its decision at the end of 1958— well over 3 years after the need for action became apparent.[18]

---

[17] Andrew Hacker, "Pressure Politics in Pennsylvania: The Truckers vs. The Railroads," in Alan F. Westin (ed.), *The Uses of Power: 7 Cases in American Politics* (Harcourt, Brace & World, 1962), pp. 323–375.

[18] Condensed from a case study in Louis J. Hector, "The New Critique of the Regulatory Agency," remarks before Section of Administrative Law, *Journal* of American Bar Association (August 25, 1959).

Who Regulates the Regulators?

The influence of the independent regulatory commissions is pervasive. The late Justice Jackson observed that the rise of these commissions "probably has been the most significant legal trend of the last century and perhaps more values today are affected by their decisions than by those of all the courts . . . They also have begun to have important consequences on personal rights." [19]

Congress has deliberately given to independent regulatory commissions the primary responsibility for restraining abuses of industrial power. As a practical matter this would not be essential. Regulatory functions can be—and are—handled by line agencies in regular federal departments under presidential responsibility. For example, the Bureau of Animal Industry in the Department of Agriculture regulates the packers and stockyards to protect farmers against arbitrary charges and other unfair practices. And wages and hours regulations are administered by a line agency lodged in the Labor Department. Nevertheless, Congress has generally preferred to make these special regulatory agencies relatively insulated from the President.

In creating each of the twenty regulatory commissions, Congress issued a broad policy directive but left it up to each commission, within the scope of its authority, to make the rules and issue the orders necessary to carry out the congressional mandate. Commissioners were given long, staggered terms; the President's power to remove them is limited; and he often must, in selecting commissioners, appoint men from both political parties. These arrangements have resulted in what some have called "a fourth branch of government."

How independent are these independent commissions? Who regulates the regulators themselves? An answer requires consideration of three quite separate but frequently confused questions. The first two questions are easiest to answer: Have the commissions operated without regard to partisan politics, and have they carried on their duties uninfluenced by improper pressures? For example, the Federal Communications Commission is supposed to decide which applicant should be licensed to use a television channel uninfluenced by personal favor, partisan preference, or the wishes even of the President of the United States. The Federal Trade Commission, in deciding if a particular company has violated the regulations concerning misleading advertising, is not supposed to be influenced by the intervention of a senator or the views of presidential assistants. Although there have been occasional incidents of improper conduct and lack of independence of the nature described, by and large the independent regulatory commissions have been insulated from partisan politics and have operated in accord with standards of propriety.

A far more difficult question is, "Have the commissions discharged their duties in terms of a broad concept of the public interest?" Obviously the independent regulatory commissions have not and cannot be made independent of politics in

[19] *FTC v. Ruberoid Co.* (1952).

the broader and more important sense of the word. No agency operating within a democracy and vested with important decision-making duties can be removed from the political system. Since independent regulatory commissions must decide big political questions calling for the adjustment of a variety of interests, their independence from the White House often makes them more dependent on the interests they regulate. For the groups most immediately affected by the decisions of a commission naturally have a more sustained interest in the regulations than does the general public. As Professor Murray Edelman has observed, "The organizational and psychological embrace of the industry around the regulatory commissioners go hand in hand. To be part of the organization in the sense of incessant exposure to its problems and decisional premises is to come to share its perspectives and values. This is not 'pressure'; it is absorption." [20]

A regulatory commission which offends a highly organized interest may discover that it is not quite as "independent" as its formal charter indicates. For the interests frequently work through the Congress and often can exert pressures on a commission more easily by moving through a congressional committee than by direct pressures on the commission. The Interstate Commerce Commission is often cited as one of the most judicial and independent agencies in Washington. It is rarely charged with showing favoritism of an improper sort or of being the tool for one railroad over another, but it is often accused of favoring the railroads over other forms of transportation. Whether this charge is true or not, the capture of a regulatory agency by the regulated interests is not unknown in Washington.

The "independence" of regulatory commissions from the President can also be exaggerated. A President may not be able and should not be allowed to influence a particular decision of a commission any more than of a court, but the general thrust of policies of an independent regulatory commission are very much a part of the President's responsibilities. A President dedicated, let us say, to a more vigorous regulation of unfair labor practices by unions or unfair methods of competition can readily make his influence felt. Despite their formal independence, it is difficult for commissions to withstand the impact of a powerful President who through his influence in Congress and the nation may bring about changes in basic statutes or alterations in appropriations. Moreover, most men do not wish to retain a position on a commission when the views they represent are inconsistent with those of the President. Thus it does not take long for the attitude of an administration to be reflected in decisions of the regulatory commissions.

Although their members are influenced by the executive, their powers derive from legislative delegation, and their decisions are subject to review in the courts, independent regulatory commissions have a scope of responsibility to the American economy that may exceed that of the three "regular" branches of government. Aside from the many operative problems of the agencies, such as delay in processing cases, increasing judicialization of procedures, overlapping jurisdiction, and lack of interagency coordination, the key issue remains—who regulates the regulators?

[20] Murray Edelman, *The Symbolic Uses of Politics* (Univ. of Illinois Press, 1964), p. 66.

25 GOVERNMENT AS PROMOTER

In recent years we have heard a great deal about the welfare state. Politicians have charged that spendthrifts in Washington have been trying to buy votes through give-away programs. Supporters of federal subsidies—which we will call here "promotion"—have denounced their opponents as heartless skinflints who would put dollars before human lives. In the heat of the argument, certain facts are sometimes ignored.

In the first place, governmental promotion is by no means a recent development in the United States. In his first annual address to Congress, President Washington called for a tariff to protect business. In his famous *Report on the Subject of Manufactures* in 1791, Secretary of the Treasury Alexander Hamilton proposed that government help develop business by giving bounties to new enterprises. Henry Clay's American System was a plan in the first part of the last century for federally subsidized roads and waterways, a strengthened banking system, and tariff protection. Parts of these ambitious programs were carried out during the first half of the nineteenth century, and after the Civil War the Republican party bestowed special-interest subsidies on businessmen, farmers, veterans and other groups.

In the second place, almost all groups have at one time or another benefited directly from government aid. During much of the nation's history, business has been the main recipient of help from Washington; but farmers and veterans have been given preferred treatment as well. Governmental promotion can be used to help any group. The main questions are: Who shall be aided? In what way? And with what consequences for the general welfare? The politics of promotion revolves around these questions.

Helping Businessmen

In the broadest sense, government assists business, as all interests, by maintaining an orderly legal and economic system. A government that protects private property and enforces contracts enables businessmen to operate in a stable situation where agreements can be enforced. A government that helps promote a prosperous economy enables businessmen to enjoy a large volume of sales and good profits. A high or low tariff can have considerable effect on the profits of individual concerns. The kind of monetary system established by government—for example, "tight" or "easy" money—is of direct interest to businessmen (see Chapter 26).

Aside from such obvious aids to business, the national government supplies a number of specific services and assists individual sectors of business.

The Department of Commerce

Occupying one of the largest office buildings in the world, the Department of Commerce in Washington is the nation's "service center for business." The Secretary of Commerce is usually a person with a business background and acceptable to the business community. Under his direction the department assists business in many ways. For example, the Office of Business Economics reports on business activities and prospects at home and abroad. The National Bureau of Standards makes scientific investigations and standardizes units of weight and measurement.

The Bureau of the Census has been called the greatest fact-finding and figure-counting agency in the world. The Constitution requires that a national census be taken every ten years, and the results of this census, and of others in between, supply businessmen with valuable information on business and agricultural activity, incomes, occupations, employment, housing, home ownership, governmental finances, crime, and many other matters. Its findings are presented in bulky volumes published by the Government Printing Office. Perhaps the most valuable of these, especially for businessmen, is the annual *Statistical Abstract of the United States*.

Another historic bureau now in the Commerce Department is the *Patent Office*. The first article of the Constitution authorizes Congress to secure to authors and inventors for a limited period "the exclusive right to their respective writings and discoveries." A patent, conferring the right of exclusive use of an invention for seventeen years, is a valuable property right. On receiving an application for a patent right, the Patent Office must study its records to see if any prior patent might be infringed and if the invention is sufficiently original and useful to be patentable; meanwhile the applicant marks his product "Patent Pending." Since decisions of the Patent Office directly involve legal rights, its rulings may be appealed to a board of appeals in the Patent Office and then to the Court of Customs and Patent Appeals or to a federal district court. Some cases even go to the Supreme Court. Although most patent problems are technical, patent policy also involves such broad problems as the stimulation of invention and the threat of monopoly and economic concentration.

The Environment Science Services Administration, an agency created in 1965, combines two long-standing service bodies, the *Weather Bureau* and the *Coast and Geodetic Survey*. The Weather Bureau not only tries to forecast the weather, but, working with private agencies, also attempts to do something about it. Staffed with over 6,000 employees, the bureau makes forecasts on the basis of data funneled in by its 325 field stations in this country and overseas. Its services are utilized especially by farmers, airlines, the resort business, and other industries. Such experiments as seeding clouds to induce rain and the use of electronic computers suggest that the Weather Bureau may have an even greater role for both civilian and military activities in days to come.[1] The Coast and Geodetic Survey charts the nation's coastlines, lake and river beds, and the ocean tides and currents along routes of commerce. Its maps and charts are used by air and sea navigators, engineers, fishermen, and others.

Other Aids to Business

In addition to the activities of the Department of Commerce, the government assists business through other agencies. One of these is the *Small Business Administration*. Created in 1953, it is an independent agency headed by an administrator, who is appointed by the President. The Small Business Administration is designed to aid small enterprises through such services as financial counseling, research, loans to victims of natural disasters,

[1] See Donald R. Whitnah, A *History of the United States Weather Bureau* (Univ. of Illinois Press, 1961).

such as floods and hurricanes, and loans for general expansion. Perhaps its major function is to insure that a fair proportion of government purchases and contracts are placed with small business.

The government also aids business through research and experimentation carried on by a variety of agencies. Annually, millions of dollars are spent for research that often directly benefits private industry. Examples include new commercial wood products resulting from basic work done in the laboratories of the U.S. Forest Service and diversified uses of bituminous coal resulting from research in the Department of the Interior.

Through a wide range of promotional services, government assists the business community not only to survive but to make the necessary adjustments to a changing economy.

Facing the World Market

From one perspective the business economy seems healthy and dynamic: The gross national product is high and continues to grow; the standard of living, reflected by our purchases of consumer goods, has also been at an all-time high; despite some unemployment, more people have been working in American industry than ever before. Some observers are content to believe that such conditions will automatically continue if we simply tend to our business at home. But dramatic changes since World War II have made that perspective dangerously narrow.

Changed world conditions have brought three essentially new external challenges to the American economy. First, it has become clearly apparent that if we are to maintain our economic growth and high standard of living we must sell our products abroad as well as at home. But unprecedented economic development in the rest of the world has introduced a new kind of foreign competition. No longer are our allies simply recipients of aid to rebuild war-devastated industries. They are keen competitors. In Europe, American business no longer faces a relatively weak and nationally fragmented competitor, but an established and growing European Common Market. This entity has a potential industrial capacity equivalent to our own, and a population—and hence a market—significantly larger than ours. Japan, which has experienced tremendous industrial expansion, already effectively competes with many American manufacturers. The question is how will American goods, often priced far above those of our free world competitors, continue to fare on the world market.

American business faces a second challenge in international trade from the Soviet bloc. As noted in previous chapters, the conflict between the free and communist worlds is not confined to the military or diplomatic spheres. The communists have already made significant industrial advances and have begun to make inroads in world trade. Undoubtedly this form of competition will be increasingly important, as the communist leaders have promised an intensified "trade offensive."

The third challenge concerns the newly emerging nations. Ambitious to secure their independence through economic and social development, these nations find themselves short of necessary human and material resources. They seek economic and technical assistance and also markets for their products. Will these countries be able to sell us their goods so that they, in return, can afford to buy ours? Many of these new nations are looking for a model. Does the American business system provide a pattern that can successfully be followed by these emerging states or will they choose economic and political systems incompatible with our own?

Of course there must be a close relationship between government and business in meeting these complex challenges. But foreign and commercial policy have long been closely connected. American goods are promoted by consular agents around the world. Commercial attachés at American embassies also look out for American business interests abroad. But the principal device used by all governments to aid their nation's business has been the *tariff*.

Congress, constitutionally responsible for the regulation of foreign commerce, has generally favored interests desiring high protective tariffs. Over the years, businesses jeopardized by foreign competition successfully petitioned Congress to curb competitive imports. By the beginning of this century, however, many industries protected by high tariffs had expanded to a point where sales in foreign markets were imperative. And Americans discovered that foreign trade is a two-way proposition—if you want people in a foreign market to buy your goods, you must be willing to buy theirs.

In spite of continuing protectionist pressures, Congress began in 1934 to lower tariffs. Through the Trade Agreements Act and its eleven extensions, the President now is empowered to negotiate mutual tariff reductions with other nations. Trade barriers have been lowered, but the protectionists have managed to place restrictions on the President in the form of elaborate negotiating procedures, limits on the percentage of reduction allowed, and exemptions for industries claiming injury from the competitive imports.

In 1962 President Kennedy moved to revise substantially trade and tariff policies. He contended that continued economic growth required expanded foreign trade at a rate impossible under current policies. Tariff reductions could, through the introduction of foreign competition, help hold down our own costs and prices and increase our total productivity, which had been lagging. Lower prices and increased productivity, the President claimed, would result in a vastly improved competitive position in international trade. He asked Congress for broadened negotiating power with authority to cut existing tariffs and with discretion to deal with general categories of products rather than on an item-by-item basis as now required. Acknowledging that there would be some adverse domestic effects, he coupled these requests with a "trade adjustment" program designed to soften the blow for industries and workers hit by foreign competition. For workers unemployed because of imports introduced by tariff cuts, he proposed a program of compensation while out of work, assistance for relocation to new job sites, and opportunities for retraining in new skills. For injured businesses, the President asked for loans, loan guarantees, tax benefits to encourage modernization or conversion, and technical assistance.

The legislative struggle for the trade expansion program reflected some unusual interest group alignments. While having some reservations on specific provisions, such strange bedfellows as the Chamber of Commerce, the AFL-CIO, and the Farm Bureau were arrayed in support of the bill. In addition to traditional protectionists, led by the textile industry, opposition arose from some groups suspicious of expanding the President's power and others wary of the long-term costs of the "trade adjustment" provisions. Despite this opposition, the President gained wide power to reduce tariffs in the passage of the Trade Expansion Act of 1962.[2]

A policy of expanded trade and tariff reduction is not in itself a comprehensive answer to the three basic challenges of the world market. Yet it can be a vital step toward an effective trade posture in dealings with both our industrialized allies and the communist bloc. In the long run, it could prove helpful in developing our commercial relations with the emerging nations of the world.

Aiding Farmers

Nowhere is the diversity of American life more apparent than in agriculture. American farmers grow an amazing variety of crops. There are big farmers employing scores of workers on many hundreds of acres of land; there are "family-sized" farmers operating farms of 100 to 200 acres with the help of one or two hired hands; there are tenant farmers working other men's farms for a share of the produce and profits; there are, finally, millions of farm laborers, many of whom move on from farm to farm as the seasons change.

This wide diversity is reflected in the highly complex set of problems commonly identified simply as the "farm problem." There are actually many inter-related problems, but the basic difficulty is that American agriculture is out of balance with the rest of society. The general features of this imbalance are these: [3]

Internal Imbalance. All farms are not equally successful. In most cases successful farms today use more capital, more land, and less labor than the marginally prosperous ones. Yet the "big" farms, which have kept pace with technological developments and have made the best use of resources, constitute a minority of farms in America. The "family" farms, while most numerous, supply only 15 per cent of the market. The lack of balance between agricultural units is related in part to their internal organization and efficiency. As is true in other economic sectors, effective competition in agriculture seems to require a large organization with modern management techniques. Most American farms are relatively small

[2] See Raymond A. Bauer, Ithiel de Sola Pool, and Lewis Anthony Dexter, *American Business and Public Policy: The Politics of Foreign Trade* (Atherton, 1963), pp. 73–81 for the broad context in which trade policy is made.

[3] The following is based on Wallace Barr, "The Farm Problem Identified," in *The Farm Problem—What Are the Choices*, No. 1 (National Committee on Agricultural Policy, 1961, pp. 1–4.

and cannot share in such advantages as large-scale purchases, improvements, and sales.

Social Imbalance. The most neglected aspect of the farm problem is the emerging imbalance between agriculture and other social institutions. Today most people live in cities, and those remaining on farms and in rural communities face special adjustments. Many rural communities are being bypassed by social and economic development. Some are hard-pressed to provide adequate schools, fire protection, and sanitation. The problem for those who are leaving these communities may be even more acute. Lacking occupational skills and unprepared for urban life, thousands of families migrate each year from failing farms to find work in the city. Too often the displaced farmers remain unemployed and their families encounter serious difficulties in adjusting to life in the city.

Economic Imbalance. The general public is probably most aware of the economic aspect of the farm problem—the imbalance between output and demand for farm products. The American farmer's enormous productivity regularly outpaces demand. The adoption of improved production methods—mechanization, fertilizers, pesticides, antibiotics, and the like—has brought sharply increased total production. But these technological advances have also brought increased costs and new demands on management. While costs have tended to increase or at least remain fixed, prices have been highly flexible and have tended to drop in response to increased output. Most farmers thus have been caught in a "cost-price squeeze." Many cannot sell their products at prices that both cover their costs and return an income comparable to similar sectors of the economy. As a result, the American farmer has not shared in the nation's economic growth. All these facts closely affect the relation of government to agriculture.

The Growth of Federal Aid

The principal agricultural role of the federal government during the nineteenth century was clearly one of promoting production. The Homestead Act of 1862 gave settlers 160 acres of public land in exchange for a promise to occupy the land for at least five years. That same year Congress granted huge tracts of land to the states for the establishment of colleges and created the Department of Agriculture. In later years agricultural experiment stations were set up, conservation and reclamation programs undertaken, and farm cooperatives encouraged.

World War I increased governmental intervention in agriculture; the prices of food, cotton, and farm land skyrocketed, and the farmers enjoyed a boom. In 1920 the bubble burst. Prices plummeted and millions of farmers were left with surplus land, unpaid for machinery, high taxes, and burdensome debts. Farmers turned to Washington and Congress responded by passing measures to *police the trading* in contracts for future delivery of agricultural commodities, to *encourage agricultural cooperatives,* and to *ease credit.* These proved ineffectual in stemming the agricultural depression.

The Great Depression simply intensified agricultural stagnation and farmers began to "raise less corn and more hell," as Populist leaders had urged them to do decades before. In response to this ferment, the new Roosevelt administration quickly secured passage of a revolutionary farm measure—the Agricultural Adjustment Act—within the first 100 days of its incumbency.

"I haven't decided which I prefer, Luke—full parity through supply-management controls, marketing quotas, and land retirement with conservative practices or. . . ." (Drawing by Stevenson; © The New Yorker, Inc.)

This new act was complicated, but its chief objective was simply to induce farmers to *cut down production* to a level low enough to force prices to rise. But how could the farmers be induced to decrease production? The answer was: Pay them to do it. So in return for cash bounties several million farmers voluntarily cut down production, plowed under part of their crops, and killed sows and pigs. Results were quickly forthcoming. Farm production decreased, prices rose, and farm income increased by over a third.

To pay for the cash benefits, the 1933 act levied a tax on processors of farm commodities, such as millers and meat packers. This provision proved to be the act's Achilles' heel, for in 1936 the Supreme Court found the measure unconstitutional on the grounds that the taxes were not levies to finance government but levies on one group to give benefits to another, and that Congress had entered a field reserved for state action under the Tenth Amendment.[4]

___

[4] *United States* v. *Butler* (1936).

Recent Farm Policy

Stunned by this decision, the administration set about formulating a new farm program. This time the strategy was to tie a control plan to soil conservation. Drought and dust storms had dramatized the need for soil conservation, and it was reasoned that the Supreme Court would not veto an act directed toward this purpose provided no processing tax was involved. Accordingly, Congress in 1936 enacted the Soil Conservation and Domestic Allotment Act. Half a billion dollars was appropriated to pay farmers for adopting good conservation methods, such as cutting down on soil-depleting crops like wheat, corn, and cotton, and growing more grasses and legumes that replenish the soil.

This act helped stabilize prices and production, but it could not cope with the immensity of the problem. Faced with continuing surpluses and low prices—and with increased political agitation in farm regions—Congress passed a new Agricultural Adjustment Act in 1938. This measure was somewhat similar to the ill-fated 1933 act, except that it carefully avoided the processing tax. Control of production was achieved by these steps: First, if in any year forecasts indicated a heavy production of basic farm commodities and a possible price break, producers of the crop involved would be asked in a referendum if they favored setting limits on production. Second, if two-thirds of the voting farmers supported limitations, each county was to be allotted a maximum acreage for growing crops under the plan. Third, if the farmer wished to grow more than his allotment, he could do so, but he would be subject to a fine if he marketed his excess production during a time of surplus conditions. Fourth, on controlled crops the farmer would receive government loans; the government would then store the surplus crops until a time of scarcity, at which point the farmer might sell them at stable prices and pay back his loan. The essential idea was a plan that would store surplus crops in time of high production and release them in years of shortage. This approach is still one of the pillars of our agricultural policy.

World War II brought an abrupt change in farm policy. The problem in the years 1942–1945 was not to restrict production but to meet the immense needs of our armed forces, our allies, and our civilian population. Postwar administrations, however, were once again confronted with the old problems of huge surpluses, rising production, and falling commodity prices. Sharp disagreement arose in the early 1950's between the Eisenhower administration and Democrats in Congress over the best way of dealing with these problems. While the Democrats were intent on maintaining *rigid* price supports of 90 per cent, the administration advocated a system of *flexible* price supports for basic commodities at a sliding scale of 82½ to 90 per cent of parity. As the farm economy weakened in 1954 and 1955, the conflict over farm policy came to a head in the 1956 session of Congress. The imminence of the election of 1956 brought an end to the stalemate, however, as leaders of both parties viewed some sort of compromise as the safest way out of this dilemma. An act was passed embodying an old conservation idea in the new form of a "soil bank." Under this plan the government pays farmers for taking certain types of land out of production. After another period of interparty conflict over farm policy Congress passed the compromise Agriculture Act of 1958, which represented a retreat from high rigid supports. It required a gradual lowering of supports for rice and cotton and ended the acreage-reserve feature of the soil bank program; but it granted more funds to the long-range conservation reserve part of the soil bank in order to take more land permanently out of corn production.

In the mid 1960's there is continuing evidence that farm policy needs major reshaping. The productivity of American farmers has shot up so far and fast that although each year the total number of acres planted decreases, the total crop output increases. Other portentous facts are the continuing decline of the small farm, the restiveness in the cities over the high cost of food, and soaring farm surpluses, which are worth between $7 and $8 billion a year and cost nearly a billion dollars each year just to handle and store. Despite presidential proposals for change, Congress seems reluctant to move either in the direction of boosting farm prices by means of strictly enforced marketing quotas or in the direction of reduced gov-

"It looks as if we'll have a good corn crop too." (Herblock in The Washington Post.)

ernmental control and a "freer" market. Meanwhile, President Johnson has indicated that principal emphasis will be on reducing the farm population by helping
those not needed in the fields to shift to other ways of making a living.

Governmental control of farm production and marketing today involves essentially these techniques:

Acreage Allotments. Government experts regularly estimate the probable demand for staple commodities like cotton, wheat, and rice. Then, using an elaborate
system that takes into account the past and present characteristics of each farm,
they break down the national acreage allotments into individual allotments.

Conservation Reserves. This is the long-term phase of the soil bank in which
lands are taken out of production for three to fifteen years. The farmers who agree
to plant their land in grass or trees receive from the government most of the costs
of planting and a "reasonable annual return." No grazing on this land is to be
permitted.

Benefit Payments. These are grants to farmers to secure their cooperation in
acreage reserves and conservation programs, in order to induce them to plan production in the light of the national and international situation and the needs of
soil conservation.

Commodity Loans. The average farmer, operating without government assistance, would have to sell his crops at prevailing prices as soon as they were har-
vested, for he would need cash to meet out-of-pocket expenses. Commodity loans
from the government, however, enable the farmer to store his crops until he can
sell them at a good price. By discouraging farm commodities from flooding into
the market after each harvest, these loans encourage orderly marketing and eliminate sharp price changes.

Marketing Quotas. These limits on what the farmer may market supplement the
acreage allotments. When production becomes high and a price collapse threatens,
farmers by a two-thirds vote may approve the establishment of marketing quotas.
Each producer is allotted his share; he pays a penalty if he markets more than his
share.

Price Supports. In its price-support program, the government buys up and stores
commodities when it appears that excess production may cause prices to fall below a certain minimum. This policy does for farmers what the Wages and Hours
Act does for labor—it puts a floor under income.

Surplus Disposal Abroad. Although for many years the government sent surplus
farm products abroad for relief purposes, a systematic program of foreign disposal
is now in effect. Known as "Food for Peace," this plan provides for long-term

credit sales, sale of surplus for foreign exchange, as well as donations of excess products through international relief agencies, such as CARE or the Red Cross. Since its adoption in 1954, this program and related ones have accounted for the disposal of over $13 billion worth of farm goods.

Surplus Disposal at Home. A relatively small amount of the farm surplus is used at home in welfare programs. Surplus food is distributed in the schools through such systems as the National School Lunch Act and the School Milk Program. Some of the surplus is available to needy families through a number of state and local programs. This domestic disposal seems to improve children's nutrition more than it reduces the surplus.

Administering the complex controls described above is the job of the *Department of Agriculture,* one of the largest and most influential civilian agencies in Washington. This is the farmer's agency; the department makes no bones about protecting his interests and promoting his welfare. The Secretary of Agriculture is usually a man from a farming state who has the respect of the leading farm organizations (see Chapter 11). Indeed, the political influence of the department in Washington is rooted in the power of the farm interests. The department also works closely with the farm bloc and the agricultural committees in Congress.[5] Aside from price and production controls, the department is responsible for many other activities. It is one of the world's great research agencies and carries on an extensive education and information program. Its Rural Electrification Administration has made low-interest loans to governmental bodies and cooperatives for the construction of electric generation and transmission facilities, for the extension of telephone service, and for the purchase of electrical appliances. The department's Soil Conservation Service promotes the development and maintenance of soil productivity. Through the Farm Security Administration, the department tries to help tenant farmers, share-croppers, and farm workers, many of whom live in rural slums. The poverty program, to be discussed later, enhances this effort by making available to low-income rural families loans administered by the Department of Agriculture.

Farm Policy: Prospects

Existing farm policies have aroused sharp controversy. Our allies complain bitterly of our dumping surpluses on the world market. Domestic critics ask why it is necessary to pay the farmer for not farming and yet storing our surplus at great expense when some of our own people are undernourished and tens of millions abroad are starving. The opponents point to abuses in the soil bank, inequities in marketing quotas, and flagrant profiteering in the huge storage program. Price supports, they argue, may help some of the farmers at the expense of pinching all the consumers. The present

---

[5] See J. M. Gaus and L. O. Wolcott, *Public Administration and the United States Department of Agriculture* (Public Administration Service, 1940).

policies are further criticized as having created a sort of Frankenstein's monster of surpluses and controls that the government can hardly handle. So far at least, production controls have not prevented surpluses, and present policy, it is said, tends to freeze existing agricultural activity, rendering it less adaptable to changing conditions.

Defenders claim that under current policies American agriculture *is* adjusting. Working conditions on the farm have been vastly improved and farm production is undeniably high and relatively stable. These facts are important, they say, not only for the farmers but also for the economic and military security of all Americans. Admitting that the machinery of administration is somewhat cumbersome, they stress the democratic nature of the program—for example, the way farmers can vote on marketing quotas. Finally, they point out that while the program has been expensive in terms of dollars, the cost has been low considering the tremendous benefits that have accrued to the farmers.

The question is largely one of the degree of support. To what extent should the federal government subsidize farmers, and in what manner? This key issue is summed up in the word *parity*. Farmers demand that their income should be roughly equal to the income of other sections of the population. Parity, they argue, means that the products the farmer sells should bring him a return roughly equal to the cost of the products that he buys. But what should parity amount to? Farmers feel that during the 1920's they were not receiving a fair income, for their costs were high while farm prices were low. The fairest ratio between farm and other prices, they say, was achieved in the period 1909 to 1914. One of the main efforts of farmers' organizations has been to induce Congress to use the 1909–1914 yardstick in establishing price supports and other controls.

Quotas, allotments, benefit payments, price supports—these and other devices have given some farmers a measure of stability and even prosperity. But the basic *imbalance* persists. One cause of the long-term problem is the constant increase in agricultural technology and productivity, as we have seen. Another problem is rural poverty. Half of the nation's farms produce only 10 per cent of the farm products. Many farmers till substandard land, lack equipment and expertness, and live in deplorable conditions. At the opposite pole are farm operators who own thousands of acres and make a good deal of money, and at the same time are receiving federal subsidies. A special problem is the lack of housing, medical, and educational facilities for the families of migratory workers. But the basic problem is this: How can we give farmers—influenced as they are by faraway events—a measure of security in an unstable economy and an unstable world? [6]

Farming is more than an occupation or a livelihood; it is a way of life. Despite the movement of millions of Americans from country to city, many people still cling to farming even when it seems almost impossible to earn a living from the land. Partly because of his wish to stay close to the soil, partly because of the very

[6] For a discussion of the complexities of this problem and a summary of the various sides to the argument, see Reo M. Christenson, *Challenge and Decision: Political Issues of our Time* (Harper & Row, 1964), pp. 72 ff.

nature of agriculture, the farmer is in a vulnerable position. Compare his difficulties with those of a businessman. When demand for his products falls, the
businessman can retrench. He lets some of his workers off, cuts down on his orders
for materials, decreases his output, and thus reduces his expenses. But most of
the farmer's expenses continue at the same level no matter what the state of the
market is. There is little he can do to cut back. So when the price of wheat, for
example, drops from $1 a bushel to 50 cents, the farmer tries to grow more wheat
to make the same income. Result: Next year, if conditions remain the same, wheat
may be down to 25 cents a bushel. Nor can farmers get together to agree to reduce production—they are too numerous and widely scattered.

What the first New Deal agricultural program tried to do for farmers was essentially what businessmen have done without governmental aid. Although plowing
under corn and killing little pigs made dramatic newspaper headlines, the same
thing was being done throughout the country by private businessmen. Millions
of automobiles, washing machines, houses, and radios were not plowed under but
were simply not produced. The first AAA was an attempt to fight agricultural depression by reducing production. Since then we have been moving, though haltingly,
in the general direction of meeting the farm problem by increasing consumption,
by creating new demand, by shifting farm production toward commodities for
which there is a good market.

From a strictly economic viewpoint, of course, we could just let farm prices
drop indefinitely until the market had eliminated all farmers who could not make
a go of it at prevailing prices. But farming is a *political* as well as an economic
matter. Farmers are politically potent in Washington and in the state capitals. And
the people as a whole, though they may grumble about the cost of farm produce,
want to protect the farmer's economic position and way of life.

Science and Government

The Founding Fathers were aware of the importance of science. Congress was
given specific authority to provide for the census, to establish weights and measures, and to encourage scientific endeavors by regulating patents. But of more
importance has been the broader power to appropriate money for the general
welfare and to provide for the common defense.

The national government has long been involved in science: the Lewis and
Clark Expedition, the Army Corps of Engineers, the National Academy of Sciences, and the Morrill Act of 1862 mark important developments. But the biggest
expansion came after World War II. Today the federal government spends more
than $15 *billion* annually on research and development ". . . of which over
three-quarters is not performed by the government at all but by industry, universities, and various nonprofit organizations." [7] About 50 per cent of the engineers in the United States and 25 per cent of the scientists are employed by the

[7] J. Stefan Dupre and Sanford A. Lakoff, *Science and the Nation* (Prentice-Hall, 1962), p. 9.

federal government either directly or indirectly. About 65 per cent of scientific research in universities and about 57 per cent in private industry is financed by the federal government.[8]

The national government conducts most developmental work in its own laboratories or through *contracting* with private industry and universities. To support science where the concern is less with immediate solution of problems, the national government makes *grants*, chiefly to university scientists. These contracts and grants are sources of competition between university research centers.[9] Although Congress provides some scientific support that has no direct national security implication, especially in connection with the health sciences, the federal government's involvement in science is still heavily weighted on the side of "hardware"—that is, science that has some immediate "payoff" in space or military benefits.

Scientific Agencies

The federal government filters support for science through many agencies, the most important being the National Science Foundation, the National Institute of Health of the Public Health Service, the Atomic Energy Commission, and the National Aeronautics and Space Administration. The *Atomic Energy Commission*, established by the 1946 act, operates a vast scientific complex, but the bulk of its work is done by contract or grants. Among the many research facilities supported by AEC is the Brookhaven National Laboratory on Long Island, a facility operated by twelve universities.

Largely in response to Soviet space success, Congress passed the National Aeronautics and Space Act in 1958. The act provided for two organizations to promote research and exploration of outer space "devoted to peaceful purposes for the benefit of all mankind." The first, the National Aeronautics and Space Administration, is an independent executive agency headed by an administrator appointed by the President with the consent of the Senate. NASA employs about 19,000 persons in functions ranging from the development, construction, testing, and operation of nonmilitary aeronautical and space vehicles to the encouragement of the widest possible participation by the scientific community in space-related research. Its facilities at Edwards, California, Huntsville, Alabama, Houston, and Cape Kennedy, are known to all Americans.

The second space organization created in 1958 is the National Aeronautics and Space Council which was placed under control of the Executive Office of the President. Headed by the Vice President, the council is composed of the Secretaries of State and Defense, the Chairman of the Atomic Energy Commission, and the Administrator of the National Aeronautical and Space Administration.

[8] Warner R. Schilling, "Scientists, Foreign Policy, and Politics," *The American Political Science Review* (June 1962), p. 288.

[9] Daniel S. Greenberg, "When Pure Science Meets Pure Politics," *The Reporter* (March 12, 1964), pp. 39 ff.

The Council is designed to furnish information and advise the President on matters of space explorations and related research programs.

The National Science Foundation, under the leadership of a director appointed by the President with the consent of the Senate and the guidance of a 24-man board of scientists (who spend only part time in this assignment), each year provides matching funds for research facilities, makes available graduate fellowships, and grants funds to thousands of scientists to support their investigations.

The Public Health Services' National Institute of Health spends millions to support the health sciences. Like NSF, the NIH is primarily an agency to support scientific work of nongovernment scientists, but it also operates its own hospitals and other research facilities.

NSF, NIH, and AEC grants have also financed the graduate education of thousands of men and women, for a grant to a university scientist also permits him to employ graduate students as research assistants. Today a substantial percentage of the research and graduate training in the natural sciences being done in our universities is supported by the federal government. Federal aid to education at this level is no longer a debated issue; it is an accomplished fact.

What are some of the consequences of federal aid to service? It has not led to intensive federal control. NSF, NIH, and other agencies have exercised extreme care to ensure that only scientific standards are used in allocating funds, although at times Congress has insisted on tests of political reliability, at least to the extent of excluding from federal support scientists whose loyalty has been questioned.

University administrators, as much as they welcome federal support, are alarmed by the fact that federal grants to the natural sciences could lead to an imbalance in university programs. Federal grants cover the direct cost of research but only partly cover the indirect or overhead costs. Hence, the universities must divert their other funds to cover this research and have less to spend on the other departments. University heads also fear that the availability of federal research support for science may tend to encourage more and more young men and women into these areas, although evidence does not support these fears. There has been a drop in the proportional number of students in the humanities, but the social sciences, not the natural sciences, have gained from this relative decline.[10] To offset the imbalances in availability of federal research funds, the National Science Foundation has expanded its support to include the social sciences, and Congress has established a National Foundation on the Arts and Humanities to begin to do for the humanities and arts what the NSF does for the natural and social sciences.

Science, Scientists, and Public Policy

Scientific considerations infuse every aspect of public policy. No federal agency today considers itself properly equipped without a science adviser. And few men have more influence than the

---

[10] Harold Orlans, *The Effects of Federal Programs on Higher Education* (Brookings, 1962), p. 43.

Director of the Office of Science and Technology, an agency within the Executive Office of the President. Not only does the Director advise the President on scientific matters, he is also head of the President's Science Advisory Committee— a group of government and nongovernment scientists, and of the Federal Council for Science and Technology—a group representing the several departments and coordinating problems that are broader than the responsibilities of a single agency.

With scientists occupying key policy-advising positions in government, a problem is coming to the fore in some ways similar to the problem of the relations between civilians and military experts.[11] With scientists now enjoying even more prestige than generals, it is difficult for the nonscientists who are publicly responsible for making policy to sort out the expert, objective advice from that which reflects the primarily personal values of the scientist. Just as military domination of civilians would undermine the democratic system, so would scientific domination of "politicians." And on the other hand, just as it would be dangerous for civilians to ignore military advisers, it would be even more disastrous for them to ignore their science advisers. Some scientists complain that the latter is happening today. Priorities, they say, are often based upon political rather than scientific considerations, such as in the moon program.

Related to the question of the role of scientific advisers in government is the increasing prominence of scientists in discussions of public policy. Especially since the atomic bomb exploded over Hiroshima, scientists have become acutely conscious of the political consequences flowing from scientific advances. Never before has man had such a potential for doing good; never before has man had such an ability for doing evil. And never before has the role of the government been so vital to the well-being and, indeed, the very survival of mankind. Prominent scientists have been active in almost every important policy debate of recent decades but, like other mortals, they often disagree with one another, even on the more narrowly scientific questions involved in the larger questions of public policy.[12] Perhaps this is one of the safeguards against the dangers to democracy that might flow from a scientific elite.

Social Welfare

There is nothing new—as the foregoing pages have shown—in the idea of governmental aid to certain sectors of the economy or to certain groups of people. For at least 160 years we have had a "welfare state," to some degree. This is certainly true of social services. As far back as colonial times, parishes and counties undertook poor relief, and later on the states set up hospitals, asylums, and other institutions. Nevertheless, until recent years American government—especially the national government—lagged far behind other countries in furnishing social services. The situation was paradoxical. On the one hand, the federal government gave

---

[11] For detailed analysis see Schilling, *op. cit.*, pp. 287–300.
[12] Don K. Price, "The Established Dissenters," *Daedalus* (Winter 1965), pp. 84–116.

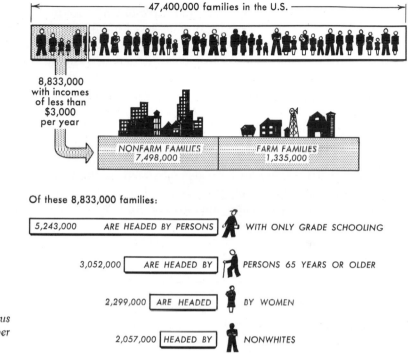

47,400,000 families in the U.S.

8,833,000 with incomes of less than $3,000 per year

NONFARM FAMILIES 7,498,000

FARM FAMILIES 1,335,000

Of these 8,833,000 families:

5,243,000 ARE HEADED BY PERSONS WITH ONLY GRADE SCHOOLING

3,052,000 ARE HEADED BY PERSONS 65 YEARS OR OLDER

2,299,000 ARE HEADED BY WOMEN

Based on Bureau of Census reports, April and December 1958.

2,057,000 HEADED BY NONWHITES

huge bounties to railroads, farmers, veterans, and other groups. On the other, Washington ignored the dire need of millions of "ill-clad, ill-housed, ill-nourished" Americans.

One reason for this paradox is that America has traditionally been a land of opportunity. The millions of acres of free land, the enormous resources, the technical advances—all helped take care of the people who otherwise might not have made a go of it. Then, too, Americans have traditionally subscribed to a philosophy of rugged individualism and devil take the hindmost. If a man failed to get ahead, people said, it was his own fault. Rather grudgingly, the state governments —mainly during the early twentieth century—extended relief to needy groups, especially old people, blind persons, and orphans. But government aid was limited, and private charity was relied on to supply most social services.

Then the nation was struck by the Great Depression. Unemployment mounted to sickening heights; in the early 1930's between ten and fifteen million men were without work. Bread lines, soup kitchens, private charity, meager state and local programs—these were pitifully inadequate gestures. In 1932 the federal government began making loans to states and localities for public relief. The Roosevelt administration established a series of relief programs designed to boost the economy by increasing purchasing power. Directed by Harry Hopkins, the famous WPA—Works Progress Administration—spent billions of dollars on local projects. The Public Works Administration, under Secretary of the Interior Harold Ickes, undertook more permanent projects—dams and roads and bridges.

Before long a reaction set in to the makeshift manner in which relief was being administered. People grew critical of useless leaf-raking projects—popularly called "boondoggles"—and of the cost and waste of the relief program. Some wanted to go back to the dole—simple handouts of food or cash by the government. But others argued for a well-planned, long-term program that would foster both the security and self-respect of the people aided. Progress was slow. The first federal attempt at an extensive security program—the Railroad Retirement Act of 1934— was declared unconstitutional by the Supreme Court.[13] Insurance companies and even certain labor groups were hostile to extensive social security programs. But over the last three decades the national government has built a social security program that has come to be widely accepted by the American people.

Broadly speaking, the program is based on the assumption that society must take care of old people, the unemployed, and the helpless. For such people are in any event a cost charged against the rest of the community. Old people are a good example. In the past, when large families were common, much of the cost of social security for the aged was borne by the family itself. The family was often large enough to bear this burden without too much difficulty, for a century ago it might be composed of father and mother, six to ten children, a grandmother, Aunt Susie, and Uncle George. Today the typical family in an urban society will consist of mother and father and two children living in a small house. It is impossible to let relatives move in. Some primitive societies kill off excess and helpless people, or let them starve. Some communities today put them in poorhouses at the expense of the rest of the citizens. Most modern democratic societies have governmental security systems that try to plan ahead and make provision for needy people in a fair and orderly fashion.

Social Security

The foundation of the social-welfare system in the United States is the Social Security Act, passed by Congress in 1935 after elaborate study, and since then frequently amended and supplemented. Today the national government's social security activities consist of several different kinds of programs.

The *unemployment insurance system* is operated jointly by the national and state governments. Until Congress acted, many states were reluctant to establish their own unemployment insurance programs for fear that the cost would place their businessmen at a competitive disadvantage with industries in states that had no such programs. Then, in 1935, Congress eliminated this source of reluctance by levying on all employers of eight persons (since amended to four) or more a payroll tax on the first $3,000 (since 1962, 3.5 per cent) paid each year to each employee. If an employer contributes to a state unemployment program that meets federal standards, he may deduct from his federal payroll tax all that he pays to the state fund, provided it is no more than 90 per cent of his federal

[13] *Railroad Retirement Board v. Alton Railroad Company* (1935).

tax. A state could stay out of the program, but none has done so because the national government levies the payroll tax in any event, and the money cannot be used by the state's unemployed unless the state adopts a plan satisfactory to Washington.

The national government helps defray the administrative costs of the programs, but each state administers its own program. Programs vary in eligibility requirements, the amount paid, the period of payment, and in other respects. All states levy a tax upon employers; several also collect from employees. Almost half the states cover firms with fewer than four workers, and since 1954 Congress has extended unemployment benefits to federal civilian employees. These employees receive the the same amounts and are governed by the same conditions as if their employer were subject to state law. In 1958 Congress extended these same benefits to all servicemen discharged since 1958. Payments to federal employees and ex-servicemen are made through state employment security agencies, but the federal government reimburses the states for payments made. Altogether, about 50 million workers earn some credits toward unemployment payments. The major groups not covered by unemployment insurance are self-employed workers, agricultural employees, domestics, and—in half the states—employees of firms that have fewer than four workers. Railway workers are covered under a separate system administered by the Federal Railroad Retirement Board. During recent recessions many jobless persons exhausted their unemployment benefits, so Congress authorized emergency assistance to states in order to allow them to extend the period of payment. A number of states have taken advantage of these provisions.

The money collected by each state is deposited to that state's account in the United States Treasury. From this fund each state pays benefits to workers who report to state public employment agencies and are willing and *able* to work, but for whom there are no jobs. Each state sets its own scale of benefits and determines who is eligible to receive them. In most states, to be eligible a person must be able to work. Indeed, if a worker is drawing benefits and becomes ill, he is no longer entitled to payments. Although states have *workmen's compensation* programs that pay disability benefits to some workers for industrial accidents or occupational diseases, most programs give no protection to those who are unable to work because of illness or accidents suffered off the job. Only four states—Rhode Island, California, New Jersey, and New York—pay unemployment compensation or workmen's compensation to workers who are unemployed because of nonoccupational illness or injury. The recent amendment to old-age insurance (see below) giving benefits to permanently disabled workers will help additional workers.

Federal-state cooperation meets local demands and keeps the program flexible. It also has disadvantages. Benefits vary considerably. Recently the average weekly benefit ranged from $55.00 in California to $30.00 in Mississippi. The number of weeks for which benefits were paid vary between 22 and 39. Administrative services in some states have proved unduly inefficient and expensive. In some states "chiselers" are able to collect payments where jobs are available, and even while holding jobs. In other states the test of unemployment is so stiff that unemployed persons find it difficult to get benefits. Because of the state-federal arrangement, administrators have sometimes had difficulty in locating jobs and steering workers to them. However, the Bureau of Employment Security in the Department of Labor, which administers the federal part of the program, does attempt to coordinate the states' efforts to place jobless workers.

Old-age, survivors, and disability insurance, unlike unemployment insurance, is run solely by the national government. By 1935 it had become clear that old age was a problem that required national action. For some time the percentage of old people in the population had been steadily increasing. Persons over 65 now number 18.7 million; their percentage of the whole population has quadrupled in the last 100 years. This social and economic problem was affecting politics, too. By 1935 the Townsend movement, clamoring for "30 dollars every Thursday" for the aged, had reached formidable proportions. The Social Security Act was in part a move to head off this political force.

The act of 1935 established a nationwide contributory retirement system under which payments to retired workers are made out of a fund built up from money collected equally from employers and employees through payroll taxes. Payments vary according to the earnings of the employee and the length of time his salary

HOW THE SOCIAL SECURITY SYSTEM FUNCTIONS

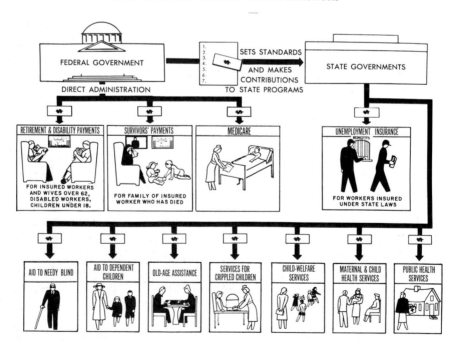

has been taxed. Since this is an *insurance* program, the plan pays for itself, except for the cost of administration, which the federal government assumes.

In 1939 old-age insurance was broadened to old-age and survivors insurance, so that not only the wage-earners but the whole family benefits. In 1960 disability benefits were added so that it became known as O.A.S.D.I., and in 1965 health care benefits were added for "senior citizens." Under present rates employers and employees each pay 4.20 per cent on the employee's income up to $6,600 a year; a self-employed person pays 6.15 per cent on his income up to $6,600. The rate is scheduled to rise gradually so that by 1987 it will be 5.65 per cent for each employer and employee and 7.8 per cent for self-employed persons.

Today the system, as recently amended, pays men and women 62 or over monthly retirement benefits that vary from $44 to $312, in accordance with the worker's contributions and the number of persons in his family entitled to secondary benefits. (If the insured has a wife 60 or over or a dependent husband 62 or over, or dependent children or disabled children whatever their ages, the family receives additional benefits.) Permanently disabled workers may retire and draw their benefits without age minimum. Full benefits are paid between 62 and 72 only if the recipients are not earning more than $1,500 a year from jobs covered by social security. Income from dividends, interests, rents, and annuities is not counted, but by a complicated formula a worker loses part or all of his retirement benefits, depending upon his earnings, if he continues to work. After age 72, however, a person is entitled to his retirement benefits regardless of his wages. Survivors' benefits for wives, dependent parents, children, and disabled children include a lump sum of money and monthly payments. For the health benefits recently made available see page 666. Benefits are subject to change by Congress, which has been liberalizing them since the system was started in 1939.

The social security insurance program now covers almost all workers, either on a mandatory or on a permissive basis. The only major professions not covered are public employees who have their own special retirement systems. Approximately 87 million workers participate, and over 11 million are now

"*Daddy's little baby must be kept warm.*" (*Courtesy D. Hesse and Mc-Naught Syndicate, Inc.*)

drawing benefits. The fact that social security has been broadened extensively under both Republican and Democratic administrations suggests that the basic system is now outside the arena of party battle.

Public Assistance

Eventually, it is hoped, social insurance will reduce the need for public assistance. But there will probably always be people who cannot support themselves. Some are not eligible for payments under the insurance programs, some cannot get along on the monthly payments, and some are physically handicapped.

The states have the primary responsibility for public assistance to needy persons. They initiate and administer the programs, but the national government helps. It makes yearly grants to the states to help support specific groups—needy aged, needy blind, needy persons who are permanently and totally disabled, and children who are in need because of the death, abandonment, or physical or mental incapacity of a parent. Unlike the insurance programs, this public assistance is essentially a charity service, for the recipients of benefits make no contributions.

Federal assistance is given to the states on certain conditions. The states must contribute some of the money, they must establish a single state agency to administer or supervise the program, and other details must meet federal minimum standards. In certain programs, the national government contributes from 60 to 75 per cent of the money. The average individual old-age assistance monthly payment varies from state to state, depending on local standards.

In addition to these programs, which are designed to assist non-institutionalized needy persons, federal grants are also available to enable states to extend their services to crippled children, health services to mothers and children, and child welfare services, especially in the rural regions. The Children's Bureau of the Social Security Administration approves state programs and distributes federal money in accordance with each state's contribution, its number of live births, its need for help, and its rural child population.[14]

Medicare

One of the most hotly debated subjects in the past two decades has been the national government's role in insuring the health of the nation's people. Democratic administrations after World War II proposed that the social security system be expanded to provide for a *national system of medical care insurance*. These proposals stirred up a hornet's nest. Leading the opposition was the prestigious American Medical Association representing over 200,000 doctors. The AMA argued in well-financed campaigns that these proposals constituted "socialized medicine" and that (1) tremendous strides had been made

[14] For an account of the problems of administration of welfare programs, see Edgar May, *The Wasted Americans* (Harper, 1964).

without governmental involvement; (2) the plans would bring politics into the traditionally private doctor-patient relationship; (3) standards might be lowered; (4) the programs would be expensive and wasteful; and (5) private plans such as Blue Cross and Blue Shield were covering more and more people.

While the program advocated by President Truman had extremely broad coverage, the proposals advanced by Presidents Kennedy and Johnson and as finally adopted centered on a limited application of the medical insurance principle—extension of the social security system to include health care insurance for the *aged*. Although enthusiastically supported by the Kennedy administration, efforts to establish the "Medicare" program failed in both the 87th and 88th Congresses.

Meantime the political battle went on. The AMA and many insurance companies supplied doctors with anti-Medicare literature for distribution directly to patients. Doctors were urged to write, not only their congressmen, but to local newspapers and other news media protesting the administration bills. The attack on medicare for the aged repeated many of the objections made to earlier proposals but particularly emphasized that it was simply "a foot in the door for socialized medicine." Opponents stated further that the plan would force young people to pay for the medical expenses of older persons who had paid nothing. Finally, some critics argued that the program was not necessary at all, since existing legislation was adequate. They pointed to the Kerr-Mills Act, passed in 1960, by which the national government provides matching grants to states to help pay medical costs for the "medically indigent"—*needy* persons over 65.

Medicare supporters claimed that the Kerr-Mills programs were not adequate and were available in less than half of the states. The Kennedy administration contended that health insurance for the aged financed through social security was the only workable method for relieving the elderly and their children from the burden of medical expenses. Statistics were cited showing that the aged had a higher incidence of illness and thus higher medical costs than the rest of the population, and that they were less capable of obtaining proper care because of their reduced incomes. It was claimed that private insurance plans provided inadequate coverage and were far too expensive for the average retired person.

Campaigning for election in 1964, President Johnson gave Medicare first priority in his proposed 1965 legislative program. The size of Johnson's electoral victory and his huge margins of support in both houses of Congress presaged the passage of Medicare in the 88th session of Congress. Sensing the mood of Congress, the President and the nation, Chairman Wilbur D. Mills of the House Ways and Means Committee—who had used the prerogatives of his position to bottle up earlier proposals—decided not to stand in the way this time after he received certain concessions from the President. After months of hearings, debate, and threats of "nonparticipation" by some doctors, Medicare became a reality in mid-summer of 1965.

This new program is administered by the social security system and extends to those 65 years or older. The cost of the benefits—which include payments for *hospital* and *nursing home care*, but not doctors' bills, as well as certain kinds of home nursing care and outpatient service—is financed by an increase in social security taxes and from general funds. The immediate additional social security tax ranges from about $14 per year for those earning $4,000 to $23.10 per year for those earning $6,600 or more; this tax will increase over the next 20 years. As a concession to Chairman Mills, this extra tax is noted separately on the workers' withholding slips so that everyone may see where his money is going. The money then goes into a separate trust fund—another concession to quell the fears of some who feel that the program might threaten the actuarial soundness of the entire social security cash-benefit system. As for the 2 million people 65 or older not covered by social security systems, their participation is financed by general revenues. Because of Republican objections, a voluntary insurance scheme was adopted to provide additional coverage for such things as certain doctors' fees, mental hospital care, and a number of types of health services. To obtain this coverage a person must pay an additional premium of $3 a month, with the remainder being financed by general revenue funds.

Thus from a rather modest beginning in which about 60 per cent of the labor force received small cash payments after age 65, the social security system has been expanded in numbers of individuals covered and levels of support, and now is called upon to insure a certain basic health-care standard for the nation's elderly. While this development has been quite spectacular, the federal government actually has been in the business of looking after the nation's health for quite some time.

Federal Health Agencies

According to the second Hoover Commission, twenty-six federal departments and agencies administer one or more health activities. The national government gives some kind of direct medical care to over 30 million people (most of them veterans) and employs about 10 per cent of the doctors, 9 per cent of the dentists, and 6 per cent of the nurses. Thirteen per cent of all hospital beds are in institutions operated by the national government, and 7 per cent of the total number of patients admitted each year enter this type of hospital. In addition, the national government makes grants to the states to construct hospitals and research facilities, to maintain medical programs, including services for maternal and child welfare and assistance to the aged. The national government also directly supports research in its own and private facilities and has special programs to meet problems such as cancer, venereal diseases, tuberculosis, mental illness, and heart disease.

Much of the responsibility for these programs rests with the Public Health Service, headed by a surgeon general and lodged in the Department of Health, Education and Welfare. The Health Service operates several dozen general hospitals, quarantine stations, outpatient clinics, and dispensaries. The service licenses the manufacture and interstate sale of serums, toxins, vaccines, and similar products. Perhaps most important for the long run, it carries on and supports basic research through its National Institute of Health. Almost $1 billion a year is granted to university scientists and physicians for basic research in health-related sciences. The service also administers grants to the states and local communities to support their research programs.

Another national health agency, which resorts to *regulation* rather than subsidy, is the *Food and Drug Administration*, also located in the Health, Education and Welfare Department. Intense popular concern over injurious food and drugs dates from early in the century, when Upton Sinclair and other muckrakers exposed the filthy practices in slaughterhouses and the evil effects of adulterated foods. Congress passed the Pure Food and Drug Act in 1906, has strengthened it in later amendments, and has passed other laws covering tea, milk, and caustic poisons. The Food and Drug Administration polices the misbranding, false labeling, and adulteration of foods, drugs, cosmetics, and therapeutic devices destined for interstate shipment. Its agents inspect sanitary conditions in factories and the processing, packaging, and labeling of products covered by the law. They keep drugstores under surveillance to prevent the dispensation of dangerous drugs without prescriptions, engage in research to evaluate the safety of goods, drugs, and cosmetics, and make studies in order to formulate definitions and standards that will promote honest and accurate labeling of foods. Before new drugs may be placed on sale in the interstate market, the Food and Drug Administration must give its approval and be assured that the drug is safe, effective, and fairly labeled. Policing of drugs was greatly strengthened by new legislation in 1962.

A War on Poverty

A generation ago Franklin Roosevelt dramatized the fact that one-third of the nation was then "ill-clad, ill-nourished, ill-housed," even though the nation generally was climbing from the trough of economic depression. Times have changed greatly, to be sure. In the 1960's signs are abundant that the United States is an "affluent society," the likes of which the world has never seen. Many take this affluence for granted, feeling that the basic economic problems of food, clothing, and housing have been solved for this society. But Americans are also being reminded that there is the "other America," one that does not enjoy the fruits of economic development. It is claimed that a sizable proportion of the American population—estimated as high as 50 million people—are poor; yet this vast group remains invisible to most Americans, since it exists in the dark slums of the city and in the mountains and valleys of rural America—off the beaten track.[15]

John Kennedy saw this face of America and attempted to apprise the country of this condition. While traveling in West Virginia during the presidential primary in 1960, Kennedy was struck by the extent of poverty, particularly in towns once

[15] Two "angry" books about this condition are Michael Harrington, *The Other America: Poverty in the United States* (Macmillan, 1962); and Harry M. Caudill, *Night Comes to the Cumberlands* (Little, Brown, 1963). For statistics on poverty see Herman P. Miller, *Rich Man, Poor Man* (Crowell, 1964).

supported by operating coal mines. He pledged that if elected he would forward a program to assist areas such as West Virginia. It became a central issue in the campaign and later a priority item in his "New Frontier" program. Immediately upon election, he mounted a major drive for corrective legislation.

The Kennedy administration proposed that the national government assist in industrial development in these "pockets of poverty," principally by inducing firms to locate their plants in high-unemployment regions and thus providing jobs. These proposals brought opposition from a number of fronts. Business groups charged that this would constitute discriminatory subsidies for some businesses and might result in "pirating"—luring industries from one community to another with the bait of a new plant. It was also claimed that such relocations would be artificial and would distort "natural" industrial development.

Despite stiff resistance a redevelopment act passed Congress in 1961 and has been extended subsequently. This program makes annually appropriated funds— in the form of grants and low-interest loans—available to eligible areas for industrial development and the improvement of related public facilities. The designation of eligible areas—at last count 1,035 counties in the U.S.—and coordination of the program is the responsibility of the Area Redevelopment Administration in the Department of Commerce. Through the creation of two advisory committees, other federal agencies whose functions impinge on the problem, state and government officials, and public representatives participate in decision-making.

The act also authorizes the Departments of Labor and HEW to establish vocational retraining programs to assist displaced workers in acquiring new skills. Grants are included to provide subsistence payments for a maximum of sixteen weeks to workers being trained for new jobs. In a broader attempt to train the "hardcore poor," Congress subsequently passed the Manpower Development and Training Act of 1962.

Appalachia

Although achieving modest success, the ARA in its short lifetime has been buffeted by congressional attacks. Part of this opposition has been due to a growing impression in Washington that the old style "pork-barrel" public works program and the pump-priming operation of the ARA are not capable of penetrating hard-core poverty. An alternative that has been offered to such "scattershot" spending throughout the United States is one which is based upon a *regional focus of federal spending*. The region that was selected for this new approach is called Appalachia, an eleven-state area that separates the prosperous Eastern Seaboard from the fertile Middle West and through which the Appalachian Mountain system winds.

Appalachia is generally viewed as the nation's largest depressed area. The general decline of the coal industry and increasing automation have rendered thousands of miners unemployed. The roads of the region are poor; roadbuilding in the mountains is nearly twice as costly as in the flatlands. Lumber companies have gutted the once rich forest stands. Industry has turned its back on a region where waterpower is largely unharnessed, flooding is prevalent, and transportation is poor, to establish itself elsewhere.

The Appalachian Regional Commission was created in 1963 representing the states affected plus all federal agencies having something to do with highways, health, education, manpower training, conservation, water pollution, economic development, flood control, and recreation. While President Kennedy established the commission, its main impetus came from the region's governors who on their own had met periodically and discussed common problems since the late 1950's and who in 1960 had formally instituted the Conference of Appalachian Governors.

The program, which received congressional approval in 1965, represents a brand new concept in cooperative federalism. A major share of decision-making as well as supervision and coordination of the various projects included in the program is delegated to the participating states represented in the *Appalachian Regional Commission*. The commission consists of the governor of each state in the region plus a federal representative designated by the President. A majority vote of the state members plus the affirmative vote of the federal representative is required for decision-making. In this way, the federal government maintains a veto power over the program, but because a majority of the representatives of the states is required to approve a project, there is a check upon federal dictation of policy. The actual operation of the aid projects comes under the direction of the appropriate federal agencies. Thus federal money will be spent on projects largely determined by the states themselves, a procedure not exactly common in the field of intergovernmental relations.

There are other novel features. Rather than employing a conventional "means test" that bases eligibility for federal aid on the extent of need, the Appalachian program utilizes the principle of "regional growth potential." The program tries to avoid raising the economic level of places with poor potential by direct injections of aid; it concentrates instead upon those cities and counties that have shown some prosperity in the face of general Appalachian poverty. The theory is that additional economic stimulation for centers possessing potential will raise the standards of the surrounding weaker areas. Huntsville, Alabama is a case in point. The city itself thrives as a university and space industry center in the middle of a depressed area. As one planner put it: "Instead of trying to build up the area to compete with Huntsville, we should try to find ways of helping the rest of the region become auxiliary to Huntsville. This could be done by improving the road network, providing sewer and water facilities for residential expansion, perhaps improving farm production and recreational opportunities in some sectors of the region." [16] There are some 50 such core cities or counties in the 360-county region.

Another novel and controversial feature of the program is its concentration on road construction. The program *in toto* carries a price tag of $1.1 billion, of which $840 million over a five-year period is earmarked for roads. The rationale for this is

[16] Jerald ter Horst, "No More Pork Barrel: The Appalachia Approach," *The Reporter* (March 11, 1965), p. 28.

that the inaccessible areas of the region must be linked to nearby cities and towns by "local access" roads and that the core cities must be linked together and with economic centers beyond the region by a system of "developmental highways." Placing so much money in road-building has, of course, drawn criticism from many who feel that the primary emphasis should be directed elsewhere, such as in education. The priority on roads, however, represents "political reality," because the political leadership of the states involved as well as the planning experts of the regional committee agreed that this is where the effort should be concentrated.

The Appalachian project will be watched closely by the President's Council of Economic Advisors, other executive agencies, and Congress to see if this approach pays off more handsomely than earlier public works programs have. If the program is relatively successful in the nation's largest economically depressed area, a similar approach will doubtless be used for attacking other "pockets of poverty."

Individual Economic Opportunity

The infusion of money, even billions of dollars, may improve the economic health of regions as a whole and of significant numbers of people within the region, but experience has demonstrated that general prosperity has a way of passing other people by. For poverty is a human condition and special provision must be made to allow the poverty-stricken *individual* to share in economic prosperity. As of late, this sharing means more than relief handouts. Rather, it requires an attempt to make the helpless less dependent on the dole and more dependent on themselves through increased education and training. The cornerstone of President Johnson's anti-poverty program which embodies these notions is the *Economic Opportunity* Act of 1964, the vehicle by which—according to the President—the nation eventually will score a total "victory over the most ancient of mankind's enemies."

Key to this billion-dollar attack on poverty is attention to youths, some 450,000 of whom are provided the opportunity to work and receive vocational education. A *Job Corps* seeks to improve the employability of youths sixteen through twenty-one years of age through education, vocational training, and work experience. Conservation camps and residential centers—over one hundred by latest count—provide work and education. Under this act the federal government is also authorized to cooperate with states and communities in establishing *work-training programs*, with Washington providing as much as 90 per cent of the funds during the first three years. In addition, a *work-study program* principally financed by the federal government assists college students from low-income families by providing part-time employment if they need the money to continue their studies.

Cooperative federalism plays an important role in the economic opportunity program. The community action organizations are local but federally assisted bodies established to operate programs helping low-income families in employment, education, vocational rehabilitation, job training and counseling, health, housing, and welfare. "Head-start" programs, for instance, were undertaken throughout the country in 1965 to provide pre-schooling experience for children from low-income families in order that they may enter the school years on a more equal basis with their classmates from more economically privileged homes. As a concession to states-rights forces in Congress, the act permits a governor to veto any project aided under the community action program. Rural America is also provided for; loans may be extended to low-income farm families to finance enterprises that would increase their incomes.

Over-all coordination of the poverty program is placed in the Office of Economic Opportunity (OEC) in the Executive Office of the President. Sargent Shriver, the Peace Corps director, was named by President Johnson to head the OEC. Under his direction a "domestic peace corps" has been established called the *Volunteers in Service to America* (VISTA). The concept behind VISTA is similar to that of the Peace Corps. Persons volunteer for a one-year period of service and after a six-week training period are sent to work in programs designed to meet the health and education needs of such impoverished groups as Indians, migratory workers, and residents of certain federally controlled areas. Other programs having high priority to receive this assistance are urban renewal project, rural education, schools for retarded children, and nonprofit mental health facilities assisted by federal funds.

Education

Only in the 1960's has education as a whole become a major promotional activity of the federal government, for education has traditionally been viewed as essentially a function of the state and local governments. The federal government has long been indirectly involved in higher education, however. Sixty-eight land grant colleges largely owe their existence to the Morrill Act of 1862, which granted federal public lands to the states for the establishment of agricultural and mechanical arts colleges.

For years federal educational activities have been remarkably broad and varied. At the elementary and secondary level, the federal government aids the school lunch program (by providing perishable foods acquired under farm price support operations), helps on problems of curriculum, and educates Indians and others. The federal government helps to construct and operate schools in local districts that have been flooded by new pupils from military bases or other federal installations. At the level of higher education, it provides research grants to colleges and universities, operates special educational projects (such as the famed Howard University, the extension service of the Department of Agriculture, and the military academies), gives annual grants for agricultural and mechanical arts education at land-grant colleges, and offers special education and training for the public services. Other activities include on-farm training and education in non-military subjects for members of the armed services. Although these activities are administered by a variety of agencies, many of them, including vocational education and assistance to land-grant colleges, are centralized in the Office of Education in the Department of Health, Education and Welfare.

Federal Aid

After World War II many Americans asked: "Is the federal government doing enough for education?" Casting a wary eye toward the low educational level of a sizable proportion of the population, the growing number of children pressing into our schoolrooms, and the increasing level of education required in the society, many felt that the state and local taxpayer would soon be unable or unwilling to provide the level of educational expenditures needed. The best alternative, some believed, was to turn to Washington for direct help for the schools. Proposals for federal aid to education, however, ran into heavy opposition stemming mainly from three sources: fear that the federal government might try to dictate what should be taught in public schools; a dispute over whether parochial schools should be eligible for benefits; and wide differences over whether federal money should be given to school districts that practice racial segregation.[17]

The interplay of these factors prevented comprehensive federal action in education for a number of years. In 1957 Russia dramatized its educational and scientific achievements by launching its first Sputnik, stimulating many to re-evaluate the state of American education and its needs. Congress responded a year later by passing the National Defense Education Act of 1958 which was primarily geared to improve the teaching of science. Attractive student loans were provided, with priority given to undergraduates preparing in science, mathematics, engineering, modern foreign languages, or teacher education. The act authorized grants to high schools and private schools to help them secure better equipment for the teaching of science, mathematics, and languages, and for the development of new teaching techniques, such as the use of television. Fellowships were made available from federal funds at universities undertaking new or expanded graduate programs approved by the Office of Education.

The new National Defense Education Act was widely hailed as a good start, but it did nothing, of course, to meet the shortage of classrooms. At the beginning of 1960 the public schools were short 195,000 teachers and 140,000 classrooms; there were over a million and a half more children attending school than the schools had room for. The United States was maintaining an "educational deficit" estimated at between $6 and $9 billion a year. In 1961, the Kennedy administration moved to broaden and extend the National Defense Education Act. Intense opposition was again encountered in Congress along the general lines that met previous educational measures. Following a protracted conflict, the act was extended without major modification. President Kennedy signed the act "with extreme reluctance" because of its inadequacies, and he promised that he would continue to press for an enlarged program.

---

[17] For a case study showing the interaction of these factors see Hugh Douglas Price, "Race, Religion and the Rules Committee: The Kennedy Aid-to-Education Bills," in Alan F. Westin (ed.), *The Uses of Power* (Harcourt, Brace & World, 1962), pp. 1 ff.

Pin-pointed Aid

The decade of the 1960's brought revolutionary thinking about general federal aid to education. Many new departures were embodied in a task force report presented to President-elect

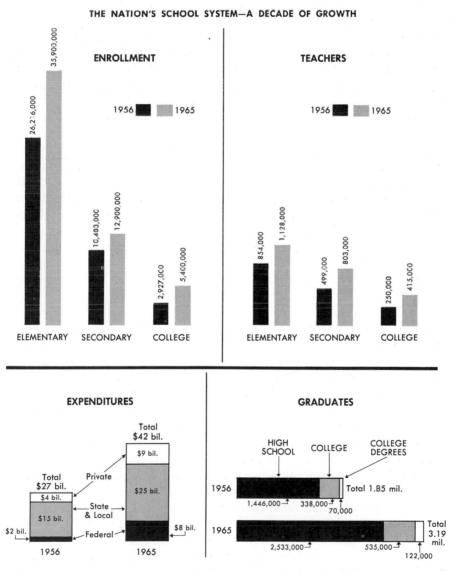

THE NATION'S SCHOOL SYSTEM—A DECADE OF GROWTH

© *1964 & 1965 by The New York Times Company. Reprinted by permission.*

Kennedy in January 1961. One of these was the notion of pin-pointed aid to locales badly in need of educational resources—the low-income states and densely populated, economically hard-pressed areas, the urban and rural slums. This idea and others were reflected in the President's proposed National Education Improvement Act of 1963, which carried a total four-year expenditure of about $6 billion. Certain problems continued to persist—such as that involving aid to parochial schools—but Congress was able to pick out of the package some significant but rather non-controversial items to consider. Shortly after John Kennedy's death, President Johnson signed into law a series of educational bills that provided for: loans and grants for the construction of academic buildings for colleges, universities and medical schools, amounting to over $2 billion during a three-year period; support for improved vocational education, raising the then current level of $57 million annually to $225 million by 1966 and each year thereafter; increased aid to college and medical students; and the broadening of the National Defense Education Act to include support for the humanities and social sciences. This flurry of congressional activity led President Johnson to laud the 88th session as the "Education Congress."

The notion of "pin-pointed" aid, which was introduced in the 1960 task force report, became the heart of the administration's education legislation in 1965. Recognizing that educational levels were lowest in poverty-stricken areas, President Johnson proposed and Congress subsequently enacted a program primarily based upon the concentration of federal school aid in the depressed areas, making it therefore an important pillar of the war-on-poverty program. Under the Education Act of 1965, over a billion dollars in grants is provided for public school districts serving economically needy children to be used as decided by local officials subject to approval by state and federal agencies. In addition to this provision, grants amounting to $100 million are authorized for text and library book acquisition for *both* public and private school children. Another $100 million is made available for the creation of "supplementary education centers" where children from *both* public and private schools can receive part of their instruction. Special stress here is placed upon up-to-date and experimental methods of teaching.

These provisions were as interesting politically as they were important in substance. By tying much of the school aid program to the war on poverty, President Johnson was able to gain congressional assent to a massive infusion of federal funds in the field of elementary and secondary education, the first time in history that federal funds were authorized for general use at these levels. Secondly, by providing direct aid to public schools and indirect aid to be available to parochial schools in the form of books and materials and in the creation of the "supplementary education centers," the President was able to blunt the church-state controversy that had plagued advocates of school aid for so many years. This may ease the way for later direct aid to the public schools. The special centers may prove additionally important for northern cities as a means by which the effects of *de facto* school segregation may be overcome even while such localities may continue their tradition of the neighborhood school. Thus by slightly altering the focus of the federal programs, interests that had previously competed for resources and through their competition had largely blocked aid at the elementary and secondary levels in particular, suddenly found themselves working in concert for a federal aid program and success was secured.

Toward a Great Society?

A cataloging of the federal government's promotional activities could be continued almost indefinitely, if space allowed. The government as promoter is not a new role. It is as old as the federal union itself. Witness the intention embodied in the preamble to the Constitution to "promote the general welfare." In the mid 1960's we are witnessing the latest of several surges of intense governmental promotion. The poverty programs, federal aid to education, Medicare—all discussed above— are the most spectacular of these developments.

Even these programs, extensive as they are, do not begin to tell the story of governmental promotion in recent years. We have said nothing about aid to the cities, for instance. Building upon past programs, there has been an expansion of the urban renewal and public housing programs. Millions of dollars in grants have been provided for metropolitan planning, the construction of new service facilities such as sewage disposal plants, and for assistance to urban areas in improving their mass transportation systems. To coordinate this vast attack on the problems of the city Congress established in 1965 a cabinet-level Department of Housing and Urban Development. Closely associated with these programs are such conservation projects as water and air pollution control, development of new parks, river and recreation areas, and a variety of projects to promote the arts and protect the natural beauty of America.

Upon the pillars of health, education, conservation, and the elimination of poverty President Johnson has envisaged the construction of the "Great Society." He would use the vast financial base of the national government and the wealth of human talent Washington can recruit to help localities attack their problems. The problems of the city, the aged, the school child are now viewed not only as the province of state and local government or the family and individual, but as ones that demand the attention of Washington as well.

Many disagree with this approach and view with distaste the bureaucracy required for this sort of society and the alleged effect this has upon individual initiative. Whether or not one shares this dim view, certain tensions and problems have already been observed. The anti-poverty program is a case in point. In Washington, inter-agency tensions have been generated over who should do what. A variety of agencies plus the Departments of Agriculture, Commerce, Labor, and HEW all have programs which impinge upon the problem of poverty. Tensions between the federal and state officials are also inevitable. In fact this sort of conflict is built into the program, since Congress specifically provided that governors may veto poverty projects in their states, a power of which some governors have already availed themselves. This veto power also compounds the natural tensions often existing between governors and large-city mayors.

At the local or "action" level tensions have been most evident, especially in the "community action phase." Welfare and other agencies that for years have struggled against poverty often object to the entrance into their communities of the new federally sponsored organizations. In many cases these groups allege that they have not been allowed to participate in the planning of the anti-poverty projects. They further charge that many of the programs are "wildly unrealistic," that paid officials of the federally sponsored programs receive excessively high salaries, and that racial discrimination is prevalent in that Negroes often have been barred from the planning stage.

Others view the poverty program as a means of organizing the previously unorganized and then challenging the current "power elite" of the community. Such objections are not entirely without foundation. In Syracuse, New York, for instance, a $314,000 federal grant under the poverty program is being used in an experimental program—patterned after the methods of the veteran and radical social organizer Saul Alinsky—to organize the poor of the city into an effective power bloc, which is then able to negotiate effectively with the city to gain more funds and greater recognition in the effort to raise their standard of living. Clearly, even such an altruistic effort as the elimination of poverty is not without its political dimension.

Will the politics of poverty prevent the "total victory" over this ancient enemy that President Johnson constantly calls for? Is the cost of the "Great Society" in all its dimensions—that of the increased role of the federal government in all our lives —too great a price to pay? Are there more effective alternatives to these programs? These are the kinds of questions that will concern us as we evaluate the workings of these policy innovations in the coming years.

26 GOVERNMENT AS MANAGER

In the last two chapters we have been looking into two of the methods by which government influences society—regulation and promotion. Through regulation, government lays down the rules controlling what men may and may not do. Through promotion, government directly or indirectly advances the interests of certain groups. There is a third method by which government influences society: *direct management* or *control*

These terms are used here in two senses. One is the *direct operation* or *management* of *enterprise*. The Post Office is a good example. Presumably the government could allow a private company to handle the mail, and it could regulate that company in the public interest, or subsidize it, or do both. Instead, the government itself took over the job long ago. The second sense in which the terms are used involves *control of the economy*. Government has come to intervene in the economy in so many ways, with such broad powers and effective instruments of control, that our political rulers are to a real extent our economic rulers as well.

Governmental management is no more recent a development in the United States than governmental regulation or promotion. What *is* new is the tremendous *increase* in governmental management during the last decade or two. All over the world, in both democratic and totalitarian countries, governments have come to direct national economies and to take over operating areas hitherto reserved for private enterprise. The trend has not been so pronounced in the United States as in Britain, Soviet Russia, Sweden, or Australia, but it has clearly shown up here too.

Some call this trend "socialism." Others call it a drift toward the "welfare state." But let us ignore this name-calling—at least for the moment—and examine just what is happening. What enterprises does our federal government directly operate? With what success? To what extent does government manage the economy as a whole? What methods does it use? What political and governmental problems does this kind of management raise?

Managing Enterprises

Americans have a curiously mixed attitude toward governmental management. On the one hand, almost all of us stolidly and unquestioningly accept the fact that the federal government fights wars, runs some hospitals and public utilities, operates parks, delivers mail, manages a huge insurance system, and during emergencies takes over private enterprises such as coal mines and railroads. On the other hand, most of us oppose governmental operation of enterprises, and we can think up pretty good reasons to support our views. We dislike socialism—but we seem willing to accept it if it comes in little chunks.

Actually, most Americans approach the question of governmental ownership on a practical, matter-of-fact basis. Nobody seriously objects to the government's management of the armed forces. Few would want the government to take over the retail stores on Main Street. It is in the vast area between these extremes that disagreements arise. In general, we feel that most enterprises should be owned and managed privately, and that the burden of proof is on those who wish to extend governmental control. Even so, the national government in recent decades has assumed direct control of important economic activities.

The types of enterprise operated by the national government range from the Forest Service to the Government Printing Office to the Hoover Dam. A survey half-way through the Eisenhower administration showed that the national government owned almost 20,000 business enterprises with assets of more than $11 billion, employing over 250,000 people. And this report did not include the Post Office.[1] A review of all these activities is impossible here. Case studies of the Post Office, the Tennessee Valley Authority, and the Atomic Energy Commission will suggest some of the major problems involved.

World's Biggest Business

The United States Post Office likes to call itself the biggest single business in the world. It is the largest non-military department of the national government, and its 586,000 employees account for almost one-quarter of the entire federal civil service. It handles over 70 billion pieces of mail every year, supervises about 40,000 post offices, and has annual cash transactions of $20 billion a year. Aside from delivering mail, it operates a postal savings system and a money-order service. It contracts for ship, rail, air, and truck transportation at a cost of many million dollars a year.

At the head of the postal service is the Postmaster General. His is a historic office; Benjamin Franklin served for twenty years as British postmaster general for the colonies, and for two years during the Revolution he ran the post-office system for the independent states.[2] The Post Office achieved Cabinet rank in 1829. For many years, however, the "PMG" has been more important politically than administratively, for it was long traditional for the President to appoint to the post the national chairman of his own party. The reason for putting a politician in this post is obvious: The PMG had thousands of patronage jobs to parcel out to the loyal party workers. Over the years, however, postal employees have gradually been brought under civil service. While perhaps 20,000 jobs are still political appointments (including some top officials and first-, second-, and third-class postmasters), postal patronage is not what it used to be.[3]

The postal service, a business agency, has only its headquarters in Washington. All but a tiny fraction of its employees work in the field. Assisting the Postmaster General are a deputy and five assistant postmasters general, and beneath them are a host of officials supervising operations in the field. Local post offices come in all sizes. Some are enormous, like that in New York with its 100 substations. The smallest are branch offices run in retail stores by small merchants. In between are the stations run by fourth-class postmasters—almost half the total number—who are appointed by the PMG partly on a civil service, partly on a political basis. First-, second-, and third-class postmasters are appointed by the President with Senate approval; these are prize patronage plums. But appointees now have to pass competitive examinations and, if they win permanent appointments, they may never be dismissed for political reasons.

[1] U.S. Code Congressional and Administrative News (West Publishing, 1956), No. 9, June 1956, p. i.

[2] See R. L. Butler, Doctor Franklin, Postmaster General (Doubleday Doran, 1928).

[3] See J. Edward Day, My Appointed Rounds (Holt, Rinehart and Winston, 1965), for an account by Kennedy's first Postmaster General.

Here is a gigantic experiment in socialism. How well has the experiment worked? In 1949 the Hoover Commission made some severe criticisms of the Post Office. The administrative structure, it said, was obsolete and overcentralized. A maze of old-fashioned practices had stifled progress. Though a business-type establishment, the Post Office lacked the flexibility essential to good business operation. Rate-making machinery was inadequate and concealed subsidies to carriers. There were still too many political appointments. Most important, the service was losing money—up to $500 million a year.[4]

The Hoover Commission report was a damaging indictment, but the Post Office had some answers ready. One reason it loses money is that it has to provide services below cost. Government officials, including congressmen, have the franking privilege under which they send official mail free. More important, a huge volume of printed matter is carried at a very low rate. The airlines are in effect subsidized at rates fixed by the CAB (see Chapter 24); rail shipping rates are not set by the Post Office but by the ICC. Postal authorities figured that almost $900 million in a recent year was lost in carrying free mail—one-half in carrying second-class mail, one-sixth in subsidizing the airlines.

Is it really feasible to apply ordinary dollars-and-cents profit standards to a government enterprise? If an efficient business firm took over our mail service, it might make a profit—but at what cost to the public? The farmer on a remote hillside would no longer, perhaps, enjoy rural free delivery. Newspapers and magazines would cost much more to distribute, and some might go out of existence. A cut in the air subsidy might impair the nation's military strength.[5]

Nevertheless, many of the Hoover Commission's criticisms could not be refuted, and attempts have been made to improve operations. A reorganization plan for the Post Office has been proposed that would give it more departmental autonomy. An advisory board, representing interested public groups, has been set up. Certain postal rates have been increased. There is little immediate prospect, however, that the Post Office will get out of the red. Attempts to run services at cost invariably arouse the opposition of groups who benefit from present below-cost services.

Harnessing a River: The TVA

During World War I, in order to produce nitrogen for explosives, the federal government bought a good deal of land, a dam, a powerhouse, and other facilities at Muscle Shoals, on the Tennessee River. After the war people began to ask what the government should do with this property. Some wanted to sell it to private interests. Others, led by a man of great vision and integrity, Senator George W. Norris, a Republican from Nebraska, urged that the federal government assume responsibility for developing the whole Tennes-

---

[4] U.S. Commission on Organization of the Executive Branch of the Government, *The Post Office* (Government Printing Office, 1949).

[5] Morton Baratz, *Economics of the Postal Service* (Public Affairs Press, 1962) weighs alternative approaches to the mail problem.

see Valley.[6] After years of controversy, Congress in May 1933 passed a comprehensive act to improve the navigability of the Tennessee, to provide for flood control, reforestation, agricultural and industrial development, and the national defense. A *government corporation,* called the Tennessee Valley Authority and headed by a board of three men, was set up. The TVA had a big job: to develop the physical, social, and economic resources of the whole Tennessee Valley, covering more than 40,000 square miles.

The TVA's achievements have been remarkable. Today it operates over a score of dams on the Tennessee and its tributaries. It produces a vast quantity of electricity, much of which is used for defense activities, as utilized in the production of atomic energy, explosives, and aluminum. It manufactures and sells fertilizers. The Tennessee is now navigable for 630 miles, and no damaging floods have swept the area since the elaborate storage system was completed. Water pollution has been reduced, malaria all but wiped out, hillsides reforested, fish and wildlife fostered, recreation areas developed. But TVA's main impact has been on the people of the valley. They benefited directly from the low electricity rates, cheap fertilizer, flood control, and construction jobs. Moreover, TVA experts have taught them how to conserve soil, use machinery, diversify their farming, improve their education and health.

All this would suggest that the TVA experiment has turned out very well and that much of the early criticism of valley socialism has disappeared. Nevertheless, a good many people are still asking questions. Some, for example, criticize the TVA's financial policies. Originally the agency was viewed as a yardstick against which private utilities would be measured. As things have turned out, the average kilowatt-hour price of TVA electricity is less than half the average cost for the rest of the country. But critics of TVA charge that this is not a fair yardstick, because TVA's rates do not include all the expenses that a comparable private utility would have to pay. They argue, for example, that TVA pays far less in taxation than private utilities (TVA does make some payments to local governments in lieu of taxes) and can borrow money at a lower rate of interest. Furthermore, they declare, too small a portion of the original investment was assessed to electric power, and the TVA has not returned from its sale of electricity enough funds to repay the original investment.

The truth has been shrouded in a confusion of charges, countercharges, and fancy figure-juggling, but it does seem clear that the yardstick idea has not worked out very well. Here again we see the difficulty of judging public enterprise in terms of private-enterprise standards. On the other hand, there seem to be wide agreements on the following:

> 1. The Tennessee Valley Authority has been run efficiently and honestly, although management by a three-man board has raised serious problems.
> 2. Politics in the narrow sense of party patronage and spoils has been kept out of the agency.

[6] See *Fighting Liberal, The Autobiography of George W. Norris* (Macmillan, 1945), esp. pp. 245–267.

3. The people in the Valley have benefited enormously with TVA's work. (Average per capita income rose from $148 in 1933 to $797 in 1947 as compared with an increase in the same period from $368 to $1,323 for the whole country.)

4. The Tennessee Valley Authority has cost a good deal of money, and much of it from the national treasury, but TVA has strengthened national defense and the whole economy. "Most of TVA's phenomenal growth in electric power took place during World War II and the Korean War . . ." [7] and it has been vital to our national defense.

TVA has also made a major contribution to the science of government, and has developed interesting new methods of cooperating with state and local officials. It has shown that the federal government can decentralize and still do its job. Above all, it has dramatized the enormous possibilities of *unified regional development*. It has proved the truth of the first Hoover Commission's judgment that "A plan for the development of a river basin cannot be devised by adding together the special studies and the separate recommendations of unifunctional agencies concerned, respectively, with navigation, flood control, irrigation, land drainage, pollution abatement, power development, domestic and industrial water supply, fishing, and recreation. These varied and sometimes conflicting purposes must be put together and integrated in a single plan of development." [8]

Will there be more TVA's? No one can say, but two obstacles may stand in the way of other unified valley authorities. One is the opposition of special interests in the valleys and of key officials in Washington. The other is the fear that if further regional authorities are created, a problem will arise of coordinating the different authorities. It is possible that future authorities—if any are created—might operate under the general supervision of the Department of the Interior.

Atomic Energy for Peace and War

Originally, the main job of the Atomic Energy Commission was to build and stockpile atomic bombs. In its two decades of existence the AEC has performed this task admirably—so much so that today the nation's military arsenal is brimming with nuclear weapons and a huge surplus of fissionable material is on hand for building even more bombs. The AEC has also overseen the development of the peaceful use of the atom; at a cost of nearly $2 billion, atomic energy is beginning to compete with electricity as a power source. In fact, through its own research and development laboratories at such places as Oak Ridge, Tennessee, and the Brookhaven National Laboratory on Long Island, and through contracts with universities and private research organizations, the AEC has assured the U.S. leadership in nearly every phase of nuclear research.

[7] Aaron Wildavsky, "TVA and Power Politics," *The American Political Science Review* (September 1961), p. 590.

[8] U.S. Commission on Organization of the Executive Branch of the Government, *Reorganization of the Department of the Interior* (Government Printing Office, 1949), p. 28.

Past successes in both the military and civilian aspects of the program have permitted expenditures for atomic energy in recent years to be decreased. This great success has been achieved under terms of the Atomic Energy Act of 1946, an act that was once described as ". . . perhaps the most radical law ever enacted in the United States"—one that virtually set up "an island of socialism in the midst of a free enterprise economy." [9] How did a conservative Congress happen to pass such a measure?

In 1945 Congress found itself in the remarkable position of being able to provide in advance for the rational control of a gigantic new resource—atomic energy. Some voices were raised in favor of private control. But most congressmen decided that the opportunity was too precious to surrender. Scientists testified that the use of fissionable, fusionable, and radioactive materials would lead to further significant discoveries, which in time would create numberless and unpredictable problems. Without some kind of central control and planning, chaos would set in. So certain was Congress of the need for government development that, in the end, it socialized atomic energy with virtually no discussion at all.

Legislative battles did break out, however, over several provisions of the bill. Civilian versus military control was the most controversial issue. As first introduced, the atomic energy bill explicitly provided that members of the proposed Atomic Energy Commission might be officers of the Army or Navy. Shortly, a new type of pressure group sprang into action—atomic scientists. Many of them had chafed under military control during the war, and they feared that such control might be authoritarian, militaristic, and harmful to the spirit of free, scientific inquiry. The scientists organized citizens' committees, testified before Congress, made speeches, put out propaganda, and lobbied on Capitol Hill. Partly as a result of this skillful political action, the bill was changed. The commission would be entirely civilian, but it would be advised on military matters by a military liaison committee.

Although the AEC's management of atomic energy has been successful, some doubt that the commission form is still administratively effective. It was originally felt that diffused responsibility was a necessary check in the new and secret field and certainly preferable to the concentration of authority in a single individual. In recent years, however, . . . "The atom has been assimilated into the affairs of the nation," as one member of the AEC put it.[10] "To an increasing extent the atomic energy enterprise has spread throughout the government and has had to be conducted by the AEC in conjunction with other agencies including the Department of Defense, State, NASA, Commerce, Interior and the Committees of Congress. Most significantly the atomic enterprise is co-ordinated at the White House level, by the President himself, by his staff members concerned with national security affairs, and by his assistants on matters of science and technology and, as usual, or more than usual, by the Bureau of the Budget." . . . The development of policy by the commission has been overseen by the Joint Congressional Committee on Atomic

[9] J. R. Newman, "America's Most Radical Law," *Harper's Magazine* (May 1947), p. 436.
[10] John W. Finney, "Is the AEC Obsolete?," *The Reporter* (November 19, 1964), p. 45.

Energy, which has taken its statutory "watchdog" responsibilities very seriously. The anomalous political position of the AEC, the wider dispersion of information about nuclear energy, the lessened need for dispersed authority, the greater involvement of private industry—all these considerations led the AEC on two occasions to recommend that the commission form be abolished and a single administrator be placed in charge. Although an independent team of consultants agreed with the AEC's diagnosis in 1962, no action has been taken to implement this proposal.

In short, owing to the increased involvement with atomic energy by other departments and agencies as well as private industry, the AEC has lost much of its previously unique status in government. Atomic energy is nevertheless still fraught with a heavy public interest because of such problems as conflict arising from overlapping federal and state safety codes, the extent of permissible competition among private atomic enterprises, the impact of this source upon other power sources, and the effects of the location of atomic facilities on the economy. The AEC's decision to concentrate the bulk of its atomic installations in the Ohio Valley, for example, stimulated the whole economy of the region and caused a major shift in population. Hence it is safe to assume that whether the AEC continues in its present collegial form or comes to be run by a single administrator, further development of atomic energy will continue to be an enterprise principally under direct governmental management.

So much for these three cases of direct management of enterprises by the national government. Will the government continue to involve itself in this way, or does there seem to be a trend away from such arrangements? The Eisenhower administration, opposing in principle federal operation of enterprises, closed down a number of federal establishments that were competing with private enterprise. But other forces work in the opposite direction—for example, technology. The Russian success in landing a rocket on the moon in 1959 climaxed an intensive program of exploring space that compelled the United States to look to its own position in the race for space. The agency responsible for catching up with the Soviets in this race is the National Aeronautics and Space Adiminstration, which quickly built launching facilities capable of handling both liquid- and solid-fueled rockets; electronic tracking systems; telemetry data receiving and recording systems; range operation and control systems; and a long-range radar tracking net. The space agency was given this vast assignment simply because no private enterprise could undertake it.

There is an important difference, however, between governmental management of space-age enterprises and their earlier counterparts discussed above. The difference is that in the space-age enterprises, the greatest share of the work is not performed within the governmental establishment by civil servants but by private industry under governmental contract. For instance, nearly 80 per cent of NASA's work is done by private industrial and university contractors. As many as 5,000 private firms have participated in the Gemini project. In the 1960's, three-quarters of the government's funds for research and development—amounting to well over $5 billion yearly—is contracted. Private concerns have been engaged for such functions as management of weapons systems, technical supervision and management of government-owned facilities, foreign technical assistance, educational activities, management analysis, and a host of additional activities.

If the space-age enterprises are valid indicators of future governmental trends, then, the movement is away from complete and direct governmental management of new enterprises and toward more cooperative ventures with private industry and universities.[11] But let us now turn to an even more important role of the government as manager—the indirect *fiscal* management of the whole economy through taxing, spending, investment, and other economic methods.

Raising the Money

Big government is expensive. In the mid 1960's, federal, state, and local governments spend over $200 billion yearly. This is between one-fourth and one-third of the income of all Americans; in short, our governments spend about 30 cents of every dollar we earn. The national government is the biggest spender of all. In recent years Washington has spent more than all state and local governments combined.

Where does all this money come from? The federal government gets most of its funds from taxes, and the rest from loans, commercial revenues from governmental enterprises, income from special fees and fines, and from grants and gifts.

Levying Taxes

"In this world," Benjamin Franklin once said, "nothing is certain but death and taxes." Tax-collecting is one of the oldest activities of government. Indeed, one of the few contacts that many people in earlier societies had with government was through the tax-collector. He was the dread figure who symbolized the demands and authority of some far-off ruler. Putting power over taxation into the hands of the people was a landmark in the rise of self-government. "No taxation without representation" has been the war cry not only of early Americans but, in effect, of people in countries the world over.

The new Constitution in 1787 clearly provided that Congress "shall have power to lay and collect taxes, duties, imposts, and excises." But duties and excise taxes had to be levied uniformly throughout the United States; direct taxes had to be apportioned among the states according to population; and no tax could be levied on articles exported from any state. Except during the Civil War, the federal government for a century relied on the tariff for most of its revenue. This hidden tax— which many people falsely thought to be a tax on foreigners—fluctuated with the rise and fall of trade and tariff levels. Congress supplemented these taxes with *excise taxes* on the manufacture or sale of certain goods. In 1894 an *income tax* law

---

[11] See Victor K. Heyman, "Government by Contract: Boon or Boner?" *Public Administration Review* (Spring, 1961), pp. 59 ff.

was enacted (such a tax had been used during the Civil War, but given up shortly afterwards). The 1894 tax was not very drastic—only 2 per cent on all incomes over $4,000—but it seemed a portent of worse things to come. The next year, in *Pollock* v. *Farmers Loan and Trust Co.*, the Supreme Court held the tax measure unconstitutional on the ground that it was a direct tax and therefore had to be apportioned among the states according to population. Twenty years later, in 1915, the Sixteenth Amendment was adopted authorizing Congress "to lay and collect taxes on incomes, from whatever source derived, without apportionment among the several States, and without regard to any census or enumeration."

Raising money is only one objective of taxation; *regulation*, and more recently promotion, of *economic growth* are also important objectives. In a broad sense, all taxation regulates human behavior; for example, a graduated income tax has a leveling influence on incomes, and a tariff act affects foreign trade. More specifically, Congress has used its taxing power to prevent or regulate certain practices. Years ago Congress laid a 10 per cent tax on the circulation of notes by state banks, immediately putting an end to such issues. Certain professional gamblers are now required to secure a federal license and pay a tax of 10 per cent on their receipts. Congress maintains a prohibitively heavy tax on sawed-off shotguns. Taxation as a device to promote economic growth will be discussed later.

Today the federal tax cake looks something like this:

Income Taxes on Individuals. Levies on the income of individuals account for over one-half of the federal government's tax revenue. Originally a low rate, the income tax was greatly increased during World War I and went to new heights dur-World War II and the Korean war. One advantage of income taxes is their flexibility. Rates can be raised and lowered, exemptions can be permitted, and the individual's ability to pay can be taken into account. In 1964 a $12 billion tax cut proved to be a healthy stimulus to the economy. The federal government—and most of the states—also levy *estate*, *inheritance*, and *gift* taxes.

Income Taxes on Corporations. These account for over one-fourth of the national government's tax dollar. As late as 1942, corporate income taxes amounted to more than individual income taxes, but returns from the latter increased relatively more rapidly during World War II.

Excise Taxes. Federal excise taxes formerly yielded about one-tenth of tax returns. These taxes were levied on liquor, tobacco, automobiles, gasoline, furs, jewelry, amusements, and a wide variety of other goods. In June 1965, Congress provided for a $4.7 billion reduction in these taxes by stages between then and January 1, 1969. All federal excise taxes will be eliminated by 1969, according to this plan, except for user, regulatory, and sumptuary levies and a 1% tax on passenger automobiles.

Customs Duties. Though no longer the main source of federal income, these taxes are far from negligible. The annual yield runs to about half a billion dollars.

While other tax returns have increased by several hundred per cent, however, customs returns have been fairly stable in recent years. The reason, of course, is that the revenue aspect of tariffs is far less important today than their relation to broad political and economic issues at home and abroad.

The Politics and Machinery of Taxation

When a young law assistant once commiserated with Justice Holmes on the taxes he had to pay, the old man replied, "With taxes I buy civilization." Most of us are less philosophical. We complain that our tax load is too heavy and that someone else is not carrying his fair share. People with large incomes naturally grumble about income taxes as high as 70 per cent or even more. Low-income people point out that even a low tax may deprive them of the necessities of life. People in the middle-income brackets feel that their plight is worst of all: Their incomes are not high but their taxes are.

What is the best type of tax? Some say the graduated *income tax*, because it is relatively easy to collect, it hits hardest those who are most able to pay, and it hardly touches those at the bottom of the income ladder. Others argue that *excise taxes* are the fairest, because they are paid by people who are actually spending money for goods—especially luxury goods—and thus obviously have money to spare. Furthermore, by discouraging people from buying expensive goods, excise taxes have a desirable deflationary effect in time of rising prices. On the other hand, excise taxes are more expensive to collect than income taxes, and in some cases, such as the tax on tobacco, they may hit the poor hardest. Most controversial of all taxes is the *general sales tax*, which resembles the excise tax except that it is levied against the sales of all goods. Labor and liberal organizations denounce this form of tax as regressive— that is, it hurts the poor man more than the rich man, because the former uses all his earnings to buy goods, while the latter may devote more of his income to buying personal services or to savings. Proponents of the sales tax stress its anti-inflationary effect and point to its successful use in a number of states.

A recent tax bill illustrated the wide impact of taxes on a variety of individuals and groups. Testifying on proposed tax changes before a congressional committee,

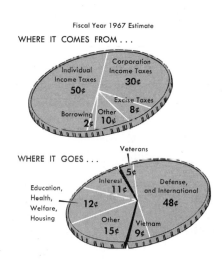

THE BUDGET DOLLAR

Fiscal Year 1967 Estimate

WHERE IT COMES FROM . . .

Individual Income Taxes 50¢

Corporation Income Taxes 30¢

Excise Taxes 8¢

Borrowing 2¢ Other 10¢

WHERE IT GOES . . .

Veterans 5¢

Interest 11¢

Defense, and International 48¢

Education, Health, Welfare, Housing 12¢

Other 15¢

Vietnam 9¢

Executive Office of the President. Bureau of the Budget.

138 witnesses expressed their views, and scores of briefs were submitted. The printed testimony covered more than 1,600 pages. Business representatives opposed new taxes on corporations. Small businessmen complained that existing taxes favored big business. Spokesmen for tobacco-growers, transportation interests, the wine and spirits industry, movies, the legitimate theater, candy-makers, telephone companies, and bowling alley proprietors argued that the proposed tax would discriminate against them. Labor demanded a lighter burden for low-income groups, higher taxes on business. Unorganized workers and consumers, however, were not represented.

Although the Constitution provides that all revenue bills must be initiated in the House of Representatives, it is usually the *President* who originates tax legislation. With the help of tax experts on his staff and in the Treasury Department, he draws up a tax program not only designed to meet the government's revenue needs for the coming fiscal year, but also taking into consideration the current and projected state of the economy. Often the representatives of interest groups are consulted while the bill is being formulated. Then the President submits his tax program to Congress, often along with his budget message. The powerful House Ways and Means Committee next holds hearings on the bill; administration spokesmen, headed by the Secretary of the Treasury, usually lead off the parade of witnesses, followed by representatives of interested groups, taxation experts, and others. Following committee consideration, tax measures go through Congress in much the same manner as other bills. Although the Senate cannot initiate tax legislation, it refuses to take a back seat on tax matters. It often differs with the House, and forces extensive changes of bills coming from the lower chamber. Sometimes Congress refuses to follow the President's recommendations and works out a tax measure largely on its own.

The Treasury Department has the job of collecting the taxes levied by Congress. One of the original departments set up in 1789, and headed by the second highest-ranking Secretary, this department today is a large agency employing about 80,000 people. The actual tax-collecting job falls mainly to the huge Internal Revenue Service. Fifty-eight district directors are located throughout the country, and taxes are paid into district offices rather than directly to Washington. The Service takes in $40 to $50 bil-

THE BIG FOUR

Under our form of federalism the taxpayer supports three levels of government. (Justus in the Minneapolis Star.)

lion a year at a cost of less than 50 cents for each $100 in returns. Customs are collected by the Treasury Department's Bureau of Customs, which maintains ports of entry, inspects the discharge of cargo, assesses the value of merchandise, and, through the services of the United States Coast Guard, prevents smuggling.

Uncle Sam, Borrower

When an individual person is suddenly faced with expenses too heavy to meet out of his regular income, he may have to borrow money. The same is true of government. During military and economic crises, the federal government has gone heavily in debt. It borrowed $23 billion during World War I, about $13 billion more during the 1930's, and over $200 billion more during World War II. Between crises, the government has tried to pay off its debts, but progress has been slow. By 1966 the federal public debt was nearing $328 billion.

Borrowing costs money. The federal government can borrow at a relatively low rate—because no security is safer than a government bond. Nevertheless, the public federal debt is so huge today that the interest alone is approaching $12 billion a year. The size of the debt itself and of the interest payments alarm many Americans. How long can we allow the debt to grow at this staggering rate? Two considerations must be kept in mind. In the first place, the government owes most of the money to its own people (rather than to foreign governments or persons); in a sense, we all owe the money to one another. Second, the economic strength and resources of the country are more significant than the size of the public debt. As we shall see later in this chapter, more borrowing may actually improve the country's economic position. Still, it is discouraging that we have failed to pay off the debt in the years between wars and depressions. The debt was reduced by about $25 billion after World War II, but then it began to go up again.

How does the government borrow money? The Constitution says that Congress may "borrow money on the credit of the United States"; it puts no limit on either the extent or method of borrowing. Under congressional authorization, the Treasury Department sells securities to banks, corporations, and individuals. Usually these securities take the form of long-term bonds or short-term treasury notes. Some bonds may be cashed in any time, others not until their maturity dates. Because the United States government backs up these bonds, they are in great demand, especially by banks and investment companies. However, the government, particularly in time of war, likes to induce as many individuals as possible to buy bonds, because individuals who buy bonds have less money to purchase goods and so will not contribute to inflationary pressures. If voluntary methods fail, the government could always require purchases by making compulsory deductions from wages and salaries.

A third source of federal funds consists of *administrative* and *commercial* revenues. The fee paid to the State Department for a passport, the fine paid by a criminal, are administrative revenues that account for a portion—though a very small portion—of federal income. More important are the funds paid to the federal government in exchange for direct services—payments to the Post Office for stamps, to the Park Service for recreation, to the Government Printing Office for pamphlets.

Finally, some public-spirited people actually *give* money or property to the government! Mr. Justice Holmes, who didn't mind taxes, left the government almost his entire estate when he died. But gifts, needless to say, are an infinitesimal source of federal revenue.

Spending the Money

All the billions of dollars the government takes in are funneled into the Treasury and then rapidly move out through hundreds of channels to points throughout the nation and, indeed, throughout the world. Nothing reflects the rise of big government more clearly than the change in the amount and methods of its spending. As recently as 1932 the federal government spent only $4 billion, about $30 per capita. In 1966 the respective figures were $98 billion and over $505. The machinery for spending has changed, too. Spending at one time was loosely administered. Records show, for example, that in an early year of the Republic one Nicholas Johnson, a Navy agent of Newburyport, Massachusetts, was handed several thousand dollars to supply "Capt. Brown for recruiting his Crew." [12] Today Mr. Johnson would have to make out detailed forms and wait for a government check.

Where does the money go? Most of it, of course, for national defense. The $99.7 billion budget estimated for the fiscal year 1966 allots about 61 per cent to the national security, international programs, and space agencies; 6 per cent to agricultural programs; 12 per cent to interest on the national debt; 5 per cent to veterans; and 16 per cent for all other services. Interesting changes have taken place even in the last two decades. In 1939 total expenditures of the federal government amounted to $9 billion. Of this, national defense took about $1 billion, interest less than $1 billion, and veterans about $600 million. It is hard to realize today that as recently as 1939 most federal expenses were for domestic relief and welfare functions. Significantly, in 1939 we spent only about 0.5 per cent of the budget on international activities. The proportion has risen manyfold as we have faced up to our global responsibilities.

The sheer fact of spending $100 billion a year is most significant of all. Years ago, federal revenues and outlays were so small that national taxing and spending had little impact on the over-all economy. But today the federal government cannot drain billions of dollars from certain areas of the economy and pump them back into other areas without its having a profound effect on the economy of the nation and of the world at large. This problem will be considered later in the chapter. First we must see how the federal budget is drawn up and made into law.

Formulating the Budget

As we have seen, Congress must authorize the spending of funds, but the initiation of appropriations is a responsibility of the President. The first step in preparing a federal budget is for the various

[12] L. D. White, *The Federalists* (Macmillan, 1948), p. 341.

departments and agencies to estimate their needs.[13] This process starts early; while Congress is debating the budget for the fiscal year immediately ahead, the agencies are making budget estimates for the year following. The estimating job is handled largely by budget officers working under the direction of the agency chiefs. The agency officials must take into account not only their needs as they see them, but also the overall presidential program and the probable reactions of Congress, especially those of the House Appropriations Committee—the "watchdog of the Treasury." [14] Departmental budgets are highly detailed, including estimates on expected needs for personnel, supplies, office space, and the like.

In the next phase of budget-making, the scene shifts to the Bureau of the Budget. A staff agency of the President, the bu-

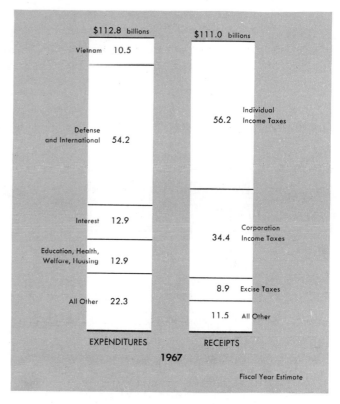

Executive Office of the President. Bureau of the Budget.

reau scrutinizes each agency budget to see if it is in accord with the President's budget plans. This job is done by experienced budget examiners who usually have been long acquainted with a particular agency, and can look over its requests with a sharp eye for accuracy, economy, and good program planning. Hearings are then held to give agency spokesmen a chance to clarify and defend their estimated needs. The Director of the Budget and his aides, who make the final decision, very frequently prune the agencies' requests rather severely.

Once again the scene shifts—this time to the White House. For months the budget director has been conferring with the Chief Executive and has been trying to keep the agencies below the budget ceilings set by the President. Finally—it is probably December by now—the director arrives at the White House with a single consolidated set of estimates of both revenue and expenditures, the product of perhaps a year's work. The President has reserved a day or two for a final review of the budget, and the two men check the consolidated figures. The budget

[13] For a discussion and graphic presentation of the budgetary cycle, see Aaron Wildavsky, *The Politics of the Budgetary Process* (Little, Brown, 1964).

[14] See Wildavsky, *op. cit.*, ch. 2; and Richard F. Fenno, Jr., "The House Appropriations Committee as a Political System," *The American Political Science Review* (June 1962), pp. 310–324.

director also helps the President prepare a budget message that will stress key aspects of the budget and tie it in with broad national plans. By January, soon after Congress convenes, the budget and the message are ready for the legislature and the people.

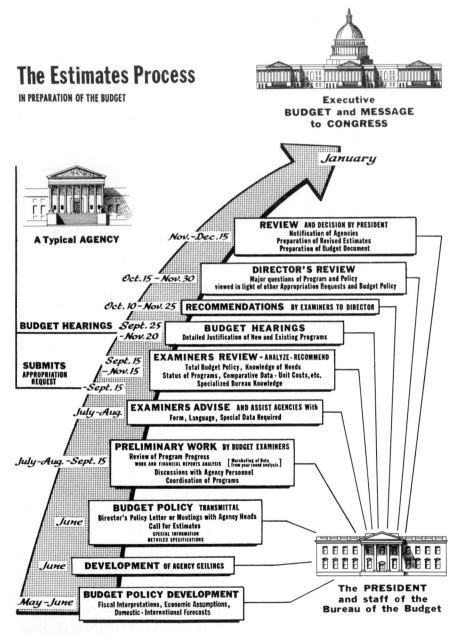

The Estimates Process
IN PREPARATION OF THE BUDGET

**Executive
BUDGET and MESSAGE
to CONGRESS**

January

A Typical AGENCY

Nov.–Dec.15 — **REVIEW** AND DECISION BY PRESIDENT
Notification of Agencies
Preparation of Revised Estimates
Preparation of Budget Document

Oct.15 – Nov. 30 — **DIRECTOR'S REVIEW**
Major questions of Program and Policy
viewed in light of other Appropriation Requests and Budget Policy

Oct. 10 – Nov. 25 — **RECOMMENDATIONS** BY EXAMINERS TO DIRECTOR

BUDGET HEARINGS *Sept. 25 – Nov. 20* — **BUDGET HEARINGS**
Detailed Justification of New and Existing Programs

SUBMITS APPROPRIATION REQUEST *Sept. 15 – Nov. 15 – Sept. 15* — **EXAMINERS REVIEW** - ANALYZE - RECOMMEND
Total Budget Policy, Knowledge of Needs
Status of Programs, Comparative Data - Unit Costs, etc.
Specialized Bureau Knowledge

July–Aug. — **EXAMINERS ADVISE** AND ASSIST AGENCIES With
Form, Language, Special Data Required

July–Aug. –Sept. 15 — **PRELIMINARY WORK** BY BUDGET EXAMINERS
Review of Program Progress
WORK AND FINANCIAL REPORTS ANALYSIS [Marshaling of Data from year round analysis]
Discussions with Agency Personnel
Coordination of Programs

June — **BUDGET POLICY** TRANSMITTAL
Director's Policy Letter or Meetings with Agency Heads
Call for Estimates
SPECIAL INFORMATION
DETAILED SPECIFICATIONS

June — **DEVELOPMENT** OF AGENCY CEILINGS

May–June — **BUDGET POLICY DEVELOPMENT**
Fiscal Interpretations, Economic Assumptions,
Domestic - International Forecasts

**The PRESIDENT
and staff of the
Bureau of the Budget**

(Source: Bureau of the Budget.)

"Well, here's another two-hundred-million debt they're saddling our generation with." (Drawing by B. Tobey © 1962 The New Yorker Magazine, Inc.)

Checking up on Expenditures

After Congress has appropriated money, it reserves the right to check up on the way the money is spent. Under the Budget and Accounting Act of 1921 the *General Accounting Office* does the national government's accounting job. The GAO is headed by a Comptroller General, who is appointed by the President with the approval of the Senate. The Comptroller General enjoys some measure of independence, however, for his term of office is 15 years, he is ineligible for reappointment, and he can be removed only for specific cause by a joint resolution of Congress.

The Comptroller General was originally intended to operate as an independent auditor serving as an arm of Congress to guard against improper and unauthorized expenditures. But as time went on he was swamped by a gigantic *accounting* job that forced him to handle administrative matters in the executive branch even though he was not responsible to the Chief Executive. At the same time, over-all management in the executive branch suffered, because daily accounting, an important instrument of administrative control, had been placed in a separate agency. Prior to 1949 the GAO imposed rigid requirements on the agencies, maintained detailed accounting records that frequently duplicated agency records, and brought tons of papers to Washington to check laboriously for irregularities.

In recent years, partly in response to recommendations of the Hoover Commissions, improvements have been made. The GAO now uses spot sampling methods to check vouchers, and makes its audits in the field rather than in Washington. Although the Comptroller General still has the authority to disallow expenditures, his approval is no longer needed prior to the disbursement of funds. Being relieved of personal responsibility for payments that may subsequently be disallowed (provided they have acted in good faith and with reasonable diligence), disbursing officers have been encouraged to make their own decisions about the legality of expenditures. Moreover, in 1950 Congress gave the departments and agencies, subject to supervision of the GAO, the responsibility and authority to set up their own internal accounting operations. Both the first and second Hoover Commissions urged that the executive departments be given even greater authority.[15] These procedures allow the Comptroller General to spend more time carrying out the vital legislative function of scrutinizing administrative fiscal practices, of making sure that laws governing appropriations are being correctly interpreted, of checking on the efficiency of accounting and other administrative practices—and of reporting on all these to Congress.

It might seem that accounting is a technical matter that could be settled without

[15] U.S. Commission on Organization of the Executive Branch of the Government, *Budgeting and Accounting* (Government Printing Office, 1949), pp. 39, 47 ff; see also U.S. Commission on Organization of the Executive Branch of the Government, *Budgeting and Accounting* (Government Printing Office, 1955), pp. 29 ff.

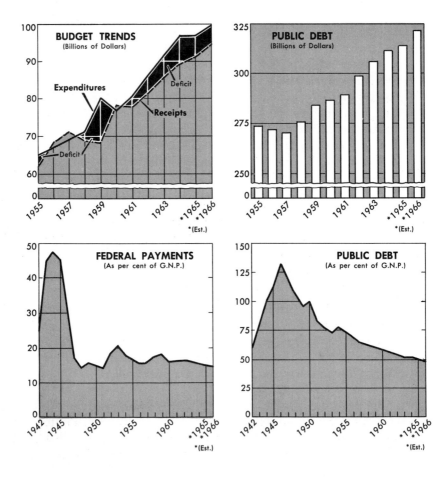

much argument. On the contrary, accounting is a political problem, too, for it reflects two struggles that go on in Washington. One is the attempt of Congress as a whole to maintain as much control as possible over the still mushrooming bureaucratic machine. The other is the struggle of individual legislators to keep and maintain a system that checks individual administrative payments.

Managing Money

Today's economy is essentially a money economy. Instead of using a system of barter—like that of South Sea islanders who swap fruit for beads—"civilized" peoples exchange commodities through a vast system of money and credit. We have seen the tremendous role the federal government plays in this system, simply because it gets and spends nearly $100 billion a year. But aside from its role as the biggest buyer and seller of goods and services, the federal government has a more direct impact on our money economy. First, it manufactures money. Second, it regulates the value of money. Third, it controls the nation's credit system.

Manufacturing money is the easiest of these jobs. The Bureau of Engraving and Printing in the Treasury Department, using carefully designed plates and special types of paper, turns out millions of dollars of bills, bonds, and postage stamps every week. This "folding-money" is fed into general circulation through the Treasury and the Federal Reserve banks. The Bureau of the Mint in Philadelphia, Denver, and San Francisco (also under the Treasury) coins the silver dollars, half-dollars, quarters, and dimes, the nickel-copper nickels, and the copper and iron pennies that together make up about one-twentieth of the country's cash.

In itself, this money is only so much paper and metal. How does the government maintain its value?

The Currency System

The Constitution gives the federal government the right to manage the nation's money system. Under the old Articles of Confederation, the national currency had consisted mainly of almost worthless paper money, and the individual states had maintained separate currencies. To correct this monetary hodgepodge, the Constitution of 1787 carefully vested in Congress authority to coin money and to regulate its value, and it carefully withheld this power from the states. Thanks partly to Secretary of the Treasury Hamilton, the early Americans scrapped the confusing British system of guineas, pounds, shillings and pence, and adopted a decimal system.

Today the United States is on the "modified gold standard" in that the money and credit supply is backed up in part with a huge store of gold at Fort Knox, Kentucky, and the unit of monetary value is defined in terms of gold. But all the currency of the United States—Federal Reserve Notes, Silver Certificates, silver dollars, and subsidiary coins—are legal tender and cannot be freely exchanged for gold. (A few United States Notes, Treasury Notes, Federal Bank Notes, and National Bank Notes are still outstanding but they are being retired.) In short, the money of the United States is freely redeemable only for other money of the United States.

Money makes up only a part of the circulating medium and is less important to our economy than *credit*. In the expansion and contraction of credit, the most important institutions are the nation's banks and the Federal Reserve System.

Banks and Lending Institutions

Although banking is a private business, it is subject to close governmental supervision. There are about 14,000 banks in the United States; 4,500 are chartered by the national government, the others by the states. The national banks, however, have 50 per cent of all bank deposits in their custody. The Comptroller of the Currency in the Department of Treasury supervises their operations. Each national bank must file reports on its financial condition at least three times a year, and must permit bank examiners to inspect its books at least twice a year—at unannounced times.

Although state authorities have the primary responsibility to supervise state-chartered banks, most of these banks are also subject to federal regulation, since their deposits are insured by the Federal Deposit Insurance Corporation. All national banks must participate in this program, and state banks that meet approved standards are permitted to do so. All but a few hundred of the 14,000 commercial bank and trust companies in the United States have their deposits insured by the FDIC, as do some of the over 500 mutual savings banks. The FDIC routinely examines banks that are not members of the Federal Reserve System (see below) and establishes rules designed to keep them solvent. In case of an insolvent member bank, the FDIC takes over its management and pays off each depositor up to $10,000.

The Federal Savings and Loan Insurance Corporation, operating under the supervision of the Federal Home Loan Bank Board, protects investors in federal savings and loan associations and those state-chartered institutions approved for participation. Like the FDIC, it guarantees savings up to $10,000 for each account.

The national government also promotes the establishment of *credit unions*, associations of persons having a common bond of occupation or residence who may secure a federal charter and receive assistance from the Bureau of Federal Credit Unions in the Department of Health, Education and Welfare. These unions, which now number about 9,500, encourage members to deposit excess funds which may then be lent to other members at relatively low interest rates.

The Federal Reserve System

In many nations a central bank owned and operated by the national government determines general monetary policies. The Constitution does not specifically authorize the national government to create such a bank—indeed, it says nothing at all about banking. But Alexander Hamilton believed some such institution was necessary; and in 1791, on his initiative, the United States Bank was incorporated by the national government and given a twenty-year charter. The United States Bank was partly private and partly public; the national government owned only a minority of the shares and had only a minority voice in its management. Jefferson and his supporters opposed the bank on monetary, political, and constitutional grounds. Nevertheless, President Madison found it necessary to have the bank rechartered for another twenty years in 1816, after the Jeffersonians had refused to do so in 1811. In 1819 the Supreme Court in *McCulloch* v. *Maryland* (see Chapter 4) upheld the constitutionality of the bank as a necessary and proper way for the national government to establish a uniform currency and to care for the property of the United States.

After the bank closed its doors in 1836, state banks, which had previously been restrained by the Second United States Bank, embarked on an orgy of issuing notes that often could not be redeemed. A military crisis forced a house-cleaning. To stabilize an economy beset with war demands and to support the desires of the "dear money" groups, Congress in 1863 authorized the chartering of national banks. These are privately owned corporations not to be confused with a central bank or an institution like the United States Bank. State banks were permitted to continue in business, but a 10 per cent federal tax on their notes quickly drove state bank notes out of existence.

The national bank system created during the Civil War was stable—indeed, so stable that it was inflexible. Financial crises during the late nineteenth century and in 1907 revealed an unhappy tendency of banks to restrict their loans, and of national banks to contract their issuance of notes, just at the times when an *expansion* of money was needed. In order to furnish an elastic currency, and for other reasons, Congress established the Federal Reserve System in 1913.

The Act of 1913 was a compromise. Some wanted a strong central bank, but many feared that this would centralize control over currency in too few hands. So a system was established that gives us a modified central banking program with considerable decentralization.

The country is divided into twelve Federal Reserve Districts, in each of which there is a Federal Reserve Bank (most Federal Reserve Banks have branches). Each Federal Reserve Bank is owned by member banks. All national banks must join the system, and state banks that meet standards are permitted to do so. Today approximately 6,100 of the 14,000 banks are members of the system; these are the largest banks and have over 85 per cent of total deposits.

Each Federal Reserve Bank is headed by a board of directors, six elected by the member banks, and three appointed by the Board of Governors (see immediately below) in Washington. Three of the directors elected by the member banks must be bankers, and three must be active in business and industry. The three directors appointed by the Board of Governors may not have any financial interest in, and may not work for, any bank. The Board of Governors designates one of its appointees to be chairman of the board of directors and this board in turn selects a president to serve as its chief executive officer.

A seven-man Board of Governors sitting in Washington supervises the entire system. These men are selected by the President with the consent of the Senate for fourteen-year terms, and the President designates the chairman, who has a four-year term. The Board of Governors, advised by the Federal Advisory Council composed of a member from each Federal Reserve district, meets in Washington at least four times a year, determines general monetary and credit policies. It has four major weapons to tighten or loosen the financial activities of the nation's banks and, in turn, of the whole economy. They are:

1. Increase or decrease within legal limits the reserves that member banks must maintain against their deposits in the Federal Reserve Bank.

2. Raise or lower the rediscount rate charged by Federal Reserve Banks to member banks. The rediscount rate is the price member banks must pay to get cash from the Federal Reserve Banks for acceptable commercial notes that the banks hold.

3. Through the Open Market Committee (composed of all members of the Board of Governors and five representatives of the Reserve Banks) sell or buy government securities and certain other bills of exchanges, bank acceptances, and so on.

4. Exercise direct control over the credit that may be extended in order to purchase securities (called "margin requirements"). From time to time Congress has given the Board of Governors temporary authority to fix terms of consumer credit.

Through these and other devices, the Board of Governors may affect the flow of circulating medium by tightening or loosening credit. For example, if inflation is threatening, the board can dampen down the economy by raising member bank reserve requirements (thus cutting down on the cash they have available for lending), by raising rediscount rates (thus forcing member banks to raise the rates for which they will lend money), by selling government securities in the open market (thus absorbing funds from the economy), and by raising margin requirements (thus reducing credit available to bid up the prices of securities.

The Federal Reserve Banks also serve as depositories for government funds, clear checks and transfer funds among member banks, and may in case of economic emergency even lend money directly to businesses.

The Federal Reserve System is intentionally isolated from influence by the President, and since it does not depend upon annual appropriations even Congress exercises little control over it. "Devised as a service agency for banking and commerce—to achieve a semi-automatic adjustment of the money supply—the Federal Reserve has become as well a policy-making institution with major responsibility for national economic stabilization." [16] And many observers feel that

---

[16] See Michael D. Reagan, "The Political Structure of the Federal Reserve System," *The American Political Science Review* (March 1961), pp. 64–76 for a detailed analysis of the present structure and policy implications of the Federal Reserve System.

it is improper to vest the important new responsibility in an agency so divorced from public accountability. The Federal Reserve Board, for example, often has to make a choice between fighting inflation, which may cause unemployment, or promoting employment at the expense of creating inflation. As Gardiner C. Means has said, "There is a good deal of question whether such a momentous decision should rest with the Federal Reserve Board." [17] On the other side, many, including most bankers, are anxious to preserve the system's independence. They believe that only an agency insulated from political pressures can take steps that are often unpopular to prevent inflation.

Today all agree that monetary policy must be considered as but one weapon to combat depression, control inflation, foster full employment, and encourage economic growth. Whether or not we can retain a system in which the central banking authorities "can legally . . . tell the head of (their) own Government to go fly a kite," [18] remains a moot issue.

Managing the Economy

So far, we have seen how the national government directly manages certain economic activities, such as the post office and TVA, how it raises and spends billions of dollars a year, and how it controls currency, banking, and credit (although the banks themselves are legally under private control). We have observed the political and governmental processes that shape the way in which government operates these controls.

Does the government have the same direct control over the national economy that it has, say, over the post office and national forests? No. Only if we had a socialized economy administered from Washington would we have a managed economy in that sense. Actually we have—and, one hopes, will always have—an economy in which a great deal of power is left to private individuals and enterprises. And yet the government keeps a firm hand on all the gears and levers that control the general direction in which the economy will move and the rate at which it will travel. These gears and levers are marked taxes, spending, credit, and the like.

If these levers were operated in a haphazard, whimsical way, they might have no effect at all on the economy. Or else they might have a catastrophic effect— as if a ship captain were to order full speed ahead and a sharp turn to the starboard at one and the same time. Operated in a carefully synchronized manner, however, they can help keep the economy on an even keel.

It is only rather recently that Americans have recognized the part that government *could* play in stabilizing and invigorating the economy. (There are still differences of opinion over the part that it *should* play.) The slow development of our understanding, the political struggle over the question of whether the federal

---

[17] Quoted by Reagan, *ibid.*, p. 75.
[18] Elliot V. Bell, quoted by Reagan, *ibid.*, p. 76.

government should take responsibility for full employment, the enactment of the Employment Act of 1946—these are fascinating episodes in the trend toward over-all control of the economy by the federal government.

Economic Groping

Austerity is a hard teacher. The depression of the 1930's had a tremendous impact on American thinking about the role of government in economic matters. We have had long, severe depressions before—for example, in the 1870's and 1890's. But by 1929 the United States had become a rich and powerful nation, and prosperity seemed here to stay. Then the Great Depression struck. Millions of unemployed, falling prices and income, plummeting production—all added up to mass misery. "One vivid, gruesome moment of those dark days we shall never forget," wrote one observer. "We saw a crowd of some fifty men fighting over a barrel of garbage which had been set outside the back door of a restaurant. American citizens fighting for scraps of food like animals!" [19]

Despite a wide range of initiatives on the part of the New Deal to cope with the depression—the NRA, AAA, PWA, WPA, social security, and wages and hour legislation—the depression hung on. Faint stirrings of recovery showed themselves in the mid-1930's, but the recession of 1937–1938 indicated that we were by no means out of the woods. Eight or nine million people were jobless in 1939. Then came the war, and unemployment was cured—for a while. Millions of people had more income, more security, a higher standard of living. Lord Beveridge in England posed a question that bothered many thoughtful Americans: "Unemployment has been practically abolished twice in the lives of most of us—in the last war and in this war. Why does war solve the problem of unemployment which is so insoluble in peace?" [20] Worried that the economy might collapse after the war, literally thousands of people came up with plans to insure jobs for all.

One school of thought was that the depression persisted because the New Deal was hostile to business and inserted government for too long and too extensively in the economic life of the nation. They urged the government to cut down on spending, lower taxes, curb the power of labor, and generally leave business and the economy alone except for traditional regulation and aids to certain businesses. Another large group, made up of economists, labor representatives, government officials, and others, took a very different tack. They said that the trouble with the New Deal was not that it had done too much, but that it had done too little. The thinking of this group was deeply influenced by the work of John Maynard Keynes, the famous English economist. In visits to the United States during the 1930's, Keynes warned that if people do not consume enough or invest enough, national income will fall. The way to increase national income is either to spend money on consumption goods (such as clothes or food or automobiles) or on investment goods (steel mills and dock facilities) or on both. Finally—and this was the

[19] Quoted in F. L. Allen, *Since Yesterday* (Harper, 1940), p. 64.
[20] W. H. Beveridge, *The Pillars of Security* (Macmillan, 1943), p. 51.

dynamite in the proposition—*government must do the spending and investing if private enterprise by itself would not or could not.* The Keynesian approach was tied in with related concepts involving governmental influence on public works, wages, prices, credit, taxation, and the like. Congress, through the passage of the Employment Act of 1946, gave formal acceptance to this latter of the two basic approaches.

The Employment Act of 1946

Congressional enactment of a measure that specifically recognized the primacy of the national government in the maintenance of full employment was bound to be difficult.[21] The bill as presented by the Truman administration embodied the viewpoint of Keynesian economists and had the support of organized labor, many senators, and members of several Senate committee staffs. Arrayed against the bill were such organizations as the NAM, Chambers of Commerce, the American Farm Bureau Federation, and a number of key conservatives in Congress. While the bill fairly easily passed the Senate in close to its original form, the conservative House Rules Committee insured that only a much weaker version would pass the lower House. Passed in February 1946, the Act declared:

> It is the continuing policy and responsibility of the Federal Government to use all practicable means consistent with its needs and obligations and other essential considerations of national policy, with the assistance and cooperation of industry, agriculture, labor, and state and local governments, to coordinate and utilize all its plans, functions, and resources for the purpose of creating and maintaining, in a manner calculated to foster and promote free competitive enterprise and the general welfare, conditions under which there will be afforded useful employment, for those able, willing, and seeking to work, and to promote maximum employment, production, and purchasing power.

If this declaration sounds like double talk, the reason may be that the bill had to be built on a series of compromises. In effect, the bill made the federal government responsible for acting in the face of rising unemployment instead of relying wholly on nongovernmental forces. Equally important, the act established machinery to carry out that responsibility. It created:

The Council of Economic Advisers. Composed of three members appointed by the President with the consent of the Senate, and located in the Executive Office of the President, this council with a small staff studies and forecasts economic trends, assesses the contribution of federal programs to maximum employment, and recommends to the President "national economic policies to foster and pro-

---

[21] For the full history of the bill, see Stephen K. Bailey, *Congress Makes a Law* (Columbia Univ. Press, 1950).

mote free competition, to avoid economic fluctuations or to diminish the effects thereof, and to maintain employment, production, and purchasing power."

The Economic Report of the President. The President must submit to Congress every January an economic report based on the data and forecasts of the council. The report must include a program for carrying out the policy of the act, and recommendations for legislation if the President sees fit.

Joint Economic Committee. This is a committee of Congress authorized by the act. Composed of seven senators and seven representatives, it must report early

MECHANICS OF THE EMPLOYMENT ACT OF 1946

THE PRESIDENT

CONGRESS

ECONOMIC REPORT

JAN. 8   FEB. 1

ON EMPLOYMENT,
PRODUCTION,
PURCHASING POWER

ANNUAL REPORT
SPECIAL REPORTS
MATERIALS FOR PRESIDENT'S ECONOMIC REPORT

COUNCIL OF ECONOMIC ADVISORS

1. Gathers information on economic conditions
2. Appraises economic programs and activities of Federal Government
3. Recommends national economic policies
4. Makes economic studies at President's request

JOINT ECONOMIC COMMITTEE

Reports to Congress its findings
and recommendations
with respect to the economic report

FEDERAL AGENCIES
PRIVATE RESEARCH AGENCIES
} SERVICES, FACILITIES
AND INFORMATION

INDUSTRY
AGRICULTURE
LABOR
CONSUMERS
STATE & LOCAL GOVERNMENTS
} ADVISORY COMMITTEES
AND CONSULTANTS

Adapted from Report of Council of Economic Advisers, *December 1947.*

in each year its findings and proposals in respect to presidential recommendations. Aside from publishing various reports, such as the monthly *Economic Indicators,* JEC is able to give Congress an overview of the economy. In this sense it is an anomaly in Congress: "a planning and theory group in a culture fiercely devoted to the short run and practical. It is committed to the panoramic view in a system that stresses jurisdictional lines. It signifies recognition that economic problems are related, in a body that deals with them piecemeal." [22]

How has the Employment Act worked in practice? Particularly under the Kennedy and Johnson administrations, the CEA emerged as a high-level presidential advisory body with its chairman serving both as an adviser to the President and as a spokesman for the President before Congress and the country. The annual Economic Report, along with the Budget Message, are major presidential statements on the role that governmental fiscal policies will play in the economy in the coming year. The JEC has played an increasingly important role in developing information on important economic problems. For example, the effects of low income were studied in the JEC years before the Johnson "war on poverty." Thus the machinery established under the act is operative and is providing both the President and Congress with the type of information and advice needed in order to shape governmental fiscal policy. [23]

The various mechanisms established by the act work, but is the information being utilized and the advice implemented? Certainly the Employment Act is more significant for the basic ideas it embodies than for the procedures it created. In the mid 1960's it is evident that the Keynesian economic underpinnings of the act have gained wide acceptance in Washington and elsewhere. Governmental fiscal policy has been used in a straightforward fashion to stimulate the economy and cope with its fluctuations. No longer, for example, is a "balanced budget" viewed by Washington decision-makers as a national goal always to be pursued. In certain instances it is better for the government actually to spend more than it takes in and to run a budget deficit. This is the widely recognized course of action when the economy is not operating at full capacity. When the economy is operating at full capacity, other measures may be called for; a budget surplus, for instance, may be required to check inflationary pressures under conditions of full employment. This sort of Keynesian rationale provided the basis for the $12 billion personal income tax cut in 1964 and the nearly $2 billion cut in excise taxes in 1965. Although unemployment in 1964 was steadily moving downward as the GNP moved upward, the economy was still not at full capacity and more stimulus from the federal government was required. The increased governmental spending and the lower taxes resulting from the 1964 cut put more money in the hands of the American public, which spent more money creating more jobs. The economy boomed. Indeed, so successful was this action that though taxes were

[22] Commission on Money and Credit, *Money and Credit: Their Influence on Jobs, Prices, and Growth* (Prentice-Hall, 1961), pp. 268, 269.

[23] For an account of performance and politics under the Employment Act, see Harvey C. Mansfield, "The Congress and Economic Policy," in David B. Truman (ed.), *The Congress and America's Future* (Prentice-Hall, 1965), ch. 6.

cut by $12 billion, $12.7 billion more was actually taken in from personal taxes in 1964. Results were so rewarding under this tax cut that the way was cleared for the excise tax cut the following year. By the mid-1960's the United States was enjoying its longest continuous period of economic growth without a major recession.

There are still practical difficulties lying between the initiation of national economic policy and its implementation. For instance, it is necessary for Congress to pass upon all revenue and expenditure proposals. This often takes time, for congressmen are called upon to deal with the very basic political problem of "who gets what." Consequently, cumbersome congressional procedures preclude the quick injection of money into the economy via a tax cut even when such a policy may be economically warranted. To remedy this it has been proposed that the President be given discretionary power to alter tax rates between certain congressionally imposed limits.[24] Keynesian thinking has not permeated the halls of Congress to the extent of sanctioning this sort of encroachment upon its constitutional responsibilities. Also, monetary policy is a tool that may be used to affect the overall performance of the economy in that the supply of money and credit may be manipulated in ways discussed earlier. The executive, however, has no means by which it can directly influence the actions of FRB, for only the latter is vested with monetary responsibilities. Consequently, it is possible for the executive and the FRB to work at cross-purposes. Proposals have been made to limit the autonomy of the FRB, making it more amenable to executive influence, but the chances for this kind of alteration are not bright.

The problem, in short, is not one of economic know-how. Hard experience and the work of both economists and men of affairs have taught us a lot about the workings and management of the national economy. The problem is not unwillingness to accept governmental responsibility for maintaining employment. The Act of 1946 specifically recognizes that responsibility. The problem is whether a governmental system such as ours can act effectively when action is needed. The true test would come if our economy took a serious turn downward after the high level of prosperity we have enjoyed for almost three decades.

The Political Economy—A Case Study

In these last three chapters we have observed that economic and political life in our society are inextricably interwoven. There are no easily discerned boundaries between private and public sectors of the economy. Some insist that government and the economy must be kept strictly separated; that government should not "interfere" in private economic affairs. Whatever its theoretical merits, this view is unrealistic. In modern American society we confront a political economy in which a decision in one area inevitably affects decisions in the other. This politi-

[24] For example, Commission on Money and Credit, *op. cit.*, pp. 133–137.

cal economy is a mixed economy—mixed in that it blends private and public enterprise, individual initiative and government promotion, personal responsibility and public regulation, federal and state governments.

We have also discovered that government regulation, promotion, and management are not really distinct approaches. Promotion may be used for regulatory purposes, regulation for promotional, and government management in the broadest sense always entails both. A single case serves to demonstrate these relationships— President Kennedy's dispute with Big Steel in 1962.

For a year the Kennedy administration had been trying, mainly through ex hortation, to induce both labor and employers to "hold the price line." Early in April 1962 the big steel companies and the labor unions had signed a contract which the President greeted with enthusiasm as noninflationary. A few days later Roger Blough, chairman of the board of the United States Steel Corporation, went to the White House late one afternoon and informed the President that his corporation was raising the price of steel. Other steel companies would follow suit, the President knew, the whole dike against inflation might be breached, and his policies of conciliation and persuasion would be repudiated. He knew that he must act, that he must act quickly, and that he must act across a wide front.

The events that occurred during the next three days at the White House have already been the subject of much scholarly and journalistic attention.[25] They can be summarized as follows:

First of all the President summoned Cabinet members, economic advisers, staff assistants, statisticians, congressional advisers to his office to plan an all-out counterattack.

Statisticians brought up to date a "fact book" on steel put out by the Eisenhower administration two years earlier—both to be armed with the "facts" and to demonstrate the continuity with Eisenhower's anti-inflation policies.

The President asked congressional leaders to publicly "register dismay" about the steel price increase. They promptly did so.

The Justice Department announced an investigation of the steel price rise for possible violations of the antitrust laws.

The Chairman of the Federal Trade Commission told reporters that his agency had begun an informal investigation to determine whether the steel companies had violated a consent decree of 1951.

The Democratic National Committee telephoned Democratic governors to ask them to issue statements supporting the President and to ask steel producers in their own states to hold the price line. But the national committee made no statement of its own so that this would not seem to be a party issue.

Before newsmen and television cameras at a press conference, the President denounced the price increase with controlled fury as a "wholly unjustifiable and irresponsible defiance of the public interest."

[25] A succinct account of this event is found in Grant McConnell, *Steel and the Presidency, 1962* (Norton, 1963).

Several liberal Republicans attacked Big Steel's action. Administration leaders with connections in high places in the business world tried to induce business leaders to pressure steel against its decision.

All this was part of the administration's tactic of mobilizing public pressure on the steel companies. But its main tactic was one of "divide and conquer." Much depended on how many other steel companies would follow the lead of U.S. Steel in raising prices. Some already had. Administration officials had networks of contacts with officials in the other companies. The government also held some economic leverage because of its huge contracts with steel companies, especially defense contracts; indeed, the Defense Department announced that it was ordering defense contractors to shift steel purchases to companies that had not raised prices. The precise nature of the negotiations between administration officials and steel company officials is not clear, but this tactic evidently turned the tide. Inland Steel and several other companies announced that they would not raise prices. Bethlehem Steel rescinded its announced increase. Soon United States Steel was left isolated, and it quickly capitulated to these market pressures. Just seventy-two hours after Blough visited the White House, he announced that his company would withdraw its price increase.

Clearly, it was a resounding immediate victory for a President pledged to "hold the price line" on behalf of the people as a whole. It demonstrated the power of the President—at least when a President felt that economically and politically his back was against the wall. Yet there were misgivings. Republican leaders in Congress, in a joint statement, said that a "fundamental issue" had been raised: "Should a President of the United States use the enormous powers of the federal government to blackjack any segment of our free society into line with his personal judgment without regard to law?" Much was made of an unfortunate action on the part of FBI agents, who routed reporters out of bed to check on the accuracy of certain statements of business officials; while there was no threat to the reporters themselves, the action smacked too much of the "early-morning knock on the door" in police states to please many observers. A few weeks later a series of sharp dips in the stock market were blamed by some on the President's action—thus linking the steel-price fight to the broader question of the government's relation to economic prosperity.

Thus, as this case illustrates, the complex relationship between government and the economy and the mutual connections between governmental techniques make policy evaluation indeed complicated. But at least we can begin with the knowledge that the goals of personal and national security are pursued in a highly political setting—a setting inevitable in a "government by the people."

PART 7

State and local government

A Problem Guide   Part Seven deals with entire systems of government at the state and local levels; hence, it raises all five sets of problems listed at the beginning of this book. Americans in their states and localities face the same challenges as they do as a nation—the challenge of making democratic government a vital and indispensable way of ruling the people; of following basic constitutional principles, such as that of checks and balances, without letting government become stymied by internal disputes; of maintaining a balance between liberty and order; of achieving democratic representation for all interests; of keeping state and local leaders accountable to the people.

State and local governments, however, pose some of these problems more sharply than others. State government, generally speaking, is the weakest link in the whole federal system. Because of gerrymandering and other distortions in the representative process, some people have a more effective voice in the state legislatures than do others. Genuine political accountability is lacking in some states because of the splintering of executive power between governors and a host of independent administrative officials. The party system is often not strong enough to knit the leaders together into a team. The disturbing problem that results from such conditions is that state governments may be unable to meet the demands of modern society and more and more functions may gradually be taken over by the federal government. This crucial question of the effectiveness of state governments is the main problem in Chapters 27, 28, 29, and 30.

What about the local governments? Here again we can recognize all our five

709

sets of problems, especially the focal problem of the capacity of local governments to carry on their functions efficiently and responsibly. It is hard to generalize about county and municipal government because of the enormous variety of systems involved. But the questions we encountered initially in studying national government keep rising at the grass roots too. How much power does the local executive have, and to whom is he accountable? Are the various interests fairly represented in government? How well can local government mobilize the two indispensable tools of administration—able men and sufficient money—to do the job? These problems are raised in Chapters 33 and 34.

The emphasis in this book has been on the *political forces*—parties, interest groups, public opinion, and so on—that shape government. This is the emphasis in Part Seven as well. To the student of American politics the states and their subdivisions are fascinating political laboratories that allow comparison among the different systems. How strong and unified is the party system? To what extent does state and local politics mirror national political tides, to what extent is it cut off (as, for example, in most southern states) from national politics? Does the state and local political system foster competition between the two parties, or does one party clearly dominate? In the latter case, how much free and open competition exists between factions *within* the dominant party? In short, does the political system help the voters make intelligent choices? Do the leaders respond to the needs and wishes of the great majority of people?

27 WHO GOVERNS— PATTERNS OF INFLUENCE

We face one great advantage and one great disadvantage in taking up the study of state and local governments. The advantage is that students who have read the earlier chapters of this book and have discussed American politics in class can consider themselves as at least apprentice political scientists by now, possessing extensive information and some skill in analyzing political problems. They understand the role of constitutions, the

711

checks and balances and division of powers in the American system, the working of interest groups, public opinion, political parties, how the executive, legislative, and judicial branches operate, and the functions of government. They have seen, in short, the interplay of ideas, interests, institutions, and individuals in national politics, and they will find these to be familiar landmarks as they turn to state and local governments.

The disadvantage lies in the sheer variety of governments to be considered. It is one thing to study a single governmental system, vast and complex though that system may be. It is something else to study 50 separate state governments, each with its own legislature, executive, and judiciary, each with its own intricate politics and varied political traditions. Moreover, the government of each state is only part of a much larger picture. To understand the government of New York one must know something about the people of New York—how they make their living, where they came from, what they believe in, into what groups they are organized, and how they are related to groups elsewhere in the United States and throughout the world. To discuss the government of Mississippi without mentioning white-Negro relations, the government of Massachusetts without noting the interactions between Protestants and Irish Catholics, the government of Texas without referring to cattle and oil, the government of Illinois without mentioning Chicago and Cook county politics, would be to ignore the dynamics of the political process. State governments, just like the national government, cannot be described meaningfully as structure or laws totally divorced from people, as organization charts rather than as systems of politics.

Complicated as the picture of the state governments might be, it is more difficult to try to understand the thousands of cities, counties, towns, villages, school districts, water control districts, and other governmental units piled up on top of one another in the states. If all states or cities or towns were alike, the job might be manageable. But of course they are not. Each city, each state is unique and we need to have more knowledge about the political life of Ashtabula, Detroit, Washington, and California, but not just to find out about these particular localities. For the study of our state and local political systems provides a fascinating laboratory for comparative analysis, for testing our hypotheses about politics and for development of new generalizations to be tested elsewhere. And while recognizing that our states, cities, and counties cannot be fit into too simplified categories, we must develop some patterns and search for the uniformities underlying all the "crazy mixed-up politics." Otherwise, our information is of limited utility. What we need are some tentative organizing concepts that will help us understand what is going on whether we live in rural Vermont or downtown Cleveland.

How, then, can we understand the operations and problems of state and local government without becoming bogged down in endless detail? We can do so by constantly returning to the core problems of this book—problems of democracy, constitutionalism, individual liberty, representation, responsible leadership. In order to focus our attention even more, we will emphasize in these chapters one "master question" that will throw light on all the above problems. The question is "Who governs?" The people, yes—but we must probe the question further. What people? Does political power in the states and localities tend to gravitate into the hands of a relatively small number of people? If so, who are these "influentials"? Do they work closely together, or do they divide among themselves? Do the same "influentials" dominate all decision-making, or do some sets of leaders decide certain questions and leave other questions to others or to chance?

This master question of "who governs?" is, of course, an ancient one, at least two thousand years old. Not only philosophers but plain people like to ask: "Who really runs things around here?" Nowhere, perhaps, has this question been asked with more fruitful results than in certain American communities in the last 40 years. In 1924 two sociologists from Columbia, a young married couple named Robert and Helen Lynd, decided that they would study a typical American city as though they were anthropologists investigating a tribe in darkest Africa. For two years they lived in Muncie, Indiana, a city then of 38,000, asking lots of questions, watching how people made their living, brought up their young, used their leisure time, joined in lodges, brotherhoods, and other groups. They reported that behind the democratic façade of "Middletown," as they disguised the name of their city, a social and economic elite was actually running things in Muncie.[1] In the mid-1940's a world famous reporter, John Gunther, studied the United States as he had previously reported Europe and Asia, "from the inside." Everywhere he went he asked people, "Who runs your state or city? What are the basic and irreversible sources of *power*—social, economic, political?" The astonishing thing, he found, was the "luxuriant variety of answers. No single person, principle, ideal, commodity, abstraction, or vested interest runs it. . . ."[2] The country was enormously conglomerate—but also interlocked.

In recent years social scientists have pressed ahead with probes of other communities and areas. Four anthropologists, analyzing a southern city of 10,000, were struck by the tenacity of old belief systems going back a century.[3] A mining town in Montana, a Connecticut suburb, a mill city in Massachusetts, provided data on the enormous variety of communal life. One of the most ambitious studies was of an old New England seaport still living off memories of its greatness in the days of the clipper ships.[4] A score of observers, using survey data punched onto cards, found an elaborate class structure, with the "old families" on top even though some of them had lost their money and were poor compared to the *nouveaux-riches*.

Following their own bent, social scientists have focused on the pattern of power in communities, and they have, of course, come up with varied findings. For example, Floyd Hunter, a sociologist at the University of North Carolina, analyzing a

---

[1] Robert S. Lynd and Helen M. Lynd, *Middletown* (Harcourt, Brace, 1929). See also their equally brilliant treatment of Muncie ten years later, *Middletown in Transition* (Harcourt, Brace, 1937).

[2] John Gunther, *Inside U.S.A.* (Harper, 1947), p. xv.

[3] Allison Davis, B. B. Gardner, and M. R. Gardner, *Deep South* (Univ. of Chicago Press, 1941). The project was directed by W. Lloyd Warner.

[4] W. Lloyd Warner and P. S. Lunt, *The Social Life of a Modern Community* (Yale Univ. Press, 1941).

southern regional city, found a relatively small and stable group of top policy-makers drawn largely from the business class. The top leaders operated through shifting groups of secondary leaders, who sometimes modified policy, but the power of the elite was almost always there.[5] On the other hand, Robert A. Dahl, a political scientist at Yale, studying his own university city of New Haven, concluded that while some people had a great deal of influence and others had very little, there was no solid, hard-core elite, but shifting coalitions of leaders who sometimes fell out among themselves and who always had to keep in mind "what the public would bear" in making their decisions.[6]

Community Power Studies—Some Research Problems

Which of these two cities, Atlanta or New Haven, is more typical of the distribution of influence in American communities? Or could it be that the difference between Hunter's and Dahl's findings stem from the questions they asked rather than from differences in the two communities? For the assumptions of the investigators and the techniques they use may produce differences in what they find.[7]

One group of investigators, chiefly sociologists such as Hunter, are mainly concerned with social stratification, for they assume that political influence is a function of the structure of the community. They try to find out who governs a community by asking a variety of citizens to identify the persons who are most influential in the community. Then these "influentials," so identified, are studied to determine their social characteristics, their role in decision-making, the interrelations among influentials and between the influentials and the rest of the citizenry. Those who use this technique generally report that the upper-socio-economic groups make up the power elite, that elected political leaders are subordinate to this elite, and that the major conflicts within the community are between the upper and the lower socio-economic classes.

Another group of investigators, primarily political scientists such as Dahl, have questioned the findings of the students of social stratification and have raised objections to their techniques. The evidence, it is contended (even that contained within the stratification studies themselves), does not support a conclusion that communities are run by a power elite. Rather, the notion of a power elite is merely a reflection of the techniques used and the assumptions of the stratification theorists. Instead of studying the activities of persons who are *thought* to have influence, one should study public policy to find out how, in fact, decisions are made. Those who make community studies in this manner usually find an open, pluralistic power structure. Some people do have more influence than others, but

[5] Floyd Hunter, *Community Power Structure* (Univ. of North Carolina Press, 1953).

[6] Robert A. Dahl, *Who Governs?: Democracy and Power in an American City* (Yale Univ. Press, 1961).

[7] See Nelson W. Polsby, *Community Power and Political Theory* (Yale Univ. Press, 1963), for the perspective of a critic of social stratification theorists (and for a comprehensive bibliography of the community power studies).

influence is widely shared and tends to be limited to particular issues and areas. Those who have much to say about how the public schools are run may have little influence over economic policies. And in many communities and for many issues there is no identifiable group of influentials; policy emerges not from the manipulation of a small group, but from the unanticipated and unplanned consequences of the behavior of large numbers of people. The social structure of the community is one factor—but not the determinative factor—of how goods and services and valued things are distributed within the community.

Here we have an example of how the questions we ask may influence the answers we find. Yet the community power studies, despite differences in approach and findings, are beginning to produce enough data about enough communities so that by a comparative analysis of decision-making we can begin to develop generalizations about how formal governmental institutions, structure of the society, economic factors, and other variables interrelate to create a political system that determines who gets what, where, when, and how.

The Stakes of the Political Struggle

Events have given the national government enormous influence over the destiny of the American people. The advent of nuclear weapons has put into the hands of one man, the President, life-and-death control of the futures of tens of millions of his fellow citizens. The assumption by the federal government of responsibility for maintaining full employment, for regulating great economic power groups such as labor and business, and for subsidizing weaker sectors of the economy, such as agriculture, has made the federal government the custodian of the nation's economic strength and security. Our economic and military aid to allies and neutrals abroad will in the long run critically shape the nature of the late twentieth-century world.

State and local governments cannot claim anything like this momentous role. But contrary to popular impression, the role of the states and localities is an increasingly large one on the domestic scene, not only in absolute terms but even as compared with the national government. Since World War II state and local governmental activities have increased much faster than the nondefense activities of the federal government. Presently, two-thirds of the fiscal burden of domestic government is carried by the states and their subdivisions.

Moreover, these governments have a far more intimate relation with the average man than does Washington. For the great neighborhood and "housekeeping" problems of Americans are closely regulated by state and local governments. The points where we come into contact with "government" most often are in school, on the highways, in a playground, at a big fire, in a hospital, in a courtroom. Some things might seem far removed from any government—for example, having a dog or a cat as a pet. But dogs are closely related to government—they need a license, a collar, and to be confined, and so on—and if anyone thinks that cats are beyond the reach of the law, he should remember the late Adlai E. Stevenson's famous veto of the "cat bill" when he was governor of Illinois. The bill would have imposed fines on cat owners who let their pets run off their premises, and would have allowed cat haters to trap them.

> "I cannot agree," said the governor, "that it should be the declared public policy of Illinois that a cat visiting a neighbor's yard or crossing the highway is a public nuisance. It is in the nature of cats to do a certain amount of unescorted roaming . . . I am afraid this bill could only create discord, recrimination, and enmity . . . We are all interested in protecting certain varieties of birds . . . The problem of the cat versus bird is as old as time. If we attempt to resolve it by legislation who knows but what we may be called upon to take sides as well in the age-old problem of dog versus cat, bird versus bird, or even bird versus worm. . . .[8]

So the governor sided with cat lovers over bird lovers, while staying neutral between bird lovers and worm diggers. But the incident illustrated how the complex working of modern society draws a maze of interests into the political vortex.

The Maze of Interests

The big interest groups described in Chapter 11 are found, in varying forms, in all the states. Even industrial Rhode Island has farm organizations; even rural Mississippi has trade unions. And the big economic pressure groups operate in the states much as they do nationally. They try to build the membership of their organizations; they lobby at the state capitol and at city hall; they propagandize the voters; they support their political friends in office and oppose their enemies. And they face the internal problems that all groups face: problems of maintaining unity within the group, of dealing with subgroups that break off in response to special needs, of maintaining both democracy and discipline within the group.

One great difference, however, is that group interests can be concentrated in states and localities whereas their strength tends to be "thinned out" in the national government. "Big Labor" does not really run things in Washington, any more than "Wall Street" does, or the Catholic Church, or the American Legion. But in some states and localities certain interests are clearly dominant because of the social and economic make-up of the area. Few politicians in Wisconsin will attack dairy farmers; a candidate for office in Boston would not shout his anti-Catholicism; as long as Negroes are denied the right to vote, white office holders in rural South Carolina can hardly be expected to take a militant stand in favor of school desegregation.

It is the range and variety of these localized groupings that give American politics its special flavor and excitement. The auto unions and manufacturers of Michigan,

[8] *Veto message,* Governor Adlai Stevenson, to members of the Senate, 66th General Assembly, Springfield, Illinois.

the corn and hog farmers of Iowa, the French-Americans in northern New England, the gas and oil interests of Texas, the sugar growers of Colorado, the aircraft employees of southern California, copper miners in the Rockies, cotton growers in the South, the "old German stock" of Ohio and other midwestern states, Pennsylvania coal miners, wool growers in Wyoming—the list of areas heavily influenced by "special" interests is endless.

Still, the power of even these groups should not be exaggerated. None is monolithic. Studying the urban politics of St. Louis, one political scientist concluded that the labor unions were sharply divided among the teamsters, building trades, machinists, auto workers, and so on; that the business community was divided between the big industrial, banking and commercial firms, on the one hand, and small downtown enterprises—shops, parking lot operators, and the like—on the other; and that such divisions had a direct impact on the governing of St. Louis.[9] Or take the case of ethnic groups in New England, where the Irish, the Italians, the Polish, and the French-Canadians have long been organized into such groups as the "Sons of Saint Patrick" and the "Columbus Society." New England politicians have long feared the power of such groups to influence elections, especially primaries. After a careful look, Duane Lockard has deflated this bogeyman. He cites many examples of "Yankees" winning in heavily ethnic areas. As against all the other considerations affecting the voter's choice the ethnic factor is very small (although a minute percentage, of course, may still be decisive in an election). Much depends on the nature of the candidate—on the other appeals he makes besides the ethnic.[10] Any group in short, no matter how strong, must cope with a variety of criss-crossing group forces, including the general sense of the "rules of the game" which say that the voter should not vote for "one of our own" on merely that ground alone.

So much for the more general interests in certain localities; let us look further at the ones that are more specialized and that have, as noted above, a close relation to local government. Many businessmen sell to the state, or perform services for it: milk dealers, printers, contractors, parking meter manufacturers, makers of playground equipment, publishers of textbooks. Such businessmen will often formally or informally organize in order to improve and stabilize their relations with purchasing officials. Another type of group intimately concerned with public policy is the professional association. The states regulate barbers, beauticians, architects, lawyers, doctors, optometrists, accountants, dentists, and many other groups performing services. Associations representing such groups are concerned with the nature of the regulatory laws and the make-up of the boards that do the regulating. They are especially concerned about the rules of admission to the profession—for example, architects' examinations and the number of years of education required—and the way in which professional misconduct is defined. Bar associations closely watch the appointment of judges and court officials.

[9] Robert H. Salisbury, "St. Louis Politics: Relationships among Interests, Parties, and Governmental Structure," *Western Political Quarterly* (June 1960), pp. 498–507.
[10] Duane Lockard, *New England State Politics* (Princeton Univ. Press, 1959), ch. 11.

The incredible profusion of groups represented in the capitol of one large state can be seen in a partial list of business activities that registered their lobbyists with the Michigan legislature during a recent session: the Upper Peninsula Dairy Manufacturers Association, the Society of Architects, the Beauticians' Aid Association, the National Association of Margarine Manufacturers, the Funeral Directors' and Embalmers' Association, the Cash-and-Carry Milk Dealers' Association, the Institute of Dry Cleaning, the Association of Private Driver-training Schools, and the Association of Civil Engineers and Land Surveyors in Private Practice.

After a survey of these and countless other lobbies in Michigan one student concluded that there was

> . . . an organization equipped to lobby for every business interest in the city, county, or state. The pattern is so complex that a particular business may be represented by an elaborate combination of groups, some with broad interests that include those of a specific calling, others dealing with a particular type of business, and the individual businessman himself may lobby before council or legislature. A supermarket chain may, for example, have its interests represented generally by the state chamber of commerce, but the company may also belong to an association of chain stores (which must parry the thrusts of the corner-grocers' lobby), to a retail-food-dealers' organization, to the package-liquor-dealers' association (if some of the stores have permits to sell liquor), and the company may itself register a lobbyist. In addition, if the chain is encountering labor problems, it may contribute to a "right-to-work" committee which lobbies against the union shop, and the executives of the company may choose to help support the state taxpayers' league. If the company owns its own fleet of semitrailer trucks or leases them, it may be represented by a company of additional groups dealing with the interests of this part of the business. A pluralistic society is simple in neither theory nor practice.[11]

Lobbyists at the State House

There appears to be a widespread conviction that lobbyists have a freer rein in state legislatures than they do in Congress, and even that bribery of state legislators by lobbyists is prevalent. There is no convincing evidence that corruption of legislators is so widespread, but the persistence of the belief that the lobbyists with the most money to spend have the most influence is itself significant.

Legitimate attempts by organized groups to influence legislation appear to have the most impact in the non-industrial, non-urban states where a single party dominates the political life of the state, and within the state legislature where party cohesion is not very strong.[12] The fifty states reflect different patterns of organized

[11] Charles R. Adrian, *State and Local Governments* (McGraw-Hill, 1960), p. 167. The list of Michigan lobbyists was also drawn from this volume.

[12] Harmon Zeigler, "Interest Groups in the States," in H. Jacob and K. N. Vines (eds.), *Politics in the American States: A Comparative Analysis* (Little, Brown, 1965), p. 114.

group interrelations with the legislative system: In a few states a single corporation or organization has considerable influence, in others there is a "Big Three" or "Big Four," in others two dominant groups of organized interests compete, but in most states there is a wide-open competition among organizations, with no single group or coalition of groups standing out. In no state does any one organization or company exercise complete control of legislative policies.[13]

Some groups have a special role both because of their relation to government and because of the size and importance of the work they are doing. Consider public school teachers, for example. They are both employees of the local government and an interest group exerting pressure on it. They must deal with many other organized groups in education: parents associated in local and state PTA's; principals and superintendents, who often have their own associations; parents of children attending private and parochial schools. Some teachers organize into unions and even use the threat to strike as a weapon for getting better wages and working conditions; all of them try to mobilize political influence as best they can. Even local school boards often band together for better representation at the state capitol, as do teachers colleges, state universities, vocational schools. The educational lobby can often put up a brave front in behalf of "educational progress," but when it comes to the specifics they may be badly divided among themselves.

Clusters of Attitudes: A Case Study

Public opinion in the states and localities confronts us with the same advantage and disadvantage as does the study of interest groups. On the one hand, the factors we noted in Chapter 9 nationally apply locally as well. The people speak with many voices; there are many publics and sub-publics; the interested public is always changing; people holding opinions vary greatly in their intensity of belief; and public opinion may be latent as well as open and noisy. And most states and communities have their own local sets of opinion-making agencies: schools, churches, newspapers, radio and television stations, as well as their share of the consumers of national television programs, best-selling books, popular magazines, nationwide newspapers like *The New York Times*, motion pictures, newspaper columnists. On the other hand, each locality has its own particular "mix" of these opinion-forming agencies, and powerful forces that may be diluted nationally may be concentrated heavily in one area.

A good example of this latter situation is the attitude toward states' rights in the South. Virtually all Americans support states' rights as a general symbol, no doubt, but in the South it has a political influence far greater than any pressure group or party. Quoted from the lips of southern heroes such as Jefferson and John Calhoun, bolstered by the trauma of civil war, resurrected in the face of northern civil rights programs and Supreme Court decisions on desegregation, states' rights has become a flaming symbol that can be evoked for a multiplicity of purposes—segregation, state control of offshore oil, local welfare standards, lower minimum wages. It is a daring southern politician who would defy this symbol, for it evokes the unity of both the

---

[13] *Ibid.*, p. 128.

community and the politicians. The combat is waged "within" the symbol—that is, over its meaning and relevance rather than between it and other political concepts.

Another local variation of public opinion raises the question of concentration of control of local media and resulting conformity of political attitudes. The enormous variety of opinion-shaping forces throughout the nation may dwindle sharply in their impact on a particular locality, especially one that is some distance from a big metropolitan area. Here again local conditions vary so widely that generalization is dangerous. Perhaps a case study of one community might raise suggestive questions for other localities.

The newspaper situation in New Haven, Connecticut, is typical of many medium-sized cities in the United States. As compared with the last century, when New Haven had three or four papers supporting different political parties, the city recently has had only two, a morning and an evening, both owned by the same family, both Republican in politics, and both heavily influenced by the family's conservative views. Almost all adults in New Haven read the evening paper, and almost all the politically active read the morning paper. Robert Dahl, analyzing the impact of the papers, concluded that their negativism and hostility to change, together with their biased news reporting, may have reduced their readers' knowledge, understanding, and concern; that they may have influenced their readers on specific policies, such as taxes; and that they probably directly influenced the attitudes of politicians who exaggerated the newspapers' influence on public opinion. The more uncertain a politician was as to the stability and intensity of his own support on some measure, the more he might defer to two newspapers that seemed to speak with a single, strong voice.

But Dahl found definite limits to the power of this newspaper monopoly. For one thing, the publisher seemed more interested in immobilizing public opinion than in mobilizing it; he was less intent on initiating new policies than in balking "spend-thrift politicians." For another, some politicians were skeptical of the newspapers' ability to influence opinion and they were confident of their own political strength. But the main reason why the newspapers had limited influence was the competition they received from many other sources. The more politically active the citizen was, the more likely he was to read an out-of-town newspaper such as *The New York Times* or the New York *Herald-Tribune*. Of the registered voters as a whole, only about four in ten said that they got more information about political affairs from newspapers than from other sources. Another four out of ten got more from radio or television, or from talking with other people. Local opinion leaders had at least as much influence as the newspapers did. Dahl was prompted to conclude:

> Word of mouth and personal experience are highly important sources of information that remain to a substantial extent beyond the reach of top leaders, . . . "The extent to which an individual gains his information from other people than from the mass media is partly a function of his own experience. In some issue-areas, many citizens have *direct* experience; what happens there is happening to *them*, in a rather immediate way. In others, only a few

citizens have any direct experience; at best the others have only derivative or vicarious experience. The more the citizens have direct experience, the more they seem to rely on talking with other people as a source of news; the more vicarious or indirect their experience, the more they seem to rely on the mass media.[14]

Direct experience, in short, was not only a persuasive teacher but could be a stubborn enemy of manipulative propaganda.

Ironically, the newspapers themselves were not monolithic organizations. As is the case with many other big newspapers, many of the reporters on the two papers were Democrats or personally friendly to politicians opposed to the publisher. Republicans sometimes complained that their stories were buried in back of the papers while their Democratic opponents got a big play on the front page. Like many a party boss or interest-group leader, the publisher found that he could not "deliver his precinct" even if he had wished to.

Nevertheless, newspapers probably have greater impact on local issues and elections than on national ones. Most citizens obtain most of their knowledge of the local political scene from the local newspaper. Voters are likely to have less rigid ideas about the merits of local candidates than about national or even state candidates. A strongly partisan Republican businessman, for example, is less open to persuasion by a Democratic candidate for Congress or the Presidency than he may be by a Democratic candidate for the city council, who might be a friend or colleague. Attitudes toward local issues are also less likely to be rigid, or to use the language of social scientists, such ideas are often less structured. And when it comes to discussions of atomic testing, federal income tax revision, medical care for the aged, the merits of Goldwater over Johnson, citizens have many sources of information, from national television to professional trade journals. But the local paper is about the only source for the local school board candidates, or the desirability of a local bond issue.[15]

In cities where political organizations are weak and authority is generally decentralized, as for example, in Detroit and Los Angeles, newspapers play a more important part in the political process than in cities where political organizations are strong, as for example, in Chicago.[16] The influence of the newspapers also appears to be related to the class structure. "As one ascends the social scale there is a greater sense of ease, intimacy, and personal relationship between the reader and his paper. It seems as though the better educated reader is more likely to view his hometown paper as an institution made up of people doing a job. . . . For those lower on the educational scale, the newspaper as a major institution of power appears more remote and impersonal." [17]

[14] Dahl, *op. cit.*, p. 262. This case study was taken wholly from this admirable study.
[15] Evidence on this question is limited; but see Reo M. Christenson, "The Power of the Press —The Case of the 'Toledo Blade,' " *Midwest Journal of Political Science* (August 1959), pp. 227–240; Harold Gosnell, *Machine Politics: Chicago Model* (Univ. of Chicago Press, 1937).
[16] E. C. Banfield and J. Q. Wilson, *City Politics* (Harvard Univ. Press, 1963), pp. 323–325.
[17] Leo Bogart, "Newspapers in the Age of Television," *Daedalus* (Winter, 1963), p. 124.

Apathy

To discuss pressure groups and opinion shapers is always to run the risk of playing up the activists and slighting the apathetic. But the political indifference that shows up as only a very general factor in a nationwide survey can be seen markedly in certain regions or localities. Nonvoting, for example, is greater in the country than in the suburbs or the city. Not only are Negroes almost wholly disfranchised in many southern rural areas, but the voting by whites is low too.

It was in the little town and village that many American political thinkers, in an earlier day, saw most hope for the vitality of American democracy. Unhappily, many such communities today seem to lack an active political life. Although the little towns may be caught up in and increasingly affected by the social and economic trends in the urban areas, the townspeople may shrink from adopting new ways of dealing with problems. Many of these small towns are slowly declining in population; their young people are leaving town for better opportunities elsewhere; their population is aging. Political decisions—such as there are—seem to be made by a relatively few people, and usually without much discussion; there is no clear confrontation of choices; politics is highly personal and much affected by family and neighborhood relationships, petty favor-swapping, and minor deals. A town that may be most in need of a searching political examination of its future, culminating in a meaningful decision, is precisely the town that may be lacking the means for such action.[18]

But big cities, too, can provide examples of apathy. Dahl found that even in New Haven, a relatively active city politically, "political indifference surrounds a great many citizens like impenetrable armor plate and makes them difficult targets for propaganda."[19] He cites as an example a strenuous campaign to revise the city charter in 1958. City politicians debated the matter vigorously; the newspapers took an outspoken position against revision; a citizens charter committee ran big advertisements; radio and television programs carried on the debate. Fliers were even distributed from door to door. The results? Only 45 per cent of those who voted in the regular election bothered to vote on the charter (and most of those opposed it). Boston affords an even more ominous case of apathy, for here the apathy stemmed directly from cynicism. Following a hotly contested mayoralty election, observers discovered that many voters disliked both candidates, thought that neither would do a good job, and were simply disgusted with politics.[20] And of course many others did not even bother to vote.

[18] Cf. A. J. Vidich and Joseph Bensman, *Small Town in Mass Society* (Princeton Univ. Press, 1958); and Laurene A. Wallace, *Carsonville: An American Village Viewed Sociologically* (Univ. of Michigan Press, 1957). See also Warner E. Mills, Jr., and Harry R. Davis, *Small City Government: Seven Cases in Decision Making* (Random House, 1962).

[19] Dahl, *op. cit.*, p. 264.

[20] Murray Levin, *The Alienated Voter* (Holt, Rinehart and Winston, 1960). See Levin's treatment of political alienation in Massachusetts, *The Compleat Politician* (Bobbs-Merrill, 1962).

State Parties: A Study in Variety

The Democratic and Republican parties virtually monopolize party activity in every state, just as they do the nation's politics as a whole. But the state political parties are not little miniatures of the national parties. Each has its own special features. Not only is the social and economic "mix" different for each state, as noted above, and hence the parties different, but also the states have reacted differently to epochal developments in American history. The Civil War left the South heavily Democratic, and portions of the North heavily Republican. The great struggle of '96 between the Democratic populist, William Jennings Bryan, and the orthodox Republican, William McKinley, left an east-west sectional split that has not wholly disappeared. And the traumatic experience of the Great Depression, combined with the coming of the New Deal, helped produce a surge of Democratic strength in the big cities that still influences politics sharply today.

The Interplay of National and State Politics

Clearly, it is impossible to separate national from state and local politics. The very structure of national party organizations, as we noted in Chapter 12 grows out of the state parties. Not only are national and state party organizations interdependent, but their fortunes and misfortunes are interdependent. Swings at the national level help produce swings at the state and local level. Whenever the Democratic party, for example, wins a presidential and congressional sweep nationally, the number of Democratic governors, state legislators, mayors, and local councilmen also tends to increase. The same is true for the Republicans (except in the South—but even in the South the Eisenhower landslides brought in local Republican victories). Moreover, the relationship is usually constant—the greater the national party sweep, the greater the local party victories. The famous coattails effect (see p. 259) is at work here, but in both directions. Strong candidates at the state level help the national candidates, and strong national candidates help those running for state and local office. John F. Kennedy said after his election to the Presidency that strong Democratic candidates had helped pull him over the top in a number of states.

The main effect of national politics on the state and local scene is sometimes to solidify sectional differences and strengthen one-partyism. In the one-party states of the Deep South, for example, the racial issue dominates all other problems. Here the state politicians, rallying around the symbol of states' rights, have smothered many of their other differences and have stood united against the rest of the nation. On the other hand, there is evidence that industrialization and urbanization are having an impact on both the rural Republican-dominated states and the rural Democratic ones, as Republican victories in the 1962 and 1964 elections suggested. Industry brings to these regions the same issues that it brought earlier to the rest of the country—employers versus workers, large industry versus small, railroads versus

truckers, and so on. These issues appear to create the same pattern of political differences that prevails in other regions and tend to move the states in the direction of two-party competition.

Sometimes, state politicians try to block off national trends. Kentucky, Mississippi,
New Jersey, Virginia, and Louisiana have complete electoral separation. They elect
their governors and all their state legislators in years when no presidential election
is being held. Nineteen other states elect their governors and some of their legislators in the off-year elections. This staggering of state elections is usually proposed as
a way of concentrating the voters' attention on state issues without the distractions
of a presidential campaign. But it is mainly a tactical device of party warfare, used
by local politicians of one party to prevent the opposition party from benefiting by
its national popularity. Of course, the tactic can backfire. Republicans in some states
managed to get Republican governors elected during the "Democratic" 1930's and
1940's by having gubernatorial elections held when neither Roosevelt nor Truman
was running; but when Eisenhower was winning in big sweeps during the 1950's,
these same Republicans regretted that they were not running their statewide candidates in presidential years, for they had lost the chance to get pulled in on Eisenhower's coattails.[21] Still, there is a general trend toward "off-year" state elections,
so that this separation of national and state politics will probably increase in coming years.

Even when presidential and state elections are held simultaneously, the impact
of national on state elections can be affected by the nature of the election ballot.
If, for example, the Republicans have as a presidential candidate an "Eisenhower
type" who has great electoral drawing power, it will be to their advantage if the
state has a party-column or Indiana-type ballot. To reduce the impact of the presidential candidate under such circumstances, the Democrats would prefer the
office-group or Massachusetts-type ballot.[22] Still, despite all the ingenious efforts of
politicians, national politics has a heavy impact on state and local government.

Party Balance and Imbalance

The impact of national political
forces on the particular social and economic "mix" of each state, combined with
local traditions and political styles, has produced important differences among the
party systems of the fifty states. The most important of these is the extent of *two-
party competition*. State parties may be classified by three types on the basis of how
the parties share *state* offices (often a state will vote for one party's candidates for
President or even senator or representative, but have an entirely different voting
pattern for party when it comes to state officers): the *two-party* type in which the
two parties share state offices rather evenly over the years, and alternate in winning

[21] Coleman M. Ransome, Jr., *The Office of Governor in the United States* (Univ. of Alabama Press, 1956), pp. 89–90; V. O. Key, *American State Politics* (Knopf, 1956), p. 38; Austin
Ranney, "Parties in State Politics," in Jacob and Vines, *op. cit.*, pp. 82–83.

[22] Angus Campbell and Warren E. Miller, "The Motivational Basis of Straight and Split
Ticket Voting," *The American Political Science Review* (June 1957), p. 306.

majorities; the modified *one-party* type, in which one party wins all or almost all the offices over the years, but the second party usually receives a goodly percentage of the votes, and surprises everybody—including itself—by sometimes winning; and the *one-party* type, in which one party wins all or nearly all the offices and the second party usually receives only a small proportion of the popular vote. From the map of State Party Systems, based on voting patterns during the period 1946 to 1963, it can be seen that the modified one-party Democratic states are mainly the border states, but so are Virginia and North Carolina. The eight one-party Democratic states are all in the South. There are no longer any one-party Republican states, since the former rock-ribbed stalwart supporters of the Grand Old Party such as Vermont, North Dakota, and Maine in recent elections have chosen some Democrats for state office.[23]

Since the end of World War II there has been an accelerating trend toward two party politics. In the South, Republicans have started to make a contest out of some general elections and the old cliché that "winning the Democratic primary in the South is tantamount to election" has lost some of its validity. Although the Republican resurgence in the South has been shown mainly in voting for candidates

---

[23] This division of states is based on Austin Ranney's adaptation of the Dawson-Robinson measure in "Parties in State Politics," Jacob and Vines (eds.), *op. cit.*, p. 65.

PARTIES IN STATE POLITICS

☒☒ One-Party Democratic

▨ Modified One-Party Democratic

☐ Two-Party

⣿ Modified One-Party Republican

Alaska and Hawaii, not shown, are both two-party states.

for President and Congress, Republicans have been elected to the state legislature in Alabama, Arkansas, Florida, Georgia, and other southern states, and Oklahoma has elected a Republican governor. Republicans still have to make significant gains before we can call most southern or border states two-party states, but the Solid South is no longer so solid, especially within the larger cities.

Outside of the South there is also a gradual spread of two-partyism with the rise of Democratic strength in formerly solid Republican states of Iowa, Kansas, Maine, New Hampshire, North Dakota, and South Dakota. "What the Democrats have lost in the South, they have regained in the rural Midwest and Northeast." [24]

What are the consequences of a fairly even party balance? When parties and their candidates compete on an even basis, each side must keep on its toes. Each side is more likely to be sensitive to slight alterations in public opinion because even the loss of a fraction of the voters might tip the scales to the other side in the next election. Party competition tends to induce leaders within each party to work more closely together, at least as elections draw near, for any defection may throw victory into the hands of the party opponents; hence competition may produce more teamwork and efficiency in government. It is notable that states having outstanding state governments—such as Connecticut, New York, and California—are among the more competitive states; whether the party system is causally related to responsive state governments is more difficult to determine.

Party imbalance may have a serious effect on the dominant party in a one-party state. Practically guaranteed a victory no matter how poor its record, the majority party may not keep itself in fighting trim. Even more important, the competition that otherwise would occur between the major parties now occurs *within* the major party. The great contests in the South, especially for control of state and local governments, are not between Democrats and Republicans in the November election, but between Democrats—sometimes a dozen or more of them—in the Democratic primary. In these intraparty fights, issues may not be clearly drawn; personalities may dominate the campaign, with little regard for issues; voters tend not to participate to the same extent as they do where there are two-party contests. Here again one has to be careful in drawing causal connections, for lack of division within the community on major issues may cause the one-party situation as much as the other way around.

But if party imbalance disorganizes the dominant party, it positively pulverizes the minority party. Almost without hope of ever winning at all, the minority party leaders do not put up much of a fight. They find it difficult to raise the money for campaigns or to persuade persons to become candidates for office. They have no state or local patronage jobs to give out in order to arouse hope within their ranks. Party workers and volunteers are slow to come forward. Young men anxious to succeed in politics tend to drift into the dominant party. And since the dominant party firmly controls the machinery of state and local affairs, the second party is likely only to be concerned with national politics and the patronage emanating from the White House. They may not even bother to nominate candidates for

[24] *Ibid.*, p. 92.

state offices or maintain local organization. For years the only Republican organization in several Deep South states was that maintained by a small group of Negroes
and whites living off patronage from the Republican national committee. Indeed,
some members of these second-party organizations have a vested interest in remaining a minority. Some may fear that if their party should become a serious contender
in the state, the insiders who have been running it would have to share their patronage and influence in national politics with other political leaders.[25]

We have been discussing *state* party imbalance, but imbalance can be found in
even more extreme form in cities and towns. Republicans practically never carry
Chicago or Boston or Albany or Hartford or Pittsburgh or a host of other cities
throughout the industrial North. Democrats have only a ghost of a chance in
numerous towns in the rural areas of the North. Indeed, one result of this imbalance
was the rapid growth, during the first half of this century, of "nonpartisanship" in
local elections. Candidates were not able to run on major-party tickets, at least
officially. The two great parties were, in effect, removed from open influence over
local politics. Adopted in the name of "good government," "nonpartisanship" had
an effect on local government that will be discussed in Chapter 32. But its effect on
the major parties was probably to weaken them further as organizations, for it
sapped them at their foundations.

We must remind ourselves again not to over-generalize in discussing a variety of
political systems. Perhaps we can test some of these generalizations by looking at
the minority party in a specific city, Elmira, in western New York. When studied
by three social scientists in the early 1950's, Elmira had been Republican since 1936.
What was the state of the *Democratic* party? Not very effective. The party did not
raise much money; it did not reach many voters outside of those already "in the
fold"; it did a poor job of interpreting the national party line in a big presidential
election (1948); it did not mobilize much of a vote on election day. Worst of all
for the Democrats, they were not attracting new leadership from the ranks of the
abler young men and women of the city. The party was run—to the extent it was
run at all—by some faithful oldtimers who could barely keep the organization from
falling apart. "Thus in 1948," the study concluded, "the Democrats of Elmira had,
not the vigorous spokesmen of a self-renewing opposition, but a leadership surviving
from the defeats of the past—a leadership of nostalgia. . . ." [26]

Party Weaknesses

Perhaps the most striking fact
about Elmira was that even the Republican party, as the dominant party, was not
very effective. The crucial fact about most states and localities is that *neither* party
is organizationally very strong. Just as the national parties tend to break into fac-

[25] The classic picture of this situation at its most extreme was drawn by V. O. Key, Jr., in
Southern Politics in State and Nation (Knopf, 1949).
[26] Bernard R. Berelson, Paul F. Lazarsfeld, and William N. McPhee, *Voting* (Univ. of
Chicago Press, 1954), p. 162. These comments on Elmira are taken wholly from this brilliant
analysis.

tions revolving around individual leaders in Congress and the White House, as noted in Chapter 12, so the state and local parties tend to fragment into groups following individual candidates and officeholders. Most of the stronger leaders have their personal organizations which often crowd the regular party organizations out of the picture. Regular party committees are supposed to remain neutral during primary fights, and often do, with the result that candidates have no feeling of obligation to the party organization once they win office. There is a tendency for every candidate in the same party to run on his own, and the devil take the hindmost. Each candidate sets up his own headquarters, puts up his own posters, sends out his own publicity, taps his own sources of funds. Sometimes a candidate may deliberately keep clear of other candidates on the same ticket and even disassociate himself from the party label. The more offices to be voted on, the more candidates, and hence the greater the fragmentation of the party. And since most states have the "long ballot," most states have fragmented parties.

What is the result of such state political systems? The late V. O. Key, Jr., of Harvard, the leading student of state politics, expressed his concern. To paraphrase his conclusions:

1. State politics combined with constitutional arrangements, especially the nature of state legislative representation (see Chapter 29 below), contributes to centralization of power in the national government by incapacitating the states for action.

2. The rapid growth of state responsibilities makes it even more important to modernize the organization of political forces within the states which at the present time is usually erratic and atomized.

3. The political system places serious obstacles in the path of popular government by making it impossible for broad popular mandates to be expressed in some situations and at some times.

4. Over the last half-century, party organization has seriously deteriorated. This decay in party organization has been associated with the rise of the direct primary. . . .[27]

In short, the problems presented at the state level by party weakness are the same as those presented at the national level—except for one thing. The national parties are roughly in balance, while state and local parties often are highly noncompetitive, where they exist at all. Many critics have suggested changes in the constitutional and administrative organization of the states, but the parties have received less attention. One reason may be that significant reforms in party structure and party balance are extremely difficult to bring about. No amount of tinkering can do much about the fact that most of the people of Kansas are Republicans and most of the people of the Deep South are Democrats. As long as strong personal factions exist within a party, preaching about the need of party cohesion will have little effect. Attitudes and political behavior change slowly and grow out of basic social, economic, and psychological conditions that reformers can do little to alter.

[27] V. O. Key, Jr., *American State Politics* (Knopf, 1956), pp. 266–267.

But to recognize that political forces are relatively stable is not to say that they are impervious to change. If institutional forces such as the long ballot help make the state and local parties what they are, institutional changes (such as the short ballot) might also affect the shape of the parties. So might changes in legislative representation or alterations in procedures for nominating candidates. Much will depend on those who take part in party activity and seek to translate democratic principles into political reality.

Elections: The Struggle for Office

The framers of the Constitution left the conduct of elections and other political matters largely in the hands of the state governments. This was one more safeguard, they felt, against too much national power. Today state control of elections is a crucial fact. For one thing, it means that each state sets up its own ways of managing elections, nominating candidates, regulating campaign contributions, preventing election fraud, and—most important—allowing or preventing people from voting. For another, it means that states also administer the election of national officials, Presidents, senators, congressmen. To be sure, Congress has certain powers, such as preventing corrupt practices and enforcing the Fifteenth Amendment. But it leaves the job mainly to the fifty states.

Nominations in the States

Almost all party nominations in the United States—with the conspicuous exception of the nomination of the President—are made in party *primaries*. As noted in Chapter 13, primaries are of different types—the closed primary, the open, the run-off, and so on. The party primary is an almost uniquely American device and has had a profound influence on the nature of state and local politics. Rather than reviewing the previously rendered information, we might here raise some questions about the primary. Why was it adopted? What effect has it had on state and local parties and on the question as to who governs? What are alternative ways of choosing party nominees?

The primaries were not always the chief means of choosing candidates. Once our parties had attained full bloom in the 1830's and 1840's, candidates for most offices were chosen in conventions. These were very much like our national conventions but in miniature. Delegates were called to order in a local hall or hotel, candidates nominated, speeches delivered, roll call votes taken, and candidates finally chosen amid huzzahs and excitement. Not only were statewide candidates, such as governor, selected in these conclaves, but also local conventions were held to select candidates for district attorney, state representative, county commissioner, and even town and city offices, such as mayor. Whatever their shortcomings, these conventions provided a vitality at the grass roots that many observers find woefully lacking today. Sometimes candidates were chosen more informally, in party caucuses or committees.

But conventions and caucuses did have their shortcomings. In the late nineteenth century, as the rise of big cities provided lucrative contracts and franchises for politicians, local and state parties fell increasingly under the domination of "bosses" who used the convention as a means of control. The bosses often handpicked the delegates to conventions, refused to seat opposing delegates or ignored them if they were seated, and even used strong-arm methods. The great safeguard against such corruption was, of course, the opposition party, which could appeal to the people against "bossism." But the creation of one-party states and districts as a result of the Civil War and the Bryan-McKinley fight of 1896 left most American states and localities with essentially one-party systems, especially in the South and the Northeast. So the great safeguard against bossism was gone.

The direct primary came largely as a result of this situation. During the "muckraking" first decade of this century, when reformers were attacking bossism, corruption, monopoly, and other conditions, the convention also came under fire. Nominations must be moved out of these boss-controlled conclaves, reformers declared, and put into the hands of the people. The means of democratizing nominations was at hand: the *direct primary*, which had first been adopted in the South. Wisconsin enacted the first state-wide primary law in 1901, and other states followed suit. Within a decade and a half—a period of progressivism dominated by Theodore Roosevelt, Robert La Follette, and Woodrow Wilson—the direct primary had been adopted for most nominations in all but a few of the states.

How has the direct primary worked out? Like most institutional reforms, it has had mixed results. On the one hand, the primary has probably diminished somewhat the power of the party leaders. It is more difficult for a boss to influence several thousand voters coming to the polls than a few score of delegates coming to a convention. But the difference has been only of degree, and varies widely from place to place. Many bosses survived the coming of the primary with ease. Participation in the primary was usually so low that they were able to control it by "delivering" the vote of their lieutenants, hangers-oners, patronage appointees, and the friends and families of all these. Still, the primaries often encouraged insurgents to challenge the bosses.

Paradoxically, however, people began to have second thoughts about the effect of primaries on party organization. After all, there were "good" party bosses as well as bad. There were party leaders who ran their organizations in a democratic fashion, tried to choose worthy candidates, and sought to live up to their other responsibilities. "Good" bosses were threatened, just as much as "bad" bosses, by factions supporting mediocre candidates and perhaps seeking to disrupt the party. The primaries had other weaknesses, some of which were noted earlier in the chapter. Primary contests were often disorganized, bewildering, and heavily influenced by local and narrow considerations. Primaries made it impossible for the parties to "balance" their tickets; for example, the Democratic party in Massachusetts, largely though by no means wholly made up of people of Irish descent, found it difficult to nominate a "balanced ticket" because the decision was made in the primaries, heavily dominated by the "Boston Irish." [28] And primaries were especially hard on

[28] Lockard, *op. cit.*, ch. 11.

the minority party; up-and-coming politicians naturally gravitated to the major party primary, and the minority-party nomination might go begging. In short, primaries seemed to militate against competitive, orderly, meaningful, vigorous two-party politics.

What is the alternative to the direct primary? One device is the pre-primary convention, as described in Chapter 13, but this is no real alternative because the final decision is still made in the primary. The only real alternative is the convention. Some states—notably New York and Connecticut—kept their conventions despite the trend toward primaries. As also noted earlier, in Connecticut anyone who receives at least 20 per cent of a convention's votes may challenge the convention-nominated candidate in a primary. Each year some primary challenges are held.[29] It is significant that both these states have "strong" party systems; that is, the parties are relatively well organized, the party leadership has been on the whole quite effective, and the parties are able to exert considerable centralized control over nominations. They are able on occasion to draft candidates; a notable example of this was in 1928, when the New York Democratic convention drafted Franklin D. Roosevelt to run for governor, as he did, successfully. Indeed, the fact that New York conventions have been able to nominate such able Republicans as Theodore Roosevelt, Charles Evans Hughes, Thomas E. Dewey, and Nelson Rockefeller, and such able Democrats as Alfred E. Smith, Franklin Roosevelt, and Herbert Lehman is a tribute to its convention system.

One thing is clear. The method of nominating candidates closely affects the organization of the party, and vice versa. The stronger the party—that is, the better led, the more vigorous and competitive and unified—the more likely it can conduct its nomination fights through conventions. The weaker the party—the more disorganized and faction-ridden and decentralized—the more the voters may wish to take nominating decisions out of the hands of the parties and trust them to voters in primaries. Hence, it is quite logical that given the fact that most state and local parties are weak, primaries are the typical method of choosing nominees. By the same token, the existence of primaries may be a major cause of the structural weakness of parties. Some day there may be a trend back toward the convention method, but for the moment the primaries rule the day.[30]

Elections: A Case Study

Perhaps the most distinctive feature of American politics is the number and variety of elections. Western Europeans, who are used to voting for one or two candidates at the national and local levels, and voting only once every two or three years, are flabbergasted by the impression they receive that Americans engage almost continuously in elections. Selection of town and local officials in the late winter may be followed by primaries to choose

---

[29] Duane Lockard, *Connecticut's Challenge Primary: A Study in Legislative Politics* (New York, Holt, 1959).

[30] The most significant work on state party systems and nominating methods has been done by V. O. Key, Jr., and his students. See his *American State Politics*, cited above, and his *Politics, Parties, and Pressure Groups* (Crowell, 1958), chs. 11, 14.

delegates to conventions, followed by primaries to choose party candidates, followed by general elections, all interspersed with special elections, special town or state referenda, and even in some states recall elections to throw some official out of office. Even more bewildering to many foreigners is the number of offices voted on at a particular election: from President to probate judge, from senator to sheriff, from governor to member of the library board. This is the "long ballot" in operation—and Europeans are more accustomed to the election of a handful of key officials who in turn appoint career officials.

While generalizing as to the nature of this enormous variety of elections would be dangerous, experienced politicians might agree on the following rules of thumb: (1) By and large, the more local the election, the less the excitement and interest aroused among the electorate, and the smaller the participation. (2) Except in areas where strong party organizations exist, candidates usually run on their own; they win through their personal organizations rather than through efforts by the party (partly because there are so many candidates running for so many offices that the party cannot give much help to any one of them). (3) Voters' familiarity with names rather than issues is of relatively greater importance in local than in state or national elections. (4) The candidate gets most of his money from his friends and from interest groups, not from his party. (5) While all kinds of propaganda are used, and often effectively, there is no substitute, especially in local campaigns, for personal contact between the candidate and the voters.

The case of a recent campaign for state representative in the state of Washington exemplified some of these rules of thumb. In 1958, in the 32nd legislative district (which includes the University of Washington), the two incumbent Republican legislators were up for re-election. Washington has the "blanket primary"—all candidates of all parties are placed on a single ballot, and the voter chooses from among them regardless of his own party affiliation. Among the Democratic candidates was a 23-year-old law student at the university, Wes Uhlman. With the help of leaders of the university Young Democrats, Uhlman vied with the two incumbents and with three other Democrats for nomination. He began by feeding stories to the newspapers; then, stepping up his effort, he and his helpers made up and posted hundreds of signs; sent out a carefully organized mailing to 1,300 Democrats in the district; mailed special letters on educational policy to the large number of teachers in the university area; conducted a tremendous "doorbelling" campaign; and climaxed their primary effort just before election by depositing thousands of fliers— "Be sure—Vote Uhlman"—on front porches. Money was so short during the primary campaign that Uhlman could not afford many newspaper ads, but his hard work paid off, for he placed first among the Democratic candidates. Running close behind him was another Democrat, an older man, who had done very little campaigning but benefited from the fact that he had the same name as two well-liked politicians in the Seattle area.

With the nomination secured, Uhlman had to begin all over again for the general election. Again he passed out literature, rang doorbells, put up signs, and put out big mailings. A massive election-eve effort to leave throw-aways on front porches ran afoul of heavy winds and rain, but a small band of the faithful were still able to distribute several thousand pieces of damp literature. The Democratic party organization, which had been neutral during the primary fight, was not very active during the general election, so Uhlman had to depend on his now expanded personal organization. The Republican candidates were active too. Backed by the university Young Republicans, they countered the Democrats by publicizing the records of the incumbent representatives in extensive newspaper advertisements. But the Republicans, too, were not very effective as a party, mainly because they had to divide their efforts among campaigns for so many other offices.

When the returns were in Uhlman, to the surprise of most observers, led the race. The next man was one of the incumbent Republicans, who thus held his seat. Uhlman's victory was credited to the hard work that he and his cohorts had done, the person-to-person contact at the polls, and his emphasis in his campaign on his name rather than on his party. Political scientists might note other facts about the election battle. Organizationally, the parties did not play a major role (though the fact that most voters were either Democrats or Republicans *was* important; third parties were not involved). The candidates mainly ran on their own, playing up their own names. Hard work—especially "doorbelling"—was the crucial element. The whole effort was also influenced by the electoral system—the blanket primary and the fact that the district had two representatives in the legislature.

Finally, and perhaps of greatest significance, this election illustrates the "openness" of the American electoral system. If the Democratic nomination in the 32nd district had been controlled by a boss, or perhaps even by a well managed convention, Wes Uhlman, as a 23-year old newcomer to politics, probably would not have won the party nod. He was able to use the primary as a way of gaining access to the inner circles of politics. Whether this openness of the system was a vice would depend much on the legislative record of Representative Wes Uhlman.[31]

Democracy or Oligarchy?

Who governs? We return to our central question after the quick look we have taken at the shape of politics in American states and localities. It would be easy to evade the question by saying again that the answer to the question varies according to the state or locality, as of course it does. But the nature of local and state political systems, as we have seen them briefly, does permit some generalization.

The striking fact is that American states and localities are characterized more by dispersion of political influence than by concentration. The tremendous diversity of elective offices gives influence to many different officials and tends to fragmentize the political parties. The primary system of nominating candidates, used in all states, further diffuses power within the parties. A newspaper publisher may have a virtual press monopoly in a city, as in New Haven, but he faces competition from many other media, such as television and radio, and he cannot even fully control

[31] This case study is from "The Election of Wes Uhlman," in Richard T. Frost (ed.), *Cases in State and Local Government* (Prentice-Hall, 1961), pp. 79–94, which was based in turn on a case study presented by the Washington State-Northern Idaho Citizenship Clearing House.

the political influence of his own newspapers. The nominating system offers wide access to the center of influence, as in the case of Wes Uhlman.

It was not always this way. In the early days of New Haven, Robert Dahl found, the city *was* ruled by a small patrician-Congregationalist-Federalist elite, which exploited its high social standing, education, and wealth to achieve key positions in the Church, the economy, and public life.[32] This small elite was powerful in *every* major decision-making area. But Dahl found the situation to have changed radically in the past century from what he calls "cumulative" to "dispersed inequalities." Different leaders hold different types of influence. The men who make the crucial decisions in education, for example, are not the same who closely influence urban redevelopment.

Roughly the same situation has been found to exist in Chicago. Formal authority in this city, Edward Banfield discovered, was divided among thousands of governing bodies.[33] There was no "small ruling elite." To be sure, the Democratic organization in Chicago was quite strong, but the mayor and the party chiefs had to bargain constantly with rebels within the organization, city officials, interest groups, and other centers of influence. Politicians and other leaders had a limited stock of power that they had to expend carefully. Everywhere there were "veto groups" that had to be placated, threatened, or given some kind of concession. The politics of Chicago was essentially a politics of bargaining and coalition-building. And always there was the voter who might ordinarily be uninformed and passive but who might always come to the polls some day and chastize some public official who had "gone too far."

Most states and localities, in short, have pluralistic systems that are a long way from oligarchy. But this does not make them systems where every voter has roughly the same influence on political decisions. Power does tend to center in separate clusters of decision-makers, and large numbers of people have very little role. The fact that under the American system they could have a more active role is not a sufficient answer, for ignorance, lack of education, and other factors keep many voters from wielding much influence. We can say only that along the broad spectrum from centralization of power to dispersion of power most of our state and local governments are found nearer the latter pole.

But in the spirit of this chapter we cannot leave the matter here. The student should look at his own state and community and ask hard questions. Who has influence and who does not? Under what conditions is influence exercised? *How* is it exercised—through authority, friendship, propaganda, deals, manipulation, coercion? What are the terms by which influence is expended—what kind of influence does a political leader sacrifice in order to get the decision he wants? [34] In short, if most of these political systems are marked by deals, bargains, and exchanges, who gains what, who loses what in the process? Does fragmented power prevent leaders from concerting efforts on behalf of the great mass of people?

[32] Dahl, *op. cit.*, ch. 1.
[33] Edward C. Banfield, *Political Influence* (The Free Press, 1961).
[34] These questions are drawn from *ibid.*

28 STATE CONSTITUTIONS— CHARTERS OR STRAITJACKETS?

"The state constitutions are the oldest things in the political history of America." [1] The early state constitutions, themselves an outgrowth of the colonial charters, were models for the national Constitution.

The people of each state, subject only to the

[1] James Bryce, *The American Commonwealth*, Vol. I (Macmillan, 1911), p. 427.

broad limitations of the federal Constitution, are free to create whatever kind of republican government they wish. And yet all state constitutions are similar in general outline. No state has established a parliamentary system; none has deprived its judges of the power of judicial review. As people moved westward across the United States, they copied the constitutions of the older states, seemingly at times without much thought. The usual pattern of the state constitutions consists of a preamble; a bill of rights; articles providing for the separation of power, a bicameral legislature, an executive department, an independent judiciary with power of judicial review, the form and powers of local units of government; an amendment article; and miscellaneous provisions dealing with corporations, railroads, finances, and numerous other topics.

State constitutions obviously tell us much about how power is distributed within our states, and from them we learn of the essential similarity in the structure of state governments. Yet it is misleading to conclude that the similarity of formal constitutions means similarity in the actual governmental process. Much else has to be considered in determining who governs our states, as the preceding chapter suggests. The constitution is but a place to start to learn.

Constitutional Rigidity and Evasion

State constitutions contain more detail and are thus *longer, less adaptable*, require *more frequent formal amendment*, and remain *effective* for a *shorter period* than does the federal Constitution.

California's much-amended constitution (over 350 amendments since 1879) goes into great detail on such things as the breeding of crustaceans and mollusks, the length of wrestling matches, and the internal organization of several major departments. Article XX, Section 2, of Oklahoma's constitution proclaims, "Until changed by the Legislature, the flash test . . . for all kerosene oil for illuminating purposes shall be 115 degrees Fahrenheit; and the specific gravity test of all such oil shall be 40 degrees." Minnesota's constitution has a route-by-route description of its highway system. Georgia's constitution details procedures to be followed by medical students in securing financial assistance. New Hampshire's sets the wages of its legislators at special sessions at a little over $3 a day. State contitutions vary in length from approximately 8,000 words in Vermont, Indiana, Connecticut, and Iowa to 227,000 in Louisiana.

Although many of these detailed provisions deal with trivial subjects, others are concerned with important matters. The federal Constitution grants powers in broad and sweeping terms, letting future generations write in the details and adapt the basic charter of government to ever-changing conditions. Not so the state constitutions. They are written in restrictive terms. Whereas the federal Constitution takes only a clause to authorize Congress to spend money, state constitutions require dozens of pages to specify the purposes for which the money may be spent, how much may be spent, and in what manner.

Constitutional Autocracy?

A written constitution, as we saw in Chapter 3, is *an instrument of government that sets forth, among other things, the terms upon which public officials are authorized to act in behalf of the sovereign voters.* The more detailed the constitution, the smaller the discretion the public officials enjoy. The earliest state constitutions had granted extensive authority to the legislatures without much restriction on how their power should be exercised. But after the legislatures gave special privileges to railroads, canal-builders, and other interests, constitutional amendments were adopted to prevent these abuses. Furthermore, reform groups, distrusting the legislatures, began to insist on having their programs incorporated into the constitution rather than settle for simple legislative adoption. In time, state constitutions became encrusted in layer after layer of detail.

What consequences does this have for democratic government? Most simply, it means that state constitutions often are less charters of self-government than straitjackets imposed on the living present by the dead past. Today's majorities find it hard to get the governmental action they wish. For example, the Delaware Bridge, linking Philadelphia with Camden, New Jersey, was delayed for five years because of restrictive clauses in the Pennsylvania Constitution. For many years the Oregon legislature could not create a state college in Portland because the Constitution forbade the founding of any new public institution outside Marion County. Portland State College was finally established in 1955 by expanding an extension unit into a four-year school.

The detailed enumeration of powers soon throws constitutions out of date. Some outdated provisions are of course harmless, but more often they are roadblocks to effective government. The fixing of salaries in the constitutions, for example, makes it difficult to keep them geared to economic conditions. Prescribing a rigid administrative organization may make government incapable of accommodating changing needs. In short, details breed more details; long constitutions spawn hosts of amendments.

Under these conditions the people's representatives—the legislature—cannot act on many problems; instead, the voters are called on regularly to pass upon scores of constitutional amendments about which they know very little. In 1954, for example, the Louisiana legislature confronted the voters with thirty-one proposed amendments. The New Orleans Bureau of Governmental Research estimated it would take five hours just to read the texts of these proposals—and the Bureau ". . . did not guarantee that reading would make them intelligible." No wonder the Bureau termed the situation "Biennial bingo—or 31 more in '54." [2]

[2] Cited in and quoted by Karl A. Bosworth, "Law-making in State Governments," in *The Forty-eight States: Their Tasks as Policy Makers and Administrators* (The American Assembly, 1955), p. 90.

GOVERNMENT UNDER THE MODEL STATE CONSTITUTION

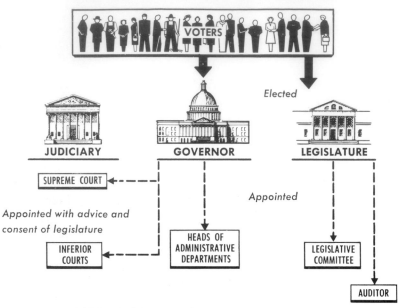

GOVERNMENT UNDER A TYPICAL STATE CONSTITUTION

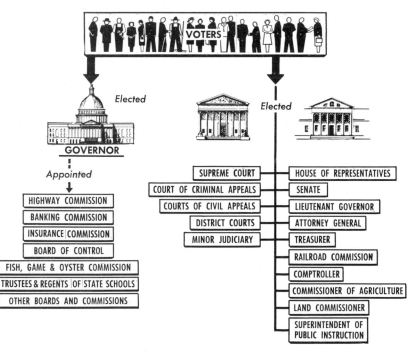

Adapted from charts prepared for the Committee on State Governments of the National Municipal League by Robert S. Bourn, based on the Texas Constitution, for the 1948 edition of the Model State Constitution, modified to reflect provisions of the 1963 edition. The set-up is typical of those states whose constitutions provide for a considerable number of popularly elected commissions and heads of departments.

Getting around the Constitution

Does all this mean that state constitutions can *forever* thwart the wishes of the majority? Not necessarily. The constitutional systems of our states, like that of the national government, include more than the formal written document. The unwritten rules, the practices, the basic statutes, the political parties, the interest groups, also shape the course of events. When large groups of people want their officials to act, they usually find some way to overcome formal constitutional barriers. Sometimes delicate tightrope-walking is called for, however. As a former Illinois Governor, the late Adlai E. Stevenson explained, "For years the machinery of our state government has been kept in motion only by continued violations of plain and positive provisions in the Illinois constitution." [3] Besides the device of simply ignoring them, constitutional barriers can be overcome through judicial interpretation. Judges can interpret the meaning of words so as to remove their restrictive force. Nevertheless, rigid state constitutions create a "constitutional autocracy" by making it more difficult for new majorities to achieve their aims.

Highly detailed state constitutions also serve to enhance the authority of the state judiciary. The more complex the constitution, the easier it is for the judges to veto legislation. In fact, one of the reasons for the growing length of some state constitutions is that formal amendments are often required to reverse unwanted judicial interpretations.

Amending the Constitution

Constitional amendments must be first *proposed* (initiated), then *ratified*. There are three ways to *propose* amendments: (1) by the legislature; (2) by initiative petition; and (3) by constitutional convention.

Proposing and Ratifying Amendments

Proposal of constitutional amendments by initiative petition from the people is permitted in approximately one-fourth of the states. Proposal of amendments by the legislature, the most common method, is permitted in all states except New Hampshire. Although the requirement varies among the states, the most general practice is to require approval of two-thirds of the elected members in each chamber of the legislature in order to initiate an amendment. Some states require approval by only a simple majority but the approval of two successive legislatures.

After an amendment has been proposed by one of these three methods, it must

[3] Quoted by Richard L. Neuberger, "States in Strait Jackets," *The American Magazine* (April 1951), p. 3.

be *ratified*. In all states except Delaware (where the legislature can ratify as well as propose amendments), ratification is by the voters. In most states, if a majority of those voting on the amendment approve it, the amendment becomes part of the constitution. In a few states, however, approval of a majority of *all* the voters *voting in the election* is required. Such a provision is a real obstacle, since many people who vote for candidates fail to vote at all on constitutional amendments.

Initiation of an amendment by the state legislature and ratification by a majority of voters voting on the amendment is the most common method of constitutional change. But in some states requirements are so stringent that it is almost impossible to get an amendment ratified, and a relatively small minority can veto the desires of the majority. In Tennessee, for example, amending the 1870 constitution proved so difficult that not a single amendment could be pushed through until 1953. One of these amendments finally adopted in 1953 slightly liberalized the amending process. Changes in the constitutional system of Tennessee have had to come by methods other than formal amendment.

Amendments usually involve piecemeal change. Many observers believe that most state constitutions are so bad that they cannot be salvaged by piecemeal improvements. Rather than patching up the old model, they advocate trading it in for a new one. The officials of the National Municipal League—an organization devoted to the cause of governmental reform—have said that "most state

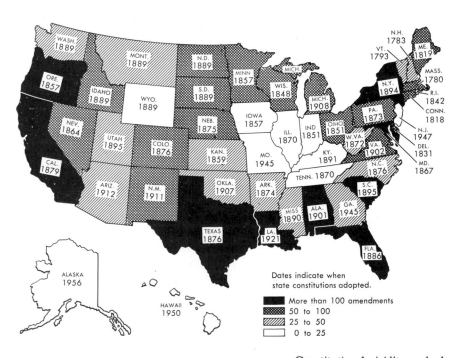

Constitutional rigidity and change

constitutions are serious obstacles to responsible and effective state and local government." How can the people get a new constitution if they want one?

Constitutional Conventions

The United States is the country *par excellence* of constitutional conventions.[4] Since the nation was founded, we have had over 200. Americans have always insisted on getting their constitutions down in writing, and on distinguishing clearly between fundamental and statutory law. A constitution is an expression of popular will; it is fundamental law binding on all public officials; and it can be changed only by prescribed methods. Hence, Americans have preferred to have their constitutions drawn up by some agency that would be more immediately expressive of popular sentiment than the legislature. The agency they have chosen most often has been a constitutional convention.

Thirty-five state constitutions authorize the legislature to submit to the voters the question of calling a convention, and in the other states the legislature is assumed to have the inherent power to do so. In ten states, the constitution requires the legislature to submit this question to the voters at fixed intervals.

If the voters approve the calling of a convention, the next step is to elect delegates. Some constitutions contain elaborate procedures governing the number of delegates, method of election, and time and place of the convention. Others leave the details to the legislature. After the delegates have been chosen for the specific job of drafting a new constitution, they assemble at the state capital.

When the convention has prepared a draft of the new constitution, it is normally submitted to the voters of the state. But first the delegates to the convention have to make a difficult choice. Should the voters be asked to accept or reject the new constitution as a whole? Or should they be given a chance to vote on each section, as though it were an amendment to the old constitution? The advantage of the former method is that one provision of a constitution ties in with another; and in order to secure all the advantages of constitutional revision, it is desirable that the entire constitution be adopted. The disadvantage is that any group that takes issue with a particular provision may vote against the entire constitution in order to defeat the offending provision. When the convention knows that one provision is highly controversial, it may decide to submit at least that provision separately. The proponents of constitutional change must look to their political fences in order to get their handiwork approved. Those states most successful in securing new constitutions have made elaborate arrangements to educate—or propagandize—the voters.

Instead of calling a constitutional convention, the legislature may appoint a

[4] Albert L. Sturm, *Methods of State Constitutional Reform* (Univ. of Michigan Press, 1954), pp. 114–115. See also National Municipal League, *Salient Issues of Constitutional Revision* (1961), and *The Constitutional Convention: A Manual on its Planning, Organization and Operation* (1961).

small *commission* to make recommendations. If the legislature approves the recommendations, it can then submit them to the voters by the regular procedures governing the proposal of amendments. Constitutional revision by commission has been used successfully in several states. Its major weakness is that since the commission is not representative of all the interests, it may fail to incorporate critically important compromises in its recommendations. The commission's work is thus rejected either by the legislature or by the voters.

In the last couple of decades only a handful of states have drawn up new constitutions. If present constitutions are so bad, one might ask, why haven't more states modernized them? The answer lies in the nature of the political process. Constitutions are not a neutral set of rules perched above the world of rough-and-tumble politics. On the contrary, constitutions significantly affect "who gets what" from government. To change a constitution in this way or that way helps or hinders various groups in gaining what they want. Present state constitutions may be "bad" from the perspective of democratic theory, but they are not "bad" for many specific groups.

To date, those who have a vested interest in present arrangements have been strong enough to prevent the calling of constitutional conventions or the establishment of commissions for revisions. Where the latter have been created, frequently they have been used as safety valves to channel demands for change into controllable hands.[5] Many people are indifferent to constitutional change; it is difficult to work up much excitement in a campaign for revising a state constitution. Hence, the "stand-patters" have a built-in advantage that, when combined with the constitutional obstacles, helps to explain the lack of action.

The political struggle does not cease once a constitutional convention has assembled. Often those who dominate the state legislature also dominate the convention. In some cases, however, the interests that dominate conventions are different from those that run the state legislature. Service in conventions usually carries greater prestige than sitting in the legislature, and many men are willing to interrupt their normal activities in order to spend some time at constitution-writing. George Romney, for example, played a vital role in the Michigan constitutional convention as President of American Motors and went from there to the governorship and national prominence. Moreover, conventions sometimes attract greater popular attention. Hence, it is possible to get from conventions changes that legislatures cannot or will not make.

Two New Constitutions—A Case Study

Early in 1950, 63 delegates representing the several islands and various ethnic groups that made up the then Territory of Hawaii met to draft a constitution for the projected state of Hawaii. Five years later, 55 men convened in a constitutional

---

[5] William C. Havard, "Notes on a Theory of State Constitutional Change: The Florida Experience," *The Journal of Politics* (February 1959), pp. 80–104.

convention in the gymnasium of the University of Alaska, and out of several weeks' effort came the constitution for what was destined to be the forty-ninth state of the Union.[6] The people of the two territories enthusiastically approved the labors of their conventions, and the proposed state constitutions were duly transmitted to Congress. Eventually Congress, as had its predecessors with each of the new state constitutions since 1789, found the Alaskan and Hawaiian constitutions to be republican in character and not repugnant to the Constitution of the United States or the Declaration of Independence, and resolutions admitting the new states were adopted by Congress and signed by the President. The necessary preliminaries to statehood were quickly disposed of and in 1958 Alaska and in 1959 Hawaii became states.

A hundred and seventy-odd years had passed since another group of 55 men met in Philadelphia to draft the national Constitution. As we have noted, these men drew heavily on the constitutions of the thirteen original states. Then the new states carved out of forest and plain as the nation moved westward borrowed from the constitutions of their older sister states as well as from the national one. With all this experience to draw on, what kinds of constitution did Alaska and Hawaii adopt?

In general the new constitution-writers followed tradition. The two newest state constitutions contain the usual preamble, bill of rights, provisions for separation of powers and a bicameral legislature, and articles dealing with local governments. But the old patterns were not indiscriminately copied. The men who wrote these constitutions were well aware of the weaknesses and shortcomings of state constitutions depicted above and they sought to avoid many of them. For example, both constitutions are relatively short. Through the avoidance of encumbering details, the legislatures have been left relatively free to respond to the changing needs of these two rapidly developing states.

Moreover, many specific proposals for improving state governments (some of these will be discussed in the next several chapters) have been incorporated in the constitutions of the two new states. For example, the problem of reapportioning legislative seats as population changes—a seemingly unsolvable problem in many states—has been met by removing the responsibility from the legislature and placing it in the hands of the governor and courts. In line with recommendations by political scientists for improving the executive branch, the number of elected executive officers has been reduced to the governor and only one other official. The organization of the judicial branch also shows the imprint of new thinking, for in both states the legislature has been left with authority to determine the organization and precise function of the lower courts. In Alaska the judges are to be selected according to the Missouri plan (page 777), and in Hawaii by the governor with consent of the state senate. In both states the chief justices serve as administrative heads of the state court systems and the supreme courts are given rule-making powers, thus laying the foundation for an integrated court structure.

[6] Paul C. Bartholomew, "The Constitution of the State of Alaska," *Southwestern Social Science Quarterly* (June 1959), pp. 40–53.

Alaska's and Hawaii's constitutions, like those of all the other states, bear distinguishing birthmarks reflecting the peculiar demands of a given time and place. Only a few can be mentioned here. Alaska, being abundantly endowed with natural resources, devotes a sizable section of its constitution to guarantees that these resources will be used in the public interest. Since Hawaii is the most racially polyglot of all our states, several provisions of its constitution deal with race relations. Discrimination in public schools and other institutions is explicitly prohibited, as are denials of civil rights because of race, sex, or ancestry. Alaska, too, guarantees the legal and political equality of all peoples. Alaska also exhibits an awareness of the threat to civil liberties that arises out of efforts to deal with disloyalty. Besides containing the familiar due process clause, its constitution specifically guarantees fair and just treatment in the course of executive and legislative investigations. One final novelty—both states have departed from the mainland tradition of setting the minimum age requirement for voting at 21 (followed by all but Kentucky and Georgia), Alaska making it 19 and Hawaii 20.

29 UNDER THE CAPITOL DOME— THE STATE LEGISLATURE

Do you know the names of the men who represent you in your state legislature? Probably not. But you probably would if you were a member of the generation that saw war and independence come to the American colonies. Indeed, you might have counted several state legislators among your heroes. One of the significant trends in our political history has been the rise and fall of the state legislatures and of the prestige that surrounds them. During the Revolution they were the focal points of the war effort, and when peace came they occupied a powerful and prestigious position in the American community. But the guns at Yorktown had hardly fallen silent when the status of the state legislatures began to decline. In fact, the adoption of the federal Constitution was a victory for those who were disappointed with, and wished to curtail, the authority of the state legislatures. In recent times, too, state legislatures have come under heavy criticism. They have been described as unrepresentative, inefficient, badly organized, and mediocre in membership.

Do the legislators deserve the criticism that is often heaped upon them? What are the defects of our state legislatures? What could be done to improve their performance? Before we turn to these problems, let us glance at the characteristic organization and procedures of our state legislatures—or assemblies, as they are often called.

State Legislatures

In all states except Nebraska, the legislature is bicameral. The lower and more numerous chamber is generally called the House of Representatives. Its size varies from a low of 35 in Delaware to a high of 400 in New Hampshire. The typical number is around 100. In most states the representatives serve for a two-year term, and are elected by counties (except in New England where they represent the town). The upper chamber, known in all the states as the senate, is composed of about 40 members elected by various kinds of districts, but most frequently on the basis of population. State senators have a four-year term in 37 of the states.

In all but 19 states (where annual sessions are held) the legislature meets in regular session once every two years (biennial sessions), usually in January of odd-numbered years. In half of the states the constitution limits the legislature to a regular session of a fixed number of days, usually 60. A dozen states stop legislators' salaries after a specified period and not often do they stay in session after their pay stops. These restrictions reflect the old distrust of government, the feeling that "the faster we get it over with the better." The governor has the power to call the legislature into special session, a power that is frequently used because of the constitutional time limitation on regular sessions. In over half the states the legislature can discuss during the special session only those matters stipulated by the governor. In another quarter of the states the legislature can call itself into special session and is not, therefore, so restricted.

The organization and procedures of the state legislatures are similar to those of Congress. A speaker, chosen by the majority party, presides over the lower house. In some states the speaker has more power to control proceedings than his national counterpart; for example, in addition to all the powers of the Speaker of the national House of Representatives, he has the right to appoint committees and exerts considerable influence in determining the rules. In most of the states, a lieutenant governor presides over the senate. In the others, the presiding officer is chosen by the majority party in the senate. The committee system prevails, as in Congress; in some states, notably Massachusetts, joint committees are used regularly to speed legislative action. But state "legislative standing committees are but pale shadows of their congressional counterparts" [1] and do not have the same power over bills as do congressional committees. Committees seldom have professional assistance, the seniority system is not as stringently followed as in Congress, turnover is high, and state legislatures meet for relatively short times so that committee members do not acquire the competence over subject-matter areas as do congressional committee members.

Although the formal structure and procedures of the legislatures are similar from state to state, this is not true of their actual operation. Some states, like New York, have strong political parties that take an active part in policy-making. Here and in perhaps a dozen other states, the party caucus is an important part of the legislative machinery. In others, the parties assume no responsibility for the actions of their legislative members. In some states, the governor leads the legislative way; in others, he is relatively unimportant. The fairly competitive two-party system found in Congress exists in not more than one-third of the states.[2] In order to describe with any accuracy the actual functioning of a particular state legislature, one must be acquainted with the entire social and political environment in which that legislature operates.[3]

What the State Legislatures Can—and Cannot—Do

What do the just over 7,700 state legislators do? A former prominent state legislator replies, "We enact the laws that set speed limits on the highways; we specify minimum salaries for classroom teachers; we fix the content of butterfat in Grade-A milk; we draw up the rules governing the purity of drinking water; and we determine whether a citizen convicted of murder in the first degree shall be gassed, hanged, shot, electrocuted, or merely clapped behind iron bars." [4]

The state legislatures have all governmental powers that are not given to some other governmental agency. The Tenth Amendment to the federal Constitution makes it clear that governmental power not given to the national government or denied to the states lies with the states or with the people. The *state* constitutions in turn give some of this reserved power exclusively to nonlegislative agencies and specifically deny some to the legislature. All that is left is inherited by the state legislatures. To be sure, some state courts have developed the doctrine of *implied*

---

[1] Malcolm Jewell, *The State Legislature* (Random House, 1962), p. 93.

[2] Belle Zeller (ed.), *American State Legislatures* (Crowell, 1954), p. 192. This is a report of the Committee on American Legislatures of the American Political Science Association.

[3] John C. Wahlke, Heinz Eulau, William Buchanan, and LeRoy C. Ferguson, *The Legislative System: Explorations in Legislative Behavior* (Wiley, 1962), is a careful and detailed analysis of the role and behavior of legislators in California, Tennessee, Ohio, and New Jersey.

[4] Richard L. Neuberger, "Tribulations of a State Legislator," *The Reporter* (January 31, 1950), p. 31.

limitations on the legislatures by ruling that when the constitution authorizes the legislature to do a particular thing, by implication it denies the legislature the power to do other things.

Although subject to all these constitutional limitations, the legislature still retains a powerful voice in the determination of the crucial political questions in the states. Among other things, the legislature levies state taxes, appropriates the moneys, creates the agencies to carry out the tasks of government, allots functions among these agencies, and investigates them to make sure that they are doing what the lawmakers intended them to do. State legislators, like their national counterparts, also participate in amending constitutions, have authority to impeach and try public officials, and exercise some appointive powers.

Quite commonly, the state constitution prescribes the *procedures* that legislators must follow in order to legislate. In addition, the rate of taxation, the kinds of tax, the subjects that may be taxed, and the purposes of taxation are often detailed in the constitution. *Special legislation*—laws dealing with particular persons or localities—is usually prohibited. Many constitutions declare that special laws are to be avoided wherever possible, and in addition they list particular subjects—divorce, chartering of corporations, licensing banks, affairs of local units of government—which the legislature is forbidden to deal with by special legislation. Such restrictions do not, however, prevent classifications, and by refined classifications (a law for cities of over 14,350 and under 15,600 population when only one city in the state fits into this category, for example) the legislatures often are able to overcome these constitutional restrictions. .

Who Are the State Legislators?

A United States senator or congressman has a full-time job for which he receives full-time pay. But a state legislator is only a part-time legislator and in most cases receives but a part-time salary. He goes to the state capitol for a short time every two years. In some states, he is paid so little that only if he were independently wealthy could he afford to spend full time as a legislator. The legislative salaries paid vary from $15,000 a year in New York to $200 a biennium in New Hampshire, with the median in the $4,000–$4,800 range for biennial salaries. Most states allow travel expenses.

James Bryce argued that legislative salaries should be abolished altogether, for they serve only to attract men who have no interest in the job except the money. While this attitude is still encountered, most observers today favor much higher salaries, arguing that inadequate pay discourages qualified candidates from seeking office. Only those with an independent source of income, or with a job that can be combined with legislative service, can afford to be legislators under persent conditions. Few businessmen, teachers, or salaried workers, for example, can interrupt their activities to attend to legislative duties, and they cannot afford to give up their jobs, and live on the salary the state will pay.[5]

[5] Alexander Cloner and Richard W. Gable, "The California Legislator and the Problem of Compensation," *Western Political Quarterly* (September 1959), pp. 712–726.

The lawyers are the largest occupational group in state assemblies, as they are in the national Congress. Many young attorneys enter the legislature in order to perform a public service, secure a reputation, and build up a practice. Farmers are the next largest group. Since farming is more or less seasonal, it can be more readily adjusted than many professions to fit legislative schedules. Salesmen, such as insurance men and real estate dealers, are also found in significant numbers. There are few women, and fewer Negroes, in state legislatures.

What kind of men and women (there are over 200 of the latter) are the state legislators? Bryce, writing at the end of the nineteenth century, stated that the average legislature had "fewer able and high-minded men among its members" than did the Congress. The reason, he believed, was that the state legislature "is surrounded by temptations relatively greater. It is guarded by a less watchful and less interested public opinion." All this is probably still true, although the late Senator Richard Neuberger, author and former member of the Oregon legislature, argued that the "voters are looking right down your throat." But as Neuberger also pointed out, it is primarily the organized interest groups that are heard at the state capitols; the unorganized public probably pays even less attention to its state legislature than to Congress in far-away Washington. When Neuberger introduced a measure to limit the number of billboards on the highways, a few men, "stung on the pocket nerve," were able to make it appear that the entire state was up in arms against the bill, although the billboard owners themselves never once appeared during the entire operation. The head of the Signpainters' Union called Neuberger an enemy of labor anxious to throw men out of work. The omnipresent widows and orphans came to the capitol and argued that they could not live without the rent they received from their roadside property. A delegation from the state advertising club charged that the Bill of Rights and freedom of speech were being jeopardized. The measure was stigmatized as communist in origin. (Actually it had been suggested by a wealthy old woman who loved scenery.) Under these pressures, the bill was defeated. Without doubt, state legislators often yield to interests which comprise an extremely small segment of the population. But this weakness—if it be such—is not peculiar to the state legislators.

The state legislator enjoys far less prestige than the national congressman, especially in states with large legislatures. Discouraged by the low salary and lack of influence, many men serve a term or two and then retire. The turnover is so large that continuity of leadership is interrupted. "Over half of the state legislators are new at each session," [6] though the practice varies widely among the states. "Factors which appear to be relevant to turnover are the rate of compensation, responsibility sufficient to make the job attractive, electoral laws and practice which favor incumbents or discourage rotation, as well as the constitutional length of terms of office." [7]

And yet there is much to be said for the state legislator. He is usually a hard-working, public-spirited citizen. Of course, those who dislike the laws that are

[6] Zeller, *op. cit.*, p. 65. See also Thomas R. Dye, "State Legislative Politics," in H. Jacob and K. N. Vines (eds.), *Politics in the American States* (Little, Brown, 1965), pp. 169, 170.

[7] Wahlke, *et al.*, *op. cit.*, p. 49.

passed, or who like the laws that are defeated, often claim that the fault lies with the intelligence of the legislators. The state legislatures probably have their share of ignorant and dishonest men, but there is no support for many of the more extreme charges directed against them. On the contrary, the general level of intelligence and devotion to the public interest displayed by state legislators is probably a fairly accurate reflection of the people who elect them.

Parties in the State Legislatures

Except in Minnesota and Nebraska, all candidates for state legislatures are nominated by political parties and elected as party members. However, the role of the parties in the management of the legislatures and in policy-making varies widely from state to state. The American Political Science Association's Committee on State Legislatures discovered strong party spirit and cohesion in seventeen state legislatures; within these states legislators in the same party tend to vote alike.[8] In eleven state legislatures the parties were found to be only occasionally or moderately strong; and in twenty, party strength was weak or nonexistent. In some states, for example, the legislature reflects a rural-versus-urban split; in others, legislators cluster in conservative or liberal coalitions; and in still others there appear to be only shifting combinations of factions. The committee also reported a fairly even division in nineteen states between the two parties in the legislature; in nine states one of the parties dominated, but the other had a sizable number of seats in the legislature; and in eighteen states one party overwhelmingly dominated the legislature.

Party cohesion and party spirit are most likely to be found in the two-party legislatures. Here it is that party caucuses are most likely to function, formulating policy that party members are expected to support in the legislative sessions. Some of the two-party legislatures, however, exhibit little party cohesion, and even where party cohesion exists, the role of the party in formulating policy may be exaggerated.

In states where a single party dominates the legislature but where the minority party has a sizable number of seats, the role of the party varies widely. In some, both the political parties are highly organized; but in others only the majority party has cohesion, and the minority party usually is weak.[9] But the most prevalent patterns in these states is for both parties to be weak. In legislatures where a single party has overwhelming control (the Democrats have traditionally held every seat

---

[8] Zeller, *op. cit.*, pp. 192 ff. Wahlke, *et al.*, *op. cit.*, supports these generalizations.

[9] *Ibid.*, p. 206. For other studies of the parties' role in state legislatures see Thomas A. Flinn, "Party Responsibility in the States: Some Causal Factors," *The American Political Science Review* (March 1964), pp. 60–71; Malcolm Jewell, *The State Legislature* (Random House, 1962); Thomas Dye, "State Legislative Politics," in Jacob and Vines, *op. cit.*, pp. 151–206. Malcolm E. Jewell, "Party Voting in American State Legislatures," *The American Political Science Review* (September 1955), pp. 773–791. For studies of particular states, see William J. Keefe, "Parties, Partisanship, and Public Policy in the Pennsylvania Legislature," *The American Political Science Review* (June 1954), pp. 450–464; and, on a more general aspect, Leon D. Epstein, *Politics in Wisconsin* (Univ. of Wisconsin Press, 1958), pp. 33–56, and Wahlke, *et al.*, *op. cit.*

in both houses in six southern states), parties are of little importance in conducting legislative business. Factions within the dominant party, however, are sometimes very active. Sometimes the factions in a one-party legislature organize around dominant personalities—the Long and anti-Long factions in Louisiana, for example.

In summary, parties are more likely to be strongest in the two-party legislatures, weakest in the one-party legislatures, and neither very strong nor very weak in the modified one-party legislatures. In a few state legislatures, parties seem to play a more prominent role than they do in Congress, but they are considerably weaker in most state legislatures. Party control of legislation, in short, is even weaker in most states than it is in Congress.

Improving Legislative Procedure

The weaknesses of some of our state legislatures are much like those of Congress, but to a greater extent. Legislative business is not conducted efficiently. Committee work is not carefully planned. Records are not always well kept. Expert information is sometimes lacking. Introducing special and private legislation is too easy. Parliamentary rules impede rather than expedite action and play into the hands of minorities. Other weaknesses are peculiar to the states. The length of sessions is unnecessarily restricted. Salaries are too low. Some legislatures lack the services needed for law-making in a complex world.

Some Specific Recommendations

Here are the recommendations made by a group of experts to improve legislative procedures in the states:

1. *Remove the restrictions on the length of regular sessions.* Constitutional provisions that give the legislators a set number of days to do their work should be abolished. These restrictions jam up the legislative business so that during the last days of each session hundreds of bills are passed in a bedlam of activity. Some authorities would go even further and provide for annual sessions, which are now held in about one-fourth of the states.

2. *Raise legislators' salaries so that competent persons can serve without financial sacrifice.*

3. *Increase the length of the term in order to provide continuity of membership.* Perhaps staggered terms should be used, as is now done in some state senates.

4. *Appoint skilled legislative employees on the basis of merit.*

5. *Reduce the number of legislative committees, equalize their work, schedule their meetings, and keep permanent and public records of their action.* Other students encourage the greater use of *joint committees* composed of members from both houses to avoid duplication of hearings and wasted effort. The joint committee has been adopted in Massachusetts, Maine, and Connecticut with great success.

6. *Provide for public hearings on all major bills.*

7. *Establish legislative councils or interim committees with adequate clerical and research facilities.* The legislative council idea, first attempted in Kansas and now found in over two-thirds of the states, calls for a small group of legislators to meet between sessions. The council, with the aid of a research staff, makes investigations and circulates reports so that the legislators who meet for a short session can still draw on the best available information.

8. *Improve legislative reference, research, bill-drafting, and statutory revision services wherever necessary.* Most states have some kind of legislative reference service, but in too many of them the service is primarily a bookkeeping and report-classifying operation. Others, however, are first-rate research organizations providing the legislators with complete information on current issues.

9. *Limit the period during which new bills may be introduced and provide for the drafting, filing, and printing of bills before the opening of the sessions.* To avoid the last-minute rush, a few states, notably California, have tried but abandoned the "split session." During the first period, bills were introduced. The legislature then recessed for a short period, and, upon reconvening, no new bills were ordinarily permitted. The split session did not work as well as many had hoped, however, for during the second session legislators tended to amend everything except the number and title of bills. Pre-session filing and the enforcement of time limits on the introduction of bills also serve to forestall a last-minute pile-up of bills.

10. *Establish permanent committees to review and revise organization, rules, and procedures.*

11. *Provide an adequate budget for legislative operations.*

12. *Delegate settlement of claims against the state to judicial or administrative agencies and give local governments greater authority to make their own laws and determine their own governmental structures.*

13. *Install electrical voting.* This device, a great time-saver,[10] has now been adopted in thirty state legislatures.

Other critics insist that the state legislatures should be smaller than they are. Some legislatures are so large that conducting business is awkward, and placing responsibility for action or inaction is difficult. There is, of course, no "right" size, and the legislature should be large enough to represent all the major interests in a state. It is doubtful, however, that the large bodies now prevalent are needed. Half as many men, paid twice as much, would probably give the public more for its money.

---

[10] Council of State Governments, *Our State Legislatures*, 1946. These recommendations were endorsed by the American Political Science Association's Committee on State Legislatures; see Zeller, *op. cit.*, pp. 26–162. For a useful survey of legislative councils, see Harold W. Davey, "The Legislative Council Movement, 1933–1953," *The American Political Science Review* (September 1953), pp. 785–797.

But will the above changes be enough? Many think not. Some others advocate more basic alterations, such as unicameralism.

Two Houses or One?

Bicameralism became the established pattern in the United States early in our history (see Chapter 2). During colonial days, the two chambers represented distinct interests—the upper house stood for royal authority; the lower house stood for the colonial cause. The desire to balance the aristocratic against the popular interest, and the belief in a government of checks and balances, led to the retention of two-house legislatures after independence had been won. During the first decades of our history, the suffrage requirements to vote for senator and the qualifications to serve in the senate were more stringent than those for the lower house. But by the middle of the nineteenth century, the same electorate was choosing the members of both houses. In many states, the two houses today represent the same people (although usually in different districts). Why then do we retain the bicameral system?

Defenders of bicameralism insist that two chambers check hasty or ill-considered legislation. But even in some states with two chambers, legislation is rushed through, especially in the closing days, with little consideration by either chamber. Sometimes the second chamber does discover unintended mistakes or errors in bills enacted by the other house and makes the necessary corrective amendments. Some bills proposed by one chamber are defeated by the other, but it is impossible to develop objective standards to determine whether the legislation so defeated was "ill-considered." Critics of bicameralism are persuaded that the governor's veto, the courts, and the electorate are better checks. They believe that too many roadblocks impede legislation, with the result that minority interests find it easy to prevent legislation desired by the majority.

Another defense of bicameralism is that it balances the interests of different groups. By enabling different groups to dominate one or the other chamber, it is argued, bicameralism provides proper balance. Defenders of unicameralism answer that if this reasoning were carried to its logical conclusion we would have a multi-chamber legislature with a separate chamber to represent each interest— one for the farmers, one for the businessmen, one for the workers, one for people living in large cities, one for people living in small towns, and so on. The interests of all groups can be fairly represented in one chamber, they insist. Moreover, bicameralism encourages buck-passing and secret legislation in conference committees, and requires elaborate committee systems. Unicameralism, on the other hand, would concentrate responsibility, encourage abler men to run for office, avoid the need of conference committees, and would be less expensive.

Under the leadership of the late Senator George Norris, Nebraska created a unicameral legislature of forty-three men elected on a non-partisan ballot. "After two and a half decades of experience, Nebraska voters appear satisfied with one house," [11] but despite consideration by several state constitutional conventions, the single-chamber legislature has not been adopted by any other state.

Whether our legislatures are composed of one house or two, we are still faced with the perplexing problem of determining the basis on which their members shall be elected.

Representation in State Legislatures

Until recently, and even today in some states, representation in the legislature reflected a "rural bias." People who live in large cities and in metropolitan suburbs elected proportionately fewer legislators than did their farm and small-town neighbors. "As of 1960 the average value of the vote in the big city was less than half the average value of the vote in the open country, so far as electing members of the state legislature is concerned." [12] Cook County, for example, had over half of Illinois' population and its residents paid more than half the state taxes, but the county elected only 24 of the 58 members of the state senate. Los Angeles County had more than 38 per cent of California's population but elected only one out of 40 senators. The 22 least populous Georgia counties combined had about the same population as Fulton County (in which Atlanta is located), but they elected 72 representatives while Fulton elected only three. Dade County in Florida (Miami) contained about

"It's a crime how those big city machines operate." (From The Herblock Book, Beacon Press, 1952.)

one-fifth of the state's population but elected only 3 out of 95 members of the lower house and only 1 of the 38 senators. In Ohio, one rural vote was equal to almost four votes from the two largest cities. The same general picture was to be found in state after state. [13]

[11] William Anderson, Clara Penniman, and Edward W. Weidner, Government in the Fifty States (Holt, Rinehart and Winston, 1960), p. 211; see also Roger V. Shumate, "The Nebraska Unicameral Legislature," Western Political Quarterly (September 1952), p. 512.

[12] Paul T. David and Ralph Eisenberg, Devaluation of the Urban and Suburban Vote (Univ. of Virginia, Bureau of Public Administration, 1961), p. 10.

[13] David and Eisenberg, op. cit. See also Gordon E. Baker, Rural versus Urban Political Power (Random House, 1955), pp. 16–17; and Manning J. Dauer and Robert G. Kelsay, "Unrepresentative States," National Municipal Review (December 1955), pp. 571–575.

Country Hicks v. Suburbanites v. City Slickers

The battle over reapportionment is more complex than just a rural-versus-city struggle. In recent decades, despite a tremendous increase in the proportion of our population living in urban areas, the largest cities have not shown much of a gain in population. In some central cities there has even been a percentage decline. Thus, as Professor Robert S. Friedman has pointed out, "The net result is that it is no longer cities which are the chief victims of underrepresentation but suburbia." [14] A few central cities are now *over*represented: for example, Boston and Baltimore.

Many who live and do business within the central city or in the suburbs, moreover, find their political interests more like those of the farmers and small-town citizens than of their city brethren. It is not unusual to find some city dwellers seeking to maintain rural supremacy in the state legislatures. For example, many business interests are fearful that more representation in the state legislature for the city and suburban voter will result in more regulation of business. In California "Privately owned utilities, banks, insurance companies and others . . . have discovered some 'cow county' legislators more responsive to their demands and less committed to contrary points of view on key social and economic questions than are urban representatives. The urban legislator is more likely to be influenced by organized labor and by the many popular movements that ebb and flow through California politics." [15]

How did this rural domination of our state legislatures come about? It was due in part to constitutional provisions. Some state constitutions fix electoral districts with no provision for reapportionment. Some state constitutions call for equal representation in one chamber for counties or towns regardless of their population. As a result of these and other constitutional provisions, people moving from farms and small cities to the suburbs and large cities left behind depopulated "rotten boroughs" where a few people had excessive voting power.

Even if the state constitution created no inequity, and even if it mandated the state legislature to reapportion representatives or to redistrict the states every ten years, as is the case in forty states, many of our state legislatures simply refused to do so. Legislators from smaller towns and farmlands naturally did not wish to reapportion themselves out of a job and their constituencies did not wish to lose their ability to control the legislature. "Any man in this legislature who doesn't fight for his own district is a particular . . . fool," candidly observed one Illinois representative during a sharp struggle over reapportionment in that state's legislature.[16] As Page has pointed out, "In perhaps no other aspect of American political

[14] Robert S. Friedman, "Reapportionment Myth," *National Civic Review* (April 1960), pp. 184–188.

[15] Dean E. McHenry, "Urban vs. Rural in California," *National Municipal Review* (July 1946), p. 350.

[16] Quoted by Gilbert Y. Steiner and Samuel K. Gove, The *Legislature Redistricts Illinois* (Univ. of Illinois Institute of Government and Public Affairs, 1956), p. 7.

life are constitutional . . . mandates so systematically honored in their breach . . . as they are in the matter of reapportionment." [17] Thus despite provisions in state constitutions calling for reapportionment, 27 legislatures as of 1962 had not been reapportioned for 25 years or more. The Vermont legislature had last reapportioned its lower house in 1793, Alabama and Tennessee in 1901, Minnesota in 1913, Mississippi in 1916, Indiana in 1921.

In some states where constitutional amendments may be proposed by the initiative procedures, reapportionment has been forced on the legislature. Where the legislature itself must initiate constitutional amendments or summon constitutional conventions into session, reapportionment by constitutional amendment has been less successful. Delegates to constitutional conventions were themselves often chosen on the same basis as the legislators. These delegates were no more likely to propose drastic changes in legislative representation than were the legislators.

To get around legislative failures to act, a few states, including Alaska and Hawaii, by constitutional provision instructed the state courts to intervene if the legislature fails to do so. In Texas, for example, if the legislature refuses to reapportion, the task is automatically assigned to a board of state officials, and the Texas Supreme Court is authorized to compel the board to act. In Alaska the governor reapportions the lower chamber and may modify senate districts after each decennial census.

How did the legislators and those who opposed reapportionment defend their failure to act? They contended that representation on the basis of population has never been consistently followed in the United States, that representation has been based on geographical areas as well as on population. The United States Senate is organized to represent states, not population clusters. If representation is based exclusively on population, they argue, the city and suburban legislators would take over, and that would be worse than country rule, for cities dominated by political organizations could maintain rigid control of their legislators. The "rural bias" that has existed in the United States at least since the days of Jefferson provided ideological backing for those who opposed equal voice in the state legislatures for city people. Although a majority of the people in the country now live in urban areas, the belief in the superior virtues of country life and country people is still strongly held. Even among city dwellers themselves, the city is often thought of as a den of iniquity and a center of un-American and radical thought.

State Legislatures v. City Officials

Conflict between the rural Republicans who run many of our legislatures and city Democrats who are trying to run most of our largest cities is a normal feature of our political landscape. City officials complain that the legislators are unsympathetic about city problems and

[17] Thomas Page, *Legislative Apportionment in Kansas* (Univ. of Kansas, Governmental Research Series No. 8, 1952), p. 1.

try to enforce rural notions of right and wrong upon their city brethren. One student of Chicago politics once noted that the office of corporation counsel of Chicago (city attorney) spent most if its time finding "ways of circumventing or changing state laws which hamper the city." [18] Frustrated by the failure to secure more equitable representation in the affairs of state governments, in recent years many cities have taken their problems directly to Washington.

George Washington Plunkitt, the Tammany Hall patriot, felt strongly about the control of the New York legislature by rural Republicans. The hayseeds, as he called them in 1905, "think we are like the Indians to the National Government— that is, sort of wards of the state, who don't know how to look after ourselves and have to be taken care of by the Republicans of St. Lawrence, Ontario, and other backwoods counties. . . . Say, you hear a lot about the downtrodden people of Ireland . . ." continued Plunkitt. "Now, let me tell you that they have more real freedom and home rule than the people of this grand and imperial city. . . . In this state the Republican government makes no pretense at all. It says right out in the open: 'New York City is a nice big fat Goose. Come along with your carvin' knives and have a slice.' " [19]

Plunkitt accused the Republican-controlled state government of levying all the taxes on liquor, corporations, banks, and insurance companies, and then spending the money for the country people. One of his fondest dreams was to see New York City withdraw from the state. But what would happen to the people upstate? "These hayseeds," he said, "have been so used to livin' off of New York City that they would be helpless. . . . It wouldn't do to let them starve. We might make some sort of appropriation for them for a few years." Plunkitt even wanted to pass a law requiring upstate politicians to get a passport before traveling south of the Bronx. He admitted that such a law might be difficult to draw up, but as he said, "With a Tammany Constitution, Governor, Legislature, and Mayor, there would be no trouble in settlin' a little matter of that sort." [20]

It is not merely the Plunkitts who have protested against what they consider to be an injustice. More recent and respectable opposition has been voiced by the U.S. Conference of Mayors and by the National Municipal League. At crowded meetings of the Conference of Mayors, the cry "Taxation without representation is tyranny!" is frequently heard. And it is reported that a president of this conference once stated that unless the cities received a fairer share of representation "there will be a tea party which will make a bigger smash than the original one in Boston." The mayors summarized their views by declaring, "Equal representation is not a mere theory or doctrine. It is a fundamental feature of democracy; and the failure of any legislative body to enforce the principle should be met with instant and vigorous protests on the part of the people affected." [21]

But no matter how much they protested, those under-represented in the state

[18] Harold Gosnell, quoted in T. Page, *op. cit.*, p. 139.
[19] W. L. Riordon, *Plunkitt of Tammany Hall* (McClure, Phillips, 1905), pp. 38–39.
[20] *Ibid.*, pp. 125–126.
[21] The United States Conference of Mayors, *Government of the People, by the People, for the People*, 1948.

legislature could find no place to apply their pressures: They had no access, no leverage. The state legislatures refused to act. The judges refused to act. Even though failure of state legislatures to reapportion violated both their state constitutions and the federal Constitution, both state and federal judges took the position that questions having to do with legislative districting were "political" and outside the scope of judicial authority.

The Federal Courts to the Rescue

In a free society formal constitutional arrangements cannot indefinitely remain far out of line with the actualities of the political system. Urban Americans would not forever allow themselves to be governed by legislators from rural areas. The 1960 census showed that state legislatures were becoming more and more unrepresentative of the people. Within some of the states pressures were so strong that legislatures made slight adjustments to give somewhat greater voice to urban and suburban districts, but without making the legislatures really representative.

In 1960 the Supreme Court ruled that the Alabama legislature had violated the Fifteenth Amendment when it redrew the boundaries of a city in order to deprive Negroes of the right to vote in city elections.[22] This ruling was not precisely pertinent to the question of legislative apportionment, but it did indicate that not all questions having to do with the drawing of election district lines were outside the scope of judicial concern. Those agitating for a

(From Government of the People, by the People, for the People, *published by The United States Conference of Mayors, Washington 6, D.C.)*

more equitable representation took heed and heart at the High Court's decision.

In Tennessee the situation was especially discouraging for city voters. The legislature had refused to reapportion since 1901 despite population shifts; residents of some rural counties had a vote worth more than twenty-two times as much as voters in Shelby County (Memphis). Nor could the city voters secure constitutional amendments, for their state constitution could not be amended except with the consent of the rural-controlled legislature. The state courts offered no hope, since

[22] *Gomillion v. Lightfoot* (1960).

the judges had ruled that legislative reapportionment was solely up to the state legislature.

Having no other place to go, some urban voters challenged the constitutionality of the Tennessee apportionment practices in the federal courts. The district judges hinted that the Tennessee legislature might be depriving urban voters of their constitutional rights, but following precedent the judges ruled that federal courts had no authority to provide relief.

When the city voters appealed to the Supreme Court, the United States Department of Justice supported their petition. In 1962, in the now famous case of *Baker v. Carr*, the Supreme Court held that urban voters *do* have standing to challenge legislative apportionment and such questions may be considered by the federal courts. The Supreme Court did not itself decide that the Tennessee legislature in fact had violated the Constitution (that had to be considered first by the district court) and it did not hold that legislative districts must be based on equal population. But it did say that "arbitrary and capricious" districts violate the Constitution and that federal judges may take jurisdiction over such cases.

Baker v. Carr started a small tidal wave. Some legislatures adopted reapportionment plans in the hopes of forestalling more drastic judicial action. In almost every state in the union under-represented voters initiated lawsuits. The Supreme Court, however, established no standards by which a system of representation could be evaluated; it merely said in the *Baker* case that federal courts would hear cases challenging representation in state legislatures as being in violation of the equal protection of the law. Finally, in 1964, the Court enunciated the standard to be applied in a case dealing with congressional representation: "... *as nearly as practicable one man's vote in a congressional election is to be worth as much as another's*.[23] Would this principle be extended to *state* representation?

The answer was yes. On the final day of the same term, in the leading case of *Reynolds v. Sims*, the Court held that it was "...

"THUMBS OFF!"

From Straight Herblock (*Simon & Schuster, 1964*).

[23] *Wesberry v. Sanders,* 1964 (italics added).

clearly established that the fundamental principle of representative government in this country is one of equal representation for equal numbers of people, without regard to race, sex, economic status, or place of residence within a state." This principle was not only applicable to the lower house of the state legislature, which was usually based upon the population basis, but also to the *upper* house, where representation was often based upon areal factors such as counties or some other governmental unit. Defenders of this pattern had strenuously argued that so long as the lower house represented population, the upper house could represent geographical units. Look at the federal system embodied in the U.S. Constitution, they said. Was not representation in the U.S. Senate based upon area? Although many thought this to be a compelling argument, a majority of the Court did not. Chief Justice Warren explained:

> Legislators represent people, not trees or acres. Legislators are elected by voters, not farms or cities or economic interests . . . the right to elect legislators in a free and unimpaired fashion is a bedrock of our political system.

The federal analogy, in short, did not hold. Political subdivisions are not and never have been sovereign entities.

The constitutional requirement was simply "one man—one vote." It did not even make any difference that a majority of the voters in a state had specifically approved of a constitutional amendment providing for the apportionment of state senators by county while specifically rejecting one that would have established both houses on the basis of population: ". . . an individual's constitutionally protected right to cast an equally weighted vote cannot be denied even by a vote of a majority of a State's electorate, if the apportionment scheme adopted by the voters fails to measure up to the requirements of the Equal Protection Clause." [24]

What are the likely effects of *Baker* and its progeny? By increasing the pace of reapportionment it will give greater representation to the urban and suburban voter and for the most part should benefit the Democratic party and liberal causes. Although there are exceptions—in Maryland, Texas, Arizona, and the South, Republican strength is suburban and often urban, so that malapportionment has hurt the Republicans—outside of the South, rural America is more Republican and more conservative than are the large cities and their suburbs. But since in the North the major benefactors will be the suburbs rather than the largest cities, and since the political differences between rural and suburban voters is less than that between rural and large-city voters, the consequence of reapportionment in the North may not be as drastic as some Republican conservatives fear or liberal Democrats hope.

In the South, however, in states such as Georgia, Florida, and Tennessee where Atlanta, Miami, and Memphis have been so grossly under-represented in the state legislatures, the impact of reapportionment will be of great significance. It is the rural areas where the Democratic party is the strongest and segregation sentiment

[24] *Lucas* v. *Forty-fourth General Assembly of Colorado,* (1964.)

the most intense. Under-representation of southern cities has permitted conservative, segregation-minded rural areas to dominate state legislatures. Reapportionment will make this more difficult; already in Georgia reapportionment has increased the voice of Atlanta's citizens in the state legislature, as reflected in the
election to that body of ten Negroes.

The impact of reapportionment on other areas of public policy is harder to predict. A comparison of legislation adopted in states that have under-represented
urban voters with that adopted in states with fairer urban representation fails to
show any significant differences in many areas of public policy. Metropolitan and
non-metropolitan legislators have seldom opposed each other in unified voting
blocs.[25] Nonetheless, it is obvious that to change the constituencies to whom legislators are accountable is to make a major change in the political system.

Certainly the legislators and their constituents who are involved in the conflict
over reapportionment have no doubt that they are battling over an important
issue. Fox Hodgdon, town representative of Granby (which has a population of
56 and replaced its oil lamps with electricity in 1963) in the Vermont legislature,
eloquently states the position of the rural forces:

> This reapportionment will have it so we'll all be governed by these city
> people without the counter-balance from the country to stop runaway legisla-
> tion. It will be quite a mess. . . . We'll fight 'em though. . . . We'll fight
> and never give up.[26]

The stakes are obviously high for Fox Hodgdon and his counterparts throughout
rural America. Generally speaking, political power is slowly shifting from rural to
urban America—a shift of which *Baker* v. *Carr* and *Reynolds* v. *Sims* are both cause
and consequence.

Direct Democracy

Some of our states have given the people themselves the power to make their own
laws. Around the turn of the twentieth century, one of the reformers' battle cries
was to "return the government to the people" through the initiative, referendum,
and recall. Give the voters the power to make or veto laws and to recall officials,
they asserted, and the political machines will be destroyed and the special interests
routed. Opponents vehemently replied that measures such as these would destroy

[25] Dye, *op. cit.*, p. 163; Herbert Jacob, "The Consequences of Malapportionment: A Note
of Caution," *Social Forces* (December 1964), pp. 256–261; David R. Derge, "Metropolitan
and Outstate Alignments in Illinois and Missouri Legislative Delegations, *The American Political
Science Review* (December 1958), pp. 1051–1065. There is some uncertainty among political
scientists about the matter: see Richard T. Frost, "On Derge's Metropolitan and Outstate
Legislative Delegations," *The American Political Science Review* (September 1959), pp. 792–795;
and Robert S. Friedman, "The Urban-Rural Conflict Revisited," *Western Political Quarterly*
(June 1961), pp. 481–495.

[26] Joe Heaney, "A Vermonter Bows to Reapportionment," Boston *Globe*, June 27, 1965.

representative government and open the way for crackpot and radical legislation.

During the first two decades of this century, about twenty states, mostly in the West, adopted the initiative and referendum, and so did hundreds of cities, especially those with commission and city manager forms of government (see Chapter 31). A smaller number of states and cities also adopted the recall.

The details of these procedures differ, but their purpose is everywhere the same. The *initiative* allows voters to enact legislation or constitutional amendments when the legislature fails to act; the *referendum* permits a majority of the voters to veto legislation or reject constitutional amendments; and the *recall* allows the electorate to eject an elected public official from his job before the end of his term.

The *referendum* is simply a way of letting the people vote on proposed measures. The referendum is required in every state except Delaware for the ratification of constitutional amendments. As applied to legislation, there are two general types of referenda, *mandatory* and *optional*. The *mandatory* referendum calls for a waiting period, usually sixty to ninety days, before legislation goes into effect. If during this period a prescribed number of voters sign a referendum petition requesting that the act be referred to the voters, the law does not go into effect unless a majority of the voters give their approval at the next election. (The legislature may sidestep this by declaring the law to be "emergency legislation" to go into immediate effect.) The *optional* legislative referendum permits the legislature, at its discretion, to provide that a measure shall not become law until it has been approved by the voters at an election.

The *direct initiative* applies in some states to constitutional amendments and to legislation. In other states, it can be used for only one or the other. In a state that permits the use of the initiative, an individual or group of voters may, on their own initiative, draft a proposed law. After the supporters have secured a certain number of signatures (often 5 to 10 per cent of the total electorate), the measure is placed before the voters at the next election.

In some states, the *indirect initiative* is used, which gives the legislature an opportunity to act on the measure before it is referred to the voters. If the legislature does not approve, the proposed legislation is then placed on the ballot, although in some states additional signatures are required.

Only twelve states provide for *recall* of state officers, but many others permit the recall of local officials. Recall also requires a petition, but more signatures are usually needed than in the case of the initiative and referendum. There are various kinds of recall election. In some, the official must stand on his record; in others, candidates are permitted to file and run against him.

30 GOVERNORS AND JUDGES

Like the national government, each state government is organized into three branches: legislative, executive, and judicial. Hence, every state is a test tube for the American experiment in government, the experiment of mingling powers among the several branches of government and of making different leaders accountable to different electorates. Each state, to a greater or less degree, makes it difficult for a simple majority of the voters to win power; each requires, to some extent, rule by concurrent majorities.

But the governmental and political systems of the states are not all alike. Formal constitutional structures may be roughly the same, but other vital aspects of government and politics—local idea-systems, interest groups, voting, parties, public attitudes, administrative arrangements—may differ widely. Indeed, the state governments dramatize the fact that constitutional *form* is only one element of government. Almost as many differences can be found between one state with a fully developed two-party system, a strong chief executive, and centralized administration, and another state with a diffused one-party system, weak governor, and decentralized administration, as can be found between our national government and that of Great Britain or France. State executives and judiciaries are a case in point.

His Excellency—the Governor

The story of the office of American governor is a progression "from detested minion of Royal power, to stepson of legislative domination, to popular figurehead, to effective executive." [1] "A strong executive is an engine of tyranny"— that was the spirit in which the office was born. Then during the period of Jacksonian Democracy, the idea spread that the people should directly elect all top officials of government, and the governor became only one of many elected officials. Nevertheless, beginning slowly and picking up speed during the last fifty years, the office of governor has grown in importance and power.

In over half the states, the governor is elected for a four-year term; in the others, for two years. The trend is toward the longer term. In about half the states where he has a four-year term (mostly southern and border states) the governor is ineligible for a second consecutive term. His salary ranges from a high of $50,000 in New York to a low of $10,000 in North Dakota and Arkansas, with the average being about $21,000. In addition, most governors receive an expense allowance.

Because of the average governor's relatively low salary, short tenure, and limited powers, we might think that it would be difficult to get able men to run for the office. But this is not so. The governor enjoys great prestige in his state. Governors of the larger states are national figures. They often control powerful political machines. The office may be an important step toward national office—the Senate or even the Presidency. [2]

[1] William H. Young, "The Development of the Governorship," *State Government* (Summer 1958), p. 183.
[2] Duane Lockard, *The Politics of State and Local Government* (Macmillan, 1963), pp. 395–398.

The Governor as Chief Executive

"The executive power," says the federal Constitution, "shall be vested in the President of the United States." Compare this flat statement with its counterpart in a typical state constitution: "The executive department shall consist of a Governor, Lieutenant Governor, Secretary of State, Auditor, Treasurer, Superintendent of Public Instruction, Attorney General," and perhaps other officials. In other words, the state governor shares the executive power with numerous other *elected* officers. Most state constitutions, nevertheless, go on to say that "the Supreme executive power shall be vested in the Governor, who shall take care that the laws be faithfully executed." And it is the governor to whom the public looks for law enforcement and the supervision of administrative agencies.

Governor Samuel W. Pennypacker, Pennsylvania's chief executive in 1903–1907, once told how he had come to office eager to insure that the laws of the state were faithfully executed. Looking around to see what instruments he had to carry out this responsibility, he discovered that the only persons to whom he could look for help were his secretary, the janitor, and his chauffeur. The prosecutors and police, locally elected and locally controlled, were subject to little or no gubernatorial supervision. The attorney general was elected by the voters and not responsible to the governor. Of course, the governor could call out the National Guard, but that is a clumsy way to enforce the law. "So," said Governor Pennypacker, "I created the state police." Today all states have a police organization. And in some states the governor has been given authority to supervise the activities of local prosecutors. Even so, most governors lack the means of seeing that "the laws are faithfully executed."

State governments, like their national counterpart, consist of a vast web of administrative agencies ranging from Departments of Finance to Bureaus of Rodent Control. How does a governor supervise this administrative structure? During the nineteenth century, as the states took on more and more new functions, new agencies were added more or less haphazardly. Boards and commissions were established, power parceled out among numerous officials, the long ballot (see page 339) created with its many elective offices, and lines of authority and responsibility hopelessly tangled. The ship of state tacked first one way, then another, and the governor had little power to control the administration.

Such was the general state of affairs until the second decade of the present century. Then in 1917 the administrative reorganization movement was born in Illinois. Following its example, state after state made some effort to unravel the tangled web that had come to characterize their administrative structure. The reorganizers hammered away at one basic formula: Reduce the number of elected officials, integrate the executive structure under the governor's direction, give the governor the executive authority he needs, and let the people hold him accountable for the effective administration of the laws. Better to make the governor the manager of the administration, they argued, than to leave the job to behind-the-scenes bosses.

The most important weapon in the governor's arsenal is his control over the *budget*. In those states in which he prepares and presents the budget to the legislature and in which he has the item veto, he can control to a considerable extent the flow of funds to the executive departments and hence, affect their activities—always assuming, of course, that he has sufficient political power to make his budget and his veto stick. Purchasing, fiscal, and personnel matters, moreover, are frequently centralized under the governor. When assisted by a strong staff, and backed by strong political power, the governor has significant control over the course of administration.

The trend toward integrated administration is still strong. In the urban states with a competitive party system such as New York, Illinois, New Jersey, Pennsylvania, Washington, and California, governors have considerable formal constitutional authority. But integrated administration is by no means an accomplished fact. In a number of states—especially southern and border states—governors have relatively little formal constitutional authority.[3] In all states the governor is still one executive among many, with only limited authority over his subordinates. He has almost no authority over the elected officials. He neither appoints them, nor can he dismiss them. If they are his political enemies, they will not accept his leadership. The governor has greater but still limited power over appointed executive officials. In most states he shares the appointive power with the senate and may remove subordinates only when they have violated the law or failed in their legal duties.

Governor's Helpers—or Enemies?

In many states the other executive officials elected by the people include the lieutenant governor, secretary of state, attorney general, treasurer, and auditor. What do they do?

The *Lieutenant Governor* does very little. He presides over the senate and, in most states, in case of the death, disability, or absence of the governor from the state, he becomes governor or acting governor. The twelve states lacking a lieutenant governor do not seem to miss him. Since the lieutenant governor is often leader of a party faction opposed to the governor, he may become a thorn in the side of the chief executive. There is a tendency, though not a marked one, to enlarge the duties of the lieutenant governor.

The *Secretary of State* is custodian of the state records and keeper of the state seal. He publishes the laws, supervises elections, and issues certificates of incorporation. In some states, he issues automobile licenses and registers corporate securities. His office is often the "dumping ground" for jobs that do not seem to

---

[3] Joseph A. Schlesinger, "The Politics of the Executive," in H. Jacob and K. N. Vines (eds.), *Politics in the American States: A Comparative Analysis* (Little, Brown, 1965), pp. 231–232. For a general discussion of the power resources of the governor, see Lockard, *op. cit.*, pp. 367–395.

belong to any existing office and are not important enough to justify setting up a new agency.

The *Attorney General* is the governor's lawyer. His office gives advice to state officials, represents the state before the courts, and supervises local prosecutors. Some attorneys general have real authority over local prosecutors and may prosecute cases on their own initiative. The attorney generalship is often a stepping-stone to the governorship, and occasionally attorneys general have made political capital out of their investigations of the state administration.

The *Treasurer* is custodian of state funds. Although in some states he has tax-collection duties, in most states his job is largely ministerial.

The *Auditor* has two major jobs: to authorize disbursements from the treasury, and to make periodic audits of officials who handle state money. Before money can be spent, the auditor must sign a warrant indicating that he is convinced that the appropriation is authorized by law and that money is available in the treasury. This is the *pre-audit,* which many students believe should be given to a comptroller appointed by and responsible to the governor. The auditing *after* the money has been spent, however, is a job that most students believe should be vested in an officer responsible to the legislature. The auditor is the one official who, even in the opinion of some of the most extreme advocates of centralized administration, should not be responsible to the governor.

As part of the trend toward integrated administration, the duties of elected state officials have generally been limited to the functions specified in the constitution, with the more critical functions given to officials appointed by the governor. The budget directors and agency chiefs under the governor in many states have more important roles than the state treasurer or the secretary of state. Yet these elected officers with their limited but constitutionally protected duties often control patronage, attract a following, and thus develop a political base from which they can attack the governor's program and administration.

The Reorganization Movement and Its Critics

The wave of state reorganizations that followed World War I was repeated after World War II under the stimulus of the national Hoover Commission. Most of the states appointed their own "Little Hoover Commissions" to recommend improvements in the state governmental structure.

Attempts to reorganize state governments have not received universal praise. In many states, the commissions get together, make studies, and submit reports— which are soon filed away and forgotten.[4] Groups that profit from the existing structure—for example, those who have a pet bureau under their influence—can be counted upon to resist changes. And so can public officials who fear loss of job or prestige. Legislators who suspect that the recommendations will make the

[4] Karl A. Bosworth, "The Politics of Management Improvement in the States," *The American Political Science Review* (March 1953), pp. 84–99.

governor too powerful are often reluctant to approve them. And politicians who have lived within the existing structure and know their way around in it are naturally reluctant to give up a good thing.

Another group of critics opposes not so much the idea of reorganization but the basic principle that has dominated the movement. This is the principle of *executive power* and *responsibility*. During the last several decades, reorganizers have plumped for the proposition that the governor should be made the manager of the executive branch. They have developed the following canons of reorganization:

1. All agencies should be consolidated and integrated into as few departments as possible, so that similar functions will be grouped together and the governor's span of control will be manageable.

2. Lines of responsibility should be fixed and definite.

3. Single-head executives are to be preferred over boards and commissions.

4. The governor should have power to appoint and remove subordinates, including officers who are now elected, with the possible exception of the auditor.

5. The governor should have control over budgeting, accounting, reporting, purchasing, personnel, and planning, and should have the staff he needs to do these jobs.

But some critics, though they agree that centralized budgeting, purchasing, and the like, are all very well, argue that conditions differ in each state and that no "cookie-cutter" pattern of administration will fit all conditions. There is little evidence, they argue, to support the proposed reforms other than the assurance of the reorganizers themselves and their citing of each other as authorities. What evidence do we have, they ask, that the people will hold the governor accountable and that the governor will devote his time and energy to administrative matters? Most governors are chiefly interested in legislative problems, not in administrative details, and are seldom judged on their executive talent. Furthermore, the critics decry the emphasis on efficiency and economy. There is a real danger, they argue, that the reorganizers are overlooking basic values in their concern with saving money. The threat of executive tyranny, they fear, is dismissed too cavalierly. As one critic put it, "Men invited to recommend a program which promises efficiency and economy for a state . . . have not only mistaken supposition for fact and hypothesis for principle; they have failed to warn their clients . . . of the enormous risk involved in creating a powerful chief executive in a state which has no responsible legislature and in many instances no effective opposition party." [5]

The reorganizers are quick to answer their critics: Of course it is ridiculous to make changes, they grant, without regard to local conditions and problems.

[5] C. S. Hyneman, "Administrative Reorganization: An Adventure into Science and Theology," *The Journal of Politics* (February 1939), pp. 74–75. For another presentation of this view, see Robert B. Highsaw, "The Southern Governor—Challenge to the Strong Executive Theme," *Public Administration Review* (Winter 1959), pp. 7–11.

But the basic idea—integrated authority, centralized direction, simplified structure—is sound. There would be little danger of dictators. In fact, it is more likely that men not responsible to the electorate will take over government when the administrative structure is cumbersome, confusing, and diffused. The legislature can more effectively supervise an administration integrated under the governor's control than one in which responsibility is diffused.[6] In actual fact, in states where the governor's formal authority is slight, special interests have found it easier to dominate administrative programs than in states where gubernatorial authority is strong.

Effects of Reorganization

What have been the results of a half century of reorganization? Again there is controversy. Some observers say that reorganization has not given us more efficient or democratic government. Others say it has. Still others say there is little evidence one way or another. Often the reorganizations result only in changes in organization charts but have no significant impact on actual operations. Large savings have been realized through centralized purchasing and the adoption of modern fiscal practices, but it is difficult to measure the results of the consolidation of departments and the strengthening of the governor's control over the executive branch.[7]

At the same time, the best-governed states do seem to be those in which the administrative structure has been closely integrated under the governor. Whether this integration has *caused* good government in those states is another, though closely related, question.

The basic idea of reorganization is to apply what we know to improve what we have. But to make reorganization pay the biggest dividends, it must be a continuous process of adjustment. Recently some states, notably Michigan and Alaska, have recognized this truth and have adopted reorganization procedures similar to those on the national level. The governor is granted authority to submit to the state legislatures reorganization proposals that if not disapproved within a certain period are automatically put into effect.

The reorganization of state administrative procedure is almost always justified in terms of efficiency and economy. Few would deny the importance of saving money, but it is doubtful if the costs of operating our state governments can be substantially reduced except by reducing their functions. To save money and to increase efficiency are important, but these are not the only objectives of government or the only criteria for judging its operations. The question must always be: reorganization for what? Not merely to save money but to strengthen democratic government.

[6] Coleman B. Ransome, Jr., *The Office of Governor in the United States* (Univ. of Alabama Press, 1956), pp. 378–386.

[7] W. H. Edwards, "Has State Reorganization Succeeded?" *State Government* (October 1938), pp. 184–185.

The Governor as Legislative and Party Chief

Just as the role of the President in determining national policy has grown over the last several decades, so has the governor become a more active participant in the making of state policy. In fact, some governors have far more influence over their legislatures than even the strongest of our presidents have had over theirs. The governor has the constitutional power to call the legislature into special session and in some states to specify what the legislators can discuss in such sessions. He is authorized to address the legislature and send messages to it. He has the responsibility in forty-three of the states to submit the budget to the legislature. Moreover, in all states except North Carolina, he has strong veto powers, usually much stronger than those of the President.

In all but nine states, the governor, in addition to the regular qualified veto, has the power to strike out—that is, *veto*—individual items in appropriations measures while approving the rest. In a few states, the governor can even reduce a particular appropriation. The *item veto*, like all vetoes can be overridden by the legislature (normally a two-thirds vote in both chambers is required), but in many states most new laws are sent to the governor after the legislature has adjourned. Thus when he vetoes bills or items of appropriations, there is no chance for the legislature to override the veto.

How much legislative influence do governors have? Although their constitutional authority varies a good deal, their actual ability to influence legislative policy varies even more widely from state to state and from time to time than a reading of the constitutions might suggest. Much depends on the governor's ability, his personal popularity, the political situation in which he operates. Some states have a long tradition of executive leadership; when the governor has the support of powerful political organizations, he can guide policy. The governors of New York and Illinois, for example, have strong constitutional positions, and they are also likely to have strong party organizations behind them and close ties with their party followers in the legislature. Furthermore, governors of these large states, and others like Ohio, Pennsylvania, and California with active two-party systems, are potential presidential candidates. These governors—men like William Scranton of Pennsylvania or Pat Brown of California—attract the national spotlight. Many of them look forward to national political careers, and each speaks with the authority of a man who might some day be President of the United States. In these states the governorship attracts able men and gives them great prestige and power. But even in states where the governor is less likely to be a national figure, he can derive power from a large popular following or a strong party organization. And we have to be cautious in making comparative statements. The governor of rural Mississippi has much less formal power than does the governor of New York, and on the national political scene he carries little weight.

Yet within his own state his control over minor jobs, contracts, and patronage may make him a pivotal figure. The governor of New York must operate through more formal machinery in a highly complex state containing many power sources able to compete with the governor on his own terms.[8] Few governors of New York have ever been able to dominate their own state legislature to the same extent as have some of the formally "weak," but politically powerful southern governors.

Emergency Powers

Emergencies enhance the authority of the executive, for they call for swift and decisive measures. The governor is commander in chief of the state's National Guard when it is not in federal service. He is responsible for using this force when the ordinary civil authorities are inadequate—in case of riots, floods, and other catastrophes. During the depression of the 1930's many governors used the Guard, not always too wisely, to handle various social disturbances. And hardly a year goes by in which the Guard of some state does not see emergency duty. In about three-fourths of the states, the governor also has a state police force at his command.

The national government has the major responsibility for providing for the national defense, but the states also have vital jobs. The governor is authorized to safeguard public safety in times of emergency—for example, to regulate supplies of fuel and electric power, or to issue orders for air-raid protection. The civil defense program places the major responsibility on the states, and in almost all cases, the states have turned the job over to the governor. He is normally advised by a civil defense council which helps him supervise and coordinate the civil defense activities of local governments.

A Judicial Function

The governor in half the states has the *pardoning power*, and in the others he shares in this heavy duty. Persons who have violated the *state* law look to the governor "to temper justice with mercy." The governor may, except in cases of certain specified crimes such as treason or in cases of impeachment, pardon the offender or commute his sentence by reducing its severity, or grant a reprieve by delaying the punishment. The governor is normally assisted by pardon attorneys or pardon boards who hold hearings and sift the evidence to determine where there are extenuating circumstances. But it is the governor who usually is faced with the responsibility of the decision. Many are the stories of governors maintaining all-night vigils when men are destined to die for their crimes. The governor as the last earthly judge has an unenviable task.

[8] Schlesinger, *op. cit.*, p. 231.

The Governor as Party Chief

Like the President, the governor is usually considered leader of his party in the state. But the governor faces more rivals for party leadership than does the man in the White House. A United States senator may dominate the state party, or a large section of it. County politics may be controlled by "courthouse rings" intent only on electing local candidates. But the most serious problems, from the governor's viewpoint, arise from the fact that the other separately elected state officials, such as attorney general, often share power over the state party just as they share the executive power.

In theory, a state party system is supposed to help integrate all the executive officials into a functioning team. In reality, it often makes for divisions within the state administration. In one-party states, the same party wins control of all the executive officers in all or most of the elections. But it is precisely in these one-party states, where the dominant party faces the weakest opposition, that the parties have the "least capacity to tie together the work of the scattered agencies of government. Whatever order and coherence develops within the administration in one-party situations must rest on some factor other than the tie of party. When one party holds both governorship and minor offices without effective challenge, the incentives for collaboration among fellow partisans are not apt to be strong." [9]

In states where parties are more evenly matched, a single party seldom carries the whole slate of executive officials. Where the Republican party tends to be stronger —as in most states outside the South and the border states—the Democrats encounter difficulty in getting a full slate elected. Although, as the lesser of the two parties, the Democrats may gather enough strength to elevate one of their men to the gubernatorial office, it takes an unusually sizable victory for them to gain control of the entire executive slate. The Republicans have the same difficulty in border and other states where the Democrats are normally the larger party.

When control of the executive departments is split between the two parties, neither party is likely to assume responsibility for over-all administration. Moreover, when the governor has to work with officials from the opposite party, teamwork, difficult under the best of circumstances, is almost impossible to achieve. It is precisely in states where party competition is keenest and party control of executive offices is divided, that we are most likely to find strongly disciplined parties. Thus, as Key has observed, we are confronted with a dilemma: In states where a party has unchallenged control of all executive positions, the party organization is apt to be too weak to impose a unified program on the several officials. But where party bonds are tight enough to impose a cohesive program, the party is often unable to win all the executive positions. (See footnote 9.)

[9] V. O. Key, Jr., *American State Politics* (Knopf, 1956), pp. 200–201.

Governors on the Spot

Not too long ago governors had it fairly easy; it was considered the best platform from which to launch a presidential career. The governor made speeches in favor of civic virtue, balanced the state budget, organized campaigns against crime, took a few well-publicized trips abroad to emphasize his knowledge of foreign affairs, and watched his rivals in the Senate lose political support because their roles required them to take stands on controversial issues.

Today the life of a governor is more difficult. People want better schools, including higher education for all; uncluttered six-lane highways that do not require condemnation of any land; adequate welfare payments; aid to local school districts; civil rights; safe cities; clean air and streams; and they expect the governor to meet all these needs without proposing higher taxes. The governor has become the major political power in the state, but he has acquired the liabilities that accompany the assets. Senators, not governors, are now leading candidates for the presidency. Of course, the situation is not quite so simple, and sometimes men leave the Senate to run for governor because of the greater ease of "standing out from the crowd." There is only one governor of the state. But governors no longer preside; they govern.

The State Judiciary

The judges of our state courts do most of the judicial business in the United States (see Chapter 19). They preside over most of the criminal trials, settle most of the disputes between individuals, and administer most of the estates. They interpret their state constitutions and apply state laws. Of course, they are required by the federal Constitution to follow the federal Constitution, federal laws, and federal treaties, "anything in the constitution or laws of any state to the contrary notwithstanding."

Except for the practicing members of the bar, many people know little about their judges, not even the name of the chief judge of their own supreme court. But these judges—perhaps even more than those of our federal courts—are important policy-makers. The legislature passes the law, but the judges interpret it. The state judges, in determining the "reasonableness" of legislative classifications, in deciding whether a state regulation of business is "arbitrary," in forcing county officials to comply with the law, in ruling whether the city council has exceeded its authority, in deciding whether the governor has the power to remove a local district attorney, play as vital a role as the other branches of government in determining who gets what, when, where, and how.

Our understanding of American government would be incomplete unless we knew how these judges operate, what is their relation to the legislature, the executive, and interest groups, what procedures they use, how they are chosen, and what groups have the greatest voice in selecting them. Our answers must be very tentative, however. Only recently have the state courts come in for serious study.[10] In the past, they tended to be obscured by the federal court system or by the other branches of the state government. Moreover, each state has its own unique court system. There is such tremendous variety in their procedures and structural arrangements that it is difficult to generalize. But for convenience, we can classify state courts into three groups: minor courts of limited jurisdiction, general trial courts, and appellate courts.

Minor and Trial Courts

W. D. Brogan, the celebrated English student of American politics, has written of one of his adventures in America:

> I had often heard of the "Jeddart justice" doled out by rural magistrates to motorists, of the iniquities of paying magistrates on a commission basis, of the insult to the law and its majesty which these methods involved. My host, whose car was moving rapidly down the great highway to the warm sun and true spring of Central Illinois after the rain, fog, and cold of the shores of Lake Michigan, had written on the subject. He had been the pupil and the collaborator of one of the greatest of American constitutional lawyers. His opinion was worth having. A car was backed off the road and a policeman signalled us in. I innocently assumed that there had been an accident, that we were being asked to take someone to hospital. How wrong I was! We were pinched for speeding. The traffic cop's not very smart uniform bore the words "Special Police." He had cartridges on his belt; they were of different colours and may have been dummies, but he was in complete command of the situation. He demanded the license which was fortunately available. He gave instructions. "Turn round and stop at the grocery store." "Can I make a U-turn?" asked my host ironically. "Sure." We entered the grocery store, and there was American justice at the receipt of custom.
>
> The magistrate was a bronzed jurist in a shabby shirt. He had one arm and no badge of office. This was not the Old Bailey. The representative of the "Senatus Populusque Illinoisensis" required no fasces, no mace to impress his customers. He duly pointed out that the accused could claim a jury trial, but that if he didn't, and pleaded guilty, the whole thing could be expedited.
>
> The policeman's complaint-sheet was produced; a conviction for speeding was duly entered in it; a receipt (a flimsy piece of paper) was issued. Ten dollars fine, $4 costs (which we believed went to the jurist). In two minutes it was all over. After all, there were other customers. My friend had "a record"; for the first time in his life he had been in an American police court.

---

[10] See Stuart S. Nagel, "Political Party Affiliation and Judges' Decisions," *The American Political Science Review* (December 1961), pp. 843–850; Kenneth N. Vines and Herbert Jacob, *Studies in Judicial Politics* (Tulane Studies in Political Science, 1963).

In a famous opinion Mr. Justice Frankfurter had laid it down that a court of the American system was not to be compared to the court of a Cadi sitting down under a tree. There was no tree, simply a third-rate village store. I recalled Mr. Frankfurter's dictum to my friend. He was not consoled. He thought of various points he might have made. The "esprit d'escalier" worked overtime. He recalled what he had written on this aspect of the American judicial system. I tried to console him by pointing out that he had got down from his ivory tower as the song suggested. He was not amused. He had got out of the ivory tower all right, but as another song puts it, "Baby, it's cold outside." [11]

Unfortunately, this story is too typical of the way justice is administered in our *minor courts.* These courts handle summary offenses or misdemeanors and civil suits involving relatively small amounts of money. They are minor only in the sense that they provide accessible forums for the settlement of small suits and for the trial of petty offenses. But it is in these courts that most disputes are settled. A $50 judgment is "small potatoes" as these things go; but to the parties involved, it is no small matter. Although decisions of these minor courts may be appealed and tried *de novo*—that is, tried all over again without reference to what happened before the minor court—few people bother.

Of course, there is another side to the story. The defendant in the above case was evidently guilty of speeding. A basic canon of justice—the separation of the prosecuting from the judicial functions—was observed. The fine was not out of proportion to the offense. Appeal to a jury was allowed if desired. To be sure, the whole proceeding was informal and undignified, but greater dignity and formality would have meant a more expensive court and probably higher costs for the defendant.

The most common type of minor courts are justice of the peace courts. The J.P., as he is popularly known, is usually elected for a two- or four-year term by the people of each township, but his jurisdiction extends throughout the county. In addition to solemnizing marriages and notarizing papers, he is the man, especially in small towns and rural places, who fines traffic violators, decides who should go to the workhouse for 30 days, and settles disputes between neighbors about who hit whom first. He usually has power to determine who should be "held over" for possible indictment by the grand jury. He sets bail and handles the preliminaries in more serious criminal matters.

The J.P. does not need to be trained in the law, and few of them are. Their lack of legal training has aroused much criticism, but a more glaring weakness is that J.P.'s are commonly paid out of the fees they collect. Plaintiffs have their choice among several justices of the peace; and in order to get as much business as possible, J.P.'s have been known to advertise quietly to plaintiffs that they should bring their cases to them to be assured that "justice will be done." Several studies have

[11] W. D. Brogan, "Down from the Ivory Tower," *The Manchester Guardian Weekly,* May 31, 1956, p. 11. See also Isham G. Newton, "The Justice of the Peace—An American Judicial Dilemma," *Social Science* (April 1959).

concluded that J.P. virtually stands for "Judgment for the Plaintiff." Even worse, despite the fact that the Supreme Court has condemned the practice, some J.P.'s get larger fees in criminal matters when the defendant is found guilty and costs are assessed against him. Even where it is not abused, the fee system leads to distrust and suspicion. The justice of the peace system is slowly losing ground. Some states have replaced justices of the peace with magistrates who are paid a standard salary and who are required to have a knowledge of the law, and five states and many counties have withdrawn all judicial powers from the J.P.'s.

In cities, there are other minor courts, some of which have more jurisdiction than the justice of the peace and handle more serious matters. Municipal courts are frequently divided into traffic courts, police courts, juvenile and domestic relations courts. A small-claims court with informal procedures is provided by some cities to handle cases for a small set fee.

Trial courts with complete original jurisdiction are variously called county courts, circuit courts, superior courts, district courts, and common pleas courts. They administer equity, criminal, common, and statutory law (see Chapter 19). Some states maintain separate courts, however, for criminal and civil matters. More commonly, there are special probate courts to administer estates and to handle related matters. Although decisions of the general trial courts may be reviewed by appellate courts, in practice the trial court has final say in approximately 90 per cent of all cases.

Appellate Courts

In most states, appeals from the trial courts are carried to the state supreme court, but fourteen states have set up intermediate appeals courts that fit into the court structure in much the same way that the United States courts of appeals fit into the federal structure.

The court of final resort is usually called the supreme court. (In New York, the Supreme Court is a trial court, and the court of last resort is called the Court of Appeals.) Unless a federal question is involved, the state supreme courts are the highest to which a case may be carried.

The appellate courts vary from three to nine in membership, with seven being the most common number. State judges have the power of judicial review and may refuse to enforce state laws on the grounds that they violate the state or national constitution. They may also declare federal laws unconstitutional, although of course such decisions are subject to review by the United States Supreme Court. All state judges take an oath to uphold the supremacy of the federal Constitution, laws, and treaties, despite anything in their own constitutions or laws.

Ten states permit the supreme court to give *advisory opinions* to the legislature or the governor upon request. These advisory opinions are not binding except in Colorado; they are regarded as the opinions of the judges rather than as court decisions.

How Are Judges Chosen?

Judges are chosen in several ways. *Popular election* is used in about three-fourths of the states. In the others—primarily eastern states—the judges are either *appointed by the governor* (with the consent of the senate or executive council) or *elected by the legislature*. Recently, some members of the bar have grown dissatisfied with the method of choosing judges by popular election. They argue that the voters are not competent to assess legal learning and judicial abilities. Popular election, they assert, puts a premium on a pleasing personality and political popularity, requires judges to enter into the political arena, and discourages many able lawyers from running for the office. Furthermore, they insist, judges are often in effect appointed by party leaders despite the elective apparatus. Lower court judges may be active members of the local political organization and gain and retain their offices because of faithful party service. At

PRINCIPAL METHODS FOR THE SELECTION OF JUDGES

Elected by popular vote, with minor exceptions in some states.

Selected by legislature.

Trial judges appointed by executive, others selected by popular or legislative vote.

Appointed by executive subject to confirmation, with minor exceptions in some states.

Modified appointment plans applicable to some or all judges.

(Source: National Conference of Judicial Councils.)

the appellate level the governor often makes an interim appointment to fill vacancies created by resignation, retirement, or death of a sitting judge; and the interim appointee as the incumbent usually wins at the next election. In fact, more than half of all judges sitting on elective courts of last resort first came to that court as appointees of the governor.[12]

Some states have turned to the nonpartisan primary for nominating judges or have held the election of judges on a separate day from the election of other officers. But these devices have not substantially altered the importance of party leaders. And those who oppose the elective system argue that the problem is not one of party but of politics. Should judges be accountable directly to the people? Should they not be indirectly responsible, so that they could better serve as a check on the popular majorities who act through the governor and the legislature? What, in short, is the role of judges in a democracy (see Chapter 19). Those who favor the popular election of judges believe that to have them appointed by the governor would destroy popular control, divorce the judges from the electorate, give the governor too much power, and encourage judges to become the governor's pawn.

Is there any alternative method? California, Missouri, and several other states have developed ways of selecting judges that are designed to eliminate the defects of popular election but still retain popular control. In Missouri, whenever a vacancy occurs in a court to which the plan applies, a special nominating commission, composed of three lawyers elected by the bar, three laymen appointed by the governor, and the chief justice, nominates three candidates. The governor selects one who serves as a judge for at least one year. The voters at the next general election are asked, "Shall Judge —— be retained in office?" If a majority of the voters answer yes, the judge gets a full new term; if not, another person is selected by the same procedure. At the expiration of his term, the judge does not have to be renominated and reappointed; he merely certifies his wish to have his name placed on the ballot, and the voters are asked whether they want to retain him in office.[13]

The dispute over the relative merits of appointive and elective systems of judicial selection has been raging for more than 150 years. Courts in appointive states seem to have generally, but not always, a higher standing among the members of the bar than those in elective states. Leaders of lawyers' groups tend to favor the appointive method. Yet there is little clear-cut evidence that the method of judicial selection makes any difference in the kinds of judicial decisions made.

[12] James Herndon, "Appointment as a Means of Initial Accession to Elective Courts of Last Resort," *North Dakota Law Review*, Vol. 38, 1962, pp. 60–73; Emmett W. Bashful, *The Florida Supreme Court: A Study in Judicial Selection* (Florida Bureau of Governmental Research and Service, 1958); Kenneth N. Vines, "The Selection of Judges in Louisiana," in Vines and Jacob (eds.), *op. cit.*, pp. 99–119; and Bancroft Henderson and T. C. Sinclair, *Judicial Selection in Texas, An Exploratory Study* (Univ. of Houston Public Affairs Research Center, 1964).

[13] Robert F. Karsch, *Essentials of Missouri Government*, 3rd ed. (Lucas Bros., 1953), pp. 113–115. See also Harry Gershenson, "Experience in Missouri," *American Bar Association Journal* (March 1960), pp. 287 ff; Richard A. Watson, Rondal G. Downing, and Frederick C. Spiegel, "Lawyers and Judicial Selection Under the Missouri Plan," paper delivered at the 1964 Annual Meeting of the American Political Science Association, September, 1964.

31 GOVERNMENT AT THE GRASS ROOTS

There are over 91,000 units of local government in the United States (about 90,000 too many, some people feel). Illinois alone has over 6,400. Rhode Island, with fewer than any other state except Alaska and Hawaii, has almost 100. Cities, counties, school districts, townships, water control districts, park districts—all are crowded together and piled on top of one another. The average citizen lives under five or six layers of government.

779

He pays taxes to all of them—federal, state, county, municipal, and others—and he is supposed to participate in the selection of the persons in charge of all these governments.

Why do we have such a patchwork of governments? The basic pattern was imported from England, like so many of our governmental forms. As the years passed, new governments were created to take on new jobs when the existing units were too small or were not up to the job. Decades of compromise and struggle among conflicting groups have given us our present system. It creaks and groans. It costs a lot of money. It is not very efficient. But there it is.

Local governments vary in structure, size, power, and relation to one another. But in a constitutional sense, they are all the same in that they all live on power "borrowed" from states. The states of our Union are basically *unitary* governments —that is, constitutionally all power is vested in the state government, with local units existing only as agents of the states and exercising power given to them by the state government.

"Little Federalism": State-Local Relations

How does the *unitary* nature of state-local relations contrast with the *federal* nature of nation-state relations? The slicing up of governmental power among the various local units and the state government leads to many of the same problems that we noted in the chapters on federalism. There is the same conflict between groups that want the state to do something and groups that fear an invasion of local rights. There is the same difficulty of constantly adjusting functions among the various units of government as economic and social conditions alter. There are the same vexing disputes over whether a local majority or a state-wide majority is to have its way. And just as the assignment of functions between the national and state governments is determined largely by the strength of conflicting interests, so it is between the state and local governments.

Since local governments, however, are created by the state legislatures and have no power in their own right, fewer constitutional obstacles and weaker pressures act against state interference in local matters than against national interference in state affairs. State officers participate in local government to a much greater extent than do federal officers in state politics. When doubt arises as to the authority of local governments, the courts have generally decided against them.

But the difference between the unitary state-local and the federal nation-state relations can be exaggerated. As in so many matters of politics, the difference is one of degree rather than of kind. Moreover, during the last several decades "home rule" amendments have been added to some state constitutions. These amendments authorize certain local governments to run their own affairs and limit the power of state officials to interfere. Thus *constitutional home rule* introduces in a small way the federal principle into state constitutions.

In the beginning, the state legislatures were given almost unlimited constitutional

NUMBER OF LOCAL GOVERNMENTS, BY STATES: 1962

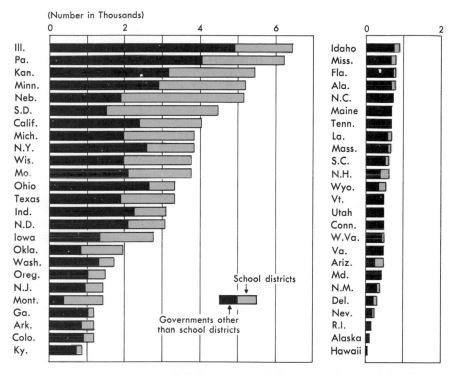

U.S. Department of Commerce, Bureau of the Census.

authority over local governments and ran them pretty much as they wished. They granted, amended, and rescinded city charters, established counties, determined city and county structure, set their debt limits, and passed ordinances for them. But by the end of the nineteenth century, many state constitutions had been amended to forbid the legislature to pass laws dealing with particular local governments, and in the place of legislative enactments, constitutional provisions determined the structure—in some cases, even the process—of local governments.

The hedging in of the legislature's power did not, however, put an end to state domination of local government; while the legislature's authority was being curtailed, the power of *state administrative* officials was being expanded. Problems once thought to be local came to be viewed as state-wide. Many local governments lacked the money to do essential jobs. They could not afford specialists. And their administrative standards were notoriously low. Moreover, the states were encouraged to enter new fields by a host of unfamiliar social and economic problems. Sometimes the states just took over a job previously handled by local people; sometimes the state offered local governments financial assistance, with certain strings attached. Gradually, state officials were given more and more authority to supervise local officials. This tendency has been especially evident in the fields of law enforcement, finance, health, highways, social security, and police (see Chapter 33).

The extent of state control over local units varies from state to state and within each state among the different kinds of local government. States supervise the activities of local governments through a host of devices that vary greatly in the amount of control they give to state officials. At one extreme—giving states the least amount of control—are requirements for reports by local officials to specified state officials. At the other extreme are requirements that local officials be appointed and removed by the state officers.[1]

Government by the People, County-Style

For those who live outside the city, the county and township (in New England, the town) are the most important units of local government. Although counties are not alternatives to city governments but merely additional layers, city people look to the city hall as the place where community affairs are managed. Where there is no city hall, the county court house stands unrivaled as the center of politics.

All states are divided into counties, though in Louisiana they are called parishes and in Alaska boroughs. With a few exceptions (such as Connecticut and Rhode Island where counties have lost their governmental function), county governments exist in all the territory of the United States. Numbering over 3,000, they vary in size and population. Some are inhabited by only a few men and lots of desert; most of them are predominantly rural.

County governments are least active in New England states where the county is essentially a judicial district; county officials do a little road-building but not much else. Elsewhere the traditional functions of counties are law enforcement, highway construction and maintenance, tax collection and property assessment, recording of legal papers, and welfare. Despite predictions that the counties are dying governments, they have within recent years taken over more jobs than they have lost. Although counties in some states have given up major responsibility for relief or highway construction, they have taken on planning, zoning, licensing of businesses, airport-building and operation, ambulance service, health services, and other new functions.

County Government and Governors

How are counties organized to do their jobs? [2] Counties, even more than municipalities, exist to enforce state laws and to serve as administrative units of state government. In general, most counties have little legislative power, but the typical county has a group of officials who act in some fashion as the governing body. These agencies have a variety of titles—

[1] Dale Pontius, *State Supervision of Local Government: Its Development in Massachusetts* (Public Affairs Press, 1942), pp. 1–9.

[2] For a comprehensive review of county and township government, see Clyde F. Snider, *Local Government in Rural America* (Appleton-Century-Crofts, 1957).

board of commissioners, supervisors of roads, county court, commissioners' court, and so on. They vary in size from one to more than fifty members. They administer state laws, levy taxes, appropriate money, issue bonds, sign contracts in behalf of the county, and handle whatever jobs the state laws and constitution assign to them.

County boards, as we shall call these agencies, are of two types. The larger boards are usually composed of township supervisors or other township officials; about 20 per cent of the smaller boards are elected from the county at large. The rural county board is the one "legislative" body in the United States in which lawyers are out-numbered by farmers. Members of county boards are often key political leaders and in some states control local affairs through their power over state patronage. Consequently, they are much more important than a mere enumeration of their formal powers might suggest. Road problems and the granting of contracts to road contractors are frequently the major topics discussed at board meetings.

The county board shares its powers with a number of other officials, most commonly the sheriff, the prosecutor, the county clerk, the coroner, and the auditor. These are generally elected officials. Often, county treasurers, health officers, and surveyors are also found on the ballot. There is seldom a single administrative head or chief executive responsible for coordinating the activities of the many officials —though sometimes the officials are coordinated by a strong party organization.

What Do County Officials Do?

Sheriff. Except in Rhode Island, where he is appointed by the governor, the sheriff is elected by the people of the county, usually for a two- or four-year term. He is charged with enforcing the law and keeping the county jail and is an officer of the county's court of record. In some metropolitan counties in the North and in rural counties in the South, sheriffs are active as law-enforcement officers, but in most counties the sheriff lets the city police do the job within the cities, and the state police in the rural areas. In some rural places, however, the sheriff and his deputies are the only ones to keep law and order. If the sheriff meets serious trouble, he can summon a posse of able-bodied men to come to his assistance.

Law enforcement is a dangerous business, and it does not pay very much. Especially in counties where the sheriff is paid on a fee basis, he is likely to spend his time on the more profitable jobs of acting as court official and keeping the jail. The sheriff serves legal processes issued by the court, summons jurors, subpoenas witnesses, and sells property to satisfy judgment. In many states he receives a fixed sum for the custody and feeding of prisoners. Some sheriffs have been known to make a substantial profit from this operation.

Prosecutor. The prosecuting attorney—also known as county attorney, state's attorney, or district attorney—is commonly elected by voters of the county. He aids the grand jury in preparing indictments, and in some states he may on his own authority bring persons to trial by what is known as "information." He prosecutes state law violators and represents the state and county in civil suits. His discretion is wide, and the decision on whether or not to prosecute is often made by him alone. The job is especially attractive to young law graduates, and it often serves as a steppingstone to higher political posts.

Coroner. This is another ancient office found in most counties. Generally elected for a short term, the coroner's main job is to hold inquests to determine the cause of accidental or suspicious deaths. In many states he selects a jury of about six men to help conduct each inquest. If the coroner and his jury believe that a crime has been committed, they turn their report over to the police and prosecutor. The coroner and his jury may actually name the person they suspect of foul play and then issue a warrant for his arrest.

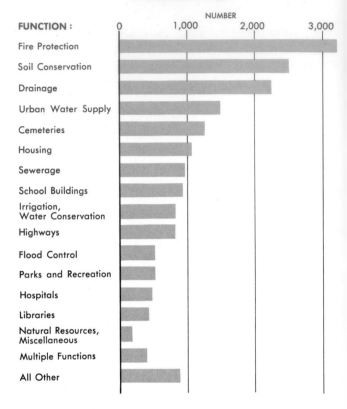

NUMBER OF SPECIAL DISTRICTS, BY FUNCTION: 1962

U.S. Department of Commerce, Bureau of the Census.

The office of coroner has been severely criticized. One student of government in rural America, Lane Lancaster, has written: "The office nearly everywhere is held in something approaching contempt. . . . In many counties it goes by default; in many others it ranks simply as a wizened and wormy fruit from the political plum tree, being held by a dreary succession of down-at-the-heel party waterboys. . . . If the coroner is wide-awake . . . he may add to his income by discreet connections with local funeral directors. Indeed it is a lugubrious fact that in a good many counties the office is held by an undertaker who thus is in a strategic position to add to his business." [3] Many authorities feel that the coroner should be replaced by an appointed medical examiner, a qualified physician with training in pathology who would be paid a set salary. The legal aspects of the work, they feel, should be turned over to the prosecutor. This is the system now used in at least seven states. Some counties are too small or too poor to support a full-time trained examiner, and it has been suggested that several counties join together to provide for a qualified official.

[3] Lane W. Lancaster, *Government in Rural America*, 2nd ed. (Van Nostrand, 1952), p. 171.

County Clerk. The office of the county clerk is found in about half the states. In other states, the *clerk of the court* often performs his jobs. The county clerk is secretary to the county board and has such miscellaneous duties as supervision of elections, issuance of hunting, fishing, and marriage licenses, and the granting of permits for operation of amusement establishments outside city limits. In some states he is also clerk of the courts of record.

County Treasurer. The treasurer, also elected by the people, receives, keeps, and distributes county funds in accordance with the law. In some counties he collects taxes for the townships and those due the state, and then remits the proper shares to these governments. Some counties have abolished the office of county treasurer, transferring his functions to other officials or designating banks to assume his task.

County Assessor. The assessor is responsible for locating property and determining its value for tax purposes, often with the assistance of a large staff. In most places, the county assessor does the job for city, township, and state tax purposes.

The "Courthouse Gang." County governments are not always as headless as it might appear. "It is safe to say that, in nine-tenths of the counties in the United States, public affairs are in the hands of what the irreverent call the 'courthouse gang.' This 'gang' may be described as a more or less permanent group of elective and appointive officeholders together with private individuals whose business normally brings them into contact with public officials." [4] Here are found road contractors, printers, purveyors of supplies, lawyers in criminal and probate work, and "ex-officials who have grown old in party service and who have become masters of the lower sorts of intrigue and so habituated to playing politics as to make residence at the county seat a psychological necessity." [5] Lancaster also points out that the county is also an electoral district and that members of the state legislature "are normally graduates of the school of courthouse politics." [6]

Frequently, one member of the courthouse elite is recognized as the boss. It may be the editor of the local newspaper, the president of the local bank, the chairman of the county farm bureau, the head of the oldest family, or the leader of a local party or faction. Particular county officials are also recognized as having general, if informal, supervisory powers. Sometimes it is the chairman of the governing body. In Indiana, Ohio, Minnesota, and South Dakota, it is often the county auditor; in Illinois, the chairman of the board of county commissioners or supervisors; in Missouri, the judge of the county court; in Tennessee, Kentucky, and Alabama, the county or probate judge.

4 *Ibid.,* p. 57.
5 *Ibid.,* p. 58.
6 *Ibid.,* p. 59.

County Reorganization

How well do the counties do their job? Not very well. In the first place, there are too many of them. When counties were first organized, the idea was to provide a county seat within a day's journey of anyone in the county. The farmer could pile his family into the wagon and head for the courthouse. While he was attending to his business, the family could shop and pick up the local gossip. They could all get home in time to do the evening chores.

Today farmers driving high-speed automobiles over modern highways can travel through ten or eleven average-sized counties in a single day. The small area and population of many counties lead inevitably to inefficiency. Study after study has shown that money could be saved and services improved by *consolidating* counties. Some state constitutions have been amended to permit such consolidations, but to date, only five organized counties have been involved in merger.

County residents take pride in their county and do not like to see it lose its identity. Officeholders, their families, and their friends do not want county jobs to disappear. Businessmen at the county seat depend on officers, employees, and persons drawn to the city by county business for much of their patronage. In view of the practical obstacles to county consolidation, "Those interested in the improvement of county government would . . . seem well advised to waste little time or effort in the support of consolidation but to concentrate on more practicable means, such as internal reorganization and the consolidation of functions." [7]

Reorganization and consolidation, however, have already demonstrated their value and practicality. Counties have joined together to provide health officers, to share equipment, to purchase materials, and for numerous other purposes. There is still great opportunity for better services through greater cooperation and consolidation of functions.

What progress has been made in reorganizing county structure? Unfortunately not enough. The headless character of county administration has long been lamented. The same arguments for integration of national and state administration have been put forth to support county reorganization. Many counties are even worse off than the states. At least, each state does have a governor who in some fashion or other does act as chief executive.

A few counties have made formal attempts to provide executive leadership. This is especially true in urban or suburban counties such as Nassau and Westchester in New York, Cook County in Illinois, and Los Angeles ·County in California. Sixteen counties have some kind of county-manager plan. More common are counties with a chief administrative officer, as in California. In several states some counties elect their executive. Among the rural counties, however, the traditional pattern still remains dominant.

Most county governments still lack merit systems or modern fiscal and pur-

[7] C. F. Snider, "American County Government: a Mid-Century Review," *The American Political Science Review* (March 1952), p. 68.

chasing methods, and auditing practices often leave much to be desired. Even such an obvious money-saving program as centralized purchasing has not been widely adopted. But progress is being made, slow as it is.

Townships

North of the Ohio River, from the Dakotas and Kansas eastward, and outside of New England, the general practice is to subdivide the county into *townships*. The township is gradually losing many of its functions either to the counties or to the cities.[8] Oklahoma, after whittling township functions down to almost nothing, recently abolished them altogether. In Iowa, townships still exist formally, but they have lost so many of their functions that the Census Bureau has stopped counting them! Where they exist, townships often handle outdoor relief, build and maintain roads, and sometimes serve as districts for school purposes. In some states, all the voters of the townships are entitled to attend an annual meeting to elect officers and to levy taxes and make appropriations. These town meetings are usually poorly attended.

A board of supervisors, a justice of the peace, and a constable are the typical township officials; all are elected. The township constable is to the justice of the peace what the sheriff is to the county courts. Since constables make their fees from court work, they do little law enforcement except for catching traffic violators.

The middle-western and middle-Atlantic townships are often confused with the New England towns. But they are essentially different types of government.

The New England Town—Direct Democracy

The town is the principal kind of rural government in New England. It is sometimes difficult for "outsiders" to understand that a New England town is an area of government that includes whatever villages there may be, plus the open country. Except where a municipality has been incorporated, the town does most of the things that a county does elsewhere.

Each town holds an annual meeting open to all voters. In the United States, this town meeting is the outstanding example of a *direct democracy* where all the voters participate directly in making the rules, passing new laws, levying taxes, and appropriating money. Before each meeting, the selectmen issue a warrant designating the time and place of the meeting and setting forth the agenda. At the appointed time, a moderator is chosen to preside. The items on the agenda are then taken up and the floor is open to any citizen who wishes to have his say. Before or during the meeting, the polls are open for the voters to choose the town officers.

The meeting may choose a board of selectmen, usually consisting of three or

---

[8] James W. Drury, "Townships Lose Ground," *National Municipal Review* (January 1955), pp. 10–13. Paul W. Wager, "Townships on the Way Out," *National Municipal Review* (October 1957), pp. 456–460, 475–476.

five members, who carry on the business of the town between meetings, have charge of town property, grant licenses, supervise other town officials, and call special town meetings. A town clerk, treasurer, assessor, overseer of the poor, constable, school board, and numerous other persons are elected by the voters or appointed by the selectmen. The town meeting often elects a finance committee to prepare the town budget.

The New England town meeting has long been a celebrated institution. The picture of sturdy and independent citizens coming together to talk over public affairs and speak their minds is a stirring one. The New England town has often been pointed to as the one place in the United States where no political bosses exist. In fact, however, a recognized group of town leaders often provides leadership. Politics is inevitable—even at a town meeting. This is not to disparage the New England town but to recognize that under conditions of freedom and diversity, groups will be formed and leaders will emerge.

Over a hundred towns, especially the more populous ones, have created the position of *town manager*. Like the city manager (see page 794), he appoints the principal administrative officials and is responsible to the voters through the selectmen. In spite of such innovations, the traditional New England town government still flourishes. Some larger towns have adopted a limited town meeting, under which the town is divided into precincts, the voters in each precinct elect a number of delegates, and the delegates in turn form the town meeting. Any voter may speak at the town meeting, but only the delegates may vote. In some larger towns, city governments would appear to be more appropriate, but the people still cling to their traditional town government.

Our Fair Cities

What does the word "city" call to mind? Bright lights, crowded streets, museums, slums, skyscrapers, and lots of people. To some of us, the city may be Main Street, Courthouse Square, the old cannon, and farm families shopping and talking on Saturdays. For a city is not merely improved real estate. It is also people, an exciting conglomerate of men and women living and working together.

In our state statutes, this exciting thing, the city, is made to sound like a dull bit of lawyers' talk. For in law a city is a *municipal corporation*; there are almost 18,000 of them in the United States. Some have millions of people, others a couple of hundred. Sometimes the smaller ones are called villages, boroughs, or towns. Although not all densely populated places are governed as a municipality, the city is the major kind of local government for the urban dweller.

Each city has two major functions. One, to provide government within its boundaries in order that the citizenry may maintain law and order, keep their streets clean, educate their children, dispose of their garbage, purify their water, create parks, and in other ways make their city a good place in which to live. But the city has a second function—it is an instrumentality of the *state* to carry out *state* functions. It is distinguished from a county, a quasi-corporation, in the greater amount of discretion given to the local officials and by the greater emphasis on their local functions. A county, on the other hand, is supposed to operate primarily as an administrative unit of the state. The distinction is of course one of emphasis.

Each city has its own charter. This may not be a single document; in some states one has to read through the state statutes to discover the organization, powers, and functions of cities. The charter is to the city what a constitution is to the national or state government. It outlines the structure of government, sets the authority of the various officials, and provides for their selection. Where do the charters come from? Who draws them up?

In about ten states the legislature writes a *special* charter for each city and may amend the charter as it pleases, although in a few of these states the charter must be submitted to the local voters for their approval. In practice, local groups often draft the charter in consultation with their legislative representatives; other members of the legislature usually defer to the legislative delegation from the city. Since legislators need local support to stay in office, in practice the groups that dominate local politics often write their own charters, even though the state legislature has the constitutional authority to do so. When the legislature is controlled by groups hostile to those in control of the city, however, a major battle may shape up.

In most states, the constitution requires the legislature to classify cities and provide a charter for each class of city. If the legislature makes refined enough classifications, it can, in effect, write a special charter for each city. And in many states the constitution specifically permits special legislation for the largest city. Many legislatures list several kinds of charter and permit the local citizenry to choose the particular kind they wish. This is known as the *optional charter plan*.

Home Rule

European cities can do anything that is not expressly forbidden; American cities have only those powers expressly conferred on them. State legislatures still exercise a great deal of control over city affairs. In addition to drawing up charters for the cities, the legislature allots functions to local officials and withdraws them at will. In case of conflict between a state law and a local ordinance, the state law is enforced. In some states, every time a city wants to put a stop light on the corner of Broadway and High, the city fathers have to get permission of either the legislature or certain state officials.

Some states have *legislative* home rule. The legislature delegates authority over certain subjects so that the cities do not have to ask permission to deal with these problems. However, any state law in conflict with a local ordinance supersedes the ordinance and whatever powers the legislature gives to the local governments it may take away.

In about one-half of the state, however, the constitution, not the state legislature, delegates to citizens of certain-sized cities authority that they may exercise regardless of the wishes of the legislature. These are the *home-rule states*. Where the constitution so permits, a few states extend this power to all municipalities, and the people of the city may elect a group of citizens who draw up a charter. After the charter has been approved by local voters (in some states it must also be approved either by the legislature or the governor, or both, to insure that it will not conflict with the constitution), it becomes the city's basic instrument of government and may be amended by local citizens. Furthermore, home-rule cities have the general power to dispose of matters of local concern without special authorization from the legislature.

Constitutional home rule thus introduces the federal principle. About two-thirds of our cities of over 200,000 population have some measure of home rule. "It would be a great mistake to think of these cities as being really independent, however." [9] Home rule cities may have some freedom in determining the general structure of their city government, but home rule has not significantly increased their substantive powers, very few items do not have some impact outside the city boundaries, and general grants to dispose of matters of local concern have been narrowly construed by the courts. Since it is the courts that determine whether a given ordinance is within the scope of authority granted to the city by constitutional home rule, the major impact of constitutional home rule seems to have been to transfer some authority from the state legislature to the state courts.[10]

Is home rule worth the struggle for it? Despite the relatively small increase in local autonomy, despite the fact that constitutional home rule introduces an element of rigidity into state-local relations and enhances the authority of judges, most reform groups favor its adoption. It frees the legislature from the necessity of dealing with local matters. More important, it gives the voters of a particular city the power to decide for themselves the general structure of their municipal government.

Forms of City Charters

The formal charters are good places to *begin* to find out how the people in our 18,000 cities govern and are governed. But to look at just a city charter can be very misleading. The actual constitutions in the sense of the rules by which our cities are governed in contrast to their legal charters vary "from the narrowest oligarchy to the freest democracy," and "from the most brutal tyranny to a near philosopher-king." [11] But until we have more comparative studies and more detailed investigation, classification of city governments by the form of their charter is still the best available.

---

[9] Edward C. Banfield and James Q. Wilson, *City Politics* (Harvard Univ. Press, 1963), p. 67.
[10] *Ibid.*
[11] Norton E. Long, *The Polity* (Rand McNally, 1962), pp. 222–241.

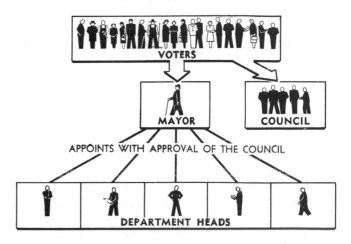

The Mayor-Council Charter

The mayor-council charter is the oldest and still the most popular charter. It predominates in the very smallest and in the very largest cities. Under this type of charter, the city council is usually a single chamber, although the bicameral form lingers on in a few cities. The size of the council varies— some have only two members, some as many as 50. Seven members is the median in cities with over 5,000 people.

Many methods are used to select the councilmen—nonpartisan and partisan elections, by small wards, by large wards, from the city at large, by proportional representation. It is artificial to isolate the method of electing councilmen from party structures, social structure, and interest groups; but the way councilmen are chosen is an important factor in determining how power is distributed in a city. Large cities that elect councilmen in partisan elections generally choose them by small districts rather than at large. This combination tends to support strong party organizations; nonpartisan at-large elections makes party organization difficult. The larger the election districts for councilmen, the more likely that city-wide considerations will be brought to bear in the selection of councilmen and the greater the influence of city-wide agencies such as the local newspaper in the election of councilmen. The larger the election districts, the less likely that racial and ethnic groups will be represented on the city council, for the voting strength of neighborhood minorities cannot be concentrated behind local councilmen. Larger districts are easier to gerrymander, but with small districts it is harder to draw lines so that a particular racial or ethnic group will have no chance of winning.[12]

The powers of the mayor vary from charter to charter (and even more widely from city to city and mayor to mayor). The mayor is elected by the people, but in some cases the charter assigns little more than ceremonial powers to him. He welcomes "visiting firemen" and gives them the key to the city. In some cities his appointive power is limited, and he shares administrative authority with other elected officials and numerous boards and commissions. This is known as the *weak mayor-council* system.

Tracing the office of mayor through various charters, one finds a general trend toward an increase in his authority. Like the presidency and the governorship, the office of mayor over the years has grown in importance. Many cities have altered their charters in order to give him the power to appoint and remove heads

[12] These generalizations are based on studies of Banfield and Wilson, *op. cit.*, pp. 89–100.

of departments and investigate their activities, to send messages to the city council, to prepare the budget, and to veto council ordinances. In other words, he has been given a share in policy-making, and city administration has been centralized under his direction. A recent development is the creation of a chief administrative officer, appointed by the mayor to assist him in directing city administration. In New York, Chicago, and Philadelphia, for example, these city administrators manage the housekeeping functions of the city government and provide professional administration, giving to these cities some of the advantages that are thought to come with the adoption of the council-manager form of government (see below).

Many people believe the *strong mayor-council* is the best charter for the large cities. This charter, they argue, gives the city a strong political leader, makes efficient administration possible, and by centering authority in the hands of a few individuals makes less likely the growth of "invisible government" by men who have power but who are not publicly accountable for its use.

The Commission Charter

In 1900, the city of Galveston was inundated by a tidal wave. Over 6,000 people lost their lives, and public and private property worth millions was destroyed. The mayor and the twelve aldermen seemed incapable of action. In the emergency, power began to fall into the hands of a group of businessmen who had been discussing methods of improving the harbor. They decided to act. After studying the charters of several cities, they went to the legislature with what was then almost a novel proposal for a new charter. They asked that control of the city be vested in five commissioners. The legislature approved.

About five years later, the attorney for the city of Des Moines, Iowa, took a business trip to Galveston. He was so impressed with

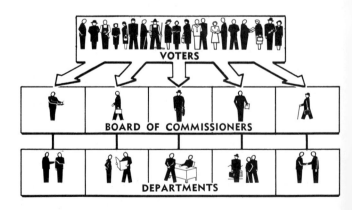

THE COMMISSION FORM

VOTERS

BOARD OF COMMISSIONERS

DEPARTMENTS

the commission government that he returned to Iowa with the proposal that the Iowa legislature permit cities to adopt commission charters.

The placing of all governmental powers in the hands of five men flew in the face of the traditional doctrine of separation of powers. Many felt that it was too dangerous to give a small group of men control over both administration and legislation. For this reason the Des Moines Plan, as it was known, included the initiative, referendum, recall, and nonpartisan ballots for primaries and elections in addition to the ideas of the Galveston businessmen. The plan became very popular, and by 1917 over 500 cities were so governed. Since that time the number has declined, although Portland, St. Paul, Memphis, and nearly 250 other cities with populations over 5,000 still have this kind of charter.

The commissioners, usually five, collectively constitute the city council; individually they are the heads of the departments of city administration. Most commissioners devote full time to their jobs and actively administer the affairs of their particular departments. One of the commissioners is designated as mayor, but he normally has little more power than the other commissioners.

The commission charter was widely heralded as an introduction of safe and sane business methods to city affairs. But after a brief wave of popularity, the new idea lost some of its glamour. The party bosses were suspicious, and the city reformers were disappointed. Although providing for more integrated control than the old mayor-council system, the city was still left without a single responsible administrative head. In fact, a commission city has five mayors. Moreover, commissioners chosen because they represent major groups within the city often leave something to be desired as administrators of departments of public welfare, public safety, and so on. By 1917, reformers had discovered a new kind of charter which they believed had greater merit.

Council-Manager Charter

The council-manager, also known as city-manager or commission-manager, plan was warmly acclaimed by James Bryce as "the latest word in municipal reform." Certainly it is one of our most significant innovations in governmental form. In 1908 the little city of Staunton, Virginia, appointed a general manager to direct the city's work. Little note was taken of this step, but Richard Childs, an advertising man active in the short-ballot movement, became very much interested.

Childs was enthusiastic about the commission plan (discussed above) because it applied two basic ideas, *unification of power* and a *short ballot*, to city affairs. But it did not go far enough. Add to this a chief administrative officer, he reasoned, and the results should be even better. So, as he said, he became "the minister who performed the ceremony that united" the commission plan with the idea of a general manager.

The city-manager plan was adopted by a few small cities but it did not receive much publicity. Then in 1913, Dayton, Ohio, had a flood. (City charters seem to owe much to tidal waves and floods.) The flood came in the midst of a campaign to select members for a charter commission. The existing city officials, like their predecessors in Galveston, demonstrated their inability to meet the emergency, and the disaster added to the strength of those who were advocating the city-manager charter. These reformers argued that the city is a corporation and should be run like any other corporation. The voters, as "stockholders," should elect a board of directors, and these directors should select a professional administrator. This is the essence of the city-manager plan, and its adoption by Dayton attracted national attention.

Almost 2,000 cities, located in almost all the states, operate under a council-manager charter and each year new municipalities adopt the council-manager plan. Although of those cities in the United States with more than half a million people only Cincinnati, Kansas City, Dallas, and San Diego have a city manager, over half the cities in the 25,000 to 100,000 class have adopted this form of city government, and over 40 million Americans live in cities governed by a council-manager.

Under the council-manager charter, the council is usually elected in non-partisan primaries and elections, either on a citywide basis or by election districts much larger than the wards in mayor-council cities. The number of council members varies, but there are usually fewer than in cities with mayor-council charters. The council appoints a city manager, supervises his activities, and fires him when he is unsatisfactory. It makes the laws, approves the budget, and—although it is not supposed to interfere in administration—it does supervise city government through the manager. A mayor is usually provided for the purpose of presiding over the council and representing the city on ceremonial occasions.

The city manager advises the council on policy and supervises the administration of city business. Since the council-manager plan envisages the selection of the best available person, most charters do not require the council to appoint a local citizen, nor do they prescribe detailed qualifications. Twenty universities now have special courses for the training of city managers. The International City Managers' Association has its own code of ethics and works to develop higher standards among its members. City managers receive substantial salaries; as more and more cities adopt this form of government, the opportunities for advancement continue to increase.

City-manager charters assume a non-political city manager who merely carries into execution policies proclaimed by the council, and councilmen who refrain from interfering with the administration of city affairs. In fact, there is no such sharp distinction between policy-making and policy-applying. Most city managers operating behind the symbol of administration are the major source within the city government for the initiation of policies and programs. "[The] city manager is a participant in the politi-

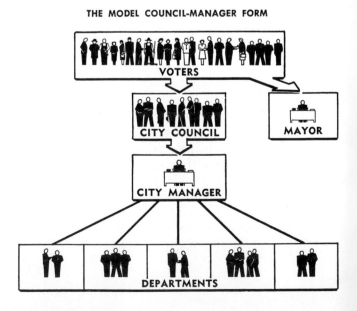

THE MODEL COUNCIL-MANAGER FORM

VOTERS

CITY COUNCIL

MAYOR

CITY MANAGER

DEPARTMENTS

cal process of the community whether he plays an active role in initiating policy, a passive role by merely drawing council attention to emerging problems, or a neutral role by refusing to commit himself publicly on a controversial question. . . . Refusal of a manager to commit himself can be interpreted by opposing groups as taking a position antagonistic to their own." [13] The unavoidable involvement of the manager in the politics of the community means that whenever there is a change in the control of the council, managers often are "fired." The dismissal of a manager is usually explained in other than political terms—he lacked sufficient management training, a personality conflict between manager or council, interference by the manager in the business of the council (or the manager may quit because of council meddling in administration). The explanations, however, are often "superficial rationalizations of the intrinsic political struggles of the community." [14]

How has the city-manager plan worked out? Although there are still some skeptics, the idea has now won the approval of most students of city government. Cities that adopted this kind of charter have generally enjoyed an improvement in standards of public employment, reduction in unit costs, and better services. Moreover, the cities have become institutions "with a broader and more vital function in the community." [15]

Adoption of a city-manager charter usually reflects an awakened interest among civic groups, and this in itself probably accounts in part for the resulting improvement in government. After all, forms of government are merely patterns for organizing the activities of human beings, and a lot depends on who those human beings are and the kind of government they want. "Many council-manager cities are upper-class or middle-class in character; few if any are predominantly lower-class." [16] City-manager government appeals to the concept of the public interest of these groups, a concept that stresses "good" disinterested government, efficiency and economy, business methods and procedures, and civic growth. The city-manager form of government, with its emphasis on nonpartisanship, thus tends to put into control of government persons who share these attitudes. In larger cities where low-income groups are not content to leave government in the hands of the business community, city-manager forms are less likely to be adopted and less likely to function in the fashion contemplated by those who seek their adoption.

Cambridge Adopts a New Charter—A Case Study

As we saw in earlier chapters, the ways in which people behave and respond to one another do not always correspond with legal institutions. In some cities, the

[13] Gladys M. Kammerer, *et al.*, *The Urban Political Community* (Houghton Mifflin, 1963), p. 5; see also by the same authors, *City Managers in Politics* (Univ. of Florida Press, 1962).

[14] *Ibid.*, p. 193.

[15] Harold A. Stone, Don K. Price, and Kathy H. Stone, *City Manager Government in the United States* (Public Administration Service, 1940), p. 260.

[16] Banfield and Wilson, *op. cit.*, p. 169.

charter gives the mayor very little power; but in reality the mayor, backed by powerful political groups, runs the city. In some cities the manager is strong and the council is weak; in others the councilmen run things and the manager serves as their handyman. Some city managers are active in local affairs, have large popular followings, and a great deal of political influence. In short, the type of charter adopted by a city tells us very little about the way the city is actually governed.

The story of how one city adopted a new charter, and of its early experiences under it, may suggest some of the political dynamics that operate at the local level.

AN ACTUAL COUNCIL-MANAGER FORM

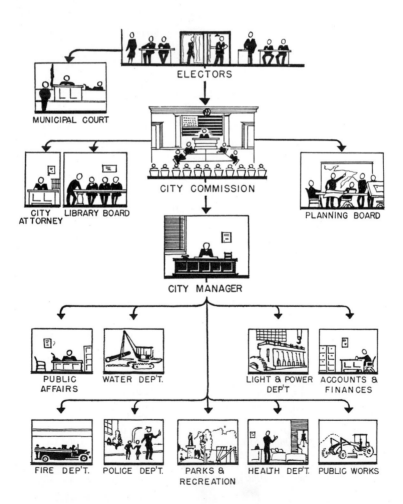

Trouble in Cambridge

In 1936 the city of Cambridge, Massachusetts, was in trouble. The tax rate was high, the city was deep in debt, and city administration was poor. The city was controlled by a Democratic organization that governed without inspiration through a charter providing for a weak mayor and a 15-man council. The worst of it was that there seemed very little that could be done to improve matters. Only a few of the 100,000 citizens of the city seemed actively dissatisfied with their plight.[17]

Moreover, the people of Cambridge are of diverse backgrounds. The Irish, the largest ethnic group, live side by side with Yankees, French Canadians, Italians, and other national-origin groups. Though known for its great universities, Cambridge also is an industrial area, part of the Greater Metropolitan Boston region. The older residents of Yankee stock have been stand-offish toward immigrant and minority groups, and there are wide extremes in wealth, housing conditions, and education. The strength of the Democratic organization was built on the grievances of the less-privileged elements and on their resentment of the Yankee "aristocrats."

Still, there was some open dissatisfaction, and soon a group of citizens was meeting to discuss plans for improvement. They became particularly interested in the city-manager idea. Under Massachusetts laws at this time, cities could choose from among four types of optional charters, but the city-manager type was not one of them. The Cambridge reformers, however, were able to induce the Massachusetts legislature to provide for a fifth charter—the city-manager form—called "Plan E."

Immediately, officers of the Cambridge Taxpayers Association called a meeting of citizens known to be dissatisfied with civic affairs. To this meeting came representatives of the Taxpayers Association, the Chamber of Commerce, and the League of Women Voters. After much discussion, the group decided to make an attempt in the coming 1938 election to get the Plan E Charter adopted in Cambridge.

What should be the strategy? Obviously the group had to be made more representative in character. It would not do to have only Republicans, businessmen, and Yankees behind the new charter. So a Plan E Committee was created. Who should be chairman? The name of Dean James M. Landis of the Harvard Law School was suggested. "He's too liberal," said some; "he's a New Dealer." "His Harvard connection," said others, "will play into the hands of the opposition, who will insist that this is merely an attempt on the part of the Harvard aristocrats to take control of the city." But it was finally decided that Dean Landis' great prestige and Democratic party affiliations would outweigh any of his alleged

---

[17] This section is drawn from F. C. Libretto, "The Cambridge City Manager," in Harold Stein (ed.), *Public Administration and Policy Development* (Harcourt, Brace, 1952), pp. 573–619.

liabilities. At least it would take the sting out of the charge that Plan E was a device inspired by wealthy Republican businessmen.

Dean Landis was a vigorous leader. He saw to it that the other leaders represented a wide range of religious, political, and ethnic affiliations. With the active help of the League of Women Voters, the necessary signatures for the referendum petition were filed with the city council.

Political Rough-and-Tumble

Under the law, the city council had to forward the petition to the secretary of state by a certain day. But as the deadline approached, the city council refused to act. The deadline was Saturday. The Harvard-Yale football game was scheduled for that afternoon, and the members of the city council were on their way to the game to occupy the special seats reserved for them. Unless they met on the resolution that day, it would be too late. At the last minute, the Plan E group found a judge of the Superior Court who was willing to act. He issued a mandamus to compel the council to meet and take the necessary action. As the council members filed into the stadium expecting to forget the problems created by the reformers and to enjoy an afternoon of football, they had a rude shock. By each of their seats stood a court deputy with a warrant from the judge requiring the council to meet immediately and transmit the petition to the secretary of state as the law required them to do.

The campaign for a city-manager charter then began in earnest, and the going became rough. Opponents charged that the council-manager form of government was dictatorial and communistic. Moreover, they said, it was a plot to turn the city over to the "Harvard-Brattle Street-Money-Taxpayer-Republican forces." The result of the election was defeat for Plan E, but by a narrow margin.

The men who continued to run city affairs apparently had not learned their lesson, however. They did little to improve matters. In fact, the failure of the mayor and council to comply with the law in preparing the city budget brought them further public attention. The city's financial plight became desperate. And then the district attorney began to investigate city services.

The reform groups returned to battle. In the 1940 elections, Plan E was again put before the voters, and this time it carried. But the battle was not over. Everything depended now on the election of the new council members under the system of proportional representation that was part of Plan E. The new city council would choose the manager and execute the new charter. If the anti-city manager forces won control of the city council, there was little chance that the new form of government would be any improvement over the old.

Despite the fact that the old mayor was convicted of bribery and that stories of corruption and inefficiency made the headlines, the Plan E group did not do so well in the election. Only four out of the nine new council members had been endorsed by the Plan E group. But the opposition, fortunately for Plan E, was split. Of the five other councilmen, only two were definitely aligned with the local party organization. The other three, though skeptical of city-manager government, had their own sources of independent political support.

A City Manager Takes Over

After sorting through a number of applications, the council finally chose as new city manager Colonel John B. Atkinson, a prominent Cambridge shoe manufacturer. The new manager faced a difficult task. He had the support of vocal and active civic groups, but these groups "represented population which was in the unenviable political position of having long been dominant in terms of wealth and social status and very much dominated in terms of numbers of voters." [18] Many people were suspicious of the concentration of so much authority in the hands of a single person. City employees were fearful for their positions. Many city councilmen were not friendly.

The city manager went to work. He straightened out the tangled financial situation, rehabilitated and cleaned up public equipment and buildings, standardized pay schedules, and generally improved the city's operations. Popular support for the new government began to increase.

The reformers who had introduced Plan E realized that they would need a permanent political organization. In 1945 they formed the Cambridge Civic Association and an affiliated Research Association. At first, the board of directors was composed of upper-class Republicans. Again the opposition charged that these people were interested only in keeping their own taxes down and in depriving the people in the "lower wards" of needed services. Finally, the Cambridge Civil Association broadened its directorship and switched from an essentially negative emphasis on economy to a positive program of civic betterment. In the ensuing years, the battle continued. City-manager government still had to fight for its existence in Cambridge.

[18] *Ibid.*, p. 590.

32 METROPOLIS: GOVERNMENT AND POLITICS

"If we forget the map of America drawn to a scale of statute miles and see only the people and their distribution," writes Scott Greer, "we find a nation of mushrooming metropolitan areas, stagnant small towns, and dying open country neighborhoods. . . . The farming areas grow increasingly prairie-like as the density of human population dwindles and the size of holding increases; many small towns lose their reason for being, changing to villages and ghost towns; the small cities become 'metropolitan areas' and the great cities expand until they form vast urban regions. . . ." [1]

Today it is metropolis, not the farm or the small town so beloved in American fact and fiction, where most of us live, and most of us who do not now live in metropolis soon will. During the 1950's over 96 per cent of our total population increase occurred in metropolitan areas. By 1980 over four-fifths of all Americans will be living in these areas. By the year 2000 the nation will find itself with several large metropolitan regions of solid settlement: the Eastern Seaboard, the West Coast, an urban Midwest uniting St. Louis, Chicago, Cleveland, Detroit, Indianapolis, Buffalo.[2]

And what is it like the world over, this urban environmental of modern man?

Circle over London, Buenos Aires, Chicago, Sydney, in an airplane or view the cities schematically by means of an urban map and block plan. What is the shape of the city and how does it define itself? The original container has completely disappeared: the sharp division between city and country no longer exists. As the eye stretches toward the hazy periphery one can pick out no defi-

[1] Scott Greer, *The Emerging City* (The Free Press, 1962), pp. 29–30.
[2] Philip M. Hauser, *Population Perspectives* (Rutgers Univ. Press, 1961).

The Growth of Urbanization, by States, 1870– 1960. From John R. Borchert, The Urbanization of the Upper Midwest: 1930–1960, Upper Midwest Economic Study, Urban Report Number 2, February, 1963, p. 2.

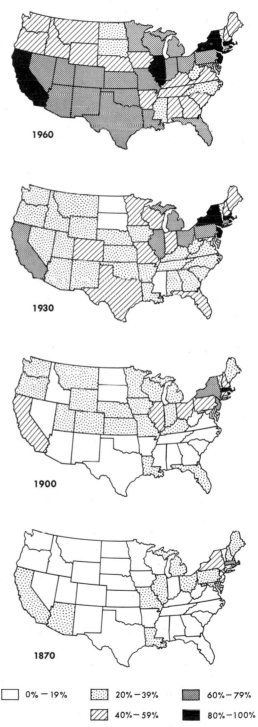

1960

1930

1900

1870

| 0% – 19% | 20% – 39% | 60% – 79% |
| 40% – 59% | 80% – 100% |

Urban Population as a Percent of Total Population

nite shapes except those formed by nature; one beholds rather a continuous shapeless mass, here bulging or ridged by buildings, there broken by a patch of green or an unwinding ribbon of concrete. The shapelessness of the whole is reflected in the individual part, and the nearer the center, the less as a rule can the smaller parts be distinguished. . . .

As one moves away from the center, the urban growth becomes ever more aimless and discontinuous, more diffuse and unfocused, except where some surviving town has left the original imprint of a more orderly life. Old neighborhoods and precincts, the social cells of the city, still maintaining some measure of the village pattern, become vestigial. No human eye can take in the metropolitan mass at a glance. No single gathering place except the totality of its streets can hold all its citizens. No human mind can comprehend more than a fragment of the complex and minutely specialized activities of its citizens. The loss of form, the loss of autonomy, the constant frustration and harassment of daily activities, to say nothing of gigantic breakdowns and stoppages—all these become normal attributes of the metropolitan regime. There is a special name for power when it is concentrated on such a scale: it is called impotence. . . ." [3]

Sprawling giantism, congestion, slums, smog, tension, rootlessness, shapelessness, loss of a sense of community, impersonal and unfriendly human relationships—all these terms have been used to describe the giant city of today. The big city has simply lost control of itself, Mumford continues. Even worse, it carries the seeds of the destruction of civilization. Historically, the city has grown from shelter to fortress to industrial center and to a mechanical way of life. *Polis*—the old Greek type of small city—gave way to metropolis and then to megalopolis and then to "tyrannopolis" and finally to nekropolis—the city of death (an idea that takes on frightening prophetic possibilities in an age of the ever-present possibility of nuclear warfare).[4]

Mumford's strictures against the city are in keeping with a long-standing tradition of anti-city bias on the part of major social critics, starting with Thomas Jefferson, running through Lord Bryce, Lincoln Steffens, Theodore Dreiser, and infusing much of American social science. These critics project the image of the city as an impersonal, cold, brutal environment in which crime flourishes and man loses his dignity.[5] The big city is contrasted with the "wholesome" small community in which men live "whole lives" of total relationships. Some of the less sophisticated critics of metropolis appear to measure the modern city against a small town inhabited by Anglo-Saxons who speak with a New England or midwestern accent and who spend their "leisure" eating Mom's apple pie or sitting around the stove at the general store engaging in high-level discussions of local politics.

[3] Lewis Mumford, *The City in History* (Harcourt, Brace & World, 1961), pp. 543–544.
[4] Lewis Mumford, *The Culture of Cities* (Harcourt, Brace, 1938), Chapter 4.
[5] Greer, *op. cit.*, p. 133 delineates the bias pro and con running through literature with respect to urban values and life. See also Anselm Strauss, *Images of the American City* (The Free Press, 1961).

But metropolis and urban values have their defenders. The big city, they contend, is not just a place of smog and sprawl. It is the center of innovation, diversity, excitement, and vitality. It is where the pluralistic social base for diversity can be found, where community pressures to conform are bearable. The large community is a meeting place for talent from all over the nation and the world, and of all types: dancers, musicians, writers, actors, leaders of the world's commerce, finance, transportation. Despite all the complaints, many people *like* living in the big city. And they point out that within metropolis there are often fairly homogeneous smaller communities that retain their identity perhaps the best known example would be Greenwich Village in lower New York City.

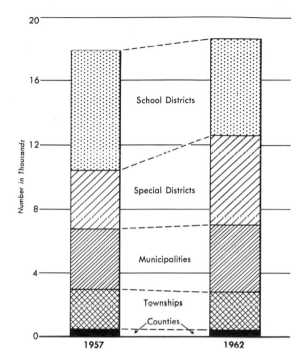

LOCAL GOVERNMENTS IN STANDARD METROPOLITAN STATISTICAL AREAS, By Type, 1957 and 1962

U.S. Department of Commerce, Bureau of the Census.

Metropolis: Core City v. Suburbs

The central fact about metropolis from the political scientist's perspective is that each is run not by a single city government but by dozens, in some cases hundreds, of governments. The sharpest political and governmental division is between the central city and the outlying suburbs.

There are many "Clevelanders"—that is, people who work in Cleveland, shop in Cleveland, sell goods in Cleveland, hire men in Cleveland, read Cleveland newspapers—who do not *live* in Cleveland. Only about half the "St. Louisans" live in St. Louis, and so it is with most of the larger American cities. The big cities and their environs suffer from serious cases of "suburbanitis." The commuter who lives in Sunnyside, or Kirkwood, or Westchester but who earns his living in the central city is well known in fact and fiction.[6]

[6] Lyle C. Fitch, "Fiscal and Political Problems of Increasing Urbanization," *Political Science Quarterly* (March 1956), pp. 71–89, and "Metropolitan Financial Problems," *The Annals* of the American Academy of Political and Social Science (November 1957), pp. 66–73.

Suburbia: Political Frustration?

In recent years suburbs have been the fastest growing units in the United States. Today most who can afford it leave the crowded and blighted business areas and move out into more pleasant living quarters. They go in search of cheaper land, lower taxes, more room, better air. New shopping centers rise in outlying communities. Industries also move from the central city in search of cheaper land, lower taxes, and escape from city building and health codes. Suburbia no longer stands for the well-to-do, but rather for the scale from "decent home-owning people up to the millionaires." [7]

Despite the fact that suburbanites often look on the politics of the central city as "dirty," something to escape from, the politics of central city are very much a part of their lives. When they read their morning papers on their way to their jobs, they find little news about the officials of their own suburbs, but much about Mayor Yorty or Mayor Daley or some other big-city mayor. Moreover, the major problems in which they are interested—transportation, crime, taxation of downtown businesses where they work—are more influenced by the decisions of the officials of central city than those of suburbia. And although the suburbanite has some influence in his central city through his business association or trade unions, he has no direct vote in electing those whose decisions vitally affect him.

What of government and politics in the suburbs? It is dangerous to generalize. Suburbs are not all alike. Some are the exclusive residences of the rich and established, with first-rate schools, governed by an efficient cluster of specialists. Others are havens for criminals. Still others are lower-middle-class neighborhoods of blue-collar workers. And others are chosen by young executives and their wives who have little interest in their community and view their surroundings as a stepping-stone from which to move with the next promotion.

Dangerous as it is to generalize, generalize we must. Some suburbanites tend to look at their local government as a device to protect their property, their schools, and their homes against "invasion" by minority groups, such as Negroes. Occasionally, suburban dwellers become aroused over major local problems like educational policy or taxation. In the absence of such explosive issues, suburban local politics tend to be trivial. Each local suburban city is so limited in its jurisdiction that it cannot cope with the major problems of urban life. As a result, even suburbanites who are active in state and national politics seldom have much interest in what happens at their local city hall. They may complain to their city officials, but since these officials deal with relatively minor issues they have little interest in their work. It is often difficult to find people to run for local office.

Scott Greer, after evaluating the various studies and surveys of local suburban politics, concludes: "Whether the election in question is for school board member or mayor of the municipality, a smaller proportion of the eligibles will turn out

[7] Greer, *op. cit.*, p. 140 ff. Also Kevin Lynch, "The Pattern of the Metropolis," in Lloyd Rodwin (ed.), *The Future Metropolis* (Braziller, 1961), p. 105.

to vote in the suburbs than will do so in the central city." [8] Of course some suburbanites are politically active, but "the small scale community of limited liability in the suburbs does not have the 'box office' appeal that major government manifests. Staying close to home, operated by amateurs and part-time politicians . . . the suburban political community has been overlooked or rejected by a substantial proportion of its citizenry." [9]

The sheer management of suburbia often makes for frustration. Each suburban city has its own city government, its own fire and police departments, its own school system, its own street cleaning equipment, its own building and health codes. Also, many of the major tasks of suburban government are bound in with those of the metropolis at large. Criminals do not stop at city boundaries. The central city usually maintains an elaborate police department with detective bureaus, crime-detection laboratories, and an elaborate communications network, but its jurisdiction stops at the city line. Suburban police are fewer, and often untrained in criminology. Or consider traffic problems. Super highways run through suburbia, with a number of access roads; these form a transportation unity, but in the midst of governmental disunity. In matters of health, too, there are often wide differences in health standards between parts of metropolis. But germs, pollution, and smog do not notice city signposts.

The Special Problems of the Central City

"He who moves from Boston to Concord or Acton, or to Weston or Needham, leaves a considerable part of his municipal burdens behind him," Cherington writes. "He leaves tremendous problems of public health and public welfare back in the central urban core, or back in the industrial soot of Cambridge or Somerville or Chelsea. He leaves Boston to solve its own street problem while he drives to work on a state supported, federally aided highway, or he may park his car at the end of the rapid transit line and ride into State Street on the Metropolitan Transit Authority's deficit. He knows that his suburban government is cheaper and in terms of his own mythology it is 'better.' He draws a State Street salary but pays a farmer's taxes. We can scarcely find a better example of having your cake and eating it too." [10]

The fundamental problem of the core city is that while many upper-income families and high-tax-paying businesses have been moving out, low-income groups have been moving in, and the need for city services has greatly expanded. In a recent six-year period, Adrian reports, retail sales rose by 20 per cent in the city of St. Louis, but by 80 per cent in St. Louis county. In one year more was

[8] Greer, op. cit., p. 141.

[9] Ibid., pp. 142–143. See also S. Greer, "The Citizen and his Local Governments: Central City and Suburban County" in J. C. Bollens (ed.), Exploring the Metropolitan Community (Univ. of California Press, 1961).

[10] Charles R. Cherington, "Pattern for Greater Boston," National Municipal Review (February 1949), p. 70.

spent for new plants and equipment in the Illinois suburbs of St. Louis than was spent in the city and St. Louis county suburbs combined. "To heap trouble upon trouble . . . the majority of migrants will settle first in the city, probably in the decaying zone of transition. Because they are culturally marginal people— that is to say, they live in the culture of a large city but still have many of the values they earlier received from a quite different rural culture—they are likely, in their isolation, resentment, or economic desperation, to create police and juvenile problems. They are insecure and confused people. . . ." [11] In the last century they were newly arrived immigrants from Europe. In this century they are migrants from the rural areas, especially Negroes and whites from the South. The center of the city tends "toward a vast ethnic ghetto, surrounding the 'white lights' and surrounded, in turn, by miles of residential streets of a shabby gentility whose residents consider the approach of the Puerto Ricans, the Negroes, the Mexicans, or the Okies," [12] and live in constant fear that their own neighborhoods will become "less desirable."

Pressing problems accumulate in the core city. The large numbers of migrants from Puerto Rico mean that the schools must be specially equipped to deal with children who may not speak English. The arrival of Negro families from the South poses new problems of race relations in the public schools. Lower-income families in general, and especially migrants from areas where medical services

[11] Charles R. Adrian, *State and Local Governments* (McGraw-Hill, 1960), p. 238.
[12] Greer, *op. cit.*, p. 31. See also Hal Bruno, "Chicago's Hillbilly Ghetto," *The Reporter* (June 4, 1964), pp. 28–31.

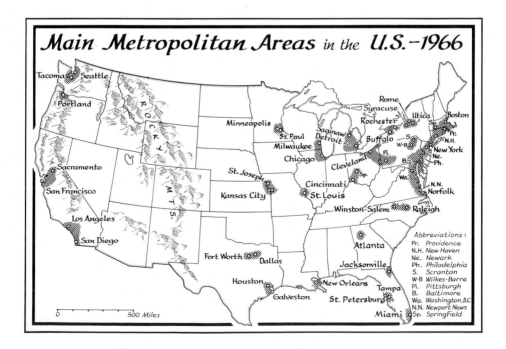

have been limited, make heavy demands on the public health facilities of the city. To meet stepped up housing needs by people who cannot pay high rents, the city moves in with big public housing programs. People who live in congested areas always require more police protection, but police problems abound when different racial and ethnic groups live closely together, with all the resulting disruption of family and community life and with the forces making for juvenile delinquency. Some cities and community and private organizations have met such challenges, but any major effort calls for a great deal of money, and this is precisely the resource that the central city often lacks.

Two Nations—Two Cultures

City and suburb confront each other as two nations each with its own culture. The suburbs' life-style is based on children, home, neighborhood, and the single-family dwelling secure in the middle of 50-foot lots. "Suburban folk tend to be of higher social rank, of white 'old American' heritage, and committed to a familistic way of life." [13] Their concept of the public interest "derives from the middle-class ethos, favors what the municipal reform movement has always defined as 'good government'—namely efficiency, impartiality, honesty, planning, strong executives, no favoritism, model legal codes, and strict enforcement of laws against gambling and vice." [14]

As we have warned, not all suburbs are of the same pattern, and many who live in the central city have the same life-styles and concepts. But speaking generally, the central cities consisting of older dwellings, high-rise apartments, and housing projects and made up of ethnic minorities and nonwhite enclaves, support concepts of the public interest that tend to identify with wards or neighborhoods rather than with the city as a whole, look to politicians for help and favors, regard gambling and vice as necessary evils, respond less to calls for efficiency and impartiality, and look to the city for material benefits such as protection for civil rights, maintenance of order, jobs, homes, and help in the face of economic adversity.

"Today many central cities find that their principal antagonist in the legislature is not the rural hinterland but an alliance of the hinterland and the suburbs." [15] The long-standing lines of cleavage between city and its suburbs persist as a major feature of political life in the metropolis.

But we must not draw too sharp a contrast between suburb and central-city problems. In the out-lying areas the suburbanites may be feeling the bite of suburbanitis. Many of them have discovered that the lower prices for land and the lower taxes are deceptive. Fire insurance rates are often higher, they have to pay more for garbage collection, they often have to build and maintain their own septic tanks, and other costs are higher. Moreover, as suburban real estate

[13] Scott Greer, *Governing the Metropolis* (Wiley, 1962), p. 52.
[14] Edward C. Banfield and James Q. Wilson, *City Politics* (Harvard Univ. Press, 1963), p. 46.
[15] *Ibid.*, p. 37.

becomes improved and as the suburb grows in size, new waterworks and other facilities are needed. The schools become crowded, the parks are inadequate, and the part-time village government is unsatisfactory.

So, common needs of government services, and the heavy expense of them, ultimately press on people both in the core city and in suburbia. This common problem raises the question of whether central city and suburbia can pool their resources in order to deal with their joint problems more effectively. We will return to this question after looking more closely at the politics and government of the core city.

Government of the Central City

The core city may be "decaying" but it remains the most important single governmental unit within metropolis. And its politics are still the dominant concern of the citizens of metropolis, even those who live in the suburbs. How are large cities governed? Like the federal and state governments, metropolitan government is divided into the executive, legislative, and judicial branches, with a large fourth branch of more-or-less independent agencies, commissions, and authorities.

The Men in City Hall

The most important and most publicized big-city official is the mayor. Some men were so effective, and indeed dramatic, in this role that they made names for themselves nationally; Fiorello LaGuardia of New York, Joseph W. Folk of St. Louis, Daniel W. Hoan of Milwaukee, Tom L. Johnson of Cleveland, James M. Curley of Boston are still remembered long after their regimes have ended.

Today the mayor must be the head of a huge bureaucracy as well as being a politician. "The profile of today's big-city mayor—with one difference—is quite similar to that of the chief executive of a large corporation," according to a recent report. "Typically, the mayor is a college graduate, usually with a legal or business background, and is now in his late fifties. He puts in hard, grinding hours at his desk, sometimes six or seven days a week, and his wife suffers as much as his golf game. The difference is in his salary: he usually makes $20,000 to $25,000. There is also a chauffeur-driven limousine and, in some cities, an expense allowance, ranging from $2,000 (Milwaukee) to $55,000 (Chicago). 'Public relations' takes a big chunk of his time. . . . Above all the mayor is a politician." [16]

The mayor of a large city thus has the same basic functions as any major executive leader. As "chief of state" he issues proclamations, receives important city visitors, appears at endless civic breakfasts, luncheons, and dinners, launches community and charity drives. As "chief executive" he appoints the heads of agencies, draws up the budget, checks up on administration, deals with sudden

[16] The Editors of Fortune, *The Exploding Metropolis* (Doubleday, 1958), pp. 87–88.

emergencies, mediates among warring department chiefs, tries to get rid of incompetents or misfits. As "chief of party" he usually dominates city organization of his party; he helps recruit candidates for office, tries to shunt aside his enemies, deals with revolts and opposition within the party, represents the party in Washington or the state capital, and perhaps works through the party to win support from state and national legislators. As chief legislator the mayor draws up proposed legislation and also makes a great deal of specific policy in "filling in the details" of general legislative enactments. Indeed, the only powers of the President that the metropolitan mayor does not hold at the city level are "commander in chief" and "chief of foreign relations"—and even in these areas the mayor has certain defense duties, such as civil defense, and he must often deal with foreign consulates and nationals, especially if he is head of a great port city like San Francisco, Chicago, or New Orleans.

The mayor shares his legislative power with the city council. Typically in the giant city the mayor has extensive power to recommend and to participate in the legislative process; he has a broad veto power, for example, over both policy measures and appropriations. But the balance of power widely varies from city to city. Much depends on the basis on which the councilmen are elected— for example, whether they are elected by the same party organization that supports the mayor, or by a personal organization of their own. The mayor finds that his relation with the legislative branch is essentially a political problem, just as the President and the governors do. Sometimes the mayor must depend on his control of the party organization to insure support in the council. For example, Chicago would seem to have a "weak" form of mayor because the city council consists of 50 members elected in small districts; but Mayor Richard Daley has been able to exercise considerable influence over the council because of his political strength in their districts.[17] Other cities may appear to have more "streamlined" executive-legislative relationships, but the mayor may be weak because he has little political influence over the councilmen.

Whatever the particular combination, the mayor and the council operate in terms of the separation of powers and the checks and balances that characterize other levels of American government. Hence he must ever deal with the problem of splintered and fragmented power, which in turn relates to the question of whether the big city can govern itself.

The Mayor as Chief Executive

The main job of the mayor is administrative in the broadest sense of that term. Under him are the big "line" agencies—police, fire, public safety, traffic, health, sanitation—and a host of special agencies, such as the board of elections, the city planning agency, and commissions that regulate particular occupations and professions. The big-city mayor usually

[17] Martin Meyerson and Edward C. Banfield, *Politics, Planning and the Public Interest* (The Free Press, 1955).

has a large staff—though usually not so large as he would like—that carries out typical "overhead" functions such as personnel, budgeting, and public relations. In this respect the mayor meets the same problems as all executives—problems of coordinating a variety of different activities, assigning responsibilities, checking up to see whether projects have been carried out, finding the ablest available administrators to take charge, allotting money through his control of the budget.

The mayor has a special problem that is found at both the national and state levels of government but not in so extreme form as in the big city. This is the *public* or *special authority*. Essentially the same as a public corporation, such as the Tennessee Valley Authority, these authorities have been set up to undertake important but specialized functions in the big cities. Examples are the Metropolitan Water District of Southern California and the Port of New York Authority. As these examples suggest, the authority oversees functions lying outside as well as inside the boundaries of the metropolitan district. It has legal authority granted it by the state (or states) to raise money, hire experts, and take over some of the big-city jobs, such as transport, water, and housing. The authority has been called "the fastest-growing division of local government" in the United States.

Why public authorities? In part because state legislatures are often hostile to big-city mayors and prefer to place important functions of metropolis outside his reach and that of his political "machine." In part because the authority has great financial flexibility; for example, it can incur debt outside the limits imposed on the city by the state. But most of all, as suggested above, because many problems, such as transportation, are simply too big, and cover too wide a geographic area, to be properly governed by the city itself. Robert Moses of New York City, himself a member of many public authorities, has summed up knowledgeably the case for this kind of device: "The nearest thing to business in government is the public authority, which is business with private capital under public auspices, established only when both private enterprise and routine government have failed to meet an urgent need, and this device is often attacked because it is too independent of daily pressures, too unreachable by the boys, and therefore essentially undemocratic." [18]

Whatever the general pros and cons of the authority—and the debate runs on and on—it poses a special problem for the big-city mayor. Not only are vital functions of metropolitan government beyond his direct control, but even worse, special authorities managing big functions like transit and sanitation constantly come into contact—and conflict—with "line" agencies dealing with closely related problems, such as intercity traffic and law enforcement. It is hard enough for the mayor to coordinate and mediate among his own agencies; it is infinitely harder to deal with independent authorities. But if the authority is a problem for the mayor, it is also a temptation. By helping to sponsor these independent agencies, he can sometimes cut down on his direct load of administration. He can tap other sources of funds and hence keep his own city's tax rate lower

[18] Fortune (eds.), *op. cit.*, p. 99.

than it otherwise would be. If things go wrong he can more easily "pass the buck" by saying that he did not have authority over a certain function and hence cannot be held responsible. But what might in certain instances make things easier for the mayor may not be necessarily good for the "metropolitan welfare"—or for the capacity of the city dwellers as a whole to govern themselves effectively.

Metropolitics: The Political Life of the Big City

The stakes and prizes of big-city politics are tremendous. Since the city government touches personal and group interests at many points, these persons and interests must continually mobilize as much influence as they can. The stakes and prizes are manifold: appointments to city offices, the incidence of taxation, regulation of businesses, professions, and other activities, the question of who gets contracts from the city, the allotment of various city benefits, like education and sanitation. Beyond all this is the "general interest" in honest, efficient, and far-seeing metropolitan government.[19]

Interest Groups in Central City

Around all these stakes and prizes interest groups tend to form in varying degrees of size, solidarity, and effectiveness. The politicians of metropolis must deal with the basic group interests found anywhere in an industrial society—with organized workers and businessmen, professional associations, good government associations, doctors, ethnic groups. But all these are much closer at hand for the city fathers than they may be for a governor or a President. The mayor of a big city is constantly operating in the eye of the political hurricane.

To a greater extent than a President or governor the mayor must deal with special types of interest groups. One of these is the "problem" group—people who share a concern over a particular city problem even though they are members of many different economic interests. Parent-teacher associations, welfare organizations such as the United Fund, and groups concerned with special problems such as "beautifying the city" or developing a park are examples of such problem groups. These interests, supported by the local newspapers, can mobilize a good deal of pressure on city hall, but once the problem is solved or somehow disappears the group may disappear with it. Another special type of interest in the big city are good government and reform groups. Some of these have enjoyed such strong leadership and wide support that they have operated virtually as political parties, as in Cincinnati. But in most big cities the reform groups are simply one more

[19] For an excellent description of the "stakes and prizes" of one city's politics, see Wallace S. Sayre and Herbert Kaufman, *Governing New York City* (Russell Sage Foundation, 1960), ch. 2.

pressure on city hall, and they are often divided among themselves. Their activities range all the way from trying to improve the whole metropolitan area, as in the case of the Greater Philadelphia Movement, to simply collecting facts and figures, as in the case of the Cleveland Bureau of Governmental Research and the Milwaukee Citizens' Research Bureau.

Another interest group of particular importance in the big city is the association or union of city employees. Police, firemen, street cleaners, teachers, and most other such employees are organized into unions, many of which are affiliated with the national AFL-CIO. Professional employees band together in voluntary associations of their own. While all these groups are more or less concerned about the city as a whole, they are mainly interested in specific matters such as their pay, working conditions, job security, and the like. Since the right of city employees to strike is often limited by law, these groups stress persuasion and bargaining in their dealings with city leaders. Some of the groups are so large—such as police and teachers—that with their families and friends they can put intense pressure on city hall. But like groups everywhere, city employees may lack unity, especially on more general issues such as taxation and the organization of city government.

Ordinarily, group interests in metropolis pursue their activities much like pressure groups anywhere; they put out propaganda, hold meetings, write letters to the mayor and council, and organize all the "pressure" they can. Occasionally, a local interest group provides a striking example of the effective mobilization of influence. In 1957, for example, the Esso Standard Oil Company, which employed 1,800 people in Bayonne, New Jersey and paid a fourth of the city's taxes, threatened to leave the city if local officials went ahead with a planned tax increase. The oil company, in combination with other businesses, concerted their efforts through citizens' and research organizations. Contending that the city's civil service was overstaffed, the businessmen asked for budget cuts as the price of their staying in the city. The five city commissioners and the school board complied by cutting the pay of city laborers, making economies in textbooks and athletic programs, and reducing various city services. Esso then announced it would continue its modernization plan. This was a case of one set of interests overcoming another set—most notably the unions and associations of city employees.[20]

The effectiveness of metropolitan group interests turns not only on their own size, unity, and leadership. It turns also on the kind of government they are dealing with. The politics and government in most of our big cities, as in the states and the nation as a whole, are pluralistic, so that group interests must deal with many centers of power and decision. "Whether a city has a loose and many-centered politics or a powerful organization or political leader dominating the scene," Lockard says, "there is always bargaining between interests, bargaining between interests and leaders in government, bargaining between interests

[20] Duane Lockard, *The Politics of State and Local Government* (Macmillan, 1963), pp. 257, 258.

and the bureaucracy. Bargaining yes, but the patterns of bargaining vary with different kinds of political systems. In a city with focused leadership bargaining goes on in an atmosphere of deference to the power potential of the leadership. Direct negotiations with the leader or his deputies become common for all interests, and while other negotiations of course continue to be carried on, the fact that there is a central source of power conditions the manner and consequences of interest group demands. In a multi-centered pattern of politics a more free-for-all kind of bargaining is common." A centrally organized set of city employees or union members, or a unified group of businessmen as in Bayonne, can sometimes multiply their power—especially to prevent action—if they deal with a loose cluster of decision-making centers.

The interest configuration of central city is in many ways similar to that of the national electorate now that this is an urban nation. However, within the city the electorate is biased in favor of the foreign-born, Negroes, Puerto Ricans, blue-collar workers. In national elections these groups support the Democratic party and these partisan affiliations hold for local politics. "Labor unions, the NAACP and the Urban League, the Sons of Garibaldi and Kosciusko, and others, including (not least) the professionals of the Democratic party," writes Greer, "are the corporate actors that contend for patronage, power, profit, and the control of the policy in the central city." But as Greer points out, to gain control of central city the politicians must also appeal to the "outer wards," populated by the middle classes with interests much like those of suburbia. Thus, politics of central city "represent most of urban America—but in a biased fashion." [21]

Who puts together these political configurations? The big city "machine."

Centralized Politics: The City Machine

At the turn of the century the boss was the typical ruler of many of our larger cities, and of some of our smaller ones. After touring the United States the famous muckraker, Lincoln Steffens, reported: "St. Louis exemplified boodle; Minneapolis, police graft; Pittsburgh, a political and industrial machine; and Philadelphia, general civic corruption." [22] Why were the big American cities boss-ridden? Many reasons were advanced: lack of public interest and the refusal of leading citizens to take part in public affairs; the influx of immigrants who found that the ward leaders and precinct men were their friends and that politics offered the main means of climbing the economic and social ladder; faulty structural organization of the city leading to such weak government that some political leader had to take charge; and finally—and this was a favorite argument of Steffens and his fellow reformers—business interests that stood behind the bosses and used them to secure favorable franchises and contracts and protection from regulation.

[21] Greer, *op. cit.*, pp. 148–149.
[22] Lincoln Steffens, *The Shame of the Cities* (Peter Smith: republished 1948; original edition 1904), p. 16.

Few strong, city-wide political machines exist today. But one that does, in Chicago, illuminates the methods of the past as well as the way that America's second largest city, until recently, at least, has conducted its political affairs. A study of the city's politics reported:

> In a formal sense, as noted above, Chicago was run by a city council consisting of 50 aldermen and by the mayor, who was its presiding officer. Actually it was run by the mayor and half a dozen of the most powerful Democratic aldermen. These "Big Boys," as they were called, controlled the rest of the aldermen by granting or denying them good committee assignments, appropriations for their wards, and other important political favors. One of the "Big Boys" was chairman of the Council's Finance Committee and hence was able to control appropriations, even to the extent of having city services reduced in some ward if its aldermen refused to "play ball." [23]

Behind this concentration of governmental power was a disciplined party. An alderman had to work closely with the party leader in his ward; often he himself was the leader. Not only was he the elected representative of the local party members; "in fact he was commonly the 'boss' of the ward; the party organization in the ward 'belonged' to him. He decided who would run on the party's ticket within the ward, he appointed and dismissed precinct captains at will, and he dispensed patronage." Sometimes aldermen rebelled against the city machine; often they formed factional alliances or geographical blocs. But rarely could an alderman fight the machine successfully. "The leaders of the Central (Party) Committee could bring him into line by withholding patronage or discharging public employees from his ward, by denying him financial support from the party's general coffers at election time, or by allowing an investigation of graft and corruption to take place in his ward." The central committee could even destroy a whole ward organization, but it usually preferred not to use such disruptive measures.

The key man in the organization was the precinct captain. A typical captain, who had spent 19 years in precinct work, described his work as follows:

> I try to establish a relationship of personal obligation with my people. . . . I spend two or three evenings a week all year round visiting people, playing cards, talking, and helping them with their problems. . . . I know 90 per cent of my people by their names. Actually I consider myself a social worker for my precinct. I help my people get relief and driveway permits. I help them on unfair parking fines and property assessments. The last is most effective in my neighborhood. The only return I ask is they register and vote. . . . I never take leaflets or conduct rallies in my precinct. After all, this is a question of personal friendship between me and my neighbors.[24]

[23] The description of the Chicago machine, including the quotations, is from Meyerson and Banfield, *op. cit.*, pp. 64–75.

[24] Quoted by Fay Calkins, *The CIO and the Democratic Party* (Univ. of Chicago Press, 1952), pp. 67–68.

The Decline of the Boss?

Aside from Chicago and a few other cities, there has been a steady decline in the number and power of city-wide party bosses since the turn of the century. This is due in small part to a steady drumbeat of criticism and opposition by reform groups. It is due mainly to more basic causes: the shrinking of patronage as more and more city jobs came under civil service; the decrease in immigration; stricter supervision of the expenditure of city funds by the state and national governments, which allot part of the funds for major functions; a more affluent society, making city dwellers less dependent on the machine; and above all, the rise of the welfare state, which supplies social security, unemployment insurance, medical assistance, and relief checks, as compared to the Christmas basket, the half-ton of coal, or the outing up the river that the organization provided free in the old days. The change should not be overdrawn. Ward bosses still dispense some of the old kind of aid, and their services are especially needed to help less educated people to get around big-city regulations, such as parking restrictions. And there are basic forces at work supporting the machines. The exodus to the suburbs is leaving the central city more and more in the hands of the less well off: Puerto Ricans, Negroes, southern whites, who are being "restricted" to the central city and who need and can profit from the help of a political machine.[25] But the trend is the other way.

What takes the place of the party machine? To some extent the personal organizations of mayors or other powerful city officials. Big-city politics abhors political vacuums—somebody must organize and govern. Mayors like Joseph Clark of Philadelphia and Robert Wagner of New York built their own "machines" that could often defeat the old type of boss, as the case study of the New York mayor will suggest. But more often the machine has been succeeded by a much less centralized system. Political influence may shift into the hands of a number of powerful and perhaps competing office holders—a few councilmen or aldermen, perhaps, or the chairman of the school committee or the head of the finance board or some other commission that controls the budget; or into the hands of state or federal officials from the metropolitan area, such as a United States senator, a congressman who may head an important committee in Washington, a state senator; or even into the hands of non-office holders such as a newspaper publisher, union head, leaders of ethnic groups, or some combination of these and others.

While the pattern of power varies widely from city to city, the problem remains the central one that has occupied us throughout this book. Granted that "bossism" is an evil, how much better off is a metropolis that has no central system of power, that may be nothing more politically than a collection of warring fiefdoms or Chinese tongs? One virtue of the boss was that occasionally he *did*

25 James Q. Wilson, "Politics and Reform in American Cities," Ivan Hinderaker (ed.), *American Government Annual 1962–1963* (Holt, Rinehart and Winston, 1962), p. 38.

want to do things for the "people" and at least he had the power to operate
through the various units of government. A divided government might be much
more honest but less effective, especially in shaping and administering programs
for the lower-income groups and for the long-run improvement of the city. To
be sure, a "strong mayor" can sometimes gather the reins into his own hands,
as we noted, but the difficulty with this is that his power is likely to last only
as long as he holds office. LaGuardia was a strong mayor who built a personal
organization in New York, as did Joseph Clark more recently in Philadelphia,
but neither man converted his personal organization into a lasting *party* organization.[26]

Party weakness is intensified by the fact that most metropolitan areas tend to
favor one party, usually the Democrats. The absence of real two-party politics
has somewhat the same effect on the city as it does on the South: One party is
so big, and wins with such little effort, that it fails to keep in fighting trim,
grows fat and sluggish, and sometimes disintegrates into factions. The minority
party is too weak to have much hope of success, fails to provide a strong opposition or meaningful alternatives, and often plays a very negative type of politics.
Just as the South is still responding to the politics of the Civil War, so the big
cities are still dominated by the depression, the New Deal action in the 1930's,
and the sympathy and help they get from the urban-oriented Democrats. If
metropolis existed by itself, as an island, its two major parties might come into
balance, one governing effectively and one opposing strongly. But the one-party
system discourages "party government" of this sort and raises the kind of basic
questions about the nature of political organization that we discussed in Chapters
12 and 20.

A Typology of Big City Politics

Because there are so many cities
and because only recently have scholars systematically studied these governmental
and political units, it is difficult to generalize about city political patterns. What
is true in Chicago may or may not be an accurate picture of Cleveland or Detroit
or Los Angeles. One scholar, James Q. Wilson, has drawn on well-supported studies
to make a tentative classification of big-city political systems.

1. *Machine politics*—Chicago and Albany, as examples. Wilson suggests that
small districts or wards based on fairly homogeneous ethnic or religious neighborhoods, a large number of elective offices, and a polyglot, lower-income population
in the city as a whole tend to promote organization or machine politics.

2. *Factional alliances or coalition of groups*—Kansas City, Boston, Cleveland, St. Louis, Jersey City, and Cincinnati. In these cities, although a single
party, usually the Democrats, wins the elections, officeholders are not bound

[26] James Reichley, *The Art of Government* (Fund for the Republic, 1959).

together by the party and are responsive to separate and independent political constituencies. One may represent a political club, another the civil servants, another the business community, another the Negro wards, and so on.

3. *Nonpolitical elite systems* where control over public policy is in the hands of newspaper publishers, businessmen, labor leaders, lawyers, bankers, and so on—Houston, Los Angeles, Detroit. In these cities the party organizations have little to say in selecting candidates, and elective officials remain aloof from party affairs. As Wilson points out in these "nonpartisan cities"—and here we refer to behavior, not to the formal charter provisions—city policies tend to favor the business community.[27]

Elements of all three types—machine, factional, nonpartisan elite—are, of course, found in all large cities. The differences are a matter of the emphasis. And of course in time the political situation in cities changes. In almost all cities there are also to be found a variety of "reform" groups, some working outside the established dominant party, some working within.

The Rise (and Decline?) of the Amateur

Old-style machine politics based on serving the needs of the masses of newly arrived immigrants and financed by undisguised graft is on the way out. New-style politics where political leaders must mediate among interests no longer satisfied merely with a few jobs on the city payroll are developing. And one facet of this new politics is the emergence of a new type, the amateur politico.

Adlai Stevenson's candidacy for President brought many of these amateurs into politics. Joining the Volunteers for Stevenson, working at doorbell ringing, and fund raising, whetted the taste for politics of these enthusiastic housewives, young public relations men, lawyers, and college professors. They organized political clubs to stay in politics.

The amateurs consist largely of highly educated, white, middle-class groups, cosmopolitan in outlook, under 45 in age, highly articulate, acting in the tradition of an earlier generation of New Deal liberals and Progressive Reformers. Concerned about the failure of the party professionals to emphasize issues—the professionals simply want to be *elected*—and the inability of party leaders to develop programmatic platforms, the new amateurs formed their own clubs, where they discussed civil rights, urban renewal, civil defense, education, nuclear policy. But they are not mere debating societies; they are also action oriented, working at the grassroots to secure the nomination of candidates, often against the leadership of the regular Democratic organizations.

Whether the reform clubs will have any staying power and will set the style for modern city politics remains to be seen. Party professionals and some political

[27] The above is drawn from James Q. Wilson, "Politics and Reform in American Cities," Ivan Hinderaker (ed.), *The American Government Annual, op. cit.,* pp. 37–55.

scientists are highly skeptical. They accuse these amateurs of being more interested in talk than in action, of preferring to be "right" rather than effective, of
intolerance toward those who do not share their own goals. The "pros" also
contend that the amateurs are unrealistic in hoping to develop programmatic,
cohesive, disciplined parties of liberal orientation within our large cities.

In fact, it is argued, the amateurs are making it difficult for the party professionals to secure the goals the amateurs profess. The great mass of the urban
population does not share these goals, but if the amateurs force elected officers to
hew the "new party line" and fail to recognize the essential compromises necessary to gain power, they will merely throw the political control of the city into
the hands of those who will exploit mass sentiments for illiberal purposes. In
time, endorsement of candidates by a club may become a political liability; the
clubs will wither away. As James Q. Wilson, a critic of the clubs, writes: "The
debate over issues becomes, in a strict sense, a spurious debate, because it is
not a responsible discussion of real policy alternatives but a device for generating
incentives for party activities." [28]

Others take a different view of the clubs. They view them as means of activat-
ing citizens who otherwise find local politics to be of no significance. The clubs
can discuss and shape party policies of much more relevance to metropolis than
traditional "bread-and-butter" issues—preserving and enhancing attractive neighborhoods, improving city planning, increasing the city's concern for artistic
and cultural activity. Moreover, even if the amateurs have a rather narrow perspective about politics and are at the moment much too rigid and unwilling to
accept political realities, they will learn in time to function as a regular party
unit.

Can the Mayor Lead?—A Case Study

The mayor is the most important and the most visible political figure in the big
city. Like the President, he is supposed to enunciate the city's goals, play the
leading role in getting them accepted by the people and adopted by the city government, and to carry them out. But like the President, he is hemmed in on
many sides. Since big cities vary widely in their politics, and mayors in their
powers, we might explore the problem of mayoral leadership by taking one
example—the mayor of New York. His job has been considered as second only
to the President's in complexity and manageability, for not only is New York
the nation's biggest city and one of the financial, cultural, intellectual, and trading
centers of the world, but it sprawls over parts of three states and hence continually faces problems of city-state-federal relationships.[29]

[28] James Q. Wilson, *The Amateur Democrat: Club Politics in Three Cities—New York,
Chicago, Los Angeles* (Univ. of Chicago Press, 1962), is a careful analysis of the goals, composi-
tion, and role of the clubs.
[29] This case study, except where otherwise noted, is taken wholly from Sayre and Kaufman,
op. cit.

The Administrative Chief?

The mayor of New York City is supposed to be the top administrative boss of the city government, and in many respects he is. For one thing, he appoints the heads of virtually all departments, such as police or fire; members of city boards and commissions, such as the Parole Commission; and city magistrates and justices. Unlike the President and most governors, he does not share his appointing power with legislative bodies. The mayor's authority to remove subordinates, despite numerous restrictions, is also fairly sweeping. In short, in his power to "hire and fire" the mayor of New York is truly "the chief executive officer of the city," as the city charter says.

In other respects, however, the mayor finds himself restricted as administrative chief. This is especially the case in the most crucial administrative area, budget and finance. "The Mayor is not the chief fiscal officer of the city; the Comptroller has greater financial powers than does the Mayor," according to Sayre and Kaufman. "Nor does the Mayor have budget powers comparable to those of the President or the Governor; he has the formal power to direct the preparation of 'the executive budget' step in the expense budget process, together with a minor role in the preparation of the capital budget, but the modification, and thus the larger elements of the administration of both budgets, belong to the Board of Estimate," [30] which agency will be described below. The mayor's power to reorganize agencies and departments is much more limited than the President's. He has an immediate staff of about 60, but this is hardly adequate for coordinating the huge and varied departments that actually run the city.

The mayor also exercises limited administrative power over the city's myriad independent authorities. Some of the heads of authorities have won such wide recognition that they are politically effective in their own right. Most notable of these by far is Robert Moses, who might well be labeled "Mr. Authority." His jobs over the past years suggest the variety of special agencies as well as the versatility of this brilliant, aggressive, and often flammable man. Moses has been chairman of the Triborough Bridge and Tunnel Authority since its inception, Commissioner of the Park Department, a member of the City Planning Commission, chairman of the Mayor's Committee on Slum Clearance, a member of the New York City Youth Board, president of the Jones Beach State Parkway Authority, among many other jobs. In all these positions he has attracted friends (and enemies) within the city's administration as well as among the public. Clearly, in dealing with Moses the mayor is dealing with an independent leader who has his own "constituency" separate from the mayor's—and relations between the two are often exacerbated because Moses is a lifelong Republican and most New York mayors are Democrats.[31]

[30] *Ibid.*, p. 670.

[31] For a provocative and colorful account of an independent authority *not* run by Mr. Moses, see Edward T. Chase, "How to Rescue New York from Its Port Authority," *Harper's Magazine* (June 1960), pp. 67–74, which describes the political context of the authority and the political controversy surrounding it.

The case of Robert Moses reminds us of a central fact of administration that we noted in Chapter 18—that administrators are *people*, that they have their own interests, attitudes, and loyalties that may conflict with those of the mayor. This is certainly the case in New York City. Even the great "line" departments such as police and fire, theoretically under the direct control of the mayor, are not composed simply of men drilled and marshaled and deployed from the top. The heads of the departments are experienced men who have worked their way up from the ranks, who have strong loyalties and obligations to their colleagues and subordinates, who may entertain professional and perhaps political ambitions of their own, and who enjoy direct access to newspaper editors, party leaders, interest groups, and professional associations inside and outside New York. The rank-and-file employees—the firemen, policemen, sanitation men, city hospital workers, guards at the city jails—have their unions or associations, desires for higher pay and shorter hours, and all kinds of internal specializations (for example, corner cops and city detectives), jealousies, and mutual defense coalitions against excessive interference from the top.

So we must forget the notion of the mayor as a real administrative "boss." He has great administrative resources, but he must ever ride herd on a collection of many thousands of human beings with crosscutting interests and attitudes. And his powers are even more limited in his other roles.

Legislative Leader?

The mayor of New York, like any other mayor, finds his policy-making power splintered and fragmented the moment he takes office. For he is working within a federal system of government that divides power among the national, state, and local governments, and among many officials at each level. Practically speaking, the mayor must often coordinate or at least clear his major policies with the President, the governor of New York, one or two United States senators from the state, several members of Congress, a host of state legislators from the city, and numerous other officials, such as the state attorney general, members of Congress from the adjoining states of New Jersey and Connecticut, and perhaps a Cabinet member or two. Within the city government his legislative power is further fragmented.

To be sure, the mayor has formal responsibility for shaping and presenting the legislative program. Indeed, formally or informally he presents it several times—to the council, to the governor and the state legislature, and to such other officials or bodies that affect his program or policies. But the formal law-making power is vested in the City Council, consisting of 25 councilmen elected by the same districts that choose state senators, and of the president of the council, who is elected on a city-wide basis. While on paper the council would appear to be virtually a "little Congress," actually it has played a rather passive role, allowing the mayor or other officials to take the leadership. The council fails to exercise the historic weapon of legislative bodies against executives—the appropriating power. It is almost monopolized by one party—the

Democrats—and hence lacks vigorous internal controversy and decision-making. Weakness begets weakness; as the council has failed to exercise its power over policy, it has failed to attract strong men who might convert it into a stronger agency.

The main fiscal control of the city is exercised neither by the mayor nor the council but by the Board of Estimate. This is a rather curious institution for a city that prides itself on modernity and "stream-lining" in so many other areas of life. Composed of eight members with varying numbers of votes (four each for the Mayor, the Comptroller, and the President of the Council; two each for the five borough presidents), the Board of Estimate is not as such elected directly by the people; its members are all elected to other positions. Still, it has the dominant role in three vital areas—the enactment of local laws, the expense budget, and the capital budget. Unlike the council, it does not pliably follow the mayor's lead; usually it prefers to fight him. Sayre and Kaufman sum up its role as follows: "It has the most generous grant of formal powers of all the city's governmental institutions; its eight members are the most influential elected officials in the city government; it has developed a mode of operation which maximizes both its formal and informal powers; the relationships of its members with the party leaders are close and usually stable; it has high prestige with the other participants (in the city's political process), particularly with those to whom it provides a public forum; and its institutional life, especially its informal processes, is surrounded by a helpful amount of mystery." [32] Like Congress on the national level, the board is the main countervailing power to the mayor.

A city legislator does not automatically need to be hostile to the mayor. The extent to which a mayor can induce cooperation from a councilman or a member of the Board of Estimate turns mainly on the extent to which the mayor can shape the political pressures working on the legislator in City Hall and in the latter's district. In City Hall the mayor can deal in jobs, favors, personal recognition, and the other usual currency of practical politics. But this may not be enough, just as it is often not enough in Washington, for the usual currency of political influence is limited, and rival political leaders have some of that currency too. Ultimately the mayor's power depends on the extent to which he can mobilize support for himself and his program that can be converted to support or threaten the councilman or member of the Board of Estimate. And this balance in turn depends on political organization.

Party Leader?

The mayor of New York is the most powerful single party leader in the city. Still, he must share his party power with a host of other officials and with party leaders. There is no single city-wide political party organization; thus Democrats are organized on the basis of county committees from the five boroughs, which in turn oversee vast hierarchies of precinct, ward, and assembly district organizations. The mayor deals not with

[32] Sayre and Kaufman, op. cit., p. 626.

a unified party organization but with five county leaders, who may be members of the United States Congress, borough presidents (who have power in the Board of Estimate), or traditional party "bosses" who hold no major office, as was the case with Carmine De Sapio, but who exert considerable influence over their county organization through the "machine." Sometimes the mayor benefits from the absence of city-wide unity, for he can follow the tactic of "dividing and conquering" the county leaders; but the party divisions may handicap him in pushing through a new program. The Republicans are somewhat more unified than the Democrats, but they lack the numbers to play competitive politics.

What a strong mayor must do is to build his own personal organization inside and outside the regular political party. This is a formidable task. He has considerable patronage, but jobs are not enough to build a political machine, for the mayor faces the classic problem, in handing out a job, of creating "nine enemies and one ingrate." Unlike the President, who can lean on the national party committee as well as his numerous personal staff, the mayor has few political aides. He must deal with party committeemen who may be much more interested in working for other candidates and office holders than for him. Usually the mayor finds that his personal organization is not enough by itself; he must supplement it by bargaining for allies among the other office holders and heads of personal organizations.

Usually the mayor and the party leaders work hand in glove; the mayor "recognizes" the party leaders through patronage and the party leaders help the mayor by insuring his renomination and helping his re-election. Occasionally the mayor and the machine have a falling out. A dramatic and suggestive example of the latter was the struggle in 1961 between Mayor Robert F. Wagner and Carmine De Sapio, head of the regular Democrats in Manhattan, better known as Tammany. In earlier decades the mayor has often been subordinated to the machine; Tammany chiefs like the nefarious William Tweed and the more genteel Charles Murphy dictated key Democratic nominations. In 1961, making full use of the personal machine that he had built up in his seven years in office, Wagner trounced De Sapio and the Tammany candidate in a bitter battle for renomination.

Wagner then announced that he would take the leadership in reorganizing and strengthening the Democratic party. Following his election he proposed new party rules under which the party would open its ranks to all interested citizens, improve its procedures for internal democracy, and play a more prominent role in drawing up and publicizing party programs. He forced some of the old party leaders out of their positions and even took on Representative Charles Buckley, long the Democratic boss of the Bronx. Yet there were many who were skeptical of any lasting improvement in the city's Democratic party. They pointed out that the mayor's real interest was in strengthening his own position in future elections, and that the reforms would wither away and the old practices would be restored as soon as he left the city's political scene. And they could point to many examples in the past to support their argument.

Leader or Head Bargainer?

The evidence is quite clear: The mayor of New York is severely restricted as a mayor, no matter how great his ability. Most of the time he must piece together a coalition out of various politicians and fragments of influence. He is less the leader who draws his sword, points out the direction, and rallies his battalions, than the horse trader who talks and swaps and persuades and compromises. His governmental role tends to be more defensive than affirmative. He is continually involved in the process of building administrative, legislative, or party coalitions, and the price of such coalitions is usually weakened programs and policies. Usually he is in the middle of the political market place; little can be done of importance without his consent. But he finds effective action along a wide front, or even long-range planning, to be very difficult.

Whether or not one approves of this situation depends on his views of the organization of political power. Some would contend that more progress comes out of loose political arrangements like that of New York City than out of a highly centralized and disciplined system. Lasting progress, they contend, comes here and there, two feet forward and one foot back, and is not dependent on direction from the top. Others hold that a city as sprawling and disorganized as New York needs a strong mayor and effective city government to lead it, and that too much bargaining and compromising will make impossible "mastery of the metropolis" by the city people as a whole.

Many New Yorkers favor moderate changes to give the mayor more leadership. They see several alternative routes. One is to change the city charter so that the mayor would have more authority and responsibility; significant charter changes in this direction have now gone through. Others believe that the mayor cannot really become a leader unless the party is reorganized; they believe in the kind of party discipline discussed in Chapter 12. Others feel that metropolitan self-government is hopeless, that the people of the giant city cannot really govern themselves, and that the job should be taken over by other governments. The election of John V. Lindsay as mayor of New York on a Republican-Liberal party ticket in 1965 offered a dramatic test of whether a reform-minded mayor could meet the challenge of metropolis.

Can We Master Metropolis?

Most of this chapter would seem to answer with a big "yes" our theme question: Have the people of metropolis lost the power to govern themselves? The division between central city and suburbia, divided executive authority, fragmented legislative power, splintered and non-competitive political parties, the absence of strong central government for the whole metropolitan region, the need for the mayor and other city leaders to bargain with a host of national, state, and local officials—

all this would seem to suggest that the people as a whole cannot master the shapeless giants that have arisen in a score of areas across the nation.

Who governs, then? In the last century reformers were afraid of boss domination. But in modern metropolis, the mayor of the central city, as we have seen, lacks authority over all the agencies within the city alone, not counting the hundreds of other units of government. Political machines do not run central city, let alone the whole metropolis. The "interests" do not control metropolis, nor does a "business elite," nor any other kind of "they." In fact, who governs metropolis? Nobody? Or perhaps everbody? For the "issue is not the manipulation of the citizenry by a small elite, but rather the inability of elites to create the conditions required for making decisions." [33] And this is the problem.

What needs to be done? Some argue that piecemeal, patchwork measures are inadequate. Metropolis is a single community, they argue, it needs a single government, a government adequate to handle the total problems of the metropolitan community. How to achieve this integration?

One suggestion is to make the county the major unit of government. Where the county covers the entire metropolitan region, real integration can be achieved. Three-fourths of all metropolitan areas are entirely within a single county. As it stands, many people pay taxes to support a city superintendent of schools and a county superintendent of schools, a city police department and a county sheriff, a city street department and a county highway department, city welfare and county relief.

Various kinds of city-county consolidations, or city-county separations, or transfer of all functions to the county, have been suggested for metropolitan regions, but they have not been widely adopted. In Virginia, however, all cities over 10,000 are separated from the county, and St. Louis, Baltimore, and several other cities have withdrawn from their counties. This move avoids duplication of effort within the central city, but it sometimes leaves the people in the county out in the cold. It can also further complicate relations between the central city and the suburbs. More successful in solving some metropolitan problems has been the transfer by cities of selected functions to the county. For example, Erie County in New York has taken over health, hospital, library, and welfare services formerly handled by the cities within the county. Los Angeles County has assumed many functions for the hundreds of communities in that sprawling metropolitan region. And in 1963 Davidson County, which includes Nashville, assumed responsibility for almost all local government functions, a most ambitious example of an attempt to govern a metropolis through the machinery of county government.

Another proposal to deal with problems of metropolitan regions is to permit the central city to *annex* all the surrounding units of government. Whatever the speculative merits of such a program, however, it is often politically impossible for the central city to take over after suburbs have established their own governments.

[33] Morris Janowitz (ed.), *Community Political Systems* (The Free Press, 1959), Preface.

Finally, many reformers advocate the "federated metropolitan" idea. They would allow each local city to retain its identity and to remain in charge of certain functions, but would create a central metropolitan government to deal with area-wide functions. Although several major cities in other nations—Toronto, London, Berlin—have moved to a federal-city plan, the only metropolitan region in the United States to try it is Dade County (Miami), Florida. (New York has some aspects of a federal city, since each borough has its own president who administers such functions as street repairs and building maintenance, but the central government of all five boroughs really governs the entire city.)

The Federal City Plan—A Case Study

Until 1957 the Miami metropolitan area was typical of many big cities—the population had mushroomed in the last couple of decades but its political structure remained unchanged. Miami, the core city, was surrounded by twenty-five separate municipalities and wide expanses of unincorporated areas. Duplication of governmental services between Dade County and the several municipalities in some areas and inadequate service in others were all complicated by an inequitable tax structure. Then in 1956 the first step toward improving the situation was taken when the people of Florida approved a constitutional amendment giving Dade County constitutional home rule. The next year the voters of the entire county adopted a home-rule charter creating a county-wide metropolitan government.

The new charter provides for a federated structure. The city of Miami and all the suburban cities retain their own identity and those functions not assigned to "Metro," the county government. "Metro" has jurisdiction over such activities as fire and police protection, slum clearance, major transportation facilities, planning, water, and sewage systems. "Metro" is governed by a board of commissioners elected on a county-wide basis who in turn select a county manager.[34]

During the first year of its operation under the new charter, "Metro" was sued 150 times by opponents of metropolitan federation, but it has won all the decisive legal battles. In 1959 a move to amend the charter to reduce the powers of "Metro" and return many functions to the separate cities was soundly defeated.[35] It is too soon to make any definitive statements on the workings of "this bold experiment," but success of the federated-city program in Dade County may serve to encourage other areas to take the plunge. Some kind of federal-city system offers real advantages, especially for the 22 large metropolitan regions that are cut into pieces by state boundaries.[36]

[34] See *The Government of Metropolitan Miami* (Public Administration Service, 1955).

[35] O. W. Campbell, "Progress Report on Metropolitan Miami," *Public Management* (April 1959), pp. 81–82. See also Reinhold Wolff, *Three Years of Progress; 1957–1960: A Report to the People, Miami Metro* (Univ. of Miami Bureau of Business & Economic Research).

[36] Daniel R. Grant, "The Government of Interstate Metropolitan Areas," *The Western Political Quarterly* (March 1955), pp. 90–107.

The Politics of Metropolitan Reorganization

In the last 30 years, 88 major surveys have been made of metropolitan governments, and today in almost every metropolitan area there is at least one official or semi-official body working to rationalize governmental structure.[37] Yet, as one distinguished student of the subject has pointed out, "So far we have accomplished little more than a world's record for words used in proportion to cures effected." [38] Why has progress been so slow? To answer this question, we must review the politics of metropolitan reorganization.

In most metropolitan regions, to combine city and suburbs would be to shift political power to the suburbs. In most northern centers it would give Republicans control of city affairs. In other cases it would enable Democrats to threaten the present Republican one-party systems in the suburbs. In any event, it would upset present political arrangements in a fashion difficult to predict exactly. Under these circumstances neither Democratic rulers of the central cities nor Republicans in control of the suburbs show much enthusiasm for metropolitan government schemes.

However, "It would be a mistake to suppose that the conflict lies altogether or even mainly between the two party organizations or among the professional politicians who have a stake in them. The party differences are important . . . , but they reflect deeper and still more important differences. Metropolitan government would mean the transfer of power over the central cities from the largely lower-class Negro and Catholic elements who live in them to the largely middle-class white and Protestant elements who live in the suburbs." [39]

Apart from these political, social, racial, and economic differences which make metropolitan reorganization difficult, the fact is that most of the residents of metropolis are not dissatisfied with the present governmental structure. Of course they want better services, but these they hope to achieve by negotiation and other special devices. There is no rebellion against the existing governmental structure.[40] Moreover, it may not be the best arrangement but it does work after a fashion.

Cooperation in Practice

Drastic alteration of the constitutional structure of metropolis seems unlikely, at least in the near future. Yet metropolis is not likely to disappear. "Rather than dwindle or collapse," writes

[37] Edward C. Banfield, "The Politics of Metropolitan Area Organization," *Midwest Journal of Political Science* (May 1957), p. 77. Most of the materials in this section are taken from this illuminating article.

[38] T. H. Reed, "Hope for 'Suburbanitis,' " *National Municipal Review* (December 1950), p. 542.

[39] Banfield, *op. cit.*, p. 87.

[40] Robert C. Wood and V. V. Almendinger, *1400 Governments: The Political Economy of the New York Metropolitan Region* (Harvard Univ. Press, 1961), Chapter 3.

Kevin Lynch, "it is more likely to become the normal human habitat." [41] And through patchwork, piecemeal, pragmatic arrangements the services the public wants and is willing to pay for are being provided.

The special metropolitan districts, such as the Cook County Sanitary District and the Metropolitan (Park) District Commission for Boston, have been mentioned. Central cities and county governments are providing services for the satellite cities. For example, thirty-three suburban communities buy water from Chicago. Los Angeles County supplies a variety of services to the smaller cities within the county on a contractual basis. [42]

The fiscal problems of metropolis are being met by two devices: Central cities are beginning to levy taxes on the earnings of all who work in the city no matter where they live. More important, the federal government by grants to states and cities is providing a large portion of the funds to deal with city planning, improvement of mass transportation facilities, urban redevelopment, hospital building and operations, and welfare.

It is not a neat system. Problems are plentiful. But as Webb S. Fiser writes, "Our difficulties derive from more than fragmentation of governmental units. . . . Creating a more desirable urban environment depends upon a combination of private and governmental action." [43] A relation between government and private interests that expedites rather than suffocates action for the general welfare is a crucial need of metropolis.

A Solution Outside Metropolis?

Many political scientists, for reasons discussed in this chapter, hold that the solution is beyond the capacity of metropolis itself. They have advanced a variety of proposals. Some favor strong controls by the federal government; and as a start they feel the setting up of the new Department of Housing and Urban Development in Washington will assist and aid megalopolis. Others believe that the job must be done by the states, which hold the fundamental constitutional power. Still others advocate bold new proposals to establish *regional* governments that would rule over huge regions embracing a host of metropolitan areas—most notably, the long stretch of congested urban areas from south of Washington, D.C., to north of Boston.

All these solutions have their opponents. Although court stimulated redistricting of congressional districts is beginning to alter the rural bias of Congress, as reflected in congressional enactment in 1965 of President Johnson's proposal for a Department of Housing and Urban Development, Congress still does not show that it is overly sympathetic to urban needs. State control? Reapportionment may

[41] Kevin Lynch, "The Pattern of the Metropolis," in Lloyd Rodwin (ed.), *The Future Metropolis* (Braziller, 1961), p. 105.

[42] Vincent Ostrom, Charles M. Tiebout, and Robert Warren, "The Organization of Government in Metropolitan Areas: A Theoretical Inquiry," *The American Political Science Review* (December 1961), p. 831.

[43] Webb S. Fiser, *Mastery of the Metropolis* (Prentice-Hall, 1962), p. 5.

make state legislatures more responsive to urban needs, but states are unable easily to deal with the problem of giant cities that stretch over state lines. New regional governments? A fascinating idea, but one that is probably beyond the reach of constitutional power and the capacity of the American people to engineer drastic governmental changes.

The issue, however, goes deeper than this—it goes back to the very heart of the question of government by the people. Can popular government best be effected through a strong executive leader of the LaGuardia or Daley type—a man who wins or builds a strong position of political power and then pulls the divided city government together behind his program? Many scholars would answer yes; they contend that progress can come only as a result of strong, central controls at the top, even though they want the leader to be willing to make concessions to particular groups and local areas. Not only can executive leadership bring about the drastic changes that may be necessary in metropolis, according to this point of view, but only through a strong mayor and a powerful organization (personal or party) can metropolitan government work for the benefit of the great majority of the people, especially low-income groups who are not fully represented in city councils or other legislative assemblies of metropolis. Just as the nation has needed Jacksons and Lincolns and Roosevelts, so the cities need popular, even charismatic, leadership.

Others disagree. Progress in the giant city, they hold, comes from piecemeal efforts, from lengthy bargaining among a multitude of leaders of all types, from community action, from exerting pressure here and there, from hammering out agreements or "treaties" among diverse groups. They grant that government-by-negotiation is often slow, and that makeshift arrangements sometimes result. But given the nature of megalopolis, it is impossible to do better. Instead of grandiose schemes of regional government and city planning and disruptive urban renewal of whole blocks, they would like to see more moderate and prudent efforts. In the process they hope to hold on to some of the values of metropolis today—the unique streets, some of the older buildings, the little houses and apartment buildings that they prefer to the great hunks of concrete and glass and steel so beloved, they feel, by the city planners and reformers.

There are many positions in between these extremes. But perhaps the extremes pose once again our crucial problem of central political control versus pluralism that runs throughout this volume.

33· STATE AND LOCAL GOVERNMENT IN ACTION

The roads we ride on, the schools we attend, the teachers we listen to, the electric light bills we pay, the purity of the water we drink, the safety of the elevators we ride in, when and whom we can marry—all these matters and many others are affected by what state and local officials do. Merely to list the activities of state and local officials would take a large book, and make a dull one.

829

And yet all these activities are part and parcel of the exciting business of politics. Listen to the debates in the state legislature, attend the meetings of the city council, watch the candidates on the stump, and you come face to face with the problems of law enforcement, education, welfare, highways. Should the city build another school building? Where? Will the voters approve a bond issue to construct a new hospital? Should the state superintendent of schools be given authority to establish minimum standards for teachers? Are the gambling syndicates being protected by the police? What can be done about the traffic jam on Main Street? Everybody—mayors, legislators, judges, ward bosses, civil commissions, unions, chambers of commerce—participates in the process of determining what the officials shall do, which ones of them shall do it, and how they shall do it.

It is obviously impossible to explore each activity of our states, cities, counties, school districts, townships, and so on. But we can at least review a few of the highlights.

"The Public Safety Is a Public Trust"

Everything government does is supposed to protect the public safety. But in its more specific sense protecting the public safety means safeguarding people and their property against law-breakers, fires, floods, and riots. It means civil defense, fire protection, disaster relief, and police protection. Probably the most important of all is police protection.

One of the government's oldest and most accepted functions is to maintain law and order. Yet the policeman has come in for relatively little attention either from the citizenry or scholars. The vital role of the man on the beat in preserving civil liberties, his wide discretion in determining whom to arrest, his responsibility for giving daily reality to the protections of our constitutions have recently been dramatized by the central role of police in the handling of civil rights demonstrations.

Perhaps the relative lack of concern about the role of the police stems in part from the fact that organized city police departments are only about a hundred years old. Until the middle of the nineteenth century, the sheriff, the constable, and the town marshal made up the police force of rural areas. In the smaller cities, citizens took turns serving on the night watch. In the larger ones, men were paid a small fee to patrol the streets during the night.

It was in the larger cities that the need for better police protection first became acute. The great city, with its guarantee of anonymity, encouraged law-breakers and made detection difficult. Furthermore, the informal methods of social control —neighborhood pressure, social ostracism, family authority—that are often effective in smaller communities lose their strength in the urban environment.

Around the middle part of the nineteenth century, cities began to set up day shifts to take over when the night watchmen went off duty. But nothing resembling a modern police department developed until the two shifts were consolidated and brought under central city control. By the third quarter of the nineteenth century, most of the large cities had police departments. At first, these departments were the haven of spoilsmen. The police force is still ridden by patronage in some cities, but in most a merit system has been adopted. The force is normally headed by a "civilian" commissioner and by an experienced chief of police appointed by the mayor or manager.

The Policeman's Lot

Many students of police science believe that proper administration requires merit systems specially tailored to the needs of police work. In some cities, civil service regulations so restrict the chief's authority that he cannot maintain discipline. Sometimes he cannot penalize or even reprimand his men except by bringing formal charges before a civil service commission. The result is that minor infractions of the rules go unpunished, discipline is lax, and general morale suffers.

The police officer, though he risks his life every day, is commonly paid only a small salary. If he is killed or disabled in line of duty, his family is often left with inadequate protection. The public is indifferent, even hostile, to improving the policeman's lot. Under the circumstances, policemen find it difficult to resist the many temptations that come their way. Many a police officer can readily supplement his income by merely looking the other way while a cigar store operates a policy game, by overlooking violations of the fire code, by permitting Mr. Jones to double-park. Some cities, however, have established first-rate police departments by raising salaries, by lifting entrance standards, by introducing training programs, and by adopting modern methods of scientific detection. As the caliber of the force has improved, the public has usually responded with greater respect and greater support.

City police and county sheriffs enforce the great body of law. These officials are officers of the state as well as of the locality and are supposed to enforce all the laws of the commonwealth in addition to local ordinances enacted by their own city councils or county governing bodies. They serve two masters—the state and the local community to which they owe their job. In case of conflict, it is obvious that the latter will win out.

Americans have been reluctant to permit control over police to pass out of the hands of the local community. They know that the centralization of police agencies is the mark of totalitarian states and that safety, if nothing else, requires decentralization of police authority. But does this mean that we must have a complex pattern of vertical and horizontal duplication? Over 40,000 separate public law-enforcement agencies, composed of 368,000 men and women (including single constables in small townships) and costing about a billion dollars a year, operate at the different levels of government. Yet our annual crime bill is about 4 million major felonies, 44,000 traffic deaths, with property damages estimated in the hundreds of millions.

People fear centralized police, but at the same time they demand better service. When local authorities fail, the cry is immediately raised for the FBI or the state police to step in. In immediate terms, it is the criminal rather than the specter of a police state that appears to be the bigger danger.

The State Police

The famous Texas Rangers started as a small border patrol when they were organized back in 1835. In 1865 Massachusetts appointed a few state constables to suppress commercialized vice, a job the local police had been unwilling or unable to do. But it was not until 1905, with the organization of the Pennsylvania State Constabulary, that a real state police system came into being. This system was so successful that other states followed suit. At present only a third of the state police organizations utilize full law-enforcement authority; twelve states restrict their police to highway traffic regulations and to the prevention of crime committed on the highways.

State police became a part of our law-enforcement system for a variety of reasons. The breakdown of rural law enforcement, the advent of the automobile demanding greater protection on the highways and a mobile force for catching up with fleeing criminals, the need of the governor to have a police force at his disposal so that he might execute his responsibilities, and the need for a trained force to maintain order during strikes, fires, floods, and other emergencies—all these factors led to the creation of state police.

Not too many years ago the state police were used to break up strikes; organized labor promptly dubbed them the "American Cossacks." Although state police have not served as strike-breakers for some time, the old suspicion of them among some labor leaders still lingers on. To be sure that state police will not be used for strike-breaking, many states stipulate by law that the state police cannot be moved into a strike situation until actual violence has taken place, and even then only with the specific authorization of the governor.

The establishment of the Pennsylvania State Constabulary marked a sharp break with traditional police methods. The force was a mounted and uniformed body organized on a military basis, with centralized control vested in a superintendent who, in turn, was directly responsible to the governor. This pattern has been followed by other states—New York, Michigan, and Massachusetts, to mention just a few. These forces are now among the most respected police organizations in the world. They are equipped with automobiles and airplanes, modern systems of communication, and elaborate crime-detection laboratories. They maintain high standards of conduct and rigid discipline.

The military organization of these forces shields them from temptations, builds morale, and helps develop an *esprit de corps* that contrasts sharply with the cynical attitude of some urban police. Because of their mobility and professional character, the state police are less accessible to "the smaller fry of urban and rural politics." Moreover, they maintain rigorous systems of recruitment and training, and exercise close supervision over personnel.

Other state police systems have developed out of the rather modest highway patrols of a few decades ago. During the 1930's traffic control in rural regions became an acute problem, and state after state organized highway patrols, usually as subordinate units of the highway or motor vehicle department. Gradually their authority was extended from enforcing the rules of the road to exercising general police powers. Generally speaking, the state police that have grown out of highway patrols do not have such effective training programs or such high standards as those that have been modeled after the Pennsylvania pattern. Even when they have statewide jurisdiction, most state police may not go into cities unless ordered by the governor or requested by local officials. Local police resent such intrusion as a reflection on their own abilities—which it often is.

State police are not the only law-enforcement agencies maintained by state governments. Liquor- and law-enforcement officials, fish and game wardens, fire wardens, independent detective bureaus, special motor vehicle-law police, and other specialized forces abound. This dispersion of functions has been widely criticized, but each department insists that it needs its own law-enforcement agency to handle its own special problems. So far, fragmentation rather than centralization of state law-enforcement agencies has been the order of the day.

Government as Educator

Centuries ago, Plato and Aristotle insisted that education was one of the vital jobs of government. Indeed, to them government itself was essentially an educational institution. Thomas Jefferson was convinced that an educated citizenry was essential to democratic government. But only during the last century has the idea become generally accepted that government should provide tax-supported schools.

Many groups opposed "free" education. They argued that it would lead to social unrest, that it would undermine the family, that it would give government control over the minds of the young, that it would require an extensive bureaucracy, and that it would result in a fatal mixture of education and politics. Was it fair, they asked, to tax people who could afford to educate their own children in private schools in order to educate others?

Today, however, *compulsory* education through the public primary and secondary schools is an established fact (although parents may, if they choose, send their children to approved private schools). A strong movement has developed to extend public education downward to kindergarten and nursery school, upward through college and adult education, outward to cover more subjects, and deeper to cover them better. Today a third of all the expenditures of state and local governments is for education—more than for any other function—with the richer states spending more on schools than the poorer states.[1]

[1] Richard E. Dawson and James A. Robinson, "Inter-Party Competition, Economic Variables, and Welfare Policies in American States," *Journal of Politics* (May 1963), pp. 286–289; Robert H. Salisbury, "State Politics and Education," in H. Jacob & K. N. Vines (eds.) *Politics in the American States* (Little, Brown, 1964), p. 353.

The Organization of Education

The city, the county, the township, or the school district has the chief responsibility for providing public education. The school district, of which there are nearly 35,000, is the basic unit. In each district the voters elect a board of education. This board levies taxes, in most cases independently of the city or county. It appoints a superintendent of schools and other supervisory personnel, hires the teachers, and runs the schools from grade one through twelve.

Each state has a superintendent of public instruction or a commissioner of education. In a little over half of the states he is popularly elected, and in almost all states he shares some authority with a state board of education. Although the immediate operation of the public schools is the responsibility of the local community, state officers have important supervisory powers. For one thing, they distribute financial assistance. State money is passed out according to many formulas, but the trend is toward the equalization of resources among the local communities, with the states giving more money to the poorer communities.

State officials often certify competence of teachers and set minimum salaries. They are sometimes consulted by local authorities, who wish to build new school buildings, to insure that the buildings meet the minimum specifications set by the state. Some state officials have the authority (subject to the state constitution and laws) to prescribe the course of study and to determine what must be taught and what may not be taught. Generally in the South and West, state authorities determine what books will be used in the schools.

Since the day of the Northwest Ordinance the national government has promoted and encouraged public education. As shown in Chapter 25, its role in financing and supervising educational programs is growing rapidly: it makes substantial yearly grants for agricultural and vocational education; for equipment, scholarships, and loans; for research; for general aid to schools in "pockets of poverty." Increasingly the Commissioner of Education who heads the Office of Education is becoming a national leader in the formulation of educational policies and programs. Although the national government conditions its grants of funds on the money being spent for the benefit of all public school students without regard to race or national origin, the state and local officials still retain primary responsibility for determining who shall teach what to whom.

The number and popularity of books, articles, and newspaper stories bearing titles like "Education at the Crossroads," "Our Educational Crisis," and so on attest to the many educational problems confronting the nation. School buildings are overcrowded and will grow even more so as the population mounts. There aren't enough competent teachers. There are still too many inefficiently small school districts; in fact, in some states there are so many districts operating small schools that school board members outnumber the teachers. However, by consolidation of school districts into more efficient units progress is being made and the little red school house, the one-room-one-teacher school, is becoming a thing of the past.

Most communities provide only for public elementary and secondary education, but some of the nation's outstanding colleges are supported by cities. States spend enormous sums of money for higher education; all operate universities and most support an array of state colleges. Today, well more than half of the students attending college in the United States go to publicly supported institutions. The fastest numerical growth in institutions of higher education has come at the junior or community college level. Many states view the community college as a key solution to the complex problem of rapidly expanding enrollments; over 400 junior colleges have been established.

Educational Politics

The methods used to oversee the operation of our schools and colleges defy classification. However, elementary and secondary schools are usually run by boards relatively insulated from the rest of the government. This isolation of elementary and secondary education from the

IMPACT OF POVERTY ON EDUCATION

Percentage of states' school-age children from families with annual income below $2,000:
Over 20%   10%-20%   Under 10%

© 1964 & 1965 by The New York Times Company. Reprinted by permission.

rest of government has been strongly backed by well-organized groups. Parent-Teachers Associations, the National Education Association, and the various state teachers' groups wield considerable political power. Furthermore, many groups of citizens are convinced that education is of supreme importance and that it must be kept out of the hands of the "politicians."

Education and educational policy are, of course, part of the democratic political process. What shall be taught, who shall teach, and so on, are hotly contested issues. Schools are favorite targets for all groups eager that the students be taught the "right" things. Patriotic groups are concerned about "un-American" doctrines sneaking into textbooks or classrooms. Labor leaders are anxious that students receive the right impression about labor and its role in society. Business leaders want the children to see the free-enterprise system in the correct light. Educators, however, try to keep the schools as isolated as possible from the demands of special-interest groups. They argue that censors, whether public or private, must be prevented from determining what the pupils should be taught.[2]

Some believe that the professional educators have too much authority over the schools. Others assert that only the educators are qualified to determine teacher competence and school curriculum. And so the debate goes on. Controversies also rage over the desirability of religious education and the virtues of "progressive" education.

Since schools are important molders of opinion, it is not surprising that different groups hold different attitudes toward the schools. The resolution of these differences is a matter for democratic politics. Educational policy, like that in agriculture, law enforcement, or any other field, is determined in our free government by the political processes available to a free people.

Despite widespread public education, private schools still flourish, especially at the college and university level, but even at the primary and secondary level 15 per cent of all students attend private, usually church-operated, schools. The same disputes over policy revolve around private educational systems as around public schools. It is this rich mixture of public and private institutions that provides one of our best guarantees that no one group can dominate the educational system of the United States. The diversity of our schools, the variety of administrative patterns, and their dependence on numerous sources for funds and support, help prevent totalitarian control by any one party, class, religion, or section.[3]

Social Services

The poor, the blind, the sick, the handicapped, the homeless children, the old—what happens to these people? How are they taken care of? Prior to the Great Depression these unfortunate groups had to rely pretty much on privately operated

[2] See in general Thomas H. Eliot, "Toward an Understanding of Public School Politics," *The American Poltical Science Review* (December 1959), pp. 1032–1051.
[3] James B. Conant, *Education and Liberty* (Harvard Univ. Press, 1953).

social agencies, charities, and haphazard systems of public relief. Today all our governments carry on extensive welfare programs. Public welfare has neither replaced private social services and charity nor lessened their importance. But it is no longer merely a depression activity. Despite the prosperity of the postwar period, state public welfare payments grew from $1.1 billion in 1946 to over $5 billion in the middle 1960's.

Not too many years ago, poverty was considered a disgrace, mental illness a moral weakness, and public assistance a waste. The state maintained a few institutions for the poor, often run by political appointees untrained and unconcerned about those under their care. But most of the needy were taken care of at the county poorhouse, where unfortunates of all kinds were crowded together—the infirm, the handicapped, drug addicts, alcoholics, mentally ill, and those who just had no place to live. Each county or township supplemented this *indoor* relief by a program of outdoor relief—that is, those unable to make their own living but who did not require institutional care were given money or goods. This basic public welfare arrangement was little improvement over the Elizabethan Poor Law of 1601.

When the American economy went down the toboggan slide in the early 1930's, local communities were swamped by persons in distress. With their facilities overtaxed, they sent out a call for help. State governments, in turn, were unable to handle the problem. The national government entered the field on a large-scale basis, first with emergency doles and work relief programs, and then with a long-range program of federally encouraged and supported social security and insurance. During the next thirty years these New Deal inaugurated welfare programs were expanded, but the basic approach was unaltered. Then, as we saw in Chapter 25, it has become clear in the past decade that despite the nation's wealth and sustained prosperity, existing programs are failing to meet the needs of the large number of Americans caught within a poverty complex—people in minority groups, often with rural backgrounds, possessing skills no longer needed because of automation and technological changes, hidden from sight, segregated geographically and culturally. The existing programs are failing to develop self-sustaining and economically self-reliant people.

As a result, the national government has started a war against poverty to supplement existing welfare programs. The emphasis is on education and training, with special attention to the needs of the young within the culture of poverty. The war against poverty through a variety of programs hopes to provide people with assistance in developing attitudes and skills to permit them to break out from the cycle of poverty.

State Programs

Every state now has some kind of department of welfare. This agency either directly administers welfare programs or, as in most states, supervises local officials, usually county officials, who actually administer the programs. The county welfare departments, which in order to qualify for federal help must also be manned by persons selected on the basis of merit, determine what individuals are entitled to assistance (appeals can be taken to state welfare departments), and deal with clients. State and county welfare departments often provide assistance beyond that established by the national social security program. And even within the limits of the federal program, each state is free to determine the size and details of its own welfare assistance.

Groups other than the aged, blind, disabled, and dependent children have been less successful in securing their own relief programs. Ordinarily, general relief programs are not as well administered or as strongly supported as categorized relief. General relief is almost entirely a state and local governmental activity. General noninstitutionalized relief is essentially a county responsibility. Some townships do this job, but most welfare workers believe that townships are too small to support adequate welfare departments. A properly administered department requires trained case workers to process applications, make home visits, and act to rehabilitate individuals and to maintain families.

The county poorhouse is still the basic institution for general institutionalized relief. Although outdoor relief programs have slightly reduced the need for institutions, there are still many who have no home of their own, who are ill, and who require care. Today county poorhouses, often renamed "county homes," are more attractive places than they used to be. The physical plant is being improved, children have special homes, and the mentally ill are being placed in state hospitals. Some counties have joined together to maintain one adequate rather than two or more inadequate homes for the chronically ill and persons of advanced age.[4]

Most states have assumed the responsibilty for insane, feeble-minded, or emotionally disturbed people, and have set up reformatories for juvenile delinquents. In some states, institutions for youthful law-breakers have been placed under the jurisdiction of welfare rather than penal authorities. Although many of these institutions are still run by incompetents, in recent years there has been encouraging progress toward trained staffs. Since distressed persons are unlikely to be politically organized, their needs are apt to be overlooked unless other citizens champion their cause.

Public Health

During a summer in the 1780's, the streets of Philadelphia were deserted. All who could afford to do so had taken their families and fled to the country. Every night the mournful sounds of the death cart echoed through the empty city. The city had been stricken by a yellow-fever epidemic. Only when cool weather returned did the disease abate and the

---

[4] See Clyde F. Snider, "The Fading Almshouse," *National Municipal Review* (February 1956), pp. 60–65.

city resume normal activity. There were few families that did not grieve the loss of a child, father, or mother.

Yellow fever, dysentery, malaria, and other dreaded scourges periodically have swept through American cities. These catastrophes were one of the hazards of city life. As late as 1878–79 yellow fever struck the South; Memphis was nearly depopulated. Drastic action seemed imperative. State after state, following the lead of Louisiana and Massachusetts, established a board of health. Spurred by the medical discoveries of Pasteur and other scientists, authorities inaugurated programs for the protection of public health. Open city sewers were covered and other hygienic measures instituted. In fact, it was not until contagious diseases had been brought under control that the large city became a safe place to live.

Today thousands of local governments—counties, cities, townships, special health districts—have some kind of public health program. Every state has an agency, usually called a department of health, that administers the state program and supervises local officials. The United States Public Health Service conducts research, assists state and local authorities, and administers federal grants to encourage them to expand their programs.

Despite the supposed virtues of country life and the supposed health hazards of city living, today it is the city people who have the best health records and the most public health protection. The bigger cities have a full-time health officer assisted by a well-staffed department. The counties have lagged behind. About 40 million Americans, most of them living in rural places, are protected either by a part-time agency or none at all. The American Public Health Association, the professional society of public health workers, recommends that counties and cities join with one another to establish health districts with at least 50,000 people, the number they believe necessary to maintain a minimum program. Again, the trend toward larger units is apparent.

Prevention and control of communicable disease is still one of the major public health activities. Doctors are required to report cases of communicable disease. Health department officials then investigate to discover the source of the infection, isolate the afflicted persons, and take whatever action seems to be called for. Most state health departments give doctors free vaccine and serum, and many local departments give free vaccinations to those who cannot afford to go to private physicians—in some cases this service is open to everybody. Since the public shows more enthusiasm for specific programs than for general disease control, some diseases have come in for special attention. The national government provides financial assistance for such activities as tuberculosis and venereal disease control. Mobile X-ray units take free X rays of school children, teachers, and the general public. Public health officials protect water supplies and see to it that waste and sewage are safely disposed of. They protect the community's food supply by inspecting hotels, restaurants, and food markets. Many cities now require domestic servants, waiters, cooks, and other food-handlers to secure a special license and undergo a health-department medical examination. Meat and milk are of special concern. Meat products shipped in interstate commerce are inspected by federal officials, but it is the job of state and local authorities to safeguard the public against dangers from the large amount of meat slaughtered locally. Some cities maintain a municipal slaughterhouse in which they require that all meat sold within the city and not inspected elsewhere be slaughtered. Most cities insist that milk be pasteurized and require the licensing, inspecting, and testing of milk, cows, and dairies.

In 1948 a lethal "smog" descended on Donora, Pennsylvania. The deaths of many of the community's residents dramatized the menace of air pollution. Since then the "smogs" of Los Angeles and other industrial areas have become notorious. Industrial waste not only infects the air we breathe but pollutes rivers and streams as well. Although there is growing concern over the critical levels of air and water pollution, a full-scale attack on this problem is yet to be mounted.

State and local public health officials work in a wide variety of fields. Health and educational officials make periodic inspections among school children and carry on educational programs. They keep vital statistics—recording births and deaths—and maintain laboratories for diagnosis of disease and for testing the purity of certain products. They enforce quarantine regulations. One of the most important public health workers is the public health nurse. Traveling throughout the community, she advises on prenatal and postnatal care, assists mothers in childbirth and in caring for their children, and in general provides nursing services for the sick.

Homes, Houses, and Slums

Today there are relatively few individuals who are ill-clothed and ill-fed, but, as we noted in Chapter 25, many are still ill-housed. According to the Bureau of the Census, some 11.4 million of our 58 million dwellings do not measure up to proper standards. The national government has supplied credit and has built some defense housing, but local officials are the most active public authorities in the housing field.

Cities have a direct financial interest in slum clearance, for the costs of education, police and fire protection, and public welfare are considerably higher in slums than in other areas. Juvenile delinquency, unemployment, and disease flourish in blighted regions. Slum areas account for 45 per cent of major crimes, 50 per cent of arrests, 55 per cent of juvenile delinquency, 50 per cent of all diseases, and 35 per cent of fires. In Atlanta it was discovered that 53 per cent of all city services went to slum regions that paid only 6 per cent of the real estate taxes. In Baltimore each acre of slums produced a $25,000 yearly deficit for the city.[5]

In addition to zoning ordinances, cities enforce building codes designed to avoid structural breakdowns, prevent fires, stop overcrowding, and protect health. Par-

[5] Donald Robinson, "Slum Clearance Pays Off," *National Municipal Review* (October 1955), p. 461.

ticularly stringent restrictions are imposed on public buildings, such as theaters, schools, office buildings, and stores. Instead of a comprehensive building code, some cities have only a mass of detailed and separate regulations dealing with construction, electrical wiring, plumbing, ventilation, heating, and safety requirements. Confusion results from vesting authority to enforce particular parts of the code in several agencies—for example, the health department enforces plumbing and sanitation regulations, the building inspector is responsible for structural regulations, the fire department for fire regulations.

Slum clearance and urban redevelopment are also a major activity of cities. Since 1937, the national government has lent money to local public housing agencies and has helped with annual subsidies. Over three-fourths of the states have legislation authorizing cities or counties to set up local housing authorities. These authorities, usually composed of five men appointed by the mayor or county board, have the power to borrow money, condemn land and buildings, and build and operate public housing projects to replace slums. Through urban redevelopment corporations cities have also encouraged private builders to invest money in slum clearance by granting tax exemptions and other concessions. The federal government through the Urban Renewal Administration makes grants to cities that develop "master plans" for urban renewal. These grants can be used to acquire, clear, and prepare blighted areas. The cleared land can then be used for public housing projects for those who have been displaced from the slums so cleared, or it can be sold to private builders.

In 1965, the federal government increased its assistance to the cities by enactment of the Housing and Urban Redevelopment Act. The urban renewal program was extended for another four years with grants totalling $2.9 billion. Grants were also made to provide an estimated 60,000 units per year of low-rent public housing. A most controversial provision provides that rent supplement payments may be made to low-income families by the administrator of the Housing and Home Finance Agency. These rent "subsidies" may be given to certain classes of individuals or families who are unable to obtain adequate housing for rents equal to or less than one-quarter of their incomes. The administrator is also authorized to make grants to local public bodies and agencies to help construct basic water and sewer facilities. The HHFA may also award grants to states and localities for the acquisition of land in and around urban centers to create "open space" areas for conservation, recreation, and scenic and historical purposes.

Planning the Urban Community

Are our smaller cities good places to live and work? Crowded shopping areas, dented fenders, shattered nerves, slums and blighted areas, inadequate parks, impossible traffic patterns—are all these evils and inconveniences necessary?

Many city people have asked these questions. Reorganization, city-manager charters, consolidated cities and counties, and the like—there are fine things, they argue, but the problem may lie deeper. Structural changes are not enough. Intelligent planning could have avoided many of the costly problems that now confront us.

For many decades, American cities were allowed to grow in a haphazard fashion. Industrialists were permitted to erect factories wherever they wanted. Towering buildings shut off sunlight from the streets below. Traffic conditions transformed drivers into malevolent maniacs, pedestrians into traumatized wrecks. Schools were sandwiched in where the land was cheap or where the political organization could make a profit on the sale.

Today many communities are attempting to bring order out of the chaos of this random growth. Most cities have some kind of *planning agency*. There are also over 400 county planning units. As noted, the problems of the urban community are the concern of all levels of government. In the 1954 Housing and Urban Redevelopment Act, Congress required cities applying for assistance to develop a master plan. Today almost all cities have one. Thus, we find increased cooperation between the national government and state, county, and local governments. One example of city-county cooperation is the Association of Bay Area Government. Organized in 1960 with 9 counties and 84 cities in the San Francisco area, it was designed to treat mutual problems both present and future. Its major current concern is the development of an effective transportation system to serve a community of more than 3 million.

The most common method of assuring orderly growth is zoning—the creation of areas and the limitation on uses to which buildings may be put in each area. A community may be divided into areas for single-family dwellings, two-family dwellings, multi-family dwellings, commercial purposes, light and heavy industry. Other regulations restrict the height of buildings or their area, or require that buildings be located a certain distance apart and a certain distance back from the front of the lot.

Zoning attempts to keep garbage dumps from being located next to residential areas, stabilizes property values, and enables the city or county government to coordinate services with land uses. A zoning ordinance, however, is no better than its enforcement. This is usually the responsibility of a building inspector who makes sure that a projected new building is consistent with building, zoning, fire, and sanitary regulations before he grants a building permit. In most cases, a zoning or planning commission or the city council can amend the zoning ordinances and make exceptions to the regulations. These officials are often under tremendous pressures to grant exceptions. But if they go too far in permitting special cases, the whole purpose of zoning is defeated.

Zoning is, however, only one phase of community planning. Until recently, planners were primarily concerned with streets and buildings. Today, many city planners are concerned with broader matters, and planning covers virtually all the activities of people. The basic job of the planners is to collect all the information they can about the city, and then prepare long-range plans. What sections of the city are growing? Where should new schools be built? Where should main highways be constructed to meet future needs? Will the water supply be adequate in ten years? Are the parks accessible to all the people?

Emphasis on planning varies from place to place. In some urban areas, planning is a small operation and even those who are responsible for it do not take it too seriously. A few cities have elaborate organizations with full-time planners, and the plans are carefully implemented by city councils and other public officials. Obviously, planning must be built upon public support. No plan, however good it looks on paper, will be effective unless it reflects the interests and values of the major groups within the community.

Government as Builder

State and local governments build highways, public buildings, airports, parks, and recreational facilities. But by far the major program is *building roads*. State and local governments spend more money on roads than they do on any other activity except education.

Until the advent of the automobile, canals and railroads were the major method of long-distance travel. Local roads, such as they were, were built and repaired under the direction of city, township, and county officials. Able-bodied male citizens were required either to put in a certain number of days working on the public roads or to pay taxes for that purpose.

By the 1890's, safety brakes and the pneumatic tire had been invented; and in the Gay Nineties, those who could not afford a carriage began to use the bicycle. Bicycle clubs began to push for the building of hard-surfaced roads. But it was not until the 1900's and the Age of the Automobile that road-building became a major industry. It is not surprising that the function of road-building gradually was transferred from the township to larger units of government—more and more to the state. But counties and townships still have important road-building and maintenance problems. Nearly four-fifths of the rural road mileage is under their control. The other one-fifth, which includes almost all the main highways and most of the hard-surfaced roads, is built and maintained by the states.

Ever since 1916 the national government has supported state highway construction, but with the Federal Highway Act of 1956 federal aid substantially increased. States do the planning, estimate the costs, get the construction done, but receive much of the money from the federal treasury. In order to receive federal support, however, states must submit their plans and have their work inspected by the Department of Commerce's Bureau of Public Roads. All federally backed highways must meet certain standards governing the engineering of the roadbed, employment conditions for construction workers, and weight and load conditions for trucks using the roads.

Under the Federal Highway Act of 1956, the states are to plan and build a National System of Interstate and Defense Highways by 1972. When completed the Interstate will consist of 41,000 miles of superhighways linking almost every city with a population of 50,000 or more. All but 7,000 miles will be of at least four lanes, grades are to be no more than a three-foot rise per 100 feet, there will be a limited number of entry roads, and the number of signs, roadside stands, or filling stations on the right of way will be regulated. The federal government pays 90 per cent of the costs, securing most of the money from user taxes—gasoline, tires, trucks—which are to be placed in a trust fund earmarked for that purpose. Funds are distributed among the states according to a formula that gives greater weight to population than has been given in other federal-aid highway programs. No federal money may be used for toll roads, bridges, or tunnels, although these may be part of the Interstate System. In 1959 Congress offered any state a bonus of one-half of one per cent of the total cost of a project if it would agree to restrict billboards along interstate highways in accordance with national standards. This "carrot" had little effect, so in 1965 Congress responded to President Johnson's recommendation to use the "stick" approach. Additional federal funds were made available for landscaping, for removing billboards, and for hiding junkyards. Beginning in 1968 states that fail to control such eyesores will be faced with the loss of 10 per cent of all federal highway funds.

Few aspects of government are more enmeshed in patronage politics than highway-building. The large sums of money spent and the army of workers needed offer many opportunities for graft and favoritism. In some states the highway department is the chief means by which a political organization maintains its power. Contractors are rewarded for their support and loyal party members are given jobs.

An array of potent interest groups supports highway development. Automobile manufacturers, tire-makers, oil companies, motel and restaurant associations, automobile and tourist clubs, trucking associations, and others join hands to protect their common cause. In most states they have been strong enough to persuade legislatures to earmark gasoline taxes, automobile drivers' license fees, trucking fees, and other user-taxes for road purposes. But there is always conflict over how the money should be spent. Farmers want secondary roads developed, but truckers and tourists favor the improvement of main highways. Merchants want the roads to come their way, and their representatives try to get top priority for roads in their districts.

The 1956 Highway Act, though sending large sums of money to the states, also adds to state officials' troubles. Because present routes are so crowded by commercial establishments, most of these new superhighways will be in new locations. It is too costly to buy out the service stations, eating places, garages, and souvenir shops in order to get the land needed to add three or more lanes with a strip of land down the middle. Congressmen report that they are being asked by constituents to tell them where the new roads will be, so that speculators can buy land for roadside services before the prices go shooting up. State highway departments feel pressures from all sides. Farmers object to having their lands cut in two, especially since they are not able to cross the highways except at the nearest exchange or grade separation, perhaps miles away. Roadside business on present routes fight loss of business. Some cities want the expressways to go through them; others do not.

Regulation at the Grass Roots

Corporations receive their charters from the state. Banks, insurance companies, securities dealers, doctors, lawyers, barbers, and various other businesses and professions are licensed, and their activities are supervised by state officials. State regulations range from stringent measures to protect the public to mere window-dressing. Both farmers and workers—especially union members—are regulated. But of all the businesses, those that we designate as "public utilities" are the most closely restricted.

Public Utility Regulation

It is easier to list than to define public utilities. Water plants, electric power companies, telephone companies, railroads, and buses are among the main ones. They are distinguished from other businesses by the fact that the government gives them certain special privileges such as the power of eminent domain, the right to use public streets, and protection from competition. In return, public utilities are required to give the public adequate services at reasonable rates. Public utilities are used to render essential services in fields where normally competitive enterprise is not suitable.

In the United States, private enterprise subject to public regulation rather than public ownership has been the more general method of providing these essential services. Nevertheless, more than two-thirds of our cities own their own water works, about 100 operate their own gas utilities, and over 50—and the number here is steadily increasing—operate their own transit systems. But other services—intercity transportation, railroads, airplanes, telephone, and telegraph—are almost everywhere provided by private enterprise subject to governmental regulation and some subsidization.

Since public utilities are not subject to the same restraints that competition brings to other businesses, the question of how they are regulated is very important. Every state has a utility commission whose responsibility is to see that utilities operate in the interest of the public they serve. In most states utility commissioners are appointed for overlapping terms by the governor with the consent of the senate, but in some southern and western states they are elected by the voters. The most common number of commissioners is three. The extent of commission regulation varies with the type of utility, but usually utility commissions have the authority to set rates, require uniform systems of accounts, approve issues of securities, pass on reorganization and merger plans, and permit abandonment of services.

Most states have only one utility commission, which combines the duties performed at the national level by the Interstate Commerce Commission, the Federal Communications Commission, the Federal Power Commission, the Civil Aeronautics Board, and (in some states) the Securities and Exchange Commission. Although the state utility commissions have broad legal powers, the general public is normally indifferent to their work and fails to give the commissions the political backing that many observers feel is necessary if they are to protect the public. On the other hand, utility managers are just as convinced that the commissions are doing a good job of regulating them—perhaps too good.

Here are some of the problems of utility regulation:

1. The requirements for a good utility commissioner are staggering. He is supposed to do everything: inspect the quality of gas and locomotives, set rates in a variety of fields, assess valuations of complex properties to protect the public interest, and listen to company grievances. Hence, a commissioner needs the technical knowledge of the accountant, the lawyer, the engineer, the economist, and the political scientist. Not many states provide either the salary or the challenge to attract that kind of man.

2. The judges have complicated the work of the commissions. Until recently, they had a habit of setting aside commission rulings, listening to the arguments all over again, and coming to their own conclusions. In 1898 the Supreme Court decided (in *Smyth* v. *Ames*) that the Constitution required utility commissioners to set rates that would allow a "reasonable return" on "the fair value of the property being used by the utility for the convenience of the public." In the view of James Bonbright, a noted utility specialist, this formula made it impossible for commissioners to develop adequate standards of regulation. Instead, it fastened on them a formula that is fatal to administration, since the controversial task of evaluating a complex utility calls for heavy expenses and time-wasting efforts.[6] Often it took ten years or more to settle a controversy, and by that time conditions had so changed that the settlement was obsolete. Moreover, this form of regulation encourages mediocrity and invites inefficiency on the part of private management. Knowing that their rates are likely to be cut if their profits seem excessive, companies have no incentive to practice economies or to make voluntary rate reductions in the hope of increasing the demand for their services.

3. Most utility commissions are understaffed—often consisting of less than half a dozen professional men—lawyers, engineers, accountants. These men are expected to process the accounts, make rate-valuations, study managerial efficiency, and so on. Since they do not have time to make studies of comparative costs or gather independent data, they may have to rely on data furnished by outside groups—including the utilities themselves.

[6] James C. Bonbright, *Public Utilities and the National Power Policies* (Columbia Univ. Press, 1940), pp. 16–17.

All the states make some attempt to isolate the utility commissions from the rest of the executive structure. James Fesler, after close study, has concluded, however, that freeing a regulatory commission from direct control of the governor may merely drive it into the hands of groups outside the executive department. To call a utility commission "independent" does not free it from "this necessity of winning friends—so as to influence legislators. The method of winning these friends varies with each state and with different periods in each state's political history." [7] Sometimes it includes a "reasonable" attitude toward the groups it is supposed to regulate.

Regulation of Employers and Employees

Despite the expanded role of the national government, state and local officials still have much to say about working conditions. Here are some of the laws they enforce.

Health and Safety Legislation. In the opening years of this century dramatic episodes like the fire in a New York plant in which hundreds of garment workers burned to death and the revelations about "sweatshop" working conditions led to corrective legislation. States now require proper heating, lighting, ventilation, fire escapes, and sanitary facilities in work areas. Machinery must be equipped with safety guards, and standards have been established to cut down occupational diseases. Health, building, and labor inspectors make tours of industrial plants to insure compliance with the laws.

Workmen's Compensation. The common law made an employer liable for the injury or death of workers resulting from his failure to provide reasonably safe conditions of work. But it also gave him three defenses that made it almost impossible for an employee or his family to win a case. The employer was not liable if he could show: (1) the employee contributed to the accident by his own negligence, (2) a "fellow-servant" caused the accident, (3) the employee had assumed the risk of injury that flowed from dangers ordinarily associated with the job.

Today all states have abolished these common-law defenses and have created workmen's compensation programs based on the belief that employees should not have to assume the costs of accidents. As with depreciation of machinery and other items, the costs of accidents are borne by the employer and, like other costs, are part of the price the consumer of the product must ultimately pay. No longer does the employee have to sue and prove that his employer was at fault. If he is injured or contracts a disease in the ordinary course of his employment, he is entitled to compensation set by a prearranged schedule.

Workmen's compensation programs vary from state to state. Most commonly, a board determines the awards. Employers either take out insurance or furnish

---

[7] James W. Fesler, *The Independence of State Regulatory Agencies* (Public Administration Service, 1942), p. 61.

proof that they are financially able to make payments when called upon to do so. In most states the insurance is sold by private companies, but about one-fourth of the states operate their own insurance programs. Although all states have workmen's compensation laws, their coverage varies. Agricultural, domestic, and temporary workers are not commonly covered, nor are those who work for a company employing only one or two workers. About half of the working force is presently protected.

Child Labor. All states forbid child labor, but laws vary widely in their coverage and in their definition of child labor. A good many states set the minimum age at just 14. Higher age requirements are normal for employment in hazardous occupations and during school hours.

Hours and Wages. Women and young people are protected by maximum-hours laws in most states. Men are covered only in certain dangerous occupations, or where the public safety is directly involved—operators of buses and trucks, for example. Sunday closing laws, and laws requiring that employees be allowed at least one day of rest in seven, generally apply to men as well as women and children.

About half the states have minimum-wage laws, but in only four do they apply to men. Since the minimums have not kept up with inflation and rising wages and prices, these laws currently have little effect.

Regulation of Unions and Collective Bargaining. National regulation of collective bargaining applies only to industries in, or affecting, *inter*state commerce. Although national law takes precedence over state enactments, states are left to impose their own regulations in many important areas of labor-management relations. Furthermore, the Labor-Management Reform Act of 1959 authorizes state labor relations boards to take jurisdiction over collective bargaining disputes in industries whose effect on interstate commerce is slight and over which the National Labor Relations Board has not taken jurisdiction.

During the 1930's state laws were patterned after national regulations and were aimed mainly at protecting the workers' right to form unions and engage in collective bargaining. Since World War II, state laws have been more restrictive of union activities. State courts have also shown a trend in postwar years to supervise picketing practices and to ban picketing whose purpose is to force conduct that is illegal or, in the opinion of the judges, would be contrary to public policy.

34 MEN AND MONEY

"Say, did you hear about that civil service reform association kickin' because the tax commissioners want to put their 55 deputies on the exempt list and fire the outfit left to them by Low [previous reform mayor]? That's civil service for you. Just think! Fifty-five Republicans and mugwumps holdin' $3,000 and $4,000 and $5,000 jobs in the tax department when 1,555 good Tammany men are ready and willin' to take their places! It's an outrage! What did the people mean when they voted for Tammany? What is representative government, anyhow? Is it all a fake that this is a government of the people, by the people, and for the people? If it isn't a fake, then why isn't the people's voice obeyed and Tammany men put in all the offices?"

This is our old friend Boss Plunkitt talking. Though we might disagree with the Sage of Tammany Hall, he did have a knack of cutting through to the heart of matters political. Plunkitt was a realist. He was interested in the tax department not merely because of the patronage involved. He also wanted to retain Tammany control over the agency that collected the city's tax dollars and turned them over to the city officials.

To Plunkitt, government was a matter of men and money. So it is today. Men must be elected and hired. Salaries must be paid and materials purchased. The cost of government depends partly on the ability of the men, and their ability to do a good job depends in part on how much money they have to spend.

Where Do the Men Come From?

When we talk about the "state," the "city," or the "county," we are simply using shorthand symbols for groups of people. Although we say that the "government" builds the roads or runs the schools, what we really mean is that a group of men whom we call public officials or public employees build the roads or run the schools. About 7 million people—engineers, clerks, governors, teachers,—work for our state and local governments. In a sense they *are* the state and local governments. How are these people chosen?

A few of them are elected, but only a very few. It is probably a safe guess to say that well over half of the rest are chosen because they know the right person and belong to the right political faction. Many of these persons are qualified, and some are among the best public officials in the nation. Nevertheless, they were chosen for patronage or party reasons, and no systematic attempt was made to choose them on the basis of merit.

State and Local Merit Systems

Thirty-two of our states—including most of the larger and more populous states—use merit systems in choosing public servants. And in all the states welfare workers who administer grants under the national social security law are selected on the basis of merit, since this is a condition attached to receiving federal money.

The most general method of administering merit systems is by a civil service commission, usually composed of three members appointed by the governor with the consent of the senate, for six-year overlapping terms. The commission prepares and administers examinations, provides "eligible" registers for various jobs from which appointments may be made, establishes job classifications and prepares salary schedules, administers a system of efficiency ratings, makes and gives promotional examinations, administers regulations having to do with sick leaves, vacations, and so on, and serves as a board of appeal for persons who are discharged by their bosses. Commissions are becoming increasingly active in providing for in-service training and other programs to improve the morale of public servants.

How well do the commissions do their jobs? Their many critics complain that they are too slow and wrapped up in red tape and cumbersome rules. Eligible lists are not kept up to date; it takes weeks to fill vacancies, they say. But a more serious charge is that civil service commissions have deprived responsible officials of authority over subordinates. There is too much emphasis, it is argued, on "keeping the rascals out" and on insulating public servants from political coercion. As a result, employees enjoy so much job security that administrators cannot get rid of incompetents. Cases have been cited where it has taken months and several elaborate hearings to dismiss secretaries who cannot type or librarians who cannot read.

It has been suggested that merit system commissions be replaced by a director of personnel who in turn would be responsible to the governor, and that administrators be given greater discretion in choosing and disciplining their subordinates. Today some states—for example, Maryland, Connecticut, Virginia, Michigan, Wisconsin, Minnesota—have what amounts to a single personnel director.

The mere passage of civil service legislation does not automatically create a merit system. Many states have put laws on the books and have appointed civil service commissions. But the commissions are nothing more than window-dressing: The patronage system still flourishes behind the scenes. Legislatures cripple the commissions by reducing their budgets and limiting their staffs. Payrolls are crowded with "temporary" or "provisional" employees. "Friendly" civil service commissioners are appointed. Employees with friends in the legislature get amendments to civil service laws that exempt their jobs from the regulations. In some states, incumbents have been able to get technical amendments that give them what is tantamount to life tenure.

The largest American cities have a merit system, and so do many of the smaller cities. Most cities over 10,000 choose their city employees by some form of merit system. In addition, some state laws require that certain kinds of employees, such as policemen and firemen, be chosen by merit. Relatively few counties maintain a merit system. School teachers are almost always chosen by school boards, but only after they have earned the appropriate certificates.

The salaries of civil servants vary tremendously from state to state, city to city, and county to county. Most jobs, however, do not pay as much as do corresponding jobs in business and industry. Many able people are thus discouraged from entering state or local government service. Perhaps even more damaging is the lack of integration in the merit systems. Each state, if it has a merit or career system at all, has its own program, each city has its own career service, and so on. A young man entering the service of a city cannot look forward to advancement up through the ranks to other cities or to the state service. If he leaves one service to enter another, he often loses retirement benefits and other privileges.

"Fallacies about Public Servants"

In 1935, a Commission of Inquiry on Public Service Personnel published a famous and influential report entitled "Better Government Personnel." [1] The commission stated: "It is apparent that the weakest link in American democracy, the point at which we fall most conspicuously behind the other self-governing peoples, is in the appointive services where the great bulk of the work of modern government is carried on." The commission concluded that the failure of our governments to attract able men to public service was rooted in certain "fallacies." What are these fallacies?

1. "The false notion that 'to the victor belong the spoils.'

2. "The mistaken idea that duties of governmental employees are, as President Jackson said, 'so plain and simple that men of intelligence can readily qualify themselves for their performance.'

3. "The false idea that charity begins on the public payroll. Too many people are elected or appointed to office because they need a job or have suffered some misfortune. The cost is poor service and lowered morale of other employees.

4. "The erroneous assumption that 'patronage is the price of democracy,' that the parties which we need for self-government cannot exist without spoils." Perhaps the commission had in mind George Washington Plunkitt's famous "syllygism." Said Plunkitt: "First, this great and glorious country was built up by political parties; Second, parties can't hold together if their workers don't get offices when they win; Third, if the parties go to pieces, the government they built up must go to pieces, too; Fourth, then there'll be hell to pay. Say, honest, now; can you answer that argument?" But said the commission, "There are, it is true, large cities, certain states, and other areas where political parties . . . are *at present* sustained by patronage. But in great sections of the United States, and in other democracies of the world, democracy exists, . . . parties thrive, without the spoliation of the appointive administrative services. The truth is, as Theodore Roosevelt once observed, that patronage is the curse of politics."

5. "The idea that 'the best public servant is the worst one. . . .'" The commission pointed out that groups who have selfish reasons for desiring bad government indulge in the vilification of public employees. "Indiscriminate vilification lessens the morale of all public officials, dissuades capable persons from entering the public service, and discredits the authority of government."

6. "The erroneous thought that 'tenure is the cure of spoils.'

7. "The superficial thought that the way to eradicate spoils and favoritism is to begin at the bottom. . . ." In many states and cities the top administrative positions are exempt from the merit system, but these are the very positions where spoilsmen can demoralize the entire service.

8. "The belief in 'home town jobs for home town boys.'" "Residence quali-

[1] *Better Government Personnel* (Whittlesey House, 1935).

fications," reports the commission, "are a benefit only to incompetent applicants and petty politicians.

9. "The notion that 'the public service is always less capable and efficient than private enterprise.'" The commission came to the conclusion that business and governments are about on a par, "what business gains through the profit motive and elasticity being apparently lost in many instances through hereditary management, labor difficulties, and outside control." Governments as a rule do not take over a job until private agencies have demonstrated their inability or unwillingness to do it themselves.

10. "The erroneous idea that the spoils system, the eleemosynary system and the other corrosive influences can be driven out of the public service through the prohibition of specific abuses. . . . What is clearly required is not negative laws, but the positive militant handling of the problem of personnel with the active backing of the public and the press." [2]

The slow progress that has been made in the years since the commission made its report indicates that these fallacies are still widely held. But progress has been made. Gradually people are coming to realize that "government is only as good as the men in it." But government needs more than able men. It needs financial resources, too.

Where Does the Money Come From?

State and local governments, like the national government, get most of their money through taxation. But the state and local governments definitely play second fiddle to the national government. In response to the demands of depression, wars, and defense, national taxes have surpassed those collected by states and local communities. National officials have been forced to search for new sources of revenue in areas heretofore reserved to the other governments. [3]

The duplication—or virtually quadruplication—of governments by which the people of the United States govern themselves complicates the tax picture. Tax policies often conflict with one another. When the national government is reducing taxes to encourage spending by the public, states may be raising taxes. When the national government increases taxes in order to reduce inflation, the states often lower taxes. Indeed, state and local governments normally spend most during periods of inflation and least during periods of deflation. Each level of government pays little attention to the tax policy of the others.

The number of taxing authorities also makes tax-gathering an expensive operation. National officials collect taxes on gasoline, state officials collect taxes on gasoline, and so do some local officials. Each maintains its own tax-gathering organization. Naturally, the taxpayer is confused. He is allowed to deduct certain

[2] *Ibid.*, pp. 16–22.
[3] H. M. Groves, *Financing Government*, 6th ed. (Holt, Rinehart and Winston, 1964).

business expenses from his federal income tax, but not from his state income tax. To complicate matters even more, changes in state laws often affect the amount of federal tax a man must pay. For example, the national government permits taxpayers to deduct amounts paid for state taxes from their federal income tax return. Thus if a state increases its taxes, the national government gets less money.

No matter who collects the taxes, however, all the money comes out of a single national economy. Each of the governments has a different tax base, and each of the taxes hits particular groups; but all government services, just as all our national wealth, rest on the productivity of the American people. And in turn that productivity is increased by many of the activities of government. With their taxes the people buy police protection, school buildings, highways, and other things that they think desirable. Who pays for these services?

What you **SPENT** largely determined your STATE tax bill

CONSUMPTION 62%
OTHERS
MOTOR FUEL 14%

What you **OWNED** largely determined your LOCAL tax bill

PROPERTY 89%
OTHER

What you **EARNED** largely determined your FEDERAL tax bill

PERSONAL INCOME 50%
ALL OTHERS

The tax bill of Illinois. (Source: Department of Finance, State of Illinois.)

Who Shall Pay the Taxes?

A good tax might be defined as one that the other fellow has to pay; a bad tax, one that I have to pay. Who shall bear the cost of state and local government is decided in the United States by politics. The people of any state are free to collect whatever taxes they wish from whomever (in that state) they wish, subject only to the restrictions imposed by the people of the United States through the federal Constitution.

The Constitution forbids states to tax exports or imports, or to levy tonnage duties without the consent of Congress; to use their taxing power to interfere with federal operation; to discriminate against interstate commerce, unduly burden it, or directly tax it; or to use their taxing power to deprive persons of equal protection of the law or to deprive them of their property without due process. Constitutional lawyers and judges spend much of their time trying to apply these generalities to concrete situations. Out of hundreds of disputes, they have decided, among other things, that states may not tax tangible property located outside the state but may tax intangible property located outside the state but owned by their own citizens, may collect sales taxes from interstate sales, may collect income taxes from persons and corporations within the state even though the income was earned from interstate businesses, but may not tax the privilege of engaging in interstate commerce or the unapportioned gross receipts from interstate transactions.

State constitutions also restrict state taxing power. Certain kinds of property are

Politically speaking, the property tax raises the loudest squawks. (Courtesy Nation's Business.)

exempt from taxation—property used for educational, charitable, or religious purposes, for example. State constitutions frequently list the taxes that may be collected, forbidding those not mentioned. The amount of tax that may be collected from various sources is also often stipulated.

The ability of people in a city, county, or other local unit to tax themselves is even more restricted. Local governments have no inherent power of taxation. Their officials can levy only those taxes, in the amount, by the procedures, and for the purposes which the state constitution or the state legislature authorizes. What kinds of tax can they collect?

General Property Tax

Widely lambasted as "one of the worst taxes known to the civilized world," the *general property tax* is still the chief revenue source for local governments. It used to be the major state tax too, but in most states it is now of minor importance. The tax is cumbersome to administer, conducive to favoritism and inequities, and takes insufficient account of ability to pay.

A hundred years ago, wealth was primarily *real* property—land and buildings. And this real property was relatively easy to value. Assessors could guess the value of the property a man owned, and this was a good test of his ability to help pay for government. Today wealth takes on many forms. People own large amounts of *personal* property—both *tangible*, such as furniture, jewels, washing machines, expensive rugs, high-priced paintings, and *intangible*, such as stocks, bonds, money in the bank. A man can concentrate a large amount of wealth, difficult to value and easy to conceal, in a small rented apartment. Real property too has changed. It no longer consists mainly of barns, houses, and land, but of large industrial plants, great retail stores, and office buildings the value of which is hard to measure.

Furthermore, property ownership is less likely these days to correspond to ability to pay. The old couple with a large house valued at $35,000 may be living on a small allowance provided by their children. They have to pay higher local taxes than does the young couple living in a rented apartment, both of whom work and have sizable incomes. Or compare the case of the man who borrows $10,000 to buy a $14,000 house and who is paying off the mortgage out of his $8,000-a-year-job, and the case of the man who owns a $14,000 house debt-free and has a $10,000-a-year job. They both pay the same tax on their homes.

Although many communities stipulate that the general property tax be imposed on all property, the tax falls in fact on limited amounts of real property. Over 20 per cent of real property in cities is exempt. Intangible personal property is seldom taxed. Some communities place a lower rate on intangible property in order to induce owners to announce their ownership. Tangible personal property, such as watches, rings, and so on, often escape taxation or are grossly under-valued. In most cities an unwritten understanding develops as to what kind of property the honest taxpayer should list. The good citizen who attempts to follow the written word of the law is kindly advised by the assessor that it is not necessary.

The general property tax is also inflexible. During times of rising prices, assessed values move up much more slowly than the general price level. Thus when governments need more money, the lagging tax basis fails to provide it. Conversely, when prices fall, valuations do not drop at the same rate. When persons cannot pay taxes, much property is thrown onto the market for tax delinquency. During the 1930's for example, the general property tax added to the miseries of many home owners and to the problems of state and local officials.

The general property tax rate is difficult to compare from community to community. The rate in one city may be only $10 per thousand as compared with another city with a rate of $40 per thousand. But in the second city, valuation may be computed only at a tenth of "real" value. Claims of local politicians that they have kept down the tax rate must be scrutinized with care.

Despite its weaknesses, the general property tax will probably remain an important source of revenue for local governments. It is especially well suited to local government because real property rather than personal property is the chief beneficiary of many local services, such as fire protection. Alternative taxes are few, and they have their own disadvantages. Moreover, some of the bad features of the general property tax can be and are being corrected by more sensible administration: elimination of duplicate assessments of the same property; upgrading of qualifications for the position of assessor; adoption of more systematic methods of appraising property; better record-keeping systems; elimination of duplicate collection.

But even with improved tax administration the general property tax is not supplying local units of government with all the money they need to render the services their citizens want. Moreover, states have tended to leave the property tax to local units and they need other sources for their funds. What other taxes do they collect?

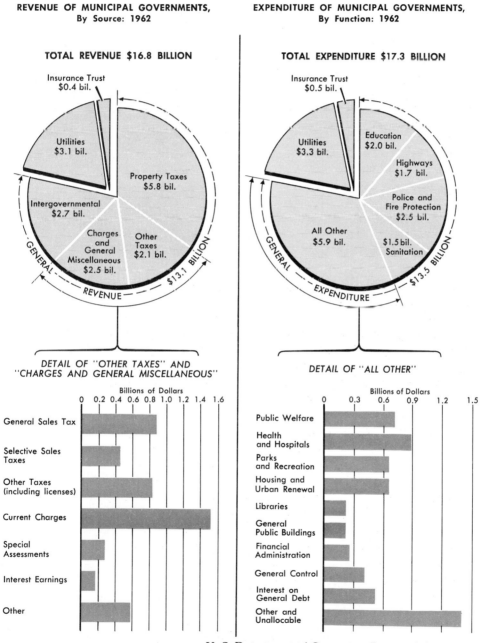

REVENUE OF MUNICIPAL GOVERNMENTS,
By Source: 1962

TOTAL REVENUE $16.8 BILLION

Insurance Trust $0.4 bil.

Utilities $3.1 bil.

Property Taxes $5.8 bil.

Intergovernmental $2.7 bil.

Charges and General Miscellaneous $2.5 bil.

Other Taxes $2.1 bil.

GENERAL — REVENUE — $13.1 BILLION

EXPENDITURE OF MUNICIPAL GOVERNMENTS,
By Function: 1962

TOTAL EXPENDITURE $17.3 BILLION

Insurance Trust $0.5 bil.

Utilities $3.3 bil.

Education $2.0 bil.

Highways $1.7 bil.

Police and Fire Protection $2.5 bil.

All Other $5.9 bil.

$1.5 bil. Sanitation

GENERAL — EXPENDITURE — $13.5 BILLION

DETAIL OF "OTHER TAXES" AND "CHARGES AND GENERAL MISCELLANEOUS"

Billions of Dollars
0   0.2 0.4 0.6 0.8 1.0 1.2 1.4 1.6

General Sales Tax

Selective Sales Taxes

Other Taxes (including licenses)

Current Charges

Special Assessments

Interest Earnings

Other

DETAIL OF "ALL OTHER"

Billions of Dollars
0   0.3   0.6   0.9   1.2   1.5

Public Welfare

Health and Hospitals

Parks and Recreation

Housing and Urban Renewal

Libraries

General Public Buildings

Financial Administration

General Control

Interest on General Debt

Other and Unallocable

U. S. Department of Commerce, Bureau of the Budget.

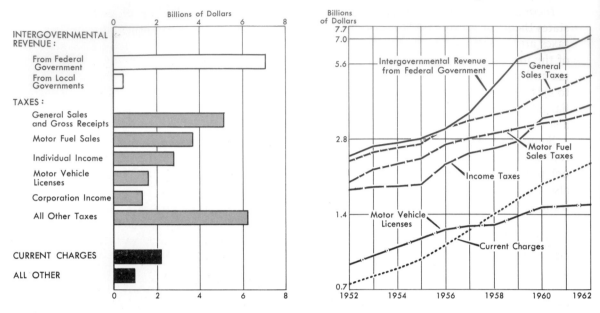

GENERAL REVENUE OF STATE GOVERNMENTS,
By Source: 1962

TRENDS IN REVENUE OF STATE GOVERNMENTS,
From Selected Major Sources:
1952 to 1962

U.S. *Department of Commerce, Bureau of the Census.*

Other Taxes

Sales Taxes. This depression-born tax is now one of the most important sources of money for many of the states. Today, 36 states impose some kind of general sales tax, normally on retail sales. City sales taxes are less common, though nearly 1,000 cities collect them. City sales taxes are readily evaded; people simply do their shopping outside the city limits. Sales taxes are unpopular with local merchants, who fear that they drive trade away. Most cities and states try to prevent evasion by imposing a *use tax* payable by persons who purchase items outside the city or state for use within the city or state. Most use taxes are, however, difficult to collect.

Sales taxes, especially those levied by the state, are relatively easy to administer and produce large amounts of revenue. Despite their regressive nature (that is, their tendency to bear hardest on the lower-income groups), their popularity is increasing. They seem relatively painless, since the consumer puts out the few cents on each item rather than paying a large tax bill at one time. Labor groups and persons with small incomes are generally opposed to the sales tax and would favor wider use of the progressive income tax. They argue that persons with small incomes spend a larger part of their budget for food and clothing than do the wealthy, and sales taxes fall heaviest on those least able to pay. In some states, food has been exempted from the sales tax. In others, passage of sales taxes has been blocked altogether, or has been coupled with an income tax.

Income Taxes. Personal income taxes are now collected in 34 states, but in most states the income tax is a less important source of money than the sales tax. Income taxes are generally progressive or graduated—that is, the rate goes up with the size of the income. State income tax rates, however, do not rise as sharply as the federal tax and rarely go over 10 per cent. In most states exemptions are generous enough to exclude large numbers of people. Corporation incomes are frequently taxed at a flat rate. Because of the importance and burden of the federal income tax, there is a strong feeling that states should go slow.

Some cities, following the lead of Philadelphia and Toledo, now collect a pay roll tax. Philadelphia imposes a relatively small flat tax on salaries of all persons and net profits of unincorporated businesses and professions. The Toledo tax applies also to corporate profits. These taxes enable hard-pressed cities to collect money from "daytime" citizens who use city facilities but reside in the suburbs.

Special Excise Taxes. All states tax gasoline and alcohol, and most of them tax cigarettes. Since many cities also tax these items, the local, state, and federal levies often double the cost of these "luxury items to the consumer. Gasoline taxes are sometimes combined with the funds collected from automobile and drivers' licenses and earmarked for highway purposes. Liquor taxes often consist of licenses to manufacture or sell alcoholic beverages and levies on the sales or consumption of the beverage. Some states own their own liquor dispensaries with the profits going to the state treasury. High taxation of liquor is justified on the grounds that it reduces the amount consumed, falls on an item that is not generally considered a necessity of life, and, through licensing, eases the job of law enforcement. If the tax is raised too high, however, liquor tends to be diverted into illegal channels, and tax revenues fall off.

This list does not begin to exhaust the kinds of tax collected by states and their subdivisional governments. Admissions taxes, stock transfer taxes, inheritance taxes, parimutuel taxes, corporate franchise taxes, and

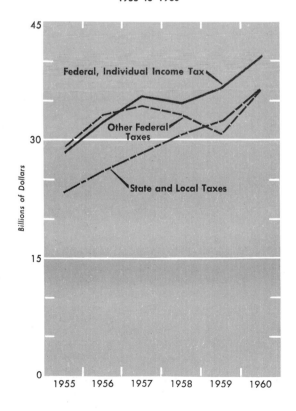

FEDERAL, STATE, AND LOCAL TAX REVENUE: 1955 to 1960

others are quite common. The severance tax on the privilege of "severing" natural resources such as coal, oil, and timber is important in some states. In Texas, New Mexico, Louisiana, and Oklahoma, for example, the severance tax on oil and natural gas accounts for more 10 per cent of state taxes.

Nontax Revenues

In addition to taxation, states derive some revenue from fees and special service charges. In fact, about 8 per cent of the money collected by the states and 10 per cent of local government revenue come from these sources. Fees are charged for building inspection, for recording of titles, for court costs, for licensing of professions, for garbage disposal, and other special services. Parking meters have become an important revenue source for many cities. Special assessments against property-owners whose property is benefited by public improvements, such as streets or sewers, are a general practice.

Some cities run business enterprises from which they make money (sometimes they lose money, too). Municipally owned waterworks or gas and light companies often contribute to the city treasury. In some cases, utility profits are large enough to make other city taxes unnecessary.

Grants from one level of government to another have become increasingly important during the last several decades. As we have noted, the national government through grants-in-aid allots large sums to the states. The states are giving more and more money to the local governments in the form of state grants to support particular programs or in the form of shared taxes. In the latter case, state officials return to local governments revenues collected from certain taxes, often without specifying the purposes for which the money shall be used.

When all the taxes and fees are added together, state and local governments collect large sums. But often they are still not enough to build the highways, or provide the amount of public assistance to the elderly, or perform the other functions that the voters have insisted upon. What then? Even as you and I, our governments often have to borrow money.

Borrowing Money

During the early years of the nineteenth century, states and cities often subsidized railroad- and canal-builders. The money for this as well as for financing other public improvements came from bonds issued by the city or state. Frequently, the standards were not high, and bribery and favoritism were common. Provision for payment of debts was inadequate. At times, the people were stuck with old debts for improvements long after the improvements had lost their value. As a result, default on obligation frequently occurred, and city and state credit fell off.

Aroused by the legislatures' abuse of their powers, voters insisted on constitutional amendments reducing legislative discretion. Today most state constitutions put elaborate restrictions on the power of state and local legislatures to borrow money or pledge credit. In large measure, therefore, the power to borrow money for a long term has been transferred from the legislatures and city councils to the voters.

Fiscal planning to insure that taxes are collected in time to cover necessary operating expenses has reduced the amount of short-term borrowing. Even so, officials sometimes need to borrow money for a short term. This "floating debt" consists of bank loans, tax-anticipation warrants, and other notes, and is paid off out of current revenues.

States and cities sometimes need to borrow money for longer periods—15 or 20 years. During the depression, money was needed for relief. Since the end of World War II many states have gone into debt in order to pay bonuses to veterans. Expenditures for highway construction, school buildings, slum clearance, and so on, are so large that it is not feasible to pay for them out of current revenue. Moreover, these improvements have a long life and add to the wealth of the community, so it is desirable to pay for them by spreading the cost. For this purpose, governments issue bonds. The best practice, and one now required by many constitutions, is to issue *serial bonds,* a portion of which come due each year and are retired out of current revenues.

State and local bonds are especially attractive to wealthy investors, since the interest received from them is exempt from federal income tax. For this reason, these governments can borrow money at a lower interest rate than can private businesses. The credit of most cities and states is good, and they readily find buyers for their bonds. Some bonds are *general obligation bonds* and are backed by the credit of the issuing governments. Other bonds, *revenue bonds,* are backed only by the income from the particular project in which the money is invested. Governments are often permitted to issue revenue bonds beyond the limitations on their general indebtedness, and this type is used wherever possible.

During World War II, with incomes high and tax collections good, many states were able to pay off much of their debt. Since the end of the war, state and municipal borrowing has increased to cover veterans' bonuses and to finance improvements that had been postponed by the emergency. Debts of state and local governments have mounted sharply in recent years, climbing from $19.3 billion in 1942 to over $90 billion in 1964, with the bulk of the increase going to education and highways.

Spending the Money

State and local governments are spending more money for more things than they did 50 years ago. Spending by state and local governments has nearly quintupled since World War II years, rising from $14.1 billion in 1946 to $69.3 billion in 1964. But the percentage of the national income taken by these governments has not materially increased. Their relative expenditures in terms of real and not inflated dollars are not much greater than they were 20 years ago, despite the fact that they have more duties than they ever had before. Even with their weaknesses—and there are many—state and local governments are giving better services than they did in the past without taking any appreciably larger part of the national income. And most citizens are probably getting their money's worth.

Who controls the purse strings? City councils, town meetings, school boards, the legislature—all share in deciding how much and what kinds of taxes shall be collected and how much and for what purpose the money shall be spent, subject to constitutional limitations. But the preparation of the budget and the responsibility for planning the state or city's program is becoming more and more the job of the chief executive. In at least forty states the governor prepares the budget; his staff reviews estimates from the various departments, correlates the program, and transmits it to the legislature. The mayor or manager has the same job in many municipalities. In other places, either the legislature or a group of officials prepares the budget.

The *executive budget* is preferred, because the governor or mayor who manages the administration can review programs from the point of view of the over-all needs of the government. Each department head is always convinced that his department needs more money, but the chief executive has to balance the needs of all the departments. The budget is prepared in much the same way as the national budget. In fact, the practice of the national government was adapted from the experiences of the states. The legislative body, normally through its committees, holds hearings and acts on the executive's recommendations. In some states and in a few cities, however, the legislature cannot increase amounts or add items to what the executive has recommended. Most governors probably have greater control over state expenditures than does the President over national. In addition to the item veto, governors often have control over the allotment of funds to departments even after appropriations have been approved by the legislature. This power over the budget makes it possible for the executive to control departmental operations, to prevent duplication and overlapping, and to require efficient management.

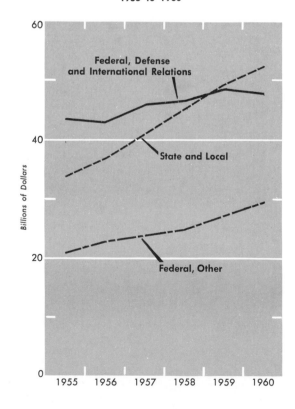

**DIRECT GENERAL EXPENDITURE:
1955 to 1960**

Federal, Defense
and International Relations

State and Local

Federal, Other

Billions of Dollars

60

40

20

0

1955   1956   1957   1958   1959   1960

EPILOGUE:
CHALLENGE
AND
OPPORTUNITY

Government by the people needs thinkers and doers, leaders who heed the injunction, "Think as men of action, act as men of thought." Government by the people also requires talents, a variety of talents not monopolized by any one individual or group. How can you put your knowledge and your belief in democratic government to good use?

863

Needed: 100,000,000 *Politicians*

College men and women do not need to be told how important it is for them to take part in politics. Since grade school, they have had this sermon dinned into their ears. Nor do they agree with Boss Plunkitt that "if you have been to college, so much the worse for you" in the rough-and-tumble of American politics. They do not feel the need to "unlearn" all they learned in college. The question is, have they learned enough?

Playing an effective part in politics depends on more than good will and interest in community affairs. It demands a good deal of political know-how. It would be pleasant to be able to say about political activity that "there's nothing to it—just learn as you go." But this would not be true. American political mechanics are a complex affair.

Many of the procedures of American politics discussed above may seem dull and difficult. So they are, until you suddenly come face to face with them in a real situation. Registration requirements, for example, seem dull matters, until someone publicly challenges your right to vote. Getting out the vote on election day seems a remote problem—until you find yourself in campaign headquarters at 2 A.M. waiting tensely for the last wards to report in. Limitations on campaign spending seem unimportant—until the opposition accuses your candidate of trying to buy the election.

Plunging in

The first step is to find the name of the local chairman of your party. Someone will know at city hall or at the court house. Calling on the chairman to tell him that you would like to help out in the campaign is the next step. Chances are that he will give you a warm welcome.

Voting lists must be checked, letters stamped, leaflets distributed, meetings arranged, publicity sent out, posters put up. Special skills will come in handy. Anyone in the advertising business can help with radio or newspaper publicity. Amateur sign painters will have ample occasion to make use of their talents. A good money-raiser can help meet the problems of campaign expenses—usually the worst headache of all. Typists, from the hunt-and-peck variety on up, are needed (with their typewriters). Good organizers are required to direct doorbell-ringing, an art and a science in itself. Cars and drivers are wanted for the countless errands that must be run.

One of the most important jobs in a political campaign is to get people registered to vote. Registration falls into two types: permanent and periodic. How does one go about getting people registered? At best, it is a chore. First, one must find names and addresses of those not registered. One way to do this is to check city directories or police lists against registration lists. Another, and more common, practice is to check the membership lists of organizations such as the American Legion or a labor union for names not on the voting lists. Then the unregistered person must be approached by mail, over the phone, or, best of all, in his home.

The unregistered voter is often an apathetic citizen. He may not see much point in voting. He will probably not know when the registration period comes. He may ask question: Will they ask me how old I am? Will they make me take a reading test? Do I have to pay anything? How long do I have to live in the area? Answers to these questions—almost always they can be reassuring ones—will be expected of anyone taking part in a registration drive. In many cases, transportation and baby-sitters also must be provided.

Another highly important job in political campaigning is to get people to vote on election day. The most effective work here is usually done by party committees and candidates. Workers are stationed at every polling booth to check off the names of persons as they vote. Then "checkers" send hourly reports to people at party headquarters, who begin telephoning voters who have not shown up. Other party workers drive voters to the polls. The success of the whole operation depends on good timing, carefully checked lists, and efficient communication and transportation.

The heart of registration and voting drives lies in approaching the individual voter in person, but the approach is much more effective if it comes as part of a general drive. This is especially true of registration drives. A nonpartisan, community-wide program is often the most fruitful procedure. The drive is carried on through the press, radio, television, posters, civic groups, trade unions, veterans' organizations, window displays, churches, schools, door-to-door canvassing, rallies— even sky writing! In some communities police cars have carried "get-out-the-vote" signs, "vote-mobiles" have toured the area with sample voting machines or sample ballots, and REGISTER TO VOTE has been stenciled on the sidewalks.

Much of this work would be simple drudgery under any other circumstances. In the heat of a campaign, however, it takes on an aura of the dramatic. Volunteers are part of a team engaged in a keen struggle. Party headquarters is always crowded; the phone seems always to be ringing. Crisis follows crisis. Candidates dash in to make arrangements for coming meetings, rush out to speak at the Odd Fellows' barbecue. Rumors flow thick and fast. And occasionally one of them may even be true.

Taking part in party politics is a rewarding business. Perhaps the biggest satisfaction comes on election day. The blinders have been taken off; the names on the ballot are those of flesh-and-blood persons. Politics has taken on a new dimension. At this stage you can feel that you are no longer an outsider, but an insider in party affairs. You have learned something of the rules and gimmicks of the political game.

After the election, what then? We will be told on all sides that "politics is now adjourned." But politics is never adjourned. It is a year-round business— at least for the professionals. The only question is whether they will have the game all to themselves.

Keeping at It

Vitally important decisions are made between elections. New members are added to local party committees, precinct captains are selected, perhaps new chairmen are elected. Members of state committees and delegates to conventions are chosen. Plans are made for registration drives, election of candidates to national conventions, future campaigns. These activities determine the shape of politics in the elections ahead. Obviously, running a party, like running a war, is too important to be left to the professionals. The period between elections is the ideal time for public-spirited citizens to make their influence felt in the party councils—an influence that will be all the greater because important party decisions are made by relatively few persons.

In most cases party workers will have no trouble gaining a foothold in the party organization. Occasionally, the old-line leaders may try to close out newcomers to keep the organization as their private preserve. They should not be allowed to succeed without a struggle. If necessary, one can often work with another part of the organization, or join or form auxiliary groups like the Young Democrats or Young Republicans.

Our mental picture of a local party leader is usually one of a ruthless boss, complete with cigar, jowls, and a taste for "honest graft." In real life the party leader usually turns out to be an amiable, honest individual who holds his position as a result of working hard and doing countless favors. Of course, unscrupulous bosses are to be found. But one should not be discouraged from taking part in politics because the local party organization seems to be controlled by a disreputable group. It is far easier to clean the organization from within than from without. Party bosses can ignore the criticism of outsiders, but they cannot resist those who outwork and outvote them within their own domain.

Let there be fair warning. Anyone going into party politics with illusions about the way the parties operate is likely to be in for a shock. On the local level, organization is often stagnant, if not moribund. Committees rarely meet and attendance is poor. Where the local organization is energetic and influential, it is usually because a leader has infused some life into it. His reward is to be called the local "boss"—whether or not he is serving private rather than public needs.

The South is spoken of slightingly as a one-party area, but in many parts of the North only one effective party organization can be found. A rival party may exist in name, but not in fact. Often, especially in the cities, one party organization is the "captive" of the other. It exists on crumbs of patronage handed out by the dominant organization, which is willing to pay for token opposition in order to prevent real competition. Real party rivalry cannot be expected in a situation like this.

Most disillusioning of all is the inglorious nature of local party operations. Any hope that men have banded together for the sake of grand principles may quickly evaporate. The main reason for party activity often turns out to be the "cohesive power of public plunder." Doubtless, local politics has been purified a bit since the days of the muckrakers, but in all too many cases, city and county organizations still are occupied with personalities and petty business rather than with the real needs of the community.

This is disconcerting to the good citizen who has gone to party headquarters to stay. The local problems worrying him concern schools for his children, lower taxes, better roads, faster snow removal in winter, a new library building. He has only one consolation, but it is a big one. The greater the need for improving the character of local politics, the larger the opportunity for him and his fellows to pitch in and do something.

"You're the boss," Mr. Edward J. Flynn of the Bronx told us reassuringly. But he added an important proviso. We're the boss only if we are willing to dirty our hands a bit at the grass roots of party politics. Never was the need greater than today.

Running for Office

For those interested in making a career of politics there are few set rules. Generalizations about the road to election-day victories are risky; the exceptions to the rules are legion. But before entering politics, the individual would be wise to reflect on his assets and liabilities. If he is sensitive to criticism, excessively shy, if he dislikes "good fellowship" and wants to lead a quiet, peaceful life, the chances are against his being successful—or at least happy—in politics. On the other hand, if he enjoys working with others, likes to speak, and can look forward without fear to countless dinners of cold peas and roast beef, then politics offers an exciting and rewarding career.

"One who enters politics must realize that he is to live dangerously," a candidate has said. "In business, the line between the red and the black divides anxiety and comfort, but a businessman can survive a bad year; in politics .1 per cent of one's biennial gross vote can mean the difference between prosperity and ruin." [1]

Some Hints from an Expert

Hugh D. Scott, Jr., a senator, former chairman of the Republican National Committee, and an experienced politician, believes that the following traits are helpful to politically active men and women:

1. Be politically informed.
2. Integrity is the most valuable tool of the trade. Despite cynicism about politics, a dishonest politician is almost always exposed sooner or later.

[1] Stimson Bullitt, *To Be a Politician* (Doubleday, 1959), p. 53.

3. "Patience is a prime political virtue," says Mr. Scott after observing that he had spent "twenty years or so of being stopped several times a day by people with something on their mind, of having my lapels seized firmly or my sleeve tugged by someone who wants something done that he feels I may be able to do, of long interviews with people with a grievance, a petition, a plan, an invention, or just a two-way ball-bearing tongue."

4. Courtesy—"on Ballot Boulevard there's no market at all for the sour stuff."

5. Gregariousness.

6. Hard work. "To know your neighborhood and to help your neighbors is a 365-day-a-year job."

7. A sense of humor. Freshman members of Congress are warned by their elders "Don't violate Rule Six." And what is Rule Six? "Don't take yourself too seriously." And Rules One to Five? "Don't take yourself too seriously." A sense of proportion, a sense of humor.

8. Courage.[2]

Politics does not offer much in the way of job security. It is, therefore, helpful if the aspiring politician has some other source of income. In American politics this has often been the case. Lawyers have more of an opportunity to combine politics and business than do doctors, teachers, workers, or others. The young graduate from law school is forbidden by the ethics of his profession to advertise, but he can run for office. If he wins, he will make valuable contacts. If he loses, he can return to the practice of law with a name that is better known to the public.

Insurance and farming are other professions that may be readily combined with politics. But one need not be a lawyer, insurance man, or farmer to enter politics. The avenues to public office are many, and the halls of Congress and the offices of the executive departments are filled with men and women who came into politics from every conceivable background and occupation.

Do's and Don't's

Here are some of the do's and don't's of politics that should prove useful to the neophyte.

1. Be a joiner. Try to join as great a variety of organizations as possible. By working for the Community Chest, becoming active in the union, the chamber of commerce, the service club, the lodges, and in church work, the candidate makes his name familiar, wins friends, and learns the skills of his trade.

2. Be one of the boys and avoid snobbish mannerisms, but be colorful.

3. Learn to remember names and faces, but don't be effusive.

4. Ignore unfriendly attacks. "Never get into an argument with a newspaper

[2] From Hugh D. Scott, Jr., *How to Go into Politics* (John Day, 1949), pp. 26 ff.

or a preacher; the newspaper always has the last word with its readers and the preacher always calls on Heaven as witness that he is right." [3]

5. Know your facts.

6. "Don't overestimate the people's knowledge or underestimate their intelligence."

7. Remember that a nice personality and a mastery of all the do's and don't's of politics are no substitute for intelligence, integrity, and conviction.

A Career in the Civil Service

Political work often leads to appointive as well as elective public positions. Lawyers who have come to the aid of their party are sometimes in line for judgeships, and others may be appointed to places in state or local government. But today more and more of the positions in the federal administrative structure are open to qualified nonpoliticians. These positions offer much to those who have a desire for public service—but little liking for politics—or for people who have administrative talents. The government needs all kinds of people with all kinds of skills. These positions offer reasonable compensation, considerable security, and an exciting challenge.

How to Get into Government

How does one go about getting a position in one of the civilian agencies of government? There are now approximately 2.5 million civilian positions in the federal government. Only 537 of these are filled by election—namely, 435 representatives, 100 senators, the President, and the Vice President. To secure one of these positions it is necessary to go into politics. The same is generally true of an appointment to the Supreme Court or a lower federal court, district attorneyship, or appointment as a first-, second-, or third-class postmaster, or a Cabinet member. These and other such positions are filled by presidential appointment with the consent of the Senate.

But well over 80 per cent of the positions in the executive branch are open to qualified citizens regardless of their politics, except that they must be loyal to the United States and not be fascists or communists. Most of these positions are filled through civil service examinations. Veterans receive preference on these examinations, which are held throughout the United States at the various regional headquarters of the Civil Service Commission. If one does not live in a city with a Civil Service Regional Headquarters, information can be secured from the Civil Service Secretary at the local post office.

Only about 10 per cent of these positions are in Washington. The rest are

---

[3] *Ibid.*, p. 32. See also Harold Gauer, *How To Win in Politics* (Humphries, 1947), and E. E. Schattschneider, Victor Jones, and Stephen K. Bailey, *A Guide to the Study of Public Affairs* (Sloane, 1952), a citizens' manual.

scattered throughout the world. Unlike English practice, American civil service examinations are for particular kinds of jobs. Positions calling for professional training are filled through unassembled examinations. Such examinations are not examinations in the usual sense, but questionnaires that enable the Civil Service Commission and the appointing agencies to learn the competence and experience of the individual.

Civil service jobs are now graded in a general schedule of 18 grades with salaries rising from $3,507 to $25,382. The work normally involves a 5-day, 40-hour week with annual vacations of from 13 to 26 days and generous sick leave. Low-cost life insurance is available, employees are entitled to unemployment compensation, and there is an attractive retirement system. The Hatch Act protects civil servants from being obligated to contribute to political funds, but it also bars them from participating in any partisan political activity.

Types of Jobs

The positions open are so many and varied that only a few can be mentioned here. Engineers, physicists, chemists, and other technical personnel are recruited through specially designed unassembled examinations. The *Federal Service Entrance Examination* is of special interest to college graduates who wish to enter the career civil service and work up to high-level assignments. This examination is designed to recruit upwards of 7,000 college-caliber people each year, and its purpose is not just to fill particular jobs, but to secure talented persons who have the ability to mature on the job. This is a move in the direction of English civil service recruitment concepts.

The Federal Service Entrance Examination is open continuously. Following are examples of the fields in which positions are filled: general administration, economics and other social sciences, agricultural sciences, communications, library science, information and records management, statistics, personnel management. Appointments are made for college graduates at a minimum beginning salary of $5,181 (Grade GS-5). Those with a year's graduate study are eligible for Grade GS-7 positions, with starting salaries of from $6,269 to $8,132.

To qualify for the Federal Service Entrance Examination, a person (1) must have completed a four-year college course, or have three years' experience in responsible work, or have a combination of education and experience; (2) must pass a written test of general abilities; (3) must be rated satisfactory in an oral interview; (4) must submit satisfactory references; (5) must be a United States citizen of undoubted loyalty; (6) must be physically able to perform the duties of the position. College seniors may take the examination and may receive provisional appointments which permit them to enter on duty after graduation. To apply for these positions, obtain Card Form 5000-AB from any post office, civil service office, or college placement bureau. The examinations are given every few months at cities throughout the nation.

Of special interest to persons of unusual ability are the management intern-ships (formerly known as Junior Management Assistant) that are offered by some of the agencies. These agencies have specially planned programs that give varied work assignments and training designed to develop persons of unusual promise. In order to obtain one of these internships, in addition to passing the Federal Service Entrance Examination, the candidate must also pass a more comprehen-sive written test on either administrative problems or public affairs and must demonstrate in an oral interview that he has the personal qualities required for higher managerial positions.

There is always room in the civil service for persons with secretarial skills. Men and women with college training or comparable experience and secretarial skills often get into the service as secretaries and then quickly move up to administra-tive positions. Persons who wish to go from agency to agency to look for civil-service positions should secure Form 57 from the Civil Service Commission and fill it out before going job-hunting. Completing this form is required procedure, and to fill it out before seeing appointing officers will save much time. Several federal agencies have their own personnel systems and are not covered by regu-lar civil service rules. The TVA, the FBI, the National Security Agency, the USIA, and the Central Intelligence Agency, for example, recruit and hire their own employees. The FBI appoints its special agents from among physically and mentally eligible lawyers (those who have graduated from an accredited law school) and accountants (with at least three years' experience). G-men receive a starting salary of $7,900, plus $1,081 for overtime, and after a probationary period are given raises and permanent appointments.

In addition to opportunities in the federal service, many attractive positions are open in state and municipal public service. Since each year the states and cities improve the conditions of their public service, opportunities are becoming more attractive for able people.

Although positions with the United Nations are difficult to secure because the American quota is usually filled, the effort may be worth-while, for service with the United Nations offers many advantages in pay and other benefits, in addition to the satisfaction of working for the community of mankind.

Entering the Foreign Service

The Foreign Service has attractions for many people. In some ways it is the glamour service of the federal government, but, as we point out in Chapter 22, much of the work is routine, and life can be dull and even unpleasant in some posts. Yet the Service has many advantages.

In order to be eligible to take the Foreign Service Officer examinations one must: (1) be at least 21 and under 31 years of age; (2) have been a citizen of the United States for at least 7½ years; (3) not be married to an alien at the time of appointment. Examinations for these positions are written, oral, and physical. The written examination is usually held in May and December in almost 300 cities in the United States, and at any American diplomatic or consulate post that candidates residing abroad may designate. The oral examinations are held in Washington, at certain regional centers in the United States, and at certain posts abroad. Persons who wish to take the examinations may receive application forms from the Board of Examiners for the Foreign Service, Department of State, Washington 25, D.C.; these applications should be completed at least six weeks before the date set for the examination.

Foreign Service Examinations

Taking a full day to complete, the written examination is composed of four parts. The first part is a General Ability test (75 minutes) designed to measure the candidate's basic learning skills—ability to read, to analyze, and to interpret data in a variety of quantitative forms, and to make simple mathematical deductions. The second part is an English Expression test (105 minutes) intended to examine the candidate's ability to recognize and use correct, effective, and well-organized written English. Each candidate is required to write on two assigned topics during the test. The third part is a General Background test (90 minutes) consisting of approximately 50 per cent social sciences, 25 per cent humanities, and 25 per cent science questions. The final part consists of Special Optional tests (75 minutes). Candidates must select one of the following four optional tests: Option A—History, Government, Social Sciences, and Public Affairs; Option B—Administration; Option C—Economics; Option D—Commerce.

The oral examination is designed to test qualities such as resourcefulness and versatility, appearance, manner, diction, and personality. The Service uses the oral interview to eliminate candidates who are "shy, aggressive, boorish, unable to defend their views, who give evidence of low standards of conduct, and who show a lack of knowledge of the United States." To test this last quality, natives of one section of the country are often questioned on other sections. Factual knowledge is given less weight than "ability to form thoughtful opinions based on the facts at the candidate's disposal, to organize his views logically, and to speak clearly and understandably." While the examinations are exacting, they are less so than formerly, and the number of positions open has recently been increased.

Service Abroad

The President, with the consent of the Senate, appoints successful candidates as Foreign Service officers (since 1956, most of them at Class 8). Their salaries range from $6,269 to $7,511; moreover, officers may work themselves up the scale until they get to the top class, where the salaries are $23,465 to $25,382. In addition, career officers may be appointed as ambassadors and ministers at higher salaries, up to $27,000. While abroad, salaries are supplemented by quarters allowances; officers receive from 13 to 26 days of annual leave; and after two years abroad they are entitled to home leave in the United States with pay and travel expenses for their families. Other attractive fringe benefits are life and family health insurance, pension, and so on. Unless an officer is promoted within a maximum period in each class, except for the top two classes, he must retire.

Before foreign assignment, Foreign Service officers are trained at the Foreign Service Institute, and throughout their careers they continue special studies. There is no single method of preparation for the Foreign Service, but persons interested in taking the examination should, while in college, learn to write clear and correct English, master a foreign language, and take enough social science, humanities, and science courses to be able to pass the examinations.

Peace Corps: Foreign and Domestic

The Peace Corps recruits from a wide range of skilled Americans for overseas work. After careful screening and intensive training, volunteers are assigned to countries requesting Peace Corps services. Applicants must be citizens of the United States, 18 years of age or older, single or married provided that applicants have no dependents under 18. Volunteers receive no regular salary payments, but receive allowances to cover the cost of clothing, housing, food, and incidental expenses so that they live at an economic level equivalent to counterparts in the host country. Upon completion of service, Peace Corps volunteers receive a separation allotment based upon time spent overseas. The payment accumulates at the rate of $75 a month. Peace Corps questionnaires are available at most colleges and universities and post offices or may be obtained by contacting Peace Corps, Washington 25, D.C.

An important component of the "War on Poverty," the Volunteers in Service to America (VISTA) is, in many respects, the domestic counterpart of the Peace Corps. Individuals volunteer for a one-year period to take their talents to the service of communities which are striving to solve their pressing economic and social problems. After an intensive six-weeks training period which stresses field experience and discussions of the nature and causes of poverty in the U.S., volunteers are sent to work in Job Corps camps, migrant worker communities, Indian reservations, rural and urban community action programs, hospitals, schools, and mental health facilities. In short, workers may be sent wherever poverty may exist, in any of the fifty states or in territories under the American flag. VISTA volunteers are paid only subsistence expenses and a modest monthly stipend and personal allowance. The program is administered by the Office of Economic Opportunity in Washington.

A Last Word

Some of you have no interest in learning about political or administrative jobs. Your future lies elsewhere. Even so, you can and should have a political career— in the party of your choice. As we have seen, our parties badly need strengthening at every level. The country needs more party politicians to hunt out good candidates and help elect them, drive workers to the polls on election day, spread the party gospel, and remind the officeholders of their responsibilities to the people.

Every individual in a democracy contributes to its success or failure. Those who, because of ignorance or indifference, try to stay on the side lines nevertheless influence the course of events, negative and destructive though their influence may be. If the 200 million Americans are to keep their free government, it will be mainly because of the activities of the people as a whole. Leaders dedicated to the principles of free government and leaders with vision and courage are essential; it is from private citizens that these leaders are recruited. The standards and values of the people determine broadly the type of leadership they get.

"Fourscore and seven years ago," said Abraham Lincoln in the midst of a crucial struggle, "our fathers brought forth on this continent a new nation, conceived in liberty, and dedicated to the proposition that all men are created equal." Lincoln saw that struggle as a test of whether government of the *people*, by the *people*, for the *people* could endure. Eighty years later another President, Franklin D. Roosevelt, could report in the midst of another great war that "the state of this Nation is good—the heart of this Nation is sound—the spirit of this Nation is strong—the faith of this Nation is eternal." Government by the people has met and mastered many crises. How well will it meet the tests to come?

Keeping Informed: Bibliography

Newspapers, radio, and television are important sources of information, but the person who depends solely on these sources will have an imperfect picture of the world around him. They give only a disconnected story of the sensational—the newsworthy—events. They tell little of the whys and wherefores. The successful negotiation of a hundred collective bargaining contracts during a day goes unnoticed while public attention is focused on the one case in which negotiations break down.

To some extent magazines supplement the news. Some give background information; others digest the weekly events for those too busy to read daily papers. *Time* and *Newsweek* with their clipped and dramatic reporting of the week's events are major sources of information for many citizens. The weekly *U.S. News & World Report* presents the news in graphic form, and is especially aimed toward influential members of the business community. While *Time*, and certainly *U.S. News & World Report* are "right of center," *The Nation*, *The New Leader*, and *The New Republic* are journals of opinion that report the week's events from left to center; the *National Review* discusses events from the conservative point of view. Though these last four have, compared to the others, only a relatively small circulation, their audience includes many leaders of opinion—clergymen, teachers, lawyers, public officials, and the like. *The Reporter*, also liberal in tone, gives less attention to the news of the week and more to extended discussion of issues of contemporary significance, especially in Washington and abroad.

Among the monthly magazines, *Harper's Magazine, Atlantic Monthly,* and *Fortune,* have relatively small audiences but great influence, since they are read by strategically placed individuals. The first two are more liberal than *Fortune,* but all three attempt to present a balanced diet. *Fortune* features materials of interest to businessmen, but it covers all phases of American society. By far the largest-circulation monthly is *The Reader's Digest,* read each month by millions of persons. In addition to features written by its own staff members, *The Reader's Digest* selects and abridges articles that appear in other magazines. It has conservative leanings.

Magazines of general circulation contain useful material, but they do not go deeply into particular questions. Where do you find a law? How do you look up a court decision? Where can you find information on the United Nations? How do you find out how your congressman has voted? What are some good books on the U.S.S.R.? Many aids and services have been designed to make such information readily available.

Important information-dispensing centers are the more than 7,500 public libraries and the many hundreds of private libraries that are open to the public. In these libraries can be found, in addition to magazines of general interest, many specialized journals such as *The American Political Science Review.* There are a number of periodical indexes of which the *Public Affairs Information Service* is especially useful since it indexes books, pamphlets, and reports, as well as articles from hundreds of periodicals on topics in a broad range of current public interest. Major political science journals are included in the *International Index.* The *International Political Science Abstracts* edited by the International Political Science Association provides précis of articles from all major political science journals throughout the world. The *Reader's Guide to Periodical Literature* includes mainly popular magazines with mass or family circulation. The *Index to Legal Periodicals* and *Business Periodicals Index* are also useful. Most of these indexes are published monthly and indexed cumulatively at the end of the year. They will help you locate materials on most subjects. The card catalogue in the library will reveal the books that are available in the library. You may be able to learn something about an author's reputation and some informed opinions about a particular book in *The Book Review Digest;* this digest, though, should be used in a limited fashion because reviews are taken from a selected list of publications and therefore a full picture of the reviews of a particular book is not necessarily presented.

One of the most useful volumes is the *United States Government Organization Manual,* an annual publication. The *Manual,* which can be obtained from the Superintendent of Documents, Government Printing Office, covers the authority, organization, and functions of all branches of the government. It has up-to-date organization charts, tells which individuals hold the higher executive positions, and gives a brief description of the work of each unit of government. If you want to know, for example, who heads the Bureau of Mines in the Department of the Interior, and what that bureau does, the *Manual* is the place to look. The *Congressional Directory*, also published each year, has some of the materials found in the *Manual*, and it includes autobiographical sketches of members of Congress, lists of congressional committees and committee assignments, election statistics for the last several congressional elections, and maps of congressional districts. The *Directory* is the place to find out the name of your congressman, a short sketch of his life, what committees he is on, and the boundaries of the district he represents.

Of special interest to persons interested in public affairs is the *Encyclopedia of the Social Sciences*, published in 1930 under the editorship of Edwin R. A. Seligman, which contains articles on various topics—political parties, sovereignty, representation, John Locke, for example—that are among the best short treatments to be found. The *Encyclopedia* is presently being revised. Although about half of the *Encyclopedia* is biography, the *Dictionary of National Biography* and the *Dictionary of American Biography* are prime sources: Included are some outstanding articles—for example, one by Carl Becker on Benjamin Franklin, found in the *Dictionary of American Biography*. In *Current Biography* you can find materials and background information on men in the news, and there is a companion set, *Biography Index* in case specific information has not been written up fully in *Current Biography* for ten years or so.

Certain important tools for quick reference to current events are available, such as *Facts on File, The New York Times Index, The Wall Street Journal Index*, and *Keesing's Contemporary Archives*.

If you want raw figures, consult the *Statistical Abstract of the United States*, another yearly publication of the Government Printing Office. Many arguments could be readily settled by resorting to this volume. The reference librarian will be able to point out other useful tools of this nature, such as the *Historical Statistics of the United States*, the *Congressional District Data Book*, and the many publications from the Bureau of the Census.

Where can you find a law? We often hear people talk about some statute without having seen it. Where can the actual text be found?

The laws of the United States as passed by Congress are first printed individually and are known as slip laws. Each law has a number; in recent years public laws are numbered according to the term of Congress in which they are enacted; the act to provide for the admission of the State of Hawaii into the Union, for example, is known as P.L. 86-3.

At the end of each year the laws are collected and published by the Government Printing Office under the title of *United States Statutes at Large*. Each year's collection is separately numbered, though there are two separate parts for each number. Part One contains *public laws*, that is, laws affecting the people generally or having to do with governmental organization. Part Two contains *private laws*, those having to do with particular groups or individuals. The laws in the *Statutes at Large* are listed chronologically, each law constituting a separate chapter. The

Taft-Hartley Act, for example, is Chapter 120 of Volume 61, on page 136. (It is cited as follows: 61 Stat. 136.)

The volumes of *Statutes at Large* are useful for research, but they include many laws of only specialized interest, such as rivers and harbors appropriations. Furthermore, many of the measures modify earlier legislation and are themselves modified by later legislation. To find *current* laws on a topic it is best to go to the *United States Code*, which contains the public laws of the United States that are in force at the present time. The official edition of the *U. S. Code* is published every six years. Supplements are issued annually between editions. The current edition is dated 1964 and embraces all laws in force on January 1, 1965. The laws are arranged according to 50 titles, each title is divided into sections, and each section into paragraphs that are consecutively numbered for each title. The 50 titles cover such subjects as Congress, Title 2; Army, Title 10; Bankruptcy, Title 11; Labor, Title 29; and so on. The *Code* is cited by title and paragraph. The citation of the Taft-Hartley Act, for example, is 29 U. S. C. 141 ff.

The *Code*, like the *Statutes at Large*, is printed by the Government Printing Office, but there are also commercially published editions known as *United States Code Annotated* (U. S. C. A.) and the *Federal Code Annotated* (F. C. A.). These annotated editions include notes on judicial interpretations of the law as well as the law itself. If available, they are more useful than the *Code* itself.

The series *Treaties in Force* is the best source of information about treaties and executive agreements. These volumes are published annually and are organized chronologically.

Where does one find the rules and regulations issued by the President and the executive agencies? Every day except Sunday and Monday the government publishes *The Federal Register* which contains executive orders, regulations, and proclamations issued by the President, as well as the orders and regulations promulgated by the executive agencies (including the independent regulatory commissions). These administrative rules and regulations are collected, codified, and kept up-to-date in the *Code of Federal Regulations*, organized on the same plan as the *United States Code*. The *Code of Federal Regulations*, *The Federal Register*, along with the *U. S. Government Organization Manual* previously mentioned, and a new publication, *Public Papers of the President*, are part of what is known as the Federal Register System. The *Public Papers of the President* contain public messages, speeches, and statements of the President.

The laws as they finally appear on the statute books give, however, only part of the story. Where do you find out what went on before the laws were passed or why certain laws were not passed? This information can, in part, be found in one of the most edifying and interesting items of American letters—the *Congressional Record*. The *Record* is issued every day Congress is in session and is bound and indexed at the end of each session. It contains everything that is said on the floors of the two chambers, plus a lot that is not said. Congress freely gives its consent to requests of its members "to revise and extend their remarks," which is a polite way of saying that congressmen are permitted to include in the *Record* statements that they did not make before Congress. These speeches are then reprinted and distributed to the folks back home. Congressmen, with the unanimous consent of their colleagues, also place in the *Record* poems, articles, letters, editorials, and other materials they find interesting. Each day's *Record* is now accompanied by a *Daily Digest* that highlights the events on both the floor of Congress and in committees.

Action on specific items can be traced by searching through the index. An easier method is to use the *Digest of Public General Bills* which gives a brief summary of all the public bills and traces their progress in the legislative assembly line.

There are several commercial services that provide convenient references to congressional activities. *The Congressional Quarterly Weekly Report* contains voting records, legislative action, reports on lobbying, and other materials about Congress in action. This is the best source for materials on lobbying activity. The materials are indexed and collected in an *Annual Almanac*. The *United States Code: Congressional and Administrative News*, and the *Congressional Index* also provide ready reference to congressional activity.

Since most of the real work of Congress is done in committees, the reports of these committees and the printed records of hearings are important sources of information. The hearings and reports may be found in any of the 550 depository libraries in the United States. (A depository library is one that receives regularly publications issued by the Government Printing Office. Of these libraries, only 125 are full depository libraries; the rest receive publications in selected categories and subjects.)

Congress is not the only branch of the federal government that keeps a record of its work. All the other agencies have their own publications, describing their work and supplying the citizen with general and specialized information. These can be obtained from the Superintendent of Documents, Government Printing Office, Washington 25, D.C., at a nominal price. They are indexed in the *Monthly Catalog of United States Government Publications*. One of the several general guides to government publications is Laurence F. Schmeckebier and Roy B. Eastin, *Government Publications and Their Use* (Brookings, 1961).

Where can you find the reports of the federal judiciary? Legal bibliography is a complex subject, but the law is too important to leave to lawyers. The decisions of the Supreme Court are published by the government in numbered volumes known as the *United States Reports*. Cases are cited by volume and page number, e.g., *Illinois et rel McCollum* v. *Board of Education*, 333 U. S. 203 (1948) means that this case can be found in the 333rd volume of the *United States Reports* on page 203 and that the opinion was handed down in 1948. Decisions of the Court prior to 1875 are cited by the name of the Supreme Court reporter. Thus, *Marbury* v. *Madison*, 1 Cranch 137 (1803), can be found in the first volume of Cranch's Supreme Court reports on page 137; the opinion was announced in 1803. Two other editions of Supreme Court opinions are commercially published and each has its own form of citation. Some of the federal district court rulings are now commercially published in volumes known as the *Federal Supplement*. Those of the federal courts of appeals are now also published by the same commercial publisher in volumes known as the *Federal Reporter*. These reports are not available in many general libraries, but in many communities a special law library, usually located in the court house, contains the reports of the cases plus other materials needed by lawyers in their professional work.

Selected Bibliography

This bibliography makes no pretense of including even all the good books pertinent to the American experiment in government by the people. Its purpose is to provide an *initial* guide to the literature. With few exceptions, the rich periodical literature is not mentioned. A number of books which in the opinion of the authors are of special importance to the general reader have been starred.

Part One: Democratic Government in America

General Sources

C. S. Hyneman, *The Study of Politics; The Present State of American Political Science* (1959). Survey of current research, problems, methods, and data.

H. D. Lasswell, *The Future of Political Science* (1963). A blueprint for the discipline by an eminent social scientist.

B. Crick, *The American Science of Politics: Its Origins and Conditions* (1959). Critical study of American political science.

R. M. MacIver, *The Web of Government* (1947). Analysis of government.

R. A. Dahl, *Modern Political Analysis* (1963). Excellent short introduction to the systematic study of politics.

A. F. Bentley, *The Process of Government* (1908; reprinted 1949). Seminal study in methodology and systematic treatment of the role of interest groups in the political process.

* D. B. Truman, *The Governmental Process* (1951). Builds on Bentley's work; analysis of political interests and public opinion.

D. Easton, *The Political System* (1953); *A Framework For Political Analysis* (1965); seeking a general theory of politics.

N. W. Polsby, *et al.* (eds.), *Politics and Social Life: An Introduction to Political Behavior* (1963). Studies of political behavior in many contexts.

J. C. Davies, *Human Nature in Politics: The Dynamics of Political Behavior* (1963). Argues that political behavior is rooted in man's organic needs.

M. Edelman, *The Symbolic Uses of Politics* (1964). Provocative analysis of the meanings of political acts.

H. J. Storing (ed.), *Essays on the Scientific Study of Politics* (1962). Critical essays on current trends in political science.

E. J. Meehan, *The Theory and Method of Political Analysis* (1965). A scientific approach to political phenomena.

V. Van Dyke, *Political Science: A Philosophical Analysis* (1960). Analysis of various approaches to the study of politics.

K. W. Deutsch, *The Nerves of Government: Models of Political Communication and Control* (1963). Toward a general theory of politics through the use of communication systems metaphor.

A. Brecht, *Political Theory: The Foundations of Twentieth Century Political Thought* (1959). Thorough analysis of "value-fact" controversy.

G. Almond and S. Verba, *The Civic Culture: Political Attitudes and Democracy in Five Nations* (1963). Presents a theory of political development and tests by sample survey methodology.

C. J. Friedrich, *Man and His Government: An Empirical Theory of Politics* (1963).

General Treatments of American Government and Society

J. K. Galbraith, *The Affluent Society* (1958). Study of American economy challenging many present assumptions.

* M. Lerner, *America as a Civilization: Life*

and Thought in the United States Today
(1957). Wide-ranging study of American
pluralism.

J. Barzun, *The House of Intellect* (1959).
Critical analysis of American culture.

M. Beloff, *The American Federal Government* (1959). Critical analysis by noted
British scholar.

A. de Tocqueville, *Democracy in America*, 2
vols. (Phillips Bradley edition, 1964, first
published in 1835). Classic study of American government.

J. Bryce, *The American Commonwealth*, 2
vols. (1888). Ranks with Tocqueville; more
descriptive and less analytical.

D. W. Brogan, *Politics in America* (1954).
Special emphasis on party system.

H. J. Laski, *The American Democracy*
(1948). Provocative interpretation by another English political scientist.

V. O. Packard, *The Status Seekers* (1959).
Popular analysis of class in American society.

W. H. Whyte, Jr., *The Organization Man*
(1956). The impact of bureaucracy on the
individual in American society.

* G. Myrdal, *An American Dilemma* (1944).
Monumental study of American society
with special attention to the problems of
Negro-white relationships.

R. M. Williams, *American Society* (1960).
Sociological interpretation.

D. Martindale, *American Social Structure*
(1960). General survey of historical antecedents and contemporary analysis of major
features of American society.

R. E. Spiller and E. Larrabee (eds.), *American Perspectives* (1961). Essays on image
of America in the twentieth century.

F. M. Joseph, *As Others See Us* (1959).
Foreign observers present their views of
American life.

D. Riesman, *The Lonely Crowd* (1953). Influential analysis of the changing character
of American society.

S. Lipset and L. Lowenthal (eds.), *Culture
and Social Character* (1961). Critical examination of Riesman's thesis.

American Political Thought

A. T. Mason and R. H. Leach, *In Quest of
Freedom: American Political Thought and
Practice* (1959).

* V. L. Parrington, *Main Currents in American Thought* (1927–1930). Interpretation
of American literature, including the writings of the major political theorists and
practitioners.

R. H. Gabriel, *The Course of American Democratic Thought*, 2nd ed. (1956). Interpretation of democratic thought from 1815
to present.

R. Hofstadter, *The American Political Tradition and the Men Who Made It* (1954).
Study of the ideology of American statesmen, emphasizing the basic agreement underlying their political conflicts.

L. Hartz, *The Liberal Tradition in America:
An Interpretation of American Political
Thought since the Revolution* (1955). Emphasizes uniqueness of American liberal
tradition.

F. G. Wilson, *The American Political Mind*
(1949). Traces the development of American thought.

H. S. Commager, *The American Mind*
(1950). An interpretation of American
thought and character since the 1880's.

C. L. Rossiter, *Seedtime of the Republic*
(1953). Political ideas of the men who
founded the Republic.

W. F. Craven, *The Legend of the Founding
Fathers* (1956). Emphasizes contributions
of the Puritans.

C. E. Merriam, *A History of American Political Theories* (1903; reissued, 1936).
Standard classic.

R. A. Dahl, *A Preface to Democratic Theory*
(1956). Constructs model of democracy
and finds Madisonian and populistic models
inadequate.

H. B. Mayo, *An Introduction to Democratic
Theory* (1960). Historical survey.

J. Tussman, *Obligation and the Body Politic*
(1960). Commitments of a democrat.

A. Downs, *An Economic Theory of Democracy* (1957). Deductive model for analysis
and investigation.

C. Frankel, *The Democratic Prospect* (1962).
An examination of democracy in an age
of science and technology.

J. S. Mill, *Representative Government*
(1882). One of the most important books
on foundations and problems of democracy.

C. L. Becker, *Modern Democracy* (1941).
Study accenting the economic basis of
democracy and the discrepancy between the
ideal and the actual.

R. B. Perry, *Puritanism and Democracy*
(1944). Study of two American ideals; has
been called a "Thesaurus of democratic
thought and an arsenal of democratic defense."

R. Niebuhr, *The Children of Light and the
Children of Darkness* (1944). Short de-

fense of democracy by one of America's leading theologians.

* A. D. Lindsay, *The Modern Democratic State* (1943). Statement of the nature of democracy, its development, its essence, and defense of it, by an English scholar.

W. Lippmann, *Essays in the Public Philosophy* (1956). Anti-parliamentarian, Burkean defense of democracy.

J. H. Hallowell, *The Moral Foundation of Democracy* (1954). Statement that democracy depends upon Hebraic-Greek-Christian tradition.

D. Spitz, *Patterns of Anti-democratic Thought* (1949). Refutation of the major critics of democracy from the "Right."

J. R. Pennock, *Liberal Democracy* (1950). Defense of democracy, major threats to it, and the limitations on the majority in democratic government.

W. Kendall, *John Locke and the Doctrine of Majority-Rule* (1941). Written by an exponent of the absolute majority rule principle.

H. S. Commager, *Majority Rule and Minority Rights* (1943). Defense of majority rule principle and attack on the limitations of judicial review.

R. Lane, *Political Ideology: Why the Ameri-*

can *Common Man Believes What He Does* (1962). Study of political belief systems.

T. L. Thorson, *The Logic of Democracy* (1962). Stimulating attempt to justify democracy logically.

S. K. Padover, *The Genius of America* (1960). Study of the leading contributors to American political culture.

N. Riemer, *The Revival of Democratic Theory* (1962). Call for renewed theoretical efforts based on the democratic premise.

Constitutionalism

W. H. Hamilton, "Constitutionalism," *Encyclopedia of the Social Sciences*, Vol. 9.

C. H. McIlwain, *Constitutionalism: Ancient and Modern* (rev. ed., 1947). Papers and essays by distinguished scholar showing the evolution of the concept of limited government.

F. M. Watkins, *The Political Tradition of the West* (1948). Traces development of modern liberalism.

C. J. Friedrich, *Constitutional Government and Democracy* (rev. ed., 1950). Analysis of relations between democracy and constitutionalism; covers all major contemporary constitutional governments.

Part Two: The Rules and How They Grew

Revolution and Confederation

D. J. Boorstin, *The Americans; the Colonial Experience* (1958). Emphasis on colonial uniqueness and its influence on the development of the American character.

J. C. Miller, *Origins of the American Revolution* (1943).

J. F. Jameson, *The American Revolution Considered as a Social Movement* (1926).

C. L. Becker, *The Declaration of Independence*, new ed. (1942).

E. Dumbauld, *The Declaration of Independence and What It Means Today* (1950). A phrase-by-phrase explanation of the Declaration, placing it in the context of the days in which it was written.

A. C. McLaughlin, *The Confederation and the Constitution, 1783–1789* (1905). Standard work.

M. Jensen, *The New Nation* (1950). Study of the Confederation, contains sharp criticism of the "chaos and patriots-to-the-rescue" interpretation.

W. N. Chambers, *Political Parties in a New*

Nation: The American Experience, 1776–1809 (1963). The development and role of the party system in a new polity.

The Constitutional Convention

W. U. Solberg, *The Federal Convention and the Formation of the Union of the American States* (1958). Documentary account.

M. Farrand, *The Records of the Federal Convention of 1787*, 4 vols., rev. ed., (1937).

A. T. Mason, *The States Rights Debate: Antifederalism and the Constitution* (1964). Antifederalist thought as seen through debates in state ratifying conventions.

J. Elliot, *The Debates in the Several Conventions on the Adoption of the Federal Constitution*, 2nd ed., 5 vols. (1835–1846). Contains the debates in the state ratifying conventions.

* J. Jay, J. Madison, and A. Hamilton, *The Federalist* (1788–1789). Basic source material, classic exposition of Constitution.

C. A. Beard, *An Economic Interpretation of the Constitution of the United States* (1913). Caused a popular furor and has had a strong influence on historians and political scientists.

R. E. Brown, *Charles Beard and the Constitution: A Critical Analysis of "An Economic Interpretation of the Constitution"* (1956).

F. McDonald, *We the People: The Economic Origins of the Constitution* (1958). Examination of Beard's thesis; concludes that economic interpretation is inadequate.

B. F. Wright, *Consensus and Continuity, 1776–1787* (1958). Another criticism of Beard, with emphasis on consensus among the framers.

J. T. Main, *The Antifederalists: Critics of the Constitution, 1781–1788* (1961). A contemporary scholar supports Beard's thesis.

J. A. Smith, *The Spirit of American Government* (1911). Spirited statement of thesis that the Constitution is the platform of an antidemocratic movement.

C. Warren, *The Making of the Constitution* (1937). Disputes the Beard thesis, contains day-by-day account of the activities of the delegates.

C. Van Doren, *The Great Rehearsal* (1948). Popularly written account of the Constitutional Convention.

W. W. Crosskey, *Politics and the Constitution*, 2 vols. (1953). Argument that framers intended to create a unitary system.

The Living Constitution

C. H. Pritchett, *The American Constitution* (1959). General treatment of our constitutional system.

J. M. Smith and P. L. Murphy (eds.), *Liberty and Justice: A Historical Record of American Constitutional Development* (1958). Collection of documents.

* E. S. Corwin, *The Constitution and What It Means Today*, 12th ed. (1958). Phrase-by-phrase explanation.

E. S. Corwin and J. W. Peltason, *Understanding the Constitution* (1964). More elementary phrase-by-phrase explanation.

C. B. Swisher, *The Growth of Constitutional Power in the United States* (1946). The Constitution as symbol, as limitation, and as grant of power.

A. N. Holcombe, *Our More Perfect Union* (1950). Defense of American constitutional principles as expounded by Madison and other Founding Fathers.

N. J. Small (ed.), *The Constitution of the United States of America: Analysis and Interpretation* (revised and annotated, 1964), Senate Document 39, 88 Cong., 1st Sess., 1964.

L. B. Orfield, *Amending the Federal Constitution* (1942). Leading book on the subject.

C. E. Merriam, *The Written Constitution and the Unwritten Attitude* (1931). Emphasizes the impact of urbanism and political parties on constitutional system.

G. Dietze (ed.), *Essays on the American Constitution* (1965).

W. O. Douglas, *We the Judges* (1956). Comparison of Indian and American law with survey of American developments.

Federalism

W. H. Riker, *Federalism: Origin, Operation, Significance* (1964). A penetrating and sophisticated study.

J. R. Schmidhauser, *The Supreme Court as Final Arbiter in Federal-State Relations, 1789–1957* (1958). Study of the Supreme Court as "umpire of the federal system."

J. J. Kilpatrick, *The Sovereign States* (1957). Presentation of states-rights position.

A. Maass (ed.), *Area and Power* (1959). Theoretical analysis of areal division of powers.

R. L. Roettinger, *The Supreme Court and State Police Power: A Study of Federalism* (1957).

A. W. Macmahon (ed.), *Federalism: Mature and Emergent* (1955). Symposium dealing with federalism throughout the world.

J. P. Clark, *The Rise of a New Federalism* (1938). Pioneering discussion of the several varieties of federal-state cooperation.

G. C. S. Benson, *The New Centralization* (1941). Interpretation of the changing nature of federal-state relations.

Commission on Intergovernmental Relations, A *Report to the President for Transmittal to Congress* (1955). Recommendations, and survey of national-state relations with emphasis on financial aspects; generally known by name of its chairman as the "Kestenbaum Report."

W. Anderson, *The Nation and the States, Rivals or Partners?* (1955). History and present status, by senior political scientist and member of Commission on Intergovernmental Relations.

L. D. White, *The States and the Nation*

(1953). Another distinguished political scientist's interpretation with somewhat different emphasis from Anderson's.

V. V. Thursby, *Interstate Cooperation: A Study of the Interstate Compact* (1952).

R. H. Leach and R. S. Sugg, Jr., *The Administration of Interstate Compacts* (1959). Review of administrative machinery and case studies of several compacts.

W. B. Graves, *American Intergovernmental Relations: Their Origins, Historical Development, and Current Status* (1964). Problems of twentieth-century federalism.

V. O. Key, Jr., *The Administration of Federal Grants to States* (1937). Administration of the grant system.

W. Anderson and W. D. Durfee, Jr., *Intergovernmental Fiscal Relations* (1956).

J. W. Fesler, *Area and Administration* (1949). Lectures on problems arising from functional and regional administration.

R. M. Hutchins, *Two Faces of Federalism* (1961). A stimulating treatment of the function of federalism as an instrument in limiting government.

R. A. Goldwin (ed.), *A Nation of States: Essays on the American Federal System* (1963).

Part Three: Civil Liberties and Citizenship

The Problem of Civil Liberty

C. Bay, *The Structure of Freedom* (1958). Concept of freedom in light of the behavioral sciences.

F. E. Oppenheim, *Dimensions of Freedom* (1961). Systematic analysis of the concept of freedom.

J. P. Roche, *Courts and Rights* (1961). Introduction to the role of the judiciary in maintaining human rights.

I. Dilliard (ed.), *The Spirit of Liberty: Papers and Addresses of Learned Hand* (1962). Distinguished jurist on the problems of liberty.

M. R. Konvitz and C. Rossiter (eds.), *Aspects of Liberty* (1959). Essays presented to R. E. Cushman on various aspects of civil liberty.

R. Pound, *The Development of Constitutional Guarantees of Liberty* (1957). Noted American legal scholar analyzes the circumstances giving rise to guarantees of liberty in England and America.

R. S. Rankin and W. R. Dallmayr, *Freedom and Emergency Powers in the Cold War* (1964). Treats the problem of preservation of liberties when strong government is needed.

R. P. Longaker, *The President and Individual Liberties* (1961). The role of the executive branch in the maintenance of civil liberties.

A. H. Kelley (ed.), *Foundations of Freedom in the American Constitution* (1958). Articles on problems of national security and constitutional liberties.

J. P. Roche, *The Quest for the Dream: The Development of Civil Rights and Human Relations in Modern America* (1963). Emphasis on political and social history with less attention to legal development.

T. I. Emerson and D. Haber, *Political and Civil Rights in the United States*, 2 vols., 2nd ed. (1958). Comprehensive collection of civil liberty materials.

L. Pfeffer, *The Liberties of an American* (1956). General discussion of Supreme Court cases dealing with civil liberties.

American Civil Liberties Union, *Annual Reports*. The state of civil liberties in the United States.

* L. Hand, *The Bill of Rights* (1958). Famous judge's statement of need for judicial self-restraint in the area of civil liberties.

* W. O. Douglas, *The Right of the People* (1958), *A Living Bill of Rights* (1961). Defense of judicial activism with regard to civil liberties by a Supreme Court justice.

W. Gellhorn, *Individual Freedom and Governmental Restraints* (1956). Recent governmental developments encroaching on freedom of the individual.

R. A. Horn, *Groups and the Constitution* (1956). Constitutional rights of groups; their role in constitutional development.

L. J. Barker and T. W. Barker, Jr., *Freedom, Courts, Politics: Studies in Civil Liberties* (1965). Problems of civil liberties placed in their political contexts.

R. A. Rutland, *The Birth of the Bill of Rights 1776–1791* (1962). Best single-volume history of origins and early years.

Freedom of Religion

P. B. Kurland, *Religion and the Law: Of Church and State and the Supreme Court* (1962).

U. S. Department of Health, Education and Welfare, *The State and the Non-Public School* (1958).

F. W. O'Brien, *Justice Reed and the First Amendment: The Religion Clauses* (1958).

A. W. Johnson and F. H. Yost, *Separation of Church and State in the United States*, rev. ed. (1948). Theory and development of American law.

J. M. O'Neill, *Religion and Education under the Constitution* (1949).

A. P. Stokes, *Church and State in the United States*, 3 vols. (1950). Encyclopedic source material.

D. E. Boles, *The Bible, Religion, and the Public Schools* (1961). The problem of religion in public education.

D. R. Manwaring, *Render Unto Caesar* (1962). A study of the flag-salute controversy.

Freedom of Speech

M. R. Konvitz, *Fundamental Liberties of a Free People* (1957). Discussion of religion, speech, press, and association.

A. Meiklejohn, *Free Speech and Its Relation to Self-Government* (1948). Attack on "clear and present danger doctrine" and defense of the absolute right of political speech.

J. C. Paul and M. Schwartz, *Federal Censorship: Obscenity in the Mail* (1960). Review and analysis of regulation of obscenity.

T. J. Murphy, *Censorship: Government and Obscenity* (1963).

* J. S. Mill, *Essay on Liberty* (1859; many editions). Famous defense of free speech.

Z. Chafee, *Free Speech in the United States*, rev. ed. (1941). Most comprehensive study of restrictions on speech during and after World War I; discussion of dangers inherent in sedition laws.

E. E. Smead, *Freedom of Speech by Radio and Television* (1959). Special problems of freedom in these areas.

Commission on the Freedom of the Press, *A Free and Responsible Press* (1947). Critical report on media of mass communication, emphasizes dangers of irresponsible economic control.

H. Brucker, *Freedom of Information* (1949). Discussion of problems; dissent from some criticism and recommendations of Commission on the Freedom of the Press.

W. E. Hocking, *Freedom of the Press* (1947). By leading American philosopher.

W. L. Chenery, *Freedom of the Press* (1955). Analysis by an editor.

J. M. Smith, *Freedom's Fetters* (1956). Study of Alien and Sedition Laws.

F. E. Rourke, *Secrecy and Publicity* (1961). The continuing problem of freedom of information in the free society.

O. J. Rogge, *The First and The Fifth* (1960). Analysis of the interrelationship between these two important guarantees.

The Battle against Subversive Conduct and Seditious Speech

Commission on Government Security. *Report* (1957). Study of the internal security program; popularly known as the "Wright Report."

H. M. Hyman, *To Try Men's Souls: Loyalty Tests in American History* (1959). Historical background.

J. H. Schaar, *Loyalty in America* (1957). Analysis of the concept of loyalty.

R. S. Brown, *Loyalty and Security; Employment Tests in the United States* (1958). Critical study of loyalty and security programs.

S. Hook, *Political Power and Personal Freedom: Critical Studies in Democracy, Communism, and Civil Rights* (1959).

S. H. Stouffer, *Communism, Conformity and Civil Liberties* (1955). Survey of American attitudes.

H. D. Lasswell, *National Security and Individual Freedom* (1950). Pressures created by cold war, with recommendations.

H. W. Chase, *Security and Liberty* (1955). Legislative and judicial handling of native communists, 1947–1955.

W. Gellhorn, *The States and Subversion* (1952). Symposium dealing with activities of six states.

M. Grodzins, *The Loyal and the Disloyal* (1956). Discussion of factors that make men loyal.

J. L. O'Brien, *National Security and Individual Freedom* (1955). Critical evaluation of our security programs.

T. I. Cook, *Democratic Rights versus Communist Activity* (1954). Defends view that it is consistent with democratic principles and practices to make communist political activity illegal.

Subcommittee on Constitutional Rights of Senate Judiciary Committee, *Hearings, Security and Constitutional Rights*, 84 Cong., 2 Sess., 1955. Testimony of officials who administer programs and of witnesses critical of the programs.

Senate Judiciary Committee, *The Communist Party of the United States*, 84 Cong., 2

Sess., Senate Doc. No. 117, 1956. "A Handbook on Operations of Communist Party."

J. E. Hoover, *Masters of Deceit: The Story of Communism in America and How to Fight It* (1958). By the Director of the FBI.

Association of the Bar of the City of New York, Special Committee on Federal Loyalty-Security Program, *The Federal Loyalty-Security Program* (1956). Critical report by this influential body.

Equality under the Law

C. Vann Woodward, *The Strange Career of Jim Crow* (1955). Account of the growth of segregation laws.

Southern School News. Periodic reports on desegregation in public schools.

Race Relations Law Reporter. Periodic presentation of court cases, legislation, orders, regulations.

A. P. Grimes, *Equality in America: Religion, Race and the Urban Majority* (1964). Essays illustrating the impact of Supreme Court decisions in modern America.

M. M. Tumin *et al.*, *Desegregation: Resistance and Readiness* (1958). Study of attitudes toward the Negro and desegregation.

R. L. Gates, *The Making of Massive Resistance: Virginia's Politics of Public School Desegregation, 1954–1956* (1963). One state's response to Supreme Court policy.

W. Record and J. C. Record (eds.), *Little Rock, U.S.A.* (1960). Materials relating to the school desegregation crisis of that city.

J. W. Peltason, *Fifty-eight Lonely Men: Southern Federal Judges and School Desegregation* (1962).

R. Harris, *The Quest for Equality* (1960). Historical and constitutional study of events leading to the Brown decision.

J. Greenberg, *Race Relations and American Law* (1959). Comprehensive coverage of legal aspects.

A. P. Blaustein and C. C. Ferguson, Jr., *Desegregation and the Law* (1957). Legal aspects of desegregation.

D. Shoemaker, *et al.*, *With All Deliberate Speed* (1957). Journalist's report on progress of school integration or lack of it to date.

V. Countryman, *Discrimination and the Law* (1965).

W. Gillette, *The Right to Vote* (1965). Politics of the passage of the Fifteenth Amendment.

B. Hays, *A Southern Moderate Speaks* (1959). Discussion of the race issue by former congressman from the Little Rock area.

L. Killian and C. Grigg, *Racial Crisis in America: Leadership in Conflict* (1964). The "sit-in" in perspective.

P. McCauley and E. D. Ball (eds.), *Southern Schools: Progress and Problems* (1959).

W. Mendelson, *Discrimination* (1962). Based on reports of the U.S. Commission on Civil Rights.

C. E. Vose, *Caucasians Only* (1959). Comprehensive discussion of Supreme Court's decisions on restrictive covenants.

C. Abrams, *Forbidden Neighbors: A Study of Prejudice in Housing* (1955).

U.S. President's Committee on Civil Rights, *To Secure These Rights* (1947).

* U.S. Commission on Civil Rights, *Annual Reports and Equal Protection of the Laws in Higher Education* (1960), *Voting* (1961), *Employment* (1961), *Education* (1961), *Housing* (1961), and *Justice* (1961). Findings and recommendations of Commission created by Civil Rights Act of 1957.

M. R. Konvitz, *The Constitution and Civil Rights* (1947). Study of civil rights in employment and accommodation in public places.

R. L. Hale, *Freedom through Law* (1952). Public control of private power.

M. R. Konvitz (ed.), *Law and Social Action* (1951). Essays on infringement of civil rights by private groups.

M. Berger, *Equality by Statute* (1952). Review of case law and analysis of work of the New York Commission against Discrimination, set in a broad social science framework.

J. Ten Broek, *et al.*, *Prejudice, War, and the Constitution* (1954). Origins, politics, and legality of Japanese-American evacuations in World War II.

M. Grodzins, *Americans Betrayed: Politics and the Japanese Evacuation* (1949). Treats what many considered a violation of civil liberties during World War II.

Rights to Life, Liberty, and Property

E. S. Corwin, *Liberty against Government* (1948). Essays on the growth and decline of substantive due process.

B. F. Wright, *The Contract Clause of the Constitution* (1938). Standard source.

D. Fellman, *The Defendant's Rights* (1958). Survey of cases and decisions on the rights of the accused from arrest to imprisonment.

A. Lewis, *Gideon's Trumpet* (1964). Exciting account of the landmark "right-to-counsel" decision from the perspective of the appellant.

W. M. Beaney, *Right to Counsel in American Courts* (1955). Survey of law and decisions.

D. Fellman, *The Constitutional Right of Association* (1963). A legal scholar looks at case law pertaining to the constitutional guaranty.

A. S. Trebach, *The Rationing of Justice* (1964). Concerns the problems of the accused, employing modern social science techniques.

Immigration and Citizenship

E. P. Hutchinson, *Immigrants and Their Children, 1850–1950* (1956). Demographic study of the foreign-born in our population.

O. Handlin, *The Uprooted* (1952). Moving history of immigration from the perspective of the immigrants.

———, *Race and Nationality in American Life* (1957).

W. Preston, Jr., *Aliens and Dissenters: Federal Suppression of Radicals, 1903–1933* (1963).

M. A. Jones, *American Immigration* (1960).

President's Commission on Immigration and Naturalization, *Whom Shall We Welcome?* (1952). Report of commission appointed by President Truman, critical of Immigration and Nationality Act of 1952.

M. R. Konvitz, *Civil Rights in Immigration* (1953). Critical study of legislation relating to admission, exclusion, deportation, and naturalization of immigrants in the United States.

Part Four: The People in Politics

Public Opinion

Two journals of special interest are: *International Journal of Opinion and Attitude Research* and *Public Opinion Quarterly*.

* V. O. Key, Jr., *Public Opinion and American Democracy* (1961). Most recent full-scale treatment of concepts and issues.

A. C. Dicey, *Law and Public Opinion in England* (1905).

G. Wallas, *Human Nature in Politics* (1919, first published in 1908). Marked a reaction from earlier over-rationalistic interpretations of politics and public opinion.

A. L. Lowell, *Public Opinion and Popular Government* (1913).

* W. Lippmann, *Public Opinion* (1922).

J. Dewey, *The Public and Its Problems* (1927).

A. O. Hero, *Opinion Leaders in American Communities* (1959). Effect of primary group communications on opinions.

S. Kelley, Jr., *Professional Public Relations and Political Power* (1956). Role of "Madison Avenue" in American politics.

R. E. Lane and D. O. Sears, *Public Opinion* (1964). Short but excellent examination of the dynamics of opinion formation.

R. Christenson and R. O. McWilliams, *Voice of the People* (1962). Survey of current issues and research in public opinion.

B. Berelson and M. Janowitz (eds.), *Reader in Public Opinion and Communication* (1953). Readings on all major phases of subject.

Public Opinion Polls

F. F. Stephan and P. J. McCarthy, *Sampling Opinions: An Analysis of Survey Procedure* (1958).

M. B. Parten, *Surveys, Polls, and Samples* (1950). Description of polling procedures.

Center for the Study of Democratic Institutions, *Opinion Polls* (1962). Comments on issues and significance of polls by Elmo Roper and George Gallup.

F. Mosteller, *et al.*, *The Pre-Election Polls of 1948* (1949). Essays by experts who investigated the reasons for the 1948 polling fiasco.

L. Rogers, *The Pollsters* (1949). Criticism of procedures, and attack upon contribution of public opinion polls.

H. Cantril, (ed.), *Public Opinion: Directory of Polls, 1935–1946* (1951). Comprehensive collection of poll data.

Media of Communication

D. Cater, *The Fourth Branch of Government* (1959). Critical evaluation of the relations of the press with the national government.

A. E. Rowse, *Slanted News: A Case Study*

of the Nixon and Stevenson Fund Stories (1957).

D. D. Nimmo, *Newsgathering in Washington: A Study in Political Communication* (1964). Interaction of government and the press.

A. O. Hero, *Mass Media and World Affairs* (1959). Study of mass media's influence on opinions toward foreign affairs.

P. F. Lazarsfeld, *Radio and the Printed Page* (1940). Role of radio described by outstanding authorities.

Z. Chafee, *Government and Mass Communications* (1947). Published under auspices of the Commission on Freedom of the Press.

F. L. Mott, *American Journalism* (1941). Standard history.

W. Lippmann, *Liberty and the News* (1920). Critical essay by one of America's famous journalists.

C. A. Siepmann, *Radio, Television and Society* (1950). Analysis of the problems of the role of radio and television in a free society.

Center for the Study of Democratic Institutions, *Television* (1962). Provocative discussion on status of and trends in television.

R. A. Inglis, *Freedom of the Movies* (1947). Under the auspices of the Commission on Freedom of the Press.

Interest Groups

H. W. Ehrmann, *Interest Groups on Four Continents* (1958). Discussions of interest groups in several countries, including the United States.

H. Zeigler, *Interest Groups in American Society* (1964). An interpretation of the role of organized interest groups in policy-making.

C. A. Beard, *The Economic Basis of Politics* (1922). The importance of economic interests in the political process.

Select Committee on Lobbying Activities of the House, *Hearings*, 81 Cong., 2 Sess., 1950. Important congressional investigation; materials on some major organizations.

D. C. Blaisdell, *Economic Power and Political Pressures* (1941). TNEC Monograph 26. Pioneering study.

L. W. Milbrath, *The Washington Lobbyists* (1963). The role of the lobbyist in the formation of public policy.

S. M. Lipset, M. A. Trow, and J. S. Coleman, *Union Democracy: The Inside Poli-* tics of the International Typographical Union (1956). Conditions of democratic and oligarchic control of voluntary organizations.

J. R. Gusfield, *Symbolic Crusade: Status Politics and the American Temperance Movement* (1963). An attempt to separate symbolic from instrumental politics.

P. H. Odegard, *Pressure Politics: The Study of the Anti-saloon League* (1928). Standard source.

J. Gaer, *The First Round: The Story of the C.I.O. Political Action Committte* (1944). Contains facsimile examples of CIO pamphlets.

F. Calkins, *The C.I.O. and the Democratic Party* (1952). Five case studies in 1950 elections by research assistant of CIO-PAC.

O. M. Kile, *The Farm Bureau through Three Decades* (1948). The official history.

P. O. Foss, *Politics and Grass* (1960). Interest group behavior relating to grazing land allocation.

S. Halperin, *The Political World of American Zionism* (1961). Interest group analysis in a broad social context.

R. Baker, *The American Legion and American Foreign Policy* (1954). Recent analysis.

J. Gray and V. H. Bernstein, *The Inside Story of the Legion* (1948). Critical of the American Legion.

R. S. Jones, *A History of the American Legion* (1946). The official history.

D. Wecter, *When Johnny Comes Marching Home* (1944). Study of return of soldiers after Revolutionary, Civil, and First World wars.

O. Garceau, *The Political Life of the American Medical Association* (1941). Pioneering study of the political activities of America's doctors.

M. L. Rutherford, *The Influence of the American Bar Association on Public Opinion and Legislation* (1937). Story of politically active profession.

B. R. Twiss, *Lawyers and the Constitution* (1942). "How laissez faire came to the Supreme Court."

L. C. Kesselman, *The Social Politics of FEPC* (1948). "A Study in Reform Pressure Movements."

L. E. Ebersole, *Church Lobbying in the Nation's Capital* (1951). The religious lobbies —the causes for which they work, and the methods they use.

D. D. McKean, *Pressures on the Legislature of New Jersey* (1938). By a political scientist and former member of New Jersey legislature.

E. P. Herring, *Group Representation before Congress* (1929). Relations between interest groups and formal institutions of government.

E. E. Schattschneider, *Politics, Pressures, and the Tariff* (1935). Case study based on mass of evidence from hearings on the Smoot-Hawley tariff bill.

E. Latham, *The Group Basis of Politics* (1952). Interplay of group pressures in basing-point legislation.

Robert Engler, *The Politics of Oil* (1961). Review and analysis of petroleum industry's political influence.

F W Riggs, *Pressures on Congress: A Study of the Repeal of Chinese Exclusion* (1950). Informing case study.

E. P. Herring, *Public Administration and the Public Interest* (1936). Interaction between interest groups and administrative machinery.

J. Frank, *If Men Were Angels* (1942). Social, economic, and psychological factors in the working of administrative agencies.

A. Maass, *Muddy Waters* (1951). Indictment of the Army Corps of Engineers as "The Lobby That Can't Be Licked."

Voting and Voting Behavior

H. F. Gosnell, *Democracy, the Threshold of Freedom* (1948). Contains discussion of several theories of citizenship, and of the theoretical premises of the right to vote.

K. H. Porter, *A History of Suffrage in the United States* (1918). Single-volume history.

R. E. Lane, *Political Life: How People Get Involved in Politics* (1958).

G. Lenski, *The Religious Factor* (1961). Thorough analysis based on survey in Detroit area.

S. M. Lipset, *Political Man* (1960). Important series of articles on political sociology.

W. Kornhauser, *The Politics of Mass Society* (1959). Analysis of difference between citizen participation and spectatorship.

E. Burdick and A. J. Brodbeck (eds.), *American Voting Behavior* (1959). Collection of essays.

S. M. Lipset, *et al.*, "The Psychology of Voting: An Analysis of Political Behavior," in G. Lindzey (ed.), *Handbook of Social Psychology*, II (1954). Survey of data.

A. Kornhauser, A. J. Mayer, and H. L. Sheppard, *When Labor Votes: A Study of Auto Workers* (1956). Detroit auto workers in the 1952 presidential election.

L. Fuchs, *The Political Behavior of American Jews* (1956).

A. Campbell, G. Gurin, and W. E. Miller, *The Voter Decides* (1954). Study of the 1952 election based on data gathered by sampling.

A. Campbell and H. C. Cooper, *Group Differences in Attitudes and Votes* (1956). Study of the 1954 election based on a nationwide survey.

* A. Campbell, P. Converse, W. Miller, and D. Stokes, *The American Voter* (1960). Analysis of 1956 election based on national sample data.

C. E. Merriam and H. F. Cosnell, *Non-voting* (1924). Pioneering study.

S. Lubell, *The Future of American Politics* (1951). Basic party and voting trends, interestingly presented.

L. Harris, *Is There a Republican Majority?* (1954). Study of 1952 election by associate in the Roper polling organization.

L. W. Milbrath, *Political Participation: How and Why Do People Get Involved in Politics?* (1965). A synthesis of research findings.

H. Eulau, *Class and Party in the Eisenhower Years* (1962). Interplay of class and voting behavior.

L. A. Froman, Jr., *People and Politics: An Analysis of the American Political System* (1962). Development of a theory of politics.

P. F. Lazarsfeld, B. R. Berelson, and H. Gaudet, *The People's Choice* (1948). Demonstrates the technique of panel interviewing on "How the Voter Makes Up His Mind in a Presidential Campaign."

B. R. Berelson, P. F. Lazarsfeld, and W. N. McPhee, *Voting* (1954). 1948 voting in a New York community, with useful summary of findings of other voting studies.

D. Bell (ed.), *The Radical Right* (1963). Eight famous social scientists view the ideas and activities of the current "far right."

* V. O. Key, Jr., *Southern Politics in State and Nation* (1949). The impact of the "Negro problem" on southern politics.

E. L. Tatum, *The Changed Political Thought of the Negro, 1915–1940* (1952). Causes and consequences of changing political allegiances of Negroes.

A. Boshoff and H. Zeigler, *Voting Patterns in a Local Election* (1964).

H. M. Bain and D. S. Hecock, *Ballot Position and Voter's Choice* (1957). Effect of candidate's position on the ballot on voting behavior.

Political Parties

* H. D. Lasswell, *Politics: Who Gets What, When, How* (1946; reissued in 1958). One of Lasswell's more popular treatments.

Eagleton Foundation, *Case Studies in Practical Politics.* Continuing series of studies of concrete political situations.

R. Michels, *Political Parties* (reprinted in 1949). Important sociological study of the oligarchical tendencies of European democratic political parties.

M. Ostrogorski, *Democracy and the Organization of Political Parties*, 2 vols. (1908). Early, classic interpretation of development of parties in the United States and England.

N. E. Cunningham, *The Jeffersonian Republicans: The Foundation of Party Organization, 1789–1801* (1957).

W. E. Binkley, *American Political Parties, Their Natural History*, 3rd ed. (1958). Stresses role of parties as coalitions of interest groups.

* F. J. Turner, *The Significance of Sections in American History* (1937). The importance of sectionalism in American politics was first projected by Turner at the beginning of the twentieth century.

A. N. Holcombe, *The Political Parties of Today* (1924), *The New Party Politics* (1933), *The Middle Classes in American Politics* (1940). Interpretation of American politics as moving from sectional to urban or "class" politics with the middle class holding the balance and preserving free government.

E. E. Schattschneider, *Party Government* (1942), *The Struggle for Party Government* (1948). Case for more centralized and disciplined parties by an outstanding scholar who has virtually developed a "school of thought" about American politics.

Committee on Political Parties of the American Political Science Association, *Toward a More Responsible Two Party System* (1950). By committee of 16 authorities under chairmanship of Professor Schattschneider; recommendations for strengthening the American party system.

E. P. Herring, *The Politics of Democracy* (1940). Interpretation and defense of present system; interpretations somewhat contrary to those of Schattschneider and the committee report mentioned above.

H. Agar, *The Price of Union* (1950). History stressing the thesis that loosely organized and undisciplined parties are essential to the preservation of the Union.

F. Greenstein, *The American Party System and the American People* (1963). A handy synthesis of recent research.

A. Ranney and W. Kendall, *The American Party System* (1956). Examination of American parties as instruments of democratic government; defense of existing party system.

A. Leiserson, *Parties and Politics, An Institutional and Behavioral Approach* (1958).

S. Neumann (ed.), *Modern Political Parties* (1956). Discussions of the party systems in several nations, including the United States.

S. Eldersveld, *Political Parties: A Behavioral Analysis* (1963).

J. M. Burns, *The Deadlock of Democracy: Four Party Politics in America* (1962). Old and new political alignments.

D. Acheson, *A Democrat Looks at His Party* (1955). By a former Secretary of State.

H. S. Merrill, *Bourbon Leader: Grover Cleveland and the Democratic Party* (1957).

R. V. Remini, *Martin Van Buren and the Making of the Democratic Party* (1959).

A. Larson, *A Republican Looks At His Party* (1956). Views of a member of the "liberal" wing of the Republican party.

H. P. Nash, Jr., *Third Parties in American Politics* (1958). Their role and history.

M. Stedman and S. Stedman, *Discontent at the Polls* (1950). Incisive account of legal, political, and other aspects of third parties.

C. P. Cotter and B. C. Hennessey, *Politics Without Power: The National Party Committees* (1964). Emphasis on the national chairman and the committee staffs.

K. A. Porter and D. B. Johnson, *National Party Platforms, 1840–1960* (1962).

Leadership

D. Marvick, *Political Decision-Makers* (1961). Diverse approaches to the study of political leadership.

A. A. Rogow, *James Forrestal: A Study of Personality, Politics and Policy* (1963). Personality study of the first Secretary of Defense.

* A. M. Schlesinger, Jr., *The Age of Roosevelt: The Crisis of the Old Order*, Vol. I (1958); *The Coming of the New Deal*, Vol. II (1959); *The Politics of Upheaval*,

Vol. III (1960). Studies by leading historian.

J. D. Barber (ed.), *Political Leadership in American Government* (1964). Excellent collection of materials on political leadership.

J. M. Burns, *Roosevelt: The Lion and the Fox* (1956). Problems and practices of FDR as a democratic leader.

A. Gottfried, *Boss Cermak of Chicago: A Study of Political Leadership* (1962).

H. Lasswell, *Psychopathology and Politics* (1930), and *Power and Personality* (1948). Through use of interviews, observations, and psychological techniques Lasswell has developed a typology of political leaders and related their public careers to their psychological characteristics.

H. H. Gerth and C. W. Mills (tr. and ed.), *From Max Weber: Essays in Sociology* (1946). Essays by famous German sociologist, pioneering student of leadership.

W. F. Whyte, Jr., *Street Corner Society* (1943). Close study of informal leadership.

S. Verba, *Small Groups and Political Behavior: A Study of Political Leadership* (1961). Experimental findings related to notions of the political process.

A. W. Gouldner (ed.), *Studies in Leadership* (1950). Essays on apathy and various kinds of leadership.

Elections

N. W. Polsby and A. B. Wildavsky, *Presidential Elections* (1964). Presents the context within which presidential elections are fought and the strategies employed.

C. A. M. Ewing, *Primary Elections in the South* (1953). Statistical study.

C. E. Merriam and L. Overacker, *Primary Elections* (1928). Standard source.

J. B. Johnson, *Registration for Voting in the United States*, rev. ed. (1946). Survey of methods used.

S. Kelley, *Political Campaigning* (1960). A study in strategy and technique.

R. M. Scammon, *America Votes*, 5 vols. (1956, 1958, 1960, 1962, and 1964). Most comprehensive collection of recent election statistics, to be kept up to date with additional volumes every two years.

L. Wilmerding, *The Electoral College* (1958). Critical analysis of its operation and of proposals for change.

Subcommittee of the Senate Committee on the Judiciary, *Hearings, Nomination and Election of President and Vice-President*, 84 Cong., 1 Sess. Testimony on several proposals to alter electoral college.

P. T. David, *et al.*, *Presidential Nominating Politics in 1952* (1954). Five-volume report undertaken by over 150 political scientists.

T. H. White, *The Making of the President, 1960* (1961). Pulitzer Prize account of the 1960 national campaign.

———, *The Making of the President, 1964* (1965). Similar treatment of 1964 campaign.

Sidney Kraus (ed.), *The Great Debates* (1962). Analysis of Kennedy-Nixon debates.

R. V. Peel and T. C. Donnelly, *The 1928 Campaign* (1931), *The 1932 Campaign* (1935). Accounts of two campaigns from nomination to election.

J. B. Shannon, *Money and Politics* (1959).

A. Heard, *The Costs of Democracy* (1960). Authoritative study of campaign finance.

President's Commission on Campaign Costs, *Financing Presidential Campaigns* (1962). Recommendations on improved financing of national election campaigns.

S. Harris, *The Economics of the Political Parties* (1962). Major parties' fiscal positions.

M. Moos, *Politics, Presidents, and Coattails* (1953). Study of congressional elections, emphasizing interaction of presidential and congressional elections.

P. T. David, R. M. Goldman, and R. C. Bain, *The Politics of National Party Conventions* (1960). Systematic analysis of the nominating process.

Part Five: Policy-Makers for the People

The Legislative Process

J. C. Wahlke and H. Eulau (eds.), *Legislative Behavior: A Reader in Theory and Research* (1959). Studies of several aspects of legislative behavior.

T. V. Smith, *The Legislative Way of Life* (1940). Defense of the legislature by an ex-congressman, ex-state legislator, philosopher, and political scientist.

H. F. Gosnell, *Democracy, the Threshold of Freedom* (1948). Contains discussion of the functions of representatives and representative assemblies.

A. de Grazia, *Public and Republic* (1951). History of who represents what and how.

Congress

* W. Wilson, *Congressional Government* (1885). Classic interpretation.

F. M. Riddick, *The United States Congress* (1949). Authoritative discussion of organizational and procedural aspects.

D. B. Truman, *The Congressional Party: A Case Study* (1959). The party system in Congress, analyzed through studies of roll calls.

L. A. Froman, Jr., *Congressmen and Their Constituencies* (1963). Focuses upon congressional elections and constituency influences upon congressional decision-making.

E. S. Griffith, *Congress: Its Contemporary Role* (1951). Favorable assessment of operation of Congress, by Director of its Legislative Reference Service.

R. L. Peabody and N. W. Polsby (eds.), *New Perspectives on the House of Representatives* (1963). Essays on the House as a political institution.

J. Burnham, *Congress and the American Tradition* (1959). Congress viewed as losing its rightful authority.

G. B. Galloway, *The Legislative Process in Congress* (1953). Organization, procedures, and problems by political scientist who played leading role in reorganization of Congress in 1946.

——, *History of the House of Representatives* (1962).

Joint Committee on Organization of the Congress, *Organization of Congress*, Senate Report 1011, 79 Cong., 2 Sess., 1946. Favorable report on Reorganization Act.

J. S. Clark (ed.), *Congressional Reform: Problems and Prospects* (1965). A Senator shows us what's wrong with the Senate.

M. E. Ridgeway, *The Missouri Basin's Pick-Sloan Plan* (1955). "A Case Study in Congressional Policy Determination."

R. Bolling, *House Out of Order* (1965). Personal account of the workings of the House by a liberal congressional reformer.

S. K. Bailey, *Congress Makes a Law* (1950). Detailed account of the enactment of the Employment Act of 1946.

T. J. Lowi, *Legislative Politics, U.S.A.* (1962). Selected readings on Congress and the forces that shape it.

D. M. Berman, *A Bill Becomes a Law* (1962). Legislative case study of the Civil Rights Act of 1960.

* B. M. Gross, *The Legislative Struggle* (1953). Probing analysis of Congress as the battleground of interest struggles.

A. Hacker, *Congressional Districting: The Issue of Equal Representation* (1963).

R. A. Dahl, *Congress and Foreign Policy* (1950). Evaluation of Congress' role in the making of foreign policy; suggestions for improving its functioning.

J. A. Robinson, *Congress and Foreign Policy-Making* (1962). Probing analysis of Congress in the foreign policy process.

J. Turner, *Party and Constituency* (1952). Measurement of relative impact of parties and constituencies upon congressional voting behavior.

W. S. White, *Citadel: The Story of the United States Senate* (1956). Readable account of the Senate with emphasis on the "unwritten rules."

W. S. White, *The Story of the U. S. House of Representatives* (1965). The journalist's attention turns to the House.

D. R. Matthews, *U.S. Senators and Their World* (1960). Study of the Senate as an institution and the behavior of its members.

J. W. Baker (ed.), *Member of the House: Letters of a Congressman* (1962). A look at Congress and congressmen through informal letters of the late Clem Miller.

F. L. Burdette, *Filibustering in the Senate* (1940). Standard source.

R. J. Dangerfield, *In Defense of the Senate: A Study in Treaty-Making* (1933). Evidence that Senate's obstruction is less serious than usually thought.

C. L. Clapp, *The Congressman: His Work as He Sees It* (1963). The House as observed by a number of its members.

J. P. Harris, *The Advice and Consent of the Senate* (1953). "A Study of the Confirmation of Appointments by the United States Senate."

S. Horn, *The Cabinet and Congress* (1960). Historical background, discussion of proposals to improve cabinet-congressional relations.

K. Kofmehl, *Professional Staffs of Congress* (1962).

Committees

D. N. Farnsworth, *The Senate Committee on Foreign Relations* (1961).

H. N. Carroll, *The House of Representatives and Foreign Affairs* (1958).

D. H. Riddle, *The Truman Committee: A Study in Congressional Responsibility* (1964). An important wartime investigating committee is examined.

Congressional investigations are covered in:

R. K. Carr, *The House Un-American Activities Committee* (1952). Balanced discussion.

T. Taylor, *Grand Inquest* (1955). Critical study of congressional investigations.

A. Barth, *Government by Investigation* (1955).

W. F. Buckley, Jr., *et al.*, *The Committee and Its Critics* (1962). Defense of the House Committee on Un-American Activities.

C. Beck, *Contempt of Congress* (1959). Discussion of a serious problem flowing from congressional investigations.

The President

W. Binkley, *The Man in the White House* (1959). Growth of the Presidency and the many facets of the office.

C. Rossiter, *The American Presidency* (1956). Analysis of the growth and uses of the Presidency.

G. A. Schubert, Jr., *The Presidency in the Courts* (1957). Study of the Supreme Court's interpretation of the office and powers.

E. S. Corwin, *The President: Office and Powers*, rev. ed. (1957). Comprehensive discussion of the historical and constitutional development.

——— and L. W. Koenig, *The Presidency Today* (1956).

S. Hyman, *The American President* (1954). Interpretative study.

R. Neustadt, *Presidential Power* (1960). Influential work on the politics of the Presidency.

H. J. Laski, *The American Presidency* (1940). Dynamics of the Presidency by famous British political scientist.

H. L. Laurin, *Presidential Transitions* (1960). Experience and problems in the transition from election to inauguration.

H. Finer, *The Presidency: Crisis and Regeneration* (1960). Analysis with provocative recommendations.

L. W. Koenig, *The Chief Executive* (1964). Up-to-date general analysis of the President performing many roles.

M. W. Childs, *Eisenhower—Captive Hero: A Critical Study of the General and the President* (1958). Readable biographical account of the man and his administration.

R. J. Donovan, *The Inside Story* (1956). Taken from notes on the Eisenhower Cabinet meetings; gives picture of this and other aspects of the Eisenhower administration.

E. J. Hughes, *The Ordeal of Power: A Political Memoir of the Eisenhower Years* (1963). A view from the inside.

L. D. White, *The Federalists* (1948), *The Jeffersonians* (1951), *The Jacksonians* (1955), and *The Republican Era, 1869–1901* (1958). Cover the early years and emphasize the administrative organization of the executive.

W. Wilson, *Constitutional Government in the United States* (reprinted 1921). Written before he became President; indicates Wilson's concept of the role and responsibility of the office.

W. H. Taft, *Our Chief Magistrate and His Powers* (1916). Presents a much more limited concept of the Presidency.

T. C. Sorenson, *Kennedy* (1965). The late President as seen by an intimate advisor.

A. M. Schlesinger, Jr., *A Thousand Days* (1965). The Kennedy administration treated in historical depth by the "resident intellectual" in the White House.

G. McConnell, *Steel and the Presidency* (1963). Story of the exciting confrontation between President Kennedy and "Big Steel."

C. P. Cotter and J. M. Smith, *Powers of the President During National Crises* (1961). Recent study.

E. R. May (ed.), *The Ultimate Decision: The President as Commander in Chief* (1961). Analysis of presidential behavior during national emergencies.

I. G. Williams, *The Rise of the Vice-Presidency* (1956). History and role.

E. W. Wough, *Second Consul: The Vice-Presidency—Our Greatest Political Problem* (1956). History and analysis of the office.

L. C. Hatch, *A History of the Vice-Presidency of the United States* (1934). Standard source.

R. C. Silva, *Presidential Succession* (1951). Study of "history, interpretation, statutory development, and practical application of the provisions . . . for presidential succession."

E. E. Cornwell, Jr., *Presidential Leadership of Public Opinion* (1962). Presidential mobilization of public and congressional support.

President as Administrator

R. F. Fenno, Jr., *The President's Cabinet* (1959). Analysis of cabinets from Wilson to Eisenhower.

L. W. Koenig, *The Invisible Presidency* (1960). A study of the President's personal advisers.

The President's Committee on Administrative Management, *Reports . . . with Studies of Administrative Management in the Federal Government* (1937). Influential studies; primary source for understanding the problems of "high-level" governmental administration.

The Commission on the Organization of the Executive Branch of the Government, *General Management of the Executive Branch*; and *Concluding Report* (1949 and 1955). Attempt to strengthen Presidency as central agency of administration, by famous Hoover Commission.

C. Silverman, *The President's Economic Advisers* (1959). A case study.

E. R. Canterbery, *The President's Council of Economic Advisers* (1962). "Study of Its Functions and Its Influence on the Chief Executive's Decisions."

Public Administration

W. Wilson, "The Study of Administration," *Political Science Quarterly*, June 1887. Classic essay marking the beginning of the modern study of administration.

F. J. Goodnow, *Politics and Administration* (1900). Another pioneering volume; attempt to isolate administration from politics as separate branch of study.

These works of the early pioneers contrast with those of modern writers mentioned below. The early students tended to divide policy and administration into separable categories.

* C. S. Hyneman, *Bureaucracy in a Democracy* (1950). Study of the control and role of the bureaucracy with special attention to the question of legislative and executive responsibilities.

J. D. Millett, *Government and Public Administration: The Quest for Responsible Performance* (1959). The control of bureaucracy.

C. N. Parkinson, *Parkinson's Law* (1957). The "laws" of bureaucratic expansion.

J. G. March and H. A. Simon, *Organizations* (1958). Study of the theory of organizations.

P. Selznick, *Leadership in Administration: A Sociological Interpretation* (1957). Study of leadership in administrative organizations.

F. M. Marx, *The Administrative State* (1957). Comparative study of bureaucracy.

E. S. Redford, *Public Administration and Policy Formation* (1956). "Studies in Oil, Gas, Banking, River Development, and Corporate Investigation."

* P. H. Appleby, *Policy and Administration* (1949). Interpretations of the dynamic aspect of administration; the interrelations between policy and administration.

H. A. Simon, *Administrative Behavior* (1950). "A Study of Decision-Making Processes in Administrative Organization."

V. Thompson, *Modern Organizations* (1961). Perceptive analysis suggestive of political applications.

P. M. Blau, *The Dynamics of Bureaucracy* (1955). Interpersonal relationships of civil servants.

D. Waldo, *The Administrative State* (1948). The theory of American public administration; survey of the various "schools" of thought.

P. Woll, *American Bureaucracy* (1963). A study of administrative responsibility in the federal government.

R. K. Merton, *et al.*, *Reader in Bureaucracy* (1951). Collection of articles by authorities in sociology and political science.

Federal Administrative Structure

O. Kraines, *Congress and the Challenge of Big Government* (1958). History of the first congressional investigation into administrative structure and organization.

General Services Administration, *United States Government Organization Manual*, published annually. Contains descriptions of legislative, judicial, and executive branches—their organization and functions, organization charts of the major agencies, select lists of government publications, and other information.

S. C. Wallace, *Federal Departmentalization* (1941). Critical analysis of the theories of federal departmentalization.

W. S. Sayre (ed.), *The Federal Government Service: Its Character, Prestige, and Problems* (1955). An American Assembly Symposium.

In addition to the Reports and Studies of the Committee on Administrative Management, other reorganization literature includes:

L. Merriam and L. K. Schmeckebier, *Reorganization of the National Government* (1939). Critical discussion of the Reports of the President's Committee on Administrative Management.

Commission on Organization of the Executive Branch of the Government (the Hoover Commission), *Reports and Task Force Reports* (1949 and 1954). Especially those on personnel and civil service.

H. Emmerich, *Essays on Federal Reorganization* (1950). Discussion of reorganization, stressing it as a continuous process.

Regulatory Administration

B. Schwartz, *The Professor and the Commissions* (1959). Story of congressional investigation of regulatory commissions and trials and tribulations of a former committee counsel.

E. Latham, *The Politics of Railroad Coordination, 1933–1936* (1959). Politics of railroad regulation during the first years of the New Deal.

H. J. Friendy, *The Federal Administrative Agencies: The Need for Better Definition of Standards* (1962). Advocates improvement in commission personnel and standards.

J. M. Landis, *The Administrative Process* (1938). Perceptive analysis.

R. E. Cushman, *The Independent Regulatory Commissions* (1941). General discussion of the independent regulatory commissions.

M. H. Bernstein, *Regulating Business by Independent Commissions* (1955). Critical study of politics of regulation.

Public Personnel Management

P. Van Riper, *History of the United States Civil Service* (1959). History of public employment in the United States; emphasis on the period since the beginning of civil service reform.

W. L. Warner, *et al.*, *The Federal Executive* (1963). Social and personal characteristics of American civil and military leaders.

F. P. Kilpatrick, *et al.*, *The Image of the Federal Service* and *Source Book of a Study of Occupational Values and the Image of the Federal Service* (1964). Companion volumes.

S. B. Sweeney (ed.), *Education for Administrative Careers in Government Service* (1958). Problems of training public administrators.

P. T. David and R. Pollock, *Executives in Government: Central Issues of Federal Personnel Administration* (1957). Problems of recruiting and keeping high-level personnel.

M. H. Bernstein, *The Job of the Federal Executive* (1958). Description of the work of top career and political executives; problems of keeping able men in government.

New York City Bar Assn., *Conflict of Interest and Federal Service* (1960). Survey and recommendations.

O. G. Stahl, *Public Personnel Administration*, 4th ed. (1956). Standard text.

W. S. Carpenter, *The Unfinished Business of Civil Service Reform* (1952). Discussion of failure "to reconcile the merit system with a method of positive administrative control by the responsible executive."

The Judges

See also the titles listed under "The Living Constitution," p. 883.

* B. N. Cardozo, *The Nature of the Judicial Process* (1921). One of the American classics in legal theory.

J. Frank, *Law and the Modern Mind* (1930). Discussion of the various factors, especially psychological, that affect men, including judges.

F. Frankfurter, *Law and Politics* (1939). Articles, book reviews, occasional papers written before the author became a Justice.

H. Jacob, *Justice in America* (1965).

V. G. Rosenbaum, *Law as a Political Instrument* (1955). The legal system as part of the political process.

G. A. Schubert (ed.), *Judicial Behavior: A Reader in Theory and Research* (1964).

J. W. Peltason, *Federal Courts in the Political Process* (1955).

W. F. Murphy, *Elements of Judicial Strategy* (1964). Judicial behavior analyzed from perspective of stratagems to maximize policy preferences.

G. A. Schubert (ed.), *Judicial Decision-Making* (1963).

T. L. Becker, *Political Behavioralism and Modern Jurisprudence* (1964).

The Supreme Court

J. P. Frank, *Marble Palace: The Supreme Court in American Life* (1958). Organization and work of the Court.

W. E. Murphy and C. H. Pritchett (eds.), *Courts, Judges, and Politics* (1961). An introduction to the organization and function of the American judiciary.

A. F. Westin (ed.), *An Autobiography of the Supreme Court: Off-the-Bench Commentary by the Justices* (1963). The judicial process as seen by the justices themselves.

H. J. Abraham, *The Judicial Process* (1962). Comparative study of U.S., English, and French systems.

R. McCloskey, *The American Supreme Court 1789–1960* (1960). Analytical history.

R. S. Hirshfield, *The Constitution and the Court* (1962). Briefs from decisions and comments.

A. T. Mason, *The Supreme Court from Taft to Warren* (1958). Interpretive history.

C. B. Swisher, *The Supreme Court in Its Modern Role* (1958).

C. H. Pritchett and A. F. Westin (eds.), *The Third Branch of Government* (1963). Eight cases which place Supreme Court decisions in their contexts.

G. G. Haines, *The Role of the Supreme Court in American Government and Politics, 1789–1835* (1944). Detailed history of the formative years.

P. B. Kurland (ed.), *The Supreme Court Review* (1959 on). Annual collection of commentary articles on Supreme Court activity.

A. M. Bickel, *The Least Dangerous Branch: The Supreme Court at the Bar of Politics* (1962). Discussion of the "proper" role of the Court in the American system.

J. R. Schmidhauser, *The Supreme Court: Its Politics, Personalities and Procedures* (1960). Internal politics of the Court.

D. Danelski, *The Appointment of a Supreme Court Justice* (1965). The story behind the appointment of Pierce Butler.

* C. P. Curtis, *Lions under the Throne* (1947). Interpretation of role of courts in the American system.

P. A. Freund, *On Understanding the Supreme Court* (1950). Analytical lectures with comments on the Supreme Court and Supreme Court commentators.

M. Shapiro, *Law and Politics in the Supreme Court* (1964).

J. B. Grossman, *Lawyers and Judges, The Politics of Judicial Selection* (1965).

G. A. Schubert, *The Judicial Mind* (1965). Attitudes of Supreme Court Justices, 1946–1963.

———, *Quantitative Analysis of Judicial Behavior* (1959). Diverse approaches to judicial behavior.

C. H. Pritchett, *The Roosevelt Court* (1948). Survey of the Court from 1937 to 1947 with statistical charts on each Justice's "batting average" on particular issues.

———, *Civil Liberties and the Vinson Court* (1954). Continuation of earlier volume during period 1946–1953.

———, *The Political Offender and the Warren Court* (1959). Analysis of Warren Court reaction to anti-communist legislation.

Senate Committee on Judiciary, *Hearings, Reorganization of the Federal Judiciary,* 79 Cong., 2 Sess. (1937). Verbatim testimony of the many people who appeared for and against President Roosevelt's Court Plan.

Senate Committee on the Judiciary, *Hearings* of Subcommittee to Investigate the Administration of the Internal Security Act and Other Internal Security Laws, 85 Cong., 1 and 2 Sess. (1957 and 1958). Hearings on the Jenner Bill, which would have curbed the power of the Supreme Court in security cases; rich source of data on public reactions to the Court's decisions.

C. H. Pritchett, *Congress versus the Supreme Court* (1961).

W. F. Murphy, *Congress and the Court* (1962). Along with the Pritchett volume useful for comprehensive coverage of the most recent "Supreme Court controversy."

Judicial Review

E. V. Rostow, *The Sovereign Prerogative: The Supreme Court and the Quest for Law* (1962). A liberal's evaluation of contemporary Supreme Court policy.

A. F. Westin, *The Anatomy of a Constitutional Law Case* (1958). Case study of *Youngstown Sheet and Tube Co. v. Sawyer,* "The Steel Seizure Decision."

C. Warren, *The Supreme Court in United States History,* rev. ed., 2 vols. (1932). Standard history, sympathetic to the Court's use of judicial review.

C. L. Black, *The People and the Court* (1960). An interpretation of modern judicial review.

C. G. Haines, *The American Doctrine of Judicial Supremacy,* 2nd ed. (1932). Balanced investigation of the role of the Supreme Court and its use of judicial review.

C. S. Hyneman, *The Supreme Court on Trial* (1963). Ramifications of the segregation rulings for the political system.

E. S. Corwin, *The Doctrine of Judicial Review* (1914). Essays including famous article on *Marbury v. Madison*.

———, *Court over Constitution*, 2nd ed. (1942). In terms of its subtitle, "A Study of Judicial Review as an Instrument of Government."

R. H. Jackson, *The Struggle for Judicial Supremacy* (1941). Critical discussion of Supreme Court, especially its activities during the New Deal period.

H. Wechsler, *Principles, Politics and Fundamental Law* (1961). A controversial interpretation of judicial review.

F. V. Cahill, Jr., *Judicial Legislation* (1952). Analytical survey of modern American jurisprudence, stressing the problem of right of the judiciary to review acts of other levels of government.

Judicial Biography

E. C. Gerhart, *America's Advocate: Robert H. Jackson* (1958).

M. D. Howe, *Justice Oliver Wendell Holmes: The Shaping Years, 1841–1870* (1957).

A. T. Mason, *Harlan Fiske Stone* (1956).

———, *William Howard Taft, Chief Justice* (1965).

S. F. Konefsky, *The Legacy of Holmes and Brandeis* (1957). Study of the constitutional philosophy of two outstanding justices.

V. Countryman, *Douglas and the Supreme Court: A Selection of His Opinions* (1959). Contains a biographical sketch of Douglas.

A. J. Beveridge, *The Life of John Marshall*, 4 vols. (1916–1919). History; has become the prototype of judicial biography.

C. P. Smith, *James Wilson, Founding Father* (1956).

D. G. Morgan, *Justice William Johnson: The First Dissenter* (1954).

C. B. Swisher, *Roger B. Taney* (1935).

C. Fairman, *Mr. Justice Miller and the Supreme Court* (1939). Contains account of the Court's work and Reconstruction politics during the critical years, 1860–1890.

C. B. Swisher, *Stephen J. Field, Craftsman of the Law* (1930). Biography of a Justice who had much to do with the development of substantive due process.

W. L. King, *Melville Weston Fuller, Chief Justice of the United States* (1950). Study of a moderately able Justice and outstanding Chief Justice; informative on the internal working of the Court.

Max Lerner, (ed.), *The Mind and Faith of Justice Holmes* (1943). Collection of Justice Holmes' speeches, essays, letters, and judicial opinions, with introduction and notes by the editor.

A. T. Mason, *Brandeis: A Free Man's Life* (1946).

S. Hendel, *Charles Evans Hughes and the Supreme Court* (1951).

M. J. Pusey, *Charles Evans Hughes*, 2 vols. (1951). Biography.

H. F. Pringle, *The Life and Times of William Howard Taft*, 2 vols. (1939). Biography of former President and Chief Justice.

G. S. Hellman, *Benjamin N. Cardozo* (1940).

S. J. Konefsky, *The Constitutional World of Mr. Justice Frankfurter* (1949). Collection of opinions with introductory notes by editor.

C. Williams, *Hugo L. Black* (1950).

J. P. Frank, *Mr. Justice Black* (1949). By leading legal thinker.

W. Mendelson, *Justices Black and Frankfurter* (1961). Conception of the Court's role in terms of the careers of these two jurists.

Part Six: Big Government in Action

Journals and Annuals

World Politics, published quarterly by the Institute of International Affairs, approaches the subject more in the framework of social science and less in terms of history and current policy than do some of the other journals.

Foreign Affairs, published quarterly by the Council of Foreign Affairs, contains articles by scholars and practicing diplomats, and emphasizes the substantive aspect of current policy and diplomatic history.

World Organization, published quarterly by the World Peace Foundation; survey of the activities of the several international organizations; articles by various authorities on world politics.

Orbis: A Quarterly Journal of World Affairs,
published by the Foreign Policy Research
Institute of the University of Pennsylvania.

The American Journal of International Law,
published quarterly by The American Society of International Law; the professional
journal for those interested in legal aspects of international affairs.

Foreign Policy Reports, published twice a
month by the Foreign Policy Association;
extended treatment of particular topics of
current significance.

Foreign Policy Bulletins, published weekly
by the Foreign Policy Association; shorter
and more popularly written than the *Reports* mentioned above.

The United Nations Bulletin, published every
two weeks by the United Nations Department of Public Information.

The Department of State Bulletin, issued
weekly; articles explaining United States
policy, speeches by officials, and documents
such as treaties and executive agreements.

Foreign Policy Briefs, biweekly news sheet
issued by State Department giving reports
on current affairs.

Foreign Service Journal, unofficial "house
organ" containing articles and reports of
foreign service published by The American
Foreign Service Institute.

*Current Developments in U.S. Foreign Pol-
icy,* published monthly by The Brookings
Institution and supplemented by a yearly
survey entitled *Major Problems of U.S.
Foreign Policy.*

The United States in World Affairs, annual
survey edited by R. P. Stebbins and the
Research Staff of the Council on Foreign
Relations.

Documents on American Foreign Relations,
annual collection published by World
Peace Foundation.

Yearbook of the United Nations, annual survey published by the United Nations.

Annual Review of United Nations Affairs,
C. Eagleton and R. V. Swift, editors.

International Politics

Here are just a few of the many general
studies of international politics that provide
the framework for understanding American
foreign policy:

* *The Worldmark Encyclopedia of Nations*
(1960). A general guide to important features of all nations, their international relationships, and the U.N. system.

J. H. Herz, *International Politics in the*

Atomic Age (1959). Problem of applicability of traditional concepts to present
conditions.

C. P. Schleicher, *International Relations:
Cooperation and Conflict* (1962). A general view.

N. J. Padelford and G. A. Lincoln, *The Dynamics of International Politics* (1962).
Overview and analysis.

S. Hoffmann, *Contemporary Theories in International Relations* (1960).

M. A. Kaplan, *System and Process in International Politics* (1957). Systematic theoretical analysis of international politics.

H. J. Mackinder, *Democratic Ideals and
Reality* (1919; republished, 1942). Seminal
study of what is too narrowly called "geo-
politics."

R. C. Snyder, et al. (eds.), *Foreign Policy
Decision-Making: An Approach to the
Study of International Politics* (1962).

American Foreign Policy

D. B. Gobel, *A Documentary Chronicle of
American Foreign Policy: 1776–1960*
(1961).

* H. S. Kissinger, *Nuclear Weapons and Foreign Policy* (1957). Influential discussion
of the strategic impact of nuclear technology and defense of policy of "limited
nuclear war."

H. K. Jacobson (ed.), *America's Foreign
Policy* (1960). Analysis of policy and prospects by leading scholars and participants.

B. C. Cohen, *Foreign Policy in American
Government* (1963). A reader focusing
upon various dimensions of foreign policy
making.

K. Knorr (ed.), *NATO and American Security* (1959). Readings.

Rockefeller Brothers Fund, *Foreign Economic
Policy in the Twentieth Century* (1958).
Discussion of economic aspects of Ameri-
can policy.

D. G. Acheson, *Power and Diplomacy*
(1958). Criticism of recent American policy.

G. F. Kennan, *American Diplomacy: 1900–
1950* (1951). By former Director of State
Department's Policy Planning Staff; important as background of American policy
of containment; has famous article, "The
Sources of Soviet Conduct."

———, *The Realities of American Foreign
Policy* (1954).

———, *Russia, the Atom and the West*
(1958). Kennan's argument for disengage-
ment in Central Europe.

S. F. Bemis, A *Diplomatic History of the United States* (1950), *American Secretaries of State and Their Diplomacy* (1957), and A *Short History of American Foreign Policy and Diplomacy* (1959).

J. W. Pratt, A *History of United States Foreign Policy*, 2nd ed. (1965).

W. A. Reitzel, M. A. Kaplan, and C. G. Coblentz, *United States Foreign Policy, 1945–1955* (1956). Brookings study in a historical and topical analysis of American policy.

T. A. Bailey, A *Diplomatic History of the American People*, 4th ed. (1950). Lively account emphasizing the role of public opinion and interest groups.

E. Lefever, *Ethics and United States Foreign Policy* (1957).

D. Perkins, *The American Approach to Foreign Policy* (1962). Topical historical analysis of American foreign policy.

N. J. Spykman, *America's Strategy in World Politics* (1942). Geopolitical analysis of American policy.

H. J. Morgenthau, *In Defense of the National Interest* (1951). Critical evaluation of American foreign policy since end of World War II.

F. Tannenbaum, *The American Tradition in Foreign Policy* (1955). Opposes "realpolitik" basis of interpretation.

L. B. Pearson, *Democracy in World Politics* (1955). By Nobel prizewinner, leader of the Canadian Liberal party.

L. J. Halle, *Civilization and Foreign Policy* (1955). By a former State Department official.

E. Stillman and W. Pfaff, *The New Politics: America and the End of the Postwar World* (1961). Survey of recent developments in foreign affairs.

How Foreign Policy Is Made

R. E. Elder, *The Policy Machine* (1960). Description of policy-making process in the State Department and related agencies.

C. O. Lerch, *Foreign Policy of the American People* (1961). Trends in formulation and execution of foreign policy.

P. W. Buck and M. Travis, Jr. (eds.), *Control of Foreign Relations in Modern Nations* (1957). Study of the machinery and methods of making and executing policy in several nations, including the U.S.

H. N. Carroll, *The House of Representatives and Foreign Affairs* (1958).

C. V. Crabb, Jr., *Bipartisan Foreign Policy: Myth or Reality* (1957). The virtues and hazards of bipartisanship.

H. B. Westerfield, *Foreign Policy and Party Politics* (1955). Role of the parties and bipartisanship in Congress.

R. A. Bauer, I. Pool, and L. A. Dexter, *American Business and Public Policy: The Politics of Foreign Trade* (1963). The political process is viewed from the perspective of foreign trade policy.

H. H. Ransom, *Central Intelligence and National Security* (1958). Study of the organization and procedures of American intelligence agencies.

A. Tully, *CIA* (1962). Popular account of the intelligence agency and the formation of policy.

* R. Hilsman, *Strategic Intelligence and National Decisions* (1956). Discussion of the place of strategic intelligence in decision-making; more critical than above volume.

A. Vagts, *Defense and Diplomacy: The Soldier and the Conduct of Foreign Relations* (1956). Role of the military in American foreign policy from a historical perspective.

H. M. Wriston, *Diplomacy in a Democracy* (1956). Discussion of the problems of foreign policy in a democracy.

S. Huddleston, *Popular Diplomacy and War* (1954). Critical comments about the impact of mass opinion on diplomacy.

* G. A. Almond, *The American People and Foreign Policy* (1950). Analysis of the effect of public, interest groups, and opinion leaders in shaping foreign policy.

B. C. Cohen, *The Influence of Non-Governmental Groups on Foreign Policy-Making* (1959). Survey of interest group patterns in the foreign-policy process.

J. N. Rosenau, *Public Opinion and Foreign Policy* (1961). Treatment of public's role in decision-making.

A. W. Macmahon, *Administration in Foreign Affairs* (1953).

J. J. McCloy, *The Challenge to American Foreign Policy* (1953). Brief discussion of problems of making and executing foreign policy, special attention to problem of civil-military relations, by former U.S. High Commissioner for Germany.

D. S. Cheever and H. F. Haviland, Jr., *American Foreign Policy and the Separation of Powers* (1952). Survey of constitutional arrangements, case studies, and recommendations for improving machinery of government.

W. Y. Elliott, *et al.*, *The Political Economy of American Foreign Policy* (1955). Policy recommendations.

H. B. Price, *The Marshall Plan and Its Meaning* (1955). Evaluation and history.

V. L. Galbraith, *World Trade in Transition* (1965).

G. H. Stuart, *The Department of State* (1949). Comprehensive history.

D. K. Price (ed.), *The Secretary of State* (1961). Examination of the office.

Report of the Secretary of State's Public Committee on Personnel, *Toward a Stronger Foreign Service* (1954). The important Wriston Report, which resulted in major organizational changes in foreign service.

W. Barnes and J. H. Morgan, *The Foreign Service of the United States* (1961). Origins, development, and functions of the diplomatic corps.

H. Cleveland, G. Mangone, J. C. Adams, *The Overseas Americans* (1960). Analysis and recommendations relating to Americans on overseas assignments.

Commission on Organization of the Executive Branch of the Government, *Report on Overseas Economic Operations and Task Force Report* (1955).

V. M. Barnett, Jr. (ed.), *The Representation of the U.S. Abroad* (1956). Study papers for a meeting of the American Assembly.

Commission on the Organization of the Government, *Task Force Report on the Organization of the Government for the Conduct of Foreign Affairs* (1949). Prepared under direction of H. H. Bundy and J. G. Rogers; generally considered one of the better Task Force Reports.

W. P. Dizard, *The Strategy of Truth* (1961). Description of U.S. Information Service.

The U.N. and World Organization

S. S. Goodspeed, *The Nature and Function of International Organization* (1959).

L. M. Goodrich, *The United Nations* (1959). Introduction to its origins, structure, and functions.

W. A. Scott and S. B. Withey, *The United States and the United Nations: The Public View, 1945–1955* (1958). American attitudes toward the organization as revealed in opinion polls.

L. M. Goodrich, *Korea: A Study of United States Policy in the United Nations* (1956).

R. E. Riggs, *Politics in the United Nations: A Study of United States Influence in the General Assembly* (1958). Study of the extent of American influence and the techniques used.

G. Clark and L. B. Sohn, *World Peace Through World Law* (1958). Outlines program for strengthening the U.N.

I. L. Claude, Jr., *Swords into Ploughshares* (1956). Analysis of the problems of international organizations.

F. S. C. Northrup, *The Taming of the Nations* (1953). "A Study of the Cultural Basis of International Policy."

C. M. Eichelberger, *UN: The First Ten Years* (1955). By one who helped prepare first American draft and believes U.N. to be a success.

C. Manly, *The UN Record* (1955). By severe critic who believes U.N. to be a failure and an instrument of subversion.

L. M. Goodrich and A. P. Simons, *The United Nations and the Maintenance of International Peace and Security* (1955). Appraisal of activity.

W. H. C. Laves and C. A. Thomson, *UNESCO: Purposes, Progress, Prospects* (1957). Account of the organization's first ten years.

C. G. Fenwick, *The Inter-American Regional System* (1949).

Commission to Study the Organization of Peace, A. N. Holcombe, Chairman, *Organizing Peace in the Nuclear Age* (1959). Discussions of the international control of atomic energy.

P. C. Jessup and H. J. Taubenfeld, *Controls for Outer Space and the Antarctic Analogy* (1959). Examination of the problems and possibilities of international control of outer space.

War and National Defense

W. R. Kintner, *et al.*, *Forging a New Sword* (1958). Study of Defense Department and recommendations for improving its operations.

E. M. Emme (ed.), *The Impact of Air Power: National Security and World Politics* (1959). Collection of readings on all aspects of air power and strategy.

* W. Millis, *Arms and Men* (1956). History of American military institutions.

W. Millis, H. C. Mansfield, and H. Stein, *Arms and the State: Civil-military Elements in National Policy* (1958). Relations of military and civilian factors in the making of recent American policy.

P. Hammond, *Organizing for Defense* (1961). Comprehensive analysis of the American military organization.

J. M. Gavin, *War and Peace in the Space Age* (1958). Critical evaluation of American military policy by a former Army Chief of Research and Development.

B. Brodie, *Strategy in the Missile Age* (1959). Effects of technical advances on military planning.

R. G. Hubler, *SAC: The Strategic Air Command* (1958). Popular account of its history, functions, and the controversy surrounding it.

E. S. Corwin, *Total War and the Constitution* (1947). Impact of war and defense requirements upon constitutional system.

S. P. Huntington, *The Common Defense: Strategic Programs in National Politics* (1961). Essays analyzing the dynamics of postwar defense policy-making.

J. R. Schlesinger, *The Political Economy of National Security* (1960). Analysis of economic factors in national security.

J. D. Singer, *Deterrence, Arms Control and Disarmament: Toward a Synthesis in National Security Policy* (1962).

Science and National Security

J. S. Dupre and S. A. Lakoff, *Science and the Nation: Policy and Politics* (1962). Appraisal of the ever-widening influence of government in science and technology.

* V. Bush, *Modern Arms and Free Men* (1949). Head of Office of Scientific Research and Development during World War II discusses the relations between new weapons and modern warfare and the conditions under which science can make its best contribution to national security.

W. Gellhorn, *Security, Loyalty, and Science* (1950). Presents the view that national security and scientific development are being jeopardized by overzealous concern for security and secrecy.

Bulletin of Atomic Scientist, published monthly; articles on science and international security.

R. Gilpin, *American Scientists and Nuclear Weapons Policy* (1962). An analysis of participation in policy-making by an important new elite.

W. L. Laurence, *The Hell Bomb* (1951). The Hydrogen Bomb—its implications, and recommendations for American policy toward its use; by *The New York Times'* science editor.

R. E. Lapp, *Atoms and People* (1956). The atomic world of the future, by a physicist.

Military and Civilian

S. P. Huntington, *The Soldier and the State* (1957). Study of civil-military relations in the United States.

J. W. Spanier, *The Truman-MacArthur Controversy and the Korean War* (1959). Case study of civil-military relationships in wartime.

Senate Committee on Armed Services and Committee on Foreign Relations, *Hearings, Military Situation in Far East*, 82 Cong., 1 Sess. (1951). MacArthur hearings contain materials on how decisions are made, the relations among the President, his military, and his civilian advisers.

L. Smith, *American Democracy and Military Power* (1951). Survey of democratic theory, constitutional law, and administrative practices, and evaluation of their adequacy to preserve civilian control of the armed forces.

A. A. Ekirch, Jr., *The Civilian and the Military* (1956). Survey of American tradition and discussion of contemporary application.

H. L. Coles, *Total War and the Cold War* (1961). Problems of civilian control of the military.

H. D. Lasswell, *National Security and Individual Freedom* (1950). Recommendations as to how to avoid the "garrison state."

Government and the Economy

M. E. Dimock, *The New American Political Economy* (1962). Challenging suggestion for reform in the American political-economic system.

A. A. Berle, *Economic Power and the Free Society* (1957). Essay on the prevailing currents in economic life and their impact on individual freedom.

T. C. Cochran, *The American Business System* (1957). Interpretive history since 1900.

L. M. Hacker, *American Capitalism* (1957). Role of capitalism in American society.

C. B. Hoover, *The Economy, Liberty and the State* (1959). Study of the relation of the state to the economy in several nations, including the U.S.

H. K. Girvetz, *From Wealth to Welfare* (1950). Interpretation of the forces that have led to the welfare state.

J. K. Galbraith, *American Capitalism* (1952). Role of government, business, and labor in modern American competitive economy, "the concept of countervailing power."

* R. A. Dahl and C. E. Lindblom, *Politics, Economics and Welfare* (1953). Patterns of economic and political power; suggests new theoretical approaches.

Although the several writers vary considerably in their beliefs, the following are just a few of the many books that in general support the thesis "the less government the better."

H. Spencer, *The Man versus the State* (T. Beale edition, 1916). Classic statement of belief in limited government by one of the most influential men of the late nineteenth century.

F. A. Hayek, *The Road to Serfdom* (1944). Attack on governmental planning.

F. H. Knight, *Freedom and Reform* (1947). By outstanding economist.

* H. C. Simons, *Economic Policy for a Free Society* (1947). Devoted to the thesis that capital and labor monopolies must be destroyed so that free enterprise can be re-established.

J. A. Schumpeter, *Capitalism, Socialism, and Democracy* (1950). Defense of the entrepreneur.

Disagreeing with views in above volumes, the following authors believe that government should perform certain welfare functions, regulate the economy for full employment, and act positively to preserve a free society.

H. Finer, *Road to Reaction* (1945). Vigorous answer to Hayek.

* J. M. Clark, *Alternative to Serfdom* (1948). Comments on the role of government; less faith in planning than the above author.

K. Mannheim, *Freedom, Power, and Democratic Planning* (1950). By famous sociologist.

Government and Business

C. Wilcox, *Public Policies Toward Business* (1960). Standard text on regulation of business.

H. J. Levin (ed.), *Business Organization and Public Policy* (1958). Readings on government's relation to business.

M. E. Dimock, *Business and Government*, 4th ed. (1961). Survey of government-business relations.

D. F. Pegrum, *Public Regulation of Business* (1959).

M. G. Glaeser, *Public Utilities in American Capitalism* (1957). Study of problems and policies of regulation.

J. Bauer, *Transforming Public Utility Regulations* (1950). Recommendations for improving regulatory activities.

J. Landis, *Report on Regulatory Agencies to the President-Elect* (1960). Policy recommendation to President Kennedy.

S. N. Whitney, *Anti-trust Policies: American Experience in Twenty Industries*, 2 vols. (1958). Analysis of the effectiveness of antitrust action.

J. W. Burns, *A Study of Anti-trust Laws* (1958). Greater emphasis on legal aspects than the above volume.

W. Adams and H. M. Gray, *Monopoly in America* (1956). Evidence to support argument that government policy in recent years tends to promote monopoly.

W. Letwin, *Law and Economic Policy in America: The Evolution of the Sherman Anti-Trust Act* (1965).

J. Scoville and N. Sargent, *Fact and Fancy in the T.N.E.C. Monographs* (1942). Critical review of TNEC reports prepared under auspices of NAM.

D. E. Lilienthal, *Big Business: A New Era* (1952). Argues for an affirmative program to help develop big business and discussion of its contributions.

S. Buchanan, *The Corporation and the Republic* (1958). The emergent role of the corporation in society.

C. D. Edwards, *Maintaining Competition* (1949). Recommendations for a governmental policy.

E. S. Redford, *Administration of National Economic Controls* (1952). Analysis of process by which policy is made and instruments through which it is executed.

I. L. Sharfman, *The Interstate Commerce Commission*, 4 vols. (1931–1937). Comprehensive study of the oldest federal regulatory agency.

J. M. Edelman, *The Licensing of Radio Services in the U.S., 1927 to 1947* (1950). Study in administrative formulation of policy.

* A. A. Berle and G. C. Means, *The Modern Corporation and Private Property* (1933). Analysis of the growth of large industry, the separation between ownership and control, and problems of social control.

R. E. Lane, *The Regulation of Businessmen* (1954). Responses of businessmen to regulation.

T. W. Arnold, *The Folklore of Capitalism* (1937). Mythology of business and trust-busting, with emphasis on its futility, by a man who subsequently became an active trust-buster.

Government and Agriculture

M. R. Benedict, *Farm Policies of the United States, 1790–1950* (1953). Origins and development of governmental policy.

M. R. Benedict and O. C. Stine, *The Agricultural Commodity Program: Two Decades of Experience* (1956). Farm program discussed in terms of specific commodities.

W. W. Cochrane, *Farm Prices, Myth and Reality* (1958). Emphasis on problems of commercial agriculture.

L. Soth, *Farm Trouble* (1957). Discussion of farm problems, especially those of the marginal farmer.

R. M. Christenson, *The Brannan Plan: Farm Politics and Policy* (1959). Study of farm politics as focused on the Brannan Plan controversy.

C. M. Hardin, *The Politics of Agriculture* (1952). Taking the field of soil conservation, the author develops methods to describe the political process.

D. F. Hadwiger and R. B. Talbot, *Pressures and Protests: The Kennedy Farm Program and the Wheat Referendum of 1963* (1965).

G. Baker, *The County Agent* (1939). Traces the work of this link between government and the farmer from 1911 to 1939.

President's Commission on Migratory Labor, *Report, Migratory Labor in American Agriculture* (1951). Latest study of this social problem.

Conservation

Popular discussions that deal with general problems are:

M. W. Straus, *Why Not Survive?* (1955).

F. Osborn, *Our Plundered Planet* (1948).

W. Vogt, *Road to Survival* (1948).

G. Pinchot, *Breaking New Ground* (1947). Autobiography of a crusader for conservation.

Other works include:

H. Jarrett (ed.), *Perspectives on Conservation: Essays on America's Natural Resources* (1958).

M. Clawson and B. Held, *The Federal Lands: Their Use and Management* (1957).

R. M. Robbins, *Our Landed Heritage* (1942). History of public land policies.

E. F. Renshow, *Toward Responsible Government: An Economic Appraisal of Federal Investment in the Water Resources Program* (1957). Critical of the program.

President's Water Resources Policy Commission, *A Water Policy for the American People; Ten Rivers in America's Future; Water Resources Law* (1950). Primary source of information; presentation of program with supporting data.

J. V. Krutilla and O. Eckstein, *Multiple Purpose River Development* (1958). General treatment of water resources.

M. Clawson, R. B. Held, and C. H. Stoddard, *Land for the Future* (1960).

W. B. Greeley, *Forests and Men* (1951). Former Chief of the Forest Service discusses problems and programs.

President's Materials Policy Commission, *Resources for Freedom* (1952). With five supporting volumes, one of the most significant studies of resources and public policy in recent years.

N. I. Wengert, *Natural Resources and the Political Struggle* (1955). History and politics of conservation.

C. McKinley, *Uncle Sam in the Pacific Northwest* (1952). Detailed study of federal government's program for management of natural resources in the area.

R. A. Cooley, *Politics and Conservation: The Decline of the Alaska Salmon* (1963). A study of pressure politics.

P. W. Bidwell, *Raw Materials: A Study of American Policy* (1958).

E. Ginzburg, *Human Resources: The Wealth of a Nation* (1958).

The Labor Movement

J. G. Rayback, *A History of American Labor* (1959).

J. R. Commons, *et al., History of Labor in the United States*, 4 vols. (1935). One of the best labor histories covering period before the New Deal.

H. A. Millis and R. Montgomery, *Organized Labor* (1945). Another outstanding labor history.

R. A. Lester, *As Unions Mature: An Analysis of the Evolution of American Unionism* (1958). Background and current problems.

S. Lens, *The Crisis of American Labor* (1959). Current issues and problems.

C. W. Mills, *The New Men of Power* (1948). Study of the leaders of organized labor, by a sociologist.

M. Karson, *American Labor and Politics, 1900–1918* (1958).

P. Taft, *The Structure and Government of Labor Unions* (1954).

M. M. Kampelman, *The Communist Party vs. the CIO: A Study of Power Politics* (1957). Study of attempted communist infiltration and union counteraction.

L. E. H. Chamberlin, *et al.*, *Labor Unions and Public Policy* (1958). Critical of the power unions now have.

C. E. Lindblom, *Unions and Capitalism* (1949). Questions the compatibility of unions and capitalism.

F. Tannenbaum, *A Philosophy of Labor* (1951). Interpretation of unions as a conservative force in modern capitalistic society.

G. Tyler, *A New Philosophy for Labor* (1959). Interpretation of labor's situation and prospects.

Government Labor Policy

S. Petro, *Power Unlimited: The Corruption of Union Leadership* (1959). Interpretation and summary of the McClellan Committee disclosures.

P. Sultan, *Right to Work Laws: A Study of Conflict* (1958). Balanced discussion of their background and arguments on both sides of the fence.

U.S. Department of Labor, *Federal Labor Laws and Agencies*, Bulletin No. 123, August 1950, periodically revised. Provides quick reference to laws and regulations.

H. A. Millis and E. C. Brown, *From the Wagner Act to Taft-Hartley* (1950). Labor policy from the New Deal to Taft-Hartley.

Social Security

J. G. Turnhill, *et al.*, *Economic and Social Security: Public and Private Measures Against Economic Insecurity* (1957). General treatment of problems and policies.

E. E. Witte, *The Development of the Social Security Act* (1962).

Rockefeller Brothers Fund, *The Challenge to America: Its Economic and Social Aspects* (1958). Sections on problems of economic and social security.

J. D. Hagan and F. A. J. Ianni, *American Social Legislation* (1957). Appraisal of problems and alternatives; sociological emphasis.

National Association of Social Workers, *The Social Welfare Yearbook*, annual collection of articles.

A. Larson, *Know Your Social Security* (1955). By former Undersecretary of Department of Health, Education and Welfare.

U.S. Social Security Administration, *Social Security Bulletin*.

Health Insurance

G. Rosen, *A History of Public Health* (1958). General review of programs through several centuries.

H. M. Somers and A. R. Somers, *Doctors, Patients, and Health Insurance* (1961). Comprehensive, balanced examination.

H. S. Mustard, *An Introduction to Public Health* (1953).

U.S. Department of Health, Education and Welfare, *Annual Report*. Useful information on current problems.

President's Commission on the Health Needs of the Nation, *Building America's Health*, 5 vols. (1953). Findings of fact and recommendations of action needed to meet the nation's health requirements.

H. E. Livingston, *National Health Insurance*, Public Affairs Bulletin 85, Legislative Reference Service (1950).

Education

* M. Mayer, *The Schools* (1961). Provocative general treatment of American public education.

* Rockefeller Brothers Fund, *The Pursuit of Excellence: Education and the Future of America* (1958). Study of needs, problems, and philosophy.

Senate Committee on Labor and Public Welfare, 85 Cong., 2nd Sess., *The National Defense Education Act of 1958* (1958). Summary and analysis of the law.

Committee on Economic Development, *Paying for Better Schools* (1960). Recommendations on educational finance.

S. K. Bailey, *et al.*, *The Economics and Politics of Public Education* (1962–1963). An eight-volume inquiry which places education in a political context.

D. M. Knight, *The Federal Government and Higher Education* (1961). Analysis of growing relationships.

C. V. Kidd, *American Universities and Federal Research* (1959). Impact of federal funds on higher education.

A. Kerber and W. Smith (eds.), *Educational Issues in a Changing Society* (1962). Discussion of current problems by experts.

Housing

R. M. Fisher, *Twenty Years of Public Housing: Economic Aspects of the Federal Program* (1959). History of federal policy and activities.

G. H. Beyer, *Housing: A Factual Analysis*

(1958). Technical information as well as information on government policy.

Housing and Home Finance Agency, *Annual Report*. Valuable factual data.

Joint (Congressional) Committee on Housing, *Final Majority Report*, Housing Study and Investigation, House Report 1564, 80 Cong., 2nd Sess. (1949).

Federal Policemen

J. N. Markis, *The Silent Investigators* (1959). Account of the U.S. Postal Inspection service.

B. Smith, *Police Systems in the United States*, rev. ed. (1949). General discussion of all police systems; special chapters on federal agencies.

M. Lowenthal, *The Federal Bureau of Investigation* (1950). Criticism of the FBI.

D. Whitehead, *The F.B.I. Story* (1956). Readable, sympathetic, and wide-ranging account.

Government as Manager

D. K. Price, *Government and Science* (1954). Shows major role of government in scientific activity.

Commission on Organization of the Executive Branch of the Government, *Report on Federal Business Enterprises; and Report on the Post Office* (1949 and 1955).

M. Thomas and R. M. Northrop, *Atomic Energy and Congress* (1956).

A. Griffith, *The National Aeronautics and Space Act* (1962). The birth of NASA.

V. Van Dyke, *Pride and Power: The Rationale of the Space Program* (1964). Careful analysis of America's program for man in space.

D. E. Lilienthal, *TVA: Democracy on the March*, rev. ed. (1953). Defense by former director of TVA as major instrument of grass-roots democracy.

C. H. Pritchett, *The Tennessee Valley Authority: A Study in Public Administration* (1943). Standard study of TVA administration.

P. Selznick, *TVA and the Grass Roots* (1949). Sociological interpretation.

Fiscal and Monetary Policy

L. H. Kimmel, *Federal Budget and Fiscal Policy, 1789–1958* (1959). General survey of policies and procedures.

P. J. Strayer, *Fiscal Policy and Politics* (1958).

J. Burkhead, *Government Budgeting* (1956). Description of the budgetary process.

A. B. Wildavsky, *The Politics of the Budgetary Process* (1964). The strategies and calculations of participants in the budget-making process.

P. H. Douglas, *Economy in the National Government* (1952). By U.S. senator; includes critical comments on budget and appropriation process.

A. Smithies, *The Budgetary Process in the United States* (1955). Surveys role of federal budget.

Bureau of the Budget, *The Federal Budget in Brief*. Published annually, summary of budget; many illustrations.

R. A. Wallace, *Congressional Control of Federal Spending* (1962). Study of Congressional role in fiscal policy.

G. L. Bach, *Inflation: A Study in Economics, Ethics and Politics* (1958).

* J. M. Keynes, *The General Theory of Employment, Interest, and Money* (1936). One of the most influential books of modern times; interpretation of economics that calls for governmental fiscal and monetary policy and public works to offset unemployment.

R. Blough, *The Federal Taxing Process* (1952). The forces at work and institutions involved in the taxing process.

R. E. Paul, *Taxation in the United States* (1954). By former high Treasury official.

H. C. Simons, *Federal Tax Reform* (1950). By distinguished anti-Keynesian economist.

G. L. Bach, *Federal Reserve Policy-Making* (1950).

E. W. Kemmerer and D. L. Kemmerer, *The ABC of the Federal Reserve System*, rev. ed. (1950).

Senate Committee on Banking and Currency, *Federal Reserve Policy and Economic Stability, 1951–1957*, study prepared by A. Achinstein, Senate Report No. 2500, 85 Cong., 2nd Sess. (1958).

The several reports resulting from the Employment Act of 1946 are primary sources for the whole problem of governmental fiscal and monetary policy. These include the President's Economic Report to the Congress, Report of the Council of Economic Advisers, and Reports and Hearings of the Joint Congressional Committee on Economic Report. These are issued regularly.

Part Seven: State and Local Governments

Many of the books mentioned in the other sections of this bibliography, especially in connection with federalism, also pertain to government of the states and their subdivisions. Except in a few cases, they will not be listed again here; nor will the standard texts be noted. Furthermore, the wealth of materials—some produced by individual scholars and some by the many research organizations connected with universities, cities, state organizations, and various associations of officials—dealing with the government of a particular state, city, county, or region or area, are not mentioned, but only the more general works.

Annuals, Manuals, and Periodicals

W. B. Graves, N. J. Small, and E. F. Dowell, *American State Government and Administration* (1949). "A state by state bibliography of significant general and special works."

D. C. Tompkins, *State Government and Administration* (1954). Selected bibliography arranged by topic with primary emphasis on legislature.

Council of State Governments, *The Book of the States*, published biennially with semiannual supplements; a basic source; contains selected bibliography of state government, short articles on current developments, charts and lists of personnel.

————, *State Government*, published monthly; articles by state officials and scholars and reports on programs of state governments.

State Manuals, published by most states yearly; usually contain directories of public officials, election statistics, descriptions of activities of various government agencies, and so on.

Library of Congress, *Monthly Checklist of State Publications*, a state-by-state list of publications.

International City Managers' Association, *The Municipal Yearbook*, published yearly; contains up-to-date information on every aspect of municipal activity.

National Municipal League, *National Civic Review* (formerly *National Municipal Review*), published monthly; the trade journal of city officials; articles dealing with problems of those who run our cities.

American City Magazine Corporation, *The American City*, published monthly; another trade journal of city officials.

U.S. Conference of Mayors, *The U.S. Municipal News*, biweekly newsletter of current events; suggests political pressures operating on mayors.

National Association of County Officials, *The County Officer*, monthly trade journal of county officials.

American Judicature Society, *Journal of the American Judicature Society*, monthly publication devoted to the cause of judicial reform and improvement in the administration of justice.

Patterns of State and Local Politics

H. Jacob and K. N. Vines (eds.), *Politics in the American States: A Comparative Analysis* (1965). Systematic comparative analysis of problems of state politics.

* V. O. Key, Jr., *American State Politics* (1956). Comparative study with important insights for understanding national politics.

D. Lockard, *New England State Politics* (1959). Politics of Vermont, New Hampshire, Maine, Massachusetts, Rhode Island, and Connecticut.

J. H. Fenton, *Politics of the Border States* (1957). Politics of Maryland, West Virginia, Kentucky, and Missouri.

* V. O. Key, Jr., and A. Heard, *Southern Politics* (1949). Brilliant studies of regional politics.

F. H. Jonas (ed.), *Western Politics* (1961). Survey of politics in the burgeoning West.

R. B. Nye, *Midwestern Progressive Politics* (1951). Historical interpretation.

* R. A. Dahl, *Who Governs? Democracy and Power in an American City* (1961). Important study of city politics.

R. A. Agger, D. Goldrich, and B. E. Swanson, *The Rulers and the Ruled: Political*

Power and Importance in American Communities (1964). Research report of decision-making in four communities.

R. Presthus, *Men at the Top: A Study in Community Power* (1964). A study of two small New York communities.

E. C. Banfield and J. Q. Wilson, *City Politics* (1963). City government is viewed in the context of the total urban setting.

O. P. Williams and C. R. Adrian, *Four Cities: A Study in Comparative Policy-Making* (1963). Who governs in four middle-sized cities.

E. C. Banfield, *Political Influence* (1961). Political patterns in Chicago.

State Constitutions

W. B. Graves (ed.), *American Commonwealth Series,* a current series of volumes on the government and administration of the states; to date, about twelve states have been covered.

————, *Major Problems in State Constitutional Revision* (1960). General treatment.

J. W. Fesler (ed.), *The Forty-eight States: Their Tasks as Policy Makers and Administrators* (1955). Symposium prepared for American Assembly conference evaluating how well the states are doing their jobs.

R. V. Peel, *State Government Today* (1948). Sprightly analysis of the ability of state governments to do their jobs.

R. S. Allen (ed.), *Our Sovereign States* (1949). Journalistic essays on the politics of some of the states.

New York State Constitutional Convention Committee, *Constitutions of the States and the United States,* Vol. III (1938). Most comprehensive and recent collection.

C. N. Callender (ed.), "The State Constitution of the Future," *The Annals* of the American Academy of Political and Social Science, September 1935. Collection of articles.

The National Municipal League has issued an excellent series in its state constitutional studies project including: *The Model State Constitution,* 6th ed. (1962), *Salient Issues of Constitutional Revision* (1961), *The Constitutional Convention: A Manual* (1961), *The Shape of the Document* (1960), *Reapportionment* (1960), *The Governor* (1960), *The Structure of Administration* (1961), and *Bill of Rights* (1960).

A. L. Sturm, *Methods of State Constitutional Reform* (1954). Monograph covering background and methods for change.

V. A. O'Rourke and D. W. Campbell, *Constitution-Making in a Democracy* (1943). Case study of a New York constitutional convention.

C. B. Swisher, *Motivations and Political Techniques in the California Constitutional Convention, 1878–1879* (1930). Study of the constitutional convention as part of the process of government.

Under the Capitol Dome

J. C. Wahlke, H. Eulau, W. Buchanan, L. C. Ferguson, *The Legislative System* (1962). Comparative analysis in four states.

J. D. Barber, *The Law Makers: Recruitment and Adaptation to Legislative Life* (1964). Theory of political recruitment and adaptation emerges from intensive interviews.

* B. Zeller (ed.), *American State Legislatures* (1954). Report of the American Political Science Association's Committee on American Legislatures.

A. C. Breckenridge, *One House for Two: A Study of Nebraska's Unicameral Legislature* (1957). Review of its operations.

M. E. Jewell (ed.), *The Politics of Reapportionment* (1962). Case studies of struggles for legislative reapportionment and congressional redistricting.

G. E. Baker, *Rural Versus Urban Political Power* (1955). Problems and consequences.

F. J. Sorauf, *Party and Representation: Legislative Politics in Pennsylvania* (1963). Sophisticated view of recruitment processes.

H. Eulau and J. D. Sprague, *Lawyers in Politics: A Study in Professional Convergence* (1964). Examination of role perceptions of lawyer-legislators.

Governors and Judges

C. B. Ransone, Jr., *The Office of Governor in the United States* (1956). Its historical development, present status, and problems.

L. Lipson, *American Governor: from Figurehead to Leader* (1939). Basic source of the development of the governor's office; special attention to the reorganization period and experiences of Virginia, Massachusetts, New York, and Illinois.

J. A. Schlesinger, *How They Became Governor: A Study of Comparative State Politics, 1870–1950* (1957).

B. Nispel, *Reform of the Office of Lieutenant Governor* (1958).

G. E. Brooks, *When Governors Convene* (1961). Study of the annual national governors conference.

W. H. Riker, *Soldiers of the State: The Role of the National Guard in American Democracy* (1957).

A. E. Buck, *Reorganization of State Governments in the United States* (1938). Comprehensive discussion of 1917–1938 reorganization movement; state-by-state survey.

J. C. Bollens, *Administrative Reorganization in the States Since 1939* (1947). Updates Buck's work.

Council of State Governments, *Reorganizing State Government* (1950). Examination of "the current situation of administrative management in the states" and a review of "the important recommendations . . . of recent . . . reorganization studies."

C. S. Hyneman, "Administrative Reorganization: An Adventure into Science and Theology," *Journal of Politics*, Vol. I (1939). One of the better-known "broadsides" against reorganization principles.

There are a number of excellent biographies and memoirs of American governors.

The State Judiciary

K. N. Vines and H. Jacob, *Studies in Judicial Politics* (1962). The role of the judiciary in state and local politics.

R. Pound, *Organization of the Courts* (1940). By leader in judicial reform movement and famous legal scholar.

A. T. Vanderbilt (ed.), *Minimum Standards of Judicial Administration* (1949). Survey by former Chief Justice of New Jersey Supreme Court of the extent to which standards of the American Bar Association have been accepted by the states, discussion of such problems as jury selection, judicial selection, pre-trial practice, and so on.

Council of State Governments, *The Courts of Last Resort of the Forty-Eight States* (1950). Comparative study of major aspects of organization and operation of the highest state courts.

———, *Trial Courts of General Jurisdiction in the Forty-Eight States* (1951). Companion report.

E. Haynes, *The Selection and Tenure of Judges* (1944). The standard history; a basic source.

J. W. Peltason, *Missouri Plan for Selection of Judges* (1945). Description of the Mis-

souri system and the activities of a judicial reform interest group.

Government at the Grass Roots

Bureau of the Census, *Governments in the United States*. Number and kinds.

J. C. Bollens, *Special District Governments in the United States* (1956). Number, kinds, and jobs done.

House Committee on Governmental Operations. *Hearings* on Federal-State-Local Relations, 85 Cong., 1 Sess., 1959, Parts 1 and 2, on state and local officials.

W. Anderson and E. W. Weidner (eds.), *Research in Intergovernmental Relations* (1950–1952). Series of ten monographs on various phases of state-local relations.

A. J. Vidich and J. Bensman, *Small Town in Mass Society: Class, Power, and Religion in a Rural Community* (1960). Sociological study.

W. E. Mills, Jr., and H. R. Davis, *Small City Government* (1962). Seven instructive case studies.

J. A. Fairlie and C. M. Kneier, *County Government and Administration* (1930). A basic work.

C. F. Snider, *Local Government in Rural America* (1957). Study of all forms of rural government.

P. W. Wager (ed.), *County Government across the Nation* (1950). Case studies of county and township government in the states.

E. W. Weidner, *The American County, Patchwork of Boards* (1946). Comments on trends and suggestions for improvement.

C. F. Snider and N. F. Garvey have published annual articles summarizing developments in field of county and township government from 1937 to 1949 in *The American Political Science Review*.

National Municipal League, *Model County Charter* (1956).

Metropolis

L. Mumford, *The City in History* (1961). Interpretative account of the emergence of the urban community.

A. Boskoff, *The Sociology of Urban Regions* (1962). Sociological discussion of major facets of urban life.

W. S. Fiser, *Mastery of the Metropolis* (1962). Approaches to the multiple problems of the metropolitan complex.

J. C. Bollens (ed.), *Exploring the Metropoli-*

tan Community (1961). Survey of social-political problems.

* Editors of Fortune, *The Exploding Metropolis* (1958). Essays on various aspects of metropolitan problems.

R. C. Wood, *Suburbia: Its People and Their Politics* (1959). Sociological and political analysis of the movement to the suburbs.

W. M. Dobringer (ed.), *The Suburban Community* (1958). Essays in the sociology of suburbia.

S. Greer, *The Emerging City* (1962). Sociological view of the modern urban setting.

V. M. Jones, *Metropolitan Government* (1942). Standard source; discussion of basic problems.

S. Greer, *Metropolitics: A Study of Political Culture* (1963).

L. H. Gulick, *The Metropolitan Problem and American Ideas* (1962). Cites failures of current approaches to "metropolitanism" and recommends solutions.

Urban Government

E. C. Banfield (ed.), *Urban Government* (1961). Selected readings.

O. P. Williams and C. Press (eds.), *Democracy in Urban America* (1961). Various approaches to the study of municipal government and politics.

G. M. Kammerer, *et al.*, *City Managers in Politics: An Analysis of Manager Tenure and Termination* (1962).

R. L. Mott, *Home Rule for American Cities* (1949). How home rule works and why it is desirable; published by the American Municipal Association.

W. S. Sayre and H. Kaufman, *Governing New York City* (1960).

N. Glazer and D. P. Moynihan, *Beyond the Melting Pot: The Negroes, Puerto Ricans, Jews, Italians and Irish of New York City* (1963). The political consequences of ethnicity.

F. M. Stewart, *A Half Century of Municipal Reform* (1950). "The History of the National Municipal League."

T. J. Lowi, *At the Pleasure of the Mayor: Patronage and Power in New York City, 1898–1958* (1964).

National Municipal League, *Model City Charter* (1948).

J. D. Crumlish, *A City Finds Itself: The Philadelphia Home Rule Charter Movement* (1959). Case study in the politics of municipal reform.

A. T. Brown, *The Politics of Reform—*

Kansas City's Municipal Government, 1925–1950 (1958).

R. A. Straetz, *PR Politics in Cincinnati: Thirty Years of City Government Through Proportional Representation* (1958).

The International City Managers' Association publishes several specialized training manuals on municipal finance, police, fire, public works, and personnel administration, municipal recreation, local planning, and "technique of municipal administration."

Public Safety

B. Smith, *Police Systems in the United States*, rev. ed. (1949). Standard source by outstanding authority in police administration.

I. Camp, *Our State Police* (1955). Examination of the varieties of state police systems.

Government as Educator

Council of State Governments, *The Forty-Eight State School Systems* (1949). Survey of school administration, finances, and other aspects of public elementary and secondary education.

V. Miller and W. B. Spalding, *The Public Administration of American Schools*, 2nd ed. (1958).

Committee on Government and Higher Education, *The Efficiency of Freedom* (1959). The relation of the states to higher education.

J. S. Brubacher and W. Rudy, *Higher Education in Transition: An American History, 1636–1956* (1958). Comprehensive single-volume history.

N. Edwards and H. G. Richey, *The School in the American Social Order* (1947). History of education and discussion of relation between educational policy and social change.

N. A. Masters, R. H. Salisbury, and Thomas H. Eliot, *State Politics and the Public Schools* (1964).

R. A. Freeman, *School Needs in the Decade Ahead* (1958). Survey of future financial needs.

H. K. Allen and R. G. Axt, *State Public Finance and State Institutions of Higher Education in the United States* (1952). Volume in series produced by a commission to study all phases of education; sponsored by the Association of American Universities.

A. Nevins, *The State Universities and Democracy* (1962). Historical evaluation.
F. Rudolph, *The American College and University: A History* (1962). Wide-ranging study.

Services

B. Y. Landis, *Rural Welfare Services* (1949).
H. E. Martz, *Citizen Participation in Government* (1948). "A Study of County Welfare Boards."
H. M. Leyendecker, *Problems and Policy in Public Assistance* (1955). General treatment.
E. C. Banfield and M. Grodzins, *Government and Housing in Metropolitan Areas* (1958).
M. Meyerson and E. C. Banfield, *Politics, Planning and the Public Interest* (1955). Case study of public housing in Chicago that emphasizes the policy-making process.
Tax Institute, *Financing Highways* (1957). Problems stemming from the 1956 Federal Highway Act.
P. N. Ylvisaker, "The Natural Cement Issue," and Herbert Kaufman, "Gotham in the Air Age," in H. Stein (ed.), *Public Administration and Policy Development* (1950). Case studies of highway and airport politics, respectively.
H. M. Somers and A. R. Somers, *Workmen's Compensation* (1954). Covers all aspects of oldest social insurance program.

Regulation at the Grass Roots

J. W. Fesler, *The Independence of State Regulatory Agencies* (1942). Discussion of existing practices, problems, weaknesses, and solutions.
D. V. Harper, *Economic Regulation of the Motor Trucking Industry by the States* (1959).

Council of State Governments, *Occupational Licensing Legislation in the States* (1952). State-by-state data.

Money and Men

H. M. Groves, *Financing Government*, 4th ed. (1955). Standard text.
A. H. Hansen and H. S. Perloff, *State and Local Finance in the National Economy* (1944). Problems of integrated national fiscal policy as complicated by federal system.
Tax Foundation, Tax Institute, and Tax Policy League, among other organizations, publish numerous monographs dealing with problems of state and local taxation, expenditure and debt.
U.S. Bureau of Census. Numerous reports dealing with state and local finances.
Municipal Finance Officers Association, *Municipal Finance*, quarterly report on current developments.
International City Managers' Association, *Municipal Finance Administration* (1949). A textbook for practitioners.
O. Eckstein, *Trends in Public Expenditure in the Next Decade* (1959).
C. Penniman and W. Heller, *State Income Tax Administration* (1960). Overview and analysis.
Civil Service Assembly of the United States and Canada, *A Digest of State Civil Service Laws*.
Civil Service Assembly, *Public Personnel Review*, quarterly journal, articles, and reports on developments.
National Civil Service League, Civil Service Assembly, and National Municipal League, *A Model State Civil Service Law* (1946). Each section is accompanied by explanatory comments.
International City Managers' Association, *Municipal Personnel Administration* (1950). Day-to-day problems of city administrators.

Epilogue: Challenge and Opportunity

Politics and You

* S. Bullitt, *To Be a Politician* (1959). An intellectual reflects on his experience in the world of "practical politics."
R. E. Merriam and R. M. Goetz, *Going Into Politics* (1957). "A Guide for Citizens."
S. A. Mitchell, *Elm St. Politics* (1959).

Former chairman of Democratic National Committee discusses the role of "amateurs" in politics and outlines how a citizen can become active in politics.
H. D. Scott, Jr., *How to Go Into Politics* (1949). By former chairman of Republican National Committee, now a senator.
J. M. Cannon (ed.), *Politics U.S.A.: A Practical Guide to the Winning of Public Office*

(1960). Insiders' advice on campaign politics.

P. P. Van Riper, *Handbook of Practical Politics* (1960). Materials drawn from many sources "to familiarize citizens with concrete ways . . . of carrying on effective political activity on the local and state levels."

National Municipal League, *The Citizen Association: How to Organize and Run It*

(1953), and *The Citizen Association: How to Win Civic Campaigns* (1953).

J. E. McLean, *Politics Is What You Make It* (1952). Pamphlet with information and suggestions on how to be an effective citizen-politician.

E. E. Schattschneider, V. Jones, and S. Bailey, *A Guide to the Study of Public Affairs* (1952). Practical guides to gathering political information.

Political Novels

Books of fiction often provide useful insights into political life. Many novelists have developed specifically political themes while others present political implications for the broader human drama. Two general studies, Joseph L. Blotner, *The Political Novel* (1955) and Irving Howe, *Politics and the Novel* (1957), discuss aspects of the interrelationship between politics and the novelist's art. Following is a brief listing of a few leading American political novels.

A. Drury, *Advise and Consent* (1960). A fictional version of the Senate's confirmation of a controversial presidential appointment.

H. Adams, *Democracy* (1880). Classic in American political fiction.

E. Burdick, *The Ninth Wave* (1956). A powerful account of applied political psychology.

J. Dos Passos, *Number One* (1943). A study in the pathology of political corruption.

S. Lewis, *It Can't Happen Here* (1936). America under a fascist dictatorship.

Robert Penn Warren, *All the King's Men* (1946). The rise and fall of a southern

demagogue in the mold of Huey Long.

E. O'Connor, *The Last Hurrah* (1955). A delightful portrait of a big-city boss and his machine.

J. G. Schneider, *The Golden Kazoo* (1956). Public relations men transform a presidential campaign.

W. J. Lederer and E. Burdick, *The Ugly American* (1959). Vignettes of several types of Americans on overseas assignments.

E. Burdick and H. Wheeler, *Fail-Safe* (1962). Policy-making and accidental war.

Pat Frank, *Affair of State* (1948). Dilemmas in the life of a foreign service officer.

A Selective Bibliography of Current Research on American Government

This is a selective list of articles relevant to the study of American government that have appeared in some of the professional political science journals between September 1962 and June 1965. These articles, of course, will be of special interest to students planning to major in political science, but they will give any student an idea of the kind of work being done by "professionals" in this area and how they report to their fellow political scientists.

The journals covered are:

The American Political Science Review (APSR)—the official journal of the American Political Science Association.

The Journal of Politics (JP)—the journal of the Southern Political Science Association.

Midwest Journal of Politics (MJPS)—the journal of the Midwest Conference of Political Scientists.

Political Science Quarterly (PSQ)—the journal of the Academy of Political Science of Columbia University.

The Review of Politics (RP)—published by Notre Dame University.

The Western Political Quarterly (WPQ)—the journal of the Western Political Science Association.

However, these are only a few of the journals in which the literature of political science is published. Others include: *Southwestern Social Science Quarterly, National Civic Review, Behavioral Science, Public Administration Review, Administrative Science Quarterly, Conflict Resolution, American Behavioral Scientist, Journal of Political Economy, Journal of Asian Studies, World Politics, Public Opinion Quarterly,* the publications of the other social science disciplines, and the many law reviews. *The American Political Science Review* carries in each issue an extensive bibliography of research in all fields of political science.

Since the titles of most articles are descriptive of their contents, the following list is not annotated. Page references indicate the first page on which the article begins. Although many of the articles are relevant to several phases of the study of American government, they are mentioned only once.

Part One: Democratic Government in America

Albert Somit and Joseph Tanenhaus, "Trends in American Political Science," APSR (December 1963), p. 933.

Robert G. McCloskey and Austin Ranney, "Political Science: The State of the Profession," PSQ (June 1965), p. 277.

Demetrious Caraley, "The Political Behavior Approach: Methodological Advance or New Formalism?" PSQ (March 1964), p. 96.

Lindsay Rogers, "Notes on 'Political Science'," PSQ (June 1964), p. 209.

Christian Bay, "Politics and Pseudopolitics: A Critical Evaluation of Some Behavioral Literature," APSR (March 1965), p. 39.

T. J. Lowi, "American Government, 1933–1963: Fission and Confusion in Theory and Research," APSR (September 1964), p. 589.

Norman Jacobson, "Political Science and Political Education," APSR (September 1963), p. 561.

Peter Bachrach and Morton S. Baratz, "Two Faces of Power," APSR (December 1962), p. 947.

———, "Decisions and Nondecisions: An Analytical Framework," APSR (September 1963), p. 632.

Charles E. Gilbert, "Operative Doctrines of Representation," APSR (September 1963), p. 604.

James N. Rosenau, "Consensus Building in the American National Community," JP (November 1962), p. 639.

Willmoore Kendall and George W. Carey, "Towards a Definition of 'Conservatism'," JP (May 1964), p. 406.

Lane Davis, "The Cost of Realism: Contemporary Restatements of Democracy," WPQ (March 1964), p. 37.

Part Two: The Rules and How They Grew

Ralph Lerner, "Calhoun's New Science of Politics," *APSR* (December 1963) p. 918.

Joseph Cooper, "Jeffersonian Attitudes Toward Executive Leadership and Committee Development in the House of Representatives," *WPQ* (March 1965), p. 45.

Ralph L. Ketcham, "France and American Politics, 1763–1793," *PSQ* (June 1963), p. 198.

Wiley E. Hodges, "Pro-Governmentalism in Virginia, 1789–1836," *JP* (May 1963), p. 333.

Gerald Garvey, "The Constitutional Revolution of 1837 and the Myth of Marshall's Monolith," *WPQ* (March 1965), p. 27.

Jacob Cohen and Morton Grodzins, "How Much Economic Sharing in American Federalism?" *APSR* (March 1963), p. 5.

Daniel J. Elazar, "Federal-State Collaboration in the Nineteenth Century United States," *PSQ* (June 1964), p. 248.

Ernest A. Engelbert, "Federal-State Relationships: Their Influence on Western Regional Growth," *WPQ* (September 1963), p. 686.

Part Three: Civil Liberties and Citizenship

Charles S. Hyneman, "Free Speech: At What Price?" *APSR* (December 1962), p. 847.

Carl J. Friedrich, "Rights, Liberties, Freedoms: A Reappraisal," *APSR* (December 1963), p. 841.

Benjamin F. Wright, "The Rights of Majorities and of Minorities in the 1961 Term of the Supreme Court," *APSR* (March 1963), p. 98.

Walter F. Murphy, "Deeds Under a Doctrine: Civil Liberties in the 1963 Term," *APSR* (March 1965), p. 64.

William W. Van Alstyne, "Constitutional Separation of Church and State: The Quest for a Coherent Position," *APSR* (December 1963), p. 865.

Walfred H. Peterson, "The American Federal System and Church-State Relations," *WPQ* (September 1963), p. 598.

Murray S. Stedman, Jr., "Church, State,

People: The Eternal Triangle," *WPQ* (September 1963), p. 610.

C. Herman Pritchett, "Equal Protection and the Urban Majority," *APSR* (December 1964), p. 869.

Kenneth N. Vines, "Southern State Supreme Courts and Race Relations," *WPQ* (March 1965), p. 5.

John C. Ries and Owen S. Nibley, "Justice, Juries and Military Dependents," *WPQ* (September 1962), p. 438.

Charles D. Tarlton, "The Mentally Ill in Criminal Cases: The Constitutional Issue," *WPQ* (September 1963), p. 525.

Robert Goedecke, "Justice Field and Inherent Rights," *RP* (April 1965), p. 198.

John P. Roche, "The Expatriation Decisions: A Study in Constitutional Improvisations and the Uses of History," *APSR* (March 1964), p. 72.

Part Four: People in Politics

Public Opinion

Herbert McClosky, "Consensus and Ideology in American Politics," *APSR* (June 1964), p. 361.

Lester W. Milbrath, "Latent Origins of Liberalism-Conservatism and Party Identification," *JP* (November 1962), p. 679.

Edgar Litt, "Political Cynicism and Political Futility," *JP* (May 1963), p. 312.

Fred H. Willhoite, "Political Order and Consensus: A Continuing Problem," *WPQ* (June 1963), p. 294.

Roberta S. Sigel and David J. Butler, "The Public and the No Third Term Tradition: Inquiry into Attitudes Toward Power," *MJPS* (February 1964), p. 39.

Douglas K. Stewart and Ted C. Smith, "Celebrity Structure of the Far Right," *WPQ* (June 1964), p. 349.

Elections and Voting Behavior

Donald R. Matthews and James W. Prothro, "Political Factors and Negro Voter Registration in the South," APSR (June 1963), p. 355.

——, "Social and Economic Factors and Negro Voter Registration in the South," APSR (March 1963), p. 24.

James Q. Wilson and Edward C. Banfield, "Public Regardingness as a Value Premise in Voting Behavior," APSR (December 1964), p. 876.

W. Ross Yates, "The Functions of Residence Requirements for Voting," WPQ (September 1962), p. 469.

Robert R. Alford, "The Role of Social Class in American Voting Behavior," WPQ (March 1963), p. 180.

John Crittenden, "Aging and Political Participation," WPQ (June 1963), p. 323.

"The American South, 1950–1970" (A Symposium), JP (February 1964), p. 3.

A. Clarke Hagensick, "Influence of Partisanship and Incumbency on a Nonpartisan Election System," WPQ (March 1964), p. 117.

Harry M. Scoble and Leon D. Epstein, "Religion and Wisconsin Voting in 1960," JP (May 1964), p. 381.

Richard S. Wells, "The Legal Profession and Politics," MJPS (May 1964), p. 127.

Stanley Coben, "A Study in Nativism: The American Red Scare of 1919–20," PSQ (March 1964), p. 52.

Paul P. Van Riper and Darab B. Unwalla, "Voting Patterns Among High Ranking Military Officers," PSQ (March 1965), p. 48.

Martha Derthick, "Politics in Voteless Washington," JP (February 1963), p. 93.

David Adamany, "The Size-of-Place Analysis Reconsidered," WPQ (September 1964), p. 477.

John H. Lindquist, "Socioeconomic Status and Political Participation," WPQ (December 1964), p. 608.

Philip E. Converse, et al., "Electoral Myth and Reality: The 1964 Election," APSR (June 1965), p. 321.

Ross D. Rice (ed.), "The 1964 Elections in the West," WPQ (June 1965), Part 2.

Lewis J. Edinger, "Political Science and Political Biography: Reflections on the Study of Leadership," JP (May 1964), p. 423.

Political Parties

Theodore Lowi, "Toward Functionalism in

Political Science: The Case of Innovation in Party Systems," APSR (September 1963), p. 570.

Donald E. Stokes, "Party Loyalty and the Likelihood of Deviating Elections," JP (November 1962), p. 689.

Samuel C. Patterson, "Characteristics of Party Leaders," WPQ (June 1963), p. 332.

Phillips Cutright, "Urbanization and Competitive Party Politics," JP (August 1963), p. 552.

Avery Leiserson, "National Party Organization and Congressional Districts," WPQ (September 1963), p. 633.

Charles Press, "Presidential Coattails and Party Cohesion," MJPS (November 1963), p. 320.

Phillips Cutright, "Activities of Precinct Committeemen in Partisan and Nonpartisan Communities," WPQ (March 1964), p. 93.

Lewis Bowman and G. R. Boynton, "Coalition as Party in a One-Party Southern Area," MJPS (August 1964).

Charles E. Schultz, "Bureacuratic Party Organization Through Professional Political Staffing," MJPS (May 1964), p. 127.

Charles E. Gilbert, "National Political Alignments and the Politics of Large Cities," PSQ (March 1964), p. 25.

Francis E. Rourke, "Urbanism and the National Party Organizations," WPQ (March 1965), p. 149.

Walter Dean Burnham, "The Changing Shape of the American Political Universe," APSR (March 1965), p. 7.

Frank Munger and James Blackhurst, "Factionalism in the National Convention, 1940–1960," JP (May 1965), p. 375.

Interest Groups

Samuel Krislov, "What is an Interest? The Rival Answers of Bentley, Pound and MacIver," WPQ (December 1963), p. 830.

Harry M. Scoble, "Political Money: A Study of Contributions to the National Committee For an Effective Congress," MJPS (August 1963), p. 229.

Samuel C. Patterson, "The Role of the Lobbyist," JP (February 1963), p. 72.

Edgar Lane, "Group Politics and the Disclosure Idea," WPQ (June 1964), p. 200.

Harry M. Scoble, "Organized Labor in Electoral Politics," WPQ (September 1963), p. 666.

Part Five: Policy-Makers

The Executive

Richard E. Neustadt, "Approaches to Staffing the Presidency: Notes on FDR and JFK," APSR (December 1963), p. 855.

———, "Kennedy in the Presidency: A Premature Appraisal," PSQ (September 1964), p. 321.

Dean E. Mann, "The Selection of Federal Political Executives," APSR (March 1964), p. 81.

Aaron B. Wildavsky, "The Analysis of Issue-Contexts in the Study of Decision-Making," JP (November 1962), p. 717.

Lewis C. Mainzer, "The Scientist as Public Administrator," WPQ (December 1963), p. 814.

Adolf A. Berle and Malcolm Moos, "The Need to Know and the Right to Tell: Emmet John Hughes, The Ordeal of Power," PSQ (June 1964), p. 161.

Stanley L. Falk, "The National Security Council Under Truman, Eisenhower and Kennedy," PSQ (September 1964), p. 403.

Avery Leiserson, "Scientists and the Policy Process," APSR (June 1965), p. 408.

Curtis A. Amlund, "President-Ranking: A Criticism," MJPS (August 1964), p. 309.

Clement E. Vose, "The Memorandum Pocket Veto," JP (May 1964), p. 397.

Earland I. Carlson, "Franklin D. Roosevelt's Post-Mortem of the 1928 Election," MJPS (August 1964), p. 298.

Congress

Floyd M. Riddick and Murray Zweben, annual analysis of work of Congress in March issue of WPQ.

Warren E. Miller and Donald E. Stokes, "Constituency Influence in Congress," APSR (March 1963), p. 45.

Lewis A. Froman, Jr., "Inter-Party Constituency Differences and Congressional Voting Behavior," APSR (March 1963), p. 57.

———, "The Importance of Individuality in Voting in Congress," JP (May 1963), p. 324.

——— and Randall B. Ripley, "Conditions for Party Leadership: The Case of the House Democrats," APSR (March 1965), p. 52.

Lee F. Anderson, "Individuality in Voting in Congress," MJPS (November 1964), p. 425.

Seymour Scher, "Conditions for Legislative Control," JP (August 1963), p. 526.

Fred I. Greenstein and Alton F. Jackson, "A Second Look at the Validity of Roll-Call Analysis," MJPS (May 1963), p. 156.

John G. Grumm, "A Factor Analysis of Legislative Behavior," MJPS (November 1963), p. 336.

T. Richard Witmer, "The Aging of the House," PSQ (December 1964), p. 526.

Charles O. Jones, "Inter-Party Organization for Congressional Seats," WPQ (September 1964), p. 461.

Raymond E. Wolfinger and Joan Heifetz, "Safe Seats, Seniority, and Power in Congress," APSR (June 1965), p. 337.

Bertrand de Jouvenal, "The Team Against the Committee," RP (April 1963), p. 147.

James D. Cochran, "Partisan Aspects of Congressional Committee Staffing," WPQ (June 1964), p. 338.

Randall B. Ripley, "The Party Whip Organizations in the United States House of Representatives," APSR (September 1964), p. 561.

Leroy N. Rieselbach, "The Demography of the Congressional Vote on Foreign Aid, 1939–1958," APSR (September 1964), p. 577.

John H. Kessel, "The Washington Congressional Delegation," MJPS (February 1964), p. 1.

Charles F. Andrian, "A Scale Analysis of Senators' Attitudes Toward Civil Rights," WPQ (September 1964), p. 488.

The Federal Courts

Paul C. Bartholomew, "The Supreme Court of the United States, . . ." an annual analysis of the work of the Supreme Court in the March issue of WPQ.

Glendon Schubert, "Behavioral Research in Public Law," APSR (June 1963), p. 433.

Wallace Mendelson, "The Neo-Behavioral Approach to the Judicial Process: A Critique," APSR (September 1963), p. 593.

Theodore L. Becker, "Inquiry into a School of Thought in the Judicial Behavior Movement," MJPS (August 1963), p. 254.

Stuart S. Nagel, "Testing Relations Between Judicial Characteristics and Judicial Decision-Making," *WPQ* (September 1962), p. 425.

S. Sidney Ulmer, "Toward A Theory of Sub-Group Formation in the United States Supreme Court," *JP* (February 1965), p. 133.

Harold J. Spaeth, "An Analysis of Judicial Attitudes in the Labor Relations Decisions of the Warren Court," *JP* (May 1963), p. 290.

Charles F. Conlon, "Judicial Views on Tax Administration," *WPQ* (March 1963), p. 5.

Kenneth N. Vines, "The Role of Circuit Courts of Appeals in the Federal Judicial Process: A Case Study," *MJPS* (November 1963), p. 305.

———, "Federal District Judges and Race Relations Cases in the South," *JP* (May 1964), p. 337.

Robert J. Steamer, "The Legal and Political Genesis of the Supreme Court," *PSQ* (December 1962), p. 546.

Chester A. Newland, "Press Coverage of the United States Supreme Court," *WPQ* (March 1964), p. 15.

Joel B. Grossman, "Federal Judicial Selection: The Work of the ABA Committee," *MJPS* (August 1964), p. 221.

Solomon Resnik, "Black and Douglas: Variations in Dissent," *WPQ* (June 1963), p. 305.

Harold J. Spaeth, "The Judicial Restraint of Mr. Justice Frankfurter—Myth or Reality?" *MJPS* (February 1964), p. 22.

Mathew Holden, Jr., "Litigation and the Political Order," *WPQ* (December 1963), p. 771.

Part Six: Big Government in Action

Lewis J. Edinger, "Military Leaders and Foreign Policy-Making," *APSR* (June 1963), p. 392.

Hans J. Morgenthau, "The Four Paradoxes of Nuclear Strategy," *APSR* (March 1964), p. 23.

J. David Singer, "Stable Deterrence and Its Limits," *WPQ* (September 1962), p. 449.

Edward A. Kolodziej, "Congressional Responsibility for the Common Defense: The Money Problem," *WPQ* (March 1963), p. 149.

Gene M. Lyons, "The Growth of National Security Research," *JP* (August 1963), p. 489.

Donald A. Strickland, "Scientists as Negotiators: The 1958 Geneva Conference of Experts," *MJPS* (November 1964), p. 372.

Wilford L. Kohl, "Nuclear Sharing in NATO and the Multilateral Force," *PSQ* (March 1965), p. 88.

David W. Tarr, "Military Technology and the Policy Process," *WPQ* (March 1965), p. 135.

Daniel Marx, Jr., "The United States Enters Export Credit Guarantee Competition," *PSQ* (June 1963), p. 245.

James W. Angell, "The United States International-Payments Deficit: Dilemmas and Solutions," *PSQ* (March 1964), p. 1.

Jacob Viner, *et al.*, "The Report of the Clay Committee on Foreign Aid: A Symposium," *PSQ* (September 1963), p. 321.

Cecil V. Crabb, Jr., "American Diplomatic Tactics and Neutralism," *PSQ* (September 1963), p. 418.

William L. Clayton, "GATT, The Marshall Plan, and OECD," *PSQ* (December 1963), p. 493.

Stephen G. Xydis, "America, Britain, and the USSR in the Greek Arena, 1944–1947," *PSQ* (December 1963), p. 581.

George Stambuk, "Foreign Policy and the Stationing of American Forces Abroad," *JP* (August 1963), p. 472.

Louis Henkin, "The United Nations and Its Supporters," *PSQ* (December 1963), p. 504.

Stephen D. Kertesz, "The United Nations: A Hope and Its Prospects," *RP* (October 1963), p. 523.

Edwin H. Fedder, "United States Loyalty Procedures and the Recruitment of International Personnel," *WPQ* (December 1962), p. 705.

Robert T. Golembiewski, "Civil Service and Managing Work," *APSR* (December 1962), p. 961.

Conley H. Dillon, "Channeling Government Contracts into Depressed Areas," *WPQ* (June 1963), p. 269.

Ray Marshall, "Union Structure and Public Policy," *PSQ* (September 1963), p. 444.

Arthur F. Burns, "Some Reflections on the Economic Act," *PSQ* (December 1962), p. 481.

Part Seven: State and Local Governments

Patterns of Influence

Paul A. Smith, "The Games of Community Politics," *MJPS* (February 1965), p. 37.

David A. Booth and Charles R. Adrian, "Elections and Community Power," *JP* (February 1963).

Thomas A. Flinn and Frederick M. Wirt, "Local Party Leaders: Groups of Like-Minded Men," *MJPS* (February 1965), p. 77.

Jack L. Walker, "Protest and Negotiation: A Case Study of Negro Leadership in Atlanta, Georgia," *MJPS* (May 1963), p. 99.

State Government

Wayne L. Francis, "Influence and Interaction in a State Legislative Body," *APSR* (December 1962), p. 953.

Jack Sawyer and Duncan MacRae, Jr., "Game Theory and Cumulative Voting in Illinois: 1902-1954," *APSR* (December 1962), p. 936.

Robert J. Huckshorn, "Decision-Making Stimuli in the State Legislative Process," *WPQ* (March 1965), p. 164.

Lester J. Seligman, "Political Change: Legislative Elites and Parties in Oregon," *WPQ* (June 1964), p. 177.

Ruth C. Silva, "Compared Values of the Single- and the Multi-Member Legislative District," *WPQ* (September 1964), p. 504.

———, "Relation of Representation and the Party System to the Number of Seats Apportioned to a Legislative District," *WPQ* (December 1964), p. 742.

Charles M. Hardin, "Issues in Legislative Reapportionment," *RP* (April 1965), p. 147.

Glendon Schubert and Charles Press, "Measuring Malapportionment," *APSR* (June 1964), p. 302.

Alan L. Clem, "Measuring Legislative Malapportionment: In Search of a Better Yardstick," *MJPS* (May 1963), p. 125.

John P. White and Norman C. Thomas, "Urban and Rural Representation and State Legislative Apportionment," *WPQ* (December 1964), p. 724.

Robert H. Simmons, "American State Executive Systems: An Heuristic Model," *WPQ* (March 1965), p. 19.

———, "American State Executive Studies: A Suggested New Departure," *WPQ* (December 1964), p. 777.

Virgil C. Stroud, "A Political Maneuver That Backfired," *WPQ* (March 1964), p. 125.

James E. Titus, "Kansas Governors: A Resume of Political Leadership," *WPQ* (June 1964), p. 356.

Albert E. Saye, "Revolution By Judicial Action in Georgia," *WPQ* (March 1964), p. 10.

Thomas A. Flinn, "Party Responsibilty in the States," *APSR* (March 1964), p. 60.

Daniel P. Moynihan and James Q. Wilson, "Patronage in New York State, 1955-1959," *APSR* (June 1964), p. 286.

Richard E. Dawson and James A. Robinson, "Inter-Party Competition, Economic Variables and Welfare Policies in the American States," *JP* (May 1963), p. 265.

Metropolis

James A. Norton, "Referenda Voting in a Metropolitan Area," *WPQ* (March 1963), p. 195.

Thomas R. Dye, *et al.*, "Differentiation and Cooperation in a Metropolitan Area," *MJPS* (May 1963), p. 145.

Robert T. Norman, "The Harvard Plan for Metropolitan Boston," *WPQ* (September 1963), p. 708.

Thomas R. Dye, "Urban Political Integration: Conditions Associated with Annexation in American Cities," *MJPS* (November 1964), p. 430.

Walter B. Watson, *et al.*, "Metropolitan Decentralization Through Incorporation," *WPQ* (March 1965), p. 198.

John B. McConaughy and John H. Gauntlett, "The Influence of the S Factor upon the Voting Behavior of South Carolina Urban Negroes," *WPQ* (December 1963), p. 973.

Local Government

Charles Press, "Attitudes Toward Annexation In A Small City Area," *WPQ* (June 1963), p. 271.

Thomas F. Hady and Clarence J. Hein, "Congressional Townships as Incorporated Municipalities," *MJPS* (November 1964), p. 408.

Thad L. Beyle, "Contested Elections and Voter Turnout in a Local Community," *APSR* (March 1965), p. 111.

The Constitution of the United States

We the People of the United States, in Order to form a more perfect Union, establish Justice, insure domestic Tranquility, provide for the common defence, promote the general Welfare, and secure the Blessings of Liberty to ourselves and our Posterity, do ordain and establish this Constitution for the United States of America.

Article I

Section 1. All legislative Powers herein granted shall be vested in a Congress of the United States, which shall consist of a Senate and House of Representatives.

Section 2. The House of Representatives shall be composed of Members chosen every second Year by the People of the several States, and the Electors in each State shall have the Qualifications requisite for Electors of the most numerous Branch of the State Legislature.

No Person shall be a Representative who shall not have attained to the Age of twenty five Years, and been seven Years a Citizen of the United States, and who shall not, when elected, be an Inhabitant of that State in which he shall be chosen.

Representatives and direct Taxes shall be apportioned among the several States which may be included within this Union, according to their respective Numbers, which shall be determined by adding to the whole Number of free Persons, including those bound to Service for a Term of Years, and excluding Indians not taxed, three fifths of all other Persons. The actual Enumeration shall be made within three Years after the first Meeting of the Congress of the United States, and within every subsequent Term of ten Years, in such Manner as they shall by Law direct. The Number of Representatives shall not exceed one for every thirty Thousand, but each State shall have at Least one Representative; and until such enumeration shall be made, the State of New Hampshire shall be entitled to chuse three, Massachusetts eight, Rhode-Island and Providence Plantations one, Connecticut five, New-York six, New Jersey four,

Pennsylvania eight, Delaware one, Maryland six, Virginia ten, North Carolina five, South Carolina five, and Georgia three.

When vacancies happen in the Representation from any State, the Executive Authority thereof shall issue Writs of Election to fill such Vacancies.

The House of Representatives shall chuse their speaker and other Officers; and shall have the sole Power of Impeachment.

Section 3. The Senate of the United States shall be composed of two Senators from each State, chosen by the Legislature thereof, for six Years; and each Senator shall have one Vote.

Immediately after they shall be assembled in Consequence of the first Election, they shall be divided as equally as may be into three Classes. The Seats of the Senators of the first Class shall be vacated at the Expiration of the second Year, of the second Class at the Expiration of the fourth Year, and of the third Class at the Expiration of the sixth Year, so that one third may be chosen every second Year; and if Vacancies happen by Resignation, or otherwise, during the Recess of the Legislature of any State, the Executive thereof may make temporary Appointments until the next Meeting of the Legislature, which shall then fill such Vacancies.

No Person shall be a Senator who shall not have attained to the Age of thirty Years, and been nine Years a Citizen of the United States, and who shall not, when elected, be an Inhabitant of that State for which he shall be chosen.

The Vice President of the United States shall be President of the Senate, but shall have no Vote, unless they be equally divided.

The Senate shall chuse their other Officers, and also a President pro tempore, in the Absence of the Vice President, or when he shall exercise the Office of President of the United States.

The Senate shall have the sole Power to try all Impeachments. When sitting for that Purpose, they shall be on Oath or Affirmation. When the President of the United States is tried, the Chief Justice shall preside: And no Person shall be convicted without the Concurrence of two thirds of the Members present.

Judgment in Cases of Impeachment shall not extend further than to removal from Office, and disqualification to hold and enjoy any Office of honor, Trust or Profit under the United States: but the Party convicted shall nevertheless be liable and subject to Indictment, Trial, Judgment and Punishment, according to law.

Section 4. The Times, Places and Manner of holding Elections for Senators and Representatives, shall be prescribed in each State by the Legislature thereof; but the Congress may at any time by Law make or alter such Regulations, except as to the Places of chusing Senators.

The Congress shall assemble at least once in every Year, and such Meeting shall be on the first Monday in December, unless they shall by Law appoint a different Day.

Section 5. Each House shall be the Judge of the Elections, Returns and Qualifications of its own Members, and a Majority of each shall constitute a Quorum to do Business; but a smaller Number may adjourn from day to day, and may be authorized to compel the Attendance of absent Members, in such Manner, and under such Penalties as each House may provide.

Each House may determine the Rules of its Proceedings, punish its Members for disorderly Behaviour, and, with the Concurrence of two thirds, expel a Member.

Each House shall keep a Journal of its Proceedings, and from time to time publish the same, excepting such Parts as may in their Judgment require Secrecy; and the Yeas and Nays of the Members of either House on any question shall, at the Desire of one fifth of those Present, be entered on the Journal.

Neither House, during the Session of Congress, shall, without the Consent of the other, adjourn for more than three days, nor to any other Place than that in which the two Houses shall be sitting.

Section 6. The Senators and Representatives shall receive a Compensation for their Services, to be ascertained by Law, and paid out of the Treasury of the United States. They shall in all Cases, except Treason, Felony and Breach of the Peace, be privileged from Arrest during their Attendance at the Session of their respective Houses, and in going to and returning from the same; and for any Speech or Debate in either House, they shall not be questioned in any other Place.

No Senator or Representative shall, during the Time for which he was elected, be appointed to any civil Office under the Authority of the United States, which shall have been created, or the Emoluments whereof shall have been encreased during such time; and no Person holding any Office under the United States, shall be a Member of either House during his Continuance in Office.

Section 7. All Bills for raising Revenue shall originate in the House of Representatives; but the Senate may propose or concur with Amendments as on other Bills.

Every Bill which shall have passed the House of Representatives and the Senate, shall, before it become a Law, be presented to the President of the United States; If he approve he shall sign it, but if not he shall return it, with his Objections to that House in which it shall have originated, who shall enter the Objections at large on their Journal, and proceed to reconsider it. If after such Reconsideration two thirds of that House shall agree to pass the Bill, it shall be sent, together with the Objections, to the other House, by which it shall likewise be reconsidered, and if approved by two thirds of that House, it shall become a Law. But in all such Cases the Votes of both Houses shall be determined by Yeas and Nays, and the Names of the Persons voting for and against the Bill shall be entered on the Journal of each House respectively. If any Bill shall not be returned by the President within ten Days (Sundays excepted) after it shall have been presented to him, the Same shall be a Law, in like Manner as if he had signed it, unless the Congress by their Adjournment prevent its Return, in which Case it shall not be a Law.

Every Order, Resolution, or Vote to which the Concurrence of the Senate and House of Representatives may be necessary (except on a question of Adjournment) shall be presented to the President of the United States; and before the Same shall take Effect, shall be approved by him, or being disapproved by him, shall be repassed by two thirds of the Senate and House of Representatives, according to the Rules and Limitations prescribed in the Case of a Bill.

Section 8. The Congress shall have Power To lay and collect Taxes, Duties, Imposts and Excises, to pay the Debts and provide for the common Defence and general Welfare of the United States; but all Duties, Imposts and Excises shall be uniform throughout the United States;

To borrow Money on the Credit of the United States;

To regulate Commerce with foreign Nations, and among the several States, and with the Indian Tribes;

To establish an uniform Rule of Naturalization, and uniform Laws on the subject of Bankruptcies throughout the United States;

To coin Money, regulate the Value thereof, and of foreign Coin, and fix the Standard of Weights and Measures;

To provide for the Punishment of counterfeiting the Securities and current Coin of the United States;

To establish Post Offices and post Roads;

To promote the Progress of Science and useful Arts, by securing for limited Times to Authors and Inventors the exclusive Right to their respective Writings and Discoveries;

To constitute Tribunals inferior to the supreme Court;

To define and punish Piracies and Felonies committed on the high Seas, and Offences against the Law of Nations;

To declare War, grant Letters of Marque and Reprisal, and make Rules concerning Captures on Land and Water;

To raise and support Armies, but no Appropriation of Money to that Use shall be for a longer Term than two Years;

To provide and maintain a Navy;

To make Rules for the Government and Regulation of the land and naval Forces;

To provide for calling forth the Militia to execute the Laws of the Union, suppress Insurrections and repel Invasions;

To provide for organizing, arming, and disciplining, the Militia, and for governing such Part of them as may be employed in the Service of the United States, reserving to the States respectively, the Appointment of the Officers, and the Authority of training the Militia according to the discipline prescribed by Congress;

To exercise exclusive Legislation in all Cases whatsoever, over such District (not exceeding ten Miles square) as may, by Cession of particular States, and the Acceptance of Congress, become the Seat of the Government of the United States, and to exercise like Authority over all Places purchased by the Consent of the Legislature of the State in which the Same shall be for the Erection of Forts, Magazines, Arsenals, dock-Yards, and other needful Buildings;—And

To make all Laws which shall be necessary and proper for carrying into Execution the foregoing Powers, and all other Powers vested by this Constitution in the Government of the United States, or in any Department or Officer thereof.

Section 9. The Migration or Importation of such Persons as any of the States now existing shall think proper to admit, shall not be prohibited by the Congress prior to the Year one thousand eight hundred and eight, but a Tax or duty may be imposed on such

Importation, not exceeding ten dollars for each Person.

The Privilege of the Writ of Habeas Corpus shall not be suspended, unless when in Cases of Rebellion or Invasion the public Safety may require it.

No Bill of Attainder or ex post facto Law shall be passed.

No Capitation, or other direct, Tax shall be laid, unless in Proportion to the Census or Enumeration herein before directed to be taken.

No Tax or Duty shall be laid on Articles exported from any State.

No Preference shall be given by any Regulation of Commerce or Revenue to the Ports of one State over those of another: nor shall Vessels bound to, or from, one State, be obliged to enter, clear, or pay Duties in another.

No Money shall be drawn from the Treasury, but in Consequence of Appropriations made by Law; and a regular Statement and Account of the Receipts and Expenditures of all public Money shall be published from time to time.

No Title of Nobility shall be granted by the United States: And no Person holding any Office of Profit or Trust under them, shall, without the Consent of the Congress, accept of any present, Emolument, Office, or Title, of any kind whatever, from any King, Prince, or foreign State.

Section 10. No State shall enter into any Treaty, Alliance, or Confederation; grant Letters of Marque and Reprisal; coin Money; emit Bills of Credit; make any Thing but gold and silver Coin a Tender in Payment of Debts; pass any Bill of Attainder, ex post facto Law, or Law impairing the Obligation of Contracts, or grant any Title of Nobility.

No State shall, without the Consent of the Congress, lay any Imposts or Duties on Imports or Exports, except what may be absolutely necessary for executing its inspection Laws: and the net Produce of all Duties and Imposts, laid by any State on Imports or Exports, shall be for the Use of the Treasury of the United States; and all such Laws shall be subject to the Revision and Controul of the Congress.

No State shall, without the Consent of Congress, lay any Duty of Tonnage, keep Troops, or Ships of War in time of Peace, enter into any Agreement or Compact with another State, or with a foreign Power, or engage in War, unless actually invaded, or in such imminent Danger as will not admit of delay.

Article II

Section 1. The executive Power shall be vested in a President of the United States of America. He shall hold his Office during the Term of four Years, and, together with the Vice President, chosen for the same term, be elected, as follows

Each State shall appoint, in such Manner as the Legislature thereof may direct, a Number of Electors, equal to the whole Number of Senators and Representatives to which the State may be entitled in the Congress: but no Senator or Representative, or Person holding an Office of Trust or Profit under the United States, shall be appointed an Elector.

The Electors shall meet in their respective States, and vote by Ballot for two Persons, of whom one at least shall not be an Inhabitant of the same State with themselves. And they shall make a List of all the Persons voted for, and of the Number of Votes for each; which List they shall sign and certify, and transmit sealed to the Seat of the Government of the United States, directed to the President of the Senate. The President of the Senate shall, in the Presence of the Senate and House of Representatives, open all the Certificates, and the Votes shall then be counted. The Person having the greatest Number of Votes shall be the President, if such Number be a Majority of the whole Number of Electors appointed; and if there be more than one who have such Majority, and have an equal Number of Votes, then the House of Representatives shall immediately chuse by Ballot one of them for President: and if no Person have a Majority, then from the five highest on the List the said House shall in like Manner chuse the President. But in chusing the President, the Votes shall be taken by States, the Representation from each State having one Vote; A quorum for this Purpose shall consist of a Member or Members from two thirds of the States, and a Majority of all the States shall be necessary to a Choice. In every Case, after the Choice of the President, the Person having the greatest Number of Votes of the Electors shall be the Vice President. But if there should remain two or more who have equal Votes, the Senate shall chuse from them by Ballot the Vice President.

The Congress may determine the Time of chusing the Electors, and the Day on which they shall give their Votes; which Day shall be the same throughout the United States.

No Person except a natural born Citizen, or a Citizen of the United States, at the time of the Adoption of this Constitution, shall be eligible to the Office of President; neither shall any Person be eligible to that Office who shall not have attained to the Age of thirty five Years, and been fourteen Years a Resident within the United States.

In Case of the Removal of the President from Office, or of his Death, Resignation, or Inability to discharge the Powers and Duties of the said Office, the Same shall devolve on the Vice President, and the Congress may by Law provide for the Case of Removal, Death, Resignation or Inability, both of the President and Vice President, declaring what Officer shall then act as President, and such Officer shall act accordingly, until the Disability be removed, or a President shall be elected.

The President shall, at stated Times, receive for his Services, a Compensation, which shall neither be encreased nor diminished during the Period for which he shall have been elected, and he shall not receive within that Period any other Emolument from the United States, or any of them.

Before he enter on the Execution of his Office, he shall take the following Oath or Affirmation:—"I do solemnly swear (or affirm) that I will faithfully execute the Office of President of the United States, and will to the best of my Ability, preserve, protect and defend the Constitution of the United States."

Section 2. The President shall be Commander in Chief of the Army and Navy of the United States, and of the Militia of the several States, when called into the actual Service of the United States; he may require the Opinion, in writing, of the principal Officer in each of the executive Departments, upon any Subject relating to the Duties of their respective Offices, and he shall have Power to grant Reprieves and Pardons for Offences against the United States, except in Cases of Impeachment.

He shall have Power, by and with the Advice and Consent of the Senate, to make Treaties, provided two thirds of the Senators present concur; and he shall nominate, and by and with the Advice and Consent of the Senate, shall appoint Ambassadors, other public Ministers and Consuls, Judges of the supreme Court, and all other Officers of the United States, whose Appointments are not herein otherwise provided for, and which shall be established by Law; but the Congress may by Law vest the Appointment of such inferior Officers, as they think proper, in the President alone, in the Courts of Law, or in the Heads of Departments.

The President shall have Power to fill up all Vacancies that may happen during the Recess of the Senate, by granting Commissions which shall expire at the End of their next Session.

Section 3. He shall from time to time give to the Congress Information of the State of the Union, and recommend to their Consideration such Measures as he shall judge necessary and expedient; he may, on extraordinary Occasions, convene both Houses, or either of them, and in Case of Disagreement between them, with Respect to the Time of Adjournment, he may adjourn them to such Time as he shall think proper; he shall receive Ambassadors and other public Ministers; he shall take Care that the Laws be faithfully executed, and shall Commission all the Officers of the United States.

Section 4. The President, Vice President and all civil Officers of the United States, shall be removed from Office on Impeachment for, and Conviction of, Treason, Bribery, or other High Crimes and Misdemeanors.

Article III

Section 1. The judicial Power of the United States, shall be vested in one supreme Court, and in such inferior Courts as the Congress may from time to time ordain and establish. The Judges, both of the supreme and inferior Courts, shall hold their Offices during good Behaviour, and shall, at stated Times, receive for their Services, a Compensation, which shall not be diminished during their Continuance in Office.

Section 2. The judicial Power shall extend to all Cases, in Law and Equity, arising under this Constitution, the Laws of the United States, and Treaties made, or which shall be made, under their Authority;—to all Cases affecting Ambassadors, other public Ministers and Consuls;—to all Cases of admiralty and maritime Jurisdiction;—to Controversies to which the United States shall be a Party;—to Controversies between two or more States; between a State and Citizens of another State;—between Citizens of different States;—between Citizens of the same State claiming Lands under Grants of different States, and between a State, or the Citizens thereof, and foreign States, Citizens or Subjects.

In all Cases affecting Ambassadors, other public Ministers and Consuls, and those in which a State shall be Party, the supreme Court shall have original Jurisdiction. In all the other Cases before mentioned, the supreme Court shall have appellate Jurisdiction, both as to Law and Fact, with such Exceptions, and under such Regulations as the Congress shall make.

The Trial of all Crimes, except in Cases of Impeachment, shall be by Jury; and such Trial shall be held in the State where the said Crimes shall have been committed; but when not committed within any State, the Trial shall be at such Place or Places as the Congress may by Law have directed.

Section 3. Treason against the United States, shall consist only in levying War against them, or in adhering to their Enemies, giving them Aid and Comfort. No Person shall be convicted of Treason unless on the Testimony of two Witnesses to the same overt Act, or on Confession in open Court.

The Congress shall have Power to declare the Punishment of Treason, but no Attainder of Treason shall work Corruption of Blood, or Forfeiture except during the Life of the Person attainted.

Article IV

Section 1. Full Faith and Credit shall be given in each State to the public Acts, Records, and judicial Proceedings of every other State. And the Congress may by general Laws prescribe the Manner in which such Acts, Records and Proceedings shall be proved, and the Effect thereof.

Section 2. The Citizens of each State shall be entitled to all Privileges and Immunities of Citizens in the several States.

A Person charged in any State with Treason, Felony, or other Crime, who shall flee from Justice, and be found in another State, shall on Demand of the executive Authority of the State from which he fled, be delivered up, to be removed to the State having Jurisdiction of the Crime.

No Person held to Service or Labour in one State, under the Laws thereof, escaping into another, shall, in Consequence of any Law or Regulation therein, be discharged from such Service or Labour, but shall be delivered up on Claim of the Party to whom such Service or Labour may be due.

Section 3. New States may be admitted by the Congress into this Union; but no new State shall be formed or erected within the Jurisdiction of any other State; nor any State be formed by the Junction of two or more States, or Parts of States, without the Consent of the Legislatures of the States concerned as well as of the Congress.

The Congress shall have Power to dispose of and make all needful Rules and Regulations respecting the Territory or other Property belonging to the United States; and nothing in this Constitution shall be so construed as to Prejudice any Claims of the United States, or of any particular State.

Section 4. The United States shall guarantee to every State in this Union a Republican Form of Government, and shall protect each of them against Invasion; and on Application of the Legislature, or of the Executive (when the Legislature cannot be convened) against domestic Violence.

Article V

The Congress, whenever two thirds of both Houses shall deem it necessary, shall propose Amendments to this Constitution, or, on the Application of the Legislatures of two thirds of the several States, shall call a Convention for proposing Amendments, which, in either Case, shall be valid to all Intents and Purposes, as Part of this Constitution, when ratified by the Legislatures of three fourths of the several States, or by Conventions in three fourths thereof, as the one or the other Mode of Ratification may be proposed by the Congress; Provided that no Amendment which may be made prior to the Year One thousand eight hundred and eight shall in any Manner affect the first and fourth Clauses in the Ninth Section of the first Article; and that no State, without its Consent, shall be deprived of its equal Suffrage in the Senate.

Article VI

All Debts contracted and Engagements entered into, before the Adoption of this Constitution, shall be as valid against the United States under this Constitution, as under the Confederation.

This Constitution, and the Laws of the United States which shall be made in Pursuance thereof; and all Treaties made, or which shall be made, under the Authority of the United States, shall be the supreme Law of the Land; and the Judges in every State shall be bound thereby, any Thing in the Constitution or Laws of any State to the Contrary notwithstanding.

The Senators and Representatives before mentioned, and the Members of the several State Legislatures, and all executive and judicial Officers, both of the United States and of the several States, shall be bound by Oath or Affirmation, to support this Constitution; but no religious Test shall ever be required as a Qualification to any Office or public Trust under the United States.

Article VII

The Ratification of the Conventions of nine States, shall be sufficient for the Establishment of this Constitution between the States so ratifying the Same.

Done in Convention by the Unanimous Consent of the States present the Seventeenth Day of September in the Year of our Lord one thousand seven hundred and eighty seven and of the Independence of the United States of America the twelfth. In witness whereof We have hereunto subscribed our Names.

.   .   .

(The first 10 Amendments were ratified December 15, 1791, and form what is known as the "Bill of Rights.")

Amendment 1

Congress shall make no law respecting an establishment of religion, or prohibiting the free exercise thereof; or abridging the freedom of speech, or of the press; or the right of the people peaceably to assemble, and to petition the Government for a redress of grievances.

Amendment 2

A well regulated Militia, being necessary to the security of a free State, the right of the people to keep and bear Arms, shall not be infringed.

Amendment 3

No Soldier shall, in time of peace be quartered in any house, without the consent of the Owner, nor in time of war, but in a manner to be prescribed by law.

Amendment 4

The right of the people to be secure in their persons, houses, papers, and effects, against unreasonable searches and seizures, shall not be violated, and no Warrants shall issue, but upon probable cause, supported by Oath or affirmation, and particularly describing the place to be searched, and the persons or things to be seized.

Amendment 5

No person shall be held to answer for a capital, or otherwise infamous crime, unless on a presentment or indictment of a Grand Jury, except in cases arising in the land or naval forces, or in the Militia, when in actual service in time of War or public danger; nor shall any person be subject for the same offence to be twice put in jeopardy of life or limb; nor shall be compelled in any criminal case to be a witness against himself, nor be deprived of life, liberty, or property, without due process of law; nor shall private property be taken for public use, without just compensation.

Amendment 6

In all criminal prosecutions, the accused shall enjoy the right to a speedy and public trial, by an impartial jury of the State and district wherein the crime shall have been committed, which district shall have been previously ascertained by law, and to be informed of the nature and cause of the accusation; to be confronted with the witnesses against him; to have compulsory process for obtaining witnesses in his favor, and to have the Assistance of Counsel for his defence.

Amendment 7

In Suits at common law, where the value in controversy shall exceed twenty dollars, the right of trial by jury shall be preserved, and no fact tried by a jury, shall be otherwise re-examined in any Court of the United States, than according to the rules of the common law.

Amendment 8

Excessive bail shall not be required, nor excessive fines imposed, nor cruel and unusual punishments inflicted.

Amendment 9

The enumeration in the Constitution, of certain rights, shall not be construed to deny or disparage others retained by the people.

Amendment 10

The powers not delegated to the United States by the Constitution, nor prohibited by it to the States, are reserved to the States respectively, or to the people.

Amendment 11

[Ratified February 7, 1795]

The Judicial power of the United States shall not be construed to extend to any suit in law or equity, commenced or prosecuted against one of the United States by Citizens of another State, or by Citizens or Subjects of any Foreign State.

Amendment 12

[Ratified July 27, 1804]

The Electors shall meet in their respective states and vote by ballot for President and Vice-President, one of whom, at least, shall not be an inhabitant of the same state with themselves; they shall name in their ballots the person voted for as President, and in distinct ballots the person voted for as Vice-President, and they shall make distinct lists of all persons voted for as President, and of all persons voted for as Vice-President, and of the number of votes for each, which lists they shall sign and certify, and transmit sealed to the seat of the government of the United States, directed to the President of the Senate;—The President of the Senate shall, in the presence of the Senate and House of Representatives, open all the certificates and the votes shall then be counted;—The person having the greatest number of votes for President, shall be the President, if such number be a majority of the whole number of Electors appointed; and if no person have such majority, then from the persons having the highest numbers not exceeding three on the list of those voted for as President, the House of Representatives shall choose immediately, by ballot, the President. But in choosing the President, the votes shall be taken by states, the representation from each state having one vote; a quorum for this purpose shall consist of a member or members from two-thirds of the states, and a majority of all the states shall be necessary to a choice. And if the House of Representatives shall not choose a President whenever the right of choice shall devolve upon them, before the fourth day of March next following, then the Vice-President shall act as President, as in the case of the death or other constitutional disability of the President.—The person having the greatest number of votes as Vice-President, shall be the Vice-President, if such number be a majority of the whole number of Electors appointed, and if no person have a majority, then from the two highest numbers on the list, the Senate shall choose the Vice-President; a quorum for the purpose shall consist of two-thirds of the whole number of Senators, and a majority of the whole number shall be necessary to a choice. But no person constitutionally ineligible to the office of President shall be eligible to that of Vice-President of the United States.

Amendment 13

[Ratified December 6, 1865]

Section 1. Neither slavery nor involuntary servitude, except as a punishment for crime whereof the party shall have been duly convicted, shall exist within the United States, or any place subject to their jurisdiction.

Section 2. Congress shall have power to enforce this article by appropriate legislation.

Amendment 14

[Ratified July 9, 1868]

Section 1. All persons born or naturalized in the United States, and subject to the jurisdiction thereof, are citizens of the United States and of the State wherein they reside. No State shall make or enforce any law which shall abridge the privileges or immunities of citizens of the United States; nor shall any State deprive any person of life, liberty, or property, without due process of law; nor deny to any person within its jurisdiction the equal protection of the laws.

Section 2. Representatives shall be apportioned among the several States according to their respective numbers, counting the whole number of persons in each State, excluding Indians not taxed. But when the right to vote at any election for the choice of electors for President and Vice President of the United States, Representatives in Congress, the Executive and Judicial officers of a State, or the members of the Legislature thereof, is denied to any of the male inhabitants of such State, being twenty-one years of age, and citizens of the United States, or in any way abridged, except for participation in rebellion, or other crime, the basis of representation therein shall be reduced in the proportion which the number of such male citizens shall bear to the whole number of male citizens twenty-one years of age in such State.

Section 3. No person shall be a Senator or Representative in Congress, or elector of President and Vice President, or hold any office, civil or military, under the United States, or under any State, who, having previously taken an oath, as a member of Congress, or as an officer of the United States, or as a member of any State legislature, or as an executive or judicial officer of any State, to support the Constitution of the United States, shall have engaged in insurrection or rebellion against the same, or given aid or comfort to the enemies thereof. But Congress may by a vote of two-thirds of each House, remove such disability.

Section 4. The validity of the public debt of the United States, authorized by law, including debts incurred for payment of pensions and bounties for services in suppressing insurrection or rebellion, shall not be questioned. But neither the United States nor any State shall assume or pay any debt or obligation incurred in aid of insurrection or rebellion against the United States, or any claim for the loss or emancipation of any slave; but all such debts, obligations and claims shall be held illegal and void.

Section 5. The Congress shall have power to enforce, by appropriate legislation, the provisions of this article.

Amendment 15

[Ratified February 3, 1870]

Section 1. The right of citizens of the United States to vote shall not be denied or abridged by the United States or by any State on account of race, color, or previous condition of servitude.

Section 2. The Congress shall have power to enforce this article by appropriate legislation.

Amendment 16

[Ratified February 3, 1913]

The Congress shall have power to lay and collect taxes on incomes, from whatever source derived, without apportionment among the several States, and without regard to any census or enumeration.

Amendment 17

[Ratified April 8, 1913]

The Senate of the United States shall be composed of two Senators from each State, elected by the people thereof for six years; and each Senator shall have one vote. The electors in each State shall have the qualifications requisite for electors of the most numerous branch of the State legislatures.

When vacancies happen in the representation of any State in the Senate, the executive authority of such State shall issue writs of election to fill such vacancies: *Provided,* That the legislature of any State may empower the executive thereof to make temporary appointments until the people fill the vacancies by election as the legislature may direct.

This amendment shall not be so construed as to affect the election or term of any Senator chosen before it becomes valid as part of the Constitution.

Amendment 18

[Ratified January 16, 1919]

Section 1. After one year from the ratification of this article the manufacture, sale, or transportation of intoxicating liquors within, the importation thereof into, or the exportation thereof from the United States and all territory subject to the jurisdiction thereof for beverage purposes is hereby prohibited.

Section 2. The Congress and the several States shall have concurrent power to enforce this article by appropriate legislation.

Section 3. This article shall be inoperative unless it shall have been ratified as an amendment to the Constitution by the legislatures of the several States, as provided in the Constitution, within seven years from the date of the submission hereof to the States by the Congress.

Amendment 19

[Ratified August 18, 1920]

The right of citizens of the United States to vote shall not be denied or abridged by the United States or by any State on account of sex.

Congress shall have power to enforce this article by appropriate legislation.

Amendment 20

[Ratified January 23, 1933]

Section 1. The terms of the President and Vice President shall end at noon on the 20th day of January, and the terms of Senators and Representatives at noon on the 3d day of January, of the years in which such terms would have ended if this article had not been ratified; and the terms of their successors shall then begin.

Section 2. The Congress shall assemble at least once in every year, and such meeting shall begin at noon on the 3d day of January, unless they shall by law appoint a different day.

Section 3. If, at the time fixed for the beginning of the term of the President, the President elect shall have died, the Vice President elect shall become President. If a President shall not have been chosen before the time fixed for the beginning of his term, or if the President elect shall have failed to qualify, then the Vice President elect shall act as President until a President shall have qualified; and the Congress may by law provide for the case wherein neither a President elect nor a Vice President elect shall have qualified, declaring who shall then act as President, or the manner in which one who is to act shall be selected, and such person shall act accordingly until a President or Vice President shall have qualified.

Section 4. The Congress may by law provide for the case of the death of any of the persons from whom the House of Representatives may choose a President whenever the right of choice shall have devolved upon them, and for the case of the death of any of the persons from whom the Senate may choose a Vice President whenever the right of choice shall have devolved upon them.

Section 5. Sections 1 and 2 shall take effect on the 15th day of October following the ratification of this article.

Section 6. This article shall be inoperative unless it shall have been ratified as an amendment to the Constitution by the legislatures of three-fourths of the several States within seven years from the date of its submission.

Amendment 21

[Ratified December 5, 1933]

Section 1. The eighteenth article of amendment to the Constitution of the United States is hereby repealed.

Section 2. The transportation or importation into any State, Territory, or possession of the United States for delivery or use therein of intoxicating liquors, in violation of the laws thereof, is hereby prohibited.

Section 3. This article shall be inoperative unless it shall have been ratified as an amendment to the Constitution by conventions in the several States, as provided in the Constitution, within seven years from the date

of the submission hereof to the States by the Congress.

Amendment 22

[Ratified February 27, 1951]

Section 1. No person shall be elected to the office of the President more than twice, and no person who has held the office of President, or acted as President, for more than two years of a term to which some other person was elected President shall be elected to the office of the President more than once. But this Article shall not apply to any person holding the office of President when this Article was proposed by the Congress, and shall not prevent any person who may be holding the office of President, or acting as President, during the term within which this Article becomes operative from holding the office of President or acting as President during the remainder of such term.

Section 2. This article shall be inoperative unless it shall have been ratified as an amendment to the Constitution by the legislatures of three-fourths of the several States within seven years from the date of its submission to the States by the Congress.

Amendment 23

[Ratified March 29, 1961]

Section 1. The District constituting the seat of Government of the United States shall appoint in such manner as the Congress may direct:

A number of electors of President and Vice President equal to the whole number of Senators and Representatives in Congress to which the District would be entitled if it were a State, but in no event more than the least populous State; they shall be in addition to those appointed by the States, but they shall be considered, for the purposes of the election of President and Vice President, to be electors appointed by a State; and they shall meet in the District and perform such duties as provided by the twelfth article of amendment.

Section 2. The Congress shall have power to enforce this article by appropriate legislation.

Amendment 24

[Ratified January 23, 1964]

Section 1. The right of citizens of the United States to vote in any primary or other election for President or Vice President, for electors for President or Vice President, or for Senator or Representative in Congress, shall not be denied or abridged by the United States or any State by reason of failure pay any poll tax or other tax.

Section 2. The Congress shall have power to enforce this article by appropriate legislation.

Proposed Amendment 25

[Submitted July 6, 1965]

Section 1. In case of the removal of the President from office or of his death or resignation, the Vice President shall become President.

Section 2. Whenever there is a vacancy in the office of the Vice President, the President shall nominate a Vice President who shall take office upon confirmation by a majority vote of both Houses of Congress.

Section 3. Whenever the President transmits to the President pro tempore of the Senate and the Speaker of the House of Representatives his written declaration that he is unable to discharge the powers and duties of his office, and until he transmits to them a written declaration to the contrary, such powers and duties shall be discharged by the Vice President as Acting President.

Section 4. Whenever the Vice President and a majority of either the principal officers of the executive departments or of such other body as Congress may by law provide, transmit to the President pro tempore of the Senate and the Speaker of the House of Representatives their written declaration that the President is unable to discharge the powers and duties of his office, the Vice President shall immediately assume the powers and duties of the office as Acting President.

Thereafter, when the President transmits to the President pro tempore of the Senate and the Speaker of the House of Representatives his written declaration that no inability exists, he shall resume the powers and duties of his office unless the Vice President and a majority of either the principal officers of the executive departments or of such other body as Congress may by law provide, transmit within four days to the President pro tempore of the Senate and the Speaker of the House of Representatives their written declaration that the President is unable to discharge the powers and duties of his office. Thereupon Congress shall decide the issue, assembling within forty-eight hours for that purpose if not in session. If the Congress, within twenty-one days after receipt of the latter written declaration, or, if Congress is not in session, within twenty-one days after Congress is required to assemble, determines by two-thirds vote of both Houses that the President is unable to discharge the powers and duties of his office, the Vice President shall continue to discharge the same as Acting President; otherwise, the President shall resume the powers and duties of his office.

Index

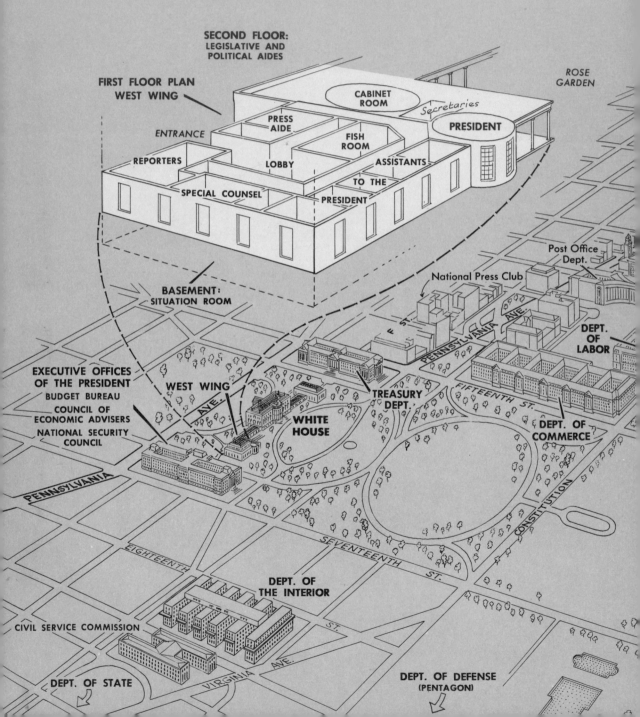

Washington —

CENTERS OF

SECOND FLOOR:
LEGISLATIVE AND
POLITICAL AIDES

FIRST FLOOR PLAN
WEST WING

ROSE
GARDEN

CABINET
ROOM

Secretaries

PRESS
AIDE

PRESIDENT

ENTRANCE

FISH
ROOM

REPORTERS

LOBBY

ASSISTANTS

SPECIAL COUNSEL

TO THE

PRESIDENT

BASEMENT:
SITUATION ROOM

Post Office
Dept.

National Press Club

DEPT.
OF
LABOR

EXECUTIVE OFFICES
OF THE PRESIDENT
BUDGET BUREAU
COUNCIL OF
ECONOMIC ADVISERS
NATIONAL SECURITY
COUNCIL

WEST WING
AVE.

TREASURY
DEPT.

WHITE
HOUSE

PENNSYLVANIA AVE.

FIFTEENTH ST.

DEPT. OF
COMMERCE

PENNSYLVANIA

SEVENTEENTH ST.

CONSTITUTION

EIGHTEENTH

ST.

DEPT. OF
THE INTERIOR

CIVIL SERVICE COMMISSION

VIRGINIA AVE.

DEPT. OF STATE

DEPT. OF DEFENSE
(PENTAGON)